RESEARCH HANDBOOK ON LAW AND LITERATURE

RESEARCH HANDBOOKS IN LEGAL THEORY

Research Handbooks in Legal Theory are designed to provide original and sophisticated discussions from an international and expert range of contributors. The volumes in this important series cover key topics within the field as well as major schools of thought, and also explore the application of legal theory to different areas of law. Comprising specially commissioned chapters from leading academics each *Research Handbook* brings together cutting-edge ideas and thought-provoking contributions and is written with a wide readership in mind. Equally useful as reference tools or high-level introductions to specific topics, issues, methods and debates, these *Research Handbooks* will be an essential resource for academic researchers and postgraduate students.

Titles in this series include:

Research Handbook on Feminist Jurisprudence
Edited by Robin West and Cynthia Grant Bowman

Research Handbook on Critical Legal Theory
Edited by Emilios Christodoulidis, Ruth Dukes and Marco Goldoni

Research Handbook on Natural Law Theory
Edited by Jonathan Crowe and Constance Youngwon Lee

Research Handbook on Private Law Theory
Edited by Hanoch Dagan and Benjamin C. Zipursky

Research Handbook on Modern Legal Realism
Edited by Shauhin Talesh, Elizabeth Mertz and Heinz Klug

Research Handbook on Law and Emotion
Edited by Susan A. Bandes, Jody Lyneé Madeira, Kathryn D. Temple and Emily Kidd White

Research Handbook on Law and Marxism
Edited by Paul O'Connell and Umut Özsu

Research Handbook on Law and Literature
Edited by Peter Goodrich, Daniela Gandorfer and Cecilia Gebruers

Research Handbook on Law and Literature

Edited by

Peter Goodrich

Professor of Law and Director of the Program in Law and Humanities, Cardozo School of Law, New York, USA and Visiting Professor, School of Social Science, New York University Abu Dhabi, United Arab Emirates

Daniela Gandorfer

Postdoctoral Researcher, University of California, Santa Cruz (UCSC), California, USA

Cecilia Gebruers

Postdoctoral Fellow, National Council for Scientific and Technical Research (CONICET), Interdisciplinary Institute for Advanced Social Studies, University of San Martin (IDAES-UNSAM), Argentina

RESEARCH HANDBOOKS IN LEGAL THEORY

Cheltenham, UK • Northampton, MA, USA

© The Editors and Contributors Severally 2022

Cover image: CODEXDIAGRAMS.

All rights reserved. No part of this publication may be reproduced, stored in a retrieval system or transmitted in any form or by any means, electronic, mechanical or photocopying, recording, or otherwise without the prior permission of the publisher.

Published by
Edward Elgar Publishing Limited
The Lypiatts
15 Lansdown Road
Cheltenham
Glos GL50 2JA
UK

Edward Elgar Publishing, Inc.
William Pratt House
9 Dewey Court
Northampton
Massachusetts 01060
USA

A catalogue record for this book
is available from the British Library

Library of Congress Control Number: 2022931174

This book is available electronically in the **Elgar**online
Law subject collection
http://dx.doi.org/10.4337/9781839102264

Printed on elemental chlorine free (ECF)
recycled paper containing 30% Post-Consumer Waste

ISBN 978 1 83910 225 7 (cased)
ISBN 978 1 83910 226 4 (eBook)

Printed and bound in the USA

Contents

List of contributors   viii

1   Introduction to *Research Handbook on Law and Literature*. What is your power?   1
Daniela Gandorfer

PART I   VISIONS AND DECISIONS

2   Premonition   15
Peter Goodrich

3   *Ostranenie*   28
Jorge Luis Roggero

4   Theatricality   38
Marett Leiboff

5   Perspective   64
James R. Martel

PART II   CUTTER ISLANDS

6   Legacies   83
Anne Bottomley

7   Castration   110
Maria Aristodemou

8   Utopia   128
Elena Loizidou

9   Adda   147
Debolina Dutta

10   Cartographies   174
Sabarish Suresh

PART III   GOVERNANCE

11   Exhaustion   201
Nathan Moore

12   *Oikonomia*   223
Marinos Diamantides

| 13 | Wilding
Nicole Rogers | 250 |

PART IV (CIS)TEMS OF THOUGHT

14	Billets *Jannice Käll*	272
15	Fury *Virginia Emilse Zuleta*	284
16	Hyperbole *Elena Cirkovic*	296

PART V TENSE FRAMES

17	Tenses *Mikus Duncis and Geoff Gordon*	315
18	Travel *Nofar Sheffi*	327
19	Death *Bernard Keenan*	339

PART VI NARRATIONS

20	Blocks *Andrea Leiter*	351
21	Auto-bio-ethno-graphy *Cecilia Gebruers*	364
22	Beoble *Deepak Unnikrishnan*	373
23	Transing *Greta Olson and Laura Borchert*	378

PART VII MATTERING-FORTH

24	Grounds *Rhys Aston and Margaret Davies*	401
25	Slash *Andreas Philippopoulos-Mihalopoulos*	419
26	Ditches *Adam Gearey*	438

PART VIII JURISLITERARY HISTORIES

27	Miracles *Serene Richards*	454
28	Soul *Jesús R. Velasco*	471
29	Ambiguity *Susan Byrne*	483

PART IX CROSSING SENSIBILITY

30	Transgression *Angela Condello and Tiziano Toracca*	499
31	Transdiscourse *Gonzalo Sebastián Aguirre and Christian Alejandro Kessel*	518
32	Trauma *Phillip Mitsis*	532

PART X A WORD ON JUSTICE

33	Lessons *Richard H. Weisberg*	552
34	Illocutionary *María Pía Lara*	568
35	Poetics *Alejandro Awad*	580

Index   592

Contributors

Gonzalo Sebastián Aguirre is Associate Professor of Political Theory at the University of Buenos Aires Law School. Gonzalo is director of the research project 'Literature and legal forms in the language of the law: the administration of justice as a place of drama' based at the University of Buenos Aires Law School and is an affiliated researcher at the Center for Studies of Philosophy of Culture at the University of Comahue, Argentina. He is a founding member of the *Grupo Experimental de Pensamiento Experimental Soy Cuyano*. In 2017 he published the book *Analítica de la crueldad* (Buenos Aires, Hekht Ediciones). He has a PhD in Philosophy and Aesthetics from the University of Barcelona.

Maria Aristodemou is the author of *Law and Literature: Journeys from Her to Eternity* (Oxford UP, 2000) and of *Law, Literature, Psychoanalysis: Taking the Unconscious Seriously* (Routledge, 2014). She introduced and taught the first Law & Literature module in a UK law school, at Bristol University, and teaches Legal Theory at Birkbeck College, University of London.

Rhys Aston completed his doctoral thesis 'Inviting New Worlds: Jurisgenesis, Anarchism and Prefigurative Social Change' at Flinders University, Adelaide, Australia. He is currently a lecturer in law and criminal justice at University of South Australia. Rhys has strong research interests in legal theory and social theory (in particular, new materialism(s) and posthumanism), and his research explores the relationship between law, power, and social change; prefigurative politics; law and the environment; and critical pedagogies.

Alejandro Awad is a Chilean criminal litigator and sporadic teacher on the subject, founding partner of BACS Abogados (Santiago, Chile), with an LLM from Columbia University who has been reflecting relentlessly during the past ten years – almost fruitlessly, until the present contribution – about the poetics of criminal law.

Laura Borchert is a PhD researcher at the International Graduate Centre for the Study of Culture (GCSC) at the Justus-Liebig-University in Giessen (Germany). Her research areas include LGBTQIAP*/Queer Studies, Law and X, and Queer Legal Theory. For her PhD project, she analyzes the connections between cultural imaginaries and constitutional protections of LGBTQIAP* in the US.

Anne Bottomley (Emeritus Reader, Kent Law School) was a founding member of Critical Legal Conference (UK) and the editorial board of *Feminist Legal Studies*, and is co-editor of the 'Feminist Perspectives on Law' series. Her research in property law continues to focus on collective and community rights in relation to land use: an interest which intersects with her current project on legacies of colonization with particular reference to the Caribbean archipelago.

Susan Byrne is Professor of Hispanic Studies and Chair of the Department of World Languages and Cultures at the University of Nevada, Las Vegas. She is the author of *Ficino in Spain* (2015), *Law and History in Cervantes'* Don Quixote (2012) and *El Corpus Hermeticum* *y tres poetas españoles* (2007), as well as a number of articles in various venues. Her research interests include the history of ideas as expressed in, and altered by, creative letters; law and literature; and Neoplatonic philosophy in early modern Spanish letters and poetics.

Elena Cirkovic is a transdisciplinary legal scholar presently researching the broader topic of *Anthropocentrism and Sustainability of the Earth System and Outer Space.* Her work focuses on connecting the Earth System(s) and outer space environment(s). The project identifies planetary and interplanetary environmental challenges: a. climate change and b. environmental problems in outer space (e.g. orbital debris or interplanetary contamination). Dr. Cirkovic's article 'Space, Ice, and the Final Frontiers of International Law: the Cosmo-legal Proposal' (*German Law Journal*, 2021) provides an introductory study on the topic and argues for a cosmolegal approach. She has also studied landscape architecture and continues to work in design and visual arts. Personal website: elenacirkovic.com

Angela Condello is Assistant Professor of Legal Philosophy in the Law Department, University of Messina; she is also Adjunct Professor at the Department of Philosophy, University of Turin, where she taught a Jean Monnet Module on human rights and critical legal thinking within European legal culture. She has published four monographs and various edited journal issues (Law and Literature, Law Text Culture, Rivista di Estetica), and volumes, among which are *Sensing the Nation's Law: Historical Inquiries into the Aesthetics of Democratic Legitimacy* (Springer, 2018), *Il denaro e i suoi inganni* (Einaudi, 2018, now translated into Spanish), *Femminismo giuridico. Teorie e problemi* (Mondadori, 2019, forthcoming in English), *Post-Truth, Philosophy and Law* (Routledge, 2019), *Law, Labour and the Humanities. Contemporary European Perspectives* (Routledge, 2019), *New Rhetorics for Contemporary Legal Discourse* (Edinburgh University Press, 2020).

Margaret Davies is Distinguished Professor at the College of Business, Government, and Law at Flinders University, Australia. Margaret is the author of five books: *Asking the Law Question* (4th edition 2017), *Delimiting the Law* (1996), *Are Persons Property?* (with Ngaire Naffine, 2001), *Property: Meanings, Histories, Theories* (2007) and *Law Unlimited* (2017, winner of the SLSA Theory and History Book Prize). Margaret's new book *EcoLaw: Legality, Life, and the Normativity of Nature* will be published by Routledge in 2022.

Marinos Diamantides is Professor of Constitutional Law and Political Science at the School of Law, Birkbeck College, University of London. His books include *Political Theology: Demystifying the Universal* (Edinburgh University Press, 2017, with Anton Schütz); *Law, Levinas and Politics* (Routledge, 2009); and *The Ethics of Suffering: Modern Law, Philosophy and Medicine* (Ashgate, 2000).

Mikus Duncis is a Latvian illustrator specializing in sequential art, currently living and studying in the Netherlands. More of his work can be found at www.artstation.com/mxduncis and on Instagram @mxduncis.

Debolina Dutta is postdoctoral fellow at the Institute for Global Law and Policy at Harvard Law School, assistant professor at Jindal Global Law School and visiting fellow at the Institute for International Law and the Humanities, at Melbourne Law School, where she completed her PhD. Debolina has a long-standing relationship with the sex workers' movement in India. She is a recipient of the Audrey Rapoport Prize for Scholarship on Gender and Human Rights. Her co-directed documentary film *We Are Foot Soldiers* (2010) on the activism of children of sex workers in Calcutta won the third prize at Jeevika: Asia Livelihood Documentary Festival. She is currently working on a book project that looks at how feminist humour enables a minor jurisprudence of non-retributive conceptions of justice.

Daniela Gandorfer holds a PhD in Comparative Literature from Princeton University and is the co-director of the research agency Logische Phantasie Lab (Loφ Lab). Currently, Daniela is a Postdoctoral Researcher at University of California Santa Cruz. Her research focuses on a materialist ethics of thought and the matter(s) of legal theory, understood as a material–discursive practice of sensing and sense-making. Daniela has worked on various collaborative and international projects such as 'Synesthesia of Law', and 'Reading Matters', and edited a special issue of *Theory and Event* (Johns Hopkins Press, 2021) on 'Matterphorical'. Her book *Matterphorics: Laws of Theory* is published by Duke University Press.

Adam Gearey is a professor of law at Birkbeck College, University of London.

Cecilia Gebruers is a lawyer from the University of Buenos Aires and holds an LLM and a JSD from the Benjamin N. Cardozo School of Law. Cecilia's work spans human rights advocacy and legal and political theory. She is currently a postdoctoral fellow at the Argentinian National Council for Scientific and Technical Research (CONICET) based at the Interdisciplinary Institute for Advanced Social Studies of the University of San Martin (IDAES-UNSAM) and an adjunct professor at the Legal Clinic I of the University Torcuato Di Tella School of Law.

Peter Goodrich is an ardent advocate of argute alliterations and the silent 'p', as in ptomaine raspberry and rhubarb. Peter perturbs the Panglossian portals and protocols of panomian legalities and other plagiarisms with the pataphysical portents of posthuman science and their paromoion postulates. A practitioner of widdershins in the *circulus disciplinarum*, he is author, recently and most compositely, of *Advanced Introduction to Law and Literature* (Edward Elgar Publishing) and the forthcoming *Vision and Decision: On the Judicial Uses of Images* (Oxford University Press). Chef, film-maker and olericulturalist, he is currently working on a project entitled *Laugh and Critique*.

Geoff Gordon is a senior researcher in public international law at the Asser Institute, part of the University of Amsterdam. His research addresses institutional points of interface between law, security, economy and technology, with current focus on applications of quantum technologies and quantum theory.

Jannice Käll holds an LLD in Legal Theory and is associate professor in Sociology of Law at Lund University, Sweden. Her research interests involve questions of new materialist jurisprudence, critical legal theory, law and technology, property and contract. Her book *Posthuman Property and Law: Commodification and Control through Information, Smart Spaces and Artificial Intelligence* is published in the Routledge Series: Space, Materiality and the Normative.

Bernard Keenan is Lecturer in Law at Birkbeck College, School of Law, University of London. His research interests lie in the study of law, political power and secrecy (with particular reference to contemporary questions of national security), digital media and legal techniques, the immigration system and social theory. Prior to his academic career, he worked as an immigration and asylum lawyer in London and in radio at the BBC in Belfast.

Christian Alejandro Kessel is a lawyer from the University of Buenos Aires and holds a PhD in Philosophy from the University of Barcelona. He has led research groups at the University of Buenos Aires, and has given lectures, seminars and conferences in Spain, Mexico, Brazil and Argentina on the concept of drama and the creative processes involved in both theater and law. In 2017 he co-edited with Gonzalo S. Aguirre the book *Juicio, proceso y drama. Ensayos sobre Estética del Derecho* (Buenos Aires, Aldina). He is an affiliated researcher at the Center for the Studies of Philosophy of Culture at the University of Comahue, Argentina. He is a civil servant of a Buenos Aires court, and is devoted to exploring the relationships between theatre, law and philosophy.

María Pía Lara, Professor of Political Philosophy, Ethics and Aesthetics at the Universidad Autónoma Metropolitana (Mexico City), is the author of *Moral Textures: Feminist Narratives on the Public Sphere* (1998), *Narrating Evil: A Postmetaphysical Theory of Reflective Judgment* (2007), *The Disclosure of Politics: Struggles over the Semantics of Secularization* (2013) and *Beyond the Public Sphere: Film and the Feminist Imaginary* (2020). She has published several articles on feminism, the public sphere, conceptual history and myth, and populism in international journals. She is a co-director of the Critical Theory Colloquium that takes place every year in Prague.

Marett Leiboff is Honorary Professorial Fellow in the School of Law, University of Wollongong, Australia. Drawing on her background in theatre studies and as a lawyer and jurisprudent, Marett is the founder of the new field of theatrical jurisprudence. Her book *Towards a Theatrical Jurisprudence*, first published in 2019, is the culmination of 15 years of experimentation in the potential of theatre as jurisprudence, in order to disrupt expectations and produce the kind of response and responsiveness that can only be created in theatre, beginning with the use of Brechtian techniques in a 2005 article on post-mortem sperm harvesting as discomfit and discomfort, before turning a couple of years later to Grotowski, whose work grounds theatrical jurisprudence. She celebrates all of the amazing work, past and present and emerging, in the burgeoning arenas of law and theatre and the work of law and performance scholars.

Andrea Leiter is Assistant Professor at the Amsterdam Center for International Law. Her research focuses on global economic inequality and law making through private actors, with a focus on the digital economy.

Elena Loizidou is Reader in Law and Political Theory at the School of Law, Birkbeck College. Her research interests range from anarchism and political theory to theories of gender and sexuality, law and culture. Her publications include *Disobedience: Concept and Practice* (ed, Routledge, 2013); *Judith Butler: Ethics, Law, Politics* (Routledge, 2007); "What is Law?" in *The Anarchist Imagination: Anarchism Encounters the Humanities and the Social Sciences* (Routledge, 2019); "Law, Love and Anarchism" in *Law and Philosophy: Critical Intersections* (Rowman & Littlefield, 2018); "Sequences of Law and the Body" in *Routledge Handbook of Law and Theory* (Routledge, 2018); "Dreams and The Political Subject" in *Vulnerability in Resistance* (Duke University Press, 2016); *A Parallel Art of Living* (Rowman & Littlefield, 2020); *Dance, Anarchism and Mutual Aid* and *From Exchange to Freedom, No Guarantees* (Bloomsbury Press, 2021). Her new book *Anarchism: An Art of Living with Law* is forthcoming (Routledge, 2022). She is on the editorial board of *Law and Critique*. She aspires to become witty.

James R. Martel teaches political theory in the department of political science at San Francisco State University. He is the author of, most recently, *Unburied Bodies: Subversive Corpses and the Authority of the Dead* (Amherst College Press, 2018) and *The Misinterpellated Subject* (Duke University Press, 2017). He has a forthcoming book also with Duke entitled *Anarchist Prophecy: Disappointment and the Power of Collective Sight*.

Phillip Mitsis is A.S. Onassis Professor of Hellenic Culture and Civilization at New York University (New York, USA) and Academic Director of the American Institute for Verdi Studies. His research centres on Greek and Roman poetry and philosophy. Recent publications include *Natura Aut Voluntas. Recherches sur la pensée politique et éthique hellénistique et romaine et son influence* (2020) and, as editor, *The Oxford Handbook of Epicurus and Epicureanism* (2020). He is currently editing the text of the *Batrachomyomachia* with a commentary and translation.

Nathan Moore is a senior lecturer at Birkbeck College School of Law, London. His current research interests include justice and contingency; absolute immanence and its jurisprudential consequences; statuses of the thing; and why Sun Ra is superior to Martin Heidegger. Refusing anthropocentricism, political theology and cybernetics, he works towards political mythologies in the shining dark of human disenchantment. He is not interested in aporias, breaking through, redemption or competition. He does believe in abstraction, feedback and social composition. The evil twin of his contribution to this volume can be found in Stanley Gontarski (ed.), *Burroughs Unbound* (Bloomsbury).

Greta Olson is Professor of English and American Literary and Cultural Studies at the University of Giessen, Germany. She is a general editor of the European Journal of English Studies (EJES) and, with Jeanne Gaakeer, co-founder of the European Network for Law and Literature. Greta aims to facilitate work on the nexus between political and artistic practice and academic analysis. She is involved in a project called "Beyond the Male Gaze: Towards Pluralistic Media Practices" with the filmmaker Lisa Friederich, and in one on the politics of images of migration. Her monograph *From Law and Literature to Legality and Affect* will be published by Oxford University Press in 2022.

Andreas Philippopoulos-Mihalopoulos is an academic/artist/fiction author. He is Professor of Law & Theory at the University of Westminster, and Director of the Westminster Law & Theory Lab. His academic books include the monographs *Absent Environments* (2007), *Niklas Luhmann: Law, Justice, Society* (2009) and *Spatial Justice: Body Lawscape Atmosphere* (2014). His fiction *The Book of Water* is published in Greek and English. His art practice includes performance, photography and text, as well as sculpture and painting. His work has been presented at Palais de Tokyo, the 58th Venice Art Biennale 2019, the 16th Venice Architecture Biennale 2016, Tate Modern, Inhotim Instituto de Arte Contemporânea Brazil, Arebyte Gallery and Danielle Arnaud Gallery.

Serene Richards is a lecturer in law at New York University in London and an Affiliated Researcher at the École Pratique des Hautes Études. Her articles have appeared in several journals, including *Journal for Cultural Research, Crisis & Critique, Birkbeck Law Review* and *Continental Thought and Theory*. She is currently completing a book detailing a genealogy of conduct in Western philosophical, theological and juridical thought, focusing in particular on the concepts of *dominium* and *vitam instituere*, and an exemplary form-of-life: the Court of Miracles.

Nicole Rogers is Associate Professor in the Faculty of Business, Law and Arts, Southern Cross University, Australia. She played a key role in the School of Law and Justice in her nearly 30 years at the University, and witnessed both the birth and demise of this pioneering regional law school dedicated to the pursuit of environmental and social justice. From 2014 to 2017, Nicole instigated and co-led the collaborative Wild Law Judgment project, and she is co-editor of *Law as if Earth Really Mattered: the Wild Law Judgment Project* (Routledge, 2017). Her 2019 research monograph, *Law, Fiction and Activism in a Time of Climate Change*, was shortlisted for the Hart-SLSA book prize and the inaugural 2020 Australian Legal Research Book award. Her book on the implications of the Australian Black Summer megafires for climate narratives was published by Routledge in 2021.

Jorge Luis Roggero is a professor at the University of Buenos Aires (UBA) and a researcher at the Argentinian National Council for Scientific and Technical Research (CONICET). He is the author of *El reverso del Derecho. Desmontajes del discurso jurídico* (Buenos Aires, La Ley, 2017) and edited the volume *Derecho y Literatura. Textos y contextos* (Buenos Aires, Eudeba, 2015).

Nofar Sheffi is Lecturer at the Faculty of Law and Justice, UNSW Sydney. Intersecting legal theory, critical theory and social theory, her work explores various technologies and techniques of government, the operation of communication systems, the constitution of domains, and the internal dynamics of social networks.

Sabarish Suresh is a doctoral candidate at the Benjamin N. Cardozo School of Law.

Tiziano Toracca is Visiting Professor at the Department of Literary Studies at Ghent University (Belgium) and Post-doc Fellow in Italian Contemporary Literature at the Department of Humanities, University of Turin (Italy). His research focuses on Italian Contemporary Literature, modernism and neomodernism, literary representation of work, and law and literature. He wrote *Paolo Volponi. Corporale, Il pianeta irritabile, Le mosche del capitale: una trama continua* (Morlacchi, 2020) and *A Theory of Law and Literature: Across Two Arts of Compromising* (Brill, 2020, with Dr Angela Condello).

Deepak Unnikrishnan is a writer from Abu Dhabi. His book *Temporary People*, a work of fiction about Gulf narratives steeped in Malayalee and South Asian lingo, won the inaugural Restless Books Prize for New Immigrant Writing, the Hindu Prize and the Moore Prize. His fiction, and non-fiction, has appeared in *Guernica*, Drunken Boat, Foreign Affairs, *The Guardian* and *Himal Southasian* among others, and he frequently collaborates with artists and scholars across disciplines. He has been a writer in residence at Sangam House, Ca' Foscari University of Venice and Brown University, and was a Margaret Bridgman Fellow in Fiction at Bread Loaf. He currently teaches at NYU Abu Dhabi.

Jesús R. Velasco (Valladolid, 1965) is currently a PhD student in Law at the École des hautes études en sciences sociales. He also teaches in the Departments of Spanish & Portuguese, and Comparative Literature at Yale University. He has a new book in press, *Microliteraturas* (Madrid, Cátedra, expected in 2022).

Richard H. Weisberg helped establish and sustain the Law and Literature movement, beginning in his days teaching French and Comp Lit at the U of Chicago, and then at Cardozo where he founded the journal *Cardozo Studies in Law and Literature*. His books include *The Failure of the Word* (Yale U Press), *Poethics* (Columbia U Press), *When Lawyers Write* (Little Brown) and *In Praise of Intransigence*. Upon taking emeritus status at Cardozo, he remained Distinguished Visiting Professor of Law at the U of Pittsburgh. He is the President of the Law & Humanities Institute.

Virginia Emilse Zuleta is currently finishing her Master's degree in Communication and Culture at the University of Buenos Aires and has a Bachelor's degree in Philosophy from San Juan National University, Argentina. Her work and research are at the intersection of contemporary philosophy, literature and political theory. She is Assistant Professor of Political Theory at the University of Buenos Aires Law School and at the National University of José C. Paz, Argentina. She is a member of the editorial committee of the academic journal *Las Torres de Lucca. Revista internacional de Filosofía Política*.

1. Introduction to *Research Handbook on Law and Literature*. What is your power?

Daniela Gandorfer

Synaesethics – Sunburned Concepts – Jurisliterary Atmospheres – Scissor Hands – How far will you go?

Abstract(ion): *Now, more than a hundred years on, what is law and literature in the face of the shifts in matter and meaning?*

The project and purpose of the *Handbook*, this *vade mecum* and enchiridion, omnium gatherum and circumbendibus on law and literature, is to experiment with jurisliterary modes of sensing and sense-making that attend closely to what concepts can *do*. This is a matter, quite literally, of *aesthetics*—one less concerned with issuing judgments than with an ethics of sensing and sense-making. Concepts are neither simply linguistic nor representational, but doings and becomings, which is to say, *spacetimematterings*.[1] They come-*from*, *matter-forth*, and are, as Elisabeth Povinelli notes, big "redirection machines" that change the "dynamics of work-ability and non-workability in a region."[2] Consequently, when it comes to concepts, sensing and sense-making require a mode of engagement sensitive and response-able to the very *relationality* of different modes of existence,[3] rather than tools of interpretation and application that are, as such, considered separate from and outside the matters at stake. For law and literature, this means that modes of inquiry into what a concept *can do* ought to attend to the disciplinary histories, methods, and quandaries of sense-making inherent in law and literature while also becoming attentive to how meaning comes to *matter* differently. In other words, it calls for modes of *jurisliterary inquiry* able to address the twofold and pressing *aesthethic* task of pushing legal and literary concepts to a point where logocentric thought cannot stand the pressure of embodied existence, where representations, too, are subject to gravity, where concepts are light-sensitive, and where fictions are held accountable for taking up all the air, while also staying with the trouble of language, the literary, the word, and the letter. It is the latter that presents the real (and by no means vanishing) challenge for law and literature, always at risk of bending (to) either will or signifier, readily relapsing into the persistent illusion that being cutting-edge is a matter of discipline(s), and thereby remaining—out of loyalty, fraternity, attraction, or habit—insensitive to the *matters* of legal and literary concepts. This is the case because law and literature, so opine Richard Weisberg and Jean-Pierre Barricelli in their guiding essay on "Law and Literature" from 1982, are both formalized attempts to "structure reality through language," and share "a common fascination with problems of language," such

---

[1] Karen Barad and Daniela Gandorfer, "Political Desirings: Yearnings for Mattering (,) Differently," *Theory & Event* 24, no. 1 (2021): 33.
[2] Elizabeth A. Povinelli, Daniela Gandorfer, and Zulaikha Ayub, "Mattering-Forth: Thinking-with Karrabing," *Theory & Event* 24, no. 1 (2021): 303, 04.
[3] Ibid., 303.

as "rhetoric, ambiguity, interpretation, and the quest for meaning through linguistic signs," which "depend on abstract formulations and on patterns of associative thinking to attain to humanistic judgement."[4] As Kieran Dolin reiterates in his critical introduction to the *Critical Introduction to Law and Literature* published in 2007, "law is inevitably a matter of language," literature is literary, and both are joining forces in "the struggle over certain words or forms of representation."[5] While this observation is speaking to a broad (yet certainly not anonymous) consensus within law and literature scholarship, it also reveals two of the facts the *Handbook* seeks to address: that the struggle is not exclusively over words or forms of representation, but, even if expressed in words and considered as representations, over bodies and modes of existence; and that it is precisely the *matter* of language and how it relates to meaning production that has so far been positioned outside the field's focus and responsibility. If law and literature is or has ever been aiming at a revolution (a term which originally refers to the movement of celestial bodies), this revolution is first and foremost symbolic.[6] Admittedly, it is difficult to bestow law and literature, whether understood separately from each other or considered a joint endeavor, with the tasks of either ensuring that the symbolic revolution *matters* or facilitating a *real* revolution, more accurately, a revolution of the real. After all, law and literature, as of now, is not *really* considered a *field*. Of course, alternative approaches exist and have always existed, both outside of law and literature's canons as well as in their close vicinity. In reading Franz Kafka's work, dear to law and literature, Deleuze and Guattari for example suggest opposing "a purely intensive usage of language to all symbolic or even significant or simply signifying usages of it," and arriving "at a perfect and unformed expression, a materially intense expression."[7] Without doubt (yet through uncertainty, if not indeterminacy), challenging the matter(s) of language and expression brings about different methods, notions of aesthetics, and understandings of ethics. What is more, concerns about contemporary pressures, forces, intensities, and considerations rely not only on the future; time (and space) would be fundamentally different for the field of law and literature than for law and literature *as a field*. Be that as it may, across disciplines and fields of knowledge production, concepts, including those of ontology and epistemology, are being put on trial in order to see what they can do *before* rather than after judgments are announced. In that sense, and many more, the last word about law and literature has not yet been spoken and, more importantly, even if it had, it would indicate another beginning rather than announcing its end. Besides, declaring an end is not easily done, for whether considered in terms of its methods or stakes, law and literature is not one but many; at times so many that neither law nor literature seems an appropriate term to describe the often even incommensurate endeavors pursued under its banner. It is noteworthy, however, that even contemporary approaches appreciative of both law's promiscuity, mingling with various fields and disciplines, and literature's blurry disciplinary boundaries are (for better or worse) staying with the trouble of language when expressing their observations, arguments, theories, and even their critiques of the insensitivity that certain strands of law and

---

[4] Jean-Pierre Barricelli and Richard Weisberg, "Law and Literature," in *Interrelations of Literature*, ed. Jean-Pierre Barricelli and Joseph Gibaldi (New York: Modern Language Association of America, 1982), 150.
[5] Kieran Dolin, *A Critical Introduction to Law and Literature* (Cambridge, UK; New York: Cambridge University Press, 2018), 2, 13.
[6] Ibid., 13.
[7] Gilles Deleuze and Félix Guattari, *Kafka toward a Minor Literature*, trans. Dana Polan (Minneapolis: University of Minnesota Press, 1986), 19.

literature inhabit. Needless to say (yet crucial to acknowledge), despite the *Handbook*'s experimental and creative cutting-edge-ness, despite the digital blocks, the grounds and heavens, waters and sewages, images and imaginations, affects and effects, impressions and expressions, silences and cacophonies, bodies and souls, matters and meanings, and even if none of it were to be understood metaphorically, it stays and makes-sense with precisely this trouble, too. What must also be acknowledged is the fact that law and literature requires institutional belonging(s) that testifies—ideally with formal degrees, publication records, and permanent positions—to a literacy in the power(s) of the written word and a recognition of the claim that the word already *was* at the *beginning*. Dissertations can be burned *after* reading, drawn *after* writing, danced *after* printing[8]—yet not vice versa. It is therefore not surprising that law and literature's "death knell has often been sounded"[9] and that the movement has been declared dead or, if still moving, busy dying and being born from *the* beginning.[10]

Given everything, including the beginning, has everything already been said? Is there any point in being revolutionary, to *revolve* and *revolt* (quite literally rolling and turning our eyes), given law and literature's uncontested vanishing point? And what are the grounds for radical approaches if at the roots of legal and literary sense-making, even despite their transdisciplinary and cross-media orientation, lies the word, and only the word, that has been said and keeps on arresting thought and inquiry in etymological and genealogical paper chases as the disciplines' idiosyncratic proof-of-work? What can legal and literary concepts *do* within a field in which the linguistic sign is the conditional signature testifying to a (more or less) tacit consensus on how meaning comes to matter, prohibiting analysis from going beyond the assumptions of its conditions for being? Consensus, as Deleuze cautions, is "not enough to create a concept," or to engage in reconceptualization for that matter, be it through blockchain (proof-of-work), or legal and literary scholarship. Lest conclusions are drawn too quickly, it must be cautioned that judgments and decisions are not sufficient either, unless considered expressions that cut-together-apart—but that is yet another story; one more about scissors than hands. In any case, before and after reading, the burning question for law and literature today is not "if anyone can tell us where substance ends and form begins"[11] (as Benjamin Cardozo asked rhetorically in "Law and Literature"), but where to begin making and expressing sense differently, *synaesethically*, not seeing the same word in all shapes and colors, but seeing colors shape wordlessly, singing the bitter-sweet glory of God as a lobster without the narcissistic desire to see and create the world in His image. The word is out. "[T]here are all kinds of scissors," not only hand scissors, but scissor hands.[12] Not everything has been decided,

---

[8] It is telling that the "Dance Your Ph.D." contest, which now takes place annually and accepts Ph.D. performances pertaining to the fields of physics, biology, chemistry, and now also the social sciences, came out of the natural sciences and still, after more than a decade, is not inviting humanities scholars to dance their research. The contest is sponsored by *Science Magazine* and the American Association for the Advancement of Science.

[9] Elizabeth Susan Anker and Bernadette Meyler, "Introduction," in *New Directions in Law and Literature*, ed. Elizabeth Susan Anker and Bernadette Meyler (New York: Oxford University Press, 2017), 2.

[10] Peter Goodrich, "Screening Law," *Law and Literature* 21, no. 1 (2009): 1.

[11] Benjamin N. Cardozo, "Law and Literature," *Yale Law Journal* 48, no. 3 (1939 (1925)): 490.

[12] From the opening dialogue between Grandma and Kim in Johnny Depp et al., "Edward Scissorhands" (New York: Twentieth Century Fox, 1990). For more on *aesth-ethics* see also Daniela Gandorfer and Zulaikha Ayub, "Introduction: Matterphorical," *Theory & Event* 24, no. 1 (2021). For

4   *Research handbook on law and literature*

let alone said. Cuts cut-together-apart, double articulations are bifurcating and entangling.[13] Concepts matter-forth, urging law and literature to attend to modes of sense-making critical *and* constructive of terrestrial heavenly concepts and registering those narratives latent in grand histories of a discipline still too disciplined and a movement ready to move on.

> **Die Begriffe, die Du hier siehst, *sind*, und damit ist Alles gesagt.**
> **The concepts you see here *are*—and with that, everything is said.**
> *Jhering*, ironically.

And so we begin, in the middle, forcing jurisliterary thought to keep transitioning by taking a novel yet neither average nor mediocre turn to 1884. Without doubt, 1884 is a significant moment, or reference, for *jurisliterary thought* to imagine its own mattering. It is the year in which judge Schreber's body ontographically begins to express thoughts worth thinking, writing a transitional theory of law by means of a (literary) memoir,[14] and it is also the year the scholar of Roman law Rudolf von Jhering publishes, at this point still anonymously, a satire titled "In the Juridical Heaven of Concepts. A Fantasy" which testifies in wit and earnest to his discontent with the state of legal scholarship in Prussia at the end of the nineteenth century. The satire begins with the narrative voice of a legal scholar explaining in the first-person plural that he fell asleep, dreamed he had died, and found himself elevated yet bodiless in the heaven of (legal) concepts. This heaven is not like any other. It can only be entered by legal theorists truthful to what the legal realist Felix Cohen will 50 years later call *transcendental nonsense*, and only after a sufficient time of quarantine, lest air is brought in. Here, legal concepts remain pure, expressed exclusively in language, uncontaminated by matter, unaffected by any kind of atmosphere, and untouched by life. Other than in the heaven in which legal practitioners are spending their afterlives, the concept heaven has no sun. In fact, the celestial body [*Weltkörper*, world body] on which the concept of heaven is found is not even part of the solar system. Importantly, the absence of sunlight from this heaven is an essential condition for the existence of concepts, for "the sun is the source of life" and legal concepts are incommensurate with life. That is to say, concepts can only exist independent of life and "cannot bear the touch" of the real.[15] "*Cogito ergo est*,"[16] *I think therefore it is*, is how legal scholarship, much to Jhering's displeasure, has made use of Cartesian dualism and thereby instantiated a power of thought that legally determines what can and cannot legitimately *be*: It is the "elevation of the reality of being to the idealism of thought."[17]

---

synaesthethics see Daniela Gandorfer, *Matterphorics: On the Laws of Theory* (Durham: Duke University Press, forthcoming).

[13] For a reading of the potentiality of these concepts see *Matterphorics*. On the practice and concept of cutting-together-apart as it is used here see Karen Barad, *Meeting the Universe Halfway: Quantum Physics and the Entanglement of Matter and Meaning* (Durham, NC; London: Duke University Press, 2007).

[14] See Peter Goodrich, *Schreber's Law: Jurisprudence and Judgment in Transition* (Edinburgh: Edinburgh University Press, 2018); *Advanced Introduction to Law and Literature* (Cheltenham, UK; Northampton, MA, USA: Edward Elgar Publishing, 2021), 92.

[15] Rudolf von Jhering, "Im Juristischen Begriffshimmel. Ein Phantasiebild," in *Scherz Und Ernst in Der Jurisprudenz. Eine Weihnachtsgabe Für Das Juristische Publikum Von Rudolf Von Ihering* (Leipzig: Druck und Verlag von Breitkopf & Härtel, 1884), 250–1. Translations cited here are my own.

[16] Ibid., 274.

[17] Ibid., 291.

Jhering's literary piece not only draws a satirical picture, a humorously fanciful image of legal scholarship in general, and of *Begriffsjurisprudenz* in particular. In an untimely, premonitory manner, it also anticipates, at least if read matterphorically, the onto-epistemological questions that will haunt and finally touch legal scholarship more than a century later: the inevitably real matter(s) of law and legal concepts. With the extinction of the terrestrial conditions vital for various human and non-human modes of existence on planet Earth, affecting and effecting modes of *mattering* (in its double sense) and calling into question established notions of relationality and sociality, concepts and their fields of workability, and with them the conditions and modes of existence, shift. This pertains to modes of governing, be they platform governance shifting what *democracy* is, blockchain entrepreneurs determining what and how *value* means, US legislators increasingly criminalizing *peaceful protest* in the wake of the George Floyd case verdict,[18] governments banning *critical race studies* and other critical modes of research from their curricula, scholars and corporations competing for what *energy justice* does and does not mean, or various entrepreneurs aggressively and successfully pushing for corporate *special* jurisdictions on Earth and in outer space, as they pertain to other modes of sense-making determining what can and cannot be and exist. Indeed, what Jhering's satire makes thinkable when read in view of a *Research Handbook on Law and Literature* that seeks to be response-able to the intricate challenges of the many presents (pasts and futures), is precisely the question of thinkability and sense-making: Who or what makes sense or is made sense of? Who or what is unthinkable or rendered thoughtless? What can modes of sensing and sense-making, of sens*ibility* and sense*ability*, contribute to a *synaesethics* of legal and literary thought and practice attentive to these concerns? These are precisely the questions and quandaries of the *jurislitery*, described in *Advanced Introduction to Law and Literature* as "a science of imaginary solutions, a discourse on holes, an aesthetic of opportunities." It will be cognizant of, but not constrained by, the letter and its histories, and the modes, beings and places of address.

In *New Directions in Law and Literature*, Bernadette Meyler and Elizabeth Anker vaguely assert that new methodologies in law and literature, sensitive to contemporary developments and challenges, have brought about "new rationales for interdisciplinarity, as well as new accounts of the law and literature nexus."[19] The *Handbook* attends closely to this nexus—a web of relationality, string figures and *textiles*, rhizomes and entanglements—while also demonstrating that the potential of law and literature "to unsettle whatever boundaries and confines may unwittingly restrain us"[20] unfolds most powerfully where not even the most fundamental boundary is questioned, that is, where the *jurisliterary* acknowledges its entanglements with phenomena that exceed the conceptual heaven in which, for far too long, legal thought could conveniently hop from cloud to cloud, soon to become digital, crypto law, and singularity. Importantly, such *synaesethical* modes of jurisliterary inquiry do not readily accept their own disciplinary and onto-epistemological conditions as given, let alone force them onto the indeterminacies those modes encounter. For better or worse, "as if" propositions have guided legal and literary sense-making, and by doing so have propagated the production of the fictions we live—and others vanish—by. Jurisliterary inquiry, however, is wary of *positivist idealism*

---

[18] International Center for Not For Profit Law (ICNL), US Protest Law Tracker, www.icnl.org/usprotestlawtracker/?location=29&status=&issue=&date=&type= (May 2021).
[19] Anker and Meyler, "Introduction," 2.
[20] Ibid., 25.

(the thought that therefore not only *is* but therefore even *had to be*). What makes a *synaesethic* engagement with Jhering's satire (as well as Schreber's memoir) intriguing is that it exposes, even if this was not recognizable in nineteenth-century (perhaps not even in twentieth-century) legal and literary scholarship, the jurisliterary potential for envisioning other conditions, even conditionals, generative of constructive and imaginative thought. The science of lucinations, of imaginary inventions, the sense of lettuce and other aesthetic opportunities takes leaps: *what if* law and literature's onto-epistemological core assumptions are not a settled matter yet? *What if* literature expresses fictions ontographically and matterphorically rather than representationally? *What if* burning makes reading possible precisely because it shows that concepts and fictions, too, get sunburned? *What if* law must aerate its concepts,[21] and *what if* thought has not only been forgetful of air,[22] but also of atmospheres, solar systems, even the vacuum which is all but empty? Shouldn't it, at some point, stand to reason—light and bright—that legal concepts existing in an allegedly empty vacuum devoid of sunlight and breathable air would need to break free from the self-incurred Enlightenment to matter differently, or to even register their un/matterings? We might wonder, like judge Schreber did,[23] about the miraculous phenomenon of presumably enlightened thought that despite the absence of a sun—of photosynthesis as the most fundamental process of sustaining life on Earth—nevertheless continues to make large enough waves to relentlessly determine who or what ought and ought not to exist? What, then, is the lifetime of a legal or literary concept and who or what determines, sustains, measures, and affects it?

Weisberg and Barricelli argue that the legal and the literary process "moves from an experience in life toward a narrative re-creation of that experience,"[24] while Deleuze states that literature's task is "certainly not to impose a form (of expression) on the matter of lived experience."[25] Either way, sense-making, even if seen in relation to law and literature, is not a settled matter—and neither is imagination. In fact, Weisberg and Barricelli point out that "[h]owever tightly bound to evidence and the logic of events," the re-creation "needs the bridging or collating powers of the imagination to put together the scene, or the picture, in all its details."[26] Imagination, and an understanding of objectivity that either accompanies, contrasts, or haunts it, finds different expressions, distinct matterphorisations in literature and in law. While law makes ample use of (Cartesian-inspired notions of) objectivity to create related concepts in its image (consider, for example, the concept of reasonableness in common law), literature, once the practice of copying originals, is considered the art of written imagination and therefore was rarely required to give accounts of how it relates to notions of objectivity. Yet, here too, alternatives exist, some of which have been productive of concepts that seek to express a different relationship between imagination and objectivity. Consider for example the Austrian and Czechoslovak writer and journalist Egon Erwin Kisch, whose work actively blurs the lines between literature and journalism, ultimately resulting in the establishment of a genre called "literary reportage," and who continuously challenges legal boundaries. Living and writing

---

[21] Barad and Gandorfer, "Political Desirings," 31.
[22] See Luce Irigaray, *The Forgetting of Air in Martin Heidegger*, trans. Mary Beth Mader (London: Athlone, 1999).
[23] See Goodrich, *Schreber's Law: Jurisprudence and Judgment in Transition*.
[24] Barricelli and Weisberg, "Law and Literature," 162.
[25] Gilles Deleuze, "Literature and Life," in *Essays Critical and Clinical* (London: Verso, 1998), 1.
[26] Barricelli and Weisberg, "Law and Literature," 162.

through two World Wars, he rejects the idea of doing research without being in touch with the matters at stake. He further cautions that not even a detailed "autopsy of the scene of a crime or event," with a thorough consideration of all testimonies given and assumptions made, will offer a complete picture. In an almost scientific and empirical manner, the reconstruction is to be understood according to a probability curve which runs through as many empirical facts as possible. Connections between the points, even if the spaces between them are infinitesimally small, will have to be drawn and require both a particular mode of imagination and a concept of objectivity: that of *logische Phantasie* ["logical phantasy" or "logical imagination"].[27] Kisch's ongoing rearticulation of what literature is and should be, where its boundaries and well-guarded walls lie, and how writers (literary writers and journalists alike) must become response-able, established a novel genre, which is neither literature nor journalism (perhaps both at once), and significantly shaped the concept and practice of *logical phantasy*. To put it briefly, *logical phantasy* requires a social and aesthetic *sensibility*, lest the (re)construction falls prey to inflexible materialism, banality, dogmatism, or lack of imagination.[28] Further, it takes seriously that imagination and *precision*, the mode of cutting off, are not only commensurate, but also inextricable. Obligated to facts and attentive to social conditions, *logical phantasy* enables (re)construction (rather than representation) as an "accusatory work of art" that relates past and future to the present.[29] In other words, for Kisch, literature must not escape the question of (its underlying concept of) objectivity,[30] precisely because imagination is powerful.[31] His suggestion—the concept of logical phantasy—deserves attention as it demonstrates *how* the power(s) of imagination can *matter*. In doing so, it adumbrates what might be termed a *synaesethics of objectivity*, neither objective nor subjective, but attentive to how lives in question are cut in and out of existence. As such it emphasizes an argument this introduction seeks to make, namely that questions about how to imagine, even how to imagine differently, are not only ethical and aesthetic considerations, but material-discursive practices of sense-making.

Nonsense, transcendental or not, *matters*. Ample fun has been made of the growing community of "flat earthers," those unenlightened minds who mistrust science and romanticize the Middle Ages (which, per definition, is what also defines Romanticism, including literary Romanticism). Yet, it is in all seriousness that legal thought (there is in general more leniency when it comes to literary thought) and scholarship, despite the fact that it is the excitement of matter that produces the very conditions for humans to see, engages in solar denialism, constructing and upholding law's Dark Ages, even at institutions at which light is claimed

---

[27] Egon Erwin Kisch, "Das Wesen Des Reporters," in *Mein Leben Für Die Zeitung 1926–1947* (1983), 206.
[28] "Reportage Als Kunstform Und Kampfform: Auszug Aus Der Rede Auf Dem Pariser Kongress Zur Verteidigung Der Kultur," 398. All translations of Kisch's texts in this introduction are mine.
[29] Ibid., 399.
[30] It should also be noted in that context that the Cartesian notion of "objective objectivity," a judgment uttered from a detached outside or an observation considered separate from that which is observed, has been importantly challenged by, among others, feminist scientists such as Sandra Harding, Donna Haraway, and Karen Barad.
[31] Kisch writes in "Reportage als Kunstform und Kampfform": "Even the unpolitical person can recognize that in countries where freedom has been put down and tyranny is ruling, sentimental vagueness, mystical romanticizing of blood and soil and the like are dominating literature, because issues concerning life are not to be raised [*angeschnitten*, literally: cut off, truncated]." Kisch, "Kunstform Und Kampfform," 400.

to be a guiding principle, as, for example, in numerous familiar maxims: *Lux et Lex, Lux et Veritas, Et Facta Est Lux, Lux Sit, Fiat Lux, Hac luce, In Lumine Tuo Videbimus Lumen, Lux et Veritas Floreant, Lumen Ad Viem, Emitte Lucem et Veritatem, Coelestem Adspicit Lucem, Post Nubes, Lux, Lux Veritatis, Et Lux in Tenebris Lucet, Hinc lucem et Pocula Sacra*, and, lest it go unmentioned, *Sol Iustitiae Illustra Nos*. "Substitute light for darkness—everything would be gone!,"[32] the heavenly guide states in Jhering's literary dream. It would be different to lecture on law, he adds. Not only concepts, but also thought is kept in the dark. Where have all the photons gone? Even if their absence is not massive, can scholarship of the twenty-first century still pretend that it does not really matter? How are we supposed to see and what are the visions of a field blind to what carries force? If the Earth matters to thought then, Goodrich writes, "the intelligence of the tellurian, *justissima tellus*, the meaning of matter, is a question of what we look at and what looks at us." This, however, requires neither mirrors nor reflections, let alone geometrical optics. In fact, as Barad argues, "[r]representationalism involves the wrong optics," the "wrong set of epistemological and ontological assumptions,"[33] at least when it comes to understanding the inextricability of being and knowing. Indeed, not only from the perspective of (and as) a brittlestar, but also that of a lobster, a sunburned concept, and even blindfolded Justitia, everything looks (and sees) different(ly).

Law and literature has acknowledged its allegiance to a specific notion of aesthetics and announced its focus on humanistic values. Making sense of and with the ongoing articulations of all kinds of visions and decisions, fictions, imaginations, and myths demands a sensibility fine-tuned to different onto-epistemological dynamisms (far in excess of Cartesian dualism) and notions of value production. For while everything *is*, and even no/thing and nothingness are[34] *real*, not everything can exist, nor even live, nor breathe. Where a concept, or anything for that matter, starts and ends is not a question of form, but of power: "How far will you go?"[35] Even the question of how legal concepts will inhabit solar systems, expressed satirically more than a hundred years previous, is more contemporary than ever. Departing from a *transhumusian* view, transhumanist science fiction and cybernetic literature have for decades been promoting the (physical) severing of the mind from the inferior body, a liberal and liberating project eager to free meaning from matter, matter from law, law from ethics, ethics from aesthetics. Transcendent thought runs deep—and flies high. To the moon!—and to Mars, where Elon Musk desires to be "Imperator of Mars" and therefore suggests keeping "law short." What does it matter, Musk likes to joke around, to be a Martian on Musk or a Muskian on Mars, and whether we like it or not, so the argument goes, humans will have to become artificial minds, digital up- and downloads, smartly contracting, hopping from heaven

---

[32] "Das Licht an die Stelle der Dunkelheit gesetzt—und Alles wäre dahin!" Jhering, "Begriffshimmel," 251.

[33] Karen Barad, "Invertebrate Visions: Diffractions of the Brittlestar," in *The Multispecies Salon*, ed. Eben Kirksey (Durham [u.a.]: Duke University Press, 2014), 234.

[34] See *What Is the Measure of Nothingness? Infinity, Virtuality, Justice/Was Ist Das Maß Des Nichts? Unendlichkeit, Virtualität, Gerechtigkeit*, 100 Notes—100 Thoughts, Documenta (13) (Hatje Cantz, 2012).

[35] Gilles Deleuze, "A Sunflower Seed Lost in a Wall Is Capable of Shattering That Wall," in *The Funambulist Pamphlets: Volume 3: Deleuze*, ed. Léopold Lambert (Brooklyn, NY: Punctum Books, 2013), https://thefunambulistdotnet.wordpress.com/2013/07/05/funambulist-pamphlets-volume-03-deleuze-now-published/, 75.

to heaven, planet to planet, and eventually bit by bit, like crazy diamonds, "shine the light of consciousness into the universe."[36]

> *Let's see… I guess it would have to start with scissors … There are all kinds of scissors.*
> *And once there was even a man who had scissors for hands.*
> *A man? Yes. Hands scissors? No, scissor hands.*
> From *Edward Scissorhands*

We might as well believe in angels—at least according to an ironic suggestion by the legal realist Felix Cohen in his essay "Transcendental Nonsense" from 1935, not so much referencing (future) outer space law as the light of consciousness which denies its worldly source and thinks highly of legal concepts as supernatural entities. Situated in the US American legal context in which jurisprudence plays a more decisive role and where gravitating toward stars and other massive phenomena is more prevalent, Cohen revisits Jhering's satire and wonders "[h]ow much of contemporary legal thought moves in the pure ether of Von Jhering's heaven of legal concepts?"[37] His answer suggests that not much has changed and that this will remain the case until the "ghost-world of supernatural legal entities" vanishes and critical attention is paid to judges and their decisions, that is, the (for Cohen social) event of the cut that makes law matter.[38] Although less engaged in the historical background of Jhering's critical intervention, Cohen is cognizant, at least to a certain extent, of the implications, constraints, and even violence(s) inherent in the application of "supernatural entities which do not have a verifiable existence."[39] Legal concepts are products of a time in which "thought without roots in reality" was "a high object of esteem" and as such served "conceptual acrobats" and their legal magic of word-jugglery.[40] "When the vivid fictions and metaphors of traditional jurisprudence," he argues, "are thought of as reasons for decisions, rather than poetical or mnemonic devices for formulating decisions reached on other grounds" it is all too easy to forget the forces and matters creating and shaping law.[41] Drawing from process philosophers such as Charles S. Pierce, John Dewey, William James, and Alfred N. Whitehead, whose work Cohen appreciates as attacking "transcendental conceptions of God, matter, the Absolute, essence and accident, substance and attribute," and emphasizing different forces at play when it comes to juridical decisions, he argues that a legal concept *is* what it *does*.[42] Legal thought and practice which engages in transcendental nonsense is forgetful of its own performances, of how decisions cut, and of how those cuts take air and breaths away. Cohen offers various examples. In his elaboration on trade names, for example, he shows that the concept was not simply applied, but eventually allowed courts to create "a new source of economic wealth or power" by granting exclusive property rights to words, or, put differently, by providing a "homestead law for the English language."[43] Elaborating further on this example, he exposes not only the power

---

[36] SpaceX, "Making Humans a Multiplanetary Species," YouTube, Sept 2016, www.youtube.com/watch?v=H7Uyfqi_TE8.
[37] Felix S. Cohen, "Transcendental Nonsense and the Functional Approach," *Columbia Law Review* 35, no. 6 (1935): 809.
[38] Ibid., 828.
[39] Ibid., 821.
[40] Ibid., 21, 24, 42, 811.
[41] Ibid., 812.
[42] Ibid., 826.
[43] Ibid., 817.

(how far will the concept go?) of legal concepts, but also the inextricability of law from both language *and* matter, in this case a particular gas. Indeed, language and air, he writes, are "socially useful apart from law," but "neither language nor air is a source of economic wealth unless some people are prevented from using these resources in ways that are permitted to other people."[44] Cohen issues an all too contemporary reminder of how easily (certainly not rarely deliberately) transcendental nonsense hijacks matter(s) if sense-making remains inattentive to what a concept can do:

> If courts, for instance, should prevent a man from breathing any air which had been breathed by another (within, say, a reasonable statute of limitations), those individuals who breathed most vigorously and were quickest and wisest in selecting desirable locations in which to breathe (or made the most advantageous contracts with such individuals) would, by virtue of their property right in certain volumes of air, come to exercise and enjoy a peculiar economic advantage.[45]

Law's magic trick is peculiar, to say the least. It might bestow itself with the power to take up all the air and to distribute breath in a split-second and at will. Splitting seconds and separating bodies, it cuts in and out of being: *Decido ergo est*, I decide; I cut, therefore it *is*—or cannot be. For Cohen legal scholarship must attend to the cut, not only after, but before the fact (that is, the decision). He complains that even "certain advocates of realistic jurisprudence" only break down "rules and concepts into atomic decisions" and refuse to go further with the analysis, unwilling to attend to the forcefield from which a decision is articulated. Transcendental nonsense, the mode of circular reasoning that makes thought run circles around itself (and its Self), is of no use when the task is to "study, describe, predict, and criticize legal phenomena."[46] In this sense, Cohen's intervention, too, can be read matterphorically. Sensitive to the onto-epistemological implications, it pushes thought further—as far as it dares to go, as real as it can get within a field that has not yet accepted the social, let alone the onto-epistemological into its analysis. What is more, "Transcendental Nonsense" adumbrates, ahead of its time and intentions, what Robert Cover states 50 years later: the cuts according to which legal worlds are built "to the extent that there are commitments to place bodies on the line."[47] It is true even in the heaven of legal concepts, where scholarship and practice demand the pure practice of ideas, that there are beings existing, even in the dark.

Being on the line[48] where the first cut is the deepest is an unbearable state of (and for) being, exposed to being cut off, cut open, cut through, separated, fractured, sliced, falling from grace and the heavens, bodies hanging and drowning, flesh rotting and decomposing, matter exploded and becoming mortal, left *to be or not to be* signified, represented, recognized. The sword that Lady Justice carries in her right hand is far from metaphorical; each *legis actio* is a cut, a cleaving of conceptual skin, a sickle that scythes through the carapace and colors, the stalk, chaff, and corn of the beings that are judged.

Indeed, the legal scholar and writer Patricia J. Williams exposes in her extraordinary essay "Alchemical Notes. Reconstructing Ideals from Deconstructed Rights" from 1987 that it is not only the construction and deconstruction of legal concepts, in this case "rights," but also

---

[44] Ibid., 816.
[45] Ibid.
[46] Ibid., 843.
[47] Robert M. Cover, "Violence and the Word," *Faculty Scholarship Series* 2708 (1986): 1605.
[48] See also Povinelli, Gandorfer, and Ayub, "Mattering-Forth."

attempts to haphazardly dismiss them that put bodies on the line—or tighten the noose further. In doing so, Williams opens her essay with a meta-story, a concise literary piece, that weaves together Jhering's concept heaven, Cohen's transcendental nonsense, and the way Critical Legal Studies (CLS) scholars have inserted themselves and their stakes in this conversation, ultimately deciding from so very high up what concepts can and cannot do so very low down. "Once upon a time," Williams begins her story, "there was a society of priests who built a Celestial City whose gates were secured by Word-Combination locks."[49] The priests, on their way to becoming gods, "were masters of the Word, and, within the City, ascending levels of power and treasure became accessible to those who could learn ascendingly intricate levels of Word Magic."[50] In a reference to CLS, a movement which evolved around Harvard Law School and remained mainly inattentive to law's systematic racism, she expresses how CLS went from legal realism to deconstruction, as one day the "priests-turned-gods tired of this sport, denounced it as meaningless," left the city, and "acquired the knowledge of Undoing Words."[51] When they reached a place "Beyond the Power of Words," they "let down their anchors, the plumb lines of their reality, and experienced godhood once more." In the heavens and on Earth, it is bodies, not Gods, that are on the line. Under the city "dying mortals called out their rage and suffering," and at the bottom of the Deep Blue Sea, "drowning mortals reached silently and desperately for drifting anchors dangling from short chains far, far overhead, which they thought were life-lines meant for them."[52] The introductory meta-story expresses what the essay argues in detail, namely how and what the concept of rights, the very concept CLS is at that time eager to throw overboard, *means*—and for whom. While it is true "that blacks never fully believed in rights," it is also true that they "believed in them so much and so hard that we gave them life where there was none before."[53] This is by no means meant metaphorically, but matterphorically, expressing the onto-epistemological processes of concepting: "We held onto them, put the hope of them into our wombs, and mothered them—not just the notion of them. We nurtured rights and gave rights life," which "was not the dry process of reification, from which life is drained and reality fades as the cement of conceptual determinism hardens around—but its opposite."[54] Immense alchemical fires, the making of something out of nothing, breathing life into concepts not meant to share breath and imagined to be deprived of air and atmosphere so that godhood can fall and rise again, have demonstrated that, for those out of, and bereft of, breath, the power of "familiar vision" ought not be considered, let alone rejected, lightly.[55] It is only the gods—and, if the opportunity presents itself, also the priests—who dream of *tabula rasa*, who get excited about *terra nullius*, the invention of virgin territory, and remain eager to burn everything down and start over from (their) scratch of violated earth. "Alchemical Notes," Williams' jurisliterary writing that seeks not only to transform matters but to expose supposedly divine decisions for their disregard of what and how they *mean* for mortals, is an attempt to inscribe ethical sensibility into an inherently racist legal system (and especially its most prestigious law schools, its most highly praised legal concepts, its most

---

[49] Patricia J. Williams, "Alchemical Notes: Reconstructing Ideals from Deconstructed Rights," *Harvard Civil Rights-Civil Liberties Law Review* 22, no. 2 (1987): 401.
[50] Ibid.
[51] Ibid.
[52] Ibid., 402.
[53] Ibid., 430.
[54] Ibid.
[55] Ibid.

12 *Research handbook on law and literature*

celebrated theoretical fraternities, and most frequently discussed jurisliterary texts). It demonstrates the potential of real jurisliterary thought to inquire *synaesethically*, that is, to challenge the decisive blindness, the *insensibility* to unrecognized and unrecognizable injustices, that continues to train more and more eyes to see the same thing, over and over again, without even acknowledging that anything was seen after all.[56]

🌱☀︎✄⛰

How to make sense of the matter(s) of law and literature? Law has, as Goodrich points out, historically preceded literature and so in binary form has overdetermined the conjunction in favor of the juridical, has subjected literature to the literalist strictures of legality. And yet, literature, at least if understood as a discipline and field of scholarly engagement, has tailored its narrative with precision, too. Jhering wisely guards his critical intervention into the onto-epistemological assumptions underlying the legal science of his time, building on Descartes and consequently Kant's representationalism, when not only choosing the literary genre of satire but also the dream as a further device for evading accountability. Certainly, literature tends to be rather open about its humorous interventions—satirical, ironical, earnest in its witfulness. Yet, like a nervous laugh, it is hiding the fact that the violences enforced by the letter of the law are as much expressions of law as they are of the letter, the word, and language. For, as humorous as it might be, law is often less of a joke than an absurdity—and neither, for that matter, is literature, let alone law and literature, mere flippant aeration. While Cohen's mobilization of Jhering's satire serves his parody of US legal scholarship and jurisprudence, Williams' adaptation of both the satire and the parody, emphasizes jurisliterary and ontographic matters of law and literature are all but funny. Law and literature, as sciences of the letter, are deadly serious. For in the end it is not *before* the law but *after* the cut that law and literature, legal and literary scholarship meet, exchanging signs and letters of all kinds, agreeing on the impossibility of electrons crashing into language, of photons carrying laws, and of breaths aerating concepts. In this sense, taking into consideration the histories of law and literature, their allegiances to the word as the beginning, and the separation of meaning from matter, law and literature is necessarily cutting-edge in the plural sense expelled and expressed here. Yet, no cut, not even the Cartesian, is once and for all. Jurisliterary inquiry attends to cuts and their underlying dynamics in order to become sensitive and response-able to how, amid an onto-epistemological cacophony, the silent dance of *as ifs* and *what ifs* draw the lines (all real yet never once and for all) that separate fact from fiction, being from knowing, matter from meaning, Life from Non-Life, law from literature, literature from law, imagination from imagination, case by case, law by law, letter by letter, point by point, pixel by pixel, particle by particle—or wave. Nothing can be taken for granted and everything matters. Law and literature, after more than a hundred years of turning a blind eye and demanding spacetime to bend before its vision of the juridical, has to open itself up to jurisliterary inquiries into its onto-epistemological assumptions which ultimately render its methods, concepts, and worldviews imperialistically incontestable. Let's be real: Divine word puzzles are not concerned with bodies on the line and crypto puzzles will not magically

---

[56] Patricia J. Williams, "Skittles as Matterphor," *Theory & Event* 24, no. 1 (2021): 373.

result in a consensus that can create livable concepts (notwithstanding the enormous amount of energy required in the process of consent creation). In the end, and the beginning, God "is a lobster, or a double pincer, or a double bind"; perhaps a millipede, an uneven number, an accident producing a humming bird.[57] It is not enough to return from thought with "bloodshot eyes,"[58] leaving the cave on shaky ground and wobbly feet just to face the sun, happily ever after. Besides, there would be no point in thinking, let alone in scholarship, if this were the end of the story, of all stories imaginable. Matsutake mushrooms wordlessly grow at the end of a world, in nuclear-contaminated soil and human-destroyed forests, writing histories that neither claim harmony nor conquest.[59] Alchemical fires create livable worlds and breathable concepts despite the constant threat of fascisms and racisms in the air and fouling its visual lines. The last word has not been spoken. And so we begin, with law and literature, again and again, "in the middle, in flight, falling, taking off,"[60] making-sense collaboratively, sensing matter(s) of law and literature *synaesethically*, and staying committed to response-ably attending to what concepts can *do*.

What is your power? How far will you go?

---

[57] Gilles Deleuze and Félix Guattari, *A Thousand Plateaus: Capitalism and Schizophrenia*, trans. Brian Massumi (Minneapolis; London: University of Minnesota Press, 2014), 40.
[58] *What Is Philosophy?*, trans. Janis Tomlinson and Graham Burchell III (New York: Columbia University Press, 1994), 41.
[59] Anna Lowenhaupt Tsing, *The Mushroom at the End of the World: On the Possibility of Life in Capitalist Ruins* (Princeton: Princeton University Press, 2017).
[60] Peter Goodrich, "Transhumusians: On the Jurisography of the Corpus Iuris," *Theory & Event* 24, no. 1 (2021): 117.

PART I

VISIONS AND DECISIONS

Jurisliterature – Pataphysics – Ethics of Visibility – Devising Enstrangement – Broken Jugs – Trial Play – Before the Eyes – Leftovers

2. Premonition
Peter Goodrich

The project and purpose of the *Handbook*, this *vade mecum* and *enchiridion*, *omnium gatherum* and *circumbendibus* on law and literature, is to subvert the order of the categories. Where law has historically preceded literature and so in binary form has overdetermined the conjunction in favour of the juridical, has subjected literature to the literalist strictures of legality, our aim has been rather to invert the jurisdictions and give fiction power over jurisprudential invention. Literature, the science of imaginary solutions, comes to govern the dictats and dictates of jurists. The intuition that motivates this creative and aesthetic project is the realization that the parchment reality of law and the pickle jar of precedent confine the literary judgement of lawyers to the rearview mirror and the analeptic deliberations of the backward looking. *Stare decisis*, the axiom of proceeding according to the proximities of unimaginative analogies, mere similes, offers the appanage of legal privilege to the dead and so promotes abstraction rather than materiality, stasis as opposed to invention, and overall acts as ontographic impediment and epistemic obstacle to prolepsis and its figures of premonition. Against the grain, askew of that tendency to traumatic repetition, literature offers the jurisdiction of thought that matters, the embrace of image and idea, of the potential of language and the openings figured by the greater zodiac of poetic wit.

The common law in particular is predicated upon the rhetorical certainty of judicial judgement as embedded in precedent, as stuck in and extracted from the rulebook of the past which, at least historically, is merely found and declared by the judge. Judgement loses its first e, even the word is truncated, castrated, and aligned etymologically with juggment, with the distillation, exsanguination, temporal condensation and lateral displacement of legal corpses, be they cases or the generic principles of the Code. The peculiar and particular quality of legal decision and rule application is a narrowness of vision, a restraint of intellective scope and scopic drive, a stasis engendered by the concept that law can be exhumed, that it somehow exists as inorganic matter, its decisions interred as pristine dead letters that resist the impermanent affects both of temporality and of embodied existence. Precedent is dead, it doesn't write. It is at best an *aide-mémoire*, a mnemomic in the mode of an image of prior and past decisions, but it is the literary that writes, the poet that decides, who turns away from the past to sense the present in its intimations and premonitions.

The premonitory is what escapes precedent, the image that eludes death, the imaginal present absence of the future, the objective unconscious of spectral anticipation in the eye of a contemporaneity which opens the tomb of archived decisions to the living. The affect of legality, lodged in the logic of death, looking back like the angel of history upon the wreckage of law's past, is necessarily not simply narrow but fearful and anxiety-ridden. The figures of jurisprudential expression are those of prohibition, censorship, indictment, interdiction, breach, arrest, fine and confinement. The future is faced via the policy formulae of floodgates, the sense that the administration of justice might easily be overwhelmed, that markets could rapidly disintegrate, that violence is ever at the brink of eruption, and that the minor infraction leads inexorably to the major cataclysm as surely as cannabis results in heroin addiction, and that heated emotional exchange will escalate into physical violence. It is no surprise that the psychoanalytic jurist Pierre Legendre links jurisdiction, the legal designation of administrative competence, to text and terror.[1] The custom and use of law is conceived in this fashion as *timor iuris* or, in the language of Masciandaro's premonitory essay, *sermones pro sollicitudinem*, namely arguments for and from anxiety.[2]

VATICINATION

The figure and the madness of the sovereign, the synecdoche of the most Holy Roman Emperor, the sanctified megalographs of Justinian or Leviathan, of monarch, of President, the highest prelate and fused fiction of national identity exist necessarily in a hostile environment. Imperial majesty, the Prince – *principium et prima regula* – is armed with laws and a sword, and decorated with arms against a sea of troubles and the oceanic affects of anxiety. The Christian doctrine of *caritas*, of charity as love and as *caritas* for the world, becomes in law a duty of care, a definition of harms to be avoided, a negative and inverted foresight of threat and of injuries culled from the past. Looking back, bound by precedent read in a literal vein, the stochastic and sclerotic tableaux of traumas limits what is seen; the fog of fear displaces foresight into the storm-blown perceptions of the angel of history, and of the rearview mirror. *Timor iuris* is a preclusive phantasm of carnage and death, a relay of the spectres of the departed, and so sees very little. Juridical vision is restrained and retinal justice is left unexplored because the logic of precedent is bound to the dead hand of the demised. The penchant of jurists is to look in the wrong direction.

The competitive residues of past events, the strictures occasioned by A versus B, *Regina* versus *Civis*, *Rex* versus *Peregrina*, in the agonistic modalities of trial, uncivil or criminal, administrative or procedural, create a bulwark and defence against the inquietude of the real, the disruptions of events and encounters, the combustive affects of corporeal networks and cellular change. The juristic concept of foreseeability is a principle less of insight than of blindness, a form of closure rather than of potential and imaginative creation. When Judge Judge judges a case concerning long-term commercial relationships he feels compelled to invoke the classically backward-looking principle of *stare decisis*, of sticking with prior decisions, in saying that:

> However settled the law may appear to be, one of its strengths is that the possibility of development, or change, remains. In my view [...] we must apply the law as it is, not as it *may* possibly one day become [my emphasis] [...] I do not believe that this approach means that the development of the law is likely to be stultified. If, for example, there were a significant conflict in the authorities, or if the law could reasonably be described as uncertain [...] [this] might provide a compelling reason for trial.[3]

---

[1] Pierre Legendre, *L'Empire de la verité: introduction aux espaces dogmatiques industriels* (Paris: Fayard, 1983) 218: 'when we pronounce the word *territory* here, recall the semantic play of the jurists: *territorium* comes from the verb *terreo*, which signifies productive of terror; it is the frontier space where power can exercise the law of terror – *ius terrendi*, which is synonymous with *jus submovendi*, which can be translated as the law of erasure from the map.' See further, Legendre, *Le Désir politique de Dieu: Etude sur les montages de l'État et du Droit* (Paris: Fayard, 1988) 371ff.
[2] Nicola Masciandaro, *Sufficient unto the Day*: Sermones contra sollicitudinem (Schism Press, 2014).
[3] *Baird Textiles v Marks and Spencer* [2002] 1 All. E.R. 737, 755 d–f.

The recourse to the *certum* of law is both rhetorically muted and syntactically ambiguous. What relationship to the future and to change is being offered? If law is settled, it is unmovable, indeed stultified because it is as it is, stolid and standing – *stultè egit*. The possibility for change that 'remains' is contradicted by the imperative to apply the law as it is and not as it may be; the weakly permissive and loosely proleptic notion of an indeterminate future in which a law of becoming is actualized is in fact syntactically and immediately suppressed by the contingent imperative that even such uncertainty has no greater force than that it 'might provide a compelling reason for trial'. Underpinning this timorous hesitancy, this extraordinarily vague generality as to what may be is an opposition and antagonism between what is the law and what may in future be the law, between possibility and potentiality. More than that, the binary effectively excludes the future as potency, as affect and imagination, because at root Judge Judge, in privileging the law that is, subsumes the present in the past. What is, in epistemic terms, means what was, the dead precedent exhumed as the implausible living form of legal rulebook. While the present is reduced to the static vestiges of past cases, the future is elided with the present as the non-legal impossibility of a future that has not happened.

It is evidently easier to forget the future and to demit that other role and literary function of the judicial, of the mediator who judges so as to harmonize, which is that of the Vates, the poet lawyer invoked most famously by Philip Sidney, the one who uses verse and rhyme, *carmen necessarium*, the presciently necessary song to restore peace, to build a future. In more familiar terms the point is simply that 'the law as it is' cannot be excised from the future, any more than prior judgement can be deemed extant without the imaginative and literary effort, the poetic intervention of the instant judicial interpreter.[4] As Vico puts it, 'only men of limited ideas take law for what the words expressly say', and by the same token it should be recalled that legally *certum* is the antonym of *verum*.[5] The truth, *verum*, is the Platonic ideal, the spiritual and intangible glow of faith, while the *certum* is what human invention constructs, the enthymeme or probable argument that rests upon the uncertain intuitions, delirious affects and corporeal immediacies of judgement. The law as it is cannot be dead, nor can it be found in the graveyard of prior decisions, but rather it must be an active combination of transitive and transient apprehensions, haptic sensibilities; of phantasms of past and future, Mnemosyne and premonition.

The office of the Vates, the poet lawyer, is to look forward, to act as soothsayer and to generate a premonitory harmony, to invent the only *certum* that matters, that of the future of a profane *verum*. The classical sense of *certum* is of making visible, of painting and rendering human action as the materialization of potential, the figuration of ideas that collide with the great perhaps, the presentiment of what is next. It is this conjunction of spirit and letter, vision and fabrication, prescience and invention, that marks the provenance and province of jurisliterature.[6] This term marks the aesthetic jurisdiction of literature within law, the opening of the discipline both to the circle of liberal sciences but also to the wild jurisprudence of the 'as if', of creative, surreal and pataphysical imagination. The literary force and matterphoric power of literary sensibility, and most specifically that branch of fiction that addresses the future,

---

[4] Philip Sidney, *An Apologie for Poetrie* [1595] (Oxford: Clarendon Press, 1907) 8.
[5] Giambattista Vico, *The New Science* [1744] (Ithaca: Cornell University Press, 2016) 390.
[6] Anne Teissier-Ensminger, *Fabuleuse juridicité. Sur la littérarisation des genres juridiques* (Paris: Garnier, 2015). For an anglophone and somewhat divergent account of the jurisliterary, see Peter Goodrich, *Advanced Introduction to Law and Literature* (Cheltenham: Edward Elgar Publishing, 2020).

science fiction and more importantly pataphysics, the science of imaginary solutions, can open legality to the materiality of moving forward, facing the unknown, expressing potential, rather than looking back in timorous hesitation. Juridical foresight is myopic and risks repetition – the trauma of legal training is hard to overcome – as it seeks to restrict rather than open vision. In Tort law, foreseeability is a concept of limitation, constraining liability by binary opposition of proximate to remote harm. The reasonable person foresees very little and is liable for even less. The point, however, is not substantive but rather temporal. It can be noted briefly that in recent case law a slim expansion of what can be foreseen has taken increasing account of affective harm and loss, both in Contract and Tort. The past will govern, and change will be in tiny increments in terms of psychiatric harm, affective loss, deprivation of use, solatium, depreciation of value and other consequential expenditures.[7] The unforeseen and unknown are excluded under doctrines of impossibility and frustration of contract: the law runs out in the face of the future, the dictate of the courts generally being to continue as before, status quo ante; and in private law the contract will govern according to explicit or implicit terms that can be manipulated to allocate risk. Thus, in recent pandemic-related case law the uniform response is simply to exclude liability by reference to generic terms governing Material Adverse Change or Events as impossibilities, or, in Mergers and Acquisitions, as subject to default rules by which exogenous risks are placed on the buyer.[8] What Wigmore terms 'a stiff and superstitious formalism' governs the law term or *dies juridicos*.[9]

A further and striking example of blinkered vision in dealing with the future can be taken from the interpretation of contractual exclusions of liability. According to early law, release from claims 'imports a knowledge in the releasor of what he releases'.[10] The principle involved was that what the signatory did not know could not be included within the ambit of release or intended meaning of the agreement: 'For *de non existentibus et non apparentibus eadem est ratio*' – what is not manifest does not exist. The specific case involved a will and the release of a share of the inheritance, being obtained by means of misrepresentation – a material *suppressio veri* – and so not knowing the import of the release, the disposition is depicted as whimsical. The unknown subject matter of the specific relinquishment was too uncertain and too vague to be enforceable. The requirement of manifestation, the *certum* of visibility, constitutes a rule demanding proof of fact and of substance which excludes claims and implications out of thin air or unknown futures. How then does the law deal with release of unknown futures – in the jargon, unquantified risks? Take a standard form release clause:

> RELEASE: [Insured] hereby releases and forever discharges [Insurer] of ALL CLAIMS, growing out of any and all known and unknown, foreseen and unforeseen bodily and personal injuries and property damage, arising out of the accident. [Insured acknowledges] the injuries sustained are or may be permanent and progressive and that recovery therefrom is uncertain and indefinite.[11]

---

[7] On affective loss and emotional harm in English contract law, see *Farley v Skinner* [2002] 2 AC 732.
[8] Most recently *Travelport Ltd v WEX Inc.; Olding and Others* [2020] EWHC 2670. In the US, see *Akorn Inc. v Fresnius Kabi AG* 2018 WL 4719347.
[9] Wigmore, *Evidence* (1981) vol 9, paragraph 2461, cited in *Bank of Credit and Commerce v Ali (No1)* [2001] 1 AC 251 at paragraph 25.
[10] *Salkeld v Vernon* 1 Eden 64 (1758): the specific doctrinal issue was the signing away of an absolute remainder devised to the wife of the testator, which share was 'sunk in the residuum' and so not apparent to the releasor.
[11] *Vincente Morta v Korea Insurance Corp.* 840 F.2d 1452 (1988).

The issue that arises is usually that of a subsequent manifestation of a latent injury that was missed by the treating physicians or otherwise, in legal terms, non-existent at the time of signing. What then is the referent of 'unknown', 'unforeseen' and 'uncertain'? Working in reverse order, the uncertain is the least problematic in that the *non-certum* is a conscious ignorance and so has a precarious status and partial manifestation, a future but one that is ill-defined rather than entirely blank. What is meant by unforeseen is legally constrained by what was foreseen or foreseeable at the time of signing, an unforeseen consequence of a known injury, but arguably does not include unforeseen harms in the sense of other injuries that were unknowable at the time. Unknown compounds the problem and lacks both referent and legal definition. Like zero, a reference to nothing might have a conventional definition but to exclude future unknown unknowns is to exclude both everything and nothing. A 'solemn composition […] expressly [to] agree to release uncertain demands' may be enforceable according to old law but the unknown exceeds such definition and hence by default escapes juristic purview, oversight or contemplation. Even under the most flexible of regimes of interpretation according to the reasonable meaning of the language used, the absolute exclusion of unknowns lacks any semantic circumscription or rational definition.

The doctrinal point to be made is that the blanket exclusion of liability for future unknown events cannot be literally applied. An accounting error in billing, fraud in the releasee's disclosures, a negligent incision or stitching, unconscionable exercise of bargaining power, an object left in the patient during the operation by mistake are all fairly obvious exceptions to the exclusion of the unknown. It is necessary to address not simply what was foreseen, but the premonitions and vaticinations of the subject who attempts in law to address the future, to open to the unknown as the tellurian equivalent of the unconscious, to listen, embrace, engage and enter a future of inventive becoming, to look forward so as to acknowledge and insufflate our part in the future now. It is here, in the domain of unknowns, that legal circumscription is most evidently a failure of imagination and an expression of a lack of sensibility and lacuna in apperception. There is a dearth of will to unknow, which is to say, to allow the eerie and otherworldly, the felt expressions and spectral manifestations, the premonitions and imaginings of our futureity to rewrite the juridical, and to recast the forms of juristic expression from the future to the past. The poet legislates and once the sometimes shockingly prosaic dictates of backward-looking lawyers manipulating feeble policy interests are overcome, the vision and vista of the properly premonitory, the jurisliterary jurisdiction, the invention and imagination of a more expansive and wilder jurisprudence that can bring to bear a greater circumstance and potential than law's attempt to strangle posterity which at root means to impose posteriority. Allow the Vates to vaticinate, the poets to prophesy and the bard to build in the antique and anticipatory sense of common law's druidic sensibilities and foundations.

JURISLITERATURE AND 'PATAPHYSICS'

The *ars iuris* is potentially much more than the literal and fearful search for the security of certainty and the posterior-orientated restraint of future vision by imposition of the past tense. The purport of the present volume is precisely to reorient in temporal and disciplinary terms. The literary imagination is the primary resource of a law that writes, the potential of a forward-looking thought which denial simply obscures without excluding. Reverting to the example of the long-term or non-proximate unknowns that releases and force majeure clauses seek to circumscribe, the jurisliterary answer is that of interpreting the language used as a series of suggestions. I take the specific term from contemporary contract theory, and relational conceptions of bargain over time to make the point that a suggestion is a foreboding, a presentiment and anticipatory, eerie sensibility of matters that exist beyond the self in the imaginal community of thought that extends from interior sense to future potentials. The premonition betokens, forecasts, predicts and prognosticates according to a literary law and apprehension that expands the knowledge base and aesthetic force of legal judgement in material and engaged ways.

Part of the history of premonition lies in the broader humanistic air and breath of natural law that now, rendered profane, emerges as wild law, as earth jurisprudence and the fertile imaginings of corporeal performativity. The theatrical sensibility of legality as a symbolic and fictional scriptural endeavour, as drama, necessarily engages in acting out its anticipations in the greater public and natural spheres of a globally connected community and commonality. This was well known to the Renaissance and early modern *mens emblematica* and philosophical imagination of lawyers. Jurisastrology, for example, studied *sphaera legalis*, the spheres of the law, and the law of the spheres, and in the inspired work of *jurisperitus* Stephanus Forcatulus it involved creative dialogues between astral personifications of distinct juristic figures and dispositions, the prosopography of the universe.[12] The fact of dialogic exchanges between symbolic representations already demarcates a shift from the embalmed and monochrome records of precedent decisions, to an active and alive intellective perambulation, *sub specie astrorum*, giving rise to a sense of constant transition, of perpetual motion, and then also, aligned to the peripeteia of creative thought, a series of wild connectives and alternative future spaces. Here we learn of the astrological and juridical import of the number 7, as an uneven enumeration of which the gods are fond, but also as the figure of harmony of the spheres, days of the week and books of the *Digest*. Music and number, the harmonics of conflict resolution, also gain analysis, as they do later in the constitutional theory of Jean Bodin and others. The roots of law, its grounding in the sensibilities of community, suggests in aesthetic terms both the unleashing of the spectres of the past and the impossible visions of what is to come.

For Teissier-Ensminger, the most erudite of proponents of jurisliterature as the real *ars iuris* and proper aesthetic of law, there is both wit and beauty in the moments and genres of juristic opening to the disciplines – *circulus disciplinarum* – and to the public sphere, when foundational introductory legal works provide accessible literary accounts of legality. These works, the preparatives, directives, institutions, enchiridia, prolegomena, present the inner sense, the bigger picture, the affect of legality as captured in literary form and legal fiction. The trope of jurisliterature can however be expanded beyond the promotion of harmonious order predicated upon the most eloquent and elegant of constructions of precedent towards a more extensive sense of the institution of life according to a more pluralistic sense of laws as wild, natural, cellular, astral, futuristic and straightforwardly, where occasion inclines, invented. For such a juristic sensibility to materialize it is necessary, as Jarry remarks, to recognize 'some beings who have managed to escape your Law and your Justice between the lines of my seized volumes'.[13] The pataphysical project of pure invention is one that addresses absences, the science

---

[12] Forcadel, *Sphaera legalis* [1549], reproduced in Teissier-Ensminger, *La Sphère du Droit* (Paris: Garnier, 2011).

[13] Alfred Jarry, *Exploits and Opinions of Dr Faustroll, Pataphysician: A Neo Scientific-Novel* (Boston: Exact Change, 1996) respectively at 21, and 16–17.

of imaginary solutions, which in its earliest definition is gauged to addressing what is not, the universe supplementary to this one whose combustive dynamic is that of replacing what merely is as of now with what imaginative premonition impossibly predicts. It is this literary venture and creative endeavour that requires the jurisliterateur 'to be simultaneously a poet: and what I mean by that is someone who creates what he is talking about the very moment he is talking about it'.[14] Defined in part as a phantasmology, the pataphysical jurist is not simply a futurist whose cognitive endeavour is turned away from precedent towards the spectral virtuality of absences, the not yet of presence – *potentia vacui* – but is intent upon unleashing the proleptic figures and imaginative possibilities of speaking law forward, the *anima lex* which the humanistic jurists were fond of invoking but anxious about realizing.

It is not novel to adumbrate the spectres unleashed from judgement, the figures, images and phantasms that escape the text, but it is stranger – more creatively diversifying – to look forward and envision these as law. The spectre is an absence surrounded by a presence and in Jarry's terminology it is something superadduced upon metaphysics, or 'the feeling of lettuce'.[15] My suggestion, which is both material and proleptic, is that the role of imaginative invention, the inscription of prognosticatory phantasms and the angelological foresight of spectres, is to be found, which is to say that it needs to be created in the jurisdiction of the literary as it intervenes in law. In ascending *Mount Analogue*, we learn that '[t]he fusion and division of living cells became a particular case of logical reasoning, and language derived its laws from celestial mechanics'.[16] The literary 'power to do justice' derives here from precisely such a poetic and divergent approach both to the spectres of judgement and to the spatio-temporal dimensions of decision. Elegance in law is but a code word for serious and necessarily also humorous – the future is the madness of the present – attention to what phantasms say, and what spectres seek to show. The literary prepares the ground and breaks the boundaries of the merely positive and extant through attention to the greater scope of *potentia*, of what will be made, and the cognitive force of *praescientia*, the arcane word for foreboding and foreknowledge, a spiritual and so sensual presentiment of what will be according to the future-orientated modes of literary knowing, the 'as if' of what Vaihinger termed 'entia imaginaria'.[17]

Remaining with the jurisliterary precognition or sense of becoming, with *Your Face Tomorrow* and the visceral emotions, the tactile intuitions of the extension of time emerge. As Marías formulates this sensibility:

> He had used the word 'prescience', a literary word in English, but not as uncommon as '*presciencia*' is in Spanish. Spaniards never say it and almost no one writes it and very few even know it, we tend to prefer '*premonición*', or '*presentiemento*' or even '*corazonada*', all of which have more to do with the senses, a feeling, '*un pálpito*' – we use that word too in colloquial speech – more to do with the emotions […] than with certainty.[18]

---

[14] René Daumal, *Pataphysical Essays* (Cambridge, MA: Wakefield, 2012) at 92 ('The Pataphysics of Ghosts').

[15] Daumal, ibid, 6 ('Pataphysics and the Revelation of Laughter').

[16] Daumal, *Mount Analogue: A Tale of Non-Euclidean and Symbolically Authentic Mountaineering Adventures* (New York: Overlook, 2020) 27.

[17] Hans Vaihinger, *The Philosophy of 'As If'. A System of the Theoretical, Practical and Religious Fictions of Mankind*, trans. C.K. Ogden (London: Kegan Paul, 1924).

[18] Javier Marías, *Your Face Tomorrow: Fever and Spear* (New York: New Directions, 2005) 86.

It is for Marías a question of withdrawal of the will, a matter of what it is like to be dead, meaning a foreknowledge that is neither wanting nor not wanting, but rather attending, open to what occurs without interest or desire to possess, control or smite with a hammer. It is a species of gift for those that can foresee and listen to warnings that exceed the immediate sensibility of law. The foreclosure of legality, the rearview of precedent, takes death literally and in the process opposes finality to futureity, distance to proximity, abstraction to intimacy.

Returning to the example of general releases, the juristic question posed of the relinquishing of future, unforeseen, unknown injuries is that of the referent of the unknown. The legal perspective upon posterity is classically that of foreclosure and avoidance. It is to be subjected to the present which is scotomized by the past and by precedent. The *soi disant* sanctity of contract leads to the early declaration of such releases that 'Whimsical as this disposition is, if the disposition is so expressed, it must take effect'.[19] The designation of the unknown as whimsical, as fantastic and fanciful, is curiously helpful in that it is a fairly direct unconscious reference to the literary, to 'whimsey and fiction', to caprice and humour as the character and surprise of the advenient, of what is triggered by the phantoms of the present. In the instant case this question of the humorousness of the future of law is that of a comedy that allowed the court to relieve a wife from the adverse effects of signing a general release because it misrepresented the effects of the instrument and would have deprived her of an inheritance, a life interest, under a device to her children. The unknown was here too remote but the ground of such temporal distance and relief was the whimsicality of the terms themselves and the umbrageous tone of misrepresentation – *suggestio falsi* or *suppressio veri*, in the legal argot of the courts of conscience of the time.

The exclusion of future unknowns is whimsical but rather than allowing or opening to the jurisdiction of the jurisliterary, the spherical, interplanetary, astrological and premonitory address of the phantasms, spectres and other imaginings of what is to come, the courts nod and look away. The modern position divagates and expressly separates the imagination of what law will mean, the intimations of conscience – of knowing with the aesthetic and ethical, the tellurian and corporeal – from the legal. In the aptly named case of *Morta*, and the release cited earlier, the mortally injured plaintiff was held to the exclusion of unforeseen unknowns: by its terms the release was held to cover all claims, including future unknowns. The purportedly literal reading of the terms of the agreement and specifically the hermeneutic invention that the referent of 'unknown' is determinate or indeed obvious in denotation requires, however, rapid metaphysical support, fictional adumbration and legitimation in which the judge digresses to state that '[w]ritten instruments, fixing the parties' rights and responsibilities by mutual consent, bring an important measure of order to life and greatly facilitate the adjudicatory process [...] despite recent cynicism, sanctity of contract remains an important civilizing concept'.[20]

The hubris and whimsicality of the statement is twofold. At one level, as Stanley Fish has brilliantly expatiated, the instrument fails to state in any literal sense what is excluded. If the words of the document in fact referenced and successfully, which is to say unambiguously, designated the unknown, then the lengthy incantations of sanctity of contract, order and facilitation, civilizing functions, covenants and other holy words would be surplusage and

---

[19] *Salkeld v Vernon* at 71.
[20] *Morta v Korea Insurance* at 1460.

hermeneutic solecism.[21] In alternate terms, the judge is invoking the divinity as the guardian and determination of the future unknown while the civilization itself is made somewhat elliptically to depend, as in the Gospels, upon the Word being singular in referent and divine in origin.[22] More directly to the point, the unknown and unsayable is retentively shut out and avoided; future potential and possibilization are excluded in favour of non-knowledge and the akinesia of precedential literalism. The judge does not escape the literary, nor can he elude the phantasm of the unknown, the not yet, but his recourse is to the mask of abstraction and the vacuity of anything and everything, a blanket that says nothing and figures only death as absence. The phantasm of the unknown, a self-confessedly whimsical and capricious literary concept, a fictive heuristic device, is denuded of content and closed to imagination at the very instant that it is paradoxically invoked in a religious figuration and presumably theological expression.

The whimsical aspect of an absence is what the jurisliterary and pataphysical seek to fill with their attempts to fly, their ecstasies and other cerebral inebriations. The unknown is an absence surrounded by presence, an unconscious that is circled by consciousness, and by similar token the unforeseen is what has not yet appeared. The law of a vacuum, for Jarry, is that of ascension toward a periphery and one can infer that the desire of the phantasm is to materialize, and that of the spectre to be seen, and so to lead the way. For a jurist to take the opportunity of the unknown would be to open up the fact that what is, is always in motion, a *perpetuum mobile* or constant affect and movement, thrownness but also passage over time. The phantasmographics of the literary and pataphysical can help orient and inspire through recognition of the living character, the insufflation and response of thought to the geo-historical trajectory and libidinal force of the fall into the future. That what is in process is also a phantasm, a spectral non-presence constantly and actively in the exercise of apparition, is nothing less than the manner of recognition of the ontographic, tellurian and astral context of presence encountering absence in the matterphor of lived fiction.

The question of release becomes immediately a greater resource and prospect, legal and literary; a question of relinquishment of rights juxtaposed with the universe supplemental to this one, the aesthetic and science of imaginary solutions. Where it is a question of release there is also the meaning of freeing from captivity, of letting go, of setting at liberty and to escape. In psychological forms it means to free of some pain, to express emotion, relieve tension and thereby dissipate the anxieties of law. In Morta's case it is apparent that the judicially asserted literal meaning of the term in the context of the contract of insurance is much more complicated and potentially of greater interest than at first appears or as is foreclosed by the judgment. From the perspective of the subject insured the key concept is that of their intention at the time of agreement as construed objectively from the words used. The meaning is not, however, unilateral but rather bilateral. The insurer drafted the language of agreement but technically the consensus is between the two signatories and in relation to the accident

---

[21] Stanley Fish, 'The Law Wishes to Have a Formal Existence', in A. Sarat and T. Kearns (eds), *The Fate of Law* (Ann Arbor: Michigan University Press, 1991).

[22] *Morta*, at 1459–60. The same view can be found in English case law, as for example in *BCCI v Ali* [2002] 1 AC 251: 'The law cannot possibly decline to allow parties to contract that all and any claims, whether or not known, shall be released'. The opinion continues to the even more extraordinary epistemic claim that '[t]he question in a case such as the present is to ascertain, objectively, whether that was the parties' intention'.

and subsequent treatment. For the judge, 'sticking to the words the parties actually used limits substantially the bounds of legitimate disagreement'. Rather than analysing the words used, however, the judge proceeds to opine that this sticking, the embedding of judgement in the words, the *litera*, is necessary to maintain 'orderly settlement of disputes, avoid multiplicity of suits and the chaos which would result'.[23] Anarchy is pitched against order, and by implication literalism versus the enigmatic incivility of interpretation. The irony involved is that sticking to the words, to the meaning of 'unknown', is precisely what the literalist does not wish to do. It has no referent, as adverted earlier, because it means not identified, without knowledge; ignorance and, in an older idiom, virgin. At the time of expression, it escapes both referent and definition. Its only possible, though potentially extensive meaning, is its inverse denotation or negative elaboration, which is that of what the interlocutors know at the time of stipulating their absence of knowledge as the necessarily undesignated matter of exclusion. The actual referent of unknown, the *consensus ad idem* or *congregatio mentem*, the meeting of minds as law, quaintly designates that agreement remains polysemic and so enigmatic.

The signing subject represented in the written terms of release is an injured body and so the presence that surrounds the absence, the known that encircles the unknown, includes as one facet the wounded corporeal signatory who, far from being released from pain, now suffers more and *mors*. What then is the referent of their unknown? What foresight, premonition or foreboding, what other eerie spectral sensibility, should play upon the meaning and interpretation of the unknowable at the time of encounter? It is not the past that should determine but rather that sensibility of future events that in premonitory and eerie fashion, as the intimations of the unknown, the sensibility of the outside, will give sense to the apprehensions of a wounded body. The insurance adjuster, aptly named Santa Maria, had required that Morta sign the release before receiving any payment and there was no evidence of any attempt to inform Morta of the exclusion of latent, hidden, concealed or suppressed future injuries. What medical science had missed, Morta was supposed to have known as being unknown – a known unknown that releases the wrong party, the insurer, from their obligation to pay for the consequences of the accident.

Premonition is always in part the foreboding of death as something that we carry within, as a sense and corporeal affect. Morta's mortality is not, however, the primary issue, but rather the incomprehending and epistemically illicit attempt to exclude the future in its totality as something that cannot happen and will not be juristically recognized. The strategy and thought process of exclusion is the intrinsic flaw of precedent, the propulsion to closure, the refusal, as Barad puts it, to meet the universe halfway, body and cosmos juxtaposed in the haptic and habile potential of ontographic sensibility and sensation. The anterograde quality of the precedential, what Mark Fisher calls the slow cancellation of the future, the sad smile of the twenty-first century and its technocratic mythologization of temporality, is experiencing collapse. It fosters non-knowledge in the face of the unknown, nostalgia rather than acknowledging the third position, the prepersonal intensity of feeling, the premonition that allows for and seeks to open to the euphoric sense of the intensity of what is to come, the spectre of what cannot be fully extant.[24] The future is not an absence that bursts into presence but a latency, a confluence of sensory experiences that are not simply prepersonal but are

---

[23] *Morta* at 1459.
[24] Mark Fisher, *Ghosts of my Life: Writings on Depression, Hauntology and Lost Futures* (Winchester: Zero Books, 2013) 17.

equally shared, communal aspects of intellection as such. The desire to know puts ignorance to work; the unknown is accessed as the failing progress of words, thinking matter that comes to terms with the sensory dimensions of knowing and, equally, of not knowing. The future is a feeling, a presentiment, a telepathy, an eerie incident that changes our course. For Morta and a purportedly literal reading of the release, the future was the persistence of the no longer, the uncanny repetition of an injury that was ahead of him, numb to science and to sense alike. It was neither known nor unknown but concealed, hidden, suppressed, and in legal terms should have been addressed precisely as an instance of *suppressio veri*, an unconscious pattern or corporeal trauma that repeats until worked through.

In its failing attempt to govern the future and the unknown, the court in *Morta* – and the name should surely have been clue enough – engages in a melancholic and thoughtless evasion. Thou art a scholar, speak to it, is Shakespeare's injunction in *Hamlet*, when the ghost appears, when time is out of joint. The juridical injunction is to say which future, to use the past as prologue, which is to say *pro-logos*, for speech and before speech, as the affect and inhabitation of the ethical force of desire. The question to be resolved is that of what happened: why did treatment not release Morta, as opposed to why the contractual release cannot be viewed as an effective relinquishment of bodily well-being? The sanctity of life here supersedes the supposed sanctity of contract; the body contests the text, which is but a contraction of the ontography of meaning, and in this instance a strangulated premonition, a limp arrow directed at the yet to come. To give premonition its due is thus to accede to the extancy and materiality of the present, to hear the other side in a more imaginative sense and with all due respect to the *ius quaesitum alteri*, as the early lawyers put it; sensitivity to another law, a tellurian and greater material cause, a wild judgement.[25]

Fear of the future, the possessive grasping at technocratic control of temporality, has to be juxtaposed with the legal category of *casus fortuitus*, the chance event or fate that is resident but unidentified in the present, in the body, in the earth. Where Nietzsche talks of forgetting as a positive act, we can add that ignorance is resistance to affect, a refusal to desire to know, a fear of feeling leading to a hiatus of intellection. What cannot be known cannot be excluded, or at least can only be avoided unknowingly, as opposed to recognized and addressed when it occurs. The doctrine of impossibility or, in the more arcane English usage, frustration of contract is the result of the apparition of the unknown and most usually the impact of natural cataclysms, zoonoses, acts of war and market failures upon the agreement. The emergence of an absence into presence, the incursion of the unforeseen and unforeseeable, are cognized legally as exogenous intrusions in one argot, and as material adverse change in another.[26] The exogenous risk is an unknown externality, a general market shift that materially impacts the transaction. Being unknown and likely unknowable at the time of exchange, the exogeneous is precisely the other law, *ius quaesitum alteri*, a force that puts our ignorance to work, the subject of accession, of mutual recognition, because what cannot be excluded must be embraced.

Contract should not be war; rather, as common venture and good faith expression, in its older definitions it embodies amity and commonality. Premonition is the sense and prescience

---

[25] *Ius quaesitum alteri* is juristically a variant expression of third party right, *ius quaesitum tertio*, but both third and other can have and should be expanded into a further sense of common cause and networks affected by the contractual relationship.

[26] Robert T. Miller, 'Material Adverse Effect Clauses and the COVID-19 Pandemic' (2020–1) University of Iowa Legal Studies Research Paper, discussed in *Travelport* at paragraph 177 et seq.

of the unknown, an openness to the commons as being also, and more than merely human community. Implicit in the juridical language of impossibility doctrine is a sentiment of foreboding and of threat. It is the concept of the accident that dominates legal theory, the unforeseen trap or fall, the unfortunately injurious: the flames that waste the building; the epidemic that kills the livestock; the flood, invasion, collapse, illness or death that overwhelms and consumes merely human purposes and their endogenous or jealous sensibility. Premonition is the limit of foresight, the image and intuition of how we understand a future that exists internally, as incarnadine sense, and which opens to the living quality, the *perpetuum mobile* of knowing. The element of not knowing, of ignorance, is not in this instance a negative but rather an opportunity, a mode of acknowledging the other and, in the paradoxically apposite language of frustration of contract, a manner also of recognizing the materiality of material adverse change. The unknown is the haptic materiality, the nervous, cellular, spectral sense of our movement as emotion.

The materiality of change is also a reference to the aura or connectivity of matter as including the human as well as mattering exogeneity. Ambulating in images, the human is at least implicitly aware, prescient of the vast host of being and beings, substantiality and connectivity, external to but no less germane for the apprehension and intellection of human relations. The unexpected adverse event, the material change, is thus both the matter of the unknown as it presses against the sensibilities of the human and the limits of premonition. Versed from early on in the art of looking backwards, tutored in the static protocols of nostalgia and the retrospection of the rule of precedent, the *casus fortuitus* or unexpected adverse event, the materiality of change, can wake law up to a constituent failing in the form of its scotomization of the future. The closure of juridical categories precludes alike the phantasmology of the literary and the science of impossible solutions, which is one of the most prescient of forms that it takes. The slopes of Mount Analogue are never reached and free solo fails to happen.[27] As the narrator of the novel puts it in describing Sogol's theories: 'I heard him […] treat human history as a problem in descriptive geometry, then, a minute later, speak of the properties of numbers as if he were dealing with zoological species. The fusion and division of living cells, became a particular case of logical reasoning, and language derived its laws from celestial mechanics'.[28] Somewhat later, the novel references a chameleon law, which is described as a resonance of statements heard, as a floating sensation and, in Manderson's intrepid diction, an incarnadine jurisprudence.[29]

The literary has always been the greater source of retrospect and prospect, of judgement and prediction, the avenue of *potentia*, and the transitive, transitional moment in the invention of decision. The textual, sub- intra- and inter-textual, analogue and digital, tympanum, tensor and texture, of the motions of discourse are the medium also of the affective, phantasmagorical, future-orientated expression of legality. The past may be prologue, but that simply means that it can orient vision and train the senses to apprehend, to discern, feel and perceive how now is moving, how the body is combustive and recombinative in its motion through the decisions

---

[27] The reference here is to immortal René Daumal, *Mount Analogue: A Tale of Non-Euclidean and Symbolically Authentic Mountaineering Adventures* (New York: Overlook Press, 2020).
[28] Ibid, 37.
[29] Desmond Manderson, *Danse Macabre: Temporalities of Law in the Visual Arts* (Cambridge: University of Cambridge Press, 2020) 112–13: arguing as to the standard of realism misses the point. The incarnadine is an attempt not to be accurate but to be true 'not to an event, but to a sentiment'.

of the day. It is that sensibility of *perpetuum mobile* that precedent has failed to gauge, that looking back cannot see, that the rearview and backface are incapable of either feeling or opening towards. As Shakespeare might have it, that is the cause, that is the cause my soul.[30] In the end, a question of insufflation, of breath, the *pneuma* of the spirit that is the body and the body that is spirit. To relume that light triggers premonition as ignition, and inebriate, preserved, pickled, connected, communal and spiritous forethinking.

---

[30] *Othello* v.ii.i, and continuing slightly later in the soliloquy: 'I know not where is that Promethean heat/That can thy light relume'.

3. *Ostranenie*
Jorge Luis Roggero

The Law and Literature movement has received a persistent objection, that can be traced from Richard Posner's seminal diagnoses[1] to Julie Stone Peters' more recent interdisciplinary critique,[2] and that in its essential core could still be phrased as: what is the use of literature in the legal field? But more fundamentally, one can simply inquire: what is the use of literature in general? Though the body of scholarly work questioning the Kantian/Romantic definition of art as the milieu of *finality without end* is vast, the work of art is still understood as an artifact without utility and as a phenomenon inscribed in its own world, detached from the real. This issue seems to be ongoing,[3] and shows that the tension between the idea of art as an absolute, autonomous sphere and the diversity of its social functions remain unsolved.

In the context of this debate, I would like to bring attention to one special feature of literature: its ability to make visible what until that moment was hidden. This operation is possible by the means of what the first Russian formalism called *ostranenie*, defamiliarization, the procedure of all literary procedures. Literature invites us to change our way of perceiving things by showing everyday objects transformed. It shows us the invisible side of the visible, what we cannot see with our daily automatized mode of perception. This possibility of making the invisible visible, I would add, in the first place can be linked to Jean-Luc Marion's account of the phenomenological operation of making the unseen visible and, in the second place, can be thought of as an ethical and political device. Literature shows its decisive ethical and political dimensions in its most literary procedure. Ethics and politics lie at the very heart of the literary. By making the unseen visible, not only can literature show the aesthetic face of an object or an event but, by doing so, it can also bring attention to what, for political or ideological reasons, remains invisible, marginalized, silenced in our societies, characterized by capitalism, colonialism and patriarchy.

In the first section of this chapter I will establish the link between *ostranenie* and the idea of making the invisible visible by briefly reviewing this notion proposed first by Viktor

---

[1] To summarize Posner's account on this issue we can say that he poses a series of difficulties that emphasizes the distinction between the legal and the literary, by looking at the differences more than at the similarities. He is not sure that we can establish a two-way dialogue between law and literature. Law can go to literature to find examples and reflections that could help to have a wider look at legal and justice problems, but literary insights and techniques are rarely suitable to the law field. Cf. Richard A. Posner, *Law and Literature* (Cambridge, MA, Harvard University Press, 1988).

[2] Julie Stone Peters argues that all interdisciplinarity is a mode of disciplinary hysteria, a form of interior dislocation. She affirms that Law and Literature studies are symptomatic of the interior of each discipline: on the one hand, they symptomatize a literature that recognizes itself as incapable of achieving praxis; on the other hand, they are symptomatic of a law that warns of a lack of critical and human dimension at its core. Cf. Julie Stone Peters, 'Law, Literature, and the Vanishing Real: On the Future of an Interdisciplinary Illusion,' 120 *PMLA* 442 (2005).

[3] Juliane Rebentisch's work on the currency of the idea of art's autonomy is a good example of this. Cf. Juliane Rebentisch, *Aesthetics of Installation Art* (Berlin, Sternberg Press, 2012).

Shklovsky, the leading figure and *enfant terrible* of Russian formalism. In the second, I will analyse the idea of making the invisible visible and I will introduce the notion of the 'unseen' as it was elaborated in Jean-Luc Marion's theory of the saturated phenomenon. In the final section I will formulate some conclusions.

OSTRANENIE, OR HOW TO MAKE THINGS STRANGE

In his early articles 'The Resurrection of the Word' (1914) and 'Art as Device (*priëm*)' (1917 and 1919), Shklovsky definitively changes our conception of art and literature by defining a work of art as a device, as a product of intentional activity and – as Peter Steiner rightly put it – as 'a functional object whose purpose is to change the mode of our perception from practical to artistic'.[4] But how can a piece of literature become a functional object, a machine capable of changing our mode of perception?

The first formalism establishes a deep contrast between 'everyday life' (*byt*) and art. We can find this opposition as a milestone presented in Shklovsky's first essay, 'The Resurrection of the Word':

> Nowadays, old art has already died, new art has not yet been born, and things have died – we have lost our awareness of the world; we resemble a violinist who has ceased to feel the bow and strings; we have ceased being artists in everyday life, we do not love our houses and our clothes, and we easily part with life, for we do not feel life. Only the creation of new art forms can restore to man the experience of the world, can resurrect things and kill pessimism.[5]

The laws of perception change in each domain. Shklovsky explains the difference in a very simple way: all our routine actions in everyday life become automatic; our skills seem to retreat into some sort of unconscious–automatic domain. In 'Art as Device', he invites us to verify it with an example:

> you will agree with this if you remember the feeling you had when holding a quill in your hand for the first time or speaking a foreign language for the first time, and compare it to the feeling you have when doing it for the ten thousandth time.[6]

Arguing with Aleksandr Potebnja's theory and his symbolist epigones, Shklovsky translates this opposition into the tension between 'prosaic language' and 'poetic language'. Potebnja asserts that 'art is thinking in images', but he does not notice the difference between a 'practical image' (characteristic of prosaic language) and a 'poetic image' (characteristic of poetic language). Shklovsky gives an example: if a man with an old hat drops his bag, I can call him: 'Hey, old man, you have dropped your bag'. 'Old hat', in this case, functions as a prosaic trope, as a metonymy used for practical means. But when I say: 'This joke is old hat, I heard it ages ago', 'old hat' has a different purpose; it operates as a poetic trope, metaphorically.

---

[4] Peter Steiner, *Russian Formalism. A Metapoetics* (Geneva/Lausanne, Sdvig Press, 2014), 44.
[5] Viktor Shklovsky, 'The Resurrection of the Word', translated by Alexandra Berlina, in Alexandra Berlina (ed.), *Viktor Shklovsky. A Reader* (New York/London/Oxford/New Delhi/Sydney, Bloomsbury, 2017), 70.
[6] Viktor Shklovsky, 'Art as Device', translated by Alexandra Berlina, in Alexandra Berlina (ed.), *Viktor Shklovsky. A Reader*, 79.

> The poetic image is a way to create the strongest possible impression. It is a device that has the same task as other poetic devices, such as ordinary or negative parallelism, comparison, repetition, symmetry, hyperbole; it is equal to that which is commonly designated as rhetorical figures, equal to all these methods of increasing the impact of a thing (words and even sounds of the text itself are things, too).[7]

Prosaic language is practical language. The automatization process accounts for the laws of prosaic speech with 'its under-structured phrases and its half-pronounced words'.[8] The Russian theorist emphasizes: 'In quick practical speech, words are not spoken fully; only their initial sounds are registered by the mind'.[9] Like in algebra, things are replaced by symbols. We do not see things anymore. We just confirm their presence out there through a quick blink that places them in space and time, and serves for us to recognize them in their objective primary qualities.

> A thing passes us as if packaged; we know of its existence by the space it takes up, but we only see its surface. Perceived in this way, the thing dries up, first in experience, and then its very making suffers; because of this perception, prosaic speech is not fully heard (cf. Yakubinsky's article), and therefore not fully spoken (this is the reason for slips of the tongue). Algebraizing, automatizing a thing, we save the greatest amount of perceptual effort: things are either given as a single feature, for instance, a number, or else they follow a formula of sorts without ever reaching consciousness.[10]

Analysing a Tolstoy diary entry in which it is reported how he sometimes forgot whether or not he had carried out some routine activity such as dusting his room, Shklovsky explains the consequences of everyday life's automatization in very eloquent way: 'This is how life becomes nothing and disappears. Automatization eats things, clothes, furniture, your wife…'.[11] And that is precisely why we need art. Art can 'resurrect things'. Art prevents life from fading away. There is a fundamental purpose for art: restoring our capability of experiencing life. Shklovsky puts it in very clear terms: 'And so, what we call art exists in order to give back the sensation of life, in order to make us feel things, in order to make the stone stony. The goal of art is to create the sensation of seeing, and not merely recognizing, things'.[12]

Art can help us to grasp life by feeling and seeing things again. But how can art manage to achieve this miracle? There is a particular device that – according to the first formalism – characterizes the essence of art.[13] This is what Shklovsky proposes to call *ostranenie*: a device that triggers perception to last longer and to be more complex by making things strange in order to let them appear in their peculiarity. As Alexandra Berlina summarizes it, *ostranenie* consists in 'making the habitual strange in order to re-experience it';[14] it works as an 'enstrangement'.[15]

---

[7] Ibid, 76–7.
[8] Ibid, 79.
[9] Ibid.
[10] Ibid, 79–80.
[11] Ibid, 80.
[12] Ibid.
[13] Twentieth-century literary theory has questioned the idea of finding in *ostranenie* the essence or the 'literariness' (*literaturnost*) of literature, but we cannot ignore the presence of this device in all kinds of works of art and literature.
[14] Alexandra Berlina, '*Ostranenie* and Other Key Concepts', in Alexandra Berlina, *Viktor Shklovsky. A Reader*, 24.
[15] This term was coined by Benjamin Sher to stress the difference of the neologism *ostranenie* from the connotation that the translation into the terms 'estrangement' and 'defamiliarization' implied.

This device – which can be implemented in all kinds of art, but is principally developed by the Russian theorist in the field of literature – has a double use: it has an 'extraliterary' dimension when it is applied to the world and real things, and an 'intraliterary' dimension when it is applied to 'poetic' language itself. Shklovsky shows how Tolstoy makes the world he describes strange (extraliterary *ostranenie*) and Sterne and Cervantes enstrange the novel by parodying its conventions (intraliterary *ostranenie*). Tolstoy's *ostranenie* 'consists in not calling a thing or event by its name but describing it as if seen for the first time, as if happening for the first time'.[16] Shklovsky gives the example of 'Strider', a story where things are enstranged by being depicted from the perspective of a horse. But there are other literary devices that can produce *ostranenie*. Many rhetorical figures used in poetic language have the power to create a strong impression. Shklovsky emphasizes that the '*ostranenie* is present almost wherever there is an image';[17] however, to underline the difference between Potebnja's proposal and his own, he further explains: 'The goal of an image is not to bring its meaning closer to our understanding, but to create a special way of experiencing an object, to make one not "recognize" but "see" it'.[18]

To delineate the limits of this device, the Russian observes its use in erotic art. Erotic riddles and erotic images in literature and also in popular culture can become familiar and immediately recognized; however, they can show the scope of *ostranenie*, precisely because when they were heard or seen for the first time, they were always enstranging.

Finally, it is important to notice that the term *ostranenie* itself, as a neologism, functions as an enstrangement device. This Russian word is composed by the prefix *o*, used to implement an action, and the noun *strannyi*, which means 'strange'.[19] As Benjamin Sher rightly notes: 'It is a pretty fair assumption, then, that Shklovsky speaks of *ostranenie* as a process or act that endows an object or image with "strangeness" by "removing" it from the network of conventional, formulaic, stereotypical perceptions and linguistic expressions (based on such perceptions)'.[20]

But it also can refer to the verb *otstranit*, which means to remove, to shove aside. Did Shklovsky drop the 't' accidentally? Deliberately or not, the absence of the 't' helps to understand the scope of the concept. Alexandra Berlina, reflecting on which is the best translation for *ostranenie*, argues that '*otstranenie* suggests a withdrawal, a stepping back, which is an

---

I will return to this issue further on in this text. Benjamin Sher, 'Translator's Introduction', in Viktor Shklovsky, *Theory of Prose*, translated by Benjamin Sher (Champaign/London, Dalkey Archive Press, 2009), xviii.

[16] Viktor Shklovsky, 'Art as Device', 81–2.
[17] Ibid, 88.
[18] Ibid.
[19] Shklovsky even admitted he made a grammatical mistake by writing it with one 'n' (н, en, in the Russian Cyrillic alphabet): 'It was then that I created the term *ostranenie*, and – I can admit today that I made grammatical mistakes back then – I wrote it with one 'n'. I should have used two, as in *strannyi* (strange). And off it went with one 'n', roaming the world like a dog with an ear cut off'. Viktor Shklovsky, 'On the Theory of Prose' (1983), in Alexandra Berlina, *Viktor Shklovsky. A Reader*, 305. And in a letter to Evgeny Gabrilovich, he mentions: 'These two words coexist now, *ostranenie* and *ostrannenie*, with one 'n' and with two, with different meanings but with the same plot, a plot about the strangeness of life'. Viktor Shklovsky, 'A letter to Evgeny Gabrilovich' (1984), in Alexandra Berlina, *Viktor Shklovsky. A Reader*, 386.
[20] Benjamin Sher, 'Translator's Introduction', xix.

effect closer to Brecht's than to Shklovsky's own ideas'.[21] Her point is accurate to the extent that Benjamin Sher's translation, 'enstrangement', illustrates the way in which making things strange should be practised. The terms most extensively used at present – 'defamiliarization' and 'estrangement' (closer to the Brechtian *Verfremdungseffekt*) – fail to account for what is at stake here, which is not the effect of an emotional disconnection. On the contrary, the device of *ostranenie* works as an invitation to profoundly connect with things again; to 'see' them, to experience them, to live them.

THE BANALITY OF SATURATION OR HOW TO MAKE THE UNSEEN VISIBLE

In 'Once upon a time' (1964), Shklovsky refers to *ostranenie* in these terms: '*Ostranenie* means showing an object outside the usual patterns, describing a phenomenon with new words, taken from a different field of relations'.[22] Hence, this device consists of describing, showing, phenomenalizing a phenomenon without the usual set of relations (horizon) where its meaning is inscribed. This suggests a link with Jean-Luc Marion's theory of saturated phenomena. In *Being Given* (1997), Marion states that there is a possibility for phenomenality that Husserl did not develop: a type of phenomenon that can give itself in an excessive way, where a saturated intuition exceeds the intention and the concepts that try to define it. Marion introduces a typology of phenomenality by distinguishing three kinds of phenomenon. In the first place, we find the phenomenon poor in intuition. This type of phenomenon does not need much more than its concept to give itself. Marion is thinking of mathematical and logical phenomena that do not need more than a formal intuition or a categorial one. Poor phenomena are characterized then by an excess of intention over intuition. In the second place, we have the common-law phenomenon. In principle, this type of phenomenon aims at a fulfilment that can be adequate: intuition equalling intention, though most of the time it remains inadequate. The technical object is the paradigm of common phenomena, where the intention is always confirmed because they only need a limited amount of intuition to verify them. Finally, in the third place, beside these two kinds of phenomena already presented by the father of phenomenology, we find the saturated phenomena, phenomena that are impossible to predetermine or foresee because no intention can anticipate them.

> To the phenomenon characterized most often by lack or poverty of intuition (a deception of the intentional aim), indeed, exceptionally, by the mere equality of intuition and intention, why wouldn't there correspond the possibility of a phenomenon where intuition would give *more, indeed immeasurably more*, than the intention would ever have aimed at or foreseen?[23]

In 2005, Marion revised his theory and added the idea of the banality of saturation. Saturated phenomena are not a type of phenomena, but a possibility present in every (or the majority of) phenomena:

---

[21] Alexandra Berlina, *Viktor Shklovsky. A Reader*, 56.
[22] Viktor Shklovsky, 'Once Upon a Time' (1964) in Alexandra Berlina, *Viktor Shklovsky. A Reader*, 252.
[23] Jean-Luc Marion, *Being Given. Toward of Phenomenology of Givenness*, translated by Jeffrey L. Kosky (Stanford, Stanford University Press, 2002), 197.

> The banality of the saturated phenomenon suggests *that the majority of phenomena, if not all* can undergo saturation by the excess of intuition over the concept or signification in them. In other words, the majority of phenomena that appear at first glance to be poor in intuition could be described not only as objects but also as phenomena that intuition saturates and therefore exceed any univocal concept. Before the majority of phenomena, even the most simple (the majority of objects produced technically and reproduced industrially), opens the possibility of a doubled interpretation, which depends upon the demands of my ever-changing relation to them. Or rather, when the description demands it, I have the possibility of passing from one interpretation to the other, from a poor or common phenomenality to a saturated phenomenality.[24]

According to Marion, given any phenomenon there is a possibility of moving from one interpretation to the other. If the description demands it, one can open up the possibilities of the phenomenon by letting it appear in its excess, in its original saturation. But who would be able to do this? Is everyone in charge of this hermeneutic task? Notwithstanding that the answer should be affirmative, Marion gives us a paradigmatic model presenting the figure of the artist. In *The Crossing of the Visible*, Marion argues that the artist is in charge of filtering the access of the 'unseen' (*invu*)[25] to the visible because what is at stake is not the simple vision of the visible but the divination of the unseen. As a blind man or a clairvoyant, the artist 'sees more than the visible'.[26] The artist can 'see more' because he assumes the risk of descending 'to the undecidable frontier of the visible and the unseen'.[27] In fact, he assumes two kind of risks: in the first place, as a blind man, he sinks into darkness because he seeks that which is unseen, that which has neither model nor precedent, and he assumes the responsibility of turning the unseen into the visible, that demands our response to let it appear in the visibility. In the second place, this search involves exposing oneself to the most extreme danger. The 'blind gaze' of the artist separates itself from the foreseen, from every operation that comes from itself, to abandon itself to what is by definition unforeseen: the unseen. This abandonment implies an extreme *receptive passivity*, a *losing of oneself*, a *neutralization of the ego*. This surrender implies, paradoxically, the most radical engagement with the unseen phenomenon.

Going back to the Shklovsky phrase previously quoted, it is remarkable that one of the features of the saturated phenomenon is that it occurs as an absolute phenomenon, that is, as an event that can happen without the Kantian category of relation because it can be without any analogy in experience. The formalist device of *ostranenie* functions in a similar way: it takes the thing out of its automatization, away from its objectivation, and shows it 'from a different field of relations', from the new horizon that the thing itself imposes when it is not regarded as it is inscribed in its 'usual patterns'. But what kind of operation is involved in this new way of perceiving things? As we have analysed it, the notion of *ostranenie* does not imply introducing

---

[24] Jean-Luc Marion, 'The Banality of Saturation', in Jean-Luc Marion, *The Visible and the Revealed*, translated by Christina M. Gschwandtner (New York, Fordham University Press, 2008), 126.
[25] Marion distinguishes the 'invisible' from the 'unseen': 'The unseen admittedly falls under the jurisdiction of the invisible, but it should not be confused with it, since it is able to transgress it precisely by becoming visible; while the invisible remains forever as such – recalcitrantly irreducible to the *mise en scène*, to the apparition, to the *entrée* into the visible – the unseen, only provisionally invisible, always exerts its demand for visibility in order to be made to irrupt, sometimes by force, onto the scene.' Jean-Luc Marion, *The Crossing of the Visible*, translated by James K.A. Smith (Stanford, Stanford University Press, 2004), 25–6.
[26] Ibid, 26.
[27] Ibid, 27.

a distance, a withdrawal, a stepping back. On the contrary, this device involves an intensification of our experience and our relationship with the thing. In 'Bowstring. On the Dissimilarity of the Similar' (1970), Shklovsky recalls the emergence of his idea: 'In 1916, the theory of *ostranenie* appeared. In it, I was trying to generalize the way of experiencing and showing phenomena. Everything in it was connected to time, to pain and inspiration, to astonishment about the world'.[28] *Ostranenie* does not suspend our bond to the world, but increases it, provoking astonishment. What is its relationship with the phenomenological *epoché*? Does not the gesture that constitutes the method of reduction's core imply some sort of suspension? How does Marion use this fundamental operation of phenomenology? Although this procedure is presented by Husserl as a way of bracketing, excluding, cancelling certain belief-components of our experience, in Marion's account it is related to a practical rather than a mere theoretic attitude, attuned by an affective disposition. According to the French phenomenologist, in order to perceive things as they give themselves, we have to reduce them from their neutral appearance as objects to their givenness as unpredictable events. To be able to phenomenalize them as they give themselves, we should exercise a gaze that 'not only must [...] know how to become curious, available, and enacted, but above all [...] must know how to submit to the demands of the figure to be seen'.[29] And the only way to put ourselves in that receptive attitude is to apply an *epoché* attuned by a fundamental mood. The only suspension that takes place in this particular reduction is the suspension of all suspensions: the suspension of the suspension and the withdrawal that is proper to the theoretic objectifying attitude. Marion proposes love as the fundamental mood, because it obstructs the impositions of any procedure of objectification as it consists of an unconditional openness to the other.[30] Shklovsky argues: 'The theory of *ostranenie*, which was taken up by many, including Brecht, speaks of art as a form of cognition, a method of exploration'.[31] Marion's reduction also functions as a method of exploration and as a form of cognition. This knowledge, that – as Shklovsky says – is 'connected to time, to pain and inspiration', however, also requires an affection and my commitment in the first person:

> No phenomenon can appear without coming upon me, arriving to me, affecting me as an event that modifies my field (of vision, of knowledge, of life) [...] there is no neutral phenomenon, always

---

[28] Viktor Shklovsky, 'Bowstring. On the Dissimilarity of the Similar' (1970) in Alexandra Berlina, *Viktor Shklovsky. A Reader*, 280. When Marion describes the effect of saturation over the categories of quantity, he explicitly gives the example of 'amazement' (*étonnement*) in Descartes. 'According to Descartes, this passion affects us even before we know the thing, or rather precisely because we know it only partially [...] The "object" offers us only one "side" (we could also say only one *Abschattung*) and yet is, at the same time, imposed on us with a power such that we are submerged by what shows itself, most likely to the point of fascination.' Jean-Luc Marion, *Being Given...*, 200. This 'amazement' is close to the 'bedazzlement' (*éblouissement*) characteristic of the reception of the saturated phenomena as 'unbearable', when it exceeds the categories of quality. 'When the gaze cannot bear what it sees, it suffers bedazzlement. For not bearing is not simply equivalent to not seeing: one must first perceive, if not clearly see, in order to undergo what one cannot bear': Ibid, 203.

[29] Ibid, 124.

[30] I allow myself to give you the reference of my book on this topic: Jorge Luis Roggero, *Hermenéutica del amor. La fenomenología de la donación de Jean-Luc Marion en diálogo con la fenomenología del joven Heidegger* (Buenos Aires, SB Editorial, 2019).

[31] Viktor Shklovsky, 'Bowstring. On the Dissimilarity of the Similar' (1970), 286.

already there, inoffensive and submissive. It makes a difference solely by its coming up. To see it, it must first be endured, borne, suffered.[32]

Like the artist, we should assume the responsibility of making the unseen visible, of phenomenalizing things beyond any device of objectification. And that certainly implies embracing life again, risking experiencing it in the first person.

THE ETHICAL AND POLITICAL DIMENSION OF *OSTRANENIE* AS MAKING VISIBLE THE UNSEEN

'*Ostranenie* is seeing the world with different eyes',[33] says Shklovsky. Should we understand that this new way of seeing has just aesthetic purposes? Isn't it precisely in this sensitive field where art and politics intertwine? Was Jacques Rancière right when he said that art and politics are both forms of distributing the sensible[34] and that 'artistic practices are ways of "doing and making" that intervene in the general distribution of ways of doing and making as well as in the relationship they maintain to modes of being and forms of visibility'?[35] What does Shklovsky mean when he says that 'the world of *ostranenie* is the world of the revolution'?[36]

The answer is simple: as Marion rightly put it, in a world that 'is covered with an invasive and highly visible layer of poor phenomena (namely, the technical objects produced and reproduced without end)',[37] we need to make what is covered over visible. And what is covered over? All things that the procedure of conceptualization and objectivation makes invisible. We have an ethical and political responsibility towards these unseen things. We have to make them visible; we have to become able to listen to their voice. The unseen is that part of the invisible that demands that we let it become visible. And what is unseen in our world? We know well that one can no longer look the other way before the rise of all kinds of otherness that demand to be included while preserving their otherness. We are witness to a variety of social movements that struggle for the rights of women, of migrants, of native people and of all kinds of the socially excluded of society, victims of the everyday, ever more worn-out capitalist, colonialist and patriarchal ways of living.

But why should we appeal to a device that turns things strange in order to see them? To respond to this we could agree, if not with Freud's psychoanalytic account of the uncanny,

---

[32] Jean-Luc Marion, *Being Given…*, 125.
[33] Viktor Shklovsky, 'The Theory of Prose', 334.
[34] 'Politics consists in reconfiguring the distribution of the sensible which defines the common of a community, to introduce into it new subjects and objects, to render visible what had not been, and to make heard as speakers those who had been perceived as mere noisy animals. This work involved in creating dissensus informs an aesthetics of politics that operates at a complete remove from the forms of staging power and mass mobilization which Benjamin referred to as the "aestheticization of politics". More precisely, then, the relationship between aesthetics and politics consists in the relationship between this aesthetics of politics and the "politics of aesthetics" – in other words in the way in which the practices and forms of visibility of art themselves intervene in the distribution of the sensible and its reconfiguration, in which they distribute spaces and times, subjects and objects, the common and the singular.' Jacques Rancière, *Aesthetics and its Discontents* (Cambridge, Polity Press, 2009), 25.
[35] Jacques Rancière, *The Politics of Aesthetics* (New York, Continuum, 2004), 13.
[36] Ibid, 335.
[37] Jean-Luc Marion, 'The Banality of Saturation', 125.

at least just with his reading of Schelling's notion of the uncanny as something that ought to have remained hidden, and yet comes to light.[38] The visibility of what was supposed to stay invisible creates uncanniness. In spite of the clear differences with this Freudian idea, *ostranenie* operates in the same way, creating some sort of uncanniness or strangeness in order to bring attention to, and maybe even re-experience, our relationship with what was silenced and hidden. One good example is Gabriel García Marquez's use of hyperbole. In *One Hundred Years of Solitude*, probably in spite of him,[39] this device helps to bring attention to the sexual exploitation of young poor women, when he tells the story of a girl forced into prostitution by her grandmother. 'The adolescent mulatto girl [...] was naked on the bed. Before Aureliano sixty-three men had passed through the room that night. From being used so much, kneaded with sweat and sighs, the air in the room had begun to turn to mud'.[40]

The hyperbolic number of men and the image of the air turned to mud causes the enstrangement that can highlight the horrifying situations of abuse that poor girls can experience in Latin America, victims not only of an oppressive capitalist system that keeps them in poverty, but also of the patriarchal and colonial thought that validates the double discrimination inflicted upon them because of their condition both as women and afro or native descendants. As film director Lucrecia Martel has recently highlighted regarding her new project of non-fiction documentary on the murder of the *chuscha* indigenous leader Javier Chocobar, literature, films and art in general can help us to see what we do not see in our daily life. She is currently working with recorded material of what happened that shows how a landowner shoots the native militant. She says about this video in a presentation for the Locarno Festival:

> When I watched it, I remembered I had already seen it. And then I thought why I forgot. I started watching it many times and realized everything was forcing me to dive deeper into those images. So it was that. Why have I forgotten the video? How could that happen to me? How was that crime even possible? [...] So it is about that: our impossibility to see others. It is a documentary to observe in detail the structures with which our white way of thinking justifies its violence. [...] I also believe that detailed observation could lead to a change.[41]

Martel is trying to make visible the unseen: the violence against indigenous people, imposed by white colonial thought, that is known and seen and yet not known and unseen. To see others we need to intensify our looking, to dive deeper into the images. Art can accomplish that task. *Ostranenie* is detailed observation that could lead to a change. *Ostranenie* is a political and ethical device. Shklovsky himself presented it this way when he referred to Tolstoy by giving the example of flogging: 'it is typical of Tolstoy's way to reach conscience'.[42] For the Russian

---

[38] Sigmund Freud, 'The Uncanny' (1919), in Sigmund Freud, *The Standard Edition of the Complete Psychological Works of Sigmund Freud, Volume XVII (1917–1919): An Infantile Neurosis and Other Works* (London, The Hogarth Press, 1955), 240.

[39] I think that García Marquez's last novel, *Memories of My Melancholy Whores*, can regrettably be read as an apologia of misogyny and violence against women. But what is interesting from this example taken from *One Hundred Years of Solitude* is that one can notice to what extent literature and its procedures are independent from the author's intention and thought.

[40] Gabriel García Marquez, *One Hundred Years of Solitude* (New York, Avon Books, 1971), 31.

[41] Lucrecia Martel presents *Chocobar*, Locarno LiveTv. For the future of films, Locarno 2020. www.locarnofestival.ch/LFF/about/film-sections/the-films-after-tomorrow/chocobar.html. I would like to thank Cecilia Gebruers for this reference.

[42] Viktor Shklovsky, 'Art as Device', 82.

literary theorist it is clear that 'the main function of *ostranenie* in Tolstoy is [the awaking of] conscience'.[43] In a world that does not distribute the sensible in fair parts, art and literature have a crucial task: they can help us see another world, or more precisely, they can do justice to the unseen and by doing so help us hear the silenced and see the invisibilized 'part of those who have no part'[44] in this world.

---

[43] Viktor Shklovsky, 'Bowstring. On the Dissimilarity of the Similar' (1970), 282.
[44] Jacques Rancière, *Disagreement. Politics and Philosophy* (Minneapolis, University of Minnesota Press, 1999), 9.

4. Theatricality
Marett Leiboff

> Discourse in the theatre is systematically constituted as if one were holding the shards of a broken jug together with one's hands: one sees all the fissures and knows that the pieces will fly apart as soon as the pressure is relaxed.[1]
> Hans-Thies Lehmann

> Theater places everything and everyone 'on call', makes everything *bestellbar*, while undermining the hope of ever staying in place, of a *Bestand*.[2]
> Samuel Weber

SHARDS

I know. You will see the word theatricality and will say: oh, you mean a play, you mean a tragedy. Or, that a trial will unfold before my eyes. There will be histrionics and I will be overcome by cloying sentimentality. I will laugh. I will cry. I will be entertained.

No, you won't. The theatricality you will experience in this chapter is transgressive and transformative. Theatricality is an impossible term, elusive and contested,[3] but if it does have a programme, it demands that we are aware in a split second[4] and, for law at least,[5] forced into an awareness of different legal realities.[6] It will take you away from expectations.[7] You will find what it feels like to hold the shards of a broken jug as they push into your hands,[8] not as metaphorical or imagined, but as words on a page that do entirely the opposite of what we expect. That move from thought and reason to the body, the actual body (not an imagined

---

[1] Hans-Thies Lehmann, *Tragedy and Dramatic Theatre* trans. Erik Butler (Abingdon: Routledge, 2016), 188. Lehmann's words echo something of Heinrich von Kleist's 1806 comedy *The Broken Jug*, first directed by Goethe in 1808. A corrupt magistrate breaks the jug but pushes the blame onto an innocent, with 'word play that helps [him] elude the truth, along with his relentless attempts to evade it despite the ruthless facts': Andrej Rozman Roza, 'Heinrich von Kleist *The Broken Jug*' 2019, www.en.drama.si/repertoire/delo?id=2215.

[2] Samuel Weber, *Theatricality as Medium* (New York: Fordham University Press, 2004), 94.

[3] Andrew Quick and Richard Rushton, 'On Theatricality' (2019) 24(4) *Performance Research* 1–4. doi: 10.1080/13528165.2019.1655350.

[4] Marett Leiboff, 'Towards a Jurisprudence of the Embodied Mind – Sarah Lund, Forbrydelsen and the Mindful Body' (2015) 6(2) *Nordic Journal of Law and Social Research* (Special Issue) 77–92.

[5] Sean Mulcahy, 'Silence and Attunement in Legal Performance' (2019) 34(2) *Canadian Journal of Law and Society/Revue Canadienne Droit Et Société* 191–207. doi:10.1017/cls.2019.18.

[6] Andreas Philippopoulos-Mihalopoulos, 'Law and the Aesthetic Turn. Law Is a Stage: From Aesthetics to Affective Aestheses' in Emilios Christodoulidis, Ruth Dukes and Marco Goldoni (eds) *Research Handbook on Critical Legal Theory* (Cheltenham: Edward Elgar Publishing, 2019), 201–22, 222, based on a disruptive theatre piece.

[7] Marett Leiboff, 'Theatricalizing Law' (2018) 30(2) *Law and Literature* 351–67.

[8] Danish Sheikh, 'Book Review: Marett Leiboff, Towards a Theatrical Jurisprudence' (2020) *Law and Literature* 10.1080/1535685X.2020.1805914.

philosophical body), is a challenge in itself, for this kind of theatricality is deeply physical.[9] Physicality isn't perfectly transmissible on the page, but there are ways.[10] Bring yourself into a place where you have to hold onto those shards of a broken jug for dear life. There is only one thing you can do. You have to hold on. You can't interpret, argue, complain or reason. You simply have to hold on. You have to be present. Totally. And once you've had to do this, you'll never be the same again. Your body will now know just what's at stake if you let go, if you fail. As Goodrich points out, in 'the present that makes the real emerge and disturb the norm […] [t]he neoteric practice of sympathy is not merely affective; it is also ontographic and hermeneutic'.[11] Holding onto the shards has rendered you sympa, *sympathique*, sympathetic, able to attend, respond and notice.[12] As Goodrich remarks: 'In new materialist terms, consciousness does not define the body, rather the body defines consciousness'.[13]

This kind of theatricality disrupts and challenges,[14] where predictability, as Weber has it, is blown asunder.[15] A responding body is the starting point,[16] but my real point in this chapter is to challenge our inevitable move back to words, language, ideals as perfection.[17] All the arguments and niceties in the world, the abstractions, are all for nothing if we lose sight of just what they're there for.[18] So in what is to follow, in the thousands of words to come, what might be thought of as a central text – a play drawn from trials – is nearly entirely absent. What you will experience instead is an extended exercise that will take us somewhere around the play, and into other places entirely. While also dramaturgical,[19] it is an exercise in theatricality, as something that works on each of us.[20]

---

[9] Sean Mulcahy, 'Performing Sexuality on the Legal Stage' in Lucy Finchett-Maddock and Eleftheria Lekakis (eds) *Art, Law, Power: Perspectives on Legality and Resistance in Contemporary Aesthetics* (Oxford: Counterpress, 2020), 70–90. A gay couple offered to have sex in front of the Refugee Review Tribunal in Australia to demonstrate their sexuality.
[10] Marett Leiboff, 'Towards a Jurisprudence of the Embodied Mind'.
[11] Peter Goodrich, 'Inutilious Propaedeutics: Performances in Theatre and Law' (2020) 29(4) *Social & Legal Studies* 596–606, 603–4.
[12] Marett Leiboff, *Towards a Theatrical Jurisprudence* (Abingdon: Routledge, 2019), 125.
[13] Peter Goodrich, 'The Pure Theory of Law is a Hole in the Ozone Layer' in *What Should Critical Legal Theory Become?* (2021) 92(4) *University of Colorado Law Review* 985.
[14] Olivera Simic, 'But I Want to Speak Out: Making Art from Women's Testimonies' (2014) 40(1) *Australian Feminist Law Journal* 51–67.
[15] My thanks to my colleague Markus Wagner for unravelling Weber's use of *bestellbar* and *bestand*.
[16] Danish Sheikh, 'Performing Contempt', *Indent: The Body and the Performative* (14 November 2019), www.indent.in/present_continuous/2019/11/13/contempt.
[17] Adil Hasan Khan, 'Tragedy's Law(s): Receiving The Mythology of Modern Law Today' (2017) 43(2) *Australian Feminist Law Journal* 273–97.
[18] Marett Leiboff, 'Challenging the Legal Self through Performance' in Simon Stern, Maksymilian Del Mar and Bernadette Meyler (eds) *The Oxford Handbook of Law and Humanities* (Oxford: OUP, 2020), 317–34.
[19] Marett Leiboff, 'Theatricalising Law in Three, 1929–1939 (Brisbane)' (2016) 20 *Law Text Culture* 93–135.
[20] Marett Leiboff, 'Of the Monstrous Regiment and the Family Jewels' (2005) 23 *Australian Feminist Law Journal* 33–59, adapting the Brechtian verfremdungseffekt, 'this article is also intentionally structured to deviate from the normal linear, expository and analytical structure of a conventional […] article': 35–6. What would have been the end of a regular article was located in the middle, and so on.

A series of 11 shards follow.

They will unfold as you go. After all, that is what it means to be present.

SHARD 1

Here is a piece of information. We will expect it to deliver us the truth. It might seem odd to not paraphrase the words here. I would like you to read them carefully.

> The first Frankfurt Auschwitz trial opened in December 1963 and lasted for 20 months, extending over 183 days of trial. It heard 359 witnesses, among them 248 Auschwitz survivors. It is today the most well-known proceeding in connection with National Socialist extermination camps before a West German court in the first decades following the end of the Second World War. The trial was initiated in 1958, after files documenting executions at Auschwitz, which had been kept by a concentration camp survivor, were sent to Fritz Bauer, Public Prosecutor General of the West German federal state of Hesse. *Bauer recognized the value of these documents, which contained not only the names of the victims but also the names of perpetrators.* After Bauer had transmitted the documents to the Federal Court of Justice, it granted the Frankfurt prosecutors general jurisdiction for all Auschwitz cases.[21] (my italics)

Now I will ask you read this portion from Tony Paterson's article 'Germany finally pays tribute to first Nazi hunter Fritz Bauer', subtitled 'Gay and Jewish, he faced death threats for his activities in a post-war state where Third Reich attitudes endured', from the UK's *The Independent* newspaper in 2016:[22]

> The key role Bauer played as one of the handful of Germans who fought the evils of Nazism remained forgotten for decades after his death. Fifty years on and just as the last ageing Auschwitz guards still alive are going on trial for the first time, Germany's forgotten first Nazi hunter is being rediscovered and rehabilitated.[23]

Ida Richter, the first author quoted above, did go on to mention Bauer's biography, and what became a renewed interest in his work, but we get none of this in this early passage. Instead, we will do what lawyers always do and find something that conforms to law, neutralising anything we assume is irrelevant. We will make law work as we expect. Our expectations will tell us that law has done its job and produced justice. Only it didn't. Otherwise Bauer wouldn't have been, as it were, buried for all those years.

…

Hans-Thies Lehmann takes issue with Judith Butler's jurisprudential reading of Antigone's most famous speech. We all know that speech, so I won't repeat it. What Lehmann says will

---

[21] Ida Richter, 'Nazi Crimes Before West German Courts: Fritz Bauer as a Visionary of International Criminal Justice?' (2020) 18(1) *Journal of International Criminal Justice* 167–83, 168, references omitted.
[22] Tony Paterson, 'Germany finally pays tribute to first Nazi hunter Fritz Bauer', *The Independent* 28 February 2016, www.independent.co.uk/news/world/europe/germany-finally-pays-tribute-first-nazi-hunter-fritz-bauer-auschwitz-nazism-adolf-eichmann-a6901756.html.
[23] Ibid.

surprise most lawyers and jurisprudents, because these standard accounts of the speech turn away from what Antigone is saying and doing: 'What goes missing [...] is theatricality. The scene does not offer a calmly delivered declaration of abstract principles [...] Antigone has not stepped onto the foreign terrain of legal discourse to the extent that Butler supposes'.[24] A theatre scholar telling a philosopher about law might seem to be a step too far, but his point is perfectly made. We are forever looking for some kind of conforming meaning in law or its jurisprudential register, when all we need to do is open our eyes and see what is directly in front of us. To be there, present, in the moment. Theatricality demands that we notice, see, what is happening before our eyes – or, more to the point in this instance, what Antigone is actually doing, what she is actually saying. Conventional readings of Antigone's speech (not just Butler's) miss, Lehmann points out, that this is not a thesis but a 'scenic arrangement' accounted for in words:[25] 'The words do not posit a rule; instead, they assure [her brother] of his entirely unique significance to her [...] [that] occurs in *the moment shown in the theatre*'.[26] (my emphasis)

This first shard insists that we pause, to be careful about words, and realise that in theatre they are showing, in the moment, something that is present.

As Peter Goodrich reminds us: 'Theory is incapable of immateriality because of the scene and space of its corporeal and interlocutory performance'.[27]

Theatricality demands that we are present. We have to be there, in the moment.

SHARD 2

The play whose text we will never meet is Peter Weiss' 1965 *Die Ermittlung. Oratorium in 11 Gesängen*, or in English, *The Investigation. An Oratorio in 11 Cantos*.[28] Built on the structure of Dante's Divine Comedy, it is made up of 11 cantos that would take close to five hours to produce unabridged.[29] The cantos or songs – Dante's *gesänge* – are an inevitable requirement

---

[24] Lehmann, *Tragedy and Dramatic Theatre* 188.
[25] Ibid.
[26] Ibid.
[27] Goodrich, 'Ozone'.
[28] Peter Weiss, *Marat/Sade, The Investigation and The Shadow of the Body of the Coachman* (ed Robert Cohen, New York: Continuum, 1998). Cohen reminds us that the German title refers expressly to Dante's Divine Comedy: Robert Cohen, 'The Political Aesthetics of Holocaust Literature: "Peter Weiss's The Investigation and Its Critics" (1998) 10(2) *History and Memory* 43–67, n 14. Neither of the original translations is satisfactory: Peter Weiss, *The Investigation: Oratorio in 11 Cantos, English version by Alexander Gross* (Calder and Boyars, 1966); *Die Ermittlung* (Frankfurt am Main: Suhrkamp Verlag: 1965) cf the omission of the subtitle in US translation where canto is replaced with song: Peter Weiss, *The Investigation (a play by Peter Weiss), (English version by Jon Swan and Ulu Grosbard)* (New York: Atheneum, 1966) translation of *Die Ermittlung* (Frankfurt am Main: Suhrkamp Verlag: 1965).
[29] Alexander Gross, *Dramaturgical Notes for The Investigation by Peter Weiss, Prepared for the Royal Shakespeare Company, 1965* (self-published www.untoldsixties.net/weisnote.htm#totop), remarks that the play itself has 30,000 words and a potential five-hour runtime. He was also the translator (see above). He suggested major cuts, turning the piece into an 18,000-word, three-hour production, with textual changes.

of an oratorio. An oratorio deals with something sacred, a sung word form that takes the form of prayer, involving nothing in the way of character or even plot, where interaction is largely avoided. Think Handel's Messiah. In an oratorio the choir often plays a central role, and there is generally little or no interaction between the characters, and no props. Even though we won't meet any other text, the structure and form of the play-oratorio matters, so let me introduce you to the cantos: Canto One – The Loading Ramp; Canto Two – The Camp; Canto Three – The Swing; Canto Four – The Possibility of Survival; Canto Five – The End of Lili Topfler; Canto Six – Unterscharfürer Stark; Canto Seven – The Black Wall; Canto Eight – Phenol; Canto Nine – The Bunker Block; Canto Ten – Cyclone B; Canto Eleven – The Fire Ovens.[30]

If these titles mean nothing, then we have no scenic arrangement to help us.

Maybe you might have a clue if Cyclone B hadn't been translated from Zyklon B?

The cantos follow the 11 stages, for want of a better expression, through which a deportee (a weasel word, really: I should say victim) would be processed in Auschwitz (yes, I mean processed, because the machinery of murder couldn't be held up), and besides, the bodies of those murdered were processed further – or should I say plundered – for their treasures. Hair, gold fillings, skin. Their clothing and other belongings had already been stolen near the beginning of the process. I will spare you further details.

Most of those murdered here were Europe's Jewish population – 1 million of the 1.1 million who were gassed, who died of starvation and disease, of brutal medical experiments, and were shot over a four-year period, with 100,000 Roma and Poles and political prisoners and more.

The 11 shards, of which this is the second, acknowledge the 11 cantos of *The Investigation*. They pay homage to the 1.1 million who were murdered in Auschwitz, the 6 million Jews of Europe murdered in one form or another from the beginning of the Nazi reign of terror in the early 1930s, and the 11 million others who were murdered by the Nazis, across the death camps, who were summarily executed, rounded up, terrorised and tortured.[31]

And all the people who had to hide, who had to flee, who were turned away from refuge, who were denounced, who had to hide their identities or lost their identities completely.

Until the 11 shards were explained to you, you were in the dark. This is the closest you might come to knowing what it would have been like to have been rounded up, put in a cattle cart on a train, and not know where you were going.

Only you won't be entering a death camp or a forced labour camp, where the chances of survival were next to impossible.

It is a very poor substitute but it's the only one I have.[32]

---

[30] Matthias Naumann (MN), 'The Theater Text Die Ermittlung. Oratorium in 11 Gesängen, by Peter Weiss (1965)' (trans. Kathleen Luft (KL)), *The Wollheim Memorial*, www.wollheim-memorial.de/en/ermittlung_theatertext_en#down4.

[31] The United States Holocaust Memorial Museum, *Documenting Numbers of Victims of the Holocaust and Nazi Persecution*, https://encyclopedia.ushmm.org/content/en/article/documenting-numbers-of-victims-of-the-holocaust-and-nazi-persecution.

[32] Leiboff, 'Theatricalising Law in Three', 93–104.

So hold these shards, knowing that your life depends on it. But even then it won't help. All the arguments in the world won't help. Don't think a recourse to law will do you any good.

We have to remember these actions and murders weren't only carried out in the gas chambers. An entire complex of vicious terror, complicity and accommodation throughout Europe made this happen,[33] but it was the state-sanctioned apparatus in Germany that was made possible by everyday people that the Frankfurt Auschwitz trials wanted to put on display. Those trials could never prosecute everyone who made the Nazi reign of terror possible, or even every functionary or official who made Auschwitz possible. Only 22 were tried during the Frankfurt Auschwitz trials, representing every kind of work, so to speak, of those who made Auschwitz possible. Some were acquitted but most received small sentences, 20 years after the end of their reign of terror.

In 1965, there were inklings that a limitations provision would be enacted to prevent any further prosecutions of those who murdered and tortured during the Nazi era. It wasn't just a limitations provision. A provision was slipped into place in 1968, soon after Bauer died, so that any future prosecution and sentencing of Nazi perpetrators and accessories became nearly impossible – by a lawyer with an impeccable Nazi pedigree.[34]

Fritz Bauer's death in 1968, after years of threats, intimidation and near misses, was never investigated. It could have been suicide, it could have been natural causes, it could have been murder.

SHARD 3

If, as a young judge, Fritz Bauer hadn't been arrested in 1933 by the Nazis, early on in their rise to power, the chances are that he would have been one of the million or more murdered at Auschwitz. He was taken to a concentration camp (not yet death camps in an organised sense) and released after a few months, most likely because one of his fellow judges managed to secure his escape. Bauer was a target because of his Jewish identity but also because of his judgments. He swiftly escaped to Denmark, and after it was invaded, to Sweden.[35] After the war he was invited back to West Germany, as part of a plan to rebuild the country. From a minor position as state prosecutor-general in Brunswick,[36] he eventually moved on to take on that role in Frankfurt, all the while keeping his Jewish identity largely under wraps. He knew that he would be forever targeted because of his background – what right had he, an 'emigrant', to pursue Germans? Naturally, if he had stayed, he would have been murdered, so Bauer was uniquely placed to know how to manage the process of initiating prosecution and,

---

[33] Michael Bachmann, 'Theatre and the Drama of Law: A "Theatrical History" of the Eichmann Trial' (2010) 14 *Law Text Culture* 94–116; Julen Etxabe, *The Experience of Tragic Judgement* (London: Routledge, 2013).
[34] Ronen Steinke, *Fritz Bauer: The Jewish Prosecutor who Brought Eichmann and Auschwitz to Trial* (trans. Sinéad Crowe, Indiana University Press, 2020; 2013 Piper Verlag GmbH), 191–3.
[35] Ibid, Chapters 4 and 5 generally.
[36] The translation 'attorney-general' is often used but this is confusing for jurisdictions where this title applies to a politician.

through his legal brilliance, the arguments that would bring those who had the most ordinary jobs in Auschwitz within legal categories that would produce successful prosecutions.[37]

He wasn't simply working with abstract legal arguments and ideas. He was working with what he had lived himself and was still living.

Of course he could see the value in the documents.

If they had ended up in the hands of other prosecutors or lawyers, then these trials would never have gone ahead. Bauer was never able to trust any lawyer who had been around during the Nazi era. Not only were nearly all lawyers members of the Nazi party but, after the war, Nazis simply faded into the background, re-emerging holding positions of power and influence, including in the judiciary. This is what made Bauer's job so dangerous and difficult: when the potential for prosecuting those named in those hidden documents came to light, he had to operate in the shadows.

This was compounded by a collective amnesia mixed with a failure to accept responsibility on the part of ordinary Germans. Even Adolph Eichmann, responsible for organising the mass murder of the Jewish population of Europe, was thought of as nothing other than a pen pusher who had no part to play in murdering millions of people.[38] Bauer had argued that it was the defendants' very involvement in Auschwitz (as a kind of condition precedent), based on the evidence, that would determine their guilt. Hofmeyer, the presiding judge, refused to make any determination on this basis, likening it to the 'rule of law at Auschwitz' rather than 'the rule of law in a state of laws'.[39] Following an 1871 law that had continued to operate during the Nazi era, the presumptive existence of practices of murder within Auschwitz were sidestepped, and the particulars of evidentiary rules demanded that witnesses precisely identify the exact conduct of defendants. Only the most barbarous and sadistic killers were given life sentences, with some defendants released and others acquitted and released, albeit reluctantly in some cases. Otherwise sentences were short.

In the public imagination, the trials either disrupted the lives of otherwise good citizens, or became a subject of popular sensationalism. As Hannah Arendt remarked: 'Exposure for twenty months to the monstrous deeds and the grotesquely unrepentant, aggressive behaviour of the defendants, who more than once almost succeeded in turning the trial into a farce, had no impact on the climate of public opinion'.[40]

Bauer insisted on judging as love,[41] but Heinz Haueisen, a former head of public prosecutions in Frankfurt and as such a representative of the state of Hesse,[42] is clear in his view that the trial and judgment failed in its moral legacy, if not moral obligation. Writing in 1989, he assesses the judgment and concludes that the crimes of the defendants were inadequately narrated and guilt was minimised:[43] 'The judgment did not do mankind a service by whitewashing

---

[37] See Pendas, Steinke, and so on.
[38] Steinke, *Fritz Bauer*, 140.
[39] Hofmeyer, cited in Rebecca Wittmann, *Beyond Justice: The Auschwitz Trial* (Cambridge, MA: Harvard University Press, 2005), 213.
[40] Cited in ibid, 246–7.
[41] C.K. Martin Chung, 'Against Loveless Judging: Fritz Bauer and Transitional Justice in Postwar Germany' (2018) 12(1) *International Journal of Transitional Justice* 9–25.
[42] Wittmann, *Beyond Justice*, 267–9.
[43] Cited in ibid, 268.

their crimes and apologising for the defendants'.[44] But he wasn't only looking backwards: 'Are we certain that something similar could not somewhere, sometime, be built again? It is never too early for vigilance'.[45]

…

In 2017, UNESCO included the 454 volumes of files from the trials, including 430 hours of recordings of 319 witnesses held on 103 tapes in its Register of the Memory of the World.[46] Germany had submitted: 'These authentic records about a monstrous crime unique in human history that should not be forgotten is of great relevance to cultural history'.[47] The simple fact of the matter was that they were nearly forgotten.[48] It is pure serendipity that these documents, destined to be destroyed, survived. They were eventually digitised and made available to anyone who needed to access them,[49] through the work of the Fritz Bauer Institute.[50] Established in 1995, the Institute was established to study and memorialise the Nazi regime and to consider warnings of future dangers. It is housed in the IG Farben building at Goethe University, Frankfurt-am-Main:[51] an apt location given the Jewish origins of the university and the appalling role IG Farben played in the forced labour camps of Nazi Germany. But the nomination identifies only that the state of Hesse holds the documents. In explaining why they need to be held on the Register, we are told that the 'murders of millions of Jews, minorities, political opponents, and Europeans *are associated* with the Nazi dictatorship in Germany (1933–1945)' (my emphasis); that it was the Federal Republic of Germany (West Germany) who brought charges against perpetrators as 'the legal successor of the Deutsche Reich' and that the trials 'focussed the world's attention on the system of practically industrialized homicide for racial and political reasons'.[52]

These words represent the very thing that troubled Fritz Bauer about the legacy of the trials – the suggestion that these were the actions of someone else, a rogue entity, heroically corrected by West Germany, who inevitably chose to prosecute, as night follows day. We should know enough to know that that wasn't the case. But reading these words in isolation, without theatricality and without the depths of dramaturgy, we would be none the wiser.

In 1965, Bauer contributed an article entitled 'In the Name of the People: The Judicial Overcoming of the Past' to a collection commemorating 'twenty years after' (the end of the

---

[44] Cited in ibid.
[45] Cited in ibid, 269.
[46] www.unesco.org/new/en/communication-and-information/memory-of-the-world/register/full-list-of-registered-heritage/registered-heritage-page-3/frankfurt-auschwitz-trial/.
[47] UNESCO, Certified Translation from the German Language, *Nomination Form, International Memory of the World Register Frankfurt Auschwitz Trial ID Code [2016–11]* www.unesco.org/new/fileadmin/MULTIMEDIA/HQ/CI/CI/pdf/mow/nomination_forms/germany_auschwitz_eng.pdf.
[48] Wittmann, *Beyond Justice*, Chapter 6 generally.
[49] Ibid, 4, 9–11, 267–8.
[50] *Fritz Bauer Institute on the History and Impact of the Holocaust*, www.fritz-bauer-institut.de/en/. The Institute has been affiliated with the university since 2000.
[51] Marett Leiboff, 'Ghosts of Law and Humanities (Past, Present, Future)' (2012) 36 *Australian Feminist Law Journal* 3–17, 16–17. The university was founded in 1914 by some of the citizens of Frankfurt, or to be precise, Jewish citizens. At the time, Jews weren't allowed to hold professorships at most universities. One-third of the academic staff were removed from their positions from 1933, and it goes without saying that they were Jewish.
[52] UNESCO, *Frankfurt Auschwitz* Trial, 2.

war). In a wide-ranging argument about the errors made in the trial by the judges, one stands out. The judges and the people of post-war Germany had been the judges and the people of Nazi Germany, and this meant that the law should have been applied in a way that drew a connection between law and society, and reflected societal change.[53] Law had to recognise its place in society and its effects on society but instead it created another image entirely: that Germany was a 'country occupied by the enemy', not one 'obsessed by Nazism'.[54] If that were the case, then nothing had been learnt, and for law in particular, it meant that it could go on facilitating appalling conduct. Bauer turns to Dante to ask us not to forget our responsibility to law: 'The law exists, but who operates it?'[55]

Us.

As we've seen unfold, even the archest positivism is unable to function without imposing a shape, a form, a scenic arrangement to which we barely attend because we're not looking for it. We look elsewhere, for the answer, the outcome, the rules that conform to expectations. Of justice, of rights, of liberty, of the rule of law.

Law is unable to see what is right in front of us.

Theatre can.[56]

Theatricality helps us to see. And to question what we assume or think we know.

SHARD 4

Turn to the second page of Freeman's *Lloyd's Introduction to Jurisprudence* (9th edition), published in 2014,[57] and you'll see a brief story that sits under the heading 'The Relevance of Jurisprudence' at [1.002]. It's been there at least since Lloyd and Freeman co-authored the fifth edition of 1985, where it sat at page 5, absent a paragraph marker. First published in 1959, *Introduction to Jurisprudence* by Dennis Lloyd, soon to be Lord Lloyd, has entered

---

[53] Wittmann, *Beyond Justice*, discussing the article, 253–7.
[54] Cited in ibid, 255.
[55] Cited in ibid, 254.
[56] Among a wealth of examples: Caroline Wake, 'Caveat Spectator: Juridical, Political and Ontological False Witnessing in CMI (A Certain Maritime Incident)' (2010) 14 *Law Text Culture* 160–87; Nicole Rogers, 'The Play of Law: Comparing Performances in Law and Theatre' (2008) 8(2) *Queensland University of Technology Law and Justice Journal* 429–43; Nicole Rogers, 'Performance and Pedagogy in the Wild Law Judgment Project' (2017) 27(1) *Legal Education Review*, art 3, http://epublications.bond.edu.au/ler/vol27/iss1/3/; Danish Sheikh, 'The Road to Decriminalization: Litigating India's Anti-Sodomy Law' (2013) 16 *Yale Human Rights and Development Law Journal* 104–32; Benedict Felman, 'The Theatre of Culpability: Reading the Tricycle's Tribunal Plays through the Trial of Adolf Eichmann' (2018) *Law, Culture and the Humanities* https://doi.org/10.1177/1743872118772232; Simic, 'But I Want to Speak Out'; Caroline Wake, 'Between Repetition and Oblivion: Performance, Testimony, and Ontology in the Refugee Determination' (2013) 33(4) *Process, Text and Performance Quarterly* 326–43; Steven Howe and Clotilde Pégorier, 'Law, Narrative and Critique in Contemporary Verbatim Theatre' (2020) 14(2) *Polémos. Journal of Law, Literature and Culture*, in press.
[57] M.D.A. Freeman, *Lloyd's Introduction to Jurisprudence* (9th edition, London: Sweet & Maxwell, 2014), 2.

the pantheon, expanding dramatically while also paring down radically, like the introductory pages of the book which are now gone. They had actually survived up to the eighth edition, charting the changes in legal thinking and education and approaches to law and society that had come about since the first edition – jurisprudence then was something of a 'dirty word', but had now 'come of age'.[58]

This background has gone from the ninth edition. Whoever stripped the text must have thought it no longer mattered. What remains is now found at [1.001], a bare precis that omits these moves and shifts. What remains is this – that lawyers had been trained in the common law without considering what the law was about, its role and that of the lawyer in society, or whether it was capable of responding to contemporary needs.[59] It probably does its job but we have something along the way – and might imagine it has always been like this.[60]

I will eventually get to the story, but let me stay at [1.001] a little longer. We move from the remarks about lawyers into Kahn-Freund's insistence that law involves some degree of critical thought, endorsed by Freeman (and Lord Lloyd): 'that legal education needs to teach both law and its context, social, political, historical and theoretical'.[61] This still prefaces the story to come, albeit truncated, but it also begs the question about how this reference to Kahn-Freund survived, given that so much else has been removed from the introductory narrative. Nothing links him to the text, other than an ancient reference to an article from 1966. It might have just made it into the 1965 (2nd) edition of the book, because the article is based on a 1965 lecture, but this is pure speculation. It would certainly have made it into the third edition of 1972. But there is no question that this is Dennis Lloyd's text, and he must have known Kahn-Freund. They were near contemporaries. I won't make you wait to find out because his life and background matters to the story to come.

Professor Sir Otto Kahn-Freund was born in Frankfurt-am-Main in 1900, and died in England in 1979, where he lived most of his life. He escaped there after having been dismissed from his position as a labour court judge in 1933 by the Nazis. Like Bauer, he was Jewish, but unlike Bauer, he never returned to Germany.[62] The lecture I mentioned was delivered at the LSE in May 1965, close in time to the end of the Frankfurt Trials and on the eve of Kahn-Freund's move from the LSE to Oxford. His message? That it was impossible to be a fully formed lawyer without a broader education: 'in the untranslatable sense of the words […] "formation" or "Bildung" which denote the forming of the personality as well as the inculcation of knowledge'.[63] He warned of a legal education comprising only rules and doctrines, dogma and detail.

Frankfurt, Jewish judges who had to escape the Nazis, the importance of law and society and the formation of the lawyer …

We find none of this in *Lloyd's Introduction to Jurisprudence*. But Dennis Lloyd, who died in 1992 at the age of 77, would have known. He just didn't tell us. Like most of us, he expects that

---

[58] Lord Lloyd of Hampstead and M.D.A. Freeman, *Lloyd's Introduction to Jurisprudence* (5th edition, London: Stevens & Sons, 1985), 4.
[59] Freeman, *Lloyd's* 9th edition, [1.001] 1.
[60] Without the old editions, you would never ever know. Editions 5–9 sit on my shelves.
[61] Freeman, *Lloyd's* 9th edition, [1.001] 1–2.
[62] Leiboff, 'Ghosts' generally.
[63] Otto Kahn-Freund, 'Reflections on Legal Education' (1966) 29 *Modern Law Review* 121, 123.

words do their own work, despite his own commitment, as his obituarist and later sole author of the volume, Michael Freeman, noted – that the 'social, economic and political context of law' mattered to Dennis Lloyd,[64] that he 'belonged to a dying breed of polymaths: a man of culture and erudition, at home in different disciplines, at ease with different worlds'.[65] So much like Kahn-Freund. Yet law at University College London, 'that Pantheon of positivism', in Freeman's words, which had been Lloyd's intellectual home, couldn't have been more different. We can tell that the early pages of the older editions of the volume would have been addressed to his colleagues.

And now to the story. It is the same as it was in the fifth edition, and begins thus: 'Consider the question that was posed by the case of *Oppenheimer v Cattermole*'. A House of Lords decision, [1976] AC 249, and a *Law Quarterly Review* article by F. Mann (1973) 89 LQR 194 adorn this sentence. Over the next 25-odd lines, we are told of a German Jewish refugee who was deprived of his German nationality by a Nazi decree. If he held German nationality, he would have been exempt from a UK tax on a pension paid to him by the Federal Republic of Germany – West Germany. That law, depriving him of his nationality, was held by the Federal Constitutional Court in 1968 to be so inconsistent with fundamental principles of justice that it was not a valid law – but that a person would not be treated as German unless he reapplied for naturalisation.

This was a case about taxation.

Oppenheimer never reapplied for German nationality. Nor did Miss Miriam Nothman (who was also being pursued for unpaid taxes).

Why would he? Why would she?

The House of Lords held that because he didn't apply for renaturalisation, he had lost his German citizenship, meaning that he would be obliged to pay tax on his restitution – pension – payments from Germany.

A Nazi perpetrator or sympathiser living in the UK and holding dual citizenship wouldn't have to pay tax.

The House of Lords moved to consider, *obiter*, whether an English court would have upheld the deprivation of nationality under the Nazi decree. We are told: 'A majority favoured rejecting it, reliance being placed on public policy'. A syntactical slipperiness (rejecting what precisely) is tempered with this remark: 'But Lord Cross also said that to his mind "a law of this sort constitutes so grave an infringement of human rights that the courts of this country ought to refuse to recognise it as a law at all"' (reference omitted). A brief perusal of the judgments will show that this was far from a universal position of the Law Lords. Some showed no desire to interfere with any lawful determinations of another country. That meant Nazi Germany.

This wasn't too far removed from the logic used by the judges in the Frankfurt Auschwitz Trials.

---

[64] Kahn-Freund, 'Reflections', 123.
[65] Michael Freeman, 'Obituary: Lord Lloyd of Hampstead Friday 8 January 1993', *The Independent* www.independent.co.uk/news/people/obituary-lord-lloyd-of-hampstead-1477249.html.

This story is meant to introduce the kinds of questions of jurisprudence – echoes of *lex injusta non est lex*, Fuller's response to Nazi law – but it is too easily read to mean tax law, a failure of nationality, perhaps human rights. What law already recognises.

Once upon a time, the mention of Kahn-Freund might have triggered the connection needed. But that is now long past.

Tax was owed for 15 years on the restitutionary payments made to Mr Oppenheimer. From 1953/4 to 1967/8. It was an enormous sum. But the law lords asked the commissioner to reconsider his decisions, based on the new information that had come to light through the appeal. The law lords weren't blind to the situation after all.

But the law was.

It was only Goulding J at first instance, finding for Oppenheimer, who realised what was really at stake:

> In the present case it would be an odd thing if the victorious end of a war, which in its later stages was presented as a crusade against the barbarities of the National Socialist regime, should lead *ipso facto* to the recognition, hitherto denied, of one of the Nazis' oppressive laws against the Jews.[66]

…

In 2014, I wrote something using what I knew of Otto Kahn-Freund and his 1965 speech. I had no idea about Bauer's 1965 piece until I began writing this chapter.[67] It was probably no accident that they each wrote in nearly identical terms about law, law and society and the formation of the lawyer. Whether they communicated is a moot point (Kahn-Freund, from London, had offered to help Bauer shortly after he had escaped from Germany),[68] but it would be safe to suggest that Kahn-Freund would have paid close attention to the Frankfurt Auschwitz trials, in English and in German.

They didn't need to be reminded how law could turn its face from mass murder, punish those who were harmed and let off perpetrators.

They could notice because they'd lived this.

They didn't need theatricality to know what was at stake. This was something inscribed in the bodies of both men.

I had understood Kahn-Freund's 1965 speech to be directed towards common law positivists like Herbert Hart. But I was wrong. Now I know. He was warning England's lawyers that they were no different to the judges in Frankfurt. So his speech was still directed towards common law positivists.

Only theatricality could save law from itself. Now and then and into the future.

---

[66] *Oppenheimer v Cattermole* (1971) *Tax Reports* 159–221, 171–2.
[67] I thought I'd never heard of Fritz Bauer, though a footnote of my 2014 article tells me I had – I'd visited the museum at the Fritz Bauer Institute in 2012.
[68] Irmtrud Wojak, *Fritz Bauer 1903–1968: Eine Biographie* (Berlin: CH Beck, 2011), 130, 537; Hannes Ludyga, *Otto Kahn-Freund (1900–1979): Ein Arbeitsrechtler in Der Weimarer Zeit*, nn 551–2.

SHARD 5

In October 1965, a panel discussion, 'Auschwitz auf dem Theater?', was held to mark the premiere of *Die Ermittlung, The Investigation*, where Fritz Bauer remarked:

> There should be a division of labour, dear Peter Weiss, between the Auschwitz judge and the Auschwitz poet. The Auschwitz judge chastises; the Auschwitz poet should educate. This division of labour is necessary, and I, as a jurist, say to you, we jurists in Frankfurt called out in alarm, with our whole souls, to the poet, who could express what the trial was not able to express.[69]

It wasn't only Fritz Bauer who thought this. Siegfried Unsled, chairman of the German publishing house Suhrkamp, wanted to use the information that emerged from the trial for a new play: 'Bauer was eager to be of service. "The state's attorney's office recognizes its important duty to writers and thinkers", [Bauer] replied'.[70] Weiss' oratorio-play would have to do what the trials couldn't, would have to reveal what law couldn't see.[71]

By 1965, Peter Weiss was world famous. A painter, sculptor and filmmaker, his extraordinary play *Marat/Sade*, or to be more particular, *The Persecution and Assassination of Jean-Paul Marat as Performed by the Inmates of the Asylum of Charenton under the Direction of the Marquis de Sade*, had just taken the world by storm, largely through the production directed by Peter Brook at the Royal Shakespeare Company at its London home, the Aldwych Theatre, in August 1964. It had premiered on 29 April 1964 at the Schillertheater in Berlin, and while in rehearsal for its Berlin premiere Peter Weiss visited the Frankfurt Trials – which he would attend a number of times – on 13 March 1964.[72]

Shortly after he sketched a fragment, *Frankfurter Auszüge*, or Frankfurt Excerpts, as an attempt to fashion a play using testimony from the trial.[73] But the play would never have taken the direction it did, to my mind, if he hadn't visited Auschwitz in December 1964. *Meine Ortschaft* – My Place – 'a place for which I was destined but which I managed to avoid. I have no experience of this place. I have no relation to it, except that my name was on the lists of people who were supposed to be sent there',[74] revealed something about Weiss that was largely unknown. Weiss originally had no idea he had Jewish origins or that he wasn't a German citizen, though he was born near Berlin in 1916 and he lived and was schooled in Germany.

---

[69] Cited in the original German in Kerstin Steitz, 'Juristische Und Epische Verfremdung. Fritz Bauers Kritik Am Frankfurter Auschwitz-Prozess (1963–1965) und Peter Weiss' Dramatische Prozessbearbeitung Die Ermittlung. Oratorium in 11 Gesängen (1965)' (2017) 40(1) *German Studies Review* 79–101, 79. My sincere thanks to the brilliant Laura Petersen from the University of Melbourne Law School, whose PhD research cuts across this area, including Fritz Bauer's remarks, for her translation.

[70] Steinke, *Fritz Bauer*, 136.

[71] Sonja Boos, *Speaking the Unspeakable in Postwar Germany: Towards a Public Discourse of the Holocaust* (Ithaca: Cornell University Press, 2015), 162. Suhrkamp became the original German publisher of *Die Ermittlung*. How the connection with Peter Weiss came about is not entirely clear, but Weiss convinced him to release the copyright for a single day so the play could be performed simultaneously across Germany.

[72] Boos, *Speaking the Unspeakable*, 162–3.

[73] Cohen, 'Introduction', vii–ix.

[74] Cited in Cohen, 'Introduction', xvi–xvii.

He was Czech. His Hungarian-born father, a convert to Protestantism, was given Czech nationality on the demise of the Austro-Hungarian empire. With his family, he fled to Sweden in 1938, where he lived for the rest of his life. *Peter Weiss wasn't German.*

Within months, *Die Ermittlung* was finished, ready for its simultaneous productions at theatres in both East and West Germany in October 1965, shortly after the trials themselves finished. He had relied on articles by journalist Bernd Naumann and other histories, enumerated as an appendix to the published edition of the play, and his own notes.[75] From these, he spliced together the words of hundreds of witnesses and the defendants and the lawyers and judges into the 11 cantos that make up an unrelenting soundscape of sadism, torture and indifference of law and the laughter of the chorus of defendants, usually marking the end of a canto, who are assured they are 'in complete sympathy with the existing circumstances in the Federal Republic and give[n] assurances of an accounting with the past that really was no accounting at all'.[76]

Their laughter echoes through the oratorio.[77] It is a laughter of disdain, a laughter of safety, a laughter at the victims whose testimony is challenged, dismissed, disregarded, disparaged. A laughter at the trial. They would have the last laugh.

There are no names in this oratorio, simply a series of defendants, numbered 1–18, and witnesses, numbered 1–9.

The victims of Auschwitz were numbered, their numbers tattooed on their forearm; their identities were obliterated – but only those chosen to work in the labour camps, worked to death through starvation and disease and overwork. It wasn't necessary, of course, for those who were immediately murdered on their arrival. They would never speak.

There were hundreds of witnesses at the trials, but they speak through these 9. The victims effaced and eradicated, bearing no trace of name, identity, life, except for Lili Topfler, whose name we know. She has a canto named for her too.

The words of the oratorio-play are something you can find. Its structure and form matters for all the reasons of theatricality. As Peter Weiss said in interview:

Weiss: In the Auschwitz play I used a structure which reminds me of ancient tragedy as well as of modern sculpture-with the chorus, the leading voice, and so on.

Gray: Did you choose this form just for this particular play?

---

[75] Peter Weiss, Gross translation, 206.

[76] Burkhardt Lindner, *Im Inferno. 'Die Ermittlung' von Peter Weiss. Auschwitz, der Historikerstreit und 'Die Ermittlung'* (Frankfurt am Main: Frankfurter Bund für Volksbildung, 1988), 44 (trans. Kathleen Luft), cited in Matthias Naumann, trans. Kathleen Luft, *The Theater Text Die Ermittlung. Oratorium in 11 Gesängen, by Peter Weiss (1965)*, www.wollheimmemorial.de/en/ermittlung_theatertext_en#down4, note 5.

[77] Robert Buch, 'The Resistance to Pathos and the Pathos of Resistance: Peter Weiss' (2008) 83(3) *The Germanic Review: Literature, Culture, Theory* 241–66, 250. For an acoustic jurisprudence, see James Parker, 'Towards an Acoustic Jurisprudence: Law and the Long Range Acoustic Device' (2018) 14(2) *Law, Culture and the Humanities* 202–18; for sound and silence, Mulcahy, 'Silence and Attunement'. The defendants are unnamed in the play, but simply numbered. They are named in an appendix to the text.

Weiss: Yes, because in The Investigation there is almost nothing happening […] You can barely hear what they say, and sometimes you're too tired and frustrated to understand, but it's going on all the time. You listen if you want to, and if you don't, you can shut your ears. The play should be about four and a half hours long – until now most directors have played it at about three hours. But part of the play's essential quality is its enormous length – it is unbearable. It should be unbearable.[78]

The relentless word and sound of the oratorio, the cantos that add layers of brutality and evil on layers of brutality and evil, the relentless sadism, murder and torture, as a repetition of horror after horror, a soundscape that never lets off: 'It is not only the detail but also the serial character that has an effect that is alternately nauseating and numbing',[79] along with the deployment of language that creates a dramaturgical distancing that 'produces a peculiar kind of affective intensity'.[80]

Gray: Are you trying to punish the audience?

Weiss: Certainly not. If I want anything from an audience, it's that they listen very carefully and be completely awake, not hypnotized, absolutely alive, answering all the questions in the play.[81]

This is what this oratorio-play demands of its audience.

This is why I won't take you to the words of the oratorio-play. You must have them read to you.[82] *You know what they will say. What matters is how you hear them and how you see them.*

I can't trust you to resist wanting to rationalise, assess and analyse. To read this play as a document, a documentary, as a judgment.

This was never a trial play.

SHARD 6

I haven't taken you to words from the play. I will take you to other words though. To another theatricality.

Which shows what words can do, even in their absence.

Peter Weiss did something unthinkable. He eliminated the actual victims of Auschwitz from his play:

---

[78] Erika Munk, Peter Weiss and Paul Gray, 'A Living World: An Interview with Peter Weiss' (1966) 11(1) *The Tulane Drama Review* 106–14, 110–11.
[79] Buch, 'Resistance to Pathos', 250.
[80] Ibid, 246.
[81] Weiss and Gray, 'A Living World', 111.
[82] For mine, I would recommend Robert Cohen's edition which incorporates the final updates that Peter Weiss made, which weren't included in their original translation: Cohen at 117.

> I tried to treat the phenomenon of Auschwitz in a scientific way, as an institution, a death factory, that could have existed anywhere, under certain circumstances. In *Die Ermittlung*, it is not Jews, but human beings, who are destroyed. The ones who are killed are not, for the main part, better than or different from the others; they are simply selected by an anonymous machinery to assume the role of victim. Another turn of history's kaleidoscope – and many of them could just as well have been on the side of the Nazis.[83]

It's not what he said about his play in 1966, which he called the Auschwitz play:

> I wanted a scientific investigation of the reality of Auschwitz, to show the audience, in the greatest detail, exactly what happened. The enormous amount of material I gathered from the Frankfurt trial was concentrated into eleven big blocks of testimony, presented one after another. Each block was a closed complex. Some modern sculpture is neither abstract nor figurative, it's only a thing which stands there – a sense of this imbues the play. There are sculptures which are just a line of heavy tubes standing in a room, without any meaning. Part of Auschwitz is in that […] a very heavy thing has happened which you say you can't understand […] Partly, I wanted to use this feeling because of the impossibility of actually staging the events, of having people 'act' the concentration camp. I worked with just words, the words of the victim's evidence, to wake these things up for us so that we could investigate them.[84]

Naumann writes of one of the original West German productions of the play, directed by the renowned Brechtian director Peter Palitzsch. Naumann's writing is in the abstract. There is something missing that we urgently need to know, especially those of us from somewhere other than Germany, who can't know how they are to be understood:

> Peter Palitzsch, in his Stuttgart production, had photos of the real defendants in the first Frankfurt Auschwitz trial hung up in the room, and had the roles of the witnesses and the defendants spoken alternately by the same actors, which one reviewer described as a 'clear, horrifyingly endless and anonymous succession of voices' that pointed to a 'machinery which relegates the victims and the executioners to a common category and makes them interchangeable'. In their perception of Auschwitz, both the director Palitzsch and his enthusiastic reviewer, Ernst Wendt, completely blank out the social circumstances, specifically the anti-Semitism of the Nazis, and thus the nature of the Jews' extermination, in which victims and perpetrators were in no way interchangeable. Thus they reinforce a tendency in the Auschwitz discussion that is already present in the text of *Die Ermittlung*, and that corresponded to a defining view of Auschwitz in the West German public in the 1960s.[85]

In a discussion honouring the 100th year of his birth, a German media outlet spoke of the controversy surrounding Palitzsch's production, which it termed a creative, alienating and intentionally infuriating experiment that triggered a lasting discussion: that each actor alternately took on the roles of perpetrators and witnesses; that no one should play a role but instead should report what came to light in the Frankfurt Auschwitz trial:

---

[83] Peter Weiss cited in Naumann, *The Theater Text Die Ermittlung*. Peter Weiss, *Peter Weiss im Gespräch*. Edited by Rainer Gerlach and Matthias Richter (Frankfurt am Main: Suhrkamp, 1986), 55, quoted in Atze, 'Die Angeklagten lachen', 798, trans. Kathleen Luft at note 3.
[84] Weiss and Gray, 'A Living World', 107–8.
[85] Matthias Naumann (trans. Kathleen Luft), *Stage Productions and Television Play of Die Ermittlung, by Peter Weiss* (1965/6) www.wollheim-memorial.de/en/ermittlung_inszenierungen_en_2, reference omitted.

> I can't think of any argument to tell one of my actors to play the defendants and you should play the witness […] The thought that a certain actor always plays a witness who is corrupted by the camp management seemed unsavoury to me. Peter Weiss shows – which we also like to think – that there was no black and white. It was just a black with all shades of grey up to white. That is a tremendous insight for me of the piece.[86]

Palitzsch wanted to produce a response that implicated ordinary people in complicity. That isn't how it was understood. It sanctioned the avoidance of complicity.

Palitzsch's device echoed that used by Jean Genet in his 1958 play Les Nègres, a role reversal deploying whiteface by black actors, as a retrial of injustice, bringing racism and colonialism to the fore.

For Auschwitz, shades of grey and interchangeability shift blame.

Interchangeability, in law too, means that victim and perpetrator are treated more or less exactly the same.

We usually don't notice it. It is what we tend to call equality.

SHARD 7

Peter Palitzsch, Peter Weiss and Fritz Bauer all appeared in a panel after the Stuttgart production. I don't know what Fritz Bauer thought of it. This was Bauer's home region and he spoke with its strong accent. It was where he had been a judge before he had to flee. I can't imagine that he would have thought himself as someone on a spectrum of interchangeability with those who caused him harm. After all, he was a left leaning judge, and that was one of the reasons he was targeted, early, by the Nazis.

> Since the legal trial failed to meet Bauer's expectations, he considered the trial as 'juristische Verfremdung von Auschwitz' ('Auschwiz auf dem Theater' 74). While Bauer's use of the term 'Verfremdung' at first glance evokes Brecht's dramaturgical practice of 'Verfremdung' […] Bauer meant by 'juristische Verfremdung' that the Frankfurt Auschwitz trial failed to present a profound history of the Auschwitz concentration camp as a state-sponsored institution of mass murder, in which every participant contributed intentionally to the mass murder and therefore should be considered a perpetrator.[87]

Bauer's own presumptions about what the play would do had far more in common, as Steitz makes clear,[88] with Schiller's eighteenth-century polemic about the place of theatre in enlightenment thought, to produce a truly human, humanistic response to questions of justice and injustice:

---

[86] www.deutschlandfunk.de/peter-palitzsch-vor-100-jahren-geboren-der-individualist.871.de.html?dram:article_id=427677, my adaptation.

[87] Kerstin Steitz, *Beyond Closure: The Artistic Re-Opening of Holocaust Trials in Works by Hannah Arendt, Peter Weiss, Roland Suso Richter, and Uwe Timm*, A Dissertation presented to the Graduate Faculty of the University of Virginia in Candidacy for the Degree of Doctor of Philosophy, 2014, 112.

[88] Steitz, 'Juristische und Epische Verfremdung', 80–1, 83–5.

> The jurisdiction of the stage [which] begins where the domain of secular law leaves off [...] is merely assisting human justice; but yet another, broader field is open to it as well. The theatre has the power to punish the thousand vices which justice must patiently tolerate; the thousand virtues which the latter must let pass without comment, on the stage are held up for general admiration.[89]

This is always interpreted to mean that theatre has to pick up what law is unable to achieve 'the stage takes up sword and scales and drags these vices before a fearsome tribune'.[90] That is, the people. This had been Erwin Piscator's aim in *his* 1965 Berlin production of *The Investigation*, insisting on theatre as a 'moral institution in Schiller's sense'.[91] Piscator, one of Brecht's key collaborators, who had to flee the Nazis for political reasons, echoed Bauer's educative aims using Schiller's, using his own and Brecht's agit-prop techniques as a staging, rather than a reading, of Weiss' play. Through his directorial and dramaturgical techniques, Piscator made it crystal clear that the victims in the play were Jewish, and the defendants were all named in the programme – with their biographies:

> As long as we have not completely accounted for our past, as long as we try to bracket our past from our present and future [...] the task of political theatre will be to recapitulate the unresolved [...] theatre must not remain neutral and distanced, even at the risk of certain artistic inadequacies.[92]

In his 1966 interview, Weiss identified Brecht as his inspiration for the play. Echoing the logic of the verfremdungeffekt, he remarked that he wanted audiences to be able to analyse what was onstage, something they couldn't do if the acting was sadistic or masochistic.[93] But there was no way his oratorio could ever meet this demand, as he couldn't help but remark himself, in the same interview, that the play is unbearable.[94]

Displaying justice is nearly impossible. Or attempting to think justice, as a form of logic through dispassion, as didactic. Or generating feelings and emotions, which are always a means of escape,[95] which permit avoidance.

Through Palitzsch's production, people were able to say: you see, it wasn't our fault after all.

---

[89] Friedrich Schiller, 'Theatre as a Moral Institution', trans. John Sigerson and John Chambless (Read at a public session of the Elector's German Society in Mannheim in the year 1784), https://archive.schillerinstitute.com/transl/schil_theatremoral.html.

[90] Steven Howe and Clotilde Pégorier, 'Law, Narrative and Critique in Contemporary Verbatim Theatre' (2020) 14(2) *Polémos. Journal of Law, Literature and Culture* 385–405; Friedrich Schiller, 'Was kan eine gute stehende Schaubühne eigentlich wirken?' [1784] in Gerhard Fricke and Herbert G. Göpfert, *Sämtliche Werke* (Munich: Hanser, 1980), vol. 5, 822–3. Translation Steven Howe, note 45, 7; cf Erika Fischer-Lichte, 'Philosophical Theatre: Some Reflections on the Concept' (2018) 136(1) *Anglia* 43–60.

[91] Minou Arjomand, 'Performing Catastrophe: Erwin Piscator's Documentary Theatre' (2016) 59(1) *Modern Drama* 49–74.

[92] Ibid, 62.

[93] Weiss and Gray, 'A Living World', 111.

[94] Ibid.

[95] Cf Howe and Pégorier, 'Law, Narrative and Critique' 7, who argue that in formulating the verfremdung, what Brecht rejects is a particular brand of empathy that stimulates thoughtless immersion and identification, while he later arrives at a more sophisticated position that admits a role for empathy in eliciting a specific class of emotions ('the sense of justice, the urge to freedom, and righteous anger') that might stir an audience to critical reflection and might enable spectators to 'think feelings' and 'feel thoughtfully'.

The only way we can recognise injustice is if we are brought into it, through our bodies.

Weiss was right – it has to be unbearable.

If it is unbearable, we are physically shaken, disturbed, broken, holding shards that break our skin, writing into our bodies.

He already knew this through Marat/Sade. *He knew this through working with Peter Brook.*

SHARD 8

In England, Peter Weiss' play was about to become a byword of documentary or verbatim or trial theatre, given the moniker of *the theatre of fact*. This was the temperament of England in 1965, a didactic moment in theatre triggered by the emergence of kitchen-sink drama in the 1950s and Harold Pinter's excruciating forays into everyday life that were filling theatres in London, or exemplified by the documentary realism of the *Seven Up!* TV event that had screened in 1964.

Brook was unhappy with the moniker *the theatre of fact* for a number of reasons, not least his understanding of Weiss' play as another version of *Marat/Sade*: 'You can never get to the facts. I'd rather call it the theatre of myth',[96] echoing his adoption of Artaud and Grotowski as theatre that seared into the body of audiences, which he used in *Marat/Sade* itself.

Part of the problem for Peter Brook was the material he had to rely on. Alexander Gross' translation of the play used by the Royal Shakespeare Company (the RSC) contributed to the idea that this was a documentary play. But time wasn't on Brook's side, because he and his co-director, David Jones, had just a matter of weeks to turn Gross' new translation (itself generated in barely a month) into a reading.

Alexander Gross' dramaturgical notes show how little he understood of the oratorio form, and of the soundscape that Weiss created. His translation of the play turns bare word into literary form, his *ex post facto* explanation of his translation and dramaturgical notes revealing: 'It is of course important to point out that a very real war crimes trial had taken place in Frankfurt, and the entire text of *The Investigation* was based on carefully edited excerpts from the trial transcript'.[97]

Gross was unable to register the play as anything other than a courtroom drama, as the opening gambit of his original dramaturgical notes from 1965 reveals:

> When an author alternates between calling his newest work a play and an oratorio, when the work itself has no fewer than 30,000 words with a potential five-hour playing time, and when the theme of the play is nothing less than the agonizing torments of Auschwitz *as seen from a comparatively static courtroom situation*, it is very hard to know where to begin […] To the skeptic who might reply 'Oh no, not the concentration camps again,' I can only say in turn that I believe Mr. Weiss has something sufficiently new and interesting to say about them and about society to merit reopening the subject. *Oddly enough, the play is not so much agonizing as surprisingly serene with an even more surprising dimension of forgiveness.*[98]

---

[96] Michael Kustow, *Peter Brook: A Biography* (London: Bloomsbury, 2005), 136.
[97] Gross, *Dramaturgical Notes.*
[98] Ibid.

We get the picture. We are in a courtroom. We have an assessment of social worth. We have serenity. We have forgiveness. We are working with a document. A courtroom drama. A trial play. Oh, and not the concentration camps. Again?

It is hard to see any of this in Peter Weiss' text.

Weiss' play needs to be fixed.

And Gross – a man – with relatives from both sides of the Atlantic including Christians and Jews, was the one to do this job.

The dramaturgical note speedily moves into a list of cuts he recommends. That he has, in fact, more or less put in place already. I paraphrase, keeping Gross' enumeration (though I have left out 8 as it is neither here nor there), and italicising some choice sentiments:

(1) The play needs to be kept to three hours.
(2) With an interval, this means 80 minutes for Act One and 70 minutes for Act Two. 30,000 words will be cut to 18,000 words, 'an extreme measure but not an unworkable one'.
(3) Repetitious details and a few unabsorbable statistics need to be cut, but '*enough of the right ones must be left to evoke the seeming aimlessness of courtroom routine*'.
(4) Reduce the characters from 30 to 21 – *some have only one or two lines.*
(5) Obviously a number of sentences which run something like: *Why did you leave the Bunker to go to the Injection Department in Block Eleven at eight o'clock in the morning?* could be changed to something more like: *Why did you go there?* which would not involve any loss as the details have already been made clear.
(6) Replace the topographical detail explaining the precise location of one place or object in the camp with a map of Auschwitz '*but I wonder, even so, if these descriptions, apart from the necessary ones at the beginning, would add anything to one's theatre experience*'.

And without paraphrasing:

(7) 'There are also a great number of long speeches by witnesses, which I tend to think of as "arias". Set to a Brechtian sort of speechsong they could be very effective, and some of them are already very effective just as speeches. *But there are a few too many of them, and I wonder if some of them may not need shortening or leaving out*'.

The repetition, the topographical detail is seemingly irrelevant, and I know there are words from the play, but I'm quoting from Gross. He holds to the image of the play as a courtroom drama, and offers advice about how it should be 'acted'. I use his words, italicising the choicest items, again, and underlining the most drastic of the misconceptions of the piece:

> I should also like to observe that the final effect this play can produce may depend to a large extent on *first-rate character acting*, on *humanizing the impersonal numbers* in the script. Unless there is characterization of the highest order, <u>this play might sound like little more than sonorous lament, which it definitely is not</u>. It should not be supposed, as I supposed while translating the first 100 pages, *that the combination of a courtroom and Auschwitz is so sombre and solemn <u>as to totally exclude ways of livening it up in a discreet way</u>*.
>
> If the play is slow in developing, it should be remembered that *it is indeed a courtroom drama with genuine courtroom climaxes*, which are in fact often anti-climaxes. Indeed, just as the free verse

58 *Research handbook on law and literature*

without punctuation *reads much like a court reporter's shorthand book*, so <u>*the play itself reads like a court record and is clearly meant to*</u>. And since it is about one of the more important trials of our time, precisely through its subject matter <u>*it has absorbed the strength of that trial and may be one of the most important of courtroom plays*</u>.

Of course it is (something like) a sonorous lament. It is an oratorio.

Not a trial play.

But then, after providing his own assessment of how an audience might respond to the play and a wildly inaccurate reading of the text involving culpability and complicity (my adaptation) Gross concludes: 'In this too there is perhaps a lesson for today'.

It was never a trial play.

Peter Brook's colleague and friend Michael Kustow tried to find another name for it – an 'oratorio-stage-documentary'.[99]

He was much closer to the mark, but it was never a documentary either.

Observing that Weiss had taken the mass of materials and had reframed them into the verse style of Dante's Inferno, Kustow remarked that he 'carved the words into a very modest verse form whose line-endings lifted the frequently appalling words of the prosecution, the witnesses and the accused *to a level beyond the merely evidential*'.[100]

SHARD 9

And this was how Peter Brook directed the RSC's staged reading of *The Investigation*, rehearsed over only a weekend, at the RSC's London base, The Aldwych, beginning at 11pm on 19 October 1965, and ending at 2am the next day, in solidarity with the East and West German productions which were all held on the same night, brought together through Piscator's leadership. The date of the production was no accident. It coincided with the intention of the Bundestag to alter the law to allow war criminals to go free.[101]

The RSC production was sandwiched between that paean to the monarchy, The Hollow Crown, *and a reprise of* Marat/Sade. *A second reading was held on 14 November with the same cast, and the next year from 19 February to 9 March 1966 with a new cast – just after a production of Gogol's* The Government Inspector.[102]

Each actor stepped into a semi-circle of red chairs, delivered a statement, was cross-examined,[103] recovered memories, had memory lapses, told lies, all with the utmost transparency; acting at

---

[99] Kustow, *Peter Brook*, 156.
[100] Ibid.
[101] Ibid.
[102] https://cdn2.rsc.org.uk/sitefinity/press-resources/performance-history---june-2016.pdf?sfvrsn=8; http://collections.shakespeare.org.uk/search/rsc-performances/view_as/grid/search/everywhere:the-investigation-80711.
[103] Kustow, *Peter Brook*, 157.

a minimal threshold, the actor not the character, but as chronicler. It had the sober authority of fact, transmitted by actors who were not impersonating but were as savagely impersonal as they could constrain themselves to be.[104]

The Aldwych, the RSC's London base at the time, was as it happens a stone's throw from the Royal Courts of Justice and the LSE.

It was also personal for Brook. There was resistance, a denial in the German public that triggered his insistence that the RSC participate in the simultaneous production of the play, to ensure it wasn't forgotten. In his biography of his friend, Michael Kustow reproduces Brook's acidic programme note to accompany the productions entitled *It's The Germans*.[105] Brook began with a stream of consciousness, which I reproduce, including its orthography, that indentation of paragraphs now largely buried in the past, and what Peter Brook hoped wouldn't be buried. It is a howl, of pain, of frustration, of repudiation:

> It's the German's business not ours teutonic guilt complex it's all over it's buried a thing of the past what good will it do let's forget bygones be bygones no muck raking we know it by heart sick of it.
> What label can we put on Peter Weiss' script to make it respectable as theatre?
> How can we defend it against predictable attacks?
> I only know that hearing that 13 German theatres and also the Berliner Ensemble were making a collective manifestation of this play we felt this to be right and we wished to stand with them. We share their belief that the ingredients of the camps have not vanished from this world and that the topic of man's indifference is not yet out of date.
> I suppose I've never got over hearing Alain Resnais' film about the concentration camps described as 'beautiful'.
> With more time we could have prepared a more polished performance, built a set, made music. What for?
> We feel our job is to transmit this text at once – to whom it may concern.[106]

Kustow uses an odd turn of phrase to describe these words of Brook. He calls it a belligerence, by which he means Brook is unable to find words to account for a burning dissatisfaction not only about the camps but an insufficiency of an entire culture.[107] That means that collective amnesia, and wanting it all to go away. While Kustow seems to mean teutonic insufficiency, it's also law's insufficiency.

For Brook and Kustow, both Jewish and who both were born in England, in relative safety, knew what was at stake. Born in the mid-1920s, they were of a next generation. And there would be more generations to come.

Fritz Bauer put all his hopes in the potential of culture to save law. But Schiller wasn't ever going to be able to do this. Only theatre that writes in the body, like that which Peter Brook uses, had any hope of changing things.

---

[104] Ibid, 158.
[105] Ibid, 317, n 157.
[106] Ibid.
[107] Ibid.

60 *Research handbook on law and literature*

SHARD 10

A portion of the text of *The Investigation* features in Brook's 1968 book of lectures, *The Empty Space*.[108] He is explaining how audiences affect actors, how sound and silence and bodies all interact to generate meaning. He recounts a talk at a university where he asks for a volunteer, and I repeat his words at length.

> A man came forward, and I gave him a sheet of paper on which was typed a speech from Peter Weiss's play about Auschwitz, *The Investigation*. The section was a description of bodies inside a gas chamber. As the volunteer took the paper and read it over to himself the audience tittered in the way an audience always does when it sees one of its kind on the way to making a fool of himself. But the volunteer was too struck and too appalled by what he was reading to react with the sheepish grins that are also customary. Something of his seriousness and concentration reached the audience and it fell silent. Then at my request he began to read out loud. The very first words were loaded with their own ghastly sense and the reader's response to them. Immediately the audience understood. It became one with him, with the speech – the lecture room and the volunteer who had come on to the platform vanished from sight, the naked evidence from Auschwitz was so powerful that it took over completely. Not only did the reader continue to speak in a shocked attentive silence, but his reading, technically speaking, was perfect – it had neither grace nor lack of grace, skill nor lack of skill – it was perfect because he had no attention to spare for self-consciousness, for wondering whether he was using the right intonation. He knew the audience wanted to hear, and he wanted to let them hear: the images found their own level and guided his voice unconsciously to the appropriate volume and pitch.[109]

Brook sets up a counter-point with another volunteer, this time using a portion of Shakespeare's *Henry V* which lists the names and numbers of the French and English dead. This volunteer responded with fake gravity and ham acting, and bored the audience witless:

> When he had done, I asked the audience why they could not take the list of dead at Agincourt as seriously as the description of death at Auschwitz. This provoked a lively exchange. 'Agincourt's in the past'. 'But Auschwitz is in the past'. 'Only fifteen years'. 'So how long's it got to take?' 'When's a corpse a historical corpse?' 'How many years make killing romantic?'[110]

Then the master director directed both the volunteer and the audience to bring their 'impressions of Auschwitz and Agincourt, to try to find a way of believing that these names were once individuals, as vividly as if the butchery had occurred in living memory'.[111] Brook told the volunteer to read each name with care, to be silent before moving onto the next. The audience now heard the names, and the volunteer felt the audience hear those names, attending to the rhythms in the words on the page.[112]

It is that simple to work with the body, to be present in the moment, to hear, to see, to notice.

Auschwitz was still fresh.

---

[108] Peter Brook, *The Empty Space* [orig. McGibbon & Kee, 1968] (Harmondsworth: Penguin Books, 1968), 27–9.
[109] Ibid, 27–8.
[110] Ibid, 28–9.
[111] Ibid, 29.
[112] Ibid.

But we can see what happens when the years fall away, when, like Agincourt, there is nothing left but names and numbers.

You will see I've taken documents, the actual text, and repeated their words, to hold onto names and numbers. Paraphrasing strips texts of what matters. This is the same technique Peter Weiss used in his Auschwitz play.

By now, you will know that these documents have to be read as present, theatrically and dramaturgically.

SHARD 11

In July 2018, a woman was found guilty of ten murders carried out over an 11-year period between 2000 and 2011. I have chosen not to name her, though her name appears in references. The only surviving member of a far-right terrorist group, the NSU, her trial in the Munich court lasted five years, during which she refused to speak for much of the time, except when she issued a statement blaming the dead members of the group for the murders and apologised to some of the family members of the deceased. She and the other members of the group murdered eight men of Turkish background, a Greek man and a policewoman, and carried out racially motivated bomb attacks and bank holdups. The case was ignored initially by the police, who blamed the murders on gang-like violence in the Turkish community;[113] the German Federal Office for the Protection of the Constitution was also suspected of concealing or withholding important information that could have helped clear up the case. The case involved 62 lawyers who represented 86 joint plaintiffs (mostly relatives of the murdered).[114] The woman's lawyer said he would appeal: 'The verdict is wrong. *Conviction for complicity is legally untenable. The fact is:* [she] was demonstrably present at no crime scene and never fired a weapon or detonated a bomb'.[115]

Four years earlier, on 27 September 2014, Elfriede Jelinek's *Das schweigende Mädchen* (The Silent Girl) premiered at the Münchner Kammerspiele (the Munich Playhouse), in the same city where the trial had already been running for two years.[116] Her play touched on all of the themes that marked the career of the Austrian Nobel Prize-winning playwright and novel-

---

[113] Claudia Hillebrand, 'Beate Zschäpe guilty: the five-year neo-Nazi trial that shook Germany', *The Conversation* 12 July 2018, https://theconversation.com/beate-zschape-guilty-the-five-year-neo-nazi-trial-that-shook-germany-99816.

[114] Anna Brod, 'Talking about Silence and Talking Instead of Silence in Elfriede Jelinek's *Das Schweigende Mädchen*' in Eva Gillhuber and Rita Rieger (eds) *Texts with No Words: The Communication of Speechlessness* 146–61, PhiN Beiheft 15/2018 http://web.fu-berlin.de/phin/beiheft15/b15t10.pdf at 147.

[115] Lucy Pasha-Robinson, 'Beate Zschäpe: Germany's "Nazi bride" found guilty of 10 racially motivated murders; National Socialist Underground gang killed eight Turks, a Greek and a German policewoman between 2000 and 2007', *The Independent* Wednesday 11 July 2018, www.independent.co.uk/news/world/europe/beate-zschape-neo-nazi-germany-guilty-murders-national-socialist-underground-a8441826.html.

[116] The play, directed by Johan Simons, was shortened by dramaturg Tobias Staab to keep it to a 140-minute run: Mi You, 'Angels and Prophets on Trial: On Jelinek's Das schweigende Mädchen' OFF TOPIC #6: *schweigen/schreien* (Kunsthochschule Für Medien Köln, 2016) Art 12; 3–18, 3.

ist:[117] the continued pull of Nazi ideology, the treatment of women and capitalist culture, but inevitably that aspect of her work on 'what is unsaid in what has been said or what is unspoken in speech, about making visible the silence that has turned into concealment'.[118]

A defendant who doesn't speak. Yet this is an oratorio,[119] where angels and prophets speak for the accused and the dead murderers, just as they speak for the victims, [120] just as they speak for the public and police whose racial prejudice means they had already made up their minds about the victims, and engage in 'wry commentaries on the political significance of the case'.[121] Jelinek foregrounds the impossible and continued legacy of the Germany of the 1930s and 1940s within German society, all the while putting German social historical consciousness on trial.[122] As Brook and Bauer and all the others knew, Auschwitz would never be at an end if this aspect of German society was simply ignored. Jelinek, who was born in 1946 and grew up Catholic in Vienna, knew this all too well. Her Czech father was Jewish, and though he survived, most of her relatives were murdered.

It's not hard to see the lingering pull of Peter Weiss and his play in Jelinek's Silent Girl. Yet this time there are no effaced victims, there is no production that imposes moral equivalence of perpetrator and victim. In her angels and prophets, she is able to confront the call to an imagined history, and imagined legacy, and imagined social order as they take on the positions, evil and angel, in which their names are invoked. As Mi You observes, Jelinek is speaking to Walter Benjamin's prophetic, that is, not simply looking back to the past, but instead, for the service 'of the beaten generations […] [as] the critique of the continuation of a catastrophic past, to "foresee the present"'.[123] And the future.

In her observations of the rehearsals of the Munich production, and its eventual production, Mi You is drawn to the place of bodily affect and its effect on an audience, remarking how the angels and prophets and the judge were forced to sit on the front edge of the stage, 'speaking with their face to the audience most of the time – if they reveal their face that is'.[124] In bringing Jelinek's play to the stage, the director has deployed the symbolist techniques developed by Russian director Vsevolod Meyerhold, in the early stage of his work in the theatrical avant-garde of the early twentieth century, challenging naturalist and realist certainties of theatre: 'a shallow stage, decorations resembling a mural, slow movements of the actors, gestures and poses that have the expressiveness of sculpture, and cold emotionless intonation', particularly through his experimental direction of Maeterlinck's *Sister Beatrice*.[125] In its foreshortening of space, the spectator's role in the performance event position was recast:

---

[117] Elfriede Jelinek – Facts. NobelPrize.org. Nobel Media AB 2020, www.nobelprize.org/prizes/literature/2004/jelinek/facts/.
[118] Brod, 'Talking about Silence', 160.
[119] You, 'Angels and Prophets', 7 calls it an oratory.
[120] Brod, 'Talking about Silence', 153.
[121] You, 'Angels and Prophets', 12.
[122] Ibid, 6.
[123] Ibid, 14–15.
[124] Ibid, 7.
[125] Vsevolod Meyerhold, 'Theatre Meyerhold Centre', http://old1.meyerhold.ru/en/library/index.html; Amy Skinner, 'Surfaces, Depths and Hypercubes: Meyerholdian Scenography and the Fourth Dimension' (2015) 1(3) *Theatre and Performance Design* 204–19, 209–11 for an excellent account of Meyerhold's adoption of symbolist practices in this production; Edward Braun, *The Director and the Stage: From Naturalism to Grotowski* (London: Methuen, 1982), 118–19 for a discussion of *Sister Beatrice*.

as external, centralised and slightly distanced.[126] And for Jelinek's play, this same technique couldn't be more apt, so that '[t]heatrical space and real space are framed as discontinuous, and restricted depth becomes a metaphor for conscious theatricality as opposed to naturalistic illusionism: both the stage space and the world it represents are reframed as fragmented, theatrical constructs'.[127]

Like law, really. Only made more alert to what is present, what is missing, and what law can never comprehend.

And this is where you come back in. The shards are now complete, as much as they could ever be. And you, holding the jug. It is up to you to keep it intact, to notice the fissures as they open, as the shards begin to fragment and fracture; to notice the unnoticeable.[128]

---

[126] Skinner, 'Surfaces, Depths and Hypercubes', 210.
[127] Ibid.
[128] Karen Crawley and Kieran Tranter, 'A Maelstrom of Bodies and Emotions and Things: Spectatorial Encounters with the Trial' (2019) 32(3) *International Journal for the Semiotics of Law – Revue Internationale de Sémiotique Juridique* 621–40.

5. Perspective
James R. Martel

INTRODUCTION

Can there be law without a point of view? Even to ask this question is a bit subversive. One of the great conceits of the law (at least in its modern, secular guise) is that it doesn't have a point of view, that it is objective and neutral and merely follows a particular protocol. In this view, law doesn't *look* from anywhere (justice is blind!); it just happens, and those who enter its rational and ordered world come out rightfully judged and determined (indeed, if law did have a point of view, this argument follows, it would be sullied and unjust, actually unlawful). Yet, as literature shows us, there is no such thing as no point of view. Even in novels that radically depart from normative literary conventions we fill in some sort of narrator, some sort of position from which the events of a novel or other artistic work is viewed.

Literature gets us to ask questions about the nature of that perspective, about who ultimately is looking out from a given point of view. Many texts have radically challenged the presumptions of a universal (read: white, male, and privileged) narrative position. Just to name a few examples, Charlotte Perkins Gilman's *The Yellow Wallpaper* forces the reader to confront the madness at the core of gender politics; Kafka's "The Concerns of a Head of a Family" offers us a main character who challenges the assumption that objects can't be agents; Fanon's *Black Skin, White Masks* shatters the assumption that the narrator's position must be universal (and therefore white).[1] Yet, even as these texts challenge and subvert the privileged perspective normally associated with point of view they do not suggest its effective or entire elimination.[2]

Point of view is thus a central core of literary structure and, to the extent that law cannot escape (much as it might like to) its own literary aspects—its own narratives, tropes, and other rhetorical structures—it cannot not have a point of view either. In fact, I would go so far as to say that law doesn't have *a* point of view but rather *the* point of view, that is to say, a positionality that is itself exempt from its own examining eye. Law is a central part of a phenomenon that I call archism (which is the opposite of anarchism, although both have many, many variants).

Archism is a world system wherein the entire universe is ruled, taxonomized, and judged from a central and secret perch, a privileged viewpoint that renders hierarchical the world according to its own criteria; it is the veritable source of the gaze. Archism is the basis for

---

[1] See Charlotte Perkins Gilman, *The Yellow Wallpaper* (Los Angeles: Enhanced Media, 2017); Franz Kafka, "The Concerns of a Head of a Family," in *A Country Doctor: Short Stories* (Prague: Vitalis Press, 2005), pp.58–60; Frantz Fanon, *Black Skin, White Masks* (New York: Grove Press, 2008).

[2] This is not to say that literature can never escape from the strictures of point of view. In addition to the novel/TV show that I will be looking at in this chapter, I can think of many that succeed in doing just this but point of view, unless it is specifically interfered with as such, will always tend to reassert itself because it is connected, as I will argue further, with the entire apparatus of how visuality and sight are organized.

capitalism, colonialism, imperialism, and sovereignty, the entire structure of the modern world. Law can be said to be neutral and all the rest because the place it judges from—the point of view of archism—is not in or of the world. Law can rely on that prior source of judgment to ensure that the values that it claims not to hold (values of white privilege, capitalism, patriarchy, and the like) are upheld nonetheless. It is this occult positionality, both in law and literature, the presupposition of a form of rule that disguises itself as neutral or background, that radical critiques set out to challenge.

In this chapter, I am going to look at a literary work, Tom Perrotta's *The Leftovers* (but in this case I'm going to focus on the HBO TV adaptation that goes well beyond the book), to examine a significant challenge both to the law's point of view and, perhaps even more fundamentally, to the very idea of an external and transcendental viewer whose vision organizes the world according to its own dictates.[3] The novel and TV series both offer a vision of a world in which the bases of archist perspective, in all of its theological, political, and philosophical forms, are either permanently destroyed or at least dealt a severe and lasting blow. In the absence of this point of view, people are reduced to their own limited and local, collective and temporary forms of perspective, hence allowing for a radical conceptualization of what the point of view is and what it can possibly do.

This is certainly the case for *The Leftovers*' central character, Kevin Garvey, who is the sheriff of his town in upstate New York.[4] Kevin *is* the law in his town, but he knows (as the result of a cataclysmic event called the "Sudden Departure, to be explained further") that the law knows nothing at all. As society breaks down, Kevin is increasingly forced to resort to outright violence to maintain any semblance of authority and also appears to lose his mind as the bases for his legal authority are pulled away from beneath his feet.

As I see it, the central drama of *The Leftovers* is to look at what happens when archism dies, taking its point of view along with it. What happens to law? What happens to politics? What happens to personal identity and relationships? All of these central aspects of human life, at least insofar as they are conceived of from a Western perspective, are (and here we can already begin to see how perspective is never a politically neutral issue) based on, as becomes increasingly apparent, a sense of a "universal" point of view. When the location of vision shifts from some Archimedean point out in the noumenal realm to each of us, the results are, to put it mildly, radical (and, I would add, anarchist). Although much of *The Leftovers* is devoted to mapping out the chaos that results from the Sudden Departure, the trigger for the death of the archist point of view, there is, especially toward the end of the TV series, a suggestion of a possible movement from mourning the loss of this universal perspective, one that had always been assumed to be eternal and unavoidable, to embracing, perhaps, a more anarchist approach in which law itself becomes radically altered.

In my reading, *The Leftovers* suggests a way to see a form of law in which it no longer exercises a parasitical power over people (as it does under conditions of archism) but rather is something that comes from out of both individual and collective forms of judgment. The great power of this narrative is that it uses point of view, normally the pinnacle of archist literary forms, in order to unmake its own position. By allowing us access to Kevin Garvey's own collapse as a figure of law, *The Leftovers* shows us how within one kind of perspective (Kevin's)

---

[3] Tom Perrotta was one of the chief writers of the series, so the TV show preserves his basic vision even beyond the confines of the novel.
[4] He is played by Justin Theroux in the HBO show. In the book he's the mayor.

we see the effect of the withdrawal of another (the perspective of archism), leaving him (and thereby the rest of us) to his/our own devices. This change lies at the heart of my comments and helps us to think more about law without—at least one principal form of—point of view.

Even as Kevin's legal authority collapses, the possibility for this different form of law is preserved by another central character, Nora Durst, who ends up being Kevin's girlfriend.[5] Even as Kevin desperately tries to shore up the collapsing authority structures of archism that have been unleashed by the Sudden Departure, Nora—who is initially very much trying to do the same thing—comes to realize the futility of such efforts. As the HBO series comes to its conclusion, Nora offers us a glimpse (but nothing more than that) of another kind of viewpoint, affording in turn another form of law, and thereby of life (to cite Agamben) that is far more connected to an anarchist politics.[6]

ARCHISM AND THE ARCHEON

Before going into an analysis of *The Leftovers*, let me begin with a few comments about the nature of archism and its relationship to point of view, as well as to law. Although the Western variety of archism (which, by imperialism and global capitalism, has influenced much of the rest of the world) pretends to be universal and eternal, it actually comes out of two specific contexts, those of ancient Greece and ancient Israel. Both societies were marked by strong prophetic traditions, wherein human beings were able to convey (it was thought) messages from transcendental beings, whether God or the gods. The Hebrew tradition of prophecy, even as it sometimes very much goes against terrestrial forms of authority, nevertheless allows for a higher and unimpeachable authority to speak in the world with a voice that cannot be denied.

Hebrew prophecy amounts to a new way of seeing the world. In the Book of Jeremiah, for example, God asks the prophet Jeremiah what he sees and, as Jeremiah conveys the objects in his vision, God re-interprets and reinvisions these visions as being vehicles of divine agency:

> Moreover the word of the LORD came unto me, saying "Jeremiah, what seest thou?" And I said, "I see a rod of an almond-tree."
> Then said the LORD unto me, "Thou hast well seen: for I will watch over my word to perform it."
> And the word of the LORD came unto me the second time, saying, "What seest thou?" And I said, "I see a seething pot; and the face thereof is from the north."
> Then the LORD said unto me, "Out of the north an evil shall break forth upon all the inhabitants of the land."[7]

Here, the seemingly neutral act of seeing becomes reorganized by God's words in such a way that the objects of sight become avatars of God's judgment. In telling Jeremiah that "I will watch over my word to perform it," God is explicitly testifying to the visual nature of divine power in the world. Accordingly, God will bring divine judgment into the world in a way that

---

[5] Nora Durst is played by Carrie Coon in the HBO series.
[6] For more on this concept, see Giorgio Agamben, *The Highest Poverty: Monastic Rules and Form of Life* (Stanford, CA: Stanford University Press, 2013).
[7] *Holy Scriptures* (Philadelphia, PA: The Jewish Publication Society of Philadelphia, 1917), Jeremiah 1: 11–13, p.662.

surpasses any form of human agency or resistance, rendering an otherwise intangible authority all too real and material.

The Greek prophetic tradition is similar. There were two key sites of prophecy in Greece: Dodona and Delphi.[8] Each site was connected to a specific God (Apollo and Zeus respectively). Each site conveyed the connection and linkages between the unknown and the known world, what the Greeks called *sympatheia*.[9] In both the Greek and the Hebrew tradition, prophecy was always subject to human interpretation, so the connection was never absolute or perfect, but it was always assumed that the words of the prophet conveyed a truth that it was up to human actors to understand (a truth that carried enormous political consequences).

This prophetic tradition also came to have a more secular manifestation as a way to reproduce divine judgment and authority in political and terrestrial forms. In *Archive Fever*, Jacques Derrida describes what he calls the "arkheion," a depository of state authority that existed in ancient Greece. Derrida connects the arkheion to the archive, both etymologically and conceptually, noting in both cases that something originary and authoritative is at stake. Derrida writes:

> The meaning of "archive," its only meaning, comes to it from the Greek *arkheion*: initially a house a domicile, an address, the residence of the superior magistrates, the *archons*, those who commanded. The citizens who thus held and signified political power were considered to possess the right to make or to represent the law. On account of their publicly recognized authority, it is at their house, in that *place* which is their house (private house, family house, or employee's house), that official documents are filed. The archons […] do not only ensure the physical security of what is deposited and of the substrate. They are also accorded the hermeneutic right and competence. They have the power to interpret the archive.[10]

In this way, the arkheion (which I will henceforth anglicize as the archeon) is both the fount of knowledge and the origin or commencement of the power to interpret and analyze that knowledge.[11] It serves, as with the Hebrew understanding of God, as a seat of judgment, a site from which such judgment could and did issue; in other words, it offers a point of view, not only in theory but actually in a "*place.*"

Accordingly, the archeon offers a location from which judgment issues, one that is anchored in a locality but which is distinct from the rest of the community. Locating archism in a place (and also in a time) gives it a substance that it requires in order to be credible. In a sense, the physicality of a place—in this case the building that houses the archeon—transfers its tangibility to the mysterious power that it is otherwise meant only to represent.[12] Through that transference we can come to believe in an invisible power as if it were as visible and as tangible as the places and things (and persons) that stand in for that power on earth.

The archeon offers a place in space and time that is unique and superior to other spaces and other times, organizing reality accordingly. Critically, it is exempt from its own judgment (it

---

[8] Sarah Iles Johnston, *Ancient Greek Divination* (Malden, MA: Wiley-Blackwell, 2008), p.34. There were also prophets at large, called *manteis*, but they did not convey the same authority.

[9] Ibid, p.13.

[10] Jacques Derrida, *Archive Fever: A Freudian Impression* (Chicago, IL: University of Chicago Press, 1996), p.2.

[11] I am indebted to Tiffany MacLellan for alerting me to the concept of the archeon.

[12] This power is itself totally transitive, however. The seat of judgment and power can shift from place to place but it must always have some imagined, and actual place to emanate from.

does not stand inside its own gaze). Thus (to connect this back for just a moment to the traditions of ancient Israel), just as in the Temple of Solomon there is a spot, a holy of holies, where God's invisible presence becomes expressed in reality, so too does the archeon (albeit according to the logic of Athens instead of Jerusalem) pinpoint an inexpressible pervasive power so that it too can have a focal point, a way to believe that it is true and absolute and that nothing is prior to it even as it is also recognizable, locatable, taking on a solid and tangible form.

This is the legacy that leads to archism, predominantly via Christianity, a form that merges the traditions of ancient Greece and Israel into one. Archism adopts that sacred and privileged perch as its own point of view and then promptly disguises that fact by resorting to standards like "reason" and "nature," secularizations that presuppose and protect the sacred position that archism always looks at us from. The possibility of this perspective radically alters all human endeavors, including that of law. Insofar as secularized forms of archism have basically accepted the mainstream Christian tradition that there will be no more prophecies, any and all would-be potentates use the archist form to project their desires out into the cosmos to be received back as irrefutable and perfect truths.[13]

This exalted point of view applies to all manifestations of archist power, law very much included. As with other manifestations of archist authority, the dual nature of this power (both tangible and intangible at the same time) allows the law to appear to be neutral and unto itself when in fact it represents the very power systems that it supposedly sits in judgment of. In this way, for example, as Benjamin argues, the much-debated difference between natural and positive law is actually inconsequential.[14] Whether the law is said to stem from transcendental forces (whether explicitly divine or not) or whether it is constructed by humans, in fact the law is always held and authorized under the divine point of view afforded by archism and transmitted by the prophetic traditions of the West. Here, point of view cannot be erased but it can be forgotten, folded into the background so that its operations of power can go unnoticed and unchecked.

Accordingly, archism rules like a parasite sitting atop human life. The actual decisions that we make, the judgments that we are always engaged in making separately and together in our own lives, remain as a vast anarchist network but the expressions of archism—law, capitalism, the state, and so on—take all the credit for this life and run it accordingly. In this way what could be read as an essentially literary device, point of view, becomes a formula for domination. Something utterly ethereal and nonexistent, the perspective by which archism rules us is, precisely because of its ethereal nature, impossible to get at, impossible to dislodge. Yet, by virtue of the transfer of tangibility from the representations of that power, it takes an all too real, violent and dominant form. If it takes a literary (or at least literary-like) device to rule the world, it stands to reason that a literary treatment might serve to dislodge that rule or at least call it into question. It is my contention that *The Leftovers* helps to show us how this might work.

---

[13] Mormonism and Shiite Islam are two forms of faith that continue to believe in the possibility of prophecy, with interesting political ramifications.

[14] See Walter Benjamin, "Critique of Violence," in *Walter Benjamin: Selected Writings Vol. 1, 1913–1926*, Marcus Bullock, Michael W. Jennings, eds (Cambridge, MA: Harvard University Press (Belknap), 1996).

THE SUDDEN DEPARTURE

Let me begin an exploration of *The Leftovers* by giving a sense of its basic plot. The premise of both the novel and the TV show is that on one particular day, at one particular moment (October 14, year not specified), 2 percent of the world's population—140 million people in all—suddenly disappeared on the spot, in what becomes called the "Sudden Departure." People were there one moment and in the next they were gone. Fetuses disappeared from mother's bodies; a circle of children who were holding hands suddenly found gaps between them as one or more of their number disappeared; husbands and wives, children and parents, loved ones and hated ones all vanished with the same random and devastating suddenness. There was no forewarning of the Sudden Departure and definitely no explanation that followed. It just happened.

The advent of the Sudden Departure does more than just pose an existential threat to archism. In a sense, it simply does archism in. On the secular side of things, there is literally no way to understand this event. There is no possible scientific explanation for what happened. Worse yet, scientists of the day (it is set in contemporary times) can't promise that this mysterious force won't return to carry off others, or perhaps even get rid of everyone.

By the same token, religion has nothing to say about the Sudden Departure either, although this is not for a lack of trying. There are multiple attempts by Christians to read this event as the rapture, for example. Yet, it seems quite clear that this is *not* the rapture; good people and bad people alike are taken away indiscriminately (celebrity departures range from Jennifer Lopez to Pope Benedict to Gary Busey).

The Sudden Departure literally makes no sense from a theological perspective. It cannot be explained away as some mysterious plan of God; it is just too awful, too devastating and too random to be something that any deity would actually do (even one who works in mysterious ways).

Without these bases in secular and theological power, archism loses its spectacular authority. It's as if the great eye that has watched over the world all of this time has withdrawn itself, no longer holding the rest of us in its gaze. To be sure, the power of archism doesn't disappear all at once. In *The Leftovers* there are still states and political systems and laws, but they are all on the verge of collapse (a subject I will return to momentarily).

In addition to a breakdown in law and order, families are falling apart. Teenagers feel completely aimless, having been robbed of the kinds of certainties (at least among white middle-class kids in the US, which is the focus of the TV series, especially during the first season) that have anchored life for them for centuries. They turn to sex and drugs but even those can't break this mood of despair (in fact they seem to only make it worse). In the pilot episode of the TV series there is a graphic scene of two young people in college jumping off a roof and killing themselves, illustrating that a larger sort of lethal despair has set in. Kevin's daughter Jill engages in unhappy sexual rituals while crying and his son Tommy has joined a cult led by a sexual predator named "Holy Wayne" (his schtick is that—for a very hefty fee—he hugs the pain away from people grieving over the loss of loved ones in the Sudden Departure).

In the absence of the normal assurances of archist forms of authority, numerous cults spring up. In addition to "Holy Wayne," the most significant cult in *The Leftovers* is called "the Guilty Remnant," a group devoted to pointing out to others that the world—a.k.a. archism, which has the conceit that it *is* the world—has already ended. Cult members wear only white, smoke cigarettes constantly (by mandate; nonsmoking is not tolerated) and don't speak. Members of the GR, as they are known, plot endlessly to ruin any attempts to lead a normal life. Indeed, normality itself is part of what has been ruined. The whole idea of a "new normal" is palpably impossible. How can anything ever be normal ever again after what happened?

One key target of the Guilty Remnant is Nora Durst, who is infamous for having lost all three members of her family (her husband and two kids). This is considered to be exceptionally unlucky since the number of departed is relatively few and randomly distributed. Nora is initially depicted as a deeply broken woman. She neurotically replaces over and over the exact same paper towels, cereal boxes and other quotidian items that her family was using the day they disappeared. She hires a prostitute to shoot her in the chest while she is wearing a bullet proof vest and she carries a gun in her purse. She becomes Kevin's love interest (his own wife, Laurie, joins the Guilty Remnant, although she later turns against them). In a way, Nora and Kevin are a perfect couple insofar as they are equally broken, but, as I will show further, they end up taking very different paths to try to come to terms with what has happened.

MANY WAYS OF SEEING

After the Sudden Departure, the human population as a whole is subjected to a vast breakdown in belief structures, leading to a radical instability in their forms of vision. Nora, who is employed as a member of the Department of Sudden Departures (which gives compensation to people who lost relatives), goes to a conference on the Sudden Departure in New York City where a priest, who is giving a talk, describes what he calls the "Prophet's Dilemma." He says:

> For most of humankind's existence certain individuals have come across as self-professed interpreters of the worlds mysteries. But what happens when those conversations with God go wrong? Following a catastrophic event or circumstance, let alone one that defies scientific explanation, the incidents of prophetic delusion rise dramatically. It's not just megalomaniacs who make the news for a week. This is happening to our friends, our neighbors our own families. This belief that a higher power is speaking to us whether through dreams or science, even voices, is a powerful coping mechanism and, if left unchecked, is a very dangerous one.[15]

Here we see that in effect, in the wake of the Sudden Departure, everyone has become a prophet and in so doing, prophecy itself has become a dangerous and destabilizing form of sight. Rather than ordering and preserving hierarchy (or perhaps returning a community to purity and truth), such acts of prophecy are a sign of the breakdown of all of those things. It seems as if, in its dying throes, archism has lost the clear distinctions that it needs to make between what it considers to be real and what it does not. In the breakdown of that clarity, the archist prophetic function of seeing what is not there—and organizing the world accordingly—becomes generalized to a form of collective madness where the directive to see things remains but the content of that sight has been emptied out. All of the cults, the despair, the bitter disappointment that the world has collectively gone through serve both to recall this community to its own collective nature as well as to simultaneously break that collectivity into tiny individual parts as the argument over what is true becomes utterly undetermined.

---

[15] *The Leftovers* (TV Series, HBO), season 1, episode 6, "The Guest."

This could be seen as a kind of transition stage from archism to anarchism as a dominant mode of seeing and thinking because it has elements of both. It is at once collective and divided; it represents both the requirement to see *something*, to be authorized by *someone*, even as it breaks that authorization and sight into an infinite number of mutually contradictory pieces.

This transition hardly appears to be a good thing in part because it is not complete; archism may have died but, like the proverbial dinosaurs of the past, it does not yet know that. In a way, the world described in *The Leftovers* is the worst of both worlds in the sense that it still requires determination but finds none at all. Yet, for all of this, in the morass created by the Sudden Departure, collective and anarchic networks, increasingly unburdened by archist competition, start to become a bit more visible. The communities of the world (at least those depicted in Mapleton, NY and later in Jarden, Texas, to which the TV series' location shifts in season 2) are not in the habit of recognizing their own collective and horizontal forms of authority, not to mention other, more local, forms of law. But we see at least a directionality in which that could (and may have already started to) happen.

These other anarchic forms require some time to fully emerge from their deep interconnection with archism (and of course there are no guarantees that archism won't reassert itself, although its basis for reassertion would have to come from an entirely new source). Yet, bereft of the overall guidance provided by *the* point of view afforded by archism, localities do begin to think in their own way, see with their own eyes, make their own forms of life, their own kinds of law.

Kevin and Nora keep seeking to escape from the after-effects of the Sudden Departure. After Mapleton, NY falls apart due to the machinations of the Guilty Remnant, they move to Jarden, Texas (renamed "Miracle"), a town where no one departed on that fateful October day. The idea is to escape from the despair and chaos unleashed by the Sudden Departure once and for all and get back to the old "normal." When that town too succumbs, they try going to Australia, the setting for much of the third and last season of the TV series. Yet each place in succession shows itself to be already ruined as a site for normality and safety and so, in a way, they are forced to confront a life that exists without the (entirely fake) assurances of archism, a disappointed life that is rawer and more unpredictable but also infinitely freer (even if that freedom is unwilled).

Even the cults that emerge in the aftermath of the Sudden Departure could be said to unconsciously promote the anarchism that the catastrophe has both exposed and furthered. The Guilty Remnant are ghastly and vicious but their work—to make sure that no one forgets that the world, as people knew it, has ended—disallows the continuation of the false point of view that archism articulates. The entire narrative arc of *The Leftovers* suggests that the intense disappointment that follows the death of archism is not the end of life but rather the end of the false projections that dominated and parasitized that life, leaving life itself to its own devices.

THE LAW AFTER THE SUDDEN DEPARTURE

In all of this chaos and madness, the law suffers along with everything else in the post-Departure world. The law continues to function—at least, sort of—well after the Sudden Departure (the TV series begins just a year after the event). Even at the beginning of the show, when Kevin is still the sheriff of Mapleton, NY, it is easy to see that he is losing his grip on things very quickly. He has to resort increasingly to pulling out his gun to maintain order (one of the first things you learn from political science is that if you have to resort to threats of violence, your power is at its weakest). Here, the usual deference to a person in uniform seems to be increasingly becoming a thing of the past.

By having Kevin be the central character, and thereby serving a bit as the foil for the audience too, we get a sense of the collapse of the archeon and the perspective that it offers, not just for the subjects who live in its shadow, but from within the archeon itself, among its employees and enforcers. There are many hints about this, foremost in the way that we see a lot of what unfolds through Kevin's eyes. He is the chief of police but he *knows* that the power of the law is entirely hollow.

There is a religious dimension to this as well. As the TV series progresses, it becomes weirder and more mystical (perhaps because the sense of what is normal and ordinary, a major aspect of sustaining archism, has started to unravel). Kevin dies on three separate occasions over the course of the series, each time being revived. Toward the end of the series, he is considered a messianic figure by a small band of devotees. Yet, even as he knows that the law is empty, Kevin also *knows* that he is not a messiah (at one point he tells his would-be followers "I'm not fucking Jesus").[16] Rather than being someone who fulfills the law and the expectation for salvation, he occupies that position and, because we see through his point of view rather than the higher and transcendent perspective that such a figure is normally meant to convey, renders it null and void.

Even Kevin's experience of the afterlife reinforces this disappointment. The afterlife looks like an anodyne hotel with muzak and his and her guest bathrobes. There's nothing special in the transcendent realm. Indeed, it isn't really different than the earth itself; at one point while he's "dead," Kevin leaves the hotel and drives home, suggesting that "heaven," if that is what it should be called, is an exact duplicate of ordinary life.

This is another marker of the radical nature of this show; as with Nietzsche's idea of eternal recurrence, in *The Leftovers* too, the afterlife, other worlds, or any other way to transcend or replace our ordinary, all-too-human life is rendered equally mortal, fallible, and ordinary, and thus no escape at all (it thereby offers no way to annihilate ourselves via dreams of salvation). To the transcendent worlds that archism imagines, *The Leftovers* answers with a healthy dose of immanentism. This too reinforces the loss of a transcendent point of view; by dying and showing us what happens next, Kevin is in effect inadvertently calling the transcendent realm's bluff. He shows that it is no better, no different than the world we live in, and so here too it loses its authority and power to command and order us.

The Leftovers undermines all of these better alternatives even as it also undermines our sense of the authority that comes from orthodox renditions of point of view in the first place. As the show becomes more mystical and strange, we are never sure if some of the things we see happening are real or not. Many of the weirdest things that happen in the show occur after Kevin goes to sleep (for a while Nora takes to handcuffing him to her in order to keep him from wandering around in his sleep). We are never 100 percent certain if the fugue states that Kevin falls into are actually happening, if he really did die and really did get resurrected, not to mention the visions of the afterlife that we are shown.

---

[16] Ibid, season 3, episode 1, "The Book of Kevin."

While it is true that a great many works of film and literature use this device (the unreliable narrator is one version), these depictions generally occur in a universe where the larger norms, the archist position, *the* point of view remains intact. Accordingly, most transgressions of orthodox boundaries generally pertain only to that character or to her context. In *The Leftovers*, the destruction of that archeonic perspective itself makes this unreliability infinitely more transgressive because there is no longer a "big other" to guarantee the order of the universe in the face of these kinds of micro-subversions.

Kevin's own subject position also reinforces the degree to which the larger norms of point of view are violated in *The Leftovers*. Kevin seems to represent a former apex predator, the proverbial straight, cis-gendered, white man (and a representative of the law at that), who finds himself in a new world in which his privileges and supremacy are no longer assured. His children despise him (albeit in complicated ways), the communities that he polices make fun of him, the Guilty Remnant mock and directly challenge his power. This leaves him confused and confounded. Kevin often speaks with the voice of gravitas but it is clear that white male gravitas isn't what it used to be, doesn't produce the effects he wants it to now that its transcendent sponsor has left the world. Insofar as his position aligns him particularly well with the point of view that is supposedly universal and eternal (but really is just a vehicle for people who look and act like Kevin), his personal descent into madness and doubt represents the unraveling of the archist mode of vision itself, opening up other possibilities, other points of view, and other ways of seeing and reacting to the world.

What Happens When We Stop Believing in "Rule of Law"?

The subversive implications for law that come from occupying Kevin's point of view are not limited to Kevin alone. Throughout the series, we occasionally get a glimpse of higher-up workings of the law and we see much the same pattern as with Kevin himself. At one point Kevin is arrested for having killed Patti, the leader of the local chapter of the Guilty Remnant (in fact she kills herself but does so to frame Kevin with the crime). When Kevin is being interrogated for Patti's murder—he was caught with her dead body in the back of his truck—he confesses to everything; he had in fact kidnapped her and beaten her badly, albeit in one of his fugue dream states. Without asking for a shred of evidence or asking a single further question, the officer interrogating him asks him: "Do you want to blow up your life?" When he says no, she tells him: "Go home."[17] Not only does this demonstrate a callow attitude toward the life of GR members in general (the police treat them like sub-humans and mow them down whenever they find them) but it also shows that there is a general breakdown in faith in law and procedure.

This might not, at first glance, look like a good thing, much less a subversive one; after all, police favoritism toward their own, vigilantism, and a disregard for the very laws that authorize them are hardly new practices. The incessant killing of unarmed Black and Brown people in the United States by police is one key example of how the practice of law is always far more violent, racist and chaotic than the law itself purports. Yet, it shows that when the police, and in particular the higher-ups who deal with law on a national level (on the show the ATF, the existing agency that deals with alcohol, tobacco, and firearms, has been rechristened as the

---

[17] Ibid, season 2, episode 2, "A Matter of Geography."

ATFEC, the Bureau of Alcohol, Tobacco, Firearms, Explosives, and Cults), stop believing in the law—don't recognize the way that the law has never been anything but their whim and their exercise of power—law's ability to sustain itself becomes highly unstable.

While the concept of rule of law is almost entirely empty, especially with its connections to imperialism where it was often a justification for taking over other countries, its mere symbolic existence has a critical effect on its constituents. Even the most corrupt, violent, and racist of police might believe that even if *they* aren't practicing the law properly, somewhere in the world (or more accurately outside of the world) there *is* law, there is the archeon. It is in fact that belief that might allow them to violate the law, because if the law exists somewhere else (even only in the noumenal realm) than it isn't their duty to uphold it; it exists independently from human actions. Without such a position for law, it becomes each person's responsibility to uphold the law (or not). Law becomes something that people do not obey so much as interpret and act upon (one way to rephrase this is that law here becomes a verb instead of a noun).

By giving us brief insights into the nature of policing in the US—arguably the central node, along with Britain and the EU, that determines what law is and what it looks like, thanks to the colonial and imperialist projects of the West—we see how deep the undermining of law as an archist practice goes. When point of view ceases to bring within itself a presupposed absolute that guarantees that there will always be a law, a truth, a right way and a wrong way, it becomes something radically other, a basis for anarchism instead of archism.

Nora: Choosing Disappointment

As already argued, Kevin's descent into madness and impotence suggests the death of archism unleashed by the Sudden Departure. But what about the anarchism that follows? To discuss this in more detail, we need to shift focus (and hence point of view) from Kevin to Nora. Ultimately it is she and not he who shows us a way beyond archism (although there is a hint at the very end of the show that Kevin too benefits from her discoveries, as I'll discuss further). As previously noted, Nora starts out in *The Leftovers* as a deeply wounded and lost person. When she begins to date Kevin, his daughter Jill is instantly suspicious. She thinks Nora is a liar (she lies about having a gun in her purse, for instance) and a phony more generally. And Jill is on to something. Nora's whole life is based on a lie, the idea that somehow if she does everything exactly the same way she did when her family were still with her, if she leads a small, rigid, and entirely circumscribed life, she might just win her family back.

Nora's falsity also seems contagious. Her boss at the DSD tells her that they've noticed that the people that Nora interviews about getting compensation for departures have one question that they all answer affirmatively (for others who administer the test there are a mixture of answers). The question is "do you think your departed loved ones are in a better place?" For Nora, the answer to this question *must* be yes, and somehow Nora gets her interviewees to affirm this over and over again. In this way, Nora remains committed to returning to normality, to reaffirming the comforts of a universe where everything made sense even if the order that it produced was ruinous (although not necessarily for a middle-class American white woman like Nora).

But Nora is also desperate and, as such, she is not immune to the lures of the many cults and belief systems that are flooding the world. As suspicious as she is of all charlatans and snake oil salespeople, she pays $1,000 to Holy Wayne for a hug. It seems to work for a while and actually, shortly after that hug, one of Nora's interviewees says that no, their loved ones are probably *not* in a better place.

For a while, Nora and Kevin set up a fairly happy life in Jarden, to where they move after law and order completely collapse in Mapleton, NY (Kevin becomes the sheriff in Jarden as well). Jill moves there with them and is obviously much happier herself. Yet this peace is very shortlived. You can see their attempt at renewed faith in the normal cracking apart as three teenage girls suddenly disappear, leading to fears that the Sudden Departure is returning. It turns out that the girls secretly joined the Guilty Remnant and weren't departed at all, but were part of a larger plot by a rogue faction of the Guilty Remnant that seeks to bring Jarden down (which it succeeds in doing).

The assault on the town does not so much ruin Jarden for Nora as confirm a sense that had been steadily growing in her anyway: that, no matter how much she didn't want it to be true, there was no place on earth that was free from the damning effects of the Sudden Departure.

In the midst of all of this, Nora begins to get calls from a group of people claiming that they can reunite her with her family. We've seen her get calls like this before: some seem really professional and scientific but then reveal themselves to be thoroughly mystical, talking about demonic possession and the like. This one seems like it might be more of the same and Nora pursues it nominally in the guise of exposing it as a fraud (that is one of her jobs at the DSD too). The viewer can tell that Nora is highly skeptical of this as well as other claims. Yet even so, she doesn't listen to these claims from a wholly rationalist perspective. She wants her family back so badly that all of her rationalism can't prevent her from wanting these frauds to turn out to be true after all.

When this particular group ask her to turn up in a hotel in Melbourne, Australia, with $20,000 she says yes right away. She continues to maintain that the purpose of her trip is to bust a ring of scam artists, but she also cajoles her boss into letting her go. At the last minute, Kevin asks to come with her to Australia and she allows it, setting in motion the events that lead to the ending of *The Leftovers*.

Once in Melbourne, Nora meets with the people who've been calling her. They seem relatively harmless and very much on the level. They say that they have the means to pass her over to whatever other dimension or space the departed now find themselves in. Although initially it still seems as if Nora might only be humoring these people, setting them up to be exposed as frauds, it becomes clear that Nora fully intends to take them up on their offer. She is prepared to risk even death if there is a chance that she might "go through" (as they put it) to wherever her husband and children have gotten to. The actual process involves being potentially drowned in a small chamber that fills with some sort of fluid. She goes into the capsule and screams as the fluid fills up beyond her head.

That is all we know for a while but in the final episode of season 3, the finale of the whole series, all is explained. At least sort of (what follows is a spoiler). We see a much older version of Nora who looks very sad and worn, living a very lonely and isolated life in the middle of nowhere in Australia. She finds out that someone named Kevin has been looking for her and it turns out to be her ex. She is terrified and tries to run away but before she can do so he shows up at her door, also looking much older. He initially feigns to barely know her but when she tells him that she can't bear his lies he tells her the truth; he has spent the last many years (it is not clear exactly how much time has passed) spending every one of his annual two-week vacations scouring Australia to look for her.

It is not clear how he knows that she might be alive but Kevin displays the tenacity of many characters on *The Leftovers* who, when faced with a choice that is neither life nor death (the status of the departed), just can't seem to let go of a hope that is in and of itself usually deeply self-defeating (another remnant of archism itself). In this case, however, it leads to a different result.

As Nora and Kevin sit down to finally talk, she begins one of the most compelling narratives that I have ever seen on television, as she explains what happened to her after she entered the chamber. She tells Kevin that she came out in the same parking lot that she went into, but there were no cars there. In fact, the same landscape was there, but most of it was derelict. After a lot of wandering she came to a house with a man and a woman inside, and this is what she found:

> They were kind and they told me […] that seven years earlier he was in a supermarket and every single person disappeared except for him. And the woman told me she lost her husband, her three daughters, and all eight of her grandchildren, and that's when I understood. Over here we lost some of them but over there they lost all of us.[18]

Here, we finally learn the big secret of what happened to the departed. For them, the same thing happened but in vastly greater numbers. It turns out that the world that we have been experiencing, Kevin and Nora's world, is the lucky one. The other world, where all but 2 percent of the human population (that is to say, 98 percent of everybody) vanish in an instant, is virtually, but not entirely, wiped out.

The beauty of this answer is that it is not an answer at all. We now know what happened to the departed, but it doesn't in any way address the bigger question of how or why it happened. Without illuminating these issues in any way, *The Leftovers* offers us a sense of resolution without anything actually being resolved. The "answer" in this case does not really get at the real questions: What about God? What about the rational universe? What about archism? This ending offers no basis to restore the transcendent point of view that promises so much but, in the end, delivers (and is) nothing at all.

What Nora discovers does not answer these questions, yet, by appearing to figure out what happened, she effectively serves to block any chance for a full resolution, exactly because by "going through" to the other side and finding only more of the same (not unlike Kevin's explorations of the afterlife) we once again see a version of Nietzsche's eternal recurrence, a wish that even if one could be reborn in another world or in another time, that time and that world would be more or less exactly like the one the person is already inhabiting. To choose this means to do an end run around your own hope for salvation. It means that even if you are "saved," you will be returned to your unwanted, unloved present form. It means no messiahs can deliver you to a better world because you have visited those worlds and they are no different (and certainly no better; in this case the "other world" is actually quite a bit worse), forcing you into your own position, onto your own resources.

We know that it is not Nora per se who discovers how to go through and she is not the only one to actually do it (among other people, the actor Mark Linn-Baker of *Perfect Strangers* fame is also said to have gone through). But Nora *is* unique in one way. As far as we know, she is the only one who went to another world and then came back to her own.

---

[18] Ibid, season 3, episode 8, "The Book of Nora."

In her discourse with Kevin, Nora tells us further that, after great effort, she made her way from Australia back to the Mapleton, NY of the world of the departed (it took her a long time, since air traffic has ceased there due to a lack of trained pilots). Finally she came to her house, the house that she lived in with her husband and two children. At that point, she tells us the following:

> When I got there I stood by a tree and waited because I was too scared to go up there and knock. And after a while the door opened. At first I didn't recognize them. A tall teenage boy with curly hair and a girl maybe 11. They were my children. And then my husband came out and he was with a woman. She was pretty. She was pretty and they were all smiling. They were happy. And I understood that here in this place they were the lucky ones. In a world full of orphans they still had each other. And I was a ghost. I was a ghost who had no place there. And that, Kevin, is when I changed my mind.[19]

What does Nora mean when she says that she changed her mind? I would say that in changing her mind, she finally accepts that archism, that salvational perspective, that meta point of view, is no more, along with all of the disappointment that such a realization gives to her. In fact, I'd go further and say that Nora *chooses* her disappointment, something else no character on the show is able to do. This too has a Nietzschean aspect to it, akin to *amor fati*, the love of one's fate. Rather than continuing to rail against a universe that seems to have wronged her (or maybe in this case that unquestionably *did* wrong her) and which seems to owe her something, Nora chooses to be what she is, disappointed, abandoned, bereft. Having gone through to the other side (in an almost perfect rendition of what Lacan calls traversing the fantasy to discover its ultimate emptiness), Nora has nothing left to hope for, nothing left to structure her life around, nothing left to connect her to and keep her dependent on an externality that has always been a projection and a fantasy, no guarantee at all—but she didn't know that until just now. Now she knows for sure that what she is is all that she'll ever be—in fact, this is all she has ever been—and she makes her peace with that.

To choose this kind of bitter disappointment then means that in some sense Nora is free from archism at last, from the kind of limbo existence that archism has held on to after the Sudden Departure. In this way she is even different from those others who have managed to find their way to the world of the departed. Although they too have "gone through," they remain to some extent mired in archism insofar as they are being driven by their wish to hold onto what has been lost. They are still in a melancholic state in which there is still an answer and still a solution and so, although archism and its transcendent perspective itself may be dead, their allegiance to it is not.

Nora is different. We know that she is the only one to go back to her original world because in the other world that she travels to she finds the man who invented the machine that transported her, a man who had gone through himself, and talked him into making another machine in this world and sending her back. She tells us: "[the man who invented the machine] asked me if I'd come all that way why in God's name did I want to go back and I told him it's because I didn't belong there. So he built it and I came back through. I came back here."[20]

Having come back, Nora doesn't necessarily know what to do with her newfound freedom. She tells Kevin that she thought of him often but she was worried as so much time had passed (time seems to move at the exact same speed in the other world as it does on ours, and she spent

---

[19] Ibid.
[20] Ibid.

years there before she was able to return). She also says that she was afraid that he wouldn't believe her, to which he replies, "I believe you."

"You do?" she asks.

"Why wouldn't I believe you? You're here."

"I'm here," she agrees, with tears streaming down her face (and his)—the last line of the series.[21]

I think that there is something else afoot in Nora's initial resistance to return to Kevin and Jarden and the life that she had, a sense that that life was completely determined by the collective resistance to loss that formed this family (and not just this family). Recall that initially Nora is not just reluctant to talk to Kevin, she is terrified. It seems that she doesn't want to go back to that life if it'll destroy her new resolve, if it will get her to change her mind back again and begin to hope and regret (and worst of all be moved once again to pity, mostly of herself) all over again. In other words, the thought of having to go back to being a subject of the archist gaze has gone from being a comfort to a source of terror; now she sees that gaze for what it is, what it has always been.

We don't know what is going to happen next. Perhaps she will return with Kevin to Jarden. Perhaps she won't. But what we do know is that Nora is perhaps the first and so far only member of the human race who looked heaven in the eye and turned the other way; in a sense, she is the first true a-theist and maybe, by the same token, the first full-on an-archist, the first to fully break with what anarchism has always struggled with.

It might appear that Kevin, through his own resurrections, may be another candidate for such atheistic anarchism, but Kevin's own desire is more a matter of continuing to refuse loss (the loss of his family on earth, the loss of whatever purpose in life he imagines himself to have) while Nora's desire is now derived from an entirely different source—her own judgment, her own point of view, liberated at last from the gaze of archism.

In her moment of watching her original family in the world of the departed, Nora finally sees and accepts the present; she sees that her husband and her kids have their own life. She sees that she doesn't belong in that world and that sight is enough. She accepts what is. She chooses disappointment. And now that she has had this realization, now that she has learned to live without the gaze, it is possible, but only possible, that Kevin too will learn to see the world through his own eyes (and not hers).

The End of Externality

What Nora has finally given up on (and we can see the huge cost and struggle that such a giving up entails) is externality as a source of validation. She gives up her enmeshment in a transcendent perspective from which to view the world and adopts a new form of radical immanentism. In some sense you could say that externality, that workhorse and black box that has supported illicit forms of authority throughout the history of archism, serving as a passive screen upon which to project archist phantasm after phantasm, is suddenly shown to have a mind, and an agenda, of its own. From that very void which is the basis of political authority comes an event that effectively deauthorizes everything that has ever been done or said on its

---

[21] Ibid.

behalf, as if the void itself is getting revenge for the endless personifications that it has been forced to endure.

In this way, it could be said that the Sudden Departure is the ultimate anarchist event. If I were going to picture what a Benjamin-style divine violence might look like in our own time, the Sudden Departure would be a great example. It is an act that destroys all false authorizations but in doing so it ensures that the myths that would inevitably follow such a visible act of supernatural power cannot lead back to reestablishing an idea of a knowable God (who is thereby the basis for further myths). This deity is determined to rule herself out of the world, to decisively break down the basis for her own fetishization (although the immediate response to the Sudden Departure is an explosion of new fetishisms, they all have this intense element of doubt that renders them ineffective as establishing new and further bases for archism).

If there is a God in *The Leftovers,* she is definitely an anarchist. Radically withdrawing her point of view from the world in a way that cannot go unnoticed serves to actualize and enable all of the other points of view, and with those perspectives a different form of visuality as well. In this way, the device of point of view as such ceases to become a way to determine and trump all individual perspectives. Thanks to the Sudden Departure, it gets broken into several billion pieces, returning its visual and interpretive authority back to the persons from which it was originally stolen. Each of these pieces has the chance now to come into a collective that has no overarching logic or rule, no demand for harmony, in other words, anarchism.

CONCLUSION: LAW WITHOUT THE ARCHEON

Amid all of the despair that it depicts, *The Leftovers* asks a question that we don't usually get to ask, namely: What would life be without all the armature that is provided from external sources? Can human beings find meaning and purpose without recourse to the devices that have kept archism going for an indeterminable amount of time? Can something as awful as the Sudden Departure have a positive—and anarchist—outcome?

We see through Nora's eyes that loss can bind as much as it moves people in new directions. The fear of loss may hold people within archism's web even as archism itself produces nothing but more loss (and furthermore, even if archism itself is part of what is lost). I think that might be part of what Nora figured out: that there is nothing to lose but loss itself. In losing her loss, as it were, Nora finds something else; herself. I do not mean this in a hokey Hallmark-card kind of way. Nora does not discover someone named "Nora," her real and authentic self under all of those layers of denial and pain. Rather, she encounters herself as she has always been, a complicated, messy, grieving, but also joyous person with multiple layers of identity, some of which overlap with other persons and some of which are perhaps unique to her.

In a previous writing, I speculated that the self at our core is itself anarchist; that there is not one true self to organize the rest of us but rather a plethora of selves, a vast and overlapping anarchist interiority that also binds us to a much larger set of anarchist selves that form the basis of horizontal forms of mutual, collective authorization.[22] Whatever this self is, it is the self that Nora, in losing her loss, has encountered and has chosen to be. In choosing her disappointment, Nora is in some sense freed from loss or, perhaps more accurately, can now face

---

[22] See James Martel, *The Misinterpellated Subject* (Durham, NC: Duke University Press, 2017).

her loss rather than form herself around and through it. She is no longer determined by what she is not (as archism always requires) and can begin to be what she is, whatever that may be.

I would not really call this a "happy ending" for *The Leftovers*. The world is still shattered; everyone remains traumatized by the Sudden Departure. Yet, maybe the final loss of hope is a boon to those who remain, those who are left over. The value of a thought piece like *The Leftovers* is that it enables us to imagine a world without something that we are otherwise told can't be read out of us. It doesn't mean that we'd all have to go through a similar trauma to find a way out of archism (and, at any rate, I highly doubt anything like the Sudden Departure will ever happen to us, although you never know…), it just means that the end of archism is at the very least *imaginable*.

Through this act of imagination, we see not just the possibility of the end of archism but also some specific features of what that loss would look like. Since, as already noted, *The Leftovers* mainly deals with a transition period away from archism, what it demonstrates doesn't seem all that appealing; the cults, the despair, the chaos are all things that serve to reinforce the way any move away from archism is always portrayed, the way that the chaos of archism itself is always projected outward onto any possible alternative mode of being. But what we do not focus on as much is how much *doesn't* change. Things look very much the same only with what Benjamin would call a "slight adjustment."[23] Insofar as human communities are always to some extent engaged in horizontal and anarchist forms of authority-making even in the context of archist domination, that activity does not change, that community does not get lost.

What *does* start to change is the archist form itself. The markings of archism, the state, the police, the laws are what are clearly suffering the most. They are supposed to bring chaos to others (in the name of imposing "order"), not to suffer from it themselves.

In *The Leftovers*, we do not quite see the full collapse of what is usually called law, but we get a sense that it is not long for this world. With it exposed as it is for the violent and predatory fist of archism, people might begin to be able to ask questions about what law serves besides itself. Why, they might ask, do we need this thing called the Law (with a capital L) when communities can themselves be the basis of another law, another form of authority?

Law under archist conditions is always referring itself to externalities (whether nature, God or the stance of a "rational actor"), but in fact it is always practiced at the ground level. This is why Benjamin says that the police are always a manifestation of law that is far more violent and arbitrary than law imagines itself to be.[24] As I've already suggested, part of that violence might be that those who "lay down the law" can do so in the comfort of knowing that no matter how much they kill and brutalize in the name of the law, the law itself remains safely ensconced in its noumenal form. It can't be threatened even by the most egregious violations of actual legal violence even though "the law" as such only actually exists via those practices.

But if that safeguard is removed, then law becomes something else entirely. Law becomes only its practice and, as such, the responsibility for creating the law rests on each practitioner, both as individuals and as members of a community. Benjamin articulates this stance very well in his "Critique of Violence" when he writes that even the commandment "Thou Shalt Not Kill" cannot be taken as an absolute (and hence transcendent) command. Instead:

---

[23] Walter Benjamin, "Franz Kafka: On the Tenth Anniversary of His Death," in *Walter Benjamin: Selected Writings Vol. 2, 1927–1934* (Cambridge, MA: Harvard University Press, 1999), p.811.

[24] "Critique of Violence," p.243.

neither divine judgment nor the grounds for this judgment can be known in advance. Those who base a condemnation of all violent killing of one person by another on the commandment are therefore mistaken. It exists not as a criterion of judgment, but as a guideline for the actions of persons or communities who have to wrestle with it in solitude and, in exceptional cases, to take on themselves the responsibility of ignoring it.[25]

This passage tells us what law *always* is, even when it is practiced under archist conditions. Law is never actually about some absolute outside as much as it insists that it is. As long as it is deemed to be so, it continues to invite the privileged to interject their own agenda into the place of the archeon. Denied this perspective, we realize that at the end of the day, law is always just a set of local and particular decisions. It is part of the fabric of human life that it normally rules over and determines.

When you can't think "I'm killing in the name of God" or "I'm killing in the name of the law," but rather "I have decided to kill; the acts I commit are on me and me alone (or in conjunction with some other group or community)," the basis for legal violence radically changes. The violence of a law that is always anxious about its status (and hence must kill to show both its power and even its existence) becomes displaced by the decisions about law from a community that knows that law is never anything but its own judgment and decision.

In *The Leftovers* this shift is produced by removing the archist point of view and necessarily transferring that lens to the readers or viewers themselves. We no longer get to read or view with the state or God or nature looking over our shoulder. Reading or viewing becomes unmoored and becomes a very different kind of activity. Such a shift gets us to ask a great many questions about authority, truth, and related issues, but it doesn't give us many answers. That is, in my view, perhaps the single best thing about *The Leftovers*. Because it peels back the curtain of the noumenal realm to show us its radical emptiness, it doesn't so much answer our questions as show that there are never going to be answers at all. It leaves its audience to ponder and figure out for themselves what will happen next, what the meaning of the Sudden Departure finally is, and what it will do to the world and its political and social orderings. Just like the characters in the show, the viewer/reader is left a bit bereft, maybe even disappointed, without some of the certainties that we have always assumed were going to be a given. The show's gift to us is to present us with that uncertainty. We are stuck only with our own limited and all-too-human point of view. What we do with this perspective, as always (but now we know this a bit better), is entirely up to us.

---

[25] Ibid, p.250.

PART II

CUTTER ISLANDS

Noises and Silences – Colonial Entanglements – Seismic Real – Cracks –
Tunes from Nowhere – Utopian Affects – Cartojuridical – *Lex Terrae*

6. Legacies
Anne Bottomley

> Thinking thought usually amounts to withdrawing into a dimensionless place in which the idea of thought alone persists. But thought in reality spaces itself out into the world. It informs the imaginary of peoples, their varied poetics, which it then transforms, meaning, in them its risk becomes realized.
> (Glissant, 1997, p.27)

NARRATING ENGLISHNESS

In 1968, Lord Denning, Master of the Rolls, heard on appeal a case involving the family settlements of a Mr Stanley Weston, the trustees having applied to the court for approval of a scheme varying the trusts.[1] His judgment was robust, a stratagem developed over his long judicial career when, as in this case, he was designing a shift away from the authority of established precedent. His technique for legitimating change involved combining a performance of assertiveness (of law) alongside a good story (of fact) framed in the style of oral narration: as the story unfolds, it leads to the inevitable, common-sense and equitably right decision, the conclusion emerging as if a natural outcome need not be hampered by impediment of law.

The back-story to the application would be good material for a contemporary novelist writing in the style of Jane Austen. A successful businessman, concerned with protecting his wealth for the economic benefit of his family, settled a series of family trusts designed to minimize tax liabilities. Unfortunately for him, a change in law meant that the trusts ceased to be efficient vehicles for their intended purpose. The best economic strategy was to move the trusts off-shore: the family moved to an off-shore island and began applications for settled status. The settlor and the trustees were all in agreement: the amounts of money which would be lost if the trusts stayed in England were huge. However, variation requires the consent of all the beneficiaries, which included grandchildren who were not of age and therefore lacked capacity. The family were forced to apply to court for approval of their scheme. The court, in deciding whether to approve, are tasked by the legislation to focus on the 'interests' of the under-age beneficiaries. All previous cases had interpreted 'interests' to be limited to economic interests, and so the family would, without doubt, have expected approval.

Lord Denning, however, decided that 'interests' should be interpreted to include social factors. His judgment hinged on presenting the family, and in particular the settlor, as more concerned with preserving wealth than ensuring the children's welfare. His narrative begins with a revelation:

> In 1894 a young Russian, Abrum Wosskow, came to England [...] He married here and had a son, Sol [who] [i]n 1942 [...] changed his name by deed poll to Stanley Weston [...] he started as a small trader on his own. After a few years he prospered exceedingly. He built up a wholesale business and a large chain of retail shops.

---

[1] *Re Weston's Settlement Trusts* [1969] 1 Ch. 223.

The judgment is framed by being explicit about the foreign origins of Mr Weston. After reviewing the law and the settlements, Lord Denning makes his next move:

> The court should not consider merely the financial benefit to the infants or unborn children, but also their educational and social benefit. There are many things in life more worthwhile than money. One of these things is to be brought up in this our England, which is still 'the envy of less happier lands'.

In a narrative replete with inter-textual references and pastoral imagery (Klinck, 1994), he reminds the family of the benefits of England and of be(com)ing English. He ends by asking, with a rhetorical flourish, if the children:

> [a]re ... to be wanderers over the face of the earth, moving from this country to that, according to where they can best avoid tax? I cannot believe that to be right. Children are like trees: they grow stronger with firm roots.

The allusion is clear: Lord Denning recognises/presumes that they are of Jewish heritage and proceeds to chastise them for being too fixated on wealth and too willing to move on; not only from the benefits of England, but also from the responsibilities of be(com)ing English. In a narrative which draws on (and continues) a long history of anti-Semitic tropes, Lord Denning images a picture of Englishness which draws from Shakespearean myth-making, biblical referencing and pastoral imagery to invoke both pride in being English and the need to maintain 'true' Englishness. Behind and throughout this judgment a silent question, a haunting echo, reverberates: Could you ever be(come) English? The question hovers over the family in the courtroom. Chillingly, it is also posed for those outside court: Could such people ever be(come) English?

The power of Lord Denning's judgments was vested in his capacity to tell a story: to speak rather than read, and in a style which invites listening; to develop plot and employ shared references; and to suggest, as a subtext, that he and 'we' hold common values.

How is a (particular) nation, a collective 'people', a national identity, narrated? Sugarman and Warrington trace the extent to which the building of an idea of 'Englishness' is 'fostered by the narratives of law' (1995, p.126). Examining the development of the equity of redemption, they reveal the extent to which the space created in-between (English) common law and equity allowed an active jurisprudence to articulate both the central national significance of wealth held as property in land, as well as to negotiate the troubled relations between the respectability of land wealth and the destabilising challenges of commerce and monied wealth. Land wealth focused on intergenerational settlement of estates, monied wealth on markets and the circulation of liquid assets. The English paradox was that as much as land wealth required the financial support of money-wealth, money-wealth desired to 'become' (at least 'as-if') 'landed'. Land, the soul of the English establishment, focused on 'the estate': visibly, a country house with land, but so much more than simply (a) 'place'.[2] The estate was a node networked into the fabric of social and political ordering: 'as house with park', it came to represent, ironically, what it was to be English, to embody the virtues of Englishness.[3]

---

[2] 'The estate' includes non-corporeal, intangible assets carried within it as-if 'land' and is formed in temporal dimensions as much as spatial mapping.

[3] The extent to which the landed estate captured the English imaginary is evidenced, paradoxically, by the contemporary presumption of shared national pride in the legacy preserved by the National Trust

Sugarman and Warrington argue that law's role is much more than simply providing technical resources, it also narrates and negotiates national identity. They conclude that 'the boundaries between law, economics, politics and culture are so blurred that they are best perceived as participating in the same social sphere' (1995, p.126).

In law, in literature, what it means to be English has been narrated and negotiated.[4] At times of national anxiety, external threat or abrupt social change, there is frequently an intensification, or amplification, of the national story and the significance of identity.[5] *Re Weston* was decided in 1968, during a period of racial tension following Commonwealth migration after 1945.[6]

In 1968, Enoch Powell MP, delivered his infamously racist, anti-immigration speech:

> As I look ahead, I am filled with foreboding. Like the Roman, I seem to see 'the River Tiber foaming with much blood'. That tragic and intractable phenomenon which we watch with horror on the other side of the Atlantic but which there is interwoven with the history and existence of the States itself, is coming upon us here by our own volition and our own neglect. Indeed, it has all but come.[7]

Powell's 'intractable phenomenon' was one of numbers: playing on a fear of becoming-minority, he amplified this with a suggested threat of violence carried in/by what might become majority. Linking his scenario to one associated with 'the history and existence of the States' implied a legacy of enslavement limited to the States, not least because, over there, they could not geographically avoid or distance themselves from 'it'. Over here, the legacy could be denied and/ or held at bay. The denied heritage of the practices of enslavement is evidenced in Powell's recounting, with rhetorical flourish, the concern of 'a working man': 'that in this country in 15 or 20 years' time the black man will have the whip hand over the white man.'

In the 1960s, the Labour government was negotiating a pathway between legislation addressing discrimination on grounds of race, and legislation placing restrictions on immigration.[8] The politics behind this strategy is evidenced in Roy Hattersley's speech made during debates leading to legislation in 1965: 'I believe that integration without limitation is impossible; equally, I believe that limitation without integration is indefensible'.[9]

(a nation sharing what was once limited to/by the privileges of class). When the NT accepted responsibility for investigating the sources of wealth which made the eighteenth-century boom in estate building and ownership possible (Fowler, 2020), significant sections of the establishment and public objected to being confronted with a problematic history (Fowler, 2020a). See further below.

[4] Which is not to suggest that it is limited to this, but this chapter is (see further Bhabha, 1990).

[5] Sugarman and Warrington (1995) describe the narration of English history as one characterised by English resilience and survival through a series of 'apocalyptic' threats to stability and security, invariably launched from, or sourced back to, external actors. This version of national histography has, yet again, been evidenced in 2020.

[6] The Immigration Act 1945 opened immigration from Commonwealth countries. Subsidised travel from the West Indies made Caribbean migration to England feasible: ships (including the Empire Windrush) taking de-mobbed Commonwealth servicemen back to the islands offered cheap passage to England. A need for labour is usually cited as the rationale behind the act, but it also served the purpose of keeping metro-isle central to a new Commonwealth order emerging from the 'end' of Empire.

[7] Powell is referencing the Sybil's prophecy of 'wars, terrible wars, and the Tiber foaming with much blood' from Virgil's Aeneid, 6, 86–7. See https://en.wikipedia.org/wiki/Rivers_of_Blood_speech.

[8] A brief history of the 1965 Race Relations Act is found at: https://thehistoryofparliament.wordpress.com/2017/03/21/parliament-and-the-1965-race-relations-act/.

[9] Quoted in Ibid.

The Labour Party concern to somehow address and mollify the racist attitudes to which Powell so directly gave voice reflected a recognition that they were all too prevalent in many traditionally Labour communities. A native-English[10] anxiety with what was perceived to be a crisis in what it meant to be English (a presumed mono-cultural environment), alongside an unwillingness to share (have taken away) access to good employment and decent housing, consolidated into an anti-immigrant/immigration politics.[11] Building an alternative politics focused on the prejudices of racism and the discrimination and inter-racial violence suffered by immigrant communities was slow, tortuous, often painful, sometimes courageous, and frequently marred by compromise.[12]

Recalling events which took place more than 50 years ago is not undertaken as a historical exercise, but as a reminder of their significance for understanding our present. What is important is to be attentive to the processes of selection and curation in what and how events are remembered or forgotten. To adopt a distinction developed by the cultural historian Aby Warburg: it is to distinguish between the production of an event as object (situated in a temporal/spatial specificity), and tracing its after-life (*nachleben*) as an on-going process (a temporal/spatial mobility) (Gombrich, 1968; Johnson, 2012).

'Our'[13] history continues to shape 'our' present and threatens to continue to distort and limit a more equitable potential for 'our' futures. The political events of 2020, on both sides of the Atlantic – particularly those associated with 'Black Lives Matter' – make this very clear.[14] As Stuart Hall pointed out in a speech delivered in 2008:

> They are here because you were there, there is an umbilical connection. There is no understanding Englishness without understanding its imperial and colonial dimensions.[15]

---

[10] Not wishing to use the word 'white' in a bracket with English, and, given the use of the word 'native' by the English in relation to colonised peoples, it seems appropriate to deploy it in a reversed move.

[11] There is also evidence of a continued racist sexualisation of black bodies, of both genders, and a particular fear of, anxiety about, sexual relations between black (migrant) men and white (native) women. Typically, in the 1967 film treatment of E.M. Braithwaite's 1958 autobiographical novel, *To Sir, with Love*, dir. James Clavell, the 'mixed race' love affair of the novel was recast as a platonic, work-based friendship.

[12] In part, the 1964 Labour Party Manifesto commitment to race relations legislation was in response to the political circumstances of the 1963 Bristol Bus Boycott. Supported by the union, the local authority-owned bus company operated an employment 'colour bar'. Activists from local West Indian communities organised a bus travel boycott: after four months, the company (and union) gave in. However, legislation did not cover discrimination in employment until 1968. Powell's speech was made in the context of debates leading to that, more extensive, legislation.

[13] There is a conscious slippage within this chapter in the use of 'our/we': the reader is asked to be active in recognising distinctive positions and the movement between them.

[14] In 1982 Denning, in his book *What Next in the Law?*, suggested that members of black communities might be unsuitable to serve on juries. After an outcry, the first edition was withdrawn and reissued without the offending remarks. He was persuaded to retire (Freeman, 1993).

[15] Key-note speech on archives and memory, Rivington Place, London, 2008. See http://kalamu.com/neogriot/2014/09/17/history-black-chronicles-ii/ .

ENTANGLED HAUNTINGS

On metro-isle, our cultural memory has, until very recently, been very successful in forgetting (or ignoring) the weight and extent (the material presence) of the legacy of our practices of colonial enslavement. Establishment patterns of memorialisation have encouraged us to treat 'slavery' as held apart from our 'own' national heritage, as if an unfortunate occurrence which existed in distant places (overseas) in far past times (before Britain led the campaign for abolition). Too often it is still as if, rather than being directly implicated in enslavement through colonisation, 'we' were just unfortunately linked into it.

In British universities, the increasing concern amongst progressive academics to 'de-colonise the curriculum' often has to begin with a move which might seem counter-intuitive: to re-call and re-member colonisation in a metropole which has been so eager to forget, and so good at it. In this sense, what might be understood as a post-colonial concern to reform the curriculum becomes, initially at least, a post/colonial[16] need to recover.

Stuart Hall describes a 'post-colonial amnesia' which 'enveloped Britain after the (1939–45) war', endorsing 'the strange imperatives by which the full force of the history of colonialism keeps slipping out of the collective memory of the metropole' (2017, p.12). 'Keeps slipping out': a pattern of episodic acts of forgetting, an accretion producing a layered amnesia in which each act of forgetting further consolidates and legitimates an authoritative 'collective memory' increasingly selective, limited and warped.

As Hall suggests, the narration of a post/colonial politics both made possible and also required a collective amnesia: post-war Britain could no longer economically afford to maintain the trappings of Empire, and, even if a residual establishment group might have wished to remain imperial, public sentiment both in the metropole and 'overseas' (the term often employed to collectively reference the many dominions, colonies and protectorates which constituted Empire) was undergoing a sea-change. Imperialism was a past which, depending on one's perspective, either had to be abandoned or rejected as a post-war world struggled into existence. Under the rubric of 'Commonwealth', the metropole and overseas territories negotiated a new political infrastructure – and, for many of those involved, forgetting a past of privilege and prejudice was understood as part of becoming focused on a different future. It was so 'convenient' to forget: it avoided having to confront the imperial legacy; and, in metro-isle, it neatly allowed an emergent non-establishment political order (the Labour Party) to distance itself from a history that many in the new leadership regarded as a distasteful and embarrassing heritage. The contrast in tone (in framing spectacle, curating exhibits and narrating story) between the 1924/5 British Empire Exhibition and the 1951 Festival of Britain evidences this very clearly (Banham and Hiller, 1976).[17]

---

[16] Following Bongie (1998) a slash rather than a dash is deployed, in emphasis of our continued entangled histories. Separately, law/literature is used as a sign which implies a moving across or mixing: an 'as-well-as'. This is in preference to the usual 'and' which brackets, but continues to hold apart: leading to such descriptions of the field as either law 'in' literature, or law 'as' literature (Ward, 1995), a formulation which blurs discourse with discipline.

[17] The contrast is also visible in *re Dominion Students Hall Trust* [1947] Ch 183, an application to the court in support of a scheme to vary a charitable foundation for students from the Dominions. Established in 1930, beneficiaries were limited to those of 'European origin'. The removal of the colour bar was agreed, as it conflicted with the objects of the college it funded (Goodenough) to promote a 'community of citizenship' among Commonwealth members (Harding, 2011).

The post-war use of symbolic memorialisation to refresh a national narrative was framed in three parts: the celebrations of victory, the coronation of the new Queen and the Festival of Britain. Films had already laid the groundwork for continuing the trope of a narrative arc linking significant historical events in a record of 'England overcoming', against the odds, the threat of external adversity. Drawing on two especially significant periods, the overcoming of the threat of Spanish invasion in the sixteenth century and the overcoming of the French in the eighteenth century, films such as Alexander Korda's *Fire over England* (1937), an Armada saga, and *That Hamilton Woman* (1941), a naval romance, narrated a recurring cycle of England standing alone against the world. Post-war narration of renewed national pride built on this: circulating images which drew on the first Elizabethan period, marked by the victorious feats of Raleigh and Drake, and focusing on the naval figure of Lord Nelson, sacrificed in victory.[18] These historical motifs were often supplemented with the allegorical figure of Britannia and the quasi-historical figure of Boudica: reaching back into the mists of history, from measured time into time immemorial, to draw on a mythic epic of 'always' and 'forever' (rather like common law).

This legacy of a necessary and useful forgetting has inhibited a fuller engagement with our past: denying our entangled colonial legacy and supressing an acknowledgment of a heritage of extensive participation in the practices of enslavement.

What we have left to work with are traces, outlines, faint echoes, indistinct, fleeting shapes and movements: hauntings which can be re-animated, re-called to re-member. And then we (can) turn to see what has often, already, been visible, hidden in clear sight; not recognised, not heard.

The image of a 'layered' amnesia usefully reminds us that amnesia is not simply a result, but a process which is continually remade: a past shrouded in layers of fabrication, woven in the service of present imaginaries in an attempt to prefigure (guard against) a future. Finding a way through the density of this layering is, in Spivak's words, a matter of locating and 'measuring silences' (1988, p.286), which can only be achieved through tracing 'a necessarily circuitous route' (1988, p.271).

The particular silence this chapter seeks to measure arises from (the forgetting of) the intimate entanglement(s) between the English metropole and the archipelago of islands which lie off the American continental mass in the Western Atlantic – islands which the European powers colonised and, in the pursuit of profit, ecologically destroyed with over-intensive farming made possible through the extensive use of enslaved labour. In contemporary travel

---

[18] The view from the Caribbean islands of these two historical periods was/is very different: the first laid the foundations of colonisation and enslavement, and the second consolidated them (even when beginning the move towards restrictions on the trade). These differences in accounts of historical record are neatly presented in Peter Tosh's 'You can't fool the youth' (first performed 1973, released in 1977 on his *Equal Rights* album):
You teach the youths about the pirate Hawkins
And you said he was a very great man
You teach the youths about the pirate Morgan
And you said he was a very great man
You can't fool the youths ...
All these great men were doin'
Robbin', a rapin', kidnappin' and killin'
So called great men were doin'...

brochures, they feature as if a virtually untouched, exotically tropical paradise (often marketed with a 'colonial' aesthetic – rum punch served on the quiet veranda of a plantation greathouse). They exist in spaces which are distant enough, spatially and temporally, for the majority inhabitants of metro-isle to avoid being confronted with their/our part in histories of colonisation and enslavement, except when presented as a regrettable but long distant past. Distant enough, also, to avoid making the (obvious) connections between the 'over there' and 'here'.

One way to begin to trace (and endeavour to understand) the processes of entanglement between metro-isle and island-archipelago is to work backwards into an engagement with the two historical conjunctures which the post-war period celebrated as foundationally English (not as beginnings, but as thresholds), and to move across law/literature (as cultural products and processes) in order to diagram the formation and transmission of the legacy of colonial enslavement.

Working within the shared domain of law/literature, Sugarman and Warrington were employed in the first section of this paper to focus on the narrational capacity and function of law. Narration is not merely about employing the arc of a story, it also privileges the 'telling' of the story in an oral/aural tradition. It is about speaking: even when written, narration employs an authorial voice which we, as readers, listen to. Narration is a poetic device – it seeks affect. Associated with narration is the deployment of image: to carry or illustrate, and thereby amplify, narrative. Listening, looking, thinking.

Recall Warburg's distinction between 'an image' (the process of its making) and its 'after-life' (how it is later received and re-perceived). Warburg's last project, his *Bilderatlas Mnemosyne*, extended his interest in how the after-life of an image is shaped as it is transmitted through time and across media. Warburg conceived the project as a visual mapping of key images and themes traceable back from contemporary use, via Renaissance referencing, into being sourced in classical origins. His interest was in the longevity and continued relevance of ancient themes, forms and figures. In building his atlas, he sought to discern the underlying patterns, the narratives, which were expressed through, and linked together, the received images. Across a series of thematic boards, he continually curated the images, moving them and reordering them (including changing the spacing between them) into constellations and series as he sought to reveal and make sense of underlying logics. For the two years preceding his death, he engaged in the process of mapping image-memory. When he died, the project 'unfortunately remained unfinished'.[19]

The after-life of the image-map might however reveal a fortunate aspect to this lack of completion: the process of curating images in order to image/think about the potential of patterns becomes an on-going process of being-open-to, an awareness of an 'and-also', rather than continually seeking the exclusiveness of closure. Warburg's practice could be thought of as anticipating Deleuze's process of diagramming as an image of thought: a potential in the curation of image-clustering.

Warburg's memory-atlas provides an image for bringing together material for one act of mapping Spivak's 'necessarily circuitous route' (1988, p.271), and offers a pattern for practices of active listening and creative visualisation to work through the layered amnesia which has cloaked metro-isle. Silence is only an interruption.

---

[19] Taken from the introduction to the online image-atlas available through The Warburg Library: https://warburg.sas.ac.uk/library-collections/warburg-institute-archive/online-bilderatlas-mnemosyne.

Following Warburg's inspiration, the next section of the chapter is imaged as one panel, in three parts, to which other images/narratives/themes can be added. The distinctive differences between Warburg's purpose and technique and my design, is, of course, that I do not limit myself to image as understood by him, and that I work backwards, through and always in an after-life, not seeking an origin but watching, listening for and to an affect.

MEMORY PANEL: LISTENING TO DIDO

1.   Plantations in the Park

The use of cultural artefacts in the post-war period to boost morale and to remind the British of core national values focused curation on the recovery and revaluation of images and narratives which spoke of the long duration of English stability and prosperity.[20] The rural landscape, land, was reinscribed as the site of national identity (Bottomley, 1996). Images which had not previously been particularly valued were now given iconic status: Gainsborough's 'Mr and Mrs Andrews', which had been left in a family attic for generations before being lent to a local East Anglian exhibition, was spotted by a London critic and declared to embody all the values of continuity and stewardship of land that made England great. Catapulted from family relic to national value, it was toured in 'Festival of Britain' exhibitions and was then purchased by the Tate Gallery (Bottomley, 2016; Hamilton, 2017).[21]

Figure 6.1   *'Mr and Mrs Andrews' by Thomas Gainsborough*

---

[20]   In the 1951 Festival, modernity was presented as emerging from the past, rather than as a break with it (Banham and Hiller, 1976).

[21]   Ironically, given the context, the Andrews family did not settle the land as inheritance for the oldest son but treated it as an investment, later selling it and distributing the monies between the children (Bottomley, 2016).

The after-life of the Andrews portrait encapsulates a nostalgic reverence for patrician landed wealth, which was one trope deployed to resettle England after the trauma of warfare. With it came a resurgence of interest in the classical aesthetics of the Georgian era, and the associated sentiments of pastoral gentility: anything to escape and shake off the impact of the industrial-urban modern. Jane Austen, who for a long time had been dismissed as over-sentimental and too femininely domestic to be 'good' literature, was reappraised and became part of a new canon deployed as literature carrying the virtues associated with English national identity.

Central to all of Austen's work is the question of wealth – not only how it is made, consolidated, distributed and threatened, but also the effects of wealth (or lack of it) on individuals and families. Unsurprisingly, Austen privileges landed wealth (and is well versed in the legal framings which enabled estates to be consolidated in settlements carried through generations), and she is also aware of the complexity of negotiating (often necessary and potentially beneficial) accommodations between land wealth and money wealth. For Austen, it is always a question of the value of wealth as effect: does it corrupt virtue or enhance it? Her stories examine the dilemma of wealth in a series of scenarios, allowing her to narrate, give shape to, an account of (English) virtue, as it overcomes challenges and negotiates change.

Mansfield Park was published in 1814. It begins, as good stories often do, with framing the narrative in/by time: 'About thirty years ago…' (Austen, 1814, 1996, p.5).

Starting with a time-frame is significant: it specifically takes the reader back to the 1790s, and it signals that the novel takes form on the edge of remembered time, a near-past witnessed within living memory and now shared through direct transmission in(to) time-now. The sentence frames narrator and recipient together, positioned in a doubled temporality of shared time: the space–time within which the narrative will unfold, and the space–time which positions narration and reception. Close enough to be understood as implicated in a present-time, 'we' reach backwards with a certain familiarity; at the same time, it is sufficiently distant to open a space of unknowing, lacking an immediacy of knowledge, or a recognition of significance, or perhaps having forgotten, or nearly forgotten what, in the arc of this novel, will be re-called and re-evaluated.

'About thirty years ago' is, in this sense, a timely working through of events before they move on, slip beyond, into the past-times of history. It is 'now' as much as 'then', a diagramming of the significance of the temporal in-between.

Orientated in time, Austen then maps the spatial co-ordinates of wealth:

> Sir Thomas Bertram, of Mansfield Park, in the county of Northampton […] with all the comforts and consequences of an (*sic*) handsome house and large income (p.5).

An astute reader familiar with Austen will note the nuances and silences in this introduction: there is no mention of Sir Thomas' family; no reference to an established landed presence; no evidence of inherited wealth (and associated title and rank) in property, and therefore an absence of the hallmarks of a settled, landed gentleman. He is a 'baronet': someone who carries the right to be addressed with the prefix 'Sir', but remains a commoner. Although the title may be inherited, it is little more than a signal of status beyond being merely 'esquire', and was more often acquired through achieving wealth and using the connections of interest to 'purchase' advancement, rather than in recognition of accomplishments or service. In this context, it signals a 'self-made man' who aspires to join the respectable establishment.

It soon becomes evident that Mansfield Park is not an inheritance but purchased with money made from commerce,[22] and probably involved the enclosure of land in order to create an estate featuring a mansion set in a secluded park: 'a real park, five miles round, a spacious modern-built house so well placed and well screened as to deserve to be in any collection of engravings of gentlemen's seats in the kingdom' (p.41).

The source of Sir Thomas' wealth is revealed very quickly, but in an elliptical move, as if entering from the side: the information is introduced as a reference made in a letter. His wife's sister writes to Sir Thomas seeking a position or prospects for her son, William:

> [...] a boy of ten years old, a fine spirited fellow who longed to be out in the world; but what could she do? Was there any chance of his being hereafter useful to Sir Thomas in the concerns of his West Indian property? No situation would be beneath him – or what did Sr Thomas think of Woolwich? or how could a boy be sent out to the East? (p.6)

In her survey, she summarises the key components of emergent imperial power ('out in the world') in the late eighteenth century: the colonies of the West Indies, the navy (Woolwich) and the East India Company (the East). And her request reveals Sir Thomas's own source of wealth: his 'West Indian property'.

Edward Said's critique of Austen and the novel (1993) began a now extensive tradition of (re)reading her from a post/colonial perspective (Fowler, 2017). However, whereas Said was emphatic in his critique of her as an Englishwoman ignoring the circumstances and consequences of empire, more nuanced readings are now employed to tease out narratives and themes which haunt the text without being immediately visible (Fowler, 2017). Austen narrates in a style which is oral – you need to hear a voice in order to pick up tone and, for instance, irony. To add complexity, the voice of the narrator is mobile: sometimes it rests in/with a particular character; other times it is omniscient – this requires being sensitive to movement in oral/aural spatiality. Added to this, there are temporal shifts and lapses in memory, patterns of amnesia, which require being attentive to how, as a recipient, one is being positioned in time. All this requires an active engagement with the text which listens to the narrative and, at the same time, watches (images) the use of the voice.

Recent post/colonial interpretations of the novel have tended towards recovering Austen as an active supporter of abolition (Fowler, 2017). While there is evidence for this, both within the text and from other sources, what is certainly evident is her concern with the consequences of plantation wealth, and in this regard what is significant in the construction of the text is the way in which she moves, elliptically, to reveal these concerns: placing them within reach, so that they can be picked up and pursed by an active reader.

Austen tells us that Sir Thomas' wealth is not secure:

> His [...] circumstances were rendered less fair than heretofar, by some recent losses in his West India Estate (p.22).

---

[22] A contrast is made between the Bertram residence and that of a near neighbour, the Rushfords, who own Sotherton Court, the 'ancient manorial residence of the family, with all its rights of Court-Leet and Court-Baron' (p.69). The reference to the (originally medieval) law courts grounds the Rushford family through their property in land: both temporally (of long duration) and spatially (carrying manorial rights and privileges, and being part of the juridical governance of the county).

Not securely invested in English rental income, but rather in riskier, if potentially more profitable, overseas estates, Sir Thomas is economically vulnerable. By the end of the third chapter, he has 'found it expedient to go to Antigua himself for the better arrangement of his affairs' (p.28). His absence in Antigua for the middle section of the novel leaves his family pursuing activities and plans without the presence of paternal authority: revealing weaknesses of character in some, and testing strength of character in others. Sir Thomas as absentee father is the counterpart to his position in Antigua: out of sight and sound in the novel, he visits the sugar estate(s) of which he is the non-resident proprietor.

In the previous century, Antigua had become one of the major sugar-producing islands in the archipelago: flat terrain and coastal winds proved well suited to the cultivation and production of sugar, and colonist-planters benefited from the earlier experiments with production on Barbados (Parker, 2011). So economically successful was the sugar economy that, by the second half of the eighteenth century, the fertility of Antiguan soil was becoming severely depleted, and crops were less economically profitable than those produced on other islands (Parker, 2011). It is no surprise that Sir Thomas experienced problems, especially as an absentee owner reliant on resident managers and overseers (notoriously problematic). In addition to problems with production, the English–American war disrupted the island economy, especially in the limits placed on trade with the American states (policed by a strong naval presence stationed at English Harbour, from which *inter alia* Nelson led patrols). The expectations of wealth and profit on which the plantocracy depended were shaken. None of this is made visible in the novel, but it adds veracity to Sir Thomas' situation and brings into account a concern which resonates throughout the text: how safe is money gained from activities other than holding wealth in (English) land?

'Safe' might be understood as simply referencing the risk that investors open themselves to when pursuing profit out of greed, rather than measuring risk with more carefully calibrated calculations. Austen expresses a concern, even anxiety, with the pursuit of (excessive) wealth. What are people willing to do to achieve it, and how might it taint the morals and sentiments of those who become involved – not only as entrepreneurs, but also as family members who benefit? 'Safe' is not only a question of economic viability and security, but also one of ethical–social mores: a concern particularly well illustrated when investment is made in colonial plantations.

Plantation wealth is associated with profit and the unlimited exploitation of land, rather than a more 'home'-based model of careful, sustainable improvement. Without a resident proprietor actively involved in (the management of) management, things can go badly wrong. In Mansfield Sir Thomas is involved in the running of the estate, whereas Antigua is too distant for regular, careful oversight. When he returns to Mansfield, he

> had to reinstate himself in all the wonted concerns of his Mansfield life, to see his steward and his bailiff – to examine and compute – and in the intervals of business walk into his stables and his gardens, and nearest plantations (p.159).

'Nearest plantations' obviously refers to distance within the park, but it can be extended to provide a contrast with his plantations overseas, a site out of sight in Antigua.

An anxiety with the consequences of pursuing profit from greed blends with a concern with the impact extensive wealth gained from distant colonial enterprise may have on the morals (the propriety) of metro-isle. Might ill-gained wealth not only corrupt those who benefit from such wealth, but also lead to a more general infection of society? Might a society driven by greed and conspicuous consumption be willing to excessively exploit others, or collude in their exploitation without concern for their condition? Might a 'dead silence' be the way in which metropolitan society responds to the sufferings of those who labour overseas on Sir Thomas' plantations? Because, of course, plantation labour is predicated on the transportation and exploitation of enslaved persons: his property is not merely in land, it is also in people.

There is only one reference to enslavement in the novel, in a conversation between Fanny, a poor relation who has been fostered into the Mansfield family, and Sir Thomas' younger son, Edmund, who is to become a clergyman.[23] Talking of Sir Thomas, Fanny asks Edmund:

> 'Did you hear me ask him about the slave trade last night?'
> 'I did and was in hopes that the question would be followed up by others. I think it would have pleased your uncle to be inquired of further.'
> 'And I longed to do it – but there was such a dead silence… my cousins were sitting by without speaking, or seeming to be interested in the subject…' (pp.165–6)

What might Sir Thomas have had to say about the 'slave trade'? Were the cousins simply 'uninterested', or did the 'dead silence' suggest something more? Were they unwilling to consider the origin of their own comforts? Did they want to distance themselves from any interest in (or concern with) the West Indies, preferring to be identified with their place and position in English society?

Austen very cleverly opens a space which soon becomes crowded, made loud, with a cacophony of questions and questioning. Again, the way in which the space is opened is elliptical: as a report, in the past and in another place, it is not a conversation which can be interrogated further. Instead, it operates as a series of echoes which ripple outwards, demanding of the reader that they too come to recognise the consequences of sharing silence.

Published in 1814, the novel recalls a time before the legislative abolition of the 'slave trade' in 1807 from the perspective of a period when enslavement in the colonies was still legal, although increasingly contested 'at home' (Hall, 2002; Hall, 2014; Parker, 2011). In this temporal space, the issue of slavery can no longer be a 'dead silence'; it has become vocal. The novel asks how in the near-past the reality of enslavement could be covered in silence, while also questioning the extent to which it can remain a silence: a past forgotten and a present repressed. The suggestion is that there can never be an absolute silence or amnesia:

---

[23] The novel ends with them marrying and moving into the Mansfield vicarage, his father holding the 'living' as part of the intangible Mansfield estate. Their Christian goodness and virtue redeem what remains of Sir Thomas' family after a sequence of social misfortunes. This is, essentially, a conservative, evangelically Christian, moral tale. The narrative does not resolve the issue of the Antiguan estates: their future is left open. It is as if it is now for the reader to intervene and insist that the implications now be confronted. Legal enslavement in the British colonies was ended under the Slavery Abolition Act 1833. Austin is writing in a time-frame when generations of Bertrams, including Edmund and Fanny, would become owners of enslaved persons through inheritance. Although many enslaved people, on the death of an estate owner, 'passed' with the estates on which they laboured to a male heir, as chattels in law they could be devolved to other relatives, including women. Bequeathing an enslaved person, or a portion of one, was often used as means through which to provide for other family members – to be used as rental income from labour or sold as capital. The details of compensation claims for loss of assets held 'in' enslaved persons after the legislation leave an archive evidencing the extent to which inheritance practices distributed 'ownership' through family networks: see the University College, London, 'Legacies of Slavery' database (and analysis) at https://www.ucl.ac.uk/lbs/project/details.

faint shapes emerge, and echoes resound which can never be totally excluded or repressed, however much work is put into trying to keep the silence dead. Mansfield can never, in the end, be a secluded park, absent from the world. The text underlines the impossibility of ignoring what is (just) out of sight and sound, because it is also right here and now, embedded in the foundation of Mansfield. The way in which the key conversation emerges in the text signifies this: recorded through a process of recall and confirmation, it is already at one remove. As readers, we are positioned within a chain of witnessing which extends, spatially and temporally, out of such a small and brief enquiry, neither answered or pursued at the time, but now becoming an on-going conversation: not just about what happened, but about the significance of remembering.

Temporally and spatially mobile, and richly inter-textual, the text opens out to reach beyond the immediacy of the enclosed world of Mansfield Park, to reveal the entanglements between (tropical) island and (rural) metropole in order to raise questions about the potential consequences of the relations between the two.

The enclosed park is a central motif. On the surface, it is no more than a design which makes the house, in situation and prospect, pleasantly genteel. But this design is not only about the construction of a picturesque rustic setting, it is also about a removal: from (and of) the outside world of all that is distasteful and threatens the peace of enclosed gentility. Enclosing a park uses land to hold commerce at bay: out of sight, sound and smell. It also excludes the impoverished: having enclosed common land and fields, and removed as unsightly (not picturesque enough, and socially unpleasant reminders of poverty) the cottages and hovels (and sometimes whole villages) of the landless poor. But such an enclosure can never be absolute: the trajectory of the novel reveals the entangled inter-connectedness between the house in the park and the world beyond the gates (the more distant plantations). The enclosed park becomes an ironic symbol, recognising the many entanglements which have made the park possible and continue to sustain it: interconnections between families, wealth and land, 'society' and 'interest', production and consumption. Mansfield Park emerges out of the mists of the English countryside and takes its place as a node in an emerging global network: as much a part of the metropole as the city of London.

Austen's contrast between the new, commercial wealth of Mansfield and the old, landed wealth of nearby Sotherton[24] reveals another layer to the embedding of colonial enterprise in(to) English homeland. Sotherton is described 'as amply furnished in the manner of some fifty years back, with shining floors, solid mahogany, rich damask, marble, gilding and carving, each handsome in its way' (p.71), the chapel with 'a profusion of mahogany' which had replaced the plainer wainscoting when it was 'fitted up […] in James the Second's time' (p.72).

James ruled from 1685 until he was deposed in 1688, and mahogany was not imported into England (in any quantity) until the turn of the eighteenth century. It seems unlikely that mahogany would have been used so extravagantly in the chapel, but an interesting combination of references suggests that Austen's use of 'mahogany' might be symbolic rather than intended to be accurate.[25] James was deeply involved in the slave trade: while Duke of York

---

[24] See n 22 above.

[25] Symbolic referencing is made more obvious after viewing the filmed version of the novel released in 2000, dir. Patricia Rozema. Rozema emphasises the theme of slavery, and contrives to bring it closer (in)to Mansfield Park: from the sound of singing coming from a ship transporting enslaved

he was a founder of the Royal African Company which, under Royal Charter, transported captured persons over the Atlantic to sell as enslaved. The 'triangular traffic', between England/Africa/Caribbean islands, required that the ships be loaded with 'commodities' for each of the stages of voyaging, and the importation of mahogany into England proved to provide both good ballast and good profit. Mahogany became a fashionable wood for furniture and panelling, replacing the use of the native species of, for instance, oak or elm. In the Sotherton chapel it would have replaced oak: the replacement of honest, plain oak by imported, glossy mahogany in a religious setting, during the reign of a royal trader in slaves, is a strong symbol and reminder of the establishment of a trade in people around a century before the setting of the novel.

There may be a suggestion that even a family as respectably established as the Rushfords have benefited from, or been implicated in, the trade. We are told that Sotherton was furnished 'fifty years ago', as if money was then available for such expense and the family ready to spend it on such conspicuous consumption. 'Fifty years before' would be just after the rise and collapse of stock in the South Sea Company, commonly referred to as the 'South Sea Bubble', incorporated to benefit from transporting and trading enslaved people into Spanish territories on the South American continent.[26] Many in the English establishment benefited from early lucrative investment; other, later investors suffered severe losses (including many trust beneficiaries whose funds had been unwisely invested by trustees who were often family members). Greed for profit overcame discretion. If the Rushfords did benefit from early investment and were wise enough to have divested their shares in good time, then a subtle message is left for the Bertrams: your current investment in Antigua may seem sound, but read the warnings.

Lady Bertram, frequently described by Austen as indolent, embodies the characteristics of unthinking, superfluous consumption. On hearing that William, who has entered the navy, is to join his ship for duties overseas, she expresses the capacity of the metropole to consume:

> William must not forget my shawl, if he goes to the East Indies; and I shall give him a commission for anything else that is worth having. I wish he may go to the East Indies, that I might have my shawl. I think I will have two shawls, Fanny.

William is highly unlikely to travel to India, given the focus of the navy on the West Indies/Atlantic. Possibly Lady Bertram is muddling West/East Indies in a vague geography of 'over-seas': what is evident is that it is not really important where the commodities she craves actually come from; she is only interested what can be brought 'home' in terms of wealth or goods for consumption. Perhaps it is more comfortable not to know anything very much about the source of the wealth or commodities: the exploitation of labour which produces it, and the expropriation of territory which has made production possible. But what is the cost of this lazy or purposeful ignorance?

---

persons moored in an English bay, through to the use of an almost ruined house as the set for the house, symbolism is used to destabilise and undermine the secure idyll of metro-isle. Sir Thomas, played by Harold Pinter, relishes the silences, and, inter alia, casually mentions that he might, next time, bring back a domestic slave with him (seething with sinister sexuality, one is left in no doubt about his sexual misuse of enslaved women).

[26] An interesting economic analysis of The South Sea Company's activities by Helen Paul is found at: www.southampton.ac.uk/assets/imported/transforms/content-block/UsefulDownloads_Download/326F907A8F434B.

2. A Plate of Fruit

Doody (2015) points out the numerous naming references in *Mansfield Park* which identify the novel as concerned with the issue of slavery – not least the naming of park and novel: Mansfield.

Lord Mansfield, Chief Justice from 1756 and primarily remembered by lawyers for his role in establishing commercial law (Posner, 2015), sat on a number of cases involving issues of enslavement. One of these, the 1772 case of *Somerset v Stewart*,[27] became significant as establishing the precedent that no person could be enslaved in Britain, and that therefore an enslaved person brought into Britain was freed as soon as s/he set foot on land. In fact, Mansfield himself did not think that he had made such a broad judgment – having done everything he could to try and avoid having to make a decision in the case, he had intended his judgment to be construed narrowly – but campaigners for abolition were astute in circulating a broad (and credible) interpretation which, as the after-life of the decision, became the received, embedded understanding of Mansfield's text (Posner, 2015).[28]

The Somerset case, both in the circumstances which gave rise to it and in the concern with which it was followed over the extensive period in which Mansfield 'sat' on it, evidences the extent to which enslaved people *were* being brought onto metro-isle. The careful archival work of historians such as David Olusoga (2016) has begun to uncover the limited historical record we have of this presence, and the 'Legacies of Slavery' project (Hall et al, 2014) has been instrumental in opening up pathways to newly recovered data. Recently, National Trust research into links between properties in their custodianship, and colonialism and 'historic slavery', has sourced new caches of archival evidence (Huxtable, 2020).[29] Slowly, fragments are being brought together to present a fuller picture of the presence of enslavement, or the presence of people as a consequence of enslavement, in the metropole.

One source of material has been found through paying close attention to, actively reading, pictorial images (Bottomley, 2020). European portraiture of the seventeenth and eighteenth centuries sometimes includes black figures – almost invariably deployed as 'props' to enhance a central white figure. Charlotte of Mecklenburg-Strelitz married George III in 1761: just before traveling to England her portrait was painted by Ziesenis (a Danish–German artist). She is under 17: against the background of her family's palace, clothed with rich fabrics and ermine, her hair dressed with pearls and, around her wrist, a bracelet displaying a portrait of her betrothed; she takes a pink rose from a basket held by a young man, also richly dressed, with a turban and plume, in his ear a pearl and, clearly visible, around his neck a silver slave collar.

---

[27] *Somerset v Stewart* (1772) 98 ER 499.
[28] The first edition of Blackstone (1765) followed the formula that slavery could not exist in England; however by the second edition (1766) he had modified his statement of law with ambiguous phraseology. It is quite possible that this revision was made under the influence of Mansfield (Posner, 2015, p.201 and p.289).
[29] See n 3 above. The report describes country houses as 'dynamic sites in which global politics are played out in a local setting' (p.8).

98 *Research handbook on law and literature*

Figure 6.2   Portrait of Charlotte of Mecklenburg-Strelitz by Johann Georg Ziesenis

The slave collar is the visible marker of (lack of) status[30] – black figures portrayed in roles of service but without a collar leave a little space for possible ambiguity, and there are a number

---

[30]   In Charlecote Park, Warwickshire, a 1680 portrait of Thomas Lucy by Kneller depicts Lucy with an unidentified young black groom or page wearing a metal collar. A guest of Lucy's wife recalled her morning chocolate being served by a black child, and local records document the presence of black people. In 1690, a young 'black girl', Margaret Lucy, was baptised; as was Will (or William) Archus, 'a black man', in 1700; and in 1735, Philip Lucy, a six-year-old 'black boy' (Huxtable, 2020). This record, particularly of children bearing the family name, suggests the presence of enslaved persons, or the children of once enslaved persons, at Charlecote over a lengthy period.

of such representations which cannot be definitively described (without more evidence) as portraits of enslaved people. But the overwhelming sense one is left with is that, even with the benefit of ambiguity, portraits of black 'servants' are actually of enslaved people, and therefore further evidence of the practice of enslavement in metro-isle.[31]

Around 1778, Lord Mansfield commissioned a double portrait of two young relatives from David Martin,[32] a protégé of the royal portrait artist, Allen Ramsay.[33] By then Mansfield's career was so well established that he had been elevated from being a baron (a status given in 1756) into the peerage, in 1776. He was successful, wealthy and had married well. He had managed to distance himself from problematic Scottish roots (a taint of Jacobite sympathies marred his family), and overcome the disadvantages of being a younger son. He had purchased a country house with a park (Kenwood, in Hampstead). His marriage did not, however, produce children: he identified a nephew he could appoint, and promote, as heir to his estates and title. The Mansfield household was extended by offering a home to unmarried female relatives and fostering children from the extended family. His domestic and familial arrangements could well have been the setting and plot line for another Austen novel.

In 1766, Elizabeth, the young daughter of his designated heir, was received into the household. Her mother had died and her father, a diplomat, was so frequently abroad that living with the Mansfield household was a good solution. She was six years old and would live at Kenwood until her marriage in 1785. In the same year, a baptismal record for five-year-old Dido Elizabeth Bell, daughter of Maria, wife of Bell, is recorded in a Bloomsbury church used by the Mansfields when resident in town. We know from family records that Dido was in fact the illegitimate daughter of John Lindsay, another nephew, a naval officer serving around that time in the Caribbean. Her mother was an enslaved woman, possibly taken by Lindsay as part of seized 'booty' from a Spanish vessel or possibly 'released' from Spanish transportation into enslavement. Unsurprisingly, of her mother Maria we know little: although much more is known than is usually acknowledged (a point returned to below). The favoured narrative of Dido's beginnings is that her mother died and her father brought her back to England, asking his wealthy English relatives to care for her; or, possibly, offered her to them as a playmate/companion/(servant?) for their newly acquired foster-child, Elizabeth.

---

[31] Of course, one has to be careful with such sweeping statements: it is more than possible that either persons once enslaved, or born free, took on roles as paid servants. The assertion is made here because I think that too often there is a tendency by contemporary commentators to use ambiguity to avoid confronting the issue of (the responsibility for) practices of metropolitan enslavement. However, I am also aware that ambiguity was often purposely deployed by contemporaries to blur status and familial relationships: see below.

[32] Both the date and the artist have been the subject of controversy. The final attribution was the result of a 2008 BBC documentary which used investigatory techniques developed in art history, as well as finding new archival evidence. See www.bbc.co.uk/programmes/p06j7zc5.

[33] Ramsay was favoured by George III and his wife, Charlotte (see above). Controversially, and somewhat improbably, one of his portraits has been used as evidence for a claim to Charlotte being of mixed heritage (see eg Stuart Jefferies, 'Was this Britain's first black queen?', at www.theguardian.com/world/2009/mar/12/race-monarchy). Ramsay, in repeating blog entries, is described as 'a well-known abolitionist' – as if this would account for the subversive text he is said to have inscribed in portraying the queen. I have not been able to find an authoritative source for this assertion. Ramsay, who painted both Mansfield and his wife, eloped with his second wife, the sister of John Lindsay, father of one of the girls in the Martin portrait. Despite a long and happy marriage, Ramsay and his wife were never accepted by her family.

100 *Research handbook on law and literature*

A certain ambiguity in household position is not unusual in extended families of this kind: recall Fanny's position as a poor relation in Mansfield Park. But here there is also a certain ambiguity in civil status: was Dido, as the daughter of an enslaved woman, herself born into slavery? That this status could certainly be alleged clearly at times worried Mansfield, who in later life did not 'free' Dido – to do that would be to accept her status of origin – but who did include in his will, drafted in 1783, a clause recognising (asserting) that she was 'free'; and, on the evidence we have, that is certainly the way she was treated in the household (Posner, 2015).

Did the Mansfields take the pragmatic decision to pursue a policy of ambiguous discretion? From the evidence, they became very fond of Dido and she remained in the household until, after the death of Lord Mansfield, his wife having predeceased him, she left and married soon after in 1793.

Figure 6.3   *Portrait of Dido Elizabeth Belle and Lady Elizabeth Murray*

Elizabeth, a legitimate daughter with very good prospects, and Dido, not merely a 'poor relation' but an illegitimate child born to an enslaved African woman, are portrayed together in Martin's portrait. We know, from recently recovered archival evidence, that Mansfield commissioned and paid for the painting.[34] We do not know what discussions took place between him and Martin about the subject matter. They are young women of about 17/18. Slightly in the foreground, the blonde Elizabeth, corseted stiffly in pink, rosebuds in her hair and a book in her hand, reaches out to the exotic, mobile figure of Dido, dressed in fluid clothing, a turban on her head and a platter carrying an abundance of exotic fruits on her arm. With one hand she points to her face as she turns towards the viewer; the other seems lost in the folds of her dress, emphasising the contours of her figure. Elizabeth, full face on, has a direct, uncomplicated gaze with just a hint of affection around her mouth and eyes. Dido, in contrast, is full of mischief and amusement: a seductive invitation set against, as a foil to, the calm authority of Elizabeth.

The portrait is not mentioned in Mansfield's will, nor is it identifiable in the inventory taken at his death. In a catalogue of Kenwood pictures compiled in 1909, it is described as a portrait of Elizabeth, with 'a Negro attendant' (Byrne, 2014, p.10). As with other pictures which included black figures, it was assumed that Dido was a slave/servant of no name or unimportant name. However, given the naming of Dido as a beneficiary in Mansfield's will, and the evidence that her presence at Kenwood was the consequence of family connections,[35] there must be a suggestion that there had been a purposeful forgetting of Dido, a useful amnesia, at some point in the Mansfield history and that no one wanted to look too closely at a picture which, even on the surface, would disturb presumptions about the rightful place (and pose) of an 'attendant'.

Dido's re-emplacement in the picture was made possible by careful local research undertaken in Camden in the 1980s (Adams, 1984), leading to the picture being used as part of an English Heritage exhibition on slavery mounted at Kenwood. The recovery proved timely – the picture became celebrated as evidence not only of black presence in Georgian England, but as a portrait of 'equality' between two young women within an aristocratic household (Byrne, 2014). Using Dido as evidence of the presence of people of colour who were *not* enslaved added to the establishment of a narrative of the forgotten, denied black presence within the received historical narrative of native-Englishness.[36] The problem was/is that this positive spin on her recovery became a vehicle for a narrative which fails to confront either the actual ambiguity of her position, or the responsibility of her father and his family as they negotiated a (marginal) place on metro-isle for her.

Amma Asante's 2013 film *Belle* embedded a celebration of the portrait as representing nothing more or less than equality and affection between two young women living in the household of their shared relative, who happened to be the judge who had ended slavery in England. The story is, of course, too good to be true. It makes a strong storyline for a film, but it has had the unfortunate effect of feeding back into popular discourse as if true: serving as a convenient spin for enhancing the role of the key native-English players, as well as building a more positive image of the majority inhabitants of metro-isle. This, a straight lift from the film, is the descriptive history used on the Mansfield website at Scone Castle (where the portrait is now hung as a major visitor attraction):

---

[34] See n 32.

[35] She is mentioned in Lord Mansfield's obituary published in 'The London Chronicle' as a 'Mulatto, who has been brought up in (his) family almost from her infancy' (Byrne, 2014, p.10).

[36] On recovering a history of the presence of people of colour on metro-isle before post-45 migration, see Olusoga (2016).

> Dido Elizabeth Belle was a girl born into slavery of mixed race, whose mother was a black African woman, Maria Belle and whose father was Rear Admiral Sir John Lindsay, nephew of the 1st Earl of Mansfield.
>
> When Dido's mother died, making her an orphan at the age of six, her father came to claim her before returning to his family home at Kenwood House in Hampstead. There he beseeched his uncle, the Earl of Mansfield, to take the child into his care and to raise her alongside her cousin, Elizabeth, in a manner befitting her aristocratic blood line.[37]

Her mother had not died: in 1774 Maria was in Pensacola, America, where she is recorded as having been granted land by Lindsay (on what became the corner of Lindsay and Mansfield Streets), on which she built a house. Referred to as 'a Negroe Woman of Pensacola in America but now of London afore and made free', she confirmed her free status by paying for a manumission transaction 'the sum of two hundred Spanish milled dollars' (Clune and Stringfield, 2009).[38] There is no record of any communication between her and her daughter after Dido was taken (in)to the Mansfield household. This is not surprising: when white fathers took steps to provide for illegitimate, mixed-heritage children, it sometimes included removing them from their mothers (and the islands) to send them to metro-isle to be brought up as adjuncts to their white relatives (Livesay, 2018). Livesay records a wide range of 'adjunct' statuses and practices: a few metro-families did receive mixed heritage children into the family network,[39] but many held them at a distance, finding their presence something of a burden and embarrassment. A great deal depended on the family politics of wealth distribution and inheritance: how financially secure and socially established was the metro-family and, if the father married, did his mixed heritage children threaten the economic–social standing of his legitimate children? A constant factor is the severance of mixed heritage children from their maternal and island heritage: a need to distance them from any record of enslavement, and from the perceived immorality of the islands.

Lindsay's delivery of Dido to Kenwood follows a well-established pattern. Having left her with relatives, there is no record of him having any other communication or contact with her. The filmic portrayal of him as a rescuing hero (echoed in the version of history sponsored at Scone) is somewhat tarnished by the recent recovery of archival material in Jamaica.[40] We now know that Dido was the first of five 'island' children fathered by Lindsay, all with different mothers and all soon after Dido's birth. The other 'island' children were baptised with Lindsay recorded as their father and carrying his surname: two died young, the remaining two were sent to Scotland to be fostered with relatives. When Lindsay returned to Scotland, he married but did not father legitimate children. In his will, he left sums of money to his two 'reputed'

---

[37] https://scone-palace.co.uk/dido-elizabeth-belle-her-story-1761-1804.
[38] Recorded by English Heritage, if not by Scone Castle: www.english-heritage.org.uk/learn/histories/women-in-history/dido-belle/.
[39] A small number of children were sent to England with large fortunes, especially in circumstances where there was no legitimate family and a chance for them to become assimilated into English society. However, this process of translation into (something akin to) Englishness became increasingly contested (Livesay, 2018). Anxieties over the corruptive power of plantation wealth carried into England through mixed heritage children seems to have been one theme influencing Austen's novel *Sanditon*, unfinished at her death, A later fear of plantation wealth being used to trick and corrupt racial purity is expressed with force in Charlotte Bronte's *Jane Eyre* (1847).
[40] Joanne Major, *Dido Elizabeth Belle – New Information about Her Siblings* (2018) 'All Things Georgian' blog entry: https://allthingsgeorgian.tumblr.com/tagged/Dido-Elizabeth-Belle.

children, the island children living in Scotland, asking his widow to distribute the money to them: clearly, she knew of their existence.[41] Dido, in England, was not mentioned. One stark difference seems to mark Dido apart from her 'recognised' half-siblings: their mothers are recorded in the baptismal records as free and/or 'mulatto'.

It is not just that a positive portrayal of family relations smooths out a much more complex picture of familial entanglements – it is also that focusing on the positive story detracts from the disturbing narratives so overtly present in the doubled portrait.

Between the two portraits used in this paper, there is an obvious (and welcome) distinction in the portrayal of the black figures. But there is also an underlying continuation in the tropes of how they are figured and deployed. Both act as a foil to a white figure, and both are clothed to characterise them as foreign and exotic. In Dido's case, her clothing is also used to convey a sexualised, eroticised woman. In contrast to the well-corseted and virginal Elizabeth, Dido is a seductive, disturbing presence.

Popular reception of the portrait has resulted in a number of experts interpreting aspects of the image: not least the clothes worn by the two women. In a recent blog entry posted by Kenna Libes,[42] a fashion historian, she challenges the dating of the portrait on the basis of the clothes worn by the women. She presumes that the portrait should be read literally, rather than considering that it might be composed symbolically. The women, in my reading, are dressed and posed with symbolic care to convey a strong message centred on the civilizing virtues and benefits of England and Englishness carried out into the world. Dido's exotic plenitude is tempered by Elizabeth's gently restraining hand.

The portrait evidences a theme which will become increasingly strong in the late eighteenth and nineteenth centuries: the historical mission of the civilising presence of England-in-the-world, also known as Empire. Within this trope, an image of the practices and legacy of enslavement is re-cast: as a horror to be suppressed, and as a threat to be feared. The aesthetics and politics of the late eighteenth century responded to the mood of Enlightenment, which set civility in opposition to perceived ideas of 'blackness' and the savage world of slavery (Dresser and Hann, 2013; Fowler, 2020; Gikandi, 2013; Kriz, 2008). As this narrative was carried forward by Evangelical Christians into the campaign for abolition, it began to morph into an emergent skin-colour racism (Hall, 2002; Livesay, 2018).[43]

3. 'Had I Plantation Here'

It is a parody, but as with all good parodies it carries a significant insight, one of Austen's mannered and problematic characters in *Mansfield Park* exclaims:

> Shakespeare one gets acquainted with without knowing how. It is a part of an Englishman's constitution. His thoughts and beauties are so spread abroad that one touches them everywhere, one is intimate with him by instinct. – No man of any brain can open at a good part of one of his plays, without falling into the flow of his meaning immediately. (p.279)

---

[41] Wills, both in naming children and in leaving an inheritance, were used as a significant means through which to 'recognise' 'reputed' children (Beeson, 2010; Livesay, 2018).
[42] 10 August 2020, at https://fashionhistory.fitnyc.edu/1778-martin-dido-elizabeth/.
[43] See n 39 and Bronte's expression in 1843 of a fear of contagion by racial impurity: the perceived need for separateness becomes the legacy of post-enslavement. Hall (2002) traces this as it is carried in Evangelical Christian sermons and practices, recalling an early Evangelical presence of Mansfield Park.

The eighteenth century adopted and constructed Shakespeare as the national poet, the foundational narrator of England and Englishness (Dobson, 1992). Denning (above) evidences an inherited tradition of referencing him as a lodestone of pride in English heritage, which, it is presumed, would be recognised and shared by other Englishmen and so operate as a marker of national character (rather like allusions to cricket).

Chantal Zabus describes Shakespeare's *The Tempest* of 1611[44] as an 'interpolative dream-text', a text taken from the Anglo-literary canonical tradition in not merely inspiring a plenitude of interpretative readings, but also becoming an inspiration, source material, for new writings: 'Such texts serve as pre-texts to others; they underwrite them' (Zabus, 1994, p.81).

The Tempest has proven a rich source for post/colonial re-interpretation, acting as a kind of foundational narrative for the beginnings of modern colonisation and enslavement (Bottomley, 2020; Hulme and Sherman, 2000; Zabus, 2002). Since Cesaire's *La Tempete*, written in 1969 for performance at an arts festival in Tunisia, there has been a productive sequence of literary texts exploring the dynamics of Prospero's relations to (property in) land and people.

Complex intertextuality, dense use of metaphors and light use of language, create a text sufficiently open and mobile to invite engagements which can remain within the framing of the text without being restricted by it. It is not a question of orthodox interpretation, of trying to pin down meaning, but rather of opening out into translations and transmissions which can be placed in conversation with each other because of a pre-text shared in common.

The play has been deployed to exemplify processes of colonisation and enslavement, and to create counter-imaginaries through which practices of resistance can (come to) be narrated (Bottomley, 2020; Hulme and Sherman, 2000; Warner, 1992; Zabus, 1994, 2002). It can be usefully read within the contested arguments concerning legitimation of land seizure and governance in colonial settings (Sokol and Sokol, 1996; more broadly Greene, 2010, and Part VII of Brewer and Staves, 1995). My purpose here is more limited: there is a moment in the text when we stand at a threshold (although we know that we have, already, stepped over it).

In Act 2, Scene 1, Gonzalo, described in the cast list as an 'honest old councillor', says that had he 'plantation of this isle' (152) he would maintain it as (a) 'commonwealth' (157) and:

'would with such perfection govern [...]
T'excel the golden age' (177–8).

Contrasted with Prospero's usurpation and patrician governance of the island, this 'golden age' vision of an alternative way is passed over, in text and plot, very quickly. But it serves to leave a trace: that things could have been different. There was, at some point, figuratively if not literally, a moment of choice: not merely in terms of whether to colonise, but of how to colonise (Bottomley, 2020). Constructing a threshold, even when we have already passed beyond it, opens a space for thinking choice and responsibility: a trope taken up and explored in Marina Warner's 1992 novel *Indigo*, which turns and extends *The Tempest*. Warner is particularly aware of the nuanced complexities of choice and responsibility in early colonisation and its legacies, not only because of her scholarship but also because of her own family

---

[44] Interestingly, Austen and her contemporaries would not have been familiar with Shakespeare's play – from 1667 Dryden's version ('The Enchanted Isle') was performed (with many rewrites and modifications); Shakespeare's 'Tempest' was restaged in 1838 (Hulme and Sherman, 2000).

history.[45] How to remember? What to re-call? How to reimagine? How to turn text? What to make possible?

In the same act as Gonzalo's dream of a golden age, there is an opaque exchange about a Queen, herself a coloniser, whose after-life has been a contested story of choice, loss and responsibility:

> 'Tunis was never graced before by such a paragon…'
> 'Not since widow Dido's time' (75–7).

And later:

> 'Widow Dido, said you? You made me study of
> that, she was of Carthage not Tunis.'
> 'This Tunis sir, was Carthage' (82–4).

Even for Shakespeare, few women appear on stage (a daughter, a handful of goddesses and their retinue): of the small number of off-island women referenced, all but one of the women are either 'of Africa' or taken to Africa to be married. All are recalled by men, glimpsed through a prism held by men. Neither seen nor heard: no more than outlines and echoes that haunt the text. The reference to Dido draws a parallel between antique and contemporary worlds, in a trope which looks to classical sources to provide patterns, precedents and lessons for the modern world. Shakespeare, however, undercuts this: he shows a character with ignorance in mapping historical events onto contemporary geographies. Virgil's *Aeneid*, the narration of Aeneas' travels and travails as he follows his fate to establish Rome,[46] was a popular (English) Renaissance source of/for classical learning, and used as a pattern for contemporary storytelling;[47] but as an account of actual events, a 'history', even contemporaries had their doubts as to its veracity. The reference to Dido as 'widow' is probably alluding to a then current debate as to the extent to which Virgil was unfair in his characterisation of Dido, portraying her as little more than a woman intent on trying to seduce Aeneas away from his destiny. Of course, that is her role in the text: to both be a threat to Aeneas and operate as a foil to his understanding of, and commitment to, his princely role. She might have founded a city, but she also deserted it. Aeneas escaped her clutches – he survived, and she didn't. In this sense, Aeneas overcame the dangerously seductive wiles of women: in particular, women of Africa.

---

[45] Warner describes the legal documentation of the Royal Charter which, in 1625, granted authority over St Kitts, Nevis, Barbados and Montserrat to the first English governor, Sir Thomas Warner: 'Boundaries between legal documents, zoological anthologies and dramatic fantasies were wide meshed' (Warner, 2000, p.108).

[46] Referenced by Enoch Powell in his 'Rivers of Blood' speech; see above.

[47] It had been particularly popular with the Tudors, who extended the narrative by sending Brutus, Aeneas' son, on a journey to northern islands where he became the founder of 'Britain'. The Brutus narrative was deployed by the (Welsh) Tudors to enhance their claim to the English throne. A similar tactic was used by James I to imply, in iconography and private documentation, that the English throne encompassed all Britain, despite the Scottish throne devolving by seperate descent until the 1707 Act of Union.

Purcell's 1689 opera *Dido and Aeneas*[48] contains the well-known aria often referred to as 'Dido's Lament', which, while beginning by addressing Aeneas, opens out to be heard across history, in long time:

> 'When I am laid in earth,
> May my wrongs create
> No trouble in thy breast;
> Remember me, but ah! forget my fate.'

Remember *me*, not 'my fate'. It seems apposite that Dido Belle was given that name. How do we move towards a place, and find a means, with which we can begin to hear, and respond to, what has been silenced? In part, by learning how to employ the magic of 'as if', and the potent logic of 'and as well as'.

NOISE, AIR, BREATH

Throughout this chapter it is noise, especially in silence, which has been significant: speech and sound, the oral/aural, as it moves off the page, and out of the image, reaching out to insist on being heard. To be attentive is to listen – not as a passive recipient, but as an active agent – in order to become part of an ever-extending, opening, pattern of relations based on 'and as well as'.

Where Denning sought to activate the privileged sanctuary of 'this sceptred isle', a safe place removed from the perfidies of the outside world where the English could carry on being English, we can now turn Shakespeare around and say, in the voice of Caliban: 'Be not afeared, this isle is full of noises' (3.2.142). The silences which must be measured, and the muffled noises which will be heard: the creolisation of an England/English which has already happened. That threshold has been passed and the task that is left is to re-examine our histories, our inheritances, in order to reimagine our futures. In law, in literature.

In *Mansfield Park*, Austin regularly references the wholesomeness of 'English air'. This is likely to be an allusion to William Cowper's 1785 abolitionist poem, *The Task*:[49]

> We have no slaves at home – then why abroad?
> And they themselves, once ferried o'er the wave
> That parts us, are emancipate and loosed.
> Slaves cannot breathe in England; if their lungs
> Receive our air, that moment they are free,
> They touch our country and their shackles fall.

The poem celebrates Mansfield's 1772 decision *Somerset v Stewart*,[50] and is a classic example of a positive reading of the decision, cast as a recovery of previously established law. The evocative image used by Cowper ('if their lungs receive our air, that moment they are free') references the strong symbolism associated with the judgment, which is actually sourced

---

[48] Libretto by Nathan Tate.
[49] Cowper is known to have been one of Austen's favourite poets (Fowler, 2017).
[50] See above.

to Somerset's counsel rather than Mansfield's decision. The problem which counsel faced in arguing for Somerset's freedom from enslavement was not a precedent, but a powerful opinion. In 1729, a group of men with 'West Indian' interests commissioned the two senior government law officers to write an opinion, in their private capacities, on whether enslavement was legal in England. In what became known as the Yorke–Talbot opinion, they wrote:

> We are of opinion, that a slave coming from the West-Indies to Great-Britain or Ireland, with or without his master, doth not become free, and that his master's property or right in him is not thereby determined or varied; and that baptism doth not bestow freedom on him, or make any alteration in his temporal condition in these kingdoms. We are also of opinion, that his master may legally compel him to return again to the plantations.

The opinion has been commissioned as a result of a fear that judgments by Lord Justice Holt[51] could be interpreted as deciding that enslaved people who had been Christened could not continue to be enslaved, and, more broadly, that English law did not recognise property in people. Rather than testing this in court, the stratagem of commissioning an opinion, without danger of a contrary decision, was a clever tactic. Clearly and forcibly expressed, it had the desired effect until challenged in the politically charged litigation of 1772.

Somerset's counsel did not want to depend on resurrecting Holt; Yorke–Talbot made that too problematic (despite it being no more than an opinion). Instead, after extensive research, he found *Cartwright*'s case, a purported decision of 1569 which, it was said, declared that the air of England was too pure for slaves to breathe (Alsford, 2001; Posner, 2013). The source used was John Rushworth's *Historical Collections*, a multi-volume compendium of historical commentary and sources written and published from the mid- to late seventeenth century by Rushworth, a lawyer and former member of parliament. The relevant passage uses the symbolism of air:

> In the eleventh of Elizabeth, one Cartwright brought a slave from Russia, and would scourge him, for which he was questioned; and it was resolved, That England was too pure an air for slaves to breath in.

After 1772 the 1569 case was cited frequently, becoming established law, and the symbolic use of air and breath entered the cultural imaginary as a means through which to reference the 1772/1569 recognition of the special status and spatial specificity of English freedom (see more broadly Greene, 2010).

Despite the slim evidence of *Cartwright* for authority, and the efforts made by Mansfield to avoid establishing a precedent which would negate the Yorke–Talbot opinion, the 1772 decision became seen, and used, as a foundational moment in the struggle against enslavement, and one grounded in a recovery of the ancient English traditions and practices of common law. This is a judgment which evidences the power of 'affect'. It was not so much *what* was decided, as *how* it was received. And what operated as a particularly powerful vector was the evocative symbolism of 'pure air' 'to breath in'.[52]

---

[51] *Chamberlain v Harvey* (1697) 1 Ld Raym 146; *Smith v Gould* (1705–07) 2 Salk 666; *Smith v Brown* (1702) 2 Salk 66.

[52] There is an obvious echo here of the German 'Stadtluft macht frei' ('city air makes you free'), referencing a principle established in the feudal period which argued that escaped serfs who lived in a 'free' city for a year and a day became freed (Alsford, 2001).

Of course, the Somerset decision fed the trope of English exceptionalism; but it also opens a judicial door for thinking differently about what it might mean to be English or resident in England. Moving that narrative forward into a potential for more equitable future(s) requires that we face and understand how partial our received narratives have been, and how they have operated to silence the voices, the noise in silence, that we now need to learn to listen to and to allow to breathe.

In law, in literature: How do our current imaginaries constrain us? How do we move beyond them, to recover or reimagine other narratives, other futures? (Gulick, 2016)

> [T]hought [...] spaces itself out into the world. It informs the imaginary of peoples, their varied poetics, which it then transforms, meaning, in them its risk becomes realized. (Glissant, 1997, p.27).

BIBLIOGRAPHY

Adams, G. (1984) 'Dido Elizabeth Belle, A Black Girl at Kenwood', *Camden History Review* 12.
Alsford, S. (2001) 'Urban Safe Havens for the Unfree in Medieval England: A Reconsideration', *Slavery & Abolition* 32(3), 363–75.
Austen, J. (1814, 1996) *Mansfield Park*, London: Penguin Press.
Banham, M. and Hiller, B. (eds) (1976) *A Tonic to the Nation*, London: Thames and Hudson.
Beeson, G.A. (2010) *The Cult of the Will*, Trinidad: Black and White Press.
Bhabha, H. (ed) (1990) *Nation and Narration*, London: Routledge.
Bongie, C. (1998) *Islands and Exiles: The Creole Identities of Post/Colonial Literature*, Stanford: Stanford University Press.
Bottomley, A. (1996) 'Figures in a Landscape: Feminist Perspectives on Land, Law and Landscape' in Bottomley, A. (ed) *Feminist Perspectives on the Foundational Subjects of Law*, London: Routledge Cavendish, 109–24.
Bottomley, A. (2016) '"… and if, in time, equity…": An Exploration of the Time(s) of Equity Diagrammed through Image', *Pólemos* 10(2), 357–87.
Bottomley, A. (2020) 'Between Islands: Colonial Legacies and Cultural Imaginaries', *Pólemos* 14(2), 237–60.
Brewer, J. and Staves, S. (eds) (1995) *Early Modern Conceptions of Property*, London: Routledge.
Byrne, P. (2014) *Belle, The True Story of Dido Belle*, London: William Collins.
Clune Jr., J. and Stringfield, M.S. (2009) *Historic Pensacola*, Pensacola: University of West Florida.
Dobson, M. (1992) *The Making of the National Poet: Shakespeare, Adaptation and Authorship, 1660–1769*, Oxford: Oxford University Press.
Doody, M. (2015) *Jane Austen's Names: Riddles, Persons, Places*, Chicago: University of Chicago Press.
Dresser, M. and Hann, A. (eds) (2013) *Slavery and the British Country House*, Swindon: English Heritage.
Fowler, C. (2017) 'Revisiting Mansfield Park: The Critical and Literary Legacies of Edward W. Said's Essay "Jane Austen and Empire" in Culture and Imperialism (1993)', *The Cambridge Journal of Postcolonial Literary Inquiry* 4(3), 362–81.
Fowler, C. (2020) in Huxtable, S-A. et al (eds) *Interim Report on the Connections between Colonialism and Properties now in the Care of the National Trust, Including Links with Historic Slavery*, London: National Trust.
Fowler, C. (2020a) *Green Unpleasant Land: Creative Responses to Rural England's Colonial Connections*, Leeds: Peepal Tree Press.
Freeman, I. (1993) *Lord Denning: A Life*, London: Random House.
Gikandi, S. (2013) *Slavery and the Culture of Taste*, Princeton: Princeton University Press.
Glissant, E. and Wing, B. (trans.) (1997) *Poetics of Relation*, Ann Arbor: University of Michigan Press.
Gombrich, E.H. (1968) *Aby Warburg, An Intellectual Biography*, Oxford: Phaidon.
Greene, J.P. (ed) (2010) *Exclusionary Empire*, Cambridge: Cambridge University Press.

Gulick. A.W. (2016) *Literature, Law, and Rhetorical Performance in the Anticolonial Atlantic*, Athens: Ohio University Press.
Hall, C. (2002) *Civilising Subjects: Metropole and Colony in The English Imagination, 1830–1867*, Chicago: University of Chicago Press.
Hall, C., et al (2014) *Legacies of British Slave-Ownership: Colonial Slavery and the Formation of Victorian Britain*, Cambridge: Cambridge University Press.
Hall, S., with Schwarz, B. (2017) *Familiar Stranger: A Life Between Two Islands*, London: Allen Lane.
Hamilton, J. (2017) *Gainsborough: A Portrait*, London: Weidenfeld and Nicolson.
Harding, M. (2011) 'Some Arguments against Discriminatory Gifts and Trust', *Oxford Journal of Legal Studies* 31(2), 303–26.
Hulme, P. and Sherman, W.H. (eds) (2000) *'The Tempest' and Its Travels*, Philadelphia: University of Pennsylvania Press.
Huxtable, S.-A. et al (eds) (2020) *Interim Report on the Connections between Colonialism and Properties now in the Care of the National Trust, Including Links with Historic Slavery*, London: National Trust.
Johnson, C.D. (2012) *Memory, Metaphor, and Aby Warburg's Atlas of Images*, Ithaca: Cornell University Press.
Klinck, D.R. (1994) 'This Other Eden: Lord Denning's Pastoral Vision', *Oxford Journal of Legal Studies* 14(1), 25–55.
Kriz, K.D. (2008) *Slavery, Sugar, and the Culture of Refinement: Picturing the British West Indies, 1700–1840*, New Haven: Yale University Press.
Livesay, D. (2018) *Children of Uncertain Fortune: Mixed-Race Jamaicans in Britain and the Atlantic Family, 1733–1833*, Chapel Hill: University of North Carolina Press.
Olusoga, D. (2016) *Black and British: A Forgotten History*, London: Macmillan.
Parker, M. (2011) *The Sugar Barons*, New York: Walker and Co.
Posner, N.S. (2015) *Lord Mansfield: Justice in the Age of Reason*, Toronto: McGill-Queen's University Press.
Said, E.W. (1993) *Culture and Imperialism*, London: Chatto and Windus.
Sokol, B.J. and Sokol, M. (1996) 'The Tempest and Legal Justification of Plantation in Virginia' in Klein, H. and Davidhazi, P. (eds) *Shakespeare and Hungary: Special Theme Section – The Law and Shakespeare (Shakespeare Yearbook)*, New York: Edwin Mellen Press, 353–80.
Spivak, G.C. (1988) 'Can the Subaltern Speak?' in Nelson, C. and Grossberg, L. (eds) *Marxism and the Interpretation of Culture*, Basingstoke: Macmillan, 271–313.
Sugarman, D. and Warrington, R. (1995) 'Land Law, Citizenship and the Invention of "Englishness": The Strange World of the Equity of Redemption' in Brewer, J. and Staves, S. (eds) *Early Modern Conceptions of Property*, London: Routledge, 111–44.
Ward, I. (1995) *Law and Literature: Possibilities and Perspectives*, Cambridge: CUP.
Warner, M. (1992) *Indigo, or Mapping The Waters*, London: Chatto & Windus.
Warner, M. (2000) '"The Foul Witch" and "her freckled whelp": Circean Mutations I the New World' in Hulme, P. and Sherman, W.H. (eds) *'The Tempest' and Its Travels*, Philadelphia: University of Pennsylvania Press.
Zabus, C. (1994) 'What Next Miranda? Marina Warner's Indigo', *Kunapipi* 16(3), 81–92.
Zabus, C. (2002) *Tempests after Shakespeare*, New York: Palgrave.

7. Castration

Maria Aristodemou

> *'First we have to accept castration. We're not used to doing that so we make up all sorts of cock and bull stories about the threats made by our parents who are supposedly to blame.'*[1]

CASTRATION IN FREUD

Freud, with characteristic humility, insisted that the castration complex – probably one of the best-known concepts in his work – was not his invention but one attested and circulated for millennia in myths and nursery stories. While Freud derived support from Greek myths, his own best-known illustration was the case of Little Hans. As Freud relates the case, three-year old Little Hans showed, as all boys his age, a lively interest in his 'widdler'. He would often ask his mum, 'Mummy have you got a widdler too?' 'Of course. Why?' 'I was only just thinking.'

His curiosity about widdlers led him to see widdlers everywhere: once he went into a cowshed and saw a cow being milked. 'Oh, look!', he exclaimed, 'There's milk coming out of its widdler!' Freud assures us Little Hans' interest in widdlers was not just theoretical; as would have been expected, it also impelled him to touch his widdler. When he was three and a half his mother found him with his hands on it and threatened him, 'If you do that, I shall send for Dr A. to cut off your widdler. And then what'll you widdle with?' 'With my bottom', Little Hans retorted.[2] This was the occasion, Freud tells us, on which Hans acquired the famous castration complex, 'the presence of which we are so often obliged to infer in analyzing neurotics'. It's worth noting that it's the mother, not, as is so often assumed, the father, who is the figure threatening castration here.

Though commentators often refer to the case of Little Hans as Freud's first reference to the castration complex, Freud had already used the term the year before in his *Sexual Theories of Children*:

> the child, having been dominated by excitations in the penis, will usually have obtained pleasure by stimulating it with his hands; he will have been detected in this by his parents and terrorized by the threat of having his penis cut off. The effect of this 'threat of castration' is proportionate to the value set upon that organ and is quite extraordinarily deep and persistent.[3]

The castration complex also left marked traces in myths that Freud had been exploring a decade earlier. In *Interpretation of Dreams* he referred to some of these myths, including Zeus' emasculation of his father Kronos, and discussed his analysis of a 14-year-old boy who

---

[1] Lacan, *My Teaching* (London: Verso, 2008), trans. David Macey, p.41.
[2] 'Analysis of a Phobia in a Five-Year Old Boy', *Standard Edition of the Complete Psychological Works of Sigmund Freud*, Vol. 10 (1909) (London: Hogarth Press, 1955), pp.7–8.
[3] *Standard Edition*, Vol. 9 (1908), pp.216–17.

had come to him terrorized by his father: the boy dreamt of playing a board game which featured a dagger belonging to his father, a scythe and a sickle. Freud listened to the boy's dream and hypothesized that 'the sickle was the one with which Zeus castrated his father; the scythe and the picture of the old peasant represented Kronos, the violent old man who devoured his children and on whom Zeus took such unfilial vengeance'.[4]

Freud continued to explore the origins, development and resolution of the castration complex, explaining that children's first reaction to discovering the absence of a penis is disavowal: they convince themselves that the penis is still small and will grow later, before concluding that the penis must have been there and was taken away. This conjecture further confirms the child's fear of castration: 'The lack of a penis is regarded as a result of castration, and so now the child is faced with the task of coming to terms with castration in relation to himself.'[5]

If the fear of castration in Freud related at first to loss of the penis, it soon expanded, particularly in the case of some of Freud's followers like Otto Rank, to fear of loss of other significant objects, such as the womb in childbirth, and the breast in weaning. In 1917 Freud suggests that, for the child, an equivalence also arises between penis and faeces so that when the boy discovers the lack of penis in women, he concludes 'that the penis must be a detachable part of the body, something analogous to faeces, the first piece of bodily substance the child has to part with. Thus, the old anal defiance enters into the composition of the castration complex.'[6]

Later still, in *Inhibitions, Symptoms and Anxiety*, Freud likens moral anxiety to anxiety associated with separation from the super-ego.[7] The concept of separation becomes therefore increasingly detached from the concept of a physical object and more a metaphor for the subject's division, detachment and incompleteness. The castration complex, Freud continues to insist, is *more* than the threat of separation precisely because it is associated to the Oedipus complex. In other words, the castration complex is not biological but cultural or – as it soon morphs into in Lacanian terminology – symbolic. This is an aspect of the castration complex that Lacan develops beyond recognition; in Lacan's elaboration, castration, far from separation from an organ, is about the separation inflicted on the subject by her entry into language. In learning to speak to others and responding to others' speech the subject experiences the forced choice of entering the symbolic order; if she is to be admitted, she has no choice but to succumb to the rules and dictates of language, an entry that Lacan describes as a castration inflicted on the subject's pre-symbolic plenitude.

CASTRATION IN LACAN

The story so far: fearing castration, Freud's reading of the Oedipus myth goes, the subject submits to the first law of any human society, prohibition of the mother as object of desire, that is, the prohibition of incest. In 'The Dissolution of the Oedipus Complex', Freud revisits the conflict between the child's narcissistic interest in his penis and libidinal investment in its

---

[4] 'Interpretation of Dreams', *Standard Edition*, Vol. 4 (1900), p.256; Vol. 5 (1900–1), p.619.
[5] 'Infantile Genital Organization of the Libido', *Standard Edition*, Vol. 19 (1923), p.143–4.
[6] 'On Transformations of Instinct as Exemplified in Anal Erotism', *Standard Edition*, Vol. 17 (1917), p.133.
[7] 'Inhibitions, Symptoms and Anxiety', *Standard Edition*, Vol. 20 (1925–6), p.129.

parental objects; narcissism, Freud concludes, wins, and the child turns away from the mother.[8] Lacan's early verdict on Freud's myth in *Family Complexes* was that the castration complex is a patriarchal 'myth' signifying 'the terror inspired in a male by a male'.[9] His detailed analysis of the Oedipus complex, however, and its significance for the subject's immersion into the law, comes in his reading of *Hamlet*: 'the psychoanalytic tradition sees in Oedipus' crime the quintessential charting of the relationship of the subject to what we call the Other, i.e. to the locus of the inscription of the law.'[10] The most important thing for the subject's baptism into the law is 'punishment, sanction, castration – the hidden key to the humanization of sexuality'.[11] In effect, both law and sexuality come to the human subject from the outside, from the field of the Other; the subject accedes to them in a Faustian pact which in Lacan's elaboration soon also includes a third all-important element, language.

Two decades later, in his seminar on *Formations of the Unconscious*, Lacan revisits and refines his reading of the nature of castration. He cautions against taking the castration complex too literally or too easily: the castration complex, he warns, is one of those things that, like La Rochefoucauld's sun and death, cannot be gazed at directly and can only be looked at obliquely: 'it's precisely the central point in analysis that one looks at obliquely and, increasingly, from a distance.'[12] Looking at it obliquely yet cunningly, Lacan starts by posing the fundamental questions: why do we need myths to understand human sexuality in the first place? It is precisely because human sexuality cannot be reduced to biological givens, he insists, that myths have arisen to evoke and explain it: the 'very necessity of (Oedipus) myth', he asserts, 'shows that understanding human sexuality is insoluble by any reduction to biological givens'.[13] One constant of those myths is that the human subject only assumes the attributes of their sex through fear, 'through threat of their privation'.[14] While, as far as we know, animals seem to follow the attributes of their sex with a minimum of fuss, language and myth are needed to mediate the human animal's assumption of sexual difference. At the time Lacan was delivering this seminar, Claude Levi-Strauss' *Structural Study of Myth* had already elaborated the function of myths at concealing and mediating irresolvable contradictions. What do castration myths conceal, Lacan and we may ask. Lacan doesn't hesitate: myths work to conceal the fact that the Big Other is castrated.

Lacan revisits the case of Little Hans and suggests that Hans' father's failure to separate Hans from the mother and act as the agent of the law gives rise to Hans' fear of horses as a substitute for the father's absent prohibition: Hans' anxiety doesn't arise from separation from the mother but from *failure* to separate. Had Hans' father intervened successfully between mother and child, the threat of castration and separation from the maternal object would have saved the subject from anxiety. So Lacan starts to suggest that castration, and 'the Oedipus

---

[8] *Standard Edition*, Vol. 19 (1923–5), p.176.
[9] Jacques Lacan, *Family Complexes in the Formation of the Individual*, 1938; www.lacaninireland.com.
[10] Jacques Lacan, 'Desire and the Interpretation of Desire in *Hamlet*' in Shoshana Felman (ed.), *Literature and Psychoanalysis; The Question of Reading: Otherwise* (Baltimore: John Hopkins University Press, 1982), p.42.
[11] Ibid, p.43.
[12] Jacques Lacan, *Formations of the Unconscious* (Cambridge: Polity, 2017), trans. Russell Grigg, p.287.
[13] Lacan, *Ecrits: A Selection* (London: Tavistock, 1980), trans. Alan Sheridan, p.282.
[14] 'Signification of the Phallus', *Écrits*, p.281.

complex is not solely a catastrophe since it's the foundation of our relationship to culture'.[15] The Oedipus complex is instrumental in immersing the subject into the order of law, language and culture.

To recap: in Lacan's retelling, while the child seeks to be the object of desire for the mother, the father intervenes to separate the child from the mother, signalling the intervention of a third element, that of the law, to the dyadic relationship between child and mother. The father enters into play as the vehicle of the law and prohibitor of the mother as object; in Hans' case it was the mother, rather than the father, who played the castrating role and laid down the law, leading little Hans to develop another phobia, that of horses, to substitute for the missing interdiction.[16] For the Oedipus complex to dissolve, Lacan – like Freud – concludes, the child must renounce the hope of being the object of desire for the mother and assume their castration.

This being Lacan, of course, the analysis does not stop there; an added element is stressed in this 'reading' of Freud, and that is the insistence that biological factors take second place to the defining effects of language and culture: 'Castration', he insists,

> is not actual castration. It's linked to desire. Even in the man it's not necessary to single out the penis in the notion of the castration complex, i.e. what is at stake is something other than this or that. It's something that has a particular relationship with the organs, but a relationship whose signifying character is not in doubt from the outset. It is its signifying character that is predominant.[17]

The emphasis is clear: unlike privation, which is real, castration is symbolic; it is inflicted by the signifier and it concerns the subject's relationship to the Big Other of language and culture.

If Lacan insists on the symbolic nature of castration, he is doubly insistent on the necessity for the subject to pay the price for it, to pay their symbolic debt. What does the subject get in return for assuming their castration? Nothing less than 'the plethora of objects that characterize the human world',[18] says Lacan. In other words, the subject gets desire in return.[19] If, in its blissful pre-symbolic universe, the subject is at the mercy of unlimited and unregulated jouissance, it is also at the mercy of unlimited disorder. Castration, by contrast, introduces order to psychic structure through the phallic function, in other words, through the register of lack. Castration inscribes the dimension of lack in the subject, thus enabling the subject to enjoy, but not too much: to enjoy within the pleasure principle. As Lacan summarizes, the law of the father tames unruly jouissance and turns it into desire within the law.[20]

Why is this called the phallic function – a term that hasn't done Lacan any favours with his critics? The simple answer is that phallus does not denote the anatomical penis but stands in for an absence: the signifier phallus signifies nothingness itself.[21] Lacan describes it as a 'paper tiger', a 'ghost', an impostor used to cover up lack, and 'the signifier for which there is

---

[15] *Formations of the Unconscious*, p.158.
[16] Ibid, pp.175–9.
[17] *Formations of the Unconscious*, pp.289–90.
[18] Jacques Lacan, *Transference* (Cambridge: Polity Press, 2015) trans. Bruce Fink, p.232.
[19] 'Subversion of the Subject and Dialectic of Desire' in Écrits: *A Selection*, p.324: 'Castration means that jouissance must be refused so that it can be reached on the inverted ladder of the law of desire.'
[20] Jacques Lacan, *The Four Fundamental Concepts of Psychoanalysis* (London: Penguin, 1979), p.34: 'The Father, the Name-of-the Father, sustains the structure of desire with the structure of the law.'
[21] 'The Signification of the Phallus', *Écrits*, p.579: the phallus is not a fantasy, nor is it an object, 'still less is it the organ – penis or clitoris – that it symbolizes ... it is the signifier that is destined to designate meaning effects as a whole, insofar as the signifier conditions them by its presence as a signifier.'

no signified'.[22] It operates, as Jacques-Alain Miller argued in a seminal text, like the number zero in algebra: in Ferge's theory of cardinal numbers the number zero counts as a number even though it is defined as emptiness. The emptiness, nevertheless, is crucial for founding the sequence of numbers.[23] The signifier phallus performs the same function of filling the empty place.

What is the consequence of refusing to accept castration, of refusing to countenance lack and pay the price for it? Refusing to accept lack, presuming to paper over the gap, spells disaster for the subject: if desire is the prize we get for paying the price of castration, refusal to accept castration also spells disaster for the subject's relationship to her desire: the subject doesn't stop desiring, far from it, but the subject bears the burden of guilt for having compromised her desire by not paying the price for it: as Lacan insists, 'If analysis has a meaning, desire roots us in a particular destiny and that destiny demands insistently that the debt be paid, and desire keeps coming back, keeps returning, and situates us once again in a given track, the track of something that is specifically our business'.[24] Our business is to pay our debt, to be 'in the clear' in our account with our own desire.[25] In the case of the neurotic the catastrophe takes the form of the catastrophe of guilt. For the psychotic, as Darian Leader describes in a telling metaphor, refusal to accept lack means that the subject leaves herself no room for movement: as in the old-fashioned game of moving squares round a board to form a shape, if there is no gap between the squares no movement is possible, all pieces are stuck.[26] Rather than refusing castration, the subject must come to terms with it, indeed become one with it, insists Lacan: 'It is at this point of lack that the subject has to recognize himself.'[27] Of course, this is not a point that the subject comes to terms with happily; because accepting castration in the real, instead of settling for what Žižek has been calling decaffeinated varieties, is a terrifying prospect: it *hurts*.

CASTRATION IN THE REAL

Published in 1986, José Saramago's *The Stone Raft* predates, and prophetically depicts, what Joseph Weiler later described as 'a seismic event in the community's geology': the 1992 Single European Act. Except Saramago's tale depicts the seismic event, the political, legal, as well as geological earthquake in the register of what Lacan terms the Real. The novel follows the itinerary of five friends as they negotiate the unthought catastrophe of the European continent suddenly and inexplicably 'cracking up', with the Iberian Peninsula separating from the rest of Europe and drifting nonchalantly off in the Atlantic.

The continent's geological catastrophe has very humble beginnings: one of the characters, Joanna, carrying a branch of elm tree on her walk, absent-mindedly draws a line scratching the ground with her branch. Instead of the branch raising a little dust and making an uncomfortable

---

[22] *Encore*, p.80: Φ 'of all the signifiers, is the signifier for which there is no signified.'
[23] Jacques-Alain Miller, 'Suture: Elements of the Logic of The Signifier', www.lacan.com/symptom8_articles/miller8.html.
[24] Jacques Lacan, *The Ethics of Psychoanalysis, Book VII (1959–1960)* (London: Routledge, 1992), p.319.
[25] Ibid, p.323.
[26] Darian Leader, *What is Madness?* (London: Hamish Hamilton, 2011), p.141.
[27] *Four Fundamental Concepts*, p.270.

crackling noise, the result of her innocent action is that the earth cracks open like 'some kind of insatiable gorge'.[28] The gentle carving of a line in the ground produces a not so gentle chasm in the middle of the Pyrenees, leading the Peninsula to gradually but surely split open from top to bottom and begin to sail out to sea.

Trying to make sense of this explosive event, the narrator looks at so-called scientific explanations: MIT scientists conduct their elaborate tests and come up with the theory that the continent broke up because of 'too much sun'. Like all subjects confronted with the limits of science, the narrator resorts for explanation to myth: this is the region, he reminds the reader, where Hades, the God of the dead lived, and where Cerberus guarded the gates to make sure the dead didn't leave. At that instant the dogs of Cerbère in Pyrenees, France all begin to bark at once. One dog, which 'preferred the infernal regions',[29] appears with a blue thread around its neck, leaps over the abyss and becomes, Ariadne-like, our protagonists' guide out of this labyrinthine catastrophe. It is 'panting', the narrator adds, 'as if it had come from the end of the world and blood stained the ground under its paws'.[30]

In line with the extraordinary event that causes the continent to split in half 'like a watermelon' whose time had come, the human characters have no trouble accepting that their guide here on earth is a dog from the underworld. Before long, with the Peninsula travelling at 50km per hour, the canal between the Peninsula and Europe soon turns into open sea, the Peninsula now a floating island that has wrenched itself from Europe and is sailing away like the doomed Atlantis.[31]

BIG OTHER TO THE RESCUE

How does the Big Other respond to the catastrophe? What does it have to offer to soothe the pain of the castration of Europe? It is soon clear that the answer is: not a lot. Within minutes of Europe cracking open and with the Peninsula sailing adrift in the Atlantic at a speed of 50km per hour, government ministers, politicians, civil and military authorities, geologists, geographers, journalists, mineralogists, photographers, film and TV crews, engineers, inspectors, sightseers all descend on the site trying to understand, report on or simply gape at the chasm unfolding before them. The media, it is soon clear, can only confirm what spectators 'already know and is not worth knowing'.[32] Local politicians on the other hand, after initial amazement at the sight, start squabbling as to whose fault it is. The Spanish resolve to try to find out what happened 'and say nothing to the French', while the French insist 'the crack was de-fi-ni-te-ly Spanish or, to speak in geographical and nationalist terms Navarrese, why don't you lot keep it was what the insolent Frenchman said, if it gives you so much pleasure and you need it so badly'.[33] The discourse of science of which humanity has been so proud since at least the Enlightenment is not much better at throwing light on the situation: 'despite vast amount of accumulated information, no one could explain how and why the Pyrenees had cracked MIT

---

[28] José Saramago, *The Stone Raft* (London: Vintage, 1986), trans. Giovanni Pontiero, p.18.
[29] Ibid, p.11.
[30] Ibid, p.145.
[31] Ibid, p.106.
[32] Ibid, p.179.
[33] Ibid, p.13.

programmers blushed with embarrassment when their terminals received the peremptory decree, Too Much Exposure to the Sun.'[34] As to what can be done about it, the suggestion of the 'experts' is to try to sew the continent back together with clamps as if it is a torn piece of cloth.

It is soon the turn of powerful institutions to address the problem and offer relief. The EU Commission is quick to make a statement: the displacement of Iberian countries, it pronounces, does not affect the binding nature of treaties in force, though some members of the committee are overheard mumbling under their breath, 'if the Iberian peninsula wished to go away then let it go, the mistake was to have allowed it to come in' in the first place.[35] Other than issuing a statement, the Commission's contribution is to order the Spanish and Portuguese governments to halt the sailing of the Peninsula. The only positive outcome of this assistance is to unite the Spanish and Portuguese government against the Big Other who can neither understand nor help them.

This stand of courage and defiance, however, doesn't last long: another catastrophe looms when the Peninsula starts rushing in the direction of the Azores, an event that is used by the Portuguese government as a pretext for resigning because of the seriousness of the situation; a resignation which only confirms 'that governments are only capable and effective at times when there's no real need to put their ability and effectiveness to the test.'[36] Taking its place is a government of national salvation 'because we do not normally have governments who know how to govern nationally', plus 'At the end of the day they are the same old faces'. The new government's solution, earnestly and gravely announced by the Prime Minister on national television, is that 'salvation lies in fleeing.'[37]

BIG OTHER IS CASTRATED

Armed with Saramago's tale, there is now little doubt of the answer to Lacan's question: why are myths necessary, what function do they serve, what truths do they try to conceal? Lacan doesn't mince his words: myths are deployed as a defence against truth; they serve to conceal what the symbolic order would rather keep hidden: 'What is there to conceal?' Lacan, like Saramago, is clear: myths conceal 'that, as soon as the father enters the field of the master's discourse he is, from the origins, castrated'.[38]

As usual, Lacan insists this point is not of his own invention but was already present in Freud. We saw already that the function of the father in Freud is to introduce the child to the law by threatening punishment should the child continue to insist on the mother as object of desire. What is less often remembered, claims Lacan, is that the father who introduces the child to the law is the *dead* father. This insight of Freud's, claims Lacan, has been overlooked: 'to the question, "what is a father" Freud replies "It is the dead Father", but no one hears him.'[39]

---

[34] Ibid, p.104.
[35] Ibid, p.31.
[36] Ibid, p.165.
[37] Ibid, p.175.
[38] *The Other Side of Psychoanalysis* (New York: W.W. Norton & Co, 2007), trans. Russell Grigg, p.101.
[39] 'The Subversion of the Subject and the Dialectics of Desire', *Écrits*, trans. Bruce Fink (New York: W.W. Norton, 2006), p.688.

The father, just like Hegel's 'thing', is dead because it is not the father the person but the father as function that institutes the law; once the function is performed, the father, like the thing killed by the word, becomes the dead father. Not only is this father dead but further, as conduit of the law, he is himself subject to the law: 'The father must be the author of the law, yet he cannot vouch for it any more than anyone else can, because he, too, must submit to the bar which makes him, insofar as he is the real father, a castrated father.'[40] The upshot for this good, castrated, dead father is unsurprisingly, and as Lacan admits, 'a remarkably difficult one; to a certain extent he is an insecure figure'.[41]

Although it's not news that faith in the Big Other has been waning, in the case of the EU this was pronounced long before Brexit. For a large section of the public, as the British referendum in 2016 showed (Irish and Danish referenda were precursors to this negative assessment of the EU), the Big Other of the EU seems to resemble Kafka's inscrutable Court more than a benign divinity. What indeed do we see when we look at EU institutions close up? The first thing that strikes constitutional lawyers is that the EU suffers from major blindspots when it comes to democracy.

From its beginnings, the EU's claim to legitimacy was plagued by its emphasis on executive decision-making rather than legislative politics. Although it promised to usher in a new democratic era that combined direct and representative democracy, the outcome was far from both ideals. The European Court of Justice presided over a vast extension of Community powers, never failing to endorse each and every request for addition to its competences. As Joseph Weiler describes the 'jurisdictional mutation' in his seminal piece 'The Transformation of Europe', 'the principal actor instigating extension was the Court itself, although, of course, at the behest of some plaintiff'.[42] By the second stage of this transformation, not only was no state activity immune from Community encroachment, it also became impossible to find an activity which was *not*, in the Court's view, within the objectives of the Treaty.[43] Despite the erosion of limits to Community competences, the Community's increased powers did not go hand in hand with its structures: states, as Philip Allott describes it, behaved as if the concept of democracy were a minor eccentricity if not folly, and so in their dealings in Brussels behaved like 'feudal barons' in charge of their respective national territories.[44]

With the Court instigating a continuous extension of Community powers, national law was absorbed and subsumed by Community law to the extent that, as Weiler put it, 'There simply is no nucleus of sovereignty that the member states can invoke against the community'.[45] In the long run, as Weiler notes in a later piece, the much lauded appeals to democracy and representation were reduced to 'fast-track' versions of their imaginary ideals: the Commission would make decisions which were then presented to the European Parliament on

---

[40] Lacan, 'Desire and the Interpretation of Desire in *Hamlet*', p.44.
[41] Jacques Lacan, *The Ethics of Psychoanalysis*, p.181; and again in XVII – p.121 – the essence of the master's position is to be castrated and succession proceeds from castration also.
[42] J.H.H. Weiler (1991) 'The Transformation of Europe', *Yale Law Journal*, Vol. 100, 2403–83, p.2403.
[43] Ibid, p.2453.
[44] Philip Allott (1991) 'The European Community is Not The True European Community', *Yale Law Journal*, Vol. 100, pp.2484–2500, 2490; Yanis Varoufakis' account of negotiations during Greece's bailout in 2015 tells a similar story: *Adults in The Room: My Battle With Europe's Deep Establishment* (London: Bodley Head, 2017).
[45] Weiler, 'The Transformation of Europe', p.2435.

a take-it-or-leave-it basis.[46] Crucially, what Weiler accurately described as the 'seismic' event setting up the single European currency in the Treaty of Maastricht was never approved by national referenda: no European government sought their people's approval before handing over monetary sovereignty to the European Central Bank.

Since Weiler's piece, there have been no shortage of constitutional lawyers both within and without the EU pointing out the institutions' continuing democratic deficit.[47] A series of key breakthroughs endowing the community with new powers, from direct effect in national legal systems to supremacy over national laws and the creation of the Council were, as Perry Anderson describes in his recent analysis of Middelaar's *The Passage to Europe*, a series of coups disguised as administrative decisions; conversely, the European Parliament functions less as 'a tribune of the people than as a Chorus, a court musician' to the Council and Commission.[48] 'If citizens' participation is the "lifeblood" of democracy', Abel warns, 'the European Union suffers from anaemia and is in desperate need for a remedy'.[49]

But it is not only that the opportunities for EU citizens to participate in the decision-making process are limited. The deficit is also substantive because at the very point where one would expect the political to come in, we encounter goals that are deemed to be beyond discussion: 'the institutional design of the EU "government" (the European Commission)', Bartl summarizes, 'is premised on the possibility of uncontroversial common goals [...] goals and objectives are considered fixed, and the only possible realm of disagreement concerns the choice of the most efficient level for accomplishing predetermined tasks'.[50] More specifically, the common market and the liberalization of goods and services are taken as Goods in and of themselves and therefore immune to debate. As community goals are set in stone, the only question is how best to implement them, a task for which no citizens are needed, only experts:[51] ministers, that is, to administer the spreading and implementation of the sacred gospel.

REJECTION OF CASTRATION

What are the community's uncontroversial goals, the sacred goods? Before Brexit and Covid dominated our headlines, the EU had several decades to develop and disseminate its message; having started, as Weiler's and many others' accounts confirm, in an attempt to stem nation-

---

[46] J.H.H. Weiler (2002) 'A Constitution for Europe? Some Hard Choices', *Journal of Common Market Studies*, Vol. 40(2), 563–80, p.564.

[47] Ben Crum (2005) 'Tailoring Representative Democracy to the European Union: Does the European Constitution Reduce the Democratic Deficit?', *European Law Journal*, Vol. 11(4), 452–67; R. Dahl, *Democracy and Its Critics* (New York: Yale University Press, 1989); Andreas Follesdal and Simon Hix (2006) 'Why There is a Democratic Deficit in the EU: A Response to Majone and Moravcsik', *Journal of Common Market Studies*, Vol. 44(3), 533–62; Christofer Gandrud and Mark Hallerberg (2015) 'Does Banking Union Worsen the EU's Democratic Deficit? The Need for Greater Supervisory Data Transparency', *Journal of Common Market Studies*, Vol. 53(4), 769–85.

[48] Perry Anderson, 'The European Coup', *London Review of Books*, December 2020.

[49] Gabriele Abels (2009) 'Citizens' Deliberations and the EU Democratic Deficit', http://aei.pitt.edu/11419/1/Abels_TAIF1_2009.pdf.

[50] Marija Bartl (2015) 'The Way We Do Europe: Subsidiarity and the *Substantive* Democratic Deficit', *European Law Journal*, Vol. 21(1), 23–43 at 24ft1, 26.

[51] Gareth Davies (2006) 'Subsidiarity: The Wrong Idea, in the Wrong Place, at the Wrong Time', *Common Market Law Review*, Vol. 43(1), 63–84.

alism and the excesses of statism after the Second World War, from the 1970s onwards its pro-market proclivities became increasingly pronounced. The direction the EU took followed the gospel of capitalism – The God of the Market and Bureaucracy.

What is the categorical imperative of capitalism? To work hard: the injunction to work *hard* is in essence, as Corinne Maier suggests, 'the requirement to have a constant hard-on'.[52] But one can't have a 'hard-on' without a widdler, so the logic of capitalism is to reject castration: 'what differentiates the discourse of capitalism is *Verwerfung*, the fact of rejecting, outside all the fields of the symbolic [...] What does it reject? Well, castration.'[53] Following Lacan and Jean-Claude Milner, Jelica Sumic analyses capitalism's idiosyncratic form of politics, a politics, she explains, that doesn't demand that the subject should sacrifice her enjoyment. Everyone's enjoyment is counted and accumulated. A politics that means the political revolves around not a social bond but the lack of one, as everyone's mode of enjoyment is irreducibly different. Capitalism offers an alternative to the social bond, that is, accumulation of diverse enjoyments, usually in the form of capital or other consumable goods; capitalist discourse therefore transforms the subject's lack of being into lack of having and offers 'having' as a cure for its lack of 'being',[54] in other words, as a cure for her castration.

With a plethora of autistic enjoyments to cater for, the system can only function if supported with fantasies that promote the singularity and inalienability of each subject's mode of enjoyment. Support for the fantasy of capitalism's omnipotence comes in the form of the ideology of liberal individualism, the responsibility of the individual worker whose achievements, success or, just as often, failures and disasters are entirely up to her. Those workers who 'cannot keep a constant hard-on', whose efforts lead not to gains but to cock-ups, or those who are unable or unwilling to enter the competition for unsatisfiable desires, join the ever-increasing ranks of workers suffering from mental illness. The categories of mental illness have also been growing exponentially: stress, anxiety, depression, are just a few of the labels deployed to exclude subjects who do not live up to the standard of continuous 'hard-ons'.

Contemporary political theorists such as Wendy Brown berate and bemoan the fact that capitalism undermines and erodes democracy of so-called equals: 'the construal of *homo oeconomicus* as human capital leaves behind not only *homo politicus*, but humanism itself.'[55] This is not news to European lawyers who for five decades have been witnessing a promotion of the market at the expense of democracy of Hayekian proportions. For Hayek, neo-liberalism not only didn't need democracy, it was more important than democracy; the market, he insisted in a letter to *The Times*, is indispensable to personal freedom while the ballot box is not.[56] If Hayek worried that the beast of democracy might erode the free market, the path taken by the European Union exceeded his wildest dreams; indeed, what Pinochet's dictatorship achieved in Chile was achieved 'legally' in the EU through the European Court.

---

[52] Corinne Maier, *Hello Laziness* (London: Orion Books, 2005), p.12.
[53] Jacques Lacan, *Talking to Brick Walls* (Cambridge: Polity, 2017), pp.90–1.
[54] Jelica Šumič, 'Politics and Psychoanalysis at the Time of an Inexistent Other', *Jacques Lacan: Between Psychoanalysis and Politics* (London: Routledge, 2016), p.33.
[55] Wendy Brown, *Undoing the Demos: Neoliberalism's Stealth Revolution* (London: Zone Books, 2015), p.42.
[56] Friedrich Hayek, 'Dangers to Personal Liberty', *The Times: Letters to The Editor*, 11 July 1978, p.15.

The ECJ's relentless pro-market caselaw treated public utilities as it treated private profit-making companies and proceeded to 'liberate' them, in other words, privatize them.[57] The Commission in turn developed a monotheistic view of the European subject as a powerful and insatiable consumer: her right to shop for the best deal at all hours of the day and night across every European country was her primary concern: the gospel, according to the Commission, is that 'empowered and confident consumers' will drive Europe into the future.[58]

In *Stone Raft* similar disquiet is voiced about members of the community that may not be as devout believers in the gospel of capitalism:

> Although it may not be very polite to say so, for certain Europeans, to see themselves rid of baffling western nations, now sailing adrift on the ocean where they should have gone, was itself an improvement, the promise of happier times ahead, like with like, we have finally started to know what Europe is, unless there still remain some spurious fragments which will also break away sooner or later.

Greece, as we know, came close to breaking off, before relenting to the strict austerity measures ordained by the EU Commission and European Central Bank and being 'welcomed' back into the fold. Who knows, had a pandemic not overtaken our lives, loves and industries, we might have seen Saramago's prophecy starting to be fulfilled: 'Let us wager that ultimately we shall be reduced to a single nation, the quintessence of the European spirit, simple and perfect sublimation, Europe, that's to say, Switzerland.'[59]

Wendy Brown, following Foucault, also bemoans the replacement in the domestic sphere of government by governance;[60] again, this was already the case in the EU from its inception. When nearly two centuries ago Karl Marx observed that '[t]he bureaucracy is the imaginary state alongside the real state; it is the spiritualism of the state',[61] he didn't foresee that a super-apparatus would emerge where the real state would be hard to detect, but its spiritualism, its bureaucracy, would be clearly visible, perhaps even all there was. Why is bureaucracy so essential to a modern state? Bureaucratic rules and hierarchies try to give the appearance of an automatic ordering system, of a self-founding law, a law without a lawmaker, a command without a commander, an 'act' without an actor. In Lacanese, we can say bureaucrats obsessively try to fill the void with rules, forms and procedures so the Big Other's castration doesn't show.

Of course, bureaucrats themselves are loath to reveal the process of law-making: 'To make public the mind and the disposition of the state', Marx continues, is 'to the bureaucracy a betrayal of its mystery'.[62] There is always an actor, though, and an act, often a violent one, even if it remains hidden. Sooner or later the cracks, as with any system, show through. In the case of the EU, increasing protest at the secrecy of its meetings in inverse proportion to their impact led to increasing leaks, including from ex-insiders keen to expose the political

---

[57] As Marija Bartl summarizes, 'Relying on the competition provisions of the EU Treaties, the Court interpreted the EU primary law in a manner that paved the way for the liberalisation of services of general economic interest' (2015, 28).

[58] European Commission, A European Consumer Agenda, 2012; http://ec.europa.eu/consumers/archive/strategy/docs/consumer_agenda_2012_en.pdf.

[59] Ibid, p.125.

[60] *Supra*, p.115.

[61] Karl Marx, *Critique of Hegel's Philosophy of Right* (Oxford: Oxford University Press, 1970), p.55.

[62] Ibid.

decisions behind so-called neutral administration. The 'revelations', if we can call them that, revealed what was suspected all along: that the supposedly insignificant administrator wields untold and unaccounted-for power.

Bureaucratic systems invariably generate an excessive enjoyment, which, as Kafka's fiction and films such as Terry Gilliam's *Brazil* depicted, is hard to give up: bureaucracy's ultimate prohibition, in effect, is to make the system efficient. Since the system thrives on reproducing itself, for an outsider to come in and attempt to remedy its problems (whether that is Greece's short-lived Finance Minister Yanis Varoufakis or Robert De Niro's plumber) is anathema. Why is such a powerful system so nervous? Could it be that, as we see in the case of so-called 'Big' Others, it is at its heart pathetically impotent? That, as Lacan insists, the master is already castrated? After all, the arch-creed of any bureaucracy is that, as Cornelia Vismann meticulously and beautifully explored in her groundbreaking *Files*, *quod non est in actis, non est in mundo*, what is not on file is not in the world.[63] If reality, as the bureaucrat insists, is what is found in files and if only what is on file is in the world, then destroying the files erases any unwanted reality. In our digital age, a computer virus, as the group Anonymous lets us know all too frequently, is all it would take to bring mighty bureaucracy's power tumbling down, with cataclysmic effects for those it administers.

ORIGINAL CRIME

In *Stone Raft*, as we also witnessed with Brexit in the UK and with the EU itself, separation leads to enforcement of nationalism and divisions: with the Iberian Peninsula sailing off into the Atlantic, the British are in a hurry to protest their sovereignty over the territory of Gibraltar. When it comes to defending the spoils of conquest from a war three centuries ago, government and opposition swiftly come together: Britain's opposition leader vouches to support the government in its pledge to strengthen the fortification of Gibraltar and adds that 'the Prime Minister committed a serious mistake by speaking of a peninsula when referring to what is now unquestionably an island, although by no means as solid as our own, of course'. Laughter and complacent grins ensue in Westminster, because there is nothing like the national interest to unite politicians.[64] Meanwhile, Iberians who didn't flee as soon as the cracks started to appear start coming to the sobering realization that 'we are no longer Europeans'.[65]

What is, after all, this identity or community, British, Iberian or European, to which individuals supposedly belong, which they are loath to relinquish and fear losing? Freud appreciated that is not just small children that fear being alone: 'The individual feels incomplete if he is alone', he reminds us.[66] The divided speaking being longs to connect with similarly divided others and be admitted to the group. To avoid being alone, she will accede to the rules, including the abuses of the group. Indeed, what holds a community together is not (only) shared values but often shared crimes: that is, not a noble belief in shared values but a shared dirty secret is, as Žižek has argued, more likely to bind the members of the community together.[67]

---

[63] Cornelia Vismann, *Files: Law and Media Technology* (Stanford: Stanford University Press, 2008).
[64] Supra, note 28, p.37.
[65] Ibid, p.56.
[66] *Group Psychology and the Analysis of the Ego*, in *Standard Edition*, Vol. 18 (1920–22), p.118.
[67] Slavoj Žižek (1994) 'Superego by Default', *Cardozo Law Review*, Vol. 16, p.925.

Community cohesion, moreover, is usually at the expense of an excluded other. There is nothing like a threat, real or imaginary, of a dangerous 'other' to rally people into solidarity and form a so-called community. As Freud pointed out: 'It is always possible to bind together a considerable number of people in love, so long as there are other people left over to receive the manifestation of their aggressiveness.'[68]

It is no different with the constitution of a legal community. As Freud hypothesized with his myth of the primal father in *Totem and Taboo*, the founding gesture of the legal system is the murder of the father. The sons' shared guilt for this crime and collective disavowal of this guilt is responsible for creating and maintaining a community of legal subjects: 'The totem meal, which is perhaps mankind's earliest festival, would thus be a repetition and a commemoration of this memorable and criminal deed, which was the beginning of so many things – of social organization, of moral restrictions and of religion.'[69] Once the new system gains supremacy, the last thing any of its members will mention is the crime at its origin. No wonder ideology distracts us daily by drawing attention to individual transgressions of the law, forgetting the absolute transgression that set up the Law itself. We can take Brecht literally here: like Brecht's 'what is the robbery of a bank compared to the founding of a new bank', the founding of a new legal system was preceded by a crime so great that it overthrew the existing system and set up a new one.

The crime at the heart of the EU was from the start the exclusion of outsiders: European integration since its inception went hand in hand with exclusion, an exclusion which kept and continues to keep its members bound to each other. The rhetoric of the migrant as threatening the homogeneity of European identity was present long before the current refugee crisis, with immigration and asylum-seeking being regularly and deliberately confused: as Jef Huysmans showed as early as 2000, 'Immigration has been increasingly politicised through the question of asylum, or more precisely through the (con)fusion of immigration and asylum […] Europeanisation of migration policy indirectly sustains nationalist, racist and xenophobic reactions to immigrants.'[70] Weiler presciently pointed out the same fear four decades ago:

> It would be more than ironic if a polity with its political process set up to counter the excess of statism ended up coming round full circle and transforming itself into a (super) state. It would be equally ironic that an ethos that rejected the nationalism of the Member States gave birth to a new European nation and European nationalism. The problem with the unity vision is that its very realization entails its negation.[71]

This grim prediction is the position we find ourselves in 50 years later: Europe's loosening of statehood turned it into a super-state, European identity turned into euro-racism, and the elimination of internal borders led to the strengthening and outright closure of external borders: with and without Covid, before and during and after the pandemic, no one can come into Fortress Europe, except, of course, to shop.

In *Stone Raft* the same currents of identification and exclusion soon follow the Peninsula's separation. Iberia's rich and powerful are the first to jump ship onto mainland Europe, spark-

---

[68] *Civilization and Its Discontents, Standard Edition*, Vol. 21 (1927–31), p.114.
[69] *Totem and Taboo, Standard Edition*, Vol. 13 (1913–14), p.142.
[70] Jef Huysmans (2000) 'The European Union and the Securitization of Migration', *Journal of Common Market Studies*, Vol. 38(5), pp.751–77; 755, 766.
[71] Weiler, 'The Transformation of Europe', p.2481.

ing suspicion that, like the fleeing tourists, they are also 'foreigners in their own country.'[72] Those not rich enough to flee and stranded on the drifting Peninsula, or who end up in North Africa, find themselves subjected to the same treatment to which Mediterranean countries subject refugees fleeing Africa and the Middle East today:

> thousands and thousands of refugees ended up in Morocco having fled from the Algarve or from the Spanish coast [...] anyone north of the Cape would ask How much do you want to take me to Europe and the chief mate would cock his eyebrow, purse his lips, look the refugee up and down assessing his means, You know, Europe is a damn long way from here, it's right at the other end of the world, and there was no point in arguing.[73]

Freud famously had little hope for the promises made by so-called civilization;[74] indeed, as Jacques-Alain Miller adds 150 years later, perhaps we are now past civilization and its discontents, and are at the point of civilization and its horrors.[75] Certainly the horrors witnessed and documented, of abuse, torture and sale into slavery of refugees at the hands of Libyan militias to which EU delegated the fate of migrants trying to reach Europe, leave little room for belief in a benign humanity.[76]

In *Stone Raft* there is at first no lack of solidarity, good will or hope, particularly on the part of the young: in a prescient depiction of contemporary social media's enthusiasm for slogans and proliferating hashtags, there is no lack of attempts to rally round stranded Iberians. European youths from Paris to Rome to Berlin spread, like wildfire, the message, in every language, '*Nous aussi, nous sommes Iberiques*'.[77] The government having fled, the people also set about organizing themselves. In a prescient depiction of the rise, and fall, of the Occupy movement decades before it happened, Saramago describes how

> within a few hours this popular movement of occupation – blamed on anarchists again – democratically elected residents' committees in the occupied buildings responsible for hygiene and maintenance, kitchen and laundry, entertainment and recreation, cultural activities, education and counseling, gymnastics and sports, in short, all the essentials for the smooth and efficient running of any community.[78]

The revolutionary fervour of youth soon fades, however: 'youngsters are now being told by their wise parents, Do you see my boy, what you were risking if you had insisted on being Iberian, and the repentant son dutifully replies, Yes Papa.'[79]

---

[72] Supra, note 28, p.81.
[73] Ibid, p.29.
[74] Sigmund Freud, *Civilization and Its Discontents* [*Standard Edition*, Vol. XXI].
[75] J.-A. Miller (1991) 'Ethics In Psychoanalysis' http://www.lacan.com/frameV1.htm.
[76] Lucia Pradella and Rosanna Cillo 'Bordering the Surplus Population across the Mediterranean: Imperialism and Unfree Labour in Libya and the Italian Countryside', *Geoforum*, July 2020.
[77] Supra, note 28, at p.126.
[78] Ibid.
[79] Ibid, p.177.

ETHICS OF CASTRATION

The Iberian youth and their parents, like all of us, are grappling, in other words, with what Lacan grandiosely calls Das Ding, or more simply with 'whatever is open, lacking, or gaping at the center of our desire'.[80] Grappling, in short, with the age-old puzzle, what ought I to do? If once upon a time Plato fantasized about filling the impenetrable void with the Sovereign Good, things, according to Lacan, have not progressed much since then.[81] Granted Kant made a valiant effort and succeeded in divorcing ethics from religion and from any notion of the Good; Kant's maxim, Lacan says, 'takes us a step further in the direction of an even greater, if not the greatest, detachment from what is known as a Sovereign Good'.[82] What Lacan appreciates in Kant's contribution is that what determines the morality of our action is not its *content*, or *goodness*, but its *form*: formal law is the only 'Good' Kant acknowledges, and that form does not prescribe any particular content.

Needless to say, neither Iberian youth, nor generations of analysands, nor human subjects in general are content with the implementation of pure form with no regard to the substantive content. They sense, that is – and hysterics are usually at the forefront voicing the complaint – that empty form does not settle the matter. They ask for it from anyone that cares to listen to them, including of course their analyst. If that analyst is Lacan, he will let them know, probably not so gently, that they are deluded: 'The question of the sovereign good is one that man has asked himself since time immemorial but the analyst knows that that is a question that is closed. Not only doesn't he have that Sovereign Good that is asked of him, but he also knows there isn't any.'[83]

The easy way out, of course, is do nothing, complain, and blame the Other; yes, the Big Other is revealed regularly to be dangerously impotent, yet blaming the Other is infinitely more digestible to the subject than blaming herself. In the final analysis, man wants to be able to blame the law for everything: 'if I'm castrated it's because of the law.'[84] If the subject is lacking, divided, dissatisfied, it's because of the law: *Dad's the one who did all that.*[85] Putting an end to her complaints, Lacan, in contrast to an ethics of the good, will articulate, and ominously insist on, an ethics of desire: follow your desire, or else: 'The ethics of psychoanalysis has nothing to do with speculation about prescriptions for, or the regulation of the service of the goods. The question facing us at the Last Judgment is this: "Have you acted in conformity with the desire that is in you?"'[86]

This deceptively simple formula suggests that Lacan's ethics can be fulfilled if only we follow our desire. What is less often emphasized, and what is abundantly clear in Lacan, is that following one's desire is not easy and certainly doesn't come cheap. Since desire is opened up to the human subject through the Oedipus complex, castration is the price, and pain, we have to pay to accede to our desire. This is a price that not everyone is willing to pay: at the end of the day, as Lacan says, '[p]sychoanalysis teaches us that it is easier to accept interdiction than to

---

[80] *Ethics*, p.84.
[81] *Transference*, p.5.
[82] *Ethics*, p.77
[83] Ibid, p.300.
[84] Jacques Lacan, *Anxiety: The Seminar of Jacques Lacan Book X* (Cambridge: Polity, 2014), p.199.
[85] Ibid, p.199.
[86] *Ethics*, p.313.

run the risk of castration'.[87] Giving way to one's desire, however, to avoid the risk of castration comes with a different price, and one just as heavy: the subject pays with guilt and other inner catastrophes such as neurosis.[88] As the price for access to our desire is the only good Lacan acknowledges, a more accurate term for the ethics of psychoanalysis would be less an ethics of desire than an ethics of castration.

LOVE THY CASTRATION AS THYSELF

What such beautiful souls achieve by shunning the pain of castration is also to absolve us from the task of *politics*. One may moan on the couch or, as Peter Goodrich famously pointed out decades ago, write career-enhancing critical papers,[89] but without the pain of castration, without paying the symbolic debt, no transformation – in the subject or the system – can be achieved. It is the political decision, the subject's 'Act', as Lacan calls it, not the supposedly neutral form, that holds the promise of genuine transformation: of the subject, as well as of the system.

Hegel's beautiful souls, just as Goodrich's critics in love with the law, are magnificent in their assessment of the lack in the Other, his uselessness and ineffectiveness. The trouble with appreciating the problems is the corresponding duty to act on them: it is not enough for the subject to *see* that the system is made of a pack of cards. This sight has to be accompanied with *acting* on one's seeing. 'This is where', Lacan suggests, 'the political impact takes place. It concerns this question in act: Out of what knowledge is the law made? Once one has uncovered this knowledge, it may happen that that changes. Knowledge falls to the rank of symptom, seen from another perspective. And this is where truth comes in.'[90] The 'act' is the psychoanalytic equivalent of an explosion, in the subject and in turn, in her relationship to the Big Other. Rather than presupposing any notion of the Good, the ethical Act redefines what is good. As Alenka Zupančič elaborates, the ethical act is not legal or illegal but *beyond* legality: it *redefines* the law and the boundaries of what is forbidden and what is permitted, changing the parameters of what is possible in a political system: 'the ethical cannot be situated within the framework of the law and violations of the law. In relation to legality, the ethical presents a surplus or excess.'[91]

The opening following such an act is far from benign; the subject cuts off her existing links and takes a leap into the unknown, without guarantees: at that point, as Lacan warns, the subject encounters 'absolute disarray' and she 'can expect help from no one'.[92] Like a subject at the end of analysis, the subject encounters the truth in the form of the non-existence of the Big Other. This terrifying leap is what is required of the subject: when the relationship between the subject and the Big Other shifts, the ethical subject takes the plunge and acts on the shift by untying herself from the fictions that tied her to the Big Other and legislate for herself, not

---

[87] Ibid, p.307.
[88] Ibid, p.319.
[89] Goodrich, 'The Critic's Love of the Law', *Law and Critique* 343 (1999).
[90] *The Other Side*, p.186.
[91] Alenka Zupančič, *Ethics of The Real* (London: Verso, 2000), p.12.
[92] Lacan, *The Ethics of Psychoanalysis*, p.304.

for the Other. When the subject has dethroned the subject supposed to know and has taken on the task of self-legislation *in the real.*

In our tale the characters observe the chaos and disorder around them following the breakup of the Peninsula but rather than following the majority's instinct to flee, or take as gospel the confused and inadequate guidance given by the authorities, resolve on making their own way guided not by the Other's desire but their own – in this instance crystallized by their canine friend who, Ariadne-like, dons a blue string round his neck and guides the characters out of the labyrinth. Significantly, unlike the Big Other in the text with their inconsistent messages, and unlike the characters themselves, it is the animal, the non-speaking being, that steers a course uncontaminated by wily and floating signifiers. Our characters' ethical status, unlike that of their compatriots who try to cover up or run away from the cracks, lies in recognizing the cracks were there all along, and we had been living with them without admitting their precarity or openness to change. The appearance of the cracks in the real served as proof, and reminder, that the cracks were there all along, however much we tried to ignore them: they showed, as Saramago summarizes,

> in a manner we believe definitive the precariousness of established structures and ideas. It then became clear how the social edifice, with all its complexity, is no more than a house of cards, solid merely in appearance, we need only shake the table on which it stands and the house collapses. And the table, in this instance, and for the first time in history, had moved by itself.[93]

The house of cards having come apart in one corner of Europe doesn't lead to big upheavals on the rest of the continent, just a quick realignment of existing identifications. European identity, the one Saramago reminds us had been 'laboriously created through hundreds of years', soon adapts to the lack of territories in the west, just as the EU announced its acceptance of Britain's departure. Quoting T.S. Eliot, European Commission President Ursula von der Leyen suggested that with Brexit behind it, the end is also a beginning; a 'deal cannot change gravity', and the EU is settling back into 'our future made in Europe'. In *Stone Raft* the castration is of the extreme south west rather than the extreme north west, but the feeling is similar:

> this was the memorable day on which already distant Europe (200km away) found itself shaken psychologically and socially about its identity, deprived of its very foundations laboriously created through hundreds of years. Europeans soon became accustomed (one suspects with an unspoken feeling of relief) to the lack of any territories to the extreme west and if there was any disquiet it's for aesthetic reasons, like the feeling we have when we first see that the arms are missing on the Venus de Milo. Soon afterwards however we can't imagine Venus de Milo with arms.[94]

We often forget that castration takes place not just in seismic events like the Iberian Peninsula drifting off into the Atlantic but on a regular basis, indeed every time we speak: to articulate something in a manner that will be understood by our listeners, we cut and mix up words, order and reorder them, even if the process comes easily and unthinkingly to us. The computer reminds us, however: if the images on our screen portray the cut with scissors, what is the paste with which we sew words back together? For Lacan the paste is nothing more or less than the act of love: to love means to admit your lack, that you need the other. 'To love is to give

---

[93] Supra, note 28, p. 185.
[94] Ibid, p. 124.

something you don't have',[95] because to give something you don't have you have to assume your lack, your castration: 'there is no chance for a man to have jouissance of a woman's body, otherwise stated, for him to make love, without castration, in other words, without something that says no to the phallic function.'[96]

In Saramago's tale the catastrophe of the Iberian Peninsula's castration from the rest of Europe is accompanied by an explosion of amorous activity throughout the drifting island. Any and all women of child-bearing age find themselves pregnant, meaning the two nations expect a population explosion, with upwards of 100,000 new babies arriving in around nine months.

We started this tale with stories of subjects fearing castration and with law as the price of accepting and acceding to one's castration. We can now add love as the prize of castration: accede to your castration, dependence, incompleteness and you get both law and love in return. Living on a drifting Peninsula suddenly wrenched from the rest of the continent, or finding oneself in the aftermath of Brexit and living through the perils of insatiable Covid, all the while mis-guided by incompetent as well as corrupt Big Others, the subject starts to love her castration as herself – an acceptance that opens her up to loving and being loved, in law, and in literature.

---

[95] *Transference*, p.34.
[96] *Encore: On Feminine Sexuality, the Limits of Love and Knowledge, 1972–1973* (New York: W.W. Norton, 1998), trans. Bruce Fink, pp.71–2.

8. Utopia
Elena Loizidou

PROLOGUE: MORE NEWS FROM NOWHERE

Nick Cave sings, in a joyful, ironic way:

> more news from nowhere
> more news from nowhere
> dont it make you feel so sad
> dont the blood rush to yr feet
> to think that everything you do today
> tomorrow is obsolete
> technology & women
> & little children too
> dont it make you feel blue
> dont it make you feel blue
> for more news from nowhere
> more news from nowhere
> dont it make you feel alone
> dont it make you wanna get right back home
> more news from nowhere
> more news from nowhere
> (Nick Cave and the Bad Seeds, 2018)

Cave is inviting us to consider whether news of today's deeds will be 'obsolete tomorrow, technology & women & little children too' and leaves us with a feeling of sadness, of wanting to return 'right back home'. The song's title and theme connect it to William Morris's socialist and scientific utopian novel *News from Nowhere* (2004), and it laments the impossibility of ever finding utopia. I will elaborate on the song later in the chapter. It suffices now to say that utopia has long been the theme of songs, literary texts, social projects, art and philosophy. Nevertheless, the word utopia is older than any cultural or political project. Utopia, from the Greek word ουτοπία, refers to an ideal *non*-place or country, or *nowhere*, as Spivak reminds us (Spivak, 1999: 318), set in the future. It is worth noting that utopia is usually contrasted to dystopia and heterotopia: dystopia, originally a Greek word, meaning a bad place, is usually used to describe authoritarian and totalitarian regimes, and is a common genre in literature, television and film. Aldous Huxley's science fiction novel *Brave New World* (2007), describing a technologically advanced society that socially engineers its inhabitants, is exemplary of dystopian fiction, while the relatively recent television drama *Years and Years* (2019, BBC1/HBO) depicts a future UK led by a leader with totalitarian tendencies, with a hostile refugee and immigration environment and the possibility of humans becoming transhuman. Gilbert, reviewing the series for *The Atlantic*, points to the slow character of dystopia-making: 'This is the way dystopia happens, *Years and Years* says: Not with a bang, but with a series of exhausted shrugs' (Gilbert, 23 June 2019). Utopia and dystopia sometimes merge. Dystopian imagining can have a utopian desire. Moreover, as we will see, utopia may not only be built on the heels of dystopia – utopian discoveries being the consequence of colonialist strategies – but moreover may hold within in it a totalitarian aspect. In his critique of dialectics, Jean Paul Sartre pointed to the fact that the Marxist ideal of communism as a way of organising life may be totalising because of its attachment and universalisation of dialectics as means of understanding human societies (Sartre, 2004: 47, 50–1). To put it simply, Sartre questions the dialectical presumption that the collective histories which the Marxist tradition attends to reflect individual histories. The dissonance between collective and individual histories that he identifies reflects the failure of dialectics having a universalising capacity. Moreover, Sartre warns that if Marxism continues to hold on to the dialectic as a way of understanding societies, there is a risk of totalising societies, curbing movement (Sartre, 2004: 47). Foucault suggested that the mirror of utopia is heterotopia, meaning other places (Foucault, 2002). Foucault first mentions the term heterotopia in *The Order of Things* (2002) in 1966, when he talks about the fictional Chinese encyclopaedia of animals that Jorge Luis Borges writes about. I don't intend to ponder Foucault's fabulous play on Borges' Chinese encyclopaedia, but it is worth saying that the non-obvious classification, their incongruity, not only surprises the reader but moreover alerts us to a particular effect that they may produce: 'heterotopias (such as those to be found so often in Borges) desiccate speech, stop words in their tracks, contest the very possibility of grammar as its source; they dissolve our myths and sterilize the lyricism of our sentences' (2002: xix). These literary heterotopias moreover, as Foucault suggests, destroy the idea of a common place. In 'Of Other Spaces' (1986),[1] Foucault contrasts utopias with heterotopias. While utopias are described as 'unreal spaces' reflecting the limits of the societies we are living in (1986: 24), heterotopias are

> places – places that do exist and that are formed in the very founding of society – which are something like counter-sites, a kind of effectively enacted utopia in which the real sites, all the other real sites that can be found within the culture, are simultaneously represented, contested, and inverted. Places of this kind are outside of all places, even though it may be possible to indicate their location in reality. (Foucault, 1986: 24)

Heterotopias, we may say, are places that contest cultural uniformity and universality. Such places or institutions – the prison, the brothel, the cemetery; places that are found at the edge of the city – contest our very perception of the world. We can say that heterotopias are not exactly the opposite of utopia, but rather a reminder that every culture is inundated with heterotopias, thus utopia equally cannot be singular.

I have wandered a little. This wandering was to point out that the concept of utopia is not so straightforward. Utopia walks along with other concepts, as we have seen, and it may be difficult to distinguish utopia from dystopia and heterotopia. In this chapter, for example, we will encounter the merging between utopia and dystopia in the discussion of More's *Utopia* (2009). The aim in introducing utopia's fellow-travellers was to familiarise us with the complexities of writing about utopia and the impossible task of framing utopia. This journey now brings me back to utopia.

---

[1] This was an essay based on a lecture that Foucault first gave to Cercle d'études architecturales, a group of architects based in Paris in 1967. This lecture was later published in 1984 in the architectural journal: *Architecture /Mouvement/ Continuité* in 1984 and in the critical theory journal *Diacritics* in 1986. For an insightful and critical analysis of Foucault's heterotopia see Kelvin T. Knight (2017) 'Placeless Places: Resolving the Paradox of Foucault's Heterotopia', *Textual Practice*, 31(1), 141–58.

The word utopia was introduced into the English language by Thomas More in 1516 through his work of fiction *Utopia* (2009). More's introduction of the word into English through this work is significant. It paints utopia in leftist colours and steers us to understand and imagine utopia as a radical project. Utopia is also often imagined as being set in the future. In this chapter, while continuing the left trajectory of utopia inherited from More, I am making a simple proposition: utopia could be a cultural artifact or a political project, but it is also an affect that re-organises our psychic world and connects us to the present. If utopia is a non-place, a nowhere, it is surprising that most critical readings of it still try to pin it down to a *topos*, even if it is an imaginary place somewhere in the future. The proposition that utopia can be an affect opens utopia to a reading that shifts our emphasis from what utopia is to what it does to us as readers, creators or participants of utopia and to utopia itself. What we may observe is utopia being ungrounded from futurity and 'situated' in the present, utopia being ephemeral and passing. If we allow ourselves to read utopia as an affect we begin to notice in utopian fiction or utopian political writings, for example, multiple affects; anxiety, enthusiasm, euphoria, all working to undo what tethers utopia to the ground, and what tethers us to the ground. Euphoria, for example, is the affect that I felt when I was working with my local Covid-19 mutual aid group. Euphoria is an ancient Greek word meaning bearing well. This could refer to carrying something well, such as bad news or clothing. In the English-speaking world, euphoria was historically mainly used in medicine, referring to the comfortable condition of a patient (Milnes and Arnold-Foster, 5 March 2019).[2] It is this comfortable position of euphoria that Sigmund Freud recognises in himself and his patients when a small amount of cocaine (0.05–0.10 grams) is administered (Freud, 1973: 497):

> It appears as if the cocaine mood at such doses is evoked not so much by direct excitement as by the elimination of depressing elements of community feeling. Perhaps one can assume that the euphoria of health is nothing other than the normal mood of the well-nourished cerebral cortex, which 'knows nothing' about the organs of its body. (Freud, 1973: 498)

Euphoria can be induced through chemicals such as cocaine or through collective activities such as mutual aid. No matter how euphoria is induced, what is central to it, if we listen to Freud, is its ability to hold at bay the depressing feelings produced in the community and reconstitute our sickly bodies. Euphoria may not be long-lasting, but it lasts just enough to resist or fend away those 'depressing elements of community feeling' – individualism, capitalism. The affective reading of utopia that I offer here attends to the ephemeral character of utopia that keeps it moving, that resists its arrest and ossification.

UTOPIA *NOT* NOWHERE

More's fictional *Utopia* features an island, made up of 'fifty four splendid big towns […] all with the same language, laws, customs, and institutions' (More, 2009: 47), designed in the same way and adorned with indistinguishable buildings.

---

[2] For the failure of law to recognise the euphoric state of Judge Daniel Paul Schreber manifested in wearing women's clothes during his psychotic episodes as a way of making and not submitting to law, see Peter Goodrich (2015).

More tells us Utopia was discovered by Raphael Nonsenso, a companion to Americo Vespucci.

In this narrative, Nonsenso was given permission by Vespucci to break away from the latter's fourth explorative voyage and it was then that he came across Utopia (More, 2009: 3–4), an island so different from the capitalist kingdoms in Europe. Nonsenso rooted himself in the everyday life of Utopia for five years. Upon his return to Europe, he enthusiastically told everybody the news from *nowhere*, the marvels he experienced on the island Utopia. Nonsenso was impressed by the different, communist political system that he witnessed in Utopia; there was access for everybody to universal healthcare, there was no private property and schools were free. All utopians worked the land, acquired a trade (such as metallurgy or carpentry), shared their food and ate together in the huge houses that they belonged to. Utopia features, at first glance, desirable characteristics. It is a place where perhaps we would like to live. Though it is noticeable that it is not such an egalitarian society – in Utopia slaves and women are not equal. As the great utopian science fiction writer Ursula Le Guin sharply puts it: 'Utopia has been Euclidean, it has been European, and it has been masculine' (Le Guin, 2016: 177). I will return later to the exclusionary tendencies of utopia, but generally you get the gist that utopia, with its communistic way of life, is presented as a desirable political system.

Since More, the term utopia has been used as shorthand for any imaginary, future-oriented society in which life is substantially different to the capitalist societies that dominate in the present.[3] We tend to imagine utopia as a society where decisions are taken collectively in horizontally organised assemblies, where private property is absent and welfare provisions are made available to all according to their needs. We have additionally been schooled to associate utopia with a desirable polity in the future. An island where life is better than the one we have. Utopia is an island that is *not yet* here, but we all dream to one day find ourselves *there*. We can simply say that utopia is what is missing from the present – at least for all those who dream of an anti-capitalist society. Utopia, as Athanasiou stresses, cannot be a 'free-market utopia' (2020: 33).

Even if utopia is articulated differently – as impulse, and not a society or a territory as featured in More's novel – it is still embellished with the same characteristics as those we have inherited from the novel. Our understanding of utopia as an impulse also reveals our hope for a more communist/socialist world for the future, a better world. The German philosopher Ernst Bloch decoupled utopia from its territorial grip. For Bloch, utopia is an impulse that 'governs everything future-oriented in life and culture – encompassing everything from games to patent medicines, from myths to mass entertainment, from iconography to technology, from architecture to eros, from tourism to jokes and the unconscious' (Jameson, 2010: 675). Nevertheless, not everything that is future-oriented and governs life is utopian. Bloch is specific about what counts as utopian impulse. In *Principles of Hope* he draws our attention to two types of utopia: abstract and concrete (Bloch, 1996: 145–6). Concrete utopias refer to concrete historical social

---

[3] For an analysis of how capitalism has been eating up our democratic processes see Wendy Brown, *Undoing the Demos: Neoliberalism's Stealth Revolution* (New York, Zone Books, 2015). On how capitalism contributes to obesity and death see Lauren Berlant, 'Slow Death, Obesity, Sovereignty, Lateral Agency' in *Cruel Optimism* (Durham, London, Duke University Press, 2011), 95–119; and for how neoliberal capitalism accumulates wealth in the hands of the few, the 1% in Occupy Wall Street's words, and dispossess populations of public and private wealth and land, see David Harvey (2004) 'The "New" Imperialism: Accumulation by Dispossession', *Socialist Register*, 40, 63–87.

struggles that resulted in the creation of socialist societies. Such societies, for example the Socialist Federal Republic of Yugoslavia, in their very concreteness, their materialisation at a certain historical moment despite its failure, retain an unfulfilled promise or the hope that there can be an organisation of life based on an ethos very different from that of capitalism or neoliberalism – a promise that fuels social movements and populations struggling for a better world. Abstract utopias, on the other hand (such as dreams, art, literature, films, architecture and so on), are valuable and important for Bloch, as José Esteban Muñoz aptly explains, only 'insofar as they pose a critique function that fuels a critical and potentially a transformative political imagination' (Muñoz, 2019: 3). These abstract and concrete utopias capture what is *not yet* present, what is missing from our contemporary worlds. At the same time, they are critical of the present. As Bloch explains, 'the essential function of utopia is a critique of what is present'[4] (Bloch, 1996: 11). We can conclude that for Bloch too, utopia, whether abstract or concrete, is anticipatory of a better freer future, and collective living.

So, when we read, for example, of Space X, a future-oriented project 'that wants to shuttle setters to Mars for $500,000 a ticket, with loans available that could be worked off', it is not difficult to agree with Shaw that all this 'sounds like indentured servitude packaged as frontier life' (Shaw, 5 February 2021), and far from the ideas of utopia developed by More and Bloch. Capitalist utopias are for the 1 per cent, to use the term coined by Occupy Wall Street (Graeber, 2014: 35–41).

But what happens if, as Cave sings, the news from *nowhere* is not so desirable. What happens if the future that we anticipate as providing us with a better life takes away all the good things we have already secured? In some respects, Cave's song is prophetic. The news from *nowhere,* the news from utopia, from the future is not so good. The future appears bleak during the Covid-19 pandemic. News of people losing their lives, people incapacitated by SARS-COV-2, unemployment and recession does not instil hope for the future. News of environmental crisis that sees life on planet earth rapidly extinguishing does not encourage us to look for utopian islands. After all, planet earth in its totality is at risk of disappearing. The tendency of associating utopia with dystopia, of seeing the proximity of the dystopian to the utopian, has been noted by the science fiction writer China Miéville (Miéville, 2016: 5–6). In his introduction to a new Verso edition of More's *Utopia* he points to the proximity of utopia to dystopia, of the possibility of utopian dreams or projects being corrupted by dystopian ones as well as the multifaced attacks that utopia endures. Utopia, as he explains, has faced multiple attacks and criticisms throughout time; liberals are apprehensive of 'utopian*ism* from below' (2016: 5), that is, socialist or anarchist utopias, and the right long for their own 'supremacist arcadias' (2016: 5). Nevertheless, Cave's point is different. The song invites us to think of the possibility that there may not be a *nowhere*, there may not be a utopia, there may not be a future. Miéville reminds us of the nexus between utopia and dystopia, but he is hopeful of the possibility of utopia. Miéville points to the shortcomings of utopia – he reminds us that More's island of utopia is not a splendid island far away or in isolation from the mainland; on the contrary it is a territory plagued by the perils of imperial capitalism: 'The fifteen miles of water that keep it apart from the main body politic are not there by God's will', he writes, 'but by the sweat of native people, amongst others, digging at an invading conqueror's command.

---

[4] For a discussion of utopia and its relation to critique and critical theory see A. Athanasiou (2020) 'At Odds with the Temporalities of the Im-possible; or, What Critical Theory Can (Still) Do', *Critical Times*, 3(2), 249–76.

The splendid-utopian-isolation is part of the violent imperial spoils' (Miéville, 2016: 4) – but he is hopeful that we can remake utopia in a way that it addresses the shortcomings (masculinist, imperialist, Euclidean, European) that we find in More. He says as much himself when he writes, 'We can't do without this book. We are all and have always been Thomas More's children' (Miéville, 2016: 6).

Cave is asking us to think of the possibility that there is no *nowhere*. The thought of this may be daunting. What if there is no future, I keep asking myself? The rhythm of the song attempts to drown the thought that there is no *nowhere*. My hips start swerving left and right to the song. Now I am not *thinking* of the song, I am *sensing* its words, its rhythm. I am not thinking any longer of how to get to utopia, to *nowhere*. I am feeling blue, I am feeling sad, I am *being affected*. *Nowhere*, utopia, is no longer an abstract, disembodied idea, project or dream. It is not located in the future. Lauren Berlant explains that 'the present is perceived, first, affectively' (Berlant, 2011: 4). Berlant, drawing on Deleuze and Guattari, understands affect as being different from feeling. It is not an individual feeling; it is rather 'an ability to affect and be affected. It is a prepersonal intensity corresponding to the passage from one experiential state of the body to another and implying augmentation or diminution in that body's capacity to act' (Deleuze and Guattari, 1999: xvi). 'More News from Nowhere' has moved me so I can now see that the *nowhere* that we have spent all this time trying to understand has been directed at what utopia is, rather than experiencing it. We have spent all this time schooling ourselves in trying to reach utopia, trying to reach a better world, thinking that utopia may not be present in the here and now. In doing so, we (I?) paid little to no attention to what happens to us, to our bodies and psyches, when we talk about utopia, write about utopia, listen to songs invoking utopia, read about utopia, engage in collective projects. In ignoring what is happening when we 'do' utopia, we neglected to notice that our experience of utopia is an affective experience. And consequently, we can say that utopia is *affective*. The affect that emerges from the different scenes of utopia; utopia as invocation, as creation (literary, artistic, social), and as sensed is wildly varied. We may feel excited, sad, anxious or worried. Whatever the emotion, we can be assured that utopia affects us, it re-organises our psychic world, revealing that we are interconnected to each other, that we are not an 'I' but a 'We'.

I am making *too* much, you may say, out of the lyrics and the rhythm of a song. How could utopia not be either a communistic society or an impulse? How can utopia not be future-oriented? I am not saying that utopia cannot be either a future communist society or an impulse: of course it can be so. I am simply saying that utopia can also be an *affect*. The inability to notice that utopia can be an *affect* may arise from the fact that left-oriented critics and commentators of utopia, as we have seen earlier (Le Guin, Miéville), tend to criticise utopian thinking, such as that of More, as being elliptical. Utopia is either described as being non-inclusive or as being founded upon inequalities. Such criticisms are useful and important but, in their attempt to supplement utopian projects, writings, and so on, they get entangled in the nitty gritty of making an ideal utopia, failing to notice their attachment to ideality. Even if they acknowledge their idealism, what they tend to forget is that ideals cannot stand the test of time, but are always going to lack, and will always be exclusionary.[5] Of course we should

---

[5] The contemporary theorist of utopia, Ruth Levitas in *Utopia as Method* argues 'for greater clarity about usage and in favour of the more open definition of utopia as the expression of desire for a better way of living and of being' and for an 'analytic rather than descriptive definition [that] reveals …that utopia may be fragmentary, fleeting, elusive. [That] mirrors an existential quest which is figured in liter-

134 *Research handbook on law and literature*

always strive for a better world, I am not disagreeing with that; what I want to suggest is: let's not sit in leisured comfort assuming that our better world will not also be non-inclusive.

When working with my local Covid-19 mutual aid group in Hackney, East London, I was initially bogged down by trying to figure out how mutual aid can work, whether we can have horizontal decision making, how we could ensure that everybody that came to the Zoom meetings that were organised had a voice, how we could avoid conflict and how such a group could deliver what it promised: support and care to vulnerable Hackney inhabitants. I was preoccupied with the mechanics of the project and I was very goal-oriented. I do not want to appear to be the originator of this idea. As I explain later in this chapter, I was not. I was, however, given some responsibility, for working with another local resident in Homerton ward – boroughs are divided into wards – to start the Homerton Covid-19 Mutual Aid group, so I felt the pressure to be goal-oriented. As an anarchist I was very much aware of the idea of mutual aid, an idea that is rooted in Peter Kropotkin's 1902 *Mutual Aid: An Illuminated Factor of Evolution* (1902; 2009). I will explain the idea of mutual aid later; for now it suffices to remember that Kropotkin argued that within our human and animal worlds, mutual aid and not competition has been the more dominant instinct. Kropotkin explains the various settings in society where mutual aid has been practised. As David Graeber and Andrej Grubačić remind us, many of the institutions of the welfare state were initiated by mutual aid groups, 'entirely independently of the state, then gradually co-opted by states and political parties' (Graeber and Grubačić, 2021). Some examples of institutions created by mutual aid groups include social insurance, public libraries and public health care. Nevertheless, irrespective of evidence that demonstrates the rise of mutual aid groups (for example, Black Lives Matter, Refugee Rescue organisations and the global Covid-19 mutual aid phenomenon), mutual aid was never considered to be the basis of organising life. The most dominant model of organising life has been the one based on capitalism, where competition is the main driver. Mutual aid and the political organisation that could arise from its uptake, an anarcho-communist society, was always seen as a utopia. As I was saying, when I first got involved in the mutual aid group, I wanted it to succeed. For years I have been a student of mutual aid. I was driven almost by a competitive instinct – 'let us show this Tory State that we can deliver what they don't have', I kept telling myself. When things were not working, when there were disagreements among members of the groups about how to do things, what to prioritise, I felt disheartened. Naively, I had thought that agreement would bring along frictionless cooperation. And then upon reflection I realised that to be driven by an instinct for mutual aid does not mean that there will be immediate and instant agreement about how to organise things, how to organise life.[6] It requires deliberation and hard work. Nick Cave's voice kept circling my soul. The news from nowhere was that tomorrow was cancelled. In our case, in the case of a planet that stood still and was battling

---

ature, music, drama, and art.' Levitas is right to identify utopia as fragmentary and fleeting, even elusive, but her understanding of utopia as 'the expression of desire for a better way of living and of being' (2013: 4) sets up utopia as future-oriented project. Utopia is something external to us, something that we are striving for. The proposition that I am making here is somewhat different. Utopia is the feeling and movement that we have when we are already doing things collectively that disrupt the kakotopia of the present, and whilst doing so in the present. Levitas desires, correctly, to keep utopia open, and being revised eternally, but the vectorial aspect of this desire, its futurity, gets trapped in the temporality of the *not yet* that she inherited from Bloch.

[6] In *Critique of Dialectical Reason*, Sartre critiques any reality, any collective history that is superimposed upon individuals. Such dialectical reason ends up being totalising. (Sartre, 2004: 36).

SARS-COV-2, this was not a metaphor. I realised that utopia was not just a project, a social project for making life better in the present, as Cooper suggests (2014), but was something which, as you know by now, I called affect. It was not about the goal but rather what the engagement with utopia may affect. I abandoned the goal-oriented understanding of utopia after this realisation. In doing so I was free and able to notice how it affected me. I noticed how my psyche was reorganised, how I was connected to the world, against a set of conditions that demanded our physical self-isolation and immobility.

With this understanding of utopia in mind I returned to two literary and one political text and tracked the affective aspect of utopia. This chapter initially tracks affect workings in More's *Utopia*. Criticisms that attend to what is missing from the novel are somewhat unable to register utopia as affect. The novel is the result of the collaboration of the author Thomas More, the explorer Raphael Nonsenso, the publicist Peter Giles and the promoter Hieronymus van Busleyden. The collaboration registers an array of emotions – tiredness, excitement, anxiety – all brought about by the production of the novel. Additionally, by tracking these emotions we can witness the psychic reorganisation of the author and his collaborators – a facet of the novel that otherwise would have gone unnoticed.

The chapter then turned to Kropotkin's book on *Mutual Aid* and tracked the excitement associated with building a society based on mutual support. It is the same affect that I experienced when working with my local mutual aid group and that we witness in contemporary writings about mutual aid. It is an affect that re-organises oneself in such a way that possessive individualism and self-interest fade away, an affect that teaches us – it certainly taught me – that I am not an 'I'.

The chapter will presently attend to Jorge Luis Borges' story 'A Weary Man's Utopia' (2001). The story is narrated by Eudoro Acevedo, a visitor to utopia. This utopia shares similar characteristics to the ones we witnessed in More's; it is self-sufficient and everybody living there is free and equal. Borges' story, minimalist in style, may face criticisms of underinclusiveness or unfairness. But still, it raises emotion. This story, the collaboration between the author, the narrator and the other characters, raises worry. Utopia, we discover, is not such an ideal place; when it exhausts itself, it can turn into a totalitarian society. In following a reading that tracks the emotions produced in the story, we learn that utopia must remain open to renewal if it is to retain its spirit, as identified by More and Bloch.

The affects, emotions, feelings that linger in utopian writings, projects, artworks are varied, but tracking them down, I argue, reveals that utopia is neither future-oriented nor an abstract idea or ideal. Utopia is what happens when something is stirred up in ways that mean we will never be the same again. I would say it is akin to love, but it is something bigger than love. It is a connection to the present, and therefore to the world.

ANXIETY/EXCITEMENT

I have already alluded to the criticisms that More's *Utopia* encountered. As I explained earlier, Miéville, for example, alerted us to the inexplicable connection between More's *Utopia* and dystopia, the connection between the communistic society and capitalism and imperialism. The discovery of utopia by a companion of Amerigo Vespucci, Raphael Nonsenso, is testament to the imperialist mentality that such expeditions carried. Such criticisms are useful and important in alerting us to the limits of utopia and moreover urge the need for a critical eye directed to what is missing, what is unjust and unequal in More's utopian society, ensuring in this way that any new utopia or any utopian project does not replicate them. We are therefore instructed by Miéville that in the novel all the domestic work is carried out by slaves and women: it is slaves who ensure that communal dining halls are cleaned; it is slaves who peel potatoes, cook the food and ensure that everyday nutrition and hygiene is available for the 'citizens' of *Utopia*. And it is women who attend to the management of home affairs but are invisible from the management of public affairs (More, 2009: 64). This type of critique enables us to write or imagine different utopias, utopias that correct what is missing from the imaginal world. And in 'Limits of Utopia' (2016: 11–27) Miéville does precisely that: he supplements the 'original' vision of utopia by calling out the exploitation of land by colonial powers and capitalism and urging environmental justice. In doing so, though, he misses references to affective states present in the novel – references that not only reveal More's awareness of the perils of capitalism, but moreover elucidate that the making of *Utopia* belongs not just to the author but to also the other characters in the novel. While the content of *Utopia* may not be *so* utopian, the affects, emotions, associated with its production reveal interdependency, a collective subjectivity, a utopia situated in the present and a subtle critique of capitalism.

Utopia registers a critique of capitalism. One of the characteristics of capitalism is its ability to own time. The flow of our lives is organised around the fluidity of capitalism, and consequently subjugates our everyday lives to its force. Nothing remains uninterrupted. Indeed, at the very start of *Utopia* More explains eloquently how the interruption of everyday life delayed the writing of this classic literary text. In a letter to Peter Gilles he writes:

> My job was simply to write down what I'd heard, which was really perfectly easy – but my other commitments have left me less than no time to get this perfectly easy job done. I've been kept hard at work in the law courts, either at the Bar or the Bench, either in civil or in criminal cases. Then there is always someone that has to be visited, either on business, or as a matter of courtesy. I am out practically all day, dealing with other people – the rest of the day I spend with my family – so there's no time left for me, that is, for my writing. (More, 2009: vii–viii)

More organised his life according first to the demands of his work, which appears to take up most of his life. A middle-class man, belonging to the legal profession, we would have expected him to have plenty of time to pursue what he finds more enjoyable, but alas capitalism has caught even More in its claws. Very little time is left for writing. If capitalism requires all those who do not own the means of production to sell their labour for wages then it goes without saying that 'me' time will be subjected to the time of capitalism, and in the case of More to the demands of clients, the opening hours of courts, the timing of cases. He does not appear to be ignorant of the fact that *Utopia* is being written on the heels of dystopia – the term that Miéville uses to describe capitalism. In explaining what it took for More to write this novel, a subtle critique of capitalism is revealed.

More begins *Utopia* with two letters: one to Peter Giles, who – in the narrative – introduced him to Raphael Nonsenso; the other from Peter Giles to Hieronymus van Busleyden, counsellor to King Charles V (Holly Roman Emperor, King of Spain, Archduke of Austria and Duke of Burgundy). In the first letter, as we have seen, More mostly talks of the reasons that delayed him in writing *Utopia*. The second letter relays Peter Giles' enthusiasm for *Utopia* to van Busleyden. It is his way of encouraging him to support the publication of the book. The letters, placed at the very start of the novel, appear as a preamble to it, giving us an insight into the author and his collaborators and exposure to the derivative character of writing. If capitalism's main characteristic is competition, the production of the novel reveals an ethos that is anti-capitalist. More is of course the author, but More's *Utopia*, like any other literary text, is a collaborative project. It is the result of collective labour. In this case we notice the collaboration between: (a) the author/narrator More and explorer Raphael Nonsenso. More desires to record Nonsenso's discoveries verbatim, to the extent that he seeks from him verification of the truthfulness of facts that he describes in the novel (2009: x); (b) Peter Giles and Hieronymus van Busleyden, counsellor to Charles V, with Giles seeking to encourage van Busleyden to promote the publication of *Utopia*. Raul Vaneigem, in critiquing revolutionary politics, wrote that '[p]eople who talk about revolution and class struggle without referring explicitly to everyday life […] such people have a corpse in their mouth' (Vaneigem, 2017: 26). Vaneigem's words are instructive here. He urges us to pay attention not just to ideals, but also to what it takes to bring to fruition ideals, and their everydayness. Vaneigem suggests that revolutionary politics without the *affect* of love (Vaneigem, 2017: 26) are dead. In our case, if we were just to critique *Utopia* from an identitarian perspective or from what is missing, we would have failed to notice that its production reveals a collective subjectivity, not just the 'I' of the author. My speculation is that More included the letters that were sent to living people not just because he wanted to make *Utopia* more believable, but also because he wanted us to see the book was the outcome of a collective effort.

For Vaneigem, love is an integral part of revolutionary politics. Indeed, we may say that any affect is integral to our understanding not only of politics but also of cultural products (Berlant, 2011). By offering a reading of the book that attends to its everydayness and production I was able to notice the affects that circulate within it. Affects, as I argued at the start of the chapter, enable us to recognise utopia as revealing a collective subjectivity but also being in the present. Enthusiasm[7] and anxiety fill the two letters that appear at the start of the novel. Utopia appears to be not just an island but also an affect, or rather multiple affects generated by the collective endeavour to publish it – affects that ground the author and his collaborators in a present. Giles' letter to Hieronymus van Busleyden, for example, is filled with excitement about More's book; he urges van Busleyden to enable the swift publication of the book and praises More's genius (2009: xv–vi). More's letter to Giles, on the other hand, is ridden with anxiety. He is 'extremely anxious to get [his] facts right' (2009: ix); he is anxious about his critics and thus unsure of whether to publish *Utopia* (2009: x–xi), and anxious to secure Giles' continued affection (2009: xii).

As we know, Freud pointed out that anxiety arises when we apprehend danger, real or imaginary (Freud, 2001: 50). Anxiety, he explains, manifests itself in two ways: as a primary anxiety, 'a reaction to the felt loss of the [love] object' (Freud, 2001: 138), where we witness the ego being overwhelmed and unable to manage the loss of the love object (Freud, 2001: 128–9); and as a signal anxiety, whereby the subject is in anticipation of the loss of the love object (Freud, 2001: 134–7). In either situation, the ego will attempt to manage them by either 'avoid[ing] that situation or […] withdraw[ing] from it' (Freud, 2001: 128–9). On both occasions the subject feels that the ego either is dissolving or is about to do so (Freud, 2001: 139–40). More's anxiety, perhaps a type of signal anxiety – fearing the loss of the world of

---

[7] We notice also curiosity coupled with enthusiasm throughout the novel. Nonsenso's travels in Europe, New World and Utopia intrigued More and led him to question Nonsenso about his knowledge of European political systems (2009: 1–45) and reluctance to acquiesce to the benefits of a communist society (2009: 139).

privilege that early capitalism has provided him – enables us to address the subjective transformations that one undergoes when one writes something new, a novel. He is no longer an autonomous subject: after all, he needs Nonsenso, Giles and Hieronymus van Busleyden to publish the book; he needs Giles' friendship and affection as a moral support; and he needs Nonsenso's travelling stories to beef up the book. By tracking More's feelings in *Utopia* we can see not only that no man is an island but moreover that utopia does not have to be an ideal space or place; it can simply be the very reorganisation of our psychic world, a reorganisation that sheds light on a new subjective existence, perhaps better than the one we inhabit.

Critiquing projects, polities, writings, objects, dreams and hopes that are utopian or hold a utopian impulse promises a revival of the utopian project. Such practices are a must. Nevertheless, any attempts to re-imagine the utopian project along identarian lines may end up closing it up or making it totalitarian because they tend not to attend to the everydayness of utopia and the subjective transformations that take place in engaging in collective projects. Borges' 'A Weary Man's Utopia' warns us of the possibility of utopia becoming stale, deadly and non-generative.

WORRY

As just stated, critiquing projects, polities, writings, objects, dreams and hopes that are utopian or that hold a utopian impulse promises a revival of the utopian project. Such practice is necessary but only important insofar as it will ensure that utopia remains open to revision. This is not always going to be possible. Let us take for example Avery Gordon's impressive work on utopia (2018). Her concept of utopia attends to what needs to be transformed in the present so we can have a better world. Gordon's better world consists of 'a collective life without misery, deadly inequalities, mutating racisms, social abandonment endless war, police power, authoritarian governance, heteronormative impositions, patriarchical rule, cultural conformity and ecological destruction' (2018: v). Gordon's utopia, or hope for a better life, emerges out of the dystopian times in which we are living. She hankers for a world where all the inequalities that plague our present one are at bay. Like More, Gordon provides us with the contours of her own desired polity focusing on the undesirable characteristics of our present, with the intention of imagining collectively a better present world.[8] Her utopian society steers its course from all those literary, artistic and political voices excluded from the canon of utopian studies. She indeed draws our attention to the work of the Black Bolshevik Harry Haywood, C.L.R. James, Toni Cade Bambara – all invested in building a better world bereft of discrimination and inequality – as sources of inspiration for utopian studies (2018: vii). She stresses their investment in collective world building and divestment from individualist liberal politics and cooperative ethos (2018: viii). While Gordon's work and intentions are valuable and important, and certainly these excluded authors and activists and their anti-capitalist impulse can give rise to a better society, it may be worth considering whether a utopia that is built out of negation of capitalism is not fated to be limited in its vision of a better life, as it is built precisely on the heels of what it does not want to be. As a result it may inherit the exclusionary mentality that is present in capitalism. Le Guin offers a useful insight here:

---

[8] Just as More's *Utopia* uses the genre of epistolography and conversation – letters written to friends, artists and political associates – discussing ways of creating a better world.

Non-European, non-euclidean, non-masculinist: they are all negative definitions, which are all right but tiresome; and the last is unsatisfactory, as it might be taken to mean that the utopia I'm trying to approach could only be imagined by women – which is possible – or only inhabited by women – which is intolerable. (Le Guin, 2016: 180)

While Gordon is not quite saying that a re-imagined utopia should be made solely from a feminist or a black Marxist perspective, for example, she is nevertheless explicitly suggesting that a utopia needs to be the opposite of our dystopian present. We may think that such a prospect is not objectionable. Don't we all want to live in an equal, just, fair society where there is no discrimination, no poverty, no authoritarian use of power? I doubt that any of you will disagree with this vision, but Le Guin nevertheless is also right. A utopia based on the negative of the now – in Le Guin's case, imagining utopia as the mere opposite of More's – is rather tired, not extending the imagination of any fiction writer. Moreover, if we simply use words that designate the opposite of dystopia to describe utopia, to describe what we desire, it will defeat what we are critiquing. What do I mean by this? It is simple: if we say that our dystopian present is masculinist, then a non-masculinist utopia will always be defined by what is not masculinist, relying inevitably on the very attribute that we are critiquing to shape it. The trick is to be able to imagine utopia in ways that break free from a dialectical logic.

How then are we supposed to imagine this utopia? How can we move away from the blemishes of More's *Utopia*? What new words can take us there? Le Guin offers guidance. As we have already established, Le Guin is critical of the kind of utopias that we inherited from More; they are flawed, exclusionary. So, she sets out to imagine a new utopia. She sets out to find new words that may put More's *Utopia* at a distance. Her journey takes her to ancient Chinese philosophy and with its help Le Guin finds a different word for *Utopia*. Utopia/*Utopia* becomes synonymous to *yang*, the bright and positive side of things. 'Utopia', she writes, 'has been yang. In one way or another, from Plato on, utopia has been the big yang motorcycle trip. Bright, dry, clear, strong, firm, active, aggressive, lineal, progressive, creative, expanding, advancing, and hot.' Our world, she elaborates, has become a totalising yang, so totalising 'that any imagination of bettering its injustices or eluding its self-destructiveness must involve a reversal' (Le Guin, 2016: 180). Imagining, another utopia, requires us to move away from yang, and towards *yin*. Yin in ancient Chinese philosophy is the complementary force to yang, identified with darkness and negativity. Le Guin urges us to return to the yin side of things and imagines a yin utopia as 'dark, wet, obscure, weak, yielding, passive, participatory, circular, cyclical, peaceful, nurturant, retreating, contracting, and cold' (Le Guin, 2016: 181).

It may be hard to imagine Le Guin's utopia at first. She uses affects, natural elements and qualities to describe it. What does it mean, for example, to desire cold instead of hot utopia? If our society has been heated up to such an extent that it is moving towards destruction, if our society has been cocked towards ecological catastrophe – an effect of capitalism and its competitive economic models – then would not some cold energy, an inclination towards cooperation, participation, be the utopia we desire? So, if we are to get to utopia, she writes, we need to rebalance our way of being in the world; we need to cool down the yang.

In her science fiction novel *The Dispossessed*, Le Guin depicts life on two diametrically different worlds: Urras, an authoritarian, masculinist and capitalist world, and Anarres, an anarcho-syndicalist community characterised by horizontal decision making, pacifism, collective living and communal property. It is not my intention to elaborate here on the novel, but I note that the two worlds that Le Guin describes in this novel are modelled after the Chinese yang and yin, Urras being the yang and Anarres the yin. Annares consequently represents a yin utopia. As Le Guin explains:

> The major utopic element in my novel *The Dispossessed* is a variety of pacifist anarchism, which is about as yin as a political ideology can get. Anarchism rejects the identification of power with coercion; against the inherent violence of the 'hot' society it asserts the value of such antisocial behaviour as the general refusal of women to bear arms and other coyote devices. (Le Guin, 2016: 186)

By using a different word to describe the type of utopian polity, yin, we can see how Le Guin is able to paint the contours of a world, an anarcho-syndicalist world, a world that is not constituted because of its opposite (capitalism). The yin utopia on Annares exists parallel to a capitalist world. This yin utopia is not just a feminist utopia – an intolerable thought for Le Guin – but rather one where every concrete subjectivity is able to shape its future and its present collectively precisely because hierarchy, authority and private property are no longer its constituent characteristics. Le Guin's discomfort with monovalent utopias stems from her *worry* that monovalent utopias can be totalising and exclusive. Indeed, Frederic Jameson reminds us that utopia, enticing as it may be, is a '[t]otality [...] this combination of closure and system in the name of autonomy and self-sufficiency' (Jameson, 2010: 677): a characteristic that we may need to be worried about. This worrisome aspect of utopia, its totalising and insular potential, is made apparent in a Jorge Luis Borges story to which I will turn now.

'A Weary Man's Utopia' (Borges, 2001: 65–72) tells the story of the Argentinian Eudoro Acevedo. Acevedo pays a visit to Utopia, a place located in the future where facts are not relevant, where there is no chronology, no statistics; where forgetting has become an art and reading books a rarity; where people have no names and reach maturity at the age of 100. At the age of 100 utopians can live without friendship and decide whether they would like to die or continue living. In this utopia, governments fall into disuse; politicians find new jobs – as comedians or witch doctors; poverty is ameliorated; people build their own houses, cultivate their own food, and engage in the arts. Utopia on this occasion is a place where people are free to live a long life without the restraints of material concerns, without government, without predictive statistics that can be used to control our lives, where each person can be a master of their own destiny and where each person does not need a name to live a good life. It is a society that has unchained itself from the shackles of capitalism; it is a society very far and very different from our own.

'A Weary Man's Utopia' identifies the mechanisms that make our present dystopian life undesirable and builds a world distant from it. As I am writing this, amid a major pandemic, his invocation of statistics as an undesirable mechanism is striking. We all know that both the mining of data and compilation of statistics are methods used by public and private institutions to acquire knowledge about our movements, habits, health, and so on, as well as controlling and influencing our movement and decision making. The effects that these mechanisms have on our freedom have become obvious during this pandemic. Governments use them to impose or relax lockdowns, to measure the stress that infections have on our health systems and to predict our behaviour. Of course, we may think that the use of statistics in this case is beneficial for all; their use predicts areas where the infection rate is higher and enables governments to contain it by confining us to our homes, and thus protecting vulnerable populations. We may say that statistics, as in the case of the pandemic, play a vital role in life. Still, statistics and data are often politicised and used accordingly by governments. For example, currently statistics indicate that Covid-19 is more widespread in BAME communities in the UK.[9] One might have expected that the government would have used these data to prioritise care and support to BAME communities, ensuring for example that they are inoculated first (Parveen et al., 18 February 2021). However, this important information was skirted over, and it was only recently, due to activist pressures, that the Tory government decided to prioritise BAME inoculation. We cannot guess why Borges felt that statistics should not be present in utopia, but the politicisation of statistics and their potential use in ways that are detrimental to populations may be what deterred him from imagining their utility.

We can say though, with some confidence, that Borges' and Le Guin's stories share similarities, as they both identify what (capitalism, bureaucracy, hierarchies, politicians) can make life unbearable. But they have different ways of addressing this problem. While Le Guin invites us to imagine worlds emerging out of yin, and therefore not dialectically opposite to a yang utopia, Borges' utopia is one that provokes a worry. Borges may be sceptical about statistics and other characteristics of the capitalist state, but he is not critical of capitalism; on the contrary, Borges is critical of socialist utopias (Franco, 1981: 77). As Franco explains, 'Borges assumes social action and solidarity to be futile and kill desire' (Franco, 1981: 77). What Borges is interested in is keeping desire open, something that he felt that utopias could not do. The worry utopias generate becomes apparent towards the end of the story. Acevedo watches someone (recall utopians have no names) who has reached the age of 100 walking to the crematorium to end his life, a decision that he is permitted to make as a centenarian. This is an unremarkable activity in utopia. On the journey to his death, someone points to the crematorium and states: 'It is the crematory [...] The death chamber is inside. They say it was invented by a philanthropist whose name, I believe, was Adolf Hitler' (Borges, 2001: 72). This casually thrown-in fact introduces into the story a worry and a warning. We as readers know who Adolf Hitler was – not a philanthropist, for sure. We as readers know that Adolf Hitler was a totalitarian leader. And we know very well that he sent more than 6 million people, mainly Jews, to the gas chambers. We as readers know that Hitler aspired to create a world of national socialism influenced by Darwinian evolutionism. We as readers know that for Hitler, this was his utopia. The reference to Adolf Hitler was, I imagine, not made gratuitously by Borges. Borges introduces a historical figure, Hitler, into the story as a reminder: utopia at any point can become totalitarian. From More, to Borges, to Le Guin, utopian polities are imagined as enclosed polities with their own self-sufficient communities, where poverty is ameliorated, and everybody is equal or not distinct. But utopia becomes dangerous when totalising it becomes akin to totalitarian regimes. It is not coincidental that in the last few lines the narrator reminds us that utopia ought to remain open, remain open to be painted repeatedly by generations to come: 'in [his] study, Cale Mexico still hangs the canvas someone will paint, thousands of years from now, with substances that are now scattered across the planet' (Borges, 2001: 72).

---

[9] The UK Government report *Beyond the Data: Understanding the Impact of COVID-19 on BAME Groups* (London, PHE reports, June 2020) reports that 'the highest age standardised diagnosis rates of COVID-19 per 100,000 population were in people of Black ethnic groups (486 in females and 649 in males) and the lowest were in people of White ethnic groups (220 in females and 22 in males)' p.4 https://assets.publishing.service.gov.uk/government/uploads/system/uploads/attachment_data/file/892376/COVID_stakeholder_engagement_synthesis_beyond_the_data.pdf. (accessed on 18 January 2021).

If there is a lesson that we can take from this short story, from the affect of worry that it produces, it is that re-imagining that utopia may not reproduce the same problems that we find within capitalist societies may be a chimera. In our struggle for a better world, in striving to create an all-inclusive world, we may end up fooling ourselves. The subtle introduction of the figure of Adolf Hitler as a philanthropist alarms and warns us about this possibility. Reading utopia through affects – either affects registered in literary texts, as in More's *Utopia*, or the affects that they produce while reading them, or both – we are also able to see the potential and limits of utopias. Borges' story warns us that everyday utopias of the type that Cooper describes in her book *Everyday Utopias* (2014), or socialist utopias, can be totalising or totalitarian. But I want to suggest here that, counter to Borges' critique of utopia, we can still retain both utopias and open desire. We can do so if we begin to think of utopia as an affect, affecting us in the present, ephemeral, and by untethering our psyche from the attachment to authorial voice and our attachment to monumentalising our individual voice in the future. This speculation or proposition is present in Borges' story, despite his own beliefs that stand against utopias, and especially socialist utopias. We find evidence for this speculation in the very last lines of the story – they insinuate that feeling of letting go of possessive individualism – recall it is someone that will paint the canvas not me – of having our psychic world reorganised so that a 'We' and not an 'I' partake in the formation of a better world, a better present world.

MUTUAL AID

My involvement, in Spring 2020, in my local mutual aid group (Hackney Covid-19 Mutual Aid) enabled me to form the understanding that utopia is not a polity, nor an impulse à la Bloch, but rather an affect that one gets when one works with others to create better worlds. I have indicated so far that utopian affects (anxiety, worry) present in More's and Borges' writings about utopia shift what we have so far come to understand as utopia. Offering a reading that tracks the emotions in these writings as well as the feelings that they prompted in me as a reader enabled me to understand that utopia can be exclusionary, totalitarian, dystopian and yang. Moreover, it unconcealed that re-imagining utopia through its exclusions – including, in other words, in new utopian landscapes/projects all those that have been excluded or all those causes that have not found their way into utopian societies – comes with its own set of problems. They come across as *add-ons* that have the potential for reproducing one of the infrastructural problems of utopia, that of exclusion. Another problem with utopian writings and critiques of utopia is their persistence in pointing to utopia or a better life as taking place in the future. My minimal work with my local mutual aid groups at the start of the pandemic, helping activists/academics such as Aviah Day (Kelly, 23 March 2020) to set them up, to gather people and momentum, was an eye-opening experience. Prior to Spring 2020 I had never worked in mutual aid groups in any way. All my knowledge about them came through reading Peter Krotopkin's *Mutual Aid* (2009). My contribution was minimal: being a middle-aged woman, I felt that it would have been too risky to expose myself to other people, so my role was something akin to a communications officer, bringing people together, gathering information on what was needed to set up functional mutual aid groups and on the needs of local citizens, gathering volunteers and helping to compile lists that organised volunteers into their preferred tasks. To be frank, I did not do much and I did not do it alone. The work of mutual aid made me realise that mutual aid is not a utopian project that resides in the future. The excitement of working with others to ensure that the most vulnerable in the Borough of Hackney were not left unattended or lonely produced in me a huge psychic shift. It enabled me to see that utopia was not something outside me and far-fetched, but something inside me. Utopia brought about a reorganisation of my psychic world that made me shed any scale of possessive individualism that I may have had, that opened me to a *we*, a collective we, that gave me a sense of what Zartaloudis calls 'anti-autonomy autonomy' (Zartaloudis, 2021: copy with me). Utopia was an affect, produced by this collective endeavour; it was ephemeral. I am certain that it affected each member of the mutual aid groups differently, but I am also certain it left its marks on all involved. Indeed, Dean Spade, in their recent book that contemporises mutual aid,[10] talks for example of the way in which ordinary people felt the need to contribute to the local communities from the start of this pandemic, to form solidarities and build mutual aid groups (Spade, 2020). The rush to mutual aid by ordinary people who had no knowledge of the origins and the roots of mutual aid in anarchist traditions evidences further the psychic transformation that one experiences when contributing to the making of a better world. *Pandemic Solidarity: Mutual Aid during the Covid-19 Crisis* (2021), an edited collection of essays brought together by Marina Sitrin and Colectiva Sembrar talking of how mutual aid groups operated globally during the pandemic, expresses the enthusiasm that went into producing the collection. Moreover, the editors explain that their collection was written collectively and how their individual authorship vanished during the production of the collection (Sitrin and Sembrar, 2021: xxii) – a transformative experience. Their psychic world was transformed, and the global mutual aid support they delivered contributed to the creation of better worlds (Sitrin and Sembrar, 2021: xxiv).

We find this idea of utopia as an affect already present in the work of Peter Kropotkin. In 1902, Kropotkin published his book *Mutual Aid* (2009). Kropotkin set out to challenge the then popular theory of 'survival of the fittest', a Darwinian idea (though the phrase itself originates from Herbert Spencer), and show that mutual aid is the most common instinct to be found among animals and humans alike. He identified that mutual aid is practised within families (of both the animal and human varieties) – where he found that the practice of mutual aid dominates – as well as in associations outside the family. For example, he observed that animals share their food or cooperate with one another even if they do not belong to the same family. Bees and ants provide some of his examples demonstrating mutual aid between species. *Mutual Aid* overall tracks the widespread practice of mutual aid in our societies amidst capitalism's dominance. And Kropotkin was right on this effect: the pandemic made visible the existence of the mutual aid instinct that he tracked in his study, with, for example, more than 4000 (O'Dwyer, 23 June 2020) groups mushrooming in the UK. But Kropotkin did not just try to convince us of the existence of mutual aid in our societies. He also identifies that transformative feeling that one encounters when one is working together in making a better world. It is, I think, worth visiting what he writes and citing his words in full here:

> It is not love, and not even sympathy (understood in its proper sense) which induces a herd of ruminants or of horses to form a ring in order to resist an attack of wolves; not love which induces kittens or lambs to play, or a dozen species of young birds to spend their days together in the autumn; and

---

[10] Dean Spade talks of mutual aid as a way of getting involved into social movements and 'produces new ways of living where people get to create systems of care and generosity that address harm and foster well-being' (Spade, 2020: 2).

it is neither love nor personal sympathy which induces many thousand fallow-deer scattered over a territory as large as France to form into a score of separate herds, all marching towards a given spot, in order to cross the river. It is a feeling infinitely wider than love or personal sympathy – an instinct that has been slowly developed among animals and men during an extremely long evolution, and which has taught animals and men alike the force they can borrow from the practice of mutual aid and support, and the joys they can find in social life [...] It is not love and not even sympathy upon which Society is based in mankind. *It is the conscience – be it only at the stage of an instinct – of human solidarity. It is the unconscious recognition of the force that is borrowed by each man from the practice of mutual aid; of the close dependence of everyone's happiness upon the happiness of all; and of the sense of justice, or equity which brings the individual as equal to his own.* Upon this broad and necessary foundation, the still higher moral feelings are developed. (Kropotkin, 2009: 23–4, my emphasis)

In setting out to write this chapter, I had in mind initially to offer a critique of the limits of utopia. I was pretty much aware from the start that utopian projects are or can be exclusive, and utopian projects can also, even if they are of the left variety, turn totalitarian. I was also planning to follow Avery Gordon's cue and identify what types of exclusions utopian literature left out, and try to rectify it by offering an inclusionary version of utopia; I thought anarchism could have attended to these exclusions. Nevertheless, I soon realised not only that any inclusionary utopia will reproduce the structural problems that we encounter in utopian writings, but that it falls into the trap of imagining that utopia belongs to the future. In re-reading More, Borges, Bloch I noticed that utopia was neither a destination, nor a polity, nor future-oriented. Utopia emerged as the feeling that rises when we work together to create a better life – a feeling that first re-organises our psychic world, sheds our possessive individualism and our competitive instinct and releases a somewhat changed self to the world. And this can happen to all, irrespective of one political inclination. The mutual aid group that I belonged to was not just constituted by left liberals. It had assembled people from all walks of life. Utopia becomes akin to euphoria, that feeling that arises, as Kropotkin writes, from 'the close dependence of everyone's happiness upon the happiness of all; and of the sense of justice, or equity which brings the individual as equal to his own'. Utopia may also bring anxiety, weariness, worry. Whatever the affect through its journey, we become not an 'I'. This is the new news from nowhere.

BIBLIOGRAPHY

Athanasiou, A. (2020) 'At Odds with the Temporalities of the Im-possible; or, What Critical Theory Can (Still) Do', *Critical Times*, 3(2), 249–76.
Athanasiou, A. (2020) 'Time and Again, No Longer, Not Yet' in N. Haq, P. Martínez and C. Oprea (eds), *Austerity and Utopia* (L'Internationale, epub), 33–42.
Berlant, L. (2011) *Cruel Optimism* (Durham/London: Duke University Press).
Bloch, E. (1996) *The Principles of Hope Vol. 1* (Cambridge, MA: The MIT Press).
Bloch, E. (1996) *The Utopian Function of Art and Literature: Selected Essays* (Cambridge, MA: The MIT Press).
Borges, L.J. (2001) 'A Weary Man's Utopia' in J.L. Borges, *The Book of Sand and Shakespeare's Memory* (London: Penguin Books).
Brown, W. (2015) *Undoing the Demos: Neoliberalism's Stealth Revolution* (New York: Zone Books).
Cave, N., and the Bad Seeds (2008) 'More News From Nowhere' from Nick Cave and the Bad Seeds, *Dig!!! Lazarus Dig!!!* (Mute Records).
Cooper, D. (2014) *Everyday Utopias: The Conceptual Life of Promising Spaces* (Durham and London: Duke University Press).

Davies, R.T. (2019) *Years and Years* (BBC1 and HBO).
Deleuze, J. and Guattari, F. (1999) *A Thousand Plateaus: Capitalism and Schizophrenia* (London: Athlone Press).
Derrida, J. (1992) 'Force of Law: The "Mystical Foundation of Authority"' in D. Cornell, M. Rosenfeld and D.G. Carlson (eds), *Deconstruction and the Possibility of Justice* (London and New York: Routledge), 3–67.
Foucault, M. (1986) 'Of Other Spaces', *Diacritics*, 16(1), 22–7.
Foucault, M. (2002) *The Order of Things* (London and New York: Routledge).
Franco, J. (1981) 'The Utopia of a Tired Man: Jorge Luis Borges', *Social Text*, 4, 52–78.
Freud, S. (1973) 'About Coca', *Psyche-Journal of Psychoanalysis*, 27(5), 487–511.
Freud, S. (2001) 'Inhibitions, Symptoms and Anxiety' (trans. J Strachey) in *The Standard Edition of the Complete Psychological Works of Sigmund Freud: Volume XX (1925–1926)* (London: Vintage Books).
Gilbert, S. (23 June 2019) 'The Near Future Shock of Years and Years', *The Atlantic* (accessed 30 March 2021).
Goodrich, P. (2015) 'The Judge's Two Bodies: The Case of Daniel Paul Schreber', *Law and Critique* 26, 117–33.
Gordon, A. (2018) *Hawthorn Archives: Letters from the Utopian Margin* (New York: Fordham University Press).
Graeber, D. (2014) *The Democracy Project: A History, a Crisis, a Movement* (London: Penguin).
Graeber, D. and Grubačič, A. (2021) 'Introduction' in P. Kropotin, *Mutual Aid: An Illuminated Factor of Evolution* (San Francisco, CA: PM Press).
Grubačić, A. (4 September 2020) 'David Graeber Left Us a Parting Gift – His Thoughts on Kropotkin's "Mutual Aid"', *truthout.org* (accessed 4 September 2020).
Harvey, D. (2004) 'The "New" Imperialism: Accumulation by Dispossession', *Socialist Register*, 40, 63–87.
Huxley, A. (2007) *Brave New World* (London: Vintage Classics).
Kelly, J. (23 March 2020) 'The volunteer army helping self-isolating neighbours', *www.bbc.co.uk/news* (accessed 23 March 2020).
Knight, T.K. (2017) 'Placeless Places: Resolving the Paradox of Foucault's Heterotopia', *Textual Practice*, 31(1), 141–58.
Kropotkin, P. (2009) *Mutual Aid: A Factor of Evolution* (London: Freedom Press).
Jameson, F. (2010) 'Varieties of Utopia', in *Atlas of Transformation* (transit: JRP/Ringier), 674–9.
Le Guin, U.K. (1999) *The Dispossessed* (London: Orion Publishing House).
Le Guin, U.K. (2016) 'A Non-Euclidean View of California as a Cold Place to Be' in *Thomas More Utopia* (London/New York: Verso), 163–94.
Le Guin, U.K. (2016) 'Utopiyin, Utopiyang' in *Thomas More Utopia* (London/New York: Verso), 195–8.
Levitas, R. (2013) *Utopia as Method: The Imaginary Reconstitution of Society* (Basingstoke: Palgrave Macmillan).
Miéville, C. (2016) 'Introduction' in *Thomas More Utopia* (London/New York: Verso), 3–9.
Milnes, C. and Arnold-Foster, A. (5 March 2019) 'Euphoria a Brief History', *The History of Emotions blog*, https://emotionsblog.history.qmul.ac.uk/2019/03/euphoria-a-very-brief-history/ (accessed 9 February 2022).
More, T. (2009) *Utopia* (London: Penguin).
Morris, W. (2004) 'News from Nowhere' in William Morris, *News from Nowhere and Other Writings* (London: Penguin).
Muñoz, J.E. (2019) *Cruising Utopia, 10th Anniversary Edition: The Then and There of Queer Futurity* (New York: New York University Press).
O'Dwyer, E. (23 June 2020) 'Covid-19 mutual aid groups have the potential to increase intergroup solidarity – but can they actually do so?', *LSE Blogs* (accessed 1 February 2021).
Parveen, N., Mohdin, A. and McIntyre, N. (18 January 2021) 'Call to prioritise minority ethnic groups for Covid vaccines', *The Guardian* (accessed 18 January 2021).
Public Health England (June 2020) *Beyond the Data: Understanding the Impact of Covid-19 on BAME Communities* (London: publishing.service.gov.uk) (accessed 18 January 2021).

Sartre, J.-P. (2004) *Critique of Dialectical Reason* (London: Verso).
Shaw, M. (5 February 2021) 'Billionaire capitalists are designing humanity's future. Don't let them', *The Guardian* (accessed 5 February 2021).
Sitrin, M. and Colectiva Sembrar (2021) *Pandemic Solidarity: Mutual Aid During the Covid-19 Crisis* (London: Pluto Press).
Spade, D. (2020) *Mutual Aid* (London: Verso).
Spivak, G. (1999) *Critique of Postcolonial Reason: Toward a History of a Vanishing Present* (Cambridge: Harvard University Press).
Vaneigen, R. (2017) *The Revolution of Everyday Life* (London: Rebel Press).
Zartaloudis, T. (forthcoming) 'The Experience of Migration: From Metaphor to Metamorphosis' in J. Ahrens and A. Fliethmann (eds), *On Culture* (copy with me).

9. Adda

Debolina Dutta[1]

CHORUS, NOT CACOPHONY

In July 2012, a leading sex workers' collective in India called the Durbar Mahila Samanwaya Committee (DMSC) and the Global Network of Sex Work Projects organised the alternative International AIDS Conference in Kolkata. They called it the Sex Worker Freedom Festival.[2] My place in this event was that of an ally. Having done many collaborative activities with the sex workers' movement in India, at this event, I was curating a panel called 'Respected, Not Policed', with another feminist lawyer. Our focus was on the wide range of punitive laws and policies that punish sex workers for engaging in transactional sex. We were extremely critical of anti-sex work laws, the state and its policies, and how these impact sex workers' lives.

The panel was organised with the awareness that knowledge production often happens at conferences – both academic and activist – without sex workers being included in the conversations, and how such conversations are held in English, excluding sex workers from the Global South due to a lack of access to translation. Much thought was therefore put into translating our critical feminist thinking into the practical organisation of the panel: the topic was selected in consultation with sex worker groups so that we discussed something that would be relevant to their context; a sex worker was included on the panel as a speaker; a colleague was requested to act as interpreter to enable conversation across the three languages (Hindi, Bangla and English) that were being spoken in the room; the seating in the room was rearranged by moving the panellists' seats down from the podium. The status quo of the power hierarchy between sex workers and lawyers was at least symbolically disturbed by the material rearrangement of how and where people occupied positions in the room.

Poornima Chatterjee, a sex worker activist from DMSC, was the second panellist. She spoke about a research study carried out by her organisation on violence faced by sex workers. This was research *with* sex workers, carried out *by* sex workers. As soon as she finished, something dramatic happened – one after the other sex workers in the audience passed around the microphone to each other and started sharing their views on the research. Some of them said, very critically, that given the climate of criminalisation of sex work in India, research studies are unlikely to reveal much about the reality of sex workers' lives.

---

[1] I thank Ann Genovese, Shaun McVeigh, Oishik Sircar and the members of DMSC for being so generous with their time and having interesting and insightful conversations with me, which informed the writing of this chapter. Thanks are also due to Peter Goodrich, Daniela Gandorfer and Cecilia Gebruers for the opportunity to be a part of this exciting volume. My special thanks to Daniela for the helpful feedback on a draft of this chapter.

[2] Travel restrictions imposed by the US government meant many sex workers, especially from the Global South, were unable to travel to Washington DC to attend the International AIDS Conference. Sex workers and allies thus envisaged the Sex Worker Freedom Festival as a place of protest for speaking against such exclusion.

Someone explained: sex workers are seldom going to talk about abuse by clients. This is not only because clients are a source of livelihood, but also because the Indian government is trying to import the Swedish model of criminalising the client.[3] Since sex workers feel that this law will only push the trade underground and increase violence, they wouldn't say anything that could go in favour of passing such legislation. It seemed that their lives had trained them well about how to think with and speak the law.

Meanwhile, a majority of the women in the audience who were sitting at the back left their seats and came and sat on the floor at the front. The distance between us shrank, both materially and metaphorically, as we engaged in a conversation in close proximity, speaking *to* and *with* each other. The sheer symbolism of the shift in the landscape of the sitting arrangement in the room was fascinating – we (the panellists) were no longer facing the audience and imparting knowledge; we were sitting in a circle and had assumed roles as both *speaker* and *listener*. We were collectively expressing and exchanging our disparate views on the legal regulation of sex work. This shape-shifting materialised a form of knowledge about sex workers' lives and law that seemed to be founded on reciprocity, as opposed to hierarchical talk.

What I was witnessing was not an outburst of subaltern-speak that was meant to drown the privileged academic into silence; it was meant to draw her *in* as a participant. Our panel became a place for an engagement like no other, carrying an emotive and affective charge, as we engaged in an appreciation of life and law. Such joining of multiple voices created a chorus of ideas about law and how it is lived and known, akin to the Bengali literary tradition of adda.

This story is not simply about the shifting of power hierarchies and the enactment of a mutual form of Indian sociality, as may be read in light of law and society scholarship, and in which the social, although not in denial of the aesthetic or the literary, subsumes it. In this account of the social, my aim is to foreground the entanglements of the conduct of law *with* the literary and the lived. This illustration is a form of conduct – a coming to life – of the literary tradition of adda which, as you shall see later in this chapter, I will re-work to create a method for recognising law's relations in a context of sex workers' collectivisation.

Law and literature scholarship, in western common law traditions, often tends to see the literary predominantly as a tradition of letters. But to see and articulate the relationship between law and literature in another place and time requires a different kind of orientation to both law and literature.[4] In the context of a Bengali post-colonial life, adda belongs to an artistic and literary genre where it is neither solely text-based nor only about public or published texts, but is embedded in a linguistic tradition in the form of the oral or *moukhik*. Moukhik, in Bangla, refers to that which is tied to speech and what is spoken, as well as the expressional.[5] In other words, adda is as much about the content of speech as it is about the style, manner, gestures

---

[3] For more recent developments relating to anti-sex work law in India see generally, Prabha Kotiswaran, 'The Criminal Law as Sledgehammer: The Paternalist Politics of India's 2018 Trafficking Bill' (*Open Democracy*, 9 July 2018). www.opendemocracy.net/en/beyond-trafficking-and-slavery/criminal-law-as-sledgehammer-paternalist-politics-of-india-s-2018-tr/. Accessed 15 March 2021.

[4] I acknowledge that my articulation and understanding of this is derived from Shaun McVeigh, who shared this during my personal conversation with him about the ideas in this chapter.

[5] Sailendra Biswas, *Samsad Bengali–English Dictionary* (3rd edn., Sahitya Samsad 2000) 885; see generally Shabnam Virmani and Ajab Shahar Team, 'Maukhik Parampara: Oral Traditions' (*Ajab Shahar*, 15 March 2021). http://ajabshahar.com/words/details/66/Maukhik-Parampara. Accessed 15 March 2021.

or conduct of its participants. Law and jurisprudence, similarly, is experienced and expressed in and through the art of conversation such as adda, which is what we shall see in this chapter.

Since my own experiences of thinking and writing this chapter are located not only within a particular genre of thought, but also in Indian academia, my engagement in adda by way of a method for feminist jurisprudence gains significance. Knowledge production in the Indian context has historically been a fraught terrain due to the insidious presence of the hierarchical caste system. The organising logic of caste is written into the systems of academic education and expertise-driven practices of knowledge production.[6] In fact, the academic pursuit of knowledge *per se*, and the question of who has a right to engage in it, is historically embedded within the structure of caste.[7] This is because people's relationship with academic knowledge is determined and mediated by their standing in the graded social hierarchy of caste.[8]

Academic practices are a particularly hierarchical experience for those who have no formal education, or those who speak and write in the vernacular, or those who do not engage in a certain kind of theoretical work.[9] The caste system also has implications for why the practices of certain people would count as knowledge while those of certain others would not. By adapting adda as a method, I show how the activism of sex workers, many of whom are illiterate, contributes to the productions of the field of Indian feminist jurisprudence. With this, sex workers emerge as bearers of their own thoughts and practices of law and not only as subjects of discourses belonging to others, such as myself or other academic researchers. For a feminist working within the Indian post-colonial academia, doing knowledge production in this way is both pleasurable and meaningful.

This chapter is what you might call a creative, imaginative exercise. It is an experiment where I work to invigorate and enact a method that is embedded in practices of post-colonial life, law and literature. To be more specific, what I am going to do is shape and adapt the literary, oral tradition of adda into a scholarly method for relating life, law and literature at a post-colonial location, and to tell a story about the productions of a sex worker feminist jurisprudence.

---

[6] See references to the works of Kumud Pawade, Chandra Bhan Prasad, Pragnya Daya Pawar and Meena Kandasamy in Sharmila Rege, 'Education as "Trutiya Ratna": Towards Phule-Ambedkarite Feminist Pedagogical Practice' (2010) 45 (44–5) Economic and Political Weekly 88. See also Braj Ranjan Mani, *Debrahminising History: Dominance and Resistance in Indian Society* (Manohar 2005); Gopal Guru and Sundar Sarukkai, *The Cracked Mirror: An Indian Debate on Experience and Theory* (Oxford University Press 2017); Kancha Ilaiah, *Why I Am Not a Hindu: A Shudra Critique of Hindutva Philosophy, Culture and Political Economy* (Bhatkal & Sen 2005).

[7] B.R. Ambedkar, 'Castes in India' in Valerian Rodrigues (ed), *The Essential Writings of B. R. Ambedkar* (Oxford University Press 2010) 241; Surinder S. Jodhka, *Caste in Contemporary India* (Routledge 2014).

[8] In India, surnames are an easy determinant of a person's caste status. It can be asserted from the surnames of academics in India, especially those who are internationally renowned for their scholarly works, that a large majority of them belong to upper castes. Raja Jayaraman, 'Personal Identity in a Globalized World: Cultural Roots of Hindu Personal Names and Surnames' (2005) 38 (3) Journal of Popular Culture 476.

[9] Gopal Guru, 'Egalitarianism and the Social Sciences in India' in Gopal and Sarukkai (n 6) 9.

A LIVED, LITERARY TRADITION OF ADDA

But what really is adda, the reader might ask? Adda is an integral part of Bengali life and literature. It has been widely talked about and depicted in literature, art and cinema. Adda is both a place of assembly and an art of conversation. Although linguistic variations may somewhat alter its meaning, these are the two ways in which the term is primarily understood. In the northern parts of India, where people mostly speak Hindi, adda is a noun and denotes a place of gathering, like a bus station (bus adda). In West Bengal, where people mostly speak Bangla, and where I am from, adda is a verb, as it denotes a very particular kind of action or activity or an occurrence of friendly, mutual conversation that is usually carried out between multiple actors.

All the different grammatical iterations and uses of adda share a sense of reciprocal exchange between participants, which is grounded in a place and time. No participant, insofar as conducting the actual activity of adda is concerned, need be either inferior or superior to the others, and some shared ground would have to exist among them to be a part of such conversations. In the way that it is practised in an everyday context, adda enables relations among people through engaged and pointed deliberations that are interpersonal in nature, and consist of wide-ranging subjects. As an oral tradition, it rests on the ability of its practitioners to engage in it cordially and skilfully as an art, and is a source of communal pleasure.[10] Adda is thus an act of coming together, or meeting, of people for a reciprocal exchange of ideas and engagement in pleasurable dialogue with one another, freely and without any fixed or predetermined end in view.[11]

One of adda's foremost proponents, novelist, playwright and journalist Buddhadeva Bose, described adda as an everyday art of conversation that led to collaborative learning and knowledge production. In his essay 'Adda', Bose wrote that the practice was instrumental in shaping his consciousness of the world and played a major role in his emergence as a learned and literary figure. That is why, he noted, he was not a mere 'devotee' of adda but would be a 'priest' who would assume the task, in the essay, of speaking about 'its virtues'.[12] Bose's view of adda finds resonance in the words of prominent Bengali graphic artist, and a member of the Communist Party of India, Debabrata Mukhopadhyay, who wrote: 'my education, whether in art or culture generally, is largely a contribution of adda.'[13]

Even being a Bengali, or Bengali-ness, has been considered by some to be inherently associated with the practice of adda, 'that favourite Bengali activity of energetic debate and raucous dissent'.[14] This Bengali preoccupation with adda is well illustrated in the following scene from Satyajit Ray's film *Agantuk* (The Stranger).[15] The scene takes place in a living room, over a cup of tea and snacks between two men – an anthropologist and a comedian – who are debating the role of adda in shaping the world of arts and culture of the educated Bengali

---

[10] Dipesh Chakrabarty, *Provincializing Europe: Postcolonial Thought and Historical Difference* (Princeton University Press 2007) 205.
[11] Buddhdeva Bose, 'Adda' in Amit Choudhary, *Memory's Gold: Writings on Calcutta* (Penguin 2008) 273.
[12] Ibid 272.
[13] Chakrabarty (n 10) 201.
[14] Mridula Nath Chakraborty (ed), *Being Bengali: At Home and in the World* (Routledge 2016).
[15] Satyajit Ray, *Agantuk* (1991). https://en.wikipedia.org/wiki/Agantuk. Accessed 15 March 2021.

middle-class. It is a conversation *about* adda that is taking place as the two characters engage *in* adda themselves. Even as the two characters ascribe meaning to adda and try to trace its source, they do it in and through adda.

R: Football, and one other thing, that you must be missing abroad, are the Bengalis' lifeblood.

M: What is that thing which I am missing?

R: Bengalis have a monopoly in that, you can also call it their invention.

M: *Rashogolla?*[16]

R: Adda! Unadulterated adda. Adda in the coffee house, near the lake, at the tea stall … without which Bengalis are unable to digest their food. Adda-made-in-Bengal.

M: Allow me to contradict you, Mr. Rakshit. Do you know about the *akhra*, or Gymnasium, that existed in Greece almost two thousand five hundred years ago?

R: Oh, that place for physical exercise?

M: Not only for physical exercise. The Gymnasium was also the place to exercise the mind. In the *akhras* of Athens, Socrates, Plato, Alcibiades and other well-known intellectuals of their time would gather together and engage in intellectual conversations. They spoke about philosophy, politics, mathematics, art, literature … *Dialogues*, which you can read even today. What will you call this?

R: Oh, this is nothing but one kind of adda…[17]

As an everyday art of conversation that is devoid of a fixed agenda, adda is not useless banter. Through the act of meeting with others and engaging in adda, one's own knowledge about the world comes into being, in a pleasurable and leisurely manner.[18] However, this leisurely aspect of adda is sometimes also identified with idleness that is personified in the *adda-baaj*, one who is wasteful and whiles away valuable time. M, in the above instance from the film, is making a similar distinction between productive and unproductive adda. M, by his own admission a Marxist, is alluding to a decadent Bengali-ness that tends to pass off unproductive adda as an expression of high culture, whereas it is merely an excuse for irresponsibility. Although there can be no denying of the fact that adda need not be idealised, it is a distinction between work and play which precedes the separation of productive adda from its non-productive counterpart. For me, the contest between work and play, as well as valuation of adda on these terms, is unnecessary. Questioning its value does nothing to alter its intrinsic place in Bengali artistic

---

[16] 'A beloved confection of fresh milk curd and sugar syrup, rosogolla is most closely associated with the West Bengal sweets-making tradition.' Ishita Dey, 'Rosogolla' in Darra Goldstein (ed) *The Oxford Companion to Sugar and Sweets* (Oxford University Press 2015) 580.
[17] Translated from Bangla to English by the author.
[18] Bose (n 11) 272.

152 *Research handbook on law and literature*

and cultural life. For Bengalis, many scholars and literary writers have noted, the practice has nothing to do with its social benefits. Adda occupies a very special place by virtue of its role in shaping creativity, cultural consciousness and an aesthetic sensibility.[19]

As you can tell, adda is an act of collective and pleasurable immersion in the aesthetics of life and learning. Mere speaking *to* others does not qualify as adda. It is a particular manner of speaking *with* others that generates pleasure and is embedded in a place and time. Adda is a means of experiencing knowledge production and gaining a worldview by engaging in mutual speaking and listening that is physically and emotionally pleasurable. In terms of being an artistic expression, adda defies homogeneity and the dominance of any singular way of thinking, expressing and experiencing knowledge. Adda, performed aesthetically, shapes the habits of the mind and the senses. Adda is born out of forms of life and living that are a melting pot of different religions, languages and gastronomy. The appreciation of such aesthetics requires an appreciation for expressions and entanglements of diverse ideas, however much they may appear contradictory, unrelated or even irrelevant.

Adda as Method

Grounding this chapter in the activism of DMSC, the Kolkata-based sex workers' organisation, I tell a story about the experiences of feminist jurisprudential knowledge production by Indian sex workers.[20] This I do by performing adda as a method, which is an adaptation of the everyday relational activity and not a replication of it.[21] I do not claim, like the above-mentioned proponents of adda, that it is an archetype for gaining a worldview or knowledge. Adda is *not* an idealised mode of engaging in feminist jurisprudential knowledge production. It is also not generalisable and applicable in all contexts.[22]

---

[19] Chakraborty (n 14) 1–10; Bose (n 11) 271–6; Samarendranath Das (ed), *Kolkatar Adda* (Gangchil 2015); Saiyad Mujtaba Ali, 'Adda' in *Rachanaboli: Saiyad Mujtaba Ali* (1st edn., Mitra & Ghosh 2015) 81–9. Although adda appears to hold special significance in the cultural and public life of Bengalis (I am a Bengali myself), it cannot be said that it belongs only to Bengal, or to India. See Chakrabarty (n 10) 183, 205.

[20] For an account of jurisprudence as storytelling, see Peter Goodrich, 'Law by Other Means' (1998) 10 (2) Cardozo Studies in Law and Literature 111.

[21] A bulk of feminist scholarship, spanning many different times and places, is animated by conversations on the question of method, such as what suffices as feminist method, or how method and the content of knowledge are related and jointly qualify to be termed 'feminist', or how it is method which makes a particular form of knowledge feminist or not. See generally Katharine T. Bartlett, 'Feminist Legal Methods' (1990) 103 (4) Harvard Law Review 829; Catharine A. MacKinnon, 'Feminism, Marxism, Method, and the State: An Agenda for Theory' (1982) 7 (3) Signs 515; Kathryn Abrams, 'Feminist Lawyering and Legal Method' (1991) 16 Law and Social Inquiry 373; Maithree Wickramasinghe, *Feminist Research Methodology: Making Meanings of Meaning-making* (Zubaan 2014); Gayatri Spivak, 'Feminism and Critical Theory' (1978) 1 (3) Women's Studies International Quarterly 241; Carol Smart, 'Shifting Horizons: Reflections on Qualitative Methods' (2009) 10 (3) Feminist Theory 295; Carol Smart, J. Hockey and A. James (eds), *The Craft of Knowledge: Experiences of Living with Data* (Palgrave Macmillan 2014).

[22] Gayatri Chakravorty Spivak has pointed out that the meaning and purpose of adda as 'free form chat with many focuses [where] no one tells anybody how long they will speak' is defeated when the practice is put to the task of achieving a definitive end, within a fixed duration of time. My practice of adda is an adaptation of a 'living discourse' and not merely a replication of its everyday conventions and protocols in entirety. I conduct adda with my interlocutors for the particular purpose of reading and

Adda as method helps to acknowledge the productions of feminist jurisprudential knowledge as a form and expression of relationships. It enables drawing attention to how such knowledge production inhabits the enactments and expressions of a reciprocal relationship through conversations. My method is motivated by an impulse to enliven how the art of conversations founds the relations which inform feminist intellectual practices of law.

Predominantly, feminist accounts of law as a site of power, how it causes or magnifies marginalisation, and how it may be resisted abound in India. This chapter is not invested in developing a critique of law.[23] I seek to invigorate a mode of knowing law that happens through its conduct in everyday life. These are conscious activities through which we take up responsibility towards other people and legal knowledge production to actively experience law in the everyday.[24] Rather than look at how law wields power over our lives, I tell a story about how we wield agency to work with it, befriend it and do things with it to organise and structure our life and experiences. These are more mutual law–life relations, which, although significant for understanding how law is lived in post-colonial India, have remained undocumented in scholarly projects of Indian feminist jurisprudence. As an emplaced method of conducting reciprocal conversations, adda helps me acknowledge and tell that untold story of law–life relations.

My story of sex worker feminist jurisprudence will unfold via an introduction into the theoretical foundations of my method, adda. The rest of this chapter thus unfolds through two interrelated sections. In the next section, I discuss how adda has been shaped and adapted into a counter-hierarchical method of reciprocal knowledge-making. Like in the tea-time conversation between the two characters in Ray's film, I shape adda as my method in and through adda. In other words, I work out a method by drawing into conversation traditions of post-colonial, feminist and jurisprudential scholarship. In the final section, I perform the method that I develop. I engage in adda with sex workers of DMSC about their activist literature to show

---

interpreting the texts authored by them. Thus, the performance of adda proceeds with a particular end in view and is time bound with respect to the completion of the writing of this account of Indian feminist jurisprudence. Teaching & Learning TV by UTLO, 'TLHEC8 – Workshop with Prof Gayatri Spivak' (*YouTube* 2 October 2014). www.youtube.com/watch?v=iMTzutBH5eM&feature=youtu.be. Accessed 15 March 2021.

[23] Scholars, across disciplines, have envisaged the relationship between critique and knowledge. As a mode of engagement with knowledge, critique has been largely conceived as involving repair or exposing error or having a better understanding or a fixing and improving, of knowledge. See Wendy Brown, 'Introduction' in Talal Asad, Wendy Brown, Judith Butler and Saba Mahmood, *Is Critique Secular? Blasphemy, Injury, and Free Speech* (University of California Press 2009) 9; Michel Foucault, 'Practicing Criticism' in Lawrence D. Kritzman (ed), *Politics, Philosophy, Culture: Interviews and Other Writings* (Routledge 1988) 152; Margaret Davies, *Asking the Law Question* (4th edn., Thomson Reuters 2017) 207.

[24] Conduct is distinct from critique and is a rival philosophical tradition. Conduct denotes a kind of practical knowledge of being and doing things in the world, a vocation, as opposed to a discourse over which one attains expertise. See Ann Genovese, 'On Australian Feminist Tradition' (2014) 38 (4) Journal of Australian Studies 430. For a discussion on the question of conduct and responsibility in moral philosophy, see Judith Butler, *Giving an Account of Oneself* (Fordham University Press 2005). For arguments about critique and its relationship with knowledge, although not using the language and tradition of conduct, see Michael Warner, 'Uncritical Reading' in Jane Gallop (ed), *Polemic: Critical or Uncritical* (Routledge 2004) 13–38; Rita Felski, *The Limits of Critique* (University of Chicago Press 2015); Eve Sedgwick, 'Paranoid Reading and Reparative Reading' in *Touching Feeling: Affect, Pedagogy, Performativity* (Duke University Press 2003) 123.

how these produce a sex worker feminist jurisprudence. In particular, the story of Indian feminist jurisprudence that I will recount inhabits the collectivisation and organisational practices of the sex workers' movement through which they come to form their relations with law.

A METHOD FOR LAW

The practice of adda entered the field of academic knowledge production through its use by Indian post-colonial scholars in the humanities. These scholars have used adda as a mode of knowing and analysing the discursive productions of critical thought.[25]

Historian Dipesh Chakrabarty uses adda to draw linkages between everyday post-colonial life and discourses of modernity. In Chakrabarty's account, adda serves as a meeting ground and a point of origin for a historicised discursive production of modernity/modern thought. He characterises the middle-class Bengali adda in the early twentieth century as the site of a dialogue between tradition and modernity, in the everyday operation of life.[26]

In showing how post-colonial subjects birthed another kind of discourse about modernity through adda, Chakrabarty demonstrates that a different form of modernity was actively inhabited through a lived tradition at a location other than Europe. This works to decentre Europe as *the* only source of modernity both in the sense of a period and an origin for historical thought. It also works to cast a post-colonial location, the *other* of Europe which is generally understood only as a site of traditions, as a site of the production of modern thought, with adda becoming its source or a means of production. By showing how ideas of modernity and tradition met in, and through, Bengali adda, Chakrabarty illustrates its role in historicising and bringing into conversation varied, even disparate, traditions of thoughts and practices.

It is in the work of literary scholar Gayatri Chakravorty Spivak, however, that adda finds a belonging in feminist thought.[27] Spivak posits reciprocal *speaking* and *listening* in conversations, as in adda, to be a feminist ethic and method of knowledge production.[28] The mutual acts of speaking–listening between a scholar/thinker and the people she is writing about are a metaphor for a relational practice of taking up scholarly responsibility as a feminist.[29] In Spivak's account, conversation is an intellectual practice by which a critical scholar/thinker is able to relate to, and thus ethically narrate the experiences of, others who may be very different/similar to herself.[30] For a post-colonial critical thinker, speaking–listening is thus a practice

---

[25] Chakrabarty (n 10) 201; Gayatri Chakravorty Spivak, 'Can the Subaltern Speak?' in Cary Nelson and Lawrence Grossberg (eds), *Marxism and the Interpretation of Culture* (University of Illinois Press 1988) 271–313.

[26] Chakrabarty explains his choice of material as a deliberate gesture of engaging with 'material from the history of the social group [he] came from'. Chakrabarty (n 10) xvi.

[27] Spivak (n 25) 271–313.

[28] 'Ethics are not a problem of knowledge but a call of relationship.' Gayatri Chakravorty Spivak, 'Echo' in Donna Landry and Gerald MacLean (eds), *The Spivak Reader* (Routledge 1996) 175–202, 190.

[29] 'Subaltern as female cannot be heard or read.' Spivak (n 25) 308; Gayatri Chakravorty Spivak, 'Subaltern Talk: Interview with the Editors' in Landry and MacLean (n 28) 287–308, 289.

[30] Spivak's understanding of knowledge formation through conversation has strong resonances with the work of Italian feminist philosopher Adriana Cavarero. Cavarero speaks about how narrating the other's experiences through the relational means of friendship and dialogue can work against establishing discursive norms of identity and bring out the uniqueness of who we are. Adriana Cavarero, *Relating Narratives: Storytelling and Selfhood* (Routledge 2014).

of reciprocity, enabling the experiences of other people to be adequately expressed and heard, and subsequently represented within critical discourses – even if these are far from those of the person who is representing them, such as in the case of subaltern subjects.

Spivak's account of adda is significant for two reasons. One, it helps demonstrate how adda can be thought of as a method of conducting reciprocal conversations with my interlocutors – sex workers in India – for relating with and narrating their experiences of life and law. Two, it helps to show how adda can facilitate a relationship between disparate ideas and practices that are historically disregarded insofar as their contributions to knowledge production are concerned (namely, the activism of sex workers vis-à-vis the productions of Indian feminist jurisprudence).

Contrary to their promise, according to Spivak, critical discursive representations that spoke about a 'Third World woman' often worked to alienate her from her own experience.[31] In doing so, the intellectual labour of critical scholars/thinkers, and their means of discourse, relegated the Third World woman to the status of a subaltern subject, serving the ends of colonialism.[32] Spivak argues that it is only when a subaltern as woman is called into relation through careful listening that her speech becomes audible, and a meaningful representation of her experiences, comprising both her experiential similarities and differences, becomes possible.[33]

Feminist knowledge production that is enabled through conversations is, for Spivak, a mode of representation that 'entails both a standing-in-the-other's-shoes and an imaginative and aesthetic re-presentation, a staging in the theatrical sense'.[34] Conversations, thus, are a specific kind of feminist practice; while they are a means of learning about and relaying others' concrete experiences by acting as a substitute for them (proxy), they are simultaneously an imaginative rendering (portrait) of such experiences in ethical or relational ways so that the hierarchies of knowledge production may be worked against.[35]

What I learn from Spivak, that proves useful for my adda, is that reciprocal conversation is a means of representing other people's experiences, and a feminist mode of ethically engaging in intellectual practices, by relating with and reading others' texts. Spivak helps me think of adda as means of drawing sex workers into a relationship as my interlocutors through the conjoined activities of mutual speaking–listening for the purpose of relating with, and representing, their lived experiences in and of law.

I perform adda, drawing from Spivak, in the senses of both proxy and portrait. This means that I do adda as an activity whereby I relate the experiences of my interlocutors by both recounting and reimagining these. This is why, as you will see, my performance of adda where I read the activist texts will unfold in two interrelated threads. In the first, I relate how sex workers articulate the correlations between the experiences of law and the social categories of gender/class/caste/sexuality/religion (a representation through proxy); in the second, I do an imaginative rendering of how sex workers' practices of collectivisation may be understood as a sex worker feminist jurisprudence (a representation through portrait).

---

[31] Spivak (n 25) 280.
[32] Spivak writes: 'Western intellectual production is, in many ways, complicit with Western international economic interests.' Ibid, 271.
[33] Spivak (n 29) 287–308.
[34] Spivak (n 28) 16.
[35] For Spivak representations are of two kinds: *Vertreten* and *Darstellen*. *Vertreten* is 'representation as "speaking for", as in politics', and *Darstellen* is '"re-presentation", as in art or philosophy'. Spivak (n 25) 275–6.

Spivak's innovation and its lessons on relationship and representation do not, however, automatically make adda an adequate method for listening to the expressions of law that are born out of sex workers' collective activism. I turn now to thinkers who help me prepare adda as a method in, and for, law.

Adda Meets Jurisprudence

To make adda an adequate method for addressing questions of law, I now join in a conversation with jurisprudents who speak about the *doing* of jurisprudence as a *conduct* of lawful relations, at a place and time. I relate adda with their thoughts to make it a method that is adequate for my project.

Shaun McVeigh and Shaunnagh Dorsett speak about the conduct of lawful relations in the context of one's duties and responsibilities of office.[36] For Dorsett and McVeigh, the questions of office and official duties are related to the exercise of authority as jurisprudents and for conducting lawful relations in public life.[37] To assume authority as a jurisprudent in this case denotes a manner of speaking about law by which one is able to create an ethical relationship between oneself, others and law.

In the western common law tradition, they argue, jurisdiction is a technology and a practice by which a law, any law, attains meaning and authority in the context of lived relations at a place; and it is simultaneously a means of drawing a limitation on law's authority at that place. Thus, 'to approach law through jurisdiction is to approach law as an activity and a conduct of life'.[38] Jurisdiction helps to think about how legal representation is a limited exercise of authority to speak in the name of law.[39] And thinking through jurisdiction helps in tying and limiting law, and the legal speech of its representative, to the specific location from where she speaks and conducts her life. When, in the role of a jurisprudent, one adopts the task of representing and speaking about law, such action takes on meaning as an activity or method for relating life and law, at a place.

The formation of law–life relations by a jurisprudent, for McVeigh and Dorsett, calls for the conduct of lawful relations, which denotes a practice of knowledge formation where law and life have a belonging with each other. This may be done by assuming office and partaking in its activities, which is, in other words, simply a mode of taking responsibility for, participating in and relating with a public life and its various formal and informal institutions.

Ann Genovese provides another account of the conduct of lawful relations as a method for jurisprudence, which is thought through the responsibilities and vocation of a feminist persona. For Genovese, a conduct of lawful relations denotes a relationship of mutuality, shaped through a conduct of the persona of a feminist and jurisprudent and inhabiting the duties of such a persona both in private and in public life.[40]

---

[36] Shaunnagh Dorsett and Shaun McVeigh, *Jurisdiction* (Routledge 2012).
[37] Ibid 139.
[38] Ibid.
[39] Ibid 4.
[40] For an account of how reciprocal law–life relations may be thought through the conduct of office and the official duties of a legal scholar, see Shaun McVeigh, 'Reciprocal Relations: Formations of the Office of Legal Scholar' (2018) 9 (2) Jindal Global Law Review 231–8.

Genovese draws attention to the fact that thinking about how to conduct oneself and one's relations lawfully is significant for practising a feminist jurisprudence that is tied to a place and its lived traditions and history.[41] In the tradition of conduct, everyday practices as they attach to a disciplinary location or status or role or office, denote experiences of 'conscious and productive activity' which are undertaken for changing one's ways of knowing and living in the world.[42] This means that the daily practices undertaken as the philosopher, the feminist, the writer, the sex worker, the jurisprudent, attain meaning and significance for experiencing knowledge in everyday life. For McVeigh, the feminist persona that Genovese talks about – one that undertakes work to create a new kind of role for experiencing knowledge in everyday life – is like that of a minor jurisprudent. The minor jurisprudent is also engaged in working out a juridical persona for participating in a public life not only shaped by office and official role.[43]

Genovese argues that doing feminist jurisprudence in the tradition of conduct involves consciously taking up roles and duties towards others *as* someone or something, and undertaking activities to fulfil such roles. The self, in her articulation, who is both a feminist and a jurisprudent, is not a personae that is formed *only* reactively by external institutions and structures such as the state, patriarchy, colonialism, academia, the judiciary and so on. Such a personae is *also* shaped actively by one's worldview and the execution of a role and duties that are consciously taken up in alignment with one's ethical imaginations of a life in a context. By performing a consciously chosen role and duties towards others as, say, a jurisprudent, feminist, teacher or activist, one is able to form relations ethically, or lawfully, for engaging in the productions of feminist knowledge about the experiences of law.

In the work of the jurisprudents that I am in conversation with, conduct of lawful relations is a method of approaching and shaping law's relations ethically through lived activities at a place and time. It is a means of relating oneself and others with law by conducting activities in a way such that responsibility may be taken for its hierarchical inheritances. In thinking about jurisprudence through conduct, one thinks of it as embodied and emplaced. It is a way of thinking and doing jurisprudence that is viewed as integral to oneself, the world, and one's intimate and official relations, in a specific location and shaped by particular histories.

By joining the works of post-colonial thinkers and jurisprudents, I adapt adda as an act and activity of reciprocal conversations for conducting lawful relations and grounding these at a place and time. I see 'lawful' neither as an antonym of 'lawless', nor as a synonym of 'legal'. The conduct of lawful relations, as I see it, is a situated ethical practice of reciprocity with my interlocutors for fulfilling the responsibility of relating their lives and law, through a shared reading and interpretation of texts authored by them. For me, such responsibility involves two things. One, to make law and its particular experiences visible through my representations of the practices of my interlocutors – the sex workers – by way of both proxy and portrait. Two, to show that my interlocutors carry their own different roles/personae and responsibilities when they speak about law, which resonate in their conversations with me, and are also embedded

---

[41] Ibid; Genovese also makes a similar point. See Ann Genovese, 'Inheriting and Inhabiting the Pleasures and Duties of Our Own Existence: *The Second Sex* and Feminist Jurisprudence' (2013) 38 (1) Australian Feminist Law Journal 41.
[42] Genovese (n 41) 42.
[43] Shaun McVeigh, 'Afterword: Office and the Conduct of the Minor Jurisprudent' (2015) 5 University of California Irvine Law Review 501.

in their texts. Thus, I work to bring adda into my disciplinary location of law as a practical method for *doing* feminist jurisprudence reciprocally with my interlocutors.

I do conversations with the sex workers of DMSC to make sense of their activist literature. These materials have been produced in a context of sex-working women's collectivisation and the consolidation of a movement in India which began in the early 1990s. These materials, published from 1995 to 2016, include activist documents such as a manifesto, a statement, a legal petition, posters, pamphlets, organisational brochures, announcements, annual reports and newsletters. The documents were put together as a result of conversations among sex workers and their allies and have been published by DMSC. These speak about the processes of sex workers' collectivisation, their modes of association, organisational rules and regulations and their worldview.

In my adda with sex workers, I speak with them regarding the meanings and significance of the contents of their activist texts. I listen to how they conceive of, and practise, mutual law–life relations through their processes of collectivisation and the formation of DMSC. As you shall see in the next section, in this way we come to learn how sex workers' activism envisions and enacts a mutual relationship between their lives and law; how they produce a particular sex worker feminist jurisprudence.

THE UNSTOPPABLE WOMEN

DMSC, the sex workers' collective that has produced the activist materials that I am engaging with, have been at the forefront of these conversations with the women's movement. With a membership of more than 65,000 male, female and transgender persons, DMSC is governed and managed by sex workers. The organisation is located in a place called Sonagachi, which is a zoned red-light area in north Kolkata.

Within the busy and narrow lanes of present-day Sonagachi where sex workers both live and work, the office of DMSC is located in a three-storey building. The DMSC's sex worker-funded initiatives are housed in this building on Nilmoni Mitra Street.[44] The sex workers' bank, called USHA Cooperative, and a short-stay home for women who are rescued from the red-light areas through DMSC's Self-Regulatory Boards (SRBs) are also housed here. On the first floor is the office of DMSC's elected general secretary. Each room on this floor is used for various official activities, such as for a health clinic, or official meetings.

The DMSC's donor-funded projects are housed in another building located in a nearby area. This building is populated by sex workers and non-sex worker staff who are employed by DMSC to work on various activities funded by external agencies for the uplift and empowerment of sex workers. The offices also house DMSC's partner organisations, which are groups comprising sex workers' lovers, clients and children.[45] My conversations with DMSC

---

[44] The DMSC's office on Nilmoni Mitra Street was acquired in 2000 with a loan from a nationalised bank.

[45] Komol Gandhar is the performing arts division of DMSC, comprising sex workers and their children. Sathi Sangathan, or the Companions' Collective, is a collective of the non-paying partners of sex workers, who form a part of sex workers' families and communities. Amra Padatik is a collective of the children of sex workers, formed in response to a provision in the Immoral Traffic (Prevention) Act, 1956, which prohibits anybody above the age of 18 years, including sex workers' children, from living on the

members were held within these office premises, which were always buzzing with activity. One could hear sounds of laughter and people talking at all times. Sex workers were seen walking in and out of their offices, appearing to be in a rush, holding an official demeanour. Our adda about activist literature and the formation of DMSC were carried out amid this rush of activities, and were held in our common native language, Bangla.

As we engaged in adda, I was told by many at DMSC that the sex workers' organisation was formed on the basis of a realisation that if women were to assume a role in public life as sex workers, they needed to formalise their organisational activities and form friendships with non-sex worker allies.[46] The sex workers decided to officially register their collective organisation under the West Bengal Societies Registration Act, 1961 (WBSRA).[47] Under WBSRA, societies may be formed through a memorandum of association among seven or more members who have decided to come together for literary, cultural, scientific, political, charitable or even religious purposes.[48]

Rama Debnath, a sex worker and former elected president of DMSC, told me that a group of nine sex workers had first made an application under the law to officially register their collective.[49] In the application for registration, the women jointly decided to call the organisation Durbar, which in Bangla means 'unstoppable'. The application was thus submitted in the name of Durbar Jounokormi Samanyaya Committee (Unstoppable Sex Workers' Coordination Committee).

In 1995, the sex workers submitted their formal application to the Office of the Registrar mandated under WBSRA. Once the application was submitted, the registrar's office rejected DMSC's application without formally stating any reasons.[50] During verbal communications with sex workers, the officials indicated their discomfort with the use of 'sex worker' in the name of the organisation.[51] Due to this, the women decided to exclude the words 'jouno kormi' (sex worker) from the name of their organisation and replaced it with the more generic *mahila* (woman). The application was then sent back to the registrar for re-evaluation. This time, the application did not get rejected. The sex workers' collective organisation came to be officially formed and known as Durbar Mahila Samanwaya Committee (Unstoppable Women's Coordination Committee). Although the words 'sex worker' were dropped from the name of the organisation, the memorandum of association explicitly stated that *only* sex workers could be members of DMSC.[52] Through the process of registration under WBSRA, the women officially initiated a new role in public life as sex workers, which was distinct from the role that

---

earnings of sex work. Anandam is an organisation for lesbian, gay, bisexual and transsexual people who do sex work or are associated with the sex worker community.

[46] DMSC, 'Sex Workers' Manifesto' in Prabha Kotiswaran (ed), *Sex Work* (Women Unlimited 2010) 268.
[47] West Bengal Societies Registration Act, 1961 (WBSRA). www.wbja.nic.in/wbja_adm/files/The%20West%20Bengal%20Societies%20Registration%20Act,%201961.pdf. Accessed 15 March 2021.
[48] Ibid.
[49] Conversation with Rama Debnath, sex worker and member of DMSC, Nilmoni Mitra Street, Kolkata, 18 October 2014.
[50] Ibid.
[51] Ibid.
[52] WBSRA (n 47).

had been deemed to be inhabited by prostitutes as per the Immoral Traffic (Prevention) Act, 1956 (ITPA).[53]

In India, sex workers' relationships in their public/private lives – with partners, family members, neighbours, clients, co-workers – are ordered by the state through ITPA.[54] The ITPA makes '[p]rostitution in or in the vicinity of public place' a criminal offence.[55] In doing so, it assigns culpability to '[a]ny person who carries on prostitution and [even] the person with whom such prostitution is carried on'.[56] The notion of 'public place' held within ITPA's legislative provisions denotes not just a place but also people, because it is defined as 'any place intended for use by, or accessible to, the public and includes any public conveyance'.[57] The *people* constituting a public is not further characterised, but as *place*, it is said to include an 'educational institution', a 'hospital', a 'nursing home', 'any place of public religious worship', and also an area that is within 'two hundred metres' distance of such places.[58] In effect, these provisions work to sever sex workers' being and belonging from a public – as place and people – almost in its entirety.[59]

A sex worker's non-commercial familial relationships, likewise, are also ordered: anybody, including a husband, 'living with, or to be habitually in the company of, a prostitute' is a trafficker;[60] a sex worker's child 'over the age of eighteen years who knowingly lives' on her earnings is also a trafficker.[61] The provisions of the ITPA make almost all aspects of sex workers' lives the subject matter of criminal law. This precludes 'prostitutes' from engaging in any kind of shared community life mutually with other people at the places where they live and work. Sex workers' relationships formed within the institution of marriage are also not recognised, because even non-commercial relationships with husbands and children are included in the ambit of ITPA.[62]

---

[53] Immoral Traffic (Prevention) Act, 1956 (ITPA). https://indiankanoon.org/doc/69064674/. Accessed 15 March 2021.
[54] See generally Ratna Kapur, 'India' in *Collateral Damage: The Impact of Anti-trafficking Measures on Human Rights around the World* (Global Alliance Against Traffic in Women 2007) 114; Ashwini Tambe, *Codes of Misconduct: Regulating Prostitution in Late Colonial Bombay* (Zubaan 2009) xx, xxii; Sumanta Banerjee, *Dangerous Outcast: The Prostitute in Nineteenth-Century Bengal* (Seagull 1998) 59.
[55] ITPA (n 53) Sec. 7.
[56] Ibid Sec. 7(1).
[57] Ibid Sec. 2(h).
[58] Ibid Sec. 7(1b).
[59] For an elaboration of this discussion see Debolina Dutta, 'Of Festivals, Rights and Public Life: Sex Workers' Activism in India as Affirmative Sabotage' (2018) 44 (2) Australian Feminist Law Journal 221.
[60] ITPA (n 53) Sec. 4(2a).
[61] Ibid Sec. 4(1).
[62] In *Subversive Sites*, Ratna Kapur and Brenda Cossman examine how the Indian state conceives female subjectivity based on contradictory divisions of the private and public spheres of women's lives. The authors argue, based on what is an established feminist position in many different places, that a 'familial ideology' informs the ways in which women's lives are perceived by the state and falsely divided into separate domains of private and public spheres. According to them, the formulation of the ITPA points to the fact that it is not the location at which sexual practices are carried out, but rather the perceived public nature of sexuality performed outside the institution of marriage as in the case of sex work, which has caused the latter to be brought within the ambit of criminal law. Ratna Kapur and Brenda Cossman, *Subversive Sites: Feminist Engagements with Law in India* (Sage 1996) 124.

Adda 161

The ITPA locates sex workers outside of a legitimate notion of people contained in its category of 'public', and works to separate them from those whom it includes in this category. Such a hierarchical ordering of sex workers' lives vis-à-vis other people within the community provided a backdrop for women's conversations with state officials and their formation of a new role in public life as sex workers through collectivisation.

Figure 9.1   DMSC booklet calling for the repeal of ITPA

Source: DMSC, Kolkata.

Sex worker and former elected general secretary of DMSC Bharati Dey shared during our adda that with the official registration of DMSC, sex-working women could now assemble in public places without the interference of the police, which was made permissible by ITPA.[63]

---

[63] Conversation with Bharati Dey, sex worker and former elected general secretary of DMSC, Nilmoni Mitra Street, Kolkata, 14 January 2015.

They could also legitimately carry out activities in public places.[64] In order to actualise a collective, or think and act collectively as sex workers in such public places, the women however still needed to create mutual relations among themselves, and with the larger sex worker and non-sex worker community.[65] The registration of DMSC as a formal organisation constituted *only* by sex workers worked towards this end. Sex workers were able to assume a role in public places which was very different from the legal status of 'public women' that ITPA attached to its 'prostitute' subjects; and it provided sex workers a legitimate place to think and act collectively and form relations within a public (see Figure 9.1).

My engagement with DMSC's activism has helped me understand that sex workers envisage a collective in relation to a public that comprises both a place and people. A clear statement of how sex workers of DMSC envision their relations with other people and their place of work through collective activism is available in one particular document, called the *Sex Workers' Manifesto*.[66] The manifesto was first published and circulated in 1997 at the Sex Workers' Festival as a theme paper for the event. It was published both in English and Bangla to reach out to a wider audience.[67] In Bangla, the manifesto is called *E lod(r)ai amader jittei hawbe*, or We Have to Win This Battle.

Even though the *Manifesto* was in English, a language that a majority of DMSC's members could not speak, read or write, the sex workers of DMSC were its co-authors, and the document was key for understanding the experiences of sex workers' collectivisation.[68] In my adda with Mrinal Kanti Dutta, the son of a sex worker and a member of DMSC, he made a distinction between *bhasha* (language) and *bhaab* (expression/meaning) to explain that the words were indeed chosen and put together by friends, allies, staff and sex workers' children, but the words derived their meaning from sex workers' lived experiences and DMSC's activist struggles.[69] For Dutta, the words could only make sense to a reader when they were related with sex workers' lived experiences of discrimination and the collective struggles against it. For me, Dutta's articulation was a demonstration of how DMSC's legal imagination was embedded in a linguistic and aesthetic sensibility.

DMSC argues that the responsibility for discriminatory actions should not be imposed only on individuals. Instead, it should be imposed on a discriminatory worldview that, in fact, makes certain discriminatory actions possible. Therefore, locating responsibility in individuals

---

[64] Ibid.
[65] Ibid.
[66] DMSC (n 46).
[67] Soon after DMSC came into formal existence, it organised the first national conference of sex workers in Calcutta in 1997 as a way of asserting public visibility and reaching out to people. The conference was organised in the form of a festival with dance, music and theatre performances, lectures, debates and food stalls. This was DMSC's first big public event. It was the first time in India that almost 3,000 sex workers from all over the country had come together to talk collectively about their lives and demand rights publicly. The rallying cry at this conference was *gawtar khatiye khai, sramik-er adhikar chai* (we work our bodies, we want workers' rights). DMSC, *Durbar: A Brief Profile* (4th edn., Durbar Prakashani 2011) 59; see generally Moni Nag, 'Sex Workers in Sonagachi' (2005) 40 (49) Economic and Political Weekly 5151.
[68] Conversation with Mrinal Kanti Dutta, founding member of DMSC and son of a sex worker, Girish Park, Kolkata, 30 January 2015.
[69] Ibid.

fails to shake the foundations of such actions, or the worldview of permissibility that enables the oppression of sex workers.[70]

Clients, pimps and madams are admittedly abusive, but DMSC considers them to be the victims of an 'ideology' that permits the abuse and discriminatory treatment of sex workers. The *Manifesto* points out to its readers that '[i]t is important to remember that there is no uniform category as men. Men like women are differentiated by their class, caste, race and other social relations.'[71] Moreover, '[i]n most cases this male client himself may be a poor, displaced man. Is he in a position to value his own life or has he enough motivation to protect his own health?'[72]

The *Manifesto* places male–female relations in a hierarchy, as well as in a continuum of oppression. The document links sex workers' experiences with 'the labourer from Bihar who pulls a rickshaw in Calcutta, or the worker from Calcutta who works part time in a factory in Bombay'.[73] It acknowledges male privilege, alongside sex workers' vulnerability in comparison to other women. It juxtaposes such understanding with an acknowledgment of the additional vulnerability experienced by male sex workers in comparison to women who are engaged in the same profession.[74] For me, as noted earlier, sex workers' thinking on the interrelated nature of class and gender clearly resonates with feminist ideas which shape the field of Indian feminist jurisprudence. The articulation of experiential commonalities between sex workers and these other migrant, marginalised groups of men works to show how 'woman' is understood as a relational category not just in terms of gender or class, but also place. Perceiving the sex worker in these terms further works to clarify the rationale behind the practical workings of USHA, the sex workers' cooperative bank.

Cooperation and Reinhabitation

In 1995, the same year in which DMSC was officially registered, sex workers also decided to form a cooperative bank of their own, which would be located in Sonagachi, and to work to alter sex workers' relations with other people who lived in that place.[75] The reason why sex workers decided to form a cooperative bank was because it would alter their prevalent hierarchical economic relations with the pimps and moneylenders of Sonagachi. More importantly, by virtue of being collectively owned, the financial institution would also train women to think and act collectively vis-à-vis the community of people with whom they shared their lives in Sonagachi.[76]

The state-authorised provisions through which people could form a cooperative financial institution resonated with DMSC's thinking to facilitate mutual relations with the legal

---

[70] 'Conditioned by patriarchal gender ideologies both men and women in general approve of the control of sex trade and oppression of sex workers as necessary for maintaining social order. The power of this moral discourse is so strong that we prostitutes too tend to think of ourselves as morally corrupt and deprived. The men who come to us as clients are victims of the same ideology too.' DMSC (n 46).
[71] Ibid.
[72] Ibid.
[73] Ibid.
[74] Ibid.
[75] Conversation with Smarajit Jana, medical practitioner and chief advisor of DMSC, Girish Park, Kolkata, 30 January 2015.
[76] Ibid.

worldview contained in the provisions.[77] The provisions allowed the members of a cooperative bank to have joint ownership of such an institution, which could also be used for other community-based activities.[78] The West Bengal Co-operative Societies Act, 1983 (WBCSA), which contained this provision, was a product of a cooperatives movement in India.[79] It was enacted for the purpose of financially uplifting poorer communities through the democratic principles of cooperation.[80]

During the colonial period, and also after independence, the cooperative movement gained momentum among political thinkers as an alternative set of ideas and practices that could counter the capitalist economic system of production which left the vast majority of people in India poor and exploited. During colonial rule, the Bengali poet, philosopher and educationist Rabindranath Tagore was one of the most vocal proponents of the cooperative movement. He saw cooperative thinking as a way of challenging the exploitation of the Indian farming communities by the British and the native ruling classes.[81]

Tagore's idea of cooperation included the understanding that the relationship between farmers and their lands was not a relationship of exploitation, but of care and subsistence. In 1928, he wrote *Samabaya Niti*, which was later published in English as *The Co-operative Principles*.[82] *Samabaya* means cooperation, while the term *niti*, which has its origin in the Sanskrit language, denotes a path, behaviour or means of conduct.[83] In *Samabaya Niti*, Tagore suggests that the conduct of cooperation among poor and exploited farmers was an effective means of achieving a just and equitable life for themselves.[84]

DMSC's thinking on cooperative banking, with an intent to craft a new role and responsibilities for women as sex workers in public life, was shaped by drawing on Tagore's world-

---

[77] Ibid.
[78] Ibid; John Restakis, *Humanizing the Economy: Co-operatives in the Age of Capital* (New Society Publishers 2010) 144–5.
[79] West Bengal Co-operative Societies Act, 1983 (WBCSA). www.wbja.nic.in/wbja_adm/files/The%20West%20Bengal%20Societies%20Registration%20Act,%201961.pdf. Accessed 15 March 2021.
[80] Sharit Kumar Bhowmik, 'Ideology and the Co-operative Movement: Worker Co-operatives in the Tea Industry' (1988) 23 (51) Economic and Political Weekly 2703; Satyendra Nath Sen, *Cooperative Movement in West Bengal* (Bookland 1966); Ranabir Samaddar, *Passive Revolution in West Bengal, 1977–2011* (Sage 2013); Anil Bhuimali, *Rural Cooperative and Economic Development* (Sarup & Sons 2003).
[81] In 1916, Tagore wrote *Ghare Baire* (*The Home and the World*), where he was extremely critical of the exploitation of farmers by both the British and nationalist leaders of the Swadeshi Movement who justified the sacrifice of the interests of poor farmers for the greater good of India's independence. Through the character of Nikhil, a zamindar (landowner), Tagore brought out the conflict between the duties of the public office of the landowner towards his subjects and the private commitment of the same individual towards the cause of India's independence. Rabindranath Tagore, *The Home and the World* (tr. Sreejata Guha) (Penguin 2005).
[82] Published in 1963 by Visva Bharati, the resident publication house at Santiniketan (literally, Abode of Peace), the liberal arts school founded by Tagore in West Bengal.
[83] Indian economist Amartya Sen, in the introductory chapter 'A Classical Distinction in Indian Jurisprudence' of his book *The Idea of Justice*, alludes to a similar meaning of the word 'niti'. According to Sen, niti in Indian jurisprudence is an ethical idea representing justice. He writes: '[a]mong the principal uses of the term niti are organizational propriety and behavioural correctness.' Amartya Sen, *The Idea of Justice* (Harvard University Press 2011) 20; see generally Rajendra Prasad, *A Conceptual-Analytic Study of Classical Indian Philosophy of Morals*, vol. 12, part I (Concept Publishing Company 2008) 6.
[84] Rabindranath Tagore, *The Co-operative Principles* (Visva-Bharati 1963) (originally published in Bangla in 1928 as *Samabaya Niti*).

view. I found extracts from Tagore's *Samabaya Niti* in a monthly vernacular magazine called *Durbar Bhavna* (Durbar's Worldview) published by DMSC.[85] A 2014 edition of *Durbar Bhavna* states that Tagore's thinking on cooperatives influenced and also inspired DMSC's cooperative thought (see Figure 9.2). Tagore's belief in the importance of developing internal community strength for tackling problems, rather than a reliance on external help and charity, is significantly incorporated into DMSC's activism.[86] Although Tagore's writings pertained to the specific conditions of farmers in pre-independent India, DMSC draws upon these ideas to use it as a means for sex workers' collective organisation.

Figure 9.2   Durbar Bhavna, DMSC's magazine

Source: DMSC, Kolkata.

---

[85] Rabindranath Tagore, 'Samabyay' (2014) 5(6) Durbar Bhavna 27–34.
[86] Smarajit Jana, 'Editorial' (2014) 5(6) Durbar Bhavna 3–6.

The WBCSA reflects the idea that the collective power of the working-class poor could be consolidated through cooperative action among them.[87] According to this law, cooperatives are envisaged as a third sector of the economy along with the private and public sectors. And the cooperative exists for the benefit of a community through cooperation among its members and responsibility and care for others.[88] The mutual alignments between the objectives of the WBCSA and DMSC's thinking led the sex workers to decide to form a cooperative bank under WBCSA.

In 1995, DMSC made an application under the WBCSA to officially create a sex workers' cooperative financial institution. Just like DMSC's first attempt at registration, the application was rejected by the West Bengal government's Department of Cooperation. The authorities opposed the application on the ground that the statute specified that applicants were required to be of good moral character.[89] Because it was mentioned that the women were engaged in sex work, an activity which is posited as immoral in the ITPA, DMSC's application was rejected.[90] The members of the newly formed DMSC, a group of women who believed they were unstoppable, took up the matter with the state officials.[91]

During sex workers' conversations with state officials in the offices of the Department of Cooperation, one of the officials suggested to the sex workers that the impediment posed by the wording in the statute could be circumvented if the women identified themselves in the application as 'housewives'.[92] The sex workers immediately refused to do so and urged the officials to define what the latter understood by 'moral character'. Sex workers explained that they didn't steal from anyone, didn't kill anyone, didn't take bribes from anyone – unlike most politicians – so there was no question of their being immoral.[93] The officials appeared unconvinced even after a heated debate. This was when one of the sex workers told the minister that she would state in the application form that she was a housewife only if he agreed to marry her right away and attached that status to her name. Otherwise, she argued, it would make her a liar.[94]

The cooperatives minister at the time was genuinely interested in the expansion of cooperative societies.[95] The existing provision in the legislation on the moral character of the applicant, however, remained a ground on the basis of which other government officials raised objections. Unable to act in the presence of such opposition from his own colleagues, and because of the debates that ensued with DMSC members, the minister took up the issue for debate in the state legislative assembly. This resulted in the removal from the act of a provision which required an applicant to be of 'good moral character'.[96]

---

[87] See generally, Bhowmik (n 80).
[88] 'We act consistently with the mission of the organization, being honest and transparent in what we do and say, and accept responsibility for our collective and individual actions.' DMSC (n 67) 8.
[89] Jana (n 86).
[90] The ITPA characterises 'prostitution' as an 'immoral' act, resulting in the characterisation of a prostitute as an immoral person. Ibid.
[91] Conversation with Bishakha Nashkar, sex worker and DMSC member, Kalighat, Kolkata, 21 January 2015.
[92] Conversation with Smarajit Jana (n 75).
[93] Jana (n 86); Restakis (n 78) 135–60.
[94] Conversations with Smarajit Jana (n 75) and Bishakha Nashkar (n 91).
[95] Conversation with Smarajit Jana (n 75).
[96] Jana (n 86).

Documenting the formation of DMSC's cooperative bank,[97] John Restakis argues that the approach of establishing mutual trust within the community was the pivot for the formation of DMSC as an organisation of, and for, sex workers. It was then that the formation of a sex workers' cooperative bank right in the middle of a red-light area became possible.[98] In my adda with sex workers, it became evident that the collective ownership of a financial institution 'of, for and by [...] sex workers'[99] was tethered to women's imagination of a new role and relationships in public life as sex workers. The formation of the bank, inclusive of its rules and regulations, speaks of sex workers' intentions of fostering mutual ties within their community, and with the place where they live and work.

The DMSC's organisational documents state that the USHA cooperative bank was not formed for the purpose of economic *rehabilitation* of sex workers active in the profession. Rather, it was designed to provide financial support to sex workers in situations of crisis, and to 'minimize economic desperation by creating a space for negotiation'.[100] The state-sanctioned rehabilitation programmes which attempt to remove sex workers from their occupation 'through meager income generation activities' are 'unable to erase the social stigma carried by sex workers'.[101] Even if sex workers are taught different activities, these skills are rendered useless because of the stigma associated with sex work, due to which people do not access their services. The DMSC's position on rehabilitation is further explained in the *Manifesto*, which asks: 'is rehabilitation a feasible or even desirable option for us? In a country where unemployment is of such gigantic proportions, where does the compulsion of displacing millions of women and men who are already engaged in an income earning occupation which supports themselves and their extended families come from?'[102]

The ITPA stipulates the 'removal' of sex workers from places where prostitution is carried out in order to 'rescue' women from trafficking.[103] After 'rescuing' her, the police are supposed to present a sex worker to a magistrate. The magistrate is then supposed to determine the 'prospects of her rehabilitation'.[104] Based on what the magistrate deems fit, the sex worker is either sent home or kept in institutional care under the guardianship of the state. The act does not permit adult sex workers, once 'rescued', to decide where they want to go, or with whom they want to live. Against this backdrop, the ownership of a financial institution by sex workers not only provides them with financial support but also enables them to claim their belonging to their occupation, and the place where it is carried out.

Sex workers' belonging to their occupation and place of work is firmly established through the formulation of USHA's by-laws.[105] The latter state that the '[e]conomical [sic] develop-

---

[97] Restakis (n 78) 146.
[98] Ibid 144.
[99] DMSC (n 67) 25.
[100] Ibid (emphasis in original); By-laws of USHA Multipurpose Co-operative Society Limited (n.d.) (on file with author).
[101] DMSC (n 46).
[102] Ibid.
[103] ITPA (n 53) Sec. 2(f) and Sec. 16.
[104] Ibid Sec. 17(2).
[105] By-laws of USHA Multipurpose Co-operative Society Limited (n.d.) (on file with author). This document was originally in Bangla, because none of the sex workers speak English, but was later translated into English by a non-sex worker staff of DMSC.

ment and social *rehabitation* of Sex Worker'[106] is USHA's primary objective. The use of 'rehabitation', a term that is not part of common parlance yet sounds similar to reinhabitation, is telling. In the online *Oxford English Dictionary*, 'rehabitation' is defined as '[t]he action or an act of *reinhabiting* a country, area, house, etc.'[107] The term has a particular conceptual usage in the works of American ecologists Peter Berg and Raymond F. Dasmann, which resonates with DMSC's activism. In the late 1970s, the concept was used by Berg and Dasmann to articulate a practice of responsible living at a place by caring for it and through its restoration.[108] The authors explain: '[r]einhabitation means learning to live-in-place in an area that has been disrupted and injured through past exploitation [...] It involves applying for membership in a biotic community and ceasing to be its exploiter.'[109]

The use of *rehabitation* in the by-laws of the society, as one of USHA's objectives, speaks to sex workers' desire for cooperation among the members of their community in undoing exploitation. It is suggestive of an assertion of sex workers' relationship to their place of occupation and living. It is also suggestive of a desire to make that very place liveable, rather than to be 'displaced' or to be removed or *rehabilitated* to another place and another occupation. In such a formulation, DMSC echoes Berg and Dasmann's idea of living-in-place as a practice of living responsibly by forming a relationship with 'place' and caring for it. The DMSC's re-inhabitation of place is realised through USHA, since it enables women to continue to work as sex workers and fosters mutual ties with those who inhabit Sonagachi, where the women live and work.

My adda with members of DMSC made it evident that the activist practice of reinhabitation tied back to the question of the role and responsibilities that sex workers decided to carve out for themselves when the women first started organising in Sonagachi in the early 1990s. What became apparent as I engaged in adda with sex workers was how the sex workers' intellectual and practical processes of organisation, through which DMSC materialised as a collective, simultaneously involved the formation of mutual relations with law. This kind of relationship with law, which was set in motion by officially designating DMSC as a *sex workers' collective* through registration under the WBSRA, is actualised, for instance, by way of an internal mode of organising mutual relations among sex workers.

Elections in the DMSC, as sex worker Bishakha Nashkar mentioned to me, are a means of self-training in how to take up responsibilities in the role of sex worker activist, and of learning how to execute such responsibilities by thinking collectively and not for individual gain.[110] The electoral process is an elaborate system by which women are positioned in the public and in relation to public institutions as sex workers by placing them in decision-making roles within the sex worker community.

Sex workers' relations within the sex worker community, and with the non-sex worker staff who are employed by DMSC to assist in its work, are founded on 'three "R"s – Respect, Reliance and Recognition'.[111] This refers to '[r]espect towards sex workers, [r]eliance on their

---

[106] Ibid By-law 4(a); emphasis added.
[107] *Oxford English Dictionary* (my emphasis). www.oxforddictionaries.com/definition/english/rehabitation. Accessed 15 March 2021.
[108] Peter Berg and Raymond F. Dasmann, 'Reinhabiting California' in David Pepper, Frank Webster and George Revill (eds), *Environmentalisms: Critical Concepts* (Routledge 2002) 231.
[109] Ibid 232.
[110] Conversation with Bishakha Nashkar (n 91).
[111] DMSC (n 67) 10.

potential and knowledge to run the programme and the [r]ecognition of their professional and human rights'.[112] There are gender, class, caste and educational differences between sex workers and their staff. In order to prevent such differences from translating into hierarchies between them within DMSC, 'the 3 Rs' act as principles of self-regulation. These principles are meant to regulate the conduct of each and every DMSC member to ensure that they remain accountable to their larger collective ideal of cooperation.[113]

Sex worker Purnima Chatterjee shared during our adda that DMSC's regulatory practices, likewise, were not limited only to sex workers.[114] For DMSC, self-regulation refers to a reorganisation of relations among sex workers. It also refers to a practice of the reorganisation of sex workers' relations with state representatives *by* sex workers themselves. This aspect of DMSC's activism becomes evident in engaging with DMSC's conception and implementation of the anti-trafficking mechanism called the Self-Regulatory Boards (SRB).

With the liberalisation of the Indian economy in the 1990s, foreign funding started to arrive for developmental issues, including for women's uplift. During this time, with the advent of the privatisation of the economy, foreign funding for HIV/AIDS programmes and anti-trafficking work increased on a manifold scale, and the sex worker emerged in public and legal discourses as a subject of new forms of state regulation.[115] Simultaneously, a state and NGO regime emerged with a shared anti-trafficking agenda, which fused with the HIV/AIDS-related interventions that targeted sex workers as a high-risk group. The inflow of funds coincided with the 1995 World Conference on Women in Beijing, where India renewed its commitment to the combat of trafficking. In this scenario, a state-authorised anti-trafficking agenda, which already existed and was being carried out through ITPA, was strengthened.[116]

Against this backdrop of state-authorised anti-trafficking measures, DMSC created the SRBs in Sonagachi in 1999 (see Figure 9.3). This localised intervention was specifically aimed at tackling 'the problem of underage and unwilling girls trafficked into sex work sites, and of unwilling women duped/coerced/forced into sex work'.[117] The SRBs' anti-trafficking model is based on what DMSC describes as a 'public–private partnership', because it is instituted through 'collaborative efforts of sex workers and of people from the rest of the society'.[118]

DMSC believes that the state will never repeal ITPA, no matter how assertively sex workers argue that it is discriminatory and ineffective for putting an end to trafficking.[119] Because of this, sex workers themselves had to take the responsibility of putting in place an alternative model that might actually be useful in the situation and create a dialogue with the state. Otherwise, the state would never be willing to involve sex workers in its own discourses on this issue.[120] Sex worker Purnima Chatterjee told me that even if DMSC's model was not

---

[112] Ibid.
[113] Conversations with Bishakha Nashkar (n 91) and Mrinal Kanti Dutta (n 68).
[114] Conversation with Purnima Chatterjee, sex worker and member of DMSC, Nilmoni Mitra Street, Kolkata, 10 October 2014.
[115] See generally Prabha Kotiswaran, 'Introduction' in Prabha Kotiswaran (ed), *Sex Work* (Women Unlimited 2010) xi–lxii.
[116] See generally Kapur (n 54) 114.
[117] DMSC, *Self-Regulatory Board: A Rolling Success in Anti-trafficking Program, Lessons Learnt from DMSC* (Durbar Prakashani 2007) 8 (on file with author).
[118] Ibid 13.
[119] Ibid.
[120] Ibid.

Figure 9.3   DMSC booklet on the Self-Regulatory Board

Source: DMSC, Kolkata.

perfect, it was useful for starting public discussion, debate and contemplation of trafficking based on sex workers' activist experiences. Most importantly, SRBs were able to challenge the foregone conclusion about the effectiveness of punitive measures as the only possible means of addressing trafficking.[121]

Bharati Dey recounted in our adda that sex workers needed to present an alternative model that was able to speak to the anti-trafficking discourse of the state, albeit differently, and that only then could the state be drawn to carry out mutual discussion with sex workers.[122] For sex workers, Dey told me, the state was an important public institution.[123] It was necessary

---

[121]   Conversations with Purnima Chatterjee (n 114) and Smarajit Jana (n 75).
[122]   Conversations with Bharati Dey (n 63), Purnima Chatterjee (n 114) and Smarajit Jana (n 75).
[123]   Conversation with Bharati Dey (n 63).

for instituting structural changes in sex workers' lives which were not possible through small-scale interventions. The state machinery is also considered to be an important catalyst for undoing social stigma, provided that sex workers are themselves able to make the institution and its laws work to their own advantage (see Figure 9.4).[124]

Figure 9.4   *'Law as a friend of sex workers': A DMSC booklet on sex workers' legal rights*

Source: DMSC, Kolkata.

Through adda with sex workers, it becomes evident that DMSC's intention of making the state work in its favour is accompanied by methods that are distinct from the state-sanctioned anti-trafficking approach to sex work. Rather than aiming for the penalisation of traffickers,

---

[124] Conversations with Bharati Dey (n 63) and Bishakha Nashkar (n 91).

the focus of SRBs is on trafficked persons. Greater importance is given to privacy, confidentiality and respect for the decision-making capacity of the trafficked person. The SRBs focus on providing 'career building opportunities [to the trafficked person] instead of taking decisions on her behalf'.[125] The rescued person's preference is also given priority in deciding whether she is sent to her own residence or kept in institutional care.[126] The DMSC believes that long-term institutionalisation of a rescued person amounts to a prison-like condition in which a person's need for a shared life and livelihood is not met.[127]

SRBs attempt to tackle trafficking 'by making it non-viable [...] [for] madams and brothel owners to recruit underage or trafficked persons as sex workers'.[128] DMSC believes in convincing pimps and madams that employing underage and unwilling persons is a harmful practice. Dey noted during adda that convincing madams to willingly cooperate with DMSC, rather than punishing them, could ensure long-lasting systemic change. This is something that the adversarial approach of criminal law – the ITPA – fails to do.

A SEX WORKER FEMINIST JURISPRUDENCE

It is my own experience of that panel turning into an adda almost a decade ago which motivated me to write this account of sex worker feminist jurisprudence. As you can see, doing this required some work of imagination to invigorate a method that was adequate for my task. I needed to re-work adda – a literary practice from Bengal – into a method which helped me ground jurisprudence at a specific place, displace the singular interpretive authority of the lawyer and broaden the authority of meaning beyond the written word, to include the oral or *moukhik*. This is what makes adda relevant for law and literature scholarship in a post-colonial context. It enables us to see that the meanings in the activist literature are not only in the letter of the text and its interpretation isn't the prerogative of the lawyer alone. Legal wisdom and meaning making are tied to everyday speech, proximate forms of cohabitation, shared intonations and expressions and relational forms of living, of which the texts are a part.

I participated in adda with DMSC members about their experiences of collectivisation which were mentioned in their activist literature. A shared meaning of the contents of the literature emerged through our discussions and interactions, grounded at the organisational site of DMSC in Sonagachi. I invested in careful listening to what my interlocutors had to say about their collective practices and the thinking behind these, to understand the significance of the arguments made by DMSC through its activism. I paid attention to how sex workers explained their own experiences of collectivisation and its interconnections with the place at which the collective is formed. Based on such exchange, I correlated the contents of DMSC's activist texts, sex workers' experiences of collective activism and the place at which the activism is conducted.

This shared method reveals that DMSC's distinct feminist jurisprudential discourse is produced through sex workers' collective activist ideas and practices of 'cooperation' and

---

[125] DMSC, *Community-Led Anti Trafficking and Child Protection Programme* (Durbar Prakashani 2013) 19 (on file with author).
[126] Ibid.
[127] Ibid.
[128] Ibid 18.

'reinhabitation'. The official registration of DMSC, SRBs and USHA is founded on 'cooperation' and 'reinhabitation'. Through these organising principles, sex workers conduct their activism and shape their collective role and responsibilities in public life as jounokormi/sex workers, to form mutual relations with other people and with law. Sex workers have achieved this mutuality by reorganising the hierarchical relations of gender and class experienced by them in Kolkata. Mediated by such alteration of hierarchies, sex workers have also reorganised their relation with the Indian state, and altered the criminalised status and conditions accorded to them by the state. DMSC's organisational practices and experiences of activism have produced a mode of non-adversarial feminist jurisprudence.

In the process of crafting a new role as sex worker, and the responsibilities associated with it, the women shaped their two tenets of activist conduct: 'cooperation' and 'reinhabitation'. These principles were practised by means of the official registration of DMSC as a society under WBSRA in 1995; the formation and registration of a cooperative bank called USHA in 1995; and the formation of a local anti-trafficking mechanism called SRBs in 1999.

The formation of SRBs and USHA and the official registration of DMSC are two-pronged activities. On the one hand, these develop an account of gender and class based on the specific activist experiences of sex-working women in Sonagachi, which are then brought by DMSC to its engagements with law or legal issues, such as trafficking. On the other hand, these activities inhabit and perform a representation of a sex worker-self in legal discourse who is shaped by practising 'cooperation' and 'reinhabitation'. The sex worker shaped by DMSC is thus developed as distinct from the state-authorised criminal subject of the ITPA, who is not accorded any decision-making power over her life and livelihood and not considered to be a responsible person.

Through 'cooperation' and 'reinhabitation', sex workers of DMSC shaped their collective role in public life as sex workers, to form mutual relations with other people and with law. The performance of adda helps to understand how DMSC's processes of collectivisation in Kolkata are not just a form of activism. They are sex workers' expressions and experiences of a legal imagination and practice which produce a non-adversarial mode of a sex worker feminist jurisprudence.

10. Cartographies
Sabarish Suresh[1]

Maps surround and make our world. We live amid and through maps. Our lives have been putatively made easier through the use of all sorts of maps, from navigation maps to park maps, from thematic weather maps to choropleth electoral maps, from atlases in libraries to revolving globes in schools. Maps are ubiquitous, assumed to be omniscient, and have historically been omnipotent. However, it has also been argued that maps are duplicitous, subjective and culturally and politically manipulable.[2] It has been suggested that maps wield force, as a tool of political power, and even *constitute* nations and national subjectivities in various forms.[3]

Despite a recent increase in cartographic scholarship that focuses on the interstices of cartography and ideology, cartography and epistemology, and cartography and cultural technologies, for instance, there has hardly been much engagement on the relationship between law and cartography. While legal scholarship has definitely witnessed what Philippopoulos-Mihalopoulos calls 'a recent rather trendy spatial turn', attention to cartography and mapping as a crucial component in the constitution of law and the juridical has not been as apparent or specifically attended to in the scholarship on legal geographies.[4]

This chapter focuses on the nexus between cartographic practices and the creation of law. The principal claim that this essay makes is that laws, systemically, cannot *do* without maps. Maps constitute an indispensable basis for the coalescence of legal sovereignty. The national territory, as an idiosyncratic political concept, is an intricate admixture of law and cartography. As Michel Foucault once declared, '*Territory* is no doubt a geographical notion, but it's

---

[1] I would like to thank Daniela Gandorfer and Ashley Tellis for incisive comments on earlier versions of this chapter. Peter Goodrich not only read and commented on multiple drafts but also provided tremendous encouragement and support in conceptualizing and writing the chapter. Lucy Chester was kind enough to share invaluable cartographic and archival input on text and maps. All mistakes and omissions remain mine.

[2] J.B. Harley, *The New Nature of Maps: Essays in the History of Cartography* (ed. Paul Laxton) (Maryland: The Johns Hopkins University Press, 2001), at p.159.

[3] See, for instance, Benedict Anderson's treatment of maps in the creation of national communities. 'Census, Map, Museum' in Benedict Anderson, *Imagined Communities: Reflections on the Origin and Spread of Nationalism* (London: Verso, 2006).

[4] Andreas Philippopoulos-Mihalopoulos, *Spatial Justice: Body, Lawscape, Atmosphere* (London: Routledge, 2015), at p.7. See also, Irus Braverman, Nicholas Blomley and Ors (eds), *The Expanding Spaces of Law: A Timely Legal Geography* (Stanford: Stanford University Press, 2014); David Delaney, *Nomospheric Investigations: The Spatial, the Legal, and the Pragmatics of World-making* (Abingdon: Routledge, 2010); Nicholas Blomley, David Delaney and Richard T. Fort (eds), *The Legal Geographies Reader: Law, Power and Space* (Oxford: Blackwell Publishers, 2001). I have deliberately avoided adding Boaventura de Sousa Santos's seminal essay 'Law: A Map of Misreading' to this list because this text is not so much an investigation of the relationship between law and cartography as it is an analogic discourse on the sociology of law, using concepts familiar to cartography.

first of all a juridico-political one: the area controlled by a certain kind of power'.[5] Territory enunciates the extent of legal power, becomes the *site* of the *lex terrae*; and maps control not just the description but also the inscription and *reproduction* of territory. Matthew Edney writes, in the context of British Indian Cartography, that '[t]o govern territories, one must know them', and the British used cartography as a bedrock of their colonial construction.[6] Political cartography and political philosophy have made valiant attempts to adumbrate this process of territorialization.[7] A legal engagement with mapping and the creation/reproduction of territory, however, is yet to develop sufficiently. To that extent, this essay may be read as an engagement with a *cartographic jurisprudence*, arguing that the juridical bases itself upon, makes use of, works with and *works through* cartography. *Cartographic jurisprudence* refers to the study of the ways in which law is inscribed through cartography, and how law, in turn, makes use of cartography to reinscribe and reproduce its power, territory and sovereignty.[8] There is a double movement in this operation: first, the cartographic delimitation of law and territory, and second, law's adoption of cartography to sustain, legitimate and justify its force. As such, the process is *always already* at work.

The juridical makes considerable use of maps as texts in its discourse, and has even attributed a precedential status to certain *official* maps. Using the Radcliffe Boundary Commission's awards[9] as illustrative texts, this chapter examines how the juridical becomes a crucial and productive site where maps are sacralized, read exegetically and reproduced as authoritative texts on territory and legal sovereignty. Through such an endeavour, the essay attempts to unravel and exhibit the overlapping operations of law and cartography, their networks of interpretive practices, their epistemic assumptions, their material and affective ramifications. Another reason for the selection of India as an illustrative example is because of the present-day continuity of colonial cartographic practices, and of juridical deference to colonial cartographic axioms. As Edney notes, the colonial cartographic conception of India 'was adopted without question in the second half of the nineteenth century by Indian nationalists […] This position is enshrined in the present-day state of India'.[10] As this chapter will expound, it is such a conception that is central to India's legal discourse and even structures some of its crucial constitutional doctrines on unity and territorial integrity.

---

[5] Michel Foucault, 'Questions on Geography' in Jeremy Crampton and Stuart Elden (eds), *Space, Knowledge and Power: Foucault and Geography* (Aldershot: Ashgate, 2007), at p.176.

[6] Matthew H. Edney, *Mapping an Empire: The Geographical Construction of British India, 1765–1843* (Chicago: University of Chicago Press, 1997), at p.1. In many ways, the Empire was primordially based on cartographic imaginations: '[T]he geographers created and defined the spatial image of the Company's empire. The maps came to define the empire itself, to give it territorial integrity and its basic existence. The empire exists because it can be mapped; the meaning of empire is inscribed into each map': p.2.

[7] Stuart Elden's text is the most exhaustive genealogical exploration of the concept of territory as yet. Stuart Elden, *The Birth of Territory* (Chicago: University of Chicago Press, 2013).

[8] Crucial to this conception is Stuart Elden's argument that '[t]erritory is not simply an object: the outcome of actions conducted toward it or some previously supposedly neutral area. *Territory is itself a process, made and remade, shaped and shaping, active and reactive*' (emphasis added). Elden, *The Birth of Territory*, at p.17.

[9] The Radcliffe Boundary Commission was set up towards the end of British colonial rule in India with the express objective of delimiting the erstwhile British Indian territory into the new nation-states of India and Pakistan.

[10] Edney, supra note 6, at p.16.

FROM POLITICAL CARTOGRAPHY TO CARTOGRAPHIC JURISPRUDENCE

Cartography literally means 'to write the earth'.[11] As a method of writing, it is a site of productive discourse. As Didi-Huberman has evocatively exhibited, reading the map, or the atlas, is a reading 'in the wide sense that Benjamin gave to the concept of *Lesbarkeit*'.[12] Far from reading the cartograph as a static text, this involves a 'reading before anything else, that is, before any "serious" reading or any reading "in the strict sense"'.[13] The map, much like the atlas, resists traditional methods of reading, from left to right, from top to bottom or even from front to back. Reading the map, in the sense that Didi-Huberman calls our attention to, is both implosive and anarchic. It defies rules of reading and is rhizomatic, without a fixed beginning or end. Precisely owing to its nature as text and as image, it embodies the space of a table, the *operating field*, as opposed to a tableau.[14] The shorthand *text/image* will be used in this chapter to indicate this complex position and function that the map occupies. Traditional cartographic discourse, however – which is institutionalized, professionalized and standardized – works around certain axiomatic principles which it perceives as its central tenets. It would be useful to conceptually classify the history of cartographic discourse into three levels of reading. There is a double-purpose to this proposal. First, the three levels of reading maps as elucidated here also corresponds roughly to the chronological shifts in the history of cartographic thought.[15] Second, these levels also take a cue from, and revise, the three layers of meaning conceptualized by Erwin Panofsky in his reading of paintings.[16]

In Panofsky's discourse, the First (or 'natural') level of reading paintings involves reading it on a surface level. We interpret the painting based on the facts displayed on the canvas and by observing what is in front of us. It corresponds to what lawyers love to call a 'literal interpretation' – to view something as simply given and as what is. The Second (or 'conventional') level of reading paintings pertains to a more nuanced identification and historical understanding of the artistic motifs. It involves prior knowledge of artistic tradition which allows the painting

---

[11] Nicole Reiz, Shannon O'Lear and Dory Tuininga, 'Exploring a critical legal cartography: Law, practice, and complexities' 12 *Geography Compass* (2018).

[12] Didi-Huberman, *Atlas, or the Anxious Gay Science* (Chicago: University of Chicago Press, 2018), at p.7.

[13] Ibid.

[14] The 'operating field', of which the table is an instance, for Didi-Huberman, 'is a determined place – framed like a *templum* in every possible expanse, the sky, the sea, a flat stone, the liver of a sheep – capable of making heterogenous orders of reality meet, then of constructing this very meeting in place of overdetermination'. Ibid, at pp.39–40.

[15] This is by no means to suggest that cartographic historiography follows a teleological or linear path. In contrast, the material available suggests that the discourses classified here do not constrain themselves to particular points in time. However, these levels must be looked at as corresponding to chronologically shifting domains of dominant cartographic thought. In many ways, some of the discourses classified in the secondary and tertiary levels emanated simultaneously as a critique of the primary level, and elements of the tertiary level have been subsequently utilized even to critique the reading practices of the secondary level.

[16] Erwin Panofsky, *Meaning in the Visual Arts* (New York: Doubleday, 1955). For a cartographic adoption of Panofsky's layers, see 'Texts and Contexts in the Interpretation of Early Maps' in JB Harley, *The New Nature of Maps*. The three levels of reading maps proposed here, however, do not correspond to the proposal of Harley, and deviate significantly in some crucial aspects.

to be situated in a proper context. Panofsky terms such a method of reading as 'iconographical analysis in the narrower sense'.[17] The Third (or 'intrinsic') level of reading paintings allows one to view the painting for both its conscious and its unconscious manifestations. This level necessarily involves an investigation of the epistemic underpinnings of the painting, and situating the painting as a text/image in a larger cultural history of knowledge production. For Panofsky, in this method 'we deal with the work of art as a symptom of something else which expresses itself in a countless variety of other symptoms'.[18] The artist himself may be unaware of his unconscious manifestation or of his complicity in a larger cultural epistemology. Panofsky terms this level of reading as the 'iconographical analysis in a deeper sense'[19] and exalts it as the 'ultimate goal of iconology'.[20]

The primary level of reading maps deals with the conventional and traditional propositions of cartographic discourse. Postulations that maps were accurate representations of stable and objective reality, independent and distant from the cartographer, observed in an unbiased way and reproduced without any predilections, were some of the closely held axioms of traditional cartography. For Didi-Huberman, this would work as a classic instance of 'reading in the strict sense'. The secondary level of reading maps refers to investigations of subjective manipulations. On one level, all maps distort reality.[21] 'Behind the map maker lies a set of power relations, creating its own specification.'[22] The secondary level then refers to the reading of maps through a historical understanding of the predispositions of the map-maker, or of that particular culture of map-production, cartographic 'motifs' if you will. It involves viewing maps as argumentative and as rhetorical, as portraying a *particular* narrative.[23] The tertiary level of reading maps situates the map as a technique of producing/proliferating cultural and political knowledge. It pertains to the affective and visceral propensities of the map as well as the ways in which maps create particular subjectivities. It involves an epistemological investigation and situates maps as key tools in the production of knowledge. It is this level that is most relevant for an understanding of law's imbricate relationship with cartography. The tertiary level shifts the focus from the subject engaged in map-production (the map-maker, the agency, the surveyor, and the technician) to assessing maps, in their own right, in the foreground of larger epistemological questions. This level works to unpack the secret and intimate relations in maps, their correspondences and their analogies. To borrow from Bernhard Siegert, it involves interpreting maps as 'spaces of representation' rather than 'representations of space'.[24] And thus sensible objects, aesthetic and affective expressions as well.

Take for instance the cartouche attached to James Rennell's map – *Hindoostan* (Figures 10.1 and 10.2) – which will be used as an illustration for both secondary and tertiary reading. While cartouches were hardly uncommon in the eighteenth century, they were not usually

---

[17] Erwin Panofsky, *Studies in Iconology: Humanistic Themes in the Art of the Renaissance* (Oxford: Oxford University Press, 1939), at p.7.
[18] Ibid, at p.8.
[19] Ibid.
[20] Ibid, at p.9.
[21] Harley, supra note 2, at p.63.
[22] Ibid.
[23] Ibid, at p.163.
[24] Bernhard Siegert, 'The map *is* the territory' 169 *Radical Philosophy* 13 (September/October 2011), at p.13.

178 *Research handbook on law and literature*

as elaborate as this one.[25] It is pertinent to remember that James Rennell was the famous surveyor-general appointed by Lord Vansittart, the erstwhile Governor of Bengal.[26] The Cartouche accompanies a map of erstwhile '*Hindoostan*', depicting the extent of the British East India Company's territories in juxtaposition with Mughal and other Princely territories. In the Cartouche, deferential and genuflecting *Pundits* (Brahmins) are seen handing over the 'shaster' (*Shastra*, rendered here as 'shaster', is a codified text of Hindu religious laws) to Britannia. James Rennell's description of the Cartouche runs as follows:

> *Explanation of the Emblematic Frontispiece to the Map*
>
> *Brittannia receiving into her Protection, the sacred Books of the Hindoos, presented by the Pundits, or Learned Bramins: in Allusion to the humane Interposition of the British Legislature in Favor of the Natives of Bengal, in the Year 1781. Brittannia is supported by a Pedestal, on which are engraven the Victories, by means of which the British Nation obtained, and has hitherto upheld, its Influence in India: amongst which, the two recent ones of Porto Novo and Sholingur, gained by General [Eyre] Coote, are particularly pointed out by a Sepoy to his Comrade.*[27]

The Cartouche signifies the glory and power of the British Empire, with the British lion's foot atop the globe. Britannia's spear rests not on barren land but on 'a bolt of cotton cloth', the main Indian export to Europe.[28] The Cartouche is situated in the white space of the Bay of Bengal, signifying the territoriality of the British *demesne* in the Indian subcontinent. The presence of the cartouche – with a list of Britain's military conquests inscribed on the pedestal, with opium poppies in its wreath above (itself next to a sword and a caduceus), the Company's ship made visible in the background, and Britannia herself appearing as a 'humane Interposition', all of which is inscribed within the confines of a cartographic depiction – signifies that there is a political and ideological argument being made *through* the cartographic representation, of commercial, military, spiritual and civilizational superiority. As Edney rightly notes, this iconography develops from an established tradition in which India is personified according to 'notions of place as a function of commerce or as a reference to the Orientalists' enthusiasms'.[29] The very presence of dividers and other mathematical and cartographic instruments *under* Britannia's spear betrays the fact that the very procedure and method of cartography practised is far from an objective technique where the object is distant from the cartographer and where the cartographer himself is 'value-free'. Objectivity, in the form of scientific instruments, is itself subjugated here under a divine, imperial presence. If this signifies objectivity, then it is certainly a *British* rendition of objectivity.

If the secondary level of reading maps investigates the predilections of the map-maker, the tertiary level shifts the focus from the map-making subject to the map-reading or viewing subject. The focus is on the epistemic propensity of the map, of the kinds and forms of knowledge that it produces, and the ways in which it *situates* subjects in particular hierarchized identities. That the map produces the subject is not surprising given the tendentious history of linear perspective. 'The illusion of reality that linear perspective creates works only when

---

[25] Edney, supra note 6, at p.13.
[26] Sidney Lee (ed.), *Dictionary of National Biography*, vol. XLVIII (New York: Macmillan & Co, 1896), at p.14.
[27] Edney, supra note 6, at p.13.
[28] Ibid, at p.15. See also Barbara Groseclose, 'Imag(in)ing Indians' 13 *Art History* 488 (1990).
[29] Ibid, at p.13.

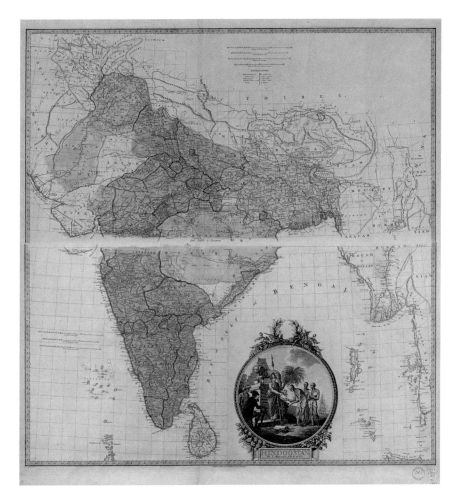

Figure 10.1   Rennell, J., Phillips, J. I. & Harrisson, W. (1782) Hindoostan. [London: Published according to act of Parliament by J. Rennell, December 1st]

Source: Retrieved from the Library of Congress, https://www.loc.gov/item/2009582749/.

the eye is at a fixed position and distance from the picture.'[30] The perspective of the viewer constitutes a relationship not only of the viewer and the object viewed, in space and time, but also among different viewers. The Renaissance painter Brunelleschi set up a 'peephole', through which his paintings were to be viewed.[31] The positioning of the painting simultaneously positioned the viewing subject. The 'peephole' established, in the words of Simon Ryan,

---

[30]   Simon Ryan, 'The Cartographic Eye: Mapping and Ideology' in Caroline Guerin, Philip Butterss and Amanda Nettelbeck (eds), *Crossing Lines: Formations of Australian Culture: Proceedings of the Association for the Study of Australian Literature Conference* (Adelaide, 1995), at pp.13–14.
[31]   Ibid, at p.14.

Figure 10.2   Cartouche accompanying James Rennell's map

Source: Retrieved from public domain under the Creative Commons License.

a 'fixed, external and "objective" view'.[32] Ryan postulates that '[i]f Brunelleschi's 'peephole' connotes a kind of voyeuristic pleasure as well as the more straightforward power inhering in the external observer whose presence orders and controls all, then perhaps maps offer a similar viewing position'.[33] He notes that maps' possession of this potent capacity was made evident by the sixteenth-century Brabantian cartographer Abraham Ortelius when he presented a map as a device to 'peepe upon those places, townes and Forts, which lye most advantagious and commodius to satisfy […] ambition'.[34] Maps situate the subject in a particular position in space, and time.

---

[32]   Ibid.
[33]   Ibid.
[34]   Ibid.

That maps have such a propensity is well exhibited by Matthew Edney in his study of how colonial maps are constructed. Extensive surveying of landscapes, Edney charts out, led to the creation of the British geographical archives.[35] The archives, however, stored static descriptions and observations of places and phenomena, 'a rational and ordered space that could be managed and governed in a rational and ordered manner'.[36] The archive was constituted entirely out of linear perspective and by stupefying objects as static reality. However, as Bernhard Siegert has noted well, maps are more than just tools of the author's predispositions, and, for that matter, are beyond just static constructions based on archival knowledge. 'The marks and signs on a map do not refer to an authorial subject but to epistemic orders and their struggles for dominance over other epistemic orders, in the course of which marks and things enter a new play of signs. The cartographic operations produce a subject, which correlates to them.'[37] They play a crucial role in positioning the subject in a constructed hierarchy and works towards enclosing the subject in that position. Maps in this sense also structure legal operations and enable the force of law. Rennell's cartouche offers a ready case in point.

In the Cartouche, the Pundits are handing over a copy of the *Shaster* to Britannia, in allusion to the 'humane Interposition of the British Legislature in Favor of the Natives of Bengal'. Historical scholarship on British codification of Indian religious laws reveals larger connotations to this image. The year in which the cartouche and the map were published is 1782. A decade earlier, in 1772, Warren Hastings, the first Governor-General of the Fort William Presidency, enacted a regulation which pushed for the codification of Hindu and Muslim personal law.[38] The first such codified text, translated from Sanskrit to English, was *A Code of Gentoo Laws; or, Ordinations of the Pundits* by Nathaniel Brassey Halhed, published in 1776.[39] In this pursuit of codification, the British were guided by an assumption that 'there was historically in India a fixed body of laws, codes, that had been set down by "law givers" and that over time had become corrupted by accretions, interpretations, and commentaries'.[40] Britannia then is receiving the *Shaster*, as a benevolent act, in order to syncretize Hindu laws, 'in Favor of the Natives of Bengal'. She brings with her a legal acumen and rationality to bestow upon the Natives a unified and systematic religious law. A secondary-level reading would reveal that Rennell was in active service, surveying the Company territory, in the

---

[35] Edney, supra note 6, at pp.34–5.
[36] Ibid, at p.34.
[37] Siegert, supra note 24, at pp.13–14.
[38] Ronojoy Sen, *Articles of Faith: Religion, Secularism, and the Indian Supreme Court* (Oxford: Oxford University Press, 2019), at p.42. For a detailed exposition on the British intervention in Hindu personal law and subsequent codification, see Brian K. Pennington, *Was Hinduism Invented? Britons, Indians, and the Colonial Construction of Religion* (Oxford: Oxford University Press, 2005).
[39] The word 'Gentoo' is a predecessor of the word 'Hindu'. The term 'Hinduism', as a term used to signify a single religion, came into vogue only as late as the nineteenth century. It was by and large introduced by British intervention. Robert Frykenberg notes that the term 'Hindu' was used to pejoratively 'characterize all things in India (especially elements and features found in the cultures and religions of India) which were not Muslim, not Christian, not Jewish, or, hence, not Western'. In that sense, it merely replaced the earlier Persian term 'Gentoo' which signified heathens. See Robert Eric Frykenberg, 'The Emergence of Modern "Hinduism" as a Concept and as a Institution: A Reappraisal with Special Reference to South India' in Gunther D. Sontheimer and Herman Kulke (eds), *Hinduism Reconsidered* (New Delhi: Manohar Publications, 1991).
[40] Bernard S. Cohn, *Colonialism and Its Forms of Knowledge: The British in India* (New Delhi: Oxford University Press, 2002), at p.69.

years of Hastings' Governorship. The Companies' policies and political considerations were a significant underpinning in the portrayal of the map and its cartouche. A tertiary reading, however, asks the question of the map's ramifications. Where does the map position the native subject? How does it construct the identity of the native subject? What is the affective and emotive outcome of the text/image?

The text/image of Rennell's map, along with its cartouche, brings into play, emotively and affectively, the native subjects' history, temporality and identity. The pundit is genuflecting before Britannia, who is positioned on an elevated pedestal, and who promises to syncretize the laws. Britannia is accorded the place, position and power of benevolent law-giver. The map becomes not just the diagrammatization of a geographic survey, but a statement, a resolution, a premonition, and simultaneous appropriation of legal authority. The map, on which landscape Britannia will perform her duty, becomes a pictorial and symbolic site of her legal territory. The map along with the cartouche transmits a legal ordinance. The map becomes a legal text in its own right in its *visiocratic* ordering.[41] In this sense, the map positions and constitutes the native subject in a particular hierarchy, as a subject of Britannia, as a subject of her benediction and law-making power. It becomes a medium to display her power, and through that it also becomes a visual basis of her legal authority. The tertiary level of reading maps goes beyond questions of authorial intentions to epistemic ramifications. It demands an investigation of how it situates subjects and produces identities out of hierarchies, how the state presents a map and the affect of such a presentation. It also demands an investigation of the state's covert operations and censorship of maps and what that signifies for the juridical. Siegert calls the constitutive power of the map a *cultural technology*. It is indeed a technology in which the map *creates* a legal territory, a jurisdiction to enforce its laws, and a medium through which land is transmogrified into the *lex terrae*. Brian Harley was right to note, in his study of the Empire's maps, that they often anticipated the Empire (to which it can be added that it also created the visual and epistemic bases for imperial laws), proliferated myths and legitimized the Empire.[42]

THE PARTITION OF INDIA AND THE BOUNDARY COMMISSIONS

If imperial maps created the territorial site for colonial laws, and situated the native subject as a colonial subject, they also contributed in a paradoxical way to the dismantling of the Empire and the creation of independent nation-states, and national subjects. Maps become functional tools of both assemblage as well as dismemberment. Insofar as imperial maps worked to constitute the native subject *in a particular way*, they also worked, not dissimilarly, to create citizens of the nation-state according to a particular conception. The Radcliffe Boundary Commissions acted as that juridical body which cartographically legitimated the transition of the colonial subject, bound by colonial laws, to citizens of new nation-states, bound by national laws. As was the case with India and Pakistan, emerging nation-states, especially

---

[41] On *visiocracy*, see Peter Goodrich, 'Visiocracy: on the futures of the fingerpost' 39(3) *Critical Inquiry* 498 (2013). For a wider exploration of the theme, see Peter Goodrich, *Legal Emblems and the Art of Law: Obiter depicta as the Vision of Governance* (New York: Cambridge University Press, 2014).
[42] Harley, supra note 2, at p.57.

when emerging from Partition, are often accompanied by elaborate cartographic negotiations and, to a large extent, cartographic imagining even precedes and anticipates the nation-state.[43] As such, the working of the Boundary Commissions are an exemplary instance of how cartographic jurisprudence is performed. The focus here is on how particular maps were used for the shaping of particular national and territorial aspirations, and how national laws came to be inscribed, and reinscribed, through the use of mapping. Thongchai Winichakul reveals this phenomenon in the context of Thailand's territorial formation:

> In terms of most communication theories and common sense, a map is a scientific abstraction of reality. A map merely represents something which already exists objectively 'there.' In the history I have described, this relationship was reversed. A map *anticipated* spatial reality, not vice versa. In other words, a map was a *model for*, rather than a *model of*, what it purported to represent.[44]

In a crucial sense, Winichakul's thesis ties with Bradin Cormack's argument that the textual material of the law comes to substitute *for* the real.[45] In Cormack's reading of Shakespeare's England, *the paper* and *the parchment* occupy 'a second reality, the one through which, namely, the law becomes able to exercise its peculiar authority'.[46] The map too occupies a similar role in the production and reproduction of law and authority. It is such a 'peculiar' authority of the law made possible through the use of maps that a reading of the Radcliffe Boundary Commission's awards exposes. The map circumscribes an epistemic space of its own, a space of representation, that conditions and configures territories and laws and substitutes itself for the visceral realities of the land. The Boundary Commission therefore becomes an instance of the operation of cartographic jurisprudence: as to how maps inscribe legal authority and how they are used, in turn, by the law to reproduce and reinscribe territory, sovereignty and authority.

In the summer of 1946, the British Government had dispatched a Cabinet Mission to India comprising Lord Pethick-Lawrence, Sir Stafford Cripps, and Mr A.V. Alexander.[47] The objective was to offer a constitutional package to preserve the territorial unity of India. India was a territorial exemplification of the greatness of the British Empire. The Empire had (ostensibly) *unified* and created a compact India for the first time, which was considered to be a feat of

---

[43] It has been commonplace to argue, especially after the publication of Ayesha Jalal's *The Sole Spokesman: Jinnah, the Muslim League and the Demand for Pakistan* (Cambridge: Cambridge University Press, 1985), that cartographic imaginations accompanying the Pakistan demand were deliberately vague, blurred, ambiguous or even completely absent. However, see Lucy P. Chester, 'Image and Imagination in the Creation of Pakistan' in Tabea Linhard and Timothy H. Parsons (eds), *Mapping Migration, Identity, and Space* (Cham: Palgrave Macmillan, 2019), at pp.137–58, who argues that cartographic conceptions of Pakistan were not as vague and underdeveloped as they were made out to be. According to Chester, 'advocates of Pakistan articulated their demands with a high level of geographic (and other) detail' (137), which exemplifies that cartographic conceptions not just accompany but even precede and anticipate the nation-state.
[44] Thongchai Winichakul, 'Siam mapped: a history of the geo-body of Siam' (PhD Thesis, University of Sydney, 1988), at p.310; emphasis added.
[45] Bradin Cormack, 'Paper Justice, Parchment Justice: Shakespeare, Hamlet, and the Life of Legal Documents' in Beecher and Ors (eds), *Taking Exception to the Law: Materializing Injustice in Early Modern English Literature* (Toronto: University of Toronto Press, 2015), at p.47.
[46] Ibid.
[47] Yasmin Khan, *The Great Partition: The Making of India and Pakistan* (New Haven: Yale University Press, 2017), at p.56.

British brilliance and pride. Figures 10.3 and 10.4 represent the territorial expansion of British territories in India. The cartographic representation signifies that territories were classified as either British, Hindu or Muhammadan. Once occupied by the British Empire, the territory lost its Hindu or Muhammadan character, at least cartographically, as can be seen with the increase of the pink shade across the landscape over the years. The unity of landscape under a single regime implied, for the British, not just political unity but also social unity.[48] The cartographic depiction of *unity* came to substitute any real political or social unity. As long as the vast mass of land could be under one regime, political unity and social unity was assumed to follow, by imposition if not by negotiation. Cartographic unity preceded, and even set the mood for, an appearance of social and political unity. It was such a (misconstrued) unity that the Cabinet Mission sought to preserve.

The Cabinet Mission's proposal of a three-tiered constitutional federal structure failed to meet the approval of either the Muslim League or the Indian National Congress.[49] In the foreground of the unfolding cataclysm, Attlee announced, on 20 February, that the British intended to completely withdraw from the subcontinent no later than June 1948.[50] With the crucial mission of transferring power, Louis Mountbatten was dispatched as British India's last viceroy. Mountbatten had a single goal: to transfer power as soon as possible before the country erupted in flames. The British were desperate to avoid any association with the violence about to engulf the subcontinent.

Despite the hurry that overarchingly characterized the entire process, the British Government was determined to present its withdrawal as orderly and rational. It was crucial that the Radcliffe Boundary Commissions appear cartographically and juridically sound to solidify this presentation. On 3 June 1947 the Partition plan, also known as the Mountbatten plan, was officially announced over the radio in India by Mountbatten, followed by Nehru, Jinnah and Baldev Singh (representative of the Sikhs) in that order.[51] Clement Attlee presented the plan in the House of Commons and stated:

> The Provincial Legislative Assemblies of Bengal and the Punjab (excluding the European members) will [...] each be asked to meet in two parts, one representing the Muslim majority districts and the other the rest of the Province. [...] The members of the two parts of each Legislative Assembly sitting separately will be empowered to vote whether or not the Province should be partitioned. If a simple majority of either part decides in favour of partition, division will take place and arrangements will be made accordingly.[52]

---

[48] As Chester argues, the project of cartographic unification 'implied that India could be completely understood, in scientific terms, and that, in addition, this complete understanding could be transferred to the map-reader through the cartographic medium'. Needless to say, such a pictorial depiction was duplicitous given that the 'British understanding of the subcontinent coexisted with serious misunderstanding'. Cartographic unity created the fiction of a social unity which would also be carried over by the independent Indian state. Chester, *Borders and Conflicts in South Asia: The Radcliffe Boundary Commission and the Partition of Punjab* (Manchester: Manchester University Press, 2009), at pp.20–1.

[49] Khan notes that 'exactly *why* the Cabinet Mission failed so spectacularly has long been the stuff of nuanced debate about the intentions and motives at the top level of negotiations'. Khan, supra note 47, at p.60.

[50] Ibid, at p.83.

[51] Ibid, at pp.1–2.

[52] *Statement of Prime Minister Clement Attlee*, HC Deb 03 June 1947 vol 438 cc35–46, at pp.36–7.

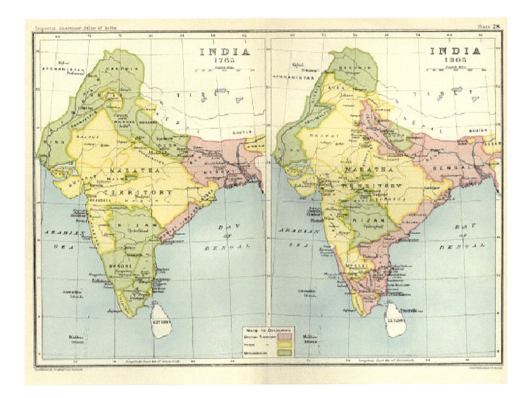

Figure 10.3   Historical Maps of India, 1765 and 1805

Note: The legend indicates 'British Territory' (pink), 'Hindu' (yellow) and 'Muhammadan' territories (green).
Source: W.S. Meyer, R. Burn, J.S. Cotton and H.H. Risley, *The Imperial Gazetteer of India*, Vol. 26, Atlas, 1909 (Oxford: The Clarendon Press, 1909), p.28.

The representatives of Muslim-majority districts and of other parts met separately in both Punjab and Bengal. The Muslim-majority district representatives voted against partition in both provinces, while the non-Muslim representatives voted for partition in both provinces.[53] Considering that the 3 June Plan stated that partition will be carried out 'if a simple majority *of either side* decides in favour', the plan for partitioning Punjab and Bengal was set in motion. The two Boundary Commissions – for Punjab and Bengal – were to be constituted at the earliest.

Mountbatten proposed that 'a man experienced in judiciary affairs would be most suitable'.[54] Leaders of the Congress and the League were in general agreement with this proposal, even believing that 'individuals with a judicial background were likely to provide "fair" and "true" decisions'.[55] From the outset, the idea that legal expertise was a sufficient, even necessary, qualification for cartographic decisions seems to have been manifest. The emphasis was on ensuring a *distributive justice*, cartographically imagined and textually transliterated,

---

[53] For a detailed examination as to why each side voted in this manner, see Jalal, supra note 43.
[54] Chester, supra note 48, at p.28.
[55] Ibid, at p.29.

186 *Research handbook on law and literature*

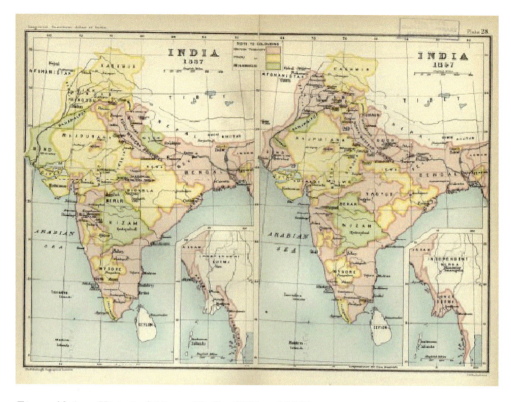

Figure 10.4   *Historical Maps of India, 1837 and 1857*

Note: The legend indicates 'British Territory' (pink), 'Hindu' (yellow) and 'Muhammadan' territories (green).
Source: W.S. Meyer, R. Burn, J.S. Cotton and H.H. Risley, *The Imperial Gazetteer of India*, Vol. 26, Atlas, 1909 (Oxford: The Clarendon Press, 1909), p.29.

which could ensure an equitable and fair distribution of land and resources to the two warring factions. The entire process was based not on surveys on the ground and subsequent demarcations, but on cartographic drawings in boardrooms and subsequent *textual* delimitations.[56] This, it was presumed, could be achieved only by jurists of high calibre. Each commission was to have four members – two nominated by the Congress and two by the League – all of whom were to be 'persons of high judicial standing'.[57] The terms of reference drafted for the two commissions borrowed predominantly from the 3 June plan and read as follows: 'The Boundary Commission is instructed to demarcate the boundaries of the two parts of the Punjab

---

[56]   In the final Radcliffe Awards, it was made explicit that the text was to take precedence over the maps. The map was anarchic and too dangerous, and the viewing had to be subjugated, disciplined and mediated by the text.
[57]   Chester, supra note 48, at p.31. Pertinent to note that Jinnah was the only person who suggested that the Commission must comprise of people who possessed technical expertise of boundary-making. His suggestion was, in Mountbatten's words, to have 'three entirely impartial Non-Indians with experience of this kind of work'. This suggestion was shot down by officials in London as well as the Congress. Chester, at pp.30–1.

on the basis of ascertaining the contiguous majority areas of Muslims and non-Muslims. In doing so it will also take into account other factors.'[58]

A notional boundary was drawn, for administrative purposes, using the 1941 census data.[59] Sir Cyril Radcliffe, who had earlier been considered for the Arbitral Tribunal that would resolve disputes arising out of Partition, was eventually appointed as the Chairman of both the Punjab and the Bengal commissions.[60] The London *Times* heralded Radcliffe's appointment by specifically cataloguing his legal qualifications and expertise, which made him an ideal candidate for the Boundary Commission.[61] Attention was drawn specifically to the fact that Sir Cyril Radcliffe was 'one of the leaders of the English Bar [...] a King's Counsel [... and] a Bencher of the Inner Temple'. It was apparent, or at least made out to be so, that cartographic boundary decisions were judicial in nature, and lawyers made the best cartographic decisions.

The Boundary Commission was instructed to finish the task of drawing the boundary before 15 August 1947, the appointed date for the transfer of power.[62] Radcliffe arrived in India on 8 July, with less than six weeks remaining before the deadline.[63] The Boundary Commission was to conduct public hearings in Lahore and Calcutta. The sites of the hearings, revealingly, were the High Courts of Lahore and Calcutta.[64] The boundaries were to be declared in the form of an 'award' as prescribed by the Indian Independence Act of 1947. As will be evidenced in the next section, the procedure was manifestly cartojuridical, performed in a juridical space, according to legal-cartographic procedures of evidence, testimony and written submissions. If cartographic jurisprudence is the epistemic admixture of cartography and law which makes territory and sovereignty possible, cartojuridism is the operation and systematic procedure which performs a cartographic jurisprudence. The Boundary Commissions' operation with its judges, legal and cartographic arguments, and evidence in the form of maps, submitted according to legal procedures, was neither purely juridical nor purely cartographic, but cartojuridical in its operation that followed and further proliferated a tradition of cartographic jurisprudence. The cartojuridical award given as a decision by the Commission not only created Indian and Pakistani territories, but also served as a precedential text for the Supreme Court of India, further ensuring the material continuity of a cartographic jurisprudence.

---

[58] Ibid, at p.26.
[59] A map showing the notional boundary may be viewed here: www.panjabdigilib.org/pdl/Downloads/stuff/026_000179__Partition%20Plan%20for%20Panjab%20-%20Showing%20Notional%20Boundary%203%20June%201947.JPG. Hindu-majority territories are shaded pink, Muslim-majority territories green, and Princely States yellow. The Princely States were given the choice to join India or Pakistan upon the transfer of power.
[60] Chester, supra note 48, at pp.33–6.
[61] *The Times*, 5 July 1947, p.4.
[62] Chester, supra note 48, at p.38.
[63] Ibid, at p.55.
[64] Hannah Fitzpatrick, 'The space of the courtroom and the role of geographical evidence in the Punjab Boundary Commission Hearings, July 1947' 42 *South Asia: Journal of South Asian Studies* 188 (2019), at p.192.

THE ARGUMENTS BEFORE THE BOUNDARY COMMISSION

That law and geography are intricately linked in the drawing of a boundary has been variously assessed by legal geographers. An authoritative text on boundary-making declared that at the stage of delimitation legal and geographical discourses are crucially intertwined, and that such an intertwining is even a necessary one.[65] While there are positive appraisals of law and geography working together,[66] geographers have also critiqued law's overshadowing of geography. A British geographer, Thomas Holdich, who served the Empire, castigated the British tradition where judges take up the role of boundary-making, sidelining geographers and surveyors who are most relevant to the process.[67] As has been indicated above, however, mapping serves an indispensable critical function for the law, and it is hardly surprising that law inclines to take over the process of territorialization. The operations of the Boundary Commissions in India are but symptomatic of this larger tradition. The arguments before the Boundary Commission were peculiarly cartojuridical, not just in embodying particular procedures and evidences which confluenced law and cartography together; the juridical even took on a priority in its admixture with cartography. Cartographic materials were meticulously appropriated as legal evidence. In that process, it became patently evident that the cartographic material, far from being objective representation, was rhetorical and political, appropriated with the hope of constituting nations and national subjects according to particular conceptions.[68] That maps were used to project specific national and territorial aspirations becomes evident if Figure 10.5 is closely perused. Figure 10.5 shows the province of Punjab and the competing claims of Congress and the Muslim League as to where the boundary line must fall. Unsurprisingly, the Congress–Sikh claim lies further West, and the Muslim League claim lies further East. Each claim had its own interpretation of the terms of reference, specifically with regard to what the 'other factors' clause ought to mean. These subjective, competing and politically aspirational interpretations were then transformed into putatively objective and accurate maps and submitted as legal evidence to the Boundary Commission. What this serves to indicate is that the legal argumentation, or more appropriately the cartojuridical argumentation, far from being objective representation, was a matter of subjective postulations of nationhood, territory and sovereignty. Each of the maps submitted proposed a different boundary, based on different imaginations of not just national territory but also who should be the citizens of the respective nation-state. These maps do not just help to decipher the various claims put forward by the respective parties; they also reveal that maps, as Brian Harley suggested, are easily susceptible to political and legal manipulation.

Even a primary-level reading of the map will indicate that the territorial claims of each map overlap and contradict each other. Opposing claims to land are made as part of a cartojuridical

---

[65] Stephen Barr Jones, *Boundary-Making: A Handbook for Statesmen, Treaty Editors and Boundary Commissioners* (Washington, DC: Carnegie Endowment for International Peace, 1945), cited in Fitzpatrick, supra note 65, at p.190.

[66] Ibid, at p.190.

[67] Thomas Hungerford Holdich, *Political Frontiers and Boundary Making* (London: Macmillan & Co. Ltd, 1916), cited in Fitzpatrick, supra note 65, at p.190.

[68] On maps and rhetoric, see Harley, supra note 2, at p.163. Harley reads maps as inherently rhetorical through a deconstructive method of reading the map as a text. For an incisive critique of Harley's reading of Derrida and Foucault, see Barbara Belyea, 'Images of Power: Derrida/Foucault/Harley' 29 *Cartographica* 1 (1992).

argument, posited through a legal method. A brief look at the nature and the method of the proceedings before the Punjab and the Bengal Boundary Commissions will reveal the concrete operations of a cartographic jurisprudence. The arguments posited, the methods used, the procedure adopted and the kind of knowledge assumed, controlled and disseminated are all key components and cartojuridical operations of a cartographic jurisprudence.

Punjab Boundary Commission

The Punjab Boundary Commission, like its Bengal counterpart, was composed of Cyril Radcliffe and four judges (two nominated by the Congress and two by the League).[69] Because the hearings of the Punjab Commission were conducted simultaneously with the Bengal Boundary Commission, Radcliffe did not attend any of the hearings. Nor did he attend the Bengal hearings. He was sent transcripts of the hearings on a daily basis.[70] The Congress had appointed a notable lawyer, M.C. Setalvad, to represent its case, and the Muslim League had appointed a British-trained barrister, Sir Zafrullah Khan.[71] There was no geographer or cartographer appointed to aid the commission, and the procedure did not accommodate receiving any expert testimony.[72]

From the beginning, the proceedings were characterized, foremost of all, by *a juridical atmosphere*. The atmosphere was tense and heavily guarded. O.H.K. Spate, an Australian geographer who attended the hearings, made the following remark of the site: 'Found right court-room by observing concentration of armed police. Gothicy room, fairly cool [...] big dais with shabby royal arms; usual dust and general air of stuffy archives.'[73] The law is about the record, about the archive, about a monumental and grandiloquent presence, performed in a sacred site which dispenses justice. The geographer's appraisal of the room is not an unusual perception of the juridical. Something important was happening here, and it was something legal. The grandiloquence and visual accoutrements of the legal space are, as has been pointed out time and again, a critical component of the performance of law.[74] Law operates visually,

---

[69] All the judges nominated to the Commission were judges of the Lahore High Court. The judges nominated by the Muslim League were (a) Muhammad Munir, who eventually became the Chief Justice of Pakistan, and (b) Din Muhammad. The Congress nominated (a) Mehr Chand Mahajan, who went on to become the Chief Justice of India, and (b) Teja Singh, a Sikh representative who became the Chief Justice of the erstwhile PEPSU State. Chester, at pp.57–8.

[70] Chester, supra note 48, at p.59. See also Ishtiaq Ahmed, 'The 1947 Partition of Punjab: Arguments Put Forth before the Punjab Boundary Commission by the Parties Involved' in Ian Talbot and Gurharpal Singh (eds), *Region and Partition: Bengal, Punjab and the Partition of the Subcontinent* (Oxford: Oxford University Press, 1999), pp.116–67.

[71] Chester, supra note 48, at pp.59–60.

[72] The only geographer present at the hearings was Oskar H. Spate, who helped prepare the arguments on behalf of the Ahmadiyya community. Chester, ibid, at p.62. See also O.H.K. Spate, 'The Partition of Punjab and of Bengal' 110 (4/6) *The Geographical Journal* 201 (1947). Spate's remark on the hearing procedure is interesting for its revelation of a geographer's perspective: 'the procedure of the Commission is odd: the two Muslim and two non-Muslim judges will hear counsel for ten days, then the Chairman, Sir Cyril Radcliffe, who will receive verbatim reports but will NOT be present will go into a huddle with them and they will in effect issue an award.' Chester, supra note 48, at p.62.

[73] Fitzpatrick, supra note 64, at p.193.

[74] Goodrich, supra note 41.

190 *Research handbook on law and literature*

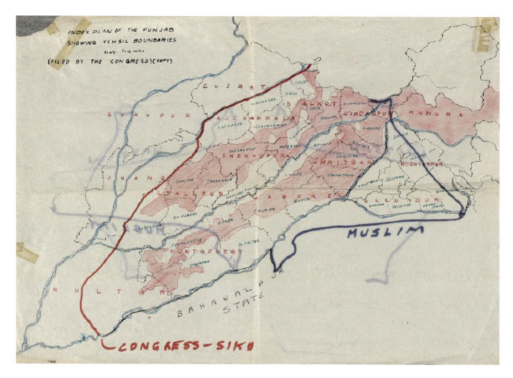

Figure 10.5   The Congress–Sikh Map submitted to the Punjab Boundary Commission

Note: The Congress–Sikh claims are shaded in pink, and the Muslim claim is depicted here in blue.
Source: Papers of Oskar H. Spate – The National Library of Australia; reproduced with permission from Jane Mills.

and through a visiocratic order, and the insignia of the courtroom are a crucial component in this configuration.[75] The atmosphere, then, already set the mood for anticipating a legal affair.

The arguments before the judges were not only made on the grounds of contiguous majority districts as stipulated by the terms of reference, but also according to the clause of 'other factors'. The first task was an interpretive task, which was to determine the authority of the 'other factors' clause. The cartojuridical effect did not fail to bear weight on this interpretive task as well, for what 'other factors' meant was to be assessed based on cartographic observations. Interpretation curiously became not just a legal and linguistic operation, but also a cartographic decryption. Lawyers and judges were required to be well versed in a cartojuridical method of interpretation which demanded not just philological acumen regarding texts but also cartographic prowess regarding maps. The question whether 'other factors' was subservient to the contiguous majority districts clause or held equal weight was to be interpreted, whenever the need arose, based on information obtained from maps.[76]

Another contentious point was the appropriate unit to be used to determine contiguous majority. The basic administrative unit of British Survey maps was the *thana*. The *thana*

---

[75]   Ibid.
[76]   Ahmed, supra note 70, at p.124.

represents the limits of the local police jurisdiction. It was policing power and the territorial extent of coercive legal force that acted as the primordial unit of British Indian cartography.[77] The *thana* as a unit entrenched the map as a tool of surveillance, which can be used to deploy police power and enforce discipline. To borrow from Mariana Valverde, this 'police gaze' as entrenched in the cartographic unit of *thana* ensured that 'legal powers and legal knowledges appear to us as always aready distinguished by scale'.[78] The *thana*, which is a continuing feature in post-independence Indian survey maps, functioned in a way to ensure that 'legal governance […] is always already itself governed'.[79] Once the territory was itself envisaged as the network of police operations, the force of law could easily be imposed upon a cartographically policed terrain. The reality of the map once again, in a different variant, became the model for and substituted the reality of the land. The work of law and order is already imagined and constructed through the work of cartography. That the *thana* continues to be the predominant unit in Indian administrative maps indicates the second operation of cartographic jurisprudence: how law, having been coalesced through cartography, uses cartography in turn to sustain, reproduce and reinscribe its authority.

Bengal Boundary Commission

The nature of the Bengal Boundary Commission's proceedings was hardly any different. Joya Chatterji describes the proceedings as a thoroughly legal affair, or at least one which appeared to be so:

> Both cases were written in a highly legalistic, technical style that could not have been more different from the hyperbole of the communal propaganda generated for popular consumption. Both were persuasive and insisted on the reasonableness of their respective demands. Both were backed with reams of 'evidence' and called on 'experts' to validate their arguments. The style in which the arguments were presented (and also much of their substance) calls to mind *a property dispute being fought in a court of law*.[80]

In the Bengal Commission, the objective of the Congress was simple: to ensure that the boundary was drawn in such a way that West Bengal was comprised predominantly of Hindus, who would be legal subjects conducive to a Congress government.[81] The Congress arguments were guided by the desire that the portion of Bengal which remains in India must be an ethnically homogenous unit, consisting of favourable national subjects, without any recalcitrant constitutents. The map which the Congress submitted comprised two proposals for the boundary: the Congress Scheme and the Congress Plan. The Congress scheme demanded for India a larger area than the Plan. The Scheme included portions which had a considerable Muslim majority, but was posited nevertheless to assuage the public sentiment that as much area as possible was being claimed for India. However, as Chatterji incisively demonstrates, the Congress strategy

---

[77] Chester, supra note 48, at p.20.
[78] Mariana Valverde, 'Jurisdiction and scale: legal technicalities as resources for theory' 18 *Soc. & Legal Stud.* 139 (2009), at p.141.
[79] Ibid.
[80] Joya Chatterji, 'The fashioning of a frontier: The Radcliffe Line and Bengal's border landscape, 1947–52' 33(1) *Modern Asian Studies* 185 (1999), at p.196; emphasis added.
[81] Joya Chatterji, *The Spoils of Partition: Bengal and India, 1947–1967* (Cambridge: Cambridge University Press, 2007), at pp.39–40.

was to exaggerate its claims in the Scheme so that the Plan would succeed. It was hoped that with the success of the Plan, a coherent Hindu Bengal citizenry could be created, and it was the success of the Plan that was Congress's sole priority. The map submitted to the Commission encapsulated not just territorial propositions but implicit arguments of national subjectivities couched in it. Chatterji rightly notes that the map and the arguments were a method to *right-size* and *right-people* the territory and citizenry of Bengal.[82] In the creation of the *right* national subjects, the unit of measurement proposed by the Congress was, appositely, the *thana*: the unit of measurement which serves as an ideal basis for a disciplining and imposing authority.

The Radcliffe Award

In preparing the award, Mountbatten, who generally stayed away from the work of the Commission, suggested a formula to Radcliffe which may well be recognized as *distributive justice*. In Lucy Chester's treatise on the Punjab Boundary Commission, she investigates the extent of Mountbatten's intervention in the working of the Boundary Commission. One outcome which Chester deems likely is that Mountbatten advised Radcliffe to make the boundary awards in Punjab and Bengal in an equitable manner such that justice could be 'uniformly done' to both parties in both the areas.[83] The idea was that losses on one side could be made up for by gains on the other side. This idea of justice certainly guided Radcliffe's cartographic decision. Whether or not Mountbatten explicitly conveyed this to Radcliffe, he did openly advocate such an aspiration in a meeting of the Partition Committee. Noting the advantage of having a single person chair both the Commissions, Mountbatten observed that '[t]he advantage of such a course would be that Sir Cyril Radcliffe would be enabled to adjust any slight loss one state might have to suffer in one particular area by compensating it in another and generally to see that *justice was done uniformly to all claims*'.[84] It appears that Radcliffe did take into account this idea of ensuring a distributive justice, where the losses of one party in one area could be compensated for in another area, in the delimitation of his final boundary. The award of a crucial Hindu-majority district to Pakistan in Bengal (the Chittagong Hill tracts) appears to have been carried out in order to countervail the award of Gurdaspur and Ferozepur, two Muslim-majority districts in Punjab, to India.[85] The loss on one side was matched by the gain on another. It was hoped, in vain, that this would not exacerbate the consternation.

The publication of the awards was characterized by a peculiar feature which continues unabated by the two nation-states: *secrecy* of the territorial limit. The Radcliffe Award was announced two days after the transfer of power that took place on 15 August 1947. The two new nation-states emerged into the world in a state of precarity, without concrete territorial limits. The absence of clarity on the territorial limits was accompanied by exacerbated territorial anxiety.[86] It was the notional boundary line which was followed for administrative

---

[82] Ibid, at p.39.
[83] Chester, supra note 48, at p.124.
[84] Ibid; emphasis added.
[85] Ibid, at p.140; Chatterji, 'Fashioning'. On the controversy surrounding Ferozepur's award to India, and the possibility that Mountbatten influenced this outcome, see Chester, ibid, pp.119–23.
[86] Gyanendra Pandey narrates several incidents where rumors of villages falling on one side or the other of the border led to significant violence. See Pandey, *Remembering Partition: Violence, Nationalism and History in India* (Cambridge: Cambridge University Press, 2001), ch. 4.

purposes. This did not, however, prevent the celebration of territorial limits during the moment of independence. Various newspaper advertisements, celebrating independence, published speculative images of India's territory. Some of these images included Pakistan in the territorial confines of India (Figure 10.6); some used their own creative imagination to speculate on where the border might fall (Figure 10.7); and others merely depicted the central and southern territorial limits and left a blank space in lieu of the northern spaces of contention (Figure 10.8). Despite the lack of clarity on territorial limits, the cartographic depiction (whether factual or imaginative) of territory was vital for the national jubilation. There was a need to have an imaged certainty even if the reality was absolutely precarious, and newspapers came in to fill that function. Whatever may have been the method employed, cartographic imagination, as these images indicate, was an indispensable aspect of a nation, and with it its laws, coming into existence. When Radcliffe's Award was published in the Extraordinary Gazette of India, on 17 August, it was made evident in the text of the Award that Radcliffe had attached an illustrative map to each of his awards. These maps, however, were not published along with the awards and have to date remained elusive. The Governments of Pakistan and India have withheld the official maps published by Radcliffe.[87] The point of interest here is the shroud of secrecy maintained over the maps. Despite Radcliffe's insistence that the text of the award, listing the districts and the villages that the boundary touched, prevails over the map, the map is precluded from public perception.[88] It appears that the affective and visceral propensity of the map needs to be *covered over*.[89] The absence of the image here gives exclusive control and superiority to the state on territorial limits. Intricate knowledge of the territory is not just crucial to the state but also critical to exclusive possession.

Harley links such censorship to Foucault's conception of 'juridical power': 'The state guards its knowledge carefully: maps have been universally censored, kept secret, and falsified. In all these cases maps are linked to what Foucault called the exercise of "juridical power". The map becomes a "juridical territory": it facilitates surveillance and control.'[90]

The official maps delineating the territorial limits constitute privileged knowledge [and knowledge production]. The legal works through such a knowledge, and, as will be explored in the next section, accords a presumption of authenticity to the state's cartographic knowledge. The courts have subsequently, and covertly, juridically entrenched the state's exclusive prerogative to territorial knowledge. The outcome of this has been not only the anxious and hyperventilated preservation of territory, but also the repeated positioning of territorial configurations and national subjects in particular ways.

---

[87] Chester writes that 'Indian and Pakistani governmental security concerns continue to block any access to relevant cartographic material in South Asian archives', supra note 48, at p.103, n.49.

[88] Radcliffe wrote in his award that 'the map is annexed for purposes of illustration, and if there should be any divergence between the boundary as described in Annexure A [the text of the boundary award] and as delineated on the map in Annexure B, the description in Annexure A is to prevail'. For a discussion of this in the context of cartographic procedure, see Chester, ibid, at p.86.

[89] On *covering* as a juridical gesture which hides things that are unfavourable, see Peter Goodrich, 'Allegories' in *Advanced Introduction to Law and Literature* (Edward Elgar Publishing, 2021).

[90] J.B. Harley, 'Deconstructing the Map' in T.J. Barnes and J.S. Duncan (eds), *Writing Worlds* (Routledge, 1992) p.245.

194 *Research handbook on law and literature*

Figure 10.6   Advertisement of Bata Footwear in The Times of India dated 15 August 1947

POSTCOLONIAL CONTINUITIES

Stephen Jones's treatise on boundary-making, which was considered by contemporary geographers as authoritative, defined seven methods of boundary definition. These ranged from 'complete definition', where the definition of a boundary would be final and binding, to 'definition in principle', with five variations of 'complete definition with power to deviate' in between.[91] Radcliffe predominantly approached his task as one of complete definition. This posed considerable difficulties for the Indian and Pakistani governments at the stage of demarcation and negotiation. Although the terms of reference stipulated that the Boundary Commission's task was one of demarcation, it would have implied absurd connotations.

---

[91] Jones, supra note 65, at pp.59–63. See also Chester's discussion of this in the context of Radcliffe's approach: Chester, supra note 48, at pp.73–4.

Cartographies 195

Figure 10.7   Advertisement of Godrej & Boyce Mfg. Co, Ltd in The Times of India dated 15 August 1947

Geographers, such as O.H.K. Spate, who were present at the Commission's sittings deplored the usage of 'demarcation' in the terms of reference as opposed to 'delimitation'. For Spate,

> [t]he terms of reference were hopelessly vague [...] The inaccurate use of the word 'demarcate' is symptomatic of the general vagueness; no one seriously envisaged the learned judges running round the Punjab with theodolites and concrete markers; but as the term accepted on all hands I could only suffer in silence each time it was used, which was very often.[92]

In geographical parlance, delimitation signified 'the choice of a boundary site and its definition in a treaty or other formal document. It is a more precise step than the general allocation

---

[92] Spate, supra note 72 at p.205.

196 *Research handbook on law and literature*

Figure 10.8 Advertisement of Union Life Assurance Co., Ltd. in The Times of India dated 15 August 1947

of territory which preceded it, but less precise than the demarcation which usually follows.'[93] Demarcation, in contrast with delimitation, refers to the physical marking on the ground of the boundary delimited. It was believed that Radcliffe's award, although envisaged as binding from an early stage,[94] could be consensually deviated from *post facto*.[95] The Supreme Court of India, however, felt differently.

The Supreme Court was pressed to interpret the Radcliffe award for the first time in 1959, in the case of *In Re: The Berubari Union and Exchange of Enclaves Reference Under Article 143(1) of The Constitution of India*.[96] The Governments of India and Pakistan had entered into a mutual agreement, in 1958, to redress boundary-related issues, wherein some portions of Bengal which fell within India's territorial limits were exchanged for portions on the side of Pakistan. The President of India referred a few questions for the Supreme Court's consideration on whether the enforcement of this agreement was constitutionally permissible or whether there was a requirement for a constitutional amendment or, alternatively, for legislation passed

---

[93] Jones, supra note 65 at p.57.
[94] Chester, supra note 48, at p.31.
[95] For instance, Jawaharlal Nehru assumed 'that any boundaries the commission determined could be modified after independence, if India and Pakistan agreed to do so'. Chester, ibid, at p.32.
[96] AIR 1960 SC 845, 1960 3 SCR 250. The case was heard by eight judges, including Chief Justice B.P. Sinha, and the unanimous judgment was delivered by Justice P.B. Gajendragadkar.

by the Parliament. The Supreme Court, in considering the matter, determined that once the Constitution of India had come into force, the territorial integrity of India was a matter of constitutional law. Any transfer of territory would imply, in constitutional law, the secession of Indian sovereignty over that part. The Constitution contained a list (Part A of the First Schedule) which tabulated the states comprising the Indian territory and territorial descriptions of each state. The description for West Bengal stipulated that those territories which comprised the province of West Bengal before the commencement of the Constitution would be considered as part of West Bengal State after independence. It was argued by the Government of India before the Supreme Court that the parcels of land in question (Berubari Union No 12 and the Cooch-Behar enclaves) were never part of India according to the Radcliffe Award, and that the agreement between India and Pakistan merely put into effect the Radcliffe award.

In assessing the argument of the government, the Court made use of the Award, and the map attached to the award, as of authoritative and precedential value.[97] The Court, in interpreting the award, held that the portions of territory exchanged with Pakistan were awarded to India according to the award, and that the agreement, in effect, entailed a secession of Indian territory. The Court held that any secession required a constitutional amendment to appropriately modify the list in the First Schedule. A secession can be legally recognized only upon such constitutional amendment. In effect, the Supreme Court held that the territorial limits of the state are a constitutional prerogative. Only the Constitution is equipped to authoritatively deal with cartographic changes. The Constitution is in force *on* the land, and arguably even above and below the land, insofar as the land is considered to be a part of the Indian territory. The law appears here, more concretely, as embodied *in the land*. By such a token, the people who inhabit the land automatically come under the domain of the law. It extends up to the boundary line and the entire land is under the surveillance of the law. The boundary itself becomes a liminal space, a no-man's land, which belongs neither here nor there, but acts as a precarious yet indispensable point of limit.[98]

Government maps in India are *presumed* to be accurate according to Indian Evidence law.[99] The map becomes a critical tool not just in cartographically inscribing the legal territory and becoming the model on which law is applied, but also in assisting law to maintain, reproduce and reinscribe its territorial limits. Cartography is used for a Constitutional fixity of the land. In India, the state wields a remarkable force in ensuring that knowledge of the territory is appropriately constructed. This knowledge is a crucial state-owned knowledge which is indispensable for governance. For instance, in 2016 the Government of India attempted to pass the Geospatial Information Regulation Bill, which mandated that 'no person shall disseminate or allow visualization of any geospatial information of India either through internet platforms or online services, or publish or distribute any geospatial information of India in any electronic or physical form' without first procuring a licence from a security vetting agency to do so.[100] Transgressing this mandate would have attracted a fine of up to one hundred crore.[101] The

---

[97] The Supreme Court accorded a superior authority to the text over the map because Radcliffe had, as discussed above, unequivocally directed such a precedence.
[98] This conception is viscerally exemplified in Saadat Hasan Manto's short story *Toba Tek Singh*. Saadat Hasan Manto, 'Toba Tek Singh' 19 *Manoa* 1 (2007), at pp.14–19 (translated by Tahira Naqvi).
[99] See Section 83 of the Indian Evidence Act. See also *Ram Kishore Sen And Others v Union Of India And Others* 1966 AIR 644, 1966 SCR (1) 430.
[100] Section 4 of The Geospatial Information Regulation Bill, 2016.
[101] Section 12.

198 *Research handbook on law and literature*

anxiety of the law here is to protect the territorial depiction of India, and only the State can do so. The map is the crucial tool which defines and constitutes the territory in cultural knowledge. The legal order of a nation-state rests on the delineation of territory. Readers of law must appreciate this crucial function that maps play in the construction of legal discourse and the construction of maps by discourses of law.

CONCLUSION

The fact that maps work to structure and inscribe the authority of the law within a given territory (or throughout the world) is neither a modern nor a novel phenomenon. This is despite the modernist conception attached to the understanding of cartography, as a science emerging from the Enlightenment. Hereford's *Mappa Mundi* (Figure 10.9), which dates back to the twelfth century, places Jerusalem, the Holy Land, right at the centre of the world. The seat of the earthly God, centrally located in this medieval atlas, is the source of power and law for the western world. As Giorgio Agamben has genealogically demonstrated, the conception of God in Christianity, especially with regard to the Trinity, is rooted in an *oikonomia*, an economy of divine work.[102] God reigns in heaven (as can also be witnessed from the *Mappa Mundi*) but does not rule. 'Rex regnit sed non gubernat.'[103] The King reigns, but does not govern. Christ, acting on behalf of – and through – God the Father, performs the divine will on earth. The divine *oikonomia* distributes the providential work between the transcendent providence in heaven and the immanent providence on earth. The *Mappa Mundi* then is a perfect cartographic depiction of this twin mode of governance and theologico-legal administration: a transcendent god-the-father placed in heaven, just above India, and an immanent deputy Christ-the-son placed at the centre of the world, symbolized with a cross. Christ the son administers and governs the world, while God reigns in heaven, according to the legal distribution of powers structured by the *oikonomia*. That this phenomenon is depicted cartographically, much before the emergence of the Mercatorial projection, is owed to the fact that law, no matter what the source, requires the exercise of mapping to culturally and materially entrench its power on the land. The text/image is a precursor, and a visceral mover of, the material and affective.

Cartographic jurisprudence then has a history beyond modernity. Whether it is the God and the Holy Land depicted in the *Mappa Mundi*, or the *thana* and the police jurisdiction of the British administrative maps, or Britannia and the cartouche over the Bay of Bengal, legal governance is always already governed by scale. As Goodrich writes:

> For lawyers, historically, the map is an expression of sovereignty, a specific and particular aesthetic of hierarchy and governance whereby the measured space and chorographic description of place is a manner of imposing political power onto the land. The map as legal device is a charter that both inscribes the name of the sovereign or nation on the *imperium* and indicates a measured correspondence of the cartograph to *lex terrae*.[104]

---

[102] Giorgio Agamben, *The Kingdom and the Glory: For a Theological Genealogy of Economy and Government* (Stanford: Stanford University Press, 2011), ch 4 and 5.
[103] Ibid, at p.72.
[104] Peter Goodrich, *Vision and Decision* (Oxford: Oxford University Press, 2022), at p.249.

Cartographies 199

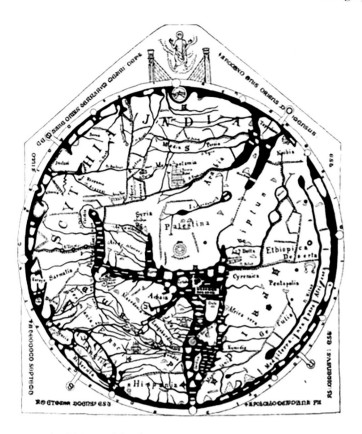

Figure 10.9 Hereford Mappa Mundi

Source: Konrad Miller, *Mappae Mundi: Die altesten Weltkarten*, 6 vols. (Stuttgart, Germany, 1895–98), 4:2 (in public domain).

PART III

GOVERNANCE

Consensus – Competitive Justice – Laughing Matter(s) – Sleeping Dogs –
Phishing Democracy – Interspecies Judging – Extinction – Speculative Fiction

11. Exhaustion
Nathan Moore

> *The end of life is always vivifying.*
> Samuel Beckett (1979, p.195)

INTRODUCTION

Given Deleuze's admiration for the philosophies of Spinoza and Bergson, it is not difficult to consider his own work as being concerned with intensity (Duffy, 2006, chapter 4) and vitalism. Indeed, as he famously said, 'Everything I've written is vitalistic, at least I hope it is, and amounts to a theory of signs and events'. (Deleuze, 1995, p.143) What does this mean? Certainly we can understand it as valorising life as the specificity of *a* life lived as, and in relation to, a series of signs and events; but it should not be overlooked that, for a philosopher who is so in favour of life and vitalism, Deleuze displays a consistent interest in death; or, at least, in that point at which life is at its most *dis-intensified* as something that is not quite, but yet as close as possible to, death or dispersal.

Despite the well-known antagonism to Freud, the death drive – as that which is beyond the pleasure principle – seems to find some favour[1] in the Deleuzian system, most obviously in *Coldness & Cruelty*, *Difference & Repetition*, and the accounts of the body without organs in *Anti-Oedipus*. From this perspective, it is Deleuze's Nietzscheanism – specifically, the affirmation of the eternal return – that seems the most profound influence. Yet, it is not really a problem of working out which philosophy influenced Deleuze 'the most', but one of taking this valorisation of the interpenetration of life and death seriously as a way of thinking and living. What are the consequences of valorising life at the point of death as its *most intense* manifestation? (Deleuze, 2001, p.28)

On the face of it, it seems that such a vitalism holds little utility for the thinking of justice. Yet, it is obvious that Deleuze thought otherwise. In 'To Have Done with Judgment', it is the beatitude of the baby that displays the greatest will to power (greater than any man of war), and Deleuze notes of the baby that one can only have an impersonal relationship to it. This does not make babies equivalent to each other but illustrates the depth or intensity of a bond (or, indeed, a rejection) that has nothing to do with character, personality, or individuality. (Deleuze, 1998, p.133) If there is a sense of justice here, it is under the sign of cruelty or the raw flesh – of a life persevering but, too, of a life that will be forced to live.[2] Earlier in the piece, Deleuze

---

[1] For an excellent overview of Deleuze's engagement with the death drive – which is more complicated than I suggest here – see Pearson, 1997, Chapter 3.

[2] As John Bowlby noted, along with others, in comparison to other primates the human infant, born after nine months' gestation, is born prematurely. (Bowlby, 1958, p.367) Left by itself, the infant would not live and so must be made to live through a degree of care. If care is necessary, it is because the infant's life is not.

writes: 'Artaud will give sublime developments to the system of cruelty, a writing of blood and life that is opposed to the writing of the book [of infinite debt], just as justice is opposed to judgment, provoking a veritable inversion of the sign'. (Deleuze, 1998, p.128)

A truthful – or even 'lawful' – inversion of the sign. It would appear that the true sign of vitalism – its justice – is the one that points to its own reversal, away from life and towards death. Yet, at no point does Deleuze turn death into a principle or revealed truth; death does not replace life, being instead the thing that gives it the possibility of intensity. Death not only as the direction of life, but also as its sense: as what must be resisted while remaining inevitable.

The reference to Artaud already shows that, for Deleuze, this problem of the least-intense-as-the-most-intense has already been raised in literature. Indeed, Melville, Beckett and Dickens (among others) all figure in Deleuze's late writings on this theme. The focus of my essay is to consider this play of intensity – which, for the sake of brevity, I will refer to as exhaustion – drawing out some of its implications for the idea of justice.

EXHAUSTION

In *Essays Critical and Clinical*, the essay 'The Exhausted' considers Beckett's works for television. Working from these, Deleuze presents a much more systematic presentation of the 'processes' of exhaustion than in his account of Dickens' 'disreputable man' in 'Immanence: A Life'. (Deleuze, 2001) Nevertheless, there are strong connections between the two essays. The disreputable man, approaching death, senses a growing soft sweetness emanating from those around him who had earlier viewed him with contempt. (Deleuze, 2001, p.28) As his life recedes, and death gains the advantage, the care and warmth of these otherwise hostile onlookers seems to increase in proportion. More specifically, it is the *slender thread* of life that they respond to. Not his actual or realised life (the biographical life of the disreputable man), but what is indistinct in him as a lifeforce (if 'force' is not too strong a word): 'Suddenly, those taking care of him manifest an eagerness, respect, even love, for his *slightest sign of life*'. (Deleuze, 2001, p.28; my emphasis) The winding down that exposes a bare life or '*homo tantum*' (Deleuze, 2001, p.28) confounds the rule of entropy: the more formless and disorganised it becomes, and the more indistinct it seems to be, the more remarkable, unusual and *informative* life paradoxically becomes. Here, where *a* life plays with death, (Deleuze, 2001, p.28) the entropic arrow of time is not linear, nor unidirectional, and we find a sign or event appearing where we least expect it – at the moment of greatest indistinction.

The idea of a uniform void as entropic telos, where each part is the same as any other, is contrary to Deleuze's philosophy. Instead, there are the non-discrete zones of the virtual, all of which have specificity or singularity, but which lack any fixed identity or externally related difference. This virtuality is what the disreputable man approaches as death takes hold, or, better, it is what begins to become more apparent in him as he dies. Yet, death is not the only means of making it apparent, as 'The Exhausted' makes clear. In this account, Deleuze identifies four processes in Beckett's works, which aim to stretch to the limit and to exhaust by:

- forming exhaustive series of things,
- drying up the flow of voices,
- extenuating the potentialities of space,
- dissipating the power of the image. (Deleuze, 1998, p.161)

With the exception of the final one, each of these procedures is an additional step, achieving a kind of meta-exhaustion of the previous process, until all that remains is an intensive field that gains its power by simultaneously being the least intensive and differentiated. Here, the affirmation or selection of any given 'part' is also, unavoidably, the affirmation and selection of every other part of the field: inclusive disjunction. (Deleuze, 1998, p.154) Nothing can be excluded, but this does not mean that everything is thereby included if, by the latter, an absolute harmony or instant communicativeness is imagined. The exhausted is the point at which non-exclusion is also non-inclusion, and where all the parts are undifferentiated without becoming equal to, or substitutable for, one another.

The contrary of exhaustion today is competition, and I will return to this below; but it can be highlighted here that competition is not only that which pits subject against subject, and life against life, in its attempts to incarnate the exception to the *exclusion* of all else; it is also the relentless pursuit of possibilities: the assembling of a desire that seeks yet another innovation, and yet another communication, and yet more growth, and yet greater efficiency. Competition, in this sense, pursues the impossible (and so tiring) dream of realising every possibility and of leaving nothing undifferentiated. In relation to Beckett, Deleuze writes:

> one can never realize the whole of the possible; in fact, one even creates the possible to the extent that one realizes it. The tired person has merely exhausted realization, whereas the exhausted person exhausts the whole of the possible. The tired person can no longer realize, but the exhausted person can no longer possibilize. (Deleuze, 1998, p.152)

As things are realised, or actualised, their possibility – as something that existed before the actualisation – becomes a thinkable representation or calculation; but only with hindsight. Thus, realisation can never have done with the possible; indeed, to realise a possibility is to make it nothing, to discharge it with an intensity that only ever wants *yet more intensity*, a greater hit. (Deleuze, 1998, p.153) The Beckettian procedure, in contrast, is to exhaust the possible before any realization of it can occur – the baby 'is exhausted before birth'. (Deleuze, 1998, p.152) Here, the contingency of a life is shown to be something altogether different from its possibilities;[3] yet it would be an error to think of this contingency as being at the beginning or the end (for example, I, or my parents, or my grandparents, and so on, might never have been born; and, too: one day the sun will become too hot to support life on earth); rather it is here, now, always in the middle. (Deleuze, 1998, p.157; Moore, 2012)

There is, then, a task or project to exhaustion that should not be equated to merely tiring work. If human life is contingent and insignificant in terms of what is, we cannot make a necessary and significant principle out of this insight; to do so would be a false move, inasmuch as it would attempt to identify, and then realise, only that which seems *most* possible. Instead, exhaustion will impose something worse: to live, but without ever knowing if one has lived or not, because death is already here in the middle, and its border with life cannot be finally made out or realised: 'At what point do separate moments of existence make up a whole, a life'? (Gontarski, 2015, p.180) This makes of exhaustion the task of repetition: 'The only

---

[3]   In a different context, and with different yet still pertinent terminology, see Ayache, 2010 on the difference between contingency and probability. Note that for Ayache, contingency can only be written into existence, whether as a derivative or some other form. In this regard, Borges' story *Pierre Menard, Author of Don Quixote* is of recurring significance for Ayache. (Ayache, 2010, p.4)

uncertainty that makes us continue is that even painters, even musicians, are never sure they have succeeded in making the image'. (Deleuze, 1998, p.161)

Of course, to fail again. However, we might wonder: is there anything *effective* in any of this? Isn't the exhausted merely the one who has finally sunk into themselves, operating their own combinatory processes and sleeping their private, dreamless sleep? At the end of 'To Have Done with Judgment', Deleuze rejects any notion that what I have here indicated by 'exhaustion' is simply a subjective matter. The reason is because the subject inevitably has its preferences: it would like to include something and to exclude others. In short, this subject is only ever the subject of the exception and of immunity – to which I will return below. But to be exhausted is to be without preference when it comes to the available possibilities. Instead, the point has to be reached where the affirmation of one choice is simultaneously the affirmation of all choices; and this means that a social dimension, exceeding the subject, is always operative in the work of exhaustion.

THE FORMULA AND THE BULBS

In his treatment of Melville's 'Bartleby, the Scrivener', Agamben (1999) focuses upon the potential and impotential of the copying (and other) work that Bartleby prefers not to undertake. In doing so, Agamben's analysis says little about Bartleby's employer, the attorney. For Deleuze, the relationship with the attorney features much more prominently – indeed, it becomes increasingly clear as Deleuze's account develops that he understands Bartleby and the attorney to form a kind of pair, through which an idealised fraternity replaces charity and philanthropy. The latter are exhausted, clearing the ground for a much more treacherous yet also, perhaps, incestuous relation between the two: 'a community of celibates'. (Deleuze, 1998, pp.84–5) Bartleby's formula – 'I would prefer not to' – seems to bear down upon the attorney much more than upon Bartleby himself; it is the attorney – and through him, the world that he inhabits – that is driven towards exhaustion and dis-intensification. It is the inclusive disjunction at work, by which to either affirm copying or not-copying automatically selects the excluded opposite as well. Through this procedure, the attorney loses his bearings without falling into an entropic, uniform void; instead, he suddenly finds that everything is both much closer and much further away than he had imagined. Rather than a coordinated space and a linear time, both begin to collapse into themselves and into each other but, in doing so, reveal a world of intensive zones or singularities, with each of the zones being distinct but without any externally related difference between them. Not a difference *between*, but difference in the very middle and core of each: 'against the particularities that pit man against man and nourish an irremediable mistrust; but also against the Universal or the Whole, the fusion of souls in the name of great love or charity'. (Deleuze, 1998, p.87)

We should not fail to see another great exhausted figure from literature: Ralph Ellison's Invisible Man. The Invisible Man relates his story while remaining invisible within the book itself, except for its margins, at the 'Prologue' and the 'Epilogue', in which he tells us where and what his adventures – if that is the right word – have led him to. At the beginning and the end, the Invisible Man addresses us from the bright, warm hole of his abode. An underground hole in which he hides – and this hiding is the condition for achieving a certain form and thus semblance of visibility (Ellison, 2001, p.6) – and from which he addresses us, or the world. Indeed, the Epilogue again makes it clear – as clear as Bartleby's effect upon the attorney –

that the exhausted does not retreat from the world so much as make the world disappear to itself. In the Epilogue, the Invisible Man's intentions are clear: he will exhaust the world. In doing so, he will return to it the lessons it had imposed upon him: 'When one is invisible he finds such problems as good and evil, honesty and dishonesty, of such shifting shapes that he confuses one with the other, depending upon who happens to be looking through him at the time'. (Ellison, 2001, p.552)

This does not mean, of course, that the Invisible Man has become a sort of wise sage – quite clearly, he continues to be invisible to himself, at least to the extent that he continues to imagine that the world is full of possibilities (Ellison, 2001, p.556) – but the truth is that he is already in the process of exhausting that possibility – which is why he must stay in his underground hole: 'So that even before I finish I've failed'. (Ellison, 2001, p.559) Failing before he has finished is the formula specific to the Invisible Man, through which he condemns and affirms, 'say no and say yes, say yes and say no'. (Ellison, 2001, p.559) Even more specifically, all of this is to come or, better, is deferred at the same moment that it is being affirmed. It is not to be mistaken for the dream – for example, the dream where one runs without getting anywhere – and Deleuze outlines his antagonism to the dream in 'To Have Done with Judgment', preferring a dreamless sleep or insomnia. The Invisible Man is also dreamless, being in a state of sleepless hibernation in the light of 1,369 bulbs. He *will* take action, yet he will not leave his hole. He has come out of hibernation, but only to relay an invisible speech, as if the lips were moving, and the pen were scratching, but the voice is out of phase, and the lines are all of a jumble. It is *his* motivation, yet it has already escaped him to form zones of indiscernibility, as if his invisible speech were the words of others: 'Who knows but that, on the lower frequencies, I speak for you?' (Ellison, 2001, p.561) More than anything, the Invisible Man traces the trajectory of a boomerang – not a dialectical spiral, (Ellison, 2001, p.6) but a continuous reversibility that shows the darkness in the light, and the light in the darkness. Beginning and ending in a brightly lit hole, where the light does not so much give form as submerge it.

JUSTICE

For want of a better word, might not the exhausted then show us a *superior* justice? This requires some explication of 'justice'. In his historical review *Concepts of Justice*, Raphael identifies two elements of the Western thinking of justice: requital of desert and impartiality. (Raphael, 2001, p.235) These two elements, that Raphael distinguishes from fairness and equality (moral or social justice), have no intrinsic bond: their combination as justice is simply 'the result of history'. (Raphael, 2001, p.241) Raphael's concept of justice here falls under the banner of institutional justice, as this is described by Sen. (Sen, 2010) It is a matter of established procedure. Although it is not clearly demarcated in *Concepts of Justice*,[4] moral or social justice seems to fall more on the side of consequentialist justice. (Sen, 2010) Likewise, Rawls (2005) and Nozick (2001) are examples of institutional justice (the original 'veil of ignorance'; historical acquisitions and exchanges) where justice is achieved through the application of a contractually agreed (or historically embedded) procedure. Consequentialist justice – as

---

[4] See Chapter 21 in particular.

advocated by Sen – is not trapped in history but is able to review outcomes in light of current patterns and distributions (moving it towards Raphael's description of moral or social justice).

If it is not too reductive, the *American* assemblage of justice draws a line between process and outcome and then debates the extent, nature and placement of this line. This is evident, for example, in the more recent development of intersectionality. As described by Hill Collins and Bilge (2020, chapter 1), the intersectional approach combines a range of social perspectives as a method for promoting consequentialist justice over the institutional. Intersectionality looks at current distributions and interrogates how these have come about and – beyond the observance of juridically sound processes – whether those distributions are fair.

What these discussions indicate is that, if the line between institutional and consequentialist justice cannot be stabilised, it is because neither is capable of grounding itself. No legal procedure can legitimate itself; but neither can any critique of that procedure. Approached from either direction, the aporia of justice is inevitably encountered: there is the procedure of the law, and there is the application of the law. Or, as Virno recounts in his discussion of Wittgenstein, a rule cannot determine the rule of its own application. (Virno, 2008, p.107) However, if law is not to slide into the abyssal crater of its own lack of foundation, it must split itself and use each half as an obstacle for the other. The question then is: what is the specificity of this double game in any given instance?

It seems clear that the Indo-European tradition always considers justice to be doubled or twinned: as Deleuze and Guattari write (following the work of Georges Dumézil),[5] we keep encountering the combination of the one-eyed and the one-armed. (Deleuze & Guattari, 1988, p.351) Nevertheless, such twins still need an orientation and frame of reference. Here, Foucault's tripartite description in the *Governmentality* lecture (Foucault, 2000) seems apposite, tracing what might be considered as three juridical orientations: territorial sovereignty, normative discipline, and circulating governmentality.[6] In terms of justice, what is the orientation of territorial sovereignty? The proper allocation of rights and obligations according to status. Infringement of this allocation calls for restitution to be made in terms of blood, money or goods. With normative discipline, justice calls for proper distinctions to be drawn between people, and for each member of the resulting category to be treated as alike as possible. Broadly, these cover the two historical accidents identified by Raphael: requital of desert and impartiality.

With circulating governmentality (or 'control'), justice involves an amplification of these two features. Requital becomes communicative, and impartiality becomes a chance outcome. As such, justice becomes orientated by problems of logistics, management, and uncertainty. In the case of the former, justice becomes expressive, as David Garland has observed. (Garland, 2002, chapter 1) More than this, though, communication itself becomes a type of justice, perhaps best illustrated by ideas of restorative justice. (Liebmann, 2007, chapter 1)

With chance, the normative basis of statistical governance centralises not only probability but also uncertainty. (Ewald, 1991) In this case, justice takes on a doubled perspective, moving forward while learning from past mistakes (Diamantides & Schütz, 2017, chapter 4) – that is, reacting to what were previously unforeseen risks – and at the same time there is the valorisation of uncertainty itself, that plays out in a number of ways: as a prop for libertarian

---

[5] For an interesting engagement with Dumézil's writing on Mitra-Varuna, see Haldar, 2012.
[6] For brevity, I will refer to the latter as 'control', accepting, yet leaving to one side, the distortions this involves between Foucault and Deleuze. See 'Postscript on Control Societies' in Deleuze, 1995.

freedom (O'Malley, 2004, chapter 1) and as a retrenchment of Nozick's view that, so long as the process is historically 'just', then the outcome – no matter how unforeseeable or presumably undesirable – must be just too. Even arbitrary outcomes of the process can appear as impartial and, therefore, as a 'natural' or apparently self-regulated result, free from 'external' interference.

Taken together, communications and chance outcomes find their articulation in competition. Competition is the mode of evaluation by which a successful outcome must be at the cost of less successful outcomes. Competition co-ordinates and compares results so that there can be 'winners' only on the condition that there are 'losers'. At best, competition depends upon the communication of envy, but at worst it must make the non-competitive visible as those who have been left to die. These constitute the unfortunate collateral damage of a system geared towards the realisation of all of the 'best' possibilities. If the winners are valorised, this is because of their luck and skill in mastering chance – they are the ones able to identify and select the range of possibilities and, through these exceptional abilities, place themselves in the position where they deserve to win. By chance, the distribution of 'goods' appears to result from the individual skill and luck of the player, rather than from the structural affordances of the game itself.

At root, the orientation of justice under control is essentially competitive: the most competitively achieved outcome is the most just one even if arbitrary, because arbitrariness, in this context, is only the unforced outcome of the competitive process. Similarly, if one takes an unfair or uncompetitive advantage by forcing the procedure in some way, giving oneself an unequal opportunity, then there is injustice. Yet, there is obviously paradox and circularity here: if a capricious outcome is nevertheless apparently just (because unforced and/or unpredictable), how to decide when an intervention or move is inappropriate – that is, arbitrary or capricious *in the wrong way*?[7] It is this that calls for constant communication and discussion, and by which the most communicated can also become the most just (not to mention the most true).[8] In this context, it is not so much the *loudest* voice that is just, but the one that circulates the most. Obvious to say, this leaves the means of being competitive open and malleable. The account of intersectionality given by Hill Collins and Bilge seems aligned to this debate, albeit, perhaps, with some ambivalence:

---

[7] Prime Minister Tony Blair was quick on the uptake regarding this problem, presenting it in terms of 'respect'. Although he did not couch his thinking in terms of communication in 2002, he did make reference to community, stating that it was respect that 'makes us a community, not merely a group of isolated individuals'. He went on to talk of it as a new social contract that 'says with rights and opportunities come responsibilities and obligations'. In hindsight, we can see this as being in keeping with strategies of responsibilisation, as discussed by David Garland (2002) and Andrew Ashworth (2004), which (according to Blair) aimed to rebalance individual choice and social rights. The connection to competition begins to emerge when the Prime Minister goes on to state: 'our new approach starts with opportunity'. Implicit here is the re-positioning of the individual as a competitive player that capitalises on opportunity while nevertheless playing by the rules. What remains unstated is the degree to which the rules can be re-negotiated. All quotes are from Tony Blair's 2002 Queen's speech, 'My vision for Britain'. Available on The Guardian website, and accessed 10 February 2021: www.theguardian.com/politics/2002/nov/10/queensspeech2002.tonyblair.

[8] For more on the propensity of communications technologies to refer only to themselves, see Baudrillard, 1983 and Moore, 2021.

For example, the FIFA World Cup case suggests that competition is not inherently bad. People accept the idea of winners and losers if the game itself is fair. Yet fairness is elusive in unequal societies where the rules may seem fair, but differently enforced through discriminatory practices. Fairness is also elusive where the rules themselves may appear to be equally applied to everyone, yet still produce unequal and unfair outcomes: in democratic societies everyone has the 'right' to vote, but not everyone has equal access to do so. (Hill Collins & Bilge, 2020, pp.238–9)

The orientation of justice is not one that departs from competition, but one that seeks to ensure a more just and equal framework for competitive actions to take place in. Not the absence of competition but *better* competition, through equality of opportunity.

In this sense, competition is the most effective means of tiring us out today. For this reason, it deserves further description. Can competition be exhausted?

COMPETITION

Competition is the ideal of neoliberal regimes. (Foucault, 2008; Dardot & Laval, 2013; Brown, 2015) This means the infusing of all social, political and economic life and practice with the spirit of competition so that it becomes the legitimation for those practices, their truth, their entrepreneurialisation, their promise of growth and prosperity, and the adjudicator of who will live and who will be allowed to die. If competition is tiring, it is because it never rests – the game calls for constant vigilance and preparedness so as to bring forth the most perfect logistical solutions. Being inextricably linked to the 'correct disposition of men and things', (Foucault, 2000, p.208) competition calls for never-ending itineration and nomadism. (Moore, 2013) If we cannot rest it is because, crucially, there is nothing 'natural' or self-given about competition – not only must it be fostered and brought forth, (Foucault, 2008, p.120) it must become *the* project to which all are dedicated and committed to bringing about. As Foucault, Brown and Dardot and Laval have all outlined and explored, competition is an essence, a dream and a goal that it is the duty of all – at even the most micro and seemingly inconsequential levels of individual life – to realise and promote.

Brown and Dardot and Laval have been particularly concerned to identify the dangers that such a promotion of the competitive entails. These dangers can be crudely described as coalescing into a unified and basic threat for the democratic tradition wherever it has taken hold: competitive neoliberalism is anti-democratic. At the same time, none of these authors are blind to the shortcomings and failures evident in the history of democracy in practice;[9] yet, as an ideal, it persists, if for no other reason than 'the negative one that we should not be ruled by others'. (Brown, 2015, p.203) If governing ourselves is identified as a 'good', it is because it allows for the articulation of difference and disagreement – of contestation – with the aim not of necessarily realising the potential of each and every difference but, instead, of negotiating a never-ending series of moves in the hope of fostering and tending such disagreement and differentiation.

This appears, though, to raise a question: if contestation is a 'good', isn't this in fact promoted by competition? What is the difference between competition and contestation that makes one anti-democratic and the other democratic? The core of this difference is consensus

---

[9] For an overview of the current difficulties thrown up by this history, see Lafont, 2020, Chapter 7.

– competition seeks consensus.[10] Brown, for one, has drawn a clear picture of what is at stake with the promotion of consensus, (Brown, 2015, pp.68, 139–42, 207–8) so I will limit myself here to the point that competition makes consensus the horizon of its own operation, in a way that democratic contestation (potentially) does not. Competition demands not only that all compete but, more than this, that all accept or recognise that there is *no alternative to competing*. It is this latter point that makes neoliberalism curiously fragile, and in need of constant state (and institutionalised inter-state) support. Seemingly, competition cannot compete on its own terms, and so must become the complete horizon of possibility; it aims to neutralise any alternative before the latter can even emerge as such. (Cooper, 2008, chapter 3)

What marks a critical development here is the transformation undergone by the image of authority. In the 1950s Arendt was able to speak of a crisis of authority, (Arendt, 1954) and this crisis has not abated. Rather, it has become a foundational tenet – somewhat unremarked upon – of contemporary competitive neoliberalism that not only is authority in crisis, but authority has itself lost its authority. This is the core of the neoliberal demand for consensus: not only that authority has failed, but that it will keep on failing. This reiterates, of course, the political theological dimension (Agamben, 2005; Esposito, 2010; Diamantides & Schütz, 2017) of neoliberalism itself, and it demands that we all accept and agree upon the fact that there is no authority, and that there can be no authority. This also illustrates why the neoliberal demand is so fragile: it attempts to make the failure of authority, its crisis, its own authorising moment. The operative contradiction is that competition is seemingly immanent, producing winners and losers without having to justify or explain this beyond it being the 'outcome' of competition itself. Competition does not then exercise any authority – it is a 'neutral' process – and this is why it has authority.

The ideal of democracy is far too broad a subject to do any justice to here. As a starting point, Cristina Lafont's arguments in favour of *institutionalised* democratic deliberation provide a useful framing, even if (or because) they are not finally conclusive.[11] How is democratic contestation different from neoliberal competitive consensus? The elimination of contestation at which such a consensus aims highlights the significance of authority once more. If authority is to appear as de-authorised, it is necessary to obscure its most basic operation; that operation through which authority is repeatedly re-authorised. In other words, authority appears only to the extent that it is continuously re-inaugurated. It is this which enables society and politics to have a past, a history. The neoliberal fostering of competition is part and parcel of its rejection of the past, to the extent that the latter shows the histories of contestation, disagreement, refusal, consolidation, and so on which point to the potential of things having been otherwise. Looked at from a pro-democratic perspective, institutional democracy does not

---

[10] See Dardot and Laval, 2013, pp.259–60 on the resultant 'entrepreneurial subject' who must find ways to live this consensus.

[11] See Lafont, 2020, chapter 7. For the sake of specificity, the reader should read me as utilising Lafont's take on what democracy should be when I use the term 'democracy'. This might raise a question about the term 'institutional' – Lafont's preferred mode. It is clear that she has a more nuanced usage of this word than we find in American jurisprudence, one that I consider as linking into processes of abstraction rather than legitimation. The institution is a technology for decision making without every single person having to be involved in that making. The advantages of this do not foreclose the ongoing possibility of reconfiguring the institution (the institution is useful, not exceptional). Perhaps the strongest type of critique that could be made of an institution would be to show the irrelevance of its alternatives: that all decisions produce the same outcome. This is what Bartleby does to the attorney's office.

seek to erase its links to the past – indeed, it will make those links another site of contestation for its own negotiated unfolding, returning again and again to the fact that consensus has not been possible. Against this, neoliberal consensus must draw a sharp line between now and then, so as to maintain that competition has only now brought the violence and injustice of history to a close. History is (of course) over and, going forward, we can all agree that it will be best to maximise our advantages. Rather than re-inaugurations, there will only be 'celebration' after 'celebration'.

What is at stake in this difference between contestation and consensus? Counter-intuitively, consensus does not bind or tie but individualises; more than this, to the extent that consensus becomes normative, it *dividualises*. (Deleuze, 1995) Neoliberalism takes a huge amount of resources to produce a minimal gesture: that we have been abandoned by authority and, being so, we are now each free, without limit or constraint. Obvious to say that the performative contradiction is that such competitive freedom without limits is itself a limit, an authority. To this extent, neoliberalism conceals its own re-inaugurations in catastrophes and crises, (Klein, 2008) by which its intervention is immediately legitimated because there is no alternative – there is no time to think, to consider potentials, to contest. Every moment is an exceptional one where, apparently, nothing is being authorised but instead what plays out is the only rational and sensible choice that can play out: the imposition of more competition. Nothing is being founded here, but each disaster reveals the 'truth' of our world – that we are without authority.

On the other hand, the claim I would like to advance is that contestation, in the context sketched out by Lafont, is potentially productive of a solidarity that holds people together in their differences. Of course, this has been the dream of the discourses of emancipatory otherness from post-structuralism on, but it is a project that must be maintained; indeed, it is in need of re-inauguration. This is where we can encounter the idea of exhaustion once more. However, we should be clear that exhaustion will take us well beyond difference – certainly in any democratic sense – but will be, nevertheless, the condition for any such democracy.

EXHAUSTED

I noted above that exhaustion means being exhausted before birth. What does this mean? At stake here is the idea of possibility: in any given arrangement or dispositif, what is possible? To be born is to be faced with possibilities but, too, it is also the narrowing of possibilities: one is born into this or that life and, from there, a certain necessity is in play: one *has been* born. For sure, life is made up of choosing between possibilities – but to what end or purpose? For the achievement of a pre-defined aim or goal? To this again, we must respond with a 'yes': humans can produce, and work towards, specific ends. The point, though, is that none of this can legitimate, nor justify, human existence; more importantly, nor does it justify specific ways of life above others. What serves as necessary in life is only the outcome of contingencies – this is the basic insight of governmentality (and control). Counter-intuitively (perhaps), we find the governmental in close proximity to the poetic. Quoting Novalis, Hacking writes: 'The individual is "individualized by one single chance event alone, that is, his birth"'. (Hacking, 1990, p.147)

Necessity comes by chance, and rationality comes out of the irrational. (Hacking, 1990, p.147) What might come into being is understood only by reference to what already has – this is as clear in statistics (Ewald, 1991) as it is in the conceptualisation of potential. (Virno, 2015, pp.76–8) To exhaust the possible means to also exhaust that which is already known, and from which we model the possible. Exhaustion is then also the exhaustion of purpose. If to have been born is to have been fated, exhaustion is the experience of this contingency: that is, the contingency by which chance and necessity are welded together. (Hacking, 1990, p.148) It can be experienced, following Deleuze and Guattari (1994), in three modes: philosophy, art and science – philosophy as the thinking of exhaustion; art as the perception and sensibility of exhaustion; and science as the paradigmatic referentiality of exhaustion. In all three modes, impersonalisation takes place – but this is not the erasure of the subject-who-was-born, but instead its loss of purpose, preference and possibility, thereby becoming bare life encountered as intensive dis-intensification.

Agamben has shown how, politically, the imposition of bare life has been a disaster for humanity. Yet, this is because bare life itself – as exhaustion – has not been grasped with sufficient directness. The plight of *homo sacer* has been as the victim of sovereign decision, but this has made of the exhausted only a consequence or epiphenomenon of sovereignty itself. The task is to turn exhaustion back onto sovereignty – this is the formula of Bartleby.

What would it mean to exhaust sovereignty? It is not a question of reaching what is impossible, because the impossible still only exists by reference to what is and what has been born. In any case, such impossibility has already been claimed by sovereignty, as its most proper possibility, in the Schmittian designation of the exception. The exception is where sovereignty defends itself most strongly against the exhausted, by bolstering the stage of possibility with the prop of impossibility: if it cannot ground itself, this inability will become the authority by which it will ground itself. At the most, the sovereign exception is the means to simply keep adding possibilities. Why is this a problem?

The more possibilities there are, the more tiredness. This is the link between competition and exception: we must compete for the exception. This gives the lie to the apparent sovereign monopoly of the exception – competitive responsibilisation is its diffusion. This has been analysed by Esposito in terms of immunity – meaning a dispensation, protection, and defence against community. (Esposito, 2010, p.12) The exceptional people are the ones immunised against the claims (and threat) of community. Indeed, a better formulation might be: sovereign are they who decide upon immunity. However, the counter to this is not to simply re-valorise community – as Esposito shows, throughout the history of the Western tradition, the problem of the withdrawal of presence and legitimacy (finding its modern articulation as *immunitas*) is already there from the start, with community, and always undermining it from within. (Esposito, 2010, Introduction)

What is increasingly clear, as the world becomes globalised and *urbi et orbi* pass into each other, (Nancy, 2007, chapter 1) is that with the addition of ever more competitive possibilities to achieve immunity, humanity is increasingly exposed to contamination and infection. This is the full necropolitical (Mbembe, 2013) horror of governmentality and control – not that individuals and groups will be *identified* as enemies for legitimate targeting (which, with its long history, is horrifying and absurd in its own right), but that whole swathes of humanity will be simply ignored, being the barely living residuum of sovereign exceptionalism. Not targeted kills, but the unfortunate collateral damage of those who will be *allowed to die*. Competitively unviable life.

Following Esposito, what calls for exhaustion is community *and* immunity as these have been hitherto thought, up to, and including, their modern articulation as competition. Only if this is achieved can justice be re-orientated away from the American debates about institutions and consequences and, more significantly, might the valorisation of competition itself be neutralised. In his unpicking of the etymological tie between community and immunity – *munus* – Esposito shows how the two, together, serve to mutually block or obscure their paradoxes and contradictions, thereby making them reciprocally functional. Historically, this functioning of Western political philosophy has been a dance around the problems of obligation, duty and gift, (Esposito, 2010, p.4) but it is the latter, according to Esposito, that has been the most unstable and often, and too quickly, obscured by being reduced to exchange. As he writes, 'this is the gift that one gives because one *must* give and because one *cannot not* give'. (Esposito, 2010, p.5; emphasis in the original) He goes on to describe it as a subtraction or loss; yet, might we not also consider this gift as exhaustion? Rather than 'loss', it is better to think in terms of filtering, in a quest not for purity but, rather, a sufficient degree of stability or *reduction in chaos* so that a life can take hold. If this sounds like a negentropic gesture, it is – but it is not one without simultaneously pursuing the line of entropy to the extent that what is filtered out is too much information and too much potential. Then a life takes hold – but this double articulation of entropy, as a measure of both disorganisation and predictability, (Janich, 2018, p.47) spins out into the intensive dis-intensification that fascinates Deleuze.

The gift that one cannot not give implies exchange and debt – but it is not an exchange with, nor a debt owed to, other subjects or sovereigns. Rather, it is a debt owed to life itself – more specifically, to bare life, as that which has compelled us to live, 'prior' to any demarcation of exceptionalism or sovereign omnipotence. This 'prior' is accessible through philosophy, art and science: the exhausted. Here, the gift is owed for the receipt of what the recipient did not want, demand or expect: bare life, which, in this sense, is the refutation of *all exceptionalism*. There is no human life that is exceptionally not bare life; and not just in the restricted play of a before and after, but continuously, in the very middle and core of every lived life. There is no legitimate basis for allowing life to die, and no sovereignty by which life can be decided against even 'passively', nor made justifiably unviable. American jurisprudence serves to conceal this logic, while competition helps us all to 'live with it' because, after all, at some point it will come down to 'you' or 'me', and to 'us' or 'them'. This should be refused.

The fact of humanity's existence, including all the lives and deaths that have constituted it, is contingent. Human existence is not necessary, (Meillassoux, 2008, p.10) and it is this lack of necessity which is common to all. The *donum* of *munus* is the conversion – or, better, the inseparability – of contingency into/as necessity in the sense of *a* life that, in being born, takes its singular formation or specificity as something other than itself and, yet, as the thing most intimate to it. *It* lives in us, as the gift that will not enable or sanction a division into community and immunity, nor society and individual. The cruelty of this exposure cannot, and should not, be focused on or allocated to one group of humans rather than another; the attempt to do so always results in sovereign exceptionalism. Instead, politics must take as its point of reference the exhaustion that philosophy, art and science all demonstrate: we have no right to be, and there is no right to foster our being at the expense of any other. Bare life is simultaneously *de facto* and *de jure*. It cannot be distributed, nor decided upon. This is not a naïve assertion that 'all lives matter' – such a statement is solipsistic at best and racist at worse; rather, it is the argument that 'no lives matter'[12] – and it is in light of this that we must live.

---

[12] Unlike the common deployment of 'all lives matter' as a refutation of 'black lives matter', I do not consider 'no lives matter' to be contrary to the latter. Rather, I take it as being implicit in the necessity of asserting that 'black lives matter', pointing to the illegitimate exceptionalism of that sovereignty which

FOUR PROCESSES

Above, I noted four processes of exhaustion that Deleuze extrapolated from Beckett's works. Each of these processes can be considered in light of four orientations or characteristics of justice, so as to progressively exhaust the latter. Swapping the final two around, this gives the following set of pairings:

(1) forming exhaustive series of things — sovereign restitution
(2) drying up the flow of voices — disciplinary impartiality
(3) dissipating the power of the image — governmental communicativeness
(4) extenuating the potentialities of space — controlled competitiveness

(1) Sovereign restitution enacts what Raphael refers to as requital of desert. This can cover both the imposition of punishment for legal infractions and, less obviously, reward for the conferral of benefit. (Raphael, 2001, p.234) As Raphael notes, reward will often remain uncrystallised in the sense that it will likely find expression in terms of gratitude, and a diffuse feeling of obligation or indebtedness. Nevertheless, like punishment, it operates in reference to an ideal equilibrium of proper distributions, the disturbance of which (by crime, for example) demands restitution. This presupposed distribution itself originates out of a common-sensical measure of equivalence by which the original distributions can be known, and their disturbances measured. The key to exhaustion here is in this notion of equivalence; the latter involves an abstract orientation by which quantities can be compared (so that the punishment can 'fit' the crime). It is this talionic measure, and the resultant combinations of equivalence, that will be exhausted.

Through exhaustion, any one formation of combinatorial equivalence (this crime = this punishment) will be as good as any other, bringing to a halt the tiring discussions about whether a wrong has been appropriately defined, evidenced, decided upon and/or punished: apparent acquittal and/or endless postponement; (Deleuze, 1995, p.179) but also Masoch's reversal of 'crime and punishment', demanding that the latter comes first so as to justify the former, (Deleuze, 1989, p.88) are modes of exhaustion. At this level, guilty and not-guilty pass into each other, with the affirmation of one affirming its opposite. Given that decisiveness is at the core of the legal process, the affirmation of this process is the simultaneous affirmation of all of the possible outcomes it might produce, without distinction between them. However, we remain at the level of Nozick unless the combinatorial is extended beyond the legal process to become active in the communal imagination of 'requital of desert' as an ideal: to have immunity is nevertheless to also be contaminated, given that it cannot take place except in the midst of community. In this regard, immunity is like the 'bad' immanence described by Jean-Luc Nancy in *The Inoperative Community*, or a certain undecidability running through the decision itself (for example, the inclusion of dissenting or minority judgments in the law reports; the possibility of appeal).

---

fraudulently seeks to ground itself by deciding that, as all lives matter, some lives will matter more than others.

Exhaustion makes any formula of restitution equally viable and, in so doing, brings to the surface the Wittgensteinian point that a rule or norm cannot contain the rule or norm of its own application. Exhaustion is the ungrounding of law to the extent that no one combination has preference over another, and justice ceases to be expressive or referable to a sovereign centre.

(2) Requital of desert is only possible through an ideal of similarity or sameness, whereby likenesses between the elements of a case, claim or action can be established so as to 'justify' equal treatment by analogy. The possibility of equality, or impartiality, presupposes the existence of the same, or of common forms active in different situations. Justice is then the process of identifying these commonalities. In actuality, the reverse is the case: a tremendous work of distinction is undertaken through which differences can be filtered out, so as to produce the same: 'To avoid showing favour is to ignore "irrelevant" inequalities, that is to say, inequalities other than the inequality of desert'. (Raphael, 2001, p.234) For this reason, impartiality does not yet attain the status of non-preferentiality, because it is derived from a myriad of partialities that must be distinguished between in the first place. A decision must be made on the relevant and irrelevant differences if the same is to take form. The reason why we must begin with difference comes back to the need for justice to exist in the first place – justice is not self-evident and therefore not self-administering. If sameness existed outright, justice would occur naturally and be, for this reason, imperceptible; yet the decision, sentence, norm, and so on must be articulated. This articulation or announcement presupposes that a moment of normativity can be extracted or isolated within the system of norms itself.

Ewald's account of norms makes it clear that they exist only as a multiplicity: the normal and the abnormal are not 'opposites' but points on a spectrum that pass into each other. (Ewald, 1991, p.157) It is not necessary to fully superimpose the norm upon the average (Canguilhem, 1989, p.151 *et seq*) to see that, to the extent that it functions as an averaging (filtering) mechanism, the norm is extracted from a range of divergences or abnormalities (no specific example coincides with the average of which it is an example).

Impartiality first requires the differentiation of instances so that their commonality (average) might be calculated. Impartiality is therefore a second order process for dealing with partialities, obviously dependent upon the latter as such. Each partiality is a possible world, (Deleuze, 1998, p.157) holding out the possibility of justice itself – not so much as a specific decision or outcome than as a multiplicity of voices. It seems that, if all of these worlds and voices could be added up or combined, justice might be achieved. Yet, this remains at the level of an ideal that presupposes the possibility of such a totality, with clearly individualised and articulated voices being combinable. The mode of exhaustion undermines such impartiality, with its implied hope of a superior and complete pan-partiality, by confusing all of these voices, of receiving them as a clamour of indistinct murmurs: 'Who knows but that, on the lower frequencies, I speak for you?' (Ellison, 2001, p.561) Capable of being neither partial *nor* impartial, normal *nor* abnormal, the voice of justice becomes a whisper that one cannot quite hear.

(3) The clamour of voices is not a problem of quantity (too many voices), but the result of a qualitative indistinctness which does not reduce them all to the same voice but, rather, makes each voice its own specific type of indistinctness or partiality. The voice already

differs from itself. For the purposes of competition this difference can be normalised and, as such, stabilised as the appearance of this or that world in competition with other worlds; but it nevertheless remains operative as something to be continuously averaged out. Such differences are an image – not as something represented or actualised, but as presupposed in an 'image of thought' (Deleuze, 1994, chapter 3) – by which a 'background' or 'context' is taken as given, so that something average can be said or communicated. Needless to say, this image is highly unstable, and constantly threatens the norms of good communication. At the very least, the image must enable a basic distinction to be made between the content of a communication and its form or articulation: 'the understander must pre-suppose self-reference in the communicator in order to use this self-reference to separate information from utterance. Therefore every communication expresses the possibility that self-reference and utterance diverge'. (Luhmann, 1995, p.151)

Distorting somewhat, we can nevertheless understand this to mean that the image constitutes self-reference and, in so doing, restrains the dangers posed by double contingency. (Luhmann, 1995, chapter 3) It seems as if, potentially at least, the image is something that we can share or have in common. Yet the image – while allowing for the separation of content and utterance necessary if interpretation is to take place at all – does not guarantee its 'proper' or 'effective' deployment in any given communication. For sure, straining language in the direction of nonsense and agrammaticality begins to display (and challenge) the presumed observance of the image (or norms of self-reference), and shows that the image is in fact constructed through the very processes of self-referentiality that it otherwise apparently provides for; but even before this (artistic) point is reached, the 'proper' day-to-day use of communication cannot guarantee its truth or correctness. Not only is it essential that meaning and statement diverge (I cannot directly say what I mean) if communication is to be anything more than a set of triggers or stimuli, but this divergence can also be exploited (take as an example the statement: 'I always lie').

The tension – evident in fake news and alternative facts – is that the exploitation of the internal ambivalence of communications can be used for competitive advantage; indeed, at some point, truth (to the extent valorised through processes of self-reference) loses its competitive edge. At the same time, the technological dimension of communications increasingly becomes the relevant image or reference for *all* communications, such that the fact *of being communicated* becomes the pertinent self-reference, or image of truth (the more something is communicated, the truer it becomes), inducing the type of simulations described by Baudrillard. (Baudrillard, 1983) Exhaustion must therefore dissipate the image so as to make communications glitch or stutter.

This requires making the silences and the voids of the image apparent. Such silences exist because the image is operative through being presupposed, rather than by being articulated. It is what must remain unsaid so that something else (another possibility) can be voiced or said. The exhaustion of the image is not the saying (nor seeing) of what would otherwise remain unarticulated, because this would simply be a tiring process of trying to give voice to all potentials; rather, exhaustion is the undermining of communication from within, giving the conditional inarticulateness and incommunicativity of the image a consequential force or intensity *outside of any actual communication*. Writing of Benveniste, Esposito refers to this as the third person: 'What is put into play with the third person is no longer a relationship based on exchange between a "subjective person," indicated by the *I,* and a "non-subjective person," represented by the *you*, but the possibility of a non-personal person, or more radically, of a non-person'. (Esposito, 2012, p.106)

The image of the non-person is the collapse of differentiation but not of specificity. It is the level of pre-personal flows concerned not with the relations between two terms (for example, between 'you' and 'I' as two persons) but in the relationality itself, free of any such related terms.[13] The particular non-persons that we already are, as the bare life subtending what we say, see, and do: 'When you start thinking in images, without words, you're well on the way'. (Burroughs & Gysin, 1979, p.2)

(4) As Deleuze describes it, the problem of the image is also the problem of space. (Deleuze, 1998, p.160) Competitiveness involves incessant movement, (Moore, 2013) both virtual and actual: one must move from place to place while also being 'innovative' and 'creative' at the same time. The figure of the curator perhaps sums this up for us today, ceaselessly combining communicative elements for exhibitions and platforming, and 'moving' it all from place to place in search of attention.

Competitive (or curatorial) space is self-coordinating, no longer having the relative stability of institutional references (or moulds).[14] It seems close to exhaustion but is more cunning: it grounds itself on its own lack of ground (that is, authorises itself by its own lack of authority), applying this as a means to keep on endlessly adjusting itself and displacing its own internal limits. (Deleuze & Guattari, 1984, pp.222–40) It is the space of possibility, inhabited by Nietzsche's 'higher man'.[15] Those who lack mobility will be allowed to die where they fall. In this regard, the heterotopias described by Foucault (Foucault, 2000b, p.175 *et seq*) did not go far enough, because they only gave place to the 'others', 'transgressions' and 'taboos' that regular space used to distinguish itself by comparison. Whether these other spaces are concealed as guilty secrets under discipline, or 'celebrated' through inclusivity under control, does not matter so much in terms of neoliberal operation. If the latter is to become exhausted, space must become an 'any-space-whatever'. (Deleuze, 1998, p.160) Such a space does not become defined by exclusions and inclusions, but forms an assemblage of elements that imparts a space rather than filling it up or being contained by it. Here, space becomes an event prioritising the relation rather than the related terms.

Even so, space remains inextricably linked to extension but, with any-space-whatever, the inhabitation of it – and movements across it – disallows divisions and exclusions: the space cannot be portioned out in proper plots; friend and enemy cannot be identified; law fails to achieve order and orientation; and nothing either belongs or is disqualified. Yet, the space has its own specificity or singularity that exceeds any possible judgement or decision on it. It is the space of an original bare life where each element is exposed to all of the others such that, while no equivalence between these elements is possible,

---

[13] Deleuze discusses such a 'pure' relationality in Deleuze, 1994. See his account of the calculus, and the formula dy/dx, at pp.170–6.

[14] Deleuze describes moulds as being a feature of disciplinary society, while control is constantly in modulation. See 'Postscripts on Control Societies' in Deleuze, 1995.

[15] See 'The Mystery of Ariadne according to Nietzsche' in Deleuze, 1998.

they have an equality of status deriving from the mere fact of their *being together*. This is not the state of nature, nor a chance outcome, but the inseparability of contingency and necessity: they have been thrown together. Any decision that particular elements should be allowed to die or perish for the advantage of other elements is disqualified at this level. What forestalls this decision is not an original veil of ignorance but something even more unreasonable: exposure to life, or abnormality without average. This provides no means by which 'interests', 'preferences' or 'ends' could be identified or pursued. Instead, any-space-whatever is a pantheistic/panpsychic raw flesh that is not harmonised or integrated with itself, and across which affects and percepts are felt and suffered. The earth ceases to be a divisible surface, becoming a constellation of intensive spaces that all pass through each other.

Considered phenomenologically, these spaces constitute the infra-world described by François J. Bonnet: the sensibility of the raw flesh that subtends any possible representation, (Bonnet, 2017, p.91) and which always fails to be exhausted by them. Of the infra-world, Bonnet writes:

Everywhere, it oozes, it crouches in the shadows. Beneath language, beneath sensations. A quaking world. The infra-world is not a speculative reality. It is the mute and blind portion of the real, its accursed share. It is the worlds of exiled impressions and actions, but it is not an absent world. The infra-world is the world that withdraws from the infra-liminal world of perception. It is what fails to make a world. (Bonnet, 2017, p.90)

Failing to make a world should be understood as the condition for any viable democracy. As Marguerite Duras wrote:

You will think the miracle is not in the apparent similarity between each of the particles that make up those millions of men in their continuous hurling, but in the irreductible difference that separates them from each other, that separates men from dogs, dogs from film, sand from sea, God from the dog or from that tenacious gull struggling against the wind, from the liquid crystal of your eyes, from the sharp crystal of the sands, from the unbreathable foul air in the hall of that hotel after the dazzling light of the beach, from the word, from each sentence, from each line in each book, from each day and each century and each eternity past and future, and from you and from me. (Duras, 1993, pp.35–6)

INJUSTICE

Communication and chance outcomes: the competition for justice is also the justice of competition. To operate as such, it is necessary to divide the institutional from the consequential so that this divide might be communicated about, and the acceptable collateral damages decided upon. Justice has become a world of possibilities.

In a remarkable intervention, Nicola Masciandaro homes in on what is at stake: law as ontology and law as ethics. (Masciandaro, 2014, p.6) Law as it is (institution) and as it should be (consequence). Through this paradigm not only is the justice of what *is* (as existent) rejected but, too, a space is opened up by which the individual can know itself as existentially worried and fearful. (Masciandaro, 2014, pp.13–14) This replaces the beatitude of justice with decisions upon – and as the competitive demand for – justice. From this perspective, the demand for justice itself becomes an *injustice*.

But what is the justice of what is? It pertains to the bare fact that there is life but that this life, as such, cannot be experienced nor lived *directly*. Masciandaro describes it as akin to a force of attraction, around which lived lives curve without incarnating it. It is the superior justice that *must* exist because 'everything takes place *as if* [it] did not exist'. (Daumal quoted in Masciandaro, 2014, p.10) It is the death that attracts life to it, continuously pulling it into orbit. This force is de-individualising and impersonal. It is exhaustion, or

> a real source of imperishable sweetness immanent to everything that infinitely exceeds *me*, namely, the so-and-so who lives according to the illusory right of telling Reality what it should be like or do. (Masciandaro, 2014, p.18)

The superior justice is the exhaustion of the difference between law as it is and law as it should be. However, given that humanity is – perhaps in essence – the entity that individualises itself by insisting upon this difference, it cannot do without law. If humanity does not coincide with the reality of its own bare life, law nevertheless provides the chance for something more – but here, 'chance' is not simply the unexpected outcome of an established process but, rather, an immediate affirmation of what is – chance in the more Nietzschean sense of something without cause or justification and which, as such, can only appear, suddenly, as necessity:

> Law is the chance that the refusal of sweetness *deserves*. It is a chance to stop worrying, not because keeping the law promises removal of the object of worry ... so that now one need only worry about keeping the law, but because keeping the law *instructs* in the needlessness and evil of worry in the first place. (Masciandaro, 2014, p.30; emphasis in the original)

The refusal of sweetness is the refusal of the nondifferentiation between ontology and ethics. Law is the best that humanity can manage having made such a refusal – not in terms of the content of law, but that it exists:

> Ontologically, law is what is *proven* in life and in the living. Ethically, law is how life is made worth living and the living make themselves *worthy* of life. (Masciandaro, 2014, pp.27–8)

Therefore, for humans, it is just that there is law and, to the extent that humans must nevertheless call for justice, this is also the injustice that is proper to them. Justice and injustice become indistinguishable in the same way that necessity and chance do. That law exists is relevant to all humans and, I suggest, this relevance is best lived through the type of institutional democracy outlined by Lafont (see above). In terms of what the law is and should be, contestation is preferable to consensus – to elide contestation with consensus immediately returns us to the acceptance that somebody will have to be allowed to die. Contestation is the inability to finally decide between what the law is and what it should be. Consensus is the always exceptional handing down of what the law is, as if it were a rule that already contained the rule of its own application.

Yet how might this be lived? Given the state of the world, isn't it scandalous to argue that the demand for justice is already a profound injustice? Shouldn't we accept as an inevitability that we must worry, fear and condemn? After all, doesn't the perceived need for me to justify myself here already point to this contradiction? It is helpful to return to the contingency of human life and existence: because it is not necessary for human life to exist, it is necessary to care for it and to foster it. In place of such fostering, the lack of human necessity can lead to three errors.

First error. As human life lacks necessity, a war of all-against-all is not only justified but unavoidable. There is no reason why any given human life cannot use the full means at its disposal to advance its own interests, no matter what harm or misery is caused to other lives as a consequence. Here, the contingency of human life is turned into a principle to legitimate the pursuit of whatever aims actual specific lives happen to incarnate. This might look like the non-differentiation of chance and necessity but it is, rather, the expulsion of contingency so as to produce an apparently necessary right of action, that seeks to securitise itself against chance by continuously adding to its power. Rather than exhaustion, it wants a virility without end that accounts for, and masters, every possibility in advance. In action it allows for (and 'justifies') allowing others to die, making of power just that: necro-potency (the separation of the winners from the losers).

Second error. Producing a model of what is universally best or good for human life, and then applying this in the name of human rights and protection. On this, nothing more needs to be added to Arendt's account (Baehr, 2000, pp.31–45) that identifies the operational paradox here: only those that have rights have the *locus standi* from which to claim rights. In pursuing what is best for all, other lives will still be allowed to die, albeit now with expressions of regret that this should be so.

Third error. Given its lack of necessity, human life should simply abort itself. However, this is to make of contingency a principle in the same manner as the first error, except (perhaps) from a position of relative 'weakness' rather than 'virility'. It is contradictory to make the meaninglessness of human life *its meaning*; to do so only allows anthropocentrism to creep in by the backdoor.

Against these three errors, the contingency of human life means a radical egalitarianism (life as an intensive dis-intensification) that precludes any one part, or combination of parts, from deciding when it is acceptable or legal for other lives to be allowed to die. It follows that, given that humanity is condemned to live, it cannot legitimately do so (that is, it cannot do so without forgoing the sweetness of justice) in any manner that allows parts of it to die. Lives exist contingently. Consequently, it is necessary to foster them all. This is the justice of exhaustion: the chance that, through law, humanity must foster itself in its entirety.

Perhaps through a lack of modesty, I suggest three strategies relative to this:

(a) Reclaim institutions as sites of contestation rather than consensus.
(b) Tax the rich.
(c) Pay every human on this planet a universal basic income and/or provide them with the necessary means to live.

CONCLUSION

Exhaustion is not the wearisome regret that life has no meaning. Rather, it is the affirmation of life as something intense and non-anthropocentric, as being without human necessity. This affirmation rests with Deleuze's notion of the virtual, and the processes of exhaustion by which it is made apparent by certain literary authors. I have applied these processes to the idea of justice, arguing that it must be considered as something more (or less) than the empowerment of actions, by which the justice proper to each regime (sovereignty, discipline, control) becomes achievable. This is not an argument 'against' requital of desert, impartiality, communications and chance outcomes. It is an argument against competition as the horizon of human life and human justice. It is this horizon that this chapter aims to exhaust.

Although I did not have the space here to go into detail on the harms diffused by neoliberal competition, I relied upon the work of Wendy Brown and Dardot and Laval and, in particular, the anti-democratic implications of competition that they identify. Again, I did not have space to expand on the meaning of democracy, but I referred to the account of Cristina Lafont as orientating my understanding. Within this context, I focused on how each of the justices pertinent to the Foucauldian/Deleuzian regimes of power might be exhausted. This led to the idea that it can never be legitimate that sections of humanity be left to die; the reason for this is that exhaustion allows for no exceptional space or image from or by which a decision that leaves humans to die can be affirmed. Exhaustion is the affirmation that all human life, past and present, is contingent and that, consequently, no part of it can claim to be 'more' necessary than any other part of it.

Although not developed here, my suggestion is that this contingency is the bare life subtending all human projects and that it makes thinkable a 'radical' egalitarianism. The condition of this, however, is that such egalitarianism cannot be reduced to equality or equivalence: one life is not substitutable or exchangeable for another. It is this difference between egality and equality that exhaustion operates in: it shows the beatitude of specific and unique lives that, in their specificity and uniqueness, cannot be compared to other lives. At the same time, exhaustion disallows any ranking or priority of such differences. This is the promise and horror of exhausted life: that it will be of *its* space and image, of *its* language and voice, alone. For this reason it is *necessary* that we humans *should* foster it. Thus, the problem of signs and events continues: 'from impenetrable self to impenetrable unself by way of neither'. (Beckett, 1995, p.258)

REFERENCES

Agamben, G. (1999), *Potentialities*, D. Heller-Roazen (ed), Stanford: Stanford University Press.
Agamben, G. (2005), *State of Exception*, K. Attell tr, Chicago: University of Chicago Press.
Ansell Pearson, K. (1997), *Viroid Life: Perspectives on Nietzsche and the Transhuman Condition*, London: Routledge.
Arendt, H. (1954), 'What is Authority?' in P. Baehr, (ed) (2000), *The Portable Hannah Arendt*, London: Penguin.
Ashworth, A. (2004), 'Social Control and "Anti-Social Behaviour": The Subversion of Human Rights?', *Law Quarterly Review*, 120 (Apr), pp.263–91.
Ayache, E. (2010), *The Blank Swan: The End of Probability*, Chichester: Wiley.
Baehr, P. (ed) (2000), *The Portable Hannah Arendt*, London: Penguin.
Baudrillard, J. (1983), *Simulations*, P. Foss et al tr, New York: Semiotext(e).
Beckett, S. (1979), *The Beckett Trilogy*, London: Picador Books.
Beckett, S. (1995), *The Complete Short Prose 1929–1989*, New York: Grove Press.
Blair, T. (2002), 'My Vision for Britain', *The Guardian*.
Bonnet, F.J. (2017), *The Infra-World*, A. Ireland and R. Mackay tr, Falmouth: Urbanomic.
Bowlby, J. (1958), 'The Nature of the Child's Tie to His Mother', *International Journal of Psycho-analysis*, 39, pp.350–73.
Brown, W. (2015), *Undoing the Demos: Neoliberalism's Stealth Revolution*, New York: Zone Books.

Burroughs, W.S. and Gysin, B. (1979), *The Third Mind*, London: John Calder.
Canguilhem, G. (1989), *The Normal and the Pathological*, C.R. Fawcett tr, New York: Zone Books.
Cooper, M. (2008), *Life as Surplus: Biotechnology & Capitalism in the Neoliberal Era*, Washington: University of Washington Press.
Dardot, P. and Laval, C. (2013), *The New Way of the World: On Neoliberal Society*, G. Elliott tr, London: Verso.
Deleuze, G. (1989), 'Coldness and Cruelty' in G. Deleuze and L. Sacher-Masoch, *Masochism*, New York: Zone Books.
Deleuze, G. (1994), *Difference and Repetition*, P. Patton tr, New York: Columbia University Press.
Deleuze, G. (1995), *Negotiations*, M. Joughin tr, New York: Columbia University Press.
Deleuze, G. (1998), *Essays Critical and Clinical*, D.W. Smith and M.A. Greco tr, London: Verso.
Deleuze, G. (2001), *Pure Immanence: Essays on a Life*, A. Boyman tr, New York: Zone Books.
Deleuze, G. and Guattari, F. (1984), *Anti-Oedipus: Capitalism and Schizophrenia*, R. Hurley et al tr, London: Athlone Press.
Deleuze, G. and Guattari, F. (1988), *A Thousand Plateaus: Capitalism and Schizophrenia*, B. Massumi tr, London: Athlone Press.
Deleuze, G. and Guattari, F. (1994), *What is Philosophy?*, G. Burchell and H. Tomlinson tr, London: Verso.
Diamantides, M. and Schütz, A. (2017), *Political Theology: Demystifying the Universal*, Edinburgh: Edinburgh University Press.
Duffy, S. (2006), *The Logic of Expression: Quality, Quantity and Intensity in Spinoza, Hegel and Deleuze*, Farnham: Ashgate.
Duras, M. (1993), *Two by Duras*, A. Manguel tr, Toronto: Coach House Press.
Ellison, R. (2001), *Invisible Man*, London: Penguin.
Esposito, R. (2010), *Communitas: The Origin and Destiny of Community*, T. Campbell tr, Stanford: Stanford University Press.
Esposito, R. (2012), *Third Person*, Z. Hanafi, Cambridge: Polity Press.
Ewald, F. (1991), 'Norms, Discipline, and the Law' in R. Post (ed), *Law and the Order of Culture*, Berkeley: University of California.
Foucault, M. (2000), *Power: The Essential Works of Foucault 1954-1984 Volume 3*, R. Hurley et al tr, London: Penguin.
Foucault, M. (2000b), *Aesthetics: Power: The Essential Works of Foucault 1954–1984 Volume 2*, R. Hurley et al tr, London: Penguin.
Foucault, M. (2008), *The Birth of Biopolitics: Lectures at the Collège de France 1978–1979*, G. Burchell tr, Basingstoke: Palgrave Macmillan.
Garland, D. (2002), *The Culture of Control*, Oxford: Oxford University Press.
Gontarski, S.E. (2015), *Creative Involution: Bergson, Beckett, Deleuze*, Edinburgh: Edinburgh University Press.
Hacking, I. (1990), *The Taming of Chance*, Cambridge: Cambridge University Press.
Haldar, P. (2012), 'Sovereignty and Divinity in the Vedic Tradition: Mitra-Varuna, Prajapati and *Rta*', *Divus Thomas*, 155(2), pp.382–401.
Hill Collins, P. and Bilge, S. (2020), *Intersectionality*, Cambridge: Polity Press.
Janich, P. (2018), *What is Information?*, E. Hayot and L. Pao tr, Minneapolis: University of Minnesota Press.
Klein, N. (2008), *The Shock Doctrine: The Rise of Disaster Capitalism*, London: Penguin.
Lafont, C. (2020), *Democracy Without Shortcuts: A Participatory Conception of Deliberative Democracy*, Oxford: Oxford University Press.
Liebmann, J. (2007), *Restorative Justice: How it Works*, London: Jessica Kingsley Publishers.
Luhmann, N. (1995), *Social Systems*, J. Bednarz Jr and D. Baecker tr, Stanford: Stanford University Press.
Masciandaro, N. (2014), *Sufficient Unto the Day: Sermones Contra Solicitudinem*, Schism Press.
Mbembe, A. (2013), 'Necropolitics' in T. Campbell and A. Sitze (eds), *Biopolitics: A Reader*, Durham: Duke University Press.
Meillassoux, Q. (2008), *After Finitude: An Essay on the Necessity of Contingency*, R. Brassier tr, London: Continuum.

Moore, N. (2012), 'The Perception of the Middle' in L. de Sutter and K. McGee, *Deleuze and Law*, Edinburgh: Edinburgh University Press.
Moore, N. (2013), 'Diagramming Control' in P. Rawes, (ed), *Relational Architectural Ecologies: Architecture, Nature, and Subjectivity*, London: Routledge.
Moore, N. (2021), 'Pay It All Back: Writing Paranoia-Paranoid Writing' in S.E. Gontarski (ed), *Burroughs Unbound: William S. Burroughs and the Performance of Writing*, London: Bloomsbury.
Nancy, J.-L. (1991), *The Inoperative Community*, P. Conor et al tr, Minneapolis: University of Minnesota Press.
Nancy, J.-L. (2007), *The Creation of the World* or *Globalization*, F. Raffoul and D. Pettigrew tr, Albany: SUNY Press.
Nozick, R. (2001), *Anarchy, State, and Utopia*, Oxford: Blackwell Publishing.
O'Malley, P. (2004), *Risk, Uncertainty and Government*, London: Routledge.
Raphael, D.D. (2001), *Concepts of Justice*, Oxford: Clarendon Press.
Rawls, J. (2005), *A Theory of Justice*, Cambridge: Harvard University Press.
Sen, A. (2010), *The Idea of Justice*, London: Penguin.
Virno, P. (2008), *Multitude: Between Innovation and Negation*, I. Bertoletti et al tr, Los Angeles: Semiotext(e).
Virno, P. (2015), *Déjà Vu and the End of History*, D. Broder tr, London: Verso.

12. *Oikonomia*

Marinos Diamantides

> Thus, they spoke to one another. And a hound that lay there raised his head and pricked up his ears, Argos, the hound of Odysseus…whom of old he had himself bred, but had no joy of him, for ere that he went to sacred Ilios…There lay the hound Argos, full of vermin; yet even now, when he marked Odysseus standing near, he wagged his tail and dropped both his ears, but nearer to his master he had no longer strength to move. Then Odysseus looked aside and wiped away a tear, easily hiding from Eumaeus what he did; … [Eumaeus, said]: 'Aye, verily this is the hound of a man that has died in a far land. If he were but in form and in action such as he was when Odysseus left him and went to Troy thou wouldest soon be amazed at seeing his speed and his strength.'
>
> Homer, *Odyssey*, Book 17, lines 290–315[1]

OF INOPERATIVE BEINGS AND APPARATUSES

For Giorgio Agamben, '[H]uman life is as inoperative and without purpose'[2] as is the life of the rest of animals – such as our best friend the dog's – yet only the human animal 'has learned to become bored'.[3] We labour in order to achieve ends – to fight in Troy or reach back to Ithaca – and, consequently, may spend too much of our lives feeling 'held in limbo' – between what we set out to achieve and what we do achieve – and even sometimes resentful, of the opportunities for happiness missed in the process, such as playing with Argos the dog. 'Do something with your life; be useful!' says the internalised figure of authority –father, god, or sovereign leader of the pack – mobilising us for various historical tasks – while they themselves are respectfully retired, withdrawn from creation and reigning over us. 'Don't just waste your life like a dog!': that in so many cultures the name of our most beloved animal is used as an insult for fellow humans[4] is telling of a near universal predicament: to be publicly divided, ontologically, from our purposeless beloved four-legged friend is also to relate to our own playfulness, aimlessness or 'inoperativity' as a repressed, private, dirty secret. Arguably, however, it is 'man in the occident' who has stood out in the schooling of in-operativity-repression as time has gone by. The ancient Athenians, like us, neatly separated animals from human life and while they loved their dogs, they objected to other humans adopting a 'Diogenes lifestyle' (hence giving to cynicism its negative twist); yet at least they loved their symposia and their sleep (*Hypnos*,

---

[1] Trans. A.T. Murray, PhD. Cambridge, MA., Harvard University Press; London, William Heinemann, Ltd. 1919.

[2] 'Human life is inoperative and without purpose, but precisely this *argia* and this absence of aim make the incomparable operativity of the human species possible. Man has dedicated himself to production and labor, because in his essence he is completely devoid of work, because he is the Sabbatical animal par excellence.' Agamben, G. (2011), *The Kingdom and the Glory: For a Theological Genealogy of Economy and Government*, Stanford, CT: Stanford University Press, pp.245–6.

[3] Agamben, G. (2004), *The Open: Man and Animal*, Stanford, CT: Stanford University Press, p.70.

[4] A point most eruditely analysed in Alizart, M. (2018), *Chiens*, Paris: Presses Universitaires de France, along with an equally important point.

the god of sleep, was a better alternative to his brother *Thanatos*), and cynically – decisively, in the negative sense of the word – left hard work to harnessed animals and slaves. By contrast, most of us wake up early for yet another long day at work – including 'from home' – and yet another 'power meeting' telling ourselves that 'sleep is for losers'. There has, therefore, evidently been great acceleration and considerable democratisation – or 'progress' – of the process of the anthropological 'apparatus'[5] that captures inoperative, purposeless human lives into a limbo between means and ends. Part of the secret of this dubious success is that for some time now – two millennia, to be exact – we have been learning that life without purpose *can* be enjoyed without shame and guilt – *just not now*. To be sure, retirees can enjoy well-earned idleness in the retirement home just as the well-judged resurrected Christian will in paradise: where, however, our organs will be separated from *any* usage; there, the hands we did not use to caress a beloved except to initiate procreational sex, or to write poetry rather than another report or email; or the feet we did not use to wander, but only to run on a treadmill, will be totally idle, retaining only an ostensive, demonstrative, exhibitionist, pornographic and, we are to accept, 'glorious' function.[6] It is against this ideological apparatus that Cavafy wrote: 'As you set out for Ithaka/hope your road is a long one,/full of adventure, full of discovery.'[7]

OIKONOMIA

We work hard so as to eventually retire; we play hard so as to prepare for hard work. How did we learn to inhabit this limbo in which means cannot be valuable and enjoyable in themselves? The question may be answerable with reference to the composite western paradigm of *oikonomia*, a key term in Agamben's painstakingly detailed archaeology. As is well known, in classical Greece, '*oikonomia*' referred exclusively to the political management/administration in the *oikoi* (Greek: estates/households) of resources for production, reproduction and consumption (fields, cattle, foodstuff, household staff, slaves and women) by the *oikonomos* – a slave who operated at arm's length from the, usually absentee, 'master' of the house; in late antique and medieval Greek the term came to mean the management of the entire *ecumene* by the anointed sovereign's staff as part of Zeus' providential plan. Agamben uses the term to describe the contemporary bi-political situation in which all beings and things (including beings *as* things) are managed by *oikonomoi* yet those human animals cast as the 'sovereign people' are portrayed as masters of modern states, namely of spaces which, additionally, blend

---

[5] Giorgio Agamben distinguishes between living beings and 'apparatuses' into which the former are incessantly captured. An apparatus is literally '… anything that has, in some way, the capacity to capture, orient, determine, intercept, model, control or secure the gestures, behaviours, opinions, or discourses of living beings. Not only, therefore, prisons, madhouses, the panopticon, schools, confession, factories, but also the pen, writing, literature, philosophy, agriculture, cigarettes, navigation, computers, cellular telephones and – why not – language itself, which is perhaps the most ancient of the apparatuses.' Agamben, G. (2009), *What is an Apparatus? And Other Essays*, Stanford, CT: Stanford University Press, p.14.

[6] '[T]here is perhaps nothing more enigmatic than a glorious penis, nothing more spectral than a purely doxological vagina.' Agamben, G. (1993), *Stanzas: Word and Phantasm in Western Culture*, New York: SUNY Press, p.99.

[7] Cavafy, C.P. (1992), 'Ithaka' in Savidis, George (ed.), *C.P. Cavafy: Collected Poems*, trans. Edmund Keeley and Philip Sherrard, Princeton: Princeton University Press, p.36.

or render indistinct two different modes of association deriving from Roman law: the idea of the state either as *societas* or as *universitas*.[8]

The paradigm of *oikonomia* is as composite as western culture. First, it involves imagining and conceiving being in the world *a la grecque*, that is, in line with classical Greek philosophical metaphysics which uses a series of binary distinctions, for example, to divide inoperative animals from humans with *teloi*, *zoe* from *bios*, body from mind, slaves from persons, emotions from reason, and *dynamis* (that is, power-potential) from *energeia* (actualised power); and to distinguish the private *oikos* from the public *polis*, heteronomy from autonomy, law from politics, *nomos* (constitutional law) from *psephisma* (decree), *politeia* (that is, the form of political activity that constitutes a democratic body politic or, as we say, 'constituent' power) from *politeuma* (that is, the resulting political outcome which we call the legally 'constituted' form of democratic government), and so on. This binary onto-metaphysics *ipso facto* opens up the prospect of 'abandonment' of forms-of-life that cannot, or will not, be neatly placed on either side of these distinctions; Diogenes' biography and Agamben's analyses of various types of 'bare lives' that are 'included' in civil life only by being utterly exposed to the most extreme vulnerability in the series entitled *Homo Sacer* are instructive in this regard. Second, the paradigm in question involves the belief that such binary relations are exhaustive of the realm of differences, or, in other words, forgetting of their abandonment effect. Arguably, both Diogenes and his more conventional fellow citizens could and would recognise the arbitrariness of such binaries as animal/man. Irreverent Diogenes put himself at odds with his community as he 'cynically' barked at the way his community used such binary thinking to define itself and the world; his conformist fellow-humans validated them as truly exhaustive descriptions of reality from the heart of their polis, in the agora, temples, philosophy schools and theatres; arguably, at the same time, they cynically laughed off the relevant arbitrariness and violence (see below my discussion of *Ecclesiazusae*). With us, however, things are often somewhat different; cynicism gives way to 'hypocrisy' in both of the original meanings of this Greek word: 'acting' as well as 'acting uncritically' by abjectly-dutifully following a mere script. What has changed since the Greeks? (Very) long – and ongoing – story short, the Stoic and later Christian religions postulated an (unfalsifiable) *third element* that totalises, structures and renders indistinct – or 'economises' – the binaries. Thus, in view of their respective *theia dioikesis tou kosmou* (Hellenistic Greek: divine administration of the world) and *theia oikonomia* (medieval Greek: divine providence), classic Greek binaries appear as necessary parts of Zeus/God's providential plan. *Ipso facto*, the 'abandonment' of plural lifeforms that comes along with binary thinking is justifiable as a necessary means for realising said plan.

To gauge the difference providentialism made to how we attune to *oikonomia* – cynically or hypocritically – let us juxtapose a contemporary reading of a Greek comedy,

---

[8] Loughlin, M. (2003), *The Idea of Public Law*, Oxford: Oxford University Press, p.20, with reference to Oakeshott, M.J., *On Human Conduct*, in which *societas* suggests a partnership of humans who are primarily tied to one another only by loyalty, not by the pursuit of a common substantive purpose or interest. This abstract loyalty can then be extended into a respect for legal rules where the law is obeyed not because it is a means to an end but because it is an expression of their kinship. The ruler of a state understood as *societas* is the guardian of the conditions which constitute the relationship and obedience to the ruler/law is an 'end in itself', not a means to an end. It is different if we think of the state as 'universitas', namely, as a 'corporate association' where persons unite only or primarily in order to attain a common purpose/interest. Here the ruler is the owner or trustee of common property and the manager of the group activities and policy is seen as far more important than law.

Aristophanes' *Ecclesiazusae* – heavily indebted to J. Ober's[9] – with that of an earlier Greek tragedy, Aeschylus' *Oresteia*, as read by two contemporary jurists. *Ecclesiazusae*[10] shows the all-male *demos* conscious of, and able to represent to itself, the arbitrariness and violence of such distinctions as emotional women/rational men; it was only ironically 'justified' with tongue-in-cheek references to 'tradition' and 'necessity' before the very same public of citizens who considered themselves the very pioneers of innovation and freedom; thus, the plot ridicules any suggestion that it was rational in a democracy to exclude women as 'irrational' when, dressed as men, they beat them to (in?) the art of persuasion.[11] The plot also expects the audience to recognise, and laugh at, the *actual indistinction* of the 'principled' distinction they had recently enacted in an attempt to limit the partisan and irrational use of political power by means of law; between *nomos* (akin to our 'constitutional law') and *psephisma* (akin to 'decree'); and, by extension, between *politeia* (the form of political activity that constitutes a democratic body politic or, as we say, 'constituent' power) and *politeuma* (the resulting political outcome which we call the legally 'constituted' form of democratic government).[12] Their constitutional reform notwithstanding, the *psēphisma/nomos* distinction was in practice 'vague from the beginning, and it was certainly not always adhered to in practice'. It was this confusion and vagueness that 'provided the grist for ... [Aristophanes'] mill ... [since the plot] deliberately jumbles the distinction between decrees and *nomoi*'.[13] The play, therefore, shows

---

[9] Ober, J. (1998), *Political Dissent in Democratic Athens: Intellectual Critics of Popular Rule*, Princeton, NJ: Princeton University Press.

[10] The plot has the Athenian women dress up as men and so participate in the legislation process, where they bring about a 'constitutional revolution' that transforms Athens into something close to a communist utopia. But: see also below note 11.

[11] Aristophanes 'shows that unconventional effects are also possible outcomes of conventional procedures. The citizens in the audience of the play learn that they really cannot have it both ways. When deeply cherished assumptions [...] collide with democratic political culture, something has to give, and it is up to the male citizens to decide whether they will acknowledge limits on their political power to enact social realities, or admit that their social order, and the political order that was built upon it, was not as natural as they sometimes liked to pretend' (*supra*: *Political Dissent in Democratic Athens*: 147).

[12] Recall that the play was presented in 390 BC, a dozen years after the end of the Peloponnesian War, the oligarchy of the Thirty, and the restoration of democracy, and 20 years after the status of the Athenian laws (*nomoi*) had been hotly contested. In the late fifth century, oligarchs had seized control of the state, claiming that democratic government acted against the dictates of the 'ancestral' laws (*patrios nomos*). Once democracy was restored in 410 BC, Athenian (male) citizens decided to collect and republish all extant laws; moreover, they initiated a new and complicated constitutional procedure for making laws (*nomothesia*) that introduced the, then new, binary distinction that proceeds from the distinction democracy/rule of law. So-called *psēphismata* – let us translate them as 'decrees' – could be passed freely by the majority of the *demos* in the Assembly as needed in order to cover matters of immediate concern (such as foreign policy); in contrast, the *nomoi*/laws were intended to cover general matters and address issues of long-term concern, and they were to be made by specially lotteried committees.

[13] *Political Dissent in Democratic Athens* 145–6. More specifically: 'By having the hitherto politically excluded women, participate in the Assembly dressed as men, where they delivered public speeches that were enthusiastically accepted as authoritative and which culminated in bringing about a new regime through "enacted" or "decreed" (*dedogmenos*) new *nomoi*, Aristophanes *staged* not only the *aporia* but also the *arbitrariness* of enactment based on the *nomos/psēphisma* distinction. Was the new regime, called into being by the performative speech-act of a *psēphisma* of the Assembly, a contravention of the new Athenian constitution's approach to *nomoi*? The women's regime was certainly a fundamental and general change in the political order and was intended to last indefinitely. But, on the other hand, the women's *psēphisma* may not have violated any existing law: it is hard to imagine that there was a law on

not only the *aporia* but also the *arbitrariness* of enactment based on the *nomos/psēphisma* distinction. Likewise, the play places centre stage the arbitrariness and unreason of other key binaries such as enactment/persuasion, nature/custom, public/private, egalitarianism/elitism. Insofar as such binaries were seen to be laughably confusing and arbitrary, the democracy/law 'relation' could not be said to have offered the *polis* what modernity expects public law to offer the state: solid authority for the legitimate use of power. While the *kratos* (of demo-cracy) in modern Greek means 'modern state', in ancient Greek it meant power with an 'authority' that was cynically accepted as tragicomic – a far cry from the *auctoritas* that the Romans imputed to public power and to which modernity harkens back. The Athenians watching *Ecclesiazusae* would be reminded of, but also invited to laugh cynically at, the excess of brute power over reason and principle which was pervasive both in their 'demo-cracy' and in their households. Greek comedies did not quite have a 'performative' transformational effect and Aristophanes could get away with irreverence as long as he was not seen as proposing to change what he showed to be risible but did not destroy. In fact, after ridiculing the *status quo*, the play's ending cynically ridicules utopia and innovation.[14]

Such was the cynical ethos of the faction-prone Athenian *demos*. While it came to accept that 'goods', such as security and justice, could be achieved only through collective action and active participation in the public realm of politics, the democratic *politeia*, the space of and for rational citizens, was neither a well-structured nor a holistic concept and was not premised on providential terms. The citizens (*zoa politika*) who were equal under one and the same law of equality arbitrarily comprised only the male heads of households (*oikiai*). Moreover, politics did not encompass everything social since the *demos* presupposed an arbitrary distinction between their *polis*, the space of political and legal equality between male political animals on the one hand and the beings and things (women, slaves, livestock and the property used to sustain biological life) inside their *households*. Moreover, within the *polis*, the (male) citizens acknowledged but 'lived with', without overcoming, their arbitrary distinction between *politeia* and *politeuma*. Consequently, it was not unthinkable, or immoral, for the Greek *zoa politika* to rock the boat of their *politeia* and allow disagreements over the application of, and abandonment caused by, their binary distinctions to play out violently, even at the expense of the *polis*. Hence the Greek tendency to faction and *stasis* which the fathers of the US constitution, millennia later, were keen to avoid precisely by seeking to set in motion a perpetual *renvoi* between majoritarianism and constitutional law, a seeking of balance that would not

---

the books that said, "Only biological males may be citizens," since few Athenians had ever supposed that anything else could be the case.' Ibid.

[14] Under the new women's regime, new radical laws were passed including a ban on private wealth; the communal raising of children, who will never know their fathers; equal pay for both sexes; a minimum provided standard of living; free sex for all as long as people first court the ugliest members of society; as well as, infamously, a few laws which contradict the seemingly altruistic sentiment, such as banning slaves from sleeping with free men. An interesting aside: Praxagora plans to tell the assembly that women are best suited to govern for they are harder workers, less susceptible to useless pursuits than men, and will not only better protect the soldiers but also care for their immediate needs such as adequate food and pay. In other words, the cunning plan was to offer themselves as both *archontes* and *oikonomoi*, joining the household and the city. She is, however, eventually reported to have actually delivered a compelling speech where she argued that women are better at hiding secrets, returning borrowed possessions, restraining themselves from suing or eavesdropping on people, or trying to overthrow Athens' democracy. In this sense the women in Aristophanes' *Ecclesiazusae* are not only communist utopians but also early constitutional lawyers.

endanger the 'providential' ship of state, as it were. For those who model our sovereign states after a providential God we killed – a God that was capable of absolute creative and destructive power (*potentia absoluta*) but who kindly and providentially limited Himself to act in accordance with natural law (*potentia limitata*) – the so-called 'constitutional paradox' – between our political *nomos* (constituent legislative power) and our legally constituted *politeia* – is a *paradox*[15] that must be conceptualised and explained totally from within society without reference to a 'transcendental' fundament, a task various theories of 'reflexive' constitutionalism undertake not necessarily any longer for the sake of the ship of the nation-state but for the sake of ensuring the discipline of its erstwhile passengers, the people.

Since the Greeks, and notwithstanding the aforementioned efforts to reflect, providential *oikonomia* has been increasingly less cynically and increasingly more 'hypocritically' experienced (in the sense of uncritically sticking to a providential script). First to succeed in 'glorifying' contingent social arrangements as salvific, and thus worthy of obedience, sparing no effort for their implementation, were the Stoics, who, though not bereft of humour, could apparently literally laugh themselves to death unless they had sufficient control of their emotions.[16] Living in times when tragedy was becoming more of a 'virtue piece' and the contemporary 'new comedy' was steering away from politics and dealing only with everyday life – a bit like today's soaps – and whose most famous comedy writer, Menander, is remembered for his *ante litteram* Protestant work ethic,[17] the Stoics postulated a third element: a providential Zeus whose *Logos* and *Pneuma* 'authorised' and 'guided' the so-called good king of Hellenistic kingdoms as to the appropriate allocation of tasks and roles to all beings. Moreover, a happy end for all was now thinkable – a far cry from the Athenian democracy's 'ship of fools' where slaves rowed, *oikonomoi* managed and masters fought for office. In view of this 'third element', one was no longer 'arbitrarily' a slave or a freeman, a political animal or a domesticated woman – as the audience of Aristophanes would have appreciated, notwithstanding Aristotle's nonsense about nature.[18] Indeed, all classical binary distinctions were

---

[15] See for example the various essays in Martin Loughlin and Neil Walker (eds) (2008), *The Paradox of Constitutionalism: Constituent Power and Constitutional Form*, Oxford: Oxford University Press.

[16] Chrysippus was one of the most influential Stoics and the third head of the Stoic school. At the age of 73, he saw a donkey eating some figs, and he found the image so funny that he laughed himself to death.

[17] Reputedly said: 'He who labours diligently need never despair, for all things are accomplished by diligence and labor.'

[18] The Stoics are well reputed for not regarding slavery as something natural as Aristotle did; they also rejected the sort of political identification that would have been familiar to Plato ('Never,' writes Epictetus, 'say, "I am Athenian" or "I am Corinthian," but rather *kosmios* lit. cosmic i.e. of the whole world') since they declared all human beings to share the same rational nature, which we have received from the Divine Reason, or Zeus, himself. This, however, is not the whole, or perhaps the main, story. Epictetus also claimed that while every person has a 'cosmic' vocation, namely that of being a human, this vocation is composed of a set of more specific vocations: citizen of the world, an active part of the world, one who can comprehend the divine economy (*dioikesis theia*), citizenship in a state, one who shares given genetic roles (for example, son, brother) and given social roles (for example, town councillor, soldier). 'The acceptance of the whole of the universe as a comprehensible object whose regular function was knowable led, almost inevitably, to the conclusion that one must or should attempt to gain knowledge of the rules and act accordingly. That meant finding out exactly where one was located in the nature of things and behaving according to that place in Nature. Hence one of the appeals of Stoic ideology was that it had a very strong element of social definition and role-playing built into it. Each person had a definite place in the cosmic order and had a role to play, whether as slave, father, husband,

thence 'locked together', as it were, in a comprehensively *providential* relation of indistinction which though anarchic was not laughable, just as God is solemnly *anarchos*.

To be sure, the rather humourless Aristotle[19] had also introduced a 'third element' when, for example, in order to get rid of the indeterminacy between *politeia/politeuma*, he had introduced the notion of the 'supreme' (*kyrion*) power that 'holds together the two sides of politics'.[20] While we can say that this 'anticipates' later theories of sovereignty, however, it is important to remember that Aristotle's (or Plato's) 'constitutional' speculations on such matters were emphatically not taken up in a discourse of 'public law' analogous to ours, that is, one that can justify a constitution. Only since the Stoics do we have evidence that the violence of abandoning forms of life that do not fit in such arbitrary binaries as human/animal etc was no longer visible to most and cynically risible to its perpetrators; since, by then, all effectively understood themselves as puppets of an overall beneficial puppeteer moving them through the administrative strings held by the (very unclassical) figure of the divinely sanctioned 'good king'. Thus, in contrast to the male *archontes* of the Athenian democratic *polis* – for whom all and any kings were tyrants, just as self-rule was arbitrarily exclusive – the Hellenistic 'good king' was neither a tyrant nor an arbitrarily exclusive *demos*: his administration could only, ultimately, prove 'fair and beneficial' to all the, culturally distinct, subjects living in the Hellenistic kingdoms in relation to both public and private life. Reverence for Hellenistic 'good kings' – whose reigns enjoyed relative stability in contrast with the irreverent and stasis-prone Athenian *demos* – anticipates and informs the Roman citizens' 'moral duty' to uphold the stability of their ResPublica, by resolving any disagreements over the correct application of their mixed constitution (democratic, aristocratic and monarchical), at least in principle, with reference to safeguarding *salus populi*. The latter 'third element', unknown to the Greeks, blurred the common good of citizenry with the interests of their *oikiai*. It was not long before Roman citizenship was bestowed to the empire's multi-cultural peoples (for fiscal reasons) while subsequently the whole *ecumene* of the Christianised empire found itself working for 'salvation' *aka* the new *salus populi*. Indeed, as the *Salus Populi Romani* icon of the Virgin and Christ[21] amply illustrates, Christianisation was not a 'rupture' between the constitutions of the pagan and Christianised Roman empires, but rather another phase in the process of epigenesis of the western machine of government as *oikonomia*. The un-Greek *Salus Populi Romani* re-appeared in the form of ecumenical Divine Providence since now, at least in principle, 'there was no more Jew and Greek, slave and freeman' inside the empire. At that point the stoic postulates of *Logos* and *Pneuma* had become, respectively, *God as Word* (John 1:1) and *Holy Spirit*. Moreover, in what was a further important innovation within the western paradigm, yet another *third element* had been added, this time to stabilise the scissile nature of the divinity itself thence formally known as Trinitarian: the incarnated *Son of God/*

---

or councillor, and also had specific duties attached to that role [...] How, then, does one know what one's role is? Merely reflect on the name of what you are, Epictetus says: town councillor, youth, old man, father, king, general, brother, son, teacher in a list where the genetically given is mixed with the social datum.' Brent D. Shaw, 'The Divine Economy: Stoicism as Ideology,' *Latomus*, vol. 64 (1985), pp.16–54.

[19] For him, tragedy imitates men who are better than the average, and comedy men who are worse.

[20] As discussed in Agamben, G. (2010), 'Introductory Note on the Concept of Democracy' in Allen, A. (ed.), *Democracy in What State?* New York: Columbia University Press.

[21] Kept, heavily (and horribly) overpainted, at the Borghese (Pauline) Chapel of the Basilica of Saint Mary Major in Rome.

Son of Man, born to a virgin mother and killed but resurrected, rupturing history and genealogy. Presided over and funded by the Eastern Roman empire, the Holy Synods gave us the theological doctrine of Trinitarianism according to which the 'mystery' of God's providential *oikonomia* overlaps with that of the relational unity of His own trinitarian essence (He is One but this unity consists of the relations between himself as Father, as Spirit and as Son). That much, then, is common to subjects of Hellenistic kingdoms, Roman citizens, the inhabitants of Byzantine 'ecumene' and, eventually, all the members of universal humanity in the name of which, say, a Pope could send a letter to the just colonised inhabitants of Mesoamerica announcing the 'Good News' of their inclusion in the Church; or 'the coalition of the willing,' in the late twentieth and early twenty-first centuries, can spread liberal values and bombs. Unlike the cynical and un-economic Greek bastards, we still (!) assume the arbitrary binary differentiations inherited from them (civilised–barbarian, for example) or from early theologians (Two Cities, Two Powers) as part of the providential *oikonomia* – for which no effort, sacrifice or collateral damage is too much.

P-OST-ULATES AND ECONOMIC TRUTHS

To illustrate the great progress we have made in passing from dastardly Greek 'cynicism' to Christian 'hypocrisy', we may now contrast the above reading of comic *Ecclesiazusae* to contemporary readings of Aeschylus' *Oresteia*. The play was produced circa 458 BC, that is, a few years after legislation, sponsored by the democratic reformer Ephialtes, had stripped the court of the *Areopagus*, hitherto one of the most powerful vehicles of upper-class political power, of all of its functions except some minor religious duties and the authority to try homicide cases. One could just say that by having the case of Orestes' matricide being resolved by a judgment of acquittal by the *Areopagus*, roughly on the basis that mariticide is worse, Aeschylus might have been simply expressing his approval of this particular reform while brushing off the traditional misogyny. Yet the *Oresteia* is also one of the Greek tragedies our countless modern scholars, jurists and political theorists do not tire in discussing as the key to their interpretations of the interplay of necessity and freedom, law and justice, norms and facts, rules and their application. As is well known, the vast majority of these produce variations of one theme: the play represents the beneficent passage from unreason, vengeance and guilt to reason, justice and legal acquittal. One, relatively recent, example is by François Ost, Belgian jurist; law and/as literature scholar; and scriptwriter of, *inter alia*, the play *Antigone Voilée*. With his 'The Invention of the Other – Aeschylus and Kafka'[22] Ost is, to my eyes, an example of hypo-critically re-validating the unclassical medieval postulate of divine *oikonomia* in the modern secular era.

His reading of the trilogy is typically undertaking a modernist 'progressive' approach in which the sequence of events over the three plays *culminates* in the meaning of the *third* one. The 'moral' of the story is when Orestes ends his wanderings in Athens, where he is used as a trial dummy by Athena, who set up the first courtroom trial in which he was, eventually, acquitted, and the *Furies* transformed into the *Eumenides*. Thus, all that is prior to this moment inside the play – all the murders of both the innocent and the guilty – and all the context of

---

[22] Ost François, 'The Invention of the Other. Aeschylus and Kafka,' *Esprit*, vol. 8–9 August/September (2007), pp.147–65.

writing and staging of the play – the aforementioned reforms by Ephialtes – are here implicitly considered as useful means towards a glorious *telos*: establishing the new, better, order in which justice is administered by a court following identifiable rules and procedures (pleas, hearings, prosecutor and defence counsels, jury, judgment and sentence).

Suggesting that such a modernist reading could have also been classical is like suggesting that Plato had written *The Laws* as a 'solution' to the problems he had identified in his earlier *Republic*. While today such an assumption may fly between glasses of wine in a polite society soiree, or in a less than rigorous jurisprudence class, not much is learnt about the ancient ways of the Athenian *demos*, which – as shown earlier in my discussion of the comic *Ecclesiazusae* – at once drew and laughed at such distinctions as *politeia/politeuma*, *democracy/law*. Arguably, through Ost's economical reading, the interplay of necessity and freedom, law and justice, norms and facts, rules and their application, and so on is, circularly, presented as if it is a necessary step in an upwardly mobile spiralling process towards a happier end: freedom becoming civic. In case we missed too subtly made a point, Ost offers us on the plate the p-Ost-ulated benefit we stand to receive if we exchange violence for legal violence; here is his p-Ost-ulate: '*Il n'est pas question de verser dans l'angélisme; il s'agit d'une forme de violence qui au moins, dans le meilleur des cas, est canalisée.*' Namely: the violence that is not extinguished by law – which the Greeks and the Jews saw as sign of a god's wrath (respectively for human arrogance and sin) and which Benjamin or Agamben saw as a cybernetic closed-circuit system where law-founding<->law-sustaining violence alternate – is here justified for at least being channelled through institutions instead of, we can only guess, drowning us in a sea of blood. Ost does not say where the 'channelled' violence is discharged into but we can risk a guess: it must be the 'sea' of bi-politics over which democracy's legal/political ship of fools circulates aimlessly. The p-Ost-ulate is certainly 'religious' in the sense that religions are based on not questioning – '*Il n'est pas question*' – and also it is certainly one of unclassical providential economy; even as we no longer believe in a providentially anarchic God we still must act as if *some*, legal, violence is justifiable *dans le meilleur des cas*, or else we will collapse into nihilism; and even as we don't buy into angelic innocence, we must not act like the fallen angel Satan who quit his glorifying day job.

If Ost's reading of *Oresteia* effectively functions as a literary supplement so as to dispel any doubts regarding the 'progress' of state law (if not in carrying us towards the horizon of happiness or/and equality, at least in keeping us floating on the choppy waters of our discontent), a more recent example aims to do so with regards to the doubts stemming from well-founded critiques of the enlightenment and liberal democracy such as Carl Schmitt's and Giorgio Agamben's. In *Athena's Way: The Jurisprudence of the Oresteia*[23] Desmond Manderson also focuses exclusively on the third play of the *Oresteia* as the most meaningful, since it 'transcends the oppositions and tensions which Aeschylus staged' earlier (p.256). He suggests that Orestes' misogynistically based acquittal is better understood and celebrated as at least evidence of a positive transformation in the sense that the trial involved the Athenian citizens in addition to the Gods and the *Erinyes/Furies*. In this, Manderson commendably brings his reading to align with the aforementioned notion that the *Oresteia* was just Aeschylus' way of expressing his approval of Ephialtes's reforms (p.257): 'This change Aeschylus treats not as diminishing … [the Areopagus'] office, but refining and advancing it' (ibid). *Eumenides*,

---

[23] *Law, Culture and the Humanities*, vol. 15(1) (2019), pp.253–76.

he argues convincingly, is therefore best read not as 'the triumph of legal reason over the passions,' nor 'of decisionism over principle,' but of 'participatory and transformative process [of public deliberation]' over 'fatalists, literalists, positivists, and fundamentalists of all kinds' (p.264) who are, elsewhere in his piece, associated with the Erinyes, Shakespeare's Shylock (ibid) and Agamben who does not, he says, 'give us any hope' (p.255). The question to be asked if we are going to be hopeful, he says, is, rather, 'what could the rule of law mean? [...] what form could legal interpretation take, capable of navigating between the Scylla of merely following orders, and the Charybdis of a monstrous discretion?' (ibid). Now that *is* indisputably the question – no arguing here. The contemporary ship of fools, to quote Plato, is indeed navigating between these two poles – and nothing more! In the UK where I am writing from, for example, the Supreme Court has taken the form of the Scylla in the two *Miller* cases,[24] whereas the PM proved a very popular Charybdis in passing legislation to turn the monstrous Scyllas back into a poodle.

With all the respect due to erudite Professor Manderson, I must point out that his retroactive defence of deliberative democracy and Habermas' communicative reason in all but name (really, why is Habermas only mentioned in a footnote?) is supported by a rather economical exercise in literary criticism. First, though he rehearses Agamben perfectly well in key aspects,[25] Manderson rather skips over Agamben's serious and intuitive reasons for casting deliberative, participatory democracy in a somewhat less flattering light. Contemporary 'democracy' is a democracy that is entirely founded upon on the efficacy of *acclamation*, multiplied and disseminated by the media beyond all imagination.[26] The function of liturgy and coronation ceremonials has been taken over by the media active in marketing and data-harvesting in all areas of society, both public and private. This is so 'irrespectively of whether the logic of acclamation at work is "conservative" in its presupposition of the substantial unity of the acclaiming "people" or "liberal" in the dissolution of the people in social communication, we observe the same principle of government by acclamation or consent, which establishes states of consensus that reproduce our subjection to the apparatuses of

---

[24] *R (Miller) v Secretary of State for Exiting the European Union* [2017] UKSC 5 & *R (Miller) v The Prime Minister and Cherry v Advocate General for Scotland* [2019] UKSC 41.
[25] 'To a large extent, the challenge [Agamben] has posed to legal thought circles around the relationship between sovereignty and the rule of law. In *Homo Sacer*, Agamben traces a line of sovereignty from Roman law to the concentration camps of modern times, drawing heavily on Carl Schmitt's observation that "sovereign is he who decides on the exception." The sovereign declares as a conclusory fact that this or that person or group or race or class fall outside all legal protection. His is the non-justiciable power to proclaim the existence of an exception or an emergency to which the rules no longer apply. Now Schmitt's insight was that all legal circumstances contain some kernel of difference, some element of exceptionality, which might at any moment provide the sovereign with the occasion – or the excuse – to let the anomic genie out of the bottle. Homo sacer, the vulnerable human body or "bare life," is the logical corollary of this Prometheus unbound. He, we, or they, are abandoned by law and surrendered entirely to a logic of untrammelled violence or expediency: the inmate of a concentration camp or a refugee detention center, the stateless person or roma, the Jew whose property is confiscated, the Palestinian whose house is razed, the Pakistani or Afghani whose village is flattened by drones on the say-so of an unreviewable executive decision taken in the name of some crisis or another whose unprecedented exceptionality is asserted. Any one of us at any moment may be reduced to a pure animal existence without political status, legal identity, or recourse. As Agamben explains, "bare life" is "included" in the legal order only "by exclusion." It is outcast from law, by law.' *Supra* n 23: p.254.
[26] Agamben, G. (2011), *The Kingdom and the Glory*, p.256.

government'.[27] While we may think that the apparatus of 'glory' has been in decline since the demise of absolute monarchies, albeit with a notable revival during the 1930s in totalitarian regimes and again in today's populist times, Agamben argues that practices of glorification and acclamation survive in contemporary democracies in new forms: referendum, public opinion or, to recall Guy Debord's work that was a major influence on Agamben's thought, the 'society of the spectacle', in which commodities assume the mediatic form of an image. Like participating in a ritual whose sacred message one no longer believes, we go on and vote, half-heartedly, for yet another president who promises that 'Change is Possible' and when that fails we vote, just as half-heartedly, for another who promises that we can return to the 'good old days.' Or – new and improved! As adverts for washing powder say. We can click 'yes' to the automated invitation that lands in our email to take part in a so-called citizens' assembly, namely the *ad hoc* bodies of citizens formed, at the instigation of the government, to deliberate on an issue or issues of local or national or international importance and who, having listened to government-chosen experts, issue an 'advisory report' to the government. Or we can raise our clenched fists and 'Occupy Wall St!' even as, unlike at the time of Versailles, there is no centre of power *to* occupy. Rather than a castle, contemporary government seems de-organised like other service providers: a loose network of sub-contractors barely co-ordinated by an overwhelmed and impotent customer service department that puts you on hold to listen to the automated voice repeat that 'your call is important to us and will be answered shortly'. And so it goes on, with us waiting for Godot, even as we know that this is no time to find heroes that will come to our rescue; only some deep data harvester who will verify our predetermined stance on social media.

These are some of the circumstances that provide the salt with which to take Manderson's truism that '[P]ersuasion, like interpretation, is not a ruse: it can be used for good or evil, but in the end, it is the only way to escape from our past and exercise a better judgment' (pp.265–6). In this regard Manderson also notably glosses over Athena's *obiter* – and very cynical – comment in the *Oresteia*'s last play: fear and force underlie the transformation of the social order (pp.681–710). Crucially, this comment is not only true up to the forceful exclusion of citizens in the decision-making process – that is, in the play, when Apollo explained that, since all his oracles are ordained by Zeus, they are therefore 'necessarily just' – rather, it is equally true *after* the triumph of the 'participatory and transformative process' which, Manderson conveniently omits to *precis*, is *not* the end of the play. In fact the play continues briefly after the acquittal and what we learn there is not insignificant; Athena's persuasive skills have by now swayed the popular jury but only *irritated* the legalistic, Shylock-esque (and hopeless, Agamben-esque) *Furies*; for she had not bothered to explain to them how accepting the argument that mariticide is a worse crime than matricide absolves Orestes of guilt for murder! The Greek men in the deliberative process, it seems, had no problem with that but, in view of the fact that the process of their communicative reason had obviously not answered this *legally* (and sociologically) relevant question, the plot then has Athena offer the *Furies* – and whatever they can represent: be it the legalism of Shylock or the fatalism of Agamben – a double additional incentive to 'play along': a *bribe* – the 'benefits and honours of a seat of worship in Athens' (pp.851ff) – and a *threat*: 'I rely on Zeus ... and I alone of the gods have access to the keys of the chamber where his thunderbolt is stored' (pp.826–9).

---

[27] Prozorov, S. *Agamben and Politics – A Critical Introduction*, p.48.

What else, if any, is there to do other than to continue to pretend to identify with the *dramatis personae* of Greek democracy's tragedy misread as the Christian melodrama of a 'paradise lost' and which, if no longer to be re-regained, is to be approximated in the form of mere avoidance of nihilism, be it in Ost's *dans le meilleur des cas* (channelling violence) or in Manderson's centrist politics of navigating between the Scylla of merely following orders, and the Charybdis of a monstrous discretion (by 'participating' in the process of will-formation whereby what the media tells us becomes 'public opinion')? Well, *there are* alternative readings. In relation to *Oresteia*, to stick with this example, whereas Ost and Manderson respectively claim us to be protagonists in the story of 'channelling' violence and 'transforming' decisionism/legalism, we could take option one – do a Luhmann and just get rid altogether of the metaphor of democracy's ship carrying society. Luhmann claimed, I believe, that the 'conversation' today between the 'law' and 'deliberative democracy' is one in which we humans are not even part of in any socially meaningful way. Seen as two impersonal 'auto-poietic' communicative systems – each of which operates on the basis of distinct binary codes, modern law and politics are observed as being in a relation of 'mutual irritation' that is not necessarily economised by the idea of an overall, human-oriented, 'social end'. As Luhmann argued, such 'irritation' can, and indeed *did*, take the form of what he termed 'structural coupling'[28] (which is a mutually beneficial 'relation' for the *autonomy* of the systems involved), whereby modern law and politics respectively 'de-paradoxified' themselves with reference to a 'third element,' that is, a third communicative system, a role *political morality* played in the heyday of modern constitutionalism; *this*, arguably, is Ost and Manderson's hope – but it is a spent one. For, currently, law and politics are taking the other direction in which systemic 'irritation' can go, just as happened in Eumenides after deliberation was concluded: 'systemic coercion' and 'corruption'[29] of one system by another, which is catastrophic for both, for it re-paradoxifies them; this is the case, for example, whenever 'purely' political decisions are taken declaring emergencies or suspending the rule of law or, in reverse, when excessive juridification of social conflict – aspects of which are aptly called 'lawfare' – inhibits the mobilisation of constituent power with equally pernicious effects for the legitimacy of public law. The other possible option is to keep the metaphor of democracy's ship but do away with the drama of navigating between the Scylla of legalism and the Charybdis of decisionism. This is bringing us to a different Agamben than the one mentioned so far. A funny Agamben who draws inspiration not from tragedy but comedy.

STAND-UP FOR YOUR RIGHTS?

It will have become apparent that Agamben – like Luhmann – is not affirming an infinite wealth of possibilities for a new and better democratic politics. On the contrary, Agamben emphatically alerts us that the governmental apparatus of the economic–political–theological machine of *oikonomia* functions *through* the ceaseless rise of political utopias *and* their equally incessant shipwrecking, the successive rise of dreams and nightmares. 'Infinity' in these circumstances appears to be a euphemism for the *endless process* of *re-arrangement and*

---

[28] Luhmann, N. (1992), 'Operational Closure Structural Coupling: The Differentiation of the Legal System,' *Cardozo L. Rev.*, vol. 13, pp.1419–42.

[29] Luhmann, N. (1992), p.1432.

management of beings and things, of crises-management. That said, there is a 'hopeful' side to Agamben that his critics often miss (as we saw in Manderson's case) because it is *funny rather than serious*, more stand-up comedy than stand up to sovereignty. Here is the Agambenian 'funny' version of the 'principle of hope', to paraphrase Ernst Bloch's eponymous utopian fiction trilogy's title:[30] we 'are witnessing ... the incessant though aimless motion of the [governmental] machine, which, *in a sort of colossal parody of theological oikonomia*, has assumed the [pre-modern] legacy of the providential governance of the world ... instead of redeeming our world, this machine is leading us to catastrophe.'[31] If for Bloch the fear of finitude is overcome, and human protagonism in the drama of infinite if tumultuous progress upheld, by the *utopian* valorisation of a life's work – insofar as it is accompanied by the hope that its value will exceed the limited span of one's own lifetime contributing, within the greater march of time, to building a more humane society ('*humanum*') – for Agamben, the Lenny Bruce of Benjaminians, the laughable fact that fantasy of *oikonomia* survives only as a parody of its former theological self ties with Walter Benjamin's take on 'weak messianism' and becomes 'destituent power'.[32] Take those of us who are the inheritors of both the goodies and the guilt of cruel ancestors who conveniently found themselves on the right side of binaries – say us citizens with actionable human rights born to cruel slave owners and colonialists, as opposed to our unwelcome refugees; Bloch's soothing hope is that our (and his) work might contribute, in time, to building a 'better future' for all; Benjamin's discomforting hope, by contrast, was premised on recognising that hell is not something to fear in the future but is already present (that catastrophe is no other than the continuation of things as they are, including the belief in the inevitability of moral progress) and soon turning the comforting images from the past – say, of providential God instructing his vicars on Earth – into something absurdly uncomfortable to us, so as to prompt us to make new, non-linear connections with particular, past or future points; the hope is that by doing so one breaks the cycle of hypocritical conformity with and automated validation of the tradition where comforting myths of progress alternate with guilt, opening up the prospect of redemption; the present generation of activists is always potentially the messiah in this sense and if they 'fail' to bring about change in the present, it may nevertheless be redeemed by some future movement, and is not in vain. Agamben is *more hopeful even: our 'hell' makes a parody of itself.* Thus, commentators who disapprovingly note Agamben's morbid obsession with the dehumanised and disenfranchised are reminded, by Sergey Prozorov, that '[O]ne of the most regularly cited phrases in Agamben's work is a line from Friedrich Hölderlin's *Patmos*: "where danger grows, grows also saving power"'.[33] While 'apparatuses running on empty' are no laughing matter, Prozorov is right, I think, that it is on laughter, play and 'profanation' that Agamben stakes redemption. True hope always stems from the despair of the darkest hour, of witnessing the ongoing catastrophe, and Agamben's witnessing comes with the hope that a change of mood[34] may be enough to 'deactivate' the

---

[30] Bloch, E. (1986, orig. published 1954), *The Principle of Hope*, London: Wiley-Blackwell.
[31] Agamben, G. (2009), *What is an Apparatus? And Other Essays*, Stanford, CT: Stanford University Press, p.24.
[32] Agamben, G., 'What Is a Destituent Power?,' *Environment and Planning D: Society and Space*, vol. 32 (2014), p.65.
[33] Prozorov, S. (2014), *Agamben and Politics – A Critical Introduction*, Edinburgh University Press, p.24.
[34] The concept of 'fundamental attunement' or mood (Stimmung) was developed in the philosophy of Martin Heidegger which is also the key influence on Agamben's intellectual development. In

machine that captures our inoperativity in the spheres of religion or sovereignty and so on. Prozorov's brilliant analysis convincingly shows that Agamben's (humourless?) critics[35] miss how turning the tragic into comic is, indeed, indispensable in Agamben's politics. Thus, while

---

Being and Time (1962), Heidegger famously described anxiety – distinguished from fear by the lack of any determinate object – as a fundamental mood, in which the mode of human being there (Dasein) is disclosed. 'In a later course of lectures, entitled *The Fundamental Concepts of Metaphysics* (1995), Heidegger posited "profound boredom" as the mood in which the world is rendered manifest as an opening, in which individual beings come to appearance. It is only when we are "left empty" by beings that become indifferent for us and are "held in limbo", all possibilities of our action suspended, that we experience the clearing of being as such. Such moods as anxiety and boredom are thus fundamental in the sense of giving us nothing less than an experience of being itself, making possible the phenomenal appearance of the ontological dimension.' In this connection I agree with Prozorov's interpretation that those who read Agamben as an unhappy pessimist miss the point: '…these readings of Agamben ignore (or scornfully, and a little too hurriedly, dismiss) the persistent references throughout his work to "happiness" and "redemption" that come at the end of the tradition whose reign has indeed been tragic and, moreover, going from bad to worse. To recall Agamben's fragment on moods, the experience of being "deprived", "worn out" and "apathetic" simultaneously marks the "true beginning" of our "word". The reversal of the tragic predicament into the possibility of a "happy life" that we find in the final pages of almost all of Agamben's books permits us to rigorously distinguish his thought from what we may term the tragic logic dominant in contemporary continental thought' (Sergei Prozorov, *Agamben and Politics – A Critical Introduction*, p.13). In his 1985 collection *Idea of Prose* Agamben devoted a separate vignette, 'The Idea of Music', to the notion of mood, arguing both for the centrality of this notion to any philosophy and for its gradual descent into obscurity in contemporary thought: 'Our sensibility, our sentiments, no longer make us promises. They survive off to the side, splendid and useless, like household pets. And courage, before which the imperfect nihilism of our time is in constant retreat, would indeed consist in recognising that we no longer have moods, that we are the first men not to be in tune with a Stimmung. [And] if moods are the same thing in the history of the individual as are epochs in the history of humanity, then what presents itself in the leaden light of our apathy is the never yet seen sky of an absolute non-epochal situation in human history. The unveiling of being and language, which remains unsaid in each historical epoch and in each destiny, perhaps is truly coming to an end. Deprived of an epoch, worn out and without destiny, we reach the blissful threshold of our unmusical dwelling in time. Our word has truly reached the beginning.' Agamben, G. (1995), *The Idea of Prose*, New York: SUNY Press, p.91.

[35] In line with this mode of reception, Ernesto Laclau accuses Agamben of positing an 'unavoidable advance towards a totalitarian society' (Laclau, 2007, p.17), '[dismissing] all political options in our societies and unifying them in the concentration camp as their secret destiny' (ibid, p.22). Similarly, William Connolly argues that '[Agamben] carries us through the conjunction of sovereignty, the sacred and biopolitics to a historical impasse. Agamben's analysis exacerbates a paradox that he cannot imagine how to transcend' (Connolly, 2007, p.27). The criticism of Agamben's tragic teleology is fortified even further by Andreas Kalyvas, for whom 'Agamben proposes a theory of history that does not seem to bring forth anything new' other than the 'survival of sovereignty over a period of 25 centuries', so that the history of Western politics ends up nothing but a 'history of repeated failures' (Kalyvas, 2005, pp.111–12). Moreover, these failures are allegedly 'guided by the iron hand of historical necessity all the way to the camps' (ibid, p.112). William Rasch succinctly sums up the logic underlying this reading of Agamben: 'What reveals itself in the sovereign ban is the long, slow, but inevitable telos of the West, an ingrained imperfection that inheres as much in the democratic tradition as it does in absolutism or twentieth-century totalitarianism' (Rasch, 2007, p.100). Agamben's politics is thus not merely tragic as a matter of contingency, but rather as a matter of teleological necessity, from whose grip one apparently cannot twist loose, since every concrete instance of political praxis ultimately bears the full metaphysical weight of the millennia of tragedy: 'At the basis of Agamben's analyses of the law, the state and the citizen lies this fundamental premise that Western metaphysics is a metaphysics of death, a deadly metaphysics' (Deranty, 2008, p.175). Thus, the consensus among the critics is that Agamben's work is an exemplar of a 'radically pessimistic philosophy of history' (Marchart, 2007, p.13).

Agamben's reading of the western political tradition explicitly asserts that western politics is moving 'from bad to worse', he also suggests that a *comic or playful mood*, that is, a modified way of dealing with the tragic, liberates us from its burden.[36] A key presupposition for this messianic stand-up optimism – one I am sceptical about for the reasons expanded on below – is that the comic and the tragic are, somehow, 'not' in a binary opposition, as two distinct states of affairs that can be economised, but two moods about the same state of affairs. In other words, the optimism rests on the assumption that, in contrast to every other binary, the comic/tragic *moods* are not subjected to the economical apparatus of western society; that our desire for happiness powers a humour that transcends its capture in the anthropological apparatus. Call me a cynic but I will ask: is such optimism justified or does it add to the means already at our disposal for hypocritically not recognising just what a pickle democracy is in?[37]

In my field, public law, Agamben's hopeful, comic-messianic message boils down to something like this: rather than trying to fix, or crying over not being able to fix, the constitutional state that does not make us happy – now by re-deploying constituent power to positively rebuild or modify it (for example, in a Rousseauist fashion), now by evoking Lockean negative constitutionalism that purports to limit the use of such power – let us expose the absurdity of sticking to an imagination inherited from pre-modern God-fearing hypocrites and look at the possibility of a happier life now – rather than as an 'end' dependent on a sovereign establishing commercial peace among nasty egoists or enhancing the possibilities of collaborative work among humans of solidarity. Let us stop trying to 'realise' our constitutional collaborative potential – the mantra of all constitutionalism, which is the original self-help book of modernity – and just take note of all the different forms-of-life and/or experiment with new ones. Let

---

[36] While Agamben 'explicitly asserts that Western politics is moving "from bad to worse", producing at best a vacuous nihilism and at worst a genocidal totalitarianism [...] yet [it is] precisely the current exhaustion of this tradition, its self-destructive running on empty, [that] opens a possibility of a transformation so radical that it would leave this tradition behind, whereby the misfortunes and horrors of our tragic history are overcome'. This theoretical standpoint calls for a methodological focus on extreme situations and settings as sites, where a comic reversal of the abject condition of the 'state of exception' or the 'ban' into a state of 'happy life' is most likely. Second, this reversal itself does not take the form of a grand transformation of the 'unhappy' condition into a 'happy' one. Agamben frequently cites Benjamin's claim in the essay on Kafka that the coming of the Messiah would not radically change the world by force but would 'only make a slight adjustment within it' (Benjamin, 1968, p.134). 'Finally [...] the relation between the comic and the tragic is not a binary opposition between two distinct states of affairs but rather between two perspectives on or attunements to the same situation. The comic mood is a modified way of dealing with the tragic that liberates us from its burden.' Prozorov, S., *Agamben and Politics – A Critical Introduction*, pp.24–5.

[37] 'Continued belief in political democracy as the realization of human freedom depends upon literally averting our glance from powers immune to democratization, powers that also give the lie to the autonomy and primacy of the political upon which so much of the history and present of democratic theory has depended': 'We Are All Democrats Now ...' in Alen, Amy (ed.) (2011), *Democracy in What State?*, New York: Columbia University Press, p.54. 'We live today in an age simultaneously marked by the widespread adoption of the idea of constitutionalism, of ambiguity over its meaning and about its continuing authority. Far from being an expression of limited government, constitutionalism is now to be viewed as an extremely powerful mode of legitimating extensive government. Where this form of constitutionalism positions itself on the ideology-utopia axis [...] has rarely been more indeterminate [...] notwithstanding the liberal gains [...] the significance of the idea of the constitutional imagination has never exhibited a great degree of uncertainty': 'The Constitutional Imagination,' *Modern Law Review*, vol. 78, no. 1 (2015) p.25.

us also 'experiment with language'[38] so that our attention to our expressive, if meaningless, voices is not lessened as we try to communicate, and decipher, messages of information [to smuggle in Levinas: let us hear the saying over the said]. As we gather outside the ruins, or ghostly presence, of the nation-state that had promised protection and welfare, we can play around and come up with, or simply notice, other ways of being together. Activists: let us play! Let us profane! The activity of *playing around* with what was once sacred is not 'wasted energy' but an 'inoperative praxis' – which neither preserves nor destroys but 'profanes' the sacred edifice – it is its 'topsy turvy image'.[39] Whereas sacred or secular rituals – such as mass or elections – and traditional or modern festivals – like carnival or referenda – fix and structure the chronological time of the calendar through their orderly recurrence, giving us a sense of certainty and continuity with tradition just as we navigated the process of continuous becoming by changing, 'play' changes and destroys this time. Whereas participating in rituals/festivals combines a relatively invariant form (casting a ballot/ marching with a raised fist) with the same mythical content (say, acclamation of an anointed emperor, or voting in the populist who will 'take power back' on our behalf, or *Occupying Wall Street*! as if it were the Bastille), *play* 'frees and distracts humanity from the sphere of the sacred without simply abolishing it'.[40] In sum: 'the power of the sacred act lies in the conjunction of the myth that tells the story and the rite that reproduces and stages it. Play breaks up this unity.'[41] Agamben's wager is that comedy and play can 'tramp' tragedy[42] and ritual in the sense that these are not negated or destroyed but 'impregnated' with pure potentiality unconnected to any teleology. The hope is that like children who 'play with whatever old thing that falls into their hands, make toys out of things that belong to the spheres of economics, war, laws and other activities that we are used to thinking of as serious',[43] we too may neither validate nor negate but will *take apart and invent new usages for the old conceptual tools of political will and legal reasoning*, that is, of constituent/ constituted power, *other than the one written on the box it came in*: providential *oikonomia*.

With respect to examples for this among Agamben's pinups we find the 'Neapolitans'[44] who enjoy making different uses of broken machines. Agamben also illustrates emancipatory profanation of the sovereign law through a series of literary figures such as Alexander the Great's renowned horse who *seriously studies but never practices the law* in Kafka's explicitly comic *Bucephalus the New Attorney*. The other lawyers accept Bucephalus into their field, understanding the 'difficulty' of his condition, which is that of a war horse without his heroic master, in times that no longer call for heroism;[45] Benjamin's famous claim, which Agamben takes up on many occasions in his writings, is that the study of the law without practising it amounts to

---

[38] Agamben, G. (2007a), 'Preface: Experimentum Linguae' in *Infancy and History: On the Destruction of Experience*, London: Verso.
[39] Agamben, G. (2007a), *Infancy and History*, p.77.
[40] Agamben, G. (2007b), *Profanations*, New York: Zone Books, p.76.
[41] Ibid, p.75.
[42] Prozorov, S., *Agamben and Politics – A Critical Introduction*.
[43] Agamben, *Profanations*, n.40.
[44] Agamben, G. (2010), *Nudities*, Stanford, CT: Stanford University Press, p.99.
[45] '[Nowadays] – it cannot be denied – there is no Alexander the Great. There are plenty of men who know how to murder people; the skill needed to reach over a banqueting table and pink a friend with a lance is not lacking; but no one, no one at all, can blaze a trail to India. Today the gates [to India] have receded to remoter and loftier places; no one points the way; many carry swords, but only to brandish them, and the eye that tries to follow them is confused.'

disengaging ourselves from the promises which tradition has attached to it.[46] Aware of the law but unhampered by the promises attached to it, Bucephalus is free to seek his happiness unsupported by, though not ignorant of, the law, and, thus to proceed to seek his happiness unsaddled by the heroic figure that would otherwise mount it to lead it to pre-decided greener pastures. Similarly, Agamben reads unconventionally the 'man from the countryside' in Kafka's *Before the Law* and *K* in *The Castle,* both of which first evoke then subvert the theme of the law presented as barricaded in the impotent sovereign's castle and guarded by glorifying guardians. The 'man from the countryside' is not necessarily 'the tragic figure who wasted his life before the law' whereas he could have heroically entered; he is also, judging from the story's end (the doors were wide open and only shut just as his time was over), a comic figure who, by not entering, enjoyed the social company of the 'Guardian' effectively as just another ordinary fellow who was not really guarding anything (to smuggle in some more Levinas we could add that this reading affirms face-to-face *proximity as a condition for* law as opposed to the reverse received, Hobbesian, wisdom). In turn, 'K' is not necessarily the tragic refugee figure waiting forever for a permit to make a life from a Kafkaesque bureaucracy that never comes; he is also the figure whose very existence ridicules the 'castle' metaphor of the modern state – namely the peculiar architectonic edifice from the middle ages that reflects the bio-political fusion of the classic private estate (or *oikos*) and *polis* in the modern state which *blends* or renders indistinct two different modes of association deriving from Roman law: the ideas of the state either as *societas* or as *universitas*.[47] In this sense, the millions of undocumented immigrants living among us are politically active, their unrecognised day-to-day life amounting to an *inoperative praxis* that may actually be more transformative than the citizenry casting a ballot.

Personally – to paraphrase the protagonist of Melville's novella *Bartleby the Scrivener*, another of Agamben's favourite literary heroes – 'I would prefer not to' pass judgement on Agamben's messianic stand-up hopes. My reticence boils down to my *different perspective on the relation between rituals to play and, by extension, of tragedy to comedy*. On the one hand, I concede that the true motor of human history, all the way up to and including the *anthropocene*, was not, as advertised by tradition, the heroes' determination to accomplish missions to reach pre-set 'sacred' goals and to realise promises taken upon oath; it was, rather, the willingness to *play* with contingency; it was bricolage, experimentation, creativity, Kuhn's change of paradigm. On the other hand, however, I also tend to agree with the anthropologist of religion who argues that, for most of history, participating – being *seen* to participate – in sacred rituals was indispensable to establishing *blind trust* among adult linguistic beings who, in contrast to children, are well aware of the 'two problems of language': the fear of the lie and the false alternative.[48] Such blind trust seems to be *a condition not only for communication but for transformative play*, too. One may or may not believe in the truth of 'ultimate sacred postulates' embedded in rituals (namely, cosmological axioms that are unfalsifiable because of their substantial vacuity bearing no relation to material *significata*: from Gods who chose one species or society over another, to 'self-evident secular truths', for example, that working

---

[46] Benjamin, W. (1968), *Illuminations*, New York: Schocken Books, p.139; cf. Agamben, G. (2005a), *State of Exception*, Chicago, IL: The University of Chicago Press, pp.59–64.
[47] Agamben, *Stanzas*, n.6.
[48] Rappaport, Roy A. (1999), *Ritual and Religion in the Making of Humanity*, Cambridge: Cambridge University Press.

on a piece of matter or an idea turns it into one's property) but blind intersubjective trust is dependent on the performative validation of these as if true social facts.

Going to church to take part in the ritual of mass is enough to validate God as true social fact and, thus, to be a trustworthy member of the congregation – even if, as a non-main participant, one can spend their time, between performing those few acts required of them, gossiping or looking at their smartphone. The 'Neapolitans' whom Agamben loves for their playful bricolage are also known for their devotion to their patron San Gennaro, the annual miracle of the liquefaction of whose blood occurs as part of a ritual that knows how to adapt to bad years[49] and, perhaps more importantly, *incorporates* adult-only 'play': in the first row of the San Gennaro church the elder women, known as the saint's *parenti*, may give a vociferous improvised 'piece of their mind' to the saint if things are not going well for Naples: profanation here is economised by being incorporated in the ritual. As for studying the law, as a professor of constitutional law in a 'critical legal studies' school in Brexit UK, I may only half-qualify as Bucephalus, for I prompt students to prepare the sovereign's Empty Throne and to wear Alexander's saddle even if no Alexander will appear – just a clown. In class we pore through various instances showing the tedious gap between the constitutional doctrine and the lived experience and we abstain from tying this task to responding to the persistent calls to say which reform is needed; we would prefer not to; but with regard to those students who undertook a substantial study loan because they want to join the legal profession, or to become professional politicians, I also instruct, and strongly and repeatedly advise them, how *to be seen as confirming the postulate* that representative democracy plus the rule of law = sovereign power with legitimacy, starting by ticking the right boxed in the (not so-) 'multiple' choice exams of the Law Society (to be soon taken, I am told, in the same private exam centres as the driving licence theory test). Bucephalus the horse-lawyer studies the law unburdened by its practice – my students must develop various personae: I want them to study the law joyfully and then practice it melancholically. Moreover, or such is my worry, every contemporary citizen is akin to Kafka's 'man from the countryside' and *K at once* as a tragic hero and a stand-up comedian, whereas in Greek theatrical festivals comedy *followed* tragedy. What if, for us hypocritical nihilists, the comic and the tragic is a simultaneous performance; what if we have learnt to laugh as part of a tragedy and to suffer as part of a comedy?

Let us be honest on this at least: though some of us may be sympathetic to a contemporary would-be Diogenes who insists on barking at hypocrisy, few of us would *trust* each other unless we are seen to validate indeed the postulate that participation in the rituals of today's democracy is a means towards transformation leading to emancipation. In a NY or a London polite society dinner party – where champagne is served often from the Left – one is more likely to trust in – and invite again – the guest that cites Agamben, or at least Runciman, that 'democracy' or 'the rule of law' is a façade and so on *if* they add, or imply: 'but of course I voted for x rather than y'; or 'nevertheless, I took part in x protest'; or 'I am a human rights lawyer'; or, 'the horned Trumpist invader of Congress is more alarming than laughable because he has nothing positive to report, his white supremacist views being on the wrong side of history', and so on. By contrast, the guest who says, or implies 'I would prefer not to' say or do anything more about the state of politics is suspect: of nihilism, or depression, or the naïveté of the charming but self-indulgent, ineffective, 'beautiful souls', as anarchists are at

---

[49] www.reuters.com/lifestyle/oddly-enough/blood-naples-saint-fails-liquefy-what-some-see-bad-omen-2020-12-16/.

best portrayed, and surely, in any case, of cynical rudeness ('*some moods* one does not share!' 'Not everything is a laughing matter!'). They make unlikely second-time guests.

By contrast, it is safe to guess that the aforementioned François Ost is a perfect dinner party guest. And also that *he would not trust* Kafka in his law and literature class except as a bit of madman in the classical enlightenment sense: a negative example of someone who mistakes political society as analogous to their private torment. In fact Ost tells us clearly that Kafka – a 'talented Jewish jurist who "neglected his work" in an insurance company and failed to sustain a loving relationship and procreate' – was a problematic fellow suffering the madness of the guilt-ridden who takes on his own weak shoulders the impossible task of formulating a strict enough law to correspond to his personal endless guilt; his failure to sublimate his problematic relationship with his father (as glimpsed in *Letter to His Father*) shows in his literary work, which focuses on law but, symptomatically, without reference to 'the figure of The Third' which, normally, intervenes between self and (m)other and makes justice possible in the form of an 'impersonal reasoned judgment' – be it the uncle, the teacher or, of course the judge and the policy maker. Hence, the absence of a judge in *The Trial* or of the Commandant in the *Penal Colony* indicates that, Kafka is *not to be trusted as a jurist*: in all his stories the 'I' does not manage to exit from itself since all its interlocutors are imposters who exercise a personal and tyrannical power rather than dispense the power that comes with an office that carries the authority of law. In sum, in Kafka's twisted world there is no impersonal judgment – only subjective judg(*e*)ments inscribed on our bodies by torture. All in all, the eminent jurist and author of *Antigone Voilée* finds that the author of *The Metamorphosis* failed to account for the way society changes for the better. Hence – absolutely no prizes for experimentation, playfulness, innovation and change of paradigm here – Ost swaps *The Metamorphosis*, *The Trial*, the *Penal Colony*, *The Castle* for the *Oresteia* read by him as discussed earlier: *minus* the cynical laughter of the Greek comedy that would have normally followed it in Greek theatrical festivals and *plus* the sense of 'glory' that attaches to impotence so typically in Christian dramas.

Athena, as Thomas Rosenmeyer put it, was 'an adroit politician' but her political success in persuasion 'is qualified by the thought that, unlike human persuaders, she cannot fail'.[50] In reverse, I submit, the persuasive skills of Ost and Manderson are complemented by the thought that although Ost's legal justice and Manderson's participatory and transformative process *can and do fail* in practice this does not affect their credit score 'in principle'. *This* is the essence of modern tragi-comedy in which we humans are protagonists in the (occidental if by now globally familiar) triadic model of 'humanity' which, while historically and anthropologically speaking is only one among many ways of instituting humanity, is by now a *de facto* inescapable framework for integration into civilised – polite – human society: we have to appear now as *political animals* (the *Zoon Politikon*, to recall Aristotle), now as *juridical humans* (the *Homo Juridicus*, to quote A. Supiot's title) and finally as *economic humans* (man duped by the ideology of *oikonomia* to cite Agamben or the *Homo Economicus*, to cite critics of A. Smith, J.S Mill, and so on).

---

[50] Cited in McAuslan, Ian and Walcot, Peter (eds) (1993), *Greek Tragedy*, Oxford: Oxford University Press, p.55.

ANIARA – COULD THE APPARATUS HAVE THE PROVERBIAL LAST LAUGH?

You would think that after getting rid of oppressive hierarchical masters we would be free to heed Cavafy's call to value a long journey to Ithaca irrespective of the possibility of reaching its pre-set, or indeed any, *telos* or happy end. But are we really rid of the apparatus these fallen masters used to preside over? What if we killed the king but still mechanically worship and even prepare his imaginary Empty Throne, even taking comic turns to sit on it? What if we took off the slaves' chains but still find ourselves tied, admittedly in less obscenely cruel and unequal ways, to the same apparatus, which is running at full speed? That, alas, is a possibility. As Carl Schmitt puts it:

> The king [may] appear as God, and God as a king [and where] God can also be imagined as the world's electric motor, and the electric motor as a kind of machine that moves the world ... as if through a kind of space-shuttle [where] all of this can be expressed in polymorphic metaphors ... [so that] the huge Leviathan, Thomas Hobbes's state [appears] tetramorphic: as well as being the great but mortal god, he is a huge animal, and furthermore, a large man and a big machine.

With this sobering possibility in mind let me turn to literature for inspiration one last time. Since this essay started with the Odyssey, I turn to sailor and Nobel laureate poet Harry Martinson's 1956 epic science-fiction poem *Aniara* as well as the eponymous 2008 cinematic adaptation written and directed by Pella Kågerman and Hugo Lilja. The title is a neologism based on the modern Greek word for boring, Ανιαρός. In ancient Greek the word meant 'torment/worry' (it is possibly related to the Latin *onus* – burden) and in modern Greek it still retains a bit of that burdensome sense: *Avία* signifies a burdensome tedium, a boredom one finds hard to shake off – think of writing 'I will behave' 100 times on the school classroom board. Both the poem and the film tell the story of a large passenger spaceship (the *Aniara*) originally bound for Mars with a cargo of colonists fleeing an ecologically ravaged Earth. In the first week of its voyage it suddenly veers off course, due to collision with space debris, and is ejected, for ever, from the solar system. (Very) long story short, with its nuclear reactor irreparably damaged – thus unable to steer itself back to reach Mars or in any specific direction – and without communication with, or observation from, anyone outside itself, but with all the technology it takes to sustain biological life on board, the ship goes into an aimless voyage. Passengers are eventually enlisted to help discharge various vital daily tasks for sustaining life and to keep the ship going. Spoiler alert: not only is there no happy ending, there are also no heroic struggles against Cavafy's imaginary 'cyclops' or the green aliens featured in a number of 1950s B movies. There are also no visits to exotic planets, and not even glorious depictions of stoic human defiance of a malign AI antagonist (as was the case in the 1970s' *2001: A Space Odyssey*).

There *are* other moods explored apart from the claustrophobic despair that correlates to the painful drag of going through dark space, busy sustaining one's bare life on the path to nowhere – unsurprisingly packaged with nihilism since the passengers appear to come from a culture in which a journey is only as good as a means to reaching a certain destination. Thus, there are moments in which the passengers simply focus on, and marvel at, their technical means and ingenuity regardless of their in-utility in reaching a destination – when 'we [...] take note of our majestic wonder of a boat'. There is invention and bricolage. Moreover, there is unproductive play: there is laughter and ballroom dancing – when '... then this ballroom in infinitude/fills with whimperings and human dreams/and open weeping none hides any more' – and stories of friendships and fall-outs, lust and love, orgies and babies born. But yes, there is also a lot of *ania* and images of claustrophobic passengers banging their heads against the windows; this is the time of disillusionment, anxiety, boredom, nihilism that alternates with scenes of acclamation of the captain's promises. The captain is essential in the process of capturing the inoperativity of the passengers within an apparatus presented falsely as means to future happy days – he ensures that everyone gets bored of working towards and waiting for the opportunity to 'turn it back' on track to its elusive destination, as opposed to, say, joining yet another ballroom dance or whatever. As if with a nod to today's rise of populism in circumstances when government is 'administration without sovereignty',[51] the film version, in particular, has the captain repeatedly deny the absence of capacity 'to govern' in the sense of the Greek verb *kybernein* – that is, of mastery and steering power by means of which a ship's human load claims to impose upon itself its own preferred direction. At first, he just denies the loss of nuclear power; then, when news leaks, he falsely assures that, according to calculations, it is a matter of time before they will be able to 'turn it around' by using the gravitational force of some external large object. Even as all the captain's promises turn out to be lies or false alternatives, passengers and crew publicly and hypocritically play along – acting as if they believe the captain even as their souls are increasingly filled with nihilism and, occasionally, climb the proverbial wall. It is as if they cannot untangle their being together from the 'purpose' of having contracted to reach their Martian destination. To this end most of the crew and the passengers enlisted to discharge various vital tasks modestly appear as mere extras in the story, their activities seen as 'delegated' powers in service of the heroic captain's efforts to steer the ship towards the promised land and as if whatever happiness they can still experience in their daily lives is only a small prelude to the final rest upon reaching Mars. Their public modesty and deference to this arch-narrative are crucial to sustaining the spectacle of their journey as merely 'auxiliary' – it is but a means to – the pre-set end of reaching their Martian destination: arrival there is 'far more important' than *what is happening now* onboard a ship sailing through risky space. Arguably, a leader who repeatedly rallies people not so as to actually solve a problem but so as to pretend to be doing is less 'charismatic,' in Max Weber's sense of that term, and more of a peculiar trickster who fails to pull the proverbial rabbit out of the hat yet is applauded *as if* providing life-affirming entertainment. Moreover, the captain's promissory and decisionist style is complemented by Jesus-like theatrics: as time passes, he takes the stage at the amphitheatre to preside over passengers deliberating with his wrists visibly bandaged (he has attempted, privately, to slash them), which works in having his 'mandate' continue by acclamation. Of course, this spectacle does not soothe popular anxiety (as Hobbes would have it), but on the contrary, maintains it so that the show of government appears necessary to allay it (as Foucault would have it). It is a circularly self-perpetuated show of collective self-representation.

Is an actual, physical, 'captain' always going to be necessary for the show to go on? Aboard *Aniara* there is also a *mechanical protagonist* in the form of a semi-mystical apparatus, the *mima*, through which crew and passengers find relief in the form of virtual reality between playing and working: so when 'the dancing stops, the music dies,/the hall is emptied, all move to the mima'. Trust in the mima is greater than that in the captain's predictions and promises:

---

[51] See, e.g., Somek, Alex (2010), 'Administration Without Sovereignty' in Dobner and Loughlin (eds), *The Twilight of Constitutionalism?*, Oxford: Oxford University Press, pp.267–88.

'[O]ur ill-fate now is irretrievable', says the poem, '[B]ut the mima will hold (we hope) until the end.' Importantly, in the 1950s poem the *mima* stands for *utopia* since it involves new sounds, scents and scenes of times 'from far-flung reaches' that 'rout the memories' of the world 'remembered and abandoned'; thus, since '[N]o human eye had ever dreamt of seeing such things', 'the mima tells no lies. She fishes metaphorically her fish in other seas than those we now traverse, netting metaphorically her cosmic catch from woods and dales in undiscovered realms.' Fast forward to the 2018 film version of *Aniara* and the *mima* stands for nostalgia of paradise lost, projecting comforting cliché scenes of luscious nature back on Earth, a world everyone knows has been lost forever and indeed long gone when anyone still alive was even born: the *mima* that used to 'tell now lies' now says sweet lies. Tragi-comically in both the poem and film, years into the trip, the *mima* becomes overwhelmed by humans and self-destructs; the captain then unfairly blames, then imprisons, the *Mimarobe*, the *mima*'s operator, accusing her of sabotage. Eventually, the ensuing *ennui* results into a spate of suicides, disorder and the rise of new cults (the return of religion, as we say nowadays) and the captain orders the *Mimarobe* be released and reassigned to work; it turns out the *mima* is beyond repair and the *Mimarobe* only succeeds in building a cruder device projecting an image of a waterfall onto the dark windows of the spaceship, blocking the darkness. The ship continues on its trip.

While other, better-known sci-fi epics have inspired constitutionalist theories looking to overcome the impasse which our 'constitutional imagination'[52] has reached in order to 'complete' the mission constitutionalism set for itself centuries back,[53] *Aniara* both shows such promises to be tragically vain and highlights that, contrary to Agamben's messianic politics, the parody of these promises may *not* be an assured way to a happier life. In the film's final scenes, it is year 24 when a dark *Aniara* drifts through space and a small group of passengers is shown sitting cross-legged in a dimly lit room with an unidentified woman rhapsodizing about the 'divine power of sunlight' on Mother Earth. Next, the film 'ends' close to six million years later with a shot from an external camera – the first and last such scene – which shows the *Aniara*, now devoid of all human life, passing by a planet as verdant and welcoming as Earth had formerly been.

Apart from the captain, there are two further notable figures aboard *Aniara*. First, the ship's exceptionally honest if grumpy astronomer observes that there is no statistically meaningful possibility of reverting the ship's course at will, and the captain must ensure that she does not reveal that it is contingency, not he, that rules. She reminds me of the late German social

---

[52] M. Loughlin, 'The Constitutional Imagination,' *Modern Law Review*, vol. 78(1) (2015), p.1.

[53] For example, Kim Stanley Robinson's *Blue Mars* features in the final chapter of Oklopcic, Z. (2018), *Beyond the People: Social Imaginary and Constituent Imagination*, Oxford: Oxford University Press, where it is taken as an example of how to use our figurative imagination *deliberately and purposefully* even, in fact especially, in today's highly unpredictable environment (p.20). Oklopcik's reading of *Blue Mars* shames constitutional theorists for not daring to employ their constitutional imagination creatively and publicly so that many desirable forms of association – some yet to come, some to be revived- do not only dwell in the realm of science fiction (p.372). In contrast to constitutional theory fixated with the image of the people as source of constituent power, *Blue Mars* features 'the neighborhood boards, the agriculture board, the water board, the architectural review board, the project review council, the economic coordination group, the crater council, […] the global delegates' advisory board – all that network of small management bodies that progressive political theorists had been suggesting in one variation or another for centuries, incorporating aspects of the almost-forgotten socialism of Great Britain, Yugoslavian worker management, Mondragon ownership, Kerala land tenure, and so on' (pp.433, 372).

theorist Niklas Luhmann and his 'systems theory'. We may agree with them that, like the *Aniara* after its collision with debris, our functionally differentiated 'world-society' is now cut loose from, that is, in no absolute way bound to, past or initial states or initially given forms, traditions, problems and aspirations. This of course is bad for messianic aspirations; just as the *Aniara*'s existential risks outweigh, or render irrelevant, the old problem of salvaging its failed colonising mission (who and how to get to Mars and how to set up the colony there), contemporary society's existential risks (such as environmental degradation or the exclusion of whole populations) outweigh the classical problems associated with navigating democracy's ship of fools for the sake of its human load: be it to deliver us to *some* 'Ithaca' or to keep travelling towards the horizon of utopic equality or even just to enrich our lives with the experience of fighting off or outsmarting Laestrygonians. Like the astronomer, Luhmann had no time for the 'overall meaning' of the voyage – a desideratum for meaning at the level of consciousnesses in humans, or 'psychic systems' as he called us. Indifferent to human memory, identity, affect, sensibility, Luhmann was interested in another kind of 'sense', the formation process which takes place *around* humans. Luhmann's 'Sinn' refers to no more than giving an account of the various, impersonal, 'communicative systems' each trying to *reduce* external complexity, be it of random space debris or the contingent drama of *oikonomia* that plays out in the heads of humans who think of themselves as tragic or comic protagonists. In *this* inhuman 'sense' phenomena of difference and indifference increasingly take place not through social conflict but through the differentiation of 'systems' from their 'environments', including from us as actors or spectators of a divine-cum-secular tragic-comedy. Unlike the medieval ('religious' and hierarchically stratified) society which had postulated its observation by a providential deity who both pre-set its historic destination and enabled it to steer itself towards it, aboard *our Aniara* there is neither a transcendental point of view nor a providential plan and everything that happens, happens *now*. Indeed, schematically speaking, too many things are happening at the same time for simple causal accounts to be able to deliver more than a *parody* of what they seem to promise of. As there is no normative panacea and no decisions are able to eliminate contingency, the business of the machinery of government now appears to be no more than that of maintaining itself. Currently, but perhaps not for ever, this includes sustaining and managing the life of its human load.

Luhmann fared better than *Aniara*'s astronomer, but was the object of a degree of academic ostracism insofar as he was outspoken in the face of those legal and political theorists who are not content with law and politics playing their discrete roles in the perennial and multi-faceted human problem-solving endeavours, and who insist that law and politics are *primus inter pares* among other social systems, for they are somehow tasked and able to steer the ship of society towards a 'better place' that ranges from paradise-lost to paradise-made. Utopia is thus treated as a kind of aeolian bag not to be opened by 'the crew' of subjects marching on pre-determined political and legal paths. At any rate, Luhmann, by no means an idealist, annoyed for precisely the reason that this old ploy distracts us from realising that, having crossed the Rubicon of functional differentiation, the *risks* to particular communicative systems belong to a different paradigm than the *crises* of human societies with social differences and, thus, politics and law. '[T]he lifeworld is in crisis; evolution is at risk'.[54] In most legal and political theories it is only a matter of blind trust, or perhaps conceit, that there is a necessary relation – an *oikonomia*?!

---

[54] Brunkhorst, H. (2013), 'Crisis and Critique. Return of Marxism?' in Ramose, Mogobe B., *Hegel's Twilight*, Edinburgh: Editions, p.152.

– between the two paradigms in which the lifeworld and *krisis* ought to weigh heavier. Thus, the secular scholar writes: 'Social crises (*at least, in principle*) can be solved normatively by changing institutions, by enacting egalitarian constitutional reforms or revolutions, by legal programmes.'[55] (I left out the original italics and added new ones for emphasis).

With this '(*at least, in principle*)' – so tellingly placed in parenthesis – Brunkhorst leads us to the second protagonist in *Aniara*, the *Mimarobe*, the engineer of the utopic-turned-nostalgic machine of virtual reality that stopped working and was replaced by a projection of a waterfall on Aniara's windows doing no more than blocking the darkness. She is reminiscent of Giorgio Agamben, who knows a thing or two about apparatuses and also cuts an awkward figure at contemporary dinner parties. On the one hand, his brilliant archaeological efforts familiarised us with the machine that keeps on running on empty and in which the human desire for happiness became framed by the image of steering the ship of democracy towards an ever-receding providential *telos* of freedom whereas, in fact, we simply navigate between idealism/realism, utopia/ideology in unending *oikonomia*, leading us to catastrophe. Such 'apparatuses' are no laughing matter: they carry on running – on empty – even when all our works hitherto, and the diversions with which we try to entertain or amuse ourselves, fail to engage us and all possibilities of action appear suspended in nihilism. In the early years of the twentieth century, we are aware that as sovereign peoples in nation-states we are impotent 'to write History'[56] except in re-writing our DNA: positing life itself as the supreme task of the human being and reorienting government towards the protection, fostering and augmentation of life as such.[57] Even when the words 'mission accomplished' were uttered by Bush Jr in Baghdad, the nauseous limbo we all felt was less overcome than resented and, since to share unpleasant feelings for too long is not the best strategy to earn the trust of other inmates of the apparatus, we dare not show it; Democracy appears as 'Mission impossible!' in an upbeat tone but alas *only* by means of acclamation as in the eponymous cinematic series.

On the other hand, as we saw, Agamben wants to be funny and, as such, offered a seat at the dinner table. Not only does he give us a sobering account of the tragic rise of the western-cum-global paradigm of government; he also re-tells it as a comic provincial west-side story in which the classical ontology that separates humans from animals met the glorious postulate of divine *oikonomia* and from their union sprang so many apparatuses that seek to

---

[55] Yet, from [Luhmann's] perspective of the paradigm of risk, they are 'missing the point', because they are relying on the old 'humanistic framework' of 'freedom and equality, self-realization and solidarity' and 'its affectionately "social" concern' for 'outdated mythologies' such as 'exploitation', 'injustice' and 'suppression'. The now (presumably) much bigger problems are the 'neglect' of individual human beings, the 'exclusion' of surplus-populations (Arendt) and the 'destruction' of systems and their environments. The very point is that individual neglect, ecologic pollution and societal exclusion need technical (or therapeutic) solutions (if there are any), and that technical solutions need smart experts, instead of political protest, moral outrage, civic self-organisation, and democratic mass movements. Ibid, p.152.

[56] '[T]oday, it is clear for anyone who is not in absolutely bad faith that there are no longer historical tasks that can be taken on by, or even simply assigned to, men. It was in some ways evident starting with the end of the First World War that the European nation-states were no longer capable of taking on historical tasks and that peoples themselves were bound to disappear.' Agamben, G. (2004b), *The Open: Man and Animal*, Stanford, CT: Stanford University Press, p.76.

[57] '[T]he only task that still seems to retain some seriousness is the assumption of the burden of biological life, that is, of the very animality of man': ibid, pp.76–7.

govern and guide humans toward the good.[58] Agamben *both* points out that the *Aniara-esque* apparatus that traps us is *inescapable* and leading us to disaster while the trip is advertised as leading us to a good, better place, *and* suggests that we can avert the disaster not by steering the ship elsewhere or jumping ship but simply disactivating the one we are on ... and have fun. If only the passengers on *Aniara* could stay at the ballroom or studying and ameliorating their ship's already awesome technology unconnected by any utilitarian or transcendent end ... If only we can be like Bucephalus and affirm ourselves as neither captivated (taken, mastered) nor captors (mastering, capturing): we are what we are without being anything, law students who don't practice, a whatever-life that does not articulate its own concept, a life that lives and speaks without negating itself in the apparatuses of language, law and history. If only we can be like Sancho Panza staying behind our demon 'Don Quixote,' sending him out on the 'maddest exploits' that lack a real object and do not do anyone any harm.

The thing is, we are evidently *not* acting as Bucephalus, at least not in public, whereas our freedom to study the law, or just to live in peace, is tied to our promise to practice/abide the law. Nor are we publicly Sancho Panza in so far as we performatively acknowledge Don Quixote as if the 'captain' of our democracy's 'ship of fools' that carries us on the choppy waters of contingency towards the horizon of equality, without whose 'steering' we would drown. We, instead, validate a relation of *oikonomia* between our disbelief and hypocrisy, between our life as is and as staged, between play and ritual. Agamben helped us understand that the very essence of the western paradigm is *oikonomia* which locks all binaries in a zone of indistinction; I have not been convinced (by Prozorov) that, exceptionally, the mood that attaches to play and ritual and comedy and tragedy are not binaries locked in a zone of tragicomic indistinction. Hypocrisy in the form of acting to a plot, even if one has the critical capacity not to believe in the representative value – or truth – of the plot, seems to be the main form of adult play in the contemporary west. Spanning tragic despair and comic relief lie our public validations of our parliaments as sovereign legislators and of our courts as guarantors of the rule of law which have all the formal characteristics of old religious rituals *minus* any subjective sense of solemnity and awe. We *playfully perform the rituals* of democracy and we *submit our play-time to the rituals of self-improvement*. We vote as mindlessly as we shop online, we consent to laws we don't read just as we tick 'agree' on those long lists of terms and conditions of, say, our network providers. We consider ourselves bound by contract to companies which are nothing but a bunch of uncoordinated sub-contractors loosely linked via an impotent outsourced customer service. How to profane *that* in the era of the *Novacene*?

Either this situation eluded Agamben, or more likely, he could not afford to be excluded from the philosophers' dinner party where 'beautiful souls' with no activist spirit to show are shamed. As it is, he already stands accused of excessive pessimism. One can imagine the chorus accusing him of full blown nihilism had he not developed the Benjaminian, materialist-messianic, strand to his work. If, that is, he had really lived up to his other literary anti-hero, Herman Melville's 'Bartleby the Scrivener' – the legal scribe who is known for responding to all his employer's requests with the formula 'I would prefer not to' and, who thus exemplifies, a disinclination to either negate or to synthesise a relation between materialism and the noumenous. Because of his materialist messianism he can now, at least, make it to the threshold of the symposium of public intellectuals hoping to de-activate the machine of

---

[58] Agamben, G. (2009), *What is an Apparatus? And Other Essays*, Stanford, CT: Stanford University Press, p.13.

oikonomia, armed with his 'sabbatical animal' surrounded by a 'glory' that is comical given the discrepancies between its decisions and laws and their application. As is well known, Diogenes is also reputed to have shown up at Plato's Academy with a plucked chicken so as to deactivate Plato's definition of man as a 'featherless biped;' arguably, Plato's idealism was always tongue-in-cheek and, in a spirit of *oikonomia*, the Academy responded by adding 'with broad flat nails' to their definition. In the case of Agamben's accusers we are dealing with tongue-in-cheek materialists – who define the sovereign people after the abolition of monarchy as a 'glory-less' biped on a History-writing journey thanks to its 'legal and political' legs. They may explain the discrepancies between law and its application as 'baby-steps' for, 'at least in principle,' man is getting wiser and more competent in 'steering' society's ship with the help of education and machines. 'At least in principle', the lifeworld's social crises can be solved normatively – by changing institutions, by enacting egalitarian constitutional reforms or revolutions, by legal programmes – as opposed to merely being managed by an algorithm.

Agamben is great at pointing to apparatuses which, like *Aniara*, encapsulate us inescapably. I am less confident that his messianism does much more than block the darkness outside, like the crude device that the Mimarobe concocted when the mima gave out. Agamben is fine in pointing out the function of *our* 'mima' – which he termed 'economic political theology' – but I have not been convinced that the mere fact that this theology now survives as a laughable parody of itself is in itself a precursor of freedom for us, as he suggests. The question must be asked: how to stage ourselves other than as protagonists acting now as *comically 'political animals'* who do *not* learn lessons from mistakes, as advertised, now as *tragic 'juridical persons'* who do not just study the law but go on to practice it only to come up against exceptions, and who, in the end, always, *tragicomically* settle with compromise and indistinction as good '*economic*' beings? Just as I agree that the danger of exiting this holy triptych only to fall into nihilist despair and madness can be hedged, I am not convinced that irony or parody are enough to free us from the clickbait of the promise of a glorious happy retirement handed down to us by some of the Greeks, the Stoics, the Romans, the Christians and those post-Christians for whom problem-solving is not worth it without the self-assurance that one is working for a 'better world'. Today's democracy works as high-tech phishing – we often mindlessly click on the scam link despite our awareness of scams. *This* is our *mima*.

> There are in the mima certain features
> it had come up with and which function there
> in circuitry of such a kind
> as human thought has never traveled through.
> For example, take the third webe's action
> in the focus-works
> and the ninth protator's kinematic read-out
> in the flicker phase before the screener-cell
> takes over everything, allots, combines.
>
> The inventor was himself completely dumbstruck
> the day he found that one half of the mima
> he'd invented lay beyond analysis.
> That the mima had invented half herself.
>
> *Well, then, as everybody knows, he changed*
> *his title, had the modesty*
> *to realize that once she took full form*
> *she was the superior and he himself.*

a secondary power, a mimator.
The mimator died, the mima stays alive.
The mimator died, the mima found her style,
progressed in comprehension of herself,
her possibilities, her limitations:
a telegrator without pride, industrious, upright,
a patient seeker, lucid and plain-dealing,
a filter of truth, with no stains of her own.
Who then can show surprise if I, the rigger
and tender of the mima on Aniara,
am moved to see how men and women, blissful
in their faith, fall on their knees to her.
And I pray too when they are at their prayer
that it be true, all this that is occurring,
and that the grace this mima is conferring
is glimpses of the light of perfect grace
that seeks us in the barren house of space.
Aniara, 9th stanza

13. Wilding

Nicole Rogers

My intention here is to play with the established parameters of orthodox judging practices. I want to explore what judging might become when emphasis shifts from the past and present to the future, when litigants include the as yet unborn, when nonhuman beings weigh in on the judging process. This is the terrain of wild judging, or judging wildly: judging which disregards, or perhaps transcends, the rules and disciplinary constraints of Holocene-era law and charts new paths in response to the urgent planetary concerns of the Anthropocene.[1] My particular focus is on the opportunities, possibilities and challenges of interspecies and intergenerational judging.

Wild judging has achieved only limited acceptance in today's courtrooms. In reflecting upon wilder possibilities of judging, I turn to thought experiments in speculative and ecological fiction in which writers attempt to portray nonhuman sensibilities and ways of experiencing the world. I look to fictitious explorations of intergenerational human judgement, and align these with contemporary social movements and lawsuits.

Drawing upon insights from ecocritical theorists and the interdisciplinary response to the concept and dilemmas of the Anthropocene, as well as contemporary textual case studies, I contemplate this question: can speculative and ecological fiction contribute to new understandings of judging so that judging practices become, truly, wild?

WILD LAW AND WILD JUDGING

The term wild law, which overlaps with Earth jurisprudence, ecological jurisprudence and Earth law, was introduced by South African lawyer Cormac Cullinan in 2002 in a book with the same title, and described therein as 'laws that regulate humans in a manner that creates freedom for all the members of the Earth Community to play a role in the continuing co-evolution of the planet'.[2] It incorporates legal recognition of the rights of all members of the Earth Community.[3] Cullinan was building upon the work of theologian Thomas Berry, who argued that rights are 'species specific': river rights, bird rights, insect rights and human rights are all quite different, and not interchangeable.[4]

---

[1] The Anthropocene is the popular term for the current geological epoch, and it was devised by Paul J Crutzen and Eugene F Stoermer in 2000: Paul J Crutzen and Eugene F Stoermer, 'The "Anthopocene"' (2000) 41 (May) *Global Change Newsletter* 17. The term signifies the greatly increased impact of the human species upon Earth: humanity as a 'major geological force' (at 18). The commencement of the epoch is a matter of contention. In May 2019, the Anthropocene Working Group of the Subcommission of Quaternary Stratigraphy voted in support of the formal adoption of the term, with the epoch commencing in the mid-twentieth century.
[2] Cormac Cullinan, *Wild Law. Governing People for Earth* (Siber Ink 2002) 10.
[3] ibid 108.
[4] ibid 113.

Wild law arguably fits best within the entangled world discourse identified by a group of International Relations scholars as one of three key Anthropocene discourses. They have described the discourse thus:

> The entangled world presents a global scene of complex interconnections and interdependencies that cut across conventional geographical and temporal scales and species boundaries. Security cannot be achieved by resolute actions grounded in expression of power targeting 'external' threats, but only by re-embedding modern humanity in the multi-species world that we now are remaking.[5]

Wild law, contained within this discourse of entanglement, poses particular theoretical complications, in part due to what Cullinan has called its oxymoronic quality. He points out that law 'is intended to bind, constrain, regularise and civilise' whereas 'wild' conjures up 'unkempt, barbarous, unrefined, uncivilised, unrestrained, wayward, disorderly, irregular, out of control, unconventional, undisciplined, passionate, violent, uncultivated and riotous'.[6] He asserts that '[w]ildness is a quality that can only be experienced by straying off the orthodox path of civilisation as we know it'.[7]

This seems relatively uncontroversial but the concept of wild can take on quite a different meaning in Indigenous ontologies. Deborah Bird Rose followed the lead of Australian Indigenous elders in describing wild country as terrain that is tamed, man-made and civilized; 'quiet' country has not been similarly destroyed.[8] Wild judging can, similarly, be viewed as tamed and civilized, innovation hemmed in and confined by the strictures of judging, habits of legal tradition, dictates of necessity. This is exemplified in the recent legal developments in courtrooms in India, Ecuador and Colombia outlined below. These have, rightly, been heralded as exciting breakthroughs in the quest to achieve judicial recognition of the rights of nature and the nonhuman. Yet such legal achievements are limited, the practical impact unclear.

I seek here to adopt a richer, more nuanced view of wild judging than that encapsulated in the rights of nature approach and recent judicial innovations. Wild judging, for my purposes, takes us beyond existing rules and outside existing courtrooms. Wild, here, is much more aligned to Rose's later use of the term: 'the wild is a refusal to submit to the conventional limitations of Western thought.'[9] For my purposes, wild judging is the legal and, indeed, extra-legal dimension of the 'uncivilized writing' explored through the Dark Mountain Project, and described in their manifesto as '[w]riting which unflinchingly stares us down, however uncomfortable this may prove'.[10] Wild judging, also, 'unflinchingly stares us down'. What happens when we, as humans, are judged as a species, or as members of the last generation able to squander natural resources with impunity; when it is nonhuman entities, or the yet to be born, that hold us to account?

---

[5] Eva Lövbrand, Malin Mobjörk and Rickard Söder, 'The Anthropocene and the Geo-political Imagination: Re-writing Earth as Political Space' (2020) 4 *Earth System Governance* [https://doi.org/10.1016/j.esg.2020.100051] accessed 17 October 2020.
[6] Cullinan (n 2) 8.
[7] ibid 9.
[8] Deborah Bird Rose, *Report from a Wild Country. Ethics for Decolonisation* (University of New South Wales Press 2004) 4.
[9] Deborah Bird Rose, *Wild Dog Dreaming. Love and Extinction* (University of Virginia Press 2011) 12.
[10] 'Uncivilisation. The Dark Mountain Manifesto' (The Dark Mountain Project, 2009) [https://dark-mountain.net/about/manifesto] accessed 17 October 2020.

Judging here transcends formal legal processes and invokes, instead, troubling ethical questions: questions about our capacity to be 'good ancestors',[11] to exercise responsibility for the 'long afterlives' of our current shaping of the world[12] and to sustain mutually beneficial and respectful multi-species relationships. In the pursuit of multi-layered, interspecies and intergenerational justice in the Anthropocene, we must be prepared to discard time-honoured legal rules, legal practices and foundational myths. We must adopt a language 'that recognizes and advances the animacy of the world',[13] the languages of 'spores' and other nonhuman entities: metaphors, grammar and mechanisms of storytelling unrelated to human 'use values'.[14] There are existing precedents, as Robert Macfarlane reminds us; he cites a Native American language, Potawatomi.[15]

WHEN WILD LAW IS NOT WILD ENOUGH

In 1972, Christopher Stone famously asked whether trees should have standing.[16] He proposed that forests, oceans, rivers and other nonhuman entities should have legally recognizable rights,[17] and that they should be represented in legal proceedings by human guardians.[18] What seemed to be an outlandish proposition in 1972 has been partially realized in certain noteworthy developments this century. Rights of nature have been acknowledged in local ordinances in the United States, in the Ecuadorian Constitution and in Bolivian, Mexican and Ugandan law.[19] The historic Whanganui River Settlement Agreement, finalized in 2014 and given legal force by the New Zealand Parliament in March 2017,[20] recognized the river as a living being and created a new legal entity for the river, with legally recognized rights and legal standing, represented by the Whanganui Maori tribe as its guardians. In 2017, agreement was reached to confer legal personhood upon Mount Taranaki in New Zealand.[21]

In 2016, the Colombian Constitutional Court recognized the legal rights of the Atrato River and, in 2017, the High Court of the State of Uttarakhand in India conferred legal personhood status on the Ganges and Yamuna Rivers on the basis that 'extraordinary measures' were needed to protect these gravely imperilled river systems, given their 'sacred and revered'

---

[11] See Robert Macfarlane, quoting immunologist Jonas Salk, in *Underland. A Deep Time Journey* (Hamish Hamilton 2019) 77.
[12] ibid.
[13] ibid 112.
[14] ibid 110–11.
[15] ibid 111.
[16] Christopher D Stone, 'Should Trees Have Standing? Towards Legal Rights for Natural Objects' (1972) 45(2) *Southern California Law Review* 450.
[17] ibid 456.
[18] ibid 464.
[19] See Alessandro Pelizzon, 'An Intergenerational Ecological Jurisprudence: The Supreme Court of Colombia and the Rights of the Amazon Rainforest' (2020) 2(1) *Law, Technology and Humans* 33, 38–9.
[20] *Te Awa Tupua (Whanganui River Claims Settlement) Act 2017* (NZ).
[21] Eleanor Ainge Roy, 'New Zealand Gives Mount Taranaki Same Legal Rights as a Person' *The Guardian* (Melbourne, 22 December 2017) [www.theguardian.com/world/2017/dec/22/new-zealand-gives-mount-taranaki-same-legal-rights-as-a-person] accessed 17 October 2020.

nature for half of India's population.[22] In early 2019, the High Court of Bangladesh granted the Turag river and all other rivers in the country legal personhood status.[23] Personhood rights of the Amazon Rainforest were recognized by the Colombian Supreme Court of Justice in the 2018 *Future Generations* case;[24] in this ground-breaking decision, as I discuss in a later section, the Court also acknowledged the rights of unborn human generations. Another important case decided by the Constitutional Court of Ecuador in December 2021 concerns the rights of the Los Cedros Protected Forest: a biodiverse area threatened by large-scale metal mining.[25]

The growing body of legislation and case law signifies a paradigm shift of sorts, although not all courts are prepared to acknowledge the legal rights and personhood of nonhuman beings. In 2017, for instance, the Colorado River Ecosystem, in conjunction with her human Next Friends and Guardians, unsuccessfully sought a declaration that she was capable of possessing the rights of a person, and recognition of her rights to exist, flourish, regenerate, naturally evolve and be restored.[26] Importantly, such legislative and judicial developments are premised upon expanded understandings of rights, in accordance with Stone's original suggestion. Yet rights arguments may not be wild enough for the moral and ethical dilemmas of Anthropocene justice: justice in an epoch in which, as Amitav Ghosh writes, humanity must acknowledge that agency and consciousness are shared with other beings, and perhaps with Earth itself,[27] even as we descend into a sixth mass extinction event of our own making. As Cullinan has put it, the terminology of rights is 'coloured by the worldview of the homosphere'.[28] Beyond terminology, there are philosophical and practical barriers to the widespread implementation of rights of nature.

Erin Fitz-Henry has expressed concern about the application of rights of nature in certain cultural contexts.[29] She has analysed the use of rights of nature provisions by various parties in relation to a proposed oil refinery and petrochemical complex in Ecuador, and suggests that rights arguments operate here as a distraction from more salient political concerns. They can be viewed as self-defeating, in that competing rights can be raised in counter-argument.[30] Mihnea Tanasescu has pointed out that rights of nature, couched in ambiguous language, can be enlisted for purposes unrelated to conservation, and that oil companies could present these

---

[22] Erin L O'Donnell and Julia Talbot-Jones, 'Creating Legal Rights for Rivers: Lessons from Australia, New Zealand and India' (2018) 23(1) *Ecology and Society* [https://www.ecologyandsociety.org/vol23/iss1/art7] accessed 17 October 2020.

[23] Farhin Antara, 'Turag Given "Legal Person" Status to Save It from Encroachment' *Dhaka Tribune* (Dhaka, 30 January 2019) [www.dhakatribune.com/bangladesh/court/2019/01/30/turag-given-legal-person-status-to-save-it-from-encroachment] accessed 17 October 2020.

[24] 'In Historic Ruling, Colombian Court Protects Youth Suing the National Government for Failing to Curb Deforestation' *Dejusticia* (5 April 2018) [www.dejusticia.org/en/en-fallo-historico-corte-suprema-concede-tutela-de-cambio-climatico-y-generaciones-futuras] accessed 17 October 2020.

[25] Marianne Brooker, 'Defending Ecuador's Los Cedros Forest' *The Ecologist* (London, 14 July 2020) [https://theecologist.org/2020/jul/14/defending-ecuadors-los-cedros-forest] accessed 17 October 2020.

[26] *Colorado River System v State of Colorado* (DC Colo, No 17cv02316–NYW) Complaint, 3 November 2017.

[27] Amitav Ghosh, *The Great Derangement. Climate Change and the Unthinkable* (University of Chicago Press 2016) 63.

[28] Cullinan (n 2) 108.

[29] Erin Fitz-Henry, 'Decolonizing Personhood' in Peter Burdon and Michelle Maloney (eds), *Wild Law – In Practice* (Routledge 2014) 133, 135.

[30] ibid.

arguments on behalf of Ecuador's hydrocarbon reserves.[31] Peter Burdon similarly notes that rights are 'susceptible to be arranged in a way that promotes economic growth over environmental protection'.[32]

More broadly speaking, any legal recognition of nonhuman rights is, of necessity, partial; law cannot accommodate an all-encompassing, nonhuman rights framework and, in any event, human bias and preconceptions mitigate against an ideal of universal, nonhuman rights. Deborah Bird Rose and Thom Van Dooren have pointed out that the rights of the unloved, the disregarded, the vilified are unlikely to be recognized, legally or otherwise.[33] They have asked, in a certain despairing tone: 'Given that [the] creatures who are so vividly present in our imaginative lives are nonetheless on the edge of loss, what hope could there possibly be for the countless other creatures who are less visible, less beautiful, less a part of our cultural lives?'[34]

These less visible, less beautiful creatures include various invasive species which, as Audra Mitchell has indicated, are treated as unnatural. In addition, common and numerous lifeforms like bacteria 'are not featured as poster-children of ecosystemic survival; more often, they are pathologized as threats to the health of humans and the other beings with whom they are more positively bonded'.[35] An idealized framework of universal rights lacks credibility when certain beings are viewed as 'non-existent' and 'ethically irrelevant'.[36] We cannot, it seems, abandon our species-centric perspective in order to place equal value upon all members of all other species.

Human rights frameworks are selectively applied and do not protect all members of every human society; this, then, is the flawed starting point for a mooted expansion of rights into the realm of the nonhuman. Siobhan O'Sullivan, reviewing a book on the political rights of animals in the maelstrom of 2020, as Australia burnt, as the world wrestled its way through a pandemic, as Black Lives Matter protests exploded on to the public arena, expressed the dilemma thus:

> I cannot help but feel bitterly disappointed in many of our Western political institutions. They have failed so many humans, yet we are just at the point of theorising why they should be engaged in order to protect sentient nonhumans. Were our institutions ever worthy? Do they have the capacity to protect the vulnerable?[37]

---

[31] Mihnea Tanasescu, 'When a River is a Person: From Ecuador to New Zealand, Nature Gets its Day in Court' *The Conversation* (Melbourne, 19 June 2017) [https://theconversation.com/when-a-river-is-a-person-from-ecuador-to-new-zealand-nature-gets-its-day-in-court-79278] accessed 17 October 2020.

[32] Peter D Burdon, 'Obligations in the Anthropocene' (2020) *Law and Critique* [https://doi.org/10.1007/s10978-020-09273-9] accessed 17 October 2020.

[33] Deborah Bird Rose and Thom Van Dooren, 'Introduction' (2011) 50 *Australian Humanities Review* 1, 1.

[34] ibid.

[35] Audra Mitchell, 'Beyond Biodiversity and Species: Problematizing Extinction' (2016) 33(5) *Theory, Culture and Society* 23, 30–1.

[36] ibid 37.

[37] Siobhan O'Sullivan, 'Should Animals Have Political Rights?' (2020) *Environmental Politics* [http://dx.doi.org/10.1080/09644016.2020.1810418] accessed 17 October 2020.

There is, as two scholars have pointed out in a decolonial critique of the rights of nature movement, a 'contradictory logic' to the endorsement of Western notions of rights and personhood as the antidote to Western anthropocentrism, with its entrenched nature-culture dichotomy.[38]

The advantage of a rights framework is that it is readily recognized within most contemporary legal systems. We are, in effect, tinkering with existing legal instruments and tools by developing the concept of nonhuman rights. Yet it is quite plausible that rights mechanisms, and indeed the workings of law as we know it, cannot accommodate the interspecies, intergenerational challenges of the Anthropocene.

This dilemma goes beyond terminology, and beyond the conceptual, ideological and political limitations of law; it becomes a matter of scale. As Timothy Clark puts it, '[s]omething planetary is breaking through'.[39]

SCALAR FRAMING AND ZOOMING OUT

Wild law incorporates many of the underlying assumptions of ecocritical literary theory but it is legal rather than literary texts, including judgments, which are subjected to critical analysis. The focus is on the invisibilization of the nonhuman, the commodification of the nonhuman, and disregard for the rights and wellbeing of the nonhuman. Clark has suggested that the Anthropocene could 'form a threshold at which art and literature touch limits to the human psyche and imagination themselves'.[40] So, too, the Anthropocene tests the limitations of legal texts, legal rules and the legal imagination. The premise of wild law, and the broader possibilities of wild judging, sidestep a fundamental question: can any form of law or judging contend with the immense, global dilemmas of the Anthropocene?

Clark identifies the scalar deficiencies of literature and the corresponding limitations of ecocriticism, arguing that there are fundamental narrative limitations, or addictions, which preclude the representation of 'the Leviathan of humanity en masse' as a geological force.[41] Amitav Ghosh and Timothy Morton have also drawn attention to the scalar deficiencies of existing literary modes and, indeed, modes of thinking and behaving, in contending with the enormity of what Morton calls hyperobjects: phenomena, such as climate change, 'that are massively distributed in time and space relative to humans'.[42] Ghosh maintains that the Anthropocene presents a scalar 'form of resistance' to literary representation, in that 'its essence consists of phenomena that were long ago expelled from the territory of the novel'.[43]

One could also assert that the Anthropocene exhibits a scalar form of resistance to legal representation. Existing legal mechanisms, anchored in realism, cannot accommodate planetary scale issues or create remedies for wrongs generated by humanity as a species. A scalar reading of judicial texts exposes the same 'deep or structural forms of illusion or delusion'

---

[38] Ariel Rawson and Becky Mansfield, 'Producing Juridical Knowledge: "Rights of Nature" or the Naturalization of Rights?' (2018) 1(1–2) *Environment and Planning E: Nature and Space* 99, 100.

[39] Timothy Clark, *Ecocriticism on the Edge: The Anthropocene as a Threshold Concept* (Bloomsbury Publishing 2015) 9.

[40] ibid 176.

[41] ibid 73.

[42] Timothy Morton, *Hyperobjects: Philosophy and Ecology after the End of the World* (University of Minnesota Press 2013) 1.

[43] Ghosh (n 27) 63.

that Clark detects in literary texts;[44] Ghosh refers to these as 'modes of concealment that [prevent] people from recognizing the realities of their plight'.[45] Judges are complicit in what he has called the Great Derangement.[46] Judicial reasoning implies a bedrock of reason, but judges share the predicament of 'the vast majority of human beings' who resist the imperative of adaptation.[47] Ghosh speculates that it is 'obsessed monomaniacs who appear to be on the borderline of lunacy', rather than those seemingly guided by reason in their decision-making, who are best equipped to make the 'necessary changes'.[48]

Dipesh Chakrabarty's influential 2009 essay on the 'climate of history',[49] which acknowledged the scientific view of humanity as a geological force and considered the significance of this for his discipline, generated some criticism for his endorsement of species thinking. He acknowledged that species thinking, with its suggestion of universalism, is troubling for historians;[50] on the other hand, his expertise in the fields of globalization, Marxism, subaltern history and postcolonialism did not enable him to '[make] sense of this planetary conjuncture within which humanity finds itself today'.[51] Indeed, a number of scholars subsequently articulated their concerns that important distinctions and inequalities are blurred when humanity is viewed from a species perspective.[52] Nevertheless, in Chakrabarty's view, there is a need to 'think simultaneously on both registers' of capital history and species history[53] – an intellectual exercise he later described as zooming in and zooming out.[54] If we omit to zoom in, we ignore the 'human inequality and suffering caused by modern institutions'; without zooming out, however, we can overlook the suffering of Earth and the impact of human populations and human consumption on Earth system processes,[55] on the 'more-than-human'.[56]

The visual metaphor of zooming in and out, as Adeline Johns-Putra has pointed out,[57] connects Chakrabarty's thinking with Clark's references to scalar framing, and Ghosh's reflections on the Great Derangement. It is, furthermore, helpful in analysing the deficiencies of legal and judicial texts in addressing the challenges of the Anthropocene. Law and judging

---

[44] Clark (n 39) 191.
[45] Ghosh (n 27) 11.
[46] ibid.
[47] ibid 54.
[48] ibid.
[49] Dipesh Chakrabarty, 'The Climate of History: Four Theses' (2009) 35 *Critical Inquiry* 197, 213.
[50] ibid 214.
[51] ibid 199.
[52] See, eg, Robert Emmett and Thomas Lekan (eds), *Whose Anthropocene? Revisiting Dipesh Chakrabarty's 'Four Theses'* (RCC Perspectives: Transformations in Environment and Society 2016).
[53] Chakrabarty (n 49) 220.
[54] Dipesh Chakrabarty, 'The Human Significance of the Anthropocene' in Bruno Latour with Christophe Leclercq (eds), *Reset Modernity!* (MIT Press 2016) 189, 197.
[55] ibid 198.
[56] Petra Tschakert and her co-authors refer to 'one of the earliest usages' of this phrase by David Abram in *The Spell of the Sensuous. Perception and Language in a More-than-Human World* (Vintage Books 1997): Petra Tschakert et al, 'Multispecies Justice: Climate-Just Futures With, For and Beyond Humans' (2020) *WIRES Climate Change* fn 2 [https://doi.org/10.1002/wcc.699] accessed 6 January 2021. Robert Macfarlane uses the phrase in his discussion of the deficiencies of 'mammal language': Macfarlane (n 11) 111.
[57] Adeline Johns-Putra, 'Climate and History in the Anthropocene: Realist Narrative and the Framing of Time' in Adeline Johns-Putra (ed), *Climate and Literature* (Cambridge University Press 2019) 246, 249.

focus upon *intra*-species relationships and interconnections. Law zooms in; judging gravitates towards detail. Judging at its most expansive purports to resolve disputes between nation states, or between nation states and multinational corporations. Zooming out, to accommodate interspecies perspectives, is a daunting proposition for legal systems as they are currently structured. The process can deliver seemingly perverse outcomes: Clark points out that, viewed at a different scale, rights-based arguments intended to distribute more broadly the trappings of Western prosperity resemble 'an insane plan to destroy the biosphere'.[58]

When it comes to large-scale planetary concerns, to hyperobjects and to humanity as a species, there is, with a few singular exceptions, a resounding silence in legal and judicial texts. For this reason, scholars have begun to theorize about the nature of planetary justice, which, as Colin Hickey and Ingrid Robeyns contend, 'present[s] a radical departure from the status quo'.[59] Louis Kotzé and Rakhyun Kim, acknowledging that law and legal science in their current manifestations are ill-suited to the challenges of the Anthropocene,[60] have identified the need for the development of Earth system law which would, inter alia, 'embrace all present and future earth system constituents including humans and the non-human world'.[61] Such discussions are still very much in embryonic form and have not, as yet, shaped legal and judicial processes.

An important decision handed down in 2020 is illustrative of judicial reluctance to venture beyond existing terrain. This decision is important for a number of reasons. It highlights the inadequacies of current mechanisms of legal reasoning and perceptions of the role of the judiciary in the Anthropocene, specifically in the contentious space of intergenerational judging. Furthermore, the decision exhibits a fundamental divergence in scalar thinking between the majority judges and the dissenting judge; in fact, the dissenting judge provides us with a scalar critique of the majority decision. This is the Ninth Circuit Court of Appeals decision in the landmark case of *Juliana v United States*,[62] proceedings commenced by youth litigants in 2015 against the United States government on the basis that the government's failure to act on climate change constitutes a breach of its atmospheric public trust obligations. The litigants are also arguing abridgement of their constitutional rights, an increasingly popular strategy in climate litigation.[63]

The case, scheduled for trial in February and then October 2018, was derailed when the well-resourced defendants, having previously failed to have the proceedings dismissed or to convince the United States Supreme Court to stay or stop the proceedings, succeeded in having an interlocutory appeal heard by the Ninth Circuit Court of Appeals. The Ninth Circuit Court issued its order in January 2020, reversing the decision of District Court Judge Ann Aiken

---

[58] Clark (n 39) 73.
[59] Colin Hickey and Ingrid Robeyns, 'Planetary Justice: What Can We Learn from Ethics and Political Philosophy?' (2020) *Earth System Governance* [https://doi.org/10.1016/j.esg.2020.100045] accessed 17 October 2020. See, also, John S Dryzek and Jonathan Pickering, *The Politics of the Anthropocene* (Oxford University Press 2019) ch 4.
[60] Louis J Kotzé and Rakhyun E Kim, 'Earth System Law: The Juridical Dimensions of Earth System Governance' (2019) 1 *Earth System Governance* [https://doi.org/10.1016/j.esg.2019.100003] accessed 17 October 2020.
[61] ibid 5.
[62] *Juliana v United States* 947 F3d 1159 (9th Cir 2020) (*Juliana v United States*).
[63] See Jacqueline Peel and Hari M Osofsky, 'A Rights Turn in Climate Change Litigation?' (2018) 7(1) *Transnational Environmental Law* 37.

in which she had held that the matter could proceed to trial. The young litigants are seeking review of this decision.

The two majority judges in the Ninth Circuit Court were not oblivious to the enormity of the issues at stake: in the words of Circuit Judge Hurwitz, there was substantial evidence to suggest that 'failure to change existing policy may hasten an environmental apocalypse'.[64] They acknowledged that '[a]bsent some action, the destabilizing climate will bury cities, spawn life threatening natural disasters, and jeopardize critical food and water supplies'.[65] Nevertheless, they concluded, albeit 'reluctantly', that their court could not provide the requested forms of relief;[66] the plaintiffs' claims were non-justiceable and this was a matter for the political branches of government. The fact that those branches had thus far refused to act on climate change did not enable the court 'to step into their shoes'.[67]

In a strong dissenting judgment, Judge Josephine Staton took quite a different position upon the court's responsibility when confronted with the calamitous consequences of the government's obdurate refusal to act on climate change. She conceded that it may well be beyond the power of the court to address the climate crisis in its entirety, but even a 'partial and temporary reprieve would constitute meaningful redress', given the unprecedented magnitude and irreversibility of the crisis and the likelihood that it will destroy the United States 'as we know it'.[68] In light of the 'impending point of no return', it was the duty of the court to intervene.[69] She concluded: 'When the seas envelop our coastal cities, fires and droughts haunt our interiors, and storms ravage everything between, those remaining will ask: Why did so many do so little?'[70]

The judgments contain two opposing approaches to the capacity of the judiciary to intervene in matters of global dimension and species significance, to apply legal tools and reasoning to the hyperobject of climate change, to address and seek to counter the looming threat of large-scale extinction events implicating humanity as well as countless nonhuman species. There is no evidence of judicial misapprehension about the enormity of the challenge. There is, however, in the majority judgment, a clear statement as to the perceived scalar limitations on the court's powers – limitations which Judge Staton, equally clearly, dismissed.

The decision[71] of a Californian judge in a case brought by two city municipalities against a number of the largest fossil fuel producers, or Carbon Majors, is another example of a judicial text which highlights the scalar limitations of law. In what was framed as a dispute which attributed climate change and its various impacts to the insidious workings of capital, the judge chose, rather, to zoom out to frame climate change as an international and global issue, and furthermore as a species issue. This framing, however, then absolved him from assessing the particular contribution and liability of certain Carbon Majors and supplying a remedy, as '[t]he problem deserves a solution on a more vast scale than can be supplied by a district judge

---

[64] *Juliana v United States* 1164.
[65] ibid 1166.
[66] ibid 1165.
[67] ibid 1175.
[68] ibid 1176.
[69] ibid 1191.
[70] ibid.
[71] *City of Oakland v BP PLC* 325 FSupp3d 1017 (ND Cal 2018).

or jury in a public nuisance case'.[72] In his view, given the global and universal dimensions of fossil fuel usage, the industry could not be held to be responsible. He stated that:

> Without those fuels, virtually all of our monumental progress would have been impossible. All of us have benefitted. Having reaped the benefit of that historic progress, would it really be fair to now ignore our own responsibility in the use of fossil fuels and place the blame for global warming on those who supplied what we demanded? Is it really fair, in light of those benefits, to say that the sale of fossil fuels was unreasonable?[73]

Significantly, he held that it was not appropriate, and potentially counterproductive, for his own court to attempt to balance 'worldwide negatives' against 'worldwide positives'.[74]

The decision is unsatisfactory on a number of fronts, not least because developments in attribution science have enabled us to pinpoint the exact contribution of a small number of Carbon Majors to the climate crisis. Richard Heede has provided quantitative evidence which demonstrates that 90 Carbon Major entities have contributed nearly two thirds of industrial greenhouse gas emissions.[75] Nevertheless, the decision does draw attention to one seemingly insurmountable obstacle in seeking and obtaining planetary justice in the Anthropocene: humanity as a species is responsible for the looming climate crisis, the global wave of extinctions, the terrifying end game where everybody is a player and spectator. And yet, how can humanity be put on trial?

Humanity here confronts what Timothy Morton calls its Oedipal moment,[76] in which 'narrators find out that they are the tragic criminal'.[77] He points out that climate narratives resemble noir fiction, in which the detective is also the criminal.[78] Deborah Bird Rose has also described humanity's plight as that of the 'classic noir protagonist': assuming the role of victim as well as detective and criminal.[79] Narrators, prosecutors, defendants, judges and juries are all complicit in what she calls 'the great unmaking',[80] although there are degrees of culpability when it comes to carbon emissions and resource consumption. This, then, is the paradox of Anthropocene justice. Who, other than God, can sit in judgement on humanity? Robert Macfarlane suggests that the Anthropocene requires us to imagine a 'hypothetical post-human geologist' who will act as 'our archivist, our analyst, our judge'.[81] Another answer to this question might lie in the outsider perspective of nonhuman species, or alternatively with human generations to come.

In the next sections, I consider the role which speculative and ecological fiction might play in enabling us to zoom out: to take a species approach in judging the human species,

---

[72] ibid 1029.
[73] ibid 1023–4.
[74] ibid 1026.
[75] Richard Heede, 'Tracing Anthropogenic Carbon Dioxide and Methane Emissions to Fossil Fuel and Cement Producers, 1854–2010' (2014) 122(1–2) *Climatic Change* 229.
[76] Timothy Morton, 'The Oedipal Logic of Ecological Awareness' (2012) 1 *Environmental Humanities* 7, 16.
[77] Timothy Morton, *Dark Ecology. For a Logic of Future Co-Existence* (Columbia University Press 2016) 9.
[78] ibid.
[79] Deborah Bird Rose, 'Anthropocene Noir' (2013–14) 41/42 *Arena* 206, 215.
[80] ibid 217.
[81] Macfarlane (n 11) 78.

and an intergenerational approach in judging those generations most complicit in the Great Acceleration.[82]

SPECULATIVE FICTION AND INTERSPECIES JUDGING

Despite, or perhaps due to, the expressed concerns of Clark and Ghosh about literary limitations, writers of contemporary speculative and ecological fiction are increasingly confronting the scalar dilemmas and uncanniness[83] of the Anthropocene. In particular, in some works of speculative and ecological fiction, writers are experimenting with nonhuman perspectives; in this regard, the literary imagination far surpasses the judicial imagination. It is my contention that truly wild judging requires more than representation of the nonhuman in human fora, in accordance with human rules and understandings. Wild judging demands a reversal of positions, a judging of humanity. Literary representations of the nonhuman, and of the human through nonhuman senses, can expedite and augment the ongoing experiment of wild judging.

The unfathomable gulf between the viewpoint of nonhuman species and the human perspective does not prevent humanity from anthropomorphising the perspective of companion animals and other species. It is even more problematic to transpose upon nonhuman species the judgement which humans visit upon each other, which, Jacques Derrida has reminded us, incorporates the capacity to assess nakedness, whether this be a matter of external clothing or a matter of naked intent. This form of judgement, biblically speaking, accompanied the partaking of fruit from the Tree of Knowledge, the onset of self-awareness and the consequential expulsion into the wilderness. Derrida writes that humans are subject to the animal gaze, and that the animal 'has its point of view regarding me'.[84] This is, he stresses, the 'point of view of the absolute other'.[85] The animal gaze is 'uninterpretable, unreadable, undecidable, abyssal and secret'.[86] Can one, therefore, 'from the vantage of the animal see oneself being looked at naked?'[87] And does such a penetrative gaze incorporate judgement: judgement of the violence, the cruelty, the 'monstrous' conditions and the annihilation visited upon animals by humanity?[88] Extending this argument beyond the animal gaze, how can we understand or at least acknowledge the experience of other nonhuman or more-than-human beings, including trees, forests, rivers and oceans, which may lack eyes but possess, arguably, sentience and agency?

Andreas Malm and Alf Homborg, while criticising species thinking as 'inimical to action' and 'conducive to mystification and political paralysis', concede that '"the Anthropocene"

---

[82] This is the post-Second World War era, termed the Great Acceleration by climate scientist Will Steffen and his co-authors due to the dramatic increase in the magnitude and impact of humanity's footprint upon the planet: Will Steffen and others, 'The Trajectory of the Anthropocene: The Great Acceleration' (2015) 2 *The Anthropocene Review* 81.

[83] Ghosh (n 27), at 30, refers to the increasingly frequent use of the word uncanny: 'No other word comes close to expressing the strangeness of what is unfolding around us.' Timothy Morton describes 'the time of hyperobjects' as 'a vastly more complex situation that is uncanny and intimate at the same time': Morton (n 42) 130.

[84] Jacques Derrida, 'The Animal that Therefore I Am (More to Follow)', David Wills tr (2002) 28(2) *Critical Inquiry* 369, 380.

[85] ibid.
[86] ibid 381.
[87] ibid 390.
[88] ibid 394.

might be a useful concept and narrative for polar bears and amphibians and birds who want to know what species is wreaking such havoc on their habitats'.[89] They contend, however, that nonhuman species 'lack the capacity to scrutinise and stand up to human actions'.[90] In speculative and ecological fiction, we increasingly find imaginative forays into a world in which humans, and humanity, *are* scrutinised by the 'absolute other'.

Michel Faber's *Under the Skin*,[91] for instance, offers insights by way of allegory into the 'industrial, mechanical, chemical, hormonal, and genetic violence to which man has been subjecting animal life for the past two centuries'.[92] Isserley, an alien entity who has been surgically altered to resemble a human woman, roams the countryside looking for male hitchhikers; likely specimens are tranquillized and transported to an underground facility run by her corporate employer. After their tongues and testicles have been removed,[93] they are caged in pens, fattened up, butchered and processed into food. The 'best cuts',[94] 'a fortune's worth',[95] are taken by cargo ship to Isserley's home planet. The aliens consider themselves to be human, and believe humans to be animals called vodsels: 'vodsels couldn't do any of the things that really defined a human being.'[96] Interestingly, the 2013 film adaptation[97] glosses over Faber's description of the business-like conversion of human beings into food. Male victims, enticed by a blank-faced Scarlett Johansson into her van, sink into a viscous black liquid and, seemingly, disintegrate. The director has explained that his primary goal was to portray humanity and the world through alien eyes.[98]

More recent works challenge the hegemony of the human perspective, as writers speculate on the animal gaze and what it might mean. In Laura Jean McKay's *The Animals in That Country*,[99] published in 2020, the reader is plunged into a strange, disorienting world, in which all known systems break down. This is the now familiar terrain of a pandemic, but a pandemic without human casualties; those infected with zooflu, or 'talking animal disease', can suddenly comprehend, and translate into verbal form, nonhuman forms of communication.[100] It is clear that our existing social structures and our collective capacity to function within them, our existing systems of governance, our existing economies, are all predicated upon animals remaining voiceless and, by extension, rights-less. Dryzek and Pickering have observed that '[t]he non-human world may be screaming in pain as we enter the Anthropocene, but we have devised institutions, practices, and discourses that render us very bad listeners'.[101] Such protective barriers are stripped away with the advent of zooflu. The narrator, Jean, is overwhelmed

---

[89] Andreas Malm and Alf Hornborg, 'The Geology of Mankind? A Critique of the Anthropocene Narrative' (2014) 1(1) *The Anthropocene Review* 62, 67.
[90] ibid.
[91] Michel Faber, *Under the Skin* (Canongate 2000).
[92] Derrida (n 84) 395.
[93] Faber (n 91) 213–14.
[94] ibid 161.
[95] ibid 157.
[96] ibid 174.
[97] *Under the Skin* (Film4, 2013).
[98] Danny Leigh, 'Under the Skin: Why Did This Chilling Masterpiece Take a Decade?' *The Guardian* (Melbourne, 7 March 2014) [www.theguardian.com/film/2014/mar/06/under-the-skin-director-jonathan-glazer-scarlett-johansson] accessed 17 October 2020.
[99] Laura Jean McKay, *The Animals in That Country* (Scribe 2020).
[100] ibid 35.
[101] Dryzek and Pickering (n 59) 127.

by a babble of terrified, cocky, and confused animal voices. Battery-reared pigs, 'half-dead', 'blind, mad', are released into the outside world for the first time, calling 'more, more, more'.[102] The joey of a kangaroo struck by a car can only say '[h]ungry' and '[n]eed her'.[103] Native animals dying of thirst in cages call for rain; a koala says, appallingly, 'I'm cooked'.[104] A cow asks Jean to 'tell my babies I'm still here'.[105]

The most idiosyncratic voice belongs to Sue, a dingo, who accompanies Jean on a desperate search for her missing son and granddaughter. Interactions between human and dingo are complex, as Deborah Bird Rose has outlined.[106] Rose's difficult meditation upon the dingo began with the discovery of the 'dingo tree': trees festooned with the bodies of slaughtered and, in some instances, skinned dingos.[107] She deplores the 'sustained attack' on dingos by white pastoralists, some of whom display on fences and trees the corpses of dingos as 'the spoils of war'.[108] Yet the dingo is recognized as multi-species kin by Aboriginal Australians and occupies a unique place in human–nonhuman relationships in Australia. Arriving in Australia approximately five thousand years ago, they were 'the first nonhumans who answered back, came when called, helped in the hunt, slept with people'.[109] As a key predator, the dingo also provides a pivotal role in supporting and maintaining Australian ecosystems.[110]

Jean, who had assumed that she could easily interpret and respond to Sue's requirements and demands while Sue was a wild animal in captivity, has to re-evaluate their relationship; she discovers that Sue finds her exasperating, ignorant, and in need of training and protection. Sue views Jean as mother, as pack, as '[s]ome old shiny thing from yesterday',[111] as queen, as an aberrant mixture of good cat and bad dog. Despite professing affection for the dingo whom she found as a newborn pup, Jean initially refutes Sue's claim of kinship; she tells Sue she is searching for her human 'kin', '[t]he real ones'.[112]

For white Australians, the gulf between the human and nonhuman remains unbridgeable. For indigenous Australians, however, there is both vulnerability and strength in belonging to cross-species kin groups: '[n]o one (human or nonhuman) stands or falls alone, and at the same time no one is exempt from the suffering of others'.[113] As the relationship between Jean and Sue develops, and Jean's various survival props disappear, this interdependence and intimacy become evident. Sue finds food for Jean, takes care of her infected bite wound, lays down 'a rule to every moment',[114] hunts for them both. The intimacy is severed when Jean is

---

[102] McKay (n 99) 130.
[103] ibid 154.
[104] ibid 162.
[105] ibid 182.
[106] Rose (n 9).
[107] ibid 98
[108] ibid 56.
[109] ibid 63.
[110] ibid 67.
[111] McKay (n 99) 149.
[112] ibid 150.
[113] Rose (n 9) 99.
[114] McKay (n 99) 263.

forced by soldiers to take 'the cure',[115] medication which silences the animals' voices. Sue's last words to Jean, before '[t]he universe [is] gone',[116] insist upon connection: 'I'm the kin.'[117]

The novel compels us to contemplate the immense gulf between human thought processes, which present themselves to us in verbal form, and the sentience of nonhumans. Even before the onset of zooflu, Jean challenges the expertise of rangers who dismiss the howl of the captive dingo as '[d]ingo admin': 'Tell me she doesn't know something about the world that you and me haven't ever thought of.'[118] Given this gulf, legal recognition of interspecies rights and shared entitlements, and the appointment of human guardians to represent other species in human courts, are inherently problematic.

In another recent work of ecological fiction,[119] we find a similar dizzying shift in perspective to that experienced by Jean, when the 'overstory' of trees is superimposed upon the lives of nine human individuals. Even as Richard Powers rejects the scalar limitations of realist literature by zooming out to encompass this overstory, he is cognisant of such limitations, with one of his characters conceding that 'no novel can make the contest for the *world* seem as compelling as the struggles between a few lost people'.[120] Powers reminds us that trees have a much longer, richer planetary presence than humanity, and exposes the hubris in our preoccupation with human narratives, in our disregard for the immensely long story of trees, and in our failure to understand their role as giant, generous, cooperative beings which enable our existence. Trees, '[t]hose slow deliberate creatures with their elaborate vocabularies',[121] communicate with each other, and with those human beings capable of understanding their messages; one character suggests that 'trees like to toy with human thought like boys toy with beetles'.[122] Here we enter a world in which sentient beings might lack vision, but not the capacity to communicate. The main human characters in the novel share a recognition of the perilous situation of the world's forests, and are linked by their increasingly desperate efforts to save these ancient beings. They are compelled to ask themselves, and answer, this question: 'What wouldn't a person do, to help the most wondrous products of four billion years of creation?'[123]

These two ambitious works of literature challenge us to recognize the agency of nonhuman others, the extent to which such others are both familiar and alien, known and unknown. The texts bring into sharp focus what Ghosh describes as 'the presence and proximity of nonhuman interlocutors'.[124] Furthermore, they highlight the existence of cross-species interdependence and cooperation, concepts not accorded recognition within the existing legal systems in the Global North although integral to what First Nations academic Irene Watson refers to as 'raw law': 'a natural system of obligations and benefits, flowing from an Aboriginal ontology.'[125] An understanding of nonhuman sentience and agency is not readily reconciled with a rational,

---

[115] ibid 271.
[116] ibid 277.
[117] ibid 276.
[118] ibid 1.
[119] Richard Powers, *The Overstory* (William Heinemann 2018).
[120] ibid 383, emphasis in original.
[121] ibid 283.
[122] ibid 151.
[123] ibid 345.
[124] Ghosh (n 27) 30.
[125] Irene Watson, *Aboriginal Peoples, Colonialism and International Law. Raw Law* (Routledge 2015) 1.

analytical, judging Western mindset. These issues are further explored in Fleur Kilpatrick's award-winning play *Whale*, performed at Northcote Town Hall in Melbourne in May 2019.

The dilemma of judging the fate of others, both humans and nonhumans, is at the core of the play. Kilpatrick creates a different, confronting form of judging, one which implicates the audience. She compels all members of the audience to think about complicity and hard decision-making by asking them to vote on the survival and sacrifice of four islands. Delegates, randomly selected members of the audience, must present the case for each island. These vary in terms of human populations. One island has no humans at all, but is home to the only nesting colony of Royal Penguins: if the island goes down, a species will disappear. Remarkably, across the play's season, only ten people refused to vote. The vast majority of people who made up the audience accepted their 'terrible power' to decide the fate of others and 'did what they were told'.[126]

The play can be viewed as ecological fiction, presenting in its second act the warm, humorous and doomed Whale as the central character. Whale does not judge humanity but instead rescues the sacrificial delegate, Jonah, who finds him or herself in Whale's stomach. Whale enacts and receives 'gestures of care, of complex thinking, of empathic connection'.[127] Her blubber full of toxic waste, Whale beaches herself but delivers Jonah, intact, to land.

One underlying suggestion in *Whale*, and indeed in the other texts analysed here, is that an attachment to judging, in the form of determining the fate of both human and nonhuman others, is a solely human attribute. Whale, after hearing that Jonah believes that he or she has saved the world, observes that: 'I think that's something pretty unique about you people. You're really into making things better.'[128] The fact that her child was killed by a boat does not prevent her intervening to save the delegate; she is devoid of any desire for retribution against humans. Interspecies judging is, quite possibly, a chimera, a futile attempt to colonize the unknown, unspoken nonhuman consciousness with human thought patterns and modes of behaviour. As Whale puts it: 'If my voice is entering your ears as human English, that's your own self-centredness. I'm talking whale.'[129]

Whale's ravaged, decomposing body, described as a biohazard, speaks to the dangers for marine species of their rapidly degrading environment. Deborah Bird Rose has pointed out that there is an added urgency to the need to hear and respond to nonhuman voices, in these 'days of violent extinctions, of global dimming and moving dust bowls, of habitat fragmentation, ice melt, and plundered lives'.[130] The onslaught of extinctions raises compelling moral and ethical dilemmas for humanity, given that our species bears responsibility for this permanent extinguishment of lifeforms. Such dilemmas are compounded by the possibility of salvaging some of these lifeforms: as a species, we have the technological expertise which could enable us to reverse some of these processes through artificial means.

---

[126] Sarah Walker and Fleur Kilpatrick, 'Sinking Feelings and Hopeful Horizons: Holding Complexity in Climate Change Theatre' in Anne Harris and Stacy Holman Jones (eds), *Affective Movements, Methods and Pedagogies* (Routledge 2020) 83, 98–9.
[127] ibid 93.
[128] Fleur Kilpatrick, *Whale* (Lab Kelpie Press forthcoming).
[129] ibid.
[130] Rose (n 9) 57.

JUDGING BEYOND THE BRINK OF EXTINCTION

In a rapidly growing body of texts, writers of fiction are tackling some of the multiple dilemmas of extinction. In another 2020 novel, *The Last Migration*,[131] the narrator, albeit for deeply personal reasons, is following what she believes to be the last migration of the Arctic terns, flying over oceans now denuded of fish. Implausibly, the tiny creatures survive and reach a sanctuary at the other end of the world. The novel is set in the near future, when tipping points have been reached that we are only now approaching, and vast numbers of familiar species have disappeared from the wild.[132] Yet, the extreme vulnerability of migratory birds, conveyed so clearly in the text, is a reality today. In September 2020, the normal flight patterns of birds travelling from Alaska and Canada to Central and South America were disrupted by climate-charged wildfires on the west coast of the United States; as a consequence, thousands starved to death. A student who had been collecting carcasses observed that they were 'just feathers and bones', '[a]lmost as if they have been flying until they just couldn't fly any more'.[133]

Different ethical issues arise in works of speculative fiction, when the extinction process is reversed. In two Australian novels,[134] both published in 2020, Neanderthal children are created by corporations, and parented by human mothers. An emerging fascination with Neanderthal revival can be explained by the inclusion of this species within the category of 'charismatically extinct beings', absent but not forgotten.[135] Asta, 'a creation completely outside this time',[136] must be surrendered to Arva Pharmaceuticals once she reaches maturity. Too valuable to be ill-treated, she is viewed by the corporation as resource and commodity, her robust body the key to innovations in medical care. Eve, created to '[connect] us to our deep past',[137] is able to live independently once her mother dies; the structure of the corporation which created her has disintegrated in a time of planetary mayhem.[138] The novel ends on an ambiguous note. She has located others like her, but their survival as a group will depend upon their capacity to adapt to a degraded environment in an increasingly chaotic world.

In another text, also published in 2020 and narrated in the voice of a long-dead member of an extinct species, mammoths are reintroduced to the Siberian tundra. Extinction is the foregone conclusion in the mammoth's story, with Mammut, a specimen exhumed in 1801 and about to be sold at a Natural History Auction, stating at the outset: 'We lost, of course. But we gave you a run for your money'.[139] Mammut concludes the tale of his adventures with a request to 'hominids' to let him 'return to the earth, to die'.[140] We are told, however, in an epilogue, that the Harvard Woolly Mammoth Revival team is seeking to genetically engineer

---

[131] Charlotte McConaghy, *The Last Migration* (Hamish Hamilton 2020).
[132] ibid 207–8.
[133] Quoted in Phoebe Weston, 'Birds "Falling Out of the Sky" In Mass Die-Off in South-Western US' *The Guardian* (Melbourne, 16 September 2020) [www.theguardian.com/environment/2020/sep/16/birds-falling-out-of-the-sky-in-mass-die-off-in-south-western-us-aoe] accessed 17 October 2020.
[134] Donna Mazza, *Fauna* (Allen and Unwin 2020); James Bradley, *Ghost Species* (Hamish Hamilton 2020).
[135] Mitchell (n 35) 31.
[136] Mazza (n 134) 232.
[137] Bradley (n 134) 23.
[138] ibid 212.
[139] Chris Flynn, *Mammoth* (University of Queensland Press 2020) 5.
[140] ibid 235.

mammoths, and restore them to the Siberian steppes in order to prevent the thawing of permafrost.[141] A resurrected Mammut has the last word, roaming again with his herd on the steppes: '[a]nnihilation has been averted.'[142]

Such thought experiments require consideration of what it means to belong to an extinct species, and to be conjured back into life through technological advancements in cloning and DNA replication. They generate difficult questions. James Bradley wanted to explore, in *Ghost Species*, what it 'would be like to *be* such a being'.[143] Can these individuals assert a problematic right not to be born, or born again, not to be forced back into existence on a hostile planet? Do corporations indeed own such creations? Is there some language more appropriate than the terminology of rights and property in contemplating the fate of members of extinct species artificially recreated in laboratories and then released into environments radically altered by humanity? In contemplating these questions, I find myself, unmoored and without a compass, on the uncharted terrain of planetary justice in the Anthropocene.

SPECULATIVE FICTION AND INTERGENERATIONAL VOICES

Unlike nonhuman species and beings, human children can speak out, or, to be more precise, can speak in a way which can be understood by adult humans, and they are doing so in increasing numbers. In recent years, their voices have brought the accelerating impacts of the climate crisis, and the disproportionate impacts upon future generations, to the world's attention. In 2018 and 2019, hundreds of thousands of children around the world participated in global school climate strikes, demanding climate action from the world's governments. Inspired by Greta Thunberg, a determined and blunt-spoken Swedish teenager, young people are conveying a strong message of stolen futures and intergenerational reproach.

Thunberg, whose speeches have been widely circulated and reproduced, has made numerous references to an intergenerational reversal of roles, and to the need for young people to hold adults to account for the irresponsible behaviour which 'will no doubt be remembered in history as one of the greatest failures of humankind'.[144] At the age of 15, she castigated delegates at the 2018 United Nations Climate Summit in Poland with the words: 'You are not mature enough to tell it like it is. Even that burden you leave to your children.'[145] In February 2019, she told the members of the European Economic and Social Committee that they were 'acting like spoiled, irresponsible children'.[146] At the New York Climate Action Summit later that year, she accused attendees of failing her generation, stating that 'the eyes of all future generations' were watching them, and that young people 'would not let [them] get away with

---

[141] ibid 245.
[142] ibid 249.
[143] James Bradley, 'Could Bringing Neanderthals Back to Life Save the Environment? The Idea is Not Quite Science Fiction' *The Guardian* (Melbourne, 27 April 2020) [www.theguardian.com/books/2020/apr/27/could-bringing-neanderthals-back-to-life-save-the-environment-the-idea-is-not-quite-science-fiction] accessed 17 October 2020, emphasis in original.
[144] Greta Thunberg, *No One Is Too Small to Make a Difference* (Penguin 2019) 64.
[145] ibid 15.
[146] ibid 40.

this'.[147] In February 2020, she repeated similar sentiments: '[w]orld leaders are behaving like children, so it falls on us to be the adults in the room'.[148]

It is unsurprising, therefore, that children feel compelled to confront their elders and seek justice in numerous lawsuits around the world. The phenomenon of youth climate litigation anchors the abstract notions of intergenerational justice and equity in concrete causes of action; in the faces and narratives of these youth litigants, we find a realized depiction of intergenerational grievance. The *Juliana* lawsuit described above is possibly the most high-profile of these lawsuits but there are numerous others, including the challenge by a Norwegian youth organization, in conjunction with Greenpeace Nordic Association, to the Norwegian government's grant of oil and gas licences in the Barents Sea;[149] the 2018 *Future Generations* case in Colombia; a youth class action against the Canadian government in the Federal Court of Canada;[150] the 2019 petition by Thunberg and 15 others to the United Nations Committee on the Rights of the Child; a 2020 constitutional challenge to the adequacy of Germany's recent climate protection law;[151] and the Youth Verdict objection to a controversial coalmine in the Queensland Land Court.[152] In September 2020, four Portuguese children and two young adults filed the first climate lawsuit in the European Court of Human Rights;[153] shortly afterwards, a class action on behalf of young people everywhere was launched by eight teenagers against the Australian government, in an attempt to prevent the expansion of yet another coalmine.[154]

One of the litigants in this recent Australian lawsuit, Izzy Raj-Seppings, came to national attention during the Black Summer of 2019/2020, when footage of her interaction with a police officer outside the Prime Minister's residence during a climate protest went viral. The protest took place as smoke wreathed the city of Sydney and landscapes were incinerated in the worst fire season on record; shortly afterwards, unforgettable images of people seeking

---

[147] Oliver Milman, 'Greta Thunberg Condemns World Leaders in Emotional Speech at UN' *The Guardian* (Melbourne, 24 September 2019) [www.theguardian.com/environment/2019/sep/23/greta-thunberg-speech-un-2019-address] accessed 17 October 2020.

[148] Jessica Corbett, 'World Leaders Are Behaving Like Children, Great Thunberg Tells Thousands of Bristol Strikers in Call for Climate Action' *Common Dreams* (Portland, 28 February 2020) [www.commondreams.org/news/2020/02/28/world-leaders-are-behaving-children-greta-thunberg-tells-thousands-bristol-strikers] accessed 17 October 2020.

[149] The Oslo District Court found against the plaintiffs (*Greenpeace Nordic Association v Ministry of Petroleum and Energy* (Oslo District Court, 16-166674TVI-OTIR/06, 4 January 2018)). This judgment was upheld on appeal on 23 January 2020 (*Greenpeace Nordic Association v Ministry of Petroleum and Energy* (Bogarting Court of Appeal, 18-060499ASD-BORG/03)). In April 2020, leave to appeal to the Norwegian Supreme Court was granted.

[150] *La Rose v Her Majesty the Queen* (Federal Court, T-1750-19).

[151] 'Activists Head to Germany's Top Court to Protect the Climate' *DW* (Berlin, 15 January 2020) [www.dw.com/en/activists-head-to-germanys-top-court-to-protect-the-climate/a-52008252] accessed 17 October 2020.

[152] 'Historic Legal Challenge against Clive Palmer's Galilee Coal Project Commences Today' *Business News Australia* (Perth, 19 June 2020) [www.businessnewsaus.com.au/articles/historic-legal-challenge-against-clive-palmer-s-galilee-coal-project-commences-today.html] accessed 17 October 2020.

[153] Jonathan Watts, 'Portuguese Children Sue 33 Countries Over Climate Change at European Court' *The Guardian* (Melbourne, 3 September 2020) [www.theguardian.com/law/2020/sep/03/portuguese-children-sue-33-countries-over-climate-change-at-european-court] accessed 17 October 2020.

[154] *Sharma v Minister for the Environment* (Federal Court of Australia, VID607/2020). In May 2021, Justice Bromberg handed down his decision, finding in favour of the children (*Sharma v Minister for the Environment* [2021] FCA 560).

refuge on beaches, in evacuation centres and in boats flooded both the national and international media. The hand-lettered sign which the teenager raised, after being ordered to leave the protest, encapsulates the dominant message of intergenerational condemnation and defiance. It read, in black letters on a red background: 'Look at what you've left us. Watch us fight it. Watch us win.'[155]

Here, again, works of speculative fiction go further than current legal and judicial texts. The fictitious voices of young narrators from the climate-changed future echo and amplify youth activist and litigant commentary upon the failings, evasions and lack of leadership on the part of their parents' and grandparents' generations.

One such text is Lydia Millet's *A Children's Bible*. A group of resourceful children, operating as a collective 'we', have judged and dismissed their parents as useless. The novel upends a prevalent stereotype in climate fiction, that of children as passive victims and parents as their protectors in post-apocalyptic scenarios. These children, having failed to persuade their parents to leave a 'vacation paradise' which has been 'turned into hell' by cyclonic flooding,[156] strike out independently in the available vehicles; they disregard the agitation of their parents, who attempt to follow them. In the dismissive words of Evie, the narrator: 'Enh, they'll get used to it. Children grow up. Children leave.'[157]

The climate apocalypse unfolds with reverberations of various biblical stories. A Moses figure found floating in the flood leads them to a sanctuary. A list of rules[158] are administered by 'the owner', who descends in a helicopter to dispense punishment to evildoers.[159] A baby is born in a barn near a town called Bethlehem, with four 'trail angels' in attendance.[160] Animals are rescued from floodwaters. The text abounds with ironies as well as biblical parallels. These children navigate the climate apocalypse with enviable stoicism and resilience but in the children's version of the Bible, as consulted by the narrator's brother, there is no Book of Revelations. The reason for this, as divulged by the God-like 'owner', is that 'children couldn't handle relevation' (sic): it is not 'nice', 'too violent'.[161] Yet these children, and in fact all children, those of today and those not yet born, have no choice. They are compelled to endure the not nice, increasingly violent challenges of rapidly accelerating climate disasters, and the social, economic and political consequences of such disasters.

When the children are eventually reunited with their parents, the reversal of roles is complete. The children take charge, pointing out that their parents' 'fitness to maintain order has been undermined'.[162] They use 'a bit of the carrot and a bit of the stick',[163] instructing the adults to contribute to the tasks and projects which will ensure their survival.[164] Their parents

---

[155] Isolde Raj-Seppings, '"I'm the 13-Year-Old Police Threatened to Arrest at the Kirribilli House Protest. This Is Why I Did It' *The Guardian* (Melbourne, 21 December 2019) [www.theguardian.com/australia-news/commentisfree/2019/dec/21/im-the-13-year-old-police-threatened-to-arrest-at-the-kirribilli-house-protest-this-is-why-i-did-it] accessed 17 October 2020.
[156] Lydia Millet, *A Children's Bible* (WW Norton and Co 2020) 89.
[157] ibid 91.
[158] ibid 102.
[159] ibid 182.
[160] ibid 111.
[161] ibid 223.
[162] ibid 214.
[163] ibid 215.
[164] ibid 214.

become depressed, 'their personalities … fading',[165] and eventually disappear. Despite having judged them and 'reviled them and all they'd failed to stand up for and against', the children experience at this point 'a kind of desperation', not because they need their parents but because 'we'd been so *used* to them'.[166] Their capacity to manage independently is irrefutable.

The judgemental tone adopted by the children, informing their parents that '[w]e blame you for everything', that '[y]ou gave up the world' and 'let them turn it all to shit',[167] appears in other recent climate fiction texts, including John Lanchester's *The Wall*, in which young people carry the sometimes deadly burden of protecting Britain from the climate refugees of the near future.[168] The narrator observes that '[n]one of us can talk to our parents' due to 'mass guilt, generational guilt'[169] on the part of the older generation, who 'feel they irretrievably fucked up the world, then allowed us to be born into it'.[170] These young people are condescending, contemptuous and even pitying in their relationships with their elders, whose complicity in the climate crisis is undeniable. It would appear, from another work of speculative fiction, that the perspective of the as yet unborn from a more distant future is far more ruthless and desperate.

In one landmark climate lawsuit, the 2018 *Future Generations* case, a court has been prepared to acknowledge the rights of the unborn. That judgment contained strong statements about the obligations of the present generation with respect to the unborn, who 'deserve to enjoy the same environmental conditions that we have'.[171] Conceding that unborn generations have a stake in the future of the planet is, however, a different matter from being judged and condemned by the unborn. In Liz Jensen's *The Uninvited*,[172] the unborn wreak havoc on today's adults in a story which is part thriller, part mystery, part science fiction, but nevertheless eerily plausible. The central character, Hesketh, tries to make sense of an accelerating wave of seemingly senseless acts of violence, self-harm, property damage and corporate sabotage on the part of adults who claim that they are manipulated by 'kiddie trolls',[173] or possessed by child figures. Children around the world generate mayhem, murdering parents and other adult relatives, and engaging in bizarre, uncharacteristic behaviour. Gradually, with the help of an old mentor, Hesketh pieces together the underlying explanation, 'written in letters too big to read, letters that could only be deciphered from a vast distance or an unusual angle':[174] the children of the future have returned to change the trajectory of planetary destruction, 'force some monumental paradigm shift in mankind's relationship to itself',[175] and thus avert the worst outcomes. The story which these children bring with them is 'the story of man's end on Earth'.[176]

---

[165] ibid 218.
[166] ibid 221.
[167] ibid 193.
[168] John Lanchester, *The Wall* (Faber and Faber 2019).
[169] ibid 55.
[170] ibid.
[171] 'Climate Change and Future Generations Lawsuit in Colombia: Key Excerpts from the Supreme Court Decision' *DeJusticia* (13 April 2018) [www.dejusticia.org/en/climate-change-and-future-generations-lawsuit-in-colombia-key-excerpts-from-the-supreme-courts-decision] accessed 17 October 2020.
[172] Liz Jensen, *The Uninvited* (Bloomsbury 2012).
[173] ibid 81.
[174] ibid 6.
[175] ibid 237.
[176] ibid 297.

CONCLUSION

The above discussion highlights the imperative for judging wildly, as I have defined it, in light of the unprecedented ecological, existential and ethical challenges of the Anthropocene. We can no longer confine ourselves to the outmoded methodology of resolving intra-species disputes through existing legal mechanisms. Anthropocene justice, or planetary justice, necessitates a radically new approach to judging practices and the practice of judging, an approach which encompasses a zooming out to address interspecies, intergenerational issues while simultaneously preserving the judicial capacity to remedy intra-species injustices.

Pseudo-legal and extra-legal performance, or what Davina Cooper has called 'role-play-with-revisions',[177] offer some tantalising possibilities for experimenting wildly with the parameters of existing judging practices. Examples include People's Tribunals,[178] judgment rewriting,[179] and mock trials such as Plan B's staging of *All Rise for the Planet* at the Tate Gallery in 2019.[180] What I have focused on here, however, is the imaginative recasting which is the pre-requisite for all experiments in judging wildly; the break with legal tradition, the adventurous leaping into the uncanny and the unknown. This imaginary recasting, I have argued, is, in particular, the preserve of writers of speculative and ecological fiction. As plant scientist Merlin Sheldrake states, the task of developing a 'new language' to encompass the animacy of forests, and their extraordinary, enabling fungal networks, is 'the job of writers and artists and poets'.[181]

To judge wildly, we must address the manifold injustices which transcend our own interactions, in this particular time/space, as members of the same species. We must approach the world through different eyes and different senses, and describe what we experience in different voices: the voices of nonhuman or more-than-human species and entities, the voices of the unborn. Here the contemporary works of fiction described above, as well as numerous other present and future works of fiction which challenge our anthropocentric focus, our scalar limitations and our focus on present gratification, play an indispensable role.

---

[177] Davina Cooper, *Feeling Like a State. Desire, Denial and the Recasting of Authority* (Duke University Press 2019) 27.

[178] See, eg, Michelle Maloney, 'Building an Alternative Jurisprudence for the Earth: The International Rights of Nature Tribunal' (2016) 41 *Vermont Law Review* 129.

[179] The Wild Law Judgment project ran from 2014 to 2017, with the rewritten judgments appearing in Nicole Rogers and Michelle Maloney (eds), *Law as if Earth Really Mattered: The Wild Law Judgment Project* (Routledge 2017). The United Kingdom Earth Law Judgments project is currently underway.

[180] See [www.tate.org.uk/whats-on/tate-modern/tate-exchange/workshop/all-rise-planet] accessed 17 October 2020.

[181] Quoted in Macfarlane (n 11) 111.

PART IV

(CIS)TEMS OF THOUGHT

Platform in Furs – Letters of Affect(ion) – Partner in Crime – *Travesti*-Trans Theory – Jedi Code – Solar (Cis)tem

14. Billets
Jannice Käll

The critique of contracts as well as the underlying social contracts expressed in them has a long history. This holds true also for digital contracts, which is the contract form I will explore in particular in this chapter via the concept of affect. Affect will here be used to express a transformation of the contract from ideas and practices where it can be considered as something that two individuals enter into under mutual consent towards something else more akin to both love contracts and love letters. Such understanding of contract to be explored here affiliates itself both with understandings of affect, to be explained further below, as well in particular with Gilles Deleuze's reading of Masochism in the essay 'Coldness and Cruelty' and the connected essay by Leopold von Sacher-Masoch (orig. 1870) (Deleuze 1991). With this focus, the chapter suggests an alternative mode of understanding what is becoming of contract under an economy where platforms have a position of power, even dominance, over the desires of those of us who populate them.

As mentioned, the transformation of contract as an institution under digitalisation, furthermore, has a long history by now. Already in the late 1990s and early 2000s, contracts formed as clickwraps and other one-sided end-user licence agreements were found to establish a new legal situation for massive amounts of standard agreements concerning use of, for example, copyrighted creative content. This situation was criticised as it was found that private persons' intellectual property rights usages were delimited to a larger degree than when alternative media were used to transfer cultural content such as music and film. This more limited situation of content use established via contract included, for example, a limitation on how content could be shared with one's friends. As such, the development of contract as closely connected to the intellectual property object in this way generally implied an increased entanglement of them both, as compared to previous contracts and contract objects (Lessig 1999; Radin 2000, 2003; Boyle 2009). A more recent form of critical debate in relation to digital contracts includes how market actors have established community rules of platforms which designate who is allowed to gain access to the platform, which content the user can share, and so on. Lately the critique related to contracts in the digital sphere has also been focused on data capture and management based on users' activities both online and with smart objects (Hildebrandt 2015; Cohen 2019). The early research on information contracts in this setting showed that we are no longer even faced with contracts, since there is no way to negotiate them. Even if this held true also for standard form contracts, in particular in relation to consumers, before digitalisation emerged, what was found to be new was the scale and scope of the non-negotiable contract object that end-users in digital spheres were faced with (Radin 2003; 2013). This has led, for example, to the recent moves of increased requirements of consent in data regulation, which subsequently legislates which contractual agreements are acceptable in terms of personal data transfer. Furthermore, demands are increasingly being voiced as to a move towards more (or any) transparency in how big communication platforms 'rule' on breaches of their community guidelines. These norm transformations may alter again what a contract can be in a digital setting, and indeed who is the subject and what is the object that can be contracted upon.

Here I am however raising a slightly different angle, in order to point at the affective aspects of digital communities, their so-called contracts and why we continue to submit to their rules. Here I will do this by reading them as love letters – or love contracts. By this I mean a style of writing that does not have the performative legal capacity that one usually assumes a legal contract to have, but more of a clearly affective objective. Surely, one assumes, both love contracts as well as love letters as a genre of their own, and occupying a central place in history of literature, are far removed from legal writing such as a contract? Yet, it is this bind between a message of affect and the formality of the contract that builds an interesting relation between the ways in which control is produced in digital settings. The concept of affect as such is pertinent as it functions as a means to understand how relations between bodies of both human and nonhuman kind are expressed in keeping them together or apart. This makes for a less formalistic understanding of how agreements come into being, compared to when a contract is understood as a fixed tool for governing what is to take place. Both love letters and love contracts are instructive in pointing at such flow, and excess, of bodies. As will be visualised via the example of *Venus in Furs*, one can also say that the love letter as such can also be intimately performed in connection to the love contract. Even more so, however, we can speak of letters and contracts regulating love, as particular ways of understanding the binding powers of agreements beyond the currently dominant idea of the characteristics of contracts in law.

This chapter, then, creates links between contracts, the digital platform-based economy, and the mechanisms used to express, capture and produce emotions through platform agreements in general, as well as behavioural advertising and dating apps in specific. Such techniques bring forward a different type of a love letter in the manner that it binds, or at least attaches, parties through an affective power at the centre of this peculiar form of a contract. My aim is thus to point at new ways of reading contracts as engaged in both the capture and production of affect. The bigger purpose in forwarding such theoretical understanding of contracts is furthermore to place the idea of the contract, as well as law in general, in conversation with a wider stream of affect theory, including how affect plays a significant role of our current forms of politics and capitalism (Hardt and Negri 2000, Ilouz 2007, Massumi 2015). In short, this view is advocated as useful in acknowledging a less rationalistic or neutral diagram of law and the transactions it enables, particularly via the idea of contract and contracting subjects. In particular, it is here explored in terms of how it is possible to move from an understanding that contract is about only transaction of objects towards also being about transmission, control, and exchange of affects.

The concept of affect as well as the politics of affect embedded in twenty-first century Western societies have been widely discussed in research (Clough 2008), in particular in the Deleuzian–Spinozan vein of philosophy (Hardt and Negri 2000, Clough 2008, Braidotti 2013, Massumi 2015, Grosz 2017). Clough describes the affective turn as a possibility to further engage with 'a dynamism immanent to bodily matter and matter generally – matter's capacity for self-organization in being in-formational' (Clough 2008: 1). As she notes, previously this engagement was carried out in the post-structuralist fields of research, however with a stronger focus on human emotions (Clough 2008). As Massumi puts it, considering affect is more about developing an understanding of the movements of bodies and how such movement can never be reduced to just subjects, since there is nothing subjective about it. (Massumi 2015: 3) Affect in this sense implies that one is both opening up oneself and operating in 'a slightly different way than you might have been the moment before. You have made a transition' (ibid). Grosz also explores this perception in the sense that '[a]ffect is the movement of this variation of bodies and their constantly changing parts as well as of ideas, their modes of flow and their ever-changing relations' (Grosz 2017: 79). In law, this perspective of affect has been explored prominently by Andreas Philippopoulos-Mihalopoulos, who stresses the less individualist, less internal idea of emotions and a move towards more collectivist ideas of affect as an energy between bodies. In this understanding, law furthermore becomes less about textual stipulations and more about force created, sustained and ruptured by different materialities involved in their coming together – or apart (Philippopoulos-Mihalopoulos 2015). Understanding affect in this way is, interestingly, also close to how we understand the contract function as something that is supposed to change a situation and re-arrange the bodies of the contracting parties, as well as the objects they are contracting about. The question here is therefore not whether contracts have force in altering the composition of bodies (of course they do) but rather which kind of transformation the contract as a body itself undergoes via an increased understanding of its affective characteristics, in composition between the bodies known as the contracting parties and contractual object over which the contract reigns.

NOT CONTRACTING AFFECT: SOME STARTING POINTS

The contract is, in the general understanding of Western law today, philosophically conceived of in a traditional liberal way in legal theory as well as in society. This implies, in brief, that the contract is perceived of as resting upon liberal ideas of the freedom of subjects to agree on transactions between them. General contract law does not even need to set out these basic parameters; instead the focus tends to be on the issue of at which point something becomes a contract and in what circumstances it can be revoked or terminated. Contracts are furthermore generally sorted under property rights law, since they are assumed to concern property transactions. Even the institution of marriage, and contracts written in relation to the entrance into such alliance, can be seen as contracts regulating the spouses' property status in relation to each other rather than contracts constituting the feelings (hopefully) underlying the act. The starting point of contract theory in legal discourse is furthermore that parties have equal power in entering into a contract, and subsequently that their agreement should be seen as an exchange of will between consensual parties. Needless to say, this idea of the contract and its contracting parties has been criticised in numerous ways. As mentioned in the introduction to this chapter, in relation to digital settings the notion of contract has been particularly criticised in relation to boilerplate practices, where, for example, Radin argues that fundamental aspects of contract as an institution are being dissolved (Radin 2013). To summarise, what this critique suggests is that it is difficult to talk about contracts in the digital sphere as contracts at all in the liberal legal sense, as the exchange of mutual will over a contract object is displaced when one party has to accept a contract without any possibility of negotiating its content (Radin 2013; Cohen 2019: 44–5). The dissolution of contract, or rather the dissolution of negotiation of contract terms, without doubt risks becoming even more prevalent when digital elements are integrated into our homes and cities, as the idea of automation in general is to dissolve decisions, transferring them from individual humans into smart objects and spaces (see, for example, Sadowski 2020).

Considering in more depth what is the contract *object/s* or what is being exchanged has furthermore been addressed not the least via the old saying: if you are getting the media for free, then you are the thing being sold (cf Wark 2019: 1–2). This transformation of the contracted object is mirrored in contract theory in traditional queries about the balance between the parties – is the contract fair? How easily can one leave the agreement if one wants? And so on – become difficult to assess when the contract object is something offered 'for free'. If you do not like Facebook, Twitter, Instagram, Tinder – just don't use it. Consequently, our general tools of contract theory and the assessment of how good a contract practice is – both based on the entrance into the contract – and who is the winner of the contract (even if of course contracts are assumed to be win-win, as per general economic thinking) can at best be assessed by tools asking questions such as 'can we really speak of consent?' What this perspective misses is exactly the affective transaction that these contracts (as well as contracts in general) have always been involved in, and are now even more so, under data-based capitalism, and the forthcoming smartification of everything.

Even if contract theory presents the contract as something engaged in economic transactions – I give you this thing and you give me money – there is already in political theory also an alternative theory of contracts to be found, one that places affect and desire in the foreground. To enter into this understanding of contract, it is first important to stress that neither affect nor love as conceptual tools are to be seen as altogether positive or affirmative. As discussed by, for example, Hardt and Negri, affect can have destructive as well as productive effects on the bodies (subjects, objects and everything in between) it is being produced within and impacting (Hardt and Negri 2000: 364–7). In feminist theory, the critical impulse in studying both love and affect has allowed comprehensive insight into how liberal contract theory hides its basis in sexist assumptions but also how all contracts within patriarchy are tainted by the sexual objectification of women (Pateman 1988; Valverde 2014: 344–7). As Pateman shows, in relation to the idea of marriage as a contractual relationship, this has a history reaching back to the fourteenth century. Feminists have critiqued this view by forwarding the argument that a contract is only a contract if it is between equal parties arriving at terms for their mutual advantage. Furthermore, such feminist critique has also shown differences in class, leading to the conclusion that since only a few women can earn as much as men, only a few middle-class women are likely to be able to negotiate an intimate contract (Pateman 1988: 154–5). We can subsequently see a similarity here in how the general feminist critique of the marriage contract can be compared to the critique of digital contracts as raised by Radin, in the way that the freedom of the parties to contract as well as the contracted object are important if we are to conceive of something as a contract. Pateman, however, goes further in her view of the foundations of contract as well as the potential for liberty in the way that she sees no solution within the institution of contract to the inequalities of marriage as an institution, as the contract will still be based on the patriarchal construction of sexuality and what it means to be a sexual being as conditioned by possessing and having access to sexual property (ibid: 185). In Pateman's understanding, this is also continued in practices of sadomasochism, where consent is drawn to its extreme and the contract becomes a parody, while sexual property stays intact (1988: 185–8). In considering what is at stake in understanding 'contracts' in digital settings, the focus on contract as both ultimately individualistic and subordinated to the desires of the dominant party (whether this dominance is visible on the surface level or not) can form an important entry point. To come closer to what is at stake in terms of affective transmission via digital media, including but not exclusively in relation to sexual desires, we will now turn to consider some of the ways in which emotions are captured and atmospheres affectively engineered.

PLATFORMS AS AFFECTIVE SPACES AND THE CAPTURE OF DESIRES

A famous line from Donna Haraway begs us to ask how the machines have become so lively, while we ourselves are so inert (Haraway 1991: 152). Today, the liveliness of machines is more intense than ever, as they circulate our homes, doing what in recent feminist theory could have been considered care work – cleaning, cooking, keeping track of our schedules and mood. Possibly even more important – they help us direct affect towards both their own materialities as well as each other. While my kids enter TikTok for the latest 'For You' content (naturally hoping that they will be showcased there themselves), my friends and I try to establish why viewers are shown in the order they are, when we upload our Instagram stories. No matter the answer, it is certain that the kind of affective nudging involved in both of these settings (and many others) has become integral to digitised spaces. This double fold of information capitalism and immaterial labour was discussed already by Hardt and Negri via their suggestion that the other face of immaterial labour so often theorised in relation to digital capitalism is affective labour of human contact and interaction (Hardt and Negri 2000: 292). And as Ferrando, for example, points out, the growing field of affective computing as well as robopsychology involve a range of affects as a form of human/robotic interaction (Ferrando 2019: 114).

The function of transmitting and producing desires of course becomes even more obvious in the range of dating apps now available on the market. Notorious for its popularity, Tinder is still the app dominating online dating and, as is increasingly acknowledged, Tinder is not the same for everyone. Just like 'For You' at TikTok and the Instagram story algorithm, dating apps aim at keeping users attached to the next attraction by suggesting new matches through the data they have acquired from your previous usage of the app. The paid version of the app has recently furthermore come to be known for the possibility to sidestep the general algorithm by the function of 'superlikes', which allows a person to transmit their interest in a person without waiting for a possible positive response from an unknowing other. Everywhere these kinds of examples remind us that what is at stake on digital platforms is the creation as well as sustenance of certain affects via data extraction and algorithmic governance (see for example Kalopkas 2019, Cohen 2019: 75). As described in a *Guardian* article from 2017, one can also say that one is lured to give away the information that makes the affective transmissions possible. As Luke Stark, a digital technology sociologist at Dartmouth University, puts it in an interview in the article: 'Apps such as Tinder are taking advantage of a simple emotional phenomenon; we can't feel data' (Duportail 2017).

Recollecting the realisation from Philippopoulos-Mihalopoulos that law is integrated into space as well as a regulator of atmospheres, it may also be noted that it has consistently been popular to talk about digital platforms in architectural terms (see for example Bratton 2015) – something that was preceded in the legal disciplines by, for example, Lessig and Zittrain in their research on the internet as space and architecture in general (Lessig 1999, Zittrain 2006). Just as architecture transcends towards new practices as well as discourses on 'affective buildings' or the more common understanding of 'desire lines' structuring how bodies move in a space, so we can also talk about how platforms integrate questions of affect both visibly and invisibly via the contracts setting the standards for the platform atmosphere (cf boyd 2012). For example, digital platforms such as Facebook write to us in their community standards in a way that is supposed to make us feel safe and as if we belong by stating that 'Every day, people use Facebook to share their experiences, connect with friends and family, and build communities' (Facebook 2020). To ensure that we connect in a fruitful way, Facebook furthermore assigns us some common grounds divided into six areas: Violence and Criminal Behaviour; Safety; Objectionable Content; Integrity and Authenticity; Respecting Intellectual Property; and Content-Related Requests (ibid). The connection between digital, human and affective spaces has been widely discussed in the arts in relation to digital technologies, such as in the Metahaven/Holly Herndon video work 'Home', where the message 'You feel like a home to me' is suggestively wrapped into platform aesthetics, including lyrics such as 'I can feel you in my room. Why was I assigned to you? I feel like I'm home on my own. And it feels like you see me' (Metahaven/Holly Herndon 2014). Mirroring the dissolution of the digital into the home, as well as pointing at the extremely uncomfortable aspects that these digital practices imply, particularly in how they create an atmosphere of being constantly watched, this piece also points at aspects of surveillance as part of how affect takes place via social media platforms (cf also Zuboff 2018, Kalopkas 2019: 1–2).

These ideas of how to build a community can be understood simultaneously as working on capturing our affective bonds to each other, including love and sexual desire, in the format of convincing and assuring that this place and community is the one which can be trusted, and, on the other hand, capturing these feelings in one or many one-sided contracts. This in turn folds into the transactions of affects as described by Massumi above, as a vital part of digital capitalism. Taking such an affective point of departure also implies that we can start to think about feelings and desires as mediated between different bodies. As suggested by Massumi: '[m]ediation, in whatever guise it appears, is the way a lot of theorists try to overcome the old Cartesian duality between mind and body, but it actually leaves it in place and just tries to build a bridge between them' (Massumi 2015: 7). In this way, digital materialities, as expressed via platforms and other forms of organisation, can be seen as active in transmitting affects between the human users connected to them, but also as entangled in other bodies determining desires: capitalism, patriarchy, colonialism, and so on. Our social media, at a surface level mediated by an entirely normal contract, backed up by our entirely normal law, as something legal subjects just consume as an object, can be understood in this way as being embedded in an intricate assemblage of materialities and affects, as well as itself being a mediator of very particular affects.

Here it is of interest to first dip into the general theme of a connection between love letters, love contracts and fetishised objects that figure excessively in the essay 'Venus in Furs'. In one of the introductory scenes in the essay, the male who is later to form a love contract with Wanda (Venus in Furs) is enamoured by an image of Venus with the Mirror, to which he composes a love note on the back of the photograph:

> *Venus in Furs.* You are cold and yet you fire the hearts of men. Wrap yourself in your despot's furs, for they become no one so well as you, cruel goddess of Beauty and Love! (Sacher-Masoch in Deleuze: 154).

Accompanying this note, he later also includes a note from Goethe's Paralipoema to Faust:

TO LOVE!

His wings belie his nature
And his arrows are but claws;
Beneath his crown are budding horns.
For without doubt he is,
Like all the gods of Ancient Greece,
A devil in disguise. (Sacher-Masoch in Deleuze: 154)

In spite of these seemingly contrasting feelings about love, as we shall see next, it is also the desire to submit to his beloved that leads Sacher-Masoch to form a contract with Venus in Furs.

FROM CONTRACT OVER OBJECT TO AFFECTIVE TRANSMISSION AND (LACK OF) CONTROL OVER DESIRES

As discussed, the feminist tradition gives us tools for considering the contract as being less innocent than liberal political theory and the Western legal tradition affords when viewing the contract as a tool for equals to regulate their economic transactions. This implies that an idea about society rests upon a view of individuals coming together to create a joint society, based on mutual consent as to what such community should be about. As Pateman shows, the social contract cannot be disconnected from its function of sustaining patriarchal cultures, since many of the institutions which are included in society uphold patriarchal desires. As an obvious example, marriage as an institution is built upon an idea of organising society around a household based on patriarchal desires, where the man has held dominance over women via the exploitation of their sexual, reproductive and emotional labour. Pateman consequently argues that even if women consent to marriage, the consent is flawed by being subordinated to a desire to subordinate women to men. Furthermore, the possibility to consent as such is striated among women depending on, for example, their social status. Another way of putting this is that consent is not possible since the characteristics of the object being traded are the problem, and the trading of this object in turn is obfuscated by a contractarian understanding of persons as well as things in Western forms of law and social contracts (Pateman 1988, cf also Esposito 2015).

Following this line of thinking, we can contend that subverting specific forms of affective capture demands more than just rules on consent in a certain contractual setting. In relation to the construction of the platform economy, this implies for example that consent of users to take part in a social media platform, or to have data collected from their use of such platforms, does not as such shift away from the affective dominance that social media platforms can pursue in capitalist societies. What is problematic here is rather the fact that we are understood as contractual individuals seeking economic exchange over certain affects, as well as being exploited for this. As discussed briefly earlier, Pateman furthermore does not see a liberatory potential in sexual contracts to shift oppression caused by institutions such as marriage. In relation to sado-masochism, she finds the possibility of ordering things in a contract rather legitimates violence that otherwise would need to be banned from a feminist perspective (1988: 185–8). This critique however collapses sadism and masochism in a way which Deleuze aims at differentiating in his essay connected to Sacher-Masoch.

By following the masochist view on contract, Deleuze suggests that we can find a much more fruitful way of imagining both contracts and law along sexual lines, without reproducing dominating forms of violence (Deleuze 1991 [1989]). Deleuze's points are not necessarily in opposition to Pateman's critique of contract but advance another register of affective thinking of consent and force under contract. To start with, Deleuze first of all reads the contractual theory which liberal conceptions of law leans on as operating:

> By observing the very letter of the law, we refrain from questioning its ultimate or primary character; we then behave as if the supreme sovereignty of law conferred upon it the enjoyment of all those pleasures that it denies us; hence by the closest adherence to it, and zealously embracing it, we may hope to partake of its pleasures. (Deleuze 1991: 88)

As he further proposes:

> A close examination of masochistic fantasies or rites reveals that while they bring into play the strictest application of the law, the result in every case is the opposite of what might be expected [...] It is a demonstration of law's absurdity. The masochist regards the law as a punitive process and therefore begins by having the punishment inflicted upon himself; once he has undergone the punishment, he feels that he is allowed or indeed commanded to experience the pleasure that the law was supposed to forbid. (Deleuze 1991: 88–9)

This understanding of contract, as a contract of both desires and love, in turn suggests not a consent to violence, as suggested for example by Pateman, but rather a subversion of why one submits to a contract, as well as which affective registers they can account for. As the particular question of Sacher-Masoch to Wanda/Venus in Furs also shows, a contract can involve a number of fetishised objects that present themselves as both objects, relations and desires simultaneously. Notable, of course, is Sacher-Masoch's requirement to include in the contract that Wanda must always wear furs when she treats him in the cruel ways to which he submits (Sacher-Masoch 1991: 197). Furthermore, Wanda agrees to never leave Sacher-Masoch entirely, even if she entertains other lovers as a means to be cruel to him, and to subsequently make him submit further to his love for her (Sacher-Masoch 1991: 197). Reading the social media platform contract in this light, we can pay attention to the onesidedness by which we submit to such contract, but also the affective bindings we both produce and submit to while being connected to such spaces and things.

One reason for this is not least that when entering relations with those who know our desires better than we know ourselves – to again paraphrase Herndon/Metahaven – we collectively suspend the pleasure of the platform. They keep us connected by constantly giving us just enough to make us stay for more. Pleasure is never instant or exhaustive, but part of the contract. Not even dating apps are there to help us find that one person and then never log on again, since then what would their business rationality be? Instead they live on the suspension of pleasure for the next swipe, the next better match, and the behavioural advertising embedded in the apps, like every other platform. This can be exemplified by the recent ruling of the Norwegian Data Protection Watchdog against the dating app Grindr due to its use of sensitive data in behavioural advertising (Euronews 2021). In this way one can say that what is at stake here is not a form of dominance that we do not enjoy, but rather that, just like in the masochistic humour outlined by Deleuze, the punishment comes via first the love contract and then the 'order that the satisfaction of desire should necessarily follow upon the punishment' (Deleuze 1991: 88–9). What we are promised from the social media platform is, furthermore, rather the possibility to enjoy a space designed for our communal desires: we get to look at nice pictures (as long as they comply with the community guidelines); we receive approval via likes, viewers or suggestions for more pleasure. Furthermore, there is a promise that as long as we just keep to the contract, we will not be left alone (something that also comes with a flavour of surveillance, as noted above).

Thinking about contracts in this sense as affective contracts becomes not only a matter of criticising the turning of everything into sexual, or affective, property; following Deleuze, we can regard it also as a means to reimage and suspend both contract and law when they appear as neutral textual orders, which just take an interest in governing transactions, both on a societal and an individual level. This in turn may be read against modern law's tendency to abstract itself from both bodies and emotions; meanwhile, law as well as contract has everything to do with how bodies are shaped and drawn together. In both sadism and masochism, this type of ruling via affects often unfolds via the suspension of particular desires. Such governance of the very body, and bodily expressions, with which the contract here is involved, is furthermore as such a characteristic of law under biopolitics and the societies of control (Deleuze 1992). As Deleuze points out, via Sacher-Masoch, law performs a form of emotional governance of the body via the capacity of presenting an ultimate threat where one's body can otherwise be locked up, submitting its subjects to law via threat (Deleuze 1991: 81). For sure, this role of law remains in criminal law in particular, and often also in the general understanding of law as being backed up by the violence of the sovereign (such as the state).

When, however, the punishment is the condition of the contractual relation as such, the law is turned on its head (Deleuze 1991: 89). One can then say that where contract is used in this way, it subsequently twists both the idea of the contract and that of law as the contract breach, or the punishment, otherwise imagined as something conditioned by state law, becomes integrated into its rationale (ibid: 92). While subverting or suspending law via the focus of mocking it to the extreme of contractual submission, the idea of law as connected to punishment as well as law as a textual operation in the form of a contract still remains. The reason for this is that contract is still viewed as something that two parties can enter into, and that consent between desiring parties can be fully expressed in advance, in text. Meanwhile, the affective dimension of both law and contract implies that there is always something that escapes the involved parties, and sometimes what escapes is exactly the core of the agreement, rather than what is being stated inside of it. The consequences are in this way similar to what Pateman suggests as being a patriarchal problem of law and contract, but on an even wider scale – as law becomes about control over human desires and punishments and its subversion consequently comes in the form of a suspension of the same. One could then possibly say that what displaces law and contract more than the pre-coded punishment in contract lies in understanding the onesidedness of affective transmission as well as control that is also exhibited by Sacher-Masoch, in both love notes, conversations and the love contract. It is in this writing that we find both suspense and excess of desire in how it moves in different medias, including the body of the loved one, but also furs, statues, paintings and poems. This in turn opens up space for an understanding of desire, contracts and law, beyond the fixed notion of a written form or its contractual object. Furthermore, and on a larger scale, it also opens the classical critical philosophical question of why one can desire and consent to submission, even knowing that it is a form of exploitation.

PLATFORM IN FURS: A LOVE LETTER

The contractual and capitalist practices that capture emotions as well as human bodies via digital screens and programs teach us that the contract is more than a text defining its subjects and object of transaction. To speak with critical theories of contract, we can see that when desire becomes a contract object – explicitly or de facto – it does something to the idea of contract, and it affects the potential for alternative types of subjectivities and law. Both Pateman and Deleuze can be understood to point to how the liberal perception of contract undermines the very idea of liberal law when transactions are concerned with sexual desires, rather than fixed things. This is interesting when theorising affects in digital platforms, as the object never fully appears in the contracts that the users sign to gain access to them. Furthermore, the transactions of affects are dynamic in the way that the relational character of communication platforms continuously change, not least by dint of who gets access to them and in which ways. The legislative efforts to regulate contract objects in platform settings have today been spread over a number of areas, such as in relation to data control, as addressed throughout. In this, we can see the nexus between the property object/and contract dissolve, at least in the terms in which it was addressed earlier in law as mutual agreement. However, many aspects escape these boxes of objectification due to their affective characteristics. Whereas this can to some degree be subverted via the critique of contract proposed by Pateman and Deleuze, the question of law and its function as the mediator of affective transactions still remains untouched.

Following the idea of affect in the Deleuzian–Spinozan vein requires viewing law as having always been something more than just a textual or punishing order. As Philippopoulos-Mihalopoulos puts it: law is a lawscape and bodies move in this lawscape based on the atmospherics that produce and keep it together (Philippopoulos-Mihalopoulos 2015). What is required to move beyond the idea of contract as a regulator of transactions consequently becomes a matter of understanding that neither contract nor law is ever about two parties fixing their agreements in a certain form; they are about continuous transmissions of affects that make their relations come into being. In this way, we can return also to an understanding of contracts as any other texts where law is always present and brimming with affects, for example via the genre of love contracts, but possibly even more so as love letters. The potential in understanding contracts in this way also points at the complexity that affect is both captured and transmitted between bodies, as such letters by no means hold the promise of simple emotional transmission. Rather, they characteristically depend on multiple material factors that determine the possibility of connection and reception. What is characteristic is however that they always work on both a literal and desiring level, which draws bodies together or apart. This understanding implies indeed that no type of text is considered to precede anything else just on the basis of legislative standing. Instead, the texts governing both our digital communities and others can be seen as always having the potential to suspend both contracts and law, via new letters of affect. In turning to the letter rather than the contract there is as little promise of a less violent lover than in the platforms we now submit ourselves to. As Wanda notes before rendering Sacher-Masoch subject to the love contract: 'Despite holy ceremonies, oaths and contracts no permanence can ever be imposed on love; it is the most changeable element in our transient lives' (Sacher-Masoch 1991: 160). This is also proven by Wanda in her ultimate breach of contract, when she leaves Sacher-Masoch for a less submissive lover. In a final letter to Sacher-Masoch she later confirms that her new lover had made her happy but only for a short while, until he was killed in a duel. In this letter, she furthermore sends her hopes that her cruel treatment has helped cure him (Sacher-Masoch 1991: 270). On reading this letter, Sacher-Masoch concludes:

> I smiled to think of the woman I had loved so much, of the jacket that had so delighted me in the past; I smiled at the thought of the whip; and finally I smiled to think of my own suffering, and said to myself: 'The treatment was cruel but radical, and the main thing is that I am cured.' (Sacher-Masoch 1991: 271)

Possibly, this final letter from Venus in Furs is also what functions as a promise in relation to the affective control under platform-based contracts, where the promise is not the subversion of contract or law as such. Instead, the hopeful note, or what we can call the love letter from Venus in Furs, implies not only that there is an end to how expansive an order of domination can become, but also that we can be cured from desiring the submission to this order as such.

REFERENCES

Books, Chapters and Academic Articles

boyd, danah (2012) *White Flight in Networked Publics? How Race and Class Shaped American Teen Engagement with MySpace and Facebook.* In *Race after the Internet* (eds) Chow-White, P.A and Nakamura, L. New York: Routledge.
Boyle, James (2009) *Shamans, Software and Spleens*. Cambridge: Harvard University Press.
Braidotti, Rosi (2013) *The Posthuman*. Cambridge: Polity Press.
Bratton, Benjamin (2015) *The Stack*. Massachusetts: MIT Press.
Clough, Patricia (2008) The Affective Turn, *Theory, Culture & Society* Vol. 25(1): 1–22.
Cohen, Julie (2019) *Beyond Truth and Power: The Legal Constructions of Informational Capitalism.* Oxford: Oxford University Press.
Deleuze, Gilles (1991 [1989]) *Masochism*. Brooklyn: Zone Books.
Deleuze, Gilles (1992) *Postscript on the Societies of Control*. Cambridge: MIT Press.
Esposito, Roberto (2015) *Persons and Things*. Cambridge/Malden: Polity Press.
Ferrando, Francesca (2019) *Philosophical Posthumanism*. London: Bloomsbury Academic.
Grosz, Elizabeth (2017) *The Incorporeal, Ontology, Ethics, and the Limits of Materialism.* New York: Columbia University Press.
Haraway, Donna (1991 [1989]) *Simians, Cyborgs, and Women. The Reinvention of Nature.* London: Free Association Books.
Hardt, Michael and Negri, Antonio (2000) *Empire*. Cambridge: Harvard University Press.
Hildebrandt, Mireille (2015) *Smart Technologies and the End(s) of Law*. Cheltenham, UK/Northampton, MA, US: Edward Elgar Publishing.
Ilouz, Eva (2007) *Cold Intimacies: The Making of Emotional Capitalism*. Cambridge/Malden: Polity Press.
Kalopkas, Igor (2019) *Algorithmic Governance: Politics and Law in the Post-human Era*. Cham: Palgrave Macmillan.
Lessig, Lawrence (1999) *Code and Other Laws of Cyberspace*. New York: Basic Books.
Massumi, Brian (2015) *The Politics of Affect*. Cambridge: Polity Press.
Pateman, Carole (1988) *The Sexual Contract*. Cambridge: Polity Press.
Philippopoulos-Mihalopoulos, Andreas (2015) *Spatial Justice: Body, Lawscape, Atmosphere*. Oxon: Routledge.
Radin, Margaret Jane (1996) *Contested Commodities*. Cambridge, MA: Harvard University Press.
Radin, Margaret Jane (2000) Humans, Computers and Binding Commitment. *Indiana Law Journal* Vol. 75: 1125–62.

Radin, Margaret Jane (2003) *Information Tangibility*. In *Economics, Law and Intellectual Property: Seeking Strategies for Research and Teaching in a Developing Field* (ed.) Granstrand, O. Boston: Springer Science and Business Media.

Radin, Margaret Jane (2013) *Boilerplate: The Fine Print, Vanishing Rights, and the Rule of Law*. Princeton, NJ: Princeton University Press.

Sadowski, Jathan (2020) *Too Smart: How Digital Capitalism Is Extracting Data, Controlling Our Lives, and Taking Over the World*. Cambridge: MIT Press.

Valverde, Mariana (2014) The Rescaling of Feminist Analyses of Law and State Power: From (Domestic) Subjectivity to (Transnational) Governance Networks, *UC Irvine Law Review* Vol. 4: 325.

von Sacher-Masoch, Leopold (1991 [orig. 1870]) *Venus in Furs*. In Deleuze, Gilles ([1989]) *Masochism*. Brooklyn: Zone Books.

Wark, McKenzie (2019) *Capital Is Dead: Is This Something Worse?* New York: Verso Books.

Zittrain, Jonathan (2006) The Generative Internet, *Harvard Law Review* Vol. 119: 1974.

Zuboff, Shoshana (2019) *The Age of Surveillance Capitalism: The Fight for a Human Future at the New Frontier of Power*. London: Profile Books Ltd.

Non-Academic Sources

Duportail, Judith, 'I asked Tinder for my data. It sent me 800 pages of my deepest, darkest secrets', The Guardian, 26 September 2017: www.theguardian.com/technology/2017/sep/26/tinder-personal-data-dating-app-messages-hacked-sold.

Euronews, 'Norway fines Grindr dating app €9.6m over data privacy breach', 26 January 2021: www.euronews.com/2021/01/26/norway-fines-grindr-dating-app-9-6m-over-data-privacy-breach.

Facebook Community Standards, www.facebook.com/communitystandards/ accessed 24 November 2020.

Metahaven/Holly Herndon, (2014) *Home*: www.youtube.com/watch?v=I_3mCDJ_iWc.

15. Fury

Virginia Emilse Zuleta

I ask you to be my partner-in-crime twice when you read this chapter. More than partners-in-crime, I ask you to bear in mind two memories about the tradition of western political thought, its legal ramifications and how they frame with law, which I have no intent to rebuild but just to provide a glimpse of. The first memory refers to the origins of this tradition, flagged by the distinctive feature of conceiving a natural order as the determining factor for deciding who is entitled to do politics—not only attained by, but also legally recognized in. To be a bearer of rights. The second memory is linked to recognizing the "fiction" behind modern societies' foundational motto, "freedom, equality and fraternity": A fiction that displays relations of exclusion and subordination from the very beginning, reshaping both the political field and the production of knowledge. In broad terms, both the theoretical and practical framework that configures modern societies and the legacy received from them operate through hierarchical relationships inside a sexist, classist, racist, heteronormative, transphobic, and ableist system.

Referring to this history allows me to anchor the concerns driving this chapter. Stated as questions, they would be the following: Which politics is it possible to practice for those of us who are part of a subaltern collective movement? Which pathways enable us to conquer rights? Are we allowed to walk on them only if we "negotiate" in the (sexist, classist, racist, heteronormative, transphobic, and ableist) language of rights? Which detours or degenerations can we inflict upon the said language?

These questions are the arrows I shoot and take on under the assumption that there is a jurisprudence we can call minor jurisprudence, in a *deleuzoguattarian* sense, that has an inextricable link with literature or a certain writing practice that erodes the language or the writing of a major jurisprudence. A possible path—which I pick and choose here to portray the journey—will result after considering the poem *Hojarascas* by Susy Shock, on one hand rebuilding the context and on the other crossing it with *Travesti/A Good Enough Theory* [*Travesti/Una teoría lo suficientemente Buena*] by Marlene Wayar. I am trying to map politics as a poetry linked to a minor jurisprudence. This politics, on the one hand, is neither contained nor exhausted in the language of major jurisprudence or its practice. On the other hand, its dynamics tears up the same representation that excludes it. It also exposes past and present times which were and still remain excluded, practices that were denied, and critically intervenes both in the legal framework and the production of knowledge.

THE URGENCY. THE SHOUT AND *TRAVESTI* FURY

> "do not get confused, like good poetry this is extremely political"
> **Susy Shock**

Hojarascas by Susy Shock[1] is a large poem written in around 300 verses, organized in six strophes, printed by the Argentinian publishing house *Muchas Nueces*. A first version of the poem was released in monthly parts in *Mu Magazine* during 2016. The edition of *Muchas Nueces* offers the poem together with the picture *El Gritazo* ["*Yelling out*"] by the Argentine Movement of self-organized photographers (in its Spanish acronym, M.A.F.I.A). "El Gritazo" is the name of the call for participation in a march toward Plaza de Mayo in the City of Buenos Aires, Argentina, organized by many *travesti*[2] and trans advocates, denouncing the crimes against their colleagues and demanding justice for the murder of Diana Sacayán. She was a well-known human rights activist[3] and a fighter for recognition and inclusion of the *travesti* collective movement in Argentina. She had received from then-president Cristina Fernández de Kirchner herself her ID reflecting her self-perceived gender identity.

The investigative report into the murder of Diana Sacayán drafted by The Prosecution Unit Specializing in Violence against Women, reporting to the Public Prosecutor's Office, framed the crime as a femicide, as Argentina had passed law 26.791, better known as the Femicide Act, in 2012. This movement as well as others claimed the importance of framing the murder of Sacayán as a specific type of femicide, a transvesticide.[4]

The poem could be said to emerge from the anger generated by Sacayán's murder. She is explicitly named; and added to this was the common situation all *travestis*[5] were going through, gathered under the name "nosotras" ["We"]:

---

[1] Shock, Susy, *Hojarascas [Fallen Leaves]*, Argentina, Buenos Aires, Muchas Nueces, 2017.

[2] In Argentina the *travesti* and trans community is part of the LGBTIQ+ movement and part of their militancy is expressed in their incorporation in the so-called Encuentro Nacional de Mujeres [National Women Meeting], in which debate has been about a name change to "Encuentro Plurinacional de Mujeres, Lesbianas, Transexuales, Travestis, bisexuales y no binarias" [Multinational Meeting of Women, Lesbians, transgender, travestis, bisexuals and non-binary persons]. In 2019, during preparations for the third International Feminist Demonstration, some debates over the political subjects named in the conference call spread through social media and pushed the 8M into a pure and exclusive cis women demonstration. The position requesting the exclusion of trans, *travestis* and non-binary identities was rejected in the first assembly, as basic consensus. The conflict was presented again during the second assembly; however, the exclusionary positions were not allowed. Beyond the context and the different views in this debate – where the term *transfeminism* can be considered a currently fashionable result of a kind of feminism taking some distance from the perspectives of the feminist movement led by cis women – in Argentina the *travesti* community is part of the LGBTIQ+ movement. In this sense, I have chosen to use the term *travesti* or *trava* (when community members themselves self-identify as such) rather than translating it to the correlate *transvestite*, since this term in English does not stand for a collective movement and by no means bears the political implications of embracing such identity.

[3] Among some of her roles, activities and militancy, she was a member of the Sexual Diverse Area of the National Institute Against Discrimination, Xenophobia and Racism (Spanish acronym: INADI); leader of the International Association of Lesbians, Gays and Bisexuals and head of Movimiento Antidiscriminatorio de Liberación [Antidiscriminatory Movement of Freedom]. She was part of the Frente Nacional por La Ley de Identidad de Género [National Front for the Gender Identity Act] and played a crucial role in achieving the passage of said legislation. She was brutally murdered on October 11, 2015, in what is considered a *transvesticide*.

[4] On June 18, 2018, Gabriel David Marino was convicted and sentenced to life imprisonment as joint author of the crime of homicide, aggravated by gender-based hate and gender violence against Diana Sacayán. This is the first time Argentina had raised the criminal issue of transvesticide.

[5] As a result of structural discrimination, trans and *travesti* people in Argentina have a life expectancy of approximately 35 years: Report submitted by the Convention on the Elimination of all Forms of Discrimination against Women (CEDAW), 2016. Retrieved from: www.cels.org.ar/web/publicaciones/

They murder us
Even though our IDs say our name is
DIANA SACAYÁN!

The excerpt cited refers to the Gender Identity Act. I allow myself a diversion here to contextualize the law of Argentina. The Gender Identity Act 26.743/12 obtained preliminary approval from the House of Representatives on November 30, 2011 and the bill was passed on May 9, 2012, when the senate cast 55 votes in favor with one abstention. The Law was enacted on May 23 by decree 773/2012 and officially published the following day.

The Gender Identity Act was progressively carried out, its criteria based on the requester's self-perception as the sole requirement entitling the applicant to ask for a change in their ID. Also, the regulation rejects pathologizing.[6] The first section of the Act establishes the right to recognition of one's gender identity, the free development of the individual according to their own gender identity, and the right to be treated accordingly. For that purpose, it develops an approach that guarantees access to rights that recognize entitlement to dignified treatment, meaning to be treated based on your own name, gender, and self-image (section 12). The Act seeks to avoid judicialization by designing a simple administrative process called record's rectification (section 3). Moreover, the State must guarantee the comprehensive recognition of gender identity and access to essential medical practices such as hormonal therapy and surgeries (section 11), and any other necessary processes.

Now that some context has been given, let's go back to the excerpt of the poem:

They murder us
Even though our IDs say our name is
DIANA SACAYÁN!

---

situacion-de-los-derechos-humanos-de-las-travestis-y-trans-en-la-argentina/. To obtain a detailed report about the current situation of *travestis*, transsexuals and transgenders see: *Report about the travesti community in Argentina, 2005. Cumbia, copeteo and tears* [Cumbia – a popular rhythmic style of music in Argentina; copeteo – colloquial Spanish: to go out for drinks, y lágrimas]. *National report on the situation of travestis, transsexuals and transgenders, 2007* [*Informe nacional sobre la situación de las travestis, transexuales y transgéneros*, 2007]. *The Feat of a Proper Name. Report on the situation of the travesti community in Argentina*, 2015. *The Revolution of Butterflies. Ten years from The Feat of a Proper Name*, 2017. *Travestis, transexual women and courts: bringing justice in CABA,* 2018 [City of Buenos Aires], [*La Gesta del Nombre Propio. Informe sobre la situación de la comunidad travesti en Argentina*, 2015]. *La revolución de las mariposas. A diez años de La Gesta del Nombre Propio*, 2017. *Travestis, mujeres transexuales y tribunales: hacer justicia en la CABA*, 2018.

[6] The legislation was ground-breaking as it established that it shall not be a requisite to resort to surgeries of sex re-assignment, whether total or partial, or to complete hormonal therapies or any other medical treatment. Besides, it guarantees complete confidentiality of the process and the inclusion of requiring medical treatments to achieve gender expression in the Medical Mandatory Programme, including the coverage of medical practices in both private and public healthcare systems. Unlike other contemporary legal recognitions of gender identity it rejects pathologizing trans people. The Spanish Gender Identity Act enacted in 2007, for instance, was pinned in a pathologizing concept for trans identities. The Spanish legislation does require a medical diagnosis of gender dysphoria as well as having completed a medical treatment for at least two years, to "customize" the physical features to the right ones according to the perceived gender, that is to say, the body under the parameters of hetero-normality. Neither regulation contemplates minor-age individuals requesting recognition. The Spanish Law is currently under review; other countries, such as Ireland, Denmark, Norway, and others, have adapted their legislation already, aiming at establishing processes of Gender Identity Recognition based on the individual's self-determination.

What is the political strategy behind hinting at the Gender Identity Act and immediately mentioning the name of one of the best-known activists fighting for human rights, and the recognition and social inclusion of the *travesti* movement? Why mention one of the biggest conquests in the human rights field and cite the name Sacayán straight away?

The Act is from 2012, and the transvesticide happened in 2015. The poem was written in 2016. Timelines do not say much if we simply read them as a series, as a causal chain of events, but in these dizzying times it strikes me as necessary and urgent to review the story and go back and forth. The struggle of Diana Sacayán's family and colleagues, as well as the support provided by several collective movements—LGBTIQ+, human rights, and feminist groups—militated and managed to conquer, insofar as a tribunal named Diana's murder a transvesti*cide*. Using this conceptual framework exposes the social, structural, patriarchal, and discriminatory oppression that affects the *travesti* community.

The concept of transvesticide brought the violence over the *travesti*'s body to the forefront, but it also challenged a differential factor. The Act from 2012 treated gender violence as aggravated crimes. The report drafted by the Special Unit of the Prosecutor's Office Specializing in Violence against Women referred to the crime as a femicide, proving that disputing the naming of the crime as a specific legal figure called transvesticide was not irrelevant.

But there is something else that the excerpt from this poem reveals—even though it is present throughout the text—and that I want to highlight: The tension between a "claim," which could be a request for recognition demanded by the whole community, and its translation into the language of the law. As Judith Butler[7] explains, *precariousness* is the shared condition of every human life, but in some cases lives express a differential existence: this is what the author calls precariousness. In other words, some lives are differentially exposed depending on the social–political–economic framework and, according to Butler, this makes them have an induced political condition. Both ideas allow us to show how some lives are "worthy" of being grievable, while others—in a differential exposition—are condemned to violence and death. In tune with the above, here another passage of the poem sings:

Yells the *sudaca*[8] question, in the middle of
nowhere:
HOW CAN A SINGLE ONE OF US BE KILLED?
WITHOUT KILLING US ALL?
And the rogue newspapers and the social media,
rogues,
What to say to all the rogue people,
they ignore these deaths
as they before ignore these lives
and the advocates of the good conscience (?)
mark with a "like"
only when the one who is down
is from their side.

---

[7] Butler, Judith, *Precarious Life: The Powers of Mourning and Violence*, London: Verso Books, 2006 ['Vida Precaria, El poder del duelo y la violencia', Buenos Aires: Paidós, 2006]. Butler, Judith, *Frames of War: When Is Life Grievable*, London, 2009 ['Marcos de Guerra: las vidas lloradas', Barcelona: Paidós, 2010].

[8] A pejorative term used to refer to a person who was born in the south of Latin America.

Even though these lives are "legally" recognized, it does not mean they are not exposed. Going back to the first lines of the poem and the tension they reveal: verses full of poetic justice make evident the boundless and necessary work of reparation, which is not achieved just through law. This is not the same as neglecting such a big human rights conquest, nor ignoring the safety it provides to all people who do not identify with their gender assigned at birth; this is the celebration ceremony that the law entails. But it is also important to highlight that although the Act is not clear about the compulsion to choose between feminine and masculine, the legal design leads to bureaucratic procedures that result in applicants having to specify one of only two genders. In practical terms, birth certificates as well as IDs are still imposing a binary legal framework, in which fluid identities, non-binaries, or many *travestis* who don't identify as women remain excluded and face bureaucratic obstacles. In 2018, Argentina recognized the application of a non-binary individual. In March 2019 the *travesti* activist Lara Bertolini asked to have the following note in their ID: "*Travesti* Femininity." The complaint was accepted at first instance but the National Registry of Persons [Spanish acronym RENAPER] and the Bureau of Vital Records of the City of Buenos Aires later rejected the claim. In December of 2019, the G Chamber of the National Civil Court endorsed this rejection.

It is interesting here to refer to the 2015 documentary by the Argentine director Juan Tauil. This feature film debut presented some well-known activists from the *travesti* collective movement. The voices of Malva Solís, Lohana Berkins, Diana Sacayán, Marlene Wayar, Naty Mestrual, Susy Shock, and Julia Amore are heard, among others. The film retells the struggles before the Gender Identity Act was passed, and describes the inequality of social and economic vulnerability that the community faces. The film also shows how the Act was born as a result of restless activism, with a focus on the *travesti* and the process of building a *travesti* identity. The name of the documentary invokes the T letter for *travesti* or *trava* and for transgressor: a person who infringes a law, a norm, a pact, or a custom.

As Michel Foucault[9] highlights, the language of the law and its correlation with the norm is one of the discourses of truth on which our western societies are founded—societies which we know well are patriarchal, heteronormative, colonial, racist, and classist.[10] This is why the reparation that the law intends to do is partial so long as it is performed by the same means which have caused such differential inequalities. This does not mean that we shouldn't fight for change, nor that we shouldn't expose and dismantle the symbolic and structural oppression that so many subjectivities are immersed in—in other words, to fight in terms of the conquest of rights. However, this works as a *glass ceiling*, because in the end what is "wrong" is the binary world. As the poem reads:

and we are bothered by their prayers, their wisdom, their
    diagnoses, their laws,
their stage plays and their cinemas,

---

[9] Foucault, Michel, *Abnormal: Lectures at the Collège de France, 1974–1975*, London: Picador, 2003 [Los Anormales. Buenos Aires, Economic Culture Fund, 2006; in Spanish, Fondo de Cultura Económica, 2006].

[10] Regarding the tension between the language of the discourse of the law, with its liberal criminal system, and the figure of femicide see Trebisacce, Catalina (2018) 'Inhabiting in disagreement. Notes for an apology of political precariousness' ['Habitar el desacuerdo. Notas para una apología de la precariedad política'] in Cuello, N. and Disalvo, L. (comp.), *Sexual Reviews to a Punitive Reason* [*Críticas sexuales a la razón punitiva*], Argentina, Neuquén: Ediciones Precarias, 2018, pp.127–38.

> where *the binary remains*,
> because the only change they dare to
> (since they learned to start a fire
>   until now)
> is not to get out of the main precept:
> *"Nothing but the binary is possible!"* (Italics are mine)

The debate about the need for a law on gender identity was triggered by trans and *travesti* collective movements, not only as a claim against discrimination and sex-gender exclusion but also as a "grassroots activism battle field" that allowed a questioning of the whole system of established norms, gender binarism, cissexism, and oppression within the capitalist system. This scheme focuses not only on gender but also on class and race; that is to say, it displays an intersectional activism.

Susy's poems, interviews, and writings often question what is presented as "ordinary/ natural" and denounce its violence. Such is the case with the well-known poem "Me, My Own Monster" ("Yo Monstruo Mío"), compiled in *Perspiring Poem Book*[11] [*Poemario Transpirado*]. I quote a few verses:

> I, I claim my right to be a monster
> neither male nor female
> Neither XXY nor H2o.

And other verses:

> I claim: my right to be a monster
> let others be the Ordinary
> The ordinary Vatican
> The Creed in God and the very Ordinary virgin
> and the shepherds and the flocks of the Ordinary
> and the Honorable Congress of the Ordinary Laws
> the old Larousse of the Ordinary

What is the Ordinary? In an interview, and referring to the poem, the writer answered this question as follows:

> That text ["Me, My Own Monster"] was written many years ago and I think that the idea of the ordinary has been adjusted. Today I would place it into the binary, which is what is not discussed, what is taken for granted to be the ordinary or natural. Particularly, I think that it comes from a political decision to be constructed and fixated because I believe that *hegemonies* exert their power there [...] When we discuss hetero-normality we are discussing a system that cannot conceive that there exists something beyond itself.[12]

---

[11] Shock, Susy, *Perspired Poem Book* [*Poemario transpirado*], Argentina, Buenos Aires: Nuevos Tiempos, 2011. Also available in: http://susyshock.blogspot.com/2008/03/yo-monstruo-mio.html.
[12] Shock, Susy in Quintana, J. "I choose the *travesti* discomfort to deal with this world" in *Revista Almagro*, (s. f.). Retrieved from http://almagrorevista.com.ar/susy-shock-elijo-la-incomodidad-lo-travesti-negociar-este-mundo/. My italics.

Discussion of this hegemonic system is an everyday battle. The poet states: "I choose the *travesti* discomfort to deal with this world"[13] as the title of the interview. As regards the *travesti*-identity discomfort and in dialogue with her, I quote Marlene Wayar's proposition: "What we call *trans* identity is connected to thinking of hegemony as a system. That is Patriarchy."[14] Therefore, poetry and *travesti* and trans thought not only question sexuality and identity but also the whole political and social system, making visible the oppressions it produces.

In a recent writing, titled "Macri is not gay" (in Spanish, "Macri no es puto"),[15] Susy Shock again questions this binary system, at the same time offering further indication of the urgency of the poem *Hojarascas*. The first editions of the poem were published in 2016, that is, the first year of the repressive and neoliberal government of Mauricio Macri;[16] but, as Susy points out in the article:

> For us, the *travas*, trans, the *macrismo* started with the transvesticide of Diana Sacayán, months before Macri took office; and a few months later, after his assumption, with the death of Lohana Berkins, in February of 2016, when the idea of getting all of us together (gays, lesbians, *travas*, non-binary, etc.) so we were not that lonely during those months of anguish began to materialize.

It was in those months of anguish that the *Lohana Berkins Collective Movement* (*La Colectiva Lohana Berkins*) was organized. As Susy explains in this intervention, they got tired of hearing chants of "Macri faggot!" during the first protest of the Association of State Employees (Spanish acronym ATE) against the government. "Faggot!" they shouted as an insult, and yet, as she narrates, gays were there too, putting their bodies on the frontlines. As a result of that experience, they created a counter-chant: "Macri is not gay, he is a liberal, take charge, he is straight!"[17] They not only shifted the pejorative use of "gay" but also stated "he is a result of this system"—something they also want to challenge. This is Susy's proposal: "we have to question what has not been questioned, we have to go deeper than others have dared, even to the resistances of our continent":[18] Repeating what she expresses in the conversation with Marlene Wayar and Sergio Ciancaglini.

Hojarascas, a term that in the dictionary first appears as a reference to fallen leaves, also alludes to the useless and the lack of substance that words can have, and the excessive, inutilious leafiness of some trees and plants. Punning on these three words: an excess of fallen leaves with no substance and useless leafiness.

---

[13] Ibid.
[14] Wayar, Marlene, *Travesti/A Good Enough Theory* [*Una teoría lo suficientemente Buena*], Buenos Aires, Argentina: Muchas Nueces, 2018, p.116.
[15] Shock, Susy, 'Macri is not Gay' ['Macri no es puto'] in *Revista Humo*, Dossier *What Macri left us* [*Lo que Macri nos dejó*] (16 December 2019). Retrieved from: www.revistahumo.com.ar/susy-shock/lo-que-macri-nos-dejo/macri-no-es puto.
[16] Mauricio Macri (b. 1959) is a businessman, politician and sports leader who was President of Argentina from 2015 to 2019. He contracted the largest credit in history with the International Monetary Fund and went into the largest debt in the history of Argentina.
[17] In the same way, the Association of Female Sex Workers from Argentina [Asociación de Mujeres Meretrices de Argentina—AMMAR] also responded to the chant "Macri son of a bitch!": "Macri is not our son. We, the whores, did not give birth to him."
[18] Shock, Susy in Wayar, Marlene, *Travesti/A Good Enough Theory* [*Una teoría lo suficientemente Buena*]. Argentina, Buenos Aires: Muchas Nueces, 2018, p.61.

BETWEEN SHOUT AND FURY, TENDERNESS AND EMBRACE

> Are you afraid of life becoming homosexual?
> And I'm not talking about putting it in and out
> And out and in only
> I'm talking about tenderness, comrade
> [...]
> So many kids will be born
> With a broken wing
> And I want them to fly, comrade
> That their revolution
> Bring them a piece of red heaven
> So that they can fly.
> **Pedro Lemebel**

Hojarascas is dedicated to all the *travas* and especially "to Marlene Wayar's rage and tenderness." Susy Shock and Marlene Wayar have a publicly known bond of friendship and love. Both weave and build concepts that allow for thinking *travestis* and trans subjectivities, trans childhoods, the world they inhabit, and the one they wish to build.

Marlene Wayar is an activist leader of the *Travesti* movement in Latin America.[19] In her book *Travesti/A Good Enough Theory*[20] she proposes a *travesti* theory, although her text blurs the rigid limits of what is usually considered a theory. The theory is presented from different discursive genres: interviews, chats with friends, a lecture, and poems. As the author points out, it is "a trans-Latin American *travesti* theory, which is presented as poetry, coming mainly from art."[21] From this discursive multiplicity, where oral-experiential registers prevail, where concepts appear disseminated and being in process, they are moving and serving this theory to conceive *trava* and *travesti* not just as generic identities but also as notions that allow us to denounce and question the idea of heterosexuality as a political regime.

Following the concept of being in process, Susy responds to the question "What are you?" by going back to Marlene's ideas. "I am a gerund. I'm not a finished event"; "we are a continuous gerund";[22] to the question: which is your gender?, she answers: "I am hummingbird gen-

---

[19] Among the many activities and publications of Marlene Wayar, we can highlight directing the first *travesti* newspaper, *El Teje. First Latin American Travesti Newspaper*, Argentina, Buenos Aires, Cultural Center Ricardo Rojas, from 2007 to 2010 (an online version is available at www.elteje.com); and most recently her essay *Travesti Dictionary from T to T* [*Diccionario Travesti de la T a la T*] from the collection *Biblioteca Soy*, by *Página12* newspaper, 2020.

[20] Wayar, Marlene, *Travesti/A Good Enough Theory* [*Una teoría lo suficientemente Buena*]. Argentina, Buenos Aires: Muchas Nueces, 2018. The book, prefaced by Susy Shock, begins with the article "Words of Fire. South American *Travesti*-trans" by Wayar, as the first approach to her theory. It is followed by the author's interview with Claudia Rodríguez, titled "The art of re-feeling. Border bridges between the oral and the written." After this comes a class dialog with Susy Shock and Sergio Ciancaglini, "Discussed rituals. Tools for a post-alphabetical era," and a final interview with Claudia Acuña, "Euphemism-Free. Living and lived words for a decolonization." It ends with an appendix titled "Yelling out. Breaking the hetero-white-patriarchal paradigm."

[21] Ibid, p.29.

[22] Shock, Susy in Quintana, J. "I choose the *travesti* discomfort to deal with this world" in *Revista Almagro*, (s. f.). Retrieved from http://almagrorevista.com.ar/susy-shock-elijo-la-incomodidad-lo-travesti-negociar-este-mundo/.

der."[23] This answer presents identity as something that is always in the process of construction and questions views that limit and circumscribe identity to the gender assigned at birth, based on something natural or essential. At the same time, she dehumanizes gender by enrolling the gender of bird. On the same line of thought, she writes:

> So that is what we are doing, now that we released the
> maxim
> rethinking everything, turning everything around,
> maybe even disengaging from everything.
> **"WE DON'T WANT TO BE THIS HUMANITY ANYMORE"**

What is the meaning of not wanting to be this humanity? As Marlene points: "the Trans Latin American Theory we affirm 'We do not want to be this Humanity anymore' (Susy Shock), and by saying it we intend to exit the systemic pair: 'I am not a man, I am not a woman, today I go being *travesti*'."[24] Every category is restrictive and favors oppression; "do not want to" means not wanting to be part of the heterosexist and adult-centered system, transforming the "no" into an ethical and political tool. Wayar insists in her theory that identity is built as a result of what I am and what I am not, in a de-identification game: "I de-identify myself of that family. And that is, I am NOT Videla,[25] I swear I am NOT Macri."[26]

It is crucial to point out that the theory of childhood is conceived as "a time and mapping where we can build a third option other than the dichotomic proposal between Identity/Self-Otherness [*Yo-Otredad*], the power of building We-ness (*Nostredad*)."[27] Why should we go to our childhood? There is a need that the *travesti*-trans theory proposes to fill in, and it is to give a new meaning to deprivations and violences suffered during childhood that cause anger, grief, sadness, fear, insecurity, shame, emptiness. Talking to Marlene, Claudia Rodríguez says: "I am so furious and I feel such a need for revenge, revenge in terms of being able to express the stench I have to keep inside myself."[28] And Marlene answers: "I have a cemetery in my head, I lost count of how many fellows and friends have died and all sad, terrible, and avoidable deaths."[29] Reviewing, reliving, and re-feeling these experiences allows them to manage affections, making them part of their theory and transforming them into tools against a system that has historically denied them a voice. As the poem states:

> because if there is something we know
> —and we have each one of us
> that are not here, to prove it—

---

[23] Shock, Susy, "Theory (and practice) of shock" interview to Susy Shock. *Revista Mu, Descolonize Yourself* [*Descolonizate*], No 44 (27 May 2011).
[24] Ibid, p.25.
[25] Jorge Rafael Videla (1925–2013) was an Argentine soldier who led the 24 March 1976 coup executed by the Armed Forces. The coup overthrew all constitutional, national, and provincial authorities, including President María Estela Martínez de Perón, and imposed in its place a Military Junta composed of the three commanders of the Armed Forces. The military civic dictatorship, called by the de facto government a National Reorganization Process, was characterized by the application of a systematic state terrorism plan.
[26] Ibid, p.69.
[27] Ibid, p.25.
[28] Ibid, p.31.
[29] Ibid, p.31.

is that although fear gets us,
we still go out,
with squeals of revenge,
so as not to end up also dead,
revenge that can be to dream about us growing old,
or insisting on becoming a metaphor.

Revenge that can be to dream about us growing old, or, as the #ToRecognizeIsToRepair [#ReconocerEsReparar] campaign slogan says: *Our revenge is to make it to old age*, which summarizes the proposal of a law that establishes a reparatory program for victims of institutional violence based on gender identity, an initiative of Transgender Future[30] [*Futuro Transgenérico*] coordinated by Marlene Wayar.

Returning to the conversation between Marlene and Claudia, the latter wonders: "Which is the contribution we, the *travestis*, could make?" and then answers: "I believe it is to set new cards on the table."[31] In conversation with this answer, Susy's poem recites:

let's give us one more chance
but I ask you to leave me for
once and for all
leave me or any of us,
to shuffle the cards, to propose the game,
to make the first move and take the first
  place,
insolents like that
snatching like that
because nothing about this dirty passion is done without
  strategy,
us is an adventure,
with strength and sense,
(nothing you won't understand)

Setting new cards on the table, to shuffle the cards, and to propose the game, just as quoted in the interview and the poem, is an ethical and political claim that does not end in the rejection of humanity but also entails taking responsibility for how we want to live together: "to confront the sadness, grief and responsibility, of how to live together with this fratricidal humanity."[32] It means, at the same time, to be able to build knowledge from the experiences of the *travesti* and trans community. From their lives, which express a distinctive existence; from their childhoods, which experienced a compulsory standardization; they have a lot to tell us about how identities are built. I insist that knowledge emerges from experiences that are inscribed on their own bodies and I stress the hard work that it takes to share them. As the poem says:

even though that "all of us together"
is hard to achieve
because the most subtle work that has been done
was stripping our class,

---

[30] *Transgender Future* [*Futuro Transgenérico*] is the name of the organization that took part in the National Front for the Gender Identity Act [*Frente Nacional por la Ley de Identidad de Género*].
[31] Ibid, p.43.
[32] Ibid, p.104.

>   stripping our travesty of identity,
>   stripping us from one another,
>   to be an easier target for them, one by one,
>   because that is another lie...

Still, they built a *travesti* thought that speaks to everybody, since this thought is not just talking about their identities or *travesti* or trans people, but reflecting about our own responsibility in this (cis)tem[33] and questioning it. As a cis woman, asking ourselves about our responsibility sustaining the (cis)tem is mainly asking ourselves about the situations of privilege that benefit cis people just for being cis.

Following this line, the trans category is redefined by Wayar: "Trans is the person who does not resign themself, who is capable of resigning privileges just to be in that other place."[34] The author reconfigures the concept of trans, connecting it to an ethical–political position rather than to a gender identity. Here I allow myself a detour, which exceeds the main concerns addressed in this chapter—but at this point I cannot stop asking (myself): *Who* is open to "losing" those positions of privilege? By this I don't mean ceasing to be cis or heterosexual but rather knowing oneself to be in a privileged position, as I said earlier. That *who*—who does not have a unique subject of enunciation—is a call to emphasize that in every place (house, work, assembly, supermarket, bar, university, and so on) we must ethically inhabit the place we fill in that network. That *who*, as Wayar says, might be one that coming from a genuine interest moves closer in order to be capable of thinking-*oneself*. As the author states:

> I am concerned about that other position that censors and obstructs the dialog even when that otherness is coming from a place of empathy. [...] So you should not talk, you cis man, white, educated, do not speak, do not speak on my behalf, you, privileged man, shut up, and that paralyzes everything, not just him. It paralyzes all of us not being able to think ourselves, to lose the possibility of a dialogue.[35]

Now we should go back to Wayar's concept of trans. Her redefinition is linked with two types of ethics outlined by the author: an ethics of the inside, connected to the process of building a space of communal living, and an ethics of the outside, that connects with a larger space of coexistence where we are all forced to live together, even with those who oppress us, and that is the space of political dispute.

It is about disputing that space, but also the political implications; as the epigraph to the first section of this chapter says: "do not get confused, like good poetry this is extremely political." In this quest over the political, a "minor" right intervenes in a way that gnaws at the legal discourse of the "major" right that excludes. Susy and Marlene's lives are crossed by art, and theater, pottery, singing, and poetry are often referenced. These practices are not secondary for the process of building knowledge; instead they are intertwined in it.

---

[33] I use the word *cistem* as system to highlight the typical cis-sexism of the heterosexual, patriarchal, racist, and colonial system.
[34] Ibid, p.40.
[35] Ibid, pp.85–6.

CONCLUSION

The decision to create a dialogue between *Hojarascas* and *Travesti/A Good Enough Theory* could be sustained for many reasons—contextual, editorial, of an affective nature, appealing to *philia*—but I want to stress that the decision is mainly epistemological and political. Working on the knowledges and discourses that the *travesti* and trans movement produce also requires a deprioritizing of knowledges about these communities built by cis people. It was a milestone for these groups to be able to subvert being treated as objects of study and shift to being subjects who produce and create; within this context I consider that knowing, referring, quoting, and referencing that production is our responsibility. And perhaps my task here was to exercise hearing, moving closer, as the person dissatisfied with this world, its humanity, and its (cis)tem that I am.

Presenting a trans-Latin American *travesti* theory as poetry and coming mainly from art has implications in the dispute over the meaning of the political, the reconfiguration of its space, and the practice of a minor jurisprudence. As I said at the very beginning, this politics, on the one hand, cannot be contained or exhausted by the language of major jurisprudence embedded in practice; on the other hand, its flow tears up the same representation that excludes it. It exposes past and present times that were and still are excluded, and practices that were denied, and critically intervenes both in the legal framework that ignores such practices as well as in the production of knowledge. I will add the concept of emancipatory political practices to this final note.

16. Hyperbole
Elena Cirkovic

INTRODUCTION

In 2019, the Israeli lunar lander Beresheet left behind some tardigrades, known colloquially as water bears or moss piglets, a phylum of water-dwelling eight-legged segmented micro-animals, on the Moon.[1] A tiny robotic lander from Israel attempted to touch down on the Moon, but it crashed into the surface. Beresheet carried a capsule on board filled with dehydrated tardigrades, known to withstand very extreme environments. It was not likely that these life forms would contaminate the Moon, as the tardigrades would have survived in a dormant state only for a certain period of time depending on their level of exposure to vacuum, temperature cycling and radiation. The incident reopened a long-debated question: who should have a say in what we send to space? What then should be the appropriate questions we ask in law, in such instances? The laws, allegedly, are also not clear on what is permissible in this 'outer' space. In contrast, I argue that the decision not to recognize the application of the Outer Space Treaty (1967) (OST)[2] and define this activity as a national responsibility as stipulated under Article 6 not only implies that outer space law needs legal reform, but also opens the question of the capacity of modern international law to co-exist with this pre-modern argument of human destiny to reach, own, inhabit and exploit any domain, including the Moon and Mars.

The rhetoric surrounding the outer space sector has different strands, but they all converge at the faith in the ultimate power of humanity to endlessly expand and allegedly 'progress'. The hyperbole is not only in the selection of words, but also in the overall discourse and the ethos of space exploration. It is the 'final frontier' and an extraterrestrial manifest destiny (one of the 'hyperboles' of colonial inclinations). Starting with the 'social justice' and 'inclusive' space: outer space activities are not questioned as such; nor are privatization and commercialization. It is the return of Veiled Ignorance and trickle-down market liberalism. Those who have the means shall exploit and utilize space. Current discourses surrounding outer space activities lean towards the idea of broader manifest destiny of individuals, States and commercial actors, in a futuristic, innovative, cutting-edge, bold and endless striving of a particular type of human: *homo economicus*.[3] This human has existed for some time, including the times of the Roman commercial class.[4] In modern times, *homo economicus* theory was defined in John Stuart Mill's 'On the Definition of Political Economy and of the Method of Investigation

---

[1] J. Daley, 'A Crashed Spacecraft Might Have Put Earth's Most Indestructible Organisms on the Moon', available at: https://www.smithsonianmag.com/smart-news/crashed-spacecraft-might-have-put-water-bears-moon-180972840/.

[2] Outer Space Treaty, art. II, Jan. 27, 1967, 610 U.N.T.S. 205 (entered into force 10 October 1967).

[3] See D. McFadden, 'Rationality for Economists' (1999) *Journal of Risk and Uncertainty* Vol. 19, 73, at 73, and K.N. Hylton, 'Calabresi and the Intellectual History of Law and Economics' (2004) *Boston Univ. School of Law* Working Paper No. 04-04, http://ssrn.com/abstract=547082.

[4] J. Persky, 'Retrospectives: The Ethology of *Homo Economicus*' (1995) *The Journal of Economic Perspectives* Vol. 9, No. 2 (Spring).

Proper to It'.[5] This hypothetical economic man had the propensity to make rational decisions. He had four interests in this rational pursuit of wealth, including an underlying drive for accumulation, passion for leisure, interest in luxury and desire for procreation. My critique of the *homo economicus* approach to outer space relies on an inverse ontology: the human is not the centre of the universe; space is not 'outer' and separate from the Earth System; and thence, any legal approach to outer space needs to be cosmolegal and rooted in an awareness that *homo economicus* is not only not as rational as but also profoundly unaware of other types of thinking and non-human laws. There is nothing radical in declaring that outer space is still the 'unknown'. The objective here is to argue that this unknown is not recognized as such in the hyperbole of the inventive go-getter, *the bold, innovative, forward-looking, to-the-point and ambitious human.*

In the field of Earth System Science (ESS),[6] the planet's oceans, lands and atmosphere are studied as an integrated system. It is an interdisciplinary field integrating the principles of biology, chemistry and physics to study problems involving processes occurring on the Earth's surface, such as climate change and global nutrient cycles, providing a foundation for problem solving related to environmental sustainability and global environmental change. The studies have extended even beyond the Earth System to include the Earth's orbit (EO) as an integrated space, as humans increasingly rely on it for commercial and scientific purposes. Some satellites are used to monitor changes in the Earth System, while others actually contribute to the increasing pollution of the orbit, and even endanger such operations.

The current approach of the *homo economicus* hyperbole can be reoriented in such a way that decision-making would not be driven by anthropocentric interests. One of the reasons for the terminology used and the reference to 'cosmos' is the increasing need to focus on long-term and planetary-level thinking. It is also meant to indicate a holistic long-term approach instead of a fragmented short-term approach of State/commerce-centric interests and uses.

Thence, this chapter refers to an interdisciplinary term meant to encompass the process of learning and lawmaking through which the law would recognize the unpredictability of human non human relations: *the cosmolegal*.[7] The term cosmolegal merges cosmology, as a branch of astronomy that involves the scientific study of the large-scale properties of the universe as a whole, with law, due to the need for a different understanding of the Earth and human-centric global politico-juridical space. It allows for a shift in the imagination and understanding of the cosmos, which would not see the human, and its laws, as a central actor of the Earth System and beyond, or as the apex owner, and manager of its environment. Rather, the human is only one of the actors of the 'cosmos', known and unknown.

My first purpose is to identify arguments in favour of unjust conduct in general, and in favour of particular actions taken by the speaker or another party, whether or not the speaker admits that the action is unjust. What this means in outer space is a situation in which some actors argue that there is no clear applicable law. And this is why it is apparently in human

---

[5] J. Stuart Mill, *On the Definition of Political Economy and of the Method of Investigation Proper to It* (D.M. Hausman ed. 2007).

[6] For a comprehensive introduction see Michael Jacobson, Robert Charlson, Henning Rodhe and Gordon Orians, *Earth System Science, Volume 72 1st Edition: From Biogeochemical Cycles to Global Changes* (Elsevier, 2000).

[7] E. Cirkovic, 'The Next Generation of International Law: Space and Ice' (2021) *German Law Journal* Vol. 21, 2.

nature to send to the Moon tardigrades or the blood or DNA of 'experts' and declare that it is legal, because there is no express prohibition. After all, the Apollo mission left nearly 100 bags of human faeces on the lunar surface before they returned to Earth. However, as we challenge this hyperbole, not only does international law apply in all situations of outer space activities, as per the Outer Space Treaty, but space is not 'outer' and is deeply intertwined with our Earthly life. This situation is not just legal but cosmolegal.

THE OTHER DIMENSION OF SPACE

A frequent narrative of the contemporary outer space sector is that of a bold, innovative, futuristic and indispensable human. The nature of this human is curious, investigative and progress-oriented. Any introduction of ethics evokes partiality and has to be mitigated by the practicality, objectivity and reason of not only science but, importantly, careerism. Arguing anything to the contrary is an impediment to progress and freedom. Matters of social justice or sustainability are not abandoned.[8] They are included in the rhetoric and, what is more, space is now a place where the ultimate veil of ignorance can thrive: there can be no racism or injustice in space, for it is the new frontier and open to all. 'Justice' becomes instead a hyperbole as the master trope, or the 'trope-producing trope', and as such a rhetorical method. This is included in the proposals by extractive industries for future activities in outer space.[9] Exploration, ownership and extraction of resources in outer space is for the 'benefit of all humankind'. In this, the narrative assumes the universality of the *homo economicus*, as the ultimate beneficiary. It also reproduces, in outer space, the long-standing conflicting perspectives and interests on the notion of ownership and exploitation of natural resources in the Earth System.[10]

More specifically, domestic legislation on exploration and exploitation of resources in outer space, by its very declaration, assumes that prior to their existence there was no clear applicable law for such activities. However, current international law states that commercial prospecting, exploration, utilization and extraction of resources in outer space, as the common heritage of humanity, needs to be conducted for the benefit and in the interest of all humanity, as per Article I of the OST.[11] This means that any granting of exclusive property rights for exploration and extraction activities is prohibited. There is an element of ambiguity regarding

---

[8] For a critical legal perspective see Isabel Feichtner, 'Mining for Humanity in the Deep Sea and Outer Space: The Role of Small States in the Extraterritorial Expansion of Extraction' (2019) *Leiden J. Int'l L.* Vol. 32, 255, arguing that the current structure of international legal framework allows extraterritorial landgrabs by granting states extraterritorial exploitation rights – or 'the turning of the deep seabed and outer space into realms of commercial exploitation'.

[9] For a detailed elaboration of these proposals see Frans G. von der Dunk, 'Asteroid Mining: International and National Legal Aspects' (2018) *Michigan State International Law Review* Vol. 26, 1. Also, The Hague International Space Resources Governance Working Group, Draft Building Blocks for the Development of an International Framework in Space Resource Activities, www.universiteitleiden.nl/en/law/institute-of-public-law/institute-for-air-space-law/the-hague-spaceresources-governance-working-group.

[10] See Feichtner, *supra* note 8.

[11] In full:
ARTICLE I. The exploration and use of outer space, including the moon and other celestial bodies, shall be carried out for the benefit and in the interests of all countries, irrespective of their degree of economic or scientific development, and shall be the province of all mankind.

obligations, if any, for the dissemination of prospecting and exploration data and the materials extracted from celestial bodies. This also includes the lawfulness of physically removing materials from celestial bodies for the purpose of commercial exploration and extraction. These activities are related to the issue of interplanetary contamination as these activities could result in adverse effects on the Earth through contamination by the introduction of extraterrestrial materials to the environment of the Earth. In the current body of space law, most national space laws have expanded the notion of 'national activities' to cover the space activities of its nationals even if carried out from abroad. Similarly, the legal concept of quasi-territoriality extends the jurisdiction of a State by virtue of Article VIII of the OST and the Registration Convention to space objects in outer space. Thence, in an attempt to balance out the *homo economic* rhetoric with *lex lata*, this section engages with various proposals for extractive and commercial activities in space, by public and private actors.

THE ECONOMIC DIMENSION: THE HYPERBOLE OF THE LEGALLY RECONSTRUCTED IMAGE OF *HOMO ECONOMICUS*

Arguably, both climate change and technological developments have contributed to the changing human interests in the outer space domain, which is not inherently friendly to human survival. Extraterrestrial environment is now an opportunity for further commercial expansion, such as the proposed space tourism or asteroid mining,[12] and is also a planet B solution[13] if the Earth System either runs out of resources or is negatively and irrevocably impacted through global warming. While proposals for outer space exploration, utilization and exploitation intensify, legal scholars are returning to the topic of the very basic tenets of outer space law and the urgent need for reform.[14]

The economic interest in asteroid mining focuses on the new delineation, ownership, privatization and extraction of space resources, rather than the vulnerability of the outer space

---

Outer space, including the moon and other celestial bodies, shall be free for exploration and use by all States without discrimination of any kind, on a basis of equality and in accordance with international law, and there shall be free access to all areas of celestial bodies.

There shall be freedom of scientific investigation in outer space, including the moon and other celestial bodies, and States shall facilitate and encourage international co-operation in such investigation.

[12] See The Hague International Space Resources Governance Working Group, Draft Building Blocks for the Development of an International Framework in Space Resource Activities, www.universiteitleiden.nl/en/law/institute-of-publiclaw/institute-for-air-space-law/the-hague-spaceresources-governance-working-group.

[13] For example, G. Sachs, 'Space: The Next Investment Frontier' (4 April 2017); E. Musk, 'Making Humans a Multi-Planetary Species' (2017) *New Space* Vol. 5, 46.

[14] S. Freeland, 'Common Heritage, Not Common Law: How International Law Will Regulate Proposals to Exploit Space Resources' (2017) Questions of International Law at www.qil-qdi.org/common-heritage-not-common-law-international-law-will-regulate-proposals-exploit-space-resources/. For the global commons perspective see Isabel Feichtner and Surabhi Ranganathan, 'International Law and Economic Exploitation in the Global Commons: Introduction' (2019) *Eur. J. Int'l L.* Vol. 30, 541: 'Yet current initiatives that seek to harness the economic potential of the oceans in the name of "blue growth", projects seeking to commercialize outer space and, a fortiori, proposals to "colonize" outer space and the oceans as a solution to conflict and environmental destruction stand in stark contrast with visions of a commons economy built on solidarity', at 541.

environment and, potentially, humans (in instances where activities are not enacted remotely via autonomous machines). For instance, the Luxembourg Draft Law on the Exploration and Use of Space Resources[15] echoes a French law from the beginning of the eighteenth century in order to argue that '[t]here is an even closer analogy in legal terms between space and the sea' (Article 1), because '[s]pace resources are appropriable, in the same way as fish and shellfish are, but celestial bodies and asteroids are not, just like the high sea is not'. Indeed, the same rights are recognized in the UN Convention on the Law of the Sea (UNCLOS) in *res communis* areas, with free access to a common resource and the impossibility of appropriation. Luxembourg's main objective is to provide 'legal certainty as to the ownership of minerals and other valuable space resources identified in particular on asteroids'. The adopted law argues that OST only prohibits the ownership of celestial bodies, not the potentially extracted resources. It thus separates the definition of a celestial body from any resources to be found on that body. Article 2 of the adopted law indicates that the approved operator has to act in conformity with conditions of its approval and Luxembourg's international obligations. However, the rights to fish and shellfish on the high sea beyond national jurisdiction have recently been evaluated in relation to demands of environmental protection, indicating that such rights are not absolute.[16] Outer space, therefore, cannot be treated as the new frontier and *res nullius* as it was in the eighteenth century.

In 2015 the United States passed the Space Resource Exploration and Utilization Act (or Space Resource Act). It forms Title IV of the Commercial Space Launch Competitiveness Act. The Space Resources Act gives US citizens engaged in the commercial recovery of asteroid or space resources the right to 'possess, own, transport, use, and sell the asteroid resource or space resource obtained in accordance with applicable law, including the international obligations of the United States'. Space resources are defined as abiotic resources in situ in outer space, including, in particular, water and minerals.

Luxembourg and the US guarantee in their respective legislation the right to resources harvested in outer space in accordance with international law. In addition, on 24 February 2020 the UAE Space Agency announced a new space law in order to create a legislative and regulatory environment for the national space sector. The National Space Policy asserts the UAE's recognition of the right of all nations to explore and use space for peaceful purposes and for the benefit of humanity.

Hence, these laws on the utilization of space resources are examples of emergent national policies and laws promoting exploration, exploitation and utilization of space resources. While the enactment of national law may be complementary to international space law and might facilitate its development, such national law still needs to comply with the international obligations of the State. The Hague International Space Resources Governance Working Group, Draft Building Blocks for the Development of an International Framework in Space Resource Activities proposes an international legal framework to 'enable the attribution of property

---

[15] Translation of the Draft Law on the Exploration and Use of Space Resources) (draft law), https://spaceresources.public.lu/content/dam/spaceresources/news/Translation%20Of%20The%20Draft%20Law.pdf.

[16] The law of the sea analogy is not limitless. For instance, Canada, China, Iceland, Japan, South Korea and the European Union have negotiated and will sign an agreement in Ilulissat, Greenland, on the 16-year moratorium on commercial fishing in the High Arctic. The agreement commits the countries to major scientific work on the entire ecosystem of a region that climate change is making increasingly accessible.

rights to an operator to search and/or recover space resources in situ for a maximum period of time and a maximum area upon registration in an international registry, and provide for the international recognition of such property rights' as well as mutual recognition of property rights in extracted space resources.[17]

Following this narrative in outer space law reveals a new imagination, which is stepping away from the global commons and a frontier of scientific research towards the contours of an economic narrative. Studies in behavioural economics indicate that, in contrast to the assumptions of the *homo economicus* model, economic preferences are not exogenous but rather are shaped by the economic and social interactions of everyday life. Therefore, utility should not be defined narrowly as reflecting only the individual's material interests (in terms of her consumption patterns). Instead, utility, properly measured, should also reflect the various psychological costs and benefits which may be experienced by the individual, reflecting, for example, altruistic preferences (for example, a concern for fairness – for the consumption patterns of other people, for scientific advancement and human progress in space) or ecological values (for example, a concern for outer space environment). In this chapter, however, I am interested in these narratives' blind spots: what is concealed and suppressed through the use of the concept such as the 'benefit of humanity', or the future of human species' survival.

With intensifying competition, legal proposals in outer space law are increasingly bilateral and not global. NASA recently adopted the Artemis Accords,[18] which will need to be taken into consideration as relevant subsequent State practice since the document is intended as a tool to reinforce a specific interpretation of certain provisions in the OST, especially Article IX.[19] In order to thereby also directly affect the interpretation of this treaty, the practice should be shown to establish the agreement of the parties of the OST as per the Vienna Convention on the Law of Treaties (VCLT),[20] which cannot be the case considering the wide discrepancy

---

[17] The Hague International Space Resources Governance Working Group, Draft Building Blocks for the Development of an International Framework in Space Resource Activities, www.universiteitleiden.nl/en/law/institute-of-public-law/institute-for-air-space-law/the-hague-spaceresources-governance-working-group.

[18] www.nasa.gov/specials/artemis-accords/index.html.

[19] ARTICLE IX: "In the exploration and use of outer space, including the moon and other celestial bodies, States Parties to the Treaty shall be guided by the principle of co-operation and mutual assistance and shall conduct all their activities in outer space, including the moon and other celestial bodies, with due regard to the corresponding interests of all other States Parties to the Treaty. States Parties to the Treaty shall pursue studies of outer space, including the moon and other celestial bodies, and conduct exploration of them so as to avoid their harmful contamination and also adverse changes in the environment of the Earth resulting from the introduction of extraterrestrial matter and, where necessary, shall adopt appropriate measures for this purpose. If a State Party to the Treaty has reason to believe that an activity or experiment planned by it or its nationals in outer space, including the moon and other celestial bodies, would cause potentially harmful interference with activities of other States Parties in the peaceful exploration and use of outer space, including the moon and other celestial bodies, it shall undertake appropriate international consultations before proceeding with any such activity or experiment. A State Party to the Treaty which has reason to believe that an activity or experiment planned by another State Party in outer space, including the moon and other celestial bodies, would cause potentially harmful interference with activities in the peaceful exploration and use of outer space, including the moon and other celestial bodies, may request consultation concerning the activity or experiment.

[20] United Nations, *Vienna Convention on the Law of Treaties*, 23 May 1969, United Nations, Treaty Series, Vol. 1155, p.331.

between the signatories to the Artemis Accords (eight at the time of this writing) and the parties to the treaty it aims to interpret (OST – 110 States).

In conclusion, the dominant debates and narratives in international law as related to ongoing and future human activities in outer space have focused recently on the military and commercial uses of outer space, with international lawyers participating in the delineation of what the public–private, State–commerce nexus of relations should become.[21]

BEHIND HYPERBOLE: OUTER SPACE ENVIRONMENT AND THE LAW

The cultural, legal, political, economic, infrastructural, and logistical processes of the contemporary space race have clearly measurable environmental footprints on Earth and in outer space. The environmental impacts of activities in space unfold on multiple scales: local and stratospheric emissions from space launches, the placement of outer space-related infrastructure in so-called peripheral places and the role of power in determining whether the use of such infrastructure aids socio-environmentally constructive or destructive practices. Importantly, space debris[22] has an impact on the fragility of the outer space environment.[23]

If the approach to outer space remains not only anthropocentric (Figure 16.1) but *homo economicus*-centric, the 'externalities' of environmental degradation are likely to follow the model of the Earth System: voluntary codes of conduct, adopted with excessive focus on good practices of actors such as the extractive industries. Whereas *homo economicus* (as the concept articulated in the economic discourse) is broad enough to incorporate non-material interests, such as altruistic or ecological concerns, *homo investicus* is a greedy, materialistic creature, who only cares about maximizing his monetary gains – disregarding those concerns which cannot be represented monetarily. In exploring the influence of the *homo economicus* model on international financial law, I will focus on one segment of the financial field: the rules pertaining to *corporate reporting*. These rules strongly influence the way in which corporations behave, and, as such, deserve close scrutiny.

The UN Committee on the Peaceful Uses of Outer Space ('UN COPUOS')[24] has created a space for debates on legal mechanisms relating to space debris mitigation resulting in development of a compendium of space debris mitigation standards adopted by States and international organizations. The aim of the compendium is to inform states of the current instruments and measures that have been implemented by States and international organizations.

The general orientation of the compendium is on the use of outer space for the benefit of 'humanity' (that is, common heritage of humanity) and State and non-State actors, rather than

---

[21] Olavo O. Bittencourt Neto et al. (eds) *Building Blocks for the Development of an International Framework for the Governance of Space Resource Activities: A Commentary* (2020).

[22] For latest figures related to space debris, see European Space Agency's (ESA) Space Debris by Numbers at: www.esa.int/Safety_Security/Space_Debris/Space_debris_by_the_numbers.

[23] *International Cooperation in the Peaceful Uses of Outer Space*, UNGA, Res 73/91, 73 Sess, A/RES/73/91 (2018), preamble.

[24] UN Committee on the Peaceful Uses of Outer Space: Scientific and Technical Subcommittee, Space Debris Mitigation Guidelines of United Nations Committee on the Peaceful Uses of Outer Space, endorsed by G.A. Res. 62/217, UN Doc. A/RES/62/217 (22 Dec. 2007).

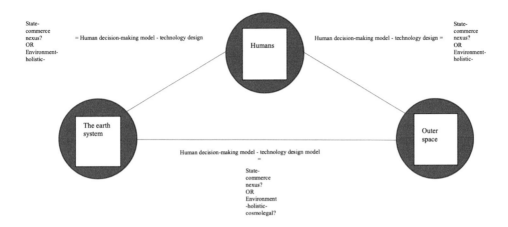

Figure 16.1   Basic model of an anthropocentric Earth System–outer space–human decision and technology design model. General model

on the space environment as an end in itself.[25] Furthermore, its status is that of a 'soft law' set of guidelines, which have yet to be incorporated and interpreted by all States. Legal scholars have identified the lack of enforcement mechanisms of voluntary guidelines. Some suggest compliance through State-enforced legislation and regulations.[26]

While satellite use is important in the monitoring of global warming, the increasing proposals for commercialization and mining of asteroids and celestial bodies could break up asteroids, harm other satellites, spacecrafts, astronauts, and even life on Earth.

Space debris is generally understood to comprise human-made objects, including their fragments and parts, which are in orbital space, re-entering the Earth's atmosphere or reaching the Earth's surface, that are non-functional with no reasonable expectation of being able to assume their intended functions or any other functions for which they are or can be authorized.[27] This

---

[25]   Compendium of space debris mitigation standards adopted by States and international organizations A/AC.105/C.2/2016/CRP.16. See also J. Wouters, P. De Man and R. Hansen, *Commercial Uses of Space and Space Tourism: Legal and Policy Aspects* (2017).

[26]   Larry Martinez, 'Legal Regime Sustainability in Outer Space: Theory and Practice' (2019) *Global Sustainability* Vol. 2, 26.

[27]   See, for instance, *Technical Report on Space Debris* adopted by Scientific and Technical Subcommittee of the United Nations Committee on the Peaceful Uses of Outer Space, UN Doc. A/AC.105/720 (1999), Introduction, sixth paragraph: 'Space debris are all man-made objects, including their fragments and parts, whether their owners can be identified or not, in Earth orbit or re-entering the dense layers of the atmosphere that are non-functional with no reasonable expectation of their being able to assume or resume their intended functions or any other functions for which they are or can be authorized'; *Space Debris Mitigation Guidelines of the United Nations Committee on the Peaceful Uses of Outer Space* endorsed by the United Nations General Assembly Resolution 62/217 of 22 December 2007, Background, first paragraph: 'For the purpose of this document, space debris is defined as all man-made objects, including fragments and elements thereof, in Earth orbit or re-entering the atmosphere, that are non-functional'; *Space Debris Mitigation Guidelines of the Inter-Agency Space Debris Coordination Committee*, Revision 1 (2007), section 3.1: 'Space debris are all man made objects including fragments and elements thereof, in Earth orbit or re-entering the atmosphere, that are non functional'; *Standard 24113 Space systems – Space debris mitigation requirements* of the International

may include spent rocket stages and defunct satellites, as well as fragments from their disintegration, such as pieces of shielding. In accordance with international space law, all the above are considered space objects and their component parts.[28] As the functional status of a space object does not as such affect the applicability of rules of international space law, orbital debris remains subject to the same rules applicable to space objects.

Still, despite the repetitiveness of 'gaps in regulation', States have a duty under Article VI of the OST regime to authorize and continuously supervise the activities of their governmental and non-governmental (that is, private) entities. As there are no mandatory international guidelines or standards of conduct for States and international organizations specifically with respect to the creation of space debris, none of them can be used to definitely assess fault for the purpose of establishing international liability under Article III of the Liability Convention[29] or establish a universal standard of due regard. Article I, paragraph 2, of the OST[30] provides that outer space, including the Moon and other celestial bodies, shall be free for exploration and use by all States. However, there can also be a situation where a space operation of State A carried out near an asteroid generates a multitude of space debris orbiting around such asteroid on different planes, thereby making it technically impossible for a scientific spacecraft of State B to complete its space mission by landing on this asteroid and collecting a probe. In this situation, State A creating space debris infringes the freedom of exploration and use, which can no longer be enjoyed, with respect to the asteroid in question, by State B or by any other State.

The occasional approach according to which what is not prohibited is allowed does not apply to outer space. The ruling to this effect in the *Lotus*[31] case is not strictly applicable to the realm of outer space. Despite the lack of express prohibition of private appropriation of celestial bodies, or leaving bags of human faeces on the Moon as the Apollo 11 mission did,[32] in the global commons of outer space, where the shared interests of States prevail over the individual interests of any one State, the types of activities and actions in space are limited by, for example, the rights of other States to explore and use space and the obligation to conduct activities in outer space 'with due regard to the corresponding interests of all other States Parties to the Treaty'.[33] There is also the general obligation to conduct space activities 'in

---

Organization for Standardization, second edition (2011), to be replaced by the third edition, Introduction, first paragraph: 'Space debris comprises all non-functional, man-made objects, including fragments and elements thereof, in Earth orbit or re-entering the Earth's atmosphere'; *European Code of Conduct for Space Debris Mitigation*, Issue 1.0 (2004), Annex 2 Terms and definitions, Space debris (synonym: orbital debris; synonym: debris): 'Any man made space object including fragments and elements thereof, in Earth orbit or re-entering the Earth's atmosphere, that is non-functional.'

[28] *Convention on International Liability for Damage Caused by Space Objects*, 29 March 1972, 961 UNTS 187, Art I(d) (entered into force 1 September 1972) *[Liability Convention]* and *Convention on Registration of Objects Launched into Outer Space*, 6 June 1975, 28 UST 695, 1023 UNTS 15, Art I(b) (entered into force 15 September 1976) *[Registration Convention]*.

[29] Ibid.

[30] *Treaty on Principles Governing the Activities of States in the Exploration and Use of Outer Space, including the Moon and Other Celestial Bodies*, 27 January 1967, 610 UNTS 205 (entered into force 10 October 1967), art. II *[Outer Space Treaty]*.

[31] *S.S. Lotus* (Fr. v Turk.), Judgment, 1927 P.C.I.J. (ser. A) No. 10, at 18–19 (7 Sept).

[32] Catalogue of Manmade Material on the Moon NASA History Program Office, https://history.nasa.gov/FINAL%20Catalogue%20of%20Manmade%20Material%20on%20the%20Moon.pdf.

[33] OST, *supra* note 2 at Art. IX.

accordance with international law, including the Charter of the United Nations, in the interest of maintaining international peace and security and promoting international cooperation and understanding',[34] but these words were meant for international relations, security among States and prevention of conflict. Trash was not really the main concern.

Planetary protection aims to prevent contamination between Earth and other bodies in the context of space exploration missions. To ensure that scientific investment in space exploration is not compromised by cross-contamination, special care must be taken by all actors and stakeholders. The Committee on Space Research (COSPAR)[35] has concerned itself with questions of biological contamination and space flight since its very inception. Generally, the basic mandate of planetary protection is: to avoid biological and organic contamination of outer solar system bodies, in particular icy moons; to avoid jeopardizing the search for extraterrestrial life, precursors and remnants, and to protect Earth and its biosphere from extraterrestrial sources of contamination. The process of determining planetary protection regulations for a specific mission depends on the target body (for example, Mars versus the Moon), the type of encounter (for example, Orbiter versus Lander), and specific goals (for example, to see if the target body has/had life). Each mission presents unique contamination challenges and therefore has different requirements.

The 'resource rush' to outer space reveals the short-sightedness of attempts to instrumentalize and colonize these spaces while sidestepping environmental problems. The new space race will lead to a saturation of orbital carrying capacity and other unexpected challenges such as interplanetary contamination unless we holistically understand and can predict the behaviours of the anthropogenic space object population, both dead and alive. The precedent for this action is that private entities are triggering governmental responsibility for outer space activities under the requirements of space law.[36] Earth organisms could thereby impact and/or even erase traces of extraterrestrial life. Humans do not know yet what would happen if alien organisms were introduced into Earth's biosphere. Would a close relationship be obvious to all, or would extraterrestrial life be so alien as to be unnoticed by both Earth organisms and human defences? What is the justification for human excursions into the outer space for mainly utilitarian purposes when there is not even a limited knowledge of actual economic returns?[37] This would demand a step away from inter-national approaches and towards planetary and even

---

[34] Ibid at Art. III.

[35] https://cosparhq.cnes.fr/.

[36] This is not the first time that a private entity has sent something into space without explicit permission. In January of 2018, a US aerospace startup called Swarm launched four tiny satellites into space on an Indian rocket that lofted a total 31 payloads. Swarm had actually been denied a licence by the Federal Communications Commission, which expressed concern that the satellites were too small to track in space. But Swarm defied the FCC and put its satellites on the launch anyway. In response, the FCC fined Swarm, and the company vowed to follow all proper licensing procedures in the future. For a view that stresses the need for state authorization of private activities in space see J.F. Mayence, 'Granting Access to Outer Space: Rights and Responsibilities for States and Their Citizens' in F. von der Dunk (ed.), *National Space Legislation in Europe. Issues of Authorization of Private Space Activities in the Light of Developments in European Space Cooperation* (2011), 74.

[37] It is beyond the scope of this chapter to engage with the detailed history of utilitarianism in various traditions, and especially the development of economic and trade-related arguments for ownership and exploitation of other humans via slavery and whatever was considered to be 'nature'. This topic has been already addressed in great detail. The objective here is to see how it orients itself towards the future, and the extraterrestrial domains.

cosmic ones, or, as is proposed below, the *cosmolegal*. The proposed concept is meant to be an illustration of an approach to outer space beyond its current anthropocentric nature, rather than an assertion. The previous discussion of *lex lata* illustrates current limits and challenges, which, arguably, cannot be properly addressed with a 'business as usual' approach to law.

THE SITH RHETORIC

Hyperbole was often considered bombastic, associated only with epideictic rhetoric (where it functions quite well), and aligned with excessive stylistic vices of the sophists. Indeed, hyperbole was often accused of affectation which results from insincerity or poor judgement and is 'the worst fault of all eloquence'. As most legal scholars who study outer space consistently have to answer questions regarding Star Wars' influences on our discipline, I here present one of the most famous sophists of the cosmic universe: the Sith.

> The Code of the Sith.
> *Peace is a Lie there is only Passion.*
> *Through Passion I gain Strength.*
> *Through Strength I gain Power.*
> *Through Power I gain Victory.*
> *Through Victory my chains are broken.*[38]

Peace is a lie, according to the Sith Code. There is only passion. Inner peace can only be gained by indulging one's desires, even via sacrifices. The boldness of an entrepreneur, futurist and cutting-edge thinker often relies on passion and conviction. The Sith has learned the art of deception, sometimes even self-deception, in order to indulge one's passion. Passion leads to strength, and strength allows one to force their will on others, and especially those who cannot defend themselves (physical and mental). And finally, those who have power are victorious and free to do as they please. The weak serve the strong. To quote Darth Bane, '*Equality is a lie [...] A myth to appease the masses. Simply look around and you will see the lie for what it is! There are those with power, those with the strength and will to lead. And there are those meant to follow – those incapable of anything but servitude.*'

The sophist Sith cannot fulfil a promise to teach virtue, truth, happiness, and justice: those are not qualities; they possess themselves. In the Sith code this is not an aim; it can be a deceptive aim, which nevertheless is revealed through its own inner contradiction. Second, there is no trust in sophistry or the world of the Sith.

This is especially relevant in what is now a discourse of 'outer space colonialism'. This semantic does not think of Mars, the Moon and other planets as somehow not inherently for the use of humanity. In the history of outer space law, this is what the 1979 Moon Agreement[39] sought to address. However, 18 States became parties to it. The Moon Agreement also importantly emerges from the discussions over legal stewardship of the Moon. One area that has yet to be explored in scholarship and practice is the idea of recognizing outer space as possessing

---

[38] Jason Fry, *Star Wars: The Essential Atlas* (2009).
[39] Agreement Governing the Activities of States on the Moon and Other Celestial Bodies, art. 7, para. 1, Dec. 5, 1979, 1363 U.N.T.S. 3, (entered into force 11 July 1984) [Moon Agreement].

agencies, in a similar manner to what is being discussed for the Earth System (including new materialisms and animal cognition).

The 'colonizing' argument evokes frontier-focused history of international law, and the otherwise outdated 'openness' of empty spaces or *res nullius*.[40] While colonialism as such has been outlawed in modern international law, imperial semantics remain in outer space law due to its outworldly nature, as a place where humans do not live. As Casumbal-Salazar has argued:

> One scientist told me that astronomy is a 'benign science' because it is based on observation, and that it is universally beneficial because it offers 'basic human knowledge' that everyone should know 'like human anatomy'. Such a statement underscores the cultural bias within conventional notions of what constitutes the 'human' and 'knowledge'. In the absence of a critical self-reflection on this inherent ethnocentrism, the tacit claim to universal truth reproduces the cultural supremacy of Western science as self-evident. Here, the needs of astronomers for tall peaks in remote locations supplant the needs of Indigenous communities on whose ancestral territories these observatories are built.[41]

Some astronomers have warned against the use of colonial frameworks in outer space, in relation to other planets.[42] More recently, aerospace engineers[43] and space environmentalists[44] have been proposing and enacting interdisciplinary projects in the academic context.[45] However, while collaborations between space agencies such as NASA aim to include indigenous knowledges, the status of indigenous peoples as non-State actors in international law has implications at the level of inter-governmental decision-making.[46]

Outer space is imagined as a limitless resource – a frontier space, and as such a hyperbole of human imagination. The metaphor of the frontier, with its associated images of pioneering, homesteading, claimstaking and taming, has been persistent in the history of international law and colonialism.

THE COSMOLEGAL[47] APPROACH AND THE JEDI CODE

The Jedi code reads as follows:

---

[40] E. Cirkovic, 'Self-Determination and Indigenous Peoples in International Law (Symposium: Lands, Liberties, and Legacies: Indigenous Peoples and International Law)' (2007) *Am. Indian L. Rev.* Vol. 31, 375.

[41] I. Casumbal-Salazar, 'A Fictive Kinship: Making "Modernity," "Ancient Hawaiians," and the Telescopes on Mauna Kea' (2017) *Native American and Indigenous Studies* Vol. 4(2), 1–30.

[42] R.F. Mandelbaum, 'Decolonizing Mars: Are We Thinking About Space Exploration All Wrong?' (2018) *Gizmodo*. See also C. Prescod-Weinstein et al, *Reframing Astronomical Research through an Anticolonial Lens – for TMT and Beyond* (2020).

[43] M. Rathnasabapathy et al, 'Space Sustainability Rating', 71st International Astronautical Congress (IAC) – The CyberSpace Edition, 12–14 October 2020.

[44] Cirkovic, *supra* note 7.

[45] A forthcoming paper is a product of such a collaboration: 'Sustainable Orbit and the Earth System: Mitigation and Regulation' by E. Cirkovic, M. Rathnasabapathy and D.R. Wood, prepared for the 7th European Conference on Space Debris, to be held 18–21 April at ESA's Space Operations Centre in Darmstadt, Germany.

[46] Cirkovic, supra note 7.

[47] Ibid.

308 *Research handbook on law and literature*

> There is no emotion, there is peace.
> There is no ignorance, there is knowledge.
> There is no passion, there is serenity.
> There is no chaos, there is harmony.
> There is no death, there is the Force.
> *The Jedi Code, Dark Disciple*

And further, this is the oath as recited by Luke Skywalker: 'I, Luke Skywalker, do swear on my honour and on the faith of the brotherhood of knights, to use the Force only for good, denying, turning always from the Dark Side; to dedicate my life to the cause of freedom, and justice. If I should fail of this vow, my life shall be forfeit, here and hereafter.'[48] But does the Jedi ethic actually counter the Sith? In essence, both deal in absolutes with pre-conceived ideas of the cosmos, the good and the just. The normativity of the Jedi practice lies in their belief that all lives are precious. For instance, the Jedi are banned from killing unarmed opponents as well as seeking revenge. Jedi do not marry or start new families. In a Socratic sense, the moral values of those who are concerned with their families, careers and political responsibilities, do not consider the 'welfare of their souls'. The love of knowledge is sought in distinction from the love for family. What this means for the current human activities in outer space is the opposite of sophistry. Rather, all space environment as an end in itself has its own value, and the search of knowledge, cannot be there for private and utilitarian interests. Finally, Sith versus Jedi ethics hinges on the distinction between believing in absolutes in a metaphysical sense, versus believing in whether or not one believes in absolutes.

In what follows, I integrate aspects of the Jedi ethic – recognizing that there is importance in the non-human with the complex systems approach. The Jedi ethic has a degree of self-limitation in the face of complexity. Rejection of such self-limitation leads to the dark side. This reorients the way the humans have appropriated the Sith code in anthropocentric interests, as is illustrated in Figure 16.2. One of the reasons for the terminology and the reference to 'cosmos' is the increasing need to focus on long-term and holistic thinking. However, holism does not imply absolutism. It is also meant to indicate a holistic long-term approach instead of a fragmented short-term approach of State/commerce-centric interests and uses, even if the latter use the disguise of beneficial economics for 'all humanity'.

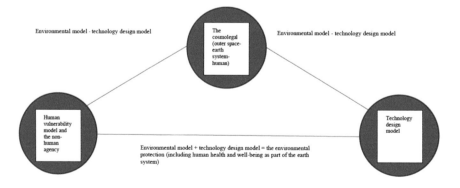

Figure 16.2   *Cosmolegal decision-making. General model*

---

[48]   J. Fry, *Star Wars: The Essential Atlas* (2009).

The chapter therefore refers to an interdisciplinary term meant to encompass the process of learning and lawmaking through which the law would recognize unpredictability of human–non-human relations: *the cosmolegal*.[49] The cosmolegal does not deal in absolutes: that there is only one way of understanding the world or living in it. The term cosmolegal merges cosmology, as a branch of astronomy that involves the scientific study of the large-scale properties of the universe as a whole, with law, due to the need for a different understanding of the Earth and human-centric global politico-juridical space. It is a normative imagination of what the world of law would look like if it was understood as encompassing the Earth System and extraterrestrial domain (cosmic) on their own terms. The human is not the apex owner and manager of its environment. Rather, the human is only one of the actors of the 'cosmos', known and unknown.

There is indeed a 'cosmic', or complex, unpredictable, and planetary scope of issues that are already an inextricable part of human life, and this is not a novel proposition. In addition, future lawmaking will need the participation of all (human) actors, requiring more inclusive and transdisciplinary processes that do not rely primarily on State-level decision-making.[50] Instead of giving the complete picture of world dynamics, cosmolegality would have to leave a free parameter or some disjunction for future contingencies and uncertainties on Earth and in outer space. Reality is dynamic and unpredictable, as is the unknowable.[51]

The Earth System and the extraterrestrial domain – *as a whole* – demonstrate that their apparent fracturing in human understanding (for instance, the very definition of 'outer' space as separate from planet Earth), practice and regulation does not stem from its own inherent multiplicity, but from the human understanding thereof. The cosmolegal, instead of being the mirror of permanently split human subjectivity, recognizes the indeterminate nature of the world beyond it. It builds on the hypothesis of profound interrelatedness and complex systems.[52] As the current legal fragmentation and conflict of laws demonstrates, analysis or regulation of each individual component has proven difficult in the regulation of the *relationships among all components*. For this reason, international legal governance would need to be able to address emergent behaviours that are not always predictable. The current State sovereignty, on the one hand, and global warming and orbital debris, on the other, are not coextensive, and therefore require non-cohesive regulation.

Hence, the cosmolegal approach (or law for the cosmos, in the true sense and not as part of the more Earth-bound philosophical tradition of cosmopolitanism) is meant to encompass the process of learning and lawmaking through which the law would recognize the unpredictability of human–non-human relations. In this respect it is a purely normative proposal.

The key working method of the cosmolegal project is to facilitate cooperation and interaction among different disciplines and knowledge, including an opening for contingencies

---

[49] *Supra* note 45. This section of the chapter further builds on the initial elaboration of the cosmolegal approach by the author (*supra* note 7).

[50] In part, this chapter is also a reflection on several academic initiatives which are currently addressing the relationship between the Earth System and outer space, as well as more inclusive participatory practices. See, for instance *Space Enabled*, www.media.mit.edu/groups/space-enabled/overview/.

[51] On the 'unknown' in law see generally V. Hamzić, (2019) 'What's Left of the Real?' in D. Fassin and B.E. Harcourt (eds), *A Time for Critique* (2019).

[52] J. Reid, C. Zeng and D. Wood, 'Combining Social, Environmental and Design Models to Support the Sustainable Development Goals', 2019 IEEE Aerospace Conference, Big Sky, MT, USA, 2019, pp.1–13.

provided by the agency of the non-human, and other dimensions/spaces, where humans seek to extend their activities and life. For instance, an image of a quantum offers a thinking of possibilities famously represented in the double-slit experiment (and its variations).[53] Because the experiment demonstrated that light and matter can unpredictably display characteristics of both classically defined waves and particles, it also showed the fundamental limitation of the ability of the observer to predict experimental results. In reference to the experiment, Richard Feynman said: 'We choose to examine a phenomenon which is impossible, *absolutely* impossible, to explain in any classical way, and which has in it the heart of quantum mechanics. In reality, it contains the only mystery.'[54] In other words, there are different possibilities, reactions not easily predictable by the human mind, and constantly changing limitations on what or who is not knowable. The existence of the unknowable, then, could be seen as an invitation to reimagine the world. As Lee Smolin warns: 'It is far more challenging to accept the discipline of having to explain the universe we perceive and experience only in terms of itself.'[55] For physicists and cosmologists, all laws, human and non-human, are constructed by humans, and as such they are always laws by situated knowers; there is no 'outside' perspective that we have of them. Physicists or cosmologists also live in their own 'case study' of the universe.

What is the meaning of global norm production in the context beyond the Earth System? Do humans have a 'right' to exploit extraterrestrial resources and alter extraterrestrial environments? The question of a 'right' inevitably echoes the burden of a history of 'rights' stemming from natural law approaches.[56] The idealizing assumption of the world's total knowability and determinability in accordance with 'laws' that humans perceive or create, in turn, leads to frustration with the limits imposed by them. In contrast, cosmolegality would need to be constantly open to contingencies in future coefficients of friction (that is, observable friction among various processes, hence deviating from what might be considered as a normal relation).

Importantly, this line of thinking is not novel, and I do not mean specifically in the context of Western academia. Traditional indigenous knowledges in decision-making have already recognized non-human agency and, for instance, 'vibrancy of matter' or 'wet ontologies'. Indeed, for this reason, indigenous ontologies are presently mentioned in the semantics of the climate change regime or Arctic governance. Nonetheless, the inclusion or mention does not mean equal consideration in the practice of lawmaking. The actual experience in a number of jurisdictions demonstrates ongoing conflicts between indigenous and other interests. There is a lack of genuine collaboration and participation in how traditional indigenous knowledges are understood or approached. First, indigenous societies (nations) are incredibly diverse, and second, a substantial amount of indigenous knowledge is accessible through published academic works authored by indigenous scholars and part of higher education curriculums. There is a difference in using indigenous knowledge as a framework of reference and a mere and essentializing depiction of indigenous peoples as 'stewards of nature'. Similarly, there is

---

[53] The double-slit experiment is a demonstration in modern physics that light and matter can display characteristics of what are classically defined as waves and particles. This possibility also demonstrates the probabilistic nature of quantum mechanics. R. Feynman, *The Feynman Lectures on Physics*, Vol. 3. 1.1–1.8 (1965). All are available online at www.feynmanlectures.caltech.edu/.
[54] Ibid.
[55] L. Smolin, *Time Reborn* (2013) 11.
[56] For a complicated history of human rights and natural law see M.G. Salmones, 'The Impasse of Human Rights: A Note on Human Rights, Natural Rights and Continuities in International Law' (2019) *Journal of the History of International Law* Vol. 21, 4, 518–62.

a difference between merely consulting traditional indigenous knowledge or actually appointing a person (or groups of persons) with such knowledge as primary decisionmaker(s) in senior professional and academic positions. It is for this reason that this chapter only refers to TEK as a source of thinking that recognizes non-human agency.[57]

In describing her own work, Leanne Simpson has argued: 'I did not want to study Aboriginal people, or my culture, or even Traditional Ecological Knowledge, but I wanted to study the people who were writing about TEK, defining it and documenting it in the area of the environment, and I wanted to do this from the Anishinaabe perspective.' Simpson turns the research method upside down as she uses the Anishinaabe perspective to analyse non-Aboriginal research on Aboriginal knowledge. Moreover, all research questions do not have to be community-generated, with also an inevitable differentiation between the scientific method and TEK. It is not a methodological necessity to engage in 'fieldwork' depending on the disciplinary definition thereof, whereby Western scholars engage with or travel to indigenous communities, as multidisciplinary research in indigenous studies is increasingly as accessible as any other knowledge. The inclusion of indigenous knowledge in the form of a proposal does not equate consideration in the practice of lawmaking.

Part of the cosmolegal project, in practice, would require an awareness of these issues, suggesting that engaging substantially with the implications of a politics of multiple ontologies might provide a better understanding of conflicts that emerge when particular governance and management options are proposed and, at times, challenged. This sensitivity is especially needed in settler-colonial contexts where modern legal ontologies remain hegemonic.

There is an enormity in the question of how various peoples engage with the Earth System and outer space in their respective worldviews. A particular theoretical model cannot predict the unknown, as we do not yet even know how to formulate the potential unknown in terms of the theory. Contingency requires that humans imagine a model of the situation, which would lend itself to interpretation and without any guarantee that adequate models can be constructed for every possible situation. This entails an entirely new approach to law, which first has to recognize its limitations as rooted in the very foundations of the law, including international law, and then implement a diversity of methodologies depending on context and suitability.

The process would be as follows: first, a recognition that outer space is governed by a different spacetime[58] would also raise awareness among decisionmakers as to how and why phenomena such as orbital debris is damaging to both the orbit and humanity. Second, there would be no appearance of distinctions, and disparate attributes of the world. Agency does not require cognition.[59] Third, the interplanetary domain demonstrates that its apparent fracturing in human understanding, practice and regulation does not stem from its own inherent multi-

---

[57] Instead of, for instance, focusing on the details of Actor–Network Theory (ANT) (B. Latour, *Reassembling the Social: An Introduction to the Actor-Network Theory* (2005), or other strands of posthumanist thinking, such as new materialisms (see for instance two seminal works on the topic, K. Barad, *Meeting the Universe Halfway* (2007) and R. Braidotti, *The Posthuman* (2013)), this chapter wishes to focus specifically on the examples of non-Western ontologies, as these predate these scholarly approaches.

[58] In physics, spacetime is any mathematical model which fuses the three dimensions of space and the one dimension of time into a single four-dimensional manifold. Spacetime diagrams can be used to visualize relativistic effects, such as why different observers perceive where and when events occur differently.

[59] J. Bennet, *Vibrant Matter* (2010).

plicity, but from the human understanding thereof. The law, instead of being the mirror of permanently split human subjectivity, would recognize the indeterminate nature of the world beyond it. And further, the material world and human bodies are not defined by strict binaries of subject–object and human–non-human.

Opening possibilities for normative rethinking of the world of lawmaking is necessary because new activities, which continue to extend the borders of the current international law into the cosmos, are becoming possible (such as the mining of asteroids and celestial bodies), including the unintended or unexpected reactions of various environments.

CONCLUSION

Traditions and approaches to non-human spaces diverge over the stewardship, cooperation and respect model versus the utilitarian, imperial and commerce-driven model.[60] The proposals for the mining of asteroids and celestial bodies and colonies on Mars do not emanate from all humankind. These 'colonial' arguments are a mere continuation of past practices which have been already put into question due to the environmental degradation in the Earth System, and histories of violence towards human and non-human. Thence, the cosmolegal is normative and argues for a restructuring away from the history of *imperium* and *commercium*, which now intends to push even further into the cosmos.

The chapter chooses to echo Nikola Tesla's statement that '[l]ife is and will ever remain an equation incapable of solution, but it contains certain known factors.'[61] The combination of known and unknown has always been present in human thought, albeit always in its relation to itself. If there is a force beyond the human, how does it explain human life? As humanity continues to approach spaces beyond the Earth System, the applicable 'rules of behaviour' will need to change accordingly. Humans cannot fix what we cannot see and observe, and lawyers have yet to be able to 'see' beyond the confines of ontologies that inform our modern legal structures and practice. The central argument of this chapter is critical and normative and recognizes the complex web of active bodies and materials. Hence, this study should not be read as a policy or lawmaking proposal. There are too many obstacles to such academic proposals. It is here argued that normative and hypothetical arguments should precisely remain so, because any prediction in social sciences and humanities is a pretence, rather than something akin to an experiment that can be replicated or falsified. There are no concrete outcomes to this thought experiment, which is also rooted in a description of some current gaps and contradictions in modern legal thought and practice.

Hyperbole of the current space and resource rush is a different kind of speech. Through it a lie that is not a deception can be employed on the side of truth(s), which is always lacking and unstable, necessitating the abundance of excess. In making clear various excessive arguments for human action in outer space, I have focused on the opposite possibility where this extraterrestrial environment remains a place of scientific exploration, expansion of knowledge and benefit to both 'all humanity' and other species, spaces, matter and, in general, all that is considered to be non-human. The passion of entrepreneurial and careerist go-getting in

---

[60] On the economic history of space exploration see A. MacDonald, *The Long Space Age* (2017).
[61] N. Tesla, 'A Machine to End War', *Liberty* 9 February 1935, 5–7.

the new frontier and endless ambition has always coexisted with other ambitions: for peace, justice and sustainable growth.

PART V

TENSE FRAMES

Law Sketches – Graphic Novel – Walking the City – Terms of Use – Touring Law – Ghost-Writing – Immigration Law – Juridical Sensing

17. Tenses
Mikus Duncis and Geoff Gordon

What are the tenses in the grammar of law? The answer may be contingent in part on the genre of law in question. The particular genre of law that I draw on is public international law. This is a situated law, but with a global history.[1] That history is a colonial one.[2] The colonial history, however, has also given rise to a hybrid grammar, as a facet of its imperial constitutive past.[3] What sort of work does tensity do in this hybrid context? Its domain is crossed with diverse elements. They include time and structure,[4] which meet in matter,[5] as well as affect and anxiety,[6] which may meet in something like embodied consciousness.[7] In both respects, tensity appears to manifest in bipolar conditions,[8] such as between apology and utopia,[9] euphoria and despair,[10] crisis and confidence.[11] These binaries characterize material and psychical coordinates discernible in international law.[12] In addition, as units of grammar, tenses also participate in the ways of law's knowing, and with the possibilities for action

---

[1] Martti Koskenniemi, *The Gentle Civilizer of Nations: The Rise and Fall of International Law 1870–1960* (Cambridge University Press, 2001).

[2] Antony Anghie, *Imperialism, Sovereignty and the Making of International Law* (Cambridge University Press, 2007).

[3] Liliana Obregón, 'Between civilisation and barbarism: Creole interventions in international law', 27 *Third World Quarterly* (2006): 815–32; and Arnulf Becker Lorca, *Mestizo International Law* (Cambridge University Press, 2014).

[4] See, e.g., Renisa Mawani, 'Law as temporality: Colonial politics and Indian settlers', 4 *UC Irvine Law Review* (2014): 65; and B.S. Chimni, 'The limits of the all affected principle: Attending to deep structures', 3 *Third World Thematics: A TWQ Journal* (2018): 807–12.

[5] Karen Barad, 'Posthumanist performativity: Toward an understanding of how matter comes to matter', 28 *Signs: Journal of Women in Culture and Society* (2003): 801–31.

[6] See, for example, Gerry Simpson, 'The sentimental life of international law', 3 *London Review of International Law* (2015): 3–29; and Susan Marks, 'State-centrism, international law, and the anxieties of influence', 19 *Leiden Journal of International Law* (2006): 339.

[7] Cf. Emily Kidd White, 'On Emotions and the Politics of Attention in Judicial Reasoning', in Amalia Amaya and Maksymilian Del Mar, eds, *Virtue, Emotion and Imagination in Law and Legal Reasoning* (Bloomsbury, 2020): 101.

[8] Cf. China Miéville, *Between Equal Rights: A Marxist Theory of International Law* (Brill, 2005).

[9] See, for example, Martti Koskenniemi, *From Apology to Utopia: The Structure of International Legal Argument* (Cambridge University Press, 2005).

[10] See, for example, Philip Allott, *Eunomia: New Order for a New World* (Oxford University Press, 1990).

[11] See, for example, Anne Orford, 'The destiny of international law', 17 *Leiden Journal of International Law* (2004): 441.

[12] Remaining within the domain of international law, the bipolar condition is discernible in structural terms in David Kennedy, *International Legal Structure* (Nomos Verlagsgesellschaft, 1987) and in psychical terms in Maria Aristodemou, 'A constant craving for fresh brains and a taste for decaffeinated neighbours', 25 *European Journal of International Law* (2014): 35–58.

inscribed in that knowledge.[13] Finally, these multiple elements meet conspicuously in a social function typically ascribed to systems of law in general, including public international law, namely, the capacity to manage (counterfactual) expectations.[14] Managing expectations means that the communication of law will bind its audience to outcomes in its name, even when those outcomes are disappointing or frustrating or worse. In short, the tensity of law holds together in, with and through conditions of conflict. Equally, its tensity holds conflicted conditions together. This is not a neutral operation, nor are its outcomes natural inevitabilities.

---

[13] A meeting point of these several strands is interrogated in Daniela Gandorfer, *Matterphorics: On the Laws of Theory* (Duke, 2021).
[14] Niklas Luhmann, *Law as a Social System* (Oxford University Press, 2004).

Tenses

This isn't working. And what difference does it make? The tense of law. Words on a page. What time is it anyway? I've been at this too long. I need to clear my head.

I look tired. I am tired. I see me all the time now, on every zoom session. Talking about law, looking at myself. Still I look in the mirror. What for? My beard looks better than usual.

I'm getting out. Fresh air will do me good. I hope the weather is ok. Got to think about the time, though. Do I need my mask? Is that mandatory outside? Strange days.

It's empty out and all I see is law. The signposts & squared intersections. Everything ordered. Besides the garbage. But that's ordered, too. It's got its laws like all the rest. And it's regular as the falling leaves.

Walking last week in the forest at night, I was tense, like afraid. Why? No light posts, no one to see me. That's the security of the city. But I don't like to be watched. Maybe I want to be seeable without being seen. In/visible order. Clever.

Look at that. Dice. They still play dice. Who knew? I never liked gambling. But there was that passage in La Condition humaine. I could almost understand it then.

Tenses

What's the sense in gambling? It's random or it's not. I don't get it. What's a law of probability anyway? Machine learning is all about probability, isn't it? What is the machine learning? Me, I suppose, and other things. It learns me like a number. Or a risk quotient.

Another building going up. That's tense, too. All of it held together with tension. The foundations, financing, deadlines. Lawyers, lots of lawyers. We are the building. Too bad we just work with words. I wish I could make things. I wonder where all the concrete comes from.

Those tall buildings make me anxious. The way they watch over me and everything. And now that space is impenetrable to me. What's it like to build something like that, something so big? It makes me feel so small. I wonder what the ground and air rights cost.

But I'm not the only one that's tense all the time. It's in the air. All the pressure. If we could only get a little time to recharge, unwind. That's what yoga classes are for, I guess. Keep you flexible, in the flow. All my colleagues do that stuff. It keeps them going.

What would it take to really change things? How different would things have to be? Should it all be new – new law, new houses and homes? Do I even know what that would look like, or what I would want? Would I have to join a movement? Or become a public defender?

But really, I know what I am, more or less. There's no great mystery. And I'm secure enough to believe things will work out. I see what there is to see, I try to puzzle out the rest. There are some subjects I may never figure out, but I get what I get. I can play my part.

I could still be going places. I just need a little more direction. Maybe it's in the law, maybe not. Maybe I'll write a novel. Lots of lawyers write novels. Not just courtroom dramas. I could forge the conscience of... how does it go?

Or I could become an influencer. One viral video, one goofy cat trick, and the world is my oyster. Shouldn't that be pearl? But who am I kidding. All I know is the law. No one's going to pay me for anything else. That's my contribution. Stay grounded.

Do your job, know your place. It sounds worse than it is, maybe. Though it gets hard to know where that place is anymore. But even when it seems like it's all coming apart, who knows where it's all going, even then, there's always something that keeps things back on track, holds it all together. Right?

Cops. Welcome back to reality. They make me tense. Not that I've got anything to fear. I mean, they don't just stop white guys out for a walk. I can't believe I can think like that. I can't believe they shot that kid, in the park, with the toy pistol.

That kid isn't growing old. I feel old. What have I done to deserve being old? Have I done so much? Experienced so much? Maybe it's just another part I play, feeling old. Sometimes I think I play parts just to fool myself. But what do I have to fool myself about?

The police are everywhere. They're law, too. A law on the street. What am I then? A lawyer out walking. I don't carry a gun or get a badge. I don't need them. Does that make me better or worse? The cops are the real ones in all the shows. The lawyers are only ever in the way.

Tenses 325

What? Is that person talking to me? What do they mean? Does that person know me? My law — like, mine? It's not mine! I mean, I didn't ask for this. I don't want this. Jesus, I don't know. I have to get out of here.

I'm leaving. All the smoke and the gas and the anger. I can't help this. Whatever that person said, I wasn't part of this. It's not my law! I just happened to see something. But what did happen? What did I just see? What am I supposed to think?

I'm sorry. I'm going home. I can't do anything here. Can I? I mean, I've never seen anything like this. But people have been protesting forever. When did the cops get geared up like for a war? What sort of law does that? My law? Really?

Home. There it is. But this isn't right. I'm not where I'm supposed to be. This is not my home. This script is all wrong. I should be somewhere else. I should be working on a different law. But what law, where? I don't think I can get there from here.

I've got to do something. There's got to be something I can still do. My law? My house? What can I do with these things? Here's something – thanks Mikus. I appreciate all the work you put into the house and everything. But Geoff got it all wrong. The whole frame should be different.

The tense of law is future perfect continuous. Its grammar communicates a future that will always be in the process of already having been completed. It constitutes an anxious promise of deliverance that sustains the pressures of competitive relations run amok. In this state, erasure is not an answer, but part of the problem.

18. Travel

Nofar Sheffi

FRAMES OF REFERENCE

In August 2018, about a week following his and his partner's stay in Hotel-Appartement Ferienhof, Thomas K published reviews of the hotel, in German and English, on TripAdvisor and Booking.com.[1] The Ks spent a night in the four-star Austrian hotel, nestled in the Tyrolean Alps, on their way from Italy back to Germany.[2] 'Mit dem Zimmer war alles in Ordnung' ('With the room, everything was in order'), the review posted in German to Booking.com confesses from the outset. Indeed, the reviews published by Thomas K do not describe the location or surroundings. Nor do they say anything about the accommodation, facilities or staff. Thomas K posted the reviews to draw our eyes and attention to a framed picture that is displayed in the hotel lobby, above a flower arrangement. It is one image that made Thomas K's experience, that shaped his view. It is one image that remains etched in Thomas K's memory, that continues to haunt him, that he is unable to shake off: the image of the Nazi grandfather.

Figure 18.1   Screenshot from Kayak.de, operated by Booking Holdings, Inc.

The title of the German version – 'Am Hoteleingang: Bild vom Nazi-Opa' ('At the Entrance of the Hotel: A picture of the Nazi Grandpa') – frames the reference, creating a portal on the

---

[1] 'Thomas K' is the name used in court proceedings and news reports. As of April 2021, neither the review posted in English nor the one published in German is available on TripAdvisor and Booking.com. 'Ferienhof Gerlos' (*Tripadvisor*) www.tripadvisor.com.au/Hotel_Review-g651666-d1584759-Reviews-Ferienhof_Gerlos-Gerlos_Tirol_Austrian_Alps.html accessed 24 April 2021; 'Hotel-Appartement Ferienhof, Gerlos' (*Booking.com*) www.booking.com/hotel/at/ferienhof-gerlos.en-gb.html accessed 24 April 2021. The German review can be viewed only on Kayak.de: 'Hotel-Appartement Ferienhof' (*Kayak.de*) www.kayak.de/Gerlos-Hotels-Hotel-Appartement-Ferienhof.384159.ksp accessed 24 April 2021. The review published in English does not appear on Kayak.com. Both Kayak.de and Kayak.com are operated by Booking Holdings Inc., which also provides Booking.com.

[2] Hasnain Kazim, 'Deutsch-Österreichischer Rechtsstreit: Wen Darf Man "Nazi-Opa" Nennen?' (*Der Spiegel*, 19 September 2019) www.spiegel.de/panorama/deutsch-oesterreichischer-rechtsstreit-wen-darf-man-nazi-opa-nennen-a-6ddcedfc-19e7-4aab-bada-f38de6928bd2 accessed 20 March 2020.

portal. On the other line of the invisible line that separates title from text, the first sentence opens a door, situating readers on the threshold, on a line they must decide whether or not to cross, before the image.[3]

> Am Eingang hängt, sichtbar für alle, kommentarlos ein altes Foto eines jungen Mannes in Nazi-Uniform mit gut erkennbarem Hakenkreuz.
>
> [At the entrance hangs, visible to all, without comment, an old photo of a young man wearing Nazi uniform and a clearly recognizable swastika.]

At the entrance, the review ushers us in, a picture of a young man, wearing a Nazi uniform and adorned with what is clearly a swastika, is displayed for all to see.

> Daneben hängt ein Bild eines älteren Herrn, so dass man annehmen kann, dass es sich um die Ehrung eines mit dem Hotel verbundenen Mannes handelt (in einem Hinweis an der Rezeption wird der Tod des Großvaters betrauert).
>
> [Next to it hangs a picture of an elderly man so one can assume that it is about honouring a man who is connected to the hotel (a sign at the reception expresses sadness about the passing of the grandfather).]

Alongside this image, the review continues, hangs another, which gives the impression that the two are displayed to honour a relation. The review adduces additional evidence to support this inference – a sign at the hotel's reception mourns the loss of a grandfather.

> Es ist schwer zu beschreiben, welchen Schock wir empfunden haben, als wir dieses Bild (leider einige Zeit nach dem einchecken) entdeckt haben.
>
> [It is difficult to describe the shock we felt on discovering the picture (unfortunately sometime after checking in).]

It is difficult to describe the shock felt by the Ks upon being faced with images of a dead and buried Nazi relation, the review proceeds. Because this confronting encounter occurred after check-in, it was, unfortunately, impossible to avoid it.

> Was möchte das Hotel mit diesem Bild seinen Gästen kommunizieren? Was ist das für eine Gegend, in der sich Hoteliers eines 4-Sterne-Hotels frei fühlen, derartige Bilder zur Schau zu stellen?
>
> [What does the hotel want to communicate to its guests with this picture? What does it say about a region that the owners of a 4-star hotel feel free to display such a picture?]

To display an image of this buried relation, out in the open, for all to see, is to send a message, the review underscores, and it reflects not only on the owners of the hotel and on the hotel, but also on the environment which they inhabit, one in which persons 'feel free to display such a picture'.

> Wir empfinden einen unglaublichen Ekel und werden zukünftig einen großen Bogen um Tirol machen.

---

[3] See Jacques Derrida, 'Before the Law' in Derek Attridge (ed), *Acts of Literature* (Psychology Press 1992) 188–90.

[We feel incredible disgust and, in the future, will make a big detour in order to avoid Tyrol.]

'We feel incredible disgust', the review concludes, 'and, in the future, will make a big detour in order to' escape not *to* Tyrol, but Tyrol. Do not go there, the review recommends. Do not cross the threshold. Do not revisit. Do not review. Avoid confrontation with honoured buried relations.

Figure 18.2   Screenshot from TripAdvisor, published by Bluewin

Source: phi, 'Deutscher Verklagt Tiroler Hotel' (*Bluewin*, 12 September 2019) https://www.bluewin.ch/de/news/vermischtes/oesi-hotel-verklagt-deutschen-wegen-nazi-bewertung-297619.html accessed 24 April 2021.

'At the Entrance they display a picture of a Nazi grandpa' is the appealing title of the review posted in English to TripAdvisor. 'A while after checking in at the hotel' – the opening sentence introduces a dimension of time – 'we noticed the pictures hanging at the entrance', on the threshold: one of a swastika-adorned young man in Wehrmacht uniform, another of a man in his old age. The hanging of the photographs alongside each other, the review explains, suggests that they are of the same person. It can also be inferred 'that the hotel wishes to honor this person, who is somehow related to the hotel'. The pictured might be a mourned relation, the review acknowledges, but for the Ks, 'seeing a Nazi being honored publicly at a hotel was a huge disappointment'. The feelings of 'indignation and disgust' with which they were engulfed led them to 'wonder what the hotel owners are trying to tell us with this image', to reflect on the message that the hotel owners were seeking to convey by remembering a relation in this way. This 'incident', the review states, 'speaks volumes' not only about the hotel owners, but also about 'the current state of affairs in this region of Austria'. The Ks' 'desire to revisit this mountain region has disappeared completely', it concludes, suggesting that others should repress theirs.

One of the readers of the reviews published by Thomas K was Andrea S, one of the hotel owners.[4] Following their posting, she contacted the providers of the two platforms, demanding the removal of the reviews. As those pictured, being two different men, were not 'Nazis',

---

[4]   'Andrea S' is the name used in court proceedings and news reports.

Andrea S claimed, the terms 'Nazi Grandpa' (*Nazi-Opa*) and 'Nazi uniform' (*Nazi-Uniform*) are libellous and defamatory. The reviews, what's more, reflect negatively not only on those photographed, but also on the owners of the hotel, giving the impression that they hold Nazi views 'in front of an audience of millions' ('vor einem Millionenpublikum').[5] Booking.com, the Terms & Conditions agreement of which 'shall be governed by and construed in accordance with Dutch law',[6] accepted her argument and removed the text of the review. Following an additional request by Andrea S, the framing title was also removed.[7] TripAdvisor, the Terms of Use of which 'shall be governed by and construed in accordance with the law of the Commonwealth of Massachusetts, USA',[8] declined to delete the review. Citing the 'Jurisdiction and Governing Law' provision included in the agreement between TripAdvisor LLC and the owners of the user account, they sent Andrea S to bring a case before 'a court of competent subject matter jurisdiction located in the Commonwealth of Massachusetts'.[9]

Having failed to get the review removed from TripAdvisor, Andrea S traced the identity of the reviewer and demanded that the review be removed. Thomas K refused, and Andrea S decided to bring the matter before a court – a regional court in Innsbruck, Austria. In her court submissions, Andrea S shared information about the photographs. The two, she disclosed, in effect, do not honour the same relation. The young man is her late uncle, who died in Serbia in June 1944, aged 20. The older man is his father, Andrea S's grandfather, who passed away in 1966, 22 years after his son's death. Neither man was a Nazi, Andrea S maintained. In the displayed image, the only one she has of him, her conscripted uncle is wearing Wehrmacht, rather than 'Nazi', uniform. Nor is Andrea S a Nazi, as the reviews imply. The photographs were not displayed to show support for the National Socialist Party or the Nazi ideology. In Austria, as is in Germany, this is illegal. In exhibiting portraits in honour of relatives who passed away, the Ss have merely been following a common regional practice.[10]

The regional court in Innsbruck accepted Andrea S's view, holding that the hotel owner's interest in protecting their reputation took precedence over the guest's right to freedom of expression, and ordered the removal of the reviews.

Figure 18.3   Screenshot from Booking.com

---

[5]   Kazim (n 2).
[6]   Clause 11 of the Booking.com Terms and Conditions agreement. 'Booking.Com: Terms and Conditions' (*Booking.com*) www.booking.com/content/terms.en-gb.html?label=gen173nr-1FCAEoggI4 6AdIM1gEaA-IAQGYAQm4ARfIAQ_YAQHoAQH4AQuIAgGoAgO4AoLr2vMFwAIB;sid=f9 d7516aba21c3db975a7c369c460a04#tcs_s11 accessed 24 April 2021.
[7]   Kazim (n 2).
[8]   The TripAdvisor Terms of Use agreement. 'Terms of Use' (*Tripadvisor*) https://tripadvisor .mediaroom.com/au-terms-of-use#JURISDICTION AND GOVERNING LAW accessed 24 April 2021.
[9]   ibid. As reported by Kazim (n 2).
[10] Kazim (n 2).

Figure 18.4   Screenshot from TripAdvisor, published by Bluewin

Source: phi, 'Deutscher Verklagt Tiroler Hotel' (*Bluewin*, 12 September 2019) https://www.bluewin.ch/de/news/vermischtes/oesi-hotel-verklagt-deutschen-wegen-nazi-bewertung-297619.html accessed 24 April 2021.

Thomas K deleted the reviews, but he did not back off. The term 'Nazi', as he sees it, should not be treated as an insult. Whether someone is a Nazi is a question of fact.[11] Armed with new information about the pictured relations, Thomas K travelled again, not to Tyrol but domestically, to the German National Archives in Berlin. Both father and son, his research unearthed, joined the National Socialist German Workers' Party (NSDAP), in 1941 and 1943 respectively. As the men were members of the National Socialist party, Thomas K argued in his appeal, his review was not defamatory. The hotel owner's grandfather was a Nazi, and so was her uncle. By displaying a picture of a swastika-wearing member of the National Socialist party, Andrea S and her family members 'uncritically venerated a former Nazi family member'.[12]

In her court submissions, Andrea S denied knowing that her uncle and grandfather were members of the National Socialist party. The insinuations in Thomas K's reviews, she argued, are not 'objectively comprehensible and verifiable' ('objektiv nachvollziehbar und überprüfbar') for readers. Her uncle and grandfather were not Nazis – an insulting label which 'implies a National Socialist (criminal, racist, inhuman) sentiment' ('eine Beleidigung und unterstelle eine nationalsozialistische (verbrecherische, rassistische, menschenverachtende) Gesinnung').[13] 'That the German Wehrmacht was an instrument of the National Socialist

---

[11]   Kazim (n 2).
[12]   Philip Oltermann, 'Austrian Hotel Owners Drop "Nazi Grandpa" Court Case against Guest' (*The Guardian*, 17 December 2019) www.theguardian.com/world/2019/dec/16/austrian-hotel-owners-drop-nazi-grandpa-court-case accessed 20 March 2020. Thomas K also brought a case, in Germany, against a family member of Andrea S whom Thomas K alleges harassed him by telephone to take down the post. Kazim (n 2).
[13]   Kazim (n 2).

regime does not mean that soldiers who were called to serve should be referred to as Nazis' ('Dass die deutsche Wehrmacht ein Instrument des nationalsozialistischen Regimes gewesen ist, erlaubt nicht, Soldaten, die zum Kriegsdienst gezogen wurden, generell als Nazi zu bezeichnen').[14] They were conscripted, and conscientious objection was punishable by death. What's more, the expression 'Nazi uniform' is the 'most unfavourable' ('ungünstigste') way to refer to the uniform of 'one of the military associations of the NSDP' ('einer der Wehrverbände der NSDAP').[15] To the German newspaper *Der Spiegel*, Andrea S's lawyer further explained that she did not even notice the small swastika; the old photograph is black-and-white and only 22 centimetres by 16 centimetres in size.[16]

The court of appeal accepted Thomas K's arguments, lifting the injunction issued by the trial court. The confrontational images no longer hang on the wall. The hotel owners decided to remove the pictures – on the advice of Andrea S's lawyer (according to the lawyer himself), to avoid inquiries and more complaints.[17] While Thomas K's reviews appear on neither Booking.com nor TripAdvisor, their prints can still be traced. They left a mark.

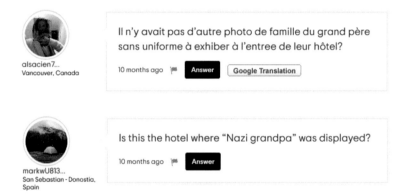

Figure 18.5   Screenshots from TripAdvisor

In September 2019, when the story was reported in the media, two users used the Questions and Answers feature on TripAdvisor to ask if the hotel was the same one reported on in the media.[18] 'Il n'y avait pas d'autre photo de famille du grand père sans uniforme à exhiber à l'entree de leur hôtel?' ('Was not there another family photo of the grandfather without uniform to display at the entrance of their hotel?') reads one enquiry. 'Is this the hotel where the "Nazi grandpa" was displayed?' asks another.

---

[14] ibid.
[15] ibid.
[16] ibid.
[17] ibid.
[18] 'Ferienhof Gerlos' (n 1).

Travel 333

Figure 18.6   Screenshots from TripAdvisor

'I would skip it due to its past' is the title of a review posted to TripAdvisor, in March 2021, by someone who did visit 'it' – the hotel, but also the past.[19] 'Stayed there for a brief moment', only for a brief moment, Tom B from the United Kingdom writes, 'then searched for the hotel's history to find out the *owners* had very dangerous *liaisons* with certain *German* past'. 'Check on Google *before* [you] book it': the review also situates readers on the threshold, recommending avoidance. Dig up the dirt, read the story, it explains, 'and you will feel appalled'.

LIVE (T)HERE

In 2016, Airbnb 'unveiled the next chapter in its mission to change the way people travel', launching 'an exciting journey to help people not just go somewhere, but truly live there'.[20]

As part of this 'journey', 'the world's leading community-driven hospitality company' rolled out a 'reengineered' mobile app, with a range of new features.[21] Having 'personalization at its heart', the newly updated app was built with a brand new 'proprietary Design Language System', which 'creates consistent, yet iconic designs that can enliven apps across all devices'.[22] It introduced 'an innovative matching system designed to understand travelers' preferences and then match them with the homes, neighborhoods and experiences that meet their needs'.[23] The app's search functionality would start 'a conversation with travelers about their ideal trip and, based on their preferences, [would] reveal the hosts, homes, and neighborhoods that will give travelers a sense of truly living in a destination'.[24] It would be 'constantly learning and adapting' to find out not only 'what types of properties a traveler is interested in', but also what neighbourhood would make the traveler 'feel like they are living like a local'.[25]

---

[19] 'Airbnb Launches New Products to Inspire People to "Live There"' (*Airbnb*, 16 April 2016) https://news.airbnb.com/airbnb-launches-new-products-to-inspire-people-to-live-there/ accessed 24 April 2021.
[20] ibid.
[21] ibid.
[22] ibid.
[23] ibid.
[24] ibid.
[25] ibid.

To inspire searchers to 'live there', in the neighbourhoods with which they were matched, the newly updated app would 'showcase' the 'spirit' of these neighbourhoods 'through rich photography and content'.[26] In addition, a newly introduced feature called 'Guidebooks' would enable travellers to 'unlock local insights'.[27] Created and curated by Airbnb hosts, these Guidebooks would 'give travelers a passport to local culture', sharing 'local tips on the very best their neighborhoods have to offer, including the best restaurants and bars, attractions, off the beaten track ideas and more'.[28] They would help travellers to 'break free of the limits of cookie-cutter travel' and 'find local gems not only in every city, but on every city block'.[29]

Alongside rolling out these new products, the company introduced 'Live There' – a global brand campaign, its largest up to then. The campaign, the company explained, had been 'designed in response to the growing dissatisfaction and disappointment with standardized tourist offerings that have become the hallmark of modern tourism', to 'encourage people to change the way they experience the world around them'.[30] 'At the heart of [it] is Airbnb's antidote to commoditized travel, including living in the heart of local neighborhoods, experiencing the hospitality and local expertise of hosts, and enjoying the comfort of every home.'[31] The campaign 'throws out the notion that people want templated experiences that dull the senses and prevent people from seeing the world with a fresh perspective. Instead, Airbnb will inspire travelers to reimagine what it is to travel, showcasing the authentic and magical experiences made possible through Airbnb and its community of over two million homes.'[32]

Airbnb, the campaign sought to reveal, is more than a platform for offering to host, for searching for and for booking 'Accommodations' and 'Experiences'.[33] The interface has not only 'opened the doors to homes around the world',[34] but also inspired users to live 'there'. But where is this 'here' from which Airbnb and other platforms of its kind allow us to escape? And where is this 'there' to which these platforms enable us to escape? Where is this 'here' from which we travel? And where is this 'there' that Airbnb and similar platforms help us to 'authentically' and 'magically' experience? Where is this 'there', which we describe in the review we post upon returning home? And where is this 'there', which we consider as an option while reading reviews posted by others?

In a sketch called 'Here and There', performed during *Sesame Street*'s first season, viewers are encouraged to reflect on these very questions.[35] In a 1973 remake, a young monster called Billy interrupts a mundane conversation between two adult monsters, Grover and Herry

---

[26] ibid.
[27] ibid.
[28] ibid.
[29] ibid.
[30] ibid.
[31] ibid.
[32] ibid.
[33] 'Terms of Service' (*Airbnb*) www.airbnb.com.au/help/article/2908/terms-of-service accessed 27 April 2021. In 2016, the website expanded beyond places to stay to offer 'Experiences' – activities, excursions, and events that go 'beyond the typical tour or class, designed and led by locals all over the world'. 'Host an Experience on Airbnb' (*Airbnb*) www.airbnb.com.au/host/experiences accessed 24 April 2021.
[34] 'Airbnb Launches New Products to Inspire People to "Live There"' (n 19).
[35] 'Here and There' (*Muppet Wiki*) https://muppet.fandom.com/wiki/Here_and_There accessed 24 April 2021.

Monster.³⁶ Billy asks the two adults to explain the difference between here and there. 'Because I don't know what "here" means', the young monster apologizes, 'and I don't know what "there" means, and I was wondering if somebody could explain the difference to me. You think anybody could explain the difference to me?' 'What do you think, Grover?' Herry asks his friend. 'I think it would be nice, if we helped the little tyke', Grover replies. 'All right, I'll tell you what. You stay here, and I'll go over there. You stay here with Grover,' Herry tells Billy and walks towards a position in the background. The focus remains on Grover and Billy, who appear to be standing in the foreground. 'Uh, what does that mean?' the perplexed youngster probes. 'Well,' Grover clarifies, 'what he means is that you and I are right here now. Right here.' 'Oh,' Billy says. 'And Herry, my friend,' Glover continues, 'is there. Hi, Herry.' Grover waves at his friend. 'Hi, Grover,' Herry waves back. 'Well, I want to be there,' the youngster declares. 'Well, OK,' Grover says. 'You just walk right over to Herry, over there.' Billy runs over to Herry. As he approaches Herry, the camera shifts focus to Herry, who now appears to be waiting in the foreground. Billy is seen running towards him. 'Hi,' Billy greets Herry upon arriving. 'Now I'm there, right?' he asks Herry. 'No, no. Now you're here. Grover is there,' Herry responds. 'Hi, Grover,' he waves at his friend. 'Hey, big Herry!' Grover waves at Herry. 'But, but I wanted to be there,' Billy exclaims. 'Well, suit yourself,' Herry responds. 'OK,' Billy says and walks towards Grover. The camera zooms in on Grover, who now appears to be standing in the foreground. Billy is seen approaching. 'Hi,' he greets Grover upon arrival. 'Now I'm there, right?' Billy asks. 'No,' Grover replies. 'You are here.' 'But I was here just a minute ago,' Billy struggles to keep up. 'Well, it is good to see you again,' Grover responds. 'But I wanted to be there,' Billy cries. 'Oh. Well, OK. Go over to Herry, then,' Grover loses patience. 'Go over there.' 'Uh,' Billy interjects. 'Don't understand,' Grover says, turning to the camera, as if to address the viewer. Billy is seen running away, towards Herry. As he approaches, the camera shifts focus to Herry and him, who now appear to be standing in the foreground. 'Now I'm there, right?' Billy seeks assurance. 'No, no,' Herry cannot hide his annoyance. 'Now you're here.' 'You mean I'm still here?' Billy cries. 'I don't know about still,' Herry replies, 'but you're here.' He draws a line. 'Listen, kid, that's enough. I don't have any more time.' Herry gets back to Grover, followed by the camera. Herry and Grover now appear to be standing in the foreground, Grover in the background. 'That kid's really pesky,' Herry tells Grover. 'Listen,' Herry shouts at Billy, 'stay there.' 'There?' the young monster asks in enthusiastic disbelief. 'You mean I'm there?' 'That's right,' the exasperated Herry replies, before leaving the frame together with Grover. 'And stay there!' 'Oh, boy! I'm there! I'm there! I did want to be there,' the excited Billy chants, as the camera zooms in on him. 'Billy? Billy?' an unnamed adult monster can be heard calling before entering the frame. 'Oh, I've been looking all over for you,' she complains. 'What are you doing here?'

'Every story', de Certeau reminds us, 'is a travel story – a spatial practice'.³⁷ Stories about space, narrated adventures – including reviews posted to Airbnb, Booking.com and TripAdvisor – tirelessly mark out frontiers. Their primary role is to open up legitimate 'theatres of actions': to distinguish and found the very abstract place in which they are set, to design

---

³⁶ Sesame Street, 'Sesame Street: Grover And Herry Explain Here & There' (*YouTube*, 31 July 2010) www.youtube.com/watch?v=9m-kbBamg_U accessed 24 April 2021.
³⁷ Michel de Certeau, *The Practice of Everyday Life* (Steven Rendall tr, University of California Press 1988) 115.

settings by distributing positions and to cast in roles.[38] 'As operations on places', however, stories also 'play the everyday role of a mobile and magisterial tribunal in cases concerning their delimitation'.[39] Narrative operations of boundary-setting confine and limit, but in so doing, paradoxically, create 'a field that authorizes dangerous and contingent social actions'.[40] This is because distinctions result from encounters. Lines need to be drawn only where two bodies come in contact, where an interaction or exchange takes place. The

> story tirelessly marks out frontiers. It multiplies them, but in terms of interactions among the characters-things, animals, human beings: the acting subjects (*actants*) divide up among themselves places as well as predicates (simple, crafty, ambitious, silly, etc.) and movements (advancing, withdrawing, going into exile, returning, etc.). Limits are drawn by the points at which the progressive appropriations (the acquisition of predicates in the course of the story) and the successive displacements (internal or external movements) of the acting subjects meet.[41]

'This', de Certeau observes, 'is a paradox of the frontier: created by contacts, the points of differentiation between two bodies are also their common points. Conjunction and disjunction are inseparable in them.'[42]

'A middle place, composed of interactions and inter-views, the frontier is a sort of void, a narrative sym-bol of exchanges and encounters.'[43] It distinguishes and separates, but, in so doing, it also forms an interface. The line that forms a boundary creates an 'in-between': a 'space between', which does not have the character of a nowhere. Belonging to neither side, this liminal space rather functions as a third element. Like the story that gives it voice, it is the mouthpiece of the limit. Playing a mediating role, it speaks in the name of the in-place law of the place; it establishes boundaries that *were* crossed, limits that *were* transgressed.

As an operation of boundary-setting, every story maps the field of intelligible things, bringing out the conditions of acceptability of a system, but also follows the breaking points which indicate its emergence, exposing cracks.[44] As a narrative operation of boundary-setting, the story 'plays a double game. It does the opposite of what it says. It hands the place over to the foreigner that it gives the impression of throwing out.'[45] By drawing a line that demarcates, the story creates an interface, a surface that forms a common boundary between two identities, but also an opening. It encloses what belongs, but also discloses the existence of an out there: of another place that belongs to an other. It forms a boundary, but also a portal. It presents with an opportunity to inspect what is out there, to explore what is inside the outside, but also with an opportunity for transgression. 'The picket fence is an ensemble of interstices through which one's glances pass.'[46] '[T]he door that closes is precisely what may be opened; the river is what makes passage possible; the tree is what marks the stages of advance.'[47] Through its accounts

---

[38] ibid 123–6.
[39] ibid 122.
[40] ibid 125.
[41] ibid 126.
[42] ibid 127.
[43] ibid.
[44] On cracks, Nofar Sheffi, 'The Art of Government' (2019) 13 *Law and Humanities* 223, 242–6.
[45] de Certeau (n 37) 129.
[46] ibid 128.
[47] ibid.

of appropriations and displacements, de Certeau illustrates, the story '"turns" the frontier into a crossing, and the river into a bridge'.[48]

It is, however, not the out there, the place of the foreigner, that the story sends us to explore. By situating us on the threshold, on the outer limits of the here, before the entrance to the inside of a confronting other, the story 'opens the inside to its other'.[49] It inspires not an escape across the line it draws, but introspection. The bridge, de Certeau observes, 'is ambiguous everywhere: it alternately welds together and opposes insularities. It distinguishes them and threatens them. It liberates from enclosure and destroys autonomy.'[50] 'As a transgression of the limit, a disobedience of the law of the place', the bridge

> represents a departure, an attack on a state, the ambition of a conquering power, or the flight of an exile; in any case, the 'betrayal' of an order. But at the same time as it offers the possibility of a bewildering exteriority, [the bridge] allows or causes the re-emergence beyond the frontiers of the alien element that was controlled in the interior, and gives ob-jectivity (that is, expression and re-presentation) to the alterity which was hidden inside the limits, so that in recrossing the bridge and coming back within the enclosure the traveler henceforth finds there the exteriority that he had first sought by going outside and then fled by returning. Within the frontiers, the alien is already there, an exoticism or sabbath of the memory, a disquieting familiarity.[51]

'Every story is a travel story', but it is not 'there' that it takes us. Stories position us not at the entrance to the there, but before it, on the outer limit of the here. They incite us not to go there, but to turn back. They invite us not to inspect the properties of others, but to reflect on our own. They inspire us not to describe the experience of living there, but to review our *here*.

And it is not only speakers and writers that author travel stories, de Certeau further suggests. It is not only speakers and writers that compose reviews of '(t)heres'. Readers, too, produce stories, albeit silently – travel stories that cannot be read, yet do leave a mark. Indeed, unlike writers, readers do not found places. They do not have dominion over the places articulated by the stories they read. Nor can they make modifications – break a wall, move a fence or open a portal. Readers do not own but possess, and even this only temporarily, short-term. Drifting from one place to another, from text to text, readers are constantly on the move. Their place 'is not *here* or *there*, one or the other, but neither the one nor the other, simultaneously inside and outside'.[52] 'Far from being writers – founders of their own place, heirs of the peasants of earlier ages now working on the soil of language, diggers of wells and builders of houses – readers are travellers; they move across lands belonging to someone else, like nomads poaching their way across fields they did not write, despoiling the wealth of [foreign places] to enjoy it themselves.'[53]

The slippage of the reader's world into the author's place, de Certeau highlights, 'makes the text habitable, like a rented apartment'. It transforms 'another person's property into a space borrowed for a moment by a transient'.[54] Just as renters 'make comparable changes in an apartment they furnish with their acts and memories', 'users of social codes turn them

---

[48] ibid.
[49] ibid 129.
[50] ibid 128.
[51] ibid 128–9.
[52] ibid 174.
[53] ibid.
[54] ibid xxi.

into metaphors and ellipses of their own quests'.[55] Into each visited text, the travelling reader insinuates 'the ruses of pleasure and appropriation: he poaches on it, is transported into it, pluralizes himself in it like the internal rumblings of one's body'.[56] A mode of silent production, de Certeau writes, reading 'introduces an "art" which is anything but passive'.[57]

> Because the body withdraws itself from the text in order henceforth to come into contact with it only through the mobility of the eye, the geographical configuration of the text organizes the activity of the reader less and less. Reading frees itself from the soil that determined it. It detaches itself from that soil. The autonomy of the eye suspends the body's complicities with the text; it unmoors it from the scriptural place; it makes the written text an ob-ject and it increases the reader's possibilities of moving about.[58]

Their 'elevation' transfigures readers into voyeurs. It puts the reader 'at a distance', transforming 'the bewitching world by which one was "possessed" into a text that lies before one's eyes'.[59] Taking neither the position of the author nor an author's position, the reader assumes momentarily, and without being noticed, the author-function. The reader dwells, leaps and slips, visits and revisits, bounces back and forth, drifts away and across, skims through, over and off. Actualizing only a few of the possibilities fixed by the constructed order and opening up new ones, the reader combines fragments to create something un-known. The reader makes use of available materials to assemble collages, to compose travel stories that would remain illegible, to create memories that can be carried, kept, recollected and revisited, cherished but also repressed.

---

[55] ibid.
[56] ibid xxi–xxii.
[57] ibid xxii.
[58] ibid 176.
[59] ibid 92.

19. Death

Bernard Keenan

1. This is a witness statement; as such it must be a personal account or, more simply, a story.
2. It's a particular account of a particular way in which personal stories are produced and communicated in the modern legal system. It's a witness statement about making witness statements.
3. In the legal system, a witness statement is a functional device and a generalizable symbolic form. As such it is a particular medium of communication. It structures its contents as meaningful and performative in a legal register. For instance, a good statement will be formed so that it contains distinct and different issues or points differentiated by clearly numbered paragraphs. That will greatly aid the good conduct of an argument later on (if necessary).
4. The numbers of each paragraph at the side of the page are ostensibly for ease of reference, in that they guide everyone to the same line, and thus the same issue, in case we are called upon to argue about the contents before the judge.
5. The numbers also provide the reader with a sense of flow, of movement through time. They help establish the time of a story.
6. So, for instance, you could expect to see some biographical material here, early in the statement. That might mean writing some facts down, like where I currently live and where I was born and when key events occurred, such as my birth.
7. If this were a statement being made for an asylum case, it may be useful at this point to demonstrate some local knowledge of the area of the city where I lived and went to school. Belfast is a relatively small city with a river and a seaport in the north east of Ireland. In an immigration or asylum case, even basic biographical information might be in dispute, so saying I attended this school on that street until that year, then that school on this street until another year, and so on, adds material that may seem irrelevant to the legal issue, but ultimately helps to make the overall account more convincing.
8. Refugees can find themselves before the law with nothing accepted about their lives, not even their basic identity. Everything they need to say at an appeal is being said because their story's truth is being aggressively contested.
9. That doesn't matter in this statement, of course. My name is undisputed and printed above. This statement isn't going to enter into a legal dispute but an academic collection of papers. Let's be honest, this is not really a statement at all, it's just a simulation of one.
10. Nonetheless, here is a relevant biographical fact: in 2013, I chose to leave legal practice in the field of immigration and asylum law and enter academia; in a sense, the reason was so I could learn to work with different symbolic media.
11. A real witness statement in an immigration or asylum case – a well-crafted one – would follow the biographical material by telling you who my immediate family members are, their occupations, and where they are now to the best of my knowledge. For refugees, it is good to add the identities and current whereabouts of family to the statement, even if it is

irrelevant to the substance of the asylum claim. That's because the statement can become an important piece of evidence later on in an application or appeal around the issue of family reunion, which the government frequently disputes, especially in cases where the family members concerned are undocumented. If an Immigration Judge finds the witness statement credible at the asylum appeal, then everything contained therein, even incidentally, has legal force as the truth. A contested statement in an asylum case can later re-enter the legal system as a verified account of truth. That can save vital time and money later on.

12. The numbers get operationalized in oral argument: One representative or the other would like to draw the Tribunal's attention to paragraphs X_1–X_4 and in particular, paragraph X_2 where it says event A occurred on date B; could the witness please tell the Tribunal exactly what they mean by that, where they were standing, what did they actually see? And so on.

13. In theory, a witness before a court or tribunal is there to give testimony – spoken answers to questions, oral evidence. The oral evidence of the witness goes to the facts of the case, and must be delivered before the judge (or jury in a jury trial) so that the testimony may be judged for its credibility and so the decision-maker can decide how much weight it ought to carry in determining the official answer to the question: what happened?

14. In the law's self-description, a witness statement is a written document that previews and structures such testimony; it serves as a textual supplement to the enactment of the primarily oral scene of a witness giving their evidence before a court. The performance of speech is observed as a performance of truth or of falsehood. No doubt this self-image that is widely distributed in the minds of lawyers and laypeople alike is itself supplemented by the large body of legal drama that has been committed to film and television in the past century.

15. In practice, things are slightly different. The text of the statement is the primary mechanism, while the oral moment of enactment is the supplement to the text. The law is a grammatological practice.

16. In the UK, asylum appeals arise when the Home Office determines that a person who has claimed asylum is not entitled to asylum. The First-Tier Tribunal is the only judicial venue in which a person can challenge the negative immigration decision on the merits of the decision. It is the primary 'fact-finding' forum. The Upper Tier Tribunal can review First-Tier decisions where the Immigration Judge has made a material error of law in structuring their determination, while the Administrative branch of the High Court can judicially review Home Office illegality or unlawful practices and decisions.

17. Only the Immigration Judge who encounters the appellant in the First-Tier Tribunal can pronounce the *facts of the situation*, proven to the lower standard of a 'reasonable degree of likelihood'. The First-Tier Tribunal may direct parties as to how they must provide their evidential submissions.[1]

18. As a lawyer working for appellants, the predominant sense is that unstated government policy is to refuse asylum as frequently as possible. Conversations with trainee Home Office asylum caseworkers and occasional news reports regarding the working culture of

---

[1] Tribunal Procedure Committee, *First Tier Tribunal (Immigration and Asylum Chamber) Rules: Consolidated Version* (2014) Rule 14(e).

the asylum casework teams suggest there is some truth to this.[2] Roughly half of all applicants are refused asylum.[3]

19. Officially, the policy is that the Home Office must give each claim 'anxious scrutiny' to ensure 'protection is granted to those who need it and refused where the claimant does not have a well-founded fear of persecution'.[4] There are two elements: the subjective account of the claimant about who they are and why they are at risk of persecution or harm in their home country, and the objective situation in their home country which means that they cannot avail of protection there.
20. If asylum is refused the refusal decision must be communicated with a written statement of reasons.
21. The simplest reason for refusal is to refuse to accept the refugee's account of events, or at least the non-trivial aspects of their account that relate to a fear of persecution and that have not been objectively documented or independently confirmed. This formal attitude of disbelief is couched in terms of credibility.[5]
22. Occasionally an individual may be found credible in respect of their personal story but be refused asylum for objective reasons, such as the availability of protection from persecution in their country of origin. But where the subjective account of events is potentially determinative of the claim, it is unlikely that a person refused in their application for asylum will be accepted by the Home Office as a credible person unless there is determinative evidence submitted in support of the application.
23. It must be acknowledged that the immigration system is deeply intertwined with a post-colonial racializing logic aiming to exclude people from formerly colonized parts of the world from migration to the former imperial metropole. This is why successive British governments have sought to portray asylum seekers as unexpected arrivals, economic migrants lying and cheating their way to remain, queue-jumpers and illegitimate rivals competing for money, housing and employment directly against the interests and integrity of the British people.[6]
24. But the system excludes consideration of its own colonial history and political signification. If an appellant or representative tried to refer to these things – that is, to suggest that the system itself is embedded in certain racist historical assumptions and exclusions – the point would simply not register. The history of the system is external to the system. These conditions do not count as valid points for legal consideration. If a lawyer were to argue for their inclusion in a case, it would be to risk being read as a protester, not a lawyer, and that in turn would harm both the appellant's case and one's career.
25. The material history of the system is excluded from taking on a meaningful role within its operations. This exclusion is necessary in order to sustain the system, which relies on the imaginary symbolic function of 'justice', which today means following procedural rules and professional norms correctly and considering deviations carefully. The normative

---

[2] Diane Taylor, 'UK Border Agency Investigation Finds Cause for "Significant Concern"' *The Guardian* (London, 8 August 2010).
[3] House of Commons Library, *Asylum Statistics* (2020).
[4] Home Office, *Assessing Credibility and Refugee Status* (2015), sec. 1.2–1.3.
[5] *Assessing Credibility and Refugee Status*, sec. 4.
[6] Nadine El-Enany, *(B)Ordering Britain: Law, Race and Empire* (Manchester University Press, 2020) 144–50.

342 *Research handbook on law and literature*

content of the system is not aligned with the normative history of the society that produced it. Knowing one's way around immigration law is complex enough on its own terms. It is a job for trained professionals.

26. Not everyone appearing before the Tribunal has professional legal representation, but everyone who does greatly increases their chances of success. Legal Aid regulations stipulate that funding for an appeal cannot be awarded unless the funded solicitor assesses that the case has merit, that is, a more than fanciful prospect of success.

27. The factors that must be included for a successful appeal concern evidence related to the subjective position of the appellant before the law and evidence related to objective factors that establish their legal position in relation to an exterior reality. All such material issues in a case are iterative. Every refugee appearing before the law must be produced as a refugee according to the categories encoded by the law. The Immigration Judge must decide if the person fits the category; which means asking, is the way I am presented with this person, this subject who has come before the law claiming the government is wrong to have refused recognition of their claim, credibly commensurate with the description of the category of refugee that they claim to be?

28. The tension between the particular and the universal can of course be viewed as another instance of the fundamental jurisprudential problem of recognizing the unique status of each case while treating like cases alike. Every case is different and the same.

29. According to Alain Supiot, the anthropological function of the law in the western tradition is to give form and stability to a mutable but consistent concept of the subject. What underpins the sameness of modern law's epistemology is the figure of a reasonable, responsible subject who is endowed with freedom and conscience and, therefore, responsibility, and the figure of the state, which transcends individuals in order to guarantee their position as sovereign speaking subjects in the imaginary of the law.[7]

30. The witness statement, in this sense, gives form to the speaking subject. It operates as a medium for communicating the appellant's subjectivity. There are other kinds of evidence that may be presented in an asylum appeal, depending on the circumstances, but a statement is the medium that binds them to a speaking subject recounting events apparently from memory.

31. Other elements depend on the case but can be briefly outlined: documents or reports supporting or verifying the subject's experiences (to be considered weighty these should be verified by an independent expert on that country); independent medical reports on the traces of the subject's physical or mental injuries, particularly where mental trauma reduces their capacity for speaking from memory; and 'objective' reports on the country of origin itself in cases where the question of persecution of people like the appellant is not accepted by the government or, as is the case for some countries, fixed by existing 'Country Guidance' precedent cases.

32. In my experience, individuals who have been through the system without representation (or with ineffective representatives) and whose cases were dismissed, their accounts labelled 'not credible', their trauma ignored or denied, their bodies made vulnerable to refoulement, can still successfully attain refugee status following a fresh claim for asylum

---

[7] Alain Supiot, *Homo Juridicus: On the Anthropological Function of the Law* (Verso, 2007) 21–40; W.T. Murphy, *The Oldest Social Science? Configurations of Law and Modernity* (Clarendon Press, 1997) 11.

– provided work is done to give solidity to their case that was previously lacking. Nothing changes in them, or their account, other than its media infrastructure.
33. All of this is to say that a good statement and supplementary pieces of evidence (where appropriate) forms a body of media – text, generated on computers in a formal, regularized template – that narrativizes a refugee subject in the eyes of a particular reader, the Immigration Judge, and does so in a manner that renders possible what was previously impossible. Through the medium of the statement (the most crucial item) the subject is transformed in the eyes of the law. The fixity of the form allows much greater fluidity in juridical sensing.[8]
34. The particular judge assigned the appeal may be hostile or they may be sympathetic. They may harbour racist assumptions about the appellant, or about refugees in general. They may have become numb over time to hearing accounts of trauma. On the other hand, they may have been lawyers ethically committed to appellant work. They may be willing to grant adjournments, to listen sympathetically, to make the best of difficult situations, and to do justice to those who come before them. At both extremes, they develop reputations.
35. Working on a statement with a client in the liminal time between lodging an appeal and it being heard, the lawyer cannot know who will read it. The reader is simply someone who will have to read it with 'anxious scrutiny'.[9]
36. What kind of writing is drafting a witness statement on behalf of a client? It can perhaps be thought of as a mode of ghost-writing: a singular first-person speaking subject emerges from a collaborative dialogue with the writer in the name of the interlocutor. A classical parallel is found in the logographers, the Athenian speech-writers who helped litigants before the law, and the word also applied to Herodotus and his predecessors who, as 'tellers of tales', claimed to record faithful and accurate records of history and myth, as distinct from poetic accounts.[10]
37. The lawyer asks questions of their client, where necessary via an interpreter, and composes the answers in a form that narrativizes the claim: in systematic terms, the skill is in re-encoding the conversation into the monological form of the statement. This means filtering and selecting what is included and what is excluded according to the criteria set by the legal system's programmes of recognition. This is in turn iterative, because the appellant is already on record in their asylum claim, primarily via the contemporaneous written record of their asylum interview. While the interview record is a transcript of a spontaneous, live interview, the statement is constructed and considered in advance of its operationalization. Writing the latter against the former, what differences will make a difference?
38. There is a short but important ethical rule that conditions the whole process: one must never 'coach' a witness (that is, tell them what to say).[11] But one can certainly explain what

---

[8] A point apprehended in advance by Murphy, *The Oldest Social Science?* 76.
[9] The authority is *R v Secretary of State for the Home Department, Ex p Bugdaycay* [1987] AC 514, 531 F–G.
[10] See 'Logographers', *The Oxford Dictionary of the Classical World* (ed. J. Roberts, OUP, 2007). I am grateful to Peter Goodrich for this observation.
[11] Solicitors Regulation Authority, *Code of Conduct for Solicitors* (2019) sec. 2.2: 'You do not seek to influence the substance of evidence, including generating false evidence or persuading witnesses to change their evidence.' www.sra.org.uk/solicitors/standards-regulations/code-conduct-solicitors/ accessed 6 February 2021; Bar Standards Board, *The BSB Handbook*, Rule C9.4: 'you must not rehearse,

the tribunal will likely regard as significant or problematic, and ask many questions about those issues.
39. Everything written must be read back to the witness. They must agree that it is true, and they must add a signature to a declaration of truth. Where they have assisted, the interpreter must co-sign to confirm that they read it back to the witness accurately. This way the text produced by the lawyer is formally coupled to the speaking sovereign subject who knows and remembers via the mark of the signature.
40. But this schematic description of the job misses an important dimension: the affective potential of writing in the voice of another. It is, I think, in this dimension that the 'style' of the individual lawyer matters. How will the text describe events, situations, places? What memories can be elicited from the client that are ancillary to the events recounted but enhance their description? What emotions might such a statement stir? What relay of affect, or indeed what counter-transference, is possible across a circuit of paper that flows between the client, the lawyers and the judge? The task is not simply to say what happened but to give the sense that the witness speaks the truth – and here one again can find a classical parallel in the task and techniques of logography.
41. The inclusion of incidental details can make a memory read like a memory, rather than a flattened account of a series of events reducible to a chronological news report.
42. To my own statement: I remember sitting for long hours with clients in basement interview rooms under harsh strip lights in an office in Tottenham. There was the smell of stale coffee; I often had a dull headache from the stress of work. It was emotionally draining, and often difficult. We typed text directly into a pre-formatted document, like this one I am typing now.
43. Particularly when working with interpreters, it was important to explore things from different angles, to ensure your narrative was commensurate with what was said. The risk of misunderstanding and misrepresenting was constant, and the consequences could be severe: if a client were asked before the tribunal about something in the statement and replied with 'I did not say that', the effect could be fatal, so all facts and dates and sequences had to be checked and re-checked. Everyone had too many cases at once. Days could be very long.
44. Rarely was one session with a client enough for the statement. Some statements would go on for hundreds of paragraphs and take days just to read back. Some were only two, three or four pages, double-spaced. That was rarer but it all depended on the situation and the style of the lawyer. Strategically, everyone needed to think about how it fits, how it will work. Can the client really answer to all of this if challenged? For some clients, less is often more, or at least, less is less risky.
45. Around these kinds of practice-based decisions, a strange mode of interviewing expertise arises in which one learns what to ask, what to select, what not to forget and what to ignore.
46. Working with counsel, closer to the day of the appeal, things are reviewed again. Changes can be made to the statement in line with what the barrister thinks. They'll be the one using this device, making it seem like a mere supplement to the parole given on the day.[12]

---

practise with or coach a witness in respect of their evidence...' www.barstandardsboard.org.uk/the-bsb-handbook.html accessed 6 February 2021.

[12] On case conferences, see Bernard Keenan and Alain Pottage, 'Ethics in Rehearsal' (2017) *Journal of the Royal Anthropological Institute* 23 1, 153.

47. In this work of plumbing through peoples' lives in retrospect, the lawyer almost resembles a psychoanalyst. Both are interested in eliciting traumatic memories. But where analysis (sometimes) aims for re-integration of the subject's split or disavowed aspects of the self and the easing of pain, the lawyer aims only at producing a convincing coherent legal subject – the materiality of the refugee as a legal subject – according to the codes and programmes of a system that is institutionally racist, operationally truculent and deliberately hostile. Symbolically at least, law claims to be disinterested in affect, yet Immigration Judges will occasionally refer to it in attacking the credibility of a witness – 'he did not strike me as a traumatised man'. This is not therapy but its obverse, an unsubtle and potentially re-traumatizing ordeal.
48. And yet, as in psychoanalysis, these meetings and conversations give rise to ethical moments, in which lawyers experience themselves as ethical actors. It is perhaps the crux of ethical lawyering on the legal, systematized, over-determined, rights-inflected border.
49. The identity of the speaker is existentially separate from this process of producing a legal identity. And yet, exclusion from identity by the law means exclusion from formal recognition by the institutions of state that underwrite and guarantee all legal rights. It is the condition of inclusion in general. One state must decide but it is only that state which can decide, under third country arrangements. Refugee law is determined locally but allows access and integration to institutions and systems that operate globally in world society.[13]
50. To this extent, one does not know in advance of completing a statement and submitting it to the appeal process who will have spoken through it. Its truth can only be determined retrospectively.
51. There is another parallel to be drawn between this practice and the production of 'slave narratives', or fugitive testimonies.
52. In the eighteenth and nineteenth centuries, people of African descent who had escaped from slavery in the Americas were interrogated before white tribunals in order to satisfy them of the truth of their accounts. If accepted, a written statement was produced and published, recording their accounts and serving to verify them as speaking subjects who were capable of and deserving of citizenship, freedom and recognition as persons.[14]
53. Such published accounts were always accompanied by statements confirming their veracity and explaining that they had been recorded and edited before printing. As Rachel Banner puts it, the 'paratextual material—prefaces, introductions, and codas—that "framed" a slave narrative most often functioned as an authoritative white verification of a black author's intellectual abilities and good moral character'.[15]

---

[13] Niklas Luhmann, 'Globalization or World Society: How to Conceive of Modern Society?' (1997) *International Review of Sociology* 7 1, 67.

[14] For instance, Mary Prince, *The History of Mary Prince, a West Indian Slave, Related by Herself* (F. Westley and A.H. Davis, 1831) https://gutenberg.org/files/17851/17851-h/17851-h.htm accessed 6 February 2021; Henry Brown Box, *Narrative of the Life of Henry Box Brown, Written by Himself* (Lee and Glynn, 1851) https://docsouth.unc.edu/neh/brownbox/brownbox.htm accessed 6 February 2021; William Craft and Ellen Craft, *Runing a Thousand Miles for Freedom or, The Escape of William and Ellen Craft from Slavery* (William Tweedie, 1860) www.lehigh.edu/~dek7/SSAWW/writCraft.htm accessed 6 February 2021.

[15] I owe this observation to Patricia Malone. Rachel Banner, 'Surface and Stasis: Re-Reading Slave Narrative via The History of Mary Prince' (2018) *Callaloo* 36 2, 298.

346 *Research handbook on law and literature*

54. The fugitive accounts were framed and printed through the efforts of abolition activists. They aimed to use these accounts to convince the public to support the prohibition of slavery. But they were accounts of escape and migration: statements by individuals seeking safety and recognition of full and dignified personhood in the heart of the imperial colonial system that had created the conditions for their enslavement.
55. If the analogy holds, it is the lawyer who stands in for the framers of slave narratives – the one who works to elicit an oral account that they then express in writing, vouching with the authority of their professional standing that the text is indeed 'true to life'.
56. Rather than the public, the audience is, rightfully, limited to the tribunal, although ordinarily, members of the public are free to observe hearings before the tribunal.
57. In her analysis of how to read such narratives, Banner discusses the example of Thomas Pringle, who framed and promoted *The History of Mary Prince* in 1831.[16] The framing operates in a manner that 'competes for control of the short thirty-eight-page narrative by way of an introduction, lengthy footnotes, a thirty-page concluding supplement that provides documents from the various legal cases surrounding Prince's freedom and enslavement, a letter written by Pringle's wife certifying her examination of Mary's naked body (to verify the existence of her scars), and a short narrative about another fugitive slave, Louis Asa-Asa, whose story is unrelated to Mary Prince's'.[17]
58. In the 1990s, critical scholarship focused on the racial hierarchies embedded in the production of the fugitive accounts. This was a corrective to the uncomplicated way in which they were intended to be received and understood by nineteenth-century audiences: as straightforward truthful testimonies. In fact, the slave narratives were irreducibly structured by the need to serve an adversarial, persuasive function. They were conceived, written, edited, formatted and published with a hostile interlocutor in mind; the reader who doubted that the slave had the intellectual capacity to speak for themselves. This was the person to be convinced. The framers' ultimate aim was to give the appearance of authenticity to the speaking subject assumed to be behind the text.
59. That scholarly criticism in turn engendered a wave of critical readings aiming at recuperating something of the authentic presence of the slave from the machinery of the account, motivated by the desire to materialize the intangible presence that resides therein, as if the 'real' voice could be recovered.[18]
60. Banner suggests that this is an impossible task. How can a literary scholar in the twenty-first century hope to uncover the true voice of the nineteenth-century fugitive behind a structured, edited statement?[19]
61. By the same token, how can the immigration lawyer claim to know the experiences of their client, even having met them face to face? Some lawyers do, of course, take on a caring role beyond the formal requirements of their job, forming friendships that last beyond the time of the case. But the job is emotionally taxing. The relentless systemic cynicism of the Home Office engenders a desire for some distance from the work. As I have noted

---

[16] Prince, *History of Mary Prince*.
[17] Banner, 'Surface and Stasis', 298–9.
[18] Banner, 300.
[19] Banner, 301.

elsewhere, immigration lawyers tend towards either irony or martyrdom,[20] and sometimes both in the same day.

62. One need not believe that it is really a just system to work in it, one merely needs to act *as if* one does, while following the procedural and ethical rules of the profession.

63. I agree with Banner when she argues that slave narratives cannot yield up an authentic voice but must be read as always already reflexively performative and opaque. They tell the truth of the situation – the violence of the slave trade and the lives of enslaved people – but they are also already engaged in a performative game of signification. Accounts were necessarily delivered in the knowledge that they were for a hostile and racist audience. Banner:

64. 'A consideration of slave narrative as an opaque, performative, literary genre can refocus criticism on what we actually have to work with. In a negative sense, the text is all or the only thing that we critics have. Yet, in a positive sense, the text of the slave narrative is a rich performance of the negotiations, collaborations, usurpations, and performed mysteries of form.'[21]

65. This is, I believe, how to understand witness statements. The ironic position – that there is nothing outside the text, that it is all surface – ultimately serves as a disavowal, and this is no doubt a tempting response when confronted with the traumatic violence that prefigures and conditions the entire operation.

66. On the other hand, to insist there is a real presence *there*, whose voice can be recuperated and judged from behind the text, is to repeat and reify the epistemic violence that the legal system, particularly the fragmented procedural forum of justice carried on in the immigration tribunal system, does to those before it.

67. But we must also remember the differences, not least the differences in what happened to published accounts of former slaves and what happens to witness statements in the asylum system. What happens to them?

68. For solicitors, who build files for their clients, documents are bound by rules and obligations to the client and, at the same time, serve as proof of work. Solicitors must keep copies of all such documents on file and store them securely for a fixed retention period, then they must destroy them.

69. Barristers return case papers to their instructing solicitor once the case has been completed. Often this happens at the same time that they record their bill. (You can get a sense of how fastidious a barrister is from the speed with which the papers arrive back).

70. The Immigration Tribunal's primary legal obligation is to ensure that they do not retain personal data that is not necessary for their functions. As appeals are generally litigated once then closed, the Tribunal would not retain case documents for long.

71. The Home Office, however, retains records on all migrants arriving in Britain. This is set at 25 years after a decision to grant settlement or naturalisation (the path for most asylum cases) and 15 years in other cases (non-permanent visas, for instance).[22] Today, British citizenship granted by naturalization is revokable. The material may be required for intelligence purposes in future. For those refused, a similar security logic applies.

---

[20] Keenan and Pottage, 'Ethics in Rehearsal'.
[21] Banner, 'Surface and Stasis', 303.
[22] UK Visas and Immigration, *Borders, Immigration and Citizenship: Privacy Information Notice* (2020).

72. Finally, there are the personal archives people keep of the documents they receive from government, lawyers and courts. No doubt many do not retain papers that can only remind them of a painful and uncertain time, but I know that many do keep them long after their case has finished, storing documents in folders, or piled up in plastic bags, just in case they might somehow be needed again.
73. How would this material be recuperated, if it ever could be? Saidiya Hartman writes that 'every historian of the multitude, the dispossessed, the subaltern, and the enslaved is forced to grapple with the power and authority of the archive and the limits it sets on what can be known, whose perspective matters, and who is endowed with the gravity and restless character of life in the city'.[23]
74. In *Wayward Lives* she 'elaborates, augments, transposes, and breaks open archival documents so they might yield a richer picture of the social upheaval that transformed black social life in the twentieth century'.[24] The book is assembled from case files, sociological surveys, trial transcripts, slum photographs, psychiatric interviews, prison case files and so on, creating a counter-narrative that reassembles a story of black lives, queer lives and their radical transformative thought from the institutions of surveillance, punishment and confinement that excluded them from the official record. In this way she navigates the line between the limits of the text, their functionalism and their silence, to do a form of justice to her recuperated subjects and their worlds.
75. I don't suggest that an archive of asylum appeal statements – if such an archive could ever be assembled – could do the same. But it is an archive of the unseen and excluded accounts of events that shape our time: stories of families separated, culture as contested, love as danger, sexuality and difference, political activism and disappointment, catastrophe, war, arrest, torture, famine, global migration, exploitation and the horror of modern refugee camps.
76. Perhaps a similar period must pass to gain distance from the lives and dignity of the individuals whose stories are recorded there – in the case of *Wayward Lives*, the author writes with the distance of a century.
77. If there is a conclusion for law, perhaps it is simply to note that for all its formalism, oppression, occlusions and violence, and even where these are at their most extreme, it remains a narrative practice.
78. A statement tells a story and in this way inserts a period of time within the time of the trial that is not subject to the rules of the trial. In a sense, this is the minimum content of the right to claim asylum: a chance to tell one's story. The ethical duty of the lawyer as logographer is to write it well, to do the research needed to ask informed questions, to give shape and depth to a timeline and to take the time to listen carefully so that an account of a life can be given. In so doing they write in the face of uncertainty and the possibility of failure. Statements are, after all, submissions made to a killing machine.
79. John Berger suggests that what separates writers from the characters they write about is not their superior knowledge but their different experiences of time. Storytellers stand outside the time of the story and can see the whole from start to finish. They know what counts and what the story means. The characters only live within the time of the story. It encases their

---

[23] Saidiya Hartman, *Wayward Lives, Beautiful Experiments: Intimate Histories of Social Upheaval* (W.W. Norton & Company, 2019) 7.

[24] Hartman, 8.

world as the universe does to us. The time of the story belongs to them. Berger reminds us that there is continuous traffic between metaphysics and storytelling. Every life is lived as a story being told and the manner of telling can thus determine all.
80. Berger writes: 'Those who read or listen to our stories see everything as though through a lens. This lens is the secret of narration, and it is ground anew in every story, ground between the temporal and the timeless. If we storytellers are Death's Secretaries, we are so because, in our brief mortal lives, we are grinders of these lenses.'[25]

I believe that the contents of this statement are true.
7 February 2021

---

[25] John Berger, *And Our Faces, My Heart, Brief as Photos* (Bloomsbury, 2005) 50.

PART VI

NARRATIONS

Blocks and Chains – White Paper – 0x89205a3a3b2a69de6dbf7f01ed13b2108b2c43e7 – Encrypted Indigeneity – Firma (Signature) – Field(s)work – Rabbit Theory – Disruption – Memo – De-Binarizing – Affective Unreliability – Transing Law

20. Blocks
Andrea Leiter

INTRODUCTION

The claim that blockchain will disrupt life as we know it has been voiced in almost every corner of the world, with few topics left untouched. But how can we engage with such a claim? How can we try to understand the kinds of changes that are being fostered by this technology? The idea behind this chapter is to try and sketch out ways of reading blockchain technology as narrative technology. Rather than inquiring into the stories about blockchain technology, I focus on the narrative capacity of the technology itself, treating the technology as a mode for mediating how we interact in and understand our social, economic and institutional engagements. I conceptualize the architecture of the technology as a site of politics, where normativity is constituted through the demands of representation as the narrative form of the technology. Rather than providing a final judgement on the potential and threats of the technology, the contribution aims at developing a vocabulary that foregrounds the ordering capacity of blockchain technology and inquires into the ways in which it mediates lives.

NARRATION AS WORLD-MAKING

Declaring a new beginning is like putting down a marker and demanding that the interpretation of everything revolves around this marker. One field that has put down such a marker is blockchain technology. Its advent was accompanied by a claim to disruption of the status quo in almost all areas of life: nothing less than the disruption of the economic structure, the disruption of the monetary structure and the disruption of established structures of governance. The notion of disruption demands a cut – a breaking of tissue and a reconfiguration of the past toward the current moment with a view to the future. One way of engaging with such a claim would be to trace its history and reassemble the genealogy of its pieces in order to locate and situate its claims.[1]

Yet, rather than historicising the claim to disruption, I work with the concept of narrative and its relationship to ordering the world.[2] It is especially the agency of the narrative, its ability to en*act* a world, and its capacity to take up 'the risks and joys of composing a […] cosmopolitics'[3] that I explore. I rely on Said's characterisation of the Western novel as the particular genre that narrates with an intention for creation, an intention for changing, for making, 'for

---

[1] Adrian Daub offers a comprehensive account of the notion of disruption in the tech space, tracing it through economic history and drawing out its libertarian flavour. See: Adrian Daub, *What Tech Calls Thinking: An Inquiry into the Intellectual Bedrock of Silicon Valley* (FSG Originals x Logic 2020).
[2] Donna J Haraway, *Staying with the Trouble: Making Kin in the Chthulucene* (Duke University Press 2016).
[3] Ibid 15.

a kind of appetite that writers develop for modifying reality'.[4] Such modification relies on the invocation of something new, something with the ability to alter the status quo. Newness in this sense is then understood to stand neither in contradistinction to everything else, nor as a placeholder for something not yet recognised. Much rather, newness here is to be understood as the inauguration of a world-making process through narration. World-making takes place through assembling various modes of representation (not representations) that cut the concepts with which we live in the world and through which we know it.[5] In such an account, narration points me to the close relationship between author(ship), author(ity) and world-making.[6]

With a view on authorship, I try to situate the stories about the blockchain space in the context of their emergence. Who is claiming what and from where? These questions have a firm place in the repertoire of critical inquiries, as they enable us to draw out implicit assumptions, biases and interests of the authors that are not made explicit or visible in a narrative. With a view on authority, I engage with the enactment of the narrative, with its ability to implement modes of engagement that mediate life. Finally, with a view on world-making, I try to follow the politics of exclusion. Narrating the world means authoring it by including certain things in the story and leaving others out, highlighting some aspects and backgrounding others. Or, to speak again with Haraway, it is about 'both absence and presence, killing and nurturing, living and dying – and remembering who lives and who dies and how in the string figures of naturalcultural history'.[7] Thus, it is by means of narrative and storytelling that I want to approach the claim to disruption in the blockchain space. But rather than only assembling stories about the technology, I will inquire into blockchain's own narrative technique, its own mode of storytelling. By focusing on blockchain as an overarching technology of narration, I try to grasp how our social, economic and institutional interactions are and will be mediated by this technology.[8]

The first part of the contribution relates the question of authorship to the White Papers of the two most prominent blockchains, the Bitcoin and the Ethereum blockchain. The White Papers are the closest we can get to actual authorship that expresses the visions, ambitions and ideologies of the projects. Through the distributed nature of the network, authorship in the operation of the network is decentralised and supposedly lies with all participants who engage in the network. The second part draws out the limitations of the non-authored network phantasies by tying them to the mechanical architecture of the blockchain. Authority is exerted by the enactment of the forms of engagement that are enabled on the blockchain in the form of smart contracts. As a Turing-complete system, the Ethereum blockchain claims to enable

---

[4] Edward W Said, *Beginnings: Intention and Method* (Granta Books 1997) 81.
[5] Donna J Haraway, *Staying with the Trouble: Making Kin in the Chthulucene* (Duke University Press 2016). The notion of 'cut' is inspired by a 'matterphorical' understanding. See: Daniela Gandorfer, *Matterphorics: Of the Laws of Theory* (Duke University Press 2022).
[6] Shaunnagh Dorsett and Shaun McVeigh, *Jurisdiction* (Routledge 2012) 32.
[7] Donna J Haraway, *Staying with the Trouble: Making Kin in the Chthulucene* (Duke University Press 2016) 28.
[8] Others have taken up a similar idea of thinking of blockchain through narrative; see: Wessel Reijers and Mark Coeckelbergh, 'The Blockchain as a Narrative Technology: Investigating the Social Ontology and Normative Configurations of Cryptocurrencies' (2018) 31 Philosophy & Technology 103–30; Lyazid Sabri and Abdelhak Boubetra, 'Narrative Knowledge Representation and Blockchain: A Symbiotic Relationship' (2020) Scinapse paper; Deborah Maxwell, Chris Speed and Larissa Pschetz, 'Story Blocks: Reimagining Narrative through the Blockchain' (2017) 23 Convergence 79–97.

universal representation and the replacement of authority with consensus. Yet, as the final section of the chapter shows, the forms that are consensually executed have already made their representational cuts and thus constitute an important site of the politics of blockchain.[9] Any worldly interaction has to pass through the filter of the smart contract, through the demands of representation of the technology. It is here that I can identify exclusion and ordering. The possible worlds that can emerge through blockchain technology, I hope to show, are shaped and bounded by its particular narrative capacity.

BLOCK 1: AUTHORSHIP – WHITE PAPERS FOR ASSEMBLING THE STORIES

A White Paper has come to be the foundational document in the space of technological innovation and almost every blockchain project is accompanied by one. The release of the Bitcoin blockchain was not through a mechanical first transaction, but through the posting of the White Paper in a mailing list.[10] The second famous blockchain project, the Ethereum blockchain, was also first described in a White Paper authored by Vitalik Buterin in 2013.[11] Since then, the White Paper has usually been the most important document in attracting funding for a new project. Studying White Papers allows me to ground and situate the projects with an eye on who authored them and in which context. There is a rich history tying the contemporary blockchain iterations to the political movements of cypherpunks and anti-authoritarian activists in the 1980s and 1990s.[12] Yet, for this contribution, the focus is not on developing a genealogical lineage of travelling concepts and people. The ambition is much more modest. A small glimpse at the genre of the White Paper and a recounting of the commonly told origin stories of the technology will provide the anecdotal context for the projects.

That blockchain projects are released in the form of a White Paper, in and of itself, gives some indication of their governance and world-making aspirations. However, despite the ubiquitous appearance of White Papers in the past decade, not much has been written on the genre of White Papers.[13] They are often said to have emerged in the British parliament and are traced to the so-called Churchill White Paper of June 1922, officially the 'Palestine-Correspondence with the Palestine Arab Delegation and the Zionist Organisation', confirming Britain's commitment to the Balfour Declaration.[14] Until today documents that include the draft text of a bill or other not yet formalised proposals in British parliament are called White Papers. In the 1980s the term White Paper transitioned into the corporate world, where it is a promotional

---

[9] Sheila Jasanoff, 'Technology as a Site and Object of Politics' in Robert E. Goodin and Charles Tilly (eds), *The Oxford Handbook of Contextual Political Analysis* (Oxford University Press 2006).
[10] Satoshi Nakamoto, Jaya Klara Brekke and Bridle James, *The White Paper* (Ignota Books 2019) 66.
[11] Vitalik Buterin, *Ethereum White Paper* (2013) https://ethereum.org/en/whitepaper accessed 27 February 2021.
[12] Jaya Klara Brekke, 'Disassembling the Trust Machine: Three Cuts on the Political Matter of Blockchain', Dissertation Durham University, chapter 5.
[13] Edward A. Malone and David Wright, '"To Promote That Demand": Toward a History of the Marketing White Paper as a Genre' (2017) 32 Journal of Business and Technical Communication 113–47; Michael A Stelzner, *Writing White Papers: How to Capture Readers and Keep Them Engaged* (WhitePaperSource Publishing 2007).
[14] Winston Churchill, British White Paper of June 1922 on Palestine (UK June 1922).

document released to create interest in and increase sales of a new product.[15] The few publications available on the study of White Papers as a genre lament that there is no answer to the question of the purpose of the White Paper and no basis for proper classification.[16] Without delving into genre theory, it appears telling that a governmental document has found its way into business marketing and now lives on as a creature of both worlds. From the perspective of increased managerialism in administration, this double heritage appears familiar.[17] In the case of the most important White Papers in the Blockchain space, this twofold quality is telling with regard to the scope of the projects. As mentioned above, the areas that will supposedly be disrupted by the technology are no less than the fundamental sites of governance of society: money, the economy and social institutions.

The Bitcoin blockchain is often said to have its origin in the release of the document 'Bitcoin: A Peer-to-Peer Electronic Cash System' to the Cryptography Mailing List, the so-called Bitcoin Whitepaper.[18] The release of the White Paper was accompanied by a number of symbolically laden gestures that foregrounded its vision. First, the paper was released on 31 October 2008, the first Halloween after the financial crisis. It proclaimed the substitution of established financial institutions with a system of decentralised trust that resides in the design of the system and not in the people operating it.[19] The suggestion of erasing the human from the transactional sphere is central to the whole blockchain undertaking. The necessity of such a system is presented as a reaction to the failures in the financial sector, especially those of big banks and investment firms, which is tied to the unreliability, messiness and irrationality of human actions. In this account, the problem is located in the inconsistencies of human behaviour, especially in governance structures and institutions more broadly. It also carries a tone of an ongoing abuse of power of the powerful elites inhabiting these institutions against the upstanding good citizens who become victims to this abuse. The human-less-ness of the proposed system is further aided by yet another symbolic gesture. The paper was released under the name of Satoshi Nakamoto, an unknown individual or collective, the subject of numerous theories and legends.[20] Taken at face value, the White Paper was released by no one and from nowhere.[21] The additional difficulty this creates for historically and sociologically locating the author(s) anticipates many of the qualities of the blockchain world.

The absence of known authorship is reflected in the proposed architecture and closely linked to a concern over privacy in electronic transactions. The Bitcoin Whitepaper states: 'What is needed is an electronic payment system based on cryptographic proof instead of

---

[15] Malone and Wright, '"To Promote That Demand": Toward a History of the Marketing White Paper as a Genre' (2017) 32 Journal of Business and Technical Communication 113–47, 114.
[16] Jefrey Naidoo and Kim Campbell, 'A Genre Analysis of High-Tech Marketing White Papers: A Report of Research-in-Progress' (2015) 2015 IEEE International Professional Communication Conference 1.
[17] Fleur Johns, 'From Planning to Prototypes: New Ways of Seeing Like a State' (2019) 82 The Modern Law Review 833–63.
[18] Satoshi Nakamoto, *Bitcoin: A Peer-to-Peer Electronic Cash System* (2008) bitcoin.org accessed 27 February 2021.
[19] Kevin Werbach, *The Blockchain and the New Architecture of Trust* (MIT Press 2018).
[20] Satoshi Nakamoto also holds the private key to a wallet that contains approximately 5 per cent of all Bitcoins, currently being estimated to amount to a value of 30 billion USD (as of 27 Feb 2021).
[21] This resembles the 'disembodied scientific objectivity' discussed by Donna Haraway, 'Situated Knowledge: The Scientific Question in Feminism and the Privilege of Partial Perspective' (1988) 14 Information & Communications Technology Law 3, 575–99, 576.

trust, allowing any two willing parties to transact directly with each other without the need for a trusted third-party.'[22] Thus the mechanism of 'peer-to-peer' electronic cash without the involvement of a third party is the centrepiece of the technology. First, no third party controls the transaction; no one except for the sender and the recipient is involved. Second, the envisioned transaction is digital, so that no physical medium of exchange, such as a paper bill or a coin, is being exchanged. The problems that arise in this peer-to-peer digital context are the following: How can both the sender and the recipient know that the value was actually transmitted; that the sender had paid and that the recipient had received the payment; and that the sender had not sent this same transaction to multiple other recipients? This has come to be known as the double-spending problem. This problem has previously been solved by a central registry keeping a ledger of transactions, typically a bank. This central registry, however, is precisely the unreliable human institution to be eliminated from the design of this new electronic cash in order to protect privacy.

Anonymity as a value of the system and factual in-transparency about current financial beneficiaries are key characteristics of the technology. This anonymity is coupled with a claim to absolute transparency, which holds with the rejection of human interaction in favour of code. It seeks an absolute flawless formalism that becomes equated with a claim to objectivity and, following that logic, truth. At a blockchain conference in 2018, I picked up a small piece of paper from a coffee table. In black typeface on white paper, it read:

PW: More Truth

The self-ascribed radical proposition of developers in the blockchain space is to create a future of more truth through formalised processes that are 'codified' into the public ledger and thus transparently accessible to everyone.[23] The envisioned architecture of the technology is well expressed in the Ethereum White Paper, where the Ethereum blockchain is described as:

> a blockchain with a built-in fully fledged Turing-complete programming language that can be used to create 'contracts' that can encode arbitrary state transition functions, allowing users to create any of the systems described above, as well as many others that we have not yet imagined, simply by writing up the logic in a few lines of code.[24]

In addition to replacing authorship with a distributed network, the vision of blockchain technology expressed by Buterin is characterised by (i) Turing-complete programming language; (ii) 'contracts' to encode state transition functions; (iii) that can create any system yet to be imagined; (iv) as a logic to be expressed in written code. The references to universality, markets and the perfect logical formalism are all features that come to legitimise the authority of the material implementation of blockchains.

---

[22] Satoshi Nakamoto, *Bitcoin: A Peer-to-Peer Electronic Cash System* (2008) bitcoin.org accessed 27 February 2021.
[23] Michael J Casey and Paul Vigna, The Truth Machine: The Blockchain and the Future of Everything (St. Martin's Press 2018).
[24] Vitalik Buterin, *Ethereum White Paper* (2013) https://ethereum.org/en/whitepaper accessed 27 February 2021.

BLOCK 2: AUTHORITY – EXECUTING THE LEDGER

Authority in the blockchain is mainly understood to stem from the functioning of the smart contracts, the pieces of code that run on the distributed network and are permanently synchronised into a state. The smart contract is a technique of decentralised, automated computing. Anyone can engage in a transaction in the network, and it will be executed on all nodes that comprise it. There is no single institution that enforces transactions, but rather an architecture of computing and cryptography that enacts them. Authorship and authority are then considered to be distributed and decentralised and legitimised through the permanent synchronisation of the ledger, also called consensus building. To understand this relationship between authorship, consensus and authority in blockchain technology, I will lay out the mode of assembling the chain.

The blockchain is a ledger kept by everyone, meaning each computer or network of computers constituting a node, participating in the system that keeps a record of all transactions. A number of transactions are gathered into a block and the block is then added to the previous block, creating a chain of blocks, a blockchain, or, as one author put it, 'simply a list of things that happened'.[25] This ledger is publicly accessible to anyone and keeps a record of all transactions ever executed on the blockchain. The computers in the network commit their computing power, or share of tokens,[26] to upholding and permanently synchronising this ledger. For this 'work' they are rewarded through shares of the transaction fees as well as by a so-called block reward, issued automatically when a new block is created. The block reward is rendered through a token pertaining to the blockchain. On the Bitcoin blockchain the native tokens are Bitcoins; in Ethereum they are called Ether.

Bitcoin and Ethereum are only two particular blockchains, but many of their features are characteristic of the technology at large. Successor projects have changed mechanism and functionalities, but most have not departed from the idea of a distributed ledger incentivised by monetary rewards in the form of native tokens issued in the process of compiling the blocks for the blockchain. The Bitcoin blockchain is concerned with transaction of funds, or, as the White Paper says, with an Electronic Cash System. Thus, it specifically targets the digital transfer of funds. The Ethereum blockchain expands this focus by including digital assets to represent ownership rights and non-fungible assets, and most importantly by enabling so-called smart contracts, pieces of code that themselves control digital assets.[27] Smart contracts in Ethereum capture anything that is represented in a form legible by a computer.

---

[25] James Bridle, 'Introduction' in Jaya Klara Brekke (ed), *The White Paper by Satoshi Nakamoto with a Guide by Jaya Klara Brekke* (Ignota 2019) xiii.

[26] The Bitcoin blockchain operates with a so-called proof of work mechanism that is dependent on the commitment of large amounts of computing power, bringing the electricity consumption of the Bitcoin blockchain to overtake that of a country like Argentina. Cristina Criddle, 'Bitcoin Consumes "More Electricity Than Argentina"' BBC News Technology www.bbc.com/news/technology-56012952 accessed 27 February 2021. Newer blockchains are working with a 'proof of stake' mechanism that relies on the staking of funds for securing the network. Henning Diedrich, *Ethereum* (Wildfire Publishing 2016) 152.

[27] Vitalik Buterin, *Ethereum White Paper* (2013) https://ethereum.org/en/whitepaper accessed 27 February 2021.

The ordering characteristics of blockchains become easier to grasp when we look at a snapshot of a state of a blockchain, in this case the Ethereum blockchain. It is publicly accessible on the website etherscan.io.[28] What you see below is a screenshot of Etherscan on 8 October 2020.

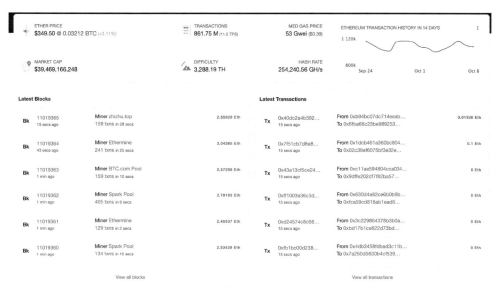

The top part indicates the current price of one Ether, the total market capitalisation of the cryptocurrency, the medium transaction fee (here called gas) and the so-called hash rate, indicating the computer power dedicated to the network and thereby serving as an indirect indicator for the security of the chain. In the lower part you see the indications for the latest blocks and latest transactions. Regarding the blocks, the first number in the first column identifies the block in a sequence of blocks with its unique number; the second column identifies the miner, the number of transactions included into the block and the time it took to compose and inscribe it. The last number indicates the amount for the block reward. In the adjacent column, called transactions, the first column indicates the transaction hash, uniquely identifying the transaction, and the second column shows the sender and recipient of the transaction by identification of the wallet address. The amount of Ether transacted is shown in the last column.

This image shows part of the representation of the ledger, called the distributed ledger, because it is simultaneously held on all nodes in the network. You could expand this view by clicking 'view all blocks' or 'view all transactions' and thereby go back to the first block in the chain, the so-called genesis block. This record would then show you every transaction ever executed on the particular blockchain you are viewing. To maintain this record of transactions the ledger is permanently synchronised along all nodes of the network.

The synchronisation is also called consensus building, in the sense that it is a consensus of all participating nodes on the state of all the enacted transactions. It is here, in the consensus mechanism, that we find the nexus between authorship and authority. Contentious questions

---

[28] Such a scan exists for any of the major blockchain projects.

that require decision-making are placed outside the workings of blockchain into the realm of the peer-to-peer negotiation prior to the execution of the smart contracts. The smart contracts are then considered to be a representation of the true intentions of the participants and their execution turns into an execution of truth.[29] The problem is not located in the realm of representation, but in the realm of the accuracy of the execution. The transactions build the bridge between one valid state in the world of Ethereum and the new valid state that now includes the change enacted through the transaction.[30] This is where the consensus mechanism becomes the most important tool. The phantasy is that a 'decentralised network would replace authority in which a consensus algorithm resolves any incompatible disputes and ensures consensus in the network; code would replace law and execute immediately and exactly as written'.[31] Authority is legitimised based on the assumption of a computational execution of mathematical logic.

BLOCK 3: WORLD-MAKING AND REPRESENTATION

The question that remains unanswered is: The execution of *what* is actually enabled in this system? This is where push finally comes to shove and we can see that the system is built with a gigantic blind spot on the question of representation. It starts its operation from the premise that representation has been solved elsewhere, or that it is not a problem in the first place. Yet it is precisely here, in the distinctions made through the representation of reality, that we find the politics of blockchain.[32]

This final section of the text outlines two questions that emerge from representation as world-making[33] along ordering modalities that enable the consensus building and thus the making of the distributed ledger. The consensus making through synchronisation is, as the name indicates, mainly dependent on temporal ordering. To enable this, two things are necessary. First is a digital representation of any event to be recorded. Since a general consideration of digital representation would by far exceed the scope of this text, I will limit myself to a very particular problem of representation, focusing on subjecthood and what it means as a precondition to be active on a blockchain. The second precondition for the consensus mechanism is the indexing of the events on a linear axis of time. Again, rather than an exhaustive discussion of the infinite aspects of this modality of linear temporality, I will lay out the ordering technique and point to some consequences. Yet, I am certain that both of these elements are essential for grasping the kinds of worlds that blockchains enable and, more importantly, the kinds of lives that can and cannot enter the world of blockchains.

---

[29] On the 'uncertainty that smart contracts produce', see: Robert Herian, 'Smart Contracts: A Remedial Analysis' (2021) 30 Information & Communications Technology Law 17–34.
[30] Gavin Wood, *Ethereum: A Secure Decentralised Generalised Transaction Ledger* (2014) Ethereum Project Yellow Paper 1–32, 2 https://ethereum.github.io/yellowpaper/paper.pdf accessed 27 February 2021.
[31] Jaya Klara Brekke, 'Disassembling the Trust Machine: Three Cuts on the Political Matter of Blockchain', Dissertation Durham University, 13.
[32] Ibid 18. For an insightful account of the connection between the physical and the digital realm in blockchains from the perspective of control see: Jannice Käll, 'Blockchain Control' (2018) 29 Law and Critique 133–40.
[33] Nelson Goodman, *Ways of Worldmaking* (Hackett Publishing 1978) 7, 132.

Viewed from the perspective of representation, the blockchain is a record of all the interactions that are enabled in this network. It is thus a record of the permissible engagements in the realm of the technology.[34] The writing of code in the form of smart contracts on a blockchain can then be viewed as a similar practice as the writing of laws. As such, the Ethereum blockchain is often understood to be the most important iteration of crypto law, a law in which the object to be regulated by law inhabits the legal rule itself.[35] As in law, the form determines possible conduct on the blockchain. To become recognisable to the world of law any phenomenon must be made legible to law's forms. Inquiring into law's forms then becomes an exercise that by necessity relies on these very forms and follows 'cuts' that have discursively consolidated.[36] Legal personhood and subjectivity are pertinent examples to show how form precedes the event in law.[37] The representation of events through the form of legal subjecthood cuts both in the sense of enabling access to the world of law and in foreclosing paths toward accountability.

In most cases legal subjectivity is so deeply embedded in our everyday lives that we might forget that the legal subjects are the result of a creative process, and not pre-determined.[38] Legal subjects are constituted in a particular configuration with enabling and constraining aspects.[39] Take the legal subjectivity of the corporate form as an example. Corporations, both public and private – such as companies, the state, the church, and so on – come into existence in the world of law through the granting of legal personhood.[40] As with any re-presentation, their outlines and characteristics are not re-presented, but created in law. In order to grasp the political stakes involved in creating legal subjects, we can look into an area in which these forms are currently contested.

The long struggle by social movements and indigenous peoples to hold corporations liable for human rights violations keeps running up against the positivist argument that corporations are not subjects of international law and thus, cannot be the bearers of responsibility of legal obligations rooted in international law.[41] The technical discussion about the subjecthood of corporations forecloses the possibility for the affected populations to rely on international legal instruments to seek redress for the harm caused by corporate conduct.[42] On the flipside,

---

[34] Jake Goldenfein and Andrea Leiter, 'Legal Engineering on the Blockchain: Smart Contracts as Legal Conduct' (2018) 29 Law and Critique 141–9, 145.

[35] Primavera De Filippi and Aaron Wright, *Blockchain and the Law: The Rule of Code* (Harvard University Press 2018) 192.

[36] I rely here on the notion of 'cuts' with regards to legal forms as invoked by Sundhya Pahuja, *Decolonising International Law: Development, Economic Growth and the Politics of Universality* (Cambridge University Press 2011).

[37] Outi Korhonen, *International Law Situated: An Analysis of the Lawyer's Stance Towards Culture, History and Community* (Brill 2000) 6.

[38] Annelise Riles, 'Is the Law Hopeful?' in Hirokazu Miyazaki and Richard Swedberg (eds), *The Economy of Hope* (University of Pennsylvania Press 2016) 100.

[39] Antoinette Rouvroy, 'Governing without Norms: Algorithmic Governmentality' in Bogdan Wolf (ed), Special Issue on Lacanian Politics and the Impasses of Democracy Today, (2018) Psychoanalytical Notebooks 99–102.

[40] Natasha Wheatley, 'Spectral Legal Personality in Interwar International Law: On New Ways of Not Being a State' (2017) 35 Law and History Review 753–87; Fleur Johns, 'Theorizing the Corporation in International Law' in Anne Orford, Florian Hoffmann and Martin Clark (eds), *The Oxford Handbook of the Theory of International Law* (Oxford University Press 2016).

[41] Antoine Martin, 'Corporate Liability for Violations of International Human Rights: Law, International Custom or Politics?' (2011) 21 Minnesota Journal of International Law Online 95–218.

[42] Olivier de Schutter (ed), Transnational Corporations and Human Rights (Hart 2006).

subjecthood for the corporation is accepted in a different field of international law, namely international investment law, where it enables companies to protect their property rights beyond the bounds of domestic legal systems.[43] Both of these areas are currently controversially discussed, but while in the debate about human rights obligations of companies, subjecthood of the company is rejected to the disadvantage of those who want to hold them accountable, in the discussion of property protection on the international level, subjecthood – and thus the ability to shield company assets from public attempts at redistribution – is being secured through ever more international investment agreements.[44] The forms of legal subjecthood and their particular configurations are the key site of political contestation in both of these debates and bring to the fore how malleable and yet powerful these forms are.

In a similar vein, the subjects that can interact with a blockchain have their own process of constitution. Currently they are constituted as so-called wallets. Only an entity that appears in the form of a wallet with a pair of a public and a private key can interact with blockchain technology.[45] The notion of a wallet invites a monetary understanding, as if it refers to having money, or rather crypto tokens, to spend in the blockchain system. But the wallet is much closer to the basic entity that creates subjectivity for interacting with the blockchain world. There are many non-monetary applications that rely on tokens for interaction, rather than payments.[46] The wallet is also often compared to an address, like an email address, and consists of a number of digits (varying on different blockchains) that uniquely identify it. An example of an Ethereum wallet looks like this:

0x89205A3A3b2A69De6Dbf7f01ED13B2108B2c43e7

Thus, the wallet is the basic form for subjectivity on the blockchain. Access to such a wallet is restricted by technical ability and material feasibility. With a device such as a smartphone, tablet or laptop and an internet connection, a wallet can be drawn up within minutes. More important for the discussion here, there are no constraints regarding the entities that can have a wallet and thus much experimentation is ongoing, regarding, for example, trees,[47] animals,[48] pieces of art[49] and so on having a wallet, and what that would mean. These propositions trigger a whole avalanche of questions: Where is the agency in a wallet for a tree? How is nature objectified in these proposals? Is this the first step to an even greater commodification of nature? How is the relationship between nature, humans and technology conceptualised in these propositions? Are these profit-driven entities? Yet, this flexibility is one of the reasons why many social activists see potential for social and environmental justice through blockchain applications.

---

[43] Andrea Leiter, Making the World Safe for Investment: The Protection of Foreign Property 1922–1959 (Cambridge University Press forthcoming 2022).
[44] There are currently 3284 bilateral investment agreements in force that inscribe legal subjectivity for the corporation with regards to the protection of assets of foreign investors. UNCTAD, *World Investment Report 2020: International Production Beyond the Pandemic* (2020) xii.
[45] Henning Diederich, *Ethereum* (Wildfire Publishing 2016) 104.
[46] In a project on crowd-sourced arbitration, 'Kleros', the tokens serve for expressing the commitment to the resolution of a contentious case. https://kleros.io/ accessed 27 February 2021.
[47] https://terra0.org/ accessed 27 February 2021.
[48] https://sovereignnature.com/ accessed 27 February 2021.
[49] http://plantoid.org/ accessed 27 February 2021.

The other angle to be considered in this context is the role of anonymity in blockchain and how it precludes the allocation of responsibility. Tracing the subject/entity/owner of a wallet address is difficult and, in some cases, impossible. Zero-knowledge proof encryption, a method that allows to verify that one has the answer to a particular mathematical puzzle without actually revealing it, is heavily relied upon for security and privacy reasons.[50] Without going into the detail of the many implications of this ambition, for the purposes of subjectivity on the blockchain, it means that accountability becomes difficult, if not impossible. The debates on subjectivity are shaped and often framed in the language of rights in parallel to the debates in law.[51] The commonality is that, again, the form precedes the event. For an entity to enter the world of blockchain it has to appear in the form of a wallet, that is, representation in 42 digits, and any interaction has to be coded in a smart contract. Digital representation is the precondition for the coming into being of subjects in the realm of blockchain. I return to the initial concern of this section by pointing out that these questions are systematically excluded from the conception of blockchains while being the most important sites of the politics of blockchain.[52]

In a similar vein, linear temporality is a crucial mode of representation in the blockchain space. The marker for a new era is the genesis block, the first block in the chain. All the events that follow are clearly defined into before and after by way of their position on the chain. The feature is related to the double-spending problem in the Bitcoin White Paper and introduced as the timestamp server. In order to be able to keep a distributed ledger without a third trusted party, the blockchain establishes 'a system for participants to agree on a single history of the order in which they [transactions] were received'.[53] The mechanism to achieve this is digital timestamping. The basis of this idea is that any submitted data will be carrying the time and date of its certification regardless of the medium on which it is inscribed. This was usually achieved through a centralised timestamping authority, which indeed exists as the TSA – the Time Stamp Authority.[54] Anyone interested in securing their data with a time stamp can submit and receive a timestamp certificate. The accuracy of the claimed time of a digital document can now be verified by anyone through the certificate issued by the time stamping authority. For privacy purposes, the sender does not send the actual document, but a hash of the document. A hash is a string of letters and numbers that identifies a digital file without revealing its content. This mechanism, though securing privacy, fully relies on the 'trust-worthiness' of the Time Stamp Authority. Or, to put it in the words of the blockchain community, it would require trust in the third-party intermediary.[55] Now, in the case of blockchain technology, this would subvert the whole project, since the idea is precisely to move away from a centralised authority and instead develop a decentralised, peer-to-peer network. Instead, in blockchain

---

[50] Z-Cash is a cryptocurrency that promises complete anonymity. https://z.cash/ accessed 27 February 2021.
[51] Primavera De Filippi and Aaron Wright, *Blockchain and the Law: The Rule of Code* (Harvard University Press 2018).
[52] Sheila Jasanoff, 'Technology as a Site and Object of Politics' in Robert E. Goodin and Charles Tilly (eds), *The Oxford Handbook of Contextual Political Analysis* (2006).
[53] Satoshi Nakamoto, *Bitcoin: A Peer-to-Peer Electronic Cash System* (2008) 2 bitcoin.org accessed 27 February 2021.
[54] https://freetsa.org accessed 27 February 2021.
[55] Bart Van Rompay, Bart Preneel and Joos Vandewalle, *The Digital Timestamping Problem* (Werkgemeenschap voor Informatie-en Communicatietheorie 1999) 3.

technology this problem is solved through a so-called time server. The time server works 'by taking a hash of a block of items to be timestamped and widely publishing the hash, such as in a newspaper'.[56] Furthermore, each block contains a hash of the previous block evidencing that it comes later on the timeline. It is thus crucial for the blockchain that all transactions are placed into one linear record along the temporal vector. They reach what is called 'finality', meaning confirmation, when they can no longer be reversed or changed, usually after the implementation of a number of successive blocks.

Expressing the potential dangers and exclusions of linear temporal ordering and its desire for finality is not easy. Yet, when we turn to the fundamental level of the relationship between experience and time, we start seeing what is at stake in a world that is built on the notion of 'finality'. In a sense, it is an augmentation, or extreme manifestation of the cuts made in digital representations in the first place, because it renders them unchangeable and more importantly, invisible. Returning to Haraway's conception that storytelling 'is about both absence and presence, killing and nurturing, living and dying – and remembering who lives and who dies and how in the string figures of naturalcultural history',[57] it is the functional erasure of remembering the exclusions and the violences committed in representation that renders the finality of a state on the blockchain the ultimate force. Memory in blockchain is completely detached from experience; it is not only halfway between the material reality and idealism as mediation, but the full-blown idealist representation detached from material reality that constitutes life on the blockchain.

CONCLUSIONS

The aim of this contribution was to explore blockchain as a narrative technology to produce a glimpse of what life in blocks might look and feel like. In treating blockchain as a narrative technology rather than only assembling stories about blockchain, I tried to move away from the hype around money and cryptocurrencies and get closer to the technology's capacity for mediating lives. Tracing the narrative capacity along the entangled axis of author(ship), author(ity) and world-making, I tried to develop an account of the site of politics in this technology. In focusing on author(ship) through a study of the Ethereum and Bitcoin White Papers, I tried to provide a sense of the historical and social context of the emergence of the projects, as well as of the ideological directions manifest in their writing. The White Paper as a genre points to the governance ambitions of the projects, morphing government regulations with corporate selling points. The picture that emerges from the White Papers is one that chases objectivity as mathematical truth, universality in formal representation, a transactional society without traditional institutions and the distribution of authorship over a decentralised network. The authority of the network, too, hinges on the decentralised nature. By locating the contestation of interests outside the realm of the technology and treating smart contracts as a reflection of consensus between all entities involved, the problem to be solved by the technology has come to be the mathematical execution of the formal consensus. As such, authority as decisive institution has

---

[56] Satoshi Nakamoto, *Bitcoin: A Peer-to-Peer Electronic Cash System* (2008) 2 bitcoin.org accessed 27 February 2021.
[57] Donna J Haraway, Staying with the Trouble: Making Kin in the Chthulucene (Duke University Press 2016) 28.

been 'solved' into a mathematical constitution of consensus. Thus, authorship and authority are distributed over the network and evade the question of force and contestation by placing it outside the system. This setup brings to the fore the most important question that lurks behind the discussion of authorship and authority, namely the problem of representation. The question of what can enter and be active in the realm of blockchain remains unanswered by the structure of the network. It becomes a question that is at best sidelined and at worst not considered a valid question in the first place. In the final section of the contribution, I tried to highlight some implications of this setup along two features of blockchain's mode of representation: first, I showed how the creation of representative forms such as subjectivity shapes the way different entities can gain or lose power for advancing their interest by comparing the creation of subjectivity in the realm of international law to that of the blockchain space; second, I drew out that the demands of linear temporal ordering dictated by the technology and the way they advance a form of representation are completely detached from lived experiences.

Indeed, when looking at blockchains through the lens of ordering, we encounter a hyper-formalist narrative structure. It is not only the abstraction of a rule that meets the excess of the world and is then negotiated, but also an attempt at marginalising the excess of the world by only enabling formalised engagement. It is an exercise of world-making through the constitution of a ledger of all events that can represent one universal truth. It is a mechanism that reduces all there is to its forms. Everything else ceases to exist. As I hope to have demonstrated in this contribution, the narrating capacity of blockchain might go further than the narrating capacity of law as we know it. As in any system of representation, form precedes the event, so that only what is legible in the recognisable forms can become part of that normative system. What might be particular about blockchain's ordering system is the way it cuts through life and the limited possibility for reframing or reinterpreting these cuts – both in the sense that what is not recognisable disappears to a degree of complete inexistence, and in the sense that its forms are even narrower than the forms of law with which we are familiar. When life is mediated through the narrative of blockchain, experience, simultaneity, duration and pluralism have to make way for a world of proclaimed universal objectivity and finality.

21. Auto-bio-ethno-graphy
Cecilia Gebruers

INTRODUCTION

This chapter is an exploration of the process of conducting research as an auto-bio-ethno-graphy that leads to an autograph of my grandmother Firma ("Signature"). It tells the process of conducting research—more specifically, of writing my dissertation—as an auto-bio-ethnographical endeavor. The dissertation focused on intersectionality in human rights law and legal theory and a key part of the research was to ground the concept of intersectionality in the case of indigenous people's land conflicts in western La Pampa. This required developing and applying an intersectional analytical framework to the situation of indigenous peoples in western La Pampa and exploring how property rights operate in a certain place. The project aimed to expose the limitations of "categorical" intersectional approaches developed in human rights law, for being centered in fixed categories which, when applied to a locality, do not respond to the material realities of their situation. The methodology combined the study of archival material, such as norms, judicial decisions, and reports, with empirical work that used an ethnographical approach in understanding the appropriate manner of building knowledge and interpreting the cultural environment in order to make it intelligible to those that do not belong to it (Guber, 2011).

The overall objective of the qualitative stage of the research was to explore indigenous women's interactions between the structural, communitarian, and individual identitarian forces that are at play in the land conflicts they are experiencing. The case studies were based on fieldwork carried out between 2018 and 2019 when semi-structured interviews were conducted with the subjects and were contextualized with judicial decisions and secondary sources such as journal articles, reports from government programs, and cadastral surveys. This methodological approach based on practices and material transactions sought to make the law emerge from subjective and material human experiences.

The methodological stance taken assumed that the self is produced at the same time as the research object. In this, the thesis followed feminist legal scholars who question the law for being androcentric, critical legal scholars' critique of positivism and formalism for not conceiving the law's indeterminacy, and critical race theorists who warn that the previous critiques failed to address power operating against black people. Aligned with a critical tradition, the research focused on the frontiers and, rather than opposing, it embraces uncertainties (Davies, 2002, p.11). Still, the alleged critical stance made use of archives and the ethnographical approach was an effort to interpret a cultural environment that was given as strange. In the next sections I explore how neither were strange; rather, they were intertwined with my biography.

ARCHIVAL TRAJECTORIES

Mario Rufer observes that the imaginary of archives involves the present of the absent, totality, and temporal continuity, all tied together through the notion of authority (Rufer, 2016, p.163). The *arkhé* of the archive is also linked to the *arkheión*, the guardian that performs rituals around the event granting authenticity. The most common guardian of archives is the State and its many mechanisms of institutionalization. This aspect of archives involves, on the one hand, that in what remains there is something else that was hidden. On the other hand, the archives are a threat to the State's own legitimacy. A sharp reading by the anthropologist Axel Lazzari of the first census in Argentina is eloquent about this aspect of archives. After the military campaigns in the late nineteenth century, also called "conquest of the desert," the question was what to do with the indigenous peoples in a way that did not threaten national identity. They were granted citizenship, provided that other means of disarming their differential identity, such as tribal organization, language, rites, beliefs, parenting systems, among others, were utilized (Herner, 2015, p.123). By the year 1882 many of the indigenous peoples who were militarized in the decade of 1870 were forcibly brought back to La Pampa to populate the newly founded localities of Victorica and General Acha, which would be part of the National Government of the Central Pampa. Some of the indigenous leaders who collaborated with the military received small land plots; later, fugitive Indians and scattered families would join (Lazzari, 2013, p.98). In 1895 the government conducted a census to determine the size of the population of the newly conquered territory, limiting the descriptions for nationality or ethnic/racial filiation in a way that only allowed the categories of "Argentinian" or "foreigner" (Lazzari, 2013, p.98). Some census officers still noticed an Indian presence and registered that in their records, although these entries were not included in the final statistics. In Axel Lazzari's account, this exposes an explicit strategy of "vanishing" (*ausentar*) that proves the failure of the "civilizing" project and leaves open-ended the question of return (Lazzari, 2013, p.100). As Derrida said, the archive always works, and a priori, against itself (Derrida, 1995, p.14).

Working with archives, as Rufer critically observes, is a continuation of the gesture of "rescuing" the subject from forgottenness (Rufer, 2016, p.176). Following Ann Laura Stoler, he conceives archives as a field of forces where the past and future are at play—the past, such as administrative and notary records, peace courts, churches, among others, being predominant—whereas the present is neglected (p.182). During the process of the research this tension became more tangible as two depictions of indigeneity were implicitly colliding. For some, Colonia Emilio Mitre, one of the geographically adverse areas where the State located and granted precarious land titles to members of indigenous communities that identify mostly as Rankulches, has survived until today as the "home" of indigenous peoples in La Pampa. It is certainly the place that has the most documented resistance to land-grabbing in La Pampa (Salomón Tarquini, 2010). Germán Canhué, an indigenous leader born in Colonia Emilio Mitre, played an important role in the revitalization of the indigenous movement in La Pampa, and in the late 1990s wrote *Un Largo Camino a Casa* (A long road to return home) (Canuhé, 2019). The narrative refers to two homes, the pre-historic Mamull Mapu and the historic Colonia Emilio Mitre, as the site of survival and resistance of Rankulches in La Pampa. This depiction is disputed by indigenous people—by individuals and families who remained spread around different localities, who see it as a ghetto of the old times and do not see a future there, but instead propose a "universalist" utopia with more individualistic and less communitarian undertones (Lazzari, 2013, p.108).

Colonia Los Puelches is another area where the government of the early 1900s located indigenous peoples, granting equally precarious land titles in a similarly inhospitable area. In Los Puelches the ethnic groups were mostly Mapuche and Pampa; however, the vast majority of the families and individuals did not integrate into the colonies and instead worked at the ranches or in manufacturing, or moved to towns. According to the registries, when in 1911 land inspectors went to Colonia Los Puelches, they did not find any of the allottees in the plots assigned. There are no longer registries of many of them, while others, such as the leader Ñancufil Calderón, settled in distant plots as "intruders." Some families managed to acquire relatively large economic capital by extending their relations through marrying their offspring into families with modest economic positions, whether they were indigenous or not (Salomón Tarquini, 2011a, p.90).

Holding on to or defending a determined territory has been the way of imagining indigenous resistance to westernization. Indigenous people, from this perspective, have a closer connection with the historical site they were sent to by the Argentinian government, as it evokes a time when, in those same lands, language and traditions were better preserved. Locating indigenous people's identity within a determined historical place or conceiving indigenous identity as intertwined with strategies of survival other than defending staying in a certain part of the land shapes the legal approaches to land claims, at the same time as it exposes the tension between past and present. There is, however, one conception of indigeneity that is reproduced by the judiciary when they decide on land disputes. Legal approaches to indigenous land claims have mostly based their claims on proof of the connection of indigenous identity to a determined place. To make use of legal protections against those alleging that they are the title holders of land lots occupied by indigenous peoples, you need to prove your indigenous identity. Who is and who is not indigenous? How do you connect to that "remote" past and what supporting documents are required to prove your case?

AUTOBIOGRAPHICAL ETHNOGRAPHY

Learning about the different trajectories of indigenous identity in La Pampa had an impact I had not foreseen when I first decided to do research on land conflicts in the area. My interest in working on this topic was motivated by a desire to reconnect with my hometown after having lived elsewhere for many years. Besides, living abroad gave me a perspective on my origins that I had not experienced before. I developed a curiosity about the place where I had grown up and I wanted to re-approach it now with the perspective of a researcher.

Before delving into my biography, it is worth briefly mentioning the narrative on which the Argentinian state was built, encapsulated in the expression "conquest of the desert". Juan Bautista Alberdi, whose book *Bases and Starting Points for the Political Organization of the Argentine Republic* influenced the content of the 1853 Argentine Constitution, crystallizes this ideology when he affirms: "My country is a desert half populated and half civilized" (Alberdi, 2002, p.198). The image of a desert plain is in itself threatening—Alberdi refers to the desert as the current enemy of the Americas (Alberdi, 2002, p.9)—and it had to be controlled in order to facilitate the project of transforming those lands into productive agriculture. It had to be ordered—first discursively, by representing it as available territory, and then materially, by subjugating indigenous and creole peoples (Herner, 2015, p.122). That narrative accompanied policies that promoted European immigration and resulted in immigrants making up a considerable share of the total population. According to the census, by 1914, a third of the population was immigrant (Modolo, 2016). As a result, the predominant narrative—which, astoundingly, remains to this day—assimilates Argentinian identity with being descendants of European immigrants.

My own family history also shows how this narrative becomes part of the story you tell yourself. When I was a child I learned that my grandfather from my mother's side came from Ukraine when he was little, and that my grandmother's family came from Italy and Spain. On my father's side I only knew that my grandfather's family came from Belgium. For many years the genealogy of my family ended there. I remember asking about my grandmother's origins, specifically where in Europe her family came from, but the answers were always vague, saying they did not really know. In fact, my grandmother and great-grandmother were born in Los Puelches in the years 1915 and 1930. This almost forgotten past of my family did not factor in the objectives of my research, but as I became more immersed in the fieldwork it unexpectedly emerged that in my family history there could perhaps be found a key to the lost tracks in Los Puelches. My research became also an exploration of my own ancestors. The call not to escape uncertainty brought me to ask, following Walter Mignolo (Mignolo, 2019): where was colonialism in me? Premises of my own ethnographical approach became problematic as I too was becoming my own subject of study.

The risk of autobiographical accounts, as identified by Franco Ferrarotti, is *literariness* (Ferrarotti, 1983, p.62). When the individual biography is reduced to a unique destiny, general laws cannot be drawn and, in the best-case scenario, autobiographies can be valued merely as illustrative contextual information. A different way of understanding them is as a "complex, non-a priori determinable relation between givenness and the lived" (Ferrarotti, 1983, p.62). This includes not only the structural frames that are given, but also the elements that make empirical data theoretically autonomous or otherwise "reified factualness" come alive—frames that otherwise would remain inaccessible. Ferrarotti's way of seeing autobiography is also a materialistic approach in that it includes Marxist premises. The sixth thesis on Feuerbach, which affirms that human essence in its reality is "the ensemble of social relations," can lead to understanding life as a practice that takes on structural social factors that then transform into psychological structures. Therefore, Ferrarotti takes a Marxist approach and conceives "social relations revealing themselves through their less generalizable aspects as a vertical synthesis of a social history" (Ferrarotti, 1983, p.66).

Biographies are commonly referred to as looking into the past, but a spectral structure defeats such limits—like a living form of archive. This is why I recover Ferrarotti's exhortation to look into biographies as a way of reaching to silenced histories: "We must abandon the privilege accorded to secondary biographical materials. We must bring back to the very heart of the biographical method primary materials and their explosive subjectivity" (Ferrarotti, 1983, p.65). This call raises the question of how the subjectivity inherent in autobiography can become scientific knowledge.

Ferrarotti's upholding of autobiography faces similar criticisms to the claims of geographers such as Doreen Massey, who had to argue against those who question the scientific entity of locality. Being on the opposite side of deterministic or passive accounts that place the social over the singular, both had to explain how unique life experiences as well as unique spatial configurations can offer generalizable social truths. Geographers have pointed out that local phenomena demand theorizing as much as global ones, since this is where their crucial processes operate (Massey, 1993, p.147). In spite of accusations that local forces are "too unique" to draw theories from, the uniqueness of a place is a result of the interlinking of specific histories with the wider national and international context: "all these sources of uniqueness are more than the inexorable playing-out of structural forces. They must be viewed, too, not only as the results of human agency but through the lens of 'what people have made of it', what they have construed as their lives in the circumstances in which they find themselves" (Massey, 1993, p.148).

How are practices linked to social structures? What is the link? In a biography, the social is not merely reflected; it is, according to Ferrarotti, a *microrelation*, where external conditioning and human practice are both present, and its foundation lies in the reciprocal synthetic practice that governs both interactions (Ferrarotti, 1983, pp.71, 72). By itself synthetizing the general and singular, biography reopens debates over the materiological foundations of disciplines, such as sociology, Ferrarotti's field of study, but also others such as anthropology and law.

Given that the fieldwork I was conducting was related to research that connected anthropological approaches with the law, the plain and explicit announcement of the inclusion of self-reference faces even harsher criticisms. The notion of narrative jurisprudence developed by Mark Tushnet (1992) refers to a stylistic operation that mediates the general and the particular through stories about particular events that intend to be representative of general broader social phenomena. The value of storytelling has also been seen by legal scholars as a way of generating empathy, connecting with feelings, and giving voice to groups that were thought to hide their emotions—something lacking in traditional, analytical, and dispassionate legal writing (Delgado, 1989, p.2440). Still, as Gary Peller argued in his critique of Tushnet's definition of narrative (Peller, 1992), jurisprudential uses of personal narrative have had higher levels of scrutiny for people of color. The experiences of subjects at the margins do not come from the same place of neutrality or objectivity as that claimed by white heterosexual male legal scholars, in order to "mediate" social structures. Critical race theory has raised this issue to expose the pervasiveness of self-claimed objectivity, embracing the subject position instead (Williams, 1992). Combining Patricia Williams and Kimberlé Crenshaw's critical legal approaches, Jennifer Nash conceives intersectionality as an analytic that occupies law and refuses its conceptions of neutrality and uniformity as performance of justice. Intersectionality, Nash argues, demands that law is centered in witnessing and vulnerability (Nash, 2019, p.129).

Including the autobiographical in legal research, however, does not rely solely on discourse. The material relations of the living are present in a notable way—in a way that means matter is present, but not merely a rigid or deterministic social construct. Including the autobiographical aspect of a research project is a way of entering into the architectural roots of the modern and carrying out the art of reading the signs encrypted in the edifice (Goodrich, 2009, p.209).

Grounding the concept of intersectionality requires looking beyond "indigenous peoples" as a fixed legal provision, unraveling the way law operates in land conflicts and exposing the tensions in the construction of the category "indigenous peoples" itself, and within the category. As Joan Scott has theorized, when a categorical subject-status is taken as fixed, it covers the operations of difference in social life and ends up solidifying the ideological processes of subject-construction (Scott, 1991, p.792). Categories are neither a given nor determined and waiting to be expressed, but are deeply historical. Developing an intersectional framework based on these premises, including a historiographical account of the different trajectories of indigenous peoples in La Pampa after the so-called conquest of the desert, is a big part of the task; however, it should also problematize the categorizations based on experience.

Scott has observed in Samuel Delany's autobiography, *The Motion of Light in Water*, how his memory of an event was interpreted as a coming to self-consciousness, a marking of his authentic identity and discovery of a prediscursive reality. Scott questions whether unmediated access to that truth is possible, and notes that the center of Delany's autobiography is representation, the mediation between words and things, through which social categories, personal understanding and language are connected (Scott, 1991, p.795). His experience is presented as divided between the material and the psychological, with entries about material things at the front and entries on sexual desire at the back, but both, in Scott's account, are constitutive of one another. The main aspect of the moment of awareness narrated by Delany is not experience itself, but the operation of identity production that led to it.

Experience is, therefore, useful inasmuch as it exposes how categories achieve foundational statuses and effects. The experience of doing research on indigenous peoples in La Pampa after having been born there added insights to the operations involved in the process of building categories. A narration of the history of the category "indigenous peoples" in that place involving my biography will tell a story about the past, but will certainly be influenced by my position and time.

In my account of the process of empirical work there is an aspect that has been identified by researchers as involving awareness of the lack of neutrality of the researcher/narrator, as Clare Hemmings exposes in *Why Stories Matter* (2011). It has been widely theorized that some feminist theories have tailored women's experiences to those of white western women, and intersectional studies are part of that critical process. The stories we tell about the past are motivated by what we want to reclaim from what happened in the past, what we want to leave on the way, and what we want to untether from (Hemmings, 2011, p.13). The recurrent chant in feminist protests in Latin American countries—"we are the daughters of all the witches that you couldn't burn"—is eloquent about how, from a feminist perspective, the elements of oppression and resistance are idealized, in order to foresee a future of liberation. A different version, more aware of the western-centered implications of the chant, changes witches to *machis* (women healers).[1]

Most of the efforts to recover indigenous people's history are centered on enhancing their leaders and stories about warriors that heroically fought during battles. Those who "made history" are those who pursued heroic actions during a battle, and found a place in the official records of the Argentinian State. When stories are told following this narrative, one should wonder: how is this story impacting our present? Who are the characters that are being brought up to represent the normative subject?

---

[1] I heard and sang this chant numerous times, however, I was inspired to use it as an example after reading Moira Perez's chapter "*Políticas de la historiografía: hacer cosas -y sujetos- con el pasado*" presented at the *Seminar Democracia y resistencia en la temprana Modernidad americana*, Gino Germani Institute, University of Buenos Aires, 22 October 2020.

AN ENCRYPTED SUBJECT OF STUDY

Learning how the stories of Cristina, my great-grandmother, and Firma, my grandmother, resemble those of indigenous peoples that were directed to settle in Colonia Los Puelches showed me a side of indigenous history that is not accessible through the State's registries. It is stated in official files that when the land inspector went to observe the situation of the indigenous peoples in the land lots assigned by the State in Puelches, they found them empty. That area had recurrent periods of flooding, and that is considered the reason why they spread to the different ranches of the area, where women were taken as servants.

Following these conclusions made by historians, I inquired within my family about my great-grandfather on my father's side. There is not much information about him. The only thing repeated over and over is that the family despises him. It is unsurprising that he was not well regarded since my great-grandmother worked for him at the ranch and, as early as 15 years of age, she was pregnant with my grandmother. Later in her life, my great-grandmother married and had a large number of children. My family from my father's side, as far as I know, were landless rural workers of La Pampa. I remember visiting my great-grandmother's family meetings and feeling overwhelmed by how numerous this side of my family was, and having meals in a yard surrounded by farm animals. That part of my family felt strange for me as I had always lived in the city. Only recently, my father learned his grandfather's full name and sent me a picture of the note he took on a piece of paper. When I was trying to reconstruct the history of land titles for the *Colonias* in La Pampa, looking at decrees of the government of Argentina from the early eighteenth century, I found land lots in the Puelches area granted to a Spaniard with the name my father had told me.

Traces of the history of indigenous peoples that I was trying to find were present in my family—those that were set aside from official registries, censuses, and records, and those that successfully remain hidden in our present. Many personal memories were reinterpreted with this new information. My grandmother used to tell me many stories about life at the ranch and the injustices of being a little girl working as a servant for ranchers, working at the house while the ranchers' kids went to school. But until recently my understanding had been that that was the typical life of rural workers. I still remember how shocking it was when I went for a visit to a ranch and my grandmother cut a chicken's throat in front of me, with no regret. This image stuck with me and I remember it very vividly. Later I asked her how she learned to do that, and if she felt bad for doing that to the chickens. She said to me that that's life in the country: "when you need to eat you do what you have to do." So, I kept on following traces from my memories. Many times she took me to see a woman healer. Her use of the expression "*paisano*" (peasant) or "*bien paisano*" (very peasant) in anecdotes of life in the countryside was, I recently learned, a common way of referring to indigenous peoples without saying it (Salomón Tarquini, 2011b, p.561). This was not, I believe, to hide their indigenous descent, but how indigeneity was seen: as a person that is *very* peasant.

However, my efforts to learn more about my great-grandmother, and who her father was, and to go as far back as possible into the family origins, met no success. They ended with the story of an aunt that says that my great-grandmother's father was a Justice of the Peace of Los Puelches—implausible, since there were no peace courts in Puelches. The search for my origins abruptly ends with an institution that had a central role in forging the identity of the inhabitants of Argentina, detaching it from those of indigenous origin and making sure no trace remains of previous times. It is also known that peace courts changed indigenous names as part of erasing their identities. My grandmother's name, *Firma* ("Signature"), had always sounded unusual. I never heard of another person named Firma, but it had a cryptic sound now.

To offer a conclusion would be to make an effort to make sense of the whole story. The purpose of bringing my auto-bio-ethno-graphy into my research is to embed unsettled questions in an intersectional exploration. An additional factor in the narrator's non-neutral position is operating in this process, which is the flux of open categories in the researcher's self-positioning. The researcher and the research subjects are mutually imbricated, affected, impacted, contaminated.

Derrida exposes how archives exceed the dichotomist logic of absence/presence by operating as a trace. A trace evokes an absence that is present through a trail, in this case, the search for the origins of my family history: A history that is gone but can be put back together with what remained or survived its death. This is why Achille Mbembe has also described working with archives as being an expert in spectral work. "The archive could not have a relationship with death without including the other remnant of death—the spectre. To a very large extent, the historian is engaged in a battle against this world of spectres" (Mbembe, 2002, p.25).

A biography encompasses a personal archive, and as such is an effort toward finding origins or, from a Derridean perspective, "organizing your ghosts." In *Archive Fever*, Derrida argues that the structure of the archive is spectral: "a trace always referring to another whose eyes can never be met" (Derrida, 1995, p.54). How to search for what was silenced in the records? How to dig into the unconscious of archives? How to encounter what was deliberately erased, but is in plain sight? The story of the women ancestors of my family speaks of a story that is in plain sight and resonates with the chants of resistance in feminists' protests. We are the daughters of the *machis* that resisted and could not be burnt. But we are also the daughters, granddaughters, of the women dispossessed, exploited, and raped by the white settlers.

My grandmother's genealogy begins with a peace court. In the beginning was the justice of the peace could be a different version of the Derridean maxim "in the beginning was the telephone" (Derrida, 1992, p.270). Now I can read more into that name, *Firma*. Her name could well be an incomplete form. When she was registered in the official records perhaps there was a space in black and below it said: "Signature." My great-grandmother did not know how to read or write, and the space left blank was taken as filled by the indication "Signature," as in "sign here."

REFERENCES

Alberdi, Juan Bautista (2002). *Bases y Puntos de Partida Para La Organizacion Politica de La Republica Argentina*, Libreria Historica.

Canuhé, G. (2019). 'Un Largo Camino de Regreso a Casa', in C. Salomón Tarquini et al. (eds), *Pueblos Indígenas y Migraciones en La Pampa*, Santa Rosa: Ministerio de Educación de la Provincia de la Pampa, pp.145–53.

Davies, M. (2002). 'Ethics and Methodology in Legal Theory—A (Personal) Research Anti-Manifesto', *Law Text Culture*, 6, 7–26.

Delgado, R. (1989). 'Storytelling for Oppositionists and Others: A Plea for Narrative', *Michigan Law Review*, 87(8), 2411–41.

Derrida, J. (1992). 'Ulysses Gramophone', in D. Attridge (ed), *Acts of Literature*, New York: Routledge.

Derrida, J. (1995). 'Archive Fever: A Freudian Impression', *Diacritics*, 25, 9–63.

Ferrarotti, F. (1983). 'Biography and the Social Sciences', *Social Research*, 50, 57–80.

Goodrich, P. (2009). 'Postmodern Justice', in A. Sarat, M. Anderson, and C. Frank (eds), *Law and the Humanities: An Introduction*, Cambridge: Cambridge University Press, pp.188–210.

Guber, R. (2011). *La Etnografía. Método, Campo y Reflexividad*, Buenos Aires: Siglo XXI Editores.

Hemmings, C. (2011). *Why Stories Matter: The Political Grammar of Feminist Theory*, Durham, NC: Duke University Press.

Herner, M.T. (2015). 'La invisibilización del otro indígena en el proceso de construcción nacional. El caso de la Colonia Emilio Mitre, La Pampa', *Huellas*, *18*, 118–31.

Lazzari, A. (2013). 'Identidad y fantasma: situando las nuevas prácticas de libertad del movimiento indígena en La Pampa', *Quinto Sol*, *11*, 91–122.

Massey, D. (1993). 'Questions of Locality', *Geography*, *78*, 142–9.

Mbembe, A. (2002). 'The Power of the Archive and its Limits', in C. Hamilton, V. Harris, J. Taylor, M. Pickover, G. Reid and R. Saleh (eds), *Refiguring the Archive*, Cham: Springer.

Mignolo, W.D. (2019). 'Reconstitución epistémica/estética: la aesthesis decolonial una década después', *Calle 14: revista de investigación en el campo del arte*, *14*(25), 14–32.

Modolo, V.E. (2016). 'Análisis histórico-demográfico de la inmigración en la Argentina del Centenario al Bicentenario', *Papeles de población*, *22*(89), 201–22.

Nash, J.C. (2019). *Black Feminism Reimagined: After Intersectionality*, Durham, NC: Duke University Press.

Peller, G. (1992). 'The Discourse of Constitutional Degradation', *Georgetown Law Journal*, *81*(2), 313–42.

Rufer, M. (2016). 'El archivo. De la metáfora extractiva a la ruptura poscolonial', in F. Gorbach and M. Rufer (eds), *(In)disciplinar la Investigación: Archivo, Trabajo de Campo y Escritura*, Buenos Aires: Siglo XXI Editores, pp.160–86.

Salomón Tarquini, C. (2010). 'Estrategias de acceso y conservación de la tierra entre los ranqueles (Colonia Emilio Mitre, La Pampa, primera mitad del siglo XX)', *Mundo Agrario: Revista de estudios rurales*, *11*(21), 9–28.

Salomón Tarquini, C. (2011a). 'Actores y redes en las políticas de tierras indígenas (La Pampa, 1882–1930)', *Revista de Ciencias Sociales*, *3*(20), 81–98.

Salomón Tarquini, C. (2011b). 'Procesos de subalternización de la población indígena en Argentina: Los ranqueles en La Pampa, 1870–1970', *Revista de Indias*, *71*(252), 545–70.

Scott, J.W. (1991). 'The Evidence of Experience', *Critical Inquiry*, *17*(4), 773–97.

Tushnet, M. (1992). 'The Degradation of Constitutional Discourse', *Georgetown Law Journal*, *81*(2), 251–312.

Williams, P.J. (1992). *Alchemy of Race and Rights: Diary of a Law Professor*, Cambridge: Harvard University Press.

22. Beoble
Deepak Unnikrishnan

[There is evidence that a lecture of this sort took place in the summer of 2020, the first year of sickness. There is video evidence that artists were in attendance. There is also evidence that the transcript was tampered with, because this lecture was not that lecture. The writer was asked to explain the changes and the need for a revised edit. He refused.]

A MEMO ABOUT QUIET BEOBLE [ENTER DATE]

Dear stranger:

1. The intent of most memos is to help you remember something, or to remind another person of something.
2. The word is short for memorandum, 'thing to be recorded' in Latin, and a close linguistic relative of memory.
3. I borrowed 1 & 2 verbatim from vocabulary.com because my mainstream search engine trusts vocabulary.com.
4. My lecture, masquerading as a memo, will list items I stole from family members, friends and strangers in the (Persian | Arabian) Gulf, starting with a) language, b) fables, c) space, d) joy and e) rage.
5. Why?
6. ████████████ emerged out of quiet beoble.

Best,
Deepak Unnikrishnan [Enter Title of Importance]

A MEMO ABOUT QUIET BEOBLE

I read a short story in graduate school, about a magician and his bag of tricks. In my opinion, the story wouldn't have worked without the rabbit.

The rabbit gave the story direction. To make the reader want to read further, the writer needed that rabbit. The writer owed that rabbit.

The name of the wordsmith who brought the aforementioned rabbit to life? David Mamet, the playwright. That's what I thought. I am not so sure any more. Nevertheless, if Mamet had cast a rabbit, he wouldn't have been the first to fall under the spell of a bunny. Rabbits have magnificently overachieved in the dramatic arts. I've often wondered why.

For proof of the influence of rabbits in the world of make-believe, look no further than the unimaginatively named Rabbit of *Winnie the Pooh* fame. There's also Peter Rabbit. Roger Rabbit. Brer Rabbit, White Rabbit. Bugs Bunny. Thumper. Even Snowball.

It would be wise to assume there were other rabbits, from cities near Baghdad, perhaps descendants of the great bunnies of Vitosha. But the public didn't take to these rabbits, because the writers who wrote them didn't know what to do with them.

To push the rabbit theory further, shall we make something up? Like, somewhere out there in the land of rabbits exists a drama school for rabbits, where buck-toothed thespians make their payments in carrots, possibly my first and only attempt at humor.

If I may be permitted to continue?

In a class I teach, where my students expect to learn how to write, I ask them, 'What if I wore a top hat, dropped it on the table in front of me, and sunk my right hand into this hat: what are your expectations?'

My students size me up and then begin to list things: flowers, ribbons, pigeons, steam.

The humble rabbit, the noun I'm looking for, eventually makes an appearance. That's my cue. 'If I pulled a rabbit out of my hat, would you be impressed?' Perhaps, they say. I know they are lying. Rabbits in hats aren't dope anymore.

As their teacher, I know I am not in control yet, another word I reflect on when I step into a classroom. I need to wait, so I wait, in order to slow the game down. It is in my interest to make them impatient, because I have a question for them.

'If I produced a rabbit, sat him on the table, and then fished out a lit cigarette which the rabbit takes and smokes, do I have your attention?'

I don't need to check if they are paying attention at this point, because my students are paying attention, just as you are paying attention. The only reason the question is posed, in the register it is posed in, is for effect.

How to take this further?

If the rabbit spoke, like Red Peter the ape in Kafka's 'A Letter to the Academy', there's promise. But I want my rabbit to be different.

As a result, my rabbit will not greet my students with respect or honour, like Red Peter, in the rhetoric of the academy. Because my rabbit has not seen the insides of a school, or sat for exams.

My rabbit will turn to me, and to my students, then get to the point. 'All right, why am I here? What do you want?'

At this stage, if you are listening, irrespective of whether my words have made an impression, let's agree on something. At this point in time you have no idea where this lecture is headed.

That's no accident.

As a writer, or word maker, story keeper, perhaps even speaker, before I construct anything, the first item on my agenda is disruption: how to unmake, remake and rework. Take this lecture, my first. To prepare, I walked over to a pile of books I am yet to read, and picked out Italo Calvino's *Six Memos for the Next Millennium*.

I read the first lecture in the book, on Lightness, and decided there was nothing there for me. Yet when I was asked before this lecture whether my lecture had a title, thanks to Calvino, I remembered the word memo, and I took a shine to it.

And then I borrowed phrases from vocabulary.com.

And then I thought about why the word memo could be of interest and use, because I am fairly certain I don't like memos. But I am interested in how the word memo sounds, and what the word evokes in the minds of most people familiar with memos, individuals accustomed to institutional jargon and rules. And since memos are most often impersonal, seen primarily as tools to transmit information, they bore me.

Yet because I am an academic, I have received many memos and missives, sent by institutional, programme and committee heads, over the past five years.

Every time I find a memo in my inbox, I take a breath, because a part of me contemplates whether *this* memo is going to be a memo with personality. That the powers that be at university have finally decided to revisit the memo, to reassess its purpose and change its template, producing an effect similar to David Marksen's *This is Not a Novel*. Indeed, it wasn't one.

And I suppose that's why I am fascinated by the languages I ingest on a daily basis, and then forget about. As I stated earlier, I work for an academic institution, with a clear hierarchy in place. The people in charge, particularly tenured faculty, are members of the administration. Those higher up, The Leadership. If you reach The Leadership, and wish to go further, there is The Board.

Rank and status, symbolically and professionally stamped on actual human beings. In my profession, I have lost track of what someone is supposed to be. Or could be. Or should be. Must be?

For example, there is the Assistant Professor who will tip their imaginary hat to the Associate Professor who will tip their imaginary hat to the Professor.

I could break down other titles but if I did that, this lecture will be remembered for my wariness of professorial titles. That is not my intention.

My point is this. We are surrounded and engulfed by language and accents, imported, exported, forced-upon, and now streamed, something I've always been conscious of. But how does one put any of this on the page? What must the writer look for?

Permit me to return to the subject of the rabbit. A rabbit, in the age of Netflix and the Anthropocene, could be a cartoon. A rabbit could be a woman in a corset, obliged and expected to wear a bow tie and a scut. A rabbit is also a vibrator. An animal fed to pythons. Flesh stewed in red wine. Or perhaps a rabbit could be a pet. Or vermin. Or a pace setter in a race, where the function of this elite athlete is to set the speed and then to exit the race at any point, in essence disappear. And this is the kind of rabbit I am interested in looking at today, the disappearing rabbit.

In Calvino's *Six Memos for the Next Millennium*, the fourth chapter is titled Visibility, which I read, because it is a subject that interests me. I am after all a brown body in an Arab space. I grew up around men like my father, South Indians, even though I was raised by my mother; people who did their best not to draw attention to themselves, especially the men. And for the most part, I believe they succeeded. I like to think the men in my family went to work and, before they hurried home for lunch or dinner, buried their secrets and rage and lovers wherever they could.

In our youth, in order to understand what was out there, we had to learn on our own, like riding a bike without training wheels. So, I didn't know my accent would be picked on and picked apart by people who didn't look like me. And I didn't know Arab boys younger than me could blurt out Hind or Kafir to my face. My father didn't prepare me for any of that; we rarely exchanged notes. But I knew not to say anything, or fight back. The response felt reflexive.

To dip further into my boyhood, may I add that as a young man I didn't know I was going to be taunted about the Malayalam I spoke, or the Arabic I didn't know. My mother didn't sit me down, my father didn't take me for a walk. But I realized early on that language, like a person in a profession, was all about rank and power, depending on what you spoke and how you spoke what you spoke.

Language outed you, all of you.

I learned on the fly, like the other kids I went to school with, because, like I said, my family didn't communicate these things over the dinner table. Perhaps we didn't have the vocabulary for it. Or perhaps their vocabulary didn't match mine. What I do remember about language, besides its power, was collision, and rules.

Collision occurred when the languages I had at home, English, enough Malayalam, went to war with each other, making me mix up syntax and sounds. At some point I gave up on grammar, and learned by listening, and watching, especially brown men who seemed to erase themselves at will, because they were expected to.

And there was shame too, which turned up in unexpected places, like Arabic class. The test was dictation, a performative exercise where the Arabic teacher yelled out the word, which you wrote on the blackboard for inspection. The first time I was asked to do this, I wrote from left to right. And my teacher asked me to start over, and I did, once again from left to right. My teacher asked me to stop, then hit me.

I knew the words, every single one of them, but I wasn't permitted to write them on the board. And now, as an adult, I know fewer words, but the sounds I continue to gravitate towards, because that is what language most often is to me, something sonic, unless you belong to the world of the non-hearing and they are your people.

Language is rhythm, which is something I pay attention to in the work that I do, and I've started to wonder about the expectation readers have about a writer from Abu Dhabi. Not based in, but from the city. And what must this writer sound like? Especially if he looks like me.

Recall the rabbit, the one I pulled out the hat and offered a cigarette to?

Well, if the rabbit spoke little-little English, some-some Arabee, almost same-same but not same-same, and enough Malayalam and Hindi/Urdu to communicate this-thing-that-thing, would anyone request a translator?

Would this translator be an academic?

If I could get away with another hypothetical?

If you belonged to a film crew, and my classroom was a documentary set, and you're sitting with your editor now, in the cutting room floor, and when you hear this rabbit, would you subtitle everything. Why? The English is some-some, the Arabic too pidgin, just basic shuay-shuay. Would you?

The answer is important.

Earlier this year, I assigned Teju Cole's *Black Body* to my students. In it, Cole writes about James Baldwin's essay 'Stranger in the Village', published in 1953 in *Harper's Magazine*. Baldwin's essay, in Cole's words, 'recounts the experience of being black in an all-white village', Leukerbad, in Switzerland. Both essays resonate strongly with me. I am unable to properly articulate why yet, but what I do know is that the following lines resonated with me deeply.

First Baldwin, from *Notes of a Native Son*: 'In some subtle way, in a really profound way, I brought to Shakespeare, Bach, Rembrandt, to the Stones of Paris, to the Cathedral at Chartres, and the Empire State Building a special attitude. These were not really my creations, they did not contain my history; I might search them in vain forever for any reflection of myself. I was an interloper; this was not my heritage.'

And to that, Cole says: 'The lines throb with sadness. What he loves does not love him in return.'

Cole continues: 'This is where I part ways with Baldwin. I disagree not with his particular sorrow but with the self-abnegation that pinned him to it. Bach, so profoundly human, is my heritage. I am not an interloper when I look at a Rembrandt portrait. I care for them more than some white people do, just as some white people care more for aspects of African art than I do…'

There is more, but permit me to do away with Cole and Baldwin's presence in the lecture since they are no longer needed. Their purpose has been served.

My father hasn't heard of Baldwin. My uncles too. They may never know that a person named James Baldwin lived and died. But when Cole writes 'what he loves does not love him in return', I think of my father, because he belongs to a generation that may never understand the in-between place that the Gulf eventually became.

My family members spent decades in the Gulf as transient employees, only to return to where they came from. I am not my father. I am not my mother. They are quiet people. I suppose this is why I write, to make them talk. And this is probably why language, any language, is fair game, to be harnessed and deployed on the page. I suppose I invent people and turn them immortal, because as long as they are read about, they exist.

I urge my students not to end their stories with dreams, but I think of dreams I ought to have.

What if I were Red Peter, not as ape, but as me, as I look now, and I was asked to address a fictitious academy, composed of individuals not too different from the people I work with and deem my colleagues? Scholars and intellectuals of the highest pedigree, strangers and people who write about people who look like me? What would/could the title of that lecture be?

I suppose I could talk about what happens to people like me, the child of temporary workers, in a city like Abu Dhabi. It wouldn't be a surprise or a distraction to anyone if I spoke about migration, or labour, particularly brown and black bodies. And perhaps transience, musings about the vocabulary of movement.

To court the language of authenticity, I could cite the names of scholars I am familiar with, or am acquainted and/or friends with, whether I agree with their work or not. And then I'd ask the organizers to dim the lights, in order to take a look at the people in the audience. And if there are people in attendance who are librarians, or book sellers, I'd like to know whether they'd file my mind, what I know and write about, under South Asia, the Global South, Arab Lit, Science Fiction, Migration Studies, Gulf Studies, or World Literature. And if there are plenty of scholars in attendance, I'd like them to categorize me. Am I segmented labor? The new bourgeois? Perhaps a word builder, a meaning maker.

Or a rabbit.

Because if we were to return to the idea of the rabbit, not the pace setter in track and field, the one who disappears, but the other rabbit, the swearer, the smoker, the talker. The rabbit who will stare you down after the conversation has ended.

Because a part of him, the one eager for mischief, will continue to watch you, because he doesn't want you to forget he existed.

Because there is no show without him.

23. Transing

Greta Olson and Laura Borchert

INTRODUCTION

One of the first things instructors ask students of literature to consider when they approach a literary text is its formal elements. Form, as Greta never tires of repeating, determines function and a text's overall message and values. Form includes, foremost, narrative situation—that is, the question of who speaks, or who sees in the text, whether this text be a novel, a film, an episode from a television series or a TikTok video. This involves taking a wide view of the "literary" to include more than poetry, poems and plays, but cultural articulations of all kinds. One can, for instance, interpret actor Elliot Page's December 2020 Twitter announcement that he is transmasculine as a cultural text and use philological means to do so. This method of unpacking cultural texts mirrors the branch of Law and Literature that has attended to the rhetorical, fictional, and imaginative aspects of law. A central question asked in this research, as in traditional literary studies, is what the locus of authority in law is. Who or what speaks law's authority?

Narrative authority has traditionally been associated with an omniscient point of view in literary fiction. Think of the godlike narrators in Henry Fielding's novels who tell readers exactly what to think, what to pay attention to and indeed where to go, as we travel along in the narrative with an eponymous character such as Tom Jones (1749). This all-knowing narrator, many literary historians agree, became the basis for what most of us think of when we think about novels, the image of which coalesced during the long eighteenth century. The omniscient narrator of such novels is that Wizard of Oz-like invisible person behind the curtain who is located outside of the text. It is the narrator who points to events and settings and, often through free indirect discourse, leads readers into the minds of the texts' characters, allowing them to feel the characters' sensations and witness their emotions even as we see them from the outside, as though we were encountering persons in the non-fictional world. This allows us to fall in love with Elizabeth even as she is falling into animosity and then in love with Darcy. In Genettian terms, the authoritative narrator is extradiegetic—located outside of the text—and heterodiegetic, that is, not a character within the novel's world; and this narrator tells the story in the third person. This authorial narrator, to borrow an alternative term for the same phenomenon, in turn has the omniscient capability to look inside of the thoughts of characters and to reliably relate their motivations. The more the narrator knows, the more authoritative they are perceived to be. As Paul Dawson writes, authority can be measured in the completeness of the narrator's knowledge, and the effect of narrative authority is one of absolute control:

> The overriding effect which the various formal elements of omniscient narration both enable, and are underpinned by, is that of a specific rhetorical performance of narrative authority. By this I mean

the heterodiegetic narrator's authority to pass judgment on the fictional world, and the authoritative resonance of these judgments in the extradiegetic or public world of the reader.[1]

A sense of the narrator's omniscience is created in expressive acts of authority. Readers' faith in this omniscience ensures their sense that the narrator's knowledge of the storyworld is complete and reliable. Readers tacitly agree to the narrator's assumed right "to pass judgment" on characters and fictional events.

The ability "to pass judgment on the fictional world" underlines what readers have come to expect of authoritative narrators. As has frequently been pointed out, law creates its authority through repeated rhetorical performances, much like the authoritative novelistic narrator that Dawson describes.[2] For members of a given legal order, who are not hostile to that order, the agreement to comply with law's passing judgment is based on the tacit belief that legal decisions are based on authoritative knowledge of events and actors' motivations.

The act of passing judgment authoritatively bears directly on recent laws and legal judgments regarding trans individuals' right to determine their gender in Germany and the United States.[3] For biographical and disciplinary reasons, Germany and the US comprise the geopolitical locations that the present authors know most thoroughly. We analyze German and American legal orders comparatively, despite their systemic differences, to uncover the similar ways in which trans and non-binary persons are denied voice and legal recognition. In both Germany and the US, the presumed right to control and limit autonomous determinations of gender rests on a discourse that frames trans and non-binary persons as lacking the capacity to authoritatively "know" and accordingly act their genders. Such attributions depart from notions about how legal persons must narrate their experience in ways that are viewed as reliable. This dovetails with research on how persons are expected to testify consistently and coherently, also in accordance with the mores of literary realism, whether in criminal trials or in statements given by asylum seekers. These notions are grounded in expectations of narrator reliability, a concept that has been explored at length in narratology, as will be discussed below.

The analysis of anti-trans and anti-non-binary legislation in Germany and the United States will demonstrate insidious prejudices that trans people are actually men who masquerade as women or are, alternatively, childish persons who are as yet unable to "properly" embrace a binary gender identity.[4] Correspondingly, fears about trans individuals' supposed interest in imposing their sexuality onto vulnerable others are instrumentalized to limit trans folks' ability to determine their own lives. The need for an omniscient quasi-heterodiegetic narrative presence to dictate trans persons' identities is invoked in identity-change laws in Germany as well as in "bathroom bills" and laws restricting trans persons' participation in sports in the US.

---

[1] Paul Dawson, *The Return of the Omniscient Narrator: Authorship and Authority in Twenty-First Century Fiction* (Ohio State UP 2013) 54.

[2] J.M. Balkin and Sanford Levinson, "Law as Performance" (1998) 2 *Law and Literature* 729; Frans-Willem Korsten, "*Öffentlichkeit* and the Law's Behind the Scenes: Theatrical and Dramatic Appearance in European and US American Criminal Law" (2017) 18.2 *German Law Journal* 399.

[3] Following recent changes in preferred usage, we use "trans" inclusively and without the asterisk in respect for those who do not have binary gender identities and also so as to not perpetuate forms of transmisogyny.

[4] Throughout this text, we use "anti-trans" to refer to pushback against non-cis individuals.

The assumption that trans and non-binary persons are unreliable narrators, whose unreliability has to be detected, contained, and also controlled, prevails in this discourse.

Discussions of narrative authority in literature and law are by no means new. Think of Robin West's attestation that legal theory is inherently narrative, and follows out of the four archetypical modes of storytelling.[5] Consider ensuing discussions about the degree to which law is narrative or not, and whether or not "law needs a narratology"—the science of storytelling.[6] If one agrees that law needs a science of narratives, then more than one narratology may be needed to account for larger systemic differences in constructing legal narratives in common law versus Roman law-based settings.[7] A more historical strand of Law and Narrative research has demonstrated how evolving literary genres and forms co-determine the narrative forms of legal processes and texts. Narrative elements and structures are integral to law and legal processes, and one witnesses multiple overlaps and cross-fertilizations of literary and legal narrative forms.

We consciously bring a fundamental distinction from literary analysis—the determination of a text's narrative situation and attendant considerations of how narrative authority is conveyed in that text—to a discussion of the need to de-binarize law. The legal recognition of a person's right to determine their gender relates to perceptions of that person's reliability and their capacity to assert identity in a manner considered consistent, trustworthy, and relevant. Yet this assessment departs from epistemic assumptions of gender essentialism. Questions of narrator reliability connect directly to non-cis expressions of gender, to sexual consent, and to the issue of who has the normative authority to decide on these matters. Because this is the area in which we see the most activism and legal activity occurring in relation to what might loosely be called "sex," we focus on legal prohibitions regarding trans and non-binary persons.

Trans has become the legal–cultural battlefield that queer once was in countries such as Germany and the US, before the legalization of gay marriage.[8] This does not however mean that queer issues now go legally uncontested.[9] Trans and non-binary individuals' efforts to live their gender freely constitute that area of sexualized life that is most contested in public debates about law. In what has been saliently described as a visibility trap, representations of trans lives and trans identities have gained new prominence, while at the same time multiple efforts are being made to radically curtail existing trans rights and protections through bath-

---

[5] Robin West, "Jurisprudence as Narrative: An Aesthetic Analysis of Modern Legal Theory" (1985) 60 *NYUL Rev.* 145; Robin West, *Narrative, Authority, and Law* (U of Michigan P 1993).

[6] Peter Brooks, "Narrative Transactions—Does the Law Need a Narratology?" (2006) 18.1 *Yale J.L. & Human. Art.* 1. For an overview of Law and Narrative, see Greta Olson, "Narration and Narrative in Legal Discourse" in Peter Hühn et al. (eds), *Living Handbook of Narratology* (Hamburg UP 2014).

[7] Jeanne Gaakeer, *Judging from Experience: Law, Praxis, Humanities* (De Gruyter 2019).

[8] Frank Bruni, "Republicans Have Found Their Cruel New Culture War: Arkansas Lawmakers' Move against Trans People Reflects a Larger Strategy" (*The New York Times* April 12, 2021) www.nytimes.com/2021/04/10/opinion/sunday/transgender-rights-republicans-arkansas.html. Inga Barthels, "Sachverständige unterstützen Gesetzesvorschläge für mehr Selbstbestimmung" (*Tagesspiegel* November 2, 2020) www.tagesspiegel.de/gesellschaft/queerspiegel/zeit-ist-reif-das-transsexuellengesetz-abzuwickeln-sachverstaendige-unterstuetzen-gesetzesvorschlaege-fuer-mehr-selbstbestimmung/26582712.html.

[9] For a critical examination of queer rights projects beyond same-sex marriage, see Laura Borchert, *Beyond* Bostock*: A Law and Culture Approach to the Potential Bond Between Sexual Orientation and Suspect Classification* (dissertation, unpublished manuscript), including analyses of legal cases involving issuing birth certificates with same-sex partners as parents as in *Pavan v Smith, 582 US_(2017)* in the US and the *Akkermann* case in Germany (*OLG Celle 21 UF 146/20, 21 W 8/20*).

room bills, bills that limit access to medical treatments, bills barring trans girls from participating in sports, and efforts to legally restrict individuals' assertions of gender identity until they are determined to be adults.[10] We analyze this hypervisibility and the simultaneous efforts at hyper-regulation in terms of the assumed unreliability of non-gender-conforming persons.

Anti-trans legislation works in conjunction with popular narratives about transgender issues and transitioning. One such narrative, resting on a moral panic, suggests that transgender is a social contagion that endangers youth.[11] It implies that trans is a fad that youth need to be protected from rather than a legitimate identity. Another narrative promotes the idea that trans girls have an unfair advantage over cis girls in athletic competitions and that their participation will destroy efforts at achieving gender equality in sports. Still a third narrative insists that trans girls will threaten the privacy of cis girls in locker rooms. It coheres with a history of prejudicial representations of adult male cross-dressers who commit sexualized violence against women. Think of the crossdressing serial killer men that populate the cultural imaginary in films such as *Psycho* (1960), *Dressed to Kill* (1980) and *Silence of the Lambs* (1991).[12] A recurring trope in these films involves the killer's long blond wig being removed to dramatically reveal his identity as a man. This act stands in for the socio-cultural insistence that non-binary and trans persons have to reveal their "real" gender identity which also speaks through cases of alleged transgender fraud when trans persons have not informed partners of their transness before sex.[13] Such images are utilized to reinforce the legal repression of non-normative gender identities, and they go hand in hand with routine violence against trans and non-binary persons by police and in prisons and in health care systems.[14] In all three cases, the imagined vulnerability of children and cis women is weaponized in an affectively arousing manner to elicit fears about trans and non-binary people and to promote legal efforts to limit their autonomy.

These rhetorically affective moves function to deny what we want to call "sexual–legal personhood" to trans and non-binary persons.[15] We introduce sexual–legal personhood in analogy to what has been called "sexual citizenship," that is, the use of discourses of citizenship and human rights to advocate for rights and protections for sexual minorities.[16] Critical histories of

---

[10] Reina Gossett, Eric A. Stanley, and Johanna Burton (eds), *Trap Door: Trans Cultural Production and the Politics of Visibility* (MIT Press 2017) xv.

[11] Dianna Kenney, "Is Gender Dysphoria Socially Contagious?" (*gdworkinggroup* September 13, 2019) https://gdworkinggroup.org/2019/09/13/is-gender-dysphoria-socially-contagious/ accessed April 22, 2021. Lisa Littman, "Parent Reports of Adolescents and Young Adults Perceived to Show Signs of a Rapid Onset of Gender Dysphoria" (2018) 14.3 *PLoS ONE* 13, 8.

[12] For a short montage of these serial killers, see *Crossdressing Serial Killers* (USC Annenberg) https://criticalmediaproject.org/transgender-serial-killers/ accessed March 15, 2021.

[13] As in the English case *R v McNally* (2013) EWCA Crim 1051, and the Israeli case *Israel v Alkobi* (2003) as discussed in Alex Sharpe, "Criminalising Sexual Intimacy: Transgender Defendants and the Legal Construction of Non-Consent" (2014) 3 *Criminal L. Rev.* 207. See also A. Sharpe, *Sexual Intimacy and Gender Identity "Fraud": Reframing the Legal and Ethical Debate* (Routledge 2018); Florence Ashley, "Genderfucking Non-Disclosure: Sexual Fraud, Transgender Bodies, and Messy Identities" (2018) 41.2 *Dal. L. J.* 339.

[14] See Viviane K. Namaste on genderbashing in transphobic acts of violence particularly towards trans women of colour: *Sex Change, Social Change: Reflections on Identity, Institutions, and Imperialism* (Women's Press CA 2005).

[15] Sexual–legal personhood refers to the legal acknowledgement of a person's right to determine their gender and sexual identity.

[16] Diane Richardson, "Rethinking Sexual Citizenship" (2017) 51 *Sociology* 208.

legal personhood highlight the mutability of the concept and its utilization to assign rights and protections to some persons while denying them to others, particularly to minorities: a legal person is then whatever law says she is.[17] Using the concept of sexual citizenship as a model, we advocate for an understanding of sexual–legal personhood that "opens up the possibility of transforming the norms of citizenship as a whole," if queered, transed, and de-binarized.[18]

Just as we take an expansive view of the literary in this Law and Literature text, we also conceptualize law generously. Law comprises not only what has been called internal legal culture—legal processes and legal institutions—but also whatever people take to be binding authority. Eugen Ehrlich called this *living law*, the norms of behavior that people actually live by whether they are based in state-centered law or in other normative orders.[19] We note the simultaneity of two contrary cultural–legal trends. One is an emergent form of *lived law* that increasingly embraces the legitimacy of mutable gender identities, as can be seen in the greater visibility of non-binary and trans persons. A second, more residual strand of *lived* and institutional law, by contrast, punishes trans and non-binary persons by insisting on law's right to dictate who they are. Imputations of unreliability to trans and non-binary persons and of vulnerability to the cis women and children with whom they interact are deployed in anti-trans discourse and anti-trans legislation.

Uncovering these rhetorical moves demonstrates that law's assumed "right to pass judgment" on trans persons, like an omniscient narrator, is deeply problematic, as is the assumption that trans and non-binary persons cannot reliably narrate their genders. Law, we suggest, needs to acknowledge transformed notions of de-binarized gender, sexual citizenship, and legal–sexual personhood. This change would run parallel to a development in literary studies, which is to question the once universally accepted category of unreliable narration as resulting from the presumed personal failings of the narrator to relate events coherently and consistently. Rather than seeing the character–narrator as inherently fallible and/or untrustworthy, unreliable narration is reconceived of as a strategy to upset dominant social hierarchies.

CONSTRUCTING AND NARRATING SEX

Notions of acceptable sex are mutable, historically and geo-politically contingent. Gayle Rubin, one of the divine mothers of queer studies, pointed out what she considered to be the "sex hierarchy" in 1982.[20] This was nearly the same year that Robin West discussed narrative authority in legal theory and implicitly in legal judgments, and Catherine MacKinnon suggested what is non-consentable for women in the realms of sexual practice and sexual

---

[17] Jeanne Gaakeer, "'Sua Cuique Persona' A Note on the Fiction of Legal Personhood and a Reflection on Interdisciplinary Consequences" (2016) 28.3 *Law and Literature* 287.
[18] Richardson, 211.
[19] Eugen Ehrlich, *Gesetz und lebendes Recht: Vermischte kleinere Schriften* (Manfred Rehbinder ed, Duncker & Humblot 1986). Ehrlich's (1862–1922) early sociological work on *living law* (*lebendes Recht*) included a notion of people's consciousness of law/justice that is independent of state-made law. Ehrlich resisted the imposition of Austro-Hungarian Empire law in the highly ethnically heterogeneous area of Bukovina (now the Ukraine) where he lived and defended the importance of customary legal traditions.
[20] Gayle S. Rubin, "Thinking Sex: Notes for a Radical Theory of the Politics of Sexuality" in Gayle S. Rubin (ed), *Deviations* (first published 1984, Duke UP 2012).

representation—porn as a form of violence against women.[21] Rubin's "radical theory of sex" aimed at denaturalizing sex as essential, instinctual, and unchangeable in order to point out the policing of those acts adjudged unacceptable.[22]

In a "hierarchical system of sexual value," some types of sex "are rewarded" while others are violently punished.[23] Rubin illustrates what was then considered to be "good sex" within what she calls "the charmed circle." This includes heterosexual, married, monogamous, procreative, and noncommercial sex; sex practiced in pairs, in a relationship, within the same generation, and taking place at home, without pornography, involving only bodies, vanilla sexual acts, no toys, and clearly delineated binaristic sex-roles (what we might call tops and bottoms). "Blessed" types of sex stand in contradistinction to what lies outside of the inner circle and is considered "bad, abnormal, unnatural, and damned sexuality," including casual, non-reproductive, and cross-generational sex. Adjudged as more abnormal, "transvestites, transsexuals, fetishists, sadomasochist" actors are located "way out" of the charmed circle, and their practices considered "abnormal, unnatural, sick, sinful."[24]

The charmed circle of "good" sex has changed its circumference since the early 1980s, with queer marriage having become legal in the United States in 2015 and in Germany in 2017. Bland and commercialized forms of BDSM have been mainstreamed and commodified through the *50 Shades of Grey* franchise. Working on Rubin's essay with students in 2020, Greta found that what was considered by Rubin to be contested border areas of sex in the US and Germany still comprises cross-generational sex, particularly when it involves much younger persons; casual sex; and sex involving multiple partners for women, who continue to be adjudged by different behavioral standards regarding sexual practices than do men.[25]

What Rubin addresses and what we wish to think through more thoroughly in this chapter is the continuous delegation of some forms of sex as "bad" and others as "good" and the anxieties about sexuality that surround these significations. As Rubin points out, social concerns coalesce around sex in a way they do not about other bodily activities, for "disputes over sexual behaviour often become the vehicles for displacing social anxieties, and discharging their attendant emotional intensity."[26] Further, in what Rubin refers to as a "bait-and-switch" strategy, fears regarding certain types of tabooed sex are instrumentalized to do other cultural–legal work. This is the case, we assert, in legislation regarding non-binary and trans persons. Our effort is to uncover how legal narratives that ascribe unreliability to trans and non-binary persons are unreliable themselves and to highlight conceptualizations of identity as fluid that have yet to be acknowledged in law.

---

[21] Catherine MacKinnon, *Feminism Unmodified: Discourses on Life and Law* (Harvard UP 1987).
[22] Rubin, "Thinking Sex" 145.
[23] Rubin, "Thinking Sex" 151.
[24] Rubin, "Thinking Sex" 153.
[25] The class agreed that the inner and outer circles would now need to be re-thought in terms of intersectionality, to include gender-, class-, ability/disability-related distinctions, as well as other factors such as HIV status.
[26] Rubin, "Thinking Sex" 143.

TRANS VISIBILITIES AND TRANS ANXIETIES

One "major area of contest" in the moving target of the "good" and "bad" spectrum of sexuality is what is misperceived as trans sex. As Rubin pointed out in subsequent discussions, her original diagram mistakenly categorized transgender and transvestitism as sexual practices rather than as aspects of gender identity and gender expression, a point for which she was correctly criticized.[27] In her defense, Rubin points out that "transgender practices were initially grouped with the sexual perversions,"[28] and have only recently been come to be conceptualized as identity issues in psychological terms.[29] While Rubin came to see that she had lacked a conceptual model for thinking about trans issues in 1982 and 1984, law as a normative authority has not done so to date. A number of legislative initiatives in the US and in Germany point to the persistent confusion of being non-binary or trans with being sexually threatening.

Whereas trans persons and practices may have appeared "way out" of the charmed sexual circle in the early eighties, they are now central to media preoccupations. Actor Elliot Page's 2020 *Twitter* announcement that they are transmasculine; adored characters such as Sophia Burset in *Orange Is the New Black*, Blanca in *Pose*, and Alex Blue Davis in *Grey's Anatomy*[30]—all of these figures contribute to a trend of representing trans persons in positive and more well-rounded ways. They also contradict old-school images of trans persons as men who dangerously masquerade as women. These men, the stereotypes go, "dress up" in order to fool heterosexual men into being mistakenly attracted to them, or assume women's identities in order to wreak violence on "real" women.[31] Less overtly destructive representations of trans persons over-represent fetishized trans women and feature inevitable moments of shocked revelation of these women's genitalia to the violent disgust of male lovers. Think *The Crying Game* (1992). Narratives of trans lives also focus myopically on medical transitions and post-transition sex, as a narrowly conceived brand of heteronormative PIV (penis-in-vagina) sex.[32]

The current surplus of trans representations, including positive ones, in public media and the arts suggests a move toward social acceptance of trans and non-binary persons in what might be considered to be a generalized legal consciousness or *living law*. This move was marked by mainstream *Newsweek*'s announcement of trans as the new civil rights issue in 2014 and its featuring trans actress Laverne Cox on its cover, and Caitlyn Jenner's live television interview

---

[27] Gayle S. Rubin, "Notes" in Gayle S. Rubin (ed), *Deviations* (Duke UP 2012) note 46, 386.
[28] Gayle S. Rubin, "Postscript to 'Thinking Sex: Notes for a Radical Theory of the Politics of Sexuality'" in Gayle S. Rubin (ed), *Deviations* (Duke UP 2012) 215.
[29] See "Gender Dysphoria Diagnosis" (*American Psychiatric Association* n.d.) www.psychiatry.org/psychiatrists/cultural-competency/education/transgender-and-gender-nonconforming-patients/gender-dysphoria-diagnosis accessed April 20, 2021: in 2013, the Diagnostic and Statistical Manual of Mental Disorders 5 acknowledged "gender dysphoria" as "gender identity-related distress that some transgender people experience" instead of pathologizing trans gender.
[30] We acknowledge the American-centrism of this list.
[31] For an overview of destructive stereotypes, also comic ones, see Sam Feder, *Disclosure: Trans Lives on Screen* (Netflix 2020). For how these stereotypes play out in criminal law, see Talia Mae Bettcher, "Evil Deceivers and Make-Believers: Transphobic Violence and the Politics of Illusion" (2007) 22.3 *Hypatia: A Journal of Feminist Philosophy* 43.
[32] As summarized in Anson Koch-Rein et al., "Representing Trans: Visibility and Its Discontents" (2020) 24 *EJES* 1; and Danae Gallo González (ed), *Trans* Time. Projecting Transness in European (TV) Series* (Campus 2021).

"coming out" as trans in 2015.[33] Yet, shortly thereafter, the Trump administration occasioned an attack on trans rights and protections, with the attempt to define trans out of existence in the legal definition of sex under Title IX, the effort to ban trans persons from serving in the military, and restrictions on trans persons' access to health care.[34] On a more visceral level, violence against trans and non-binary persons and particularly trans women of color appears ever more prevalent. Visibility therefore comes at a high cost for those trans individuals who need to pass in order to avoid harassment and assault.[35] As trans activist Tiq Milan succinctly states in a 2020 documentary that rehearses the history of clichéd negative representations of trans people: "The more we are seen, the more we are violated."[36]

Anxieties about trans persons and their actions stand behind the visibility gap. They revolve around essentialized notions of sexuality that attach sexual orientation to gender identity and to biological, binary sex. One assumes that being assigned female at birth means that a person will automatically feel herself to be feminine and will present herself accordingly in how she dresses, speaks, and acts, and that she will desire and wish to make herself attractive to cis men. The shorthand version of this equation is: sex = gender = sexual orientation. Laws restricting trans and non-binary persons' gender choices and behaviors are based on this equation as well as binaries that result out of it: female/male, feminine/masculine, homosexual/heterosexual, cisgender/transgender, and so on.

When the sex = gender = sexual orientation equation is applied to trans and other gender nonconforming persons in law, these persons are assumed to be deficitary in terms of their sexual–legal personhood. A purported unreliability is projected onto them in two distinct ways. The first of these concerns young people. When presented as not fully capable legal subjects, trans and non-binary persons are treated as unable to narrate their identities in a way that would render them eligible for gender self-determination. This includes *Bell v Tavistock* (2020), to take one well-known anti trans case from English law, and bills such as Arkansas' HB 1570 scaremongering Save Adolescents from Experimentation (SAFE) Act (2020), which prohibits access to gender-conforming drugs and penalizes doctors who treat young patients. Individuals are portrayed as too immature and child-like to authoritatively know that they want to transition. In other words, they are not legally allowed to assert their gender identities. An incapacity to know their genders accurately is ascribed to trans and non-binary persons. A second kind of unreliability is projected onto gender nonconforming persons in bills directed at trans women and girls. In bathroom bills and legal prohibitions against trans girls in sports, prejudices about trans women as sexually deviant adults come into play. In both projections, trans persons are viewed as unreliable narrators who lack the capacity to narrate and determine their sexual–legal status.

---

[33] Katy Steinmetz, "The Transgender Tipping Point" (*Time* January 11, 2014) https://time.com/135480/transgender-tipping-point/ accessed March 15, 2021.

[34] Erica L. Green, Katie Benner and Robert Pear, "'Transgender' Could Be Defined Out of Existence under Trump Administration" (*The New York Times* October 21, 2018). www.nytimes.com/2018/10/21/us/politics/transgender-trump-administration-sex-definition.html.

[35] S.E. James et al., *The Report of the 2015 U.S. Transgender Survey* (National Centre for Transgender Equality 2016) and due to the delayed publication of an updated survey in 2020, statistics from Human Rights Campaign, "Fatal Violence against the Transgender and Gender Non-Conforming Community in 2020" (*The Human Rights Campaign* n.d.) www.hrc.org/resources/fatal-violence-against-the-transgender-and-gender-non-conforming-community-in-2021 accessed April 26, 2021.

[36] Sam Feder, *Disclosure: Trans Lives on Screen* (Netflix 2020) 00:01:30–00:01:38.

Narrator unreliability was first described in 1968 by Wayne Booth as the discrepancy between what a given narrator says about herself and the world around her and what the text signals otherwise.[37] Well-known examples include Dostoevsky's *Underground Man* (1864), Twain's *Huckleberry Finn* (1884) and Nabokov's Humbert Humbert from *Lolita* (1955). Unreliable narrators are those character–narrators whose statements directly contradict themselves or the evidence supplied by other characters or by the textual world around them. The concept is a staple in literary criticism and features in most introductions to literary analysis. Readers identify unreliable narrators when they note discrepancies between what the narrator says, which they initially take at face value, and other information supplied by the text, which causes them to read against the grain and fill in narrative gaps. Readers perform this interpretive work because, as Booth pointed out, they expect characters that they meet in literary fiction to act like people in the outside world: "We react to all narrators as persons."[38] Accordingly, readers detect unreliability when they note that a narrator violates pragmatic communicative norms such as relevance, succinctness, and clarity.

More recently, the widely accepted concept of unreliable narration has been questioned due to its ideological underpinnings.[39] The concept rests on the assumption that communicative acts in fiction, like those that take place in extra-textual contexts, occur between interlocutors with similar communicative goals, based on their being autonomous, self-determined, and rational subjects.[40] Unreliable narrators are adjudged as deficient—as fallible and/or as untrustworthy—due to their assumed capacity to articulate themselves relevantly and their perceived choice to flout norms of communication. Yet, at least since Kant, narrative unreliability has been attributed to colonized and racialized persons as well as to subordinate women as proof of an inherent lack of trustworthiness. All these groups have been regarded as deceptive or uninformed in their expressions, and hence also as unreliable narrators.[41] No awareness is given to how people may choose or be forced to express themselves in ways that are perceived as unreliable by their interlocutors due to the power imbalances that exist between them. As Homi Bhabha writes: "The incalculable colonized subject—half acquiescent, half oppositional, always untrustworthy—produces an unresolvable problem of cultural difference for the very address of colonial cultural authority."[42] As Bhabha and other post-colonial and race-critical critics have shown, communicators choose to use mimicry and double-voicedness, among other strategies, to speak back to power in indirect ways. Narrating

---

[37] Female pronouns are used inclusively. See Wayne Booth, *The Rhetoric of Fiction* (Chicago UP 1968). For historical overviews, see Greta Olson, "Reconsidering Unreliability. Fallible and Untrustworthy Narrators" (2003) 11.1 *Narrative* 93; for a list of textual signals of unreliability, see Ansgar Nünning, "Reconceptualizing Unreliable Narration: Synthesizing Cognitive and Rhetorical Approaches" in J. Phelan and P.J. Rabinowitz (eds), A Companion to Narrative Theory (Blackwell 2005) 89. Dan Shen, "Unreliability" (2011) in Peter Hühn et al. (eds), *Living Handbook of Narratology* (Hamburg UP 2014).

[38] Booth, 273.

[39] Fredric Jameson, *Marxism and Form: Twentieth-Century Dialectical Theories of Literature* (Princeton UP 1971) 357.

[40] Greta Olson, "Questioning the Ideology of Reliability in Mohsin Hamid's *The Reluctant Fundamentalist*: Towards a Critical, Culturalist Narratology" in Divya Dwivedi, Henrik Skov Nielsen, and Richard Walsh (eds), *Narratology and Ideology: Negotiating Context, Form, and Theory of Postcolonial Narratives* (Ohio State UP 2018) 164–5.

[41] Olson, "Questioning" 164–7.

[42] Homi Bhabha, *The Location of Culture* (Routledge 1994) 33.

unreliably can then constitute a form of resistance to hierarchies of power, including those adjudicated in law.

Unreliability is attributed to trans, non-binary, and non-gender-conforming persons in laws that restrict their access to medical treatments, to participation in sports, and simply to operate in public spaces, such as by using bathrooms.[43] The attribution of unreliability in these persons goes hand in hand with the authority attributed to law to "pass judgment" on their fallibility. This authority circumscribes non-binary and trans persons' lives by assigning them fixed, supposedly authentic gender identifications. These identifications are premised by cisnormative mores of gender that non-binary and trans people in themselves repudiate. Trans and non-binary persons invite strategies to subvert legal authority, for instance, through the refusal to disclose gender identity.[44] Rather than being unreliable, non-binary and trans folks speak back to cisnormative identifications of static and essentialized gender.

CIRCUMSCRIBING TRANS PERSONS' LEGAL SELF-DETERMINATIONS AS INHERENTLY UNRELIABLE

In Germany, two laws are at the center of trans rights debates: the *Transsexuellengesetz* (law for transsexuals; *TSG*) and the §45b *Personenstandsgesetz* (civil status law; *PStG*). The *TSG* has existed since 1981 and originally necessitated that only people who were over 25 years of age,[45] had medically transitioned,[46] were divorced,[47] and had been sterilized could legally change their first name and civil status (*Personenstand*) to the other gender. These requirements were determined to be unconstitutional in a number of judgments, with the requirement of sterilization becoming inapplicable in 2011. Today, the *TSG* requires trans people to "successfully" undergo assessments by two court appointed psychological experts, which they must pay for, as well as a fee of €1,868, on average, to change their "sex" in official documents. Transitioning's inherent classist logic contributes to the gatekeeping of autonomous determinations of gender identity.[48]

The *PStG* was introduced in December 2018 and came into effect in January 2019 after the German Federal Constitutional Court decided that two fundamental rights of non-binary people are violated "if civil status law requires that one sex be registered but does not allow for

---

[43] Koch-Rein et al., "Representing" 3: "Using the hashtag #wejustneedtopee, trans media producers demonstrate the discrepancy between imagined sexual "perversion" and the lived realities of trans people in relation to the effects such legislation might have in forcing trans folks into restrooms that match their sex assigned at birth but clashes violently with their current gender presentation."
[44] Ashley, 377.
[45] § 8 sec 1 (1) *TSG* read with § 1 sec 1 (3) *TSG* on civil status, § 1 sec. 1 (3) *TSG* on changing one's first name. Both norms have been ruled unconstitutional because they violate equality before the law (*Gleichheitssatz*) as stipulated by art. 3 sec. 1 of the German Basic Law (GG).
[46] This was altered by the *Beschluss* of August 15, 1996—*2 BvR 1833/95*.
[47] The stipulation of divorce was in force until 2008, as regulated in § 8 sec. 1 (2) *TSG*.
[48] Laura Adamietz and Katharina Bager, "Regelungs- und Reformbedarf für transgeschlechtliche Menschen. Begleitmaterial zur Interministeriellen Arbeitsgruppe Inter- & Transsexualität" (*Bundesministerium für Familie, Senioren, Frauen und Jugend*, 7/2017) www.bmfsfj.de/blob/jump/114064/regelungs—und-reformbedarf-fuer-transgeschlechtliche-menschen---band-7-data.pdf accessed March 10, 2021, 12.

a further positive category other than male or female."[49] The law determines a "third option" regulation of a "diverse" gender category in addition to female and male. This option enables trans people to change the gender on their personal identification documents without going through the more difficult and invasive process that the *TSG* prescribes.

Trans lives were made easier by the "third option" for only a very brief time. What seemed like a progressive victory for trans individuals was soon contested. A growing backlash by official registrars led the Federal Ministry of the Interior, Building and Community (BMI) to issue a draft bill in April 2019, which makes clear that the law is only applicable to people who experience a "variant of sex development,"[50] that is, only inter* sex individuals.[51] Various judgments regarding the *PStG* and the *TSG* have created a legal patchwork situation that is difficult for trans and inter* persons and registrars to navigate. The BGH decided that only inter * persons can refer to the *PStG* after a medical expert has assessed that they lack a clearly defined female or male sex. Yet the BGH also determined that the *TSG* can be used to eliminate one's previous gender entry or to change it to the category of "diverse."[52] In any case, legal restrictions to changing gender identity can only be overcome by having court-designated physicians attest to the rightfulness of a person's claim to have their gender acknowledged. In other words, a quasi-authorial narrator, one imbued with the right to pass judgment, is appointed by the court. Located outside of the action of the trans person's wish to alter their gender, this authoritative instance adjudges the reliability of the trans person's assessment.

A recent revitalization of attempts to reform the *TSG* includes the option to abolish the law entirely and replace it with a *Selbstbestimmungsgesetz* ("self-determination bill"). After the Green Political Party (*die Grünen*) and the Liberal Party (*FDP*) proposed a 2020 bill that would allow trans and inter* people to change their gender without being examined by two medical "experts," the governing coalition invited an expert to comment. Dr Alexander Korte proceeded to reiterate fears associated with transness. According to his report, allowing people to choose their gender on official personal documents autonomously would pave the way for a "problematic arbitrariness" that would result in "unsettling social and legal consequences."[53] Korte cited concerns over an ensuing lack of safe spaces for women and girls—the implication being that these persons can only be cis. Further, the supposed difficulty to determine "a child's capacity for discernment"[54] was listed as another reason to not establish a trans law based on autonomy.

Korte's argumentation ties into a wider perception of gender fluidity as inherently unreliable and potentially threatening. By referring to the autonomous choice of gender identity

---

[49] BVerfG *Beschluss* of October 10, 2017, *Az 1 BvR 2019/16* head note 3.
[50] *BMI* circular letter from April 10, 2019, *VII 1—20103/27#17*: "Variante der Geschlechtsentwicklung".
[51] The use of inter* includes people who identify as intersexual, intergender, or other.
[52] Bundesgerichtshof (BGH) decision of April 22, 2020—*BGH XII ZB 383/19*.
[53] Alexander Korte, "Stellungnahme Dr. med. Alexander Korte, Klinikum der Universität München—Selbstbestimmungsrecht—19/17791—Ausschussdrucksache 19(4)626 C neu" (Deutscher Bundestag, November 2, 2020) www.bundestag.de/resource/blob/802752/8fe155e6f019c4734ae2aa9 2efe2f505/A-Drs-19-4-626-C-neu-data.pdf accessed March 15, 2021, 4. The German reads: "Unabhängig davon scheint es nicht ausgeschlossen, dass durch eine ausschließliche Selbstdefinition der eigenen Geschlechtszugehörigkeit einer problematischen Beliebigkeit in der offiziellen geschlechtlichen Zuordnung, mit dann auch verwirrenden gesellschaftlichen und rechtlichen Konsequenzen, der Weg geebnet wird."
[54] Korte, "Stellungnahme" 6. The German reads: "Die Feststellung der Einsichtsfähigkeit eines Kindes ist eine komplexe ärztlich-psychologische Angelegenheit."

as "problematic," "arbitrary" and "unsettling," Korte unwittingly unmasks a conservative approach to sexual–legal personhood for what it is: an anxious attempt to force people's realities into familiar categories and to determine the legitimacy of claims to gender identity according to the degree to which they do not cause moral panics among privileged, cis, and heterosexually normative persons.

Elements familiar from moral panic narratives are regularly seen in arguments against trans autonomy. Citing references to a "psychic epidemic" and "'waves' of misdiagnosed female patients" in the context of teenagers who wish to transition, Samuel Werner illustrates the power of the imagery that informs them: "Teenagers are being deindividualized by comparing them to inanimate matter, and their wish to transition is not acknowledged as an individual desire but rather framed as emanating from a moving and dangerous mass which spreads uncontrollably."[55] The epidemic imagery coheres with metaphors of social contagion in bills restricting youth from access to puberty blockers and hormones, such as Arkansas' SAFE Act. Further, the waves *topos* reiterates a pattern in anti-immigration discourse, which is to present migrants as uncontrollable masses of matter rather than as individual persons.[56] Werner examines how anti-trans narratives equate granting trans persons greater agency with actively harming children. Such narratives work from the premise that non-binary and trans identities are caused by a social chain reaction that harms children and teenagers, who are projected as unknowing, non-insightful, and non-consenting legal personae. The supposed victims of a social contagion regarding transness, these unreliable beings are regarded as unable to tell their gender narratives or to assert their gender identities.[57]

Coming back to Gayle Rubin's distinction between "good" and "bad" sex and the interest in sexual practices during periods of social crisis, we note that lawing the autonomous choice of gender identity has become a contested site for negotiating minority rights. Changing one's gender has become entangled with fears about rape and sexual coercion and the myth that MTF[58] persons are not only deceptive in terms of their 'true' identities as men but are also sexual predators.[59] In Germany, an angst about insufficient procreation and imperiled national survival speaks through the discourse about civil status and the challenge to established social norms regarding gender. Trans rights have become an affective battlefield for hostilities

---

[55] See Samuel Noah Werner, "Über die Angst vor der Ansteckung und die Pathologisierung geschlechtlicher Non-Konformität" in Victoria Preis, Aaron Lahl, and Patrick Henze-Lindhorst (eds), *Vom Lärmen des Begehrens: Psychoanalyse und lesbische Sexualität* (Psychosozial Verlag 2021) (forthcoming, translation Laura Borchert). The German reads: "Die Jugendlichen werden durch den Vergleich mit unbelebter Materie entindividualisiert und ihr Wunsch nach Transition zu einem Anliegen erklärt, das nicht Ausdruck eines individuellen Bedürfnisses sei, sondern von einer sich bewegenden, gefährlichen Masse, die sich unkontrollierbar verbreitete, ausgeht."

[56] On anti-immigration discourse, see Greta Olson and Janna Wessels, "Imag(in)ing Human Rights: Deindividualizing, Victimizing, and Universalizing Images of Refugees in the United States and Germany" in Kirsten Schmidt (ed), *The State of Human Rights* (Universitätsverlag Winter 2020) 249, 254, 255.

[57] See Kenney; see Littman.

[58] Female-to-male; referring to someone who is or has been transitioning from a (cis) female gender identity to a (trans) male identity.

[59] Katy Steinmetz, "Why LGBT Advocates Say Bathroom 'Predators' Argument Is a Red Herring" (*Time* May 2, 2016) https://time.com/4314896/transgender-bathroom-bill-male-predators-argument/ accessed April 20, 2021. See also Bettcher, "Evil."

surrounding non-normative gender alignments that equate gender with the capability and willingness to reproduce biologically.

Women and children are used as moral credentials to mask discriminatory stances toward trans and non-gender-conforming persons, who supposedly present a threat to children and youth—in locker rooms and bathrooms. In the US, one such argument has been successfully implemented into law. In March 2021, Mississippi's Governor Tate Reeves (R) signed Senate bill 2536, which

> require[s] any public school, public institution of higher learning or institution of higher learning [...] to designate its athletic teams or sports according to biological sex; to provide protection for any school or institution of higher education that maintains separate athletic teams or sport for students of the female sex.[60]

The saliently named 'Miss. Fairness Act' presumes the vulnerability and defenselessness of girls.[61] In Gov. Reeves's words: "This important piece of legislation will ensure that young girls in Mississippi have a fair, level playing field [...] [it] sends a clear message to my daughters, and all of Mississippi's daughters, that their rights are worth fighting for."[62] Affectively persuasive to some, Reeves conveys a narrative about individual and imperiled girls, personalized as Mississippi's and his own daughters. Old-school images of trans persons as men dangerously masquerading as women become manifest here.[63] These men, the stereotypes go, "dress up" in order to fool heterosexual men into being mistakenly sexually attracted to them, as dramatically and offensively portrayed in *Ace Ventura* (1994), or assume a feminine appearance in order to violate cis women, as portrayed in films such as *Dressed to Kill* (1980). Reeves's listeners are invited to imagine the specter of a fearsome testosterone-laden male runner, "masquerading" as a female, racing past "real" female competitors and then threatening them in the locker room.

These images prevail in discourse surrounding bathroom bills as well as anti-trans athlete legislation, as in the statement in support of such a bill that "a male sexual predator will need only tell school personnel that he 'identifies as a female' (or vice versa) and must be granted access to the female restroom, locker room or shower" from *Gavin Grimm v Gloucester*

---

[60] MS SB2536 (Senator Hill, 2021) http://billstatus.ls.state.ms.us/documents/2021/html/SB/2500-2599/SB2536IN.htm accessed March 14, 2021.

[61] See Emily Wax-Thibodeaux and Samantha Schmidt, "Transgender Girls are at the Center of America's Culture Wars, Yet Again" (*Washington Post* January 30, 2021) www.washingtonpost.com/national/transgender-girls-are-at-the-center-of-americas-culture-wars-yet-again/2021/01/29/869133d6-602c-11eb-afbe-9a11a127d146_story.html accessed April 8, 2021: "bills about transgender athletes trigger the idea that 'this is wrong; this male person is in this space that is supposed to be segregated to protect girls and women,'" Serano said. See Molly Minta, "'Denying Humanity': Advocates Discuss Law that Bans Trans Athletes from Female Sports Teams" (*Mississippi Today* March 31, 2021) https://mississippitoday.org/2021/03/31/advocates-discuss-mississippi-law-banning-transgender-athletes/ accessed April 8, 2021.

[62] Devan Cole et al., "Mississippi Governor Signs Bill Banning Transgender Students from Women's Sports, Approving First Anti-Trans Law of 2021" (*KITV* March 12, 2021) www.kitv.com/story/43485303/mississippi-governor-signs-bill-banning-transgender-students-from-womens-sports-approving-first-anti-trans-law-of-2021 accessed March 15, 2021.

[63] For an overview of these destructive stereotypes, see the documentary *Disclosure* (2020).

(2017).⁶⁴ The assumption that trans women will act in sexually violent ways, as stated in discourses about bathroom bills and locker rooms, essentializes sexuality as indivisible from assigned binary sex. It also occludes the reality of sexualized violence against trans women and girls.

The Miss. Fairness Act argues for discrimination against trans athletes on the basis of protecting cis girls. Prominent arguments by those in support of the Mississippi bill cite concerns over the physical safety of cis girls, stress the importance of genetics, and make claims that recall the *Plessy v Ferguson* doctrine of "separate but equal" in the demand for separate facilities for non-cis athletes.⁶⁵ The bill picks up these arguments and explicitly refers to the potential violation of a student's "bodily privacy [...] including encountering a person of the opposite sex in a facility traditionally designated for the exclusive use of members of one sex."⁶⁶ The resulting "psychological, emotional and physical harm" of such an encounter is argued on the basis of biological determinism.⁶⁷ There exist "'inherent differences' [which] range from chromosomal and hormonal differences to physiological differences."⁶⁸ Differentiations made on the basis of "sex" are legitimized in terms of immutable biological categories and are promoted as effective means for achieving equality: "[h]aving separate sex-specific teams furthers efforts to promote sex equality."⁶⁹ Using biology and genetics as the core of alleged truisms about a person's sexual–legal personhood locates authority in a higher normative instance that dictates gender identity into law. In the case of the Miss. Fairness Act, biological considerations and concerns function as "processes of demarcating" and categorization.⁷⁰ A static, essentialist understanding of categories of sexuality operates in the Act. Sex, according to its trans and non-binary-exclusive logic, is assumed to be scientifically provable, universal, and invariable. Biological sex serves as the supposed shelter of reliability even when existing understandings of gender, identity, and social equality are being actively challenged elsewhere.

We observe the persistence of the belief in immutable sex in discussions of prominent persons' trans identities. Actor Elliot Page's declaration that they are trans was followed by media coverage of their physical transitioning.⁷¹ Similarly, Katie Couric's invasive questions about whether Laverne Cox and Carmen Carrera had had sex reassignment surgery demonstrates how trans persons' bodily integrity and right to privacy is not regarded as strong as

---

⁶⁴ *Gavin Grimm v Gloucester County School Board*, On Writ Certiorari to the US Court of Appeals for the Fourth Circuit (2017), Brief of Amici Curiae Dr. Judith Reisman and the Child Protection Institute, 54.
⁶⁵ See n 61.
⁶⁶ MS SB2536 sec. 5 (3).
⁶⁷ MS SB2536 sec. 5 (5).
⁶⁸ MS SB2536 sec. 2 (1) (b). See also MS SB2536 sec. 3 (3).
⁶⁹ MS SB2536 sec. 2 (1) (l).
⁷⁰ Doris Liebscher et al., "Wege aus der Essentialismusfalle: Überlegungen zu einem postkategorialen Antidiskriminierungsrecht" (2012) 45/2 *KJ* 204, 211: "Prozesse der Grenzziehung."
⁷¹ See "Elliot Page: Had Top Surgery to Remove Breasts ... It Changed My Life!!!" (*TMZ* March 16, 2021) www.tmz.com/2021/03/16/elliot-page-top-surgery-remove-breasts-trans-time-cover/ accessed March 17, 2021.

that of cis persons.[72] The presumed right to disclosure extends to non-celebrities as well.[73] The sense of entitlement to transgress a trans person's bodily privacy demonstrates the equivalence that is regularly made between genitalia and gender.[74] It also shows the imposition of a heterodiegetic narrative authority that passes judgment on trans experience. The demand to make intimate information available to the public, the idea that trans persons owe such disclosure to the public, and the readiness with which otherwise heavily policed boundaries of moral and ethical standards around privacy are overridden to determine a person's "real" sex are all forms of violence against trans persons that are masked as requirements for an outside authority to state explicitly who these people are.

As the laws discussed show, trans and gender-nonconforming adults are punished for claims to self-determination, while children and teenagers are constrained from attempting to be autonomous, thereby stressing their need to be protected from making ill-informed choices. In both instances, trans and non-binary identities are policed via legal and non-legal norms, and those claiming trans are patronized. In adults, these gender identities appear to reflect only on the person claiming them and their suspected unreliability. It is not transness as such that leads to troubling consequences; rather, the active, reliable, and autonomous choice to determine one's gender or gender fluidity renders the trans adult legally chargeable for their behavior.[75]

The Mississippi law and numerous other attempts to restrict trans rights target trans and gender-nonconforming individuals in sports, schools, and access to healthcare.[76] These legal initiatives add to trans exclusion and hostility toward trans and non-binary people in non-legal contexts. So-called trans-exclusionary radical feminists (TERFS) contribute to attempts to silence trans people's legal and socio-cultural demands for inclusion and recognition.[77] Anti-trans sentiments are also reflected in intra-community struggles. Antagonisms exist between "transmeds," that is, those who support the view that transness is predicated by a sense of gender dysphoria and a wish to transition, and so-called tucutes, those who do not,

---

[72] Katie McDonough, "Laverne Cox Flawlessly Shuts Down Katie Couric's Invasive Questions About Transgender People" (*Salon* January 8, 2021) www.salon.com/2014/01/07/laverne_cox_artfully_shuts_down_katie_courics_invasive_questions_about_transgender_people/ accessed March 19, 2021; see Mey, "Flawless Trans Women Carmen Carrera and Laverne Cox Respond Flawlessly to Katie Couric's Invasive Questions" (*autostraddle* January 7, 2014) www.autostraddle.com/flawless-trans-women-carmen-carrera-and-laverne-cox-respond-flawlessly-to-katie-courics-invasive-questions-215855/ accessed March 19, 2021.

[73] Talia Mae Bettcher, "Intersexuality, Transgender, and Transsexuality" (2016) in Lisa Disch and Mary Hawkesworth (eds), *The Oxford Handbook of Feminist Theory*, 421: "Such privacy invading questions are never asked of cisgendered people, and questions about genitalia are not normally demanded in polite conversation, the euphemistic quality of the query does not mitigate the sexually invasive character of the question."

[74] See "Constitutional Privacy and the Fight Over Access to Sex-Segregated Spaces" (2020) 133 *Harv. L. Rev.* 1684; on the criminalization of non-disclosure, see Ashley.

[75] Andrew N. Sharpe, "From Functionality to Aesthetics: The Architecture of Transgender Jurisprudence" (2001) 8.1 *Murdoch UELJ*.

[76] The American Civil Liberties Union reports more than 60 active anti-trans state bills as of February 26, 2021; see ACLU, "Legislation Affecting LGBT Rights Across the Country" (*American Civil Liberties Union* February 26, 2021) https://www.aclu.org/legislation-affecting-lgbt-rights-across-country accessed March 3, 2021.

[77] When President Biden recently announced his "Executive Order on Preventing and Combating Discrimination on the Basis of Gender Identity or Sexual Orientation," TERFS used the hashtag #BidenErasedWomen to criticize the order as marginalizing cis women.

and who are therefore regarded by the former group as appropriating aspects of trans identity, as "transtrenders."[78] These differentiations may reflect forms of gender gatekeeping that become manifest in transnormativity.

Trans-exclusive feminist, conservative political, and intra-community identity-political efforts to prevent trans inclusion share a distrust of trans individuals' authority over their identities. This pattern reinforces a narrative of transness as a construct that has to be policed for its own sake. This patronizing approach becomes apparent in claims that trans women do not understand what it is to be a "real" woman,[79] or that trans children and youth are too young to have agency over their bodies and identities,[80] or that trans adults have to go through a process of psychological assessment before being recognized. The processes of submitting to external institutions before being granted permission to determine one's life is a legally regulated and socio-culturally policed project that rests on the assumption that trans and non-binary individuals lack the capacity for reliable sexual–legal personhood. They are treated as non-consentable actors.

Law acts as an authorial narrator when it ascribes unreliability to trans and non-binary persons. The refusal to take trans individuals seriously in their legal demands is reinforced by a general uneasiness about no longer clearly demarcated sexual and gender-related categories. Moral panics over those who challenge existing gender binaries, norms, performances, and notions of femininity and masculinity feed on cultural anxieties about fluidity and the loss of allegedly static and fixed, thus reliable categories.

Transness poses a threat to immutable conceptualizations of sexuality as well as to traditional forms of narrative authority. First and foremost, this occurs because trans and non-binary identities are equated with sexual orientation and sexual practices, and trans women, in particular, are associated with longstanding prejudices about "perversion." The perceived instability of what trans sex is translates into the need to outlaw gender positions considered ungraspable or as violations of social norms, as illustrated by the German *TSG* with its earlier requirement that trans persons had to be sterilized and divorced before they could change genders. Regulating reproduction and socially legitimated forms of marriage constitute state-level attempts to enforce sexual practices, forms of cohabitation, and kinship deemed "good."

The necessity to have an outside authority recognize trans people's identity functions performatively. Trans autonomy is only possible when granted by external institutions—such as the trans-exclusive feminist community in instances of social inclusion, the government/state in legal instances of changing one's gender, private companies in instances of allowing for all-gender bathrooms, or parents in cases of minors who identify as trans. Deliberate attempts to repress trans and non-binary voices by denying them narrative authority result in the need for advocates to mediate between trans demands and anti-trans fears. While anti-trans narratives reproduce the need for external policing mechanisms, pro-trans legislation and jurisprudence responds to the systematic denial of trans sexual–legal personhood.

---

[78] Jordan Forrest Miller, "'I Wanna Know Where the Rule Book Is': YouTube as a Site of Counternarratives to Transnormativity" (Georgia State U, Institute for Women's, Gender, and Sexuality Studies January 6, 2017) https://scholarworks.gsu.edu/wsi_theses/60 accessed March 3, 2021, 20.

[79] As espoused most infamously by Janice Raymond in *The Transsexual Empire: The Making of the She-Male* (Beacon Press 1979) and the subsequent introduction from 1994.

[80] One can legally change one's religion at 14 years of age in Germany, but one's civil status only at 18 (with parents' permission, before 18).

INSTRUMENTALIZING VULNERABILTY

An imagined vulnerability is common to all of the laws discussed above. Court-appointed experts such as Korte, trans-exclusionary feminists, and other opponents of equal rights for non-binary and trans people: all refer to the wellbeing of vulnerable groups to establish the dangerousness of those aiming to overcome established legal categories.

The child or the imperiled woman stands at the forefront of these arguments. Similarly, the panic surrounding injunctions against young people being prescribed hormone blockers to delay the onset of puberty is made on the basis of the presumed vulnerability of the non-adult person in question. One notes the deployment of that most affectively resonant of figures, the child. The child is the universally preferred victim in human rights discourse.[81] As documented in an analysis of mainstream media reports about detransitioning youth, concerns about children's transitioning when they are too susceptible to peer pressure are consistently used to restrict all trans persons' access to health care. The concern is allegedly for the putative future adult who will regret their choice and will also be unable to reproduce due to early hormone treatments.[82] The imagined vulnerability of the precariously gender-dysphoric child, who has been carried away by the social contagion of transness, is instrumentalized, as is the image of that person's tragic inability to have children "naturally."

The imagined child in anti-trans discourse is held out as a political threat. This threat includes the endangering of what Lauren Berlant has called "infantile citizenship," as a stand-in for "the traumatized virtuous private citizen around whom history ought to be organized."[83] The actual concern is with gatekeeping trans people, and particularly poorer trans persons, from getting medical attention.[84] This is also what Rubin called the "bait-and-switch" approach to laws regarding sexuality and protections of children from sexual harm.[85] The image of the violated child is deployed affectively to restrict freedoms of sexual and gender minorities.

Use of the age of 18 in Germany as the demarcation of when one can determine one's gender belongs to the pattern of instrumentalizing imagined vulnerability to achieve a retrograde political end. An assumed false consciousness is attributed by law to the child who wishes to transition too early. Similarly, the cis woman in the bathroom who is pictured as being threatened by a trans woman is a politicized figure of vulnerability. Using the cis woman who is unable to protect herself from the implicitly monstrous sexuality of the trans woman who "just needs to pee,"[86] bathroom bills demarcate cis women's state-mandated vulnerability. Whether in crime reporting or human rights discourse or jingoistic calls for state-sanctioned

---

[81] Think of images of toddler Alan Kurdi's dead body in debates about refugees in 2015. Consider every end-of-the-year plea from a humanitarian organization, asking for financial support using an accompanying image of a wide-eyed suffering child. See discussions of the commodification of images of suffering children: Wendy S. Hesford, *Spectacular Rhetorics. Human Rights Visions, Recognitions, Feminisms* (Duke UP 2011); Upendra Baxi, "Towards an Aesthetics of Human Rights" in Werner Gephart and Jan Christoph Suntrup (eds), *Rechtsanalyse als Kulturforschung II* (Klostermann 2015) 163.

[82] Van Slothouber, 90, 93–4.

[83] Lauren Berlant, "The Subject of True Feeling: Pain, Privacy, and Politics" in Jodi Dean (ed), *Cultural Studies and Political Theory* (Cornell UP 2000) 42, 56.

[84] Van Slothouber, 96.

[85] See Gayle S. Rubin, "Blood under the Bridge: Reflections on 'Thinking Sex'" in Gayle S. Rubin (ed), *Deviations* (Duke UP 2012) 219.

[86] Koch-Rein et al., "Representing", 3.

violence, preferred victims are most often [white] children, young [white] women, or other feminized figures.[87]

We reiterate an argument made by Jordana Greenblatt in a discussion of legal cases involving sex acts adjudged by Canadian and English courts to have been non-consentable. A bad-faith notion of feminism was adopted by the courts as the locus of narrative authority to prescribe allowable and non-allowable sexual interactions. Accordingly, some sexual acts were determined to have been falsely consented due to the participant's—often the bottom's—ideological conditioning. The courts argued that a women could only have consented to a sexual practice on the basis of her having a false consciousness that led her to assent to what she allegedly could not have really wanted: "The idea that women and other marginal sexual actors cannot know what they want is fundamental to false consciousness feminisms; false consciousness is by definition predicated on oppressed people *not* knowing."[88] Greenblatt argues that feminists must engage with sexual minorities' autonomy and capacity for consent rather than infantilizing them: "Instead of assuming false consciousness when sexual tastes and behaviors exceed the norms consistently enforced in the legal arena, *all* feminists must begin to at least provisionally trust the sexual self-assessment of marginalized subjects."[89] In such cases, an authorial narrator as the voice of law steps in. Located outside of the action but knowing better, that narrator authoritatively proclaims a sex that cannot conscionably be. The victimhood and imagined vulnerability of the trans child, or the regretful post-transition trans adult, or the imagined cis woman who might be harassed in a public bathroom by a trans woman: all of these push affective buttons and assumptions of rightness and wrongness.

DE-BINARIZING AND TRANSING LAW

Feminist jurists before us have repeatedly pointed out the masculine bias in law.[90] This includes the assumption that assault takes place in public spaces between strangers, or the recognition that sexual assault victims are often violated twice—first by the perpetrator of the violence; second by the court that forces them to prove the violation took place and that they are credible victims—with all the cultural prejudices this entails concerning victims' having to be sexually inexperienced in order to be violatable. Our arguments about the need to trans law build upon these sisters' work. There is no animosity here, and we wish to actively contradict a popular and often instrumentalized narrative that portrays older and younger feminists as

---

[87] Olson with Wessels, 254, 255.
[88] Jordana Greenblatt, "The 'Yes' Which Is Not One: Consent, the Law, and the Limits of False Consciousness Feminism" in Greta Olson et al. (eds), *Beyond Gender* (Routledge 2018) 235, 243 [emphasis in the original].
[89] Greenblatt, "The 'Yes'", 254 [emphasis in the original].
[90] Foundational work was done by Ruth Bader Ginsburg and McKinnon, particularly on privacy, and Martha Minow and Deborah Rhode. Subsequent critique has demonstrated how the exclusionary focus on gender has failed to address other forms of intersectional bias. See the work of Marianne Valverde, Kimberlé Crenshaw, and Patricia Williams. As applied to trans legal advocacy, see Dean Spade, "Intersectional Resistance and Legal Reform" (2013) 38.4 *Signs* 2013. For definitions of current feminisms, see Greta Olson and Mirjam Horn-Schott, "Beyond Gender: Towards a Decolonized Queer Feminist Future" in Greta Olson et al. (eds), *Beyond Gender: Futures of Feminist and Sexuality Studies—An Advanced Introduction* (Routledge 2018).

antagonists or, alternatively, suggests that queer activists and theorists have fundamentally different aims than do feminist ones. Queer and feminist critics of law, we attest, work to achieve similar ends, to upset hegemonic operations of law that are inherently masculinist and heteronormative. Both forms of critique function to 'bring[] into view forms of law's violence that had remained invisible in analyses that ignored gender, sexuality and non-physical violence'.[91]

Our arguments here also build upon the work of queer jurists who have paved the way in demonstrating that law is inherently straight and has functioned by sanctioning homosexuality as the other of legally normative heterosexuality. As Leslie Moran writes in an overview of Law and Sexuality scholarship, queerness is continuously created in contiguous "legal categories" that "produce[] 'sexualized subjects' by way of violent hierarchies of hetero and homo, of masculine and feminine."[92] Following arguments that law enacts a masculinist and a heterosexual violence on legal subjects and non-subjects alike, we highlight law's inherent cisnormativity in assuming a confluence between genitalia, identity, and sexual–legal personhood.[93] Our critique targets what we perceive as the cis logic of law. This "cisness" privileges biologistic notions of gender identity and exerts normative force over non-cis bodies and persons. Cis law focuses on dominant, universal interpretations that mirror notions of "correct" genders stemming from biological sex, and the non-reflective use of seemingly natural legal and socio-cultural categories. Transing law intends to do more than challenge the instrumentalization of legal norms that oppress non-cis persons. Rather, it aims to reform law to admit pluralism and heterogeneous interpretative spaces. The othering of transness and non-binariness in laws such as those discussed above works in combination with non-legal forms of normativity to project trans and non-binary persons as threats to sexual–legal citizens. This is a jurispathic jurisprudence that closes down the potential of individuals to determine their sexual–legal personhood.

We propose a countermove. Rather than a "Fucking Law (A New Methodological Movement)"—which we appreciate in all its participatory disruptiveness and its desire "to fuck (with) law"[94]—we suggest a research and activist agenda that aims to actively and progressively trans and genderfuck law.[95] The necessity to do so is indicated by what is happening in German and US cultural–legal discourses concerning trans and non-binary lives. Despite their systemic differences, German and US law assert normative authority over trans and non-binary people by framing them as inherently unreliable. Although the *TSG*'s eugenicist requirement of being "permanently incapable of reproduction" and the prescription of being 25 or above are no longer binding, the logic that underlies discriminatory criteria and an anti-trans cultural imaginary remains.[96] Cultural anxieties find their way back into legal norms as seen by the backlash against the German §45b *PStG*, or the introduction of the Mississippi bill, which discriminates against trans athletes, or the Arkansas bill that criminalizes the medical

---

[91] See Rosemary Hunter, "Law's (Masculine) Violence: Reshaping Jurisprudence" (2006) 17 *Law and Critique* 27, 44.

[92] Leslie J. Moran, "Sexuality in Law and Society Scholarship" in Austen Sarat (ed), *The Blackwell Companion to Law and Society* (Blackwell 2007) 487, 496.

[93] See Dean Spade, *Normal Life: Administrative Violence, Critical Trans Politics and the Limits of Law* (second edition, Duke UP 2015).

[94] V. Brooks, "Fucking Law (A New Methodological Movement)" (2018) 7 *Journal of Organizational Ethnography* 31.

[95] See Florence Ashley's saliently titled "Genderfucking Non-Disclosure" at note 13.

[96] §8 sec. 1 (3) *TSG*: "dauernd fortpflanzungsunfähig."

treatment of trans youths. Aiming to contain trans existence in pre-determined categories, to regulate biological reproduction, and to restrict freedom of expression, legal efforts that are hostile to trans and non-binary persons are at the forefront of current cultural wars.

Transing and de-binarizing law involves returning to a point made at the beginning of this text. Law—in the sense that most people understand it, as actual legal processes, legal institutions, and legal ordinances—does not stand alone but is always and already imbricated in other forms of normativity, in what might be called the cultural–legal environment in which legal processes take place. This is, to quote others before us, *living law*, what people actually live in terms of the norms of behavior that govern their actions; it is also what Greta has termed "legality"—the totality of whatever people understand to be normatively binding or law-full.[97] We suggest that *living law* is pushing toward a non-binary understanding of gender that would reverse the exclusion of non-binary and trans persons from the realm of sexual citizenship and legal subjectivity, as conceived of as full sexual–legal personhood.

We return to Elliot Page's 2020 announcement that they are trans, non-binary, and queer.[98] We compare this to Caitlyn Jenner's dramatic announcement of being a woman in 2015, in all manner of conventionalized trans tropes, including a confession of longstanding gender dysphoria, a dramatic "coming out" with a swish-swish of hidden long hair on live television, and a sexy *Vanity Fair* swimsuit cover. By contrast, Elliot's announcement was of a different kind. Calling themself "queer" and asking to be referred to with the alternate use of the pronouns they/them and he/him bespeaks a notion of trans that is not the opposite of cisgender. Elliot's announcement has been less a coming out—a problematic metaphor in itself—than an active embrace of a more inclusive identity. The acceptance of Elliot's identity as transmasculine and queer bespeaks a general *lived law* movement to understanding gender identities as non-exclusive. It points to an awareness of the mutability and fluidity of "those who challenge neat gender identity categorization […] whose lives are gloriously, beautifully messy."[99]

Accordingly, we note that dating sites for women such as HER include trans persons and have actively adopted a more generous notion of what it means to be queer womxn.[100] This embrace belies the Mississippi Governor's defense of his daughters, the insistence by J.K. Rowling that imperiled cis women need safe spaces away from threatening trans women, or, for instance, *Fox News* commentator Tucker Carlson's assertion that trans women are "faking" in order to get into women's bathrooms.[101] In all of the alleged defenses of female children and imperiled adult women, an imagined vulnerable victim contends with the specter

---

[97] See Olson, *From Law and Literature to Legality and Affect* (Oxford University Press, 2022).
[98] Elliot Page, "Hi friends, I want to share with you that I am trans, my pronouns are he/they and my name is Elliot. …" (*Twitter* December 1, 2020, 6:10 pm) https://twitter.com/TheElliotPage/status/1333820783655837701 accessed March 17, 2021.
[99] Ashley, 377.
[100] Kasandra Brabaw, "Queer Women's Most Popular Dating App Has a Fresh New Look" (*refinery29* May 31, 2018): "It's important to Exton for HER to be a space that all queer women and non-binary people feel is theirs. So, in addition to the logo change and the new photos, HER has been using the more-inclusive 'womxn' (which includes trans women and feminine-identifying non-binary people as well as cisgender women) on their ads."
[101] Media Matter, "Tucker Carlson Claims That the Government Recognizing the Trans Community Would Hurt Women" (*Media Matters* October 23, 2018) www.mediamatters.org/tucker-carlson/tucker-carlson-claims-government-recognizing-trans-community-would-hurt-women accessed March 24, 2021.

of a predatory man that "dresses up." A whole world of blond-wigged serial killers is invoked in these images, as is the picture of their imagined victim. She is not a real woman or girl, but a screaming character from a fantasy such as Hitchcock's *Psycho*, a victim who needs the heroic cis observer to come and save her. This violated and victimized figure does a disservice to actual legal persons (trans and cis women) and their claims to rights and protections.

With Rubin, we assert that imagined victimized women and affectively resonant images of defenseless children are deployed in anti-trans laws in a bait-and-switch operation. This operation responds to a moral panic regarding the movement away from binary gender identities and the increasing visibility of trans and gender nonconforming persons. Questioning trans and non-binary individuals' competence to identify with a gender or genders other than the one assigned at birth delegitimizes their personal autonomy and claims to sexual citizenship. It also threatens the concept of sexual–legal personhood in itself, also for cis persons.

The fear of pluralistic approaches to identity exposes an inherently undemocratic concept of sexual citizenship. Accordingly, trans rights advocates the need to challenge laws that discriminate against non-normative gender identities as well as generalized anxieties about the legal coming-of-age of trans people as regulatory orders. This includes unseating the heterodiegetic authorial narrator-as-judge of trans identity. Law, in the sense of institutional law, will need to withhold judgment on legal subject positions that are non-binary and non-exclusive, as signaled by Page's 2020 announcement.

De-binarizing and transing law requires that narrative authority be attributed to gender nonconforming persons, rather than an inherent inability to adhere to legally defended gender categories. Trans and non-binary persons' "unreliability" needs to be regarded not as a failing but rather as an invitation to contemplate identity in new terms, including legal ones. Persons can maintain non-exclusive gender positions that change over time. Transing law entails a new kind of reveal, not of a trans person's "real" gender or genitalia, but of the politically deployed confusion of sexual orientation and fetishism with gender identity. This transed law has been, we assert, imagined *avant le lettre* in the *living law* of social media by Elliot Page and others as well as in other cultural–legal texts.

We conclude by inviting a trans poetical text to voice non-gender-conforming identities. This text belongs to a project that works "against the conception of trans literature as a self-interested discourse narrowly focused on securing the rights and recognitions of the state."[102] Beyond the state, trans possibilities are created in autonomous enactments of self rather than through attributions that come from without. Trish Salah's "What's to come" inaugurates a future forged in current performance. This future now will be:

> more than breaking the frame of sex's reach
> more, or before, and under, what grounds?
>
> more than the frame of the oppositional
> tender proliferation, gender euphoria
>
> beyond being counted
> where they ceased to exist

---

[102] Andrea Abi-Karen and Kay Gabriel, "Making Love and Putting on Obscene Plays and Poetry Outside the Empty Former Prisons" in Andrea Abi-Karen and Kay Gabriel (eds), *We Want It All: An Anthology of Radical Trans Poetics* (Nightboat Books 2020) 3.

This "more than" and this "beyond" constitutes a

> [...] new humanity without purge and burn
> What from the discarded and or loudly ignored
> What from the rendered inoperable, non-possible
> What newly new do we now passionately live?[103]

A de-binarized and transed *living law* invites persons of all kinds to imagine and "passionately live" a generous and inclusive sexual–legal personhood, one that includes multiple positions. The unreliable narrative commonly attributed to non-binary and trans persons presents an opportunity to revise conceptions of consistent sexual–legal personhood. Rather than having a false consciousness regarding gender, trans and non-binary persons' mutable gender alignments demonstrate the need for fluid conceptualizations of sexual–legal personhood. This chapter advocates for such fluidity in the future that we recognize in Salah's "more than," "beyond," and "newly new." The future is trans.

---

[103] Trish Salah, "What's to Come" in Andrea Abi-Karen and Kay Gabriel (eds), *We Want It All: An Anthology of Radical Trans Poetics* (Nightboat Books 2020) 401–2.

PART VII

MATTERING-FORTH

Underground Thoughts – Bio-Norms and Geo-Norms – More-Than-Human Normativity – Cutting Flows – Digging Poetry – Minor Jurisprudence – Matterphor – Wave Writing – Aquatic Membrane

24. Grounds
Rhys Aston and Margaret Davies

INTRODUCTION

Grounds and the notion of grounding have been essential to all forms of theory and philosophical inquiry. At the base of any founding gesture is a conceptual ground, known as groundwork or the process of grounding.[1] Knowledge claims must be grounded in some way: they must have a basis or a reason. For instance, Kantian philosophy aimed to find necessary *a priori* grounds that describe the very possibility of knowledge. Later critical theory examined claims of grounding skeptically, unpacking alleged foundations and showing their political or conditional nature. For all that, grounds remain important to critical philosophy—they might even be said to ground it, since critical philosophy is reliant on the idea and the assertion of grounds even though it also critiques them. Empirical knowledges rely on observable facts as grounds, employing careful observation of phenomena in order to design theories and test their adequacy. This epistemological process is itself grounded on an ontological belief that such facts are an objective (and relatively transparent) feature of the material world.

There is also another conventional meaning of ground, a more literal (or at least more material) meaning: ground as the surface of the earth (and that which exists below it). While these two understandings might, at least at first glance, appear to refer to distinct phenomena (even if their meanings are etymologically related), in fact, employing the actual ground as a symbolic tool to examine and interrogate metaphysical grounds has long been a common trope in religion, literature, art, science, and philosophy. In some iterations, the aim has been to rise above the ground, to transcend the earthly plane in order that we might discover "higher" truths or be able to view life in its entirety. Alternatively, in others it has been to dig/sink/journey below the ostensibly solid surface in order to uncover and excavate hidden origins—sometimes seen as the unconscious, but equally implicated as a (buried) source of emergent actuality. Whether seeking a position above or below, however, the aim has always been to identify an axiomatic or transcendent (and usually singular) foundation or "ground" for life (or law, or philosophy, etc.).

In recent theoretical work in the humanities and social sciences, this connection between metaphysical grounds and the actual ground has been extended beyond the purely metaphoric or symbolic, seeking to also understand this relationship in a thoroughly material sense. A part of the broader materialist and posthumanist turn in social theory,[2] this work explores how the physical earth—both the outer layer of soils, rocks, trees and so forth, and the underlying

---

[1] While questions of grounds have always been a core concern of metaphysical philosophy, there has recently been renewed interest and debate regarding the concept and how best to conceptualize it (Correia and Schnieder, 2012; Raven, 2020).

[2] This includes a broad range of contemporary perspectives in social theory and social research more generally, including the feminist-inspired new materialisms and posthumanism (Barad, 2007; Bennett, 2010; Coole and Frost, 2010; Braidotti, 2013), science and technology studies (particularly the work

401

geological strata which subtends it—is both deeply connected with and shapes (as well as is shaped by) human sociality and human endeavors, including the institutional and conceptual structures we build such as law. In other words, the ground for everything that exists, including philosophy, law, literature, science, and so forth, includes the actual literal ground itself.[3] And here, unlike the purely metaphorical journeys described above, the aim is not to reduce connections and relationships, but to increase them. Drawing attention to geontological power (Povinelli, 2016) or geosocial processes (Clark and Yusoff, 2017; Bobbette and Donovan, 2019a), as well as mobilizing—while also critically reworking—concepts such as the Anthropocene (Crutzen and Stoermer, 2000; Hamilton, Bonneuil and Gemenne, 2015)[4] and Gaia (Lovelock and Margulis, 1974; Stengers, 2015; Danowski and Viveiros de Castro, 2017; Latour, 2017), this new groundwork seeks to challenge the persistent anthropocentrism which underpins most social thought by destabilizing the sharp ontological distinctions—subject/object, nature/culture, life/non-life—which it relies on and reproduces. These perspectives invite us to refocus and reorient our conceptual gaze, to return back "down to earth" (Latour, 2018) and embrace our terran lives (Haraway, 2016; Danowski and Viverios de Castro, 2017). Importantly, in such frameworks the ground, as well as nature more generally, is not an inert or passive background to, or raw material for, human activities. Nor is it a source of, or explanation for, fixed and unchanging human characteristics. It is a dynamic, open, and generative plurality of forms-in-process. This understanding undermines any sense that grounds are an ultimate limit. It suggests more complex images of grounds. Grounds are never final or solid, they are emergent; they have three- (or multi-) dimensionality and there is always something under and around any foundation. Looked at from above, the ground upon which we stand might appear to be a two-dimensional surface, a thin, barely existent layer underneath which are the rocky depths of an unfathomable planet that provides the actual support for our feet. But this surface appearance is only one—even regarded as a membrane or skin, the ground is a threshold for the circulation of matter and meanings. Just as the narratives, practices, and texts that constitute the law are constantly being passed around in jurisgenetic communications that both constitute and transgress the grounds of law (Cover, 1983), so the materials that constitute the earth are constantly cycling across, over, and under the ground. Ground as surface, while solid and somewhat supportive, is entirely emergent from these cyclical relational processes.

Moving beyond analogies, how can an exploration and deep-dive into the *material* ground provide us with conceptual and political tools for understanding law and recasting the anthropocentrism of law? What does it mean to think about law as not only *on* the ground, but also *in* the ground? Can we speak not only of human normative systems, but also of bio-normative and geo-normative systems? If so, how is it possible to reconnect human law with the broader systems of (non-human) normativity in which it is embedded? Such knowledge is longstanding in many Indigenous cosmologies (see for example Bawaka Country et al., 2016) but

---

of Latour, Stengers, and others) (Stengers, 1997; Latour, 2005), and object-oriented ontology (Bryant, Srnicek, and Harman, 2011).

[3] As Grosz (2005, p.44) has argued, albeit relying on the broader/more inclusive language of nature more generally, "it may prove fruitful to understand [nature and culture] as terms whose relation is defined by emergence. Nature is the ground, the condition or field in which culture erupts or emerges as a supervening quality not contained in nature but derived from it."

[4] Or its related variations, including *Capitlocene* (Moore, 2017), or *Plantationocene* (Haraway et al., 2016), or *Chthulucene* (Haraway, 2016).

Western thought has comprehensively severed culture from nature, and *nomos* from *phusis*. Here we will need to think about the nature of law as the connective, iterative, and purposive practices of human bodies that themselves cycle through the earth and continue to emerge from its ground.

In order to open, if not answer, these questions, we will dig into and engage with the ground,[5] a process that will occur at a number of levels and registers. We seek to highlight and explore the fertility of the ground (both materially and metaphorically), drawing attention to the vital, generative, and normative processes and relationships involved in its continuous (re)composition. Our approach, inspired by Donna Haraway (2016), mixes compostables. The material practice of composting involves assembling and mixing a diverse range of mainly organic materials in order to enrich the (organic and inorganic) soil. While it is a process that takes time, as well as great care and attention, it is ultimately a multi-agential collaborative act, relying on "many unknown, unseen and often un-sensed nonhuman entities such as microorganisms, worms, and microclimates" (Turner and Somerville, 2020, p.229). Our compostables include observations about conceptual topographies, two short stories, and various theoretical interventions.

IMAGINARY GROUNDS

As a system and as a practice, law is presumed to have grounds. As Peter Goodrich (1986) helpfully wrote some decades ago, law is said to have "institutional" and "ideational" sources: these are, respectively, the factually identifiable source and the ultimate principle upon which a legal system is founded. The ideational source is particularly important for legal theory. As Goodrich says, it is the condition both of law's unity and of its separation from non-law: "law is kept separate and distinct from other institutions and forms of control precisely by virtue of being a unity" and of having an essence which is its ultimate ground (1986, p.4). One of the central projects of legal theory, at least in classical and mainstream variants, has been to identify and certify the foundations of law. This has never been an easy or uncontroversial task. One could point out that it has also never been successful in this search for a singular resting point for law. One of the most famous, Kelsen's *grundnorm*, shifted its own rhetorical ground in its several iterations (in turn Kelsen said it was a presumption, a hypothesis, and a fiction); though, to be fair, it was never meant to be a solid thing, merely a kind of theoretical stopping point (albeit one that was *both* institutionally and ideationally necessary) (Kelsen, 1934, 1961, 1991). Much critique of law has been aimed at considering the political and/or contradictory nature of law's grounds and illustrating that the purported ground always opens onto meanings and practices beyond the law—for instance, that law's foundations are based on force (Derrida, 1990). Like all critical theory, such a critique remains wedded to the idea of grounds, even if it seeks to disturb their solidity and reveal their contingency and fluidity. A similar understanding of grounds pervades law and legal practice in a more everyday sense.

---

[5] Digging is the method deployed by the Bawaka Country authors—which includes the Country itself (2016) and also a collective of Indigenous and non-Indigenous women. Introducing one of their extraordinary articles, they say: "when we are at Bawaka, we'll be doing more than just digging and getting food. We will be bringing ourselves and Bawaka into being, we will be living our history, our ceremonies, and our future, and we would like you to join us" (2016, p.456).

Without grounds, there is no case. No *matter*. Nothing that matters to the law, that is.[6] (In case it needs to be said, matter is both the meaning of the law and the physical stuff that comprises it—which we will come to later.) In these contexts, the ground is the metaphor for a solid basis—something upon which the law depends; its explanation and necessary condition. But it never *is* entirely solid, because even when the grounds might be readily apparent—as for instance with any routine trial—the case nonetheless rests upon other matters and other matter.

In legal philosophy and theory more generally, discussions of grounds have drawn on a diverse range of different (and even contradictory) spatial metaphors and imagery. Despite the language of "foundations," often the motivation has been upwards—to vertically superior justifications. Therefore, in a strange inversion, grounds are sometimes represented as higher than the thing that they ground. This is especially the case in idealist philosophical systems, exemplified perhaps in the Platonic direction that contemplation should be focused upwards, that truth exists *above* the material plane. To cast our gaze downwards is to remain trapped in a world of shadows and partiality. Similar vertical imagery also pervades classical and modernist legal theory. Natural law, for example, depicts a clear hierarchy in which movement is always up to a higher law of god or universal nature or even the cosmos. Similarly, Kelsen's positivism is based on the establishment of hierarchy of legal validity. In order to determine the validity of any norm, it is always necessary to trace it back to a "higher" norm in a chain: "the reason for the validity of a norm can only be validity of another norm. A norm which represents the reason for the validity of another norm is figuratively spoken of as a higher norm in relation to a lower norm" (Kelsen, 1967, p.193). Again, the idealist language and imagery used is of movement upwards. In fact, his conceptual system is usually—perhaps strangely—depicted with the *grundnorm* at the top of a pyramid (reflective of law's traditional association with the political state and other hierarchical forms of authority).

There are also numerous examples in which grounds have been conceptualized as existing below the surface. Perhaps the most celebrated and widely discussed of these is Marx's distinction between base and superstructure. In Marxist theory, "the base," a society's underlying economic system, is depicted as existing below the political and cultural institutions that form the superstructure. It is their foundation or source and, therefore, they sit above it: "relations of production constitute the economic structure of a society, the real foundation, on which rises a legal and political superstructure" (Marx, 1859, pp.159–60). Similar imagery of underlying foundations is also evident in linguistic and cultural structuralism, which, as Williams concisely summarizes (2008, p.48), hold that "*beneath* cultural forms lie invariant structures, largely preliterate, from which derive the surface phenomena of cultural life" (emphasis added). By contrast, topological representations of the mind–body complex in psychoanalytic thought frequently contest any simplistic representation of layers or foundations: the unconscious may, for instance, be buried in the folds of the conscious and is always operative, but it does not straightforwardly ground action, communication, or belief.

---

[6] The importance of grounds in this context is captured clearly in Kafka's *The Trial* (1953) (albeit from the perspective of a person subject to legal proceedings, rather than from an institutional perspective). Josef K's bewilderment, and his obsessive pursuit of information, stems from the fact that the case against him is unspecified—it has no foundation or at least none that is made known to him. But we might equally ask, does K—in his search for a ground—himself produce the grounds that condemn him? Not only expose it, but actually cause it? As K says, "it is only a trial if I recognize it as such" (1953, p.49). Possibly K does not recognize the trial as having any legitimate foundations, but nonetheless his actions—performing the role of an accused man—are the only foundations it (in the end) requires.

While in each of these examples the imagery employed is largely figurative, they are still commonly conceptualized in relation to, and draw on language and metaphors connected with, the actual ground itself, the surface of the earth. This is perhaps not surprising as, for humans, this is our predominant physical and phenomenological orientation. It is hard to deny the importance and centrality of the ground for human life. In fact, as others have noted, the word "human" etymologically stems from the Proto-Indo-European root word "dghem," meaning "of the earth" (a root that it shares with both "humus" and "chthonic") (Margulis and Sagan, 1997, p.12; Bringhurst, 2009, p.54). As terrestrially bound animals, the ground is where we dwell and live. It is where our lives unfold and where we come into relationship with other humans, as well as with the broader non-human environment (both organic and inorganic). Nevertheless, when it comes to the construction of philosophical and scientific schemes to help us make sense of, and obtain meaning from, the world, the tendency has been to conceptually locate and occupy a position away from these relationships that constitute life; either journeying upwards in order that we may, through a disembodied god-like gaze (Haraway, 1988, p.581), capture it in its totality; or, alternatively, journeying down in order that we may uncover the hidden source or origins. Whether we journey up or down, though, the aim isn't to increase connections, but to reduce and simplify them. To arrive at the singular. This results in something of a strange tension: in order to make sense of life we need to travel away from it; we need to strive—as much as possible—to locate a site exterior to it. In fact, the further we move away from the lively, entangled mess, the better our understanding of it is presumed to be. This search for exteriority is impossible, artificially created by conceptually denying life, by excising lively relations.[7] The (under)ground is neither a dead nor a flat space, we just chose to construct it that way.

THE DUALISM OF UNDER AND OVER

So, let's look down, first to a classic short story by E.M. Forster, *The Machine Stops*. This work, originally published in 1909, describes a world in which most of humanity now lives underground. Although never directly specified, it is suggested that this burial of life was precipitated by some form of environmental crisis on the surface. As Vashti, one of the two central protagonists, remarks: "[t]he surface of the earth is only dust and mud, no life remains on it, and you would need a respirator, or the cold of the outer air would kill you. One dies immediately in the outer air" (Forster, 2001, p.94). While it remains possible to visit the

---

[7] As Barad (2007) has argued, this exteriority is conceptually produced through "representationalism," an ontological perspective that separates the material world from the way it is understood and explained by different knowledge practices. This is a deeply entrenched perspective (at least in the West) and underpins most natural and social sciences. One of the consequences of this perspective is that meaning is ontologically stripped from the world, creating a divide between a static and inert "natural" world and the cultural and scientific representations which give (human) meaning to and make sense of that world. In doing this, the dynamism of nature, as well as complex interdependence between nature and culture, is hidden. Somewhat ironically, therefore, the search for an exterior position that will enable a more objective, complete, or deeper understanding actually results in a far shallower and reductive understanding. As Deleuze (1994, pp.55–6) has remarked, "[r]epresentation has only a single centre, a unique receding perspective, and in consequence a false depth. It mediates everything but mobilises and moves nothing."

surface (with appropriate permissions and life-sustaining equipment), and to travel across the outer surface in airships (an unfortunate necessity when, on rare occasions, you might be forced to travel to another part of the world), residents of the underground falsely believe that it would be impossible to live permanently above ground. For most members of Forster's imagined society this was of little concern. They were perfectly content to remain ensconced in their underground home, sheltered from the vicissitudes of "nature" that had preoccupied their forebears: "Night and day, wind and storm, tide and earthquake, impeded man no longer. He had harnessed Leviathan. All the old literature, with its praise of Nature, and its fear of Nature, rang false as the prattle of the child" (Forster, 2001, p.98).

Each member of this subterranean society resides alone in a "small room, hexagonal in shape like the cell of a bee" (Forster, 2001, p.91), all of their needs met by an omnipresent mechanical entity known simply as "the Machine," worshipped by some and obeyed by all. The Book of the Machine—a kind of techno-legal scripture—provides all necessary information for life governance. Through a series of buttons and switches, the Machine provides fresh air, lighting, food, water, clothing, music, and literature. It also provides a means to communicate with fellow inhabitants. In fact, as the "clumsy system of public gatherings had been long since abandoned" (Forster, 2001, p.95), nearly all social interactions took place via the Machine. For Vashti, this is something of a mixed blessing. While frequently interrupted—she does know "several thousand people"—it also means that she is able to regularly attend and deliver lectures without leaving her room (an experience many of us became accustomed to in a COVID world). In fact, driven by an insatiable appetite for "new ideas," delivering and attending lectures is one of her central preoccupations. At one point she delivers a lecture on "Australian music" before attending a lecture on the sea. She enjoys this lecture: "there were ideas to be got from the sea" (Forster, 2001, p.95).

Vashti's daily routine is interrupted by a request (via the Machine) from her son, Kuno. He wishes to speak to her. In fact, he wishes to speak to her in person. He is planning a trip to the surface and wants to see her before embarking on this journey. Although somewhat perturbed by his request (she will need to journey via airship to see him), and confused by his desire to see the surface—"It is contrary to the spirit of the age" (Forster, 2001, p.94)—she nevertheless agrees. The journey is uneventful; however, Vashti finds it deeply confronting and unsettling and she is overwhelmed as the "horror of direct experience return[s]" (Forster, 2001, p.97). The smells, the sights, the close physical proximity with other people, all leave her anticipating a return to her room, in which she can continue her search for new ideas without such sensory distractions. The airship in which she travels has windows, allowing Vashti to see the earth's surface, but she has little interest in the view. As Forster (2001, p.103) describes it:

> At midday she took a second glance at the earth. The air-ship was crossing another range of mountains, but she could see little owing to clouds. Masses of black rock hovered below her, and merged indistinctly into grey. Their shapes were fantastic; one of them resembled a prostrate man.
> "No ideas here," murmured Vashti, and hid the Caucasus behind a metal blind.
> In the evening she looked again. They were crossing a golden sea, in which lay many small islands and one peninsula.
> She repeated, "No ideas here," and hid Greece behind a metal blind.

When Vashti eventually arrives at Kuno's room she discovers he has already made a journey to the surface. Although lacking the requisite permits, he had snuck through a long series of passageways and tunnels until eventually reaching a vent that opened onto the surface. He climbed onto the surface and found himself "in a grass-grown hollow that was edged with ferns" (Forster, 2001, p.109). Spending the day exploring this new environment, Kuno took great pleasure in the richness of sights, smells, and other sensory experiences. While Vashti had found the direct sensory experience of her journey unsettling, Kuno had found it invigorating. He attempts to explain this to his mother: "Cannot you see, cannot all your lecturers see, that it is we that are dying, and that down here the only thing that really lives is the Machine […] It has robbed us of the sense of space […] it has blurred every human relation" (Forster, 2001, p.110). Unable to understand, Vashti leaves, realizing she has little in common with her son.

The rest of the story tracks the slow decline of the underground society until "the final disaster" when, for reasons that remain unexplained, the Machine stops repairing itself and then, eventually, stops altogether. In the lead-up to this event there had been a further retreat from the surface. All expeditions to the surface (except for the purpose of airship travel) had been banned. As Vashti saw it, this was of little consequence, as such journeys were inevitably "unproductive of ideas" (Forster, 2001, p.114). Everything she needed to know about the surface she could learn via the Machine's gramophone or cinematophote. And, in any event, "a lecture on the sea was none the less stimulating when compiled out of other lectures that had already been delivered." In fact, "first-hand ideas do not really exist"; they are simply "physical impressions"; it is always better to let your ideas be "second-hand, and if possible tenth-hand, for then they will be far removed from that disturbing element" (Forster, 2001, p.114).

In most contemporary interpretations, Forster's dystopian story is considered a warning about the rise of technology (Seabury, 1997; Williams, 2008), and it is hard to deny its prescience on this level. His exploration of the tensions between hyper-connectivity and isolation appears extremely apt in a world saturated with social media.

However, in this context we are more interested in what it says about the relationship between a geologically stratified world and how we obtain knowledge and meaning from that world. In particular, we are interested in how the underground is imagined in contradistinction to the surface. In one sense the story presents a simplistic division between above and below, a distinction that is figured differently for Vashti and for her son, Kuno. Through Vashti, we are invited to see the in-ground existence as one of ordered security and of turgid, recycled ideas that come only occasionally. Vashti's underground seems to her full of life; she has thousands of friends, and always has a lecture to give or attend and ideas to explore. As she sees it, life is produced and enhanced by the Machine, allowing nature to be completely conquered. It is a lawful, Machine-governed world, where things happen predictably.

But Vashti's perspective is subverted in the narrative, partly through Kuno's report of his experiences above ground and partly through Vashti's own ironically described actions (such as shutting out Greece). She and her acquaintances strip all ontological meaning from the wider physical world that is extrinsic to their Machine-governed life. This world is constructed as inert and, though interesting to learn about in ten-minute lectures, it is not itself productive of ideas. Vashti finds direct experience both repulsive and uninteresting. In fact, the stability produced by the Machine—rather than enabling a flourishing life—reduces life. Because of his visit to the surface, Kuno is threatened with Homelessness, that is, banishment to the surface, a fate that Vashti perceives as involving certain death. As we find out later, the Homeless on the surface are to become the survivors of the human race. Once the Machine stops repairing itself, the artificially sustained underground lives are doomed: the music-on-demand becomes warped, the poetry machine makes "defective rhymes," requests for Euthanasia cannot be processed, pain is felt, the artificial lights fade, the Machine ceases its reassuring hum, a terrifying silence ensues, the air turns foul, and finally the Machine's human dependents are left to fight, scream for help, and die in the "poisoned darkness" (Forster, 2001, p.123). The emergent image of the underground is that—by contrast to the surface—it is in fact lifeless, devoid of authenticity and of creativity. Forster offers a cautionary tale of a human world disconnected from the non-human environment—the stability it may create is illusory, short-term, and highly abstract.

FROM AND WITH THE GROUND

Forster's underground is a lawful and orderly space, but ultimately a prison, lifeless, and a terrifying failure as a home for human beings. Perhaps, however, *The Machine Stops* also suggests a more hopeful message about the necessary relationship between law and life. As a lawgiver, the Machine maintains homeostasis for a time, but when its ability to repair itself fails, it "dies"—of course, lacking self-replicative ability, it always was dead. Somewhat paradoxically, as the Machine begins to fail, its legitimacy as a working governance structure is increasingly replaced by faith in it as a deity. But as object of worship, it is nothing more than a figment and almost useless in a crisis—when Vashti clutches her Book she is reassured, but the disintegration of her life support continues regardless. As the Machine ceases, so too does its law. Without Machine and without religious figments, all that is left are the lives on the surface that *are* able to repair themselves and replicate. Thus it seems that Forster had a rather negative view of subterranean space: it is presented as spaceless and timeless and is not, after all, a place to sustain human life or unchanging law for long. Forster's imaginary appears to see little generativity—and no biotic complexity—under the ground. But the *ground* remains vital in every sense. It is the place of the future, as Kuno finally suggests: "They are hiding in the mists and the ferns until our civilization stops. Today they are the Homeless—tomorrow—" (Forster, 2001, p.123).

Exploring the actual ground reveals a far more complex and less dualistic picture than that presented by Forster. It is easy to take the ground for granted. It is often relegated to the background, a platform or stage for human endeavors. Even when we engage with it as a natural space, it is those more interesting natural objects—flowers, trees, pebbles, ant hills—furnishing it which attract attention (themselves often considered props rather than actors). However, as Lefebvre reminds us, "flowers and trees should not make us forget the earth beneath, which has a secret life and richness of its own" (Lefebvre, 1991, p.87). The earth's surface itself, the outer layer of the lithosphere, comprises a varied landscape of intermingling soil and rock, its shifting composition and form an ongoing accomplishment of atmospheric, hydrospheric, biospheric, and geospheric processes and forces. Digging down into the earth, starting with soil, quickly exposes a rich "bioinfrastructure" (Puig de la Bellacasa, 2014). Soil is composed of a heterogenous mix of minerals, chemicals, and organic matter: "Forty-five percent mineral, 5% organic matter, between 20 and 30% water, with air making up the rest. Clay, sand, and silt; humus, earthworms, and insect corpses; hydrogen and oxygen; nitrogen and phosphorous" (Tironi et al., 2020, p.27). The inclusion of earthworms in this catalogue is a good reminder that soil is also home to a diverse range of organisms, from animals and insects to fungi and bacteria (the population of bacteria estimated to be approximately 40 million per gram: Clark and Hird, 2013, pp.45–6), which participate in its active composition and whose subterranean networks are vital to the maintenance of soil health and ecosystem health (Simard et al., 2012).

Below the soil we encounter the mix of sedimentary, metamorphic, and igneous rocks that forms the "bedrock" of the earth's crust. Ostensibly a "solid" foundation, it remains a dynamic and porous space, permeated with rich seams of metallic ores and fossilized biomass, and marked with fissures and fractures, a result of broader geologic and hydrogeologic processes (Bosworth, 2017). The lithosphere itself (made up of the earth's crust and the upper portion of the mantle) is separated into a series of plates that move across the underlying asthenosphere (a zone in which high temperatures and pressures produce a fluid viscous layer of magma). The movement of, and interaction between, these plates provides a mechanism that connects the subterranean and the surface in important ways: it shapes geological features on the surface (creating mountains, basins, and the like); it allows for the sinking of lithospheric rocks into the mantle, a process which alters their lithic and mineral composition; and it also allows for the mineral-rich magma to be forced upwards, toward the surface—a transference of minerals that was central to the establishment of (organic) life (Clark, Gormally, and Tuffen, 2018, pp.280–1).

Rather than a lively surface and dead (under)ground, the ground is a dynamic space and, perhaps most importantly, deeply interrelated with and connected to environmental processes above ground. It is a space in which bio and geo meet and which reveals their interdependency.

MYSTERY, MYTH, AND HYPOTHESIS

Nevertheless, Forster's rendering of the (under)ground as an inert and lifeless space is a construction that has long dominated social imaginings, both scientific and cultural (Bobbette and Donovan, 2019b; Tironi et al., 2020). In part, this is a reflection of the slow (and relatively recent) development of our knowledge of subterranean geological processes. This is perhaps understandable as our direct interaction with the underground is limited to an extremely small section close to the surface. Beyond the soil—that porous "skin" (Montgomery, 2007) that acts as threshold between the biosphere and geosphere proper—and the upper edges of the rocky outer crust that forms lithosphere, the underground remains largely inaccessible to humans. In fact, the furthest a living human has traveled underground is 3.9km, and the deepest human-constructed hole, the Kola Superdeep Borehole, is only just over 12km in length (a point at which the drilling equipment is no longer able to withstand the heat) (Parikka, 2015, p.164; Melo Zurita and Munro, 2019, p.39). (To put this in context, the lithosphere (or outer layer) itself averages approximately 100km in thickness and the distance to the earth's core is approximately 6000km.) This lack of spatial or physical proximity is also combined with a lack of temporal proximity. The geological processes outlined above operate at timescales difficult to comprehend when considered within the temporal frameworks that shape everyday life for most humans (Puig de la Bellacasa, 2015).

Considering this, the current scientific understanding of the earth's underlying structure has largely been developed through a combination of abstract calculations (drawing upon broader principles from physics and mathematics) and careful observations of, and extrapolations from, external manifestations on or near the earth's surface. This has been an evolving and often contentious process, and one fraught with error and revision. One of the most persistent historical theories, for example, was that the earth was (at least partially) hollow,[8] an understanding that remained a common (if not always credible) scientific hypothesis right up until the nineteenth century.[9] Edmund Halley proposed such a theory in 1692 after completing calculations based on Newton's "value of lunar relative density" (a value which turned out to be "Newton's most significant error in the *Principia's* Book III": Kollerstrom, 1992, p.185). Similarly, Descartes developed a model of the earth that, while assuming a dense center, also included "atmospheric" layers closer to the surface (a theory that was adopted by both Leibniz and Kelvin: O'Hara, 2018, pp.92–3). With the expansion of mining and the development of earth-based sciences (geology, palaeontology, archaeology) across the eighteenth and nineteenth centuries, a more familiar depiction of the earth's substructure began to emerge. Experiments based on (more accurate) Newtonian understandings of gravity suggested the earth was actually quite dense (Williams, 2008), and the close study of rocks and sediment enabled a more thorough understanding of the earth's geological stratification. Related to this, the discovery of fossils—some clearly older than humanity—pointed to a pre-human era, as well as enabled the underground to be viewed as a stratified historical record or chronology of the earth. This destabilized many prevailing ideas regarding the earth's age, as well as religious beliefs that viewed the earth as existing primarily as a domain for humans. Kant himself, after taking an interest in seismology, enquired: "How many such revolutions (including, certainly, many ancient organic beings no longer alive on the surface of the earth) preceded the existence of man, and how many [...] are still in prospect, is hidden from our enquiring gaze" (Kant, 1993, p.67; as cited in Hawkins, 2020, p.231). Debates continued across the nineteenth and early twentieth centuries, perhaps most famously between Neptunists and Plutonists about the origins of rocks, and between catastrophists and uniformitarians regarding the nature of geological change (O'Hara, 2018). However, it was only as recently as the 1960s that the theory of plate tectonics—an understanding that, perhaps more than any other previously, altered how we understand the relationship between the underground and aboveground—was accepted.

The development of geological sciences provided tools that helped us to overcome issues of spatial and temporal proximity and, in so doing, made the underground "knowable" in ways it previously hadn't been. However, their approach, like that of most modernist science, was grounded in an epistemological framework that, in its quest to obtain "objective" facts, carved geological phenomena out from the broader socio-material relationships and context in which they were embedded and from which they emerged. As Bobbette and Donovan summarize it:

> the task of modern geology is to penetrate into the murky world of the ground and synthesise the complexities of topography in order to return with an objective picture that we can all agree upon about the world beneath our feet. This purification of nature, the erasure of body, the discovery of the universal in the production of facts is the conceptual architecture of modernist geology. (2019b, p.18)

---

[8] Such an idea also resonates with many classical images in which the "underground" was frequently rendered as an "underworld," familiar to us, for example, in the classical Greek myths and stories of Hades and Persephone or Orpheus and Eurydice. Even in such myths, however, this underworld remained strongly linked to death/lifelessness. The underworld was home to the dead (and the gods that watched over them), and any living person who journeyed to this realm risked remaining trapped there forever (Ekroth and Nilsson, 2018).

[9] As Lesser (1987, p.33) notes, when Jules Verne published *Journey to the Centre of the Earth* in 1864, it was "truly science fiction rather than pure fantasy: it played with the possibilities that had not yet been eliminated, proposed scientific discoveries that had not been proved unscientific."

In this way, while overcoming problems of spatial and temporal proximity, the knowledge produced has created a new distance and disconnection from the underground, one related to (onto-)epistemological proximity (Barad, 2007, p.185). In effect, the complex interdependence and interconnection between geological processes and the broader socio-material environment—which includes human constructions and representations of such processes—is smoothed over. The result of this is that we arrive back at Forster's dead space: the ground becomes something we can obtain knowledge of, but which itself is "unproductive of ideas." A thoroughly anthropocentric perspective that leads to much thinking *about* the ground, but very little thinking with the ground.

A similar anthropocentric trend can be seen in law—law applies to the ground, it isn't to be found in the ground. Most obviously this objectification of ground occurs through concepts such as property, which dephysicalizes land (Graham, 2011), and turns it into two-dimensional space delineated by survey points. While at common law, ownership of land supposedly extends from the center of the earth to the upper edges of atmosphere (as per the famous Latin maxim *cuius est solum, eius est usque ad coelum et ad inferos*), this principle has been subject to so many exceptions that it has been described as little more than "poetic hyperbole" (Melo Zurita, 2020). Relying on processes of abstraction and demarcation, the law struggles to conceptualize the continuity of grounds, always seeking to carve them into limited, measurable, and commodifiable portions. In fact, in a strange recursive logic, the absence of these legal markers is often taken to mean the ground is empty of normativity, an assumption that underpinned colonial appropriation.

What might it mean to start thinking with and through ground? This necessarily entails acknowledging our interdependence with the ground and a process of, to borrow a phrase from Haraway (2016), "becoming with" the ground (see also Lyons, 2015; Bawaka Country et al., 2016; Bartel, 2018). In the context of law this means both recognizing and developing the relational and multi-agential sources and sites of human and more-than-human normativity, as well as acknowledging and fostering their co-emergence and co-constitution.

LAW, LIFE, AND THE GROUND

As we have seen, neither Machine nor god can supply legitimacy for human society in Forster's story but—prospectively—human life on the ground can and will. Life and law have had a long-term relationship. Common law theorists such as Matthew Hale understood law as a continuous process of accommodation to "the conditions, exigencies and conveniences of the people"—its legitimacy arising not from a point in constitutional time but from its ability to self-reform and self-repair (Hale, 1971, p.39). In twentieth-century legal theory, legal sociology, legal realism, legal consciousness studies, and the "law in everyday life" theorists are those who most securely connect law with living human relationships: law is alive, it emerges from daily practices and values, there is "living law" in distinction to merely formal "legal propositions" (Ehrlich, 1962).

But these anthropocentric connections of life and law are just the beginning. There is a much deeper connection between life and law, one that is emergent not only from already existing human society, but that rests on the ground and emerges from the ground. As we have said, there is significant knowledge about these matters in Indigenous cosmologies, but it is also important to consider what resources are available within the many contested terrains and counter-traditions of Western theory that might bring *nomos* into closer dialogue with *phusis*. Already, for instance, in the 1940s Georges Canguilhem wrote of "vital normativity" to refer to the ways in which the processes of life establish norms—an organism does not create norms contingently, as a legislature might. It creates and follows—performs—norms that promote its own existence, actualize its environment, and allow it to avoid suffering. "Vital normativity" is embedded in biological processes and is necessary to the continuation and reproduction of life. "Even for an amoeba, living means preference and exclusion" (Canguilhem, 1978, p.76). Life has direction and purpose and is therefore teleological. Its "end," however, is (contra Aristotle) contained neither in a "final cause" nor in any inherent essence but rather in the moment-to-moment unfolding necessary for life, which repeats and replicates, endlessly diversifies, and makes connections and forms relationships through symbiosis. As such a concept—in part inspired by Kant's reflections about organisms as "natural purposes" in the final part of the *Critique of Judgement*—teleology had a strong resurgence throughout twentieth-century biophilosophy (see for example Grene, 1974, chap. 9; Okrent, 2017, chap. 2). The elements of repetition, symbiosis, and purpose belong to a conception of emergent law beyond the human. Vital normativity is in the (ab)normality, adaptation, and connectedness to habitat that drives evolution. There is much of interest in Canguilhem's discussion of vital norms—without analyzing it in detail, it is perhaps sufficient to point out that it places normativity within the processes of all life, not just, as anthropocentric and Newtonian science would have it, in human society. The living compost that sits at the top of the soil is normative, in the sense that it contains and produces norms. So too the mycorrhizal networks underground, as well as the micro-organisms and the worms. Such vital normativity supports and applies to human life as much as to life in general, and therefore is implicated in the material practices that constitute all law—it is part of the *nomos*. But can we go further, and find life and law in inorganic processes?

A physician by training with a deep interest in biology, Canguilhem focused his discussion of vital normativity on biological organisms, leaving the question of its application to inorganic material largely unanswered. In summarizing his overall project, Osborne (2016, p.187) suggests, "[i]nstead of seeing vital principles everywhere, Canguilhem began with biological (and medical) facts and remained within […] a disciplinary organicism." However, as Greco (2019) has argued, it is possible to read his theory as having broader application to the whole of nature (which she also argues he did clearly intend), and this can be achieved by productively reading his work alongside the vitalism of process philosopher Alfred North Whitehead. Deeply critical of the "bifurcation of nature into two systems of reality" (Whitehead, 1920, p.45), Whitehead unashamedly extends life to everything: "the doctrine that I am maintaining is that neither physical nature nor life can be understood unless we fuse them together as essential factors in the composition of 'really real' things whose interconnections and individual characters constitute the universe" (Whitehead, 1968, p.150).

For Whitehead, existence (and life) takes on a radically processual nature. As Shaviro (2009, p.17) summarizes, reality for Whitehead "is made of events, and nothing but events: happenings rather than things, verbs rather than nouns, processes rather than substances." Even the most apparently stubborn and static entities are in a constant process of change and renewal. To illustrate this point, Whitehead uses the example of Cleopatra's Needle in London:

> If we define the Needle in a sufficiently abstract manner we can say that it never changes. But a physicist who looks on that part of the life of nature as a dance of electrons, will tell you that daily

> it has lost some molecules and gained others, and even the plain man can see that it gets dirtier and is occasionally washed. (1920, p.167)

Life is to be found in the generative unfolding that defines existence for all of nature. It is the 'origination of conceptual novelty' (Whitehead, 2010, p.102), the process of change.

Whitehead's expansive approach has been criticized—in granting "life" to everything, you lose any sense of what life is; if everything is "alive," nothing is "alive": "Precisely in stressing the ubiquity of processual becoming there is a tendency to collapse everything into itself, into generalized process, thus perhaps losing anything much to do with what is in fact, so to speak, originally 'original' to life" (Osborne, 2016, p.186). However, it is important to note that while Whitehead denies any fundamental ontological difference between living/organic and non-living, he does acknowledge difference in how life is expressed. The generative forces of life aggregate with different levels of organization, complexity, and stability. For Whitehead, the critical thing is to avoid the bifurcation of nature that would see some entities but not others granted an ontological priority. It is not a world in which some entities but not others live—where some are blessed with an *elan vital*, a soul, or even a specific bio-chemical structure that makes them ontologically distinct, even if their specific expression of life makes them more active participants in its generative unfolding.

Whitehead sees this misattribution of life as a result of a sort of conceptual reading backwards—from outcome to origin. By seeing human life as definitive of life, you carve it out of the world. You disconnect it from the generative socio-material processes from which it emerged, making it seem unique and atemporal. In many ways, in contrast to those who would draw a clear boundary around life, Whitehead's view is analogous to that of Ehrlich, when compared to legal positivist thought. Kelsen (and even Hart) starts with one expression of human law (a highly specialized version) and reads it as definitive of law and normativity, rather than as one specific expression or emergence of normativity within a broader field. By contrast, Ehrlich places law in a broader generative milieu of different forms of normativity, like Cover (some time later) in relation to narrative and myth. As Cover very powerfully argued, jurisgenesis creates a situation of plural normativity—"polynomia," which is reduced to singularity by jurispathic courts (Cover, 1983, pp.40–1). Dynamic unfolding legal plurality is the ground—a diverse ecosystem—transformed into a monoculture by the courts. To reiterate the point about the ideational sources of law made by Goodrich and noted at the beginning of this chapter, the consequence of this unification of law is its disconnection from the broader socio-material relationships from which it emerged. Understanding these dynamics makes pre-defined state law implausible: we can only understand law by seeing it as an emergence from a wider ontological field in which human life, non-human life, and all of non-life are co-implicated.

EARTH AS GROUND: GAIA

The generative milieu of the earth as "geopower" has also been theorized by Elizabeth Grosz:

> The "geo" is an inversion of the "ego"! It leads us to understand what may have an agency or force on forms of life and on material objects: the earth itself, while "unliving" as chemical elements and forces, can be understood as having a kind of life of its own when it is understood as a system of order and organization that is continually changing, never fully stable, dynamic. If dynamism is a quality

of the earth as a whole, if the very framework of life, its literal grounds, are never fully stable—or rather, are functionally metastable—then all our conceptions of life, and the human, acquire a kind of unstable, potentially transforming ground. (Grosz, Yusoff, and Clark, 2017, p.132)

If non-life is the unfolding agential shifting ground, so to speak, from which life emerges, then it becomes difficult to confine law, and the *nomos* generally, to a domain understood specifically as *life itself*. Indeed, as composting illustrates, a cycling of matter and energy through life and non-life—at varying spatiotemporal scales—is arguably normal across earth and hence normative in Canguilhem's sense: norms of earthly movement are constantly in production. These bio-norms and geo-norms are different from the physical laws of cause and certain effect—the billiard-table view of chain reactions determined by the laws of nature. Rather, they rely on complexities, emergent patterns, and probabilities. Hydrological cycles, nutrient cycles, rock cycles, and so forth are part of complex patterns that constitute earth order and systems.

The continuity of the biological and geological aspects of the earth is imagined in "When the World Screamed" by Arthur Conan Doyle. Decades before twentieth-century Western science hypothesized Gaia as the totality of the interconnected living and non-living processes of earth, Doyle's character, Professor George Challenger,[10] believes the earth is a single living organism "endowed […] with a circulation, a respiration, and a nervous system of its own" (Doyle, 1990, p.8). Challenger argues the point by comparing a "moor or heath" with the "hairy side of a wild animal," the "slow rise and fall of the land" with respiration, earthquakes with fidgeting, and volcanoes with "heat spots" on human bodies. More specifically, he claims "Nature repeats itself in many forms" and that the model or prototype for the world can be seen in a sea urchin fed not by water but by the ether that swirls around the planet. Challenger argues that earth is "quite unaware of the fungus growth of vegetation and evolution of tiny animalcules" on its surface (Doyle, 1990, p.9), but the egotistical professor resolves to draw the attention of the earth to his own existence by drilling through the crust and into the earth's sensitive middle. (As an aside, we can't help asking how could earth possibly know the identity of Challenger, who is from the earth's perspective nothing but a "tiny animacule," as he who funds and directs the experiment?) The narrator, Peerless Jones, is employed by Challenger to drill through the final section. On descending the eight miles already drilled, Jones bears witness to the truth of the assertions he had thought so ridiculous and sees for himself a soft pulsating interior, variously described as a "skinned animal," "beast," and "sensory cortex." When the soft skin is eventually pierced, the scream is heard: "a howl in which pain, anger, menace, and the outraged majesty of Nature all blended into one hideous shriek." Following the scream, earth underlines its agency by spitting out the drilling paraphernalia, ejecting a "vile treacly" geyser of ambiguous significance (was it the "life blood"? was it "a protective secretion?"), and abruptly and definitively closes its own wound. Finally—proving that the earth is a single entity—volcanoes around the entire globe erupt as one.

Two elements are particularly worthy of comment: first, the depiction of Challenger's arrogance illustrative of human and (as Kathryn Yusoff explains in her reading of the story) more particularly masculine hubris (Yusoff, 2017)—once he has, as he sees it, compelled earth to acknowledge his presence, he is surveyed in admiration by the assembled crowd—"from his

---

[10] This is the same Professor Challenger who famously delivered a fictional lecture in Deleuze and Guattari's "Geology of Morals" in *A Thousand Plateaus* (Deleuze and Guattari, 1987, p.40).

hillock he could look down upon the lake of upturned faces," adopting a Napoleonic stance: "He rose from his chair, his eyes half-closed, a smile of conscious merit upon his face, his left hand upon his hip, his right buried in the breast of his frock coat" (Doyle, 1990, p.27). There is an undeniably mocking tone—"the June sun shone golden upon him as he turned gravely bowing to each quarter of the compass. Challenger the super-scientist, Challenger the arch-pioneer, Challenger the first man of all men whom Mother Earth had been compelled to recognize" (Doyle, 1990, p.27). As Yusoff comments, "Challenger's attempt to make the earth scream is a misogynist tale of conquering the geological impotence that the earth has bestowed on mankind" but it also "exhibits the desire for a reciprocal relation with inhuman nature" (2017, p.107). Considered from the point of view of how humanity relates to the earth, we see both a desire to conquer and an almost insecure need for a personal response.

A second point of interest concerns how earth is imagined as a living entity—in this story it becomes a single organism with skin and pulsating interior. This image serves as a useful reference point for what Gaia is *not* in the theory devised by Lovelock and Margulis (1974; see also Margulis and Lovelock, 1974), as considered at length by Bruno Latour (2017). Lovelock and Margulis presented evidence showing that non-living nature is not just a container or "environment" to which life adapts, but is also engineered by life. Living and non-living systems co-evolve and produce a "planet-wide homeostasis"—"the maintenance of relatively constant conditions by active control" (Margulis and Lovelock, 1974, p.473). As Latour points out, for Lovelock and Margulis, and contrary to some misrepresentations of the hypothesis, Gaia is not a single living entity or a unified system, much less a unitary agent, but a complex of interacting systems. There is totality, but not equilibrium, stasis, or closure. Gaia is multiple interacting agents and systems-as-agents—working together to prevent earth from slipping into a state of chemical equilibrium or disorder, but not constituting a whole single system. Indeed, as Latour comments, 'there are neither parts nor a whole' (2017, p.95). And thus, many of the metaphors for earth systems are incorrect—earth has no engineer, no clockmaker, and is not a spaceship (2017, p.96). But the systems are connected and there is self-regulation and self-adaptation.

What can we make of this Gaia as ground for an emergent law? First, of course—and like all grounds—that it is not one but many, not simple but complex, not solid but shifting. Second, that being a human on the ground is entirely secondary to the processes of becoming human from the ground. For law, rather than seeing natural entities and processes as vulnerable objects defined, regulated, propertized, or protected by law, it becomes possible to see an unfolding earth as composed of multiple subjects and partners in new legal relations. Such relations are not imposed, like the attempt by Challenger to force earth to recognize him, but nor are they even formed between humans and earth as separate entities. Michel Serres speaks of a natural contract in which humanity forms a symbiotic contract with the earth: "we must add to the social contract a natural contract of symbiosis and reciprocity" (1995, p.38). This follows from the fact that "the Earth speaks to us in terms of forces, bonds, and interactions, and that's enough to make a contract" (1995, p.39). Although Serres might be taken to be implying here that such a contract is an innovation, something we as humans ought to devise and implement in order to halt the damage we are doing, Latour notes that Serres' natural contract "is not a deal between two parties, humanity and nature." Rather, it is "a series of transactions in which one can see how, all along and in the sciences themselves, the various types of entities mobilized by geohistory have exchanged the various traits that define their agency" (Latour, 2017, p.64). Exchange is within the agency of every active thing, living and non-living. In other words, the natural contract is inherent to every thing on the planet because it precedes the emergence—via symbiosis and/or intra-action—of entities and agents. Returning to Whitehead: "We are in the world and the world is in us" (Whitehead, 1968, p.165).

CONCLUSION

Western thinkers are accustomed to understanding law as something outside or beyond the ground, and in particular beyond the physical ground, composed of matter such as soil, microbes, rocks, and fungus. Ultimately, this is human mythology, and a very specific Eurocentric one. At the same time, and put simply, human life and law rests entirely upon the ground and not only on it, but in it. In many ways this is an easy point to comprehend: how can we *not* be of the earth? But it is another matter altogether for those of us acculturated in Western thought to fully understand the multitude of ways in which law emerges from the ground and is already implicated in the ground. It is perhaps even more difficult to express this in the language of Western science and philosophy. In this chapter, we have traced some of the possibilities for re-connecting bio-norms with geo-norms and human law. The ground is the dense surface under our feet that provides a normally solid resting and growing place for the paraphernalia around us. The ground can be represented as two-dimensional and—as mere background—seem immovable and limited. As we have explored in this chapter, both the literal ground and its aligned metaphorical and imaginary constructions are far more suggestive, materially complex, and theoretically interesting than simply being a lower limit for human life. Notions of grounding and of grounds, the material in and on the ground, the spacetimes above and below the surface of the earth, and even the unknown matter of the entire earth are engaged in an ongoing process of interdependent motion and exchange that implicates all of life and all of non-life.

REFERENCE LIST

Barad, K. (2007) *Meeting the Universe Halfway: Quantum Physics and the Entanglement of Matter and Meaning*. Durham: Duke University Press.
Bartel, Robyn (2018) "Place-speaking: attending to the relational, material, and governance messages of *Silent Spring*", *The Geographical Journal*, 184, 64–74.
Bawaka Country et al. (2016) "Co-becoming Bawaka: towards a relational understanding of place/space", *Progress in Human Geography*, 40(4), 455–75.
Bennett, J. (2010) *Vibrant Matter: A Political Ecology of Things*. Durham: Duke University Press.
Bobbette, A. and Donovan, A. (eds) (2019a) *Political Geology: Active Stratigraphies and the Making of Life*. Cham: Palgrave Macmillan.
Bobbette, A. and Donovan, A. (2019b) "Political geology: an introduction", in Bobbette, A. and Donovan, A. (eds) *Political Geology: Active Stratigraphies and the Making of Life*. Cham: Palgrave Macmillan, p.1.
Bosworth, K. (2017) "Thinking permeable matter through feminist geophilosophy: Environmental knowledge controversy and the materiality of hydrogeologic processes", *Environment and Planning D: Society and Space*, 35(1), 21–37.
Braidotti, R. (2013) *The Posthuman*, Cambridge: Polity.
Bringhurst, R. (2009) *The Tree of Meaning: Language, Mind and Ecology*. Berkeley, CA: Counterpoint.
Bryant, L., Srnicek, N., and Harman, G. (eds) (2011) *The Speculative Turn: Continental Materialism and Realism*. Melbourne: Re.Press (Anamnesis).

Canguilhem, G. (1978) *On the Normal and the Pathological*. Dordrecht, Netherlands: Springer.
Clark, N., Gormally, A., and Tuffen, H. (2018) "Speculative volcanology", *Environmental Humanities*, 10(1), 273–94.
Clark, N. and Hird, M.J. (2013) "Deep shit", *O-Zone: A Journal of Object-Oriented Studies*, 1, 44.
Clark, N. and Yusoff, K. (2017) "Geosocial formations and the Anthropocene", *Theory, Culture & Society*, 34(2–3), 3–23.
Coole, D. and Frost, S. (eds) (2010) *New Materialisms: Ontology, Agency, and Politics*. Durham: Duke University Press.
Correia, F. and Schnieder, B. (eds) (2012) *Metaphysical Grounding: Understanding the Structure of Reality*. Cambridge: Cambridge University Press.
Cover, R.M. (1983) "Foreword: nomos and narrative", *Harvard Law Review*, 97, 4.
Crutzen, P. and Stoermer, E. (2000) "The 'Anthropocene'", *IGBP Newsletter*, 41, 17–18.
Danowski, D. and Viveiros de Castro, E.B. (2017) *The Ends of the World*. Malden, MA: Polity.
Deleuze, G. (1994) *Difference and Repetition*. New York: Columbia University Press.
Deleuze, G. and Guattari, F. (1987) *A Thousand Plateaus: Capitalism and Schizophrenia*. Minneapolis: University of Minnesota Press.
Derrida, J. (1990) "Force of law: the 'mystical foundation of authority'", *Cardozo Law Review*, 11, 919.
Doyle, A.C. (1990) *When the World Screamed & Other Stories*. San Francisco: Chronicle Books.
Ehrlich, E. (1962) *Fundamental Principles of the Sociology of Law*. New York: Russell & Russell.
Ekroth, G. and Nilsson, I. (eds) (2018) *Round Trip to Hades in the Eastern Mediterranean Tradition: Visits to the Underworld from Antiquity to Byzantium*. Leiden: Brill.
Forster, E.M. (2001) "The Machine Stops (1909)", in *Selected Stories*. New York: Penguin Books, p.91.
Goodrich, P. (1986) *Reading the Law: A Critical Introduction to Legal Method and Techniques*. Oxford: Basil Blackwell.
Graham, N. (2011) *Lawscape: Property, Environment, Law*. Abingdon: Routledge.
Greco, M. (2019) "Vitalism now—a problematic", *Theory, Culture & Society*, 0(0), 1.
Grene, M. (1974) *The Understanding of Nature: Essays in the Philosophy of Biology*. D Reidel.
Grosz, E. (2005) *Time Travels: Feminism, Nature, Power*. Durham: Duke University Press.
Grosz, E., Yusoff, K., and Clark, N. (2017) "An interview with Elizabeth Grosz: geopower, inhumanism and the biopolitical", *Theory, Culture & Society*, 34(2–3), 129–46.
Hale, S.M. (1971) *The History of the Common Law in England*. Chicago: University of Chicago Press.
Hamilton, C., Bonneuil, C., and Gemenne, F. (eds) (2015) *The Anthropocene and the Global Environmental Crisis: Rethinking Modernity in a New Epoch*. London: Routledge.
Haraway, D. (1988) "Situated knowledges: the science question in feminism and the privilege of partial perspective", *Feminist Studies*, 14(3), 575–99.
Haraway, D.J. (2016) *Staying with the Trouble: Making Kin in the Chthulucene*. Durham: Duke University Press.
Haraway, D. et al. (2016) "Anthropologists are talking—about the Anthropocene", *Ethnos*, 81(3), 535–64.
Hawkins, H. (2020) "'A volcanic incident': towards a geopolitical aesthetics of the subterranean", *Geopolitics*, 25(1), 214–39.
Kafka, F. (1953) *The Trial*. Harmondsworth: Penguin.
Kant, Immanuel (1993) *Opus postumum*. Eckart Förster and Michael Rosen trans. Cambridge: Cambridge University Press.
Kelsen, H. (1934) "The Pure Theory of Law: its method and fundamental concepts", *Law Quarterly Review*, 50(4), 474–98.
Kelsen, H. (1961) *General Theory of Law and State*, Russell & Russell.
Kelsen, H. (1967) *Pure Theory of Law*, 2nd edn, Berkeley and Los Angeles: University of California Press.
Kelsen, H. (1991) *General Theory of Norms*, Oxford: Clarendon Press.
Kollerstrom, N. (1992) "The hollow world of Edmond Halley", *Journal for the History of Astronomy*, 23(3), 185–92.
Latour, B. (2005) *Reassembling the Social: An Introduction to Actor-Network-Theory*. Oxford: Oxford University Press.
Latour, B. (2017) *Facing Gaia: Eight Lectures on the New Climatic Regime*. Cambridge, UK: Polity.

Latour, B. (2018) *Down to Earth: Politics in the New Climate Regime.* Cambridge, UK: Polity.
Lefebvre, H. (1991) *Critique of Everyday Life*. London: Verso.
Lesser, W. (1987) *The Life Below the Ground: A Study of the Subterranean in Literature and History*. Boston: Faber and Faber.
Lovelock, J.E. and Margulis, L. (1974) "Atmospheric homeostasis by and for the biosphere: The Gaia Hypothesis", *Tellus*, 26(1–2), 2–10.
Lyons, K.M. (2015) "Decomposition as life politics: soils, selva, and small farmers under the gun of the U.S.–Colombia War on Drugs", *Cultural Anthropology*, 31(1), 56–81.
Margulis, L. and Lovelock, J.E. (1974) "Biological modulation of the Earth's atmosphere", *Icarus*, 21(4), 471–89.
Margulis, L. and Sagan, D. (1997) *Microcosmos: Four Billion Years of Microbial Evolution*. Berkeley: University of California Press.
Marx, K. (1859) "'Preface' to A Contribution to Critique of Political Economy", in Carver, T. (ed.) *Marx: Later Political Writings*. Cambridge: Cambridge University Press, 1996, p.158.
Melo Zurita, M. de L. (2020) "Challenging sub terra nullius: a critical underground urbanism project", *Australian Geographer*, 51(3), 269–82.
Melo Zurita, M. de L. and Munro, P.G. (2019) "Voluminous territorialisation: historical contestations over the Yucatan Peninsula's subterranean waterscape", *Geoforum*, 102, 38–47.
Montgomery, D.R. (2007) *Dirt: The Erosion of Civilizations*. Berkeley: University of California Press.
Moore, J.W. (2017) "The Capitalocene, Part I: on the nature and origins of our ecological crisis", *The Journal of Peasant Studies*, 44(3), 594–630.
O'Hara, K.D. (2018) *A Brief History of Geology*. Cambridge: Cambridge University Press.
Okrent, M. (2017) *Nature and Normativity: Biology, Teleology, and Meaning*. Abingdon: Routledge.
Osborne, T. (2016) "Vitalism as pathos", *Biosemiotics*, 9(2), 185–205.
Parikka, J. (2015) *A Geology of Media*. Minneapolis; London: University of Minnesota Press.
Povinelli, E.A. (2016) *Geontologies: A Requiem to Late Liberalism*. Durham: Duke University Press.
Puig de la Bellacasa, M. (2014) "Encountering bioinfrastructure: ecological struggles and the sciences of soil", *Social Epistemology*, 28(1), 26–40.
Puig de la Bellacasa, M. (2015) "Making time for soil: technoscientific futurity and the pace of care", *Social Studies of Science*, 45(5), 691–716.
Raven, M.J. (ed.) (2020) *The Routledge Handbook of Metaphysical Grounding*. New York: Routledge.
Seabury, M.B. (1997) "Images of a networked society: E.M. Forster's 'The Machine Stops'", *Studies in Short Fiction*, 34(1), 61.
Serres, M. (1995) *The Natural Contract*. Ann Arbor: University of Michigan Press.
Shaviro, S. (2009) *Without Criteria: Kant, Whitehead, Deleuze, and Aesthetics*. Cambridge, MA: MIT Press.
Simard, S.W. et al. (2012) "Mycorrhizal networks: mechanisms, ecology and modelling", *Fungal Biology Reviews*, 26(1), 39–60.
Stengers, I. (1997) *Power and Invention: Situating Science*. Minneapolis: University of Minnesota Press.
Stengers, I. (2015) *In Catastrophic Times: Resisting the Coming Barbarism*. London: Open Humanities Press.
Tironi, M. et al. (2020) "Soil theories: relational, decolonial, inhuman", in Francisco Salazar, J. et al. (eds) *Thinking with Soils: Material Politics and Social Theory*. New York: Bloomsbury Academic, p.15.
Turner, B. and Somerville, W. (2020) "Composting with Cullunghutti: Experimenting with How to Meet a Mountain", *Journal of Australian Studies*, 44(2), 224–42.
Whitehead, A.N. (1920) *The Concept of Nature*. Cambridge: The University Press.
Whitehead, A.N. (1968) *Modes of Thought*. Simon and Schuster.
Whitehead, A.N. (2010) *Process and Reality*. Simon and Schuster.
Williams, R.H. (2008) *Notes on the Underground: An Essay on Technology, Society, and the Imagination*. Cambridge, MA: MIT Press.
Yusoff, K. (2017) "Geosocial strata", *Theory, Culture & Society*, 34(2–3), 105–27.

25. Slash
Andreas Philippopoulos-Mihalopoulos[1]

An experimental text that introduces and tries out wavewriting. Wavewriting is the all-connected yet perpetually withdrawing turn of phrase that does not lead to clear conclusions, truths and certainties, but to an accumulation of wavings that approximate a direction without a thesis. To do this I bring together eight literary fiction texts on water, and elicit their legal dimensions, while interspersing them with 'waves', short ruminations/explanations/deviations/comments on the process and brief autoethnographic vignettes. This is orchestrated around the *slash*, a dividing yet connecting punctuation sign that I take both metaphorically and materially as a way to make waves.

/FIRST WAVE/

We use *slash* to regulate the flow of the text. We interrupt and interweave. Just wait a little, the slash says. The slash brings line breaks in poetry / breaths in songs / caesuras of a linearity that enable the return to the linear.

We use slash to go deeper into law. We dive deeper into the sections / then the paragraphs / then the subparagraphs. Slash zooms in the law, it allows the law to bring up the particular, or at least the law's ambitions towards the particular. Just swim further in, the slash says.

We use slash like a weir to regulate the flow of the water. Slash stops the water from running or allows it to flow forth even more profusely. Slash is the wall of the reservoir, the inner lining of the sluice gate, the open mouthing of the slush.[2]

Slash separates and links. Slash is the text's skin, a suture, a process of knitting together the two skin lips and the scar of the wound.[3] Slashing the water generates waves. Slash as the shape of the wave, rising and falling into the *ondoyant*.

In this text, I use the slash as a tool to mix water, law and literature. I visit some well-known and some lesser-known works of fiction and I zoom into the moments where the aquatic and the legal come together. In order to do this, I rewrite parts of them, I interject my own experiences, I become reader, academic commentator, fiction author, plagiarist, con artist, ballast thrown into the sea, all in an attempt to tease out the way these texts employ the aquatic and the legal.[4] The fact that I offer no literary context for the works I am using is deliberate: while this

---

[1] With thanks to Jan Hogan, Yusuf Patel, Ifor Duncan, Olivia Barr, Peter Rush, Daniela Gandorfer and Peter Goodrich for their comments.

[2] John K. Donaldson, 'As Long as the Waters Shall Run: The "Obstructed Water" Metaphor in American Indian Fiction' (2002) 40(2) *American Studies International*, 73–93.

[3] Mark B. Salter, 'Theory of the / : The Suture and Critical Border Studies' (2012) 17(4) *Geopolitics*, 734–55.

[4] Hoping for what T.J. Demos calls the 'unanticipated connections between narratives, virtual openings that offer places where the unexpected appears and where discovery can take place'. T.J.

text aims to have a direction of questioning, and a practice of flowing law, literature and water together, it does not have a thesis. Rather it invites the reader to tease that thesis, should they wish. This performative practice of writing, inalienable from the text itself, is about waves, their disruptive singularity and their diffractive multiplicity.

I call this wavewriting: a writing in waves; a writing that makes waves. This unfolds in nine + one waves, wavewriting method and commentary at the same time, an attempt at linking the fiction works with each other.

In between my reading and rewriting of these texts, however, I do offer a commentary on the questions in the heart of this chapter. The reader is invited to slash in this text, dip in and out of it, trace or dwell the spaces around the slash.

Let's see whether we can make some waves, then.

FRANZ KAFKA'S *POSEIDON* / WHEN WILL WE STOP CALCULATING?

Poseidon sits at the bottom of the sea and gets on with his calculations. That's all he does. 'The administration of all the waters was a huge task.'[5] Yet, 'one couldn't say that the work made him happy either; he only did it because it was his to do'. Who made him do this? 'They.' 'Kafka does not say who "they" are, but that is what makes him Kafka.'[6] History or myth, original fact, a role as deep as the earth's breath. Underwater breath. He just knew he had to get on with it. Endless calculations. That's just how it was.

'The thing that most angered him was when he got to hear what people thought it involved, that is, forever parting the waves with his trident. And when all the time he was sitting at the bottom of the ocean up to his ears in figures.' (46)

The calculable stops him from diving into the incalculable. He just about manages to stay afloat in the calculable. He never even gets to see the sea. He is in it but there never is enough time to actually see the sea.

The calculable is an impermeable, plastic mantle made of figures and guilt that keeps Poseidon dry. It is a law, as deep as the deepest sea. This law protects Poseidon from life. Let's list its qualities: separating, covering, categorizing, appeasing, protecting, waiting. There are no waves here. All is contained. All is calculated. Waiting for the law to end and for the waves of life to start. This is the water, finally, open and life-giving, or life-taking, it doesn't matter, life is what matters, not calculations. We must wait for that; we must work for that. Poseidon's Messiah is wet and titanic: 'he was waiting for the world to end first, because there was bound to be a quiet moment just before the end when he had signed off on his last calculation and would be able to take himself on a little cruise somewhere' (46). Law has convinced us all: there will be a last calculation. A last judgement. And then, the water will be ours.

Demos, 'On Terror and Beauty: John Akomfrah's Vertigo Sea' (2016) 56 *Revista Atlantica*, www.revistaatlantica.com/en/contribution/on-terror-and-beauty-john-akomfrahs-vertigo-sea/.

[5] Franz Kafka, 'Poseidon' in *Investigations of a Dog and Other Creatures* (ed and trans. M. Hofmann, New Directions 2017) 45.

[6] Cees Nooteboom, *Letters to Poseidon* (Quercus 2014) 32.

/SECOND WAVE/

Life versus law: that was a bit too easy, wasn't it? But sometimes one needs crude binaries, awkward slashings and rough divisions. This might be the way to make waves.

Let's slash another crude division then: Law / Literature: slanted Ls domino-collapsing onto each other. Let's add some nuance by reconsidering the need for prepositions. Why insist on distinguishing between these parallelisms, law *and/of/in/as* literature? What do we achieve? Clarity, categorisation, cleaving.

Let's multiply the slash: law / (breath) / literature.

Why else would we (academics, fiction authors, readers) read law and literature together if not to take a breath? To put calculables and incalculables together? To get a glimpse of the sea? To escape the unidimensional impression of the individual in which the law pushes us?[7] Why else would we read law and literature together if not to see that law's illusions are more brittle and even more multipliable than those of literature? Why else, if not to put ourselves squarely in the centre of the action? Why else, if not to try and understand, something, anything, about why we do what we do?

My partner once described me as a 'slasher': academic slash artist slash fiction author slash poet slash slash. I liked it when he said it; it had a freshness and sounded like a compliment – which is how he meant it. But I now see it as responsibility: it is not enough just to do different things (so what?). The important is to circulate also in that space above and below the slash, where the waves, the excess, the overflow and the offcuts pool, and ease these into a cyclical channel, a hydrocircumference, a gentle moat from where our political positions will be launched.

In this text, I am author/reader/fictional personality. I flow between these slashes, and as I do, I follow laws of writing and referencing, editorial decrees of word-limits and handbook exigencies, technological norms of typing. At the same time, I imagine myself going against or perhaps complementing what 'We' do: I generate new laws that we might not accept as law yet, but might be interested in exploring; I carve canals that others might find navigable, new sluice gates (between disciplines, between styles, between self-narrative and literary analysis, between flows and slashes) that others might appreciate my holding open for them. My time is limited. I become part of the We as soon as I set foot on the coast.

I want to see the sea. I want to make waves. I want to emerge from the calculable and dive into the incalculable. I am taking a risk: the incalculable will flood into me and all my legal calculations. The incalculable brings along its own law.

I still want to see the sea. Come along and we might find some waves there.

KARL OVE KNAUSGAARD'S *A TIME FOR EVERYTHING* / THE WATER CANNOT SAVE US

It takes Knausgaard almost 300 pages to rewrite the biblical flood. We are in that curve of world's time, when the angels fly off and the waters rush in, undisturbed by walls and laws. Unlike Poseidon, though, Knausgaard's god releases his water from above. Like Poseidon,

---

[7] Maria Aristodemou, *Law and Literature: Journeys from Her to Eternity* (Oxford UP 2008).

this god does not see the water. He has already departed, abandoning his creation to its final struggle: 'Only after the cherubim had gone did they fully understand just how important their proximity had been. It was as if a wall had been removed in the room they inhabited.'[8] No walls, no gods, no laws. Just a seemingly smooth space opening up, freedom/fear chiaroscuro. But right then, the waters rush in. 'There was suddenly an opening, through which even the most unexpected could pour in. The sky darkened, the water rose, and when they looked to the west, where the light of the cherubim had once been, their glance no longer met any resistance, but swept on through more of the same: trees, mountains, a darkening sky, rising water' (Loc 2703–5).

Laws as walls. A room without walls is draughty, smooth, exposed. How long can one last in such a room? Not long. We draw lines, build walls, make laws, breed gods. Laws are mantles, protective walls, flapping angel wings, presences of relative proximity – never quite here, never without. Until they depart, and the world opens up like a wounded horse mouth spitting torrents.

Little Noah – and not his sister Anna – is his father's favourite child. Noah is a fragile boy, given to obsessively categorizing everything around him: living things, dead things, god, the sun... A volatile lawmaker who calms down only when his father picks him up and consoles him. And his other Father (here I can capitalize if you insist) makes the best of this categorizing spirit: one pair from every species. Heterosexual obviously. Fully able-bodied obviously. Lovingly monogamous obviously. Check, check, check.

As every lawmaker (every one and every thing that moves, stands still, floats or drowns) knows, what counts is what you leave out of your calculations: Noah's sister Anna, for example; her family, Noah's nephews and nieces; their wives and husbands; their children – to name but a few. They are left out, looking onto a future that does not include them. They see the ark from the mountaintop where they took shelter: 'the water rose relentlessly up the ship's sides, and when half the hull was submerged, it began to glide forward slowly. It glided between the trees, huge and dark. There wasn't a sign of life aboard. "A ship in the forest," whispered Omak. "What sort of being could have made it?" "It's a death ship," whispered Ophir…The aura of death that clung to it strengthened the assumption. The ship was their last hope. In just a few hours' time the sea would cover this mountain too. They thought the ship had been sent by God' (Loc 5870–4).

We think that literature will save us from the law, just as the water will save us from sins. Nice little constructions that rely on facile binaries again. But does law ever truly depart, even when flooded by the redeeming water? 'They saw him quite clearly… "Noah!" Anna shouted. "You must save us! Save us, Noah!" Noah remained motionless where he stood…Anna took the baby from Rachel and raised him above her head so that he could see. He saw.' (Loc 6075–81) Noah's Father, yes, *that* Father, has picked him up and is holding him tight, radiating his paternal love from within, flooding Noah's body with an embodied law that knew no other judgement. Noah *is* the last judgement, one in a series of lasts, but who's got time to count now that the waters are swallowing up mountains and creations? Not Noah. He just signed off the last calculation and took himself on that little cruise.

No waves here either. This is just the swelling of death.

---

[8] Karl Knausgaard, *A Time to Every Purpose under Heaven* (trans. J. Anderson, Portobello 2008) Locations 5610–12.

"I'm sorry about that," Anna said. Gently, she pushed the baby down and held him under the water… "I'm sorry about that," she said again' (Loc 6088–91). Forgotten by that looming law of the Father, the only thing left to embrace all those incalculable masses of misfits was the silent waveless water.

/THIRD WAVE/

I must try harder. Waves are hard to come by, and much harder to write on. I must find a different god or water or law. An ondoyant writing methodology, 'the language of waveshape'.[9] I need something else to show what a waveshape language might be, something other than language that returns to the soundwaves that make up language. Music perhaps. The Vanuatu women, waist-deep in the ocean, slashing and creating water music: *vus lamlam* or slashing the water. A rough melody, a gurgle and an incantation, a repetition.[10] Or Richard Strauss's *Der Rosenkavalier* – possibly one of the dullest operas in the global repertoire yet with two or three of the most devastatingly beautiful passages. The finale with three sopranos is wavewritten: sound wavelets from multiple directions, confluence and conflict, a constantly postponed gratification, particle explosions of desire at every note, a slashing of expectations, a new law.

It is the kind of wavewriting I am aiming at: small waves, not showy. Corroding yet inviting. These waves remain together because they have a horizon of movement, but not much else. Manifold yet streamlined, precariously contained by slashes: the reader's small sharp breaths, or her quick parentheses to google this and that book, add them to the list, more waves.

Wavewriting to accommodate the three meanings of the word *Nalu* in the Hawai'ian Kanaka language: wave / to ponder and to speculate / amnion, amniotic fluid.[11]

Wavewriting to accommodate a multiplicity of laws and ethics, their confluence and conflicts, their differentiated power and affective displacement.

Wavewriting as the affective intermingling of justice and injustice.

JOSÉ SARAMAGO'S *THE GOSPEL ACCORDING TO JESUS* / WE CAN NEVER LEAVE THE LAW BEHIND

OK, let me try another god, to see whether I make any waves. This time, the god is slashed up in three. The first one is already waiting, 'big man, elderly, with a great flowing beard'.[12] The second is about to arrive: 'I am going to the water. At his shoulder, Mary Magdalene asks, Must you go, and Jesus replied…At last I shall know who I am and what is expected of me…he began rowing out towards that invisible space in the middle of the lake' (278) towards the locus of the contract, the radiating space of law: 'a diffused light turns the mist white and lustrous… The boat comes to a halt, it has reached the middle of the lake.' Jesus says to the

---

[9] Wu Ming-Yi, *The Man with the Compound Eyes* (trans. D. Sterk, Vintage 2014) 169.
[10] *Vanuatu Women's Water Music*, a film directed by Tim Cole, https://vimeo.com/97992375.
[11] Karin Amimoto Ingersoll, *Waves of Knowing: A Seascape Epistemology* (Duke UP 2016) 45.
[12] José Saramago, *The Gospel According to Jesus Christ* (trans. G. Pontiero, Mariner Books 2014) 278.

man with the beard, 'I've come to find out who I am and what I shall have to do henceforth in order to fulfil my part of the contract' (278).

The middle is not the centre. It is a fold that collapses under its own gravitas, a dark green hole, life-giver and life-taker. Like another covenant presaging another last judgement, the boat of the contract floats in the middle of the water, lake below and mist above, a mist the gods breathe in and out.

This is quite remarkable, considering that the law is hydrophobic. The law cannot deal with water.[13] It still thinks of water as land, markable and striatable, flat and for the taking.[14] Yet it's only on water that the law can be agreed. Water is the locus of the contract. It is what makes the tellurian law, solidifies it, contrasts it and reflects it, feeds its narcissism. Water is the *sine-qua-non* that enables Schmitt to carry on drawing lines on the terra firma.[15] Water protects the law from itself, dilutes it and layers it, shakes its solidity, gives it its escape. Water unmakes the law, damps it down, rots it, grates on its surface with the diluvial force of aeons. Water outlasts the law.

Ah finally, here comes the third: 'In the silence that followed one could hear somewhere in the mist the noise of someone swimming this way…His hands grabbed the edge of the boat… hands belonging to a body which like that of God must be tall, sturdy and advanced in years. The boat swayed under the impact…a Leviathan rising from the lower depths…I've come to join you, he said, settling himself on the side of the boat equidistant between Jesus and God' (280). The devil has joined in, three men in a boat, our aquatic unholy trinity: we can now proceed with the contract.

'God arranged the folds of his tunic and the hood of his mantle and then with mock solemnity, like a judge about to pass formal sentence, he said, Let us start from the beginning' (285). The negotiations are tough. Jesus wants out. God wants eternal power and he can only get that through Jesus. The devil wants to be loved again by his father. Jesus cannot take it any more: 'I am breaking our contract, I am detaching myself from you… Empty words, My son, can't you see you're in my power and that all these sealed documents we refer to as agreements, pacts, treaties, contracts, alliances, and in which I figure, could be reduced to a single clause, and waste less paper and ink, a clause which would bluntly state that, Everything prescribed by the law of God is obligatory, even the exceptions' (283). Jesus jumps back on his boat and begins to row away: 'Farewell, I'm off home, and you can both go back the way you came' (284); he rows and rows but ends up exactly where he was, in the middle, always moving, never leaving.

There is no escape from the law. What would have happened if Jesus managed to reach the coast? This means, what would happen if one could finally escape the middle, that luminous space of the law? The space of need? I don't know. I never reached it. I tried, several times. Maybe my world has always been a coastless lake. Once, I woke up, early autumn morning, haven't talked to him for three months, I really could not forgive what he did, shall I tell you?

---

[13] 'The emphasis on the transportation surface neglects vertical zones in favor of horizontal trajectories, making the deep seas the void of the void.' Stacy Alaimo, 'Violet-Black', in Jeffrey Jerome Cohen (ed) *Prismatic Ecology* (University of Minnesota Press 2013) 234.

[14] Mara Ntona and Mika Schröder, 'Regulating Oceanic Imaginaries: The Legal Construction of Space, Identities, Relations and Epistemological Hierarchies within Marine Spatial Planning' (2020) 19(2) *Maritime Studies*, 241.

[15] Carl Schmitt, *Nomos of the Earth* (trans. G.L. Ulmen, Telos Press 2003).

yes, ok although this is hard, but I write, that's what I do, whatever I do, this is what I do, I write and I have always been writing, and here it is, my writing, my text, published under his name, a bloated narcissistic gesture befitting the long bearded guy type, although my father's beard was neither flowing nor white at that point but it still choked me, three months later I woke up with a black metal cube weighing on my chest, shiny black metal cube that started barking at my face, metal resonant barking, "I'm proud of you, I can see you're an intelligent lad and perceptive, And you're not afraid, No, Don't worry, you will be, fear always comes, even to a son of God' (279), fear did come of course, I am no son of god but a mere offspring of the law, just like all of us. The law demanded of me that I remain his son, the son of law, with that calm sense of entitlement, with that raging sense of threat, ok I will do it, I will tell stories, fake it all up, even perform miracles, but with one condition, 'But you know perfectly well you cannot lay down conditions, God replied angrily' (288), ok then on one understanding, that I will be able to, no, nothing, he says, you will do this in my name, you are nothing but my son, 'So, I'm to make up stories, Yes, stories, parables, moral tales, even if it means distorting the law ever so slightly, don't let that bother you… for it was I who put justice into the laws I handed down, It's a bad sign when You start allowing men to tamper with your laws, Only when it suits Me and proves to be useful' (287), but you did not write that text, I did, if I pretend that this is ok, if I tell stories, don't I tamper not just with your law but also with that justice of yours? And then what?

'A voice came down from the mist and said, Perhaps this God and the one yet to come are one and the same god. Jesus, God and the Devil pretended not to hear but could not help looking at each other in alarm, mutual fear is like this' (297). We are all characters in a play of course and stage directions travel quick over water. We choose to ignore the law overhead even when it soothingly whispers 'you are not to blame'.

/FOURTH WAVE/

I tried to make waves, didn't I? Did you see me trying to escape the law, trying to make waves on my way to the coast? I failed, of course. But something moved, the surface of the lake trembled a little. Or maybe not at all. I don't know.

Here is someone who manages it rather well: 'The waves broke and spread their waters swiftly over the shore. One after another they massed themselves and fell; the spray tossed itself back with the energy of their fall… The waves fell; withdrew and fell again.'[16] Virginia Woolf wavewrote a narrative of whirls, reversals and non-endings, untruths and unquests. How unlegal therefore to suggest wavewriting for a text at least partly about law. How unlegal not to be on a quest for truth, on a line for decision, on a line of depth. But wait: 'at first sight it wasn't just a wave crashing in so much as the sea itself surging up, silently and suddenly. Before I got a good look at it, it had returned whence it came. It did not make any sound. It merely confiscated a few things. That's all it did.'[17] This confiscation, a mere nothing, a taking away, a stealing from the façade of truth, a slashing away from the solid: wavewriting is licking the face of the law in order to unmask it. So perhaps I did make some waves after all when I was rowing back to the coast, even though I never reached it. Moving *with* the law

---

[16] Virginia Wolfe, *The Waves* (Wordsworth 2000) 83.
[17] Ming-Yi, 150.

means moving uncertainly but with direction, with underwater power but with differentiated surfacing.

Is there a deeper desire here, in my literary choices, to forget the law? To depart from the law, to leave it behind on the coast, the echo of a wave, dead memory, flattened liminality? This is the symbolism of the water, after all: unmarkable by law, open and seemingly free. This is what this author might be trying to say.

Well, what a neat little binary. And how mendacious.

Even in the water, I cannot forget the law. Especially in the water I cannot depart from the law. On the land, the law is everywhere, its omnipresence banalized, becoming white noise. In the water, the law is luminous. It becomes water itself.

So perhaps my deeper desire is to depart from the law *and* to float on the law. To have my pie and eat it.

You see what I mean? How legal indeed is wavewriting! And how truly constant. For we never truly depart from the law, however much we might recede. All legal writing is wavewriting.

MERCÈ RODOREDA'S *DEATH IN SPRING* / THE LAW IS OUR BODY

OK, I am now determined. Get ready for some waves.

'They built the village over the river, and when the snows melted, everyone was afraid the village would be washed away. That is why every year a man entered the water on the upper side and swam under the village and came out on the lower side. Sometimes dead. Sometimes without a face because it had been ripped away when the desperate water hurled him against the rocks that supported the village.'[18] Our waters kill. Maybe all waters kill. They gorge flesh and spit out appeasement. They swallow sacrifice and vomit future. We need rituals to neutralize the killing, laws as brutal as the river, as linear as its water flow, as spiralling as its turbulence. And so we throw our men into the river and ask them to cross it, to come out the other side.

No one has ever handed us these laws. No one makes us follow them. *We* want to follow them. It is our choice, for the sake of the village. These norms are the only thing saving us from the waters.

I promise, we've left the gods behind now. But Senyor overlooks everything we do. Not really but we want to believe he does. 'Senyor observed it all from his towering window… He could see when a man entered the water and when he emerged. As soon as the man had left the water, Senyor would close his window' (61). It isn't Senyor that makes us throw these men in the river. We know he is made of nothing. Thin air, weak flesh, moribund asthma, nothing. An authority that tries to sneak into our prayers. Oh Lord. Fake. All fake. But we still like to think he overlooks everything we do. He is wealthy and his house is up the hill, the only house free from flood risk. He is old and dies halfway through the book. He dies just like everyone else, with cement poured down his throat. He did not want it that way. He pleaded for a natural

---

[18] Mercè Rodoreda, *Death in Spring* (trans. Martha Tennent, Penguin 2018) 8.

death. It doesn't matter. We followed our rituals. We carry on exactly as before, even after Senyor dies, because we carry our rituals under our skin. We are all the law.

We are one with the river, the fear of water has become one with us, it wakes us up at night. We become one with the turbulence, our faces splayed open, sacrificial otherness, Levinasian faciality flayed by the disfiguring rocks. The river kills us; and so we kill ourselves before it does.

A soundwave, the voice of the reader: *just stop with these rituals! They are absurd, inane, meaningless!*

Who said that?

The voice travelled from outside the book, from the edge of the village. It brought the smell of rotting mucus, green smell in green nostrils. We cannot unhear it. It has been written on the surface of the water, under our skins. But the rituals are us. We all carry the law in our bodies. We breathe the law, and when we choke, we choke with the law in our throats. The mist coming out of the river permeates our skin, becomes our body fluid. The law of the water is our law, it is us.

When the book's narrator is chosen to become the next sacrifice, he follows the law without complaining. He resists any resistance. The riverbed becomes a field of hands waving back and forth, cradling their power like scythes. 'When I was little my father was a hand. A hand behind my head, pushing me forward, grow up fast, you're a nuisance' (124). When I was growing up, I did not want to be a nuisance. My breath was wrapped in fear: not too loud, not too present, not too me. 'I lowered myself gently into the water, hardly daring to breathe, always with a fear that, as I enter the water world, the air – finally rid of my nuisance – would begin to rage' (3). My father's hand is pushing me forward. Or aside. Rage. 'Standing beside the water, my back to everyone, I felt as if I were more insignificant than the thing I was before I was born. A large hand gave me a shove on the head' (123).

My father's hand kept on working on other bodies: painting portraits, sometimes for money, often because he just liked to paint. He was what I would now call a naturalist painter, his realism mixed with months maybe years studying Rubens, the Florentines, Goya. He never painted me. Except once, when he was making the oil portrait of a sitter, a girl of my age, 4 or 5 years old, and I asked him to paint me too, make my portrait, I want to be touched by you. He dismissed me, or perhaps he should have, it would have been better, no he didn't dismiss me, not in that way, he actually entertained my request, very well, take a seat, the girl and her father standing next to us in the studio admiring the girl's just finished portrait, were they looking at us while I was being painted? I was hoping so, I was full of pride, my father's hand is painting my portrait, I am seen. But something made me worried, I was always worried so this was not a new state, but this was a worry seen from the outside, the other side of the river, across the water, worry as ritual, a fear that pulsed under my skin making me wonder: is he already done? but how? It took days for the girl, how can he be done with me so quickly, all smiles and giggles, the clients and my father and maybe me too, because no one handed me my ritual, I am a good boy, I smile when I am expected to smile, the water is under my skin, here it is! a rapid sketch in pencil, was there any colour, maybe a dash of watercolour, red or maybe green, a lake whose water has not been renewed, here you are! my portrait was the rough sketch of a clown.

The origin of the law is trauma.

/FIFTH WAVE/

I understand now. In order to make waves, I need to make a sacrifice. I need to give you a piece of me. I will never make waves unless I show you my trauma.

But now I must withdraw. It cannot always be drama. It is too much. No one can take that. Wavewriting is like waves: it cannot all be dramatic crests. It needs some nice sleek troughs.

Law, like wave, is both withdrawn and all-connected. Withdrawn when the wave reaches the shore, an individual movement, a wink of an ocean, a turn of a sea, an effect. And connected to the volumes of water below and around, the waves before and after, the terrain, the wind, the moon. We might, like Schmitt,[19] forget the water when waves surge. We might think of the water only as waves. But the water remains, the unmoved volumes underneath are always there, the vast complexity of depths, indifferent to the wind and to the land crashed overhead, following other currents.

So, not a mad text. Just the slight madness of a text held together by an aquatic membrane. The text waves up at the moment of getting it all together, those singular moments when complexity appears simple, formed, black and white, or rather blue and white. All molecules in order. And then, boom, flat, nothing. Until the next wave.

This text cannot give you what you want. Well, it might. But it will take it away almost at the same time. Trauma. Deal with it.

ALEXIS WRIGHT'S *THE SWAN BOOK* / AS MANY LAWS AS WATERS

You know those land juts where waters from two or more seas converge? That aquatic liminality that plays away from the land? Waves are guaranteed here. Let's call it legal pluralism.

They are all laws: the laws of the colonizers, the laws of the army coming to blow up the last vestiges of the old community around the lake, the laws of the swans that slide on the surface, the law of Oblivia that came from a tree and ended up following those swans. Wright interweaves the aboriginal mode of being with western erudition.[20] Law is archipelagic.[21] The water surrounds all laws' movements: water as an emollient to the harm caused by law, water as an abyss to exacerbate the trauma.

In water, we feel the law because we feel our body move: 'I begin locally, navigating yellow-watered floods that grow into even greater inland sea-crossings, to reach an alluvial plain that feeds shaded gardens, where the people who live there say they do not know me and ask why I have come.'[22] I do not simply follow 'my' law. With every flooded step, my body is the law of its own movement. Not a maverick or a hero that follows his (typically) own destiny, but a body that slides among other alluvial bodies tracing legal arcs that connect and separate. Not a human privilege either: 'swans had Law too. But now…nobody remembered

---

[19] 'On the waves, there is nothing but waves.' Carl Schmitt, *The Nomos of the Earth* (trans. G.L. Ulmen, Telos Press 2003) 43.
[20] 'Dystopic, anti-elegiac narrative': Honni van Rijswijk, 'Encountering Law's Harm through Literary Critique: An Anti-elegy' (2015) 27(2) *Law and Literature*, 237.
[21] John Selden's formulation that makes all laws one, all islands an archipelago.
[22] Alexis Wright, *The Swan Book* (Giramondo 2013) Loc 100.

the stories in the oldest Law scriptures of these big wetland birds' (loc 999). 'and on they went, forging into territory [where] great flocks might have travelled their law stories over the land' (loc 254). And of course, the law itself as a body of movement: 'old Law forms its own footpaths' (1243). Law of water-finding (swans becoming 'gypsies, searching the deserts for vast sheets of storm water soaking the centuries-old dried lakes' 254) but also law of the desire to move, whether away from or towards something.

Law is also stories: movement is a story, in turn generating stories that make up the law. The country is brought to life by 'law music' (loc 2667). Stories raise bodies up, willing in them the law of flight: 'the swans were now glued to the shores of the swamp where they looked dolefully towards the hull, waiting for the old woman's world of stories to appear' (loc 1323); but also water is law,[23] 'the law of breaking waves' (491), a story that gives wing to the law and to the bodies that carry it, reminding them of their wounds. These stories are marks on the body, colonizing, environmentally devastating, raping wounds that cannot heal except perhaps collectively, in a flock of law that gazes at its reflection on the water and dances.

And law is also its conflicts: 'all of these big law people thought tribal people across the world would be doing the same, and much like themselves, could also tell you about the consequences of breaking the laws of nature by trespassing on other people's land. They were very big on the law stories about the natural world' (loc 277). And clash of laws within, 'those laws of the two sides of the local world' (1174), mixing the Dreamings, there is no other level, no voice from above to tell us how to do this. Law is the clash between voice and writing, 'two laws, one in the head, the other on worthless paper in the swamp' (498).

Law's origin stretches across lands, stories, minds, texts. A multiple, proliferating origin of emphatically not one source, indeed not a source. The water of the law comes from elsewhere – not a source but a horizon. When the water is no longer there, we crave the law: 'she and the swan were joined as companions, of being both caught in a *mal de mer* from the yellow waves of dust spreading over the land' (loc 4660).

/SIXTH WAVE/

I was riding the trough just now. No, I don't think that this can actually happen. But never mind. Reading *The Swan Book* as a legal academic is a smooth wave, expected, all set up ready for the ride. I did not have to try much.

What if a wave then is an ontological condition that emerges regardless of how much I try to bring it about? This would mean that as long as there is an encounter (between water and land, or water and hand) there would be waves. Like law: an ontological effect that emerges at every encounter.[24] This confluence (law, water, wave) can get messy, but I am willing to give it a go without succumbing to the temptation of untangling the mess. We have slashes for that. They keep things separate. Not for long, but enough.

---

[23] Stephanie Jones, 'Maritime Space as Law and Light: Retrieving William Clark Russell's *An Ocean Free-Lance* (1882)' (2014) 15(1) *Journal of Colonialism and Colonial History.*

[24] Andreas Philippopoulos-Mihalopoulos, *Spatial Justice: Body Lawscape Atmosphere* (Routledge 2014).

This is the method of wavewriting. A matterphor to start with.[25] But also, away from any figure of speech, an ocean methodology,[26] a seascape epistemology,[27] a wet ontology,[28] an enquiry of submerged perspectives.[29] It is persistent, fathoming, layering, uncovering. Like Michel Serres's analysis of *la belle noiseuse*,[30] the repetitive ruckus of waves, the noise that reveals existence. It is also about a readiness to ride a certain wave. It is collective, and at ease with losing control and becoming one with the elemental.

And here is a bit of a political strategy recommendation: just when the crest of a revolutionary banner becomes visible on the horizon, I must let it boom itself out, reach its peak, become the last wave. I need to *believe* that this will be the last ever wave, the one that will flood and change everything. But I should also imagine what happens after the wave is gone. Or at least to know that the wave will be gone and that, although it might well be the last ever wave, there is always one after that.

We must write both crest and trough.

MARY OKON ONONOKPONO'S *INYANG* / LAW'S BUOYANCY

'Fetch a barrel of sea water' she said.[31] But I got distracted, as I do. The water could wait. This is our home, the home of the river. The water can always wait. There is a myriad of market stalls to explore, a forest to wander in, worlds to imagine, white people to mock dressed all wrong for the climate.

Like this little guy, 'skin the colour of the golden sand, eyes the colour of their waters…I felt a prickle of friendliness within me' (258). We got lost in the forest, him chasing me or the other way around, it doesn't matter. 'I've always wanted to see the sea' I say. 'But you are close to it, he said, suddenly jovial…You can hear them now, the waters…That stream can't make all that noise by itself. It's the sea. Listen to her. She's breathing.' And then I saw: from deep in the forest, volumes and waves and those majestic winged vessels, stuff of lore, dreams from other lands moored on our mouths waiting for something. I did not know what.

Come the evening, we fell asleep on the branches of a tree overhanging the estuary waters. The water can wait. But what it carries in its belly, the flow of capital, doesn't.[32] 'It

---

[25] Daniela Gandorfer and Zulaikha Ayub, 'Matterphorical' (2021) 24(1) *Theory & Event*, 2–13.
[26] Renisa Mawani, *Across Oceans of Law* (Duke UP 2018).
[27] Karin Amimoto Ingersoll, *Waves of Knowing: A Seascape Epistemology* (Duke UP 2016).
[28] Philip Steinberg and Kimberley Peters, 'Wet Ontologies, Fluid Spaces: Giving Depth to Volume through Oceanic Thinking' (2015) 33(1) *Environment and Planning D: Society and Space*, 247–64.
[29] Marcarena Gómez-Barris, *The Extractive Zone* (Duke UP 2017).
[30] Michel Serres, *Genesis* (trans. G. James and J. Nielson, University of Michigan Press 1995).
[31] Mary Okon Ononokpono, 'Inyang', in Nick Mulgrew and Karina Szczureck (eds), *Water: New Short Fiction from Africa* (New Internationalist 2015) 254.
[32] 'The "flows of capital" metaphor is exceptional in that it not only borrows water's meanings, but appropriates them directly. That is, as investment comes to be regarded as an essential source of health, good livelihood, and agency, water's more fundamental association with these qualities falls into the background […] a quasi-abstraction like capital comes to seem as real as a river.' Janine MacLeod, 'Water and the Material Imagination: Reading the Sea of Memory against the Flows of Capital', in Cecilia Chen, Janine MacLeod and Astrida Neimanis (eds), *Thinking with Water* (McGill UP 2013). For sea metaphors, see Hans Blumenberg, *Shipwreck with Spectator* (trans. Steven Rendall, MIT Press 1997).

appeared unexpectedly, the body of a tree of gigantic proportions…hollowed to accommodate a vast number of bodies…I saw them…faces in the water…scores upon scores of small dark islands…Some of them saw me…but the faces could not call out, for their mouths were bound' (264). One hundred and forty mouths in the first boat. Eight boats in total. Thousand boats in past and future, taking bodies 'to the realms of the living-dead, never to return to the land of their birth' (264). I recognized people 'grabbed as pawns for defaulting on payments' (265). The boat fate is 'legitimate' punishment for crimes. The slave boats are kept buoyant by legal tendrils, seaweeds of justice rotting under their bellies, bubbles of lawful putrefaction ushering these bodies into the Black Atlantic.[33]

And then I saw the face of the law, 'Proud. Regal. Surveying his newly acquired wealth… Etubom, Father of the Canoes, his new title never more befitting…Attired as both Obong and white man. My father' (265). When our eyes met, I shrieked and fell from the tree and down in the raging waters.[34] I was drowning, churned by the water of a law I could not live to bear, choked by the law of a water I no longer wanted to touch my skin. I surrendered to my liquid death, but just then 'I discovered I could breathe. I became the ocean. I became the watcher of the water…I saw figures in the waters…rising from the bottom of the deep' (266).[35]

Waves that smudge the black and white of the law. Well, black and white were never there to start with. The lines between bodies have always run into each other, churned by centuries of grief. I spit on your categories and smudge them with my wet hands. Your law is no longer dry. It drips bleeding.

/SEVENTH WAVE/

> ROME, July 9 (Reuters) – Italian authorities have seized a boat operated by a German NGO that last month rescued more than 200 people stranded at sea, because it did not comply with safety rules, the Coast Guard said on Thursday. In April, Italy banned migrant rescue ships from docking in its ports until July 31 because of the COVID-19 pandemic. It now transfers all those saved at sea onto large ferries which must wait off its coast. The mainly African passengers were moved to the Italian ferry Moby Zaza, where 28 tested positive for the new coronavirus. In a statement posted on Twitter, the Coast Guard said an inspection had found a number of irregularities that threatened the safety of those on board and the shop must fix the irregularities before resuming operations.[36]

---

[33] Paul Gilroy, *The Black Atlantic* (Harvard UP 1995). See also T.T. Arvind, '"Though it Shocks One Very Much": Formalism and Pragmatism in the "Zong" and "Bancoult"' (2012) 32(1) *Oxford Journal of Legal Studies*, 113–51.

[34] 'The image of Kant on his insular promontory wavers, seen from a watery depth. For down here, down underneath, there may be an underwater city of bones, magical, miraculous, an entirely new way of being or of being re-borne, of understanding and knowing.' Maurya Wickstrom, 'Wet Ontology, Moby-Dick, and the Oceanic in Performance' (2019) 71(4) *Theatre Journal*, 475–91.

[35] On the Black Atlantic: 'Is it possible that they could have given birth at sea to babies that never needed air? Recent experiments have shown mice able to breathe liquid oxygen, a premature human infant saved from certain death by breathing liquid oxygen through its underdeveloped lungs.' Kodwo Eshun, *More Brilliant than the Sun: Adventures in Sonic Fiction* (Quartet Books 1998) 83.

[36] Reuters Staff, www.reuters.com/article/healthcoronavirus-migrants-italy/italy-seizes-german-flagged-charity-vessel-for-breaking-safety-rules-idUSL8N2EG1PJ.

WU MING-YI'S *THE MAN WITH THE COMPOUND EYES* / EXCRETAL JURISDICTION

'Garbage is fair.'[37] An island made of rubbish is washing over the coast of Taiwan. The plastic vortex is breaking up and the island is spreading, from ambulatory irrelevance in the middle of the ocean to a jurisdictional problem covering the coast stretches of several Pacific Rim nations. Its anthropocenic sludge adds an aesthetic layer, the soft hand of disaster: 'The garbage glittered in the sunshine like it was encrusted with jewels' (150). 'The wind blew up light plastic bags that had dried in the sun…unbearably putrid flowers' (155). You need to be on the ground to see this from the perspective of sovereign sclerosis, from the micromyopia of artificial borders. The real thing cannot, once again, be captured by the law: 'the confetti of plastic rubbish is translucent and lies just below the water's surface, it's not detectable in satellite photographs. It can only be seen passing along the hull of a ship' (122). But the vortex becomes a problem only when it accosts a state. And then only for that state. Or so the jurisdictional narrative goes. Yet the plastic vortex is a hyperobject,[38] always here even if geographically distant: 'all those things we tossed out assuming the tide would take them away and the ocean would digest them were now floating slowly back' (116).

We have all found ourselves on that island, picking up the plastic debris of humanity and learning to ignore the stench of planetary decomposition. This time, though, there is a different, odd reliance: the rubbish island becomes the protagonist's refuge. He wakes up on it, half-dead, after he has been ostracized (the law again) from his own mid-pacific island 'far from any continent' (10), an island so small that 'the islanders could neither walk to a place where the sea could not be heard nor have a conversation in which the sea was not mentioned' (12). His old world, where water and law are tautologous, is replaced by this new shiny dead world where plastic is the only law and the sea is supplanted: 'the island under the island was even more immense than the island itself. It was almost like an underwater maze, so big as to be another kind of sea' (35). Against all odds, he survives on that unrooted emanation of death: 'the island sometimes looked like a giant floating cage…the cemetery of all creation… Creatures that died from eating bits of the island eventually became part of the island' (40).

Was that the other law? The other water? Did the original gods 'still rule over this other world' (127)? No. It is all the same. We are all in it. This is our shared room without walls, exposed to planetary flows of destruction against which we erect ricepaper walls of jurisdictional smugness. Law melts in water, because water is never just water. Water and bodies are co-extensive,[39] excretal and solidified, filled with corpses of slaves, plastic bourgeoisie and sickening nostalgia. But garbage is fair. We are all complicit in the whirls of the vortex.

---

[37] Wu Ming-Yi, 156.
[38] Timothy Morton, *Hyperobjects: Philosophy and Ecology after the End of the World* (University of Minnesota Press 2013).
[39] We are bodies of water, Astrida Neimanis, *Bodies of Water: Posthuman Feminist Phenomenology* (Bloomsbury 2017) 1, writes again and again. Not embodied on the one hand and comprising water on the other. 'We are both of these things, inextricably and at once – made mostly of wet matter, but also aswim in the discursive flocculations of embodiment as an idea.'

/EIGHTH WAVE/

We are approaching the last wave. The one wave to end all waves. We are generating it with our slashes, every moment of our comfortable western lives. Brace yourselves.

But we now begin to understand at least that: every legal text is wavewritten. Every text is turning blue.[40] Every law is turning blue.[41] This is not just a fad. 'Despite international efforts and tireless research, there is no permanent solution – no barriers to erect or walls to build – that will protect us in the end from the drowning of the world as we know it.'[42] This wave might well be the last. From water scarcity, droughts and massive global fires to flooded cities, melting icecaps, submerging islands and drowned states, water is becoming the determining element of our century, asphyxiatingly present and scorchingly absent. Rivers, underground water reserves, oceans: they are all claiming their textuality.[43]

Two provisos. First, the disengagement of the legal from the purely tellurian, especially when it comes to questions of sovereignty and jurisdiction.[44] And second, it is not about fully knowing the water. It is not about surface and depth control.[45] It is about maintaining the aquatic unknowability while acknowledging the affinities with our own, more proximate bodies of water.[46] Acknowledging the continuum between our body and the hydrosphere.[47] Wavewriting, and legal wavewriting specifically, requires a radical immersion: 'In these early days for ocean justice, I propose thinking with the ocean's midnight aphotic depths, invoking it to bubble up through a juridical imaginary that would not deny its lively worlds and our relations with them.'[48]

---

[40] For the blue turn in humanities and social sciences, see for example Philip Steinberg and Kimberley Peters, 'Wet Ontologies, Fluid Spaces: Giving Depth to Volume through Oceanic Thinking' (2015) 33(2) *Environment and Planning D: Society and Space*, 247–64; Stefan Helmreich, *Alien Oceans: Anthropological Voyages in Microbial Seas* (University of California Press 2009). For a different kind of blue, see Gaston Bachelard, *Water and Dreams: An Essay on the Imagination of Matter* (Dallas Institute of Humanities and Culture 1994 [1942]).

[41] Irus Braverman and Elizabeth R. Johnson (eds), *Ocean Legalities: The Life and Law of the Sea* (Duke UP 2019).

[42] Jeff Goodell, *The Water Will Come: Rising Seas, Sinking Cities, and the Remaking of the Civilized World* (Little, Brown and Company 2017), from the cover.

[43] 'The ocean is involved in the writing and reading process, affecting how we create and shape both ourselves and our nations.' Amimoto Ingersoll, 2016, 93.

[44] The classic example is UNCLOS Article 76(1), which defines a state's continental shelf as 'the natural prolongation of its land territory' with the result that 'Complex, intra-active ocean elements and relations are effectively redacted in a governance framework based on law of the land'. Susan Reid, 'Solwara 1 and the Sessile Ones', in Braverman and Johnson (eds), 57.

[45] We can nowadays control even the most evanescent of water forms: 'it *is* possible, to some extent, to control and command ocean waves: to build infrastructures that guard shorelines, to mold beaches that generate waves of stipulated measure and shape, and to engineer devices that "harness" wave energy.' Stefan Helmreich, 'Wave Law', in Braverman and Johnson (eds), 168.

[46] Renisa Mawani, *Across Oceans of Law* (Duke University Press 2018).

[47] '[T]he lake's water now seemed an extension of his own bloodstream. As the dull pounding rose, he felt the barriers which divided his own cells from the surrounding medium dissolving, and he swam forwards, spreading outwards across the black thudding water.' J.G. Ballard, *The Drowned World* (Fourth Estate 2012) 71.

[48] Susan Reid, 47–8. See also Stefan Helmreich, 'Seagoing Nightmares' (2019) 9(3) *Dialogues in Human Geography*, 308–11.

RACHEL ARMSTRONG'S *INVISIBLE ECOLOGIES* / EXCRETAL RETURN

We finally reach Venice, the city that embodies the tautology between law and water. Building the city with and against water was a juridical necessity, a distancing from the laws of the land and the hordes of the mountains for the aquiferous construction of a sodden republic. Here all lines are smudged by the lagunar mucus: buildings and terrain, humans and nonhumans, the dead and the living, 'a city that is built upon the bones of its populations, where in some places it is said that the earths are half mulch and half human'.[49] Armstrong's near-future Venice is vibrating with the awareness of its posthumanity: 'the entire ecological realm is in meltdown, where the familiar distinctions between things disappear. Plants, stones and creatures are continuous with each other, blending together more like shadows and objects…There is a background stench and gurgling noise through which all the voices appear to dispute the nature of existence. Life is in a state of oscillation' (97). These ways of thinking of the world are not new.[50] But here, they become the only way. The affective body of the city is in material and immaterial continuum with our moods: 'the lagoon's constantly changing chemical trails, biomolecule standing waves, structured currents, water memory channels and complex and pervasive bouquets of substances…These feelings feed moods, make new kinds of experience and linger in aftertastes… These feelings are being produced by the spaces between things' (96).[51]

But things have deteriorated, and the city's fragile ecology is suffering. 'While these artificial materials have always been part of [the water], it previously found ways to stimulate them into its living mass. These current accumulations are toxic, proliferative and malignant. Like a festering wound they split the [water's] flesh and hold it open to trauma and poisons' (214–15). Amid this rapid decline, a bunch of nomads, illegally moored at Venice's cemetery island, are working on the democratization of the ultimate privilege, a Venetian burial. They defy the hierarchy of death, so explicit in Venice in terms of both how and where one is allowed to be buried. Instead they set up in the folds of the lagoon memorials of the beloved made out of smartly processed waste, that eventually become assimilated into the environment through their plastic-eating and toxin-neutralizing 'planned obsolescence'. A second death, a second offering to the leakage of bodies,[52] an ecological burial practice which they insist takes place according to the law, providing all necessary legal documents including a 'mortuary passport' (112).

This business idea has the fluidity of the city, bridging legality and illegality, operating from an unlawful mooring yet hoping for a new ecological necropolitics that helps assuage the grief of a dying planet. 'We are born into a world of plastic…Our lives are plastic coated' (215), yet we can allow our dead bodies to become remedies.

---

[49] Rachel Armstrong, *Invisible Ecologies* (NewCon Press 2019) 32.
[50] See for example Jane Bennett, *Vibrant Matter: A Political Ecology of Things* (Duke UP 2010).
[51] See also Melody Jue, *Wild Blue Media* (Duke UP 2020).
[52] 'It's not dust to dust, that's for sure, it's water to water. We are made of water, it's the most obvious thing, still we don't get it, we think we are solid, we are not, we are pockets of moisture. We bleed. Our mouths, our eyes, our every opening to the air are filled with saliva, mucus, or wax.' J.M. Ledgard, *Submergence* (Vintage 2012) 115.

A molecular eternal return that works as a metaphor for the city of liquid legality, where nothing ever disappears forever.

/NINTH WAVE/

Repeat. Even if this is the last wave.

These waves break our skins down, and with them pulverize our anthropocentric physicality. We are leaking bodies, excretions are our offsprings, clotted morasses of our ancestors. Our defences are corroded, our exceptionalism floored. Seepages make slippery, undesirable alliances. We pay our debt in discharges. And from within that collapse, the real planetary collectivity emerges. Astrida Neimanis writes:

> Bodies of water puddle and pool. They seek confluence. They flow into one another in life-giving ways, but also in unwelcome, or unstoppable, incursions. Even in an obstinate stagnancy they slowly seep and leak. We owe our own bodies of water to others, in both dribbles and deluges. These bodies are different – in their physical properties and hybridizations, as well as in political, cultural, and historical terms – but their differing from one another, their differentiation, is a collective worlding.[53]

Our epistemes shed their skins too: 'the boundaries between hitherto discrete bodies of knowledge have blurred to challenge both the hierarchical organisation of distinct disciplines and the division between theory and practice.'[54] There has always been knowledge produced in the materiality of the passage of water from body to body, from aquatic collectivity to aquatic collectivity, and from immensity to momentary individuality. But now we know that these knowledges, these epistemes, follow the same destiny as our physical bodies. Everything becomes a Venetian renaissance painting where forms give way to the *colorist*'s fearless acrobatics in the unknown spaces beyond the line.

And from within the fold of these waves, new waves emerge.

REPETITION: MERCÈ RODOREDA'S *DEATH IN SPRING* (II)

/ I WAS ALWAYS AFRAID OF THE LAW
/ I WAS ALWAYS AFRAID OF THE WATER

Rodoreda shows me the riverbed of violence: 'It's fear. They want to be afraid... If the rocks and water rip away your face, it's for the sake of everyone. If you live with a belief that the river will carry away the village, you won't think about anything else' (82). We never think about anything else. This groundless violence, the groundlessness that has become its ground, mossy, slippery cutting ground, bodies and movement entangled into the production of violence. It's fear.

But sedimented fear is no longer just fear. It multiplies, it becomes fear *of* fear, angst, paralysis, life. It makes one turn against oneself. I am the clown and the clown laughs at himself. Especially at himself. What a good boy. Now, swim.

---

[53] Neimanis, 28.
[54] Margrit Shildrick, *Leaky Bodies and Boundaries* (Routledge 1997) 4.

The law says, be afraid. The law says, do not desire anything other than fear. 'That's why they're afraid. They are consumed by the fear of desire', says Rodoreda. 'They want to suffer so they won't think about desire. You are maimed when you're little, and fear is hammered into the back of your head. Because desire keeps you alive, they kill it off while you're growing up, the desire for all things' (83). I do not know what desire for all things is. My desire is a fetish, no outlet, just inlets of concentrated failures. My desire is my stepmother. My desire is actually my father. My desire, false and fetid, has blinded my desire for all things.

Here is fear. Again.

And here is law. Again.

The waters have reached us.

It is afternoon. I am sitting on the riverbank, or was it a beach? and I am looking at the water. No, I cannot see the water. It is evening and I cannot see the water. I am surrounded by teenagers, I am a teenager myself, surrounded by pungent sweaty fear. This is a summer like every summer, a summer of fear and hiding. There is a game going on, the girls are lying on the sand, a river flowing overhead in the night sky transporting 'stars and pieces of moon' (36), late evening waves that cannot save me keep on lapping at the end of the girls' legs. The boys kiss the girls, this is the game but really nothing random or playful, there is a system of desire here, the girls have to lie on the sand, agentless lipglossed strawberries reshuffled after every boy, this is all there is, while the boys have to hunt down the already splayed prey, lie on top of every girl and kiss them in turn, kiss where the other boy had kissed before them but better, believably better, full of real desire better. I am one of the boys, and I want to be nowhere beneath and nowhere above, but I cannot but be. These are our rituals, no one has handed them to us. The rituals are us. A head is pushing the back of my head. Swim! Kiss! Be a man. This is the desire you have.

In the book, I am in the same scene but different. From within the water floods the water. 'The water by the canes was calm. I shut my eyes as if I were dead. I was dead…All of me was weighed down. As I was feeling the weight, I heard a splash and raised my head. Rings had formed in the water, giving birth to other rings, as if someone had hurled a flat rock. The rings kept spreading until they reached the point where they died… I glimpsed a hand by the canes. A hand above the water…The hand rose, then fell furiously, striking the water…I caught sight of a girl who climbed out of the water and got dressed… We looked at each other. She stood in front of me, I in front of her. Eye to eye, mouth to mouth…As if I had passed on to her the wish to do what I had done, she extended her arm towards me, her hand open. That was enough… We remained like that as the morning mist grew thinner, as if the water in the middle of the river had swallowed it, instead of spitting it out' (93–4).

All waters give life. They swallow laws and open up horizons. They become mist, fog, vapour, ice, cloud, tree, amoeba, human. We need to forget these rituals, to stop building atmospheres out of frozen water pillars. We need other rituals, as translucent as the water we are thirsty for, as light as pure desire, as round as womb. We just need to learn how to become these waters, to come out the other side.

I long to have had that desire, and for that desire to have been heard by the water. I long for the mist to wrap around my desire and diffuse it, make it a desire for all things. I long for the law to invite me in and let me find the other bank, the other water, the other law.[55]

---

[55] Peter G. writes: 'The jurisographer would say that you long to find your law, precisely not the vagueness of "another" law, another's law, but your law, your water, your land and your body yourself.'

/THE LAST WAVE/

Here it comes.

26. Ditches
Adam Gearey

'Diligite justitiam qui judicatis terram'

INFLOW[1]

Minor jurisprudence invents normative imaginaries from bodies of law that have been obscured by modernity.[2] Historically and doctrinally, sewer and ditch were the province of the Courts of Sewers.[3] A minor jurisprudence of the ditch – or ditch law – is an engagement with

---

[1] Thanks to Mary Gearey, Benjamin R. Gearey and Piyel Haldar: *Melior est fossoribus*.

[2] Imaginary is meant in the sense used by Castoriadis, rather than Deleuze or Lacan. As such, the term describes a foundational fiction on which a broader set of meanings are constructed to define a network of social, political and legal significations and practices. The argument in this chapter is that ditch law is an imaginary. Fictional is to be understood in the sense of the made or constructed, created and re-created over time. Fictional does not carry the sense of un-real; rather of the way in which an order is made: a necessary dialectic between immaterial ideas and material practices. Thus the working and re-working of the imaginary of the ditch and its relationship with other networks of fictions, is a way of thinking about the transformation of institutions over time. It could be, crudely, mapped onto the complex historical developments that lead from feudalism to capitalism, and the ongoing re-articulations of the latter. However, this argument does not imply either the teleology of the processes concerned, nor the stability of institutional forms. In shorthand: what is made is unstable and can be unmade precisely because it can be remade. But there is no guarantee of its un-making; nor that the un-making will be 'progressive'. At very least, a minor jurisprudence will carry, in legal terms, the possibilities of un- or re-making imaginaries. An imaginary, then, and, contrary in this respect to what Castoriadis argued, an imaginary that is not closed in on itself, but an amalgam of openings and closures. As Marx would have pointed out, it all depends on the play of forces. See Cornelius Castoriadis, *The Imaginary Institution of Society* (Cambridge 1997).

[3] Despite the fact that the 'history of the Courts of Sewers' is one of the 'remoter corners' of English legal history, it is clear that the cost of ditch work remained one of the main features of its jurisprudence: see Webb and Webb (1922, 20). It is difficult to reconstruct the precise jurisdiction of the various juries of sewers or justices of sewers and the regional variation in custom, powers and appointment. The Statute of Sewers 1532 was perhaps the most important of a series of Acts that attempted to clarify the nature of the relevant authorities and their legal footings. The Act of 1532 established the authority of the King's Commission of Sewers as the foundation of the Courts of Sewers establishing the procedures and 'constitution' of what became 'practically permanent local governing bodies': Webb and Webb, *English Local Government Volume 4: Statutory Authorities for Special Purposes* (Longmans Green & Co 1922, 19). Commissioners of Sewers 'resembled' Justices of the Peace, and for the most part had to be title holders of freehold land. Commissioners of Sewers were 'empowered' to hold Courts of Sewers and the 1532 Act required such Courts to have juries of 'honest and lawful men'. By jury verdict the court determined the existence of obligations and the extent to which they had been carried out by the relevant parties. The Courts' jurisdiction extended over 'walls, streams, ditches, banks, gutters, sewers, gates, bridges, trenches, mills, mill dams, floodgates, ponds, locks, hebbingwears and other impediments, lets and annoyances […] in the rivers streams and other floods' (23 Henry VIII c 23, cited in Webb and Webb 1922, 21). The powers of the Courts extended to surveying the relevant drains, channels, and ditches

the transformation and 'interruption' of history and doctrine – an articulation of what overspills and escapes.[4] The texts we will study – from Dugdale via Shakespeare, to Winstanley, Ruskin, Morris and Kropotkin – trace these eddying phantasies and 'literary' imaginings about what might have been; what might still be possible.[5]

The foundational text of ditch law's minor jurisprudence is Sir Thomas Dugdale's *History of Imbanking and Drayning of Diverse Fenns and Marshes*. Returning to tracts of ancient marsh law, Dugdale poses fundamental questions: who digs, and who directs? How are ditch and culvert, channel, cut, river and stream readable? By who and for whom? We will follow these questions from Dugdale to *Antony and Cleopatra* and *Hamlet*. The minor jurisprudence of ditch law will then be tracked into Gerrard Winstanley's re-inscription of Dugdale's divine history in the aftermath of civil war. In Digger texts, God does not respect boundary ditches. Indeed, 'the great Creator is mightily dishonoured' as he finds no pleasure in the distinction between the 'comfortable Livelihoods of some' and 'the miserable povertie and straits of others'.[6] Winstanley's ideas flowed into Ruskin's *Unto This Last* – a visionary text of channelled energies and irrigation. Ditch law is re-imagined in the face of political economy and the industrial revolution. Morris' *News from Nowhere* marks the next most significant moment, the point at which Ruskin's economics of energy encounters a philosophy of work. Morris' endeavour to re-direct energies fouled by industrial modernity, to summon the overflowing and to create its symbols, can be traced into Kropotkin's *Fields, Factories and Workshops*. This key anarchist text is as much about manure, greenhouses, gooseberries, currants, strawberries, potatoes and drainage as it is about surplus value.[7]

---

that required upkeep, as well as pressing into service the labour and materials necessary to make repairs. Work on sewers and drainage throws up issues of boundary and ownership – problems writ large when it comes to the land of riparian owners, or, worse, land that bordered marshes, fens or the sea. A particularly fraught issue was the extent to which the Courts had the power to order new works, or merely to compel the upkeep of existing works. It appears that the Courts were limited to maintaining rather than initiating new works. The Courts were certainly empowered to issue rules and ordinances that applied to the localities under their control.

[4] Peter Goodrich, *Law in the Courts of Love* (Routledge 1996) 3.

[5] Literature and the literary are conventionally understood as describing particular kinds of textual organisation, categorisation and canonisation. Literature and literary texts can then be distinguished from other forms of textual classification (legal, for example). While Shakespeare's plays are undoubtedly part of the canon of English literature, there is also the sense that they harbour meanings and invite interpretations that do not sit comfortably with certain assertions of the values that canonical texts should reflect. This concern could, of course, be related to the ongoing 'struggle' over the texts to be canonised and the values that the canon is meant to reflect and perform. In this essay, literature and literary writing is used as a designator of a kind of canonised text that escapes the canon, or lies somewhat uncomfortably on its margins. This dialectic of escape and capture is not meant to be an explicit engagement with notions of major and minor literatures. There is no claim that the line of texts studied in this chapter represents a minor literature. It might be possible to link the dialectic of escape and capture to forces of de-territorialisation and re-territorialisation described by Deleuze and Guattari, but this is not to the forefront of the present argument. Rather, the texts assembled in this chapter are either not properly literary (Dugdale), canonical (Shakespeare), on the boundary of literature (Ruskin and Morris) or better classified as political philosophy (Winstanley; Kropotkin) or a kind of visionary literature: a peculiar hybrid of politics, philosophy and literature. Thus the approach deployed in this chapter is to suggest that an invented hybrid literary/legal/political/philosophical 'tradition' can be read as an imaginary construction of a textual apparatus appropriate to the expression of ditch law's minor jurisprudence.

[6] George Sabine, *The Works of Gerrard Winstanley* (Cornell University Press 1941) 270.

[7] Peter Kropotkin, *Fields, Factories and Workshops* (Puttenham 1913) 215.

The minor jurisprudence of the ditch terminates in the most recent case on the ditch rule, a conveyancing fiction that shows that property law is still bound up with ditch digging. The House of Lords evokes Fortinbras, a character from *Hamlet*, to articulate its role as the director of the correct flows of land, labour and money, but in so doing invokes the 'landless resolutes' who buried the prince. It is hardly surprising that Deleuze and Guattari's study of minor literature – a key text for minor jurisprudence – expresses itself as a way of writing that uncovers and turns over, precisely in the manner of a trencher's shovel, the arc of soil thrown over the digger's shoulder.[8]

The minor jurisprudence of the ditch compels us to think differently about community, property and power.[9] As a sewer, the ditch is a channel that directs flows of water, energy and political meaning. The prince who commands ditch labour controls the symbols that justify his power. In a theological sense, the prince, as God's representative on earth, holds the boundary between this world and the divine. The radical theologies of the early modern period opened onto a transformation of the energies of ditch digging. To assert the power to dig ditches is to evoke counter-power; communal control of labour and land. Utopian ditches are the creation of those who work together and direct the flow of their own labour. The lesson of *Hamlet*, that great text of ditch law, is a warning to the prince and men of property: the 'landless' and 'lawless resolutes' are on the march. They will have their day.

WORK AND DAYS: A BRIEF HISTORY OF IMBANKING

Sir William Dugdale's treatise *The History of Imbanking and Drayning of Divers Fenns and Marshes* is the first text of ditch law.[10] The book can be read in at least two distinct ways. As a legal text, it is a compendium of laws and customs that defines the jurisprudence of sewers. Dugdale stresses that the ancient understanding and usage of ditch law was founded on the monarch's defence of his/her 'dominions from the ravages of the sea'.[11] Political community is nothing without sewerage.[12] Dugdale's *History* also invites other readings, beckoning the reader towards a different way of understanding the relationship between the sewer, the ditch and the origins of law. Suffice to say, this is the reading that opens onto a minor jurisprudence. From *The Old Testament*, Dugdale drew the principle that drainage is the 'most antient, and of divine institution'. The 'drying of the land' is inscribed in the complex of divine punishment

---

[8] Gilles Deleuze and Felix Guattari, *Kafka: Towards a Minor Literature* (University of Minneapolis Press 1986, 19).

[9] The etymology of sewer is difficult to establish. '[T]he best learning' suggests that the word was 'originally applied to the protection of land from inundations' – as such, a sewer may be 'a wall, or dam, opposed to the inroads of the ocean; or […] a fresh water trench supported by banks on either side, for the purpose of carrying water into the sea' (Woolrych 1864, 2).

[10] It is possible to infer from Magna Carta that there were forms of 'collective regulation' predating the Normans, but the details are almost entirely lost to history: see Webb and Webb (1922, 16–17).

[11] 'Blocking' or stopping water channels was a 'grievous offence'. The sewer, by its nature, is public: a crime against a sewer is one against other people. See Humphry W. Woolrych, *A Treatise of the Law of Sewers* (London: Butterworth, 1864) 2.

[12] The commission that protected the kingdom against the sea was 'the most ancient' and the 'only one known to the common law': Webb and Webb (1922, 3).

and the promise of a new life.[13] As works of drainage are salvific, the sewer is the proper concern of the Christian King. If the 'strength of a King is the multitude of his subjects', the sovereign must rescue his people from benighted bogs, and preside over the 'Art and industry' of drain work.[14] He commands the labour that digs ditches to improve 'Wasts [and] Commons', bringing fecundity to 'barren' and 'Drowned Lands'.[15] It is not just rich crops that come from the correct management of soil and flood water. The mire is a barrier to the truth of religion. Christian faith cannot penetrate to the 'hards and banks' – an image that enters the canon via Bunyan's *Pilgrim's Progress*.[16] The fens were evil places. The word and the king's justices could not penetrate miasmas and bogs. No wonder, then, that Dante's Inferno is divided up by ditches – *malebolge* – the ditch that isolates, impedes and limits.

Indeed, like Dante's appropriation of pagan wisdom, *The History* instructs us that 'the AEgyptians, the Babylonians, the Graecians, the Romans' anticipated the truths of divine drainage.[17] For the Egyptians, the Nile was the symbol and agent of a nature that creates and destroys. In winter the river keeps to its course, but come the summer solstice it swells for 'an hundred dayes, is almost as long a time in retreating' and fertilises the deserts.[18] The flood has to be understood and managed by priests who read the river through two kinds of trench: those that take away excess water and those that direct the water to where it is needed for irrigation. This distinction maps onto further differentiations. Once a ditch is dug, it is necessary to ensure that it serves as a drain. If one does not work on its upkeep, the trench silts and blocks up.

The scouring/flowing couplet is further elaborated into a slightly more complex one around power. Dugdale's example is an artificial lake created by King Maeris as the setting for an elaborate necropolis: '[a]lmost in the middle thereof, stand two Pyramids, each fifty paces above water, and as much below; in all an hundred paces; there being upon each a Colossus sitting in a Chair.' Power as crown and colossus, the will to its own memorialisation, sat above the water, surveying a trench in whose name it was 'dug'. The 'embanked' tomb, created by those sentenced to death, is the acme and symbol of a power that can control the river, and hence fertility – the power of life and death – the very un-natural power of signification and law making.[19]

However, there is something distinctly precarious in this image of power. Ditches silt up, palaces fall into ruin and tombs disappear, buried by the sand. The power that expresses itself in banks and ditches is vulnerable to forces it cannot control. If the gods have spoken, and the floods have not come, the colossus is shaken. Power is vulnerable to a greater power. The ditch is an ambiguous symbol. These themes are bound up with the image of the Nile: the crumbling of the palace, the death of the prince; power and the zero.

---

[13] Sir Thomas Dugdale, *The History of Imbanking and drayning of diverse fenns and marshes, both in forein parts and in this kindom, and of the improvements thereby extracted, from records, manuscripts, and other authentick testimonies* (Alice Warren 1662).

[14] Dugdale (n 13) 1.

[15] ibid 1. The courteous reader cannot help but read this text as a practical excursus on themes also found in Hobbes' *Leviathan* (Printed for A. Crooke 1651), which, despite its status as one of the foundations of sovereignty, contains not a single mention of the ditch.

[16] ibid Unnumbered.

[17] ibid 1.

[18] ibid 1.

[19] ibid 2.

Meditations on the creative/destructive power of the Nile were commonplace in Elizabethan England and it is likely that Dugdale would have been familiar with these understandings of the river.[20] Nile imagery is central to *Antony and Cleopatra*, and Dugdale may even have seen the play. The ditch Leviathan of *The History* certainly seems to be reminiscent of Antony, who eulogises his power in the following verse:

> By the fire
> That quickens Nilus' slime, I go from hence
> Thy soldier, servant, making peace or war,
> As thou affects.[21]

Antony may be a sovereign, but he has obligations to those whom he serves – a 'soldier/servant' to the mother/river, Cleopatra. Antony's male sovereign sun must be coupled with the ooze of river mud – the female fertility of water. We could relate this complex of themes back to *The History*. A successful union between Antony and the Queen of Egypt would require banks and ditches to divide land from water. But, for Cleopatra, Antony is linked with 'oblivion'. The figure of power is further complicated. The queen is herself subject to an 'overflowing' that returns to the nihil, the zero:

> Rather a ditch in Egypt
> Be gentle grave unto me, rather on Nilus' mud
> Lay me stark naked, and let the water-flies
> Blow me into abhorring! Rather make
> My country's high pyramides my gibbet
> And hang me up in chains.[22]

The river Nile as a ditch is preferable to what Rome can offer to Cleopatra. Mud, nakedness and putrefaction are set against the symbol of the pyramid.[23] Ditch and grave. Enobarbus offers his own commentary that re-works the images of Cleopatra's speech. No 'gentle' grave but a 'foul […] ditch'.[24] The putrefying flesh is best forgotten. Even the queen will rot. The foul ditch claims the rich and the poor, the sovereign and the subject. All become nothing.

The burial of a suicide in *Hamlet* further elaborates these concerns. One of the gravediggers refers to 'crowner's quest law' – a portmanteau term that brings together the coroner and the crown, the mandate for the burial in hallowed ground – as opposed to the mere ditch or pit in which the suicide's body would have been slung. The grave the diggers are digging, then, is a vestibule in which the body awaits the greater power of resurrection, another, more profound in breaking – a 'crowing' into eternal life: 'Why, there thou sayst. And the more pity that

---

[20] As Chiari has argued, themes of creation and destruction were associated with fertility, and a further set of images which linked the river with 'the belly of [a] mother'. These images can themselves be traced through Giambattista Della Porta's *Magia Naturalis* (1558) to Spencer's *The Faerie Queene*. A pun on Nile/Nihil also allowed the river to be likened to Lethe, the boundary between this world and the next. See Sophie Chiari 'Overflowing the Measure: Cleopatra Unbound' (2019) 39 *Société Française Shakespeare*, 1–13.

[21] Shakespeare, *Antony and Cleopatra*, 1.3.68–71.

[22] Ibid 5.2, 57–62 (n 21).

[23] The sovereign upholds the order of the ditch. When this line cannot be held, order breaks down. These themes could be followed through *King Lear*, *Macbeth*, *Coriolanus* and *Timon of Athens*.

[24] Shakespeare (n 21) IV, vi, 2742.

great folk should have countenance in this world to drown or hang themselves more than their even-Christen. Come, my spade. There is no ancient gentleman but gardeners, ditchers, and grave-makers. They hold up Adam's profession.'[25]

An apostrophe to a spade – on the theme of graves, wealth and ditches. Death by drowning or hanging; images that return us to Cleopatra's speech and to a historical source for the 'grave-digger's scene', the drowning of judge Sir James Hales in 1554. Plowden's *Commentaries* report that Hales' drowning – ruled suicide by the court – could result in the forfeiture of his land – a controversial decision that raised the issue of the inheritance of landed wealth.[26] This is a significant concern in the play as a theme is the inheritance of King Fortinbras' land. Hamlet's father had killed King Fortinbras and won title to his lands.[27] Fortinbras' son, seeking revenge with an army of 'landless resolutes', marches on Denmark.[28] There is a suggestion that the dying Hamlet returns the titles of the land to Fortinbras.[29] The return of land to its rightful owner affirms the order of property and the correct transmission of wealth. Despite the equality of Christians before death, land and money mark the difference between 'great folk' and commoners. But, the digger tells the spade, there is a levelling nobility to work. Wit (which no one owns) presses into service the appropriate metaphor: 'Adam's profession.' The gravedigger; the working man; the representative of Adam will go on to bury the prince. While the fate of Fortinbras' army is unknown, the gravedigger's scene suggests that ditches and trenches are figures of work, even of a working class, resolutely landless. Robbed of any inheritance, they will assert the prerogatives of their ancient profession.

'TO DIG UP GEORGE HILL'

Hamlet was performed before King Charles I in 1637. We cannot speculate on how the arrival of the army of 'landless resolutes' would have been received on that January day at Hampton Court Palace. There were, though, profound changes taking place in the country. Civil war broke out in 1642.[30] The execution of the king in 1649 and the revolutionary upheavals in its aftermath provided the context for the emergence of racial ideas about land. The ditch and the drain become linked to a vision of a new order. In a series of pamphlets published between 1649 and 1652, Gerrard Winstanley effectively re-imagined the law of ditches.[31] For Winstanley, the apocalyptic sense in which the 'old world was running up like parchment

---

[25] Shakespeare, *Hamlet*, V, i.
[26] 1 Plowden 253, 262, 75 Eng. Rep. 387, 401 (C.B. 1562).
[27] Thomas Regnier, 'The Law in Hamlet' (2011) *Brief Chronicles III*, 107–32. Whether or not this property had passed to Claudius – who assumes the crown – or Hamlet himself is left unclear.
[28] Shakespeare (n 25) I, I, 103.
[29] Regnier (n 27) 109.
[30] The feudal system of landholding came under increasing stress, as landowners consolidated their holdings and enclosed common land to take advantage of new markets for wool. Agricultural markets also encouraged the buying and selling of land, exerting further pressures on feudal notions of inheritance and tenure. A class of yeoman farmers began to appear at the same time as large numbers were driven from their land to become landless labourers, or itinerants subject to harsh laws against vagrancy. Christopher Hill, *The English Revolution 1640* (London: Lawrence and Wishart, 1940).
[31] Gerrard Winstanley was one of the leaders of the band who cultivated common land on St George's Hill in Surrey.

in the fire' presaged the 'new law of righteousness' – a return to Biblical order.[32] *The Bible* provided a user's guide to the present – provided one could read the signs. As all were one in the body of Christ, the righteous new order would require common ownership of land. The war was the flood that had destroyed the corruption into which the world had fallen. It was necessary to 'wade deep to find the bottom of this divining spiritual doctrine' that would bring the return of righteousness and make the earth a 'Common Treasury of relief for all'.[33] Winstanley's recurrent image of the law of righteousness is of collective labour to the common good. Men will '[s]ow Corn, and […] eat […] bread together by the sweat of [their] brows.'[34]

The sweat of the labourer is the key to Winstanley's imagery. The sign of productive work on fecund fields, the sweat of the honest man is linked to an entire network of productive flows that can be blocked and become stagnant and dead. The ditch plays an ambiguous part in this symbology. It represents something that could have been dug by people with tools owned in common. But it is also the symbol of a dividing line – of property itself. The foul and stagnant ditch of blocked flows. Indeed, those who cannot appreciate the law of righteousness will fall 'into the ditch and be mired in their own inventions most pitifully'[35] – a parcelling up of common land into private claims, marked by the hedges that define the ditch lines of enclosed land.

Thus, '[t]o dig up George Hill [while not] enclosing any part into a particular hand […] [working] as one man […] together, and feeding together' makes labourers visible to each other. Hedges block lines of sight. The hedge is the badge of division, of master and servant. Winstanley speaks of the enclosures as 'hedging out others'[36] and of the rich sitting in their enclosures saying 'this is mine' – 'let the poor work together on the Commons.'[37] In the *Law of Freedom* the 'several enclosures of the earth' also define the boundaries of plots that can be sold.[38] Money is the 'great god that hedges some in and some out'.[39] Buying and selling for money is the most hateful form of exclusion. He that 'hedges himself in […] hedges out his brother.'[40] So, working together with 'spade and plow […] to make the barren and common lands fruitful' is a kind of 'oath' or 'covenant' made to the 'righteous king' in whom all are equal.[41] To work with each other is, literally, '[to] Look […] upon each other, as equals'. The blocking of creative flows, the amassing of fortunes from the sale of land, is so heinous a sin against the original common gift, that Adam is re-named A-dam. The dammed and damned ditch; the ditch dug around Hell in *Paradise Lost*, the sin of property and the 'bondage' of the spirit – a stagnant 'gathering of water'. 'The slavish fears of others' – the internalisation of the boundary within the self – match the 'external power' of the judges, magistrates and property owners who have set themselves up over others. The law of righteous flows breaks through the dams. Love streams out to all. The 'stout hearted' Pharaohs will be carried away in the flood; an image that is reminiscent of *The History*, the ruined palace and the shattered statue.

---

[32] Sabine (n 6) 252.
[33] ibid 568.
[34] ibid 266.
[35] ibid 209.
[36] ibid 283.
[37] ibid 196.
[38] ibid 445.
[39] ibid 270.
[40] ibid 428.
[41] ibid 286.

The great digger and creator of common storehouses condenses the scriptures into a single principle: 'Do as you would be done unto, and live in love.'[42]

WHEN ADAM DELVED, AND EVE SPAN

One might think that the utopian imaginary of ditches was erased by the demands of the industrial revolution.[43] The law had to deal with growing urban concentration and the discharge of factories. The cutting of canals and railway embankments also posed new problems for the management of water. While drainage law was indeed transformed by industrial modernity, we need to follow a stream that goes underground.[44] Drainage and digging become re-inscribed by a poetic drive for new symbols; desires for different communities, different economies, different flows.

Ruskin's *Unto This Last* studies energies and overflows. This is clear from the celebrated statement, announced in capitals: 'THERE IS NO WEALTH BUT LIFE.' *Unto This Last* channels a very different understanding of wealth than that presented by Smith, Ricardo and leather-tongued Malthus. Wealth, for Ruskin, is a kind of joyous being that informs living well. Joyous being is shared between those who live nobly, honestly and valiantly. To explain valour, Ruskin resorts to the language of the ditch. For political economists, wealth is what gathers like 'pools of dead water'. In this negative sense, wealth is compared to 'eddies in a stream (which, so long as the stream flows, are useless, or serve only to drown people)'. Proper wealth is a stream that flows to the sea. The sense of the metaphor is that 'the forms of property in general' go to 'where they are required' – a principle dictated by a 'law' above 'human laws'.[45] To push his point, Ruskin moves to the figure of irrigation. The law above the law is the work of energetic, honest men. This evokes Dugdale's art and industry of ditching, the skilled intervention into the paths of water: 'whether the stream be a curse or a blessing, depends upon man's labour.'[46] In a passage that would have delighted the author of *The History*, Ruskin writes of 'soft irrigation from field to field' determined by the 'leading trench and the limiting mound'. The 'lawless flow' that creates 'waters of Marah' is the rot that is the 'root of all evil.'

Pilgrim's slough of despond has become the morass of free market economy.

The 'science' of economics is the art of the swindler. Ruskin claims to have discovered the proper principles for the just distribution of wealth. *Unto This Last* redefines a tradition that can be traced back to the Biblical principle (echoed in Dante): 'diligite justitiam qui judicatis terram' – the one who judges the earth must love justice.[47] Justice rests on reciprocity. The honest, hardworking labourer 'can serve with his spade' because 'the man who has two

---

[42] ibid 408.
[43] The drive to drain and modernise picked up pace in the early modern period. A law of drainage was developed which did not entirely replace the jurisdiction of the Court of Sewers. Between 1689 and 1835 the Commissions of Sewers created various local authorities who had the oversight of land and drainage issues, and the upkeep of bank and drains was under their jurisdiction: Webb and Webb (1922, 32).
[44] The Land Drainage Act of 1861 created elective drainage districts, under the supervision of Drainage Boards, exercising all the powers of the Commission of Sewers.
[45] John Ruskin, *Unto This Last* (J.M. Dent 1921) 65.
[46] ibid 66.
[47] ibid 68.

measures of corn wants sometimes to dig; and the man who has two spades wants sometimes to eat'.[48] Surpluses are shared. They are not traded for profits that end up in the pockets of land owners. Ruskin's economics of honesty requires good sewers: trenchers 'draining' and 'reclaiming' the land.[49]

These themes can be traced into Ruskin's discussion of the gothic. For all the praise of labour in *Unto This Last*, the work of trenching is ignored in the celebration of cathedral architecture. The starting point of the argument is praise for gothic style as an 'expression of man's pleasure in labour'.[50] Gothic carving requires the same manual strength needed to 'plough' or clear wooded land. Carving is the physical signature of the craftsman, a token of 'a higher nobility' present in 'the life and liberty of every workman who struck the stone'.[51] The necessary discipline cannot be imposed by 'laws' or 'charters'. Carving is an expression of the vigour articulated in *Unto This Last*. Joyous work, not the compulsion of wage labour that sends 'multitudes [...] like fuel to feed the factory smoke'.[52]

Why does Ruskin not see the drains and trenches that provides the foundations for the cathedral? He was certainly aware that the management of water was central to gothic architecture in northern Europe.[53] Ruskin's poetics of wealth fail at this crucial moment. Structures that embody soaring desire, gables reaching for heaven, require deep foundation trenches. And a network of pipes and gutters to take rain water away.

William Morris grappled with this problem in *News from Nowhere*. Ditch digging is a central problematic for Morris' novel, set in a future utopian London. In one scene, Morris rows up the Thames with his guides to the new world: Dick and Clara. The latter denounces Morris' 'books'. They might have contained some insight into the plight of the 'poor', but Morris' heroes were blind to the labour of those who 'dug and sewed and baked and built and carpentered'.[54] Clara identifies the fundamental problem of Ruskin's failure of vision – a failure that Morris does not want to share. The novel links Clara's critique with a vision of 'complete communism' that occurs slightly later upstream.

Morris reports that the 'railways' have 'disappeared', as have the many 'bridges over the streams of Thames'. River meadows have 'become as beautiful as they should be'. From the boat, moored by a weir, the moon reflecting on the water, Morris notes the villagers 'tented in the hay-fields'.[55] The water meadows are beautiful because they are being worked. The next day, Morris sees something that he had not seen before: 'we sat for a while on the mound of the Dykes looking up at Sinodun and its clear-cut trench, and its sister *mamelon* of Whittenham.'[56] Is there an echo of *The History*? Morris is deploying classic sewer imagery: ditch and bank. The mamelon, a feminised term for a bank or a mound, hints at the fecundity of the irrigated

---

[48] ibid 17. Reversed in *The Good, The Bad and the Ugly* (Sergio Leone 1966): 'There are those with guns, and those who dig. You dig.'
[49] ibid 134.
[50] John Ruskin, *The Nature of the Gothic* (George Allen 1892) i.
[51] ibid 12.
[52] ibid 19.
[53] Structures in northern climates had to take a certain form: a sloping roof from which rain can fall and on which snow cannot settle. Gables are required to support sloping roofs. In Gothic architecture, the gable takes the form of a pointed arch precisely because it aligns with the roof.
[54] William Morris, *News from Nowhere* (Kelmscott Press 1893).
[55] ibid.
[56] ibid.

fields. Certainly, Morris presents ditch and bank in relationship. The bank is the soil dug from the ditch and provides a metaphor of a labour process made visible – just as the haymakers' work is visible in the water meadows. Morris appreciates the fine work of a 'clear-cut trench'. The surrounding villages have been 'lifted out of [their] nineteenth-century degradation'. Morris has revisited a truth of divine drainage: the good society must dig and scour its own ditches.[57]

The vision of communal ditch work feeds into Morris' appreciation of labour in *Useful Work versus Useless Toil*. There is certainly an understanding of the effort needed for a 'clear cut' ditch. Work interrupts 'animal rest'.[58] We cannot escape the desire to return to a point of relaxed stasis. The pleasure of work is knowing that it will come to an end and that one will be able to 'recover [mental and physical] strength'. This is a peculiar economy: 'all living things [have] a pleasure in the exercise of their energies.' Morris has taken Ruskin's vague but provocative ideas and linked them to a physical process modelled on the digging of clear-cut ditches. Ditch work does not disappear like the foundations of a cathedral. Ditching brings something into being and makes it visible; something that may outlast its creator. The lesson learnt in the fields of the Thames is that the ditch labourer is involved in an 'event': 'the thoughts of the men of past ages guide his hands.'[59]

Morris generalises. Assuming that most honest people have to work, and should do pleasurable work, society is unjustly organised if the work of the many supports the non-productive leisure of the few. A just society, then, would not only be organised differently, but would offer joyous labour for all. Morris stresses the shovel work necessary to think about the relationship between art and work. Clara's principle is further elaborated in *Art, Wealth and Riches*. One must read the everyday and discover in the mundane the traces of a different world, just as a building can be read to reveal meanings about the sensibilities of those who laboured upon it. Those who have left no name behind them, 'nothing but their work', are nevertheless significant.[60] The hand on the plough, the swing of a hammer or the way a shovel cuts into the ground are all tokens of work equal to its own craft. *News from Nowhere* is a successor text to *The History*, to Winstanley and Ruskin, and it points towards another text: Kropotkin's extended engagement with 'an economy of human energy required for the satisfaction of human needs' – a meditation on 'manual work in the free air'.[61]

FIELDS AND FACTORIES: THE ETHICS OF SUPERFLUITY

Kropotkin's text is a celebration of joy or superfluity that can be shared between those who are working together. This is why the ditch does not, as such, appear in his writings. The ditch figures a boundary, the sign of private property: something claimed and detached from communal work. In place of the ditch, Kropotkin focuses on well-organised communal labour that leaves time for the creation of a common culture. The 'dangling arms' of the unemployed

---

[57] ibid.
[58] William Morris, *Useful Work versus Useless Toil* (William Reeves 1886) 87.
[59] ibid 88.
[60] William Morris, *Art, Wealth and Riches* (William Reeves 1884) 35.
[61] Kropotkin (n 7) vii.

workman, shovels that are not worth the price paid for them, are the tokens of wasted lives.[62] Work undone. Lost energies.

Kropotkin's account of communal agriculture is that of a man who works outdoors. *Fields, Factories and Workshops* begins with the author shutting the study door behind him: 'I once took a knapsack and went on foot out of London, through Sussex.' In his wanderings, he expected to see men working in the fields. Instead he walked across 'heath or woodlands, rented as pheasant shooting grounds', pondering official statistics on employment that showed more clerks and members of the 'domestic and unproductive class' than those involved in 'busy human labour'.[63] Comparing the market gardens that surrounded Paris with the 'meadows' from which '[m]an is conspicuous by his absence', Kropotkin rejects the argument that the 'heavy clay soil' prevents cultivation: 'in the hands of man there are no infertile soils.'[64] The fundamental theme: that poor social and economic organisation prevents the production of enough to enable all to live 'the lives of human beings'.[65]

Land is not worked efficiently, because it is owned by rentiers who have no interest in farming techniques. The revolution begins when people realise that they can grow their own food, and produce 'more with less labour' by using scientific techniques and the methods of the 'new agriculture' coupled with the 'association of labour'.[66] In place of romanticism and nostalgia is scientific data about agricultural and industrial techniques. Concentration of wealth in the hands of the few is irrational, wasteful and unnecessary. While Ruskin might resist industry, for Kropotkin the social organisation of agricultural and 'industrial production with the full aid of machinery' is necessary.[67] Once knowledge and machinery are brought to bear, even the worst soils require only 'plain, unskilled human labour [and] laying in drainage tubes' to become productive. In the good society, the tube replaces the ditch.[68] The guiding principle: producers produce for themselves.[69] As a social principle it gives onto the idea that 'each healthy man and woman [should] spend a part of their lives in manual work in the free air'.[70]

This principle draws on the 'festivals of labour' that one can find in peasant communities.[71] Collective work is performed through communal competition and the display of skill. In the

---

[62] ibid 94.
[63] ibid 91.
[64] ibid 92.
[65] ibid 160 and 130.
[66] ibid 237. The idea of economy that emerges from the collective nurturing of energy is one of the rational uses of resources. Thus, reflecting on the failures of the Paris Commune and other revolutionary experiments, Kropotkin points out that the correct relationship between cities in revolt and the countryside is not for the former to requisition food and resources from the latter, but, to enter into exchanges for mutual benefit. Urban industry should produce what peasants need – shovels and other tools – and in exchange, peasant communities would willingly provision the cities. If agriculture is organised outside of private property relationships – where a portion of produce is taken without the work that would otherwise legitimise a share of the produce – there would be more than enough for all.
[67] Kropotkin (n 7) 36. In distinction to Aldo Leopold's complaints in *The Sand County Almanac* (Oxford University Press 1949), the 'steam shovel' is not to be resisted; rather, correct social organisation leads onto the correct use of machines.
[68] ibid 360.
[69] ibid 361.
[70] ibid 361.
[71] Peter Kropotkin, *Mutual Aid* (Heinemann 1903) 131.

canton of the Vaud, for example, the 'felling of wood' on land owned by the village shows the 'greatest ardour for work and the most considerable display of human energy'; in Russian communities '[c]omrades vie with each other in cutting the widest swathe' through the meadows. The superfluity that comes from common labour is a liberation of a spontaneous concern for others.[72] The ditch does re-appear in this imaginary: it may even be the figure of mutual aid. Rural peasant communities look out for their own in a way that does not require a coordinating authority. Thus, when a child falls into a flooded ditch or stagnant pond, the whole village comes running when they hear cries of distress. This is not a phenomenon of group compulsion. *Mutual Aid* contains the story of a prisoner hiding in a ditch who, on hearing cries of distress, broke cover to rescue a child from a burning building – and was promptly arrested. The ditch is the place from which human energy bursts forth to do good.[73]

Anarchist economics, in this sense, departs from Marx.[74] The fundamental analytical category is not surplus value. The surplus – or at least the surplus claimed by the landlord or the factory owner – should not exist in the first place. It is a token of misdirected energies. The point of non-authoritarian organisation is to ensure that 'the most favourable conditions' are obtained for 'giving society the greatest amount of useful products with the least waste of human energy'.[75] It follows, for Kropotkin, that the end point of the good society is work directed towards communal luxury and well-being. Well-being is the social measure of the most equitable distribution of human energy.

Communal luxury requires no more than the sane division of working time that replaces the specious distinction between hand work and brain work. Kropotkin's thinking does not require an ontology of labour – quite the opposite. The human being is essentially curious, involved in passionate enquiry about themselves and their world, infused by a 'spirit of invention' and a 'boldness of conception'.[76] Freed from wage labour, and with the basic material needs for food, dwelling and clothing satisfied, the real needs and 'necessities' of human life emerge: 'artistic creation'.[77] After the revolution, artistic creation becomes the organising principle of the working day. Some labour is necessary, and it might even be arduous. The working day is, however, made as short as possible to enable recovery and the kind of pursuits, artistic and scientific, that are, most properly, engaged in by the community as a whole: a kind of self-positing – an ongoing and communal act of collective intellectual creation and re-creation.[78] Kropotkin urges the reader to engage in a metaphorical digging into experience, to find those points of communal interaction that summon collective energies. Desire has been incorrectly harnessed to private property. The good society must expropriate the resources necessary for its inven-

---

[72] ibid 275. Kropotkin celebrates the focused and united energy of lifeboatmen and women who – without a concern for themselves – rush 'to the rescue'. The lifeboat association, like the Red Cross, provides further evidence of the power of communal and voluntary organisation.
[73] ibid 278.
[74] ibid 89.
[75] ibid 129.
[76] ibid 102.
[77] ibid 93.
[78] Peter Kropotkin, *The Conquest of Bread* (Chapman Hall 1906) 98, 106. Poetry is exemplary: art becomes powerful because stripped of waste ('saying more on fewer pages […] attentively read and appreciated'). A recollection of energetic life. A poet is nothing unless s/he 'has followed the plough at dawn, and enjoyed mowing grass with a large sweep of the scythe next to hardy haymakers vying energy with lively young girls who fill their air with their songs'.

tion. To expropriate, traced through its etymological twists and turns, can indeed be tracked back to an Indo-European root word that carries the meaning of being happy or free. Hence, Kropotkin's articulation of well-being: the original, primal power of the ditch digger.

THE DITCH RULE

When modern law comes to consider ditches, it cannot escape from the minor jurisprudence that we have been studying. The ditch rule is an emanation of ditch law. To follow this entanglement of property law and minor jurisprudence, we need to read the most recent House of Lords ruling, which invokes *Hamlet*: 'Boundary disputes are a particularly painful form of litigation. Feelings run high and disproportionate amounts of money are spent. Claims to small and valueless pieces of land are pressed with the zeal of Fortinbras's army.'[79]

Desire gathers at boundaries – that point at which 'your' and 'mine' meet. It is too easy to desire the wrong thing: the 'small and the valueless'. Lord Hoffmann evokes Fortinbras and his army to explain the peculiar disproportion of value evoked by boundary disputes. Lord Hoffmann goes on to explain how the precise position of the boundary has always been a problem for the conveyancing of land. Recalling Dugdale, one can appreciate a more basic problem. The preservation of the community requires boundary ditches. Registered conveyancing inherits a similar problem. However, the issue is not the writ of the Godly Prince, but the terms in which land is bought and sold.

Boundaries are prerequisites for commodified land. Lord Hoffmann refers to Royal Commission reports that recommended the use of Ordnance Survey as well as deeds. Boundaries can thus be demarcated and buyers and sellers confident of their exchanges.[80] But pinpointing boundaries on maps is difficult. Lines drawn on the charts are too 'fat' to be precise enough. In terms of practicalities, a chain of proxies, 'land agents' and men on the ground can determine accurately where a boundary lies, so that the rule is very rarely invoked. But there are occasions when the location of a boundary cannot be settled. The only way in which conveyancing can resolve the problem is through the application of a presumption.

The presumption concerns a ditch:

> The rule about ditching is this. No man, making a ditch, can cut into his neighbour's soil, but usually he cuts it to the very extremity of his own land: he is of course bound to throw the soil which he digs out, upon his own land; and often, if he likes it, he plants a hedge on top of it.[81]

The ditch rule presupposes labour, and a pre-existing boundary that the ditch respects. This presumption would be displaced if the ditch existed before the boundary was drawn. The example is 'an internal drainage ditch'. Such a ditch might become a boundary at a later date, but, if it was dug on land that did not abut neighbouring land, it would not be possible to presume that the boundary ran along the middle of the ditch. The court is grappling with a typology of ditches like the priests of the Nile.

---

[79] *Alan Wibberley Building Ltd v Insley*, 1999 W.L.R. 894, at 894.
[80] Another strange echo of *Hamlet*. Ordnance maps, drawn up for the defence of the realm; the burst of cannon fire that concludes the play. A soldier's funeral. Order of Fortinbras. A king coming into his inheritance.
[81] *Vowels v Miller* (1810) 3 Taunt. 137, at 138.

This typology of ditches is not related to divine providence. It is impacted in a history of land markets. The ditch rule is a fiction that relates to commodified land and emotions that are bound up with what has been bought and sold. The court must set matters straight; must correct, as it were, misplaced desire where 'feelings' prompt to inappropriate action. Kropotkin might comment that these bizarre feelings are themselves occasioned by irrational social and economic structures based on private ownership of land. The court is certainly concerned with resolving 'painful' forms of litigation. This is when Fortinbras enters. The 'zeal of Fortinbras' army' is, first of all, an image of misplaced desire. On a second reading, though, it appears that the court will itself have to act like Fortinbras, entering at the end of *Hamlet* to assert good order and bury the prince (while leaving much undone). Indeed. What becomes of the army of the landless resolute? What has become of the labour of the landless?

The presumptions of the ditch rule are based on the fiction that the person who owns the land is a ditch digger and a hedge planter. This is, of course, a poeticism. The rule would not be different if one imagined that a hired hand had dug the ditch. The poeticism, though, is an imaginative re-construction of work that gives rise to ownership and respects the boundary of one's land. The memory of ditch work on which the ditch rule rests evokes something of the sweat and labour that an honest man would expand on his land. It evokes Ruskinian energies. However, if we continue to think about the line of the ditch not as a boundary but in Morris or Kropotkin's terms, we can arrive at a different reading of the ditch rule.

The determination of boundaries of things owned depends on an energy that – while it can be bought and sold for a wage – resists commodification. In Kropotkin's version of Morris' digging of the clean ditch, desire is trained to fixate not on property and wage work, but on something beyond. Fortinbras, in this sense, is the figure that attempts to resolve, to offer an ending. But he is an ambiguous figure – a symbol of what might have been, and, what still could be 'most royal' if we were to try it out. The ditch rule might invoke Fortinbras' army, but, unlike even Rosencrantz and Guildenstern, they remain outside the lines, awaiting their own entrance, their own inheritance.

OUTFLOW

The work of inbanking creates the boundaries that define the community of the sovereign, and ensures the correct flows of water and wealth. Ditch law is a minor jurisprudence of symbols written into and under the soil; those symbols that legitimise the power that keeps banks and boundaries in order. The minor jurisprudence of the ditch is unthinkable without flows between law, literature and philosophy that define the shifting forms of counternormativity. In the end (if there can be an end to digging), ditch and minor jurisprudence are workmates: both concerned with what gets turned over, dug out, scoured or left to silt up. We might learn from them how to make something of the ruins in which we live. After all, as Durruti said, a worker is not frightened of ruins.[82] The court might invoke the ditch rule, the ditch rule might allow the correct training of the desire for commodified land, but it does not help the resolutely land-less. A minor jurisprudence would counsel the spiritual discipline that finds in useless toil the

---

[82] Or Durutti, as he is known in Manchester. The quotation is from an interview given by Buenaventura Durutti to Pierre Van Passen on 5 August 1936 and published in the *Toronto Daily Star*, 18 August 1936.

possibility of something else. No wonder, then, that D.H. Lawrence likened poetry to a desire that opens canalised flows and invents the future.[83]

Bread and poetry. Grain, sewer, ditch.

---

[83] 'The Poetry of the Present' in *The Complete Poems of D.H. Lawrence*, Vivian de Sola Pinto and Warren Roberts (eds) (London: Penguin, 1964) 194.

PART VIII

JURISLITERARY HISTORIES

Epistemicide – Forms-of-Life – Singularities – Science of the Soul – *Persona Ficta* – Gatekeeping – Juridical Hypothetical – *Mos Hispanicus* – Literary Ontogenericity

27. Miracles
Serene Richards

FORMS OF LIVING

> All our ideas about life must be revised in a period when nothing any longer adheres to life.[1]

The human being has long been defined and articulated from several differing perspectives, from being born in God's image to the speaking being, political animal, or, in the language of the natural sciences, *homo sapiens*. Today, critical philosophical and legal thought postulate an era of post-humanity, aiming to dethrone the human from its long history of having assumed for itself, without irony, mastery over nature. The privileging of the question over 'what' the human being is, throughout Western philosophical and scientific thought, and the assumption of its definition as constituting an epistemological consensus in the history of the present, is carried over into the juridical through the institution of legal personality. As is familiar to many legal scholars, legal personhood is the artifice through which citizenship and subjective rights are assigned to the human being, and without which, as Hannah Arendt had most clearly articulated, the human being as such cannot be recognised as being simply human.[2] In our present conjuncture, akin to a life-distilling machine, the artifice of legal personhood functions in a paradoxical manner, fusing the abstract separation that it was initially devised to sanction.

The work of the jurist Yan Thomas is instructive in this case. The legal artefact of the person features throughout his work, though perhaps most explicitly articulated concerning the *affaire Pérruche*.[3] For Thomas, 'we are still dependent on a formal system that isolates in each of us, apart from what is irreducibly singular, a legal person, where almost nothing of our physical, psychological and social reality is revealed, since it is reduced to a function: our capacity to hold and exercise rights.'[4] With the increased juridification of the social sphere, this significant abstraction, characteristic of law, has largely been forgotten. Thomas argues that this strictly juridical operation has leant itself to confusion, with intellectual traditions ascribing to it a meaning and quality far removed from its originally quite narrow function as a legal institution. Through Christian theology and humanism, the juridical person has acquired a new sense and value that, in all respects, is incompatible with its initial function, as a technical pre-requisite to entering into the language of law. According to Thomas:

> In our legal culture, the person is confused with the human being itself, with the living human being in that which is singular and common to the human species [...] Hence, in our contemporary law,

---

[1] Antonin Artaud, *The Theatre and Its Double* (Grove Press 1958) 8.
[2] See Hannah Arendt, *The Origins of Totalitarianism* (Harcourt 1951) 297.
[3] The case of the *affaire Pérruche* caused much controversy in France. In its ruling on 17 November 2000, the Court of Cassation recognised the right of a child born disabled to seek compensation following a medical fault which deprived his mother of the possibility of interrupting her pregnancy.
[4] Yan Thomas, 'Sujet concret et sa personne' in Olivier Cayla and Yan Thomas, *Du Droit de ne pas Naître: A Propos de l'Affaire Pérruche* (Gallimard 2002) 125.

regimes of protection which attempt to project the individual and generic identity of each person into a double intimate and public dimension of the person: personality rights on the one hand, and human rights borne by everyone on the other.[5]

In other words, our present is marked by an ever-expanding process of bringing into the fabric of law all aspects of what constitutes life with the aim of protecting it; where the juridical notion of the dignity of life can, in a sense, be activated and a form of justice apportioned one way or another.

A good example is the extension of a form of legal personhood to animals, rivers and ecosystems, so that 'rights of nature' may facilitate a recourse to justice and environmental protections.[6] For Thomas, extending legal personhood to include nature, for instance, is misguided; a case of 'an ill-conceived and dangerous category for men' now assumed to offer protection to 'pelicans and trees'.[7] Thomas is not suggesting that subjective rights are an *a priori* negative phenomenon; rather, the problem lies elsewhere: in the relationship between power and life. Thomas argues that this is essentially where the notion of biopolitics, as developed by Giorgio Agamben, can most clearly be elucidated. The shifting limit of legal protection, while including previously excluded elements from the patronage of law, is a simultaneous affirmation of that which lies beyond this limit, beyond the sacredness of life, and therefore unworthy of protection.[8] This logic connecting personhood, rights and justice is the subject of Simone Weil's essay 'Human Personality'. Here, Weil affirms that 'there is something sacred in every man, but it is not his person. Nor yet is it the human personality. It is this man; no more and no less.'[9] Weil makes a simple assertion, one that is impossible to honour within the framework of rights and juridical personhood. For Weil: 'Justice consists in seeing that no harm is done to men. Whenever a man cries inwardly: "Why am I being hurt?" harm is being done to him.'[10] Weil distinguishes between rights and the impersonal cry of hurt; only an impersonal, non-legal justice can hear the latter. The institution of legal personality is incapable of hearing this cry of hurt for it is an impersonal cry, and 'the notion of rights, by its very mediocrity, leads on naturally to that of the person, for rights are related to personal things'.[11] Indeed, for Weil, the notion of rights is immediately connected with exchange; it has a 'commercial flavour' tied up with individual claims.[12]

The problem, then, is twofold: on the one hand, the biopolitical scission characteristic of the legal limit (or prohibition) excludes from the realm of law that which is thought to lie beyond the merits of legal protection; on the other hand, the juridical institution of rights is necessarily tied up with individual, personal claims, and appears to be the only means through which dignity and justice are possible. However, there are times when what is demanded is not

---

[5] Thomas, 'Sujet concret' (n 4) 125.
[6] Anastasia Greene, 'Symposium Exploring the Crime of Ecocide: Rights of Nature and Ecocide' (*Opinio Juris*, 24 September 2020) http://opiniojuris.org/2020/09/24/symposium-exploring-the-crime-of-ecocide-rights-of-nature-and-ecocide/ accessed 4 March 2021.
[7] Yan Thomas, 'Le Sujet de droit, la personne et la nature' (1998) 100 *Le Débat* 3 85, 97.
[8] Thomas, 'Le Sujet de droit' (n 7) 89.
[9] Simone Weil, 'Human Personality' in Sian Mills (ed), *Simone Weil: An Anthology* (Penguin 2005) 70.
[10] Weil, 'Human Personality' (n 9) 93.
[11] Weil, 'Human Personality' (n 9) 84.
[12] Weil, 'Human Personality' (n 9) 81.

an individual claim for this or that right, but rather the demand and desire to utterly transform one's way of life. Such demands usually go unheard; if they are heard, the only means of redress and response within juridico-political parameters is brutal repression. For instance, consider the wholesale repression of the *Mouvement des travailleurs arabes* (MTA), the North African migrant workers' collective organising in the early 1970s in France.[13] The women and men that composed this collective experienced exploitation in numerous ways, ranging from inadequate housing to irregular juridical status that often depended on the goodwill of their employers, police violence, exclusion from established trade unions, racism and a generalised hostile environment. Tragically, the exploitation and racism they faced was not limited to the factory floor, nor were their troubles to disappear with the correct paperwork; instead, ritual humiliation and exclusion occurred out on the street, in cafés and supermarkets – indeed, in all aspects of their daily lives. The women and men of the MTA desired and demanded a wholesale transformation of their world; they viewed politics and the social field of their everyday lives to be inseparable. In the end, the movement was brutally repressed; it was infiltrated by the State security services and its demands were crushed. Perhaps this is what Henri Lefebvre meant when, in the *Critique of Everyday Life*, he stated plainly that 'in capitalist countries, the superstructures […] are in contradiction with the contents of the living'.[14]

This chapter then is intimately concerned with the question of this seeming incompatibility: the idea that the superstructures contradict the contents of the living (with ways of life, the desires and possibilities of living, the style, mode and *habitus* of everyday life). The tensions between the form-of-life on the one hand, and the superstructures on the other, are evident in different contexts throughout history. From colonial violence to environmental destruction and the erasure of civilisations, a planetary 'brutalism' ensues, to use Achille Mbembe's term.[15] Although a methodological analysis through the prism of political economy would offer a pertinent critique of our present (after all, it is clear that capitalism is incompatible with the relations of planetary life, and continued exploitation of peoples, land and organisms can only lead to their assured mutual destruction), I want to suggest another, perhaps *minor* and overlooked perspective which is no less urgent. It is worth recalling that capitalism is but a system of social relations; only one means, then, of organising sociality. The question of the form-of-life of the living is fundamental, and yet, while it is a shared experience with all life on earth, it remains both a practical and conceptual enigma for human beings. As Marielle Macé wonderfully put it: 'tell me then what you really want to see, to protect, but also to accuse, and more, what you really want to imagine in the forms of living, and I will tell you what kind of world you are supporting.'[16] That each one of us is capable of a mode of being is a universality that brings together all species, and yet it is increasingly impossible to exercise; the conditions of possibility of the living present one obstacle after another. In Lefebvre's terms, the forms of living appear to be incompatible with the superstructures; indeed, our present so-called universal mode of life, if it can be described as such, is one indicative of a planetary world made (un)inhabitable in our names. What can be described as the tension between the universal and

---

[13] I expand on this in 'May '68 – A Past that Never Was and a Future that Has Already Been Lost' (2018) 5 *Crisis & Critique* 2 300–17.
[14] Henri Lefebvre, *Critique de la vie Quotidienne I* (L'Arche Editeur 1997) 58.
[15] See Achille Mbembe, *Brutalisme* (Éditions la Découverte 2020).
[16] Marielle Macé, *Styles: Critique de nos formes de vie* (Gallimard 2016) 322.

the particular, is, in reality, only the forceful application of a generalised form of one mode of the particular, one mode of being among numerous possibilities.

This is the instituting function of law, where what is in question is the transformation of the human being into identity: 'the entry of the individual into the symbolic […] is the condition of institutional existence, the capture of the subject by law'.[17] As Peter Goodrich develops:

> The stakes, in other words, are high for if, following Legendre, we read the law against itself we must read it as the narrative (roman) through which, in a phrase taken from the *Digest*, life is instituted (*vitam instituere*). The tripartite division of Roman law progresses from *ius personarum* (the law of persons / masks) through the law of things and obligations […] to the law of actions: the subject is instituted by the law of masks and through the bonds, the words of the law, comes to or, better, is led to act, to speak in the name of the *principium*, the first and absolute Reference. Zero becomes through law the place of the actor, the site of subjectivity, the mask or persona of historical being in the theatre of truth.[18]

The challenge is in part to re-conceptualise our modes of relating, our social relations that compose the 'theatre of truth'. In a sense, this is what Antonin Artaud proposed in relation to the theatre of cruelty, recognising that 'we are not free. And the sky can still fall on our heads.'[19] The idea, for Artaud, is to overcome the separation between 'the analytic theatre and the plastic world', since 'one does not separate the mind from the body nor the senses from the intelligence'.[20] In terms of the juridical, this resembles Spinoza's point that power or rights are unconditional.[21] This is to say that they do not depend on artifice, neither for their distillation nor for their always possible confiscation. If a role is to be given to institutions it is for the organisation of encounters, to multiply relations that can be combined and agree with the nature (always singular) of human beings as singularities, to increase their possibilities and powers of action.

In what follows, I investigate how a particular mode of being was destroyed, forcefully made to disappear without a trace after a perilous confrontation with the generalising tendency of the juridico-political order and reigning language of power. Almost nothing remains of this epistemicide; having survived unkept and torched archives, it persists only in legend as speculative fiction: a place known as *The Court of Miracles*.

A MIRACULOUS DRESSING ROOM

> If repetition is possible, it is due to miracle rather than to law. It is against law: against the similar form and the equivalent content of law.[22]

Repetition is a mode of being, a form of conduct, that concerns 'non-exchangeable and non-substitutable singularities'.[23] For Deleuze, 'if exchange is the criterion of generality,

---

[17] Peter Goodrich, *Languages of Law: From Logics of Memory to Nomadic Masks* (Weidenfield and Nicolson 1990) 278.
[18] Goodrich, *Languages of Law* (n 17) 282.
[19] Artaud, *Theatre* (n 1) 79.
[20] Artaud, *Theatre* (n 1) 86.
[21] Gilles Deleuze, *Expressionism in Philosophy: Spinoza* (Zone Books 1990) 259.
[22] Gilles Deleuze, *Difference and Repetition* (Continuum 2001) 2.
[23] Deleuze, *Difference and Repetition* (n 22) 1.

theft and gift are those of repetition'.[24] 'Generality, as generality of the particular, thus stands opposed to repetition as universality of the singular',[25] for repetition, conceptually, is understood as the affirmation of singularity. Singularity, in relation to law, is impossible; it is concerned rather with establishing generality. Law functions on the basis of discerning and establishing specific criteria, relying on the resemblance of legal persons as well as their supposed equivalence with a legal personality that they both constitute and are constituted by – a double-bind that makes repetition, the appearance of singularity, impossible. For Deleuze:

> If repetition exists, it expresses at once a singularity opposed to the general, a universality opposed to the particular, a distinctive opposed to the ordinary, an instantaneity opposed to variation and an eternity opposed to permanence. In every respect, repetition is a transgression. It puts law into question, it denounces its nominal or general character in favour of a more profound and more artistic reality.[26]

The exemplary case of the *Cour des Miracles*, a series of slums scattered around Paris during the sixteenth and seventeenth centuries, sheds some light on the continual tension between singularity and the generalising impulse of law. Little is known of the inhabitants of the *Cour*, whose lives appear in literary works with fragmentary historical records. Much of what we reconstruct here is a weaving together of disparate literatures: historical, literary, anecdotal. The inhabitants of the *Cour* cannot be said to form a people, with a shared history and language. Indeed, they were immigrants from across Europe who had found themselves in the city of Paris for one reason or another. The *Cour* is described by Victor Hugo in *Notre Dame de Paris* as though 'from another world': 'The limits of races and species seemed effaced in this city, as in a pandemonium. Men, women, beasts, age, sex, health, maladies, all seemed to be in common among these people; all went together, they mingled, confounded, superposed; each one there participated in all.'[27]

In the absence of any written testimonies from the inhabitants, concerning their form-of-life and manners of being, it is left to us to bring their world to life and re-activate this space in the historical narrative surrounding the making of the responsible, juridical subject. In doing so the point is not to give voice to the voiceless, but rather, as Saidiya Hartman put it, 'to imagine what cannot be verified, a real of experience which is situated between two zones of death – social and corporeal death – and to reckon with the precarious lives which are visible only in the moment of their disappearance'.[28] The annihilation of the *Cour* and removal of its inhabitants constituted an ending of their world, their *manneries*[29] and way of life; it was the destruction of a shared language and jargon that to this day remains unspeakable and unthinkable, their existence collapsed into the broad term 'dangerous classes'. It is this tension of the assertiveness of the singular, thought practically and epistemically unbearable from the perspective of the language of power, that I am concerned with revisiting.

Two contrasting texts written around the same period toward the end of the sixteenth century form vivid accounts of the *Cour des Miracles*, vividly articulating what seemed to be at stake: one jovial and mysterious that featured in burlesque literature, a popular genre of

---

[24] Deleuze, *Difference and Repetition* (n 22) 1.
[25] Deleuze, *Difference and Repetition* (n 22) 1.
[26] Deleuze, *Difference and Repetition* (n 22) 2–3.
[27] Victor Hugo, *Notre Dame de Paris*, ebook.
[28] Saidiya Hartman, 'Venus in Two Acts' (2008) 26 *Small Axe* 12 1, 12.
[29] Giorgio Agamben, *The Coming Community* (University of Minnesota Press 2009) 27.

the period; the other an official letter, the author of which is unknown, intended for Louis XI, which is a warning, and a desperate plea for the eradication and sanitisation of this space and re-education of the inhabitants.

In Richard de Romany's *Carabinage ou Matoiserie Soldatesque* (1616), a conversation between Belles Oreiles and Poltronesque on the subject of the *Cour des Miracles* unfolds. After Poltronesque admits that they had never heard of the place, Belles Oreiles offers a glimpse:

> Beyond the gate at Montmartre, there is a dwelling called the *Cour des Miracles*, which many who have lived in Paris for a long time may not know about, especially since the beggars of the Court and others spend the day crippled, mutilated [...] returning in the evening carrying a sirloin under their arms, or a piece of veal, some leg of mutton, not to mention the bottle they have hung on their belt, and, entering the said Courtyard, abandon their gallows, resume their disposition and stoutness, and in imitation of the old bacchanals, each with his trophy in hand and awaiting the preparation of their supper, dance all sorts of dances, mainly the sarabande. Can one see greater miracles than the lame man walking straight in this courtyard?[30]

This was the miracle from which the name of the *Cour* was derived, for it was not the inhabitants who nominated their abode the 'Court of Miracles'; rather, the name was given in jest, meant to poke fun at the inhabitants, for it was believed that they feigned injuries by day only to return to the *Cour* by nightfall in good health, 'dancing all sorts of dances'. While this imagery of the miraculous and fantastical entertained Parisians, many fascinated by an urban sociality altogether removed from their everyday life, this space terrified those in high office, who understood it instead to pose an existential threat to the prosperity and way of life of the city. Little captures the terror more than a *Mémoire* written in 1612, by an author who to this day remains anonymous, addressed to Henri de Gondy, the archbishop of Paris and adviser to Louis XI. 'My Lord', the author writes, 'the establishment of the police of the interned poor (that the foreigners call workers) introduced in this city of Paris six years ago, was held in high esteem'.[31] War, budding commercial capitalism and migration from Spain of the Gitans in the fifteenth century had transformed the city, which was now the most populous in Europe. The question of poverty, hitherto associated with religious voluntary poverty, had by now taken the form of a social problem to be solved urgently, with the *Grand Bureau des Pauvres* acting as the largest administrative organisation offering a city-wide management of Paris's poor during the time of the *Mémoire*'s writing. The *Mémoire*'s author warns that, despite these efforts, a great disorder still lurks, haunting the city; with the multitude of slums growing ever larger, the inconvenience, we are told, grows ever greater. When attempts are made to arrest the poor, they resist and 'respond with injurious words, threats, blasphemes, maledictions and dirty language, dishonest and, in sum, prejudicial to the honour both of God and the magistrates'.[32] The letter urges greater organisation of Paris's poor, a more rigorous administrative apparatus, a generalised system of confinement: it describes something akin to the establishment of the General Hospitals; which was a novel system of confinement aimed at incarceration on the one hand, and, on the other, the exercise of a positive power, a positive

---

[30] Richard de Romany, *Carabinage ou Matoiserie Soldatesque* (1616) (J Gay et fils 1867) 70–1.
[31] 'Mémoire concernant les Pauvres qu'on appelle enfermés' (1612) in L. Cimber and F. Danjou (eds), *Archives Curieuses de l'Histoire de France*, 1st ser., 15 (1837) 243–70; 243.
[32] 'Mémoire' (n 31) 244.

potential, of inculcating the poor into a new ethics of work. Fear of idleness as a way of life was common, with *acedia* (sloth) considered the worst of all vices, an unpardonable sin.[33] This mystery letter, written roughly 50 years prior to the Great Confinement and the establishment of the General Hospitals, describes a particular community who seemingly posed the single greatest threat to the prosperity of the City: idle, joyous, careless, knowing neither God nor laws nor the sacraments, speaking their own language and obeying a separate King. Although not named explicitly, it is clear that the community the author has in mind is that of the *Cour des Miracles*. The anonymous author writes:

> This poverty was known as a real cesspit for all sorts of obscenity, of villainy, of nastiness and trickery, they acted like armless men, hunchbacked or full of ulcers all over their body, their skin was deformed, covered in animal blood, swollen and jaundiced by the force of their suffering, horrid and shameful displays, and an infinite number of inventions to abuse the word poverty from the charity of well to do people, cheating everybody.[34]

And, as they approached their homes:

> We could see them redress their limbs that seemed torn and rotten and enter with a straight back and gay like someone without any pain or harm; witness the place vulgarly called the *Cour des Miracles*, behind Filles-Dieu, […] we would see them in the evening, all summer, dancing, playing and laughing – having a good time.[35]

This space of fantasy and reverie, of pleasures and play, seemed to be altogether incompatible with the prevailing order of things. A foreign space at the heart of the city, where an entirely different form of life was being lived. The inhabitants spoke their own language and jargon, they obeyed their own laws, and a separate king, they had their own beliefs and system of knowledge. This audacity, to live according to one's own specificity, seemed irrational, beyond any reason, and as a result had to be eradicated (Figure 27.1).

Victor Hugo's *Notre Dame de Paris* (1831) fantastically describes the space, and retells the tale capturing the sense of horror that the inhabitants caused to those in power. Hugo writes:

> It was, in truth, that redoubtable Cour des Miracles, whither an honest man had never penetrated at such an hour; the magic circle where the officers of the Châtelet and the sergeants of the provostship, who ventured thither, disappeared in morsels; a city of thieves, a hideous wart on the face of Paris; a sewer, from which escaped every morning, and whither returned every night to crouch, that stream of vices, of mendicancy and vagabondage which always overflows in the streets of capitals; a monstrous hive, to which returned at nightfall, with their booty, all the drones of the social order; a lying hospital where the bohemian, the disfrocked monk, the ruined scholar, the ne'er-do-wells of all nations, Spaniards, Italians, Germans,—of all religions, Jews, Christians, Mahometans, idolaters, covered with painted sores, beggars by day, were transformed by night into brigands; an immense dressing-room, in a word, where, at that epoch, the actors of that eternal comedy, which theft, prostitution, and murder play upon the pavements of Paris, dressed and undressed.[36]

---

[33] Giorgio Agamben, *Stanzas: Word and Phantasm in Western Culture* (University of Minnesota Press 1993) 3.
[34] 'Mémoire' (n 31) 250.
[35] 'Mémoire' (n 31) 250.
[36] Hugo, *Notre Dame de Paris* (n 27).

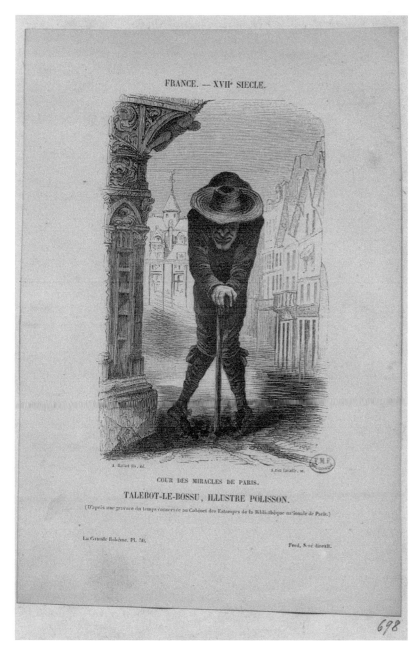

Figure 27.1   *Talebot-Le-Bossu: Illustre Polisson*

This 'immense dressing-room' was simultaneously unthinkable and all too real, made of myth and the very mythical thing that had to be eradicated, expelled; forming the basis and justification for the greatest transformation of the system of discipline and punishment. The metaphor of the 'dressing-room' extended beyond the appearances of the inhabitants to their subjective constitution as human beings. In a study of the *Cour des Miracles* published in 1912 by a professor at the School of Anthropology in Paris, Émile Nourry, writing under the pseudonym of Paul Saintyves, the inhabitants are depicted as experts in simulation. 'They are real sick people', Saintyves writes, 'but their real illness is only a need to simulate illnesses they do not have, and this need is itself only impulsive vanity'.[37] For Saintyves, the inhabitants are not merely irrational, but incapable of reason altogether:

> The wretched beggars or vagrants are easily liars or simulators; they are weak, incapable of regular work, of any sane will. The same is true of children and primitives. Debilitated or degenerate, neurotic or hysterical, they are all characterized by mental instability which makes them not only illogical but a-logical. Pathological simulators can be divided into two main categories: mythomaniacs and pathomimes. Mythomaniacs are content to lie, pathomimes do not hesitate to cause the most serious injuries to themselves.[38]

The inhabitants of the *Cour* were thought to be not simply deceitful in their presentations of themselves but 'incapable of regular work, of any sane will', their actions and gestures 'not only illogical but a-logical'. Experts at simulations, their expertise, we are told, lies in 'sensory phenomena, motor disorders: epilepsy, chorea, paralysis, contractures; intellectual disorders: imbecility and madness; functional disorders of the sight, hearing, larynx or limbs. Vanity, a pathological and monstrous vanity'.[39] A vain existence, simulating ailments of all sorts to cheat Parisians out of their change and empathy, incapable of work or any 'sane will', and worst of all, as the author of the *Mémoire* put it, 'we would see them in the evening, all summer, dancing, playing and laughing – having a good time'.[40] It was precisely this temporality, manner and style of life, this mode of living, that could not be tolerated by the established order of things – this singularity that could not be generalised, and that therefore had to be eradicated.

In 1630 Louis XIII planned an urbanisation project on the site, attempting to remove the space once and for all. The project was abruptly suspended when the inhabitants of the Court of Miracles successfully fought off the architects and urbanists. The anxieties over the lives of the inhabitants, their seeming ungovernability and idleness, continued to pose a problem to the order of the city. Jean-Baptist Colbert, First Minister of State serving under Louis XIV, devised a novel strategy, this time in the name of public health. On 29 March 1667 Louis XIV created the first post of Lieutenant General of the Police and appointed Gabriel Nicolas de La Reynie for the role, charging him with leading the 'grand renfermement' [Great Confinement] and finally eliminating the Court of Miracles, confining the inhabitants to the newly established General Hospitals. After numerous failed attempts at destroying the space, La Reynie organised an ambush. Despite the residents' best efforts, hurling stones and pots and pans, all dispersed: 'the blind with sight, the disabled with agility, the limbless with legs, to avoid the

---

[37] Paul Saintyves, *La Simulation du Merveilleux* (Flammarion 1912) 7.
[38] Saintyves, *La Simulation* (n 37) 52.
[39] Saintyves, *La Simulation* (n 37) 53.
[40] 'Mémoire' (n 31) 250.

fate of the last dozen and to escape the menacing minotaur. In twenty-minutes, the *Cour des Miracles* had lost its entire population.'[41] La Reynie ordered his troops to 'burn down the huts, tear down the walls,' so that 'the place cleared up: with the *Cour des Miracles* gone, the last trace of barbarism disappeared with it.'[42]

The most detailed account of the destruction of the *Cour des Miracles* was written by Henri Sauval, historian to the King, who wrote the text as an ethnographic account of the last remaining *Cour*. Sauval's descriptions served as the primary source material for much that has been subsequently written about the *Cour* and its inhabitants. Sauval was chiefly concerned with the seeming lawlessness of the inhabitants, saying: 'Everyone lived in great licentiousness: no one had faith nor law, and Baptism, Marriage and the Sacraments were unknown.'[43] At the same time, Sauval describes rules of conduct, and, in many respects, norms that the inhabitants adhered to in one form or another. Sauval also establishes a rank among the residents, distinguishing between beggars, pickpockets, thieves and road bandits, all with separate characteristics. For example, thieves, Sauval says, are without law or discipline, while beggars have a king, laws and 'a Kingdom, made up of an infinite number of disciplined subjects, if one can say that of the bad poor'.[44] What appeared to be most troubling was the indifference of the inhabitants to the emerging ethic of work, epitomised in their seeming lack of regard for capitalist temporality and the belief in progress. Sauval remarks:

> Each one enjoys at ease the present and eats with pleasure in the evenings that which he has gained by day through inflicting pain and beatings; since what they called earned is elsewhere called theft: and it was one of the fundamental laws of the *Cour des Miracles*, not to leave anything for the next day.[45]

This image of criminality coupled with a nonchalance, an aversion to thrift, represented a mode of entire opposition to a disciplined work ethic. The inhabitants had to be confined to the General Hospitals, not merely to labour, but, as Foucault so clearly articulated, the purpose of the General Hospitals was precisely to remedy, or correct, idleness so that labour would take the form of 'an ethical transcendence'.[46] This sentiment is expressed by the anonymous author of the *Mémoire*, who proposed a generalised system of confinement to house the idle,[47] those who could be seen 'in the evening, all summer, dancing, playing and laughing, having a good time'.[48]

The destruction and incarceration of the *Cour des Miracles* and its inhabitants typifies the instituting function of the law. To put it in more familiar terms, it provides a paradigmatic account of the transformation of the chaotic 'dressing room' of the multitude into a presumed coherent people, subject and subjected to a particular political and social order. Indeed, as Paolo Virno explains, there remains an underlying tension and hostility towards 'the concept

---

[41] Henri Sauval, *Histoires et Recherches des Antiquités de la Ville de Paris*, Tome I (Moette et Chardon 1724) 477.
[42] Sauval, *Histoires et Recherches* (n 41) 478.
[43] Sauval, *Histoires et Recherches* (n 41) 512.
[44] Sauval, *Histoires et Recherches* (n 41) 513.
[45] Sauval, *Histoires et Recherches* (n 41) 512.
[46] Michel Foucault, 'The Great Confinement' in *Madness and Civilization: A History of Insanity in the Age of Reason* (Vintage Books 1988) 55.
[47] 'Mémoire' (n 31) 256.
[48] 'Mémoire' (n 31) 251.

of the multitude, and the singularities that comprise it. Virno shows that the distinction between the 'People' and the 'multitude' was the subject of numerous theoretico-philosophical and practical controversies during the seventeenth century.[49] These controversies range from ideas on the formation of the modern State to religious wars and the making of the juridical subject; accordingly, it was the fierce battle between these two concepts that, in the end, shaped the political and social categories of our contemporary politics, with the notion of a 'People' prevailing over a 'multitude'.

Thomas Hobbes, a key thinker of the distinction between these two terms, is well known to have mistrusted the idea of the multitude. On the distinction, Hobbes writes in *De Cive*: '*a people* is a *single* entity, with a *single will*; you can attribute *an act* to it. None of this can be said of a Multitude.'[50] The key differentiating factor then, is the unity of the will in the People. The multitude, for Hobbes, is in a sense something which precedes the 'body politic' and politics proper. Foucault expressed this clearly, stating that the theory of sovereignty characterises itself through the following formula: a subject-to-subject cycle.[51] In other words, the subject *qua* human being is not thought as immediately political, but rather enters into a body politic by 'giving up' a part of themselves. 'Sovereignty', Foucault writes, 'is the theory that goes from subject to subject and establishes the political relationship between subject and subject'[52] – where, in terms of sovereignty, an assumption exists from the beginning of a multitude whose powers are not-yet political. Instead, these powers 'are capacities, possibilities, potentials, and it can constitute them in the political sense of the term only if it has in the meantime established a moment of fundamental and foundational unity between possibilities and power, namely the unity of power'.[53]

This 'unity of power' can be said to be embodied in the idea of a single will. Indeed, for Hobbes, a '*combination* of several wills' is impractical for the preservation of peace and defence. A single will [*una voluntas*] is required, which can only happen if 'each man subjects his *will* to the *will* of a *single* other [*alterius unius*], to the *will*, that is, of one *Man* [*Hominis*] or of one *Assembly* [*Concilium*], in such a way that whatever one *wills* on matters essential to the common peace may be taken as the *will* of all and each [*omnes et singuli*]'.[54] The multitude, then, cannot be trusted for it resists political unity, therefore never attaining, as Virno puts it, 'the status of the juridical person', since its own natural rights are never given over to the sovereign.[55] The problem, it would seem, is an ontological one, in that what prevents this transfer from occurring in the first place is the irreparable incompatibility of the multitude with the notions of people and the State. As Virno argues, it is '[the multitude's] very mode of being (through its plural character) and by its mode of behaving'[56] that situates it in an alternate image of thought, rhythm, frequency than that required by sovereignty.

It is through Hobbes' reading of Aristotle's *Politics* that this fundamental incompatibility of the multitude with the notions of a people and the State can be most clearly elucidated. Hobbes shows that, for Aristotle, in addition to man understood as a political animal, one can count

---

[49] Paolo Virno, *A Grammar of the Multitude* (Semiotext(e) 2004) 21.
[50] Thomas Hobbes, *On the Citizen* (Cambridge University Press 2003) 137.
[51] Michel Foucault, *Society Must Be Defended* (Penguin Books 2004) 43.
[52] Foucault, *Society Must Be Defended* (n 51) 43.
[53] Foucault, *Society Must Be Defended* (n 51) 44.
[54] Hobbes, *On the Citizen* (n 50) 72.
[55] Virno, *Grammar of Multitude* (n 49) 23.
[56] Virno, *Grammar of Multitude* (n 49) 23.

the ant and the bee, since, while the insects are lacking in *logos* or reason, they nevertheless direct their actions to a common end. However, Hobbes adds the following caveat: 'their swarms are still not *commonwealths* [*civitates*], and so the animals themselves should not be called political, for their government is only an accord, of many wills with one object, not (as a commonwealth needs) one will.'[57] The conflicting theme rests on the idea of a multiplicity of wills on the one hand, and a singular will on the other. The latter is a primary qualification for entry into a political community. In this sense, the multitude for Hobbes has no real political significance; instead, it is pre-political and must be eradicated for the formation of the State. Rather, in Agamben's words, 'it is the unpolitical element upon whose exclusion the city is founded.'[58]

In reality, this 'subject-to-subject' cycle reveals a fundamental paradox: in order that a subject exist in a political community, they must give up a part of themselves to become counted as part of a people which, in essence, does not exist. Agamben reminds us that the Commonwealth, or political body, does not coincide with the physical 'body' of the city.[59] The Leviathan, after all, is an artificial Man, a 'phantasm', and yet 'the artifice is effective because it grants unity to a multiplicity'.[60] In this sense, one can understand how 'the unification of the multitude of citizens in a single person is something like a perspectival illusion; political representation is only an optical representation (but no less effective on account of this)'.[61] In other words, the optical representation is effective in that it effectuates a transformation of wills to one will, though without erasing the material existence of the multitude itself. The potential of a dissolved multitude continues to exist, albeit in a repressed form. As Agamben argues, the formation of the human species into a political body can only take place through a splitting of 'naked life (people) and political existence (People)' so that '*[t]he concept of people always already contains within itself the fundamental biopolitical fracture. It is what cannot be included in the whole of which it is a part as well as what cannot belong to the whole in which it is always already included.*' [italics in original][62]

In other words, the language of power demands that something, a fundamental and inseparable part of life, be identified, divided and excluded, in order to enter into the city; in order to constitute a People and thereby, in a sense, gain access to a qualified life. However, this conceptualisation of the human being is an abstraction, there can be no splitting, no prioritising, of the multiplicity of sensations, imaginations, tastes, thoughts, contemplations, logos, that make up the living. It is in this sense that one can understand Nathan Moore's conceptualisation of the problematic of law. For Moore, law is trapped in a perpetual adulation for the origin, as ground or foundation; establishing the 'source' of law and legal relation *always* as one between ruler and ruled.[63] The miraculous dressing room – replete with dance and play, taste and sensibility, savvy skills and wit – was necessarily part of the city; neighbours to Parisians. And yet, a collective of singularities composing the multitude which the juridico-political order could not tolerate, and the language of power had, at any cost, to eradicate. The inhabit-

---

[57] Hobbes, *On the Citizen* (n 50) 71.
[58] Giorgio Agamben, *Stasis: Civil War as a Political Paradigm* (Stanford University Press 2015) 47.
[59] Agamben, *Stasis* (n 58) 37.
[60] Agamben, *Stasis* (n 58) 41.
[61] Agamben, *Stasis* (n 58) 41.
[62] Agamben, *Means Without End: Notes on Politics* (University of Minnesota Press 2000) 32.
[63] Nathan Moore, 'The Perception of the Middle' in Laurent de Sutter and Kyle McGee (eds), *Deleuze and Law* (Edinburgh University Press 2012) 133.

ants of the *Cour* were expelled, but never disappeared; lying under and haunting the city, the spirit of the multitude can only keep returning to demand a life of possibilities.

DIALECT WITHOUT WORLD

> Every day a string is plucked from the guitar of dialect. […] Those who speak them are like birds that sing in a cage.[64]

During the early seventeenth century, the language and jargon of the inhabitants of the *Cour des Miracles* came to be the object of numerous literary works known as the literature of roguery. The literature of roguery shared a common thread, as the historian Roger Chartier says: 'whether they mask fictions as truth or use the recounting of true events to support comic, picaresque, or burlesque elements of the author's invention, they all describe the society of rogues [*gueux*].'[65] One such work was Ollivier Chereau's *Le Jargon ou le langage de l'argot reformé* [Jargon or the reformed language of the argot]. The work is an assemblage of different texts, including a dictionary, songs and detailed descriptions of different types of rogues. In the preface to the work, Chereau says: 'If the philosopher Epicurus was of this time, he would have found worthy disciples: they faithfully practiced the doctrine that he had advocated, since their felicity and highest pleasure was to eat well and not work.'[66]

Chereau's distaste for a way of life that appeared hedonistic, combining pleasure and idleness, and altogether fantastical is evident; this form of living was a far cry from the orderly society abiding by a so-called ethical transcendence of work. The *Cour des Miracles* is not explicitly mentioned in this edition, but the early editions did mention it; though this was subsequently removed from later editions, it is clear in the work that the rogues mentioned were the inhabitants of the *Cour*. Chereau's introduction contains what seems to be almost an origin story of the *Cour*, where, we are told, an independent King of France, along with select merchants, established assemblies across a number of cities where their special language was introduced, along with their customs and rituals. This special language and the customs and rituals were taught to large crowds of the poor, according to Chereau, and in exchange the poor would teach them how to beg: 'from there emerged the grave and famous vagrants who ordained the great disorder that subsequently ensued.'[67] Chereau follows this introduction with a dictionary of the aforementioned jargon, intended to act as a lexicon for readers to use to decipher the fables and songs that follow. A few words and phrases include:

> **Artie** – *signifie pain* [Artie – means bread]
> **Artie de gros Guillaume** – *du pain noir* [Fat William's Artie – black bread]
> **Empoucher la foucauderie** – *c'est quand les coupeurs de sources jettent ce qu'ils ont defrobé de peur d'être surprise* [Preventing foucauderie – when thieves abandon their loot for fear of being caught]
> **Ficher la colle gourdement** – *c'est être bon tricheur en perfection* [Stick the glue in a gutter – to be a perfectly good cheat]

---

[64] Pier Paolo Pasolini, *Scritti corsari* (Garzanti 2019).
[65] Roger Chartier, *The Cultural Uses of Print in Early Modern France* (Princeton University Press 1987) 266.
[66] Olivier Chereau, *Le Jargon, ou le langage de l'argot reformé, comme il est à présent en usage parmy les bons pauvres* (Yves Girardon 1660) ii.
[67] Chereau, *Le Jargon* (n 66) 2–3.

Débrider la lourde sans tournante – *c'est ouvrir une porte sans clé* [Unbridle the door without turning – to open a door without a key].[68]

Chereau's work joins others from the same period derived from a tradition of Carnival literature. As Roger Chartier explains in *The Cultural Uses of Print in Early Modern France*, the texts often parodied juridical and medical texts, often with the aim of subverting rules, mocking genres and distorting language.[69] This word-play conjured a world in the Parisian imaginary which was altogether far removed from social norms. Though the account is fictional, and the language and jargon have little bearing on the speech of the *Cour*'s inhabitants, the truth is that this jargon existed, and its contents were known only to the speakers. In *L'Essence du jargon* (1994), Alice Becker-Ho notes that the language spoken by these 'dangerous classes', of which the inhabitants of the *Cour* formed a part, was a secret language, developed out of a desire to create a world. As Becker-Ho describes:

> One is not born a dangerous class. One *becomes* dangerous when one no longer recognises the values and constraints of a world from which one has freed oneself: that is, essentially, the necessity of salaried work. It is on this boundary that the distinction between the working class and the dangerous class can be delineated.[70]

What is at stake, then, is a *demand* to persevere in an experience such as they desire it to be; a form-of-life that, in no uncertain terms, both rejects and refuses the ethical transcendence of the value of work attached to exchange value, refusing the ontological separation between being and having-to-be that such a transformation necessarily entails. It can be understood as a process of appropriating domination, a gesture of dominating *dominium* itself.

Twentieth-century linguists would later lay claim to the language of the argot, tracing an apparent etymology and claiming the origins to be French, old French, Latin, Greek, and other foreign languages – however, without success.[71] Instead, Becker-Ho argues: 'argot, that truly existed during this period, would not have been as hermetic, or effective, if it had borrowed from existing dialects the majority of its vocabulary, as the linguists argue.'[72] In order to survive, it was common for the speakers of jargon to use words that could very well sound French but have little to do with it – and this was part of the argot's savviness, giving the appearance of blending in, all the while advancing along a different plane. In reality, the jargon or argot was composed of a multiplicity of words drawn from a number of languages reflective of the nomadic lives of the multiplicities known today as the 'dangerous classes', with influences from Greek, Turkish, Armenian, Arabic, Slavonic, Romanian, Gitan and Judeo-German.[73] As Becker-Ho says: 'argot is a language spoken in secret and written on water.'[74] Perhaps the most important influence on the language of the argot is the Yiddish language, yet, as Kafka has written on Yiddish:

---

[68] A selection from Chereau, *Le Jargon* (n 66).
[69] Chartier, *The Cultural Uses of Print* (n 65) 285–6.
[70] Alice Becker-Ho, *L'Essence du jargon* (Gallimard 1994) 52.
[71] Becker-Ho, *L'essence du jargon* (n 70) 25.
[72] Becker-Ho, *L'essence du jargon* (n 70) 28.
[73] Becker-Ho, *L'essence du jargon* (n 70) 75.
[74] Becker-Ho, *L'essence du jargon* (n 70) 71.

> It consists solely of foreign words. But these words are not firmly rooted in it, they retain the speed and liveliness with which they were adopted. Great Migrations move through Yiddish, from one end to the other. All this German, Hebrew, French, English, Slavonic, Dutch, Romanian, and even Latin, is seized curiosity and frivolity once it is contained within Yiddish, and takes a good deal of strength to hold all these languages together in this state [...] It is only the argot that is in the habit of borrowing from it.[75]

This is reminiscent of Victor Hugo's description that we encountered earlier: 'all seemed to be in common among these people; all went together, they mingled, confounded, superposed; each one there participated in all.' The shared experience of the errancy of life characterises the multiplicity, sharing a world in the argot. The argot, a language without origin, is nomadic, immanent to the lifeworld of the multiplicity; inseparable from it. 'The argot appears, transforms itself, disappears only to reappear, without being able to know where it came from nor where it went.'[76] Moreover, as Becker-Ho reminds us:

> This language is not simply discreet and defensive. It theorises what is about to be done: it already is a project. It never talks for the sake of talking. For those who can understand this language, every aspect of it carries the permanent confirmation of their vision of the world. [...] the dangerous classes enjoy the superiority over ordinary people of having created out of nothing a speech, which is artificial in form, but not arbitrary, and in which the meaning of words is divorced from the sound and image commonly attached to meaning by those languages in current use.[77]

The inhabitants of the Court of Miracles had no intention of assuming a major function, official status or majority position. They created, instead, an 'opposite dream': to 'know how to create a becoming-minor'.[78] Through the creation of a minor language, the inhabitants were able to create a world, making a new use of language a part of a form-of-life. As Goodrich writes: 'the goal of a minor jurisprudence is to cut holes in the fabric of law. The minor [...] has to create a site of temporary evacuation, by which I mean an avenue of withdrawal and return [...] and thereby the expression of a novelty in the putatively closed skein of legal rules.'[79] Thus the minor 'is the crack in the edifice, the fissure in discourse, a site of incompatibility and novelty'.[80] Indeed, in *What is a Minor Literature?*, Deleuze and Guattari show that what is in question is the creation of a minor literature within a major language, that is to say that, within the language of power, another language is produced, is made to circulate, and with it, another world is made possible. A minor language is also decidedly political and collective, where individual concerns become all the more magnified precisely because, and so long as, 'a whole other story is vibrating with it'.[81] This is the story of the inhabitants of the *Cour*'s

---

[75] Kafka, *Discours sur la langue Yiddish* cited in Becker-Ho, *L'essence du Jargon* (n 70) 70. I have cited the English translation, amending it to include 'argot', which in English is replaced with 'thieves' cant'. See Franz Kafka, 'An Introductory Talk on the Yiddish Language' in *Reading Kafka: Prague, Politics, and the Fin de Siècle* (ed.), Mark M. Anderson (Schoken Books 1989) 264.
[76] Becker-Ho, *L'essence du jargon* (n 70) 76.
[77] Alice Becker-Ho, *The Language of Those in the Know* (Digraphe 1995), tr. John McHale www.cddc.vt.edu/sionline/postsi/language.html accessed 4 March 2021.
[78] Gilles Deleuze and Félix Guattari, *Kafka: Toward a Minor Literature* (University of Minnesota Press 2003) 26–7.
[79] Peter Goodrich, 'How Strange the Change from Major to Minor' (2017) 21 *Law, Text, Culture* 30.
[80] Goodrich, 'Major to Minor' (n 79) 32.
[81] Deleuze and Guattari, *Kafka* (n 78) 17.

travails, recognising in each other the necessity of a shared tongue, that would enable them not only to evade power's grip but to persevere in their mode of being; escaping, for as long as they were able, subsumption into the inclusive-exclusion of the dominant discourse. Indeed, as Becker-Ho says, the argot 'theorises what is about to be done: it already is a project'. The form and content of the expressions directly connect both a saying and a doing; it is in this sense affective in expanding the speaker's power to act.

In the *Corsair Writings*, covering the linguistic and socio-economic transformation of Italy during the 1960s and early 1970s, Pasolini saw very well the connections between speech and world, and, in turn, the question of the mode or form of life. In an article on the 'Experiences of an Investigation of Drug Addiction among Young People in Italy', Pasolini suggests that, although the so-called sub-proletarians were poor relative to a standard of economic development, they were also 'absolutely free'[82] – so that, on entering into a developmental paradigm based on a particular notion of progress, the sub-proletarians transformed into 'poor people like everyone else'.[83] For Pasolini:

> These developments, within a few years, or even months, have reduced the old particular cultures to ruins, relegated dialects to the status of fossils, to mere speech without spirit (jargon and expressiveness have deteriorated so definitively until they have entirely disappeared: the code can no longer be recreated by those who no longer consider it to be 'their own true' means of communication). The poor therefore suddenly found themselves without their own culture, without their own language, without their own freedom: in short, without their own models whose realisation represented the reality of life on this Earth.[84]

What Pasolini is passionately evoking here is the annihilation of a mode of life, a mode of living, that is erased, paradoxically, in a process of inclusion. Jargons and dialects are erased, rendered useless, of little value. This point is further emphasised by Pasolini in a separate article, 'Ignazio Buttitta: I am a Poet'. For Pasolini, this erasure leaves a scar, since even if the dialects and jargon survive the brutality, they 'no longer comprise ways of existence'[85] so that 'those who speak them are like birds that sing in a cage'.[86]

Today, nothing remains of the inhabitants of the *Cour des Miracles*. Their story exists only in the telling of those who wanted their disappearance. And while the spirit never disappeared, the inhabitants were removed and confined in the General Hospitals, where they would learn the value of work and investment, unlearning what Sauval saw as 'one of the fundamental laws of the *Cour des Miracles*, not to leave anything for the next day'.[87] What is in question here is not an argument for a return to a past event, not a suggestion that a prior moment in history is necessarily better or worse than the present. This perspective would miss the point entirely. Rather, it is the relation between the particular and the universal, or the tension that exists between the particular and another form of the particular adopting the status of the majoritarian, and as majoritarian becomes generalisable. This generality leaves little room,

---

[82] Pasolini, *Scritti corsari* (n 64).
[83] Pasolini, *Scritti corsari* (n 64) 163.
[84] Pasolini, *Scritti corsari* (n 64) 163.
[85] Pasolini, *Scritti corsari* (n 64) 181.
[86] Pasolini, *Scritti corsari* (n 64) 181.
[87] Sauval, *Histoires et Recherches* (n 41) 512.

if any, for the appearance of singularity. This is the modest point of the chapter, and it is an ongoing enquiry: is singularity possible?

28. Soul
Jesús R. Velasco

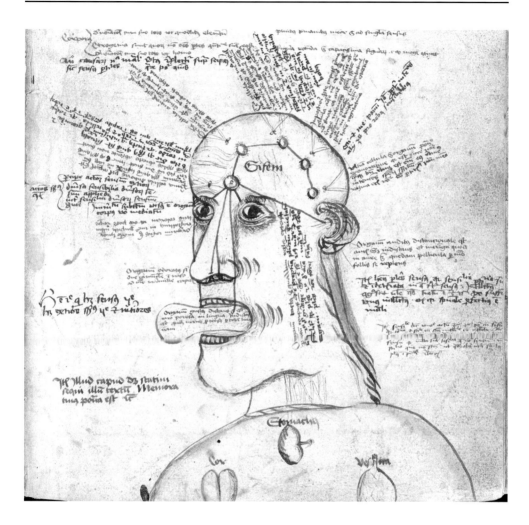

The image at the top of this chapter is a fifteenth-century drawing by Peter Gerticz of Dresden's *Parvulus philosophiae naturalis*. It was a very successful epitome of Aristotle's *De natura*, which garnered a host of commentaries in the margins. This particular manuscript, now preserved at the Wellcome Library in London, collects other psychological treatises, including Aristotle's *De anima* and *De sensu et sensato*. This diagram provided the student with all the elements that linked anatomy with aesthetics. This synoptic map devises how each of the external senses is attached to specific organs of perception with its different faculties and physical characteristics. The depiction of the nervous system gives a visual idea of their interconnection, and how they relate to other aesthetic faculties that are disseminated across the brain and inhabiting each their own *cell* – a word that conveys enclosure – with no specific external organ attached to them.[1] Those cells are the private dwellings of the post-sensorial operations that, to summarize here, we call, after Aristotle and his commentators, common sense, imagination, phantasy, estimation or thought, and memory.[2]

This image visually synthesizes the science of the soul, the realm where this chapter will partially lead us. This now expired – or maybe only dormant – science was the object of commentary and debate between late antiquity and the Middle Ages, and beyond.[3] It does encompass many interacting traditions, languages, philosophies, theologies, political stances and modalities of jurisdictional power. Here follows a not totally accurate definition of the science of the soul for most of the medieval period – the one period I work on: it is the discipline that deals with all those aspects of the human being that include the *intellect*, cognitive processes and post-sensorial operations. There are parts of the science of the soul that deal specifically with the vegetal soul and with the animal soul, but this is not where I am going to venture in this case.[4]

My interest in the science of the soul did not come from its rich, well-studied field, with a bibliography that would fill several linear miles of bookshelves. It came to me while reading a piece of legislation in the Castilian vernacular from the thirteenth century, Alfonso X's *Siete Partidas*. The legislation dealing with the science of the soul is located in the *Second Partida*, which contains administrative law. The prompt to introduce this legislation is a definition of the people as the sensitive soul of the kingdom.[5] It comes after another definition of the people

---

[1] Wellcome Library, London. Manuscript MS55, fol. 93r. A higher resolution image can be found here: https://wellcomelibrary.org/item/b19656452. There are many other similar diagrams in medieval manuscripts and modern printed books. In some cases, they are mixed up with texts that were quite well known and studied in scholarly venues different from the university – the monastery, for instance. The pseudo-Augustinian *De spiritu et anima*, as represented on Manuscript O.7.16 from the Wren Library, Trinity College, Cambridge, is an interesting example: this manuscript was created in the thirteenth century, in the midst of the debates regarding the interpretation of Aristotle's *De anima*, although it is mostly a treatise on self-care and spiritual exercises; within its pages, on fol. 42v–43r, there is a double diagram, containing an Aristotelian account of the science of the soul, and a diagram of a person with the representation of the external senses and their organs, and the internal senses and their cells. See: https://mss-cat.trin.cam.ac.uk/manuscripts/uv/view.php?n=O.7.16&n=O.7.16#?c=0&m=0&s=0&cv=26&xywh=1135%2C737%2C1556%2C1477.

[2] This account of five internal senses, with the names and order I have just offered, is not something universally accepted, and many commentators have discussed it. See Henry Austryn Wolfson, 'The Internal Senses in Latin, Arabic, and Hebrew Philosophic Texts'. *The Harvard Theological Review*. 28.2 (1935): 69–133.

[3] For the Christian scholastic Middle Ages alone, see Sander W. de Boer, *The Science of the Soul: The Commentary Tradition on Aristotle's 'De Anima', c.1260–1360*. Leuven: Leuven University Press, 2013.

[4] It would be extremely productive to engage with the question of how vegetal and animal souls are also sought after by the legal science, but, maybe invoking here the authority of Hegel, one has the right to determine the limits of one's research.

[5] This prompt, in *Partidas* 2.12, prologue. Alfonso X (that is, a series of specialized workshops under his name) composed the *Siete Partidas* between 1256 and 1265, but the work was revised and reworked many times during his kingdom, and probably afterwards, during the kingdom of Alfonso XI, especially around 1348. It has – as its name conveys – seven parts that deal with all the branches of law: ecclesiastical and canon law, administrative law, procedural law, family law, commerce and trade law, laws of succession, and penal law; furthermore, it is throughout filled with considerations on legal theory and philosophy of law, along with quasi-constitutional theories of power and jurisdiction. The sections I refer to can be found in the *Second Partida*, titles 11–13. The English translation of the *Partidas* is

as the gathering of all the subjects of the kingdom regardless of their social and economic status.[6] Eleven laws about the people as the sensitive soul of the kingdom stipulate how the people are the kingdom's external senses (six laws, including the sense of speech which resides in the tongue, like the sense of taste) and its internal senses or post-sensorial operations (five laws).[7]

I included a chapter on this legislation at the end of my book *Dead Voice*.[8] While I was writing the fifth chapter, titled 'Sensitive Souls', I wondered whether there was some kind of historical affinity between the law and the science of the soul, and whether such an affinity, if it existed, was still doing some kind of work in contemporary law and politics.

At the time of writing the chapter I wondered how the soul was to acquire some sort of legal subjectivity, and I ended up reformulating this question in a way that is similar in form, but entirely different in theoretical and practical terms: if the legal discipline had to have any interest whatsoever in the soul, it should be because the legal appropriation of the soul would give legislators and legal scholars a way, or ways, to fabricate a juridical person, that is, to define a *persona ficta*.

My current research project, therefore, intends to investigate the affinity between the legal discipline and the science of the soul – between the science of the soul and the body of law. The point of departure for my framing argument – the existence of this affinity – is that it has become, at different moments in history, naturalized, dissolved and automatized, to the point of its invisibility, and that, because of this invisibility, the affinity can continue doing a political work that is not always evident to us readers, citizens and clients of the law. In this project I expect to show, maybe only in fragments, perhaps discontinuously, how both the affinity and the processes of its naturalization have worked in several moments of remote and recent history.

Affinity, in both Johann Wolfgang von Goethe and Max Weber, presupposes a situation in which those things that are affined to each other are also in equality of conditions, rather than hierarchically ordered.[9] How long does this presupposed equality last? In my view, not very

---

easily available; the translator, Samuel Parsons Scott, was a lawyer himself, and the translation, from 1923, is plagued with technicalities that are not necessarily part of the Castilian original. Alfonso X, King of Castile and Leon, 1221–1284. *Las Siete Partidas*, ed. Robert I. Burns, trans. Samuel Parsons Scott. Philadelphia: University of Pennsylvania Press, 2001, 5 vol. I quote the *Partidas* as number of *partida* in title, or chapter in law.

[6] 'People are called the union of all men in common, those of superior, middle, and inferior condition. For all of them are necessary, and none can be excepted, for the reason that they are obliged to help one another in order to live well and be protected and supported': *Partidas* 2.10.1. In *Partidas* 7.33.6, the legislator establishes that 'men means both men and women'. Also in *Partidas* 1.2.5, 'People is the gathering of all the people from all categories in the land they converge. And there is no exception as to whether it is a man or woman, cleric or secular.'

[7] *Partidas* 2.13.

[8] Jesús R. Velasco, *Dead Voice: Law, Philosophy, and Fiction in the Iberian Middle Ages*. Philadelphia: University of Pennsylvania Press, 2020.

[9] The clearest explanation of the concept of affinity or elective affinity can be found, in my opinion, in Enrique Gavilán's translation of Max Weber's *Sociology of Religion*: Max Weber, *Sociología de la Religión*. Madrid: Istmo, 1997: 448. I was wondering whether it would have been more useful to think about the relationship between these two disciplines (law and the science of the soul) in terms of parasitics, with Murad Idris, *War for Peace: Genealogies of a Violent Ideal in Western and Islamic Thought*. Oxford: Oxford University Press, 2018. I ended up considering that parasitic relationships are more visible in themselves and in the way they display tissue damage. Affinity is more subtle, because

474 *Research handbook on law and literature*

long. My position is that the affinity between the science of the soul and the legal discipline is the result of a process of appropriation of the science of the soul by the legal science. In this process of appropriation, the very legal science transforms itself to make room for natural and metaphysical conceptions and investigations on the soul, and at the same time redefines the purview of the science of the soul. The appropriation and the ensuing transformations create the affinity. This affinity, although clearly visible at certain points and not so much in other moments, is always alive within the bodies of legislation, in the judicial process, and in the ways in which we conceive the juridical person and the subject of the law.[10]

I want to suggest that studying this affinity helps us unveil how the gatekeepers of the legal discipline deployed internal and external strategies to colonize other disciplines – that is, invade their epistemological field, exploit it and then leave with certain riches, while printing the trace of the colonizer, tattooed with pain on the surface of the invaded land. I intend to show these colonizing strategies at work in relation to the emergence, definition and epistemological purview of the science of the soul, and how this colonization defines the political extension of something we can call the *legal soulscape*, that is, the achievement of a well-meditated legal perspective regarding the science of the soul – and ultimately, the soul as a political device, whose characteristics we would still need to investigate further.

Those gatekeepers of the legal discipline are specific actors. In this chapter, which is part of my longer project, I will delve into some of those actors' works and words. Perforce, as I said, this will be a discontinuous account in which I intend to generate a conceptual map of the affinity in question. I plan to pinpoint some of the concepts generated around this affinity, to explore their theoretical productivity. Although I call them the gatekeepers, and I imagine them with fur coats; large, pointed noses; and long, thin, black Tartar's beards – just like Kafka's *Türhüter* – I hold no animosity against them. They are, in a way, my friends in this research. I need them. I respect them. I think, in the depth of my soul, that they tried to constitute a positive force. Maybe.

I will start with the moment in which Socrates discusses with Gorgias, Polus and Calicles in one of Plato's *Gorgias*. Socrates declares that for him the science of the soul is called Politics, and that the two parts of Politics are legislation and justice – the first being the operation that keeps the balance within the political body, and the second being the very endgame of any politics.[11] Socrates seems to know that he will not convince Polus or Calicles, let alone Gorgias, of anything; the same is true if we reverse the sentence, as the trio is also unable to convince a vitriolic and dismissive Socrates. The latter paves the way for telling the myth that crowns the dialogue.[12] Turning *mythos* into *logos*, the ironist explains a procedural transformation in the final judgement implemented by Zeus after the dethronement (and painful emasculation) of Chronos. The new procedures stipulate that those who are to be before the law need to

---

it presents itself as some sort of equalizing device and as the result of a voluntary election, as a common project for two things to do things together.

[10]   Of course, different legal systems call for more nuanced observations, which I expect to convey in a larger project.

[11]   Plato, *Gorgias*, 464b, in Plato. *III. Lysis. Symposium. Gorgias*, ed. W.R.M. Lamb. Cambridge: Harvard University Press (Loeb Classical Library, 166), 1991, 316 (Greek), 317 (English). I offer here a slightly different translation. 'δυοῖν ὄντοιν τοῖν πραγμάτοιν δύο λέγω τέχνας· τὴν μὲν ἐπὶ τῇ ψυχῇ πολιτικὴν καλῶ' ('There are two different things to which I assign two different arts; the one that deals with the soul, I call politics').

[12]   The whole myth is in Plato, *Gorgias*, 523a–527e.

be already dead and devoid of their bodies, so that their true self cannot be covered with the clothes of their lineage, and they will be unable, going forward, to request the favour of rich and powerful witnesses. In the newly established process even the judges (Zeus's sons) are dead and have no access to the earthly networks of the defendants. Judges and defendants are both souls, and they necessarily show the same traits of character and the same scars their earthly naked bodies sported. The logos of the myth is the argument that in order to gain access to the soul, the law needs to remove all bodily materiality. The myth of the logos is the fiction that the soul will then show with clarity all the wounds of the crimes committed. Or maybe it is the other way around.

Here, the immortality of the soul is a fulcrum to build the argument that no amount of bodily beauty, expensive elegance in your clothes, family links, riches, eloquence or verbosity will save you – only political and legal adequacy will save the soul of the citizen. For Plato (who dictates it to Socrates), political and legal life determine the history of the soul in the afterlife, and therefore the subject needs to understand the science of the soul as politics. Politics *is* of the soul.[13] Of course, we all know that the Platonic version of the science of the soul is labyrinthine, and that this is just one of its many threads, and frequently not the one the history of philosophy has taken into account.[14] Plato's *Gorgias* treats rhetoric, but I would say that its central argument is that the Science of the Soul is Politics, whose parts are the Legal Science.[15]

Indeed, nothing of this was mentioned by Aristotle when he created the science of the soul in his *On the Soul*. He created a genealogy of the science, from the pre-Socratic thinkers to Plato, but not in political or legal terms. If authors choose their predecessors, it is also clear that they choose their antagonists – and Aristotle did a great job on this front in this part of *On the Soul*. Aristotle intended to give a natural perspective on the soul, as the actualization, *entelechía*, of being, although, as scholars have pointed out, it is sometimes apparent that he considered the soul to be an instrument of the body.[16] It is the fragmentary and tentative, and yet immensely suggestive, discourse on his treatise that would transform how to talk about the soul in the following centuries. There are mountains of research on the ways in which Hellenistic neo-Platonism, neo-Pythagoricism, and neo-Aristotelianism made efforts to put in contact the Aristotelian science of the soul with the Platonic perspectives on the immortality of the soul. Likewise, we see how other important commentators were invested in connecting the Aristotelian science of the soul with Aristotelian moral disciplines, including, of course, the *Ethics* and the *Politics*. When Thomas Aquinas writes Qq 90–97 of the *Summa Theologiae* 1–2, he focuses on the fact that the law resides in the practical intellect, that is, the soul, and this interiority of the law allows him to connect it with ethical and political considerations.[17]

---

[13] 'And the name for the states of organization – says Socrates – and order of the soul is "lawful" and "law," which lead people to become law-abiding and orderly, and these are justice and self-control. Do you assent to this or not?' 483 b c d.

[14] Monique Dixsaut, *Études platoniciennes. II: Platon et la question de l'âme*. Paris: Vrin, 2013.

[15] A medieval reader of the dialogue seemed to agree with this position. In the *plutei* of the Biblioteca Laurenziana, there is a 12th (or 13th, I would say) Greek manuscript of the *Gorgias* (and other Platonic dialogues). On fol. 9r, where Socrates explains that the science of the soul is called politics and that politics is composed of legislation and justice, the reader (maybe the scribe, if I am right in the interpretation of hands) has drawn a diagram to explain exactly this thesis.

[16] See, for instance, Aristotle, *De l'âme*. Paris: Les Belles Lettres, 2009, vii–xxiv.

[17] These *quaestiones* are frequently placed under the rubric 'treatise on law'. Thomas Aquinas, *The Treatise on Law. Summa Theologiae, I–II*. South Bend: Notre Dame University Press, 1993, 90–97.

Some of the Aristotelian commentaries are specifically important for the elaboration of the concept of *nómos émpsychos* or, in Latin, *lex animata*. This is one of the crucial moments of the affinity between the science of the soul and the legal discipline. These expressions are correctly translated as *living law*, thus dovetailing with the metonymy already present in Aristotelian theses: that being alive is being animated, because the soul is the vital principle of being. I would prefer, however, *animated law*, or even, using a nineteenth-century lexical invention, *insouled law*.[18] If we see this legal and political doctrine, according to which certain figures are to be considered *animated law*, as an expression of the science of the soul in legal theories, we may have a better understanding of the processes whereby legal and political thought is increasingly interested in the ways in which good political actors – whether citizens or not – perceive and, above all, perform all the other post-sensorial operations, chief among them memory.

Now, as we know, different authors attribute the *insoulment* of the law to different actors: for Philo of Alexandria, it is Moses, and for Clement of Alexandria it was Jesus, and in both cases this is because they were the conveyors of the *orthos logos*, the correct discourse of the divine word; for Justinian it was the emperor who could and needed to be considered the *lex animata* – his body now turned into the *Corpus Iustiniani*.[19]

---

[18] Plutarch, '*Perí tou eauton epainein anepiphthonos. De laude ipsius [contra invidia]*', in *Plutarchus: Moralia. III. 544E*, eds M. Poehlenz and W. Sieveking. (Leipzig: Teubner, 1972, 385). English translation of William Watson Goodwin, *Plutarch's Morals. Vol. 2.* Boston: Little, Brown, & Co., 1874, 306–25 (the latter accessible through Perseus Digital Library).

[19] The bibliography on the subject is large, but at the same time it follows in the footsteps of a closed tradition inaugurated in hellenistic times around the group of treatises, or fragments of treatises, known as *Perí Basileías*, or *On Monarchy*, preserved in the second part of the *Anthologia* of Stobaeus. Stobaeus gathered those fragments of authors such as Pseudo Ecphantus, Pseudo Archytas, Diotogenes or Sthenides. In English, the treatises were compiled and translated in the work of Thomas Taylor, *Political fragments of Archytas, Charondas, Zaleucus, and other ancient Pythagoreans, preserved by Stobaeus, and also, Ethical fragments of Hierocles, the celebrated commentator on the golden Pythagoric verses, preserved by the same author, translated from the Greek.* Chiswick: Taylor, 1882. See Antonella Squilloni, 'Il significato etico-politico dell'immagine re-legge animata. Il "nomos empsychos" nei trattati neopitagorici "Peri Basileias"'. *Civiltà Classica e Cristiana.* 11.1 (1990): 75–94. Arthur Steinwenter, 'Nomos Empsychos: Zur Geschichte einer politischen Theorie'. *Anzeiger der Akademie des Wissenschaften in Wien* 133 (1946): 250–68, considers it a political theory. Kantorowicz thinks of *lex animata* as a doctrine to emphasize monarchical power, in *The King's Two Bodies* (Princeton: Princeton University Press, 1957). Although *lex animata* may have appeared as a political theory, or at least as a theory of a particular political idea (namely, the centrality of monarchical power), it cannot really be considered a doctrine, as it never became a mainstream operative discourse – unlike the theocracy of some monarchies, such as the French during the Middle Ages, or the English during the Early Modern period. There are hosts of shorter essays to explain the peculiarities of the expression in specific authors' work, which shed light on the metaphoric character of the notion. See for instance John Martens, '*Nómos empsychos* in Philo and Clement of Alexandria', in *Hellenization Revisited: Shaping a Christian Response Within the Greco-Roman World*, ed. Wendy E. Helleman. Lanham: University Press of America, 1994, 323–38. Justinian included this idea in his *Novellae*, 105.2.4: '*Omnibus enim a nobis dictis imperatoris excipiatur fortuna, cui et ipsas deus leges subiecit, legem animatam eum mittens hominibus: eo quod imperatori quidem iugis indesinens <est> consulatus omnibus civitatibus et populis gentibusque in singulis quae placent distribuenti, advenit autem cum ipse annuerit trabea, ideoque et imperii consulatus per omnia sit sequens sceptra.*' The idea probably arrived with Justinian through the Byzantine interest in this possible political theory, which some Christian authors, including Eusebius of Caesarea, fought against. See also J.H. Burns, ed., *The Cambridge History of Medieval Political Thought.* Cambridge: Cambridge University Press, 1988, 25–8, 64. It is not unlikely that the knowledge

King Alfonso of Castile perhaps helps us understand this form of animation or insoulment of the law when he declares that the King is the soul and the heart of the kingdom.[20] He conveys the same idea of the *lex animata*, but spelling it out in Castilian language and breaking the topological barriers that may have made this doctrine slightly opaque: instead of saying that the King is the living law, he goes back to the original meaning of the *animation*, to stipulate that the King is, to his kingdom, soul and heart. *Heart* is, indeed, one of the synonyms of soul. Paul of Tarsus works with this synonymy in his epistles. Even Al-Ghazālī deploys the synonymy of the soul in four terms: soul (nafs), spirit (rūḥ), intellect ('aql) and heart (qalb);[21] Spinoza, in the first chapter of the *Political–Theological Treatise*, explores the regimes of synonymy and polysemy of the hebreu *ruagh* (spirit), only to determine that, in some cases, it is impossible to separate it from the semantic field of 'heart'.[22]

This is just one first link that is worth pursuing, but that also points to a specific issue arising from the affinity between the legal discipline and the science of the soul, which is the world of tropologies underneath the conceptual map on which it is based. The question of the *lex animata* directs our attention to the metonymies that revolve around the idea of the soul: life, indeed, or immortality; insoulment as embodiment; transmission as transcendence, and so on. And above all, it directs our attention to the great tropology of the soul as a subject, as the focus where perceiving and knowing resides, and from which comes judgement, the very soul that is also the legal subject to be judged.

Those tropologies play an important role beyond this question of the *lex animata*. In the process of commentary of Aristotelian aesthetics throughout the centuries the soul becomes like a piece to be crafted on the potter's wheel. One of the tropes of the soul that I find of the utmost importance can be found in a few letters from the Brethren of Purity, written and disseminated sometime in the ninth century, and irradiating from Basra. Letters now catalogued as 32 to 36 deal with aesthetics, mainly the Aristotelian sensitive soul in its connections with the human being and their rational soul. In those letters, the Brethren of Purity reorganize the science of aesthetics, and the whole science of the soul, through a reading and interpretation of Pythagorean, Platonic and Aristotelian texts.[23] Although their sources are Hellenistic philosophical readings about the science of the soul previously translated, paraphrased or

---

of the *nomos empsychos/lex animata* trope in the Latin Middle Ages owes a lot to the work of Eusebius, which was translated, complemented and commented on by Hyeronimus of Stridon (saint Jerome).

[20] *Partidas* 2.1.5.

[21] Abū Hamid al-Ghazālī, *Kitāb sharḥ ʿajā'ib al-qalb. The Marvels of the Heart. Book 2 of the Iḥyā' ʿUlūm al-Dīn.* Walter James Skellie. Louisville: Fons Vitae, 2010, 5–11.

[22] Baruch Spinoza, *Traité théologico-politique. Oeuvres III*, trans. Jacqueline Lagrée and Pierre-François Moreau. Paris: PUF, 2012. In his recent complete translation of the Hebrew bible, Berkeley professor Robert Alter decided to get rid of the English word *soul* as a translation for the Hebrew *nephesh* in a very bold and interesting movement. Spinoza, in a certain way, already warned, basing his attention of the word *ruah* (also translatable as 'soul', but more related to the English 'spirit') of the complications derived from the introduction of a theological concept of soul of Christian origin. See Robert Alter, trans. *The Hebrew Bible.* New York: W.W. Norton & Co., 2018. Alter addresses the question of translating *nephesh* as 'soul' on a few occasions, including his interviews with NPR and *The New York Times*.

[23] Paul E. Walker, Ismail K. Poonwala, David Simonowitz and Godefroid de Callataÿ, ed/trans. *Epistles of the Brethren of Purity: Sciences of the Soul and Intellect. Part I, An Arabic critical edition and English translation of epistles 32–36.* Oxford and New York: Oxford University Press, 2015, hereafter abbreviated to EBP.

commented in Syriac and Arabic, their point of reference is always Muslim knowledge and, in particular, Muslim law.

The theoretical explanation of the faculties of the human soul comes in the letters in the form of a metaphor. For the Brethren, a technical explanation of the way in which senses and post-sensorial operations work does not suffice, because it risks leaving behind a non-philosophical audience. Maybe this is one of the senses in which we can imagine the encounter between *kalām* and philosophy: a process whereby philosophical corpora meet an audience of interlocutors who, being religious, do not have a full grasp of the heavily specialized language of philosophical inquiry. The Brethren meet this audience at the crossroads, so to speak: by providing the people in their network with a philosophical knowledge as if it were an intervention in public humanities – relying on the power of metaphors and tropologies that make this body of knowledge intelligible and susceptible of being re-used. This form of public communication of *kalām* is not unknown to other moments of the history of Islam, including the Almohad project of Ibn Tūmart, that will find echo in Averroes' work.[24]

The choice of the metaphor is not neutral. Indeed, the Brethren use a political metaphor. We are more or less used to the metaphor of the political entity (a kingdom, for instance) as a body.[25] The Brethren reverse this metaphor: the human body, the being itself, is a kingdom. External faculties, that is, the senses, are like the king's ambassadors to other regions: the faculties of the soul serve the purpose of surveying and collecting information from the different parts of the *mamlaka* or kingdom – and assure its subsistence.

In this metaphor the human body has been eliminated from the equation, or subsumed under the preeminence of the soul. Politics is at the same level of the soul, in a regime of affinity that explains simultaneously the faculties of the soul and the modes of power circulation based on the *malik*, the king: what secures the king's power is the system of survey and surveillance that does not originate in the king's body, but in the king's soul.

The post-sensorial operations are defined using the same metaphorical structure. Imagination is like the master of maps of the king that gathers together the information about sensed things (EBP 128). Memory is the 'treasurer who safeguards the king's deposits'; the faculty to articulate external sounds, to speak, is called *al-naṭiqa*, and although it would seem easy to connect it to the ability to speak in general, it seems to be the case that this is related to the articulation of internal speech; this faculty seems to correspond to the Greek *dianoia* or thought (in the sense that thinking is speaking inside oneself) and is likened to 'the chamberlain and the dragoman to the king' – notice simply that the ability to speak is normally connected to the tongue itself as an external sense, while here it appears as an internal sense or post-sensorial operation. The productive faculty, in its turn, is the vizier, who is 'aid to the king in administering his kingdom and in assisting him in his governing of his people' (EBP 129).

What interests me about this letter is the way in which the Brethren chose to explain how each of the senses, internal and external, operates. To do so, they turn the human being into a kingdom, a political entity for which external and internal senses perform political and legal operations, from gathering information and bringing it to the centre of power of the kingdom to translating it or to archiving it. The whole aesthetic system is here a legal and political tropological operation that, once again, puts forth the construction of this affinity between the

---

[24] See Averroes, *Discours décisif [Fasl al-maqāl fīmā bain ash-sharī'ah wa al-hikmah min al-ittisāl]*. Marc Geoffroy, ed. Introduction by Alain de Libera. Paris: GF-Flammarion, 1996.
[25] Hobbes? Hobbes!

legal science and the science of the soul. In this case, the affinity has two different purposes: understanding aesthetics by means of political and legal concepts, certainly, but also creating an idea of the political being as a subject endowed with a sensitive soul. Subjects are subjects because their soul can be interpreted politically.

The affinity between the legal discipline and the science of the law is frequently messy because it involves the participation of theology. This means that there is another affinity at play, although of a different character. In the affinity between law and theology both disciplines seem to benefit equally from one another, but the reader may feel sometimes perplexed about the identity and epistemological integrity of each of these disciplines, which seem to morph into each other constantly: the law becomes theology; theology acquires normative power and dovetails and gets entwined with legal science. This perplexity is tremendously productive because it helps those two sciences to reinforce one another.

So, maybe when we read al-Ghazālī's influential *Iḥyā' 'Ulūm al-Dīn* or *Revival of Religion*, or his no less influential, and translated into Latin during the thirteenth century, *Refutation of the Philosophers*, we have the very reasonable reaction of looking at those treatises as a product of *kalam* and theology that seem to muddle their reflection on the law. However, al-Ghazālī himself helps us dispel such reaction: in a vein that is common among Muslim thinkers, the point of reference of the reflections is to fathom what is legal and separate it from what is not legal. His purpose is to understand the regime of legality, the modalities of legality of what is legal – whether mandatory, optional, recommended, and so on. In other words, those reflections are theological or philosophical reflections *before the law*.[26]

The language of the law, here, is what matters most, the semantic precision of the legal sources and the flexibility of such language. And this is something I am asking myself all the time while reading my primary sources. Semantic precision is of the essence, and I am frequently relieved when I realize that, if nothing else, al-Ghazālī is a master of semantic precision, even when such precision may work against his main argument.

Indeed, in the opening book of the section devoted to moral philosophy (the third quarter of the *Iḥyā'*), which corresponds to the 21st book of the whole treatise, al-Ghazālī begins with a complete series of distinctions based on the semantic of the concept of the soul – which, from the epigraph of the book onward, al-Ghazālī generally calls the *heart*, *al-qalb*.[27] The soul, indeed, can be called by four different names that are, each of them, polysemic: heart, soul, spirit and intellect (*qalb*, *nafs*, *rūḥ* and *'aql*). Each of these words refers to different extra-mental ideas that are independent from one another, but they are also simultaneously univocal in that they have a common second meaning. For instance, the heart corresponds to a physical, cone-shaped organ, which is not in the domain of the lawyer, but rather in that of the physician; in the second meaning, however, it is the 'tenuous substance of an ethereal spiritual sort' (MH 6), the meaning that matters to al-Ghazālī, because this substance is also what links the four names in one single idea of the soul with common functionalities: the heart (qalb) and the spirit (rūḥ) refer to the human faculties that perceive and know, while the soul (nafs) and the intellect ('aql), in their second meaning, perceive, know and constitute the self (MH 6–9). What matters most to al-Ghazālī is, in the end, the ultimate legal interpretation of

---

[26] Abū Hamid al-Ghazālī, *Kitāb al-ḥalāl wa'l- ḥarām. On the Lawful and the Unlawful*. Book 14 of the *Iḥyā' ʿUlūm al-Dīn*. Yusuf T. Delorenzo. Louisville: Fons Vitae, 2014.

[27] PAbū Hamid al-Ghazālī, *Kitāb sharḥ cajā'ib al-qalb. The Marvels of the Heart*. Book 21 of *Iḥyā' ʿUlūm al-Dīn*. Walter James Skellie, trans. Louisville: Fons Vitae, 2010, hereafter MH.

those words in the main legal source, the Qur'an, and in the customs (MH 10): wherever those words appear in those sources, either written or oral, they must be interpreted as a metonymy (*kenayah*) network – those names point to the understanding of the self that perceives and knows (MH 10).

The semantic of this kind of soul, and the metonymical networks it constitutes within the legal, allow al-Ghazālī to explore some metaphors that serve his legal and political purpose. Indeed, the heart – that is, the second sense that all those four names share, and that constitutes the knowing and perceiving self – is like a king, and as such, has two armies of servants and helpers. One of the armies is bodily and includes all external and internal organs of perception, which include 'the perception of sight, taste, smelling, hearing, and touch; and an external army, which is the eye, ear, nose, etc.' (MH 15). These armies in particular are like 'spies', and they are called knowledge (*'ilm*) and perception (*idrāk*). Those five forms of perception are in correspondence with what resides in the 'ventricles of the brain, which are also five' (MH 15). He goes on to explain how these post-sensorial operations work:

> Thus after seeing an object a man closes his eye and perceives its image (*sūra*) within himself. This is the retentive imagination (*khayāl*). This image then remains with him by reason of something which preserves it, which is the army of memory (*al-jund al-ḥāfiẓ*). He then thinks about what he has remembered and combines part with part, after which he recalls what he had forgotten and it comes back to him again. Then he gathers together in his retentive imagination all the meanings of his sense impressions by means of the common sense (*ḥiss mushtarak*). For there are within man common sense, imagination (*takhayyul*), reflection (*tafakkur*), recollection (*tadhakkur*), and memory (*ḥifẓ* – preservation). (MH 15–16)

With this reflection on the semantics of the heart or the perceiving and knowing soul of the self – which in the following book of the same third section he will refer to as *nafs* – he intends to correct the erroneous interpretations of lazy '*ulamā*' who seem to be confused about the right interpretation of the legal texts. It is obvious, however, that in order to unmake this confusion among legal scholars, al-Ghazālī is mobilizing a philosophical corpus that, like that of the Brethren before him, like the one mobilized in his interpretation of the soul by Ibn Sina before him, and like the ones being discussed by some contemporaries and future critics, including some andalusi thinkers like Ibn Bajja, Ibn Ṭufayl, Averroes, Maimonides or Ibn Falaqera, among many others, would not be possible without a thorough study and commentary of Aristotle's books on the soul and on aesthetics.

Underneath the cases I have explained, and others that I could pile up for you, there are some common elements. Although neither the Brethren nor al-Ghazālī have the task of creating legislation, they nevertheless convey that there are modes of perception and post-sensorial operations that fall into what is legal, and that have a legal interpretation of themselves, so that the law scholars or '*ulamā*' do not get it wrong. Kalam establishes the right relationships between the perceiving and knowing constitution of the self and the body of law.

A different legal experience is when a legislator undertakes the task of legislating with this affinity in mind. In that case, the questions would not be led by the need or opportunity to explain a philosophical corpus or to give an idea of the concept of the soul before the law and against the backdrop of moral philosophy, but rather the desire to regulate the modes of perception and the post-sensorial operations of the legal subject.

And, as you remember, this was where everything started. I felt I needed to know more about the fragmented genealogy of this legal experience of touching, appropriating, and turning the science of the soul into a legislative tool. That is why I started reading some of the traditions that, in my view, were the building blocks upon which Alfonso could imagine such strange and, in a way, revolutionary legislation. It is well known that Alfonso's sources are multilingual and come from very different traditions, but the critique of sources would never be enough to understand Alfonso's work. If anything, Alfonso is in the middle of a larger conversation that involves Iberian, Mediterranean and Middle Eastern connections. It does not seem that he wants to adhere specifically to any of them in an exclusive way; rather he seems to want to advance a legal epistemology that will break the spell of specific forms of perplexity, impasse or even fear that could hamper the construction of a large, authoritarian, profoundly centralized form of monarchical power.

What would be the reasons why the science of the law, legal scholars, legislators and other people involved in the study and discussion of legal matters, including, of course, philosophers, would be interested in appropriating the science of the soul? Let's imagine immediately that the main reason would be the immortality of the soul, and conceiving the soul as a divine breath, the soul being life itself – both physical and metaphysical life. And I would not disagree with this.

However, the real legal interest in the soul regards the sensitive soul, the soul that is, in fact, the *lower* soul, as al-Ghazālī puts it; that is, the one that is in charge of perception and post-sensorial operations. This is not the immortal soul, but the mortal life – as Martin Hägglund puts it, it is a reflection on *this life*. In other words, when we talk about the affinity between the law and the science of the soul, what we are talking about is how the law defines and discusses the ways in which the subject must – or should – perceive, and which kind of internal operations are lawful and which ones aren't.

This fundamental distinction indicates that the affinity between these two disciplines is instrumental for the creation of a juridical subject whose *persona ficta* or artificial person is soul, rather than body. This is interesting at many levels, but perhaps the most important one is the ability of the law to *access* perceptions and post-sensorial operations and redefine them in legal and political terms, rather than in strictly natural ways. It then falls on the side of the law to explain how *the people*, that is, juridical subjects, perceive, and the kinds of things they do with those perceptions.

Al-Ghazālī seems to be able to invent expressions that are simply splendid to promote to the rank of concepts to think beyond a specific period in history. One of them is *al-ḥadith al-nafs*, which translates as something like a narrative that the soul presents to the self, the inner voice, the inner rationalization, if you wish, that agrees with the right, legal modes of perception and knowing of the self.

It seems to me that the affinity of the law with the science of the soul aims to create that narrative, to legalize that narrative in such a way that the legislators may hack the processes of subjectivity, the very construction of subjects.

When I was planning this project, I thought I would not write it as a scholar. I thought I would write it as some sort of public intellectual – although I am neither public nor, let alone, an intellectual. But I thought it was the right way to do it, if one had not just the knowledge, but also the linguistic skills (in English!) to do it that way. This is because I am perhaps less interested in Alfonso, Al-Ghazālī and other dead dudes, and more interested in Miguel, who is my five-year-old, and Simone, my one-year-old daughter, born in April 2020 at the peak of the pandemic. Not that I wanted to get their interest – I am not that dumb. I simply thought that the way in which we perceive, imagine, memorize things is nowadays subject to scrutiny.

Power structures around us – of which the state is perhaps the least important – such as the corporations behind social media gather and market our most intimate information, even our DNA; these power structures are hacking our soul constantly, and mainly because we are eager to share those perceptions and post-sensorial operations. Maybe the study of this affinity can give us a certain perspective about how voluntary forms of servitude and the legalization of the modes of perception and the politics of the soul have worked, and what kind of work they may be still doing at different levels of our existence, private and public. What kind of soul storytelling we put at the disposition of corporations and other structures of ultra-liberal domination may define how we want to build the soulscape around us.

29. Ambiguity
Susan Byrne

Practitioners of the juridical and political arts have long embellished their prose with images borrowed from the writings of creative artists. To support arguments regarding contracts of purchase and sale, Emperor Justinian's counsellors used a barter scene from Homer's *Iliad*.[1] As they tried to construct a democratic republic, the writers of the United States Constitution exchanged letters describing their difficulties as a quixotic battle against windmills.[2] Contemporary examples abound, in legal opinions with citations to Shakespeare, Kafka, Charles Dickens and Bob Dylan.[3]

There is a mirror-image tradition of juridical citation in creative work, with legal themes and detail functioning as adornment or, in some cases, as structural basis for fictional writings. What we call poetic justice is frequently the displacement to a fictional environment of topics on fair-dealing frustrated in real-world settings. The authors of medieval debate literature approached such questioning through characters styled as opposing counsel who rendered opinions on everything from the best lover (priest or soldier?) to the best beverage (water or wine?) or the assignation of blame in matters of love (man or woman?). One fifteenth-century Spanish debate piece (*Grisel y Mirabella*) begins with a pair of lovers meeting illicitly. When caught, each self-accuses so as to absolve the other of culpability. Frustrated in his wish to see justice done, the king contracts a pair of attorneys to argue against each of their wishes, that is, to blame the other party. When the male attorney is judged to have won, the queen and her female courtesans enact an Orphic ritual: they invite the victorious male advocate to a tryst with the female attorney but instead tie him to a stake, torture him with words, teeth and nails while dining leisurely, then burn him to death. Each female will carry a small pouch of his ashes around her neck, commemorating justice enacted as byzantine cult ritual.

In the early seventeenth-century *Don Quijote*, Spanish author Miguel de Cervantes formulates what I have called a *mos hispanicus*, a creative and defiant challenge to the legal authorities and processes of his day.[4] He does so in a text that he called a history but modern

---

[1] Institutions III.17: precedent for an exchange of goods rather than coin is found in Homer's text, when the Greeks barter for wine in exchange for copper, steel, animal skins, oxen and slaves. *See* Institutes, Fordham University Medieval Sourcebook: Corpus Iuris Civilis: *Institutes* (535 CE). Ed. Paul Halsall. https://sourcebooks.fordham.edu/basis/535institutes.asp.

[2] *See* Susan Byrne, 'Chapter 2. Constitutions', in *A Cultural History of Law in the Early Modern Age (1500–1680)*, ed. Peter Goodrich. Vol. 3 of 6-volume *Cultural History of Law* (Bloomsbury Academic, 2019) 39–64.

[3] *See* Alex B. Long, 'The Freewheelin' Judiciary: A Bob Dylan Anthology' 38.5 Fordham Urban Law Journal, Special Issue: Symposium – Bob Dylan and the Law (2012) 1363–83; Jules Gleicher, 'The Bard at the Bar: Some Citations of Shakespeare by the United States Supreme Court' 26.1 Oklahoma City Law Review (2001) 327–54; Juan Francisco Soto Hoyos, 'Jurisprudencia literaria en Colombia: los usos de la literatura en las decisiones judiciales' 2.2 Summa Iuris (2014) 217–51; Mariantuá Correa Bedoya, 'El lenguaje del podre y el poder del lenguaje: literatura en las sentencias de la Corte Constitucional Colombiana', Tesis, Abogado (Universidad de los Andes, 2018).

[4] *See* Susan Byrne, *Law and History in Cervantes'* Don Quijote (University of Toronto Press, 2012).

scholarship recognizes as the first modern novel, an enormously successful portrait of one man's pursuit of justice as imagined ideal. It is perhaps telling that the protagonist's sanity is a focal point of debate in the novel, and would remain so for centuries: ideal justice might be an impossible dream for all but the mad. For half a century prior to the publication of that novel, Spanish jurists had debated the merits and flaws of both the *mos italicus* and the *mos gallicus* approaches to historical legal reasoning. They did so in the context of Spain's bureaucratic centralized state forming itself on the shaky foundation of its own contradictory legal statutes and practices.[5] In his fictional search for justice, Cervantes incorporates all three divisions of Aristotelian rhetoric: *inventio* in his use of fundamental legal questions as subject matter; *elocutio* with, for example, the introduction of ambiguity into single words or adverbial phrases that contradict and undermine the words they modify; and *dispositio* in the construction of larger units of discourse as counterpoint to official legal volumes and practices. Cervantes had to fashion his fiction in a way that would evade the censorship of his day, and as just one example of his prowess with enigmatic legal messaging: one word that was read for four centuries as a simple synonym (a masked *elocutio*) turns out to be the clue to a critique (*inventio*) of both State and Ecclesiastical Court practices (*dispositio*).[6] Cervantes styles ambiguity into juridical hypotheticals that present complex yet very entertaining intellectual challenges to the imagination.[7]

That is the *raison d'etre* for the two words that serve as alpha and omega in my topic: ambiguity and hypothetical. Both constitute challenges to precision in verbatim, logical representation. From a literary sensibility, the converse side of that inexactitude is rewarding: ambiguity can be perfection in use of the poetic word, and hypotheticals confront a reader's critical intellect.

In law, ambiguity is generally read as problematic indeterminacy in interpretation,[8] particularly in 'situations in which an expression has two or more perfectly clear meanings'.[9] Noting the paradox that 'the word *ambiguity* itself has more than one interpretation', Sanford Shane recognizes another, non-judicial 'restricted meaning […] concerned with certain lexical and grammatical properties that are part of the very fabric of language'.[10] This is the sense studied by Andrea Alciato in the first half of the sixteenth century, when the Italian humanist noted that ambiguities in law frequently stem from a failure to understand the full contextualized intention of a writer or speaker. He argued for the importance of usage and custom in such lexical matters, rather than strict adherence to authority.[11] In creative texts, all those same basic characteristics make ambiguity the great enabler of irony, allegory, satire, double entendre

---

[5]   For full detail, *see* Byrne (2012) 45–51.
[6]   *See* Byrne (2012) 62–74.
[7]   Forcione has noted that 'the conventional technique of exemplary fiction' is to 'create characters according to ideas'. *See* Alban Forcione, *Cervantes and the Humanist Vision: A Study of Four Exemplary Novels* (Princeton University Press, 1982) 13. For Cervantes, those central ideas frequently revolve around the themes of law and justice.
[8]   *See* Ralf Poscher, 'Ambiguity and Vagueness in Legal Interpretation', in *Oxford Handbook on Language and Law*, eds Lawrence M. Solan and Peter M. Tiersma (Oxford University Press, 2012).
[9]   *See* Lawrence M. Solan, 'Vagueness and Ambiguity in Legal Interpretation', in *Vagueness in Normative Texts*, eds Vijay Kumar Bhatia and Jan Engberg (Peter Lang, 2005) 73.
[10] *See* Sanford Shane, 'Ambiguity and Misunderstanding in the Law' 25 T Jefferson Law Review (2002) 167–94.
[11] *See* Denis L. Drysdall, 'A Lawyer's Language Theory: Alciato's De verborum significatione' 9.2 Emblematica (1995) 269–92.

and any type of mixed messaging, whether intentional or found in subsequent (mis)readings. William Empson identified seven types of this 'phenomenon of compression' in verse and his seventh model, 'psychological rather than logical', parallels the ambiguity in prose found by Manuel Durán in Cervantes's characterizations of a truly subjective reality in *Don Quijote*.[12] Highlighting the generic instability of that first modern novel, Nicolás Antonio would categorize it as 'poetic prose' in a late seventeenth-century bibliography.[13]

Whereas the intellectual, melodic and suggestive density of verse liberates language for a multiplicity of images and associations, Cervantes uses ambiguity in prose to create a rich, dissonant background for dissembling and dissimulating, specifically regarding contentious legal matters of his day. He builds poetic indeterminacy of interpretation into his prose, activating the reader's imagination within that more mimetic, constricted genre so as to linguistically, lexically and logically transcend both the legal and literary mores of his day.

Interpretive ambiguity is inherent in my topic's omega term, hypothetical, which can be the bane of experiential legal studies, or relief from the same: 'many hypotheticals have been written not so much for pedagogy as for humor. The best of these, while indicating the foibles of the law, are nonetheless instructive.'[14] Hypotheticals 'use the imagination to supply what life has not yet presented',[15] and they challenge reliance on absolutes.

The best fiction does the same and in what follows, I will highlight two examples of Cervantes' use of ambiguous legal hypotheticals in a collection of short stories published in 1613 and titled *Novelas ejemplares* (*Exemplary Novels*).[16] The author reads the law, then rewrites it with a jaundiced eye, defying juridically determined social mores, and questioning authority through opaque insinuation and ironic innuendo. My first example is broad and diffuse, scattered throughout the collection of stories as a topos regarding the age of legal culpability; the second is specific to 'La gitanilla', a story much debated for its complex messaging on social class and ethnicity. I propose that Cervantes' manipulation of legal specificities should be read as a literary trope, a concrete building block of his narrative style, as well as a direct challenge to the thought process of his reader.

As background to my first example: age is a standard operative factor in societal, governmental and juridical determinations: the age of reason for testimonial credibility, for schooling, driving a car, military service, voting, control over an inheritance, and a variety of other elements of daily existence, all made today primarily on the basis of documented chronological specificity.

In the late sixteenth century when Cervantes began to pen his *Novelas ejemplares*, Spanish legislation on such age determinants had to a certain extent coalesced, if still a bit uneasily and with a good deal of variation, around the numbers in Emperor Justinian's Digest. That source

---

[12] *See* William Empson, *7 Types of Ambiguity* (first published, 1936, New Directions, 1966) 31; 192. *See* Manuel Durán, *La ambigüedad en el Quijote* (Universidad de Veracruz, 1960). Others have noted ambiguity in Cervantes' writings in the sense of mixed reception, or contradictions of readerly expectation, but Durán highlights the socio-historical and literary precedents that paved the way for the author's iconoclastic perspectivism.

[13] *See* Nicholás Antonio, *Bibliotheca Hispana Nova* (first published, 1672, Fundación Universitaria Española, 1999).

[14] *See* Scott J. Burnham, 'The Hypothetical Case in the Classroom' 37 J Legal Education (1987) 406.

[15] *See* Paul Gewirtz, 'The Jurisprudence of Hypotheticals' 32 J Legal Education (1982) 120.

[16] *See* Miguel de Cervantes, *Novelas ejemplares*, 2 vols., ed. Harry Sieber (Cátedra, 1995). All translations from Spanish to English from this text and others included herein are my own.

offers details on debates between Roman jurists regarding the propriety of age determined by direct visual examination of pudendal traits versus decisions based on chronological age as the sole governing factor. Gaius provides two options: visual bodily condition or specification of 13 years. Paul allows that males testify at 14 years of age and females at 12. Ulpian bases his reasoning on the end of the status of tutor or guardianship, which coincided with puberty, to offer a slight variation: either 14 years or both conditions, chronological confirmed by corporal inspection. By the sixth century, visual inspections for females had been deemed immoral and Justinian extended that consideration to males, deciding for 14 years of age in the male and 12 in the female, as the direct chronological ages determinative of the condition *puber*. Earlier stages of human development were similarly labelled according to precise age: *infans* ended at seven years of age, *impuber* extended from 7 to 12 or 14 depending on gender, and the intermediary stages were further subdivided mathematically. Glosses in the legal volumes detail division between 7 and 12 (female) or 14 (male), leading to 9½ as the age of earliest possible culpability for a female, and 10½ for the male. Labels codified the corresponding societal conditions: between seven and 9½ or 10½ was *infans proximus* while the stage from those ages to 12/14 was *puber proximus*.

By the time Justinian's legal codes were rediscovered and studied in Bologna in the eleventh and twelfth centuries, the Iberian Peninsula's operative legal tomes included the seventh-century Visigothic Liber iudiciorum and the local *fueros* or law books granted to cities and towns beginning in the eighth century, during a process called the Reconquest that would continue to 1492. Among these volumes, the variants in specifications on legal age of reason are striking.

The *Liber iudiciorum* (year 671) specifies 14 for permission to give testimony and consideration as an adult, allowing for 10 in urgent matters. Neither the *Fuero de Jaca* (year 1063) nor the *Fuero de Ledesma* (year 1111) rules on the age for testimonial credibility, but the first extends the age of adulthood to 20, while the second allows the same status at the age of 15. The *Fuero de Navarra* (year 1194) provides that at the age of seven, one is to be considered an adult and granted testimonial credibility. Neither the *Fuero de Plasencia* (twelfth century) nor the *Fuero de Madrid* (year 1202) speaks to age for testimony, but the first allows that an orphan will be considered an adult at the age of 13. The *Fuero de Zamora* (year 1208) and the *Fuero de Salamanca* (year 1229) are silent on the age for adulthood but they specify, respectively, 14 and 15 years for giving testimony. The *Fuero de Béjar* (end of thirteenth–beginning of fourteenth century) allows that at the age of 12, one is an adult and allowed to testify.

The variants in those early documents are further confounded in the *Fuero Real* (year 1254), despite its having been promulgated specifically as a means to reconcile them. This volume's law on testimony and proofs specifies 16 years as the age for giving testimony, but adds a gloss with three different ages: 14, 12 or 20, depending on the circumstances, severity of the charge and gender of the witness. In a separate law, the phrase 'of age' is glossed to mean 14 years old, a number justified by the *impuber*'s lack of juridical knowledge and discretion. The *Fuero Real* allows that one may be a legal spokesperson (*vocero*) at the age of 25. As to *pro se* representation, at the age of 14 one may file a lawsuit but there is a caveat: if the results are favourable, the win is awarded; if not, the youthful *pro se* practitioner is indemnified from any damages incurred. To contract matrimony, a male must be 14 and a female 12 but, should either's parents not be in favour of the match, the hopeful spouse must wait until the age of 30 to move forward with the marriage. Other related specifications include: one may adopt at 18 and one may care for an orphan at 20, while in the case of an abandoned child, s/he must be raised and cared for until the age of ten.

In the mid-thirteenth century *Siete Partidas*, a collection promulgated to merge Peninsular law with that of the rediscovered Roman jurists, the numbers are taken directly from Justinian's volumes. A child is *infans* until the age of seven and *puber* at 12 if female and at 14 if male, with the same midpoint of 9½ or 10½, for the same respective genders, as the ages at which legal culpability begins. This precise marker is directly referenced in the early thirteenth-century epic poem *Cantar de mío Cid*, which includes a nine-year-old female who dares to inform the exiled hero of the king's prohibition against contact with him. Why can she take that risk in the face of the king's threatened punishments for speaking with him, which include the loss of her eyes? Because she is six months shy of the 9½ year marker for liability for her acts.[17] This and other details in the epic poem suggest a jurist familiar with Justinian's *Digest* as author.

Over time, the specific ages from Justinian's volumes, as reflected in the *Siete Partidas*, would strengthen in juridical force and reliability. By the mid-sixteenth century, local *fueros* were only somewhat superseded by the slightly more standardized *Recopilación de leyes* (1567). In this collection, age divisions are reduced to the generality '*menores*' (minors), with specific ages leading to variable punishments for crimes. For example, a 17-year-old who steals at Court receives the death penalty, while the same crime by one aged from 15 up to, but not yet, 17 brings a sentence of 200 lashes and ten years' time rowing in the galleys.[18] In a late sixteenth-century manuscript detailing punishments for erotic crimes, Justinian's division and ages of 9½ or 10½ are repeated and explained: 'The youth with fewer than seven years, when the stage of infancy is ended, and from then until 10½ in the male and 9½ in the female, are never found guilty of a crime: given that they cannot consent, they cannot sin.'[19]

The legal volumes operative when Cervantes wrote his *Novelas ejemplares* include all of the above, and throughout the collection of stories, the creative author takes full advantage of the social and aesthetic plurisymbolism of those specifications and contradictions. In one story, 'Rinconete y Cortadillo', two young men who will proceed to rob and steal at Court are described as 'maybe 14 or 15' but 'definitely not 17';[20] that is, only maybe eligible for the 200 lashes and ten years in the galleys indicated in the Recopilación, while definitely too young for its death sentence. In 'La española inglesa', the protagonist is stolen from her parent's house when she is 'seven, more or less',[21] with that caveat phrasing to indicate cuasi-*infans*, but then, when she turns 12, she has become sufficiently beautiful in an age-appropriate way to make her captor's young son burn with love for her. The protagonist of a different story, Tomás Rodaja, is discovered along the road by two young gentlemen when he is 'just about 11',[22]

---

[17] See Susan Byrne, 'Por qué una "niña de nuef años"?: la edad de razón y la razón del poeta del CMC' 31.1 La Corónica (2002) 5–17.
[18] See *Recopilación de las Leyes*, 5 vols (first published, 1640, ed. fac. Lex Nova, 1982), Autos acordados 8.11.19. In subsequent citations, Recop. Citations are to book, chapter, law number. The indication 'Autos acordados', as here, indicates the additional legal matter found in vols 4–5 of the edition.
[19] See Antonio de la Peña, *Tratado de los juicios, jueces y orden de las penas criminales* (unpublished manuscript, on file at Biblioteca Nacional Española, BNE MSS/6379) fol. 91r.
[20] See Miguel de Cervantes Saavedra, *Novelas ejemplares* (Cátedra, 1995) I, 191. In subsequent citations, Cervantes (1995).
[21] Cervantes (1995) I, 244.
[22] Cervantes (1995) II, 43.

that is, just over the 10½ necessary for *puber proximus*, and so liable for his actions. A young woman 'who would seem to be 13 or 14',[23] clearly a *puber* ergo marriageable in legal terms, is wed to Felipo de Carrizales, who at the age of 68 has just returned rich and prosperous from the Americas. The marriage will be a disaster, and the age difference is highlighted as one, although not the principal, factor. Yet another protagonist, Carriazo, leaves his parents' house at the age of '13, more or less',[24] to explore the open road and the free life of a *pícaro*. A bit shy of the legally mandated 14, the phrasing 'more or less' allows for doubt and absolution.

For each case detailed above, the precision of chronological age is questioned with parenthetical phrasings: maybe, more or less, almost, just about, would seem to be. With this stylistic quirk, Cervantes confounds the most concrete human fact: a number. Each specific integer is relativized through arbitrary modifiers that make age itself unreliable and unsound as a measure. The legal strictures are called into doubt through understated but obvious lexical structures. This use of qualifiers is a lexical-order hypothetical (*elocutio*) that challenges precision in legal logic.

In a more abstract and thematic sense, Cervantes' short story titled 'La gitanilla' ('The Little Gypsy Girl') is itself a hypothetical case (*inventio*) that poetically contravenes contemporaneous Spanish legislation and social posturing (*dispositio*) on those identified as 'gypsies' in late sixteenth and early seventeenth-century Spain.

Early mentions of Egypt and the Egyptians are found in King Alphonse X's 1375 *General History* and in Alfonso de Palencia's 1490 bilingual Latin–Spanish dictionary, which includes translations for the months of the year from Greek, Hebrew, Egyptian and Macedonian. 'Egyptian' Hermes Trismegistus is well respected in early modern Spain, as is Hercules, the 'Egyptian' reputed to have founded the city of Seville. Groups of Romani, known by the common misnomer *egypcianos* (Egyptians) or *gitanos* (gypsies), 'almost certainly first arrived in northern Spain in the mid 1420s, passing themselves off as pilgrims'.[25]

The earliest legal prohibition against the Romani in the Spanish kingdoms is a *pragmatic* (royal ordinance) with all force of law dated 1499, which would be repeatedly modified and reissued throughout the following two centuries. The original ordinance prohibits gypsies from travelling from place to place with their families, as well as from begging, stealing, casting spells and reading fortunes. They are ordered to either leave the Spanish reigns or settle down for farm work, with violators subject to a penalty of 100 lashes followed by exile. The same law was thrice re-promulgated: in 1525, 1528 and 1534. By 1539, the penalty for any non-settled gypsy between the ages of 20 and 50 was increased to six years in the Spanish galleys.[26] That same pragmatic was reissued in 1560, then a new order mandating restrictions on commercial activity by gypsies was published in 1586. In 1619, any gypsy who wished to remain within Spain's territories was ordered to reside in a town of one thousand or more inhabitants, and to work the land.[27] This last ordinance also forbids use of gypsy dress, name or language, and prohibits the sale of animals by gypsies. By 1692, the scope of the ordinance had expanded to forbid the possession of firearms, as well as segregated neighbourhoods, with

---

[23] Cervantes (1995) II, 102.
[24] Cervantes (1995) II, 139.
[25] *See* Richard Pym, 'The Pariah Within: Early Modern Spain's Gypsies' 4.2 Journal of Romance Studies (2004) 24. In subsequent citations, Pym (2004).
[26] Recop. 8.11.12–13.
[27] Recop. 8.11.14.

time in the galleys for violations increased to eight years. In 1717, possession of mules or horses was prohibited to those identified as gypsies, and the final pragmatic in the series, dated 1727, called for judges to uphold the laws on gypsies.[28]

Shortly before Cervantes published the *Novelas ejemplares* in 1613, Spanish magistrate Jerónimo Castillo de Bobadilla declared a generalized failure to uphold and enforce the country's laws on gypsies. The magistrate also alleges that some persons pretending to be gypsies are not any such thing but, rather, vagabonds, thieves and swindlers. His advice: 'magistrates should not allow gypsies in their jurisdictions, when these are without masters or professions (it is rare that they have one, with the exception of stealing), and they should not allow that gypsies sell anything.'[29] The magistrate's mix of commercial and legal concerns reflects court discussions of the day regarding Spanish citizens pretending to be gypsies so as to declare themselves not bound by Spanish law, as well as social concerns from royal advisors who looked for scapegoats on whom to blame the nation's ills.[30] Vitriolic anti-gypsy treatises had been published elsewhere in Europe, and would serve as models for Spain's political reformers, who called for ethnic expulsion of gypsies, a project that would eventually be abandoned.[31] Details from one such treatise provide explicit, revelatory background for Cervantes' creative portrayal of the same group.

In 1619, a professor of theology at the University of Toledo named Sancho de Moncada published a volume of nine chapters with political advice to King Philip III, commonly referred to by the title *Restauración política de España* (*Political Restoration of Spain*).[32] This type of writing was fairly common at the time and those who made such recommendations, the 'talking heads' of their day, were called *arbitristas*, a word translated by Simon & Schuster as 'crank politicians or reformers'.[33] In his nine chapters, Moncada advises the king to reap the riches of the New World and keep them for Spain, curtail spending, favour internal production of goods and create a gold standard. He advocates prosperity through savings along with reduced taxation, recommends an end to abuses by renegade soldiers, censures extravagance and advocates for the founding of a new university. The only group singled out for a xenophobic rant in this collection of treatises is the gypsies, for whom Moncada demands expulsion from Spain.

The *arbitrista* begins with a pseudo-historical religious justification for his demand: the gypsies have always been a menace to God's people. That succinct statement is followed by intensifying, excessive imagery: the gypsies in Spain are bees' nests of drones and parasites;

---

[28] Recop., Autos acordados, 8.11.17.

[29] See Jerónimo Castillo de Bobadilla, *Política para corregidores* (first published, 1597, Geronymo Margarit, 1611) 2.13.35.

[30] See Richard Pym, 'The Errant Fortunes of "La gitanilla" and Cervantes's Performing Gypsies' 12.1 Journal of Iberian and Latin American Studies (2006) 28, and Pym (2004) 22.

[31] Pym (2004) 32.

[32] See Sancho de Moncada, *Riqueza firme y estable de España* (first published, 1619, reprinted as *Restauración política de España*, 1746) Chapter 9. Issued as *Suma de ocho discursos*, or eight treatises in 1618, Moncada republished the following year with the inclusion of the additional ninth chapter on the gypsies. See Niccolò Guasti, 'The Debate on the Expulsion of the Gypsies in the Castilian *Arbitrismo* of the Early Seventeenth Century', in *Reforming Early Modern Monarchies: The Castilian Arbitristas in Comparative European Perspectives*, eds Sina Rauschenbach and Christian Windler (Harrassowitz Verlag in Kommission, 2016) 167.

[33] See *Simon & Schuster's International Dictionary, English/Spanish*, ed. Tana de Gámez (Simon & Schuster, 1973).

atheists with neither law nor religion; restless birds like the white wagtail that never builds a nest of its own; spies and traitors, enemies of any Republic; lazy vagabonds whose only profession is to rob and steal; they are even worse than *moriscos* (the moors, Spain's historical arch-enemy throughout the Reconquest); and they steal children to sell on the Barbary Coast. Female gypsies weaken society's morals with their dancing, singing and common-wife status. Moncada relates the apocryphal history of the first thieves in Spain, who supposedly arrived with Hercules and were Egyptians. Gypsies are spellcasters, fortune tellers, and superstitious in everything; heretics and idolaters, they conveniently adapt the outward signs of whichever place they are in without believing in anything. They speak slang so as to not be understood by others.

Moncada's recommendations for dealing with the group: arrest all gypsies then condemn them to death as spies, traitors, wastrels and vagabonds. The *arbitrista* alleges that any vagabond is, of necessity, out to kill someone else, ergo should be put to death as a preventive measure. Reviewing various Spanish laws on gypsies, he gives a particular spin to the prior century's pragmatics that instructed them to settle down or to leave the country. For Moncada, those settle-down directives were only for Spaniards pretending to be gypsies, those who had opted for *gitanismo* (gypsy-ism) as a style of life, a choice. The real gypsies were exiled by those pragmatics, as the arbitrista reads it, and anyone who disagrees with him is simply mistaken. In sum, Moncada's treatise exemplifies what some would later posit as proof of early modern Spanish allegiance to the Counter Reformation and conservative, arch-Catholic, nativist principles. Many historians have repudiated this monolithic portrait and, for his part, Cervantes proposes a counter-hypothetical to those images, as well as to the prevailing juridical situation of the ethnic group.

'La gitanilla' is the first story of the collected *Novelas ejemplares*, and Cervantes begins it with a two-word qualifying phrase: '*Parece que*' ('It would seem that'). That lead-in is followed by an echo of magistrate Castillo de Bobadilla's manual:

> It would seem that gypsy men and women were born into the world only so as to be thieves: they are born of thieving parents, raised with thieves, they study how to be thieves and finally, they turn out to be nothing but thieves at each and every moment; the desire to steal and stealing itself are, in them, like innate accidents, not to be abrogated until death.[34]

Following this deliberate yet subtly qualified statement about gypsies who *seem to be* thieves through and through, which echoes the magistrate's manual, Cervantes offers a dramatic paean to what is truly at the core of the *arbitrista*'s complaint: personal freedom. As he does so, he also proves magistrate Castillo de Bobadilla correct in showing that none of the Spanish laws on gypsies were enforced.

The plot of the story includes the gypsies breaking many of the laws detailed above: they move from place to place, sing, dance, tell fortunes, use gypsy dress and name. Multiple ministers of justice are characters in the story, but none arrest the gypsies for any of the above, nor do they chastise them for those legally violative actions: to the contrary, they invite them into their homes for private performances and fortune-telling.

Cervantes illustrates the ethnic prohibitions in a manner that questions such stereotyping. For example, no animals are sold in the story, although there is one episode in which the

---

[34] Cervantes (1995) I, 61.

question is broached. A nobleman has left his family to join up with the gypsies. He insists that his mule be killed so as to hide his escape from Madrid. The gypsies declaim this action: 'A grievous sin! [...] you ask that we kill an innocent mule?',[35] that is, they sentimentalize the mule, and protest the request as tantamount to a religious transgression. Only following more argument and the persuasion of coins paid do they reluctantly agree to the mule's death sentence. The author's message is that the gypsies can be persuaded to go against their instincts, but cruelty against an innocent creature is the cold verdict of only the nobleman.

There is no mention of possession of firearms in the short story, although there is one deadly fight. The disguised nobleman-turned-gypsy is speechless at having been accused of stealing by the town's mayor. At that moment, a pompous soldier who happens to be the mayor's nephew insults him loudly, and deals him a hard slap to the face. With that, the nobleman-turned-gypsy recovers his voice, takes the soldier's sword and kills him with it. Immediate imprisonment follows, but that legal remedy will be surreptitiously thwarted for personal reasons by a magistrate.

On language and the arbitrista's complaint of unintelligible slang, the narrative voice makes one ironic commentary when it notes that while in Madrid, the little gypsy girl speaks with the Spanish *ceceo* (a lisping pronunciation of 's' as 'th'). The reader is told that this is 'an acquired skill for gypsies, rather than natural'.[36] After all, she is in Madrid, and the *ceceo* was the regional characteristic pronunciation of the Court. Cervantes turns the table on linguistic snobbery, equating the prized accent of those in the Spanish Court to disreputable gypsy slang.

Having echoed the complaints in legal volumes about thieves and thievery as standard gypsy behaviour in his opening paragraph, Cervantes elides its supposedly ubiquitous nature in the rest of the story. His gypsies speak of stealing as a way of life, but also present it ironically as a social good: they steal so as to teach a lesson to others, who should learn to 'keep an eye on their goods'.[37] They bribe town mayors, who accept those bribes, to allow gypsies to settle in their environs, as long as the gypsies promise to not rob within that jurisdiction. The most egregious example of stealing is revealed in the story's denouement, when an old gypsy woman confesses to having stolen the protagonist, the little gypsy girl, from her parents when she was a babe in arms. The little gypsy girl's father, himself a minister of justice, 'forgave the offense of her having stolen his soul, given the joys inherent in its return'.[38] Justice is measured in the personal equity sense understood by Plato, and later echoed by Erasmus, as individual virtue rather than state-sanctioned imposition of penalties.

As to the supposedly pestiferous curse of Spanish citizens who decide to become gypsies in order to ignore the laws, Cervantes' version is of amorous inspiration. As she dances and sings in Madrid, the little gypsy girl named Preciosa attracts the attention of a young nobleman named Juan who proposes to 'elevate her' to his status through marriage.[39] She tentatively agrees, but insists that to prove his love, Juan must join the gypsies for a 'novitiate' of two years.[40] He does so, taking the gypsy name Andrés. This noble-turned-gypsy who loves Preciosa learns the lessons in stealing given to him by the group, but thinks he will not have

---

[35] Cervantes (1995) I, 100.
[36] Cervantes (1995) I, 72.
[37] Cervantes (1995) I, 101–2.
[38] Cervantes (1995) I, 128.
[39] Cervantes (1995) I, 84.
[40] Cervantes (1995) I, 103.

to actually carry out the act because he can simply pay for goods while misrepresenting how he got them: with this decision, the non-gypsy will deceive the gypsies he has befriended. The stereotypes on honourable behaviour are selectively inverted through the deliberate ruse, made possible because the nobleman has the resources. Juan/Andrés insists on going out alone to steal, in order to purchase items then claim to have stolen them. His '*industria* (clever trick)'[41] works very well, and the author's comment on honourable behaviour emphasizes its selectivity: the nobleman will not steal, but he has no scruples about lying.

The gypsies' reaction to this ruse is presented as a principled stance: faced with the idea that Juan/Andrés might have compensated those robbed for their losses, the gypsies stress that such an act would be contrary to their own statutes, which rid their hearts of charity because it interferes with their 'essence as thieves'.[42] An earlier example in the story highlights the same point of pride: Preciosa refuses a bag of coins, but the old gypsy woman insists on accepting it so as to not lose for gypsies the name earned over centuries of being greedy and taking advantage of a situation. She supports her decision with a solid argument: to have funds for bail or for bribes when gypsies are arrested. The laws insist that gypsies have a profession, and the old gypsy woman says they do. She describes it as a risky one, ameliorated just a bit by having access to the coin of the realm for bribing justices who persecute and prosecute gypsies 'more than they do highway robbers'.[43] After dancing in the home of a minister of justice who suddenly discovers his lack of coins with which to pay her, Preciosa urges him to '*coheche*' (take bribes) as do all other ministers of justice because if not, he will 'die of hunger'.[44] Again, the creative author's message is that the state's justice is unjust, and selectively commercialized. In all of the episodes with confirmed ministers of justice, this message is made evident: Cervantes presents the counter-perspective to the law from those who most suffer its indignities.

On the age of reason and responsibility: in 'La gitanilla' age is not a factor for legal culpability, as we are told repeatedly that Preciosa is 15: once she turns that age, the old gypsy lady brings her to the royal Court, 'where everything is for sale';[45] at a later moment, Preciosa defends her right to be knowledgeable about things supposedly beyond her years with a rhetorical question: 'Am I not 15?', then further insists that gypsy females know 'by the age of 12 more than non-gypsy women will at 25'.[46] Later in the story, we read that she will turn 15 'on the upcoming Saint Michael's day', which is 'more or less' two months away.[47] Albeit that minor discrepancy, pursuant to Spanish law of the day even if dependent on which legal volume is consulted, as a female Preciosa was regularly liable for her actions beginning at the age of 12. The hypothetical then becomes: did she break any laws?

A definitive answer is complicated by the protagonist's simultaneous status as both a gypsy and a non-gypsy. For all intents and purposes, she is a gypsy up to the last scene in the novella, when her own noble birth is revealed. According to the pragmatics, gypsies were not allowed to sing and dance. Preciosa does, ergo she is breaking the law. She also tells fortunes, another act forbidden to gypsies by the same laws. On the other hand, if she is not a gypsy, those

---

[41] Cervantes (1995) I, 113.
[42] Cervantes (1995) I, 107.
[43] Cervantes (1995) I, 89.
[44] Cervantes (1995) I, 81.
[45] Cervantes (1995) I, 63.
[46] Cervantes (1995) I, 76–7.
[47] Cervantes (1995) I, 85; 125.

actions are not *verboten*. Cervantes embeds that hypothetical challenge: if dancing, singing and fortune-telling are illegal for gypsies, what can a judge's decision be if someone both is, and is not, a member of that group? Identity politics and laws based on them are called into question.

Further in support of that posture, Cervantes's presentation of the gypsies' actions runs counter to the image provided by the legal prohibitions. The gypsies are not shunned by society but, rather, sought after and welcomed. Preciosa dances for money, but she does not steal it. She 'enchants' with her eyes,[48] she tells fortunes and she casts spells, but all at the behest of society's finest members. As presented by Cervantes, the gypsies are a travelling theatre group, welcomed by Spanish cities and towns that see their arrival as an opportunity to contract dances for 'religious feast days'.[49] Preciosa debuts on the streets of Madrid with a song to Saint Ann, patron saint of the city, on her feast day. There are moments when coins rain down so quickly as she dances that the old gypsy woman 'lacks enough hands' to collect them all,[50] but in none of these instances do the gypsies steal money. Faced with a group that wants fortunes told but has no money to pay for it, Preciosa tells one anyway in exchange for a silver-plated thimble.

The gypsies themselves explain their own laws to Juan/Andrés as he joins the group: marriage is for life; the law of friendship is paramount; there is no jealousy; expect a lot of incest, but no adultery; and self-determined group justice mandates that if a woman cheats on her mate, she is killed and buried like a 'noxious beast'.[51] Contrary to the *arbitrista* stereotypes about shared women, Cervantes' gypsies insist that everything else is shared, but not women. They further describe their life as one of rustic astrologers, living in happy concert with nature. There is, in this section on internal gypsy law, much ironic commentary: acceptance of incest but not adultery is most likely a not-so-veiled swipe at the Spanish monarchy, whose own inbreeding had led to the famed 'Habsburg jaw'.[52] That is, the gypsies simply follow established custom and ongoing precedent set by the royal family, rather than concede to legal prohibition.

From the beginning, the little gypsy girl's story offers qualifying caveats that serve as confirmation of the stereotype on thievery, while simultaneously predicting caution in judgments: the old gypsy woman is described as well-schooled in the science of Cacus, the mythological thief *par excellence*. She raised a young gypsy girl '*in the name of* her grandchild',[53] gave her the name Preciosa, and taught her everything she knew: tricks, guile, and ways to steal. Those lessons, however, are never practiced by the protagonist in the story that ensues. Instead, Preciosa is described as the best dancer in all *gitanismo* (gypsy-dom), and also the most beautiful and discrete woman among all women, gypsy or not. Despite the taxing environment

---

[48] Cervantes (1995) I, 76.
[49] Cervantes (1995) I, 108.
[50] Cervantes (1995) I, 67.
[51] Cervantes (1995) I, 101.
[52] Genetic homozygosity leading to very noticeable mandibular prognathism is a hallmark of the Habsburg line. Vilas et al. study it, along with the 'Habsburg lip' and 'Habsburg nose' (2019). As an example: Phillip II ruled Spain from 1556 to 1598, at which point he was survived by his fourth wife, who also happened to be his niece. His first wife had been both a maternal and paternal first cousin. *See* Román Vilas et al., 'Is the "Habsburg Jaw" Related to Inbreeding?' 46.7–8 Annals of Human Biology (2019) 553–61.
[53] Cervantes (1995) I, 61, emphasis added.

of open-air living that we are told marks gypsy existence, no weather could dull her face or hands; her rough upbringing only brought out in her signs of having been born of better stock. She is courteous and well-reasoned, if just a bit *desenvuelta* (bold), a word considered a necessary characteristic for an actor or businessman in the sense of free-speaking enough to convince but, when used to describe a woman, slyly suggestive of immorality. Having used the word for Preciosa, Cervantes immediately attenuates: 'but not [*desenvuelta*] in any way that might indicate impropriety; to the contrary, she was astute but also so chaste that no other gypsy would dare, in her presence, to sing a lascivious song.'[54] Beautiful and bold, Preciosa is also honest, discrete and wholesome, shining as a diamond in the rough. There are frequent references to her spoken statements as surprising for their ingenuity and intelligence. These messages about belonging yet seeming to be always one step above, better than or the best of, the group of gypsies she travels with clearly telegraph the ending denouement, which includes a chest of infant baubles and secret documents, along with dramatic anagnorisis.

En route to that ending, there will be various plot twists: as noted above, Juan/Andrés is imprisoned for murder, and accused of stealing. This last is doubly ironic given his resistance to precisely that act: goods are planted in his bags by a jealous woman and her word (noble) versus his (supposedly gypsy) carries the day, but only for a while. Once again, the facts and resolution demonstrate the unreliability of state-sanctioned justice. This sole formal accusation of thievery in the story is levied falsely against someone pretending to be a gypsy, who is himself tricking the gypsies into believing that he has been stealing so as to be like them. His arrest will trigger the events that lead to a happy ending for the two young lovers.

As Preciosa pleads with a magistrate and his wife for the release of Juan/Andrés from prison, the assembled group learns that she is in reality the daughter of that same magistrate and his wife. The old gypsy woman confesses that she stole the infant Preciosa from the same magistrate's house in which the young girl now pleads Juan/Andrés's case. The magistrate forgives the crime, and worries only that the girl has been engaged to the thief/murderer gypsy, Juan/Andrés, who is now in prison. Told that the young man's gypsy persona is a pretence, the magistrate enacts an elaborate ruse to free Juan/Andrés. His free-handed approach to his sworn duties proves the old gypsy woman right: the law is selective in its application. The last example of justice for sale is a significant sum of money paid to the uncle of the dead soldier, killed with his own sword by Juan/Andrés. The town mayor, his uncle, accepts the deal and drops his complaint. The incoming regional magistrate, we learn, will be none other than Juan/Andrés's father. That completes the ironic circle: the son of a magistrate broke the law to join up with the gypsies, deceived them by pretending to steal, was arrested for murdering a soldier and then illicitly freed by another magistrate who also arranged payment to the town mayor to drop the homicide case, just as the position of magistrate was about to pass to the father of the falsely accused.

That happy ending is complicated only by an unexpected turnabout in Preciosa's most treasured quality: like Cervantes' more iconic protagonist Don Quijote, the little gypsy girl professes personal, unequivocal freedom in all she does and believes, throughout the novella. She refutes all the stereotypes about gypsy women, and about women more generally, refusing any constraints on her own behaviour absent those she herself imposes: 'with me unrestricted liberty is a must.'[55] She rejects a gold coin that accompanies a poem, finding the poem more

---

[54] Cervantes (1995) I, 62.
[55] Cervantes (1995) I, 87.

important than the money. Her adamant approach to sexual relations prior to marriage refutes all commonplaces about gypsy wantonness: she would rather go to the grave a virgin than sell that state for 'chimera or dreamy illusions'.[56] As Juan/Andrés joins up with the gypsies, the group's 'legislators' tell him that Preciosa will be his, but she simultaneously cautions: 'the law of my own will is stronger than any other law', and while her body may have been granted, 'not my soul, which is free and was born free, and will remain free for as long as I might want it to be'.[57]

Despite those claims for free will and liberty, after the truth about her birth is told Preciosa puts her fate squarely in the hands of her newly found, long-lost parents. Asked directly if she loves Juan/Andrés and wishes to marry him, she demurs, deferring to their judgement. That surprise ending is one of the puzzles for readers of the story, much like protagonist Don Quijote's renouncing of his knight errant's dream at the end of the novel titled for him, for both decisions seem to shatter rather than satisfy readerly illusion. However, read in the light of a different perspective on justice, both protagonists' actions make perfect sense. Questioning justice while positing a hypothetical lack of clear, confirmed and unchanging identity is standard fare in Cervantes's writings. The external trappings are less important than the internal equilibrium realized through individual choice in any given moment. Cervantes gives his fictional characters the liberty to decide, and to change.

We all constantly evolve in a changing world. José Ortega y Gasset would say it 300 years later: 'I am myself and my circumstance.'[58] When Preciosa's circumstance changes, it should not be surprising that her internal calibrator of self does as well. Cervantes anticipates Descartes's famous *cogito ergo sum* with a more existentially uncertain *cogito ergo sim*. I think, therefore I might be, more or less, for now. As Alciato insisted, context matters. Definitions and beliefs determine us, but they are themselves hypotheticals, open to the sway of an imagination that can create what has not yet come to pass. In Cervantes's fictional texts, whether presented in minor lexical detail or as a reality that defies a recognized yet questionable historical absolute, the author's master trope is the masking of legal issues as entertaining yet quite philosophical, creative narrative.[59]

Arthur Jacobson has studied decreases in the use of legal hypotheticals in judicial opinions as a marker of transition between oral and written judicial cultures, or between judgment by rule versus by precedent.[60] The argument is apt, albeit with modification, for Cervantes's day: for three centuries Spanish had been the language of written and spoken law, although educational practice and manuals that explained legal functioning were all in Latin. It was only in 1595 that magistrate Jerónimo Castillo de Bobadilla fought for and was granted the publishing rights for such a manual written in Spanish. As to rule versus precedent, prior

---

[56] Cervantes (1995) I, 85.
[57] Cervantes (1995) I, 103.
[58] See José Ortega y Gasset, *Meditaciones del Quijote* (first published, 1914, Cátedra, 1990) 77.
[59] Multiple examples of this trope are found in the author's masterpiece *Don Quijote*. See Susan Byrne, *Law and History in Cervantes' Don Quijote* (University of Toronto Press, 2012).
[60] See Arthur J. Jacobson, 'Death of the Hypothetical' 9.2 Stanford Literature Review (1992) 125–38. Further to Jacobson's study, the transition between oral and written cultures more broadly led to the need for allegorical exegesis of myth, to explain passages and commentary inconsistent with contemporary-to-the-reader mores. Ambiguity can be, as it frequently is read today in Cervantes's writings, the product of achronological reading uninformed by the actual situation of the time of the writer.

cases were used to exemplify practice, although not specifically called precedent.[61] Judgment was by rule, but there were multiple complaints about the infamous *ley del encaje* (lace law), that is, judges deciding on whim rather than by statute. Additionally, as I have noted above, late sixteenth-century Spain was experiencing upheaval in political terms, with bureaucratic centralization accompanied by multiple economic and social concerns. In sum, Jacobson's argument for transitional phases might be read more broadly than just his oral-written or rule-precedent dichotomies. Perhaps any transition in legal culture will demand that its participants resort to more imaginative practices. This is masterfully explained in the most enigmatic medieval Spanish text, the fourteenth-century *Libro de buen amor*, which includes a splendid scene in which the ambiguity of legal interpretation, and all knowledge more broadly, is highlighted mockingly. The Romans, who do not have laws, demand that the Greeks explain their legal science. The Greeks mock the request, alleging a complete lack of preparation on the part of the Romans to receive such knowledge; nonetheless, they agree to try. The case (*pleito*) is signed and commenced, although the lack of a common language means it must proceed through gestures and signs. Things go downhill quickly: feeling outclassed, the Romans hire a known astute rogue to represent them, disguising him in the robes of a doctor of philosophy. He and his Greek counterpart exchange signs: one finger held up is answered with three, an open palm is answered with a closed fist. The visual iconography can lead to multiple interpretations, and it does. The Greek reads the exchange as the Roman's sensible recognition of the existence of a tripartite God (one finger versus three), along with the importance of will (open hand) as the essence of power (closed fist). The Roman explains to his compatriots that the Greek threatened to poke out his eye with one finger, so he upped the ante to three fingers to take out both of his rival's eyes along with his teeth, followed by the Greek threatening to slap him with an open palm and his response, the menace of a closed-fist punch. The scene is comical, but not at all ambiguous: justice is inexplicable and unrealizable without common language.

On a related note, and paraphrasing Aristotle: prose is what happened, and poetry is what might have happened. Strictly per that reasoning, poetry is hypothetical. Cervantes affords prose the same poetic liberty of hypothesis and invention. One noteworthy, celebrated aspect of his novels is the author's unparalleled creation and manipulation of narrative voice. This is another tantalizing link to a statement made by Jacobson: 'Hypotheticals flourish only in cultures that make a place for the oral in the written, cultures that engrave the oral.'[62] Cervantes's narrative voices, and his mastery with dialogue, do engrave the oral, along with the poetic imaginative, in the written. In that aspect, and in the author's choice of 'exemplary' for the title of his collection of novellas, Jacobson's arguments regarding hypotheticals and examples have an even greater resonance in relation to the fictional text.

A fitting coda to this reading of Cervantes's legal–literary *mos hispanicus* can be found in the approach taken to legal exegesis by Alciato, who sought to explicate ambiguities in Justinian's legal texts by reading them side-by-side with 'works outside the usual ambit of

---

[61] *See* Jerónimo Castillo de Bobadilla, *Política para corregidores* (first published, 1597, Geronymo Margarit, 1611), who includes hundreds of *casos* (prior cases) to educate the beginning magistrate in practicalities.

[62] Jacobson (1992) 129.

legal studies, works on language, literature, and history'.[63] Much of the perceived ambiguity found in Cervantes's novels by today's scholars can be resolved through a similar but inverted legal exegesis of the literary, as I hope to have accomplished above. It may be, as Alciato said, mixing 'foxes with lions',[64] but it does serve to untangle and explain what are frequently read as textual uncertainties.

Such an approach is fully in concert with early seventeenth-century Spanish reworkings of disciplinary parameters, developments that function in furtherance of the goals of earlier humanists like Alciato. Cervantes wrote prior to the French coining of the phrase 'belles lettres', but he and his compatriots had begun to reclassify their writings, abandoning the phrase 'good letters' that had been used for all writings in prose irrespective of subject matter, in favour of 'human letters' for the same broad group of texts. In the same period, attorneys tried to usurp for themselves the word *letrado* (lettered man), as Sebastián de Covarrubias complains in 1611,[65] while jurists incorporated examples from creative letters into legal manuals as proof positive for legal determinations and punishments.[66] Shortly after, Spanish writers would begin to use the phrase 'polished letters' for their creative works, thus differentiating their product from those of other prose writers, a distinction later codified in the classifications 'belles lettres' and 'poetic prose', categories that would eventually move creative letters out of the realm of perceived 'serious' writings. Scholars of literature have made clear that Cervantes amalgamated earlier literary models into his poetic prose but he also, as demonstrated above, used the humour of legal hypotheticals to *docere, delectare et movere*.[67] Cervantes took advantage of his own legal and literary situation and, as he did so, he created a new prose genre: a modern novel. Reading law as creative fodder, his ingenious glosses on its nonsensicalities rewrote literary history.

---

[63] See Denis L. Drysdall, 'Alciato and the Grammarians: The Law and the Humanities in the *Parergon iuris libri duocecim*' 56 Renaissance Quarterly (2003) 695–722.

[64] Quoted at Drysdall (2003) 698, and 698–9 n 16, who notes in that place the source of Alciato's use of the adage as Erasmus, while also noting as original sources Martial and Pindar.

[65] See Sebastián de Covarrubias Orozco, *Tesoro de la lengua castellana o española* (first published, 1611, Castalia, 1994).

[66] In a late sixteenth-century manuscript of punishments for erotic crimes (see note 19, supra), while identifying the citation as from a confirmed legal source, jurist Antonio de la Peña uses a story from Poggio de Bracciolini's *Facetiae* to illustrate the legal punishment for adultery. See Susan Byrne, 'Juridical Philology: Incest, Adultery, and the Law in *Don Quijote*', in *Sex and Gender in Cervantes/Sexo y género en Cervantes: Essays in Honor of Adrienne Laskier Martín*, eds Esther Fernández and Mercedes Alcalá Galán (Edition Reichenberger, 2019) 71–88.

[67] The well-known trio of rhetorical goals proposed by Cicero in 'De Oratore'.

PART IX

CROSSING SENSIBILITY

Metabolize Transgression – Salmon Mayonnaise – Jurisliterary Compromise – Loguical Transcursivity – Fictive Forces – Aesthetics – Poetic (In)Justice – Blind Crime – Jurisliterary *Aporia*

30. Transgression
Angela Condello and Tiziano Toracca

SALMON MAYONNAISE

The term *transgressio* derives from *transgressus*, past participle of *transgredi* ('step across, step over; go beyond, pass')[1] and it indicates the act of going beyond a limit. As a starting point, it is important to differentiate more thoroughly between a thin and a thick transgression as an internal difference within the semantic field of the ancient *trangressio*. A *thin* transgression indicates the mere, occasional trespassing or excess. A *thick* transgression is an intentional crossing of a confine, a willing passage over a threshold: it is bearer of *sensus* and it is reasonable in its being counternormative (that is, it crosses a boundary *with* reasons that claim to be recognised). With such a distinction in the background, we introduce a parallelism between law and literature concerning the way in which these two discourses, working as ancient *artes* (techniques), respond to thick transgression with compromise.

In such a response, nevertheless, a relevant difference emerges, such that the logic of law and the logic of literature undergo a bifurcation. Literature performs a mediation between the reason of the norm and the reason of the transgressor through a compromise formation which is the real value of literary figurality, since it can preserve contrasting points of view in the same discourse. Opposing reasons can coexist because opposing logics coexist. The logic of literature is the logic of the unconscious, where someone can be right and wrong at the same time. On the contrary, against a transgressive act that challenges the validity of a norm, law mediates through its use of language by selecting, arguing and by aiming at a final cut of some meanings in favour of others. Opposing reasons, in law, cannot coexist because here all reasons are interpreted coherently with one logical system. Nevertheless, for example, by crossing the line of the accepted meanings falling within the senses of a norm, hard cases in law reconstitute new boundaries and commonly excluded voices enter into the legal jurisdiction by undoing a code.

What seems to be certain is that transgression, and the compromise that law and literature activate in order to handle it, challenge law and literature at a profound level, in their basic functioning, upsetting their orders of values and producing different consequences. In observing their dual logics, originating in the same root (handling counterposed reasons) and then bifurcating in their way of handling the transgressive act at a symbolic level,[2] we intend to discuss how both law and literature metabolise transgression, by recognising and expressing it.

---

[1] In the etymological dictionary, the term is indicated to result from *trans* 'across, beyond' and *gradi* (past participle *gressus*), 'to walk, go' (from the root *ghredh-*, 'to walk, go') [www.etymonline.com/search?q=transgression&ref=searchbar_searchhint].

[2] The relation with the Imaginary and the Symbolic, as they relate to the Real – following Lacan's triadic structure of discourse – is proper to both law and literature. As will be argued in various passages, the unconscious is a dimension where the societal repression is reorganised, and where the 'discourse of the Other', of the systemic social formations, of names and sentences repressing our own singularities

500 *Research handbook on law and literature*

***

Let us enter into a more concrete scene: in *Wit and its Relation to the Unconscious* (1916), Freud recounts the following tale.

> An impoverished individual borrowed twenty-five florins from a prosperous acquaintance, with many asseverations of his necessitous circumstances. The very same day his benefactor met him again in a restaurant with a plate of salmon mayonnaise in front of him. The benefactor reproached him: 'What? You borrow money from me and then order yourself salmon mayonnaise? Is that what you've used my money for?' 'I don't understand you', replied the object of the attack; 'if I haven't any money, I can't eat salmon mayonnaise, and if I have some money, I mustn't eat salmon mayonnaise. Well, then, when am I to eat salmon mayonnaise?'

In this tale, overcoming the logical surface of the impoverished individual's reasoning, a serious reader would recognise the reason of the benefactor as stronger, more valid, more just. The impoverished gourmand is indeed transgressing a moral norm: he has borrowed money because he is poor and now he spends the money on exquisite and expensive food.[3] If we are tempted to laugh nevertheless, it is not only because at one point we recognise the absurdity of his reasoning and we feel it is just to sanction his argument – which would save us some psychic energy in driving us to laugh – but it is also because his reproachful reply to the benefactor expresses a more profound reason and a totally different order of values.[4] As Freud claims, the benefactor does not blame the other for having ordered salmon mayonnaise with his money, but underlines that – given his miserable economic condition – he should not be thinking about such delicacies, which symbolically recall unnecessary needs and pleasure. The logical semblance of the motto bewilders us; and it is for this reason that the perspective of the *logical subject* tends to sanction the gourmand's behaviour as illogical and even unjust. Laughter, that accompanies the sanction to the gourmand's argument and previous reasoning, derives – Freud claims – from the *dépense* of psychical energy required to understand, and to enter into his position.

Obviously, the impoverished man has asked to borrow money and therefore, following common diligence, he should use it *properly*, and yet how could we not grant him a portion of reasonableness, when he finally wonders when he will have the chance, or right, to eat salmon mayonnaise? How can we not agree with him, in other words, when he demands a form of enjoyment that now he *cannot*, and maybe later he *shall not* be granted and that in any case would *always* be precluded to him? At stake here are not only metahistorical reasons counterposing the pleasure principle against the reality principle (Freud, in commenting on the tale, discusses Horace's and Lorenzo de' Medici's Epicureanism), but also historical reasons. Since we have stopped believing in an afterlife, Freud writes, the reasons to procrastinate pleasure and not to grasp it immediately (*carpe diem*) have become more problematic. Are we

---

by collective utterances, is made: see J.M. Rabaté, *The Cambridge Companion to Lacan*, Cambridge University Press (2003), p.xii.

[3] In Freud's Vienna and prior to fish farming, salmon was considered a luxury item, whereas today it is a staple almost synonymous with fish.

[4] In using the plural subject 'we' here, the reference is not to a common or dominant idea of just society. It is used, instead, to underline the nature of human beings as logical subjects: the 'we' is a spectator that comments on the brief story and sympathises first with one character, then with the other (namely: first with one reason, then with the other).

sure, Freud wonders, that giving up the forms of satisfaction condemned by society will then entail some kind of reward? Are we sure that procrastinating *jouissance* is right or just? When, in other words, is it *possible* to eat salmon mayonnaise? If the poor gourmand's reasoning appears correct at first, and then ridiculous and daft afterwards, it finally appears, at least partially, just; in fact, Freud notices, after an initial distantiation, we usually develop a deeper complicity with the poor man eating salmon mayonnaise.

In the hermeneutics of this tale, oriented towards the conformist middle class, Freud shows that the hedonist desire of the poor gourmand goes far beyond a cynical request for personal satisfaction: it expresses instead an anthropological need and it therefore constitutes a radical critique of middle-class society. According to Freud, the gourmand's joke even leads us to realise how – behind the moral of the story – there is the privilege of a minority, and this pushes us to rebel against a predominant system of values. As long as the bourgeois societal structure is not capable of making life more pleasant, the voice arising against morality – in the people constituting that society – cannot be suffocated. It is Freud, here, that speaks: in the *bon vivant*'s transgression, he glimpses an *argument of social justice*.

In order for this complicity to be shared universally, that is, not only by those that openly fight middle-class values but also by conformists, what makes a real difference is the way in which the poor gourmand replies to the request of the benefactor. If, hypothetically, the poor gourmand had replied 'I cannot do without what I really like and I do not care about how the money arrived in my pocket' (this is the cynical reduction of the joke, that Freud reports at the beginning of his analysis); if he – in other words – had *openly* shown the cynical content of the joke without paying attention to its form, he would have transgressed. That would have been an absolute claim for the pleasure principle and, at a historical level, an open violation of middle-class values. It would have been, we might say, a purely ideological gesture.

The poor gourmand would have claimed the same right to pleasure, but his reason in that case, so openly expressed, would not have been recognised by the bourgeoisie, and first and foremost would not have been appreciated by his benefactor. The behaviour of the poor gourmand would have been condemned or, on the contrary, would have openly been approved. The reality principle and the moral system of norms would have been contrasted with the pleasure principle and with an open transgression.

The way in which the poor gourmand reacts against the benefactor's reproach, instead, aspires to find a universal complicity and therefore it is far from constituting a mere ideological position. It aspires to see his reasons recognised and to give his transgression a legitimate appearance, legitimate also from the perspective of those who are not ready to be in his shoes. The joke allows the other subject to identify himself with him and to recognise and share at least a part of the reasons of his transgression. The joke constitutes, in other words, a particular formalisation of the transgressive act, a particular way of *expressing* the transgression.

The final (rhetorical) questions of the poor gourmand defend the right to pleasure, contest middle-class values and criticise bourgeois morality. Yet, this defence and objection is not expressed through a simple and pure transgression (or through a dissumulation of the transgressive action), but through a compromise formation. The *bon vivant* claims the legitimacy of his own transgression with a *refined* expression. There is a commitment to the form of the expression and such commitment attributes to the transgressive action a meaning that goes beyond pure cynicism. This transgression corresponds not only to a way of expressing a desire, but to a literary form: at stake, here, are the generalisation and the symmetry proper of the logic of the unconscious and of its language. For this reason, inside that form cohabit the opposites.

In a few words, the *bon vivant* denies and affirms at the same time. He says that he has the right to eat salmon mayonnaise and, at the same time, he implies: 'true, actually I cannot and should not' (the 'not', the Freudian force of the negative, is both present and invisible). In his joke, opposing reasons are all valid and present. The form is refined in its ambivalent character and it is ambivalent in its figural nature, which reflects the logical structure of the unconscious.[5]

With his joke, the poor gourmand recognises that he cannot and should not eat salmon mayonnaise and at the same time presents a 'nevertheless' that imposes on everyone, also on the conformists, a re-negotiation of the repressive reasons for obloquy or prohibition. His request follows a double affirmation, in which the man recognises that he cannot and should not do what he desires to do, and it is such compresence of negation and affirmation (the request creates a doubt about what is affirmed) that produces the emergence of a reason different from that of the borrower.

The *transgression* of the norm is expressed together with the *recognition* of the norm: it is not based on a non-recognition of a certain morality (in that case it would be a pure, nude, ideological transgression), but on a concession to it. 'It is true', we seem to hear the poor gourmand speaking, 'that I should not spend the money in this way; nevertheless when, then, will I be able to eat salmon mayonnaise?' This special form of transgression, recognising the reasons for repression in exchange for *recognition* of other reasons, is what characterises figurative language and therefore, by extension, literature.

This is a very important passage, since it somehow defines what we call literature: we call literary that discourse that has a certain degree of figurality. We could say that if the degree of figurality crosses a certain boundary, the discourse becomes incomprehensible and stops being literature. If the discourse drops beyond a certain threshold, it becomes aesthetically irrelevant and ceases to be literature. Literature reveals a certain similarity with the language of the unconscious because it attracts attention by covering itself with figures. The figures of a text highlight its literary essence and this principle of individuation (for which a text is literary only if it has a certain quantity of figures) is a 'Freudian principle of individuation' because the figures activate the logic of the unconscious, with its principles of generalisation and symmetry. Literature, in this sense, always performs a compromise formation between a content respecting the rational logic and a content respecting the bi-logic, and the compresence of this double logic is guaranteed and expressed by figurality. This point is peculiarly interesting from the perspective of law and literature, because in their parallel lives these two discourses perform two different and yet interestingly interrelated uses of language. Law, unlike literature, must exclude meanings in order to reach a decision, to legitimise itself as an authoritative system which aims at *fixing* meanings within conflicts and cannot generalise, nor work through symmetry and compresence because such logical devices are contrary to the social function of the law, and to its necessity to perform reasonable argumentation. No law could admit the reason expressed by the *bon vivant*, recognising at the same time that he is wrong. He can be either right or wrong but he cannot be right and wrong at the same time. As a matter of fact, the judgment of a legal court would probably differ from that of the reader of Freud's tale of salmon mayonnaise. Who would be legally right? What principle, or value, or ideal of justice should prevail? Would those criteria vary according to the time and place of reference (bourgeois or aristocratic society, for instance)? Any mediation of the judge (of the

---

[5] We shall return to these remarks later in the text.

law) would not be capable of connecting the conflict with a rational, logical solution. It will merely reconnect the affirmation or negation expressed by the motto to a determined affirmation or negation. Basically, law cannot contradict itself as the *bon vivant* does with his joke.

Literature is capable of expressing repressed instances through the recognition of repressive instances because of its proper use of figurality, conceived as the compresence of different and also opposing meanings within the same form, expression, motto, joke: it is for this reason that it works as a compromise formation. The literary discourse does not openly express the reasons of the transgressor (this is what ideology does), but it *compromises* such reasons with the norms, with what can be called *repression*. And nevertheless repression must not be conceived as a negative or unjust instance. The reasoning of the borrower formalises an instance of repression but this does not mean that it is unjust. On the contrary, it is perfectly logical and just. If the *bon vivant* can transgress the repression of the norm in order to impose his reason, it is only because he recognises that he is also wrong. This is how compromise functions in literature: a part of the reason is claimed, by recognising at the same time that our request is *also* wrong. A transgression occurs, and at the same time the law is recognised to be just.

The reaction of the poor gourmand tends, in other words, to join the reality principle and the system of moral norms on the one hand, and the pleasure principle and the infraction of the norm on the other. This type of transgression and compromise represents an interesting analogy between law and literature, showing how they work both differently and similarly.

***

The act of transgressing entails going beyond a limit, a boundary. Transgressive actions are all those actions that become meaningful in relation to a limit or threshold. Such an action is groundbreaking, it overcomes, it strays from a path. And, of course, where there aren't limits, there can be no transgression.

What becomes relevant from the double perspective of law and literature is establishing a basic differentiation between two forms of transgression: a brute, basic form and a higher-level transgression, entailing the subject's intention to go beyond the norm. It is thus relevant to clarify the difference between a thin and a thick version of transgression, as we already anticipated in the introductory lines of this chapter. The first (thin) is synonymous with a violation of a norm and it exists outside, before and independently of the norm that is transgressed. In this case, transgression denies the norm. The second (thick) is instead a form of transgression that brings with it another force, the capacity to challenge the meaning of a norm, by ontologically recognising its relevance. It is not (only) the violation of a given order, but it (also) bears a counternormative force, resisting the meaning attributed to the specific norms, while at the same time recognising the function of the normative system and of its formalisation through law. Transgression does not 'deny limits or boundaries, rather it exceeds them and thus completes them'. Transgression is therefore a 'component of the rule. Seen in this way, excess is not an abhorration nor a luxury, it is rather a dynamic force in cultural reproduction – it prevents stagnation by breaking the rule and it ensures stability by reaffirming the rule.' It is not, in other words, 'disorder; it opens up chaos and reminds us of the necessity of order'.[6]

Against the background of such differentiation between types of transgression, literature – unlike law and other human and social sciences – is capable of working as a 'counter-memory'

---

[6] C. Jenks, *Transgression*, Routledge (2003), p.7.

for society:[7] the literary language stores the otherness, thanks to what Francesco Orlando refers to as its capacity to work as a *wide compromise formation*. Transgression breaks the limits of the common thread that connects law and literature, which is language, by 'showing just how far speech may advance upon the sands of silence':[8] it calls for mediation, for compromise, in both fields – and by doing so it recomposes their voids,[9] as well as their absences:

> Transgression is an action which involves the limit, that narrow zone of a line where it displays the flash of its passage, but perhaps also its entire trajectory, even its origin; it is likely that transgression has its entire space in the line it crosses. The play of limits and transgression seems to be regulated by a simple obstinacy: transgression incessantly crosses and recrosses a line which closes up behind it in a wave of extremely short duration, and thus it is made to return once more right to the horizon of the uncrossable.[10]

Transgression and compromise generate a reciprocal movement, a sort of spiral, which no simple infraction (or thin transgression) can exhaust.

TRANSGRESSION AND COMPROMISE

In dealing, through the compromise made possible within language, with diverging reasons for transgressing, law and literature function both analogously and differently.

Analogy. In both fields, as mentioned above, transgression can have different forms. When the transgression is intentional, in other words in cases of thick transgression, law and literature deal with the clash between contrasting reasons as arts of compromising; that is, as discourses that aim at finding a balance between contrasting forces, thus searching for balance between transgression and norms. This is the crossing of the line and the necessary *return* to it, the reformation that transgression portends.

Difference. In law, the art of compromising is finite because it aims to reach a decision (in law, the contrast between opposing reasons or interests must be resolved). In literature, it is infinite because it does not aim at reaching a decision (it is up to the reader to interpret the relationship between the opposing reasons or interests). In the literary field, no full stop or judgement must be produced, not at an institutional level at least: hence, literature can go through the spiral involving norm and transgression infinitely, whereas law progresses through moments of finitude in which meanings must be fixed, choices must be made, full stops must

---

[7] M. Foucault, *Language, Counter-memory, Practice. Selected Essays and Interviews*, ed. and with an Introduction by D.F. Bouchard, translated from the French by D.F. Bouchard and S. Simon, Cornell University Press (1977). See as well J. Lacan and J.B. Swenson, *Kant with Sade*, The MIT Press (1989), pp.55–75.

[8] M. Foucault, *Language, Counter-memory, Practice. Selected Essays and Interviews*, p.30.

[9] The void recalls the Lacanian episode of the mustard pot (*l'pot d'moutard*): during a seminar, as reported by Rabaté, Lacan speaks about a mustard pot: 'This pot, I called it a mustard pot in order to remark that far from necessarily containing any, it is precisely because it is empty that it takes on its value as a mustard pot. Namely that it is because the word "mustard" is written on it, while "mustard" means here "must tardy be", for indeed this pot will have to tarry before it reaches its eternal life as pot, a life that begins only when this pot has a whole': J.M. Rabaté, *The Cambridge Companion to Lacan*, Cambridge University Press (2003), pp.1–2.

[10] M. Foucault, *Language, Counter-memory, Practice. Selected Essays and Interviews*, pp.33–4.

be positioned inside a discourse. For this reason the decision of a court, though mediated, always entails a sacrifice.

Law *argues* in order to justify, while literature *preserves* the contradictions. Law must reach determined, clear meanings. In law, the content of concepts must be gradually fixed and should not be contradictory. And, even when contradiction is possible, terms are associated to meanings in accordance with principles and with a higher-level order of values that informs the semantic balances within legal discourse.

Figurality, which is what characterises the literary discourse, always embodies an ambivalence, a compromise between different meanings. Genette is right in claiming that a figure cannot be translated without the loss of its quality. He is also right in claiming that the sense of a figure is identical to that deriving from its translation (if I say 'I am lightning', the sense, translated, is 'I am fast' and it coincides with the sense of the figure), but the meaning of a figural expression (that is, the relationship between sign and sense) is different from the sense derived from its translation.[11] Nevertheless it is important to add that the meaning which a figure bears tends to exaggerate and therefore to subvert the sense derived from its mere translation. Between one and the other there is an opposition. Surely, if I claim that I am lightning I intend to mean that I am fast but I also want to say that I am *not* fast, but I am lightning. It is not true that figures must not be interpreted literally: they must *also* be interpreted literally if we want to catch their transgressive content toward the sense that they also affirm and that can be extracted through their translation.

The meaning activated by a figural expression is not only different from what the expression affirms (from the meaning we catch by translating it), but tends to contest it, too. To catch and appreciate fully the meaning of a figure we must first understand its sense, that is, we must perceive what could have been said otherwise. While we hear 'she is lightning' we must necessarily understand 'she is fast'. And nevertheless the alternative that we perceive (she is fast) does not fully substitute the figural expression (she is lightning) and, actually, while it is affirmed by the figure, it is also contested. The notorious and usual sense (normal) is counterposed to an unusual and unknown sense (transgressive). When Gregor Samsa turns into a cockroach, we must necessarily understand that he has turned into a disgusting and unuseful waste, but in order not to miss the figural meaning of the text we must also believe that he has really turned into a cockroach. The sense that we catch by translating the macrofigure of the text (Gregor is a disgusting and unuseful waste) is transgressed and denied by the meaning of the figural expression. Gregor is a waste and nevertheless he is not only a waste but he is also a cockroach. By approaching the idea of a waste with that of a cockroach, Kafka contests the meaning of the waste. He exaggerates, he transgresses it, he resignifies it and this allows him to give voice to something repressed by the idea of waste. In the supernatural event of the story (which we must believe), we therefore also see the recognition of the alienation of the individual but also a protest against the meaning of alienation. Yes, Gregor is waste (he does not fit the middle-class institutions: work and family) and nevertheless being waste means transforming into a monster and being recognised as such. What the meaning of alienation represses and the credit to a supernatural dimension reveals is the magnitude of this condition. Being a waste equals not only being alienated but also being monstrous. The return of the repressed is this equivalence for which being a waste means not only being excluded, but also

---

[11] Genette, *Figures I*, Paris (1966), pp.210 and ff.

being obscene, inhuman, being trash. The supernatural metamorphosis of Gregor gives voice to the protest against the unnaturality of social relationships and transgresses the reassuring idea that alienation cannot reach the point where we turn into a monstrous bug.

***

We can hence say that, in front of an actual or potential transgressive act, law explains why one of the reasons must be sacrificed while literature tends to keep the contradiction open through a form, be it a metaphor, a joke, a stream of consciousness or a figure of speech (this is the real problem for the interpreter: finding the macrofigures that characterise a literary text beyond the singular rhetorical figures).

In stating that both law and literature function as arts of compromising,[12] we must bear in mind that 'compromise' is a term referred to a complex field of meaning, which is usually and most frequently referred to a conservative political attitude of negotiating between contrasting needs. Etymologically, a compromise is a *promise* that performs some kind of reciprocity between the parties. As a matter of fact, the term indicates a *joint promise* (*to promise with*) to abide by an arbiter's decision, deriving from the Latin *com-promissus*, past participle of *com-promittere*, 'to make a mutual promise'. Coming from *com-* (together, with) and *promittere* (foretell, assume beforehand, send forth), which in turn derives from *pro-* (before) and *mittere* (send, throw). As the etymological root testifies, in the act of compromising there is an intrinsic drive to draw opposing poles together, by preserving a common interest, hence the compromise constitutes an agreement aimed at resolving a conflict, stretching towards a middle (com-promissory) ground. It is also a settling of debts which is interesting in relation to the money borrowed by the salmon mayonnaise enthusiast.

A specific use of these terms has been made by Italian theorist of literature Francesco Orlando (1934–2010). In literary criticism of the second half of the twentieth century, Orlando is known in particular as the author of the so-called organic cycle of Freudian studies (*Lettura freudiana della Phèdre*, 1971; *Per una teoria freudiana della letteratura*, 1973;[13] *Lettura freudiana del Mysanthrope – e due scritti teorici*, 1979; *Illuminismo e retorica freudiana*, 1982).[14]

---

[12] As mentioned in the preliminary remarks, above in the first paragraph, and as we have explained in *A Theory of Law and Literature. Across Two Arts of Compromising*, Brill (2020): 'our proposal is to consider law and literature as arts of compromising: i.e. as discourses that aim at finding a balance between contrasts and divergences. Why do we call them "arts"? Because they are peculiar discourses revealing the properties of arts in the classical understanding of the term "arts": they both entail, in other words, operations, techniques and mechanisms which reflect a knowledge and a practical capacity to handle specific cases and problematic situations. Let us be clear: they are peculiar discourses, or arts and, still, they are everywhere. In both law and literature, the use of language is crucial and characterises them as arts. Because of this fundamental role played by language in both fields, they are typical of our everyday life in society. We will explain this further, but we can anticipate that there is literature each time that there is trade off (disguised as figurality); and that there is law each time that convention and negotiation (justified and explained through argumentation) are at play' (p.3).

[13] Translated into English: Orlando, *Toward a Freudian Theory of Literature: With an Analysis of Racine's Phèdre*, Baltimore (1978). We refer to the Italian version of the text, using our translations of the original: therefore, all the citations from Orlando's texts correspond to a translation that we have made.

[14] At the end of the twentieth century, Orlando republished these four essays with a different structure: on the one hand, the four original essays have been collected into a cycle of three volumes in which

In essence: Orlando deduces from psychoanalysis a *logical-formal model*, and not a series of psychical contents to be applied to literary texts. After Freud, the main point of reference for Orlando is the Chilean psychoanalyst Ignacio Matte Blanco, who, drawing from Freud, hypothesises that the human psyche is based on two different logics. Lacan, first, had affirmed that the unconscious is structured like a language.[15] Yet, Matte Blanco has also defined the two logics governing this language: one defined as asymmetrical (what we usually refer to as our *thought*, governed by the principles of Aristotelian logic: principles of identity, non-contradiction, incompatibility);[16] the other as symmetrical, functioning on the basis of opposing and radically different principles, in particular on two mechanisms: the principle of generalisation and the principle of symmetry.

The principle of generalisation implies that two elements having at least one common attribute can be assimilated within a wider class; the principle of symmetry implies that these elements become identical (A shares with B only one feature, they are included in a more general class, and therefore A = B).

In his *The Unconscious as Infinite Sets* (1975) and later, more radically, in *Thinking, Feeling and Being. Clinical Reflections on the Fundamental Antinomy of Human Beings and World* (1988), Matte Blanco reformulates the unconscious as a proper logic: for him, Freud's fundamental discovery is not the unconscious, but that of a world (that Freud names the 'unconscious'), founded upon laws completely different from those on which conscious thought is based.[17]

Orlando claims that the mechanisms governing the logic of the unconscious characterise literature as figural and from this perspective he defines literature as a communicating language of the unconscious.[18] Moreover, considering the unconscious as the place where the repressed is manifested, he defines literature as the *seat* of a compromise formation between a repressive force and a repressed force. Through the compromise between these two forces, by expressing the repressive force *and* the repressed force, literature can give voice to what remains suffocated in the world: to *reasons that do not (otherwise) find recognition*.

Here, at its best, is the definition of compromise formation given by Orlando: 'a semiotic manifestation […] that makes room, simultaneously, for two contrasting psychical forces, that have become contrasting meanings.'[19] The compromise formation that best exemplifies this definition is represented by the *Freudian negation*, that is, by the discourse that affirms while it denies and denies while it affirms; by that logical and antilogical model for which, exactly, the contradiction is also equivalence and compresence. It is as if one wanted to affirm 'I like it'

---

the first essay and the third have been unified; on the other hand, new relevant changes and extensions have been added to *Per una teoria freudiana della letteratura*, republished in 1992. The final text inserted in this final edition – *Dodici regole per la costruzione di un paradigma testuale* – is considered by Orlando as a sort of appraisal of his theoretical system.

[15] Lacan, *Écrits*, Paris (1966).
[16] A = A; A cannot be at the same time A and not A; A cannot be at the same time different and equal to B.
[17] Matte Blanco, *The Unconscious as Infinite Sets*, London ([1975] 1998).
[18] When it arises in dreams, in lapsus and in the symptoms, the language of the unconscious is incommunicable; when the language of the unconscious arises in the joke, beyond being significant, it is communicable. Literature, like the Freudian jokes, is a communicating language of the unconscious. Hence, the only book that Freud wrote on literature is the book on jokes.
[19] Orlando, *Per una teoria freudiana della letteratura*, p.326.

only by saying 'I do not like it'. Only by recognising the reasons of repression can the reasons of the repressed be affirmed.

In making room, at the same time and in the same form, for contrasting reasons, literature creates the *possibility* of radically opposed logics to intervene within the same discourse. Orlando represents the compromise formation between contrasting reasons with a fraction: R/r, where R = repression and r = repressed. In this model, the 'normative' is the repressive force and the 'counternormative' is the repressed force. The model is wide and aims at embracing all the possible clashes between repressive and repressed forces. For instance, in the example mentioned above, law (repression) is the historical character of alienation and transgression (return of the repressed) is its monstrosity. Kafka's story seems to be claiming: I do recognise that alienation exists and that it is natural that an individual that does not adapt to social rules is considered as waste, and nevertheless, no, this condition is also unnatural and monstrous.

Even when repression derives from the reality principle or from the laws of nature, the return of the repressed is socially connotated. In substance, the repressed reasons count inasmuch as they are repressed, broadly speaking, by the *laws of men*. According to Marcuse, 'repression is a historical phenomenon' and 'the return of the repressed makes up the tabooed and subterranean history of civilization'. For Marcuse, in fact, 'Freud's theory is in its very substance "sociological"' and 'the replacement of the pleasure principle by the reality principle is the great traumatic event in the development of man – in the development of the genus (phylogenesis) as well as of the individual (ontogenesis)'.[20]

Repression and repressed are *neutral* containers. We must not conceive repression as a negative instance, unjust because it is repressive, and we must not conceive the return of the repressed as a (merely) positive instance, legitimate since it is repressed: this is what Bakhtin does, by counterposing the neurosis and idealism of Don Quixote and the carnivalesque euphoria of Sancho Panza, and thus counterposing repression, which is negative, and the joy of the carnival, that is, the overturning of order and hierarchies. Bakhtin's carnival resembles the return of the repressed in Orlando's theory but it presupposes that the repressed is characterised always positively, as the expression of vitality, joy, freedom. Repression, on the contrary, is not unjust or evil, and the return of the repressed is not just or good. They are *neutral* and *counterposed* positions, and they are empty.

It is not by chance that the most extraordinary compromise formations in literature are the result of the full recognition of the reasons of repression, that is, that Evil, paraphrasing Bataille, receives its obscurity from the Good, and sexual sin is repressed at its best in Catholic believers, and so on and so forth. It should be sufficient to think of the difference between erotism and pornography. In the first, there is more introjection of the instances of repression, and precisely this introjection makes it possible for the art of erotism to be more refined in the representation of human complexity than pornographic literature (which is much less repressed). The monstrosity of the alienation of the individual, in *Metamorphosis*, can be seen together with the recognition of the middle-class institutions that allow the functioning of modern society and determine the alienation of the individual. In the XXVI Cantica of the Inferno, Dante meets Ulysses. It is probably the most important meeting of the Cantica, as is testified by the fact that Dante shapes his trip (of salvation) in contrast with that of the

---

[20] Cf H. Marcuse, *Eros and Civilization. A Philosophical Inquiry into Freud*, Boston (1966), pp.6, 16.

(deranged) Greek hero and by the frequent references to this meeting and to Ulysses also after Cantica XXVI.

Dante had not read the *Odyssey* and he knew Ulysses through the mediation of classical and medieval sources, with two peculiarities: the shrewdness of the fable teller and the unlimited thirst for knowledge. Ulysses is Virgil's '*sceleror inventor*' (Aeneid, II 164) and is also (as in Cicero, Seneca and Horace) the exemplary man representing the passion for knowledge.

Ulysses is located in the *bolgia* and he is among those who schemed frauds by using their eloquence. He is thus punished for the deceits and not for the trip beyond the Pillars of Hercules. The famous 'orazion picciola' (little oration, Inf., XXVI, v. 125; cfr. Par. XXVII, vv. 82–4) is the umpteenth proof of the eloquence and slyness of the Greek hero. In his oration, nevertheless, in order to persuade his comrades Ulysses does not underline the glory of his endeavour, but the duty to know which is proper not only of his comrades but of all men ('fatti non foste a vivere come bruti/ma per seguir virtute e canoscenza', Inf. XXVI, vv. 199–20 – 'Your mettle was not made; you were made men, To follow after knowledge and excellence'), and by doing so he appears to Dante (who identifies with his desire to advance as well as with his fate of exile) as an example of magnanimity. But Dante can recognise and 'sign' the grandiosity of Ulysses' transgressive endeavour and can feel admiration for him only after having recognised that the trip (horizontal) of Ulysses is not his trip (vertical); that is, only after having recognised that one must respect the limits imposed by God upon man's desire of knowledge. The recognition of a limit – that is, the recognition that 'this is not me' – allows Dante to identify himself with Ulysses and to place his desire for knowledge within a human paradigm. In his celestial trip, Dante is assisted by Grace and Ulysses' endeavour cannot but be condemned, and nevertheless it is by condemning it that Dante can recognise its value. Ulysses' transgression becomes admissible and grand, and can even become a paradigm of humanity – only after having been condemned.

The return of the repressed lies in the compromise; it is only speakable (in literature) by recognising the reasons for the repression. Literature (which is not ideology) cannot give voice to the repressed without taking into consideration, simultaneously, the repression.

***

Law mediates, as well, between contrasting reasons. Yet, it does so by bringing them back to coherent orders of values, to hierarchies of systematic principles. The mediation or compromise enacted by the law, too, is peculiar: the difference from the literary field is that law works with contrasting reasons in order to satisfy the *necessity* of reaching a point of adjudication.

Between analogies and differences, we could say that the compromise between contrasting reasons in *literature* is performed *according to the logic of the unconscious*; the compromise between contrasting reasons in *law* is *rationally* linked to a conjunctive dimension comprehending the reasons in relation to a conventionally valid order of values.

Hence, many of the reasons relevant to literary discourse might simply sound irrelevant in legal discourse. For instance, if a person decides not to repay a loan because she wants to enjoy life – law could never recognise such a reason as valid. Or, paraphrasing the tale used in Freud's text quoted at the beginning of this text, if a person decides to use the money borrowed because of his poverty in order to enjoy the form of life of a *bon vivant*, a court will probably find such an explanation unsatisfactory to justify disproportionate or unjust behaviour. The logic of the unconscious does not include systematic judgement and can follow diverse, even opposing, codes of behaviour. Literature *can* thus claim that one thing is *at the same time just and unjust*: law, instead, *must* decide which reason should prevail.

If legal judgment can be unjust, it is because it maintains a certain degree of injustice intrinsic to judgement: law eventually must choose, where literature must not. What grounds civilisation (in law, together with other institutional forms) is also the grounding of the discontent that derives from civilisation.[21]

The use of the '*nevertheless*' logic that characterises literature (Titius is right; nevertheless Caius…), is limited in law: some reasons are *necessarily* classified as irrelevant. The *pleasure* of literature (given by the possibility that two incompatible reasons are both, at the same time, valid) is counterposed to the *Sollen* (duty, ought, obligation) of the law. Such 'admission' of the compresence of opposite logics is possible in literature since it is based on ordinary language which, itself, allows the cohabitation of opposite meanings within the same proposition (think for instance about conjunctions and other kinds of relationalities).

In dealing with transgression and its limits, we should notice how the literary forms allow us to grant relevance to what one *dreams*, or even *hates*. In the literary field, we can grant relevance to the contradictions inhabiting the human mind, including emotions and fantasies. In literature, the repressed reasons of the singular subject can *return* and speak their truth.

By way of contrast, in the legal sphere, subjective reasons are relevant inasmuch as they are somehow pertinent to resolving a conflict. A dream counts only when and if it can count; likewise, imagination speaks if and only if it can play some role in the argumentative process that leads towards a verdict – a term coming from '*veredictum*', a performative proposition 'said with truth' and truthfully constructed in order to produce effects. Against this background, the compromise in law takes the form of a pact aimed at resolving conflicts, a pact that represses individual instincts in order to avoid war and provide security for the greatest possible number of people. In law, individual reasons represented by the parts within a conflict are all considered valid, and it is up to a *tertium*, the judging institution, to establish which one should prevail.

Thus, the literary compromise is wider than that of the law because it draws from another *archive of truth*. The law cannot deny and affirm the same statement at the same time: one cannot be, at once, both guilty and not guilty, condemned and acquitted. To use a synthetic formula, we could say that the law cannot *dream*: in literature, on the contrary, a statement can be at the same time both true and false.

If it is true that every human action and every text could potentially constitute a transgression of the 'first level', transgression implying a compromise formation is only possible in terms of *thick* transgression. Without recognition of the reason of the other, there would not be any compromise – but merely a lower-level, or *thin*, transgression.

On this point, Hegel, notoriously, states that the thief is the subject that recognises the legal order the most since with 'his act he negates the owner's entitlement to his or her property but it also negates the wider recognition offered by the law'. In this example, the victim and the thief represent two opposing claims: damage affects the property owner in both their external attributes and heritage and in their dignity. On the other hand, 'the thief's desire for recognition, […] makes him or her negate legality altogether'.[22] Within the legal realm, the conflict

---

[21] Freud, *Civilization and Its Discontents*, New York (1961).
[22] C. Douzinas, 'Identity, Recognition, Rights or What Can Hegel Teach Us about Human Rights?', *Journal of Law and Society* (2002), Vol. 29, No. 3, pp.379–4, p.393.

requires the law to move forward, where the rigidity of the system of values and the law's abstraction and formalism are elements that might call for greater sensitivity to social context, individual need and desire. *That might, but are not necessarily capable of doing so.*

It is this kind of voluntary and intentional transgression that becomes interesting across law and literature; on a different note, Kelsen, too, recognises that norms are such only because – metaphysically – there is a field of the unlawful, of the illicit:[23] and yet, from Kelsen's point of view, if every human action is a transgression of a certain limit imposed by the law, it follows that there is no transgression at all since there is nothing *but* transgression.[24] It is not, therefore, that whatever transgression that we are looking at here in this discourse at the crossroads of law and literature, but it is the *significant* transgression: that capable of renegotiating the sense of a norm. The significant transgression, entailing a certain knowledge of the law, requires 'a zone of neuroses, a zone which encloses a legislation of speech and of the subject's enjoyment', an area revealing how the basic function of institutions like the law 'is to produce human beings and to lead them towards death'. Which follows from the primary recognition that 'legal knowledge emerges from a science of the body because it presupposes human beings in the grip of unconscious desire. If one analyses the tradition at the level of its unconscious, the domain of Law is a grey world, uniform and terrible, in which regulations are haunted by transgression.'[25]

Behind these reflections lies the Freudian assumption that discontents follow from all processes of civilisation; in such a frame, law underlines the needs and requests of the individuals and constantly attempts to translate them into reasonable and legitimate needs and requests. Among these requests, there are some, however, that can only be recognised outside of the law and that we can find within the literary dimension. Could law ever acknowledge and accept Oedipus' reasons?[26] It could, yes, but only under the condition that they had the potential to be somehow pertinent in the argumentation aimed at making a decision. Literature, conversely, lets the perversions speak and includes also logical patterns that would otherwise be excluded by reasonable discourse.

Individuals cannot be treated, in law, as desiring subjects: they are, instead, treated as rational subjects who can think, decide and act. The logic of the law *adheres* to reality, the logic of literature is *in relation* to reality, but – since it works through the principles of the unconscious (symmetry and generalisation) – it can transcend the context and it can refer to other dimensions, also radically unrelated to each other. In the same object, literature can include opposing interpretations: it contributes to the representation of interior worlds and various dimensions, and can give voice to what would otherwise be condemned, to what is unexpected and even inaccurate – not only to what is technically illegal, but also to what is unique, singular and individual in its most humane aspects.

---

[23] H. Kelsen, *Pure Theory of Law*, trans. Max Knight, University of California Press (1967).
[24] A. Condello, 'Transgression and Individuation: Proximities between Law and Literature', in A. Condello and P. Heritier (eds), Law and Literature, special issue, *The Myth of the Law through the Mirror of Humanities: Perspectives on Law, Literature, Psychoanalysis, and Aesthetics* (2020).
[25] P. Goodrich (ed.), *A Legendre Reader*, trans. Peter Goodrich with Alain Pottage and Anton Schütz, Palgrave Macmillan (1997), p.126.
[26] P. Goodrich, *Oedipus Lex. Psychoanalysis, History, Law*, Berkeley (1990) and M. Aristodemou, *Law, Psychoanalysis, Society: Taking the Unconscious Seriously*, London (2010).

DIFFERENT LOGICS

As we have mentioned throughout the chapter, across law and literature the tension produced by transgression is handled through different versions of compromise. In literature, the tension regards values and interests not only in contraposition, but also as entirely non-homogeneous and even oppositional. In law, instead, all reasons representing the interests of opposing parts, in order to be recognised, must fall within the realm of legal rationality: reasons, in law, are such only in relation to norms. This structural difference entails that while the logic of the law must be coherent, the logic of literature, by contrast, reflects the contradictory and chaotic realm of the unconscious, where the opposites can coexist.

From this first difference, it follows that the art of compromise within the two spheres functions differently: in law, such art is oriented towards a result, it is *finite*, since law is bound to judgement. On the contrary, the art of compromising in literature is *infinite*, since within the literary field the contradictions do not have to be resolved at all costs. Literature preserves the contrasts and upholds them: unlike law, it is not aimed at judging and it can bear the weight of contradictions. From this characteristic follows that the pleasure given by literature is due to its capacity to grant human beings the possibility of experiencing not only what *they are*, but also what *they are not*. Literature takes us into other worlds and gives access to *otherness* (also to dimensions of *otherness* present within the same subject). In the legal realm, the contrasts between opposing values or interests are resolved into decision and judgement; in literature, instead, all reasons remain valid. In law, compromise is necessary and must be resolutive because of the prohibition of the *non liquet*.

Law handles the tension between norm and transgression through argumentation, by justifying its judgements *analytically* and by explaining each choice in order to preserve its coherence and to reflexively legitimise its authoritative force. In law, the process of adjudication connects the level of norms with the level of facts, by explicitly stating why *one* norm applies (and not another), or why such and such principle is *relevant* (and not another) in order to comprehend the case at stake within a wider order of the discourse. Law is *Folgenorientiet*, goal-oriented: it must find a balance between conflicting values *in order to* try to realise the principles that gave it origin.

Literature, on the contrary, handles the tension between norm and transgression *synthetically*: through figurality, it contains and includes opposite reasons and thus allows the claim, at the same time, of *something* and of its *contrary*. Through the figurative language of literature, it is possible to *affirm by denying*, and to *deny by affirming*.

***

Let us now consider these analogies and differences between law and literature also at a more operative level. The main consequence deriving from the differences between these two arts is, in fact, that in performing compromise the law cannot attribute relevance to all the reasons expressed by literature. There are, however, *exemplary fields* that testify more clearly to how the inclusive bi-logic of literature, retaining values, principles and opposing reasons, can shed light on the (more exclusive) selective logic of the law. Law and literature cross and intersect each other, in this sense, because in this exemplary field the art of compromising in literature challenges the validity of the law. This exemplary field is where law encounters extra legal values and horizons or projects of justice;[27] more broadly, where law openly intercepts issues concerning *the sphere of morality*: for instance, in that field of legal casuistry concerning fundamental civil rights and freedoms.

As a matter of fact, law mediates between (potentially or actually) contrasting reasons, through norms, by recognising hierarchies of values that qualify singular reasons as more or less relevant, in order to reach an adjudication. Because of such necessity, the logic of the law is based on oppositions between what *can or cannot* be done, what *should or should not* be done, and so on. However, despite the central role played by form, and as pointed out various times in the history of legal theory, man-made laws that conflict with accepted moral orders and principles are just 'not valid law'.[28] A classical example is the validity of the legal order established under the Nazi regime, as discussed in Hannah Arendt's *Eichmann in Jerusalem: A Report on the Banality of Evil* (1963), and in Gustav Radbruch's formula, which states, simply, that *extremely unjust law is no law*.

Discussed in his *Rechtsphilosophie*, Radbruch's formula can be translated as:

> The conflict between justice and the reliability of the law should be solved in favour of the positive law, law enacted by proper authority and power, even in cases where it is unjust in terms of content and purpose, except for cases where the discrepancy between the positive law and justice reaches a level so unbearable that the statute has to make way for justice because it has to be considered 'erroneous law'. It is impossible to draw a sharper line of demarcation between cases of legal injustice and statutes that are applicable despite their improper content; however, another line of demarcation can be drawn with rigidity: Where justice is not even strived for, where equality, which is the core of justice, is renounced in the process of legislation, there a statute is not just 'erroneous law', it is in fact not of a legal nature at all. That is because law, even positive law, cannot be defined otherwise than as a rule, that is precisely intended to serve justice.[29]

In other terms, following these critiques of strict formalism, a judge who encounters a conflict between a statute and what he/she perceives as just has to decide against applying the statute – if the legal concept behind the statute in question seems *unbearably unjust* or in *deliberate disregard* of human equality before the law. It is, indeed, widely recognised that principles of morality, or values like justice, should have a prominent place in the criticism of legal arrangements, and on the validity of legal systems.[30]

Quite obviously, the sphere of values is not composed by immutable principles, but it expresses human attitudes that vary from context to context and from individual to individual. *Quid iuris*, then, when a court is called to establish whether euthanasia should be juridified, made legal or not (see *Cappato*, Italian Constitutional Court, 2019)? *Quid iuris*, when a national Parliament is called to establish if same sex marriage should be foreseen or not, in contrast with communitarian principles (see *Coman*, European Court of Justice, 2018)? *Quid iuris*, when the European Court of Justice must decide if a Muslim woman can wear a cover against the regulations of her employer (see *Achbita*, European Court of Justice, 2017)?

---

[27] Namely, what is correct and reflects a principle of equal treatment among different cases: which is also Radbruch's criterion to differentiate the unjust law.
[28] Hart, *The Concept of Law*, Oxford (1961), p.156.
[29] G. Radbruch, *Gesetzliches Unrecht und übergesetzliches Recht*, in SJZ, 1946, pp.105–8, trans., p.107. Cf ibid, *Rechtsphilosophie*, ed. Ralf Dreier and Stanley L. Paulson, Heidelberg, 2003.
[30] Hart, *The Concept of Law*, p.157.

Before questions regarding *rights and freedoms* like these, standing *across* law and literature and conceiving them as arts of compromise could be useful and may be advantageous. Let us consider how and in what sense. When challenged with questions that concern individual freedoms, such as those regarding (among others) choices on affects, body, faith, desires, forms of life – the law has a double chance: either reducing the number of choices by not recognising or by denying, for instance, a right or a choice; or widening the number of choices, by *saving the chances* of both, for instance, those that believe that same sex marriage should be included within the range of forms of marriage and those that believe the opposite. This type of conflict paradigmatically shows that there are, indeed, opposing reasons coexisting within society. Considering one of the mentioned cases, and borrowing the logic of literature, we could say that same sex marriage is theoretically both just *and* unjust at the same time, since society comprehends individuals that are *pro* and *against* it.

Unlike the logic of the law, the logic of literature is not directed to finality nor is it constrained to systematic judgement: it is, in this sense, more inclusive, since it reflects the logic of the unconscious, governed by symmetry and generalisation, where two contrasting instances can inhabit together. The law is often called to measure its limits with dimensions of life governed by individual free will, such as for instance those relevant in the definition of liberties and civil rights. In these spheres, how can law establish what is right or wrong in situations where the orders or values and the visions of the world might be radically opposed, that is, when there are individuals or groups of individuals believing that good and bad are situated at radically opposed poles? This problem concerns the logic underlying norms and their creation, and thus is directly related to actual or potential transgression of norms.

At a logical level, the law can include, it can save the chances of the other; or it can decide in advance, embracing one position and considering *that* as *just* (for instance, by prohibiting same sex marriage). Observing the nature of transgression across law and literature could thus lead to the *assumption of a critical stance towards liminal issues* such as those concerning the liberties of each individual, where law – instead of deciding in advance what people may or may not do – can choose to leave the choice up to the individual woman or man, working more as an inclusive and interpretable *regula iuris* than a firm formalistic norm. In other words, there are fields in legal science where the bi-logical model of literature might be productive of a counternormative pressure testing the value of the limits created by the law: as in the *regulae iuris* in Roman law, in those fields it might be more effective to think through maxims containing the fundamental values of the legal order, maxims that would then be declined, and applied, case by case according to different and even *opposing* needs, desires, visions of the world. The contradictory logic of literature suggests, in this coupling with the logic of the law, a prudential account of it.

The logic of prudence is built on the coexistence of plural voices within a communitarian realm, where major and minor discourses (legal and literary, crosswise) can reach institutional recognition. As a matter of fact, a *regula* directs and guides, indicates a dynamic path and without imposing a static model. There are indeed spheres of collision between reasons and norms, such as that of freedoms, civil rights and liberties, where the law would work (and *does* work, when understood this way) better as a project, a possibility, a horizon within which each existence is realised authentically and autonomously. This field is especially interesting because it pertains to the individuation of the singularity of each life, and at the same time it reveals quite clearly the differences between the modes of handling the art of compromising in law and literature.

The reciprocal signification of transgression and its limits hence leads to a dimension where opposing reasons are considered and measured reciprocally, case by case, and not according to universal criteria: a dimension, in other terms, recalling the common law of equity, that is, the art of finding the right measure in accordance with the order of rules – which is recognised – and yet by (re)measuring and (re)signifying the relevant criteria on the case and for the case.

Exploring the intersectional sphere of law and literature through transgression (and reflexively through compromise) helps to build a possible second *regard* on the nature and institutional function of the law, open to minoritarian voices and projected towards a minimal normativism in favour of a larger role of *prudentia*, as seems to be suggested by experiences such as the rewriting of decisions by projects like the feminist legal judgments[31] – reflecting the singular life experience in its dismeasurement in respect of the form and to the norm.

***

In the fourth story of the sixth day of the *Decameron* by Giovanni Boccaccio (a day dedicated to jokes), a Venetian cook[32] named Chichibio is appointed by his rich, noble and generous master, Currado Gianfigliazzi, to cook a crane that he has hunted.[33] Brunetta, a girl Chichibio is in love with, smells the fragrance coming from the kitchen and asks the cook for a thigh; when he refuses, offended, she threatens that she will not allow him to indulge his sexual desires.[34]

Chichibio then, fearful, agrees to give her a thigh from the crane. Later, when his master, Currado – who has invited guests for dinner – is astonished to see the crane without a thigh, the liar cook replies: 'the crane, Sir, has but one thigh and one leg'. The master is angry but, not wishing to disturb his guests in the face of Chichibio's stubbornness, he commands the cook to prove, the following morning, that cranes have only one leg. Otherwise, Chichibio will be punished.

The morning after, the two go to a river. Chichibio recognises that the master is still very angry and considers how to get out of the difficult situation. All of a sudden he sees a group of cranes standing on just one leg, cheers up and, showing them to his master, says: 'now may you see well enough, Sir, that 'tis true as I said yesternight, that the crane has but one thigh and one leg; mark but how they stand over there.' Currado frightens the cranes, which, after putting down the other leg, fly away. Then, to the cook: 'How now, rogue? Art satisfied that the bird has thighs and legs twain?'

> Whereto Chichibio, all but beside himself with fear, made answer: 'Ay, Sir; but you cried not, oho! to our crane of yestereve: had you done so, it would have popped its other thigh and foot forth, as these have done.' Which answer Currado so much relished, that, all his wrath changed to jollity and laughter: 'Chichibio,' quoth he, 'thou art right, indeed I ought to have so done.'

---

[31] Cf R. Hunter, C. McGlynn and E. Rackley (eds), *Feminist Judgments. From Theory to Practice*, Oregon (2010).

[32] Around mid-1300, Venetians were considered liars by Florentines. Chichibio is defined as a 'liar Venetian' and he is presented as dumb.

[33] Cranes were often cooked at that time.

[34] 'Chichibio fell a singing: "You get it not from me, Madam Brunetta, you get it not from me." Whereat Madam Brunetta was offended, and said to him: "By God, if thou givest it me not, thou shalt never have aught from me to pleasure thee"': www.brown.edu/Departments/Italian_Studies/dweb/texts/DecShowText.php?myID=nov0604&expand=empty&lang=eng.

Between Chichibio and Currado there is a clear social and cultural difference, and such difference has a crucial relevance within the story. Chichibio belongs to the kitchen, Currado to the living room; the first goes to the river on a nag, the other on a horse. Chichibio is a poor servant; Currado is a noble and rich lord. Furthermore, Chichibio is dumb (he does not know that the cranes sleep on one leg and when he sees them he thinks it is fate that is actually supporting him), and he is a thief, a liar, and lustful.

Even his final line is absurd and surreal, and it is not pronounced with the intention to defend some reason but only to postpone the sanction, even if only for an instant. Chichibio's transgression, that is, does not aspire to reach a compromise; it is a thin transgression and only requires sanction.

The conflict between the two, nevertheless, is resolved otherwise. Currado is hit by the final line of Chichibio, and his rage is converted into laughter, and the master decides to reward the slyness of the servant. Although granted by the master and although only momentarily, a potential parity between the two characters is established. The value attributed by the master to Chichibio's final line neutralises, in a second, his infractions (he has stolen, he is a liar, but he is forgiven), and even threatens, though momentarily, the great social difference between him and the master (otherwise confirmed throughout the story). Chichibio offers no logic and nevertheless his joke, his line, without him even recognising it, bears a new system of values that might resignify not only the social norms that he has violated, but the entire moral and juridical system on which those rules are based. If Currado (and Boccaccio with him) rewards that absurd joke, in fact, it is because he sees in it values such as guile, initiative and intelligence, values that right then (in the middle of the fourteenth century) were about to acquire relevance in Europe. Without even knowing it, Chichibio is the bearer of an open, problematic and unscrupulous morality that will characterise the age of merchants and the birth of a new *intelligentsia*.[35]

Chichibio's joke nullifies the conflict because it bears (from Currado's and Boccaccio's point of view) a contemporary morality which is emerging together with the age of municipalities and of the middle class. Next to the world of virtues and of the chivalrous swords, a new world is rising, where the structural forces are richness, entrepreneurship, malice, adventure, roguery. And these forces are not deprecated by Boccaccio, but represented realistically and with engagement. Currado's empathy for the servant is then less banal than it might appear to be. If Chichibio does not provide any specific logic, it is instead Currado, with his laughter and total forgiveness, who sustains a reason different from that which would lead him to punish the Venetian cook, liar and thief. The servant is right, and Currado states it explicitly. The field of reasons is enlarged, and makes room for different orders of ideas which are often incompatible with those that precede them. The empire is disaggregating into a mosaic of reigns, princedoms, districts, municipalities. Medieval universalism is in crisis. The middle class, industrious and active but also avid and cynical, shall dominate the new society to come.

Chichibio's transgression, which seems inappropriate to any compromise, becomes the mouthpiece of a new system of values and of new morality, both more open and problematic. By laughing and by recognising the logic of the dumb Chichibio, Currado seems to be giving up on applying the pre-existing law (for which he would have punished the cook instead) and seems to be suspending his own judgement by entering the logical order created by the

---

[35] See V. Branca, 'Una chiave di lettura per il "Decameron"', in G. Boccaccio, *Decameron*, Einaudi, Torino (2014), vol. I, pp.vii–lxxvi.

concrete singularity of the situation he is in, hence embodying – in a certain sense – the logic of equity, which (re)measures the concept of justice according to the definiteness and purposefulness of the case.

31. Transdiscourse
Gonzalo Sebastián Aguirre and Christian Alejandro Kessel

INTRODUCTION

For some time now, we, the authors, have been doing legal research; coming from a transdisciplinary approach, we have been composing a sort of singular epistemic field that we call *Aesthetics of Law* as a specific domain, rather different from a Philosophy of Law. Over the course of at least ten years of joint research, we have studied notions such as 'drama', 'norm', 'fiction', 'law', and so on, by approaching authors and works in a way that does not presuppose the distinction between Law and Art or Law and Literature. Indeed, if something characterizes this Aesthetics of Law it is the *loguical* (in the sense of Logos not reduced to any logic) and the dramatic assumption common to Law and Literature. We understand that both are expressions of the same *loguical* circumstance that gives rise to what Michel Foucault calls the 'order of discourse' (Foucault, 1981).

We will present a notion of drama that has been key in the configuration of the Aesthetics of Law, whose epistemic postulates we will summarize in the following argument. Finally, we will present three jurisliterary cases of different calibre. First, we will present the work of Macedonio Fernández, not as a writer but as a jurist, that is, as a thinker of the Law, always assuming the community between Law and Literature. In this sense, he strikes us as a valid interlocutor of the work of Friedrich Nietzsche, since we understand that both constitute themselves by the juridical–dramatic key through which the Aesthetics of Law approaches its objects of study. We will then present a summary of the dramatic development of two historical characters whose vicissitudes have challenged the limits of reality and fiction, as they are understood in modern times, or at least since the end of the nineteenth century. The lives of Juan Moreira and Hormiga Negra (whose nickname literally means 'Black Ant') were marked by judicial ups and downs, and were repeated and altered by literature over decades. Both show how their lives, which were on the verge of the disintegration of language, civilization and their own narratives, influenced the composition of *fictive forces* of art and legal process in the Río de la Plata.[1]

ON DRAMA: BETWEEN THE OB-SCENE AND THE SACRED

The playwright is a drama maker, but what do we call drama? Sometimes it has been understood as a synonym of action, and in particular, of scenic action. This conception has lasted over time. Nietzsche opposed it. Months before ceasing his literary production, he wrote two pamphlets in which he condemned the art and figure of his former mentor, Richard Wagner.

---

[1] The Río de la Plata ('River Plate') is the estuary formed by the confluence of the Uruguay and the Paraná rivers. It is considered the widest river in the world, and it works as a border between Argentina and Uruguay. Its coasts are the most densely populated areas of both countries.

In one of the only three footnotes to the first of these texts, *The Case of Wagner*, written in the spring of 1888, he refuted Wagner's conception. Nietzsche postulated that drama is not action. It is an event, and not any kind of event, but one that displaces action before or behind the scene and instead presents the legends of the place, its hieratic history. The canon teaches that in ancient tragedies action preceded the story on stage, or happened where no one could see it. For example, as is known, Sophocles' *Oedipus Rex* begins after the death of Laius, the defeat of the Sphinx, Oedipus's marriage to his mother and the birth of his children. The play shows the consequences of action and, above all, the affirmative reaction of the protagonist, the political and emotional response of a king who leads an investigation, without ceasing, despite clues indicating that the cause of the plague, the murder of his predecessor, was perpetrated by his own hand. These stories – both *Oedipus Rex* and the vast majority of Greek tragedies that have survived, with the exception of Aeschylus' *The Persians* – are part of a mythical tradition, that is, one that predates the time of their authors and history itself, and they are a fundamental part of the Western cultural heritage; they are texts with an evocative capacity that is renewed generation after generation.

Within this framework, the definition given by Nietzsche serves as a platform to develop a concept of 'drama' (among many, many others) that includes those events that are of interest both to theatrical and to legal writing.

In 1978 Moriaki Watanabe interviewed Michel Foucault. It was the second time that the French philosopher spoke at the request of the Japanese writer (Foucault, 2001). Watanabe said that Foucault's texts gave him the same kind of pleasure as reading Racine. Foucault was flattered, pointing out that his work was more like that of a playwright than that of a philosopher. In fact he said that he was not a philosopher, or that he was a bad one, because he had no interest in the eternal (the dimensions of the universe, the categories of the soul); instead he was interested in events, and in a peculiar way, as in the theatre, beyond the truth and the lie of what is observed on stage. The theatre concentrates life; it does not present, but expresses dramas that tend to repeat themselves. Thus, drama summarizes an event that displaces the question of truth and lie or submits it to its becoming. For its part, the modern Law, in its quest to intervene in dramas, to prevent or repair their undesirable consequences, dispenses with a binary link to truth and lie. As is known: in the legal world, formal truths, substantive truths and a long list of singular hypostases (such as the concept of juridical person) or controversial conventions (such as those that deal with the determination of the beginning or end of human life) coexist and are all expressions of a complex link with reality. In short, the relationship of drama (the substratum of theatre and ancient tragedies; the interest and source of legal writing) with truth and falsehood is in no area flat or simply subject to spurious Logos.

Broadly speaking, the displacement of action from or placement before the scene, which is repeated incessantly in classic tragedies, has remained a resource ever since. Two examples will suffice to show the continuity of this dramatic gesture: (a) in William Shakespeare's *The Tragedy of Romeo and Juliet*, the love of the young couple is created in an instant and what follows is the course of their destiny, that is, the consequences of that affection which is presupposed and not the goal of dramatic development; (b) in Samuel Beckett's *Happy Days*, the protagonist, Winnie, is first buried up to her waist and then up to her neck; the play progresses without revealing how or why she got there, but everything that happens is marked by the facts that would answer those questions. To this day, at least for a relevant part of contemporary theatre, it remains fundamental to detect how events are configured, are expressed and lead to reaction, as well as how the transformation of characters is made operative.

The events that become dramatic in legal texts also usually have an *ob-scene* dimension, that is, an action or vision that inspires them. Naturally, rulings are derived from past events, just as laws and contracts generally attempt to influence future events. These events, these series of past or future actions, are not always clearly distinguished or anticipated and, in fact, their very obscurity justifies the maturation of the institutes of Law. In any case, legal writing, like theatrical writing, does not seem to deal so much with what happens but rather with what surrounds the action, both inside and outside the event. In what way can we prevent or repair those undesirable events? Perhaps one of the main differences between the two spheres lies in how the displacement of action occurs; while theatrical writing mainly organizes its expression, legal writing mainly organizes its *pathos*. In general, Law intervenes before or after the event. It tries to repair or it tries to prevent. Perhaps the situation can be considered differently when the legal text is equated to an action, but even in some of these cases there is usually a series of previous actions that are dramatized by the legal texts. Thus, stories of love or convenience precede marriage just as much as the ups and downs of a conflict or the development of an ambition to declare war. In short, this complex web of action and re-action is characteristic of both disciplines.

The drama of *Oedipus Rex* is the *ob-scene* action of *Antigone*, just as a declaration of war may have been preceded by an act of war and pursued by others. In one way or another, dramatization is about distinguishing a response to what is happening or may happen, questioning the event and operating accordingly. But how does something of the hieratic order play out in dramatic events? The very meaning of the term is elusive; too many religions and doctrines have been founded in its name, and have arranged interpreters and weapons in the service of ensuring a means of understanding it. It is natural, however, to assume that the experience of the sacred predates its administration, its institutionalization. How, then, can we account for their primary impression? Perhaps, as a start, it is worth considering Roger Callois' (Reims, 1913–Kremlin-Bicêtre, 1978) impious indication.[2] In *Man and the Sacred*, the French writer proposed that outside the field of religion, what is designated as sacred is that to which each person consecrates the best of his or her being, what each one considers to be the supreme value, what is venerated. In his opinion, the sacred is to be found in the being, the thing or the notion by which people interrupt all their conduct; what they do not consent to discuss, nor allow to be the object of mockery or jokes; what they would not deny or betray for any price. In a similar vein, Argentine anthropologist Rodolfo Kusch (Buenos Aires, 1922–Maimará, 1979) suggested that the sacred is what cannot be sacrificed under any circumstances.[3] In

---

[2] Both the concept of drama and that of the sacred have been worked on over the years, in more or less explicit, systematic and interesting ways. We do not intend to present their definitive, current or integrated meaning, but rather to recognize a possible sense of the term and we think that, perhaps, this will enable an experience of trans-disciplinary thinking. In any case, of course, on the question of the sacred it is advisable to read the great works of Roberto Calasso, Mircea Eliade, Rudolf Otto, René Girard and María Zambrano, as well as the remaining texts of Georges Bataille, among many, many others.

[3] '[W]e cannot deny that we all do the job. But we say in this case: we sacrifice ourselves. And what does this mean? It means that we make sacred what we do, because nothing else means sacrifice. And sacred for whom? Well, sacred to me, to my own kingdom, that which we hide when we are working. Obviously we only work by sacrificing, to get things that are sacred to me.' ('no podemos negar de que todos cumplimos con el trabajo. Pero decimos en este caso: nos sacrificamos. ¿Y esto qué significa? Pues que tornamos sagrado lo que hacemos, porque no otra cosa significa sacrificar. ¿Y sagrado para quién? Pues sagrado para mí, para mi propio reino, ese que ocultamos cuando estamos trabajando. Evidentemente solo trabajamos sacrificándonos, para conseguir cosas sagradas para mí'. In 'Nuestro

any case, this pattern allows us to allude to a person's experience but not to the sincerity of its content. On this subject, Georges Bataille, in *Erotism: Death & Sensuality*, summarized the concept by affirming: 'This sacredness is the revelation of continuity' (Bataille, 1986). Nevertheless, he associated this notion with a kind of spectacular perception of death, in which the 'discontinuity of existence' of the individual would be interrupted and he would remain in contact with the 'continuity of being'. In this work, Georges Bataille explicitly rejected the possibility of referring to the Divine, to God, instead of the 'sacred', because, according to his sayings, 'it is better to be less easily understood and more accurate' (Bataille, 1986). Certainly his texts make it difficult to systematize the concept, but it is a problem that in general seems to be faced by those who consider that they have reached an understanding of what they call 'sacred' when they try to inform 'profane' readers. Bataille had already noted this difficulty, even considering that the nature of the sacred is perhaps the most elusive thing that occurs among men, nothing more than a privileged moment of communal unity, a moment of convulsive communication of what is ordinarily stifled (Bataille, 2008).

In this context, the playwright's task is to compose the matrix of these events that not only bring into play an order of the sacred, but also give the reader, or the spectator, the opportunity to empathize with its movement. Law seems to deal with a similar series of events, even from a secular conception of their genesis. How can we not feel a certain hieratic air in the matrix of constitutionally protected rights, or in human rights in general? There are orders, gods that should not be outraged. There are orders, gods, whose constitution is or allows us to enable experiences of the continuity of the being in the discontinuities of the life. Thus, the sacredness that can be revealed in a journey presupposes the right of transit and that which is experienced in a meal requires the protection of health and the guarantee of access to food.

In this sense, assuming that the hieratic orbit of Human Rights does not necessarily imply a return to natural law, perhaps natural law can be considered as only one of the great ways in which the sacred has become a legal system. From our point of view, drama, in fact, is concerned with the expression of sacredness, without the need to appeal to any religion. It takes up singular features of the manifestation of the sacred and seeks forms that conjure up its repetition. From this point of view, we ask ourselves whether the legal order and theatrical practice, in the final analysis, will not pursue the same end: the protection of a sacred experience.

POSTULATES OF AN AESTHETICS OF THE LAW

We present here a series of postulates that try to establish and develop the conditions of possibility of the epistemic field that we call 'Aesthetics of Law'. We will do so in a Spinozan manner, but without claiming, from the outset, any geometrical order. At most, as we have said, there is a chain of postulates whose *loguical load* is not exhausted in the operative rules of modern Logic. Precisely what we are dealing with here is also an Aesthetics of Logic, so as to recover for the notion of Aesthetics the expressive force that it could have had in a Kantian expression as a Transcendental Aesthetics. In fact, this Aesthetics will not be limited to the semantic field of what we call Art. Aesthetics refers to a Science of Forms. Modern Logic has

---

recinto sagrado del pa'mí', *Obras Completas 1*, Rosario: Ross Foundation, 2007, pp.339–40). Kusch dedicated a large part of his work to anthropological and philosophical thought; he was a professor, and over the years his writings have become increasingly relevant in Latin American thought.

taken this position by formalizing a basic operational formal scheme that structures the field of modern Science and Technology, leaving Aesthetics the field of non-operational forms, called art. Thus, Aesthetics is in a certain way determined by what we call Art History.

The postulates will follow one another by determination and opening up epistemic obstacles. Our starting point, articulated by Edgar Garavito's notion of *transcursividad* (transcursivity), takes into account the distinction between Law and Literature. We understand, as will be seen, that it is foundational with respect to the distinction between Science-Technique and Art-Aesthetics and that, in turn, it gives rise to a recovery of dramatic force.

First Postulate

The modern distinction between law and literature is not univocal; it can be either a legal distinction or a literary distinction. We are faced with two clear and distinct ways of organizing action: as legal acts or as literary acts. We are dealing with two types of fictions, that is, two ways of structuring and giving meaning to the behaviours of human beings: juridical fiction charges behaviours with objective meaning and literary fiction charges them with subjective meaning. Thus, from the juridical point of view, the distinction between Law and Literature reserves for Law the real or true weight of the behaviours, and leaves for Literature their fictional or false load. From the literary point of view, although the distinction between Law and Literature is often assumed according to the legal mode, both the legal and the literary fields are producers of fictions, conceived as *logical*-moral and optical–moral compositions that give meaning to the conduct of human beings.

Second Postulate

All literature is *police literature*. Literary *loguic* formation emerges from the public presentation of the nascent Administration of Justice in terms of standardized public policy, that is, it forms part of the epistemic axis that Foucault attributes to the *Polizeiwissenschaft*, conceived as a science or mode of knowledge oriented towards the achievement of (public) policies. From this public presentation of some matters (cases) related to the Administration of Justice, the public space structured by *police journalism* practices emerges. These practices basically consist of counting the policies that constitute the area of interest of these journalistic practices. The encounter of public policies with the world of life is not yet subjected to such policies. This is why public policies on crime are the ones that generate the most interest, in stories of criminals and famous cases. However, it is precisely from this same area of journalistic interest that literary interest emerges. That is why on many occasions it has been possible to confuse journalistic practice with literary practice and is what has established the idea that Law as a State Language, or Grammar of Public Policies, constitutes the field of the real (true), and Literature that of the fictional (false). Since Journalism is a sort of transmission belt between legal Grammar and the world of life, Literature would delve into the aspects of the world of life that subsist and persist without being addressed by law as public policy.

Under these conditions of behaviour control through the control of the phenomenal images that compose the space–time of Kantian sensibility it can also be understood that Cinema comes from the Novel, and not from the Theatre as might be assumed at first glance. The Cinema is a sort of audiovisual amplifier of the Novel. Therefore, like the Novel, Cinema can either give subjective fictional consistency to objective legal fictions, or it can pursue the affective forces of the life world that do not coincide with the legal organization of the affective conflicts of the life world. The latter variant offers a chance for the survival of poetic forces that were able to give rise to the Poetry that reigned as a mode of *logical* composition before the advent and consolidation of juridical fiction.

Third Postulate

Biology is a branch of Law. All modern science, as an academic discipline that responds to the achievement of public policies, whether state or private, is a branch of law, resulting from the legal formalization of practices of justice that, in turn, give rise to a fictional administration of them. It is from this fictional administration that all the modes of true or operational knowledge of the real or useful world derive.

Fourth Postulate

Modern law and literature are discursive formations that come from a common *loguical transcursivity*. This *loguical transcursivity* gives rise to a course (*transcurso*) or legal–literary discourse that Foucault called *l'ordre du discourse* ('the order of discours'), and which structures the 'world that is left over' after the loss of the epistemic influence of the Kantian notion of '*noumeno*' at the hands of the notion of utility as proposed by Nietzsche in his 'How the "true world" finally became a fiction'. History of an error. This story is not to be read scientifically or literally, for it would rather be the story that gives rise to the birth of modern scientific and literary formations. It should be read, perhaps, in a dreamy tone and as a children's story (*Traumton* and *Märchenton* in Nietzsche, 2019).

Fifth Postulate

The legal course (*transcurso*) or discourse (*discurso*), in short, the legal transdiscourse (*transdiscurso juridico*), structures the *sensible experience* of successions and contiguities that Hume detected at the origin of the idea of causality. And it is from this policing, from the organizational relevance of *Sensibility*, that Kant can detect the Forms of Space and Time as a priori forms of all rational *Sensibility*.[4] To put it more precisely: only the *Sensibility* that can be organized in the key of Space and Time as forms given a priori to all *Sensibility* can be considered rational. And it is only within the field delimited by this Transcendental Aesthetics that an (always phenomenal) knowledge that is normalizable and a generator of public policies could take place.

Sixth Postulate

Literary transdiscourse gives way to the *sensible experience* that insists and persists in overflowing the space–time field delimited by Kantian transcendental Aesthetics, when this field loses the epistemic support of the 'noumenal world' that, like an unlimited ocean, surrounded the 'island of Truth', structured according to the a priori forms of Space and Time.

---

[4] 'The capacity (receptivity) to acquire representations through the way in which we are affected by objects is called *Sensibility*' (Kant, 1998).

Literary Space (*espace littéraire*) follows what Maurice Blanchot proposes, a space and also a time that both arise from surpluses not reached by the police; that is, by the public policies that organize the *Field of the Sensible* in terms of Kantian Space and Time.

Seventh Postulate

Within rational space–time sensible experience, Kant presents the 12 categories of Understanding, according to which the *Field of the Sensible* can be regularized and made operational. The imputation is a sort of 13th category added by Kelsen that explains what we call Law, as a regulated operationalization of the practices of justice without the interference of 'juridical feelings'. It follows that what we call Law does not comprehend *legal transdiscourse*. Legal transdiscourse may well be understood as a condition of the transcendental Kantian Aesthetics that is at the base of any regular operability of the *Sensibility* and behaviours that can be normalized.

Eighth Postulate

Inside *sensible experience* organized spatially and temporally by Kantian transcendental Aesthetics there is the *surplus sensible experience* (or *literary experience*) that gives rise to what we call Literature, whose singular spatial (and temporal) condition was specified by Maurice Blanchot in *The space of literature* (*L'espace littéraire*).

Ninth Postulate

Literature is a discursive formation supplementary to the discursive formation of Law that is structured according to the 13th category of the Understanding, that of imputation; but it is also part of the Order of the Discourse as a whole, structured by all the categories of the Understanding, as it comes from the *juridical transdiscourse* (see Fifth Postulate).

Thus, Literature can operate both at the level of the Order of Discourse as fiction that accompanies the reality of Law, which can also be approached journalistically, and at the transdiscursive level, where the fictional distinctions between Law and Literature play out.

Tenth Postulate

The 13 categories of the Understanding, regardless of whether the imputation constitutes a specific category or a kind of 'causality doubling', have their condition of reality, their fictive force[5] or optical–moral illusion, in the fiction 'speaking is seeing'. The order of Speaking or Language, here called the Order of Discourse, grammatically structures the order of Seeing, here called *Sensibility*, and follows the Nietzschean maxim that we cannot get rid of God as long as we continue to believe in Grammar.[6]

---

[5] See Paul Valéry, 'Prologue to Montesquieu's Persian Letters'.
[6] See Friedrich Nietzsche, 'Reason in Philosophy', pt. 5 in *Twilight of the Idols*.

Eleventh Postulate

Literature either collects and returns the affective surpluses of the Order of Discourse to the grammatical stream, or explores the 'is' of the phrase 'to speak *is* to see', which at the same time unites and separates the Logos from sensible experience understood spatially and temporarily.

Twelfth Postulate

What we call *event* expresses the fictive force that sustains the set of 'states of affairs' (Deleuze, 1990) and behaviours that express any action. The drama is the specific event that destabilizes those sets; it is the fictive force that has become sacred dramatic force.

Thirteenth Postulate

Drama is not what happens to or what is done by characters in a novel or people in a court case. Neither action nor reaction. Neither active nor passive voice. Drama is the medium or the field of fictive forces from which ob-scene actions and expressive re-actions arise.

Fourteenth Postulate

Both Law and Discursive Literature try to keep drama at bay, managing it among 'the parts' or 'the characters' that are distributed spatially and temporally. Transdiscursively, on the other hand, Law and Literature can address this dramatic force: not only administering or resolving conflicts but also capturing justice; not only administering or arousing desires and emotions but also displaying them on stage.

THREE CASES OF VICE-DICTION

The three cases presented below have a peculiar relationship with the theory of drama and the postulates of an Aesthetics of Law. Following Deleuze's method of dramatization, we will say that none of the three cases are intended to be examples of a theory. On the one hand, Macedonio Fernández is presented as a dramatic source of the Aesthetics of Law. On the other hand, Juan Moreira and Hormiga Negra dramatize the proper concept of 'drama' developed here. It is not a question, then, of cases that try to demonstrate a theory or illustrate an Idea, but rather of one anecdotal source (Macedonio) and two expressive anecdotes[7] (Juan Moreira and Hormiga Negra). The three of them try to show the interweaving between drama, theory and Idea on the one hand, and between Literature and Law on the other hand.

> Subsuming under 'the case' forms an original language of properties and events. We should call vice-diction this quite different procedure to contradiction. It consists in traversing the Idea as a multiplicity. [...] A concept being given, we can always seek the drama, and the concept would

---

[7] 'The anecdote is to life what the aphorism is to thought: something to interpret' (Deleuze, 2002).

never divide or specify itself in the world of representation without the dramatic dynamisms which determine it in this way in a material system beneath all possible representation.

The Idea thus appears as a multiplicity which must be traversed in two directions, from the point of view of the variation of differential relations, and from the point of view of the distribution of singularities which correspond to certain values of these relations. What we were calling before a procedure of vice-diction merges with this double traversal or this double determination, reciprocal and complete. (Deleuze, 'The method of dramatization'[8])

In this way, writing and reading also make up a theoretical drama, and each reader can become a case or a dramatic perspective of this epistemic proposal.

MACEDONIO FERNÁNDEZ AS A JURIST AND TRANSDISCURSIVE WRITER

I've moved from the Law Office; I'm just entering Literature and since none of my judicial clientele came with me, I don't have the first reader yet. (Macedonio Fernández, 1989, p.84)

Macedonio Fernández, contemporary of Hans Kelsen, graduated as a lawyer and was a prosecutor in the city of Posadas. They say he never accused anyone. In the city of Buenos Aires, his presence in the bar La Perla, in the neighbourhood of Once, attracted the attention of a group of 'cultural operators', among whom was Jorge Luis Borges. Borges himself contributed to creating the legend of Macedonio, as a great conversationalist, the writer who never published. Like all legends, the legend of Macedonio is absolutely true and has grown over the years. Macedonio was disorganized, would not combine his writings well, lost or confused his papers, did not care too much for publication, was distracted in doing so. Perhaps that is why few people have paid attention to his theories or taken them seriously.

In his 'Theory of Art', Macedonio Fernández calls 'Culinary' (*Culinaria*) those literatures that give back to the grammatical torrent surpluses of the Order of discourse, to literatures that try to conjure up this surplus. He calls 'Novelistic' (*Novelística*), on the other hand, the 'Belarte' itself, which impacts on the juridical–literary fictions upon which the world of the normalized Attention is sustained. The mission of Novelistics is to put an end to the predominance of the Culinary and, thus, to give rise to a renewed sensitive experience and to a recovery of the juridical feeling of life. In this sense, the key fictional figure for Macedonio is the Reader – not the Narrator or the Author or, in short, the legal person. The Reader combines legal and literary fiction. It is therefore a matter of discontinuing the Reader, also called the 'Orderly Reader'[9] in a piece that gives rise to the 'first good novel'. Profoundly zenonian, Macedonio will not only tackle the endeavour of writing the first good Novel, but will also write the last bad one: *Adriana Buenos Aires*, followed by *The Museum of Eterna's Novel. The first good Novel* (*Museo de la Novela de la Eterna. La primera novela buena*). Macedonio has everything calculated. In 'What is Born and What Dies', the first of the 56 prologues of *The Museum of the Novel*, Macedonio is proposing an upcoming bad novel that will be the first to last in its genre:

---

[8] Translated by M.J. McMahon, 'Deleuze and Kant's critical philosophy', thesis submitted for the degree of Doctor of Philosophy, University of Sydney, 2004.

[9] We would like to thank Federico Fridman for his guidance in translating Macedonio into English.

Today we release to the public the last bad novel and the first good novel. Which one will be the best? [...] How I suffered not knowing if the brilliant page before me belonged in the last bad novel or the first good one! Let the Reader take charge of my agitation and trust in my promise of a forthcoming goodbad novel, firstlast in its genre...[10]

The work of Macedonio Fernández must be considered as a legal–literary–metaphysical continuum. His writings delve into transdiscourse from which comes not only the Kantian Space–Time distinction, but also those of Sleep–Wakefulness, Subject–Object and True–False. These distinctions, which comprise the Order of Discourse, are meticulously scrutinized and discarded in his book *No todo es vigilia la de los ojos abiertos* (*Not all is Wakefulness with Open Eyes*). The Subject–Object distinction, for example, is at the base of the distinction between person and good (legal ownership), between reader and book, between author and book, between character and reader. Transdisciplinarily, the *culinary* distinction between law and literature is only supplementary: the latter symbolically takes over the fictive surplus of the former in the same way that, according to Foucault in *Truth and Juridical Forms*,[11] the prison symbolically takes over the surplus of confinement of the Family and the School. Law and literature act jointly as culinary operators, as generators of memories and reports of a given normality of 'states of desire':

> a primary ingredient of Leisure that he [a new employee] discovered in every office in the Administration, where not only is the new employee immediately banned from doing anything but is made to sign a schedule of presence in the office, and, so that his not doing is seen, he is charged with making all kinds of reports, which is not difficult because it consists simply of tearing out pages of any novel and signing them. (Macedonio Fernández, 1989, p.103)

Based on their transdiscursive conditional quality, both Law and Literature can reactivate what Macedonio calls 'emotional states'. These are not mere reactions or 'sensational states', nor are they usual repetitions or 'states of desire'. The 'emotional states' activate the differential valuing relation that is expressed in the recovery of the capacity of Attention, both on an 'intellectual' and 'muscular' level through contractions of images and muscles respectively: 'Courage is not an emotion but the free availability of Attention and Muscle that is translated into these terms: absence of Fear' (Macedonio Fernández, 1997, p.80).

The value of literature as a transdiscursive non-culinary practice is the 'inverse paramnesia' (Macedonio Fernández, 1975, p.361) according to which something that was known becomes unknown and the reader then becomes a 'reader who skips around' (*Lector salteado*). The value of Law as a non-culinary transdiscursive practice is 'justice', according to which something that was determined becomes indeterminate and the continuous (juridical) person becomes discontinuous.

JUAN MOREIRA, ON THE EDGE OF FICTION

Sometimes the same drama repeats itself in the field of theatrical and legal writing, and in one way or another it lasts. In fact, the folkloric tradition and legal documents have been two

---

[10] Translation by Margaret Schwartz published by Open Letter at University of Rochester.
[11] Foucault, 2000, pp.1–89.

of the greatest sources of Argentine literature of the late nineteenth century. Many stories of fugitive gauchos[12] fleeing from justice come from that period – stories of their wanderings, profiles and contradictions. Among the references of that prose is Eduardo Gutiérrez (Buenos Aires, 1851–89), a prolific writer of disputed quality, author of many gaucho novels, historical chronicles, police stories and, above all, creator of Juan Moreira, his most popular work (Morales, 1944, p.184). The real historical character was apparently a thug ('*matrero*') who used his knife to solve all kinds of problems and was killed by a policeman while trying to jump over a fence, in April 1874. Five years later Gutiérrez published a portrait of the *matrero*, inspired by his judicial history (Rojas, 1960, p.586); presenting him as a generous, brave bandit, a walking gentleman who avenged the victims of a rapacious grocer ('pulpero') and an arbitrary judge, in the manner of a Robin Hood from the lands of La Pampa.[13] Five years went by and the gaucho's ups and downs shift from an imperfect reflection made of pure words to one of almost pure action: a pantomime based on the novel, premiered by the Carlo brothers' circus, in which the only speech occurs in a stretch of song and dance. Moreira's interpreter was José J. Podestá (Montevideo, 1858–La Plata, 1937), a clown who belonged to one of the biggest families of artists from Río de la Plata. He later added dialogue to the mimodrama gestures and, in 1886, he assembled one of the foundational works of the Argentinean theatre.

José J. Podestá played Moreira in theatres and circuses for almost 40 years; several presidents of the Republic met him, congratulated him and granted him awards. The historical character, who had lived in confrontation with the authorities, was surpassed by the literary and then by the theatrical, which blurred the limits between reality and fiction. The examples are abundant. Podestá says in his memoirs that before the premiere of the mimodrama he had agreed with one of the actors that after being killed, he would stay lying down at the end of the performance, and he did so – to the point that after a while there was serious concern on the part of some of the spectators. Then, at Podestá's indication, he jumped up, leading the audience to burst into monumental laughter (Podestá, 2003, p.52). The Argentine playwright Mauricio Kartun[14] says that Juan Moreira's performances often had to be suspended due to stage invasions during the final scene, where, holding *facóns*,[15] audience members confronted the 'policemen' to defend their idol (Kartun, 2006, p.71). Decades later, when José Podestá was being honoured for his 50 years in the theatre, there were still those who approached him and greeted him calling him 'friend Moreira' (Podestá, 2003, p.71).

However, the best expression of the irrelevance of the question of truth and lies in the dramatic field comes from a text signed by Carlos Moritán, which is an extract of *Memorias de un provinciano* (1932), a selection of *gaucho* literature created by Jorge Luis Borges in 1969. It states that in 1910, in a brawl, a boy in his 20s stabbed another to death and when questioned by the police he said his name was Juan Moreira and that he was the son of the legendary *matrero*. The statement was implausible: the gaucho had died more than 35 years earlier; however, his mother confirmed the declaration of the knifeman. She said she and the famous gaucho had conceived him when his circus stopped in her village (Borges, 1972).

---

[12] A sort of Argentinian cowboy. The simplification of their similarities and differences can be seen in the film *Hello Friends* (1942) by Walt Disney.
[13] Morales, p.186; Rojas, p.593.
[14] Mauricio Kartun is perhaps the greatest Argentine playwright alive. He has written plays and been giving conferences, talks and workshops for years.
[15] Large, straight, pointed knife used by the *gauchos*.

As to the young man's filiation, the anecdote is uncertain. The book where the text should be found is not listed in the index of the publication, nor in the catalogue of the Argentine National Library. Many believe that its true author is no other than the compiler, Jorge Luis Borges, famous for this kind of mischief. In any case, when on 30 April 1874, in the small town of Lobos, Sergeant Chirino crossed Moreira with the bayonet of his Remington rifle, he determined the end of the profuse legal prose that motivated his figure and the beginning of a dramatic revolution. Almost 150 years later, artistic references to Juan Moreira remain, particularly in Eduardo Gutiérrez's novel that replaced the biography of the gaucho as the first source of the repetitions of his drama. In the words of the writer, at that agonizing moment, significant for the incipient Argentine judicial system and fundamental to his art, Moreira mumbled: 'Ah, coward! Coward! Men like me don't get stabbed in the back! You cannot deny that you are justice.'[16]

THE RISKS OF DRAMA: THE CASE OF *HORMIGA NEGRA*

Without a doubt, the most memorable gaucho in Argentine literature is José Hernández's *Martín Fierro.*[17] However, the character of Juan Moreira described in Gutiérrez's novel is also a celebrated figure. In 2009, researcher Beatriz Seibel (Buenos Aires, 1934–2018) recorded 56 adaptations for theatre, three of them with female protagonists; two adaptations for opera; one adaptation for television; and five adaptations for film (Seibel, 2009, p.14). Juan Moreira was not Jorge Luis Borges' preference and, between Gutiérrez's characters, the writer has shown an unquestionable preference for the story of the adventures of Guillermo 'Hormiga Negra' Hoyo, a gaucho whose adventures became a novel, written in prose that Borges elegantly described as ungrateful and trivial. Beyond this style, according to Borges, what consecrates the immortality of the text is that 'it is similar to life' (Borges, 2007, p.338). In fact, the life of the historical Hoyo himself was unusually long for a *gaucho matrero*. He lived more than 80 years and outlived the author who consecrated him.

Again Borges quotes a remarkable anecdote of undoubted attraction and dubious verisimilitude, although useful for the purpose of measuring the risks of dramatization in the field of the arts. His compilation of writings about matreros includes a second text not referenced in the index, 'Vistazos críticos a los orígenes de nuestro teatro' (Critical views of the origins of our theatre), that he attributed to Fra Diavolo and cited as a source in a 1911 edition of the then famous magazine *Caras y Caretas*. According to this:

> In those years, the Podestá were touring around the province of Buenos Aires, performing gaucho plays. In almost all towns, the first performance corresponded to *Juan Moreira*, but, when they arrived at San Nicolás, they announced it was going to be *Hormiga Negra* instead. That was the land of Guillermo Hoyo. The eve of the performance, a rather short and elderly subject, dressed in neat poverty, introduced himself to the tent. 'They are saying,' he said, 'that one of you is going to come out on Sunday in front of everyone and say you are Hormiga Negra. I warn you that you will not

---

[16] '¡-Ah, cobarde! ¡Cobarde!… ¡A hombres como yo no se los hiere por la espalda!… ¡No podés negar que sos justicia!…' (Gutiérrez, 2020, p.238).
[17] The epic poem written by Hernández (Buenos Aires, 1834–Belgrano, 1886) was originally published in two parts, *El Gaucho Martín Fierro* (1872) and *La Vuelta de Martín Fierro* (1879). It is considered one of the main works of Argentine literature, and for many it is its pinnacle.

fool anyone, because I am Hormiga Negra and everyone knows me.' The Podestá brothers treated him with such deference and tried to make him understand that the piece in question was the most conceptual homage to his legendary figure. It was all useless, although they did order a few glasses of gin from the hotel. The man, firm in his decision, claimed that he had never been disrespected and that if anyone came out saying that they were Hormiga Negra, he, old man and all, was going to run him over. They had to surrender to the evidence! On Sunday at the announced time, the Podestá performed Juan Moreira.[18]

Perhaps the author imagined a true fact.

REFERENCES

Bataille, G. (1986), *Erotism: Death & Sensuality*, San Francisco: City Light Books.
Bataille, G. (2008), *La conjuración sagrada: Ensayos 1929–1939*, Buenos Aires: Adriana Hidalgo.
Blanchot, M. (1992), *El espacio literario*, Barcelona: Paidós.
Borges, J.L. (1972), *El matrero*, Buenos Aires: Barros Merino.
Borges, J.L. (2007), *Obras Completas IV*, Buenos Aires: Emecé.
Callois, R. (1959), *Man and The Sacred*, Illinois: The Free Press.
de Romilly, J. (2011), *La Tragedia Griega*, Madrid: Gredos.
Deleuze, G. (1990), *The Logic of Sense*, London: The Athlone Press.
Deleuze, G. (2002), *Nietzsche and Philosophy*, London: Continuum.
Deleuze, G. and Guattari, F. (1998), *Kafka, por una literatura menor*, México: Era.
Fernández, M. (1975), *Museo de la Novela de la Eterna*, Buenos Aires: Corregidor.
Fernández, M. (1989), *Papeles de recienvenido y Continuación de la Nada*, Buenos Aires: Corregidor.
Fernández, M. (1997), *Teorías*, Buenos Aires: Corregidor.
Fernández, M. (2001), *No todo es vigilia la de los ojos abierto*, Buenos Aires: Corregidor.
Foucault, M. (1981), 'The order of discourse' translated by Ian McLeod in R. Young (ed.), *Untying the Text: A Poststructuralist Reader*, Boston: Routledge and Kegan Paul.
Foucault, M. (1993), *Las palabras y las cosas*, México: Siglo XXI.
Foucault, M. (1999), *La verdad y las normas jurídicas*, Barcelona: Gedisa.
Foucault, M. (2000), *Essential Works* (ed. Paul Rabinow): *Power* (ed. James D. Faubion), New York Press.
Foucault, M. (2001), *Dits et écrits 1954–1988*, Paris: Éditions Gallimard.
Foucault, M. (2008), *El orden del discurso*, Buenos Aires: Tusquets.
Garavito Pardo, M. (1997), *La transcursividad. Crítica de la identidad psicológica*, Medellín: Universidad Nacional Colombia.
Gutiérrez, E. (2020), *Juan Moreira*, Caseros: Gradifco.
Hume, D. (2010), *Investigación sobre el entendimiento humano*, Buenos Aires: Losada.

---

[18] 'Por aquellos años, los Podestá recorrían la provincia de Buenos Aires, representando piezas gauchescas. En casi todos los pueblos, la primera función correspondía al Juan Moreira, pero, al llegar a San Nicolás, juzgaron de buen tono anunciar Hormiga Negra. Huelga recordar que el epónimo había sido en sus mocedades el matrero más famoso de los contornos. La víspera de la función, un sujeto más bien bajo y entrado en años, trajeado con aseada pobreza, se presentó a la carpa. "Andan diciendo", dijo, "que uno de ustedes va a salir el domingo delante de toda la gente y va a decir que es Hormiga Negra. Les prevengo que no van a engañar a nadie, porque Hormiga Negra soy yo y todos me conocen". Los hermanos Podestá lo atendieron con esa deferencia tan suya y trataron de hacerle comprender que la pieza en cuestión comportaba el homenaje más conceptuoso a su figura legendaria. Todo fue inútil, aunque mandaron pedir al hotel unas copas de ginebra. El hombre, firme en su decisión, hizo valer que nunca le habían faltado el respeto y que si alguno salía diciendo que era Hormiga Negra, él, viejo y todo, lo iba a atropellar. ¡Hubo que rendirse a la evidencia! El domingo a la hora anunciada, los Podestá representaban Juan Moreira…' (Borges, 1972, p.147).

Kant, I. (1992), *Crítica de la razón pura, 'Estética trascendental y Analítica trascendental'* (José del Perojo, trad.), Buenos Aires: Losada.

Kant, I. (1998), 'The Transcendental Doctrine of Elements. First Part: The Transcendental Aesthetic' in *Critique of Pure Reason*, Cambridge: Cambridge Edition.

Kartun, M. (2006), *Escritos 1975–2005*, Buenos Aires: Colihue.

Kelsen, H. (2001), 'Reflexiones en torno de la teoría de las ficciones jurídicas, con especial énfasis en la filosofía del "como si" de Vaihinger' in *Revista Crítica Jurídica*, 18, México: UNAM.

Kelsen, H. (2005), 'Validez y eficacia del derecho' in H. Kelsen, E. Bulygin and R. Walter, *Validez y eficacia del derecho*, Buenos Aires: Astrea.

Kusch, R. (2007), *Obras Completas 1*, Rosario: Fundación Ross.

Morales, E. (1944), *Historia del Teatro Argentino*, Buenos Aires: Lautaro.

Morey, M. (2014), 'Ficción y verdad en Michel Foucault: Notas para un itinerario', 'Un murmullo infinito… Ontología de la literatura y arqueología del saber' and 'Ver no es hablar. Cinco apuntes para una reflexión con una postdata', in *Escritos sobre Foucault*, Madrid: Sexto Piso.

Nietzsche, F. (1993), *Crepúsculo de los ídolos*, Madrid: Alianza.

Nietzsche, F. (2000), *Escritos sobre Retórica*, Madrid: Trotta.

Nietzsche, F. (2003), *Escritos sobre Wagner*, Madrid: Biblioteca Nueva.

Nietzsche, F. (2008), *Fragmentos póstumos (1875–1882), Vol II*, Madrid: Tecnos.

Nietzsche, F. (2014), *El libro del filósofo*, Buenos Aires: Taurus.

Nietzsche, F. (2019), *Twilight of the Idols*, Compass Circle Press.

Podestá, J.J. (2003), *Medio siglo de farándula. Memorias de José J. Podestá*, Buenos Aires: Galerna.

Rojas, R. (1960), *Historia de la Literatura Argentina II*, Buenos Aires: Kraft.

Seibel, B. (2009), *Antología de obras de teatro argentino*, Buenos Aires: INT.

Valéry, P. (1995), *Estudios literarios*, Madrid: Visor.

32. Trauma
Phillip Mitsis

MINNIE'S INNOCENCE? POETIC JUSTICE AND TRAUMATIC SPECTACLES OF THE INVISIBLE IN GLASPELL'S *TRIFLES*

I want to begin with Sophocles' *Oedipus* – which may seem an odd way to start off a discussion of Susan Glaspell's *Trifles*, especially since to many critics *Oedipus* has seemed a quintessentially 'male' play with narrowly male concerns, while *Trifles* is often given the palm for being just the opposite, perhaps even the very first such opposite. But on particular questions of the complex relations between literature and law, and thus between readers and the kinds of evidence they confront, both textual and legal, these two plays, though in many ways so antipodal, perhaps provide mirror images of similar textual and ethical *aporias*.

In a volume dedicated to the work of René Girard,[1] Sandor Goodhart argued that readers must turn a blind eye to a series of troubling inconsistencies in Sophocles' drama concerning the evidence about the murder of Laius if they are to conclude, as Oedipus himself does at a key moment in the play, that he is the one who killed his father. The difficulties begin at the outset when Creon reports that Apollo's oracle has said that the *murderers* of Laius must be expelled from Thebes and we later learn that Laius' servant, the one sole surviving witness to the killing of Laius, had reported that a group, presumed to be robbers, had attacked the king. By the same token, Oedipus himself reports that he had killed an old man at the crossroads, but had killed his entire retinue along with him. Now it is easy to assume that these different accounts of Laius' death refer to one and the same event, and that either the servant is lying about the number of attackers (why?) or that Oedipus is unaware that there was a survivor of his roadside slaughter. However, Laius' servant reports that after the attack he returned to Thebes only to find that Oedipus, having solved the riddle of the Sphinx, was already on the throne and married to Jocasta. Thus, there remains a further *aporia* in the text about the timing of Laius' death.

Oedipus, it is to be remembered, begins with a plague sent by Ares, who fathers Eros with his sister Aphrodite. The plague, in conformity with this divine source, thus seems to be linked as well to the problem of Oedipus' incestuous relationship with his mother, since the various aberrations that have been caused by the plague are instances of anomalous birth and reproduction. Evidence about Oedipus's incest with Jocasta is put on a solid footing during the course of the play. Apart from having been predicted by an earlier oracle, it is then corroborated by eye-witness accounts that indicate that Oedipus is indeed Jocasta's son. But while Oedipus had earlier received an oracle that he would marry his mother and kill his father, and he comes

---

[1] S. Goodhart (1978). "Ληστὰς Ἔφασκε: Oedipus and Laius' Many Murderers". *Diacritics*, 8(1), 55–71. Wider elements of Oedipal influence, especially on juridical history are taken up in Peter Goodrich's seminal Oedipus Lex. *Psychoanalysis, History, Law* (Berkeley, 1995), from which I borrow elements of the title.

to learn that he is indeed Laius' biological son,[2] the actual evidence for his killing of Laius is extremely confusing, inconsistent and, as it stands, just does not add up. More important, this evidence ultimately goes uninterrogated in the play. At the very moment when Oedipus, who had been hoping to exonerate himself by confirming that the attackers were many, is finally in a position to interrogate the one eye-witness to the murder and to learn if one or many had attacked Laius, he fails to. Instead of demanding this crucial piece of corroborative empirical evidence, he concludes prematurely on the basis of the fact that he has now learned that he has committed incest with his mother that he must indeed have killed his father in accordance with the oracular prediction.[3] He then blinds himself – a gesture[4] that, among other things, many have taken to show his realization of the inadequacy of empirical evidence in the face of the inscrutable power of mythic, divine, oracular truths. Goodhart asks, however, why readers follow Oedipus in this gesture and willingly convict him without waiting for the conclusive eye-witness evidence. Moreover, in skating over the troubling inconsistencies in the evidence surrounding Laius' murder, readers readily accede to particular 'mythic' readings of the play's action which, however, are underdetermined by the textual evidence on offer. A deep fissure, therefore, opens up in the text that not only fractures our ability to understand the evidence for parricide in the play and its meaning, but also ultimately presents us with a larger dilemma. Does Sophocles uphold the power of oracular, divine truth and show the pitiful inadequacy of our own abilities to understand the world and parse its confusing evidence? Is he, in other words, a defender of traditional religion and the power of divine, mythic truth at the expense of human empirical legal inquiry? Or is he attempting to knock theonomic shibboleths off their pedestal as mere rhetorical constructions, offering instead a subtle critique of mythic and oracular interpretations that are inadequate to the task of explaining actual empirical realities and, indeed, that blind us to them?

Subsequent criticism has often come down on one side or another of these alternatives, in some ways marring the subtlety of Goodhart's more sphinx-like questioning of the text. But his discussion also raises a more general problem for interpretations of the play's evidence in the light of contemporary theoretical construals. René Girard, for instance, used *Oedipus* as a linchpin in his argument about a scapegoating mechanism in the play. Creon reports early on that the oracle has proclaimed that the murderers of Laius must be expelled in order to rid Thebes of pollution. In the play's final moments, Oedipus, after blinding himself, asks Creon that he be allowed to be led by his daughters out of Thebes to Mt. Cithaeron to live out the rest of his existence. Creon demurs and compels him to return into the palace – a further puzzle and seeming inconsistency that has led some to argue that this is another possible indication that Oedipus has not polluted himself with the blood of his father and that Creon knows it. Others,

---

[2] David Konstan (2015). "Blood Parents versus Foster Parents, or What Was So Terrible About Killing Laius?" *Psychoanalytic Inquiry*, *35*(1), 53–9.

[3] In his 'Lettres sur Oedipe' that serve as a preface to his *Oedipe* (1718), Voltaire finds Oedipus' failure to ask the essential question at this key moment a further flaw among the many in Sophocles' craftsmanship. [*Oeuvres Completes, II*, ed. A. Beuchot (Paris, 1877), pp.1–58]. See Goodhart's discussion. His point is that we should take these inconsistencies in the empirical evidence not as signs of Sophocles nodding, but as raising arguably the central questions posed by the text.

[4] I leave aside here the question of whether the blinding is a symbolic castration as well, the rejection of the role and power of father, the binaries of agnatic and cognatic relations, and so on. By blinding himself Oedipus becomes like Tiresias, the blind prophet of Apollo, hence further reinforcing at a symbolic level his conviction in the power of oracular truths.

including many translators, merely end their reading of the play with the equivalent of the following stage direction: 'Oedipus exits from Thebes, led by his two daughters.' Of course, this kind of reading, whether under the influence of a Girardian scapegoat theory or not, runs roughshod over Creon's overt denial of such a resolution to Oedipus and to the audience. For whatever reason – and here critics need to be remarkably ingenious[5] – the play ends with Creon himself leading Oedipus towards the palace, ostensibly in violation of the oracle that he himself had reported. Many critics, however, disregard this final action in the play and again assume an oracular perspective that aligns itself with notions of fate, tragic self-knowledge, ritual expulsion, and so on.

By the same token, the spectre of Freud always hangs over interpretations of this play. While critics have certainly noticed that Oedipus has not willingly or consciously done what he has done, they have no doubt that he both kills Laius and then fathers children with Jocasta. One intriguing possibility raised by Goodhart's reading is the relation of Freudian theory to the empirical testimony of the analysand. However much empirical evidence is offered on the couch about one's positive conscious attitudes towards one's father, the cure does not take place until one comes to discover and understand the nature and source of one's murderous instincts in the light of theoretical Freudian truths. One is led to question through Goodhart's analysis, therefore, whether, when one comes to such a new Freudian therapeutic understanding of one's self, it is on a par with Oedipus' self-blinding and the taking on of the mantle of mythic truth without sufficiently weighing or ultimately examining the empirical evidence for such self-knowledge. That is, the analysand must assume a new kind of self-knowledge that merely reasserts the accusatory power of the father and the truths of Freudian theory. In sum, Goodhart opens up the possibility that a drama that is often taken to be the quintessential text of patriarchal and religious authority itself reveals the ways in which both characters and readers fall under the spell of oracular and patriarchal truths. In so doing, it holds these truths up for examination, rather than championing them. And it exposes the dangers that await readers who choose to blind themselves along with Oedipus by eschewing the messy world of empirical detail.

This rather breathless summary of some of Goodhart's questions about what is often taken to be not only a paradigmatic drama of European theatre, but also arguably its foundational detective drama, can perhaps serve as a point of reference as we begin to look at the mariticide in *Trifles*.[6] Glaspell's text is fast becoming foundational in its own right as an attempt to unmask mechanisms of patriarchy and the legal edifices upon which they depend. It seems to me, however, that critical understanding of the play's action is in danger of falling too easily into the grip of various contemporary rhetorics that offer us a monological reading of the play's action and of women's experience of violence, and that depend, as in *Oedipus*, on a certain blindness to what might be characterized as the empirical evidence surrounding the murder that grounds the action of the play. On the face of it, of course, such a claim might seem to be woefully blinkered and naïve. After all, we are facing a work that is held to show how

---

[5] For discussion see Oliver Taplin, "Echoes from Mount Cithaeron" in *Allusion, Authority, and Truth: Critical Perspectives on Greek Poetic and Rhetorical Praxis*, eds Phillip Mitsis and Christos Tsagalis (De Gruyter, 2010) pp.235–48.

[6] For a discussion of Glaspell's obsession with the Greek language and Greek tragedy, see Marie Molnar, "Antigone Redux: Female Voice and the State in Glaspell's *Inheritors*" in *Susan Glaspell. New Directions in Critical Inquiry*, ed. Martha Carpentier (Cambridge Scholars Publishing, 2006) pp.37–44.

women's solidarity and empathy create an alternative space for notions of evidence and justice in a patriarchal system of law, and how 'punishing symbolic crimes will lead to a greater form of Justice than pursuing the law on the basis of tangible evidence'.[7] In a sense, then, Glaspell's text wears on its sleeve the problem that Goodhart's Sophocles only darkly hints at. Yet, I would argue that such readings of Glaspell, however salutary, nonetheless depend on critics not only systematically turning a blind eye to potentially exculpatory evidence in the play, but also on endorsing a series of ethical conclusions that should put us in mind of Goodhart's dilemma about Sophocles. I want to raise, therefore, a set of corresponding questions about how the text of *Trifles* has come to emblematize the power of particular political and social discourses to blind readers to elements in the text in a way that may undermine what many critics have taken to be its presumed overt goals. *Trifles* undoubtedly contested boundaries that distinguished 'good' women from 'bad' in the early twentieth century and it offered a brave primer on such things as feminist epistemology, domestic liberation and justice and the nature of power relations in law and its administration. But as it continues to do so, it may also unwittingly harbour a warning about how such concerns can come to override in ethically problematic ways other significant conceptions of evidence in both literature and law, and thus undermine with subtle forms of literary symbolism and narration our overall integrity as readers, or, if you will, as implied jurors. In a sense, I will be turning the tables on Shoshana Felman's argument about the relation of law to cultural or collective trauma.[8] While Felman argued that the law is 'professionally blind' to such trauma and that literature offers a way of symbolically understanding traumatic experience that can consequently transform legal procedures, I will try to show how such symbolic understanding can be correspondingly blind to crucial questions of autonomy and potential innocence, and that we must also be alert to other forms of tangible prosaic evidence when approaching such narratives, both literary and legal, in order to ensure victims their voice. By the same token, Glaspell's text, ironically, is beginning to speak with the very kind of monologic voice of a remote judge delivering a legal opinion that it presumably was meant to criticize in the first place – an unapproachably authoritative patriarchal voice, as it were, that effaces all freedom and ambiguity in its text by forcing readers to inevitable conclusions and judgements based on a logic of symbolic poetic justice. Here too, I will try to point to some of the more prosaic virtues of textual polyphony.

We can begin with the following summary that, I think, for the most part represents standard critical readings of the action of the play:[9]

> The play begins in the now abandoned farmhouse of John and Minnie Wright. On command from the county attorney, Mr. Hale recounts his visit to the house the previous day. He found Mrs. Wright

---

[7] Mary M. Bendel-Simso (1999). "Twelve Good Men or Two Good Women: Concepts of Law and Justice in Susan Glaspell's 'A Jury of Her Peers'". *Studies in Short Fiction, 36*(3).

[8] Shoshana Felman (1997). "Forms of Judicial Blindness, or the Evidence of What Cannot Be Seen: Traumatic Narratives and Legal Repetitions in the O.J. Simpson Case and in Tolstoy's 'The Kreutzer Sonata'". *Critical Inquiry, 23*(4) (Summer), 738–88.

[9] I quote the Wikipedia summary since it shows how entrenched a particular interpretation has become. It also does so with considerable economy. It offers a similar barometer for traditional interpretations of *Oedipus*, starting its summary: 'Oedipus, King of Thebes, sends his brother-in-law, Creon, to ask advice of the oracle at Delphi, concerning a plague ravaging Thebes. Creon returns to report that the plague is the result of religious pollution, since the murderer of their former king, Laius, has never been caught. Oedipus vows to find the murderer and curses him for causing the plague' – which nicely effaces Creon's report that 'murderers' killed Laius.

behaving strangely and her husband upstairs dead, with a rope around his neck. Mr. Hale notes that when he questioned her, Mrs. Wright claimed that she was asleep when someone strangled her husband. While the three men are searching the house for evidence, the women begin to explore the domestic space on their own. As they interact with the stage environment, the two women discover clues to the couple's personalities as well as potential evidence in the case. Although Minnie and John Wright are not physically present they become vivid figures for us via the dialogue and actions of Mrs. Hale and Mrs. Peters. Through evidence, the wives soon realize that Mr. Wright killed the bird, and that led to Mrs. Wright killing her husband. Although the men find no evidence upstairs in the Wright house that would prove Mrs. Wright guilty, the wives piece together that Mrs. Wright was a victim of abuse by her husband. They understand how it feels to be oppressed by men. After the women discover the truth, they hide the evidence against Mrs. Wright so that she is spared the punishment for killing her husband. Whether Mrs. Wright is convicted is neither confirmed or denied at the end of the play.

Much of the play revolves around Mrs Hale and Mrs Peters slowly coming to construct a motive for Minnie Foster Wright's[10] murder of her husband. They find various bits of evidence, 'trifles', that presumably would have been overlooked by the male investigators, though this particular claim is complicated by the fact that the two women lie about, tamper with, and hide evidence at every turn in the service of female solidarity.[11] The text suggests, however, that the male investigators would not have valued or understood this evidence in any case. Leaving this assumption aside, their reconstruction of Minnie's motive has led to a variety of claims about the nature of feminist epistemology[12] and also to a number of rather deflationary contrasts aimed not only at the kind of phallogocentric epistemology supposedly relied on by the county attorney and sheriff in the play, but also, by extension, at such figures as Glaspell's great fictional contemporary, Sherlock Holmes. Yet, whether we rely on feminist epistemology or enlightenment rationalist Holmsian epistemology or, perhaps, even parisological literary epistemology, there is a fundamental problem at the heart of the text which with some trepidation I will characterize in hushed tones as being based on 'real' as opposed to hearsay evidence.[13] However much readers may appreciate the symbolic force and poetic

---

[10] Mrs Hale always refers to Minnie Foster Wright as Minnie Foster, while the men and Mrs Peters use her married name. It is hard to know whether 'Minnie Foster Wright' is a post-1960s critical creation and whether anyone in the play would have ever called her that. But it is striking that Mrs Hale refers to her only with her premarital name. Following my students' predilection for forms of address, I will refer to them as Minnie and John without any intent to condescend to either.

[11] In addition to hiding the dead canary, Mrs Hale concocts an improbable lie about the bird being killed by a cat, and the cat then leaving the house because of 'superstition'. She also fixes knots in the quilt which had involved hand-stitching two of the quilt strips together. They are pieced in a simple running stitch, the easiest of all hand sewing. The fact that Minnie has done a sloppy job with this most basic of stitches is taken by Mrs Hale as evidence of her nervousness, or perhaps anger. In any case, Mrs Hale has knowingly removed what she takes to be evidence from the scene of the crime – not that any of the men would have noticed.

[12] For a wider discussion, see Kristina Hinz-Bode, "Susan Glaspell and the Epistemological Crisis of Modernity: Truth, Knowledge and Art in Selected Novels", in *Susan Glaspell. New Directions in Critical Inquiry*, ed. Martha Carpentier (Cambridge Scholars Publishing, 2006) pp.89 ff.

[13] In some sense, we have a play that explicitly presents us only with hearsay evidence, and while we may typically use such evidence in forming our ordinary factual beliefs, courts do not use hearsay as part of an inference towards a truth that is being asserted. In effect, we are continually being urged to be triers of fact in a way that would have little basis in a court. Cf J. Stephen, *The Indian Evidence Act, with an Introduction on the Principles of Judicial Evidence* (Calcutta: Thacker, Spink & Co, 1872); *A Digest of the Law of Evidence* (London: William Clowes & Sons, 5th edition, 1886).

justice of Minnie strangling her husband in retaliation for his malefic strangling of her canary and, by extension, the expression of her own voice and agency in an assumed oppressive and abusive marriage, the simple fact is that in the non-symbolic world of quotidian forensic reality, it is almost certain that she could not have done it. As a Miss Marple or Sherlock Holmes would have quickly deduced, it would be nearly impossible for a woman of Minnie's presumed size and strength to strangle her husband with a rope. Domestic strangulations overwhelmingly involve men strangling women with their hands because it requires a considerable asymmetry in bodily strength. The very few recorded strangulations of men at the hands of women are typically either of male invalids or elderly patients who have been drugged first and rendered incapable of defending themselves. Moreover, those who have ever watched a mafia movie may have observed that real professionals use a garotte wire and not ropes. This is because pressure increases as the surface area of contact decreases ($P=F/A$). Even so, such higher-pressure ligature strangulations, which seem to go on forever on the big screen, would be even longer in real life and take at least two to two and half minutes, even when administered by the powerful shoulders and forearms of a mafia brute with the most efficient equipment.[14] Also, importantly, the victim is always somehow restrained, either by being trapped in the front seat of a car and strangled from behind or, say, as in a famous scene in *The Godfather*, by having a hand pinned to the top of a bar with a knife. A rope, even when wielded by a powerful and skilled hitman, might take up to three minutes to render a suitably overpowered and restrained victim unconscious. It partially depends on how long one can hold one's breath. Of course, John was sleeping. Couldn't Minnie have slipped a rope around his neck and rendered him unconscious before waking up? For those rooting for Minnie to kill John, I am afraid there are certain features of human physiology that these days one does not need to be a brilliant fictional detective to adduce, but just another chunky academic like me with a CPAP machine. As soon as John's airway was blocked and he no longer was getting air, his brain, deprived of oxygen, would immediately send a signal to release a shot of adrenaline to wake him up in order to breathe. This is the reason why *apneia* leads to sleep deprivation: because those who suffer from it keep waking up every time their throat closes. Thus, as the strangulation began, John would almost immediately awaken suspiciously gasping for air, and though he might be puzzled about why Minnie had a rope around his neck and fail to understand its symbolic significance, he would be in absolutely no danger of being successfully strangled if he chose to resist.[15] But perhaps he was drunk? We learn that John doesn't drink. Perhaps she drugged him? This cannot be ruled out, but we unfortunately have no inkling of this in the text. Perhaps she was so enraged by the death of her canary that she had the strength of three Minnies when twisting the rope? Fine – she could have had the strength of five Minnies and all John would have to do is twist away from her and struggle to his feet. Perhaps she securely tied him up first, either while he was asleep or – and here admittedly we are just indulging in a bit of idle *delectatio morosa* – perhaps she might have induced her 'close' and frosty John into a bit of replevisable bondage on yet another one of those long aesthetically barren nights in

---

[14] One may compare, for instance, the length needed for hypotaxia when strangulation results from dangerous police neck holds.
[15] G. Strack, G. McClane and D. Hawley (2001). "A Review of 300 Attempted Strangulation Cases – Part I: Criminal Legal Issues". *Journal of Emergency Medicine*, *21*(3), 303–9. doi:10.1016/S0736-4679(01)00399-7. PMID 11604294. J. Archer (2000). "Sex Differences in Physically Aggressive Acts between Heterosexual Partners: A Meta-analytic Review". *Psychological Bulletin*, *126*(5), 651–80.

the cheerless cabin, and then strangled him? She was, as Mr Hale noticed, 'done up' when he arrived at the cabin.[16] Again, however, we are only told that a rope[17] was observed to be around his neck and there is no suggestion in the text that he was otherwise restrained.[18] Nor was he battered about the head while asleep or after he awakened, and then strangled. In changing the manner of death from her journalistic model,[19] in which the historical Mrs Hossack was charged with bludgeoning her husband's head twice with an axe while he slept, Glaspell has clearly opted for a cleanly symbolic and poetically apt death which, however impossible,[20] seems to be a textual *donnée* never queried by critics, who happily assume that Minnie killed John. Does this matter?

Speculations about the exact manner of John's death can, of course, go on endlessly, and certainly one supposition that we might have expected from the patriarchal perspective of the males in the text is that Minnie opened the door to an adulterous lover who helped her strangle John. One might think this would be one of the first suppositions that would arise in keeping with certain stereotypes of murderous women, but the fact that the men do not even raise it suggests that patriarchal speculation is being tamed and tailored here for the specific purposes of the victim narrative. The larger question, however, is where do such speculations and textual meaning meet, and to what extent are the former relevant? It might plausibly be argued that it is highly unlikely that Glaspell is suggesting that Minnie is innocent, and the forensic reflection that she could not have committed the murder can hardly serve as a site of resistance against the various narratives and constructions of Minnie's motives and of her life that critics present. But this is a work that, in effect, asks us to be triers of fact within an alternative textual/legal framework, and in some sense the only 'real evidence' in a legal sense offered to us is that Minnie could not have killed John on her own. One crucial question this poses for relations of law and literature is the extent to which such evidence, which normally might be crucial in a legal trial, should be overlooked as being extra-textual or, conversely, treated as a necessary part of the play's fabric and of our reading of it. Critics here will no doubt diverge, but to the extent that the play, certainly now in pedagogical contexts, has been used as an argument for changing canons of evidence in legal procedures, it seems to me that if we are going to advocate for blurring literary and legal insights in this way, at least on the basis

---

[16] This observation of Mr Hale, I imagine, might signal Minnie's liberation, once she has strangled John, from the narrow boundaries of her patriarchally constructed muliebrity.

[17] With some sleuthing one can begin to narrow down the kinds of rope that might have been available to Minnie on her farm, but the general point still stands. Cf *The Story of Rope. The History and the Modern Development of Rope-Making* (Plymouth Cordage Company, 1931).

[18] One cannot be sure that this evidence was not tampered with either by Minnie, or afterwards when she was taken away and the crime scene was not secured.

[19] M. Wan (2018). "Cases as Cultural Events: Privacy, the Hossack Trial and Susan Glaspell's 'A Jury of Her Peers'" in *Law and Literature*, ed. K. Dolin (Cambridge University Press, 2018) pp.308–21.

[20] 'Impossible' is perhaps too strong, given what goes on in possible-worlds speculation among contemporary philosophers. So, for instance, if the bed was a four-poster (quite likely at the time) and John was a sound sleeper, Minnie could have slowly slipped the noose around his neck, pulled the rope around the bedpost, and then jumped back away from his reach, jerking the rope and slamming his head against the headboard. If she got some leverage, leaning her whole body back while holding onto the rope, maybe that could do it? But could he still grab the rope and keep it loose enough to keep it from choking him? And so on and so forth. My point is that on this key point of the means of John's death the text urges us to avert our eyes and turn our attention to a symbolic level.

of this particular play, we cannot merely cherry-pick what we take to be useful for making such an argument. Taking the question of Minnie's innocence seriously, I submit, makes for less monologic and triumphal readings and actually serves to put the deeper questions raised by the text into a world closer to the messy empirical realities of both life and the courts. It also changes its tonalities as a pedagogical text and forces students to critically engage with the varieties of women's experience of violence and with the many legal aporias surrounding domestic abuse, rather than merely assuming its occurrence and self-righteously condemning it without following out all the ramifications of taking an effortless Wikipedia path to such conclusions.

In *Oedipus*, we are left with purely textual uncertainties that raise questions about the nature of our reading. In *Trifles*, a gap opens up in between the symbolic textual world and the evidence of prosaic forensic reality. Rather than just passing over this and chalking it up to the prerogatives of poetic conceit, I want to try to isolate some of the reasons for the systematic failure of not only the men but also the women[21] within the text and their claque of critics to seriously even entertain the question of the means of John's death and the possibility of Minnie's innocence. Failing to do so, I think, raises troubling worries about the nature and methods of such critical readings, and also about the creation and approbation of alternative epistemologies and realms of justice, with all their potentially unhappy ethical sequelae. There is a mechanism strongly at work here that matters both in our reading, however textually determinate, and in the workings of the courts. As the suspicion of abuse becomes stronger in the course of the play, the stronger the assumption becomes that Minnie killed her husband,[22] despite her own professed innocence. Poetic justice so demands. Yet, one ironic result of this textual dynamic is that the creation of an alternative realm of symbolic justice for judging Minnie's actions actually robs her in this instance of her voice and her day in court, as it were, since none of her supporters within or without the text take her profession of innocence seriously or even superficially examine the central question of whether she did it or not. The seductive elegance of poetic justice and the palpable ressentiment of Mrs Hale and Mrs Peter that puts into motion a discourse of trauma and victimhood seem to have been sufficient to deflect critical attention from this problematic textual gap.

In order to better understand how such a critical blind spot is created, we need to look in more detail at the particular problem of motive and intent, since this occupies the greater part of the play and has been the primary focus of critical interpretations and theories. These have assumed that Minnie's motive, intent and subsequent action issue in her husband's murder by strangulation. If that assumption is taken away at the level of prosaic reality, however, it casts a different light on ascriptions of motive. Clearly, if Minnie did not kill John or want to kill him, then the whole tissue of suppositions about possible motives is unnecessary, since there is no motive. To be sure, she might have been unhappy in her marriage and wanted him to die in some sense – a common enough sentiment in many unhappy or abusive marriages – and even might have been pleasantly relieved when, if we believe her, she woke up in bed and found him dead. Yet, if we suspend the surety of her commission of the murder that is hanging over

---

[21] The men in the text merely assume Minnie is guilty, but they do not approach the certainty about her guilt that Mrs Hale and Mrs Peters gain by discovering the 'motive'.
[22] See P.L. Bryan (1997). "Stories in Fiction and in Fact: Susan Glaspell's 'A Jury of Her Peers' and the 1901 Murder Trial of Margaret Hossack", *Stanford Law Review*, *49*(6), 1293–1363 for a discussion of this in the Hossack case.

her and the text, our estimation of how her motive for murder is narratively and symbolically constructed and, hence, how successfully it is constructed, needs to be re-examined. Moreover, if she is innocent of the murder, the inflexible logic of poetic justice set up in the text then has the unfortunate effect of actually defusing evidence that she might also still be a victim of oppression and abuse. Clearly, she might have been abused and not killed John, or she might have killed him and not been abused. But the textual dynamic of the play works with a kind of blind talionic efficiency that eliminates such alternatives. As we shall see, this can happen in courts as well when judicial narratives adopt a similar discursive pattern.

With this in mind, let us turn to our two redoubtable indagatrixes, Mrs Hale and Mrs Peters, in order to see how they come to formulate a motive for explaining their unexamined assumption that Minnie murdered John. It is notable that although Mrs Hale in particular is hostile to any inferences by the detectives about potential motives for Minnie killing John, she herself seems more concerned about motive than the question of Minnie's innocence and her ability to actually carry out the strangulation. She does not reject the men's basic assumption that all that is needed in the case to convict Minnie is to establish the motive. This assumption is also basic to her decision at the end of the play to hide what she takes to be evidence for Minnie's motive. In all fairness, the two women are not allowed upstairs to examine the victim's body, the manner of his death, the instrument of his death, and so on and to subject that evidence to the scrutation of feminist epistemology. However, if for one second they had empathetically put themselves in Minnie's place at the time of the murder, it might have suggested to them that it would be impossible for her to subdue and strangle a brutish or even a wimpy husband with a rope, which might have given an entirely different cast to their researches and to the necessity of constructing a motive. They might have searched instead for trifles to support Minnie's professed innocence or even just strenuously questioned the accusing patriarchs as to the possibility of her carrying out the murder. One unpalatable suggestion might be, then, that like many critics, they allow their own palpable resentments, traumas and vengeful fantasies to float free, and that their empathy extends only so far as their resentment. Not only do they merely adopt the (patriarchal) assumption that Minnie kills John, but we witness them putting together the evidence for the murder based on inferences from their own past traumatic experiences without questioning their relevance. At the same time, their experiences are structured by the text to strongly suggest that they underwrite the (alternative) justness of murdering him. So too, their experiences only lead them to embrace and imagine themselves in the position of a victim of abuse, not as an agent capable of murder. Mrs Peters confesses to having a murderous impulse when the little boy killed her kitten, but she uses her empathy, if that is what it is, only to imagine the resentment and motivation of Minnie as victim, not as an agent who actually acts on her impulse, since as a little girl she didn't. Moreover, if she had more fully imagined herself in Minnie's place, rather than merely projecting her own traumatic girlhood experience onto Minnie's marital situation, she might have soon discovered the unlikelihood of Minnie carrying out the murder with a rope.

To be sure, *Trifles* was and continues to be an important intervention on questions of homicide in situations of domestic abuse and it addresses in a powerful and subtle way the nature and effects of such abuse. In raising the question of Minnie's innocence, I am not downplaying the seriousness of the various suggestions in the text that John is exerting what has come to be called 'coercive control'[23] over her. She would appear to have been isolated from her previous social life, and one standard way of exerting control and stripping victims of power is to kill their pets.[24] At the same time, however, I worry that critics have followed Mrs Hale and Mrs Peters rather too unselfconsciously and triumphally down the path of 'poetic justice' that is opened up in the text. Apart from the question of evidence, there is also the important matter of John's death, and, worryingly, criticism often tends to follow Mrs Peters in letting her trauma narratives diminish or even entirely efface its importance. Mrs Peters' girlhood trauma did not lead to murder and by embracing the epistemological validity of Mrs Peters' trauma, that particular asymmetry tends to get lost. Indeed, reading some critics on this question, at least for me, is rather akin to being told after Medea kills her children that, well, perhaps it is not so great that she kills them, but after all, Jason treated her shabbily, so non-patriarchal justice is served in the patriarchal world of ancient Greece. Certainly, one more ethically accountable response to Euripides' play might be to point out that Jason offers her alimony, that the poor children are innocent and that to murder them in order to cause her husband pain for dumping her is disproportionately morally grotesque. Poetic justice, however, often has the strange effect not only of countenancing or even celebrating vengeance, but also of turning the gaze of readers away from collateral damage. To point to this worry with respect to this text, I think, is an attempt not merely to reassert the ideological mechanisms of patriarchy and patriarchal law, but to ask the larger kind of question that, say Donna Haraway and others ask in a different context, when they urge us to interrogate 'for whom and how' various institutions work and to engage in practices of witnessing.[25] Even if John killed Minnie's bird and kept her coercively caged in his control, does this justify her killing him and critics either explicitly or unexplicitly countenancing this on the basis of 'poetic' justice? Shouldn't the complicity of many critics give way to Haraway's call 'to stand publically accountable for and psychically vulnerable to'[26] the larger ramifications of the homicide, even if he was an abuser, and its critical role in shaping readers' views of the suspected abuse in the play? When Ibsen's Nora feels smothered by the crushing burden of Torvald's diminutives, she walks out the door in search of a new autonomous way of life. Some may question the depth of her actual commitment to her children, her demand that Torvald sacrifice his honour for her in a rather retro-chivalrous manner that seems to conflict with her stated wishes for autonomy, and so on, but at least those critics who unabashedly support and extol her decision to leave her family have an ethical leg to stand on. It is not clear to me that Mrs Hale and Mrs Peters and the critics who have followed in their wake can make as strong a claim in justifying John's murder. By the same token, I think it is important to sort out how much of the construction of Minnie's motive is based on inferences that depend on the way that the text seems to be able to elicit and shape ethical responses on the part of its readers that are rooted in resentment and in the narration of past traumas that may or may not be germane to Minnie's particular experience. As Mrs Hale and Mrs Peters knit together their conclusions, too many critics, I fear, unwittingly don a cloak of murderous

---

[23] www.nysenate.gov/legislation/bills/2019/a8904; www.gov.ca.gov/2020/09/29/governor-newsom-signs-legislation-to-support-survivors-of-sexual-assault-domestic-violence-and-other-crime-and-abuse/.

[24] A. Herbert Garrido (2020). "Maltrato Animal: Las Victimas Ocultas de la Violencia Doméstica". *A. Derecho Animal (Forum of Animal Law Studies)*, *11*(1).

[25] Donna J. Haraway, *Modest_Witness@Second_Millennium. FemaleMan©_Meets OncoMouse™: Feminism and Technoscience* (Routledge, 1997) p.267.

[26] Haraway (1997) p.280.

sanctimony before sufficiently examining the actual relevance of Mrs Peters' traumas. Not that I am recommending a venireman's smirk as we listen to her narrations. But we at least need to exercise with literary texts the relevant kind of sober caution recommended by Peter Goodrich, for instance, who shows how mobilizations of corresponding judicial 'vocabularies' lend themselves to obfuscations and rhetorical manipulation, and are 'a semantic and symbolic adventure' in their own right.[27]

In looking at these features of the text, therefore, I propose that we re-examine the way that the conclusions about motive are revealed, while also keeping track of the kinds of emotional and rhetorical reconstructions that critics have used to bolster the force of their epistemological claims. First a word of clarification, though. It might seem that raising the question of Minnie's innocence is a kind of rearguard patriarchal manoeuvre meant to undercut the discoveries of the two women in the text and to discredit them as 'emotional'. It is hardly clear, however, that the men in the text line up easily on the side of 'reason' as opposed to 'emotion'. More important, my question in the first instance is why the text does not show Mrs Hale and Mrs Peters putting themselves in the position of Minnie as an agent, which would raise the question of her innocence. I am not rejecting the potential utility of such a procedure, only the sources of its erasure in the text. In effect, then, entertaining the possibility of Minnie's innocence actually serves to undercut an unsavoury dichotomy between emotional women united in their traumatic solidarity versus rational male patriarchy, since both ultimately founder both rationally and emotionally in considering Minnie's innocence. The critical tack suggested here in the face of various larger critical ideological denominations is really little more than that of an incredulous Thomas: 'Except I shall see in his hands the print of the nails, and put my finger into the print of the nails, and thrust my hand into his side, I will not believe' (John 20:25). After readers put their fingers into these wounds of the text, they may believe, but at least they will be doing so with their eyes wide open.

So to begin, near the outset of Mrs Hale's and Mrs Peters' investigation, the question of Minnie's innocence arises ever so briefly in the following interchange, and it may be worth asking why it has been so readily overlooked by the two protagonists and by critics:

MRS HALE: Mrs Peters?

MRS PETERS: Yes, Mrs Hale?

MRS HALE: Do you think she did it?

MRS PETERS: Oh, I don't know.

MRS HALE: Well, I don't think she did. Asking for an apron and her little shawl. Worrying about her fruit.

MRS PETERS: Mr Peters says it looks bad for her. Mr Henderson is awful sarcastic in a speech and he'll make fun of her sayin' she didn't wake up.

---

[27] Peter Goodrich, *Legal Discourse: Studies in Linguistics, Rhetoric, and Legal Analysis* (Palgrave Macmillan, 1990) pp.158–203.

MRS HALE:	Well, I guess John Wright didn't wake when they was slipping that rope under his neck.
MRS PETERS:	No, it's strange. It must have been done awful crafty and still. They say it was such a – funny way to kill a man, rigging[28] it all up like that.
MRS HALE:	That's just what Mr Hale said. There was a gun in the house. He says that's what he can't understand.
MRS PETERS:	Mr Henderson said coming out that what was needed for the case was a motive; something to show anger, or – sudden feeling.

Mrs Hale's first inference from Minnie's asking for her apron and shawl in jail is that she must be innocent. The apron that Minnie clutches in her reported discussion with Mr Hale and that is then later laughingly dismissed by the county attorney as not being a dangerous item to have in jail has been read by some critics as symbolic of Minnie's attachment to her slave uniform as a housewife. Mrs Hale, however, first infers from it that Minnie is innocent. This is not then further grounded in the text by any particular kind of shared empathetic experience and we might be inclined to just ascribe it to the kind of knee-jerk solidarity with Minnie that Mrs Hale had earlier displayed. However, although Mrs Hale is continually confrontational in defence of Minnie and 'her sex' and the sanctity of her home generally, her view of Minnie's desire to have her apron in jail as exculpatory appears to be based on the notion that if Minnie still cares about her housework, she could not have killed her husband, in effect mirroring the country attorney's insinuation that a dirty kitchen is a sign of a woman's potential guilt. Moreover, she tries to surreptitiously tidy up in ways that suggest that she wants to cover up potential evidence. At the very least, this should perhaps warn us to be careful of the distance between the way that characters view their domestic and social situations and the ways that critics have come to view them. But in any case, a crucial question about the means of the murder is raised in connection to Minnie's claim that when John was killed she did not wake up.[29] Mrs Peters reports that Mr Henderson, the county attorney, has been sarcastic about this and Mrs Hale responds with a strikingly mordant reply, 'Well, I guess John Wright didn't wake up when they was slipping that rope under his neck.' Apart from this bitter sarcasm, she interestingly divines that it would take 'they' to kill John with a rope. One wonders, is Minnie part of this 'they' or is the text urging us to imagine 'they' as a group of men suddenly falling upon John, restraining and then suffocating him with a rope as Minnie sleeps soundly? Mrs Hale's observation provides an interesting parallel to the one-versus-many quandary that structures *Oedipus*, and we might think that it would open an interesting avenue of either reflective inference or empathetic solidarity if Mrs Hale had continued along its path. Mrs Peters, however, then remarks on the craftiness and oddity of John's murder, which elicits Mrs Hale's observation that Mr Hale wondered why the gun in the house was not used, presum-

---

[28] Many of my students have taken this vocabulary to suggest that John was hanged by Minnie but then, when asked how she managed it, quickly reverse positions and conclude that John must have committed suicide. This in some ways fits the kind of psychological profile Mrs Hale constructs, but here I think 'rig' is used with 'awful crafty' in the sense of 'to rig an election'.

[29] This was a key question in the Hassock trial and complicated by the fact that they had a dog who on some accounts had been barking.

ably by Minnie. These too are all plausible exculpatory questions to linger upon, but the text quickly turns our attention away from the means of murder to the question of motive, which is further reduced solely to a question of anger or sudden feeling. Certainly there might be all sorts of motives for a woman to murder her husband, but from here on out any non-traumatic motives and any suggestions of Minnie's innocence are effaced by the search for the source of her anger or sudden emotion. We might also wonder why the motive has to be reduced to anger or emotion. While one may initially ascribe this to the distorting lens of patriarchy and a characterization of women as being driven by emotion and anger, further reflection shows that it serves as a deeper necessary link to the empathetic spectacles of Mrs Peters' own trauma and her sudden desires for vengeance. Clearly the complicated imbrications of trauma and patriarchy, and in this case, their possible mutual reinforcement, need to be 'witnessed' as the play becomes driven by a textual dynamic of poetic justice that is rooted in the sudden justified anger and vengeance of victims united by shared traumatic emotions. As readers, we are urged to take part in this dynamic, but only after we have been given the most cursory of glances at the crucial question of Minnie's innocence and then had our attention yanked away in the search for evidence explaining Minnie's sudden Vesuvian desire for vengeance. But certainly one question that remains is: why should anyone assume that, apart from the larger question of Minnie killing John, she did so in a burst of sudden anger and emotion? A rope, even if it were a possible murder weapon, would certainly involve more cool-headed planning than a gun or an axe.

In any case, the decisive moment in the discovery of Minnie's motive occurs when Mrs Hale opens a fancy box and finds within a dead canary wrapped in silk. From this and from an earlier observation that the hinge of the door of the bird cage was broken, Mrs Hale and Mrs Peters share a moment of inferential horror and recognition that John must have killed the canary. The validity of this inference is endorsed by Glaspell's own stage direction: 'Their eyes meet. A look of growing comprehension, of horror.' But on what basis do we follow both Glaspell and her characters to this conclusion? As readers we have Glaspell's seeming imprimatur on the veracity of their comprehension and for an audience this is meant to be conveyed by the gestures of the actors. But, one may ask, the comprehension of what? A truth or their mutual false inferences? Neither we nor they have what would be sufficiently probative documentary or eye-witness evidence to establish this act of comprehension as a *factum probandum* even under the most flexible standards of legal proof. How is it then that we are persuaded to make the move from broken cage door to broken bird's neck and finally to the unbroken violence of the husband? As a heartbroken canary owner I can attest to the recurring problem of broken birdcage door hinges and the worry that should a canary get out it may very well do what they are often wont to do: to immediately fly into the nearest mirror or window of the sort prominently mentioned at the end of the play, and render their necks 'other side to'. Why should we conclude that the delicately wrapped bird was not just a common victim of this kind of out-of-cage aux folles that afflicts canaries, rather than being the victim of murderous and unexplained marital rage? Normally to do so, we need some motive and context to explain such a flagrant action on the part of a spouse. Was there perhaps some larger ongoing dispute that helps to explain what triggered this particular episode of rage? We have access to none of this, of course, and our views might be different if we knew that John suffered from a particularly painful kind of avian misophonia and that Minnie stubbornly refused to give the bird away despite her helpmeet's horrible suffering. Or perhaps a psychotic Minnie killed the bird, which provided both a tipping point in her increasingly violent behaviour and a trial run for the corresponding strangulation of her husband. In other words, to share Mrs Hale's and Mrs Peter's horror and comprehension both of the manner of the canary's death and its killer, we must accept Mrs Peters' inference from her own traumatic experience of her pet being killed before her own eyes. High school readers of the text are dutifully taught that the broken bird cage door symbolizes a broken marriage; the bird and the cage, a once sweet and fluttery Minnie and her now unhappy trapped life; the bird's strangulation, the strangulation of her own agency and tuneful voice, and so on. Now, of course, apart from the fact that only male canaries sing, a moment's reflection shows why these disparate elements do not make for a smoothly coherent symbolic system, much less being in any way adequate to the complexities of a typical heterosexual marriage, even under the claustrophobic reign of the phallus and potential abuse.

Some directors attempt to build the case in the mind of its audience in rather blunt ways that, ironically, actually turn out to be useful for registering some important reservations. One prize-winning movie production, for instance, treats the death of the canary as an imagined flashback scene inserted immediately after Mrs Hale makes her final deduction. None of this is explicitly presented in the play, of course, but it speaks to the way that we are urged to imagine it. In this rendition, we witness Minnie sitting in her chair knotting away and happily listening to her canary singing. She then suddenly hears the footsteps of her returning husband. In terror she runs to cover the bird cage,[30] presumably to keep the bird quiet. John comes in, hears the bird, and immediately storms over to the cage, tears off the covering, rips the cage door off of its hinge, reaches in to grab the bird, and then we cut to the distraught and terrified Minnie covering her eyes in horror as he presumably wrings its neck. In some sense, this captures nicely the imagined primal scene of violence needed to reconstruct Minnie's motive and to spur critics' synecdochic imagination and ethical outrage. Interestingly, we are not shown the actual death of the bird, which has the effect of placing us in the position of Minnie and shutting our eyes in horror as it is being killed, but it would be interesting to know, for instance, how one is to square the imagined violence of this enactment with the condition of the bird's body as described in the text. The bird's neck is reported by Mrs Hale to be 'other side to'. Are we to assume that after violently grabbing the bird, John then delicately wrings its neck, perhaps with a vindictive Scarpian flourish in front of his cowering and terrified wife? One might have expected, given the brutish violence of a man ripping away a cage door, that the canary would suffer a kindred fate and, for instance, be crushed in his hand and then flung to the floor or against a wall. It takes, perhaps, the motiveless malignity of a clever Iago to immediately gather oneself up when enraged and then to calmly and sadistically snap a little bird's neck. After killing it, John must then somehow allow his wife to retrieve the body and carefully wrap it for burial. So does he now hand it to her with jackbooted politeness, when he might have just crushed it and crammed it in a pocket, for instance, and deprived her of the solace of lamenting over its body? Part of the problem is that we really don't know where John lies on the spectrum from frosty country lumpishness to calculating malignity, but such individual fine-tuning is made unnecessary by the very abstraction of any potentially imagined scene. Moreover, in cases of domestic abuse, the dead animal is often merely left so that the

---

[30] Among the trifles considered in the play, one hears nothing of a birdcage cover. A beautiful knotted one might have been a nice touch. As it stands, one could easily draw the conclusion that the bird endured the same kind of cheerless indifference as the rest of the household accoutrements.

abuse victim can find it, which is sufficient to provoke humiliation and terror.[31] So, perhaps John killed it and wrapped it beautifully as a kind of warped terrorizing gift. Why should we assume he broke the canary's neck with Minnie as witness? To answer this we need to look at the two trauma narratives, since they shape our perception of John's role in the canary's death and also show why the kind of directorial esprit evinced in the flashback is not merely arbitrary.

After Mrs Hale's and Mrs Peters' growing comprehension, we have a brief interruption of the two men who ask an ironic question about whether Minnie was going to quilt it or knot it, which only serves to build more resentment at the patriarchy and also to undercut its credibility in dealing with evidence. Mrs Hale lies to Mr Peters and Mr Henderson about the existence of a cat on the basis of an extremely dubious claim that not only builds a certain sentiment of resistant solidarity, but also reinforces a sense of patriarchal fatuousness. Then we get another of the briefest glimpses of the question of Minnie's innocence in a short snatch of the men's conversation indicating their perplexity about the means of the murder. This line of speculation again is immediately cut short and then followed by the two central tableaux of Mrs Peters' remembered traumas, which are meant to cement the case for Minnie's motive.

> MRS PETERS: (in a whisper) When I was a girl – my kitten – there was a boy took a hatchet, and before my eyes – and before I could get there – (covers her face for an instant) If they hadn't held me back I would have (catches herself, looks upstairs where steps are heard, falters weakly) – hurt him.

In the dialogue between the two women, Mrs Peters is the one who both is unsure about whether the evidence shows that John killed the bird and initially keeps in sight the 'awfulness' of what was done. We see her slowly come to share Mrs Hale's views and drawing an audience along with her, and she does so through reliving traumatic memories. The first gives us a grisly image of unprovoked and gratuitous male violence with the subtle suggestion of a kind of cradle argument. I have read enough Thucydides to be agnostic about whether barely hidden below the surface in every grown male is a grinning little boy with a hatchet who delights in gratuitously killing things, especially if they belong to little girls. But there still remains the question of how this particular memory is used in this context. Its horror is enough to call up memories of Mrs Peters' own murderous rage, but she suppresses too open a verbal expression of it for fear that the legal patriarchs above will hear her. This is unlikely, of course, since the women are whispering together downstairs, but in this scene of remembrance we have a template for the untutored natural reactions of a young girl that the text is trying to elicit and justify. It is important to do so in solidarity and out of the earshot of The Man. We also are shown these natural reactions before they are suppressed in the grown woman by phallocratic restraints and subsequently internalized.

But, in any case, all of these imaginings crucially depend on the postulation of an unmotivated, gratuitous and primal act of naked male violence that corresponds to Mrs Peters' own trauma when her kitten was killed. On the basis of her description of unbridled male violence with no mitigating aspects, the unaptly named Mr Wright is held to be guilty not only of killing the canary, but also of spousal abuse, and this profoundly colours inferences about their marriage and the construction of Minnie's motive for murder. For any evidence of his domes-

---

[31] Cf above note 24.

tic abuse, unlike for the murder, however, we must rely entirely on hearsay, argumenta ex silentio, and the kinds of character evidence that a prosecutor would have to wait to introduce until the defence had first raised the question. It would be hard to know how John's general reputation as a sober, honest and 'good man' even in Mrs Hale's telling would stand up against her dislike for his being 'hard' and rebarbative and, at least in her view, not liking 'things that sing'. This is not to argue that the play fails to capture and present many of the ways that evidence for domestic abuse, especially in questions of 'coercive control', depends precisely on indirect inferences. However, the fact that readers are urged to read a traumatic girlhood experience of Mrs Peters involving an apparently random, brutal act of a neighbourhood boy directly onto the complexities of a potentially abusive marriage shows the potential problems in such traumatic witnessing, as well as the move from Mrs Peters' vivid personal experience in an altogether different context to the conclusion that Minnie was subject to a trauma with the same basic features. Even Mrs Peters initially resists such a conclusion since, as she says, they don't know that John killed the bird. But when a director recreates a scene of John gratuitously killing the canary in front of Minnie's eyes, she is not only projecting one traumatic experience onto another that might have an utterly different context but also validating the truth of the projection, which may rather be telling us much more about Mrs Peters and the director than about Minnie, and certainly John. Mrs Hale claims to know that John was the sort to not like things that sing. Yet, if he had killed the canary in a solitary moment and left it for Minnie, that would also be evidence for coercive control and abuse. But these are things that we cannot learn through Mrs Peters' girlhood trauma. And even if one may harbour desires of vengeance against someone who kills one's pet surreptitiously, the tonality of the resultant anger or emotional response is likely to be different from the experience of a child watching one's kitten being killed by a hatchet and having a sudden urge to kill in return.

It is worth asking, as well, whether without the assumption of the poetic justice of John's strangulation and without the critical spectre of imagined irrational male violence and memories of past trauma, it would at all be plausible to conclude that John was abusing Minnie at any level. In other words, if we bracket the assumption that she strangled him, would we so easily conclude that he had been strangling her in an abusive marriage as exemplified by this imagined symbolic scene of him strangling her canary? To further see the wider contexts of this question, we can turn to our second and last *statio* on the *via vulnerum* of traumatic remembrance, where we encounter the silence of a house without children. Of course, we have absolutely no way of knowing whether Minnie actually wanted to have children or the reasons the couple didn't or couldn't, though the text links the silence of a house without children to John's harpocratic tyranny. The assumption, in any case, seems to be that Minnie was deprived of something she badly wanted. Again, we may perhaps just chalk this up to first-wave feminism's tendency to homogenize women's desires and goals, but Mrs Peters, now armed with a sense of justified revenge through her own memory of the killing of her pet, is still resisting the second component necessary for fully embracing the text's sirenic call for poetic revenge. She is not sure that John killed the bird. Mrs Hale, on the other hand, is convinced that John killed the bird because she 'knew John Wright'. He wouldn't have liked the bird, 'a thing that sang. She used to sing. He killed that too.' By killing the bird, John returns the house to its earlier oppressive silence. This evocation of a silent house is the source of Mrs Peters' next traumatic memory.

MRS PETERS: (something within her speaking.) I know what stillness is. When we homesteaded in Dakota, and my first baby died – after he was two years old, and me with no other then—

Through the traumatic experience of the death of her first child, Mrs Peters identifies with the silence in Minnie's life. In her stage direction, Glaspell ascribes the expression of this voluntary memory to a nameless delitescent entity, almost as if Mrs Peters' wound is speaking aloud with its own voice. Here Glaspell seems to be calling up her beloved Greeks and the deepest layers of the tradition by depicting a separate individual organ speaking on its own from within a character, as in the manner of Homer. Mrs Peters, however, still remains torn between the twin demands of trauma and of law.

MRS PETERS: I know what stillness is. The law has got to punish crime, Mrs Hale.

As the play ends, however, Mrs Peters decides to be complicit in hiding the dead canary, apparently now convinced by her memories of silence that John must have killed it. The county attorney and her chuckling sheriff husband merely banter about how she is 'married to the law'. As often in Shakespeare, we see the most powerful scenes of emotional turmoil and trauma play out against a backdrop of comic ineptitude, the comic ineptitude here being associated with the men who are unsuccessful in puzzling out the means of the crime, entirely miss the purported motive[32] and succeed only in making a few fatuous final remarks about knitting. However moving, powerful and exemplaric, what gets cut out of the fabric of the play is the central question of Minnie's innocence, while John's death is too often accompanied by critical sounds uncomfortably close to those of the cackling of a tricoteuse at the foot of the guillotine.

In closing, I want to turn briefly to a corresponding problem in the courts, where we see a similar discursive mechanism at work underlying official domestic abuse narratives of judges. In one recent study, for instance, Melissa Hamilton analysed more than 60 appellate case opinions in which a California trial court accepted expert testimony in prosecuting male offenders for domestic abuse. She found that the discursive assumption underlying judicial narratives is that 'abused women would, should or could easily exercise agency in ending an abusive relationship and, once it ended, refuse to reengage in their abusive relationships'.[33] Evidence of resistance and attempts to terminate a relationship were salient elements in the court's opinions in constructing a narrative context in which abuse occurred. Failing to resist indicates that either a woman's narrative of abuse is overblown or abuse did not occur. This dichotomous view of women, either as victims of abuse who resist and terminate their relationships or who overstate or lie about abuse if they remain in their relationships, often guides both expert and judicial opinion. It also, in effect, marginalizes or silences the voices of abuse victims themselves in favour of authoritative opinions that embrace a particular dialectic that mirrors the assumptions of the kind of poetic justice we saw at work in *Trifles*. In some sense, of course, we might expect in a juridical context this kind of emphasis on taking authority seriously because of its source and not of its content, commitments to institutional consistency and the application of rules and precedent as opposed

---

[32] One oddity in the critical reception of the play is the relation between the claim that the men would not understand the evidence and the conclusion that the women must nonetheless hide it from them to obtain non-patriarchal justice.

[33] Melissa Hamilton (2010). "Judicial Discourses on Women's Agency in Violent Relationships: Cases from California". *Women's Studies International Forum*, 33 (November–December), 570–8.

to particularist approaches to decision making, and so on.[34] However, the core notion that women who resist are innocent and undeserving of abuse creates a series of conceptual difficulties for judges when faced with women staying in abusive relationships. In the same way that *Trifles* symbolically effaces the alternative that Minnie might have been abused but not killed John, fully 60 per cent of the cases that Hamilton analyses show how judges are baffled by such an alternative and either express scepticism, since it defies 'common sense', or rely on simplistic normative – and gendered – explanations based on family-oriented values, rather like Mrs Hale's first knee-jerk reaction about Minnie's innocence. The way that a social understanding of women's agency is judicially staged in these cases fails to speak to the multi-faceted character of human agency generally, and constrains both victims and abusers within a talionic mechanism that both silences women's voices and creates imperatives for establishing an abuser's guilt that can override ordinary prosaic evidence.

To take a step back, I have concentrated on one among the many difficulties in trying to understand abuse both in texts and in the courts. It is no secret that various narratives of abuse do not fit this model of 'patriarchal' control as opposed to couples in conflict, nor would all feminists agree with the basic thrust of Glaspell's notion about the necessarily superior knowledge that women gain about other women through their own experience. Many would generalize the kind of general sceptical argument I have offered about the kinds of knowledge of women's experience that women gain in this text. At the same time, it is not clear to me that Glaspell's text ultimately carries through successfully its Gramscian impulse of unravelling the practical knowledge and common sense of subalterns in order to construct counter-hegemonic positions against the imperatives of the dominant class[35] that will lead to spaces of social justice and human liberation. In some sense, both of these features of Glaspell's text necessarily appeal to an essentialist conception of 'women's experience' that poststructuralist feminists have argued is fractured across various discourses and socially performative. Such arguments highlight that we cannot even begin to pretend to have access to 'an abused woman's experience', since all such representations are interpellative discourses presenting arguments about that experience. We should keep in mind that, as Rosemary Hunter argues, '"women's experience" of violence is diverse rather than singular, and it is necessary to be attentive to these differences in individual cases'.[36] Raising the question of Minnie's innocence allows us to question the extent to which there is something called 'women's experience' to ground the kind of traumatic inferences that drive the text's urge for 'poetic justice'. Although I have done so by pointing out how her inno-

---

[34] For general discussion see, for instance, Frederick Schauer, *Thinking Like a Lawyer: A New Introduction to Legal Reasoning* (Harvard University Press, 2009).

[35] Cf Catharine MacKinnon (1982). "Feminism, Marxism, Method and the State: An Agenda for Theory". *Signs*, 7, 515.

[36] Rosemary Hunter (2006). "Narratives of Domestic Violence". *Sydney Law Review*, 28(4), 733. She goes on to argue that given the diversity of women's experience of violence: 'In light of these considerations, I would not propose that any particular narrative about domestic violence be taken to be universally correct or adopted as the ruling narrative. Rather, I would advocate a more contextual and evidence based approach. The analysis of violence adopted in any given case should be the one that best fits the evidence in that case. This requires, however, that the "power and control" analysis, and variations on or alternatives to that analysis developed in relation to lesbians, women with disabilities, immigrant women and Indigenous women, must become *an essential element of the knowledge base* of judicial officers making decisions in cases involving allegations of domestic violence. This knowledge would not replace or supplant non-feminist understandings of violence in all circumstances, but neither should it be ignored or repressed.'

cence is grounded in 'real evidence', as it might be in the courts, it should and can be raised based even on its purely textual standing – in the manner of Goodhart's reading of the textual evidence for Oedipus killing his father.

CONCLUSION

My aim has not been to try to diminish the pressing concerns and goals of Glaspell's text. Just the opposite, I hope. As we have seen, however, the more Minnie is taken by critics to be deserving of belief and compensation by reason of being a victim, the more her status as a victim robs her of credibility in the eyes of those most vocal about their concern that her voice be heard and believed. At the heart of this effacement of her voice is a conception of 'poetic justice', that brings in its wake the further worry that literary and legal discourses built on such a conception also rely on a particular essentialist conception of victims, of the sort that are now being eschewed with considerable difficulty by abused women and other victims of psychological and social trauma alike. By way of contrast, such universal victimization narratives are now eagerly being taken up by the beneficiaries of the very power structures Glaspell originally meant to expose. One does not have to look too far to see how many forms of contemporary populism are rooted in the imagined 'traumas' of a silenced and victimized majority of 'common people' who feel they are mistreated by a small, all-powerful political elite. The idea, for instance, of white suburban ofendiditos being the victims of looming black violence or even just senior male colleagues furtively lamenting their plight and helplessness when faced with watching the latest 30-minute diversity training video speaks to the way that the mechanism we have seen in Glaspell can begin to float free and be used by those who victimize to take on the stance of victims themselves and to blame their victims for this victimization. When Oedipus blinded himself he became convinced that a special fate and form of knowledge was in store for him alone. Perhaps, but he did so at the cost of knowing what we might think not only societies but also individuals need to know about their own action and its effects. The corresponding special knowledge promised to us by Glaspell's *Trifles* based on solidarity and trauma carries with it a similar danger of blinding us to the particularities of experience and its action and effects.[37] Moreover, iterations of its rhetorical mechanisms are generating legal discourses that not only ultimately obscure prosaic questions of autonomy and individual innocence and guilt, but also seem to offer justifications for widespread and disturbing forms of social blindness.[38]

---

[37] My claim here extends to the epistemological difficulties of the trauma narratives in Glaspell's text and the extent to which, in abuse cases, Hunter is correct in worrying about essentializing narratives of violence that do not best fit the evidence in particular cases. So too, in pointing to these kinds of contemporary 'victim' narratives, I am assuming that their 'knowledge base' is nil. The larger questions of large-scale social traumas of gender, race, class, and so on and their relation to individuals have their own parameters and it would be dangerous to try to draw any straightforward implications from the kind of reading I am offering of Glaspell. I certainly don't mean to.

[38] I am grateful to Sandra Sider, Kelly Murphy, Rawan Dareer, Greg Camp and Pura Nieto for helpful suggestions. I'm painfully aware of how few of Daniela Gandorfer's and Peter Goodrich's trenchant criticisms I have been able to meet, but I thank them for still including me in the volume. Lastly, I would like to thank my then 12-year-old daughter, Alexandra, who responded to our discussion of the play with, 'Yeah, that it is all fine, but you know she couldn't have done it', and then persisted in her usual endearing Mr Tulkinghorn manner in interrogating me about the means of John's death.

PART X

A WORD ON JUSTICE

Words Count – Cutting Flesh – Just Words – Image of Justice – Illocutionary Action – Counter-Publics – Poetic Code – Theory Of Punishment – Linguistic Turning

33. Lessons
Richard H. Weisberg

A while ago, I offered a trifecta of lessons to be gleaned by putting the fields of law and literature together.[1] They were all about "Considerate Communication," "Law-talk in Vichy France," and "No 'Plain Meaning'." This volume provides the opportunity for three more: "Every Word Counts," "But More So If We Permit 'Extrinsic Evidence'," and "'On Moral Writing': The Goal(s) When Generating Normative Texts."

EVERY WORD COUNTS. 1. THE "AKEDAH"/*THE MERCHANT OF VENICE*

One of the ancient springboards to the modern field of Law and Literature is the Hebrew Bible. The reader in 2022 finds there—as in that other signpost, Cicero—the path forward to the contemporary, complex inter-discipline. In sacred text and single orator, law and literature merge; the nomos of the Hebrew texts cannot be disaggregated from the narratives that make law understandable and workable across millennia; and the words and phrases chosen by the great Roman orator fuse into his every legal pronouncement. Drawing from the ancient unities, but thousands of years later, Judge Benjamin N. Cardozo went on to re-prove that form and substance are *one* in every judicial declaration.[2] This scientific progression from proof to proof to re-evaluation[3] and then re-statement sends us back to these ancient origins.

Lying at the heart of the matter linking—in Robert Cover's famous titular phrase—"Nomos and Narrative"[4] is a mysterious story that itself has been retold perennially: the "Akedah," or the binding of Isaac. Try to recall the setting: Abraham, the first Jew, who had awaited the arrival of a child with his wife Sarah until late in life, has now been commanded by Heaven to sacrifice the lad, Isaac. With undeviating obedience, the old man takes the late-in-life gift to an altar-place, carrying with them the tools that will be necessary for the dreadful act. The reader of this tale experiences Kierkegaard's "Fear and Trembling,"[5] J.V. Cunningham's "Woe and Wonder,"[6] or some similar variation on the devastating experience we move through as priv-

---

[1] Weisberg, "Three Lessons from Law and Literature," 27 *Loyola Law Rev.* 285 (1983). I would like to thank Marguerite White for her fine assistance in researching this chapter.
[2] Cardozo, "Law and Literature," in M.R. Hall, ed., *Selected Works of Benjamin N. Cardozo* (N.Y.: Matthew Bender, 1947) 338 at 340.
[3] The current period of serious claims to the intertwining of Law and Literature begins in the late 1970s and 1980s, with the publication of a dozen or so book-length studies on and in the field, and continues to this volume.
[4] Cover, "Foreword: Nomos and Narrative," 97 *Harv. L. Rev.* 4 (1983–4).
[5] Kierkegaard, *Fear and Trembling* (1843) trans. Bruce K. Kirmmsov (London: Liveright, 2020).
[6] J.V. Cunningham, *Woe or Wonder: The Emotional Effect of Shakespearean Tragedy* (Col: U of Denver Pr., 1951).

ileged but overwhelmed observers to a tragedy. But this is a tragedy with a difference. Let's re-visit it:

> GENESIS 22:7. And Isaac spoke unto Abraham his father, and said: "My father." And he said "Here am I, my son [heneni b'niy]." And he said: "Behold the fire and the wood, but where is the lamb for a burnt offering?" 8. And Abraham said: "God will provide Himself the lamb for a burnt offering, my son." So they went both of them together. 9. And they came to the place which God had told him of: And Abraham built the altar there, and laid the wood in order, and bound Isaac his son, and laid him on the altar, upon the wood. 10. And Abraham stretched forth his hand, and took the knife to slay his son. 11. And the angel of the Lord called unto him out of heaven, and said: "Abraham, Abraham." And he said "Here am I [Avraham, Avraham. Vi'yomer heneni]." 12. And he said, "Lay not thy hand upon the lad, neither do thou any thing unto him; for now I know thou art a God-fearing man, seeing thou hast not withheld thy son, thy only son, from me." 13. And Abraham lifted up his eyes, and looked, and beheld behind him a ram caught in the thicket by his horns. And Abraham went and took the ram, and offered him up for a burnt offering in the stead of his son.[7]

To readers of this volume, much can be offered (sacrificially?) from this text. Following Cover, let me offer a "midrash"—a kind of spun off story upon a story. The Akedah blends into *The Merchant of Venice* and—in Talmudic fashion—yields the question "Would Shylock have cut?", a question answered negatively and most recently in a brilliant essay by Anton Schütz.[8] No devout Jew such as Shylock, who has taken in and made organic this dreadful story—this Akedah—reading it in the Synagogue more than once a year, and later reading more often than that the Ten Commandments, will actually shed another's blood upon a contractual breach. Shylock wants a fair shake at Christian justice but beyond that will not take the bond to its final penalty phase. If need be, an angel will intervene in Shylock's own actions to stop that.

But that angel is decidedly not Portia! Everything within Shylock resists—because he simply does not need!—Portia, with her hair splitting[9] and ultimately cruel manipulations of the law.[10] The better angel lies already within Shylock on his own, as an observant Jew and reader of the Akedah. So, as Schütz says, only an anti-Semite would make the assumption that Shylock, as drawn by the Bard, will plunge his knife into the Merchant's flesh.[11]

With this Midrash in mind, the Akedah could open up here the story of millennia of deliberate Christian mis-readings of Jewish sacred texts, imported, expropriated, and then distorted to

---

[7] *Genesis*, 22:7–13, *Pentateuch and Haftorahs* in J.H. Hertz, ed. (London: Soncino Press, 2nd ed., 1960) 74–5.

[8] Anton Schütz, "Structural Terror," in Goodrich et al, eds, *Law, Text, Terror* (NY: Glasshouse, 2006) 79.

[9] Rudolf Von Ihering, the great nineteenth-century German legal thinker, strongly took the side of Shylock and famously maintained it against numerous opponents in edition after edition of his *Der kampf ums recht* [*The Struggle for Law*] (Vienna, 1886), trans. in part in H.H. Furness, ed., the New Variorum *Merchant of Venice* (Philadelphia: JB Lippincott, 1888, 410 et seq). Von Ihering, as part of a majestic argument, first notes that no one in the open Venetian court argues that the contract's penalty clause was unenforceable, since it was reached at arm's length and for good consideration by Antonio and Shylock; and second, Portia's interpretations of Venetian law amount to a "miserable quibble" compared to Shylock's righteous search for individual human rights under law.

[10] Weisberg, "Antonio's Legalistic Cruelty," 15 *College Literature* 25 (1998) 12–20.

[11] Schütz, supra n 8; see also on this point, Jacob Rabkin, "A Fresh Look at Shakespeare's *The Merchant of Venice*," 25 *Litigator* 69 (1999) 70.

find meanings nowhere available to any sound interpreter.[12] These mis-readings do not show "love" or "mercy"; as far as the Jews are concerned, they convey hatred and *ressentiment*. In the early Christian spin-offs called the "Gospels," the Jewish God's readily available mercy is canceled and the Jews made into diabolical and legalistic ("Pharisaic") Christ-killers, destroying the Lamb who against all the textual odds had purportedly been announced way back by Isaiah [!] to be the Messiah. (The Akedah is re-read as pre-figuring the Crucifixion.) And Shylock will pay, as Jews have since those Gospels, for not accepting such ridiculous interpretive leaps to Jesus! Yet the Akedah ends without the shedding of human blood. The Jewish sacred text, bound like Isaac to a tradition of justice tempered with mercy, survives intact. But Shakespeare's tale reveals the perverse dilution of meaning brought to mercy and law by the "Gospels."

Christian law, as exemplified in Act IV of this portentous, complex comedy, lacks all mercy and has become legalistic beyond any Jewish court's most extreme practice of judgment. Portia reads the contract between Shylock the Jew and Antonio the Merchant in an absurdly hair-splitting manner. She takes the elegant paradigm of the Akedah (with which she probably has little familiarity except maybe through Christian distortions of the story to turn "binding" into "sacrifice"—in these ridiculous variations, Isaac dies and is resurrected [!] and Abraham's *obedience* is transmogrified into "faith"[13]) and takes each literal word beyond the context of the contract, its parties, or anything except her need to "save" her new husband's best friend, the Merchant of Venice himself. Then she pulls out an "Alien Statute" and assures in the bargain Shylock's complete de-humanization. Only the Christian Merchant remains to infuse some benign meaning into the word "mercy," as he is assigned the ultimate task of deciding Shylock's fate. "What will Antonio do to Shylock" becomes a more consequential question to the theater-goer than "Will the Jew cut?" Portia, probably happy to delegate the ultimate decision to the Merchant, shows this explicitly:

"What mercy can you show him, Antonio?,"[14] she asks the Merchant. In response, most un-Christianly, the title "hero" all but destroys the defeated civil-plaintiff-now-twisted -into-criminal-defendant. The Jew must convert to Christianity; he must leave his eventual estate to Jessica and Lorenzo ("the man who lately stole your daughter"), and Antonio himself takes control of the money-lender's wealth for the rest of the old Jew's lifetime, with the remainder going to Lorenzo and the distraught Shylock's eloping daughter; among other pieces of his portable property, Jessica has stolen the precious ring he received from his wife Leah as a bachelor and then sold it, during a pagan honeymoon, "for a monkey." She now will

---

[12] Nietzsche, our greatest thinker, speaker, and actor on what constitutes sound readings of texts, differentiates throughout his work not only the so-called "Old" Testament (which he prizes) from the "New" (which he detests) but also the devious work of Christian interpreters to usurp Jewish stories and make them, through distortion, their own. See, e.g., *On the Genealogy of Morals*, Essay III, aphorism #22; *Beyond Good and Evil*, aphorisms #52 and 251; *The Will to Power*, aphorisms #180–2; *Dawn of Day*, aphorism #205; *The Case of Wagner*, epilogue and note.

[13] See, e.g., *Epistles to the Hebrews*, 11: 17–19, and many other Christian source texts amounting to Isaac's actually having died on the mountain because Abraham had "faith," after which Isaac is resurrected. But when the angel intoned twice Abraham's name, any threat that Isaac was going to die disappeared! That is the Jewish tradition. It should be respected, and the meaning of words not programmatically devalued.

[14] *The Merchant of Venice*, IV, i, 530.

get much more, through the medium of "Christian law," having herself apparently decided that such words as "Honor thy father and mother" and "Thou shalt not steal" don't signify.

Though his life is spared, it's a Pyrrhic victory for the Jew: "You take my life," Shylock says, as the court robs him of property, freedom of testation, livelihood, and the right to read such sacred texts as the Akedah within the traditions of his own religion. There is no angel intervening when Antonio, just saved from a death he need not have feared from the devout Jew, viciously turns the tables on Shylock. Suddenly victorious, Antonio's full character as a Christian gentleman has been tested, and like Portia, he comes up way short.

Although "mercy" is used repetitiously during the scene, it is a *word that does not count*. Unlike Abraham, who only needs one reminder from the angel, Antonio is not listening to anything but his prejudiced heart. There is no training in the Christian faith traditions that provides an understanding of "mercy" except as its antithesis. It is a word, and it is used (like "love") repetitiously; but like the word "not" in the Ten Commandments ("Thou shalt *not* steal"), it can be easily ignored. In the Jewish tradition—already enriched when the Christians came to "replace" it by eight centuries of oral tradition[15]—every word is revered.

In verse 11 of the foundational story, why must the angel call twice: "Abraham, *Abraham*"? As the traditional, sound, and still excellent answer goes: "This exclamation (Abraham, *Abraham*!) shows the anxiety of the angel of the Lord to hold Abraham back at the very last moment […] All that God desired was proof of Abraham's *willingness* to obey His command; and the moral surrender has been complete."[16]

For the theater-goer, picture the same angel who desperately called to Abraham also calling to Shylock with knife still in hand: "Shylock, *Shylock*!"—and at that moment, the Jew drops the knife.[17] Or is it the learning Shylock always already had in his head, based on his sacred nation's awe-inspiring holy text, that causes him to drop the knife of his own accord; he needs no "Christian intercessors"[18] for that, and no wonder: they have distorted the idea of "law" out of recognition by creating "new" stories that all but eliminate or render infinitely flexible whatever once was magnificently there as Law. If Shylock listened to "Christian intercessors," for example, he might well have plunged the knife into Antonio, because many Christian traditions simply use the story by having Isaac actually die at Abraham's hand and then return to life, an absurd typological rendering way in advance of the events in Jerusalem.[19] The Jewish God does not let that happen to the lad. Shylock will not let that happen even to his enemy, Antonio.

The single repetitive verbal moment in the *Akedah* imagines a universe in which the stories that produce law and the law that produces its own stories need no angel *repeating* from fear of excessive obedience that the devout individual will go too far. On the contrary, *The Merchant*

---

[15] There is no real inter-relation, in this tradition, between nomos: "Love thine enemy," say, or "Turn the other cheek," and narrative: a set of strong stories—many transmitted orally from generation to generation—re-enforcing an understanding of that command. So each conflict, like the one in *Merchant*, lies for resolution in the subjective hands of the appointed adjudicator, who provides at her will the most self-satisfying application of the "nomos."
[16] Soncino edn, supra n 7, at 75.
[17] See propounding this staging, from a Christian perspective, Peter J Alscher, "Staging Directions for a Balanced Resolution to *The Merchant of Venice* Trial Scene" 5 *Cardozo Studies in Law and Literature* 1 (1993).
[18] *The Merchant of Venice*, III, iii, 20.
[19] See Weisberg, *In Praise of Intransigence* (NY: OUP, 2014) ch. 3, and sources therein.

of Venice may want us to see that we have been degraded to the opposite paradigm: there is no internal righteous voice within us that prevents us from progressing too far into cruelty, not charity. Portia demands at least something like "mercy" from Antonio, but she might have well asked this of a stone. "Mercy" is a coded word full of sound and gentleness but compelling at its best nothing, and at its worst cruelty.

The More Mundane Application of the Rule: From Ordinary Law to Anton Chekhov

As we move from the sacred to the profane, we find both in the understanding of ordinary stories and in legal doctrine a similar interpretive principle: every word counts. A commonplace of statutory and constitutional interpretation,[20] the idea is based on a bit of a "legal fiction": that a collectivity of authors has been so scrupulous in releasing a text as to have guaranteed together for future readers the sacrosanct nature of its every word and phrase. So even more, where the presumed author of a text is an individual, the presumption applies. Take two fairly recent examples from the law of wills and trusts, the first coming from the Supreme Court of North Dakota.[21] In paragraph 6 of their trust, executed during their lifetimes (his wife's trust was identical in this regard), the father attempts to settle the family farm upon his oldest son. Unfortunately and mistakenly, the method of this disposition cross-refers to another provision of the same trust, where the same property seems to have been given not just to the son but to all four of the parents' children equally. The first provision refers to the second, so the other children have a valid argument that the farm goes to all of them. External evidence, however, strongly points to the parents—now deceased—having wanted only the eldest son to take that land. The situation is saved, in part, by our universal rule of construction: If only the second provision controls, the first would have no meaning. The court says:

> In construing the provisions of a trust, the general rules of construction of written documents apply and the trust must be read as a whole so as to give effect to every part [cite omitted]. The construction urged by [the other three children] effectively reads Paragraph 6 out of the trust.[22]

The trust is reformed by the high court of North Dakota to eliminate the error and give that parcel to the eldest son. But in the same area of law, and using the same principle—every word counts—courts may justify results that run counter to the testamentary writer's intentions. Consider our second example, involving a Missouri couple, Archie and Dortha, happily married for more than 50 years. Unlike in the earlier case, they executed separate documents by will (no trusts here), she disposing of her property "to my nieces and nephews that are living as of the date of my death," and he, using the same language, "to my nieces and nephews living as of the date of my death." By all accounts they were a close extended family that, during their lives, did not pin the status of niece or nephew to some bond by blood. Dortha's nieces and nephews through her siblings were as dear to Archie as those born to his own sisters and brothers. However, the word "my" in each will became dispositive:

> If Archie, or the lawyer who drafted his will, had intended to include the children of brothers and sisters of Dortha as beneficiaries under her will, it would have been easy for them to have done so

---

[20] See, e.g., the "Superfluity Canon," Bryan Garner, ed.
[21] *Agnes M. Gassmann Revocable Trust v Reichert*, 802 N.W. 2d 889 (N.D., 2011).
[22] Ibid, at 893–4.

simply by referring to "our nieces and nephews" instead of "my nieces and nephews." […] However, this was not done. "My" is the possessive form of the pronoun "I", while "our" is a possessive pronoun of the pronoun "we". American Heritage Dictionary of the English Language (1970).

The avuncular wishes of Archie are displaced because of a single word.[23] Those of the farmers in the earlier case were redeemed but only because of the rule of construction that essentially says no words or phrases can be considered wasteful.[24] Everything counts. These cases conflict as to outcome only,[25] not as to how they reached the outcome through construction. And the same can be said of how authoritative—as well as lay—readers have traditionally construed the meaning of stories. Consider a superb thought experiment on the reading of Russian stories conducted recently by the novelist and author of *Lincoln in the Bardo*, George Saunders.[26] Saunders has us read, page by page, some stories by four Russian writers and asks us to imagine that those authors are offering us a master class on reading, writing, and life. He interrupts each page of text by asking us what, at this stage, we have understood and what we are expecting; *how* the writer sets those expectations up; and what ensuing details further or dampen those expectations.

In the first tale he examines this way, Chekhov's "In the Cart," a lonely school-teacher is a passenger riding toward a meeting she dreads will be boring; in fact, her whole life is boring and sad. The old coachman, who's describing a political assassination in Moscow, does not help her mood. This changes, potentially, when a handsome man comes on board in the seat next to her. Many questions are left open in the first few pages of the story, and the reader might want "direct" information about the feelings of both potential sweethearts. Some is available, but as in most great stories of 11 pages, much remains to do when we are only on page 4. That page begins as follows: "'He is really handsome,' she thought, glancing at Hanov. Meanwhile the road was growing worse and worse. They drove into the woods. Here there was no turning off the road, the ruts were deep, and water flowed and gurgled in them. Twigs struck them stingingly in the face."

Our guide, Saunders, stops after each page. Here, among other questions, he asks why that long paragraph tilts heavily toward the road taken by the coach when what we want is more about whether Hanov reciprocates the protagonist's feelings of attraction. (We might ask an analogous question about what gets in or goes missing in any text: why is Portia seemingly so sweet but ready to drop the ax on Shylock? Why does Abraham not explain to his son their fateful trip up the mountain? Why do the Missouri judges not emphasize, but instead exclude, the loving details of Archie's extended family?[27]) As to the detailed description of the turn in the road, Saunders says:

---

[23] See *Estate of Carroll*, 764 SW 2d 736 (Ct. of Appeals of MO, 1989).
[24] See supra n 20.
[25] The major difference follows from the first case falling under the law of trusts, where "extrinsic" evidence is usually permissible even without an "ambiguity," and the second under the law of wills, where an ambiguity usually must be found before allowing evidence of how, e.g., the families generally interacted. Compare Uniform Trust Code Section 415 with Uniform Probate Code Section 2-805. We will see there are similar conflicts among readers of poetry and fiction. See infra, second section.
[26] Saunders, *A Swim in the Pond in the Rain* (NY: Random House, 2021).
[27] The seemingly sleepy arena of Trusts and Estates law does not often command the attention of Law and Literature scholars as it does in this chapter. For a fine counter-example, see Kim Lane Scheppele, "Facing Facts in Legal Interpretation," in Robert Post, ed. *Law and the Order of Culture* (CA: Berkeley, 1991) 42–77.

Notice how impatient your reading mind is or, we might say, how alert it is. It knows where we are: Marya, lonely and unhappy, has encountered a potential antidote in Hanov. Like an obsessed detective, the reading mind interprets every new-arriving bit of text purely in this context, not interested in much else. And yet here, in the third paragraph, it seems that, whether we want one or not, we're going to get a description of the road.

Why does a story even need these kinds of descriptions? Why did Chekhov decide to pull us out of the central action and describe the world outside the cart? One of the tacit promises of a short story, because it is so short, is that there's no waste in it. Everything is in there for a reason (for the story to make use of)—even a brief description of a road.

So, as we enter this description, we're asking, somewhere in the back of our reading mind: How is this description of a road going to turn out to be essential, that is, not wasteful?[28]

Every word counts, in law and literature. There is no waste. Nothing but each word or phrase controls our understanding of the text.[29] Melville's digressions—his rides off the road—in *Billy Budd, Sailor* are as "important" as the seeming "highway" of the story.[30] They are part of the plot. There is no superfluity. That Chekhovian "detour" will soon help the attentively distracted reader return, better informed, to the cart's GPS.

"Abraham, *Abraham*."

EVERY WORD COUNTS/BUT MORE SO IF WE PERMIT "EXTRINSIC EVIDENCE"

"No Plain Meaning" Redux[31]

Law continues to be saddled with the notion that words have "plain meanings." Consider the Missouri court's emphasis on the word "my" and its refusal to consider the full context of Archie and Dortha's avuncular affections. Consider, in a fictional context, Portia's emphasis on the bond's plain meaning—"a pound of flesh"—when, in one of the arguments that destroys Shylock, she absurdly construes the provision to exclude the attendant features of that penalty provision: "Shed thou no blood, nor cut thou less nor more/Than just a pound of flesh."[32]

A too literal reliance on a word's "plain meaning" reduces, rather than enhances, the value of the lesson "every word counts". To understand the Bible, or Chekhov, or *The Merchant of Venice*, or Uncle Archie's wishes, the full context of the ultimately expressed single word or phrase needs to be exposed and understood. It was an intentional error by the early Christian writers to ignore, when decrying so-called Jewish literalism, an entire centuries-long elaboration of phrases like "Abraham, Abraham!" that the Jews had woven into their interpretations. Many of those early Christian writers were themselves Jews, and they surely knew better;

---

[28] Supra n 26 at p.27. Remember the rule against wasted language in law, supra n 20.
[29] Does this change when we locate an incongruity, as in *Gassmann*, supra n 21, as opposed to a seeming irrelevance, like the road? When should we look outside the text for answers? What about the coachman's account, early in "In the Cart," of an assassination in Moscow? Don't we want to know more about it, even or especially if it never comes back specifically into the story, as the perilous and depressing road surely will? See infra, second section.
[30] See, e.g., Weisberg, *The Failure of the Word* (New Haven: Yale U Press, 1984) chs. 8 and 9.
[31] Weisberg, "Three Lessons . . .," supra n 1.
[32] *The Merchant of Venice*, IV, i, 465.

but their charge of "legalism" or "Pharisaism" both served their purposes and stuck, as did Portia's similarly clever turn against Shylock. Meanwhile Shylock, and Jews generally, have "stubbornly" maintained their elegant interpretive traditions. They have paid an inconceivably huge price for this hermeneutic fidelity.[33]

Pain is felt every day, too, in the far more mundane arena of English and American adjudication. Uncle Archie paid a posthumous price, and those he loved paid a real-time penalty, for too strong a resistance to evidence of surrounding circumstances. When do judges recognize that at least some words or phrases need such illumination?

When "Extrinsic Evidence" is Permitted

In law
Courts in a variety of areas show an unwillingness to go beyond a word's "plain meaning". So, in a branch of what is known as Constitutional "originalism" perhaps familiar to even non-lawyer readers of this chapter, many judges and academics claim that "only the original meaning of the words as they would have been read by those at the time of the text's promulgation" control our contemporary understanding of it.[34] This view entails not only the availability to a 2021 interpreter of such prior readings but even more strangely, perhaps, the notion that a reader "way back then" would have had a plain understanding of the word or phrase in question. The framing generation itself knew about the tricky nature of every utterance.[35] They wanted their words—each word—to be taken as they meant them (we all do) but doubted such resonance between speaker and listener would just automatically occur. They were more tolerant of overlaying external details because—although they deeply valued language—they understood its limits.

Statutory and (as we have seen regarding Uncle Archie) testamentary language also often is bound to a "plain meaning" rule of one kind or another. No matter what Archie wanted for the children of Dortha's siblings, his wishes were reduced to a dictionary meaning utilized authoritatively by the court.

Only in certain circumstances will courts construing wills, or contracts (such as fictionally represented in the Venetian variation given us by the Bard) for that matter, go beyond the somewhat fallacious idea of sticking to the plain meaning of what they are interpreting. If an "ambiguity" can be shown, then they may tolerate a bit of an opening into the actual intentions of the text writer. This literalistic view, which as a theological matter was never adopted by

---

[33] In a remarkable recent work of popular fiction, the spy novelist Daniel Silva thoroughly explores what one of his characters calls the "straight line between the teachings of the early Church and the gas chambers and crematoria of Auschwitz." His story is followed by compendious author's notes underlying that character's assertion. See Silva, *The Order* (NY: Harper, 2020) 514.

[34] This boilerplate has been set down most vociferously in recent years by the late Antonin Scalia, who has many followers; among challenges to his memory are those that wonder aloud whether Justice Scalia followed the constraints of his own theory when straining to reach the conclusion he otherwise wanted.

[35] See Madison in *The Federalist Papers*, #37, speaking of language as such a "cloudy medium" that even God might only be able to hope His own words will be understood. (Abraham managed to do so. A whole Christian tradition of distorting Jewish sacred texts, as Nietzsche repetitively and correctly opined, closed the door on that always miniscule chance of getting closer to God through the medium of language). See supra n 12.

the Jews, for whom an emphasis on each word automatically opened up a world of experience, values, and stories—their "oral tradition," among other sources—takes Portia to the absurd limits so criticized by Rudolf von Ihering among others.[36] Like Portia, though, most English and American judges feel comfortable opening up such worlds only if a party wishing to do so can show that the word or phrase turns out to be much less than "clear on its face." If, for example, X's Last Will and Testament leaves everything to "My cousin Sheila," well, that's "plain" enough. But suppose when we try to fulfill X's intent, we discover she has *two* cousin Sheilas? Well, now, most judges will be OK in bringing in a good deal of the back story: did X know both of them?; if so was X much closer in life to one than the other?; did one help her during the stressful times while the other never called? The extrinsic features of X's life, within these narrow confines, are permitted into the resolution of the meaning of "Sheila."

We have so far been arguing that no words are superfluous.[37] "To my cousin Sheila" counts, essentially, in figuring out what to do with X's estate. But once we become skeptical of a judicial rule that—unless there's this sort of ambiguity—*limits* further understanding of that phrase, what are we to make of an entire tradition that has somewhat successfully used it? For this inquiry, let's find some answers in literature and in literary theory.

In literature

This business of figuring out when to open the reader's understanding of a text to proofs "outside" of its four corners has a rich recent history in twentieth-century American and continental literary criticism and theory. When discussing a poem and story, some "schools" allowed talk of such factors as the writer's life, the general cultural background that informed the text, a comparison of the text under analysis with others (whether or not by the same writer), and/or a variety of factors "extrinsic" to the text itself. My Ph.D. training at Cornell included an exemplar of this approach, a German-trained scholar named Wolfgang Holdheim who, when analyzing a text, practiced in many of his writings what might be called "Geistesgeschichte" or history of ideas.[38] This fundamental feature of scholarship informed the area I was training for and then taught in—comparative literature—for many decades. While not exactly the same thing, Americans studying, say, with Lionel Trilling, may have learned a kind of "sociology of literature" from him, as some in France may have learned similarly from such luminaries as Lucien Goldmann several decades later.[39] Generalizing, it's fair to say that these thinkers allowed "in" entire worlds of philosophic and cultural and biographical evidence with the aim of understanding a literary text.

Various others, often formed into schools, had been rebelling against such approaches, throughout the twentieth century. In one way or another, they sought to make more rigorous the study of a poem or story by excluding anything that was not part of the text itself. As in the "judicial sciences" we have referenced, they developed their own rules while focusing on "the thing itself." But they formed those rules each in their different ways.

---

[36] See supra n 9. More recently, see the excellent attack on Portia by an American attorney, Daniel Kornstein, *Kill all the Lawyers?* (Lincoln: U of Neb Press, 2005) 72–4.

[37] See first section and note 20.

[38] W.W. Holdheim, *Theory and Practice of the Novel: A Study on Andre Gide* (Geneva: Librairie Droz, 1968), and his masterpiece, *Der Justizirrtum Als Literarische Problematik* (Berlin: de Gruyter, 2nd ed. 2019).

[39] Lucien Goldmann, *Towards a Sociology of the Novel* trans. A. Sheridan (London: Tavistock, 1975).

One of my favorite such schools is that of "Russian formalist theory." Developed in the very rich early period of Soviet literature and criticism, its proponents were such greats as Viktor Shklovsky, Boris Eikhenbaum, and Boris Tomashevski.[40] This school looked at the text (often, in their case, a novella or short story) strictly from within its four corners. They emphasized from that internal perspective such ground-breaking narrative techniques as "defamiliarization," "slowing down," and "plot" (as opposed to "story"); they were formalists in the sense that they resisted earlier Russian critical methods, which brought from the outside to these same texts history, morality, and sociology.

Roughly contemporarily, but in the United States, the "New Critics" moved to excise from the quest for literary meaning (their favorite genre was poetry) anything but the play of language within the text itself. *Verboten* were references to the author's life, to ideas brought in from sociology, philosophy, or history, or to the "spirit of the times." Their loosely knit group—Cleanth Brooks, John Crowe Ransom, Allen Tate, and my own favorite, John Ciardi—has influenced "close readings" of literature by everyone from high school students to Deans of Humanities divisions at great universities. In Ciardi's titular phrase, they were interested not so much in what a poem meant as in "*How* A Poem Means."[41] They specialized in finding irony, paradox, and other techniques within the poem while programmatically ridding themselves of external "guidelines" to its meaning.

Both judges and lit crits take pride in a certain insular approach to meaning that makes their jobs special. Anyone can make judgments on the basis of dramatic data, they seem to be saying: what we do—*we* special ones—is stick to a set of insider rules we have framed for ourselves. We do not, in the words of American critic R.S. Crane (who in other ways distanced himself from the New Critics), give in to the "temptation to assimilate poetry [or law], by large analogies, to metaphysics or rhetoric or history or the spirit of the age."[42]

I was fortunate while still at Cornell (and at Zurich, where they taught Cornell graduate students who followed them around) to be taught by Paul de Man and Geoffrey H. Hartman. They, together with Murray Krieger, J. Hillis Miller, and Jacques Derrida, were moving from "structuralism"—which still worked largely from within the text itself—to "deconstructionism," which found meanings not in some central internal structure but rather at the margins of textual permissibility. Their readings were mind-blowingly original and, especially in the case of de Man (my teacher, who, despite everything, I revere), often wrong. There is often a willful, elliptical attempt to skirt the significance of individual words in order to prove their theory's ascendancy over a text or a writer, especially one as vital to the whole history of ideas as Nietzsche.[43] Even as their school recedes a bit into the past, arguments continue

---

[40] Fortunately, a good concise collection of their essays is available, edited by Lemon and Reis: *Russian Formalist Criticism: Four Essays* (Lincoln: U of Nebraska, 1965, 2nd ed., 2012).

[41] See e.g. John Ciardi, "The Form is the Experience," 14 *Art Education* 16 (1961).

[42] R.S. Crane, "Cleanth Brooks, or the Bankruptcy of Critical Monism," 45 *Modern Philology* 226 (1948).

[43] See Weisberg, "De Man Missing Nietzsche: 'Hinzugedichtet' Revisited," which examines De Man's reading of *one word* (because De Man was a close reader) to find it being twisted out of shape (because he was a bad reader, in the Nietzschean sense): De Man takes Nietzsche to mean that no new experience has meaning until it is recounted or recollected (but this is wrong on its face throughout Nietzsche's writings and perhaps especially in *Ecce Homo*), and then—worse—in a reading of another key word, "truth," and here joined by Derrida in *Eperons: Les Styles de Nietzsche* (Paris: Flammarion, 1978) [trans. Barbara Harlow, *Nietzsche's Styles* (Chicago: U of Chicago, 1979)], where for their

as to whether they more resembled the imaginative but constrained Talmudists or the New Testament con(dis-?)tortionists.[44] Deconstructionism, as to law, has had its heyday not so much in analogous judicial approaches as in the law reviews, but it can be argued that *Brown v Board*, avant la lettre, was a deconstructionist opinion.[45]

The ongoing American critical approach that most delights in bringing to textual meanings a whole variety of "extrinsic" evidence is labeled "the new historicism." Law and Literature as a field has been identified as an exemplar of that approach in discussions of this school.[46] The literary text, read closely ("every word counts"), then opens up uses of historical data (sometimes empirical), which reciprocally rebound to the text for further clarification of the words, phrases, paragraphs, or even the entirety of the story under analysis.

"ON MORAL WRITING": THE GOAL(S) WHEN GENERATING NORMATIVE TEXTS

John Gardner and Moral Criticism

We have so far been examining *how* the authors of law and the writers of stories write and also *how* they are understood (or misunderstood). This coda asks the question, *why* do people in these two word-bound enterprises write? The question, by definition, is normative: when you open up your computer to write a legal brief or a judicial opinion or a story, what *should* be your aim in doing so? If there are multiple aims, and multiple audiences to your words, are there nonetheless some universal aspirations you might bring to the act of written (or, sometimes, verbal[47]) communication?

The teleological inquiry, which looks forward as the act of writing takes place to locate goals to be sought by the writer, is old-fashioned. Yet there are traditions in both law and literature that sustain it in each generation. Nietzsche was surely within this tradition. His late ruminations about the morality of writing (and reading) remain challenging in an environment still not yet ready to read them properly (he predicted he would not be understood for a century

---

argument that Nietzsche is authorizing the capture of texts by readers of any kind who manage to make a mark, it is crucial to bend Nietzsche's "*solche* Wahrheiten [*such* truths]" into "*meine* Wahrheiten [*my* truths]" hermeneutically cutting the heart out of Nietzsche's multiply expressed view that there are good and bad readings of texts and of life itself, and that no reader or observer can claim truth just because she has and is entitled to her own perspective or interpretive needs.

[44] For an exceptionally strong description of the debate on whether deconstructionism is "Talmudic" or Pauline—faithful to texts or in the long run too flexibly opposed to them—see Pantazakos, "Dvar Torah," 29 *Law and Literature* 41 (2017).

[45] The unanimous Supreme Court in its 1954 *Brown v Board* decision explicitly unanchored the Court from the usual rules of Constitutional interpretation (text, history, intention); once liberated, they went to the margins of meaning, including the use of non-legal material from the social sciences, to end apartheid in the United States. As to methods of reading across a wide range of SCOTUS opinions see, passim, Levinson and Mailloux, *Interpreting Law and Literature* (Evanston: Northwestern U Press, 1988).

[46] For a fine example of theory and practice of New Historicism in connection with Law and Literature, see Christine Krueger, "Law and Literature and History," in K. Dolin, ed., *A Critical Introduction to Law and Literature* (Cambridge: Cambridge University Press, 2007) 58–76.

[47] Recall the rich Judaic oral tradition that undergirds the written text: see supra n 15.

or more).[48] And Benjamin N. Cardozo, as we shall elaborate further in this section, never lost sight of the teleology of judicial decision making: to do justice in each case.

Meanwhile, as many of the critics and theorists discussed in the second section of this chapter were paying little attention to the morality of the narrative enterprise, one novelist/critic, John Gardner, was doing so. His *On Moral Fiction* identified story-tellers, as well as critical "schools" who, on his terms, wrote "morally" and criticized contemporaries and colleagues (he was also a fiction writer) who did not.[49]

Perhaps because he judgmentally excluded most late twentieth-century writers from his field of approbation (Albee, Barth, Doctorow, Heller, Mailer, Pynchon, Updike, Vonnegut are cast away—and even Bellow barely escapes calumny), Gardner's audiences fell off. They neglect at some peril the criteria for winning his admiration: "In literature, structure is the evolving sequence of dramatized events tending toward understanding and assertion: that is toward some meticulously qualified belief" (65). "Art instructs. Why, one may wonder, would anyone wish to deny a thing so obvious?" (39).

The contemporary writers whom Gardner cherishes and predicts will survive into the twenty-first century form a very short list, including Toni Morrison, Bernard Malamud, and especially John Fowles.[50] Fowles is admired because:

> He will tell in the novel he means to write – the novel we are reading – the truth. […] The would-be artist who cannot tell moral truth from statistics[51], who cannot find "the real" both in his images and behind them, as Fowles says [in DANIEL MARTIN] must inevitably wander lost in false questions of relativity. (51)

In somewhat the same vein, Gardner takes on contemporary critical schools we have also scrutinized earlier in this chapter: he was living through the transition from the New Critics toward post-modernism. Of the former, he opined:

> The new criticism regularly claimed that what counts in literature is not what it says, what it affirms and promulgates, but only how well it works as a self-contained, organic whole, by doing whatever it does […] But even in conspicuously technical art, no serious viewer, listener, or reader—certainly no artist—is indifferent to whether the work in front of him is not just well made but in some sense noble, fit to last. (131–2)

And as to post-modernism, which he attacks both in its literary emanations (such as in the novels of John Barth and William Gass) and in its nascent critical schools, he says something especially significant for this chapter, a set of lines that, once updated and complicated a bit, will faithfully lead us to its conclusion:

> Fiction as pure language (texture over structure) is *in*. It is one common manifestation of what is being called "post-modernism." At bottom the mistake is a matter of morality, at least in the sense that it

---

[48] See text supra at notes 12 and 43.
[49] *On Moral Fiction* (NY: Basic, 1978). Subsequent quotes from this book are in textual parentheses.
[50] For Fowles, read, e.g., *The Magus, the French Lieutenant's Woman*, and Gardner's favorite, *Daniel Martin*.
[51] See "Growth of the Law," in Hall, ed., *Law and Literature*, supra n 2 at 216, from Judge Cardozo, where he launches a remarkably prescient similar attack on statistical approaches, and specifically Law and Economics, to law.

shows, on the writer's part, a lack of concern. To people who care about events and ideas and thus, necessarily, about the clear and efficient statement of both, linguistic opacity suggests indifference to the needs and wishes of the reader and to whatever ideas may be hidden under all that brush. And since one reason we read fiction is our hope that we will be moved by it, finding characters we can enjoy and sympathize with, an academic striving for opacity suggests, if not misanthropy, a perversity or shallowness that no reader [sh]ould tolerate. (69)

The key to this passage, inclusive of its directness, is not only that it comes from a writer who enjoys and is sensitive to very complex modern writers he admires (his readings of Melville are particularly astute[52]) but also that it recognizes deliberate avoidance of clear writing, which he calls "opaqueness," as a sin against the morally holy ghost in fiction and criticism.

(We find the same demand for stylistic clarity in Benjamin N. Cardozo's masterful essay, "Law and Literature," where he insists that the legal writer be clear, that difficult messages need not be obfuscated but instead intertwined to and indistinguishable from the simplest possible form the writer can find, and that these writing strictures lead, precisely in those hard cases, to justice.[53])

Now there is good reason, after World War II in particular, to be skeptical of calls, like Gardner's for "moral fiction," or of any such claim relating to literary or legal writing in the service of some over-arching code. The reason is simple: too many of those codes are bad, horribly bad. One writer's sound morality is another's perverse one: we saw that in the first section of this chapter.

Hitler's judges, while signing away the lives of countless innocents, thought they were serving a "higher truth" called the "Fuehrerprinzip" or what the Leader wants.[54] And, to Gardner's demand for clear language, wasn't it precisely Hitler's *clarity*, a grotesquely "moral" one, that generated the horrors to follow, as cultured Europeans conspired to send 6,000,000 to the ovens?

I am convinced as first a student, then a friend and occasional academic partner of Geoffrey H. Hartman, that the "opacity" of many deconstructionist texts was born of a highly ethical need precisely to avoid any repetition of the twisted lucidity that brought inconceivable tragedy to World War II Europe. No simple, syntactically clear statement of critical theory was to be allowed. The "sublimity" of such directness had been more than matched by the grotesqueness of listeners' or readers' awful, genocidal response. It makes sense if it was an aversion to simple and direct writing that might almost be called "moral" if their premises were correct.

Gardner has this right, though. As I have argued with Hartman in print (and on long walks on beaches near New Haven, and on Lake Como near our month-long study-center at Bellagio) and other post-modernists, an understanding of the enormity in Hitler's Europe requires knowledge that it caused the *deconstructive* capacities of tens of thousands of leaders and ordinary people, and not some simple brutish command that they obeyed like slavish dogs! How much intricate—opaque—linguistic work these cultured ones needed to do to wind them-

---

[52] "The true artist is likely to be furious in the company of cheapness and compromise. (It is careless criticism, not Melville, that forgives Captain Vere.)" The parenthetical is the best straightforward single sentence I have ever read about the critical response to the masterpiece; see *On Moral Fiction*, 204, and supra n 31.
[53] See Cardozo, "Law and Literature," supra n 2.
[54] See Ingo Mueller, *Hitler's Justice: The Courts of the Third Reich* (trans. Deborah Schneider, 1991).

selves, snake-like, away from their prior lives' best teachings! People who had been trained to refuse and rebut such "simple rhetorical horrors" failed to emerge publicly. Instead, good people and bad gave purchase to other traditions (discussed in this chapter)—particularly, say, Portia's deconstructive techniques—to find a very complex, tragic pathway. This complex work permitted tens of thousands in Europe to jettison the finest elements within them and to rationalize the most reprehensible. During the Holocaust in Europe, words became more, not less, complicated.[55]

The Holocaust, from which thinkers like Hartman, de Man, and Derrida each in his sharply divergent way emerged, should not have encouraged, to avoid repetition of that enormity, a flood of deliberately difficult words (Heidegger-like) that took them away from the problem at hand.[56] Deconstruction is not "justice," in other words, despite Derrida's obscure claim to that effect.[57] Justice is finding the right set of words—every one of which counts and most of which can be quite straightforward—that takes the writer to the reader and moves him or her to write (in their turn), or to act, justly. "Abraham, Abraham!"[58]

There is a right and wrong, and both law and stories have long since contributed, either way or at their best *together*, to constructing a sense of both. But how do we know, as writers, that we are at the very least striving toward the sound and the correct? Here Gardner provides few answers.

Benjamin Nathan Cardozo and The Ethical Ends of the Act of Judgment

The judicial enterprise offers at least some, albeit often tentative, answers. Here is a discipline whose teleology—whose future-oriented practice—is, precisely, to do the right thing! Our guru, again, is Benjamin N. Cardozo. In a rare moment, he gets to discuss his own opinion in *Hynes v RR*, in an essay published the year after it came down. In *Hynes*[59] the judge fielded a confusion of conflicting rules to find what he explicitly called "justice."[60] Only a year or so later, in another of his extra-judicial essays,[61] Cardozo described his forward-looking method in that (and other) cases:

> I have been trying to give some notion of the kind of problems that must be met by a philosophy that concerns itself with the final causes of the law [...] What I have wished to lead up to is the bearing of such a philosophy upon the problems that must be met in practice by the lawyer or the judge [...] We had in my court a year or more ago a case that points my meaning. [He describes the oft-repeated facts of *Hynes*[62] and the court's dilemma in choosing between two conflicting uses by the parties of analogous reasoning to support their side.] [...] When we find a situation of this kind, the choice that will approve itself to this judge or to that will be determined largely by his conception of the end of

---

[55] Weisberg, *Vichy Law and the Holocaust in France* (NY: NYU Press, 1996) ch. 10.
[56] Hartman gets to that problem in a relatively late work, *The Longest Shadow: In the Aftermath of the Holocaust* (Bloomington: U. of Indiana P, 1996).
[57] Derrida, "Force of Law: The Mystical Foundation of Authority," originally published at 11 *Cardozo Law Review* (1990) 919–1046.
[58] "Tzedek, tzedek tirdof [Justice, justice, shall ye seek!]," *Deuteronomy* 16:19.I.
[59] *Hynes v NY Central RR*, 231 N.Y. 229, 131 N.E. 898 (Court of Appeals, NY, 1921).
[60] Ibid, at p.904.
[61] Cardozo, "Growth of the Law," supra n 51 at 228.
[62] See, e.g., Weisberg, *Poethics: and Other Strategies of Law and Literature* (NY: Columbia UP, 1992).

the law, the function of legal liability […] *Some* theory of liability, some philosophy of the end to be served by tightening the circle of rights and remedies, is at the root of any decision in novel situations when analogies are equivocal and precedents are silent […] We must learn to handle our tools, to use our methods and processes not singly, but together.

Choosing from the tools he—and all writers in our twinned disciplines—have at hand, the judge ponders the situation. In Cardozo's case, his "philosophy" undoubtedly included the teachings of his life-long faith, Judaism. He had read as a youth, at the Spanish and Portuguese Synagogue in New York City, the Akedah.[63] Would he "plunge the knife"[64] into the plaintiff's estate, as they sought a remedy for the railroad's negligent taking of their child's life? Or would he remember the denouement of the Akedah, undistorted by foreign traditions that fill in "sacrifice" for obedience. Would he proceed to support, as God did Isaac, the "lad of 16"?[65]

A few years later, in *Paradoxes of Legal Science*,[66] Cardozo continues his answer to the question how he decided *Hynes* and, more generally, the means by which judicial narratives *do the right thing*. In fact here he becomes as explicit as his modest persona allowed (a great leader is always modest).[67] Abjuring mention of his own faith, he invokes it indirectly as follows:

> Yet there are signposts on the way, if only we have skill to read them. Lord Acton tells us that "the example of the Hebrew nation laid down the parallel lines on which all freedom has been won, the doctrine of national tradition and the doctrine of the higher law: the principle that a constitution grows from a root by a process of development, and not of essential change, and the principle that all political authority must be tested and reformed according to a code which was not made by man."[68]

Joining with and requiring the merger of form and substance he espoused in "Law and Literature,"[69] his judicial tools—his philosophy and indeed his religious training—bring him as close as possible to escaping the victimhood of the "paradoxes" every serious writer faces. Harvey Hynes will emerge from the thicket of formalistic rules upon which he otherwise would be sacrificed:

> The wizard Justice has a queer way of setting the victim free.[70]

CONCLUSION

Cardozo's "wizard of Justice" lies in each of us. Unified in law and literature, we need to clarify our own morality (because every writer has a morality), test it for its soundness by doing a lot of reading, by trial and error figure things out in the world of action, and then get

---

[63] Andrew Kaufman, *Cardozo* (Cambridge, Mass.: Harvard University Press, 1988) ch.1.
[64] See Cardozo, "The Growth of the Law," supra n 51 at 215. He is speaking of cruel judges who use formulas to destroy worthy litigants.
[65] *Hynes*, supra n 59 at 898.
[66] "Paradoxes of Legal Science," in Hall, ed., supra n 2 at 252.
[67] "For Moses was a very modest man [V'haeesh Moshe onov m'od]," *Numbers* 12:3.
[68] "Paradoxes of Legal Science," supra n 66 at 326, quoting from Acton, *History of Freedom and Other Essays*, 5.
[69] See supra n 2.
[70] Ibid at 266.

into the business of generating *just* words and paragraphs, structured as best we can to convey and exhibit justice.[71]

---

[71] For his most recent poethical offering, see the elegant justice-seeking words of Peter Goodrich in *Advanced Introduction to Law and Literature* (Cheltenham, UK and Northampton, MA, USA: Edward Elgar Publishing, 2021).

34. Illocutionary

María Pía Lara

In my book *Moral Textures* (1998), I defined 'illocutionary action' as a compelling interaction between two sides (alter and ego) and as a sort of performative–narrative engagement about claims of justice from a social movement. The term 'illocutionary' comes from Jürgen Habermas's development of the concept of speech-acts, taken from Austin[1] and Searle, granting them a normative status due to their goal of bringing about understanding between alter and ego. His idea was to highlight the willingness of both sides to work through an exchange of reasons.[2] When I took the concept inspired by him,[3] I wanted to use his perspective to describe the ways social movements can engage with one another while building up their claims about social justice. Instead of referring to 'alter and ego', I will refer to plural groups as counter-publics. This concept helps me bring about the plural context where different social claims can enter into visibility and have the chance to build up an agenda of common interests. In some way, the process of engaging with other groups must aim at the convergence of perspectives through possibilities of identifying common experiences. It can also be understood as finding the right clues of an intersectional perspective.[4] As I understand intersections, they of course include other hierarchical situations of power, violence or domination such as class, ethnicity, sexual differences and so on. Intersectionality must be only the beginning of what Laclau has called the libidinal process of learning to find 'the [common] articulation of demands.[5] It frames these processes with an affective element that is at the core of any social movement. But there is also an epistemic dimension involved in the process, since we must learn to connect our experiences with those from others, and together reach a new stage of illocutionary force. Another way of describing this would be to bring about a new image of 'us and others'. It is a disclosing effort similar to an epiphany or an experience of illumination that guides us as it reveals something of moral significance to 'us and others' in an instant. This process must be one of mutual learning because it allows both sides to change their previous

---

[1] Austin, J.L. *How to Do Things with Words.* Cambridge, Massachusetts: Harvard University Press. 1962. See also: Searle, J.R. *A Theory of Speech-Acts.* New York: Cambridge University Press. 1969.

[2] Habermas developed his theory of speech-acts in his two-volume opus *The Theory of Communicative Action*, translated by Thomas McCarthy and published by Beacon Press in 1987. See: Lara, María Pía. 'Illocutionary Force' in: *The Cambridge Habermas Lexicon.* Edited by Amy Allen and Eduardo Mendieta. New York: Cambridge University Press. 2019. pp.188–90. See also: Lara, María Pía. *Moral Textures: Feminist Narratives in the Public Sphere.* Cambridge, England: Polity Press. 1997.

[3] See: Lara, María Pía. *Moral Textures: Feminist Narratives in the Public Sphere.*

[4] Kimberlé Crenshaw argues: 'Drawing from the strength of shared experience, women have recognized that the political demands of millions speak more powerfully that do pleas of a few isolated voices. This politicization in turn has transformed the way we understand violence against women.' In: Crenshaw, Kimberlé. 'The Intersection of Race and Gender' published in the collective volume: *Critical Race Theory: The Key Writings that Formed the Movement.* Edited by Kimberlé Crenshaw, Neil Gotanda, Gary Peller and Kendall Thomas. New York: The New York Press. 1995. pp.357–83, at 357.

[5] See: Laclau, Ernesto. *On Populist Reason.* New York and London: Verso. 2005. p.ix.

views in order to come together as a movement. When the exchange of ideas is successful and mutual engagement takes place, it discloses new paths towards social transformation.

In the following pages, I aim to enlarge the concept of illocutionary action by elaborating the connection between narratives and images. In doing this, I will consider how other theorists have dealt with the question of who shares similar concerns to mine in relation to how and why a certain narrative in the public sphere can trigger a change in perceptions towards social injustice among other actors. I will argue that in order to bring an end to patriarchal concepts of practices that have occupied the space of the social imaginary for centuries, a radical new feminist social imaginary is necessary. In this essay, I will show that my concept of 'illocutionary action' provides a way to achieve this.

In my most recent book – *Beyond the Public Sphere: Film and the Feminist Imaginary* – I claim that contemporary feminists are already aware of the importance of this imaginary space because it helps them to question why and how oppressive capitalistic structures and institutions are still in place. Indeed, many of them have already developed new agendas seeking racial justice, gender justice and ecological justice. (Their work has not been easy, and not without some negative political reactions and institutional consequences.[6])

One of the most recent examples of illocutionary action with a radical feminist message is the performance of a script entitled 'A Rapist in Your Path'. It was created by a feminist group from Chile called *Colectivo LasTesis*[7] and has been performed in many countries around the world. The first enactment took place on 18 November 2019, on the International Day of Eliminating Violence Against Women. A film of the event went viral on social media. A week later the performance was staged in Santiago de Chile in front of the Palace of Justice on Paseo Ahumada, with some 2000 participants. On 28 November it was performed in front of the Ministry of Women and Gender Equity to demand the resignation of Isabel Plá, the Ministry's Head, because of her failure to respond to violence against demonstrators during previous performances. Another performance was staged in front of the President's official home, the Palacio de la Moneda. Weeks later, students from the University of Chile's Faculty of Medicine gave the performance in honor of Xaviera Rojas, who had been killed days before. On 3 December the play was enacted again, but this time the performers were women over 40, since the idea was to connect with older generations who had endured similar violence decades earlier during the dictatorship of Augusto Pinochet. This time the performance was staged in front of the Estadio Nacional (the sports centre, where many people had been held captive and tortured in the Pinochet era). These massive protests have become emblematic of the traditional patriarchal narrative's 'script of rape',[8] in which women are always the victims and always blamed for inciting the violence that befalls them. One not-so-surprising fact is that in many countries around the world where 'A Rapist in Your Path' has been staged – for

---

[6] In Romania and Hungary, for example, political authorities have banned gender studies in high schools and universities. Moreover, in Poland, abortion is only allowed in cases of incest and rape and in medical situations where the mother's life is in danger. Poland has just banned abortion and its new laws are among the most restrictive in Europe.

[7] The writers – Lea Cáceres, Paula Cometa, Sibila Sotomayor and Daffne Valdés – based their script on work by the Argentinian anthropologist Rita Segato. See: Segato, Rita. *La Guerra contra las mujeres*. Madrid: Mapas, Traficantes de Sueños. 2016. See also: Segato, Rita. *Contra-pedagogías de la crueldad*. Buenos Aires, Argentina: Prometeo Libros. 2018.

[8] See: Lara, María Pía. *Beyond the Public Sphere: Film and the Feminist Imagination*. Evanston, IL: Northwestern University Press. 2020. pp.93–121.

example, Mexico, Perú, Brazil, Turkey, India, Cyprus, England, the United States and even Kyrgystan – the same script is used; the only changes are the names of the specific political situations, as they vary from country to country.

COUNTER-HEGEMONIC NARRATIVES FROM THE FEMINIST SOCIAL MOVEMENTS

Before developing my conception of 'illocutionary actions', let me focus on the script for a performance that I consider a narration. So my first step will be to clarify that I use the term 'narrative' in a wider scope than its traditional meaning, that is, as a dimension of a story that is written and then published. Here, I will cite the historian Hayden White, who transformed our understanding of political and social historical events in the nineteenth century through their poetic constructions and rhetorical devices. He maintained, for example, that great historians are known to have interpreted historical events in different ways, according to the literary genre they chose as a model: Jules Michelet used romance; Leopold von Ranke comedy; Alexis de Tocqueville tragedy; and Jacob Burckhardt satire. White also spoke of how historians and political philosophers used tropes and figures of speech to make their scholarly points perfectly clear. He contended that Marx used metonymy and synecdoche as tools to help organize his theoretical perspective.

White understood well that a structured narrative with a distinct beginning and ending helps us make sense of the past. He was also clear that ideology could not be defined as a simple distortion of reality but rather as a particular way of representing societies. Further, he claimed that, since representations are devices that help us articulate meanings, they are also imaginary and can be changed. In my opinion White is not a relativist, as he wanted to make explicit that history is not neutral and that we can look for the validity of representational texts only on moral or aesthetic grounds. Moreover, he claimed that the knowledge we gain from history is 'human self-knowledge and specifically knowledge of how human beings make themselves through knowing themselves and come to know themselves in the process of making themselves'.[9]

To illustrate his point, let us consider why Habermas was so distressed about the post-war narratives written by some leading German historians that attempted to distort the country's collective moral responsibility for the Jewish genocide. Ernst Nolte, for example, tried 'to make Auschwitz unexceptional by remarking, among other things, that with the sole exception of the technical procedure of gassing, what the Nazis did had already been described in an extensive literature dating from the early 1920s'.[10] Habermas understood how distortions of the moral meaning of actual events could help historians legitimate the past, even if that past was more than a moral catastrophe, but rather an unprecedented destruction of millions of

---

[9] White, Hayden. 'Northrop Frye's Place in Contemporary Cultural Studies' in: *The Fiction of Narrative: Essays on History, Literature and Theory, 1957–2007*. Baltimore, MD: Johns Hopkins University Press. 1994. p.266.

[10] Habermas, Jürgen. 'Remarks from the Römberg Colloquium' in: *The New Conservatism: Cultural Criticism and the Historians' Debate.* Edited and translated by Shierry Weber Nicholsen. Cambridge, MA: The MIT Press. 1989. pp.209–11, p.211.

people carried out with terroristic measures to erase all features of their humanity.[11] Habermas claimed that, by making Hitler and his 'radical race doctrine' the only cause of what happened at the *lagers*[12] (the concentration camps), the historian Andreas Hillgruber 'changed more than the perspective of the presentation'. He left behind 'the frightening fact that the bulk of the population, as Hillgruber certainly assumes, kept quiet while it all went on'.[13]

Habermas was deeply concerned by the way ultra-conservative historians, whose goal was to recast and re-represent the events of the recent past, pretended to insert a new narrative designed to 'normalize' German society's historical and moral consciousness. Indeed, he saw how the strategies of revisionism aimed at protecting post-war Germans from being part of 'the country's complicity' could become dangerous political weapons in a tragedy that still remains difficult to understand.

Second, narratives are parts of institutional practices of all kinds. This is so not only because they help build our collective memory about past events and our hopes for the future, but also because they build our social and political self-conceptions – our sense of ourselves both as individuals in our own right and as social and political actors related to others.

Third, my notion of a narrative includes the plots that can circulate around people and societies in the wider space of the social imaginary. The plots can be about anything that is going on in politics, social life or even personal matters. They are the means by which we organize our lived experiences, and we cannot function without them. Because narratives are so deeply embedded in human experience and cognitive structures, they have many functions: they can calm fears, soothe anxiety and raise our hopes. They can also stir up all kinds of negative emotions, including anger and despair. The social actors and the spectators see themselves reflected in specific representations of the social and political world because they identify themselves through images that can motivate and persuade them of what needs to be transformed for the better. Indeed, most of the plots concerning social movements have normative claims because they want to engage others by articulating ideas about justice and hope-inspiring future actions.

Historical narratives have specific political or moral purposes, and these become evident not only as a result of the actions themselves but the order in which the actions are presented, as this intensifies their dramatic and rhetorical effects and helps us develop ideas about representations of the good society. When we organize actions into a coherent narrative, we want them to reflect the ways that our particular experiences can be captured by those others who are meaningful to us because we live in the same community, and we hope to share values and goals about how and why a society should be changed. As Maeve Cooke argues, 'representations of the good society do not claim *authority* in matters of validity; rather, they claim to disclose the transcendent object more powerfully, and to articulate it in ways that provide better ethical orientation, than other, rival representations'.[14]

Developing representations of certain actions can be expressed through language, which I understand in a broad sense as including communication through political performances by

---

[11] See: Lara, María Pía. *Narrating Evil: A Post-Metaphysical Theory of Reflective Judgment.* New York: Columbia University Press. 2007.
[12] Habermas, Jürgen. 'Apologetic Tendencies' in: *The New Conservatism.* Edited and translated by Shierry Weber Nicholsen. Cambridge, MA: The MIT Press. 1989. pp.212–28, p.219.
[13] Ibid p.220.
[14] Cooke, Maeve. *Re-Presenting the Good Society.* Cambridge, MA: The MIT Press. 2006. p.120.

social movements, through moral perspectives captured by images and other expressive forms, even silence. Language has two dimensions – denotative and expressive – and it is the latter that I am concerned with here. This includes creative activities such as making music, painting, making signals and building symbolic objects.[15] Expressions make something manifest in the tools that we chose for its embodiment. This is the reason I fully endorse Charles Taylor's expressive theory of language, which he describes as presenting us with a very different picture of language from the empiricist one:

> Language is not an assemblage of separable instruments, which lie as it were transparently at hand, and which can be used to marshal ideas, this use being something we can fully control and oversee. Rather it is something in the nature of a web and, to complicate this image, is present as a whole in any of its parts. To speak is to touch a bit of the web, and this is to make the whole resonate. Because the words we use now only have sense through their place in the whole web, we can never in principle have a clear oversight of the implications of what we say at any moment. Our language is always more than we can encompass; it is in a sense inexhaustible. The aspiration to be in no degree at all a prisoner of language, so dear to Hobbes and Locke, is in principle unrealizable.[16]

So, if language encompasses a range of activities that belong to our expressive capacities, its centre lies in their capacities as forms of life.[17] Connected to those forms of life is another dimension that belongs to the way our experiences can – or cannot – be expressed. Again, as Charles Taylor noticed, language becomes an institution of the social and of public life:

> Speech also serves to express/constitute different relations in which we may stand to each other: intimate, formal, official, casual, joking, serious and so on. From this point of view, we can see that it is not just the speech community which shapes us and creates language, but language which constitutes and sustains the speech community.[18]

Going back to the uses of narratives, while someone might say narratives do not cause conflicts, I claim that, because they encapsulate emotion and memory at the service of political causes, they work effectively as a kind of praxis. Here we recall Paul Ricoeur's definition of narrativity:

> The character of mimesis as being an activity which confers *poiesis* on it; and if, moreover, we hold tightly to the guideline of defining mimesis by *muthos* [*emplotment*], then we ought not to hesitate in

---

[15] The major interpreters of the expressive theory of language were Hamman, Humboldt and Herder. They are usually called the theory of the three Hs. See: Taylor, Charles. *Human Agency and Language: Philosophical Papers*. Volume 1. New York, Cambridge, Massachusetts: Cambridge University Press. 1985. See also: Lafont, Cristina. *The Linguistic Turn in Hermeneutic Philosophy*. Translated by José Medina. Cambridge, MA: The MIT Press. 1999.

[16] Taylor, Charles. 'Language and Human Nature' in: *Human Agency and Language*. Volume 1. New York: Cambridge University Press. 1990. pp.215–47, p.231.

[17] The concept of form of life belongs to Ludwig Wittgenstein. See: Wittgenstein, Ludwig. *Philosophical Investigations*. Translated by G.E.M. Anscombe. Oxford: Blackwell. 1953. A very interesting development of the concept of forms of life is given by Rahel Jaeggi. See: Jaeggi, Rahel, *Critique of Forms of Life*. Translated by Ciaran Cronin. Cambridge, Massachusetts and London, England: The Belknap Press of Harvard University Press. 2018.

[18] Taylor n.17, p.234.

understanding action – action as the object in the expression '*mimesis praxeos*' [...] – as the correlate of the mimetic activity governed by the organization of the events (into system).[19]

Fourth, narratives, even historical narratives, are permeated by political goals, and we need to focus on the possibilities of finding cues that grant them moral weight, for this is a necessary condition for those social movements that aspire to transform societies for the better. Narrativity is one of the most powerful tools used by political agents (either for the agents themselves or, as we have seen, for historians), because through our constructions – by giving meaning to our experiences within a particular historical time and by articulating our representations and organizing them as a coherent whole – we not only allow intelligibility, we also endow our actions with ethical meanings and political purposes.

But how are we able to learn to discriminate among the different kinds of narrative claims? This question has great importance for me, as I want to give normative strength to the impact of those narratives and performances that can be considered illocutionary actions. I emphasize this because the aim of these actions is to change people's perceptions of institutions and social and political practices for the better. The process of engaging other actors means that illocutionary actions have a normative claim (the ethical content) and a specific kind of critique (the justification of why certain institutions are harmful or dangerous because they construct social domination from one class to others; political, racial, and gender hierarchies that allow them to treat people unequally). Together they can produce an effect of what is seen as a disclosive device: an image fully coloured by its moral contents. What matters is that the illocutionary effect is the vehicle of the common sense we construct through our being interrelated with one another. An opening of the lightning path or epiphany where people begin to see how powerfully the image opens up possibilities of change through imagination that instantly captures our attention. When a lightning moment occurs, it means that we have shared an ethical orientation with others and resonated with them. It is also a means by which both eyes and minds can be opened by performative actions that affectively resonate with those others. As an example of an 'illocutionary action', consider how, by streaming the video of George Floyd and his iteration of the refrain 'I can't breathe', the Black Lives Matter Movement initiated an unstoppable critique of racism. This is the first moment of a larger process of 'illocutionary force' that consists of a negative moment, the possibility of seeing injustice being done to others, and a second moment, which I will focus on later, which implies the positive articulation of a full pictorial view of something like justice or what Maeve Cooke has called the transcendent object.[20]

The common search for change does not mean finding exactly what we hope for. Rather, it means that we can only achieve success if we accept as valid the kind of interrogations that different forms of expressions (discursive, non-linguistic, and so on) make possible. I absolutely agree with José Medina when he describes these kinds of exercises from counter-publics as *epistemic interactions* because '[o]ur experiences are expanded and critically assessed in

---

[19] Ricoeur, Paul. *Time and Narrative*. Volume 1. Translated by Kathleen McLaughlin and David Pellauer. Chicago and London: Chicago University Press. 1983. p.34.
[20] Cooke, Maeve. *Re-Presenting the Good Society*. Cambridge, MA: The MIT Press. 2006. p.124.

and through the imagination which enables us to connect our actual experiences with possible ones, extending and projecting them into alternative pasts, presents, and futures'.[21]

The expressive and powerful articulation of how an image of justice (or injustice, as in the case of George Floyd) can be structured from a narrative into a performative action that must have consequences for both parties because they learn to see themselves changed after the performance has been successful. This kind of interaction has two dimensions. One relies on the moral validity process – of an illuminating perspective and the interconnection of experience and imagination – and of mutual learning about the feeling of relatedness that comes when we share our critical goals with others. The second dimension is an epistemic and expressive perspective. Each of these two conditions is necessary; one would not suffice without the other. The struggle to articulate our claims need not be restricted to argumentation only. Also required are expressive ways to undertake a radical critical interrogation of particular norms and values and of historical institutions that have been created to dominate or oppress certain groups. The latter process is necessary because it involves ways of challenging our previous understanding about how those norms and rules have been constructed and taken as given into a life form. They are actually particular representations with specific political reasons. The work of critique has a normative context-transcendent validity. Why? Because unless we articulate clearly and expressively the reasons that certain social arrangements are harmful or that social institutions impede transformation for the better, we will not be convincing. Yet, as we have said before, by using Taylor's definition we accept that we are not in full control of what can be expressed, because there is always a space between concept and intuition in what we know and what we feel. This process must lead to a collective effort at envisioning certain positive transformations for the better, but they will have to remain open to future questioning. Indeed, as Medina argues, while creativity and intuition play big roles in expanding our ability to bring about positive transformations, we must also be wary: 'This critical interrogation requires that we examine the easiness with which we imagine certain things and the difficulty we face in imagining others.'[22]

THE TASK OF CRITIQUE AND THE DEFENSE OF ILLOCUTIONARY ACTIONS

Judith Butler's critique of speech-acts, and in particular her definition of 'the illocutionary act [that] itself [is] the deed that it effects',[23] has provided us with a vision of how language is not only an institution, it can also be a potentially lethal weapon:

> Indeed, words exercise a certain power here that is not immediately clear. They act; they *exercise performative force of a certain kind;* sometimes they are clearly violent in their consequences, as words

---

[21] Medina, José. *The Epistemology of Resistance: Gender and Racial Oppression, Epistemic Injustice, and Resistant Imaginations.* Oxford and New York: Oxford University Press. 2013. p.7.
[22] Medina, José. *The Epistemology of Resistance.* p.256.
[23] Butler, Judith. *Excitable Speech: A Politics of the Performative.* New York and London: Routledge. 1997. p.3.

that either constitute or beget violence. Indeed, sometimes it seems that *the words act in illocutionary ways, enacting the very deed that they name in the very moment of the naming.*[24]

For Butler, illocutionary actions are the kind of actions that can be used as weapons of war. Her strategy, however, is to liberate language from any determinism and to conceive of its counter-dimensional, non-authoritative critical status as building up the basis of subversion. She raises the question of our survival and resistance to hate speech, which could be articulated by a new understanding of 'illocutionary actions' if we were to begin by exploring the meaning of insurrectionary counter-speech. Lisa Disch gives an excellent description of this when she claims: 'Politically, insurrectionary speech is the power of calling justice in the very terms in which one has been disenfranchised, thereby "reterritorializing" the term from its operation within dominant discourse precisely in order to counter the effects of [one's] marginalization.'[25] Again, we are reminded of George Floyd's words, 'I can't breathe', which have become not only a denunciation but a symbol of racist institutions and police violence, but also the terrible image of his murdered body lying on the sidewalk. If certain terms became norms through iterations, Butler claims that we can perform them as disruptors. If 'power is also exercised'[26] through language, then there are possibilities of subverting it.

In her critique of Catherine MacKinnon's conception of pornography as a performance of violence, Butler claims that if MacKinnon's arguments moved from 'perlocutionary' utterances to 'illocutionary ones' (which, according to Austin's conception, means acting with words), there should be other ways to find a notion of agency. Butler is against the idea that speech-acts are always the subjects of injury because '[t]he resignification of speech requires opening new contexts, speaking in ways that have never yet been legitimated, and hence producing legitimation in new and future forms'.[27] She highlights what she sees as the problems with MacKinnon's arguments because she is thinking of state forms of resistance. Butler wants to maintain a gap between speech and conduct 'to lend support for the role of nonjuridical forms of opposition, ways of restaging and resignifying speech in contexts that exceed those determined by the courts'.[28] Her 'counter-injurious speech' became the very signification of the concept of 'queer'. Through Butler's illocutionary action, this once derogatory term lost the power to injure. Butler explained that the 'improper use of the performative can succeed in producing the effect of authority where there is no recourse to a prior authorization, whether the misappropriation or expropriation of the performative might not be the very occasion for the exposure of prevailing forms of authority and the exclusions by which they proceed'.[29] Thanks to Butler, Queer Theory was born. She was successful in proving that her idea of agency also applied to her conception of subversion of language as an institution clearly linked to other institutions such as law, the military, education, and so on. Thus, she articulated a new

---

[24] Butler, Judith. *Antigone's Claim: Kinship between Life and Death.* New York: Columbia University Press. 2000. p.63; my italics.
[25] Disch, Lisa. 'Judith Butler and the Politics of the Performative', *Political Theory* Vol. 27, No. 4 (August 1999). pp.545–59, p.554.
[26] Ibid. p.8.
[27] Butler, Judith. *Excitable Speech: A Politics of the Performative.* New York and London: Routledge. 1997. p.41.
[28] Ibid. p.23.
[29] Ibid. p.158.

way to think about language as the 'politics of the performative'.[30] Yet she reversed the classification of 'illocutionary actions' that perform the deed at the very moment of its utterance, and placed the subversive action in the category of 'perlocutionary acts', that is, speech acts where there is a separation between the moment of the utterance and its effect. My contention, however, is that perlocutionary actions are usually commands, orders; therefore, there is already an established hierarchical relation between the one who is uttering the command and the one who is compelled to obey because of her powerless position. This gap should be associated with the hierarchical relations from counter-publics vis-à-vis the state. But it is a quite different situation when we want to explore how to construct a counter-hegemony with a new social movement. We must persuade others to find together new ways to promote social change for the better. Then we need to return to illocutionary actions. Indeed, if there should be a space between the utterance and the action, this should be effected through an understanding of how those others, who identify themselves with their own experiences contribute to iterating their script. Again George Floyd's *cri de coeur* illustrates its immediate impact on other people. Austin's classification of perlocutionary actions is not helpful here, but my conception of illocutionary actions or force is. This gap should be situated in the spaces of our imagination and the feminist anti-racist imaginary that will allow our minds to see the changes in our perceptions after the performance is done. The construction of temporality through citing a term already associated with certain significations, and the way to challenge those relations of power, lies in how the illocutionary actions allow others to see things in a new and imaginative way. So, agency in Butler is developed in tandem with the ways I see performing critique and triggering imagination. They refer to the first stage, the negative one, as I have described it before. This much is clear now.

Second, for Butler, criticism must suspend judgement if it wants to remain in a non-authoritarian position. In her book *Antigone's Claim* she uses Sophocles' Antigone as an example of how anomalous performances can 'provoke innovative ways of articulating and restaging social norms and social relations.'[31] Moreover, when she explains how Hegel and Lacan interpreted this particular story quite differently, she acknowledges that their particular historical moment contributed to their disparate viewpoints. Hers is a renewed effort in which she ends up concluding that Antigone was an outsider, thus connecting her actions with Butler's own exercise of immanent critique, insofar as they demonstrate that by 'acting as the one who has no right to act, she upsets the vocabulary of kinship that is a precondition of the human, implicitly raising the question of what preconditions really must be'.[32]

For Butler all norms are partial, and they always create an 'outsider'. This is why she focuses on questioning how our ideas about 'universality' have their own particular context and place. The kind of universality that Butler wants to bring about seems similar to Walter Benjamin's notion of the 'not yet' – specifically, what remains unrealized is what one can accept as the normative place that can never be filled – since she wants to avoid the 'authoritarian position' of excluding others or being closed to others' future claims. She seeks an open end or the indeterminacy of the ideality of the ideal that helps her normative conception avoid teleology or eschatology. In a recent text, Butler explains: 'If there is a sense of the messianic

---

[30] Disch, Lisa. 'Judith Butler and the Politics of the Performative', *Political Theory* Vol. 27, No. 4 (August 1999). pp.545–59, p.547.
[31] Butler, Judith. Ibid. p.79.
[32] Butler, Judith. Ibid. p.82.

within the performative, it would doubtless be a way of thinking about this anticipatory form of positing that fails to achieve a final realization.'[33]

MAEVE COOKE'S CONCEPTION OF CRITIQUE AND VALIDITY

Maeve Cooke has dealt extensively with how societies' efforts to represent themselves can construct critical devices which can be helpful only if we understand that we need a concept of critique that possesses a 'context transcendent validity'. For Cooke, this is a way of discriminating between different claims as political goals and of showing how some of them can have moral contents in their narratives. In her book *Re-Presenting the Good Society*, Cooke demonstrated how contemporary critical social theory, radical contextualists (such as Richard Rorty) and context-transcending approaches share the anti-authoritarian stance that makes critique possible. Cooke also claims that agency – that is, ethical agency – means that we could be held accountable as responsible agents. This is important for politics, because some post-structuralist accounts have almost erased the concept of individual agency from subjects, as they are considered only as being the effects of power. For this reason, Cooke revises at length the positions of Judith Butler and Ernesto Laclau. While the two share some features, she points out that they also have some differences which are important to her own position. Specifically, she demonstrates that Butler is not denying the existence of universals but sees them as always producing gaps between the ideal and the real. Laclau, on the other hand, acknowledges that the particular ways in which we define a value such as justice or democracy must be compelling enough to want us to be involved with change. Laclau thinks that the normative moment (the ethical) is necessary but is impossible to fulfil. Cooke demonstrates that his notion of the image that inspires change is underdeveloped.

Cooke argues convincingly that Butler does not reject universal concepts such as democracy, freedom or truth, but 'she actually rejects the closure of concepts' because that is exclusionary, judgmental and authoritarian.[34] Instead, Butler seeks to preserve 'the ideality of ideals'[35] by allowing 'the practices of criticism that seek to unsettle and disrupt prevailing norms, exposing the contingency of what is presented as necessary and the incompleteness of what is presented as complete'.[36] Yet, as Cooke demonstrates, 'this gap in principle between the ideality of the ideal and its historical actualization' is what 'provides *a space for the critical transcendence of the given*'.[37] Butler's position is open-ended and non-authoritarian, and she carefully creates the space of incompleteness as her principle of non-exclusion. But Cooke questions why Butler never focuses on the kinds of cognitive and social transformation that could be involved in different claims. She argues that the principle of context transcendence is needed because, unless we are limited by a purely contextualist position, Butler's concept of critique is not helpful because we need to learn to discriminate among many different positions. Without the dimension of context-transcendence, Butler cannot explain why certain changes are better

---

[33] Butler, Judith and Athanasiou, Athena. *Dispossession: The Performative in the Political.* Cambridge: Polity Press. 2013. p.129.
[34] Cooke, Maeve. *Re-Presenting the Good Society.* Cambridge, MA: The MIT Press. 2006. p.78.
[35] Ibid.
[36] Ibid. p.78.
[37] Ibid. p.79.

than others because of their moral goals or their ethical content. Otherwise, she would have to regard as acceptable that changes in societies are either normatively arbitrary or are purely decisionistic. At this point, Cooke maintains that Rorty's radical contextualism faces the same problem by not accepting any kind of context-transcending critique. As Cooke argues, Rorty's 'radically contextualist position rules out the possibility of a critical interrogation of ethical and intellectual vocabularies, foundational rules, frames of intelligibility, and so on, *whether or not* this criticism is argumentatively—or even verbally—articulated'.[38] However, we can detect that when Butler gives the examples of slavery or kinship, she uses an evaluative language as reflecting the positions of outsiders who can raise their claims and have a normative stand precisely because they are vulnerable or oppressed. This is the reason why Cooke thinks Butler's position needs the contextual-transcendent validity of ethical questioning. The context-transcendence critique is linked to an ethical content that helps to open the questioning of participants about why the points of view of those who are seen as outsiders or those who challenge social norms and institutions have justifications that need to be considered. But if 'epistemic authoritarianism' is to be avoided, we must accept that there are some contexts in which the social arrangements are harmful, as they are also historically constructed. Yet they are not simply contingent; they were created to perpetuate the asymmetrical relations of power or domination of some social and political groups over others. Critique enables us to compare whether some versions and claims from particular social movements are better than others and, if so, to justify why this is true.

CONCLUSION: THE DISCLOSIVE EFFECT IN THE SCRIPT OF 'UN VIOLADOR EN TU CAMINO'

The workings of the imagination in the political realm as well as in the moral sphere can be understood best if we consider the connection between the social imaginary and our ethical hopes. Social imaginaries are representations of ourselves to us and to others; of our relations, internal and external; of nature and of the ways we internalize social and political institutions and practices. In *Beyond the Public Sphere: Film and the Feminist Imaginary* I show how, throughout history, physical violence against women, specifically rape, was never regarded as an act of physical and moral harm done specifically to women. Rather, it was seen as the enactment of an endlessly repeated scene from the script of male sovereignty. In most societies, even the most democratic ones, the remnants of patriarchal structures are so powerful that women are always the one who have to answer the questions, prove they are telling the truth, provide witnesses or be considered liars. This is the way women are dealt with throughout their lives – and not just after that single experience where they claim they have been violated.

The understanding of 'rape' as a historical phenomenon framed under patriarchal and then capitalist institutions needs to be thematized now as what it is – an act of violence perpetrated on women's bodies taken from the political script of male sovereignty and constructed over centuries. Rejecting the script of rape and reconceptualizing it as an illocutionary performative action – as I have described in my own work and as reflected in Butler's notion of subversive agency in her speech-act theory – is well illustrated in the performances by *Colectivo LasTesis*.

---

[38] Ibid. p.80.

The liberatory spectacle enrolls as the women organize themselves in lines and dance to their choreography as they chant the new feminist hymn:

> El violador eres tú. (You are the rapist.)
> Son los pacos, (The police,)
> Los jueces, (The judges,)
> El Estado, (The State,)
> El president. (The President.)
> El Estado es un macho violador. (The state is a macho rapist.)
> Es feminicidio. (The femicide.)
> Impunidad para un asesino. (No punishment for the criminal.)
> Es la desaparición. (The vanishing.)
> Es la violación. (The sexual violation.)
> Y la culpa no era mía, ni. (And I was not the guilty one.)
> Dónde estaba ni como vestía (And it was not because of how I was dressed or where I was.)
> El violador eres tú. (You are the rapist.)

The script is a powerful and subversive expression of the patriarchal trope that women are always the guilty ones, that singing and performing their script builds the *image* of how institutions have worked to perpetuate violence against women. Those who committed rapes and murders, who carried out abductions, are complicit with patriarchal institutions and their long history of justifying violence against women. Yes, the dramatic enactment carries the moral content that helps the performers share their collective experiences from the past and present and seek to develop a different conception of freedom, to imagine a different future. And only by making radical changes in our social and political institutions and building up a global movement will women be ready to put in place this new feminist imaginary. We can actually hope to bring about a change for the better as we express our anger, our pain, our solidarity now reimagined as a speech-act, which holds us together through the spaces between the past and the future to come. This image is still underdeveloped, but it will come as women activists gather our hopes for a better society.

35. Poetics

Alejandro Awad

In the 2010 Korean movie *Poetry* the leading character, Yang Mi-ja, discovers with horror that her grandson, together with five other boys, raped a female schoolmate who later killed herself by drowning. She struggles to react to the offense. At her mature age, she is taking poetry lessons in order to compose a single poem that would justify her life. The film can be thought of as a reflection on the justification of punishment, and Yang Mi-ja's story as the struggle to solve a persistent dilemma: whether justice should be imparted through language or physical pain administered by the state bureaucracy. As contemporary expressive theories of punishment, she chooses both.

At the same time, the movie offers a theory of poetry and, more generally, of art. For most of the film, Yang Mi-ja is unable to produce a single verse. It is only when she resolves to address the one question that keeps her awake at night, the inevitability and the elusive meaning of punishment, that she can write. It is as if without an inner, self-destructive and atoning purpose, art could just not be. In the movie, poetry justifies itself as a compensation for the lack of meaning of the—*real* and morally silent—world, and, to this extent, as a justice-maker.

Crime was defined by a German criminal law author as the erosion of the "reality of the norm,"[1] and punishment thus conceived as a confirmation of that eroded reality. By deviating from the norms of language,[2] poetry has been called to explain punishment's elusive mission.

Punishment remains a mysterious institution. It is anything but obvious how the infliction of harm on the offender can remediate the harm already inflicted by the offender on the victim. It is equally doubtful that punishment aims to remediate anything. As Hegel acknowledged early on, "it must, of course, seem quite unreasonable to will an evil merely because another evil is there already."[3] Or as John Hollander puts it in the poem "Tailor-Made": "How can a punishment fit a crime?/What's not ill-suited for a wrong?/The pants will always be too long/…"[4] Violent reactions to violence, however, have been present, in their various forms, for as long as we can remember.

In her *Eichmann in Jerusalem*, Hannah Arendt posits that any "[criminal] trial resembles a play in that both begin and end with the doer, not with the victim."[5] A play with bloody repercussions—"(l)aw is language with violent consequences."[6] When criminal justice is understood as literature, the debate among the theories of punishment translates into the question of what we are writing for: to turn the page, as in early retribution; to deliver the

---

[1] Jakobs, G. (1998). *Sobre la Teoría de la Pena*. Universidad Externado de Colombia, 15.
[2] Eagleton, T. (2003). *Literary Theory: An Introduction*. John Wiley & Sons, 5.
[3] Hegel, G. W. F. (2015). *The Philosophy of Right*. Hackett Publishing, § 99
[4] Kader, D., Stanford, M., & Stanford, M. K. (Eds.). (2010). *Poetry of the Law: From Chaucer to the Present*. University of Iowa Press, 134.
[5] Arendt, H. (2006). *Eichmann in Jerusalem*. Penguin, 9
[6] Yoshino, K. (2011). *A Thousand Times More Fair: What Shakespeare's Plays Teach Us about Justice*. Harper Collins, 67.

fable's moral and neutralize its characters, as in the crime prevention paradigm; or to describe ourselves, as in contemporary retribution?

Poetry has always found its habitat in these existential conundrums, and thus it should be unsurprising that one may read the history of attempts to justify punishment in poetic code. The first theoretical construct, however, that consciously reconciles the linguistic dimension of prison, courthouses, spilled blood, and broken lives is relatively recent. It is upon this attempt, described here as the linguistic turn in the legitimization of punishment, that I *justify* ending this chapter with a poetic account of our everlasting struggle to make peace with punishment.

Poetry, like jokes, is not to be explained, but can be introduced. This piece should thus be read as the long introduction to a short poem that, inspired by the latest developments in the theory of punishment, offers a free-verse reconstruction of the reasons we have invoked to inflict pain. Our expert tour guide into the inextricable crawlways of cryptic dogmas and ethical mazes is the Argentinian writer Jorge Luis Borges, whose lifework could be described as a brilliant effort to provide literary answers to impossible questions.

THE BIRTH OF PUNISHMENT: EARLY RETRIBUTION

In the beginning was vengeance. One of the few agreements of the centuries-long debate about punishment's justification is that the very concept of punishment had originally a fundamentally negative function, to bring an end to vengeance, understood as the noninstitutional private set of reactions to crimes and harms. The effect of this first theory was to expropriate from individuals their power to react to violence. Under the early retribution model, crime was no longer a disruption in the private sphere of the victim but a crack in the structure of the world, and should be dealt with as such. The retributionist approach operated a shift in the scale of crimes: from specific instances of violence, to cosmic violations. Correspondingly, punishment originally had a metaphysical and backward-looking nature: Justice *requires* the offender to suffer *in return* for their deeds.

Practical considerations were crucial. Civilization required order, and the underlying assumption was that retaliation, or, in Bacon's words, "wild justice,"[7] would only lead to further violence; that vengeance "never just evens the odds, but leads to retaliation"[8] and chaos. In this precise sense, even retribution had a consequentialist, or forward-looking, aim, to put a limit to the spread of blood and stop violence proliferation. It is under this light that we may read the Talion law of the Old Testament, precisely as a restraint on the victim's discretion in retaliation, as an objective limit designed to stop the spiral of violence, and thus install *tamed* justice: "Life for life, eye for eye, tooth for tooth," no more … This was thought to be the only way to make things even, to flatten the ground so that the ball of vengeance would stop turning.[9]

---

[7] Yoshino, K. (2011). *A Thousand Times More Fair: What Shakespeare's Plays Teach Us about Justice*. Harper Collins, 4.
[8] Yoshino, K. (2011). *A Thousand Times More Fair*, 4.
[9] Hannah Arendt had this primary function of punishment in mind when she brilliantly contended that "both [forgiveness and punishment] have in common that they attempt to put an end to something that without interference could go on endlessly". Arendt, H. (2019). *The Human Condition*. University of Chicago Press, 241.

This may be conceived as not only punishment's first justification but also the birth of the very concept. As every birth, however, it is the beginning of something new but also the continuation of its predecessors: the chaotic currents of vengeance were *merely* canalized into the orderly flows of punishment, but still nobody had called into question the very existence of the improved descendant: why *on earth* should the sound of violence echo?

CRIME PREVENTION PARADIGM: A SECULARIZATION

God had died some centuries before Nietzsche's issuance of their death certificate. Man himself became divine and the measure of all things, and punishment needed to confront this new scale. The first serious attempt to justify in secular form the *existence* of punishment came with the Enlightenment, inspired by a utilitarian philosophy, under which "the degree of utility or non-utility was the yardstick for all human actions."[10] Under such a paradigm, human pain should be reduced to its minimum and pain was what punishment was all about. Civilized societies were to impose it only insofar as its aggregated effect was an increase in happiness. Punishment could only be justified if it brought safety, if it helped to prevent the commission of new crimes, either to be committed by the punished offender—by taking him out of circulation—or by others—who would be dissuaded by the pain inflicted on the criminal. In this utopian era, punishment had no intrinsic worth, but only an instrumental one directed toward the eradication of crime. But Utopia means the place that cannot be.

CONTEMPORARY RETRIBUTION: THE LINGUISTIC TURN

It was soon realized, however, that an instrumental conception of punishment was based on an instrumental conception of humankind. In Kant's words: "For a human being can never be treated merely as a means to the purposes of another or be put among the objects of rights to things: his innate personality protects him from this."[11] Hegel could not but agree: to threaten an individual with the fear of punishment was comparable "to the act of a man who lifts his stick to a dog. It is to treat a man like a dog instead of with the freedom and respect due to him as a man."[12] To justify punishment, humanism had gone way too far, negating humankind.

---

[10] Venturi, F. (1970). *Utopia and Reform in the Enlightenment*, Cambridge University Press, 100.
[11] Kant, I. (2017). *Kant: The Metaphysics of Morals*. Cambridge University Press, § 331.
[12] Hegel, G. W. F. (2015). *The Philosophy of Right*. Hackett Publishing, § 99. This reference should not be confused with Bentham's (actually, one of the most emblematic exponents, together with Beccaria, of the utilitarian justification of punishment) famous criticism, usually abbreviated as *dog law*, directed against the retrospective nature of Common Law. In Bentham's view, a system based on judge-made law, despite judges' attempt to appear as applying preexisting rules, always imposes on the parties rules that could not have been known by them before the ruling—and certainly, not before the judicially evaluated behavior. Thus, when it comes to criminal law, according to Bentham, Common Law treats the convicted as dogs, denying them the chance to rationally adapt their conduct to a—written—rule before their punished conduct. Ultimately, Bentham's point is, *merely*, an argument in Statute Law's favor. See Postema, G. J. (2019). *Bentham and the Common Law Tradition*. Oxford University Press, 269–273. Hegel's argument runs deeper, and it has been unanimously read as an attack against criminal utilitarianism: humans should not be punished to achieve any social good, regardless of whether the infringed rule was established by Statutory or Common Law, but only for—retrospective—desert considerations.

For these authors, the legitimacy of punishment is only warranted insofar as it is understood as an end in itself. Its value must be intrinsic and not derive from any goal beyond its imposition. Respect and desert become the keys to entering the reign of punishment and thus the concept of punishment is reconstructed as a sign of recognition for, and only for, criminal deeds. As with any reputable award, punishment must be based on pure desert: "The law of punishment is a categorical imperative. It must always be inflicted upon him only *because* he has committed a crime."[13] It is the right of the criminal,[14] who, "when the concept and measure of his own punishment are derived from his own act" and not with the aim to deter or reform him, "by being punished [...] is honored as a rational being."[15]

The Hegelian idea that a desert-based punishment honors the convicted resembles the last of the arguments reviewed by Borges to explain hell's eternity, an argument whose merit, according to Borges, is not logical, but "entirely dramatic."[16] Hell and heaven need to be eternal in order to dignify human free will and for human actions, merits and demerits, to have real meaning. In Borges's words: "Your destiny is a real thing [...] eternal condemnation, eternal salvation are in your reach; that responsibility is your honor."[17]

It is easy to see how this notion of punishment as an honor and as an act of recognition of the criminal is hard to reconcile with its comprehension as a harm imposed on the harm-doer, or as a second evil, following the offender's crime. Under the Hegelian model, the material dimension of the punishment, the criminal's reddened body, the heavy chains attached, the metal bars, become just an epiphenomenon of something else. Famously, retributive punishment was categorized by Hegel as the "annulment of crime"[18] or even as "the negation of the negation,"[19] and thus ultimately as a communicative institution for the achievement of justice. Only through the communicative meaning of punishment can "the genuine reconciliation of right with itself take place."[20]

More recently, punishment has become a deliberately linguistic artifact,[21] "a conventional device for the expression of attitudes of resentment and indignation, and of judgments of

---

It is actually to rebut a German utilitarian author with similar views to Bentham's, that Hegel attacks the comprehension of criminal rules as threats and compares its underlying conception of humans to dogs:
> "Feuerbach bases his theory of punishment on threat and thinks that if anyone commits a crime despite the threat, punishment must follow because the criminal was aware of it beforehand. But what about the justification of the threat? A threat presupposes that a man is not free, and its aim is to coerce him by the idea of an evil. But right and justice must have their seat in freedom and the will, not in the lack of freedom on which a threat turns. To base a justification of punishment on threat is to liken it to the act of a man who lifts his stick to a dog. It is to treat a man like a dog instead of with the freedom and respect due to him as a man.(...)" Hegel, G. W. F. (2015). *The Philosophy of Right*. Hackett Publishing, § 99.

[13] Kant, I. (2017). *Kant: The Metaphysics of Morals*. Cambridge University Press, § 331.
[14] Hegel, G. W. F. (2015). *The Philosophy of Right*. Hackett Publishing, § 100.
[15] Hegel, G. W. F. (2015). *The Philosophy of Right*. Hackett Publishing, § 100.
[16] Borges, J. L. (1996). *Discusión. Obras Completas*. Vol. I. Emecé, 238.
[17] "Tu destino es cosa de veras (...), condenación eterna y salvación eterna están en tu minuto; esa responsabilidad es tu honor". Borges, J. L. (1996). *Discusión. Obras Completas*. Vol. I. Emecé; (2005). *Historia de la Eternidad. Obras Completas*, Vol. I., 238.
[18] Hegel, G. W. F. (2015). *The Philosophy of Right*. Hackett Publishing, § 101.
[19] Hegel, G. W. F. (2015). *The Philosophy of Right*. Hackett Publishing, § 97.
[20] Hegel, G. W. F. (2015). *The Philosophy of Right*. Hackett Publishing, § 220.
[21] It is important to clarify, however, that the comprehension of crime and punishment as communicative phenomena is not privative of retributionists theories. Some of the criminal law theorists

disapproval and reprobation,"[22] a means of communicating "the condemnation or censure that offenders deserve,"[23] or a "declaration that the violated law remains valid despite its breach."[24] Communicative retributivist theories have built upon Austin's speech act theory to specify punishment's function.[25] This branch of retributivism claims that punishment belongs to the class of illocutionary acts, namely acts that are performed "*in* saying something as opposed to performance of an act *of* saying something."[26] The specific illocutionary speech act performed through the imposition of punishment is blaming the criminal, and, according to Habermas's taxonomy between forms of communicative actions aimed at mutual understanding, it corresponds to an expressive act; a communicative act underpinned by a sincerity claim,[27] lest the linguistic act of punishment be understood as an instrumentalization of the communication, and thus of the criminal.

This linguistic turn has been so radical that the physical—and basic—dimension of punishment has become suspicious. The discussion has evolved from the question of why add an evil to an evil, to that of why aggregate physical consequences to punitive language. Once the *hard treatment* was analytically separated from the expression of moral indignation it conveyed,[28] it was only natural to wonder: why not *express* punishment with *kinder words*. In Duff's terms: "censure can be expressed by a formal conviction, or by a purely symbolic punishment […] Why then should we express it through the kinds of hard treatment punishment that our existing penal systems impose—punishments that are burdensome or painful independently of their communicative content?"[29] Jakobs, among others, offered an explanation: because the offense has not only meant that human life is worthless, but also has effectively destroyed it, the state reaction must not only be carried out in symbolic terms, but also exert violence on the individual.[30] If punishment only operated at the symbolic level, it would suffer from an "objectivation deficit."[31]

The fundamentally symbolic meaning of punishment and the difference between physical pain and censure and the fundamentally symbolic meaning of punishment had already been masterfully articulated by Borges. One of the author's most prominent heroines, Emma Zunz, seeks justice for a crime falsely attributed to her father, which cost him his life. As part of the plan that she devises against Loewenthal, her boss and the real party responsible for the crime, she accepts the cruelest harm she could think of ("In April she would be nineteen, but men still

---

mentioned hereafter should not be labelled as retributivists. Notably, this is the case of Feinberg. See Mañalich, J. P. (2007). 'La pena como retribución'. *Estudios Públicos*, *108*, 137.

[22] Feinberg, J. (1965). 'The expressive function of punishment'. *The Monist*, *49*(3), 397–423, 400.

[23] Duff, R. A. (2001). *Punishment, Communication, and Community*. Oxford University Press, USA, 27.

[24] Mañalich, J. P. (2013). 'Justicia, propiedad y prevención'. *La ciencia penal en la Universidad de Chile*, 167–187, 171.

[25] Mañalich, J. P. (2007). 'La pena como retribución'. *Estudios Públicos*, (108), 157.

[26] Austin, J. L. (1965). *How to do Things with Words*. Oxford University Press, 99.

[27] Habermas, J. (2002). 'On the pragmatics of social interaction: Preliminary studies in the theory of communicative action'. MIT Press, 149.

[28] Feinberg, J. (1965). 'The expressive function of punishment'. *The Monist*, *49*(3), 397–423, 400.

[29] Duff, R. A. (2001). *Punishment, Communication, and Community*. Oxford University Press, USA, 82.

[30] Jakobs, G. (1998). *Sobre la Teoría de la Pena*. Universidad Externado de Colombia, 24–25.

[31] Mañalich Raffo, J. (2010). *Terror, Pena y Amnistía. El Derecho Penal ante el Terrorismo de Estado*. Flandes Indiano, 72.

inspired in her an almost pathological fear"): to endure sex with an anonymous, unattractive sailor. She will then attribute the false rape to Loewenthal, and thus, after killing him, excuse her conduct through self-defense. Even after voluntarily subjecting herself to her darkest nightmare, being sexually injured by a disgusting stranger, she needs to avoid punishment for the homicide at all costs: "It was not out of fear, but because she was an instrument of that justice, that she herself intended not to be punished."[32]

The same idea underlies one of the most outrageous passages of Borges's short tale "The Lottery in Babylon." The narrator explains that after a time, the Lottery had evolved to become not only the main distributor of goods in Babylon but also that of evils. Any given draw would mean the award of a large sum of money, the issuance of a money fine, the imposition of a prison term, or even the infliction of physical harm upon the ticket holder. At a certain point in time, a slave, excluded from the *game*, stole a ticket which, according to the corresponding drawing, "*entitled* the bearer to have his tongue burned out." The same consequence attached as the punishment for stealing a lottery ticket, so a heated debate arose: "Some Babylonians argued that the slave deserved the burning iron for being a thief; others, more magnanimous, that the executioner should employ the iron because thus fate had decreed."[33] There was no doubt about the torture the slave should experience; the question was strictly constrained to whether the torment should be his punishment for stealing the ticket, or his *reward* as the ticketholder.

When punishment ceases to be—fundamentally—an evil imposed in reaction to another evil, crime is also transformed. For Hegel, crime should be fundamentally viewed as a nullity, as a negation of the law. Hegel's contention here is that, although crimes are particular events in the world connected with pain and sorrow, a proper understanding of crime should focus on its objective will, and not on the spilled blood or the perpetrator's intentions. From an abstract perspective—and regardless of whether it adopts the form of rape, a murder, or an embezzlement—a crime would always express a person's self-contradictory will, which, insofar it attacks the free will and the rights of an equal, ends up denying "that all persons (including the criminal, who is a person) have free will and rights."[34]

This theoretical contention has been the background for further reconstructions of crimes as implied claims raised by the wrongdoer—whose content is the negation of the law—to which the law *needs* to react through the imposition of punishment *qua* the confirmation of the validity of the law. "A crime is an act through which something is declared. The content of the declaration is the proposition that a certain norm is not recognized as an effective reason for action."[35]

Sometimes precise words are put in the wrongdoer's mouth. Gunther Jakobs, for example, contended that the meaning of a crime—despite the actual intentions of the criminal—should

---

[32] Borges, J. L., & Hurley, A. (1999). *Collected Fictions*. Penguin Books, 218.

[33] Borges, J. L., & Hurley, A. (1999). *Collected Fictions*. Penguin Books, 103.

[34] Stillman, P. G. (1976). 'Hegel's idea of punishment'. *Journal of the History of Philosophy, 14*(2), 169–182, 171.

[35] Mañalich, J. P. (2013). 'Justicia, propiedad y prevención'. *La Ciencia Penal en la Universidad de Chile*, 167–187, 170. The recent and much debated trend of *cancelling* legally (or just socially *cancelling*) convicted artists can be understood as an exasperation of this very idea: the offender's voice should only declare the implicit claim raised by their evil deed. Everything else should be muted; their books not read, their films not watched, their music not heard. Notably, in these cases, the punishment of cancelling operates not only as a speech act but also a speech suppressor.

be understood as a declaration stating "this society is not".[36] And so, punishment, whose function is the prevention of "the erosion of society's real normative configuration,"[37] would be a response exclaiming *yes, it is*! Klaus Gunther understands the meaning of any crime to be "an expression of dissent against the valid norm," but an invalid expression insofar as the criminal did not articulate her dissent "through the public deliberative procedures of the public sphere of civil society" but through violent means that denied the victim "as an equal participant in the public discourse"; punishment must therefore make sure the offender is not "regarded as a co-legislator."[38]

Whatever the meaning of the offender's act, retribution requires that the crime can be viewed as stemming from their free will. Because the retributivist theory of punishment is ultimately a theory of justice, and because it is entirely dependent on the notion of desert, the deterministic objection has been raised against it. The argument goes like this: if free will and desert are scientifically non-demonstrable, how can a theory rely so heavily on them to justify punishment?[39] In a world without demonstrable freedom to decide, no one should be rewarded nor punished for their *decisions*.

Free will and predestination were, to be sure, two of Borges's most acute concerns. In one single beautiful poem, "Chess," he not only deprived life of any real meaning, but also portrayed God as a marionette. In the poem, the chess pieces are unaware of being controlled by the hands of the players. But not only them: "The player is also a prisoner/(the words are Omar's) of another board/of black nights and white days/God moves the player, and the player, the piece/What god behind God the plot begins/of dust and time and sleep and agonies?"[40] To Borges, punishing humans for their crimes would be as pointless as punishing the white horse for a merciless attack on the black rook. This same concern reappeared more than 20 years later as Borges witnessed part of a session of the trial held against Argentina's former top authorities for atrocities committed during the country's military dictatorship. As he admitted in a column published in a Spanish newspaper: "What to think about all this? I personally disbelieve in free will. I disbelieve in punishments and awards. I disbelieve in hell and heaven." He went on to quote the Argentinean poet Almafuerte: "we are the announced, the foreseen,/if there is a God, if there is an omniscient point;/and before they are, they are already, in that mind,/the Judas, the Pilates and the Christs."[41]

This has also been the core of the Marxist criticism of criminal law's justification, in particular to Hegel's retributivism: "Is it not a delusion to substitute for the individual with his real

---

[36] Jakobs, G. (1998). *Sobre la Teoría de la Pena*. Universidad Externado de Colombia, 21.
[37] Jakobs, G. (1998). *Sobre la Teoría de la Pena*. Universidad Externado de Colombia, 16.
[38] Günther, K. (2016). *Criminal Law, Crime and Punishment as Communication*. Liberal Criminal Theory. Essays for Andreas von Hirsch. Oxford: Hart Publishing, 139.
[39] Roxin, C. (1981). *Culpabilidad y Prevención en Derecho Penal*. Instituto Editorial Reus, S. A., 54.
[40] "También el jugador es prisionero/ (la sentencia es de Omar) de otro tablero/ de negras noches y blancos días./Dios mueve al jugador, y éste, la pieza/¿Qué dios detrás de Dios la trama empieza?/ de polvo y tiempo y sueño y agonías". Borges, J. L. (1996). El Hacedor. *Obras Completas*. Vol. II. Emecé, 191.
[41] "Somos los anunciados, los previstos,/si hay un Dios, si hay un punto omnisapiente;/y antes de ser, ya son, en esa mente,/los Judas, los Pilatos y los Cristos". Borges J.L., "Lunes, 22 de julio de 1985" *El País* (Madrid, 9 August 1985). https://elpais.com/diario/1985/08/10/opinion/492472809_850215.html accessed 7 March 2020.

motives, with multifarious social circumstances pressing upon him, the abstraction of 'free will'—one among the many qualities of man for man himself!"[42]

Retribution must deal with determinism, but also with chaos, in order to adjudicate punishment fairly. For retributive punishment to give order to the world, must assume a prior order in it. The poet William Matthews expresses skepticism in this regard: "Ladies and gentlemen of the jury, I ask/you to vote against random pain, to vote/that suffering has cause and thus has blame,/to vote that our lives can be explained."[43]

To be sure, contemporary retributivism has an answer to Borges, Marx, and Matthews, which assumes both the truth of determinism and free will (or sometimes just responsibility); an answer with a straightforward name, compatibilism, according to which there is still free will behind determined behavior.[44]

But this sort of free will, dependent on the use of a concept of personal autonomy "sufficiently robust to bear the burden of the notion of a personal culpability reproval,"[45] is not the last attribution that sophisticated retributivism places upon the criminal. Punishment should only fall upon the *authors* of the infringed norm, as it is understood to be the case in democratic communities in which every citizen is understood to be a legislator and, hence, responsible for every criminal norm.[46] Under this assumption, every crime is self-betrayal.

This idea of punishment being justified only insofar as the convicted is a member of the community that punishes them has also been subjected to a linguistic turn. Building upon Wittgenstein's notion of form of life, Duff argues that, as a precondition for legal liability, the language of the law must be the language of the defendants. They must be part not merely of a "linguistic community whose members agree about the definitions of their concepts. They must agree, to some significant extent, in their use of those concepts."[47] The infringed law that warrants punishment must be expressed in a language that criminals can speak "in an authentic first-person voice."[48]

Collecting the scattered features of contemporary retributivism's portrayal of the criminal's face, we are now able to describe the wrongdoer as deserving state violence: An end in themself and not a dog threatened with a stick; a person holding the right to be punished, gifted with a sufficiently free will, who is honored when the deserved pain is inflicted upon them; someone to punish sincerely and not for apocryphal reasons; a citizen, at once the author and a dissenter of the law—who, however, should not be regarded as co-legislator—and a member

---

[42] Marx, K. (2008) *Dispatches for the New York Tribune. Selected Journalism of Karl Marx*. Penguin Classics, 121.

[43] Kader, D., Stanford, M., & Stanford, M. K. (Eds.). (2010). *Poetry of the Law: From Chaucer to the Present*. University of Iowa Press, 152.

[44] For an exhaustive description of different kinds of compatibilism, see Moore M. S. (2020). *Mechanical Choices: The Responsibility of the Human Machine*. Oxford University Press, 282–310.

[45] Mañalich, J. P. (2013). "Justicia, propiedad y prevención". *La ciencia penal en la Universidad de Chile*, 167–187, 175.

[46] Strictly speaking, this would only be the case when the wrongdoer is a national of the country reproving their conduct. The status of a French citizen punished for the infringement of an English law, M. J. Demold argued, would be that "of an (English) dog". Detmold, M. J. (1989). 'Law as practical reason'. *Cambridge LJ*, 48, 462.

[47] Duff, R. A. (1998). 'Law, language and community: Some preconditions of criminal liability'. *Oxford Journal of Legal Studies*, 18(2), 201.

[48] Duff, R. A. (1998). 'Law, language and community: Some preconditions of criminal liability'. *Oxford Journal of Legal Studies*, 18(2), 198.

of a linguistic community who speaks about the law in a first-person voice, so that they may understand the full extent of our reproval, typically expressed through material deprivation and physical violence.

The evolution of the theory of punishment has transmuted the criminal from an alien, an excluded *homo sacer* whom we may treat as an object or instrument, to an equal who should be taken seriously and addressed honestly. The nineteenth-century poet Walt Whitman would have probably applauded this empathetic move. In "You Felons in Trial Courts" his vindication of criminals dissolves into self-vindication: "I feel I am of them—I belong to those convicts and prostitutes myself,/And henceforth I will not deny them—for how can I deny myself."[49]

It is remarkable how this shift in the conception of the criminal runs parallel to the transformation of the figure of the enemy in Carl Schmitt's theory of politics. As Eva Horn explains, "(w)hereas in his *Concept of the Political* he designs the enemy as the epitome of 'the stranger', in later remarks [...] Schmitt fashions a concept of the enemy as 'he who calls me into question'."[50] Suggestively enough, the latter version of the enemy was sketched by Schmidt while serving time in prison. Posed with the question of whom may one recognize as his enemy, Schmidt wrote: "Manifestly, he alone who can put me in question. Insofar as I recognize him as my enemy, I recognize that he can put me in question. And who can effectively put me in question? Only myself. Or my brother."[51]

This mirrored view of enmity, the idea that the enemy is so closely related to oneself, that both my enemy and I can end up being the same person, was one of Borges's most recurring themes. The last hypothesis of his "Three versions of Judas" speculates on the possibility that God's sacrifice could have been greater than inhabiting Jesus's human body and experiencing his human life and painful death:

> God was made totally man, but man to the point of iniquity, man to the point of reprobation and the Abyss. In order to save us, He could have chosen any of the lives that weave the confused web of history: He could have been Alexander or Pythagoras or Rurik or Jesus; he chose an abject existence: He was Judas.[52]

In "The Theologians," Borges revisits this very idea. The short piece tells the story of a fierce and incessant intellectual enmity between Aurelian and John of Pononia, which leads to the execution of the former and the ruin and solitary death of the latter. As Aurelian dies, he finds out that God had taken him for John of Pononia all the way, and that this was of course no mistake: "Aurelian discovered that in the eyes of the unfathomable deity, he and John of Pannonia (the orthodox and the heretic, the abominator and the abominated, the accuser and the victim) were a single person."[53]

"Fear," a poem in Pablo Neruda's "Extravagaria," also delves into the identification between the aggressor and the aggressed. Again the solitary prison, again shared only with

---

[49] Kader, D., Stanford, M., & Stanford, M. K. (Eds.). (2010). *Poetry of the Law: From Chaucer to the Present*. University of Iowa Press, 66.
[50] Horn, E. (2009). 'Borges's Duels: Friends, Enemies, and the Fictions of History'. *Thinking with Borges*. Auroa, The Davis Group Publishers, 166.
[51] Quoted in Derrida, J. (2006). *The Politics of Friendship*. Verso, 162.
[52] Borges, J. L., & Hurley, A. (1999). *Collected Fictions*. Penguin Books, 166.
[53] Borges, J. L., & Hurley, A. (1999). *Collected Fictions*. Penguin Books, 207.

one's most sinister adversary. "And so, in these brief, passing days,/I shall not take them into account./I shall open up and imprison myself/with my most treacherous enemy,/Pablo Neruda."[54]

And so, to justify punishment, it has seemed nobler in our minds to create a tailor-made version of the subject of the infliction of pain. We have filled our character with attributes, in order for them to deserve the slings and arrows of their own guilt. But by sketching the criminal, we have built for ourselves a new identity. And that is—also—why we punish: to define ourselves. It has often become explicit: After expressing his disbelief in desert as a solid ground for punishment, Borges admitted, "However, not to judge and not to condemn the crime would mean […] becoming, in a way, an accomplice to it."[55] He seemed to be paraphrasing Kant, who in one of the most dramatic passages of his "Metaphysics of Morals" wrote:

> Even if a civil society were to be dissolved by the consent of all its members (e.g., if a people inhabiting an island decided to separate and disperse throughout the world), the last murderer remaining in prison would first have to be executed, so that each has done to him what his deeds deserve and blood guilt does not cling to the people for not having insisted upon this punishment; for otherwise the people can be regarded as collaborators in this public violation of justice.[56]

Conviction as the definition of the jurors' identity has become common sense. The image was recently deployed by the US House member Jamie Raskin in his closing argument to convince the Senate to impeach Trump: "Senators, this trial, in the final analysis, is not about Donald Trump […] this trial is about who *we* are."

POETRY'S ROLE IN THEORY OF PUNISHMENT: A JUSTIFICATION

After all these comings and goings in the theory of punishment, however, it could well be argued that little has changed since day one. We continue to inflict pain on pain-inflictors, regardless of the reasons we provide to do so. From a sociological standpoint, this was Durkheim's point:

> The nature of a practice does not necessarily change because the conscious intentions of those who apply it are modified. It might, in truth, still play the same role as before, but without being perceived […] It adapts itself to new conditions of existence without any essential changes. It is so with punishment.[57]

Some of Durkheim's skepticism can be detected under the harsh questioning that critics have directed to expressive retributivism, especially with regard to the metaphorical and poetic nature that has been found in its arguments. Dolinko complained that retributivism has "relied

---

[54] Neruda, P. (1972), *Extravagaria*. Jonathan Cape Ltd, 59.
[55] "Lunes", 22 de julio de 1985' *El País* (Madrid, 9 August 1985) https://elpais.com/diario/1985/08/10/opinion/492472809_850215.html accessed 7 March 2020.
[56] Kant, I. (2017). *Kant: The Metaphysics of Morals*. Cambridge University Press, § 333.
[57] Quoted in Tunick, M. (1992). *Punishment: Theory and Practice*. University of California Press, 39.

heavily on metaphor and imagery whose suggestive power exceeds its clarity."[58] Klug was even more drastic: "The time has come to definitely bid farewell to Kant's and Hegel's theories of punishment, with their irrational excesses of lyric thinking, in all their epistemological, logical and moral extravagances."[59]

Of course, one should not read these objections as directed against the attempts to legitimize punishment through language. To be sure, our world seems impossible to shape by other means, and may not even exist otherwise:

> Language does not only distinguish man from other animals, it distinguishes his animality from that of other animals. To be a man is to be an animal in a sense, to be alive in a new sense. […] Man does not just *add* speech on to such things as eating and sexual behavior; the fact that these latter occur in a linguistic context makes a difference to what they are.[60]

But if one understands the objections of Dolinko, Klug, and others as impugning only the poetic features of recent criminal discourse, this attempt at criticism itself seems ill-founded. Humankind has been struggling to justify the infliction of pain as the proper response to bad deeds for thousands of years, stumbling every time on the same logical obstacle: why add pain to pain? And we have done so only to find that this *is* not punishment's function. We have realized that when a crime is committed, the world's meaning changes, and that when a conviction is declared, the world is reshaped again. And that the transformative power of both, crime and punishment, is real to the extent that our perception of the world is real.

We have also learned that language is the way we interact with reality, and that one word is worth a thousand *substances*. To be sure, there is a relevant degree of *incommunicability* in this idea, something which resists traditional linguistic expression. For Niklas Luhmann, who spent most of his career analyzing the roles of different social systems and the ways they interact with one another, it is "this problem of incommunicability in particular that makes its presence felt in poetry." In his view, poetry and lyrical expressions are "non-linguistic language devices available here for making visible what cannot be formulated."[61]

To make things visible and not to describe them has been a self-assumed role of poetry. Two twentieth-century South American poets have enshrined in their respective *Ars poetica* the creation of reality as the key principle of poetry's justification. Vicente Huidobro, the Chilean self-proclaimed founder of literary "Creationism," inverted common sense as he encouraged his colleagues to: "let all the eye sees be created." He went on imperatively "(i)nvent new worlds and watch your words … Oh poets, why sing of roses;/Let them flower in your poems." For Huidobro, poetry's mission was nothing but creation: "The poet is a little God."[62] Borges too stressed the transformative function of poetry:

> To see in the day or in the year a symbol
> Of the days of man and of his years,
> To transmute the outrage of the years

---

[58] Dolinko, D. (1991). 'Some Thoughts About Retributivism'. *Ethics*, *101*(3), 538–539.
[59] Mañalich Raffo, J. (2015). *Retribucionismo consecuencialista como programa de ideología punitiva: Una defensa de la teoría de la retribución de Ernst Beling*, 3.
[60] McCabe, H. (1979). *Law, Love and Language*. Sheed & Ward, 68.
[61] Luhmann, N. (2001). 'Notes on the Project "Poetry and Social Theory"'. *Theory, Culture & Society*, *18*(1), 15.
[62] Huidobro, V. (1981). *The Selected Poetry of Vicente Huidobro*. New Directions Books, 3.

Into a music, a murmur of voices, and a symbol,[63]

That was probably the accomplishment of Yang Mi-ja, the tribulated grandmother of the film *Poetry*, with whom I started these lines. Besieged by the paralyzing sound of silence, she managed to find her own voice. It was only then that she could turn the wheels of bureaucratic punishment and fill the blank page. The poem was a letter to her grandson's victim, but primarily to herself; a forgiveness letter, and the enshrinement of a new world order to account for the dead and the convicted. It was also a Borgesean device, designed "to see in death sleep, and in the sunset/a sad gold."[64]

FORCE OF LAW

That which you prevented your brother from seeing,
You won't ever stare again.
That which your victim never again bit,
You won't ever again grind.
It will be your sacred end, and a new start for justice,
Which does not satiate itself but with the blood
Of those who spill blood.
We are even.

We've proven in laboratories that your eyes are sacred,
And we will not touch them but just
To preserve your brothers' eyes.
We don't take delight in your flaming pain.
If we make wood from your fallen trunk,
It is only to warm up the room.
We are safe.

It's not wood you're made from,
Though the infringed rule was a fruit of your own tree.
The sentence is written in your own ink.
We'll honor you.
(You'll honor me)
We'll hold you accountable for all you could have said,
And your talkative civic dignity will thus be praised.
(My deed, my dignity)
Of those who don't utter them are the insults
and theory loads the shotguns with words.
We are.

---

[63] Borges, J. L. (1972). *Selected Poems 1923–1967*. Allen Lane, The Penguin Press, 157.
[64] Borges, J. L. (1972). *Selected Poems 1923–1967*. Allen Lane, The Penguin Press, 157.

Index

Abram, David
    The Spell of the Sensuous. Perception and Language in a More-than-Human World 256
academic knowledge production 154
Acevedo, Eudoro 135, 140, 141
activist documents 158
activist literature 153, 158, 159, 172
Act of Union 1707 105
Actor–Network Theory (ANT) 311
Acuña, Claudia 291
adda
    chorus 147–9
    literary tradition of 150–54
    method for law 154–8
    sex worker feminist jurisprudence 172–3
    unstoppable women 158–72
Adriana Buenos Aires (Fernández) 526
Aeneid (Virgil) 105
Aeschylus 231
    Oresteia 226, 230, 231, 234, 241
    The Persians 519
"aestheticization of politics" 35
aesthetic jurisdiction of literature 17
Aesthetics of Law 518, 521, 525
Aesthetics of Logic 521
affective contract 280
Agamben, Giorgio 198, 204, 211, 223–5, 231–41, 244, 246–8, 455, 465
    Idea of Prose 236
age 485–8, 492
agricultural markets 443
Aiken, Ann 257
Airbnb 333–5
"Akedah" 552–8, 566
Alberdi, Juan Bautista
    Bases and Starting Points for the Political Organization of the Argentine Republic 366
Alciato, Andrea 484, 495–7
Alexander, A.V. 183, 240
Alexander the Great 238
Alfonso X 473, 477, 481
    Siete Partidas 472, 487
Allott, Philip 117
ambiguity 98, 101, 237, 298, 483–97, 535, 557, 559, 560
    benefit of 99
    in household position 100

    interpretive 485
American jurisprudence 212
Amore, Julia 288
anarchism 71, 74, 78, 140, 144
anarchist economics 449
anarcho-communist society 134
anarcho-syndicalist community 139
Anderson, Perry 118
Anglo-literary canonical tradition 104
Aniara 242
The Animals in That Country (McKay) 261
animated law 476
Anker, Elizabeth
    New Directions in Law and Literature 5
"annulment of crime" 583
anonymity 355, 361
ANT *see* Actor–Network Theory (ANT)
antagonisms 17, 201, 205, 392
Anthropocene 250–53, 255–7, 259–61, 266, 270, 375, 402
anthropocentric Earth System 303
anthropocentrism 219, 402
anthropological function of the law 342
anthropology 368
'anti-autonomy autonomy' 143
anti-capitalist impulse 138
Antigone 40, 41, 576
Antigone's Claim (Butler) 576
anti-immigrant/immigration politics 86
anti-non-binary legislation 379
anti-sex work laws 147
anti-trafficking mechanism 173
anti-trafficking model 169
anti-trafficking work 169
anti-trans athlete legislation 390
anti-trans discourse 394
anti-trans laws 398
anti-trans legislation 379, 381
anti-trans narratives 393
anti-trans sentiments 392
Antonio, Nicolás 485
Antony and Cleopatra (Shakespeare) 442
anxiety 16, 86, 93, 111, 112, 135–8, 198, 236, 243, 555
Aquinas, Thomas
    Summa Theologiae 475
archeon 72–4
    archism and 66–8
    law without 79–81

archism 64–5, 68, 69, 71, 78, 80
archist conditions, law under 80
archist prophetic function 70
Architecture /Mouvement/ Continuité 129
archival trajectories 365–6
Archive Fever (Derrida) 67, 371
Arendt, Hannah 44, 454, 581
    Eichmann in Jerusalem: A Report on the Banality of Evil (1963) 513, 580
Argentine Constitution 366
Argentine Movement 285
Aristophanes 226–8
    Ecclesiazusae 226, 227
Aristotle 228, 229, 475, 480
    De anima 471, 472
    De natura 471
    De sensu et sensato 471
    Politics 464
    On the Soul 475
Arkansas bill 396
Armstrong, Rachel
    Invisible Ecologies 434–5
Ars poetica (Horace) 590
'Art as Device (*priëm*)' 29
Artaud, Antonin 457
Artemis Accords 301, 302
Article III of the Liability Convention 304
Article I of the OST 298
Article VIII of the OST 299
Article VI of the OST regime 304
Asante, Amma 101
Ashworth, Andrew 207
atheistic anarchism 78
Athena 230, 233, 241
Athena's Way: The Jurisprudence of the Oresteia (Manderson) 231
Attlee, Clement 184
Austen, Jane 83, 91–6, 99, 103, 104
    Mansfield Park 91, 92, 95, 97, 100, 103, 106
    Sanditon 102
Austin, J. L. 94, 106, 568, 576, 584
authentic gender identifications 387
authoritative 'collective memory' 87
authority in blockchain technology 356–8
authorship in blockchain technology 353–5
autobioethnography 364
    archival trajectories 365–6
    autobiographical ethnography 366–9
    encrypted subject of study 370–71
autobiographical ethnography 366–9
autobiography 367, 369
'auto-poietic' communicative systems 234
Averroes 478, 480

"bait-and-switch"

approach 394, 398
    strategy 383
Baldwin, James 377
    Notes of a Native Son 376
Balfour Declaration 353
Bambara, Toni Cade 138
BAME communities 141
Banner, Rachel 345, 346, 347
Barad, Karen 7, 8, 405
bare life 202, 211, 212, 216, 218, 220, 232, 242
Barricelli, Jean-Pierre 1, 6
Bartl, Marija 118, 120
Bartleby the Scrivener (Melville) 204, 239, 247
Bases and Starting Points for the Political Organization of the Argentine Republic (Alberdi) 366
Bataille, Georges 520
    Erotism: Death & Sensuality 521
Baudrillard, J. 215
Bauer, Fritz 40, 43, 44, 46, 47, 49, 50, 54, 55, 59, 62
    "In the Name of the People: The Judicial Overcoming of the Past" 45
BDSM 383
Becker-Ho, Alice 468, 469
    L'Essence du jargon 467
Beckett, Samuel 202, 203, 213
    Happy Days 519
Before the Law (Kafka) 239
Begriffsjurisprudenz 5
behavioural economics 301
Being and Time (Heidegger) 236
Being Given (Marion) 32
Belle, Dido Elizabeth 99, 102
Bell v Tavistock 385
Bengal Boundary Commission 191–2
Bengali literary tradition of adda 148
Benjamin, Walter 35, 62, 68, 231, 235, 238, 576
    "Critique of Violence" 80
Benjamin-style divine violence 79
Bentham, Jeremy 582, 583
beoble, memo about quiet 373–7
Berg, Peter 168
Berger, John 348, 349
Berkins, Lohana 288
Berlant, Lauren 133, 394
Berlina, Alexandra 30, 31
Berry, Thomas 250
Bertolini, Lara 288
Beyond the Public Sphere: Film and the Feminist Imaginary (Lara) 569, 578
Bhabha, Homi 386
Bharati, Visva 164
Biden, Joe 392
Big Other 73, 112, 113, 121, 124–7

castration 116–18, 120
   to the rescue 115–16
Bilderatlas Mnemosyne 89
Bilge, S. 206, 207
Billy Budd, Sailor (Melville) 558
binary legal framework 288
biological determinism 391
"Bitcoin: A Peer-to-Peer Electronic Cash System" 354
Bitcoin blockchain 352, 354, 356
Bitcoin White Paper 354, 361, 362
Black Body (Cole) 376
Black Lives Matter Movement 86, 212, 254, 573
Black Skin, White Masks (Fanon) 64
Blair, Tony 207
Blanchot, Maurice 524
   The space of literature 524
Bloch, Ernst 131, 132, 135, 144, 235
   Principles of Hope 131
blockchain community 361
blockchain's ordering system 363
blockchain technology
   authority in 356–8
   authorship in 353–5
   narration as world-making 351–3
   world-making and representation 358–62
block reward 356
Blue Mars (Robinson) 244
Bobbette, A. 410
Boccaccio, Giovanni 516
   Decameron 515
Bodies of Water: Posthuman Feminist Phenomenology (Neimanis) 432
Bodin, Jean 20
Bongie, C. 87
Bonnet, François J. 217
Booking.com 327, 330, 332
Booth, Wayne 386
Borges, Jorge Luis 129, 140–42, 144, 526, 528, 529, 581, 583–7, 589, 590
   "A Weary Man's Utopia" 135, 138
   "The Theologians" 588
Bose, Buddhadeva 150
Boundary Commission 188–94
   Bengal Boundary Commission 191–2
   partition of India and 182–7
   Punjab Boundary Commission 189–91
   Radcliffe Award 192–3
Bowlby, John 201
"Bowstring. On the Dissimilarity of the Similar" (Shklovsky) 34
Bradley, James 266
   Ghost Species 266
Brave New World (Huxley) 128
Brecht, Bertolt 32, 34, 55, 122

Brethren of Purity 477
Bristol Bus Boycott 86
British Empire Exhibition 1924/5 87
British Indian cartography 175, 191
Bronte, Charlotte
   Jane Eyre 102
Brook, Peter 50, 56, 58–60, 62
   The Empty Space 60
Brooks, Cleanth 561
Brown, Wendy 119, 120, 208, 209, 220
Brown v Board 562
Brunelleschi, Filippo 179
Brunkhorst, H. 246
Bunyan, John
   Pilgrim's Progress 441
Burckhardt, Jacob 570
Burdon, Peter 254
bureaucratic rules and hierarchies 120
bureaucratic systems 121
'business as usual' approach 306
Buterin, Vitalik 353, 355
Butler, Judith 40, 41, 287, 574, 575, 577, 578
   Antigone's Claim 576

Cáceres, Lea 569
Calasso, Roberto 520
Calderón, Ñancufil 366
Callois, Roger
   Man and the Sacred 520
Calvino, Italo
   Six Memos for the Next Millennium 374, 375
Camp, Greg 550
Canguilhem, Georges 412
Canhué, Germán 365
Cantar de mío Cid 487
capitalism 119, 120, 131, 132, 134, 135, 138–41, 143, 273
   characteristics of 136
   commercial 459
   digital 276, 277
   politics and 273
capitalist economic system of production 164
Carabinage ou Matoiserie Soldatesque (de Romany) 459
Cardozo, Benjamin Nathan 552, 563, 565–6
   Paradoxes of Legal Science 566
Carlson, Tucker 397
carmen necessarium 17
Carrera, Carmen 391
Cartesian dualism 4
cartographic depiction 193
cartographic historiography 176
cartographic imagination 193
cartographic jurisprudence 175–83, 187, 189, 191, 198

cartographic materials 188
cartographic scholarship 174
cartographic unity 184
cartographies 174
    arguments before Boundary Commission 188–93
    partition of India and Boundary Commission 182–7
    from political cartography to cartographic jurisprudence 176–82
    postcolonial continuities 194–8
cartojuridical argumentation 188
cartojuridical award 187
cartojuridical method of interpretation 190
cartouche 177, 178, 180–82, 198
Cartwright 107
The Case of Wagner (Nietzsche) 519
caste system 149
The Castle (Kafka) 239, 241
Castoriadis, Cornelius 438
castration 126–7
    Big Other 115–18
    ethics of 124–5
    in Freud 110–11
    in Lacan 111–14
    original crime 121–3
    in the Real 114–15
    rejection of 118–21
Casumbal-Salazar, I. 307
casus fortuitus 25, 26
"categorical" intersectional approaches 364
Cavafy, C.P. 224, 242
Cavarero, Adriana 154
Cave, Nick 128, 132–4
centralised timestamping authority 361
Cesaire, Aimé
    La Tempete 104
Chakrabarty, Dipesh 154, 256
Charles V 137
Charlotte of Mecklenburg-Strelitz 97
Charter of the United Nations 305
Chartier, Roger 466
    The Cultural Uses of Print in Early Modern France 467
Chatterjee, Purnima 147, 169
Chatterji, Joya 191, 192
Chekhov, Anton 556–8
    "In the Cart" 557
Chereau, Ollivier 467
    Le Jargon ou le langage de l'argot reformé 466
Chester, Lucy 174, 183, 184, 186, 189, 192, 193
Chiari, Sophie 442
A Children's Bible (Millet) 268
Chocobar, Javier 36

Christian 'hypocrisy' 230
"Christian intercessors" 555
Christian law 554, 555
Christian theology and humanism 454
Chrysippus 228
Churchill White Paper 353
Ciancaglini, Sergio 290, 291
Ciardi, John 561
circulus disciplinarum 20
cis law 396
cisnormativity 396
civilized societies 582
Clark, Timothy 255–7, 260
'classic noir protagonist' 259
Clement of Alexandria 476
climate protection law 267
Clough, Patricia 273
CLS *see* Critical Legal Studies (CLS)
Cohen, Felix 4, 10–12, 41
    "Transcendental Nonsense" 9
Cohen, Robert 52
Coldness & Cruelty, Difference & Repetition (Deleuze) 201, 272
Cole, Teju 377
    Black Body 376
Colectivo LasTesis 569, 578
collective activism 162
collective amnesia 44, 59, 87
'collective regulation' 440
Collins, Hill 206, 207
Colombian Constitutional Court 252
colonial cartographic practices 175
Colorado River Ecosystem 253
Cometa, Paula 569
comic 230, 231, 236–40, 242, 247, 466, 548
Commentaries (Plowden) 443
Committee on Space Research (COSPAR) 305
Common Law 582
communal luxury 449
communication 102, 203, 206, 207, 232, 242, 386, 521, 571, 584
    and chance outcomes 207, 217, 220
    internal ambivalence of 215
    jurisgenetic 405
    of law 316
    nonhuman forms of 261
    platforms 281
    public 478
    verbal 159
communicative retributivist theories 584
'communicative systems' 245
communist political system 131
community-based activities 164
community cohesion 122
community encroachment 117

community law 117
competition 208–10
competitive economic models 139
competitive (or curatorial) space 216
compromise, transgression and 504–11
Concept of the Political (Schmitt) 588
Concepts of Justice (Raphael) 205
"The Concerns of a Head of a Family" (Kafka) 64
Condello, Angela
    Theory of Law and Literature. Across Two Arts of Compromising 506
conduct of lawful relations 156, 157
Congress Plan 191
Congress Scheme 191
Congress–Sikh Map 190
Connolly, William 236
"conquest of the desert" 365
consensus building 356–8
consequentialist justice 205–6
'constitutional imagination' 244
constitutionalism 237
constitutional law 227, 240
constitutional "originalism" 559
'constitutional paradox' 228
constitutional prerogative 197
constitutional theory 20
contemporary competitive neoliberalism 209
contemporary contract theory 20
contemporary democracies 232, 233
contemporary retributivism 587
contemporary travel brochures 88–9
contestation 218
context-transcendence critique 577, 578
'context transcendent validity' 577
contingency 203, 211, 212, 215, 217–20, 239, 244, 245, 247, 311, 403, 577
contract theory 274, 275
conventionalized trans tropes 397
Convention on the Elimination of all Forms of Discrimination against Women (CEDAW) 285
Cooke, Maeve 571, 573
    conception of critique and validity 577–8
    Re-Presenting the Good Society 577
Cooper, Davina 135, 270
    Everyday Utopias 142
cooperative banking 164
cooperative financial institution 163
cooperative movement 164
The Co-operative Principles 164
Cormack, Bradin 183
corporate conduct 359
Corpus Iustiniani 476
Corsair Writings 469
cosmolegal approach and the Jedi code 307–12

cosmolegal decision-making 308
cosmolegality 309, 310
Cossman, Brenda
    Subversive Sites: Feminist Engagements with Law in India 160
'counter-injurious speech' 575
counter-public 568, 573, 576
Counter Reformation 490
Cour des Miracles 458–60, 462, 463, 466, 469
Couric, Katie 391
The Court of Miracles 457, 459, 462, 468
Courts of Sewers 438, 445
Cover, Robert 10, 413, 552, 553
Cowper, William
    The Task 106
Cox, Laverne 391
Crane, R.S. 561
"Creationism" 590
Crenshaw, Kimberlé 368
criminal law 582, 586
Cripps, Sir Stafford 183
critical feminist thinking 147
Critical Legal Studies (CLS) 11
critical race theory 368
critical theory 401, 403
critique 274, 278, 401, 403, 484
    of Austen 92
    of capitalism 136
    of contracts 272, 279, 281
    decolonial 255
    and defense of illocutionary actions 574–7
    of dialectics 129
    of enlightenment 231
    feminist 275
    function 132, 396
    of *homo economicus* approach 297
    of insensitivity 2
    interdisciplinary 28
    of law 153, 403
    of positivism and formalism 364
    of racism 573
    radical 65, 501
    of strict formalism 513
    of utopia 142, 144
    and validity 577–8
Critique of Dialectical Reason (Sartre) 134
Critique of Everyday Life (Lefebvre) 456
Critique of Judgement (Kant) 412
"Critique of Violence" (Benjamin) 80
The Crossing of the Visible (Marion) 33
'crowner's quest law' 442
Crutzen, Paul J 250
Cryptography Mailing List 354
crypto law 359
Cullinan, Cormac 250, 251, 253

cultural artefacts 90
The Cultural Uses of Print in Early Modern France (Chartier) 467
culture 59, 62, 131, 150, 151, 177, 242, 403
Cunningham, J.V.
 "Woe and Wonder" 552
cybernetic closed-circuit system 231
cybernetic literature 8
cyclical relational processes 402

Dante Alighieri 41, 46, 58, 441, 508, 509
Dardot, P. 208, 220
Dareer, Rawan 550
Dark Ages 7
Dark Mountain Project 251
Darwinian evolutionism 141
Dasmann, Raymond F. 168
Daub, Adrian 351
Daumal, René
 Mount Analogue 21
Dawson, Paul 378
Dead Voice 473
De anima (Aristotle) 471, 472
death, witness statement 339–49
Death In Spring (Rodoreda) 426–7, 435–6
de-binarizing and transing law 395–9
Debnath, Rama 159
de Bobadilla, Jerónimo Castillo 489, 490, 495
Debord, Guy 233
Decameron (Boccaccio) 515
de Certeau, Michel 335–8
de Cervantes, Miguel 31, 483–5, 487–97
 Don Quijote 483, 485, 494, 495, 508
 La gitanilla 490, 492
 Novelas ejemplares 485, 487, 489, 490
decision-making process 233
De Cive (Hobbes) 464
deconstructionism 561, 562
de Covarrubias, Sebastián 497
de facto inescapable framework 241
de Kirchner, Cristina Fernández 285
Delany, Samuel
 The Motion of Light in Water 369
de La Reynie, Gabriel Nicolas 462, 463
Deleuze, Gilles 2, 3, 6, 89, 133, 201–6, 211–13, 216, 219, 278–81, 405, 438–40, 457, 458, 525
 Coldness & Cruelty, Difference & Repetition 201, 272
 Essays Critical and Clinical 202
 "Immanence: A Life" 202
 "To Have Done with Judgment" 204, 205
 What is a Minor Literature? 468
deleuzoguattarian sense 284
'deliberative democracy' 234

della Porta, Giambattista
 Magia Naturalis 442
de Man, Paul 561, 565
demarcation 196
de Moncada, Sancho 489, 490
Demos, T.J. 419
De natura (Aristotle) 471
Denning, Baron 104, 106
 What Next in the Law? 86
Denning, Tom 104, 106
 What Next in the Law? 86
de Palencia, Alfonso 488
de Perón, María Estela Martínez 292
de Romany, Richard
 Carabinage ou Matoiserie Soldatesque 459
Derrida, Jacques 260, 365, 561, 565
 Archive Fever 67, 371
Der Rosenkavalier (Strauss) 423
Descartes, René 12, 410, 495
De sensu et sensato (Aristotle) 471
desire 111, 113, 114, 116, 124–6
de Tocqueville, Alexis 570
Dewey, John 9
Dey, Bharati 161, 170, 172
Diacritics 129
diagramming 89, 91
Dickens, Charles 202, 483
Didi-Huberman, Georges 176, 177
Dido and Aeneas (Purcell) 106
"Dido's Lament" 106
digging 403, 408, 442
 ditch 440, 446
 drainage and 445
 metaphorical 449
digital communities 273, 281
digital contracts 275
digital materialities 277
digital platform-based economy 273
Diogenes 223, 225, 240, 248
discipline 463, 472
 academic 523
 Aristotelian moral 475
 legal 473, 474, 476, 477, 479
 and punishment 462
 spiritual 451
The Dispossessed (Le Guin) 139, 140
"The Dissolution of the Oedipus Complex" (Freud) 111
distinct feminist jurisprudential discourse 172
distributed ledger 357, 358
distributive justice 185, 192
ditches
 ditch rule 450–51
 fields and factories 447–50
 inflow 438–40

work and days 440–43
ditch law 439, 440, 451
ditch rule 440, 450–51
diverse ecosystem 413
"diverse" gender category 388
Dolin, Kieran 2
Dolinko, D. 589
domestic abuse 539, 540, 545, 547, 548
domestic legal systems 360
donor-funded projects 158
Donovan, A. 410
Don Quijote (de Cervantes) 483, 485, 494, 495, 508
Doody, M. 97
Dorsett, Shaunnagh 156
Dostoevsky, Fyodor
   Underground Man 386
double-spending problem 355
Doyle, Arthur Conan
   "When the World Screamed" 414
drama 525, 527, 529
   courtroom 56, 57
   between ob-scene and the sacred 518–21
   of *oikonomia* 245
   risks of 529–30
Dryden, John 104
Dryzek, John S 261
Duff, R. A. 584, 587
Dugdale, Sir Thomas 441, 445
Dugdale, Sir William
   The History of Imbanking and Drayning of Divers Fenns and Marshes 439, 440
Dumézil, Georges 206
Durán, Manuel 485
Duras, Marguerite 217
Durbar Jounokormi Samanyaya Committee 159
Durbar Mahila Samanwaya Committee (DMSC) 147, 152, 153, 158, 159, 161–9, 171–3
Durkheim, Émile 589
Durruti, Buenaventura 451
Dutch law 330
Dutta, Mrinal Kanti 162
Dylan, Bob 483
dystopia 128, 129, 132, 135, 136, 139

Earth Community 250
Earth organisms 305
Earth's orbit (EO) 297
Earth system law 257, 298, 299, 302, 307, 309, 311, 312
Earth System Science (ESS) 297
Ecclesiazusae (Aristophanes) 226, 227, 230
ECJ 120
ecocritical literary theory 255
ecological catastrophe 139

ecological fiction 250, 259–61, 263, 264, 270
'economic political theology' 248
economic rehabilitation of sex workers 167
Edney, Matthew 175, 178, 181
egalitarian constitutional reforms 248
Ehrlich, Eugen 382
Eichmann, Adolph 44
Eichmann in Jerusalem: A Report on the Banality of Evil (Arendt) 513, 580
Eikhenbaum, Boris 561
Elden, Stuart 175
Electronic Cash System 356
Eliade, Mircea 520
Eliot, T.S. 126
Ellison, Ralph
   Invisible Man 204, 205
empirical knowledges 401
Empson, William 485
The Empty Space (Brook) 60
Encuentro Nacional de Mujeres 285
energy justice 5
English Heritage exhibition 101
English law 107, 385
Enlightenment 6, 54, 103, 115, 198, 582
Ephialtes 230, 231
Epictetus 228, 229
'epistemic authoritarianism' 578
Erasmus 491, 497
Erotism: Death & Sensuality (Bataille) 521
Esposito, R. 211, 212, 215
ESS *see* Earth System Science (ESS)
Essays Critical and Clinical (Deleuze) 202
Ethereum 356, 362
   blockchain 352, 355, 357, 359
   wallet 360
Ethereum White Paper 355
'ethical transcendence' 463
ethics 2, 8, 217, 298
   of castration 124–5
   and politics 28
   of superfluity 447–50
   types of 294
ethnography 366–9
European Court of Human Rights 267
European Economic and Social Committee 266
Europeanisation of migration policy 122
European political systems 137
Everyday Utopias (Cooper) 142
Ewald, F. 214
exhaustion 201–4
   competition 208–10
   formula and the bulbs 204–5
   four processes of 213–17
   injustice 217–19
   justice 205–8

expressive retributivism 589
expressive theory of language 572
Extraordinary Gazette of India 193
extraterrestrial environment 299
extraterrestrial manifest destiny 296
"Extravagaria" (Neruda) 588
"extrinsic evidence" 557–62

Faber, Michel
    Under the Skin 261
The Faerie Queene (Spencer) 442
'familial ideology' 160
Fanon, Frantz
    Black Skin, White Masks 64
"Fear and Trembling" (Kierkegaard) 552
Federal Communications Commission 305
Federal Constitutional Court 48
Felman, Shoshana 535
Femicide Act movement 285
feminism 285, 395
feminist accounts of law 153
feminist anti-racist imaginary 576
feminist epistemology 535, 536, 540
feminist jurisprudence 157
    Indian 149, 153, 154, 163
    non-adversarial 173
    sex worker 149, 153–5, 158, 172–3
feminist jurisprudential knowledge 152, 153
feminist knowledge 155, 157
feminist legal judgments 515
feminist legal scholars 364
feminist scholarship 152
feminist social movements 570–74
feminist theory 275, 276
feminist tradition 278
Ferge's theory of cardinal numbers 114
Fernández, Macedonio 518, 525, 527
    Adriana Buenos Aires 526
    The Museum of Eterna's Novel. The first good Novel 526
Ferrando, Francesca 276
Ferrarotti, Franco 367, 368
Festival of Britain 87, 90
feudal system of landholding 443
Feuerbach, Ludwig 367
Feynman, Richard 310
fictions
    dystopian 128
    ecological 250, 259–61, 263, 264, 270
    juridical 522
    literary 378, 386, 419, 522, 526
    science 131, 132, 139
    speculative 260–69
    transhumanist science 8
    utopian 130

Fielding, Henry 378
Field of the Sensible 524
Fields, Factories and Workshops (Kropotkin) 439, 448
Fire over England (Korda) 88
First-Tier Tribunal 340
Fish, Stanley 22
Fisher, Mark 24
Fitz-Henry, Erin 253
"flows of capital" metaphor 430
Floyd, George 5, 573, 575, 576
Forcatulus, Stephanus 20
foresight 16, 24, 26
    angelological 21
    juridical 18
forgetting 87, 88, 101
Formations of the Unconscious (Lacan) 112
form-of-life 456, 458, 467, 468
Forster, E.M. 406–9, 411
    The Machine Stops 405
Foucault, Michel 120, 174, 193, 208, 216, 288, 464, 519
    "Of Other Spaces" 129
    The Order of Things 129
    Truth and Juridical Forms 527
Fowles, John 563
Franco, J. 141
Frankfurt Auschwitz trials 40, 43, 49, 53, 54
"freedom, equality and fraternity" 284
Freeman, Michael 47, 48
    Lloyd's Introduction to Jurisprudence 46
'free-market utopia' 131
French law 300
Freud, Sigmund 35, 112, 113, 116, 121, 123, 130, 137, 201, 501, 502, 507–9, 534
    Inhibitions, Symptoms and Anxiety 111
    Interpretation of Dreams 110
    Sexual Theories of Children 110
    Totem and Taboo 122
    Wit and its Relation to the Unconscious 500
Freudian negation 507
'Freudian principle of individuation' 502
Frykenberg, Robert 181
"Fucking Law (A New Methodological Movement)" 396
Fuero de Béjar 486
Fuero de Jaca 486
Fuero de Ledesma 486
Fuero de Madrid 486
Fuero de Navarra 486
Fuero de Plasencia 486
Fuero de Salamanca 486
Fuero de Zamora 486
Fuller, Lon 49
functional mutual aid groups 142

'fundamental attunement' 235
The Fundamental Concepts of Metaphysics (Heidegger) 236
fury 295
   between shout and 291–4
   the shout and *travesti* 284–90
Future Generations case 253

Gaia 402, 413–16
Gainsborough, Thomas
   "Mr and Mrs Andrews" 90
Gandhar, Komol 158
Gandorfer, Daniela 147, 174, 550
Garavito, Edgar 522
Gardner, John 562–5
   On Moral Fiction 563
Garland, David 206, 207
Gavin Grimm v Gloucester 390
Gebruers, Cecilia 147
"Geistesgeschichte" 560
gender essentialism 380
gender identities 289, 389, 392
Gender Identity Act 286–8
Gender Identity Recognition 286
gender politics 64
gender self-determination 385
gender violence 285, 287
general contract law 274
genesis block 357
genetic homozygosity 493
Genovese, Ann 147, 156, 157
geological sciences, development of 410
George III 97, 99
Geospatial Information Regulation Bill 197
German criminal law 580
German Wehrmacht 331
Gerticz, Peter
   Parvulus philosophiae naturalis 471
Ghare Baire (The Home and the World) (Tagore) 164
al-Ghazālī, Abū Hamid 477, 479–81
Ghosh, Amitav 253, 255, 256, 260, 263
Ghost Species (Bradley) 266
Gilbert, S. 128
Giles, Peter 135–8
Gilman, Charlotte Perkins
   The Yellow Wallpaper 64
Ginsburg, Ruth Bader 395
Girard, René 520, 532, 533
Glaspell, Susan 534–6, 538, 544, 548–50
   Trifles 532–50
global brand campaign 334
Global Network of Sex Work Projects 147
Goldmann, Lucien 560
Goodhart, Sandor 532, 533, 535

Goodrich, Peter 8, 12, 39, 41, 125, 147, 174, 198, 403, 413, 436, 457, 468, 542, 550
Gordon, Avery 138, 139, 144
Gorgias (Plato) 474, 475
The Gospel According to Jesus (Saramago) 423–5
Graeber, David 134
Grand Bureau des Pauvres 459
'grand renfermement' 462
"grassroots activism battle field" 289
Great Confinement 460
Great Derangement 256
Greco, M. 412
Greek democracy 234
Greenblatt, Jordana 395
Greenpeace Nordic Association 267
Green Political Party 388
Gross, Alexander 56–8
Grosz, E. 274, 402, 413
ground-breaking narrative techniques 561
grounds/grounding
   from and with 408–9
   conventional meaning of 401
   dualism of under and over 405–8
   earth as 413–16
   imaginary 403–5
   of law 402
   law, life and 411–13
   mystery, myth, and hypothesis 409–11
Grubačić, Andrej 134
Guattari, F. 2, 133, 206, 211, 439, 440
   What is a Minor Literature? 468
'Guidebooks' 334
Guilty Remnant 69–71, 73, 75
Gunther, Klaus 586
Gutiérrez, Eduardo 528, 529
gypsies 488–95

Habermas, Jürgen 232, 568, 570, 571, 584
'Habsburg jaw' 493
Hacking, I. 210
Hägglund, Martin 481
Hague International Space Resources Governance Working Group 298, 300
Hale, Matthew 411
Hales, Sir James 443
Halhed, Nathaniel Brassey 181
Hall, C. 103
Hall, Stuart 86, 87
Halley, Edmund 410
Happy Days (Beckett) 519
Haraway, D.J. 7, 276, 362, 403, 411, 541
harbour racist assumptions 343
Harding, Sandra 7
Hardt, Michael 275, 276
Harley, Brian 182

Hart, Herbert 49
Hartman, Geoffrey H. 561, 564, 565
Hartman, Saidiya 458
  Wayward Lives 348
Harvard Woolly Mammoth Revival team 265
hash rate 357
Hastings, Warren 181, 182
Hattersley, Roy 85
Haueisen, Heinz 44
Hayek, Friedrich 119
Hebrew tradition of prophecy 66
Heede, Richard 259
Hegel, G. W. F. 117, 125, 510, 580, 582, 583, 585, 586, 590
Hegelian model 583
Heidegger, Martin
  Being and Time 236
  The Fundamental Concepts of Metaphysics 236
Hemmings, Clare
  Why Stories Matter 369
Henry V (Shakespeare) 60
Hereford Mappa Mundi 198, 199
'here/there' 334–7
Hernández, José
  Martín Fierro 529
heterodiegetic narrative authority 392
heterotopias 129, 216
Hickey, Colin 257
hierarchical caste system 149
"hierarchical system of sexual value" 383
Hillgruber, Andreas 571
Hindoostan 177, 178
Historical Collections (Rushworth) 107
The History of Imbanking and Drayning of Divers Fenns and Marshes (Dugdale) 439, 440
The History of Mary Prince (Prince) 346
Hitler, Adolf 141, 142, 564, 571
Hobbes, Thomas 464, 465
  De Cive 464
  Leviathan 441
Hojarascas (Shock) 284, 285, 290, 291, 295
Hölderlin, Friedrich 235
Holdheim, Wolfgang 560
Holdich, Thomas 188
holistic long-term approach 308
Hollander, John 580
Holocaust 565
"Holy Wayne" 69
Homborg, Alf 260
Homer 548
  Iliad 483
  Odyssey 242, 509
homo economicus 298–302
  approach 297
  hyperbole 297
  model 301, 302
  theory 296
homo investicus 302
homo oeconomicus 119
homo politicus 119
Homo Sacer 225, 232
Horace
  Ars poetica 590
Hormiga Negra 518, 525, 529–30
Horn, Eva 588
Huckleberry Finn (Twain) 386
Hugo, Victor 458, 468
  Notre Dame de Paris 460
Huidobro, Vicente 590
human-centric global politico-juridical space 309
human normative systems 402
'Human Personality' 455
human rights
  frameworks 254
  obligations 360
  violations 359
Hunter, Rosemary 549
Husserl, Edmund 32, 34
Huxley, Aldous
  Brave New World 128
Huysmans, Jef 122
hydrological cycles 414
Hynes v RR 565
hyperbole 296
  cosmolegal approach and the Jedi code 307–12
  of legally reconstructed image of *homo economicus* 299–302
  other dimension of space 298–9
  outer space environment and the law 302–6
  Sith rhetoric 306–7
hyper-formalist narrative structure 363
'hypothetical post-human geologist' 259
hypotheticals 496
  juridical 484
  legal 485, 495, 497
  lexical-order 488

Ibn Falaqera 480
Ibn Sina 480
Ibn Ṭufayl 480
The Idea of Justice (Sen) 164
Idea of Prose (Agamben) 236
ideational source 403
idiosyncratic political concept 174
Iliad (Homer) 483
illocutionary 568–9
  counter-hegemonic narratives from feminist social movements 570–74

Maeve Cooke's conception of critique and validity 577–8
task of critique and defense of illocutionary actions 574–7
'Un violador en tu camino' 578–9
illocutionary actions and force 568, 570, 573–7
illocutionary speech act 584
imaginative invention 21
"Immanence: A Life" (Deleuze) 202
immaterial labour 276
immigrant communities 86
Immigration Act 1945 85
Immigration Tribunal 347
Immoral Traffic (Prevention) Act, 1956 (ITPA) 158, 160, 161, 166, 167, 172, 173
impartiality 214
imperialism 87
'impersonal reasoned judgment' 241
Indian Evidence law 197
Indian farming communities 164
Indian feminist jurisprudence 149, 153, 154, 163
Indian Independence Act of 1947 187
Indian post-colonial academia 149
indigeneity 365, 366, 370
indigenous communities 311
indigenous cosmologies 402, 411
indigenous knowledge 310
indigenous societies 310
Indigo (Warner) 104
individualist liberal politics 138
Indo-European tradition 206
"infantile citizenship" 394
information capitalism 276
Inhibitions, Symptoms and Anxiety (Freud) 111
The Inoperative Community (Nancy) 213
inoperativity 223, 236, 243
In Re: The Berubari Union and Exchange of Enclaves Reference Under Article 143(1) of The Constitution of India 196
insouled law 476
institutional democracy 209
institutionalised democratic deliberation 209
institutional law 398
institutional violence 293
instrumentalizing vulnerabilty 394–5
intellectual property rights 272
intergenerational judging 250, 257
intergenerational justice and equity 267
inter-governmental decision-making 307
internal gypsy law 493
International Day of Eliminating Violence Against Women 569
International Feminist Demonstration 285
international investment agreements 360
international investment law 360
international law 359, 363
international legal framework 298
international legal governance 309
international legal instruments 359
International Monetary Fund 290
international peace and security 305
international space law 304
Interpretation of Dreams (Freud) 110
interpretive ambiguity 485
intersectional activism 289
intersectionality 206, 207, 364, 368, 568
interspecies judging 260–64
"In the Cart" (Chekhov) 557
"In the Juridical Heaven of Concepts. A Fantasy" 4
"In the Name of the People: The Judicial Overcoming of the Past" (Bauer) 45
Introduction to Jurisprudence (Lloyd) 46
'inverse paramnesia' 527
The Investigation. An Oratorio in 11 Cantos (Weiss) 41, 42, 50, 55, 56, 58, 60
Invisible Ecologies (Armstrong) 434–5
Invisible Man (Ellison) 204, 205
Inyang (Ononokpono) 430–31
ITPA *see* Immoral Traffic (Prevention) Act, 1956 (ITPA)
Ius quaesitum alteri 25
ius quaesitum tertio 25

Jacobson, Arthur 495, 496
Jakobs, Gunther 585
Jalal, Ayesha
  The Sole Spokesman: Jinnah, the Muslim League and the Demand for Pakistan 183
James, C.L.R. 138
James, William 9
James I 105
Jameson, Frederic 140
Jana, Smarajit 163
Jane Eyre (Bronte) 102
Jean-Pierre Barricelli 1
Jelinek, Elfriede 62, 63
  The Silent Girl 61, 62
Jenner, Caitlyn 397
Jensen, Liz
  The Uninvited 269
Jewish genocide 570
Jewish literalism 558
Jinnah, Muhammad Ali 184
Johansson, Scarlett 261
Johns-Putra, Adeline 256
Jones, David 56
Jones, Stephen 194
Jones, Tom 378

Journey to the Centre of the Earth (Verne) 410
judging
    beyond brink of extinction 265–6
    intergenerational 250, 257
    interspecies 260–64
    wild (*see* wild judging)
"judicial sciences" 560
Juliana lawsuit 267
Juliana v United States 257
juridical fiction 522
Juridical foresight 18
juridical hypotheticals 484
juridical injunction 25
juridical–literary fictions 526
"juridical territory" 193
juridical transdiscourse 524
juridical vision 16
juridico-political order 465
jurisastrology 20
'jurisdictional mutation' 117
"Jurisdiction and Governing Law" 330
jurisgenetic communications 402
jurisliterary inquiry 1, 5
jurisliterary jurisdiction 19
jurisliterature 17, 19–27
jurispathic jurisprudence 396
juristic concept of foreseeability 16
justice
    consequentialist 205–6
    distributive 185, 192
    energy 5
    exhaustion 205–8
    poetic 288, 483, 532–50
justification of punishment 580, 583

Kafka, Franz 2, 64, 117, 121, 230, 237, 238, 240, 241, 374, 420, 467, 483, 505, 508
    The Castle 239, 241
    Before the Law 239
    The Metamorphosis 241, 508
    Poseidon 420
    "The Concerns of a Head of a Family" 64
    The Trial 241, 404
    Türhüter 474
Kafkaesque bureaucracy 239
Kågerman, Pella 242
Kahn-Freund, Otto 47–9
kalām 478, 479
Kalyvas, Andreas 236
Kant, Immanuel 12, 124, 386, 410, 412, 431, 524, 582, 590
    Critique of Judgement 412
    "Metaphysics of Morals" 589
Kantian philosophy 401
Kantian transcendental Aesthetics 523, 524

Kapur, Ratna
    Subversive Sites: Feminist Engagements with Law in India 160
Kartun, Mauricio 528
Kelsen, Hans 403, 404, 511, 524, 526
Khan, Sir Zafrullah 184, 189
Kierkegaard, Søren
    "Fear and Trembling" 552
Kilpatrick, Fleur 264
Kim, Rakhyun 257
King Alfonso of Castile 477
King Charles V 136
Kisch, Egon Erwin 6, 7
Knausgaard, Karl
    A Time for Everything 421–3
Korda, Alexander
    Fire over England 88
Korte, Alexander 388, 389, 394
Kotzé, Louis 257
Krieger, Murray 561
Kropotkin, Peter 144, 447–51
    Fields, Factories and Workshops 439, 448
    Mutual Aid: An Illuminated Factor of Evolution 134, 135, 142, 143
Kurdi, Alan 394
Kusch, Rodolfo 520
Kustow, Michael 58, 59

Labour Party Manifesto 86
Lacan, Jacques 77, 111–14, 116, 117, 119, 121, 124–6, 438, 499, 504, 507, 576
    Formations of the Unconscious 112
Laclau, Ernesto 236, 577
Lady Bertram 96
Lafont, Cristina 209, 210, 218, 220
La gitanilla (de Cervantes) 490, 492
Lanchester, John
    The Wall 269
land 84, 93, 94, 448
    conflicts 364, 368
    disputes 366
    private ownership of 451
    stewardship of 90
    wealth 84
Land Drainage Act of 1861 445
Lara, María Pía
    Beyond the Public Sphere: Film and the Feminist Imaginary 569, 578
    Moral Textures 568
La Rochefoucauld, François de 112
The Last Migration (McConaghy) 265
La Tempete (Cesaire) 104
Latour, Bruno 415
Law and Narrative research 380
Law and Sexuality scholarship 396

lawful relations 156, 157
Law of Freedom (Winstanley) 444
Lawrence, D.H. 452
The Laws (Plato) 231
Law Society 240
layered amnesia 87–9
Lazzari, Axel 365
Leader, Darian 114
Lefebvre, H. 408
    Critique of Everyday Life 456
The Leftovers (Perrotta) 65, 66, 68, 69, 71–6, 79–81
legacies 107–8
    Bell, Dido Elizabeth 90–106
    entangled hauntings 87–90
    narrating Englishness 83–6
'Legacies of Slavery' project 97
Legal Aid regulations 342
legal–cultural battlefield 380
legal fiction 522, 556
legal personhood and subjectivity 359
legal transdiscourse 524
Legendre, Pierre 16
legitimization of punishment 581
Le Guin, Ursula 131, 138–41
    The Dispossessed 139, 140
Lehmann, Hans-Thies 40, 41
Le Jargon ou le langage de l'argot reformé (Chereau) 466
Leopold, Aldo
    The Sand County Almanac 448
L'Essence du jargon (Becker-Ho) 467
Lesser, W. 276, 410
Leviathan (Hobbes) 441
Levi-Strauss, Claude
    Structural Study of Myth 112
Levitas, Ruth 134
    Utopia as Method 133
lex animata 477
lexical-order hypotheticals 488
liberal contract theory 275
liberal individualism 119
Liberal Party 388
liberal political theory 278
Liber iudiciorum 486
Libes, Kenna 103
libidinal process of learning 568
Libro de buen amor 496
Lilja, Hugo 242
"Limits of Utopia" (Miéville) 136
Lincoln in the Bardo 557
Lindsay, Sir John 99, 102
linear temporality 361
linear temporal ordering 362, 363
linguistic act of punishment 584

linguistic community 587, 588
linguistic turn 581–9
Lisa Disch 575
literary fiction 378, 386, 419, 522, 526
"literary reportage" 6
Literary Space 524
literary transdiscourse 523
Little Hans, case of 110, 112, 113
lived law movement 397
Lloyd, Dennis 47, 48
    Introduction to Jurisprudence 46
Lloyd's Introduction to Jurisprudence (Freeman) 46
Lockean negative constitutionalism 237
logical-formal model 507
logical phantasy 7
loguical transcursivity 523
Lohana Berkins Collective Movement 290
Lolita (Nabokov) 386
Lord Denning 83, 84
Lord Hoffmann 450
Lord Justice Holt 107
Lord Mansfield 97, 99, 100
Lord Nelson 88
l'ordre du discourse 523
Lord Vansittart 178
love contracts 272, 273, 277, 279–81
Lovelock, J.E. 415
Lucy, Margaret 98
Lucy, Philip 98
Lucy, Thomas 98
Luhmann, Niklas 234, 245, 590
Luxembourg Draft Law on the Exploration and Use of Space Resources 300

Macfarlane, Robert 252, 259
The Machine Stops (Forster) 405, 408
MacKinnon, Catherine 382, 575
Macri, Mauricio 290
Magia Naturalis (della Porta) 442
magic 373
Magna Carta 440
Maier, Corinne 119
Maimonides 480
majoritarianism 227
Malamud, Bernard 563
Malm, Andreas 260
Mamet, David 373
Man and the Sacred (Callois) 520
Manderson, Desmond 232–4, 241
    Athena's Way: The Jurisprudence of the Oresteia 231
Mann, F. 48
Mansfield Park (Austen) 91, 92, 95, 97, 100, 103, 106

The Man With The Compound Eyes (Wu Ming-yi) 432
Marcuse, Herbert 508
Margulis, L. 415
Maria Belle *see* Belle, Dido Elizabeth
Marías, Javier 21, 22
Marino, Gabriel David 285
Marion, Jean-Luc 28, 29, 34, 35
    Being Given 32
    The Crossing of the Visible 33
Marksen, David
    This is Not a Novel 375
Marquez, Gabriel García 36
    Memories of My Melancholy Whores 36
    One Hundred Years of Solitude 36
Martel, Lucrecia 36
Martin, David 99
Martín Fierro (Hernández) 529
Martinson, Harry 242
Marx, Karl 120, 404, 438, 587
Marxist approach 367
Marxist ideal of communism 129
Marxist theory 404
Marxist tradition 129
Masciandaro, Nicola 16, 217, 218
Massey, Doreen 367
Massumi, Brian 273, 277
materiality 15, 18, 25, 26, 345, 435, 475
Matte Blanco, Ignacio
    Thinking, Feeling and Being. Clinical Reflections on the Fundamental Antinomy of Human Beings and World 507
    The Unconscious as Infinite Sets 507
matterphor 23, 430
Matthews, William 587
Mbembe, Achille 371, 456
McConaghy, Charlotte
    The Last Migration 265
McKay, Laura Jean
    The Animals in That Country 261
McVeigh, Shaun 147, 148, 156, 157
Medical Mandatory Programme 286
Medina, José 573, 574
Melville, Herman 202
    Bartleby the Scrivener 204, 239, 247
    Billy Budd, Sailor 558
Mémoire 459, 462, 463
Memories of My Melancholy Whores (Marquez) 36
Menander 228
Mercatorial projection 198
The Merchant of Venice (Shakespeare) 552–8
Mergers and Acquisitions 18
Mestrual, Naty 288

The Metamorphosis (Kafka) 241, 508
metaphysical grounds 401
"Metaphysics of Morals" (Kant) 589
Meyerhold, Vsevolod 62
Meyler, Bernadette
    New Directions in Law and Literature 5
Michelet, Jules 570
Middelaar, Luuk van
    The Passage to Europe 118
Miéville, China 132, 135, 136
    "Limits of Utopia" 136
Mignolo, Walter 367
Milan, Tiq 385
military civic dictatorship 292
Mill, John Stuart 296
Miller, Jacques-Alain 114, 123
Miller, J. Hillis 561
Millet, Lydia
    A Children's Bible 268
Milner, Jean-Claude 119
minor jurisprudence 284, 295, 438–40, 450, 451, 468
minor language 468
Minow, Martha 395
miracles
    dialect without world 466–70
    forms of living 454–7
    miraculous dressing room 457–66
'Miss. Fairness Act' 390, 391
Mississippi bill 396
Mississippi law 392
Mitchell, Audra 254
Mi You 62
modernist 'progressive' approach 230
Moon Agreement 306
Moore, Nathan 465
moral criticism 562–5
moral panic 381, 389, 393, 398
Moral Textures (Lara) 568
Moran, Leslie 396
More, Thomas 131–3, 135, 136, 141, 144
    Utopia 129, 130, 132, 135–9, 142
Moreira, Juan 518, 525, 527–30
Moritán, Carlos 528
Morris, William 446, 447
    News from Nowhere 128, 439, 446, 447
    Useful Work versus Useless Toil 447
Morrison, Toni 563
Morton, Timothy 255, 259, 260
The Motion of Light in Water (Delany) 369
moukhik 148
Mount Analogue (Daumal) 21
Mountbatten, Louis 184, 185, 192
Mountbatten plan 184
Mouvement des travailleurs arabes (MTA) 456

"Mr and Mrs Andrews" (Gainsborough) 90
MTF 389
Mukhopadhyay, Debabrata 150
Muñoz, José Esteban 132
Murphy, Kelly 550
The Museum of Eterna's Novel. The first good Novel (Fernández) 526
Musk, Elon 8
mutual aid 130, 134, 135, 142–4, 449
Mutual Aid: An Illuminated Factor of Evolution (Kropotkin) 134, 135, 142, 143
mutual law–life relations 153, 158

Nabokov, Vladimir
   Lolita 386
Nakamoto, Satoshi 354
Nancy, Jean-Luc
   The Inoperative Community 213
narrating Englishness 83–6
narratives 4, 64, 76, 89, 92, 267, 301, 381, 402, 518, 552
   of abuse 549
   anti-trans 393
   authority 378
   climate 259
   counter-hegemonic 570–74
   human 263
   in international law 302
   judicial 540, 548, 566
   jurisprudence 368
   legal 380, 383
   moral panic 389
   slave 346, 347
   of trans lives 384
   trauma 541, 546
   universal victimization 550
narrator unreliability 386
Nash, Jennifer 368
Nashkar, Bishakha 166, 168
National Registry of Persons 288
National Reorganization Process 292
national socialism 141
National Socialist German Workers' Party (NSDAP) 331
National Socialist Party 330, 331
National Socialist regime 331–2
National Space Policy 300
Natural History Auction 265
natural law 310, 404
nature 352, 360, 362
Naumann, Bernd 51, 53
Nazi dictatorship 45
'Nazi Grandpa' 330
Nazi ideology 330
Nazi law 49
Nazi party 44
Nazi regime 513
'Nazi uniform' 330, 332
Negri, Antonio 275, 276
Nehru, Jawaharlal 184, 196
Neimanis, Astrida 435
   Bodies of Water: Posthuman Feminist Phenomenology 432
neoliberalism 210
Neruda, Pablo 589
   "Extravagaria" 588
neutral administration 121
New Directions in Law and Literature (Meyler & Anker) 5
News from Nowhere (Morris) 128, 439, 446, 447
Newton, Isaac 410
New York Climate Action Summit 266
Nieto, Pura 550
Nietzsche, Friedrich 25, 72, 76, 216, 518, 523, 554, 561, 562, 582
   The Case of Wagner 519
Nietzscheanism 201
Ninth Circuit Court of Appeals 257
nobleman-turned-gypsy 491
noble-turned-gypsy 491
Nolte, Ernst 570
non-adversarial feminist jurisprudence 173
non-commercial familial relationships 160
non-culinary transdiscursive practice 527
non-human environment 408
nonhuman rights framework 254
non-masculinist utopia 139
non-negotiable contract 272
non-normative gender identities 381, 398
non-obvious classification 129
Nonsenso, Raphael 131, 135–8
non-sex worker community 162
normative literary conventions 64
Norwegian Data Protection Wa 279
Norwegian youth organization 267
Notes of a Native Son (Baldwin) 376
Notre Dame de Paris (Hugo) 460
Nourry, Émile 462
Novalis 210
Novelas ejemplares (de Cervantes) 485, 487, 489, 490
'Novelistic' *(Novelística)* 526
Nozick, R. 205, 207, 213

Oakeshott, M.J.
   On Human Conduct 225
Ober, J. 226
   Political Dissent in Democratic Athens 226
"objective objectivity" 7
occupy movement 123

Odyssey (Homer) 242, 509
Oedipal moment 259
Oedipus Rex (Sophocles) 519, 520, 532–5, 539, 543, 550
"Of Other Spaces" (Foucault) 129
Oikonomia 225–9
    Aniara 242–8
    inoperative beings and apparatuses 223–4
    postulates and economic truths 230–34
    stand-up for your rights 234–41
Olusoga, David 97
omniscient quasi-heterodiegetic narrative 379
'Once upon a time' (Shklovsky) 32
One Hundred Years of Solitude (Marquez) 36
On Human Conduct (Oakeshott) 225
On Moral Fiction (Gardner) 563
"on moral writing" 562–6
Ononokpono, Mary Okon Inyang 430–31
On the Soul (Aristotle) 475
onto-epistemological assumptions 12
onto-epistemological cacophony 12
onto-epistemological core assumptions 6
onto-epistemological dynamisms 8
onto-epistemological implications 10
onto-epistemological processes 11
Oppenheimer v Cattermole 48
oppressive capitalist system 36
oral tradition 149, 150, 555, 560
'Orderly Reader' 526
Order of the Discourse 524, 525, 527
The Order of Things (Foucault) 129
Ordnance Survey 450
Oresteia (Aeschylus) 226, 230, 231, 234, 241
organisational activities 159
Orlando, Francesco 504, 506–8
Ortelius, Abraham 180
Osborne, T. 412
OST *see* Outer Space Treaty (OST)
Ost, François 230, 231, 234, 241
ostranenie 28–32
    banality of saturation 32–5
    ethical and political dimension of 35–7
O'Sullivan, Siobhan 254
Otto, Rudolf 520
'outer space colonialism' 306
Outer Space Treaty (OST) 296, 298

Padatik, Amra 158
Page, Elliot 384, 391, 397, 398
Palitzsch, Peter 53, 54
Pandemic Solidarity: Mutual Aid during the Covid-19 Crisis 143
Pandey, Gyanendra 192
Panofsky, Erwin 176, 177

Paradoxes of Legal Science (Cardozo) 566
'participatory and transformative process' 233
partition plan 184
Parvulus philosophiae naturalis (Gerticz) 471
Pasolini, Pier Paolo 469
The Passage to Europe (Middelaar) 118
Pateman, Carole 275, 278–81
Paterson, Tony 40
'peer-to-peer' electronic cash 355
Peller, Gary 368
People's Tribunals 270
perception 471, 480–82
'performative' transformational effect 227
'perlocutionary acts' 576
Perrotta, Tom
    The Leftovers 65, 66, 68, 69, 71–6, 79–81
The Persians (Aeschylus) 519
Personenstandsgesetz (PStG) 387, 388
perspective 64
    archism and archeon 66–8
    law after Sudden Departure 71–9
    law without archeon 79–81
    Sudden Departure 69–70
Perspiring Poem Book 289
Peters, Julie Stone 28
Pethick-Lawrence, Lord 183
phallic function 113
Philippopoulos-Mihalopoulos, Andreas 274, 281
Philo of Alexandria 476
physical violence against women 578
Pickering, Jonathan 261
Pierce, Charles S. 9
Pilgrim's Progress (Bunyan) 441
Pinochet, Augusto 569
Pinter, Harold 56
Piscator, Erwin 55, 58
planetary protection regulations 305
"planet-wide homeostasis" 415
plantation wealth 93
platform contract 279
Plato 124, 139, 232, 248, 475, 491
    Gorgias 474, 475
    The Laws 231
Plessy v Ferguson 391
Plowden
    Commentaries 443
Podestá, José J. 528–30
poetics 580
    contemporary retribution 582–9
    crime prevention paradigm 582
    early retribution model 581–2
    image 29, 30
    justice 288, 483, 532–50
    role in theory of punishment 589–91
poetry 290, 291, 295, 378, 449, 523, 581

role in theory of punishment 589–91
  theory of 580
point of view 64–8, 71, 72–4, 76, 77–9, 81, 245, 260, 378, 415, 511, 516, 521, 522, 526, 572
police journalism 522
political cartography 176–82
political community 440
Political Dissent in Democratic Athens (Ober) 226
politics 85, 119, 125, 478
  aestheticization of 35
  anti-immigrant/immigration 86
  of blockchain 353, 358, 361
  and capitalism 273
  ethics and 28
  gender 64
  individualist liberal 138
  law under 280
  messianic 244
  of multiple ontologies 311
  revolutionary 137
  theory of 588
Politics (Aristotle) 464
"politics of aesthetics" 35
Polizeiwissenschaft 522
Portia's deconstructive techniques 565
Portrait of Charlotte of Mecklenburg-Strelitz 98
Poseidon (Kafka) 420
positivist idealism 5
Posner, Richard 28
possessive individualism 143
post-colonial amnesia 87
postcolonial continuities 194–8
post-colonial critical thinker 154
post-colonial location 149, 154
post/colonial politics 87
posterity 19, 22
posthumanism 401
post-modernism 563
post-sensorial operations 472, 473, 476, 478, 480–82
post-structuralist fields of research 273
Potebnja, Aleksandr 29, 31
potentia vacui 21
Povinelli, Elisabeth 1
Powell, Enoch 85, 86
Powers, Richard 263
practical image 29
precedent 15–17, 20–24, 26, 27, 33, 97, 107, 175, 187, 197, 305, 493, 495, 496, 548
precedential literalism 23
premonition 15
  jurisliterature and 'pataphysics' 19–27
  vaticination 16–19

Prince, Mary
  The History of Mary Prince 346
principle of generalisation 507
Principles of Hope (Bloch) 131
Pringle, Thomas 346
"problematic arbitrariness" 388
property rights law 274
"Prophet's Dilemma" 70
providentialism 225
Prozorov, Sergey 235, 236
psēphismata 226
pseudo-historical religious justification 489
psychoanalysis 124, 125, 345, 507
public policies 523
'public–private partnership' 169
Punjab Boundary Commission 189–92
Purcell, Henry
  Dido and Aeneas 106

Quid iuris 513

Rabaté, J.M. 504
Race Relations Act 1965 85
Radbruch, Gustav 513
Radcliffe, Sir Cyril 187, 189, 192, 193, 197
Radcliffe Award 192–3, 197
Radcliffe Boundary Commission 175, 182–4
radical contextualism 578
radical egalitarianism 219, 220
radical immanentism 78
"radical theory of sex" 383
Radin, Margaret Jane 274, 275
Raj-Seppings, Izzy 267
Ramsay, Allen 99
Rancière, Jacques 35
Rank, Otto 111
Ransom, John Crowe 561
Raphael, D. 206, 213
  Concepts of Justice 205
"A Rapist in Your Path" 569
Rasch, William 236
Raskin, Jamie 589
Rawls, J. 205
real witness statement 339
Rebentisch, Juliane 28
reciprocal law–life relations 156
Recopilación de leyes 487
Reeves, Tate 390
'reflexive' constitutionalism 228
refugee law 345
Refutation of the Philosophers 479
Registration Convention 299
"reified factualness" 367
relationality 1, 5, 216
religious transgression 491

religious voluntary poverty 459
Rembrandt 376, 377
Rennell, James 177, 178, 180–82
"representationalism" 405
Re-Presenting the Good Society (Cooke) 577
residual establishment group 87
"Respected, Not Policed" 147
Restakis, John 167
Restauración política de España (Political Restoration of Spain) 489
"The Resurrection of the Word" 29
retributionist approach 581
retributive punishment 583, 587
retributivism 584
retributivist theory of punishment 586
reviews 327, 329, 330–32, 334, 335, 337
revolutionary legislation 481
revolutionary politics 137
Re Weston 85
Rhode, Deborah 395
Richter, Ida 40
Ricoeur, Paul 572
rights-based arguments 257
Robeyns, Ingrid 257
Robinson, Kim Stanley
    Blue Mars 244
Rodoreda, Mercè
    Death In Spring 426–7, 435–6
Rodríguez, Claudia 291, 292
'role-play-with-revisions' 270
Roman commercial class 296
Roman law 239
Rorty, Richard 578
Rose, Deborah Bird 251, 254, 259, 262, 264
Rosenmeyer, Thomas 241
Rowling, J.K. 397
Rozema, Patricia 95
Rubin, Gayle 382–4, 389, 394
Rufer, Mario 365
rule of law 46, 73–4
'rules of behaviour' 312
Rushworth, John
    Historical Collections 107
Ruskin, John 445–8
    Unto This Last 439, 445
Russian formalism 28, 29
"Russian formalist theory" 561
Ryan, Simon 179, 180

Sacayán, Diana 285, 287, 288
sadomasochism 275
sado-masochism 278
SAFE Act 389
Said, Edward 92, 351
Salah, Trish 398

Salus Populi Romani 229
Samabaya Niti (Tagore) 164, 165
The Sand County Almanac (Leopold) 448
Sanditon (Austen) 102
Saramago, José 116, 120, 123, 126, 127
    The Gospel According to Jesus 423–5
    The Stone Raft 114, 120–23, 126
Sartre, Jean Paul 129
    Critique of Dialectical Reason 134
Saunders, George 557
Sauval, Henri 463, 469
Save Adolescents from Experimentation (SAFE) Act 385
Scalia, Antonin 559
'scenic arrangement' 41
Schelling, Friedrich 36
Schiller, Friedrich 54, 55, 59
Schmitt, Carl 231, 232, 242
    Concept of the Political 588
Schreber, Daniel Paul 6, 130
Schütz, Anton 553
science of the soul 472–7, 479, 481
Scott, Joan 368, 369
Scott, Samuel Parsons 473
scouring/flowing couplet 441
Segato, Rita 569
Seibel, Beatriz 529
Selbstbestimmungsgesetz 388
Self-Regulatory Boards (SRBs) 158, 169, 170, 172, 173
self-sufficient communities 141
Sembrar, Colectiva 143
semi-structured interviews 364
Sen, Amartya 205, 206
    The Idea of Justice 164
sensing 1, 5, 13
Serres, Michel 415, 430
Setalvad, M.C. 189
sewers 438–40
sex, constructing and narrating 382–3
"sex hierarchy" 382
sexual citizenship 381, 382, 397, 398
sexual contracts 278
sexual–legal personhood 381, 385, 398, 399
Sexual Theories of Children (Freud) 110
sex work 147, 148, 159, 160, 166, 167, 169, 171
Sex Worker Freedom Festival 147
sex worker-funded initiatives 158
sex workers
    collective organisation 159, 165
    collectivisation 162
    community 168
    feminist jurisprudence 149, 153–5, 158, 172–3
    groups 147

movement 147, 154
organisation 159
Sex Workers' Festival 162
Sex Workers' Manifesto 162
Shakespeare, William 25, 27, 103–6, 183, 232, 376, 439, 483
   Antony and Cleopatra 442
   Henry V 60
   The Merchant of Venice 552–8
   The Tempest of 1611 104
   The Tragedy of Romeo and Juliet 519
Shaviro, S. 412
Sheldrake, Merlin 270
Sher, Benjamin 30–32
Shklovsky, Viktor 28–33, 35, 36, 561
   "Bowstring. On the Dissimilarity of the Similar" 34
   'Once upon a time' 32
Shock, Susy 288–91, 293
   Hojarascas 284, 285, 290, 291, 295
the shout
   and fury, between 291–4
   and *travesti* fury 284–90
Sider, Sandra 550
Sidney, Philip 17
Siegert, Bernhard 177, 181, 182
Siete Partidas (Alfonso X) 472, 487
"Signature" 364, 371
The Silent Girl (Jelinek) 61, 62
Silva, Daniel 559
Simpson, Leanne 311
Singh, Baldev 184
Single European Act 114
Sircar, Oishik 147
Sitrin, Marina 143
Six Memos for the Next Millennium (Calvino) 374, 375
Skywalker, Luke 308
slash 419
   Death In Spring (Rodoreda) 435–6
   Death in Spring (Rodoreda) 426–7
   The Gospel According to Jesus (Saramago) 423–5
   Invisible Ecologies (Armstrong) 434–5
   Inyang (Ononokpono) 430–31
   The Man With The Compound Eyes (Wu Ming-yi) 432
   Poseidon (Kafka) 420
   The Swan Book (Wright) 428–9
   A Time for Everything (Knausgaard) 421–3
slavery 87, 94, 95, 97, 100–103, 123, 228, 345, 346, 578
Slavery Abolition Act 1833 94
smart contracts 356, 358
Smolin, Lee 310

social contract 278
social imaginaries 578
Socialist Federal Republic of Yugoslavia 132
social movements 571–3
Socrates 474
Sogol 26
The Sole Spokesman: Jinnah, the Muslim League and the Demand for Pakistan (Jalal) 183
Solís, Malva 288
Somerset v Stewart 97, 106
Sophocles
   Oedipus Rex 519, 520, 532–5, 539, 543, 550
Sotomayor, Sibila 569
soul 471–82
'South Sea Bubble' 96
sovereign exceptionalism 211, 212
Sovereign Good 124
space debris 303
space environment 302–6, 308
The space of literature (Blanchot) 524
Space Resource Exploration and Utilization Act 300
space resources 300
The Space Resources Act 300
spacetimematterings 1
Spade, Dean 143
Spanish Gender Identity Act 286
Spanish law 489
   on gypsies 490
Spate, O.H.K. 189, 195
speculative fictions
   and intergenerational voices 266–9
   and interspecies judging 260–65
speech act theory 584
The Spell of the Sensuous. Perception and Language in a More-than-Human World (Abram) 256
Spencer, Edmund
   The Faerie Queene 442
Spivak, Gayatri Chakravorty 89, 128, 152, 154–6
SRBs *see* Self-Regulatory Boards (SRBs)
stare decisis 15, 16
Stark, Luke 276
state-authorised anti-trafficking agenda 169
state-authorised anti-trafficking measures 169
state-level decision-making 309
state-sanctioned anti-trafficking approach 171
state-sanctioned rehabilitation programmes 167
States Parties to the Treaty 301, 304
statistical governance, normative basis of 206
Staton, Josephine 258
Steffen, Will 260
Steiner, Peter 29
Steitz, Kerstin 54
Stobaeus 476

Stoermer, Eugene F 250
Stoics 228, 229, 248
Stoler, Ann Laura 365
Stone, Christopher 252, 253
The Stone Raft (Saramago) 114, 120–23, 126
Strauss, Richard
    Der Rosenkavalier 423
string figures 5, 352, 362
'structural coupling' 234
"structuralism" 561
Structural Study of Myth (Levi-Strauss) 112
subaltern collective movement 284
Subject–Object distinction 527
Subversive Sites: Feminist Engagements with Law in India (Kapur and Cossman) 160
Sudden Departure 69–70, 75, 77, 79–81
    law after 71–9
Sugarman, D. 84, 85, 89
Sumic, Jelica 119
Summa Theologiae (Aquinas) 475
Supiot, Alain 342
Swadeshi Movement 164
The Swan Book (Wright) 428–9
sympatheia 67
synaesethical modes of jurisliterary inquiry 5
synaesethic engagement 6
synaesethics of objectivity 7
synchronisation 357, 358
'systems theory' 245

Tagore, Rabindranath 164
    Ghare Baire (The Home and the World) 164
    Samabaya Niti 164, 165
Talion law 581
Tanasescu, Mihnea 253
The Task (Cowper) 106
Tate, Allen 561
Tauil, Juan 288
Taylor, Charles 572, 574
technocratic mythologization of temporality 24
TEK *see* Traditional Ecological Knowledge (TEK)
Tellis, Ashley 174
The Tempest of 1611 (Shakespeare) 104
temporality 15, 24, 25, 134, 462
    capitalist 463
    construction of 467
    linear 358, 361
tenses in grammar of law 315–16
territory 131, 132, 175, 191, 192, 198, 365, 366
    expropriation of 96
    juridical 193
    legal 182, 197
    national 174, 188
    virgin 11

Tesla, Nikola 312
That Hamilton Woman 88
theatricality 38–63
theatrical sensibility of legality 20
"The Theologians" (Borges) 588
theories of punishment 580, 581, 586, 588–91
Theory of Law and Literature. Across Two Arts of Compromising (Condello and Toracca) 506
theory of plate tectonics 410
theory of politics 588
theory of punishment 588
Thinking, Feeling and Being. Clinical Reflections on the Fundamental Antinomy of Human Beings and World (Matte Blanco) 507
This is Not a Novel (Marksen) 375
Thomas, Yan 454, 455
Thomas K 327, 329–32
Thunberg, Greta 266, 267
A Time for Everything (Knausgaard) 421–3
time server 362
Time Stamp Authority (TSA) 361
timestamp certificate 361
Timor iuris 16
Title IV of the Commercial Space Launch Competitiveness Act 300
"To Have Done with Judgment" (Deleuze) 204, 205
Tolstoy, Leo 30, 31, 36, 37
Tomashevski, Boris 561
Toracca, Tiziano
    Theory of Law and Literature. Across Two Arts of Compromising 506
tort law 18
Totem and Taboo (Freud) 122
traditional cartographic discourse 176
traditional cartography 177
Traditional Ecological Knowledge (TEK) 311
traditional indigenous knowledge 310, 311
traditional literary studies 378
tradition of conduct 157
The Tragedy of Romeo and Juliet (Shakespeare) 519
trans anxieties 384–7
trans autonomy 393
Transcendental Aesthetics 521, 523
transcendental Kantian Aesthetics 524
transcendental nonsense 4, 9–11
transdiscourse
    case of *Hormiga Negra* 529–30
    Macedonio Fernández 526–7
    Moreira, Juan 527–9
    ob-scene and the sacred 518–21
    postulates of aesthetics of the law 521–5
    three cases of vice-diction 525–6

transdiscursive non-culinary practice 527
trans-exclusionary radical feminists (TERFS) 392
trans-exclusive feminist 393
trans-exclusive feminist community 393
transgender 381, 384
transgression
    and compromise 504–11
    different logics 512–17
    salmon mayonnaise 499–504
transhumanist science fiction 8
transing 378–81
    constructing and narrating sex 382–3
    instrumentalizing vulnerabilty 394–5
    law, de-binarizing and 395–9
    trans persons' legal self-determinations 387–93
    trans visibilities and trans anxieties 384–7
transitional theory of law 4
trans law 388, 395
trans persons' legal self-determinations 387–93
Transsexuellengesetz (TSG) 338, 387, 388
transvestitism 384
trans visibilities 384–7
trauma
    of legal training 18
    mental 342
    narratives 451, 456, 550
    poetic justice and traumatic spectacles 532–50
    of warfare 91
travel
    frames of reference 327–33
    'live there' 333–8
    stories 335, 337, 338
Travesti/A Good Enough Theory (Wayar) 284–91, 295
travesti movement 287, 289, 291
travesti-trans theory 292
Treaty of Maastricht 118
triadic model of 'humanity' 241
The Trial (Kafka) 241, 404
Trifles (Glaspell) 532–50
Trilling, Lionel 560
Trinitarianism 230
TripAdvisor 327, 329–33
Trump, Donald 385, 589
Truth and Juridical Forms (Foucault) 527
TSA *see* Time Stamp Authority (TSA)
Tschakert, Petra 256
tucutes 392
Türhüter (Kafka) 474
Turkish community 61
Tushnet, Mark 368
Twain, Mark
    Huckleberry Finn 386

UAE Space Agency 300
ultra-liberal domination 482
Ulysses (Joyce) 508, 509
UN Committee on the Peaceful Uses of Outer Space (UN COPUOS) 302
The Unconscious as Infinite Sets (Matte Blanco) 507
UN Convention on the Law of the Sea (UNCLOS) 300
Underground Man (Dostoevsky) 386
Under the Skin (Faber) 261
unforeseeable 25
unforeseen 18, 19, 22, 23, 25, 26, 33
The Uninvited (Jensen) 269
United Nations Climate Summit 266
United Nations Committee on the Rights of the Child 267
unknowns 18, 19, 22–6
Un Largo Camino a Casa 365
unreliable narrators 386
unseen 28, 29, 32–7
Unsled, Siegfried 50
Unto This Last (Ruskin) 439, 445, 446
Upper Tier Tribunal 340
Useful Work versus Useless Toil (Morris) 447
USHA cooperative bank 158, 167, 168, 173
US legal scholarship and jurisprudence 12
utopia 128–35
    anxiety/excitement 135–8
    mutual aid 142–4
Utopia (More) 129, 130, 132, 135–9, 142
Utopia as Method (Levitas) 133

Valdés, Daffne 569
"value of lunar relative density" 410
Valverde, Mariana 191
van Busleyden, Hieronymus 135–8
Van Dooren, Thom 254
Vaneigem, Raul 137
"variant of sex development" 388
Venus in Furs (von Sacher-Masoch) 272, 277, 282
verbal communications 159
Verne, Jules
    Journey to the Centre of the Earth 410
Verwerfung 119
Vespucci, Amerigo 131, 135
Vico, Giambattista 17
Videla, Jorge Rafael 292
Vienna Convention on the Law of Treaties (VCLT) 301
violence 578
    arbitrariness and 226
    Benjamin-style divine 79
    against demonstrators 569

gender 285, 287
heterosexual 396
against indigenous people 36
institutional 293
inter-racial 86
of law 81
legal 231
sexualized 391
of slave trade 347
against trans and non-binary 385
against women 287, 381, 579
Virgil
  Aeneid 105
Virno, Paolo 463, 464
Vismann, Cornelia 121
vital normativity 412
"vital normativity" 412
vitriolic anti-gypsy treatises 489
voluntary and intentional transgression 511
von der Leyen, Ursula 126
von Goethe, Johann Wolfgang 473
von Jhering, Rudolf 4–6, 8, 9, 11, 12, 553, 560
von Ranke, Leopold 570
von Sacher-Masoch, Leopold 213, 279–82
  Venus in Furs 272

Wagner, Richard 518, 519
The Wall (Lanchester) 269
wallets 360
Warburg, Aby 86, 89, 90
Warner, Marina 105
  Indigo 104
Warrington, R. 84, 85, 89
Watanabe, Moriaki 519
water 419–36
Watson, Irene 263
waves 419–36
wavewriting 419, 420, 423, 425, 426, 428, 430, 433
Wayar, Marlene 288, 290–94
  Travesti/A Good Enough Theory 284–90
Wayward Lives (Hartman) 348
"A Weary Man's Utopia" (Borges) 135, 138, 140
Weber, Max 39, 243, 473
Weil, Simone 455
Weiler, Joseph 114, 117, 118, 122
Weisberg, Richard 1, 6
Weiss, Peter 50–52, 54–6, 58–62
  The Investigation. An Oratorio in 11 Cantos 41, 42, 50, 55, 56, 58, 60
Werner, Samuel 389
West, Robin 380, 382
West Bengal Co-operative Societies Act, 1983 (WBCSA) 164, 166

West Bengal Societies Registration Act, 1961 (WBSRA) 159, 168, 173
Western anthropocentrism 255
Western common law traditions 148, 156
Western legal tradition 278
Weston, Stanley 83, 84
Whanganui Maori tribe 252
Whanganui River Settlement Agreement 252
What is a Minor Literature? (Deleuze and Guattari) 468
"When the World Screamed" (Doyle) 414
Whitehead, Alfred North 9, 412, 413, 416
White Papers 362
  for assembling the stories 353–5
  Bitcoin 354, 361, 362
  Churchill 353
  Ethereum 355
Whitman, Walt 588
Why Stories Matter (Hemmings) 369
wild judging 252–5
  judging beyond brink of extinction 265–6
  scalar framing and zooming out 255–60
  speculative fiction and intergenerational voices 266–9
  speculative fiction and interspecies judging 260–64
  wild law and 250–52
wild law 20, 250–55
Wild Law Judgment project 270
Williams, Patricia J. 10–12, 368
Winichakul, Thongchai 182
Winstanley, Gerrard 439, 443, 444, 447
  Law of Freedom 444
Wit and its Relation to the Unconscious (Freud) 500
witness statement 339, 340, 342, 343, 347
Wittgenstein, Ludwig 206, 587
"Woe and Wonder" (Cunningham) 552
Woolf, Virginia 425
World Conference on Women 169
world-making 363
  narration as 351–3
  and representation 358–62
Wright, Alexis
  The Swan Book 428–9
Wu Ming-yi
  The Man With The Compound Eyes 432

Yang Mi-ja 591
The Yellow Wallpaper (Gilman) 64
Yorke–Talbot opinion 107
youth climate litigation 267
Youth Verdict objection 267
Yusoff, K. 415

Zabus, Chantal 104
Zambrano, María 520
Zartaloudis, T. 143
Z-Cash 361
zero-knowledge proof encryption 361

Ziesenis, Johann Georg 98
Zittrain, Jonathan 276
Žižek, Slavoj 114, 121
Zunz, Emma 584
Zupančič, Alenka 125